Experience PSYCHOLOGY

Fourth Edition

Laura A. King

University of Missouri, Columbia

EXPERIENCE PSYCHOLOGY, FOURTH EDITION

Published by McGraw-Hill Education, 2 Penn Plaza, New York, NY 10121. Copyright © 2019 by McGraw-Hill Education. All rights reserved. Printed in the United States of America. Previous editions © 2016, 2013, and 2010. No part of this publication may be reproduced or distributed in any form or by any means, or stored in a database or retrieval system, without the prior written consent of McGraw-Hill Education, including, but not limited to, in any network or other electronic storage or transmission, or broadcast for distance learning.

Some ancillaries, including electronic and print components, may not be available to customers outside the United States.

This book is printed on acid-free paper.

1 2 3 4 5 6 7 8 9 LWI 21 20 19 18

ISBN 978-1-260-39710-9 (bound edition)
MHID 1-260-39710-6 (bound edition)
ISBN 978-1-259-91103-3 (loose-leaf edition)
MHID 1-259-91103-9 (loose-leaf edition)

Senior Portfolio Manager: *Nancy Welcher*
Director, Product Development: *Meghan Campbell*
Lead Product Developer: *Dawn Groundwater*
Senior Product Developer: *Cara Labell*
Marketing Managers: *Augustine Laferrera; Olivia Kaiser*
Lead Content Project Managers: *Sandy Wille; Jodi Banowetz*
Senior Buyer: *Susan K. Culbertson*
Senior Designer: *Matt Backhaus*
Content Licensing Specialist: *Ann Marie Jannette*
Cover Image: *©republica/E+/Getty Images*
Compositor: *Aptara®, Inc.*

All credits appearing on page or at the end of the book are considered to be an extension of the copyright page.

Library of Congress Cataloging-in-Publication Data

Names: King, Laura A. (Laura Ann), author.
Title: Experience psychology/Laura A. King, University of Missouri, Columbia.
Description: Fourth edition.|New York, NY : McGraw-Hill Education, [2019]
Identifiers: LCCN 2018013909|ISBN 9781260397109 (alk. paper)|ISBN 1260397106 (alk. paper)
Subjects: LCSH: Psychology.
Classification: LCC BF121 .K536 2019|DDC 150–dc23 LC record available at https://lccn.loc.gov/2018013909

The Internet addresses listed in the text were accurate at the time of publication. The inclusion of a website does not indicate an endorsement by the authors or McGraw-Hill Education, and McGraw-Hill Education does not guarantee the accuracy of the information presented at these sites.

mheducation.com/highered

Laura A. King

Laura King did her undergraduate work at Kenyon College, where she began studying toward an English major. In the second semester of her junior year, she declared a second major in psychology. She completed her A.B. in English with high honors and distinction and in psychology with distinction in 1986. Laura then did graduate work at Michigan State University and the University of California, Davis, receiving her Ph.D. in personality psychology in 1991.

Laura began her career at Southern Methodist University in Dallas, moving to the University of Missouri in 2001, where she is now a Curators' Distinguished Professor of Psychology. In addition to seminars in the development of character, social psychology, and personality psychology, she has taught undergraduate lecture courses in introductory psychology, introduction to personality psychology, and social psychology. She has also taught the Psychology of the Good Life for the community at large. At SMU, she received six different teaching awards, including the "M" award for "sustained excellence" in 1999. At the University of Missouri, she received the Chancellor's Award for Outstanding Research and Creative Activity in 2004.

Her research, which has been funded by the National Institute of Mental Health and the National Science Foundation, has focused on a variety of topics relevant to the question of what it is that makes for a good life. She has studied goals, life stories, happiness, well-being, and meaning in life. In general, her work reflects an enduring interest in understanding what is good and healthy in people. In 2001, her research accomplishments were recognized with a Templeton Prize in Positive Psychology. In 2011, she received the Ed and Carol Diener Award for Distinguished Contributions to Personality Psychology. Laura's research (often in collaboration with undergraduate and graduate students) has appeared in many outstanding publications, including *American Psychologist, Journal of Personality and Social Psychology, Personality and Social Psychology Bulletin,* and *Psychological Science.*

Laura has served as editor of the *Journal of Personality and Social Psychology: Personality and Individual Differences* and the *Journal of Research in Personality.* She has also served as associate editor of *Personality and Social Psychology Bulletin,* the *Journal of Personality and Social Psychology,* and *Social and Personality Psychology Compass,* as well as on numerous grant panels. She has edited or coedited special sections of the *Journal of Personality* and *American Psychologist.* In 2015, she received the award for outstanding service to the field from the Society for Personality and Social Psychology.

In "real life," Laura is an accomplished cook and enjoys listening to music (mostly jazz vocalists and singer-songwriters), running with her faithful dog Bill, and doing math homework with her son, Sam.

about the author

For Sam

brief contents

connect |PSYCHOLOGY   McGraw-Hill Education Psychology APA Documentation Style Guide

contents

9 Motivation and Emotion   325

10 Personality   363

14 Health Psychology 518

connect PSYCHOLOGY McGraw-Hill Education Psychology APA Documentation Style Guide

preface

Experience Psychology

Some Students Take Psychology . . . Others Experience It!

Informed by student data, *Experience Psychology* helps students understand and appreciate psychology as an integrated whole. The personalized, adaptive learning program, thought-provoking examples, and interactive assessments help students see psychology in the world around them and experience it in everyday life. *Experience Psychology* is about, well, experience—our own behaviors; our relationships at home and in our communities, in school, and at work; and our interactions in different learning environments. Grounded in meaningful real-world contexts, *Experience Psychology*'s contemporary examples, personalized author notes, and applied exercises speak directly to students, allowing them to engage with psychology and to learn verbally, visually, and experientially—by reading, seeing, and doing. Function is introduced before dysfunction, building student understanding by looking first at typical, everyday behavior before delving into the less common—and likely less personally experienced—rare and abnormal behavior. *Experience Psychology* places the science of psychology, and the research that helps students see the academic foundations of the discipline, at the forefront of the course.

With *Experience Psychology*, students do not just "take" psychology but actively *experience* it.

Experience a Personalized Approach

PERSONAL NOTES FROM THE AUTHOR THAT PROMOTE UNDERSTANDING

Experience Psychology emphasizes a personal approach, with an abundance of personal pedagogical "asides" communicated directly by author Laura King to students to guide their understanding and stimulate their interest as they read. Some of these notes highlight important terms and concepts; others prompt students to think critically about the complexities of the issues; and still others encourage students to apply what they have learned to their prior reading or to a new situation. These mini-conversations between the author and the reader help develop students' analytical skills for them to carry and apply well beyond their courses.

This is very "meta," but you're reading one right now. Think of it as a chance to nudge the reader's attention. And also to say thanks for taking on Intro Psych!

A PERSONALIZED EXPERIENCE THAT LEADS TO IMPROVED LEARNING AND RESULTS

Students study more effectively with Connect and SmartBook.

How many students *think* they know everything about introductory psychology but struggle on the first exam?

- SmartBook helps students study more efficiently by highlighting what to focus on in the chapter, asking review questions, and directing them to resources until they understand.

- Connect's assignments help students contextualize what they've learned through application, so they can better understand the material and think critically.

- SmartBook creates a personalized study path customized to individual student needs.

- Connect reports deliver information regarding performance, study behavior, and effort so instructors can quickly identify students who are having issues or focus on material that the class hasn't mastered.

Experience the Power of Data

Experience Psychology harnesses the power of data to improve the instructor and student experiences.

BETTER DATA, SMARTER REVISION, IMPROVED RESULTS

For this new edition, data were analyzed to identify the concepts students found to be the most difficult, allowing for expansion upon the discussion, practice, and assessment of challenging topics. The revision process for a new edition used to begin with gathering information from instructors about what they would change and what they would keep. Experts in the field were asked to provide comments that pointed out new material to add and dated material to review. Using all these reviews, authors would revise the material. But now, a new tool has revolutionized that model.

McGraw-Hill Education authors now have access to student performance data to analyze and to inform their revisions. These data are anonymously collected from the many students who use SmartBook, the adaptive learning system that provides students with individualized assessment of their own progress. Because virtually every text paragraph is tied to several questions that students answer while using SmartBook, the specific concepts with which students are having the most difficulty are easily pinpointed through empirical data in the form of a "heat map" report.

POWERFUL REPORTING

Whether a class is face-to-face, hybrid, or entirely online, McGraw-Hill Connect provides the tools needed to reduce the amount of time and energy instructors spend administering their courses. Easy-to-use course management

THE HEAT MAP STORY
APPRECIATING THE POWER OF STUDENT DATA

STEP 1. Over the course of three years, data points showing concepts that caused students the most difficulty were anonymously collected from SmartBook for *Experience Psychology, 3e.*

STEP 2. The data were provided to the author in the form of a *Heat Map,* which graphically illustrated "hot spots" in the text that impacted student learning.

STEP 3. Laura King used the *Heat Map* data to refine the content and reinforce student comprehension in the new edition. Additional quiz questions and assignable activities were created for use in Connect Psychology to further support student success.

RESULT: Because the *Heat Map* gave Laura King empirically based feedback at the paragraph and even sentence level, she was able to develop the new edition using precise student data that pinpointed concepts that caused students the most difficulty.

tools allow instructors to spend less time administering and more time teaching, while reports allow students to monitor their progress and optimize their study time.

■ The **At-Risk Student Report** provides instructors with one-click access to a dashboard that identifies students who are at risk of dropping out of the course due to low engagement levels.

■ The **Category Analysis Report** details student performance relative to specific learning objectives and goals, including APA learning goals and outcomes and levels of Bloom's taxonomy.

■ **Connect Insight** is a one-of-a-kind visual analytics dashboard—now available for both instructors and students—that provides at-a-glance information regarding student performance.

■ The **LearnSmart Reports** allow instructors and students to easily monitor progress and pinpoint areas of weakness, giving each student a personalized study plan to achieve success.

Expand each category to see scores.

APA Outcome	Questions	Students submitted	Category score (*Best assignment attempt*)
1.1: Describe key concepts, principles, and overarching themes in psychology	315	34/35	89.15%
1.2: Develop a working knowledge of psychology's content domains	459	33/35	88.75%
1.3: Describe applications of psychology	132	35/35	90.5%
2.1: Use scientific reasoning to interpret psychological phenomena	299	28/35	78.9%
2.2: Demonstrate psychology information literacy	304	34/35	83.5%
2.3: Engage in innovative and integrative thinking and problem solving	1	35/35	85.5%
2.4: Interpret, design, and conduct basic psychological research	16	34/35	81.7%
Apply ethical standards to evaluate psychological science and practice	6	33/35	92.5%
Apply psychological content skills to career goals	35	29/35	73.8%
5.2: Exhibit self-efficacy and self-regulation	24	33/35	81.6%

Expand each category to see scores.

Bloom's	Questions	Students submitted	Category score (*Best assignment attempt*)
	38	30/35	78%
Analyze	214	32/35	87%
Apply	8	29/35	86%
Create	24	31/35	92%
Evaluate	257	35/35	93%
Remember	238	34/35	89%
Understand			

Challenge YOUR THINKING

Does Birth Order Matter to Personality?

Alfred Adler's ideas about birth order strike a chord with many people. You might have some beliefs about this issue yourself. Ask yourself, what is the typical firstborn, middle, or youngest child like? Common beliefs about birth order include that firstborns are natural leaders; "babies of the family" are indulged; middle children are neglected (like Jan Brady). Chances are, if you have siblings (and even if you do not), you have some hypotheses about the way birth order relates to personality. Do these naive theories have a kernel of truth? The answer to that question might surprise you. Let's take a look at the data.

Impressive contemporary research examining the relationship between birth order and personality characteristics has included very large samples: nearly 400,000 U.S. teenagers (Damian & Roberts, 2015a) as well as over 5,000 U.S. adults, nearly 5,000 British adults, and over 10,000 German teens and adults (Rohrer, Egloff, & Schmukle, 2015). For each sample, participants completed measures of personality characteristics. Information was collected about birth order, family size, socioeconomic status, and other potential "third variables." In addition, the studies compared individuals across different families (for example, comparing all firstborns to all secondborns) as well as within families (comparing siblings to each other).

Because the research used very large samples, included a host of potential confounds, and employed the most sophisticated analytical tools, the investigators were very well positioned to find links between birth order and

personality, if those links existed. The results? For all of the samples, the relationship between birth order and personality was, essentially, zero. Birth order was unrelated to personality characteristics. For example, firstborns were not more likely to have leadership characteristics nor were they more responsible (Damian & Roberts, 2015a; Rohrer, Egloff, & Schmukle, 2015). The lack of associations held as well across genders: Whether older brothers or sisters were compared to younger brothers and sisters, no systematic differences in personality characteristics were found.

The results were very clear-cut, yet the intuition that birth order matters to personality seems to persist. In fact, some researchers refer to the idea that birth order predicts personality as "zombie theory," one that should die but somehow simply won't (Damian & Roberts, 2015b). Perhaps the biggest mystery of all is why the idea that personality is linked to birth order is so compelling.

©Natalia Lebedinskaia/Shutterstock

What Do You Think?

● Are you convinced that birth order bears no relationship to personality? Why or why not?

● Where do your beliefs about personality and birth order originate?

Experience an Emphasis on Critical Thinking

Experience Psychology stimulates critical reflection and analysis. The **Challenge Your Thinking** features involve students in debates relevant to findings from contemporary psychological research. Thought-provoking questions encourage examination of the evidence on both sides of a debate or issue. For example, the Challenge in the "Motivation and Emotion" chapter considers whether streaming TV can contribute to optimal well-being (it might). The Challenge in the "Personality" chapter invites students to consider whether birth order matters to personality (it does not).

INTERSECTION

Personality, Developmental, and Cross-Cultural Psychology: Why Do We Grow Up, Psychologically?

Experience Psychology's **Intersection** features are also designed to spark critical thought. Showcasing studies in different areas of psychological research that focus on the same topic, the Intersections shed light on the links between, and the reciprocal influences of, this exciting work, and they raise provocative questions for student reflection and class discussion. For example, the selection for "The Science of Psychology" chapter brings together personality, development and cross-cultural psychology by reviewing recent research on how people mature.

Each chapter of *Experience Psychology* includes a **Psychology in Our World** section that demonstrates the relevance of psychology in a variety of real-world contexts, including the workplace, the media, and current events. For example, in the "States of Consciousness" chapter, the Psychology in Our World section focuses on the urgency of appropriately responding to the opioid crisis. In the "Human Development" chapter, the Psychology in Our World feature reviews the changing landscape of gender identities. Psychology in Our World seeks to open the students' eyes to the presence of psychological science all around us.

In addition, the **Psychological Inquiry** features draw students into analyzing and interpreting figures and photos by embedding a range of critical thinking questions within the caption.

FIGURE 12 **The Brain in Different Species** This figure compares the brain of a rat, a cat, a chimpanzee, and a human being. As you examine the illustrations, remember that each organism's brain is adapted to meet different environmental challenges.
> What structures are similar across the species? > Why do you think there are some common features, and what does this commonality tell us about these brain structures? > Why don't rats have a large cerebral cortex? > How might life be different for a rat or a cat with a human brain?

Do It!

Go on a caffeine hunt. Check out the ingredient lists on your favorite beverages, snacks, and painkillers. Which of these contain caffeine? You might be surprised by how much caffeine you consume every day without even knowing it.

Experience Active Engagement

Experience Psychology offers several ways to actively engage with the course content. Through **Do It!,** a series of brief, recurring sidebar activities linked to the text reading, students get an opportunity to test their assumptions and learn through hands-on exploration and discovery. Reinforcing that the science of psychology requires active participation, Do It! selections include, for example, an exercise on conducting an informal survey to observe and classify behaviors in a public setting, as well as an activity guiding students on how to research a "happiness gene." Such exercises provide vibrant and involving experiences that get students thinking like psychologists.

McGraw-Hill Connect offers several ways to actively engage students. New to the fourth edition, **Power of Process** guides students through the process of critical reading and analysis. Faculty can select or upload content, such as journal articles, and assign guiding questions to gain insight into students' understanding of the scientific method while helping them improve upon their information literacy skills.

Concept Clips help students comprehend some of the most difficult ideas in introductory psychology. Colorful graphics and stimulating animations describe core concepts in

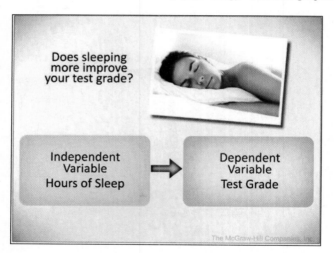

a step-by-step manner, engaging students and aiding in retention. Concept Clips can be used as a presentation tool in the classroom or for student assessment. New in the fourth edition, Concept Clips are embedded in the ebook to offer an alternative presentation of these challenging topics.

Interactivities engage students with content through experiential activities. New and updated activities include: Perspectives in Psychology; Correlations; Neurons; The Brain and Drugs; The Stages of Sleep; Levels of Processing; Maslow's Hierarchy of Needs; Naturalistic Observation; Observational Learning; Defense Mechanisms, Stereotypes and Prejudice, Heuristics, Personality Assessment, and First Impressions and Attraction.

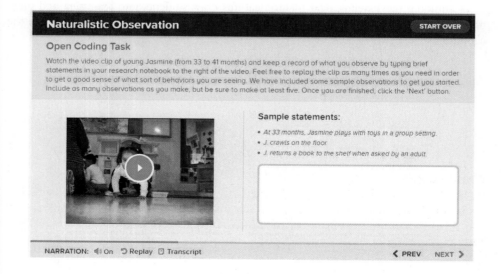

Through the connection of psychology to students' own lives, concepts become more relevant and understandable. **NewsFlash** exercises tie current news stories to key psychological principles and learning objectives. After interacting with a contemporary news story, students are assessed on their ability to make the link between real life and research findings.

At the Apply and Analyze levels of Bloom's taxonomy, **Scientific Reasoning Activities** found in Connect offer in-depth arguments to sharpen students' critical thinking skills and prepare them to be more discerning consumers of psychology in their everyday lives. For each chapter, there are multiple sets of arguments accompanied by auto-graded assessments requiring students to think critically about claims presented as facts. These exercises can also be used in Connect as group activities or for discussion.

New in this edition, **brain and nervous system "tours"** are embedded in the ebooks to encourage learners to engage with key structures. These tours provide students with practice in grasping key biological structures and processes that are essential to an appreciation of the role of science in psychology and success in the course. The digital tours are also available in the instructor's materials to be used as presentation resources.

Psychology at Work videos, assignable and assessable within McGraw-Hill Connect, highlight careers in which knowledge of psychology is beneficial in the workplace. Each video introduces a person at work, who specifies how knowledge gained from taking introductory psychology in college is applied to the work environment.

Experience the Course You Want to Teach

SUPPORTING INSTRUCTORS WITH TECHNOLOGY
With McGraw-Hill Education, you can develop and tailor the course you want to teach.

 McGraw-Hill Campus (www.mhcampus.com) provides faculty with true single sign-on access to all of McGraw-Hill's course content, digital tools, and other high-quality learning resources from any learning management system. McGraw-Hill Campus includes access to McGraw-Hill's entire content library, including eBooks, assessment tools, presentation slides, and multimedia content, among other resources, providing faculty open, unlimited access to prepare for class, create tests/quizzes, develop lecture material, integrate interactive content, and more.

With **Tegrity,** you can capture lessons and lectures in a searchable format and use them in traditional, hybrid, "flipped classes," and online courses. With Tegrity's personalized learning features, you can make study time efficient. Its ability to affordably scale brings this benefit to every student on campus. Patented search technology and real-time learning management system (LMS) integrations make Tegrity the market-leading solution and service.

With McGraw-Hill Education's **Create**, faculty can easily rearrange chapters, combine material from other content sources, and quickly upload content you have written, such as your course syllabus or teaching notes, using McGraw-Hill Education's **Create.** Find the content you need by searching through thousands of leading McGraw-Hill Education textbooks. Arrange your book to fit your teaching style. Create even allows you to personalize your book's appearance by selecting the cover and adding your name, school, and course information. Order a Create book, and you will receive a complimentary print review copy in three to five business days or a complimentary electronic review copy via email in about an hour. Experience how McGraw-Hill Education empowers you to teach *your* students *your* way. **http://create.mheducation.com**

TRUSTED SERVICE AND SUPPORT
McGraw-Hill Education's Connect offers comprehensive service, support, and training throughout every phase of your implementation. If you're looking for some guidance on how to use Connect, or want to learn tips and tricks from super users, you can find tutorials as you work. Our Digital Faculty Consultants and Student Ambassadors offer insight into how to achieve the results you want with Connect.

INTEGRATION WITH YOUR LEARNING MANAGEMENT SYSTEM

McGraw-Hill integrates your digital products from McGraw-Hill Education with your school LMS for quick and easy access to best-in-class content and learning tools. Build an effective digital course, enroll students with ease and discover how powerful digital teaching can be.

Available with Connect, integration is a pairing between an institution's learning management system (LMS) and Connect at the assignment level. It shares assignment information, grades and calendar items from Connect into the LMS automatically, creating an easy to manage course for instructors and simple navigation for students. Our assignment-level integration is available with **Blackboard Learn, Canvas by Instructure,** and **Brightspace by D2L,** giving you access to registration, attendance, assignments, grades, and course resources in real time, in one location.

Instructor Supplements

Instructor's Manual The instructor's manual provides a wide variety of tools and resources for presenting the course, including learning objectives and ideas for lectures and discussions.

Test Bank By increasing the rigor of the test bank development process, McGraw-Hill Education has raised the bar for student assessment. A coordinated team of subject-matter experts methodically vetted each question and set of possible answers for accuracy, clarity, effectiveness, and accessibility; each question has been annotated for level of difficulty, Bloom's taxonomy, APA learning outcomes, and corresponding coverage in the text. Organized by chapter, the questions are designed to test factual, conceptual, and applied understanding. All test questions are available within TestGen™ software and as Word documents.

PowerPoint Presentations The PowerPoint presentations, available in both dynamic, lecture-ready and accessible, WCAG-compliant versions, highlight the key points of the chapter and include supporting visuals. All of the slides can be modified to meet individual needs.

Image Gallery The Image Gallery features the complete set of downloadable figures and tables from the text. These can be easily embedded by instructors into their own PowerPoint slides.

Chapter-by-Chapter Changes

All chapters are updated with current research and data, when available. The author utilized anonymous data from SmartBook to pinpoint "hotspots" where learners struggled with particular content and revised content with this in mind.

CHAPTER 1: THE SCIENCE OF PSYCHOLOGY

- New opening vignette: Unlocking the Secret of Heroism
- New Intersection on why we mature
- Expanded treatment of replication
- New treatment of the Replication Crisis
- New research example of Demand Characteristics
- New Challenge Your Thinking on authenticity in social media

CHAPTER 2: THE BRAIN AND BEHAVIOR

■ New opening vignette: The Empathic Brain

■ New research example of managerial experience and brain structure and function

■ New Intersection: Neuroscience and Environmental Psychology: How Does Spending Time in Nature Affect the Brain?

■ Expanded coverage of acetylcholine, glutamate, and oxytocin

■ Updated treatment of neurogenesis

■ New Challenge Your Thinking: Could Neuroscience Help Identify the Right Brain for the Job?

■ Updated Psychology in Our World: Protecting the Athlete's Brain

■ New discussion of challenges of genome wide associations and linkage studies

CHAPTER 3: SENSATION AND PERCEPTION

■ New opening vignette: Those Potato Chips Sound Delicious

■ Further differentiation between sensation and perception

■ New discussion and example of the Influences of Top-Down Expectations, including research on how people miss "gigantic" objects

■ New Challenge Your Thinking: Why Does a Cell Phone Look Like a Gun?

■ New research discussion of biological responses to information presented outside of awareness and priming

■ New detail on Feature Detectors

■ New example of Binding

■ New Intersection: Sensation and Social Psychology: Why Do Some People Literally Feel What Others Feel? reviewing mirror-touch synaesthesia

■ Updated research discussion on gender differences in pain perception

CHAPTER 4: STATE OF CONSCIOUSNESS

■ Updated opening vignette: When the Human Mind is a Buried Treasure

■ New discussion of Brain Wandering and the Default Mode Network

■ New Challenge Your Thinking: Are There Benefits to Mind Wandering?

■ Updated naming of the sleep stages (W, N1, N2, N3, R)

■ New information about GABA's role in sleep

■ New Intersection: Sleep and Neuroscience: Does Sleep Deprivation Affect Neurons?

■ Updated and expanded treatment of opioids (including fentanyl)

■ New Psychology in Our World: Responding to the Opioid Crisis

CHAPTER 5: LEARNING

■ New opening vignette: Frida: Labrador and Life Saver

■ New discussion of classical conditioning and mindless habitual behavior

■ New Intersection: Learning and Health Psychology: Can Classical Conditioning Help Combat Obesity?

- Revised presentation of Timing and Consequences of Behavior (operant conditioning)
- New example of observational learning
- Revised and updated Challenge Your Thinking: Do Learning Styles Matter to Learning?

CHAPTER 6: MEMORY

- New opening vignette: The Ubiquitous Selfie, Memory, and Meaning
- New Intersection: Cognitive Psychology and Developmental Psychology: How Does Reminiscing Affect Our Relationships and Our Development?
- New coverage of Executive Attention
- New Challenge Your Thinking: Why Is the Pen Mightier Than the Keyboard?
- Replaced priming examples from studies that have not replicated

CHAPTER 7: THINKING, INTELLIGENCE, AND LANGUAGE

- Updated opening vignette: The Value of a Really Good Idea
- New Intersection: Cognitive and Health Psychology: Does thinking fast relate to living longer?
- New research example of "intelligence" genes
- New example of delayed language exposure
- New coverage of socioeconomic status and language development
- New Challenge Your Thinking: Can Reducing the "Word Gap" Lead to Better Outcomes for Disadvantaged Children?

CHAPTER 8: HUMAN DEVELOPMENT

- New opening vignette: The You You Used to Be
- Expanded discussion of pruning
- New research example of telomere length and stress
- New section on the Information Processing Approach to Cognitive Development
- New Intersection: Developmental Psychology and Cognitive Psychology: Do children engage in wishful thinking?
- New research example of cross-cultural parenting styles
- New extended example of Marcia's identity statuses theory
- New discuss sexual and gender minority youth and bullying
- New coverage of Gender Identity and Sexual Orientation in the context of gender development
- New Psychology in Our World: Human Identities and the Changing Gender Landscape
- New coverage of children and prosocial behavior
- New Challenge Your Thinking: Are children natural helpers?

CHAPTER 9: MOTIVATION AND EMOTION

- New opening vignette: What Would You Do If You Won the Lottery?
- New example of social context and eating

- New coverage of Mindless Eating

- New Psychology in Our World: What's on the Menu and Why It Matters

- Revised coverage of Sex Education

- New information on frequency of sexual behavior

- Updated coverage of biological factors and same sex attraction

- New examples of Self-Determination Theory

- New Challenge Your Thinking: Can Watching TV Shows Contribute to Optimal Well-Being?

- New research example of association between intrinsic and extrinsic motivation, and work factors

- New Intersection: Motivation and Neuroscience: Can We See Intrinsic Motivation in the Brain?

- Replaced suspect research by Wansink with more rigorous findings from other investigators

CHAPTER 10: PERSONALITY

- New opening vignette: "So much time has passed but it hasn't changed a thing"

- New discussion of Reaction Formation

- New Psychology in Our World: What's Your Type?

- Revised and updated descriptions of the Big Five Factors of Personality

- New Intersection: Personality and Sleep Science: Are You a Morning Person or an Evening Person and Does It Matter?

- Revised section on the Study of Traits in Animals

- New review of links between neuroticism and the HPA axis

- Expanded coverage of Personality Neuroscience

- New coverage of neuroticism and avoiding punishment

- Updated coverage of the TAT

CHAPTER 11: SOCIAL PSYCHOLOGY

- New opening vignette: Can one hour change a life?

- Integration of Social Neuroscience throughout Social Cognition section

- New research example of Person Perception

- New coverage of the role of the brain in first impressions

- New research example of physical attractiveness and achievement

- New research example of Self-Fulfilling Prophecy

- New expanded example of how social perceivers treat attractive people

- New Challenge Your Thinking: Do We Look Like Our Names?

- Expanded coverage of stereotypes

- New coverage of the brain and fundamental attribution error

- New coverage of the brain and cognitive dissonance

- Expanded coverage of Resisting Persuasion

- Expanded discussion of video games and aggression

- Expanded coverage of long-term relationships

- New example of Group Influence

- New research findings of Ingroup Favoritism in Infants and Children

- New coverage of Discrimination and Health Disparities

- Intersection: Social Psychology and Health Psychology: What Is the Physical and Psychological Cost of Prejudice and Discrimination?

- New section on Breaking the Prejudice Habit

CHAPTER 12: PSYCHOLOGICAL DISORDERS

- New opening vignette: Making castles from life's stones

- New coverage of definitions of risk factors and comorbidity

- New major section, Neurodevelopmental Disorders, covering ASD and ADHD

- New Challenge Your Thinking: Can Adults Develop ADHD?

- New Intersection: Clinical Psychology and Cognitive Psychology: How Does PTSD Affect Autobiographical Memory?

- New Psychology in Our World: Sexual Victimization on Campus

- Expanded coverage of GAD and the brain

- New coverage of Social Anxiety and Beliefs about Social Failure

- Coverage of PTSD and Dissociative Disorders moved to Trauma and Stress-Related Disorders section

- New coverage of brain structure and schizophrenia

- Updated suicide coverage with more appropriate less stigmatizing language

- New, brief, overviews of treatments for most disorders

- New advice for talking to a friend with a psychological disorder

CHAPTER 13: THERAPIES

- New opening vignette: The Immense, Invisible Burden of Secrets

- New Intersection: Clinical Psychology and Social Psychology: Can Authentic Interactions Help Those with Social Anxiety?

- New research example of the effectiveness of Neuroleptics

- New coverage of Transcranial Stimulation

CHAPTER 14: HEALTH PSYCHOLOGY

- New opening vignette: The importance of listening to your body

- New coverage of Social Support

- New coverage of the role of physical activity in longevity

- New Intersection: Health Psychology and Emotion: How Do Negative Feelings Fit in the Healthy Life?

acknowledgments

The quality of *Experience Psychology* is a testament to the skills and abilities of so many people, and I am tremendously grateful to the following individuals for their insightful contributions during the project's development.

Anthony Adamopoulos, *Missouri Southern State University*

Kathryn Alves-Labore, *Forsyth Technical Community College*

Jeff Anderson, *Oklahoma City Community College*

Renee Babcock, *Central Michigan University*

Marina Baratian, *Eastern Florida State College–Melbourne*

Pam Bradley, *Sandhills Community College*

Nicole Brandt, *Columbus State Community College*

Amy Buckingham, *Red Rocks Community College*

Kevin Burns, *Shelton State Community College*

Cindy Campbell, *Ivy Tech Community College of Indiana–Indianapolis*

Bernice Carson, *Virginia State University*

Myra Cox, *Harold Washington College*

Patricia Crowe-Rubino, *Hawkeye Community College*

Sara Dolan, *Baylor University*

Lauren Doninger, *Gateway Community College*

Sundi Donovan, *Liberty University*

Jennifer Ducz, *College of Staten Island*

Laura Edwards, *Ivy Tech Community College of Indiana–Indianapolis*

Celeste Favela, *El Paso Community College, Valle Verde*

Desi Franks, *Northeast Wisconsin Tech, Green Bay*

Linda Freeman, *Valencia College East*

Janice Frum, *Columbus State Community College*

Nathan Gandy, *Crowder College*

Drew Gleitsmann, *Ivy Tech Community College of Indiana–Indianapolis*

Jeff Green, *Virginia Commonwealth University*

Mark Healy, *De Anza College*

Brett Heintz, *Delgado Community College, City Park*

Debora Herold, *Indiana University, Purdue University Indianapolis*

Carmon Weaver Hicks, *Ivy Tech Community College of Indiana–Indianapolis*

Zachary Hohman, *Texas Tech University*

Rebecca Howell, *Forsyth Technical Community College*

Sandra Hunt, *College of Staten Island*

Michael James, *Ivy Tech Community College of Indiana–Bloomington*

Yuthika Kim, *Oklahoma City Community College*

Kristin Kwasny, *Sinclair Community College*

Claudia Lampman, *University of Alaska, Anchorage*

Lee Ann Lucas, *Sinclair Community College*

Theresa Luhrs, *DePaul University*

Shawn Matthews, *Forsyth Technical Community College*

Donna Marie McElroy, *Atlantic Cape Community College*

Hayley Nelson, *Delaware County Community College*

Tori Norris, *Calhoun Community College, Tanner*

Andrew Pollack, *Brookdale Community College*

Michael Poulakis, *Ivy Tech Community College of Indiana–Indianapolis*

Diana Powers Willard, *Iowa Central Community College*

Cynthia Rickert, *Ivy Tech Community College of Indiana–Indianapolis*

Shelly Rogers-Sharer, *McClennan Community College*

Lauren Ruffin, *Mott Community College*

Carlos Sandoval, *Cypress College*

Amy Skinner, *Shelton State Community College*

Stephanie Smith, *Indiana University Northwest, Gary*

Emily Stark, *Minnesota State University, Mankato*

Margaret Staton, *Valencia College East*

Marla Sturm, *Montgomery County Community College*

Laura Talcott, *Indiana University, South Bend*

Kenneth Texeira, *Quincy College at Plymouth*

Lora Vasiliauskas, *Virginia Western Community College*

Peter Vishton, *College of William & Mary*

Jennifer Wentz, *Leigh Carbon Community College*

Samantha Wolfe, *Grand Rapids Community College*

Virginia Wood, *Kennesaw State University*

James Wright, *Forsyth Technical Community College*

Brandy Young, *Cypress College*

Personal Acknowledgments

Returning to *Experience Psychology* for this fourth edition has been quite an adventure. I very much appreciate all those at McGraw-Hill Education who brought their characteristic levels of innovation, enthusiasm, and encouragement to bear. I especially wish to thank Cara Labell for her efforts in conveying the information from LearnSmart heat maps to inform this revision, making it as responsive to students' needs as possible. A very special thank you as well to Margaret Haywood whose painstaking copyediting was invaluable and whose hard work made a difficult year much easier; and to Sandy Wille and Matt Backhaus who, respectively, managed the production process and design development with expertise. Thanks as well to Christopher Greene for his outstanding proofreading.

A special thanks goes out to the many students and faculty I visited around the country the last few years. Those visits were rejuvenating and stimulating. It meant so much to me to have students come up, take selfies with me, and chat about psychology. I treasure the times I have heard you say, "You sound just like you do in the book!" That's what *Experience Psychology* is all about, and nothing could be more gratifying. It has been an honor to share your introductory psychology experiences with you. Thanks to Nancy Welcher, A. J. Laferrera, and Ann Helgerson for finding innovative ways for me to reach out to faculty and students, whether in person or through technology.

Thanks to my colleagues at the University of Missouri, for their enthusiasm, advice, patience, and support. I owe special debts of gratitude to Sarah Ward, Jake Womick, and Chris Sanders, my graduate students, who have patiently endured having an advisor who is often very busy while generating their own very exciting scholarship. A heartfelt thank-you goes to my family and friends who have supported and inspired me, especially Lisa and Sam.

In closing, I acknowledge a mother who reached out to me last year. One of her sons died by suicide and the other happened to be taking a course that used *Experience Psychology*. With great courage, she sent me an email respectfully pointing out that the language in the treatment of suicide was outdated and problematic. She kindly offered guidance on a better way. Thank you so much, Christine.

1 The Science of Psychology

Unlocking the Secrets of Heroism

n every life there are turning points: Moments when everything hinges on a single, crucial choice. On May 27, 2017, three men on a Portland, Oregon, train faced such a moment. Like others on the train, they witnessed a man harassing two teenaged girls, one of whom was wearing a hijab, a traditional veil worn by many Muslim women. The man was berating the women because of their religious faith (Flaccus, 2017). Unlike the other passengers, these three men took action, placing themselves between the attacker and his victims. The attacker had a knife and killed two of the men, leaving the third seriously injured (Zarkhin, 2017).

How can we understand such heroic action? These three men were very different from each other. Ricky John Best, who died at the scene, was a 53-year-old army veteran and city employee. Taliesin Myrddin Namkai Meche, who died later at a hospital, was just 23 and a recent college graduate. Finally, Micah David-Cole Fletcher, the sole surviving hero, was 21, a college student and a poet whose work protested bigotry (Zarkhin, 2017). All three of these men took action when others stood by. They were heroes, risking their very lives for the well-being of strangers.

Reflecting on this incident, many questions pop to mind. How can we understand such courageous action? How can we understand the behavior of those who did not intervene? What motivated the attacker to harass the young women, eventually turning his hatred toward the defenders? These are the kinds of questions psychologists might ask about this remarkable heroism.

Although psychologists are interested in extraordinary moments like this one, they are also interested in everyday experiences. The science of psychology is about *all* human behavior. In fact, ordinary human behavior can become extraordinary when viewed in the right light, with a close lens. Psychologists are scientists who look at the world with just such a lens. Right now, thousands of dedicated scientists are studying things about you that you might have never considered, like how your eyes adjust to a sunny day or how your brain registers the face of a friend. There is not a single thing people do that is not fascinating to some psychologist somewhere.

This chapter begins by defining psychology and reviewing the history of the field. Next we survey seven broad approaches that characterize psychological science today. Then, in sequence, we examine the elements of the scientific method, review the different kinds of research psychologists do, and consider the importance of conducting psychological research according to ethical guidelines. We conclude with a look at applications of psychology to daily life—a central focus of *Experience Psychology*.

1 Defining Psychology and Exploring Its Roots

What is your definition of psychology? When you think of the word psychology, what first comes to mind?

Formally defined, **psychology** is the scientific study of behavior and mental processes. Let's consider the three key terms in this definition: *science, behavior*, and *mental processes*.

As a **science,** psychology uses systematic methods to observe human behavior and draw conclusions. The goals of psychological science are to describe, predict, and explain behavior. In addition, psychologists are often interested in controlling or changing behavior, and they use scientific methods to examine interventions that might, for example, help to reduce violence or promote happiness.

Researchers might be interested in knowing whether individuals will help a stranger who has fallen down. The researchers could devise a study in which they observe people walking past a person who needs help. Through many observations, the researchers could come to *describe* helping behavior by counting how many times it occurs in particular circumstances. They might also try to *predict* who will help, and when, by examining characteristics of the individuals studied. Are happy people more likely to help? Are women or men more likely to help? After the psychologists have analyzed their data, they also will want to *explain* why helping behavior occurred when it did. Finally, they might be interested in changing helping behavior, such as by devising strategies to increase helping.

Behavior is everything we do that can be directly observed—two people kissing, a baby crying, a college student riding a motorcycle to campus. **Mental processes** are the thoughts, feelings, and motives that each of us experiences privately but that cannot be observed

psychology
The scientific study of behavior and mental processes.

science
The use of systematic methods to observe the natural world, including human behavior, and to draw conclusions.

mental processes
The thoughts, feelings, and motives that people experience privately but that cannot be observed directly.

behavior
Everything we do that can be directly observed.

Behavior includes the observable act of two people kissing; mental processes include their unobservable thoughts about kissing.
©Visual Ideas/Nora Pelaez/Blend Images/Getty Images Plus

directly. Although we cannot directly see thoughts and feelings, they are nonetheless real. They include *thinking* about kissing someone, a baby's *feelings* when its mother leaves the room, and a student's *memory* of a motorcycle trip.

The Psychological Frame of Mind

What makes for a good job, a good marriage, or a good life? Psychologists approach these big life questions as scientists. Psychology is a rigorous discipline that tests assumptions, bringing scientific data to bear on the questions of central interest to human beings (Leavy, 2017; Passer, 2017). Psychologists conduct research and rely on that research to provide evidence for their conclusions. They examine the available evidence about some aspect of mind and behavior, evaluate how strongly the data (information) support their hunches, analyze disconfirming evidence, and carefully consider whether they have explored all possible factors and explanations. At the core of this scientific approach are four attitudes*: critical thinking, curiosity, skepticism,* and *objectivity.*

critical thinking
The process of thinking deeply and actively, asking questions, and evaluating the evidence.

Like all scientists, psychologists are *critical thinkers.* **Critical thinking** is the process of thinking deeply and actively, asking questions, and evaluating the evidence (Lack & Rousseau, 2016; Stanovich, 2013). Critical thinkers question and test what some people say are facts. They examine research to see how soundly it supports an idea (Passer, 2017). Critical thinking reduces the likelihood that conclusions will be based on unreliable personal beliefs, opinions, and emotions. Critical thinking also comes into play when scientists consider the conclusions they draw from research. As critical thinkers who are open to new information, scientists must tolerate uncertainty, knowing that even long-held views are subject to revision.

Critical thinking is very important as you read *Experience Psychology.* Some of what you read might fit with your beliefs, and some might challenge you to change or reconsider them. Actively engaging in critical thinking is vital to making the most of psychology. As you study the field, think about how what you are learning relates to your life experiences and your assumptions about human behavior.

Scientists are also *curious.* The scientist notices things in the world (a star in the sky, an insect, a happy person) and wants to know what it is and why it is that way. Science involves asking questions, even very big questions such as where did the earth come from, and how does love between two people endure for 50 years? Thinking like a psychologist means opening your mind and imagination to wondering why things are the way they are.

In addition, scientists are *skeptical.* Skeptical people challenge whether a supposed fact is really true. Being skeptical can mean questioning what "everybody knows." There was a time when "everybody knew" that women were morally inferior to men, that race could influence a person's IQ, and that the earth was flat. Psychologists, like all scientists, look at assumptions in new and questioning ways. Psychology is different from common sense because psychologists are skeptical of commonsensical answers.

Psychological research often turns up the unexpected in human behavior. Such results are called *counterintuitive* because they contradict our intuitive impressions of how the world works. To get a sense of what counterintuitive means, consider the saying, "Work before pleasure." Many people believe that it is best to get work done prior to engaging in leisure activities. Ask yourself, would you rather enjoy a relaxing trip to a spa before midterm exams or after them? Many people think that the spa will be less enjoyable if you know you have exams "hanging over your head." Does unfinished work detract from our enjoyment of pleasurable activities? Recently, researchers sought to answer this question. First, they conducted a number of studies showing that, indeed, people generally believe that a fun activity will be less fun if there is work waiting to be done (O'Brien & Roney, 2017). That means that "intuitively," people believe that having work waiting to do will spoil pleasant experiences. Second, in a series of clever experiments they compared groups of people who either predicted how much fun they would have at a pleasurable experience (such as spending time in a spa they set up in their lab) or actually had the experience, either before or after they completed a task

*You might be wondering about the names and dates in parentheses. They are **research citations** that identify the authors of particular studies and the year each study was published. If you see an especially interesting study, you might look it up in the References at the end of the chapter and check it out online or in your school's library.*

involving hard work (such as midterm exams). The results showed that although people believed that having work hanging over their heads would spoil a good time, in fact it did not. The "experiencers" enjoyed the fun experience just as much even when there was still working hanging over their heads (O'Brien & Roney, 2017). This set of studies shows how sometimes our intuitions can be mistaken. Knowing if what we think we know is true requires scientific evidence.

Last, practicing science also means being *objective*. Being objective involves trying to see things as they really are, not just as the observer would like them to be. Scientific knowledge ultimately is based on objective evidence. It also means that sometimes knowledge changes in the face of new evidence. Thinking like a scientist means being open to that new evidence even when it challenges our assumptions.

To gather objective evidence, scientists rely on empirical methods. The **empirical method** involves gaining knowledge by observing events, collecting data, and reasoning logically. For scientists, objectivity means waiting to see what the evidence tells them rather than going with their hunches. Does the latest herbal dietary supplement really help relieve depression? A scientist would say, "That's an empirical question," meaning that hard evidence is required to answer it. An objective thinker insists on sound evidence before drawing conclusions. Like critical thinking, relying on evidence to provide the foundation for conclusions means being open to uncertainty. Empirical evidence provides the best answers to questions at any given moment.

This is why researchers often say that a study 'supports' a particular prediction, but rarely if ever say that it 'proves' anything.

empirical method Gaining knowledge through the observation of events, the collection of data, and logical reasoning.

Once you start to think like a psychologist, the world begins to look like a different place. Easy answers and simple assumptions will not do. As you can probably imagine, psychologists, as a group, are people with many different opinions about many different things. If a number of these critical thinkers were to gather around a table, it is a safe bet that they would have a lively conversation.

Indeed, as you will see throughout *Experience Psychology,* there are many things about which psychologists disagree, and psychology, like any science, is filled with debate and controversy. We will address many of these controversies in sections called *Challenge Your Thinking.* Each of these boxes will give you a chance to think critically about a topic.

So, debate and controversy are a natural part of thinking like a psychologist. Psychology has advanced as a field because psychologists do not always agree with one another about why mind and behavior work the way they do. Psychologists have reached a more accurate understanding of human behavior because psychology fosters controversies and because psychologists think deeply and reflectively and examine the evidence on all sides. A good place to try out your critical thinking skills is by revisiting the definition of psychology.

Psychology as the Science of All Human Behavior

As you consider the general definition of psychology as the science of human behavior, you might be thinking, okay, where's the couch? Where's the mental illness? Psychology certainly includes the study of therapy and psychological disorders. Clinical psychologists are psychologists who specialize in studying and treating psychological disorders. By definition, though, psychology is a much more general science (Leavy, 2017; Woody & Viney, 2017), practiced in several environments in addition to clinical settings (Figure 1). In fact, the most common place to find psychologists is in academic settings (colleges or universities). How did we end up with the idea that psychology is only about mental illness? Surely, psychological disorders are very interesting, and the media often portray psychologists as therapists. Yet the view of psychology as the science of what is wrong with people started long before TV was even invented.

When they think of psychology, many people think of Sigmund Freud (1856–1939). Freud believed that most of human behavior is caused by dark, unpleasant, unconscious impulses pressing for expression. For Freud, even the average person on the street is a mysterious well of unconscious desires. Certainly, Freud has had a lasting impact on

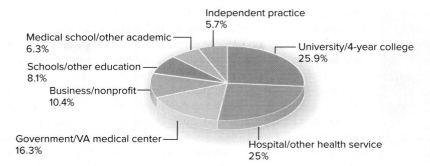

FIGURE 1 **Settings in Which Psychologists Work** This figure shows where individuals who have recent Ph.D.s in psychology work. As you can see, many are employed in higher education and medical contexts.

SOURCE: Adapted from D. Michalski, J. Kohout, M. Wicherski, & B. Hart (2011), 2009 Doctorate Employment Survey (Table 3).

psychology and on society. Consider, though, that Freud based his ideas about human nature on the patients he saw in his clinical practice—individuals who were struggling with psychological problems. His experiences with these patients, as well as his analysis of himself, colored his outlook on all of humanity. Freud once wrote, "I have found little that is 'good' about human beings on the whole. In my experience most of them are trash" (1918/1996).

You have probably heard of a 'Freudian slip.' Freud's name has become part of our everyday language.

Freud's view of human nature has crept into general perceptions of what psychology is all about. Imagine, for example, that you are seated on a plane, having a pleasant conversation with the woman, a stranger, sitting next to you. At some point you ask your seatmate what she does for a living, and she informs you she is a psychologist. You might think to yourself, "Uh oh. What have I already told this person? What secrets does she know about me that I don't know about myself? Has she been analyzing me this whole time?" Would you be surprised to discover that this psychologist studies happiness? Or intelligence? Or the processes related to the experience of vision? The study of psychological disorders is a very important aspect of psychology, but it represents only one part of the science of psychology.

Psychology seeks to understand the truths of human life in *all* its dimensions, including people's best and worst experiences, and everything in between. Research on the human capacity for forgiveness demonstrates this point (Balliet, Li, & Joireman, 2011; Costa & Neves, 2017; Harper & others, 2014; McCullough, Kurzban, & Tabak, 2011, 2013). Forgiveness is the act of letting go of anger and resentment toward someone who has done something harmful to us. Through forgiveness we cease seeking revenge or avoiding the person who did us harm, and we might even wish that person well (Lin & others, 2014; Tuck & Anderson, 2014).

In October 2006, after Charles Carl Roberts took 10 young Amish girls hostage in a one-room schoolhouse in Pennsylvania, eventually killing 5 of them and wounding 5 others before killing himself, the grief-stricken Amish community focused not on hatred and revenge but on forgiveness. As funds were being set up for the victims' families, the Amish insisted on establishing one for the murderer's family. They prepared simple funerals for the dead girls, and the community invited the killer's wife to attend. The science of psychology has much to offer to our understanding not only of the violent acts of the perpetrator but also of the forgiveness by the victims.

The willingness of these Amish people to forgive this horrible crime is both remarkable and puzzling. Can we scientifically understand the human ability to forgive even what might seem to be unforgivable? A number of psychologists have taken up the topic of forgiveness in research and clinical practice (Costa & Neves, 2017; Lander, 2016; Worthington & others, 2011). Michael McCullough and his colleagues (McCullough & others, 2010) have shown that the capacity to forgive is an unfolding process that often takes time. For the Amish, their deep religious faith led them to embrace forgiveness, while many others might have been motivated to seek revenge and retribution. Researchers also have explored the cognitive skills required for forgiveness (Pronk & others, 2010; van der

The murder in 2006 of five Amish schoolgirls evoked feelings in the community not of hatred and revenge but of forgiveness.
©Matthew Cavanaugh/EPA/REX/Shutterstock

Wal, Karremans, & Cillessen, 2014), the benefits of forgiving oneself (Peterson & others, 2017), and even the potential dark side of forgiveness, which might emerge, for example, when forgiveness leads an abusive spouse to feel free to continue a harmful behavior (McNulty, 2011; McNulty & Russell, 2016).

Some psychologists argue that the field has focused too much on the negative aspects of humanity and neglected topics that reflect the best of human life (Johnson & Wood, 2017; Seligman, 2016; Seligman & Csikszentmihalyi, 2000). Others insist that psychology would benefit more from studying human weaknesses (Lazarus, 2003). The fact is that to be a truly general science of human behavior, psychology must address all sides of human experience. Surely, controversy is a part of any science. Healthy debate characterizes the field of psychology, and a new psychological perspective sometimes arises when one scientist questions the views of another. Such ongoing debate is a sign of a lively discipline. Indeed, the very birth of the field was marked by debate. Great minds do not always think alike, especially when they are thinking about psychology.

Psychology in Historical Perspective

Psychology seeks to answer questions that people have been asking for thousands of years—for example:

- How do we learn?
- What is memory?
- Why does one person grow and flourish while another struggles?

The notion that such questions might be answered through scientific inquiry is relatively new. From the time human language included the word *why* and became rich enough to let people talk about the past, we have been creating myths to explain why things are the way they are. Ancient myths attributed most important events to the pleasure or displeasure of the gods: When a volcano erupted, the gods were angry; if two people fell in love, they had been struck by Cupid's arrows. Gradually, myths gave way to *philosophy*—the rational investigation of the underlying principles of being and knowledge. People attempted to explain events in terms of natural rather than supernatural causes.

Western philosophy came of age in ancient Greece in the fourth and fifth centuries B.C.E. Socrates, Plato, Aristotle, and others debated the nature of thought and behavior, including the possible link between the mind and the body. Later philosophers, especially

Wilhelm Wundt (1832–1920)
Wundt founded the first psychology laboratory (with his two coworkers) in 1879 at the University of Leipzig in Germany.
©bilwissedition/imageBROKER/REX/Shutterstock

René Descartes, argued that the mind and body were completely separate, and they focused their attention on the mind. Psychology grew out of this tradition of thinking about the mind and body. The influence of philosophy on contemporary psychology persists today, as researchers who study emotion still talk about Descartes, and scientists who study happiness often refer to Aristotle (Synard & Gazzola, 2017; Ward & King, 2016).

In addition to philosophy, psychology has roots in the natural sciences of biology and physiology (Schultz & Schultz, 2016; Woody & Viney, 2017). Indeed, it was Wilhelm Wundt (1832–1920), a German philosopher-physician, who put together the pieces of the philosophy–natural science puzzle to create the academic discipline of psychology. Some historians like to say that modern psychology was born in December 1879 at the University of Leipzig, when Wundt and his students (most notably E. B. Titchener) performed an experiment to measure the time lag between the instant a person heard a sound and when that person pressed a telegraph key to signal that he had heard it.

What was so special about this experiment? Wundt's study was about the workings of the brain: He was trying to measure the time it took the human brain and nervous system to translate information into action. At the heart of this experiment was the idea that mental processes could be measured. This focus ushered in the new science of psychology.

Wundt and his collaborators concentrated on discovering the basic elements, or "structures," of mental processes. Their approach was called **structuralism** because of its focus on identifying the elemental parts or structures of the human mind. The method they used in the study of mental structures was *introspection,* which literally means "looking inside." You have likely engaged in introspection when you have thought deeply about your feelings or have sought to quietly monitor your own responses to some event. For Wundt's introspection research, a person sat in a laboratory and was asked to think (to introspect) about what was going on mentally as various events took place. For example, the individual might be subjected to a sharp, repetitive clicking sound and then might be asked to report whatever conscious feelings the clicking produced. What made this method scientific was the systematic, detailed self-reports required of the person in the controlled laboratory setting.

Although Wundt is most often regarded as the founding father of modern psychology, it was psychologist and philosopher William James (1842–1910), perhaps more than anyone else, who gave the field an American stamp. From James's perspective, the key question for psychology is not so much what the mind is (that is, its structures) as what it is for (its purpose or function). James's view was eventually named *functionalism.*

Structuralism emphasized the components of the mind. In contrast, **functionalism** probed the functions or purposes of the mind and behavior in the individual's adaptation to the environment. Whereas structuralists were looking inside the mind and searching for its structures, functionalists focused on human interactions with the outside world to understand the purpose of thoughts. If structuralism is about the "what" of the mind, functionalism is about the "why."

A central question in functionalism is, why is human thought *adaptive?* When we talk about whether a characteristic is adaptive, we are concerned with how it makes an organism better able to survive. So, the functionalist asks, why are people better off because they can think than they would be otherwise? Unlike Wundt, James did not believe in the existence of rigid structures of the mind. Instead, James saw the mind as flexible and fluid, characterized by constant change in response to a continuous flow of information from the world. Not surprisingly, James called the natural flow of thought a "stream of consciousness."

Functionalism fit well with the theory of evolution through natural selection proposed by British naturalist Charles Darwin (1809–1882). In 1859, Darwin published his ideas in *On the Origin of Species.* He proposed the principle of **natural selection,** an evolutionary process in which organisms that are best adapted to their environment will survive and, importantly, produce offspring. Darwin noted that members of any species are often locked in competition for scarce resources such as food. Natural selection is the process by which the environment determines who wins that competition. Darwin asserted that organisms with biological features that led to survival and reproduction would be better represented in subsequent generations. Over many generations, organisms with these characteristics would constitute a larger percentage of the population. Eventually this process could change an entire species. If environmental conditions changed, however, other characteristics might become favored by natural selection, moving the process in a different direction (Dennett, 2017).

If you are unfamiliar with Darwin's theory of evolution, it is helpful to consider the simple question, why do giraffes have long necks? An early explanation might have been that giraffes live in places where the trees are very tall, and so the creatures must stretch their necks to get their food—leaves. Lots of stretching might lead to adult giraffes that have longer necks. This explanation does not tell us, though, why giraffes are *born* with long necks. A characteristic cannot be passed from one generation to the next unless it is recorded in the *genes,* those collections of molecules that are responsible for heredity (Cummings, 2016).

According to evolutionary theory, species change through random genetic mutation. That means that, essentially by accident, some members of a species are born with genetic

structuralism
Wundt's approach to discovering the basic elements, or structures, of mental processes.

functionalism
James's approach to mental processes, emphasizing the functions and purposes of the mind and behavior in the individual's adaptation to the environment.

natural selection
Darwin's principle of an evolutionary process in which organisms that are best adapted to their environment will survive and produce offspring.

Introspection has its limits. Many behaviors are hard to explain using introspection. Think about talking, for example. You somehow know where you are heading even as the words are tumbling out of your mouth, but you cannot say where those words are coming from.

William James (1842–1910)
James's approach became known as functionalism.
©Historia/Rex/Shutterstock

characteristics that make them different from other members (for instance, some lucky giraffes being born with unusually long necks). If these changes are adaptive (for example, if they help those giraffes compete for food, survive, and reproduce), they become more common in members of the species. So, presumably long, long ago, some giraffes were genetically predisposed to have longer necks, and some giraffes were genetically predisposed to have shorter necks. Only those with the long necks survived to reproduce, giving us the giraffes we see today. The survival of the giraffes with long necks is a product of natural selection. Evolutionary theory implies that the way we are, at least partially, is the way that is best suited to survival in our environment (Buss, 2016; Johnson, 2015).

It turns out that giraffes don't eat food from tall trees. Instead, they use their long necks to fight!

Darwin's theory continues to influence psychologists today because it is strongly supported by observation. We can make such observations every day. Right now, for example, in your kitchen sink, various bacteria are locked in competition for scarce resources in the form of those tempting food particles from your last meal. When you use an antibacterial cleaner, you are playing a role in natural selection, because you are effectively killing off the bacteria that cannot survive the cleaning agents. However, you are also letting the bacteria that are genetically adapted to survive that cleaner take over the sink. The same principle applies to taking an antibiotic medication at the first sign of a sore throat or an earache. By killing off the bacteria that may be causing the illness, you are creating an environment where their competitors (so-called antibiotic-resistant bacteria) may flourish. These observations powerfully demonstrate Darwinian selection in action.

If structuralism won the battle to be the birthplace of psychology, functionalism won the war. To this day, psychologists continue to talk about the adaptive nature of human characteristics. Indeed, from these beginnings, psychologists have branched out to study more aspects of human behavior than Wundt or James might have imagined. We now examine various contemporary approaches to the science of psychology.

self-quiz

1. Which of the following statements is correct?
   A. There are many controversies in the field of psychology.
   B. Psychologists on the whole agree among themselves on most aspects of the field.
   C. Psychologists do not engage in critical thinking.
   D. There are few controversies in the field of psychology.

2. Of the following, the characteristic that is *not* at the heart of the scientific approach is
   A. skepticism.
   B. critical thinking.

C. prejudging.
D. curiosity.

3. Charles Darwin's work is relevant to psychology because
   A. Darwin's research demonstrated that there are few differences between humans and animals.
   B. Darwin's principle of natural selection suggests that human behavior is partially a result of efforts to survive.
   C. Darwin stated that humans descended from apes, a principle that allows psychologists to understand human behavior.
   D. Darwin created functionalism.

APPLY IT! 4. Two psychologists, Clayton and Sam, are interested in studying emotional expressions. Clayton wants to determine whether emotional expression is healthy and if it has an influence on well-being. Sam is interested in describing the types of emotions people express and building a catalog of all the emotions and emotional expressions that exist. In this example, Clayton is most like _____ and Sam is most like _____.
   A. Wilhelm Wundt; William James
   B. William James; Wilhelm Wundt
   C. Wilhelm Wundt; Sigmund Freud
   D. Sigmund Freud; Wilhelm Wundt

2 Contemporary Approaches to Psychology

In this section we survey seven different approaches—biological, behavioral, psychodynamic, humanistic, cognitive, evolutionary, and sociocultural—that represent the intellectual backdrop of psychological science.

The Biological Approach

Some psychologists examine behavior and mental processes through the **biological approach,** which is a focus on the body, especially the brain and nervous system. For example, researchers might investigate the way your heart races when you are afraid or how your hands sweat when you tell a lie. Although a number of physiological systems may be involved in thoughts and feelings, perhaps the largest contribution to physiological psychology has come through the emergence of neuroscience (Lenshinskaya & Caramazza, 2016; Qiu, Mori, & Miller, 2015).

Neuroscience is the scientific study of the structure, function, development, genetics, and biochemistry of the nervous system. Neuroscience emphasizes that the brain and nervous system are central to understanding behavior, thought, and emotion (Kasemsap, 2017; Khan, Schmidt, & Chen, 2017). Neuroscientists believe that thoughts and emotions have a physical basis in the brain. Electrical impulses zoom throughout the brain's cells, releasing chemical substances that enable us to think, feel,

Magnetic resonance imaging allows scientists to get a view of different "slices" of the brain in a living person.
©AkeSak/Shutterstock

and behave. Our remarkable human capabilities would not be possible without the brain and nervous system, which constitute the most complex, intricate, and elegant system imaginable. Although biological approaches might sometimes seem to reduce complex human experience to simple physical structures, developments in neuroscience have allowed psychologists to understand the brain as an amazingly complex organ, perhaps just as complex as the psychological processes linked to its functioning (Halldorsdottir & Binder, 2017).

The Behavioral Approach

The **behavioral approach** emphasizes the scientific study of observable behavioral responses and their environmental determinants. It focuses on an organism's visible behaviors, not thoughts or feelings. The psychologists who adopt this approach are called *behaviorists*. Under the intellectual leadership of John B. Watson (1878–1958) and B. F. Skinner (1904–1990), behaviorism dominated psychological research during the first half of the twentieth century.

Skinner (1938) emphasized that psychology should be about what people do—their actions and behaviors—and should not concern itself with things that cannot be seen, such as thoughts, feelings, and goals. He believed that rewards and punishments determine our behavior. For example, a child might behave in a well-mannered fashion because her parents have rewarded this behavior. We do the things we do, say behaviorists, because of the environmental conditions we have experienced and continue to experience.

Contemporary behaviorists still emphasize the importance of observing behavior to understand an individual, and they use rigorous methods advocated by Watson and Skinner (Gray & Diller, 2017). They also continue to stress the importance of environmental determinants of behavior (Martin & Pear, 2014). However, not every behaviorist today accepts the earlier behaviorists' rejection of thought processes, which are often called *cognition* (Bandura, 2016a, 2016b).

The Psychodynamic Approach

The **psychodynamic approach** emphasizes unconscious thought, the conflict between biological drives, such as the drive for sex, and society's demands, and early childhood family experiences. Practitioners of this approach believe that sexual and aggressive impulses buried deep within the unconscious mind influence the way people think, feel, and behave.

Sigmund Freud, the founding father of the psychodynamic approach, theorized that early relationships with parents shape an individual's personality. Freud's theory (1917) was the basis for the therapeutic technique that he called *psychoanalysis,* which involves an analyst's unlocking a person's unconscious conflicts by talking with the individual about his or her childhood memories, dreams, thoughts, and feelings. Certainly, Freud's views have been controversial, but they remain a part of contemporary psychology. Today's psychodynamic theories tend to place less emphasis on sexual drives and more on cultural or social experiences as determinants of behavior (Blass, 2017).

Sigmund Freud (1856–1939)
Freud was the founding father of the psychodynamic approach.
©Ingram Publishing

The Humanistic Approach

The **humanistic approach** emphasizes a person's positive qualities, the capacity for positive growth, and the freedom to choose one's destiny. Humanistic psychologists stress that people have the ability to control their lives and are not simply controlled by the environment (Maslow, 1971; Rogers, 1961). They theorize that rather than being driven by unconscious impulses (as the psychodynamic approach dictates) or by external rewards (as the behavioral approach emphasizes), people can choose to live by higher human values such as *altruism* (an unselfish concern for another person's well-being) and free will. Many aspects of this optimistic approach appear in research on motivation, emotion, and personality psychology (Chen & others, 2015; Keltner & others, 2014; Rassakazova, Ivanova, & Sheldon, 2016).

humanistic approach
An approach to psychology emphasizing a person's positive qualities, the capacity for positive growth, and the freedom to choose any destiny.

According to humanistic psychologists, warm, supportive behavior toward others helps us to realize our tremendous capacity for self-understanding.
©Blend Images/Alamy Stock Photo

The Cognitive Approach

According to cognitive psychologists, your brain houses a "mind" whose mental processes allow you to remember, make decisions, plan, set goals, and be creative (Slotnik, 2017). The **cognitive approach,** then, emphasizes the mental processes involved in knowing: how we direct our attention, perceive, remember, think, and solve problems. For example, cognitive psychologists want to know how we solve math problems, why we remember some things for only a short time, but others for a lifetime, and how we can use our imaginations to plan for the future (Feitosa-Santana, 2017; Xie & Zhang, 2017).

cognitive approach
An approach to psychology emphasizing the mental processes involved in knowing: how we direct our attention, perceive, remember, think, and solve problems.

Cognitive psychologists view the mind as an active and aware problem-solving system. This view contrasts with the behavioral outlook, which portrays behavior as controlled by external environmental forces. From the cognitive perspective, an individual's mental processes are in control of behavior through memories, perceptions, images, and thinking.

The Evolutionary Approach

Although arguably all of psychology emerges out of evolutionary theory, some psychologists emphasize an **evolutionary approach** that uses evolutionary ideas such as adaptation, reproduction, and natural selection as the basis for explaining specific human behaviors. David Buss (2016) argues that just as evolution molds our physical features, such as body shape, it also influences our decision making, level of aggressiveness, fears, and mating patterns. Thus, evolutionary psychologists say, the way we are is traceable to problems early humans faced in adapting to their environments (Cosmides, 2011).

Evolutionary psychologists believe that their approach provides an umbrella that unifies the diverse fields of psychology (Lewis & others, 2017; Witherington &

evolutionary approach
An approach to psychology centered on evolutionary ideas such as adaptation, reproduction, and natural selection as the basis for explaining specific human behaviors.

Lickliter, 2017). Not all psychologists agree with this conclusion, however. For example, some critics stress that the evolutionary approach provides an inaccurate explanation of why men and women have different social roles, and it does not adequately account for cultural diversity and experiences (Eagly & Wood, 2013). Yet keep in mind that even psychologists who disagree with the application of the evolutionary approach to psychological characteristics still agree with the general principles of evolutionary theory.

Human beings originally evolved long ago in a very different environment than we occupy today. The survivors were those who were most able to endure extremely difficult circumstances, struggling to find food, avoid predators, and create social groups. What do you think were the most adaptive traits for these early people? To what specific environments are humans adapting even now?

The Sociocultural Approach

sociocultural approach
An approach to psychology that examines the ways in which social and cultural environments influence behavior.

The **sociocultural approach** examines the influences of social and cultural environments on behavior. Socioculturalists argue that understanding a person's behavior requires knowing about the cultural context in which the behavior occurs (Blaine & McClure, 2018). (*Culture* refers to the shared knowledge, practices, and attitudes of groups of people and can include language, customs, and beliefs about what behavior is appropriate and inappropriate.) The sociocultural approach often includes *cross-cultural* research, meaning research that compares individuals in various cultures to see how they differ on important psychological attributes. Cross-cultural research is important for testing the assumption that findings for one culture also generalize to other cultural contexts, and as such it allows psychologists to test for the possibility that some characteristics are universal (Bai & others, 2017).

The sociocultural approach focuses not only on comparisons of behavior across countries but also on the behavior of individuals from different ethnic and cultural groups within a country (Hou & others, 2017; Shankar & Hinds, 2017). In light of rising cultural diversity in the United States in recent years, there has been increasing interest in the behavior of African Americans, Latinos, and Asian Americans, especially in terms of the factors that have restricted or enhanced their ability to adapt and cope with living in a predominantly non-Latino White society (Blaine & McClure, 2018; Duncan, Magnuson, & Votruba-Drzal, 2015; Sanchez & Awad, 2016). The influence of culture on behavior has led to important findings about psychological processes and especially about the role of culture in the psychological experience of our own sense of self (Han, 2016).

Summing up the Seven Contemporary Approaches

These seven approaches to studying psychology provide different views of behavior, and therefore each may contribute uniquely valuable insights. Think about the simple experience of seeing a cute puppy. Looking at that puppy involves physical processes in the eyes, nervous system, and brain—the focus of the biological approach to psychology. The moment you spot that puppy, though, you might smile without thinking and reach down to pet the little guy. That reaction might be a learned response based on your past learning with your own dog (behavioral perspective), or unconscious memories of a childhood dog (psychodynamic perspective), or conscious memories that you especially like this breed of dogs (cognitive perspective), or even evolutionary processes that promoted cuteness to help offspring survive (evolutionary approach). You might find yourself striking up a conversation with the puppy's owner, based on your shared love of dogs (humanistic perspective). Further, sociocultural factors might play a role in your decision about whether to ask the owner if holding the puppy would be okay, whether to share those warm feelings about the puppy with others, and even whether (as in some cultures) to view that puppy as food.

These broad approaches are reflected in the variety of specialties within which psychologists work (Figure 2). Many of these specialties are represented by chapters in *Experience Psychology*.

Specialization	Focus of Specialists
Behavioral Neuroscience	Behavioral neuroscience focuses on biological processes, especially the brain's role in behavior.
Sensation and Perception	Sensation and perception researchers focus on the physical systems and psychological processes of vision, hearing, touch, and smell that allow us to experience the world.
Learning	Learning specialists study the complex process by which behavior changes to adapt to shifting circumstances.
Cognitive	Cognitive psychology examines attention, consciousness, information processing, and memory. Cognitive psychologists are also interested in cognitive skills and abilities such as problem solving, decision making, expertise, and intelligence.
Developmental	Developmental psychology examines how people become who they are, from conception to death, concentrating on biological and environmental factors.
Motivation and Emotion	Researchers from a variety of specializations are interested in these two aspects of experience. Motivation researchers examine questions such as how individuals attain difficult goals. Emotion researchers study the physiological and brain processes that underlie emotional experience, the role of emotional expression in health, and the possibility that emotions are universal.
Personality	Personality psychology focuses on the relatively enduring characteristics of individuals, including traits, goals, motives, genetics, and personality development.
Social	Social psychology studies how social contexts influence perceptions, social cognition, and attitudes. Social psychologists study how groups influence attitudes and behavior.
Clinical and Counseling	Clinical and counseling psychology, the most widely practiced specialization, involves diagnosing and treating people with psychological problems.
Health	Health psychology emphasizes psychological factors, lifestyle, and behavior that influence physical health.
Industrial and Organizational (I/O)	I/O psychology applies findings in all areas of psychology to the workplace.
Community	Community psychology is concerned with providing accessible care for people with psychological problems. Community-based mental health centers are one means of delivering such services as outreach programs.
School and Educational	School and educational psychology centrally concerns children's learning and adjustment in school. School psychologists in elementary and secondary school systems test children, make recommendations about educational placement, and work on educational planning teams.
Environmental	Environmental psychologists explore the effects of physical settings in most major areas of psychology, including perception, cognition, and learning, among others. An environmental psychologist might study how different room arrangements influence behavior or what strategies might be used to reduce human behavior that harms the environment.
Psychology of Women	Psychology of women stresses the importance of integrating information about women with current psychological knowledge and applying that information to society and its institutions.
Forensic	Forensic psychology applies psychology to the legal system. Forensic psychologists might help with jury selection or provide expert testimony in trials.
Sport	Sport psychology applies psychology to improving sport performance and enjoyment of sport participation.
Cross-Cultural	Cross-cultural psychology studies culture's role in understanding behavior, thought, and emotion, with a special interest in whether psychological phenomena are universal or culture-specific.

FIGURE 2   **Areas of Specialization in Psychology** Psychology has many overlapping subfields.

As you read, keep in mind that psychology is a science in which psychologists work together collaboratively to examine a wide range of research questions. Indeed, many times scholars from different specialties within psychology join forces to understand some aspect of human behavior. It is the purpose of the Intersection feature to review research that represents a collaboration among scientists from different specialties to answer the same question.

3 Psychology's Scientific Method

Science is not defined by *what* it investigates, but by *how* it investigates. Whether you study photosynthesis, butterflies, Saturn's moons, or happiness, the *way* you study your question of interest determines whether your approach is scientific. The scientific method is how psychologists gain knowledge about mind and behavior. A key theme in the scientific method is that knowledge comes from empirical research.

It is the use of the scientific method that makes psychology a science (Passer, 2017). Indeed, most of the studies psychologists publish in research journals follow the scientific method, which may be summarized in these five steps (Figure 3):

1. Observing some phenomenon
2. Formulating hypotheses and predictions
3. Testing through empirical research
4. Drawing conclusions
5. Evaluating conclusions

1. **OBSERVING SOME PHENOMENON** The first step in conducting a scientific inquiry involves observing some phenomenon in the world. The critical-thinking, curious psychologist sees something and wants to know why or how it is the way it is. Inspiration for scientific inquiry can come from contemporary social problems, current events, personal experiences, and more. The phenomena that scientists study are called variables, a word related to the verb *to vary*. A **variable** is anything that can change.

Science is defined not by what it studies but by how it investigates. Photosynthesis, butterflies, and relationships among people all can be studied in a scientific manner. (butterfly) ©Albert Tan photo/Flickr RF/Getty Images; (couple) ©George Doyle & Ciaran Griffin/Stockbyte/Getty Images

variable
Anything that can change.

1

Observing Some Phenomenon

We feel good when we give someone a gift. However, do we genuinely feel better giving something away than we might feel if we could keep it? Elizabeth Dunn, Lara Aknin, and Michael Norton (2008) decided to test this question.

2

Formulating Hypotheses and Predictions

These researchers hypothesized that spending money on other people would lead to greater happiness than spending money on oneself.

3

Testing Through Empirical Research

In an experiment designed to examine this prediction, the researchers randomly assigned undergraduate participants to receive money ($5 or $20) that they had to spend either on themselves or on someone else by 5 P.M. that day. Those who spent the money on *someone else* reported greater happiness that night.

4

Drawing Conclusions

The experiment supported the hypothesis that spending money on others can be a strong predictor of happiness. Money might not buy happiness, the researchers concluded, but spending money in a particular way, that is, on other people, may enhance happiness.

5

Evaluating Conclusions

The experimental results were published in the prestigious journal *Science*. Now that the findings are public, other researchers might investigate related topics and questions inspired by this work, and their experiments might shed further light on the original conclusions.

FIGURE 3 **Steps in the Scientific Method: Is It Better to Give Than to Receive?** This figure shows how the steps in the scientific method were applied in a research experiment examining how spending money on ourselves or others can influence happiness (Dunn, Aknin, & Norton, 2008). The researchers theorized that although money does not typically buy happiness, the way we spend it might well predict happy feelings.

(gift) ©Stockdisc/PunchStock; (multiple faces) ©Flashpop/Getty Images; (woman with money) ©Jupiter Images/Brand X/Alamy Stock Photo

> **For each step in the process, what decisions did the researchers make, and how did those decisions influence the research?** > **Are the findings counterintuitive or not?** > **This study was inspired by the saying "It is better to give than to receive." Does the study do a good job of evaluating that cliché? How else might a researcher have addressed this question?**

For example, one variable that interests psychologists is happiness. Some people seem to be happier than others. What might account for these differences? As scientists consider answers to such questions, they often develop theories. A **theory** is a broad idea or set of closely related ideas that attempts to explain observations. Theories seek to explain why certain things are as they are or why they have happened. Theories can be used to make predictions about future observations. For instance, some psychologists theorize that the most important human need is the need to belong to a social group (Leary & Guadagno, 2011; Reitz, Motti-Stefanidi, & Asendorpf, 2016). This theory would seek to explain human behaviors through the need to belong.

> *A scientist must be able to anticipate being wrong and remain open to that possibility.*

A key characteristic of a scientific theory is that it must be *falsifiable*, meaning that even a scientist who believes that a theory is true must be able to generate ideas about research that would prove the theory wrong and test those ideas. This is what separates scientific theories from beliefs and opinions.

theory
A broad idea or set of closely related ideas that attempts to explain observations and to make predictions about future observations.

2. FORMULATING HYPOTHESES AND PREDICTIONS The second step in the scientific method is stating a hypothesis. A **hypothesis** is a testable prediction that derives logically from a theory. A theory can generate many hypotheses. If more and more hypotheses related to a theory turn out to be true, the theory gains in credibility.

hypothesis
A testable prediction that derives logically from a theory.

So, a researcher who believes that social belonging is the most important aspect of human functioning might predict that people who belong to social groups will be happier than others, or might hypothesize that individuals who are excluded by a social group will be more aggressive. Each of these hypotheses would lead to specific predictions within a particular empirical study.

3. TESTING THROUGH EMPIRICAL RESEARCH

The next step in the scientific method is to test the hypotheses by conducting empirical research—that is, by collecting and analyzing data. At this point, it is time for the researcher to design a study that will test his or her predictions. We will review the specifics of various research methods for testing predictions later in this chapter. Whatever the method used to test a prediction, the first thing a researcher needs in order to conduct a study is a concrete way to measure the variables of interest.

An **operational definition** provides an objective description of how a variable is going to be measured and observed in a particular study. Such a definition eliminates the fuzziness that might creep into thinking about a problem. Imagine, for example, that your psychology class is asked to observe a group of children and to keep track of kind behaviors. Do you think that everyone will define "kind behaviors" in the same way? An operational definition allows the class to be sure that everyone agrees on what a variable means. To measure personal happiness, for example, prominent psychologist Ed Diener and his students (Diener & others, 1985) devised a self-report questionnaire that measures how satisfied a person is with his or her life, called the Satisfaction with Life Scale. You will get a chance to complete the questionnaire later in this chapter. Scores on this scale are then used as measures of happiness. Research using this scale and others like it has shown that certain specific factors are strongly related to being happy: marriage, religious faith, purpose in life, and good health (Diener, 1999; Diener & Chan, 2011; Pavot & Diener, 2008; Tay & others, 2013).

Try operationally defining the following variables: generosity, love, aggression, liberal, conservative, exhaustion, stress, attractiveness. What are some things that you find interesting that you think a psychologist should study? How might you operationally define these variables?

Importantly, there is not just one operational definition for any variable. For example, in a study that examined happiness as a predictor of important life outcomes, Lee Anne Harker and Dacher Keltner (2001) looked at the yearbook pictures of college women who had graduated three decades earlier. They coded the pictures for the appearance of *Duchenne smiling*—that is, genuine smiling, the kind that creates little wrinkles around the outer corner of the eyes. Duchenne smiling has been shown to be a sign of genuine happiness. (If you want to see whether someone in a photograph is smiling genuinely, cover the bottom of the person's face. Can you still tell that he or she is smiling? A genuine smile can be seen in the eyes, not just the mouth.) So, while Diener and colleagues operationally defined happiness as a score on a questionnaire, Harker and Keltner operationally defined happiness as Duchenne smiling. Harker and Keltner found that happiness, as displayed in these yearbook pictures, predicted positive life outcomes, such as successful marriages and satisfying lives, some 30 years later.

Coming up with operational definitions for the variables in a study is a crucial step in designing psychological research. To study anything, we must have a way to see it or measure it. Clearly, to devise an operational definition for any variable, we first must agree on what it is that we are trying to measure. If we think of happiness as something that people know about themselves, then a questionnaire score might be a good operational definition of the variable. If we think that people might not be aware of how happy they are (or are not), then facial expression might be a better operational definition. In other words, our

Researchers have identified Duchenne smiling (notice the wrinkles) as a sign of genuine happiness.
©maridav/123RF

conceptual definition of a variable must be set out clearly before we operationally define it. An operational definition is how a variable is defined in a particular study. Whether that operational definition fully captures the variable of interest outside the study may be an important matter of debate.

Because operational definitions allow researchers to measure variables, they have a lot of numbers to deal with once they have conducted a study. A key aspect of the process of testing hypotheses is *data analysis*. *Data* refers to all the information (all those numbers) researchers collect in a study—say, the questionnaire scores or the behaviors observed. Data analysis means "crunching" those numbers mathematically to see if they support predictions. In other words, data analysis involves applying mathematical procedures to understand what the numerical information means (Carlson & Winquist, 2018). Many psychology students are surprised to learn that much of psychologists' work relies heavily on sophisticated *statistics,* numbers that help them describe what the data have to tell them.

Let's pause and examine an example that demonstrates the first three steps in the scientific method. One theory of well-being is *self-determination theory* (Ryan, Huta, & Deci, 2008; Ryan & Deci, 2011). This theory states that people are likely to feel fulfilled when their lives meet three important needs: relatedness (warm relations with others), autonomy (independence), and competence (mastering new skills).

One hypothesis that follows logically from this theory is that people who value money, material possessions, prestige, and physical appearance (that is, extrinsic rewards) over the needs of relatedness, autonomy, and competence (intrinsic rewards) should be less fulfilled, less happy, and less well adjusted. In a series of studies entitled "The Dark Side of the American Dream," researchers Timothy Kasser and Richard Ryan asked participants to complete self-report measures of values and of psychological and physical functioning (Kasser & Ryan, 1993, 1996; Kasser & others, 2004). Thus, the operational definitions of values and psychological functioning were questionnaire scores. The researchers found that individuals who value material rewards over intrinsic rewards do indeed tend to suffer as predicted, and similar findings have emerged in nations throughout the world (Kasser, 2011).

4. DRAWING CONCLUSIONS

Based on the results of the data analyses, scientists then draw conclusions from their research. If the results of a study (or a series of studies) support predictions, then a theory may gain credibility. A theory, however, is always open to revision. Before a theory is accepted or changed, the scientific community must establish that the research can be replicated, or repeated, by other scientists using different methods. **Replication** means that one scientist tries to reproduce a study to see if they get the same result. The replicator can be the same scientist who originally produced the results or a different scientist altogether. If a particular research finding is demonstrated again and again across different researchers and different methods, it is considered *reliable*—in other words, it is a dependable result. Whether the results of psychological experiments are typically replicable has been a recent issue in the field and one that we will return to later in this chapter.

replication
The process in which a scientist attempts to reproduce a study to see if the same results emerge.

5. EVALUATING CONCLUSIONS

The final step in the scientific method, evaluating conclusions, is one that never ends. Researchers submit their work for publication, and it undergoes rigorous review. Afterward, the published studies are there for all to see, read, and evaluate continually.

Because scientists are skeptical and critical thinkers, published studies often lead to alternative theories and hypotheses that are themselves tested.

Although the published research literature represents the current state of scientific knowledge about various topics and areas, the research community maintains an active conversation about this knowledge and constantly questions conclusions. Inspired by published studies, a scientist might come up with a new idea to be tested, one that will eventually change the thinking on some topic. Steps 3, 4, and 5 in the scientific method are thus part of an ongoing process. That is, researchers go back and do more research, revise their theories, hone their methods, and draw and evaluate their new conclusions.

1. Any changeable phenomenon that a scientist studies is called a
   A. differential.
   B. predictor.
   C. variation.
   D. variable.

2. The statement "I believe this research will demonstrate that students who study in groups will get better grades than those who study alone" is an example of
   A. a theory.
   B. an observation.
   C. a conclusion.
   D. a hypothesis.

3. The last step in the scientific method, and one that never ends, is
   A. drawing conclusions.
   B. evaluating conclusions.
   C. testing through empirical research.
   D. running a statistical analysis.

APPLY IT! 4. Paul believes that physically attractive people are selfish. He conducts a study to see if he is right. He goes up to five people he thinks are good-looking and asks them for spare change. They all turn him down. Paul concludes, "Aha! I knew it all along." The operational definition of selfish in Paul's study is

A. physical attractiveness.
B. whether people gave Paul spare change.
C. whether Paul thought the person was attractive.
D. asking for spare change.

BONUS: As you practice thinking like a scientist and learn about research design, give further thought to Paul's study. Can you spot at least four big problems with it?

4 Types of Psychological Research

The five steps of the scientific method are reflected differently in three types of research commonly used in psychology. *Descriptive research* involves finding out about the basic dimensions of some variable (for example, what is the average level of happiness of men in the United States?). *Correlational research* is interested in discovering relationships between variables (for instance, are married men happier than single men?). *Experimental research* concerns establishing causal relationships between variables (if men smile, do women perceive them as more attractive?). Let's examine each of these types of research.

Descriptive Research

Just as its name suggests, descriptive research is about describing some phenomenon—determining its basic dimensions and defining what this thing is, how often it occurs, and so on. By itself, descriptive research cannot prove what causes some phenomenon, but it can reveal important information about people's behaviors and attitudes (Leavy, 2017). Descriptive research methods include observation, surveys and interviews, and case studies.

Public opinion polls are a type of descriptive research.

OBSERVATION Imagine that you are going to conduct a study on how children who are playing a game resolve conflicts that arise during the game. The data that are of interest to you concern conflict resolution. As a first step, you might go to a playground and simply observe what the children do—how often you see conflict resolution occur and how it unfolds. You would likely keep careful notes of what you observe.

This type of scientific observation requires an important set of skills. Unless you are a trained observer and practice your skills regularly, you might not know what to look for, you might not remember what you saw, you might not realize that what you are looking for is changing from one moment to the next, and you might not communicate your observations effectively. Furthermore, it might be important to have one or more others do the observations as well, to develop a sense of how accurate your observations are. For observations to be effective, they must be systematic. You must know whom you are observing, when and where you will observe, and how you will make the observations.

Also, you need to know in advance in what form you will document them: in writing, by sound recording, or by video.

SURVEYS AND INTERVIEWS

Sometimes the best and quickest way to get information about people is to ask them for it. One technique is to interview them directly. A related method that is especially useful when information from many people is needed is the *survey,* or questionnaire. A survey presents a standard set of questions, or *items,* to obtain people's self-reported attitudes or beliefs about a particular topic.

Although surveys can be a straightforward way to measure psychological variables, constructing them requires care (Fielding, Lee, & Blank, 2017). For example, surveys can measure only what people think about themselves. Thus, if we are interested in studying a variable that we think is unconscious, like a psychodynamic drive, we cannot use a survey. Furthermore, people do not always know the truth about themselves. If you were answering a survey that asked, "Are you a generous person?" how might your answer compare to that of a friend who is asked to make that same rating about you? One particular problem with surveys and interviews is the tendency of participants to answer questions in a way that will make them look good rather than in a way that communicates what they truly think or feel (Peterson & others, 2011). Another challenge in survey construction is that when questionnaires are used to operationally define variables, it is crucial that the items precisely probe the specific topic of interest and not some other characteristic. The language used in surveys therefore must be clear and understandable if the responses are to reflect the participants' actual feelings.

Surveys and interviews can cover a wide range of topics, from religious beliefs to sexual habits to attitudes about gun control. Some survey and interview questions are unstructured and open-ended, such as "How fulfilling would you say your marriage is?" Such questions allow for unique responses from each person surveyed. Other survey and interview questions are more structured and ask about quite specific things. For example, a structured question might ask, "How many times have you talked with your partner about a personal problem in the past month: 0, 1–2, 3–5, 6–10, 11–30, every day?"

Mahatma Gandhi was the spiritual leader of India in the middle of the twentieth century. Erik Erikson conducted an extensive case study of his life to determine what contributed to his identity development.
©Universal History Archive/UIG/REX/Shutterstock

CASE STUDIES

A **case study** or **case history** is an in-depth look at a single individual. Case studies are performed mainly by clinical psychologists when, for either practical or ethical reasons, the unique aspects of an individual's life cannot be duplicated and tested in other individuals. A case study provides information about one person's goals, hopes, fantasies, fears, traumatic experiences, family relationships, health, or anything else that helps the psychologist understand the person's mind and behavior. Case studies can also involve in-depth explorations of particular families or social groups.

An example of a case study is the analysis of India's spiritual leader Mahatma Gandhi (1869–1948) by psychodynamic theorist Erik Erikson (1969). Erikson studied Gandhi's life in great depth to discover insights into how his positive spiritual identity developed, especially during his youth. In piecing together Gandhi's identity development, Erikson described the contributions of culture, history, family, and various other factors that might affect the way other people form an identity.

Case histories provide dramatic, detailed portrayals of people's lives, but researchers must be cautious about applying what they learn from one person's life to other people. The subject of a case study has a unique genetic makeup and personal history that no one else shares. Case studies nevertheless can be very valuable at the first step of the scientific method, in that they

case study or case history
An in-depth look at a single individual.

often provide vivid observations that can then be tested in a variety of ways in psychological research.

THE VALUE OF DESCRIPTIVE RESEARCH
Descriptive research allows researchers to get a sense of something but cannot answer questions about how and why things are the way they are. Such research can nonetheless be intriguing, such as descriptive research on the experience of happiness in different cultures. Before reading about that research, complete the measure below. Using the 7-point scale below, indicate your agreement with each item that follows.

1	2	3	4	5	6	7
Strongly Disagree	Disagree	Slightly Disagree	Neither Agree Nor Disagree	Slightly Agree	Agree	Strongly Agree

1. In most ways my life is close to my ideal.
2. The conditions of my life are excellent.
3. I am satisfied with my life.
4. So far I have gotten the important things I want in life.
5. If I could live my life over, I would change almost nothing.

You have just completed the Satisfaction with Life Scale (or SWLS; Diener & others, 1985), one operational definition of happiness. To find out your score, add up your ratings and divide by 5. This average rating could be considered your level of general happiness. A broad range of studies in many different countries have used this scale and others like it to measure happiness levels. Based on such research, Ed and Carol Diener (1996) concluded that most people are quite happy because they score above the midpoint, 4, on the scale you just completed. However, research on happiness in various cultures has generally centered on relatively industrialized countries. What about nonindustrialized cultures?

One study examined levels of happiness in groups of people who have not generally been included in psychological studies (Biswas-Diener, Vitterso, & Diener, 2005). The research included three groups: the Inuits of Greenland, the Masai of southern Kenya, and American Old Order Amish. All three groups completed measures essentially the same as the one you just did.

The Inuit tribe studied—the *Inughuits*—live at 79 degrees latitude (very far north), in the harshest climate inhabited by a traditional human society. The landscape consists of rocks, glaciers, and the sea. Farming is impossible. The Inughuits have some modern conveniences, but they generally adhere to a traditional hunting culture. It is not uncommon to find an Inughuit hunter carving a seal or caribou on the kitchen floor while children watch TV in the next room. Most of us might feel a little blue in the winter months when gloomy weather stretches on day after day. For the Inughuits, however, the sun never rises throughout the winter months, and in the summer, it never sets. How happy could an individual be in such a difficult setting? Pretty happy, it turns out, as the Inughuits averaged a 5.0 on the Satisfaction with Life Scale.

The Masai are an indigenous (native) African nomadic group who live in villages of about 20 people, with little exposure to the West. The Masai are fierce warriors, and their culture has many traditional ceremonies built around a boy's passage from childhood to manhood. Boys are circumcised between the ages of 15 and 22, and they are forbidden from moving or making a sound during the procedure. Girls also experience circumcision as they enter puberty, a controversial rite that involves the removal of the clitoris and that makes childbirth extremely difficult. The Masai practice child marriage and polygamy. Masai women have very little power and are generally expected to do most of the work. How happy could an individual be in this context? Masai men and women who completed the measure orally in their

Notice that these first two studies involve examining two different cultures, while the last one focuses on a culture within a culture. These studies exemplify the sociocultural approach.

native tongue, Maa, averaged a 5.4 on the Satisfaction with Life Scale (Biswas-Diener, Vitterso, & Diener, 2005).

Finally, the Old Order Amish of the midwestern and northeastern United States belong to a strict religious sect that explicitly rejects modern aspects of life. The Amish separate themselves from mainstream society and travel by horse and buggy. The women wear bonnets, and the men sport beards, dark clothes, and dark brimmed hats. The Amish farm without modern machinery and dedicate their lives to simplicity—without radios, TVs, CDs, DVDs, iPods, smartphones, washing machines, and cars. Still, the Amish are relatively happy, averaging 4.4 on the 7-point happiness scale (Biswas-Diener, Vitterso, & Diener, 2005).

Like a host of other studies in industrialized nations, these results indicate that most individuals are pretty happy. Such descriptive findings provide researchers on well-being a foundation for further examining the processes that lead to feelings of happiness in different cultural settings. If a researcher wanted to examine, for example, what predicts happiness within these different groups, he or she would use a correlational design.

How does your score compare with the score of the Inughuits, the Masai, and the Old Order Amish? Is the Satisfaction with Life Scale a good measure of happiness? Why or why not?

Correlational Research

correlational research
Research that examines the relationships between variables, whose purpose is to examine whether and how two variables change together.

We have seen that descriptive research tells us about the basic dimensions of a variable. In contrast, **correlational research** tells us about the relationships between variables, and its purpose is to examine whether and how two variables *change together*. That is, correlational research looks at a co-relationship. For instance, if one of the variables increases, what happens to the other one? When two variables change together, we can predict one from the other, and we say that the variables are correlated (Carlson & Winquist, 2018).

Correlational research is so named because of the statistical technique, *correlation,* that is typically used to analyze this type of data. The key feature of a correlational study is that the variables of interest are measured or observed to see how they relate. If we wanted to know whether shy people are happy, we might give the same people two questionnaires, one that measures shyness and another that measures happiness. For each person we would have two scores, and we would then see whether shyness and happiness relate to each other in a systematic way.

The degree of relationship between two variables is expressed as a numerical value called a *correlational coefficient,* which is most commonly represented by the letter *r*. The correlation coefficient is a statistic that tells us two things about the relationship between two variables—its strength and its direction. The value of a correlation always falls between -1.00 and $+1.00$. The number or magnitude of the correlation tells us about the *strength* of the relationship. The closer the number is to ±1.00, the stronger the relationship. The sign ($+$ or $-$) tells us about the *direction* of the relationship between the variables. A positive sign means that as one variable increases, the other also increases, or as one decreases the other does as well. When variables are positively correlated, they change in the same direction. A negative sign means that as one variable increases, the other decreases. Negatively correlated variables change together but do so in the opposite direction. A zero correlation means that there is no systematic relationship between the variables. Examples of *scatter plots* (a type of graph that plots scores on the two variables) showing positive and negative correlations appear in Figure 4. Note that every dot in this figure represents both scores for one person.

CORRELATION IS *NOT* CAUSATION Look at the terms in bold type in the following news headlines:

Researchers **Link** Coffee Consumption to Happiness in Women

Scientists Find **Connection** Between Ear Hair and Heart Attacks

Psychologists Discover **Relationship** Between Marital Status and Health

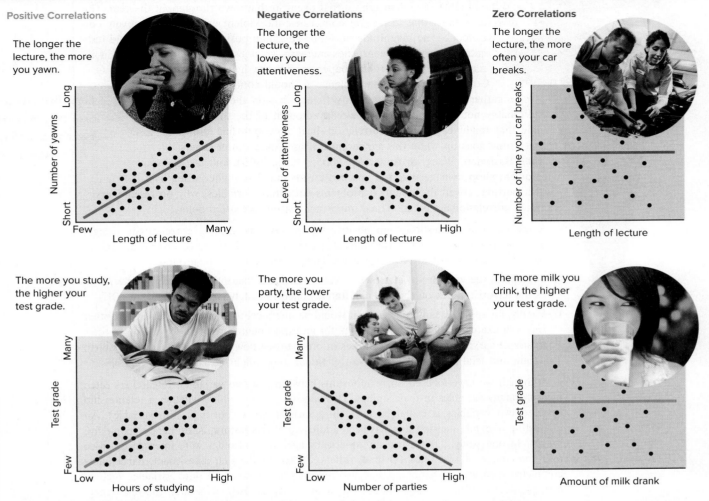

Positive Correlations

The longer the lecture, the more you yawn.

Number of yawns (Short → Long) vs. *Length of lecture* (Few → Many)

The more you study, the higher your test grade.

Test grade (Few → Many) vs. *Hours of studying* (Low → High)

Negative Correlations

The longer the lecture, the lower your attentiveness.

Level of attentiveness (Short → Long) vs. *Length of lecture* (Low → High)

The more you party, the lower your test grade.

Test grade (Few → Many) vs. *Number of parties* (Low → High)

Zero Correlations

The longer the lecture, the more often your car breaks.

Number of time your car breaks vs. *Length of lecture*

The more milk you drink, the higher your test grade.

Test grade vs. *Amount of milk drank*

FIGURE 4 **Scatter Plots Showing Positive and Negative Correlations** A positive correlation is a relationship in which two factors vary in the same direction, as shown in the two scatter plots on the left. A negative correlation is a relationship in which two factors vary in opposite directions, as shown in the two scatter plots on the right. Note that each dot on these graphs represents one person's (or one class's) score on the two variables of interest.

(yawning) ©Doug Menuez/Getty Images; (attentiveness) ©Ariel Skelley/Blend Images; (mechanics) ©ColorBlind Images/Getty Images; (male test) ©andreypopov/123RF; (group test) ©Stockbyte/Punchstock; (female test) ©JGI/Blend Images LLC

For each graph, consider these questions:
> How might one of these variables cause the other? Can you imagine a way that the causal direction could be reversed? > What is a possible third variable that might account for these relationships? > Identify two variables that you think are positively correlated and two that are negatively correlated. > What would the graphs look like if the two variables were not systematically related?

From these headlines a reader might conclude that coffee causes happiness, ear hair causes heart attacks, and so on. The words in bold type are synonymous only with correlation, however, not with causality. *Correlation does not equal causation.* Remember, correlation means only that two variables change together. Being able to predict one event based on the occurrence of another event does not necessarily tell us anything about the cause of either event. Sometimes some other variable that has not been measured accounts for the relationship between two others. Researchers refer to this circumstance as the **third variable problem.** Third variables are also known as *confounds.*

third variable problem
The circumstance where a variable that has not been measured accounts for the relationship between two other variables. Third variables are also known as *confounds.*

To understand the third variable problem, consider the following example. A researcher measures two variables: the number of ice cream cones sold in a town and the number of violent crimes that occur in that town throughout the year. The researcher finds that ice cream cone sales and violent crimes are positively correlated, to the magnitude of +.50. This high positive correlation would indicate that as ice cream sales increase, so does violent crime. Would it be reasonable for the local paper to run the headline "Ice Cream Consumption Leads to Violence"? Should concerned citizens gather outside the local Frosty Freeze to stop the madness? Probably not. Perhaps you have already thought of the third variable that might explain this correlation—heat. Research has shown that crime goes up when the temperature rises (Anderson & others, 2000; Bushman, Wang, & Anderson, 2005; Mares, 2013), and, as any ice cream shop manager will tell you, ice cream sales are higher when it is warm outside. Given the potential problems with third variables, why do researchers conduct correlational studies? Three important reasons are listed below:

Crime, then, is probably also "linked" to air conditioning sales and repair profits, as well as swimsuit sales.

- Some important questions can be investigated *only* by using a correlational design. Such questions may involve variables that can only be measured or observed, such as biological sex, personality traits, genetic factors, and ethnic background.

- Sometimes the variables of interest are real-world events that influence people's lives, such as the terrorist attack on the Ariana Grande concert in Manchester, England, in 2017.

- Finally, for some research questions it would be unethical to do the research in any other way. For example, it would be unethical for an experimenter to direct expectant mothers to smoke varying numbers of cigarettes in order to see how cigarette smoke affects birth weight and fetal activity. Instead a correlational study might measure these variables.

Although we have focused on relationships between just two variables, researchers often measure many variables in their studies. This way, they can examine whether a relationship between two variables is explained by a third variable (or a fourth or fifth variable). An interesting research question that has been addressed in this fashion is, do happy people live longer? In one study, 2,000 Mexican Americans aged 65 and older were interviewed twice over the course of two years (Ostir & others, 2000). In the first assessment, participants completed measures of happiness but also reported about potential third variables such as diet, physical health, smoking, marital status, and distress. Two years later, the researchers contacted the participants again to see who was still alive. Even with this many potential third variables taken into account, happiness predicted who was still living two years later.

Correlational studies are useful, too, when researchers are interested in everyday experience. For example, some correlational researchers use the *experience sampling method (ESM)* to study people in their natural settings. This approach involves having people report on their daily experiences in a diary a few times a day or to complete measures of their mood and behavior whenever they are beeped by an electronic organizer or smartphone.

LONGITUDINAL DESIGNS

One way that correlational researchers can deal with the issue of causation is to employ a special kind of systematic observation called a **longitudinal design.** Longitudinal research involves observing and measuring the same variables periodically over time. Longitudinal research can suggest potential causal relationships because if one variable is thought to cause changes in another, it should at least come before that variable in time (Grimm, Davoudzadeh, & Ram, 2017).

One intriguing longitudinal study is the Nun Study, conducted by David Snowdon and his colleagues (Mortimer, Snowdon, & Markesbery, 2009; SantaCruz & others, 2011; Snowdon, 2003; Tyas & others, 2007). The study began in 1986 and has followed a sample of 678 School Sisters of Notre Dame ever since. The nuns ranged in age from 75 to 103 when the study began. These women completed a variety of psychological and physical measures annually. This sample is unique in many respects. However, some characteristics render the participants an excellent group for correlational research. For one thing, many potential extraneous third variables are relatively identical for all the

longitudinal design
A special kind of systematic observation, used by correlational researchers, that involves obtaining measures of the variables of interest in multiple waves over time.

women in the group. Their gender, living conditions, diet, activity levels, marital status, and religious participation are essentially held constant, providing little chance that differences in these variables can explain results.

In one study, researchers examined the relationship between happiness and longevity using this rich dataset. All of the nuns had been asked to write a spiritual autobiography when they entered the convent (for some, as many as 80 years before). Deborah Danner and her colleagues (2001) were given access to these documents and used them as indicators of happiness earlier in life by counting the number of positive emotions expressed in the autobiographies (note that here we have yet another operational definition of happiness). Women who included positive emotion in their autobiographies when they were in their early 20s were two-and-a-half times more likely to survive when they were in their 80s and 90s.

Longitudinal designs provide ways by which correlational researchers may attempt to demonstrate causal relations among variables. Still, it is important to be aware that even in longitudinal studies, causal relationships are not completely clear. For example, the nuns who wrote happier autobiographies may have had happier childhood experiences that might be influencing their longevity, or a particular genetic factor might explain both their happiness and their survival. As you read about numerous correlational research studies throughout *Experience Psychology,* do so critically, and with some skepticism, and consider that even the brightest scientist may not have thought of all of the potential third variables that might have explained his or her results. Keep in mind how easy it is to assume causality when two events or characteristics are merely correlated. Think about those innocent ice cream cones and critically evaluate conclusions that may be drawn from simple observation.

To appreciate the kinds of conclusions that can be reached using correlational and longitudinal designs, see the Intersection.

Experimental Research

To determine whether a causal relationship exists between variables, researchers must use experimental methods (Nelson, 2017; Passer, 2017). An **experiment** is a carefully regulated procedure in which the researcher manipulates one or more variables that are believed to influence some other variable. Imagine that a researcher notices that people who listen to classical music seem to be of above-average intelligence. A correlational study on this question would not tell us if listening to classical music *causes* increases in intelligence. In order to demonstrate causation, the researcher would manipulate whether or not people listen to classical music. He or she might create two groups: one that listens to classical music and one that listens to pop music. To test for differences in intelligence, the researcher would then measure intelligence.

If that manipulation led to differences between the two groups on intelligence, we could say that the manipulated variable *caused* those differences. In other words, the experiment has demonstrated cause and effect. This notion that experiments can demonstrate causation is based on the idea that if participants are randomly assigned to groups, the only systematic difference between them must be the manipulated variable. **Random assignment** means that researchers assign participants to groups by chance. This technique reduces the likelihood that the experiment's results will be due to any preexisting differences between groups. The logic of random assignment is that if only chance determines which participants are assigned to each group in an experiment, the potential differences on other characteristics will cancel out over the long run. So, for instance, in the example of classical music and intelligence, we might wonder if it is possible that the groups differed on intelligence to begin with. Because participants were randomly assigned, we assume that intelligence is spread across the groups evenly.

Random assignment does not always work. One way to improve its effectiveness is to start with a relatively large pool of people. Let's say that you decide to do that study—examining

experiment
A carefully regulated procedure in which the researcher manipulates one or more variables that are believed to influence some other variable.

random assignment
Researchers' assignment of participants to groups by chance, to reduce the likelihood that an experiment's results will be due to preexisting differences between groups.

Personality, Developmental, and Cross-Cultural Psychology: Why Do We Grow Up, Psychologically?

Early adulthood can be a time of great change. Consider all the choices that are made and all the events that occur: Leaving home, going to college, graduating, starting a career, finding a life partner, perhaps starting a family. These many events, experiences, and life changes, often clustered in a person's 20s and 30s, have important ramifications throughout the rest of life. Another type of change that occurs during this same time period is personality change. Specifically, between the ages of 18 and 40, people are likely to become more conscientious (responsible, reliable, and hardworking), more agreeable (kind and compassionate), and more emotionally stable (less worrying and prone to distress). That's right: Research shows that over time, people tend to become more mature (Milojev & Sibley, 2017). This pattern of personality trait change has been termed the maturity principle because it appears that, on average, people are growing-up, psychologically (Roberts, Wood, & Caspi, 2008). It would seem to be great news that young slackers can grow up to be conscientious members of society. But a fascinating question is, what drives these changes? Why do many people show this pattern of personality change? Answering this question requires scientific evidence from a diverse array of sources, including personality psychology, life-span development, and cross-cultural psychology (Bleidorn, 2015).

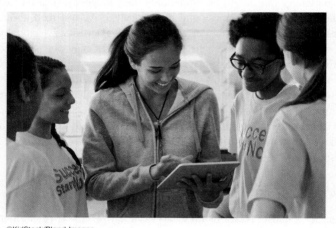
©KidStock/Blend Images

Psychologists have suggested two main sources of maturation in young adulthood. A first approach, suggested by the leading trait theorists, is that these changes are largely controlled by biological or genetic processes (McCrae & Costa, 2006). These scholars believe that, regardless of experience, growing up, psychologically, is just what people do. An alternative perspective suggests that these trait changes are a response to the roles people occupy in young adulthood (Roberts, Wood, & Smith, 2005). When a person becomes a spouse, an employee, or a parent, social expectations for their behavior change drastically (van Schippengen & others, 2016). From this perspective, we grow up, psychologically, because life demands it.

Which perspective is correct? A fascinating way to resolve this issue is to examine personality maturation across different cultures. The strong genetic argument would predict little to no cultural variation in personality trait change over time. If maturation is driven by an unfolding biological process it should not be affected by cultural differences. In contrast, if social roles trigger maturation, we might expect greater cultural variability in the timing of trait changes. A study of over 880,000 young adults from 62 different countries (Bleidorn & others, 2013) showed that, across cultures, age was associated with higher levels of conscientiousness, agreeableness, and emotional stability. That means that regardless of country, young adults tended to show maturation, providing support for the strong genetic argument. However, and interestingly, experience did matter to the timing of these changes. Strikingly, the most important experience precipitating personality changes was employment. And in nations where young adults take on the role of full time employee sooner (for example Pakistan and Malaysia), changes in personality happened faster. In nations such as the United States and the Netherlands, where young adults delay full-time employment, the trait of conscientiousness in particular changed more gradually.

So, why do we grow up, psychologically? Maturation appears to be an unfolding of biological process that occurs in and is affected by social demands. Many of us may have the capacity to become more responsible, considerate, and emotionally stable, but we may need the roles we occupy to push us toward that better, more mature self.

\\ **What experiences have made you "grown up" psychologically?**

---

whether listening to classical music (as compared to no music) prior to taking an intelligence test leads to higher scores on the test. Although you wisely use random assignment, you begin with just 10 people. Unbeknownst to you, there are two geniuses (people with extraordinarily high IQs) in that small pool of participants. Each person has a 50-50 chance of ending up in either group, so there is a 25 percent chance that both geniuses will end up in the same group, meaning there is a 25 percent chance that your groups will differ systematically in intelligence before you even start the study. In contrast, if your study had begun with, say, 100 people, intelligence scores will likely be more evenly spread in the overall pool. When these individuals are randomly assigned, differences in intelligences would be much more likely to cancel out across the two groups. That is why it is important that random assignment is allowed to work its magic on a larger pool of people.

©Fuse/Getty Images

To get a sense of what experimental studies, as compared to correlational studies, can tell us, consider the following example. Psychologists have long assumed that experiencing one's life as meaningful is an important aspect of psychological well-being (Frankl, 1946/1984; Steger & Frazier, 2005). Because surveys that measure meaning in life and well-being correlate positively (that is, the more meaningful your life, the happier you are), the assumption has been that experiencing meaning in life causes greater happiness. Because the studies involved in exploring this relationship have been correlational, however, the causal pathway is unknown. Meaning in life may lead people to be happier, but the reverse might also be true: Happiness might make people feel that their lives are more meaningful.

To address this issue, Laura King and her colleagues (2006; King & Hicks, 2012) conducted a series of laboratory experiments. The researchers had some people listen to happy music and other participants listen to neutral music. Participants who listened to happy music rated their lives as more meaningful than did individuals who listened to neutral music. Note that participants were randomly assigned to one of two conditions, happy music or neutral music, and then rated their meaning in life using a questionnaire. In this case happiness was operationally defined by the type of music participants listened to, and meaning in life was operationally defined by ratings on a questionnaire. Because participants were randomly assigned to conditions, we can assume that the only systematic difference between the two groups was the type of music they heard. As a result, we can say that the happy music caused people to rate their lives as more meaningful.

INDEPENDENT AND DEPENDENT VARIABLES
Experiments have two types of variables: independent and dependent. An **independent variable** is a manipulated experimental factor. The independent variable is the variable that the experimenter changes to see what its effects are; it is a potential cause. Any experiment may include several independent variables or factors that are manipulated to determine their effect on some outcome. In the study of positive mood and meaning in life, the independent variable is mood (positive versus neutral), operationally defined by the type of music participants listened to.

independent variable
A manipulated experimental factor; the variable that the experimenter changes to see what its effects are.

Sometimes the independent variable is the social context in which a person finds himself or herself. Social psychologists often manipulate the social context with the help of a **confederate,** a person who is given a role to play in a study so that the social context can be manipulated. For example, if researchers are interested in reactions to being treated rudely, they might have a confederate treat participants rudely (or not).

confederate
A person who is given a role to play in a study so that the social context can be manipulated.

A **dependent variable** is the outcome—the factor that can change in an experiment in response to changes in the independent variable. As researchers manipulate the independent variable, they measure the dependent variable for any resulting effect. In the study of mood and meaning in life, meaning in life was the dependent variable. The similarity in their names has plagued students of psychology forever, but independent and dependent variables are very different things. Independent variables are manipulated. Dependent variables are measured.

dependent variable
The outcome; the factor that can change in an experiment in response to changes in the independent variable.

EXPERIMENTAL AND CONTROL GROUPS
Experiments can involve one or more experimental groups and one or more control groups. In an experiment, the researcher manipulates the independent variable to create

The independent variable and dependent variable are two of the most important concepts in psychological research. You should memorize their meanings now. Remember that the independent variable is the cause, and the dependent variable is the effect.

these groups. An **experimental group** consists of the participants in an experiment who receive the treatment that is of interest to the researcher, or a particular drug under study—that is, the participants who are exposed to the change that the independent variable represents. A **control group** in an experiment is as much like the experimental group as possible and is treated in every way like the experimental group except for that change. The control group provides a comparison against which the researcher can test the effects of the independent variable. In the study of meaning in life above, participants who listened to happy music were the experimental group, and those who heard neutral music were the control group.

Coming up with a good control group can be a challenge. Say you want to do a study on the influence of smiling on social behaviors. Your experimental group will interact with a confederate who smiles a lot during the experiment. What will you have happen in your control group? Will the confederate keep a blank expression? Frown? Smile just a little?

Within-Participant Designs

One way to ensure that a control group and an experimental group are as similar as possible is to use a *within-participant design,* in which the participants serve as their own control group. In such a design, rather than relying on random assignment to produce equivalent groups, a researcher has the same group of participants experience the various conditions in the study. Let's say that a researcher predicts that the presence of other people (the independent variable) decreases math performance (the dependent variable). She might have participants complete math problems first while alone and then with others, and compare performance in the two conditions to test her prediction. The advantages to a within-participant design include requiring only half the number of participants and knowing that the groups are the very same people in each condition. The disadvantages include concerns about whether the two math tests are really equivalent and how the order of the conditions might influence their effects on performance.

When the participants who are in the experimental and control groups are different people, the design is called a between-participant design.

Quasi-Experimental Designs

Another approach to experimental research is to use a *quasi-experimental design.* As the prefix *quasi-* ("as if") suggests, this type of design is similar to an experiment, but it is not quite the same thing. The key difference is that a quasi-experimental design does not include random assignment of participants to a condition, because such assignment is either impossible or unethical (Reichardt, 2009).

Quasi-experimental designs might be used for studies that examine the differences between groups of people who have had different experiences—say, soldiers who have seen combat versus those who have not, or children whose school was destroyed by a tornado versus those in a neighboring town whose school was not affected. In a quasi-experimental design, a researcher examines participants in varying groups, but their assignment to groups is not determined by random assignment.

For example, a researcher interested in the influence of using online learning tools on performance in introductory psychology classes might compare students from two different sections of a class—one that uses online tools and one that does not. Of course, students typically choose what section of a course they take, so the experimenter cannot randomly assign them to sections. Examining differences between the groups might provide information about the merits of online learning tools. However, there might be confounds (for instance, whether students are morning people or not) that account for differences between the groups. Although quasi-experimental designs are common, it is important to keep in mind that they do not allow for the strong causal conclusions that can be drawn from experiments.

The late Donald Campbell, an eminent psychologist, referred to quasi-experimental designs as "queasy experimental designs" because of the way they often make hard-core experimentalists feel.

SOME CAUTIONS ABOUT EXPERIMENTAL RESEARCH

Validity refers to the soundness of the conclusions that a researcher draws from an experiment. Two broad types of validity matter to experimental designs. The first is **external validity,** which refers to the degree to which an experimental design really reflects the real-world issues it is supposed to address. That is, external validity is concerned with the question, do the experimental methods and the results generalize—do they apply—to the real world?

Imagine, for example, that a researcher is interested in the influence of stress (the independent variable) on creative problem solving (the dependent variable). He or she randomly assigns individuals to be blasted with loud noises at random times during the session (the high-stress or experimental group) or to complete the task in relative quiet

experimental group
The participants in an experiment who receive the drug or other treatment under study—that is, those who are exposed to the change that the independent variable represents.

control group
The participants in an experiment who are as much like the experimental group as possible and who are treated in every way like the experimental group except for a manipulated factor, the independent variable.

validity
The soundness of the conclusions that a researcher draws from an experiment. In the realm of testing, the extent to which a test measures what it is intended to measure.

external validity
The degree to which an experimental design actually reflects the real-world issues it is supposed to address.

(the control group). As the task, the researcher gives all participants a chance to be creative by asking them to list all of the uses they can think of for a cardboard box. Counting up the number of uses that people list, the researcher discovers that those in the high-stress group generated fewer uses of the box. This finding might indicate that stress reduces creativity. In considering the external validity of this study, however, we might ask some questions: How similar are the blasts of loud, random noises to the stresses individuals experience every day? Is listing uses for a cardboard box really an indicator of creativity? We are asking, in other words, if these operational definitions do a good job of reflecting the real-world processes they are supposed to represent.

Quasi-experimental designs tend to be high on external validity.

The second type of validity is **internal validity,** which refers to the degree to which changes in the dependent variable are due to the manipulation of the independent variable. In the case of internal validity, we want to know whether the experimental methods are free from biases and logical errors that may render the results suspect. Although experimental research is a powerful tool, it requires safeguards (Nelson, 2018). Expectations and biases can, and sometimes do, tarnish results (Rosnow & Rosenthal, 2012), as we next consider.

internal validity
The degree to which changes in the dependent variable are due to the manipulation of the independent variable.

Experimenter Bias   **Demand characteristics** are any aspects of a study that communicate to the participants how the experimenter wants them to behave. One such influence is experimenter bias. **Experimenter bias** occurs when the experimenter's expectations influence the outcome of the research. No one designs an experiment without wanting meaningful results. Consequently, experimenters can sometimes subtly communicate to participants what they want the participants to do. For example, consider research on the effects of oxytocin, a neurotransmitter that is sometimes considered a "love drug," in interpersonal trust. In one study the researchers showed that those randomly assigned to receive oxytocin in a nasal spray (the experimental group) were more trusting than a group who received a control substance (the control group) (Mikolajczak & others, 2010). However, when these investigators tried to replicate this study they failed to get the same results (Lane & others, 2015; 2016). The reason? The research team realized that, in the first study, the experimenter who interacted with participants was aware of the condition assignment the participants had received. Apparently, even without intending it, those who interact with participants can influence participant behavior.

demand characteristics
Any aspects of a study that communicate to the participants how the experimenter wants them to behave.

experimenter bias
The influence of the experimenter's expectations on the outcome of research.

In a classic study, Robert Rosenthal (1966) turned college students into experimenters. He randomly assigned the participants rats from the same litter. Half of the students were told that their rats were "maze bright," whereas the other half were told that their rats were "maze dull." The students then conducted experiments to test their rats' ability to navigate mazes. The results were stunning. The so-called maze-bright rats were more successful than the maze-dull rats at running the mazes. The only explanation for the results is that the college students' expectations affected the rats' performance.

Often the participants in psychological studies are not rats but people. Imagine that you are an experimenter and you know that a participant is going to be exposed to disgusting pictures in a study. Is it possible that you might treat the person differently than you would if you were about to show him photos of cute kittens? The reason experimenter bias is important is that it introduces systematic differences between the experimental and control groups, so that we cannot know if those who looked at disgusting pictures were more, say, upset because of the pictures or because of different treatment by the experimenter. Like third variables in correlational research, these systematic biases are called *confounds*. In experimental research, confounds are factors that "ride along" with the experimental manipulation, systematically and undesirably influencing the dependent variable. Experimenter bias, demand characteristics, and confounds may all lead to differences between groups on the dependent variable that threaten the validity of experimental results.

Research Participant Bias and the Placebo Effect   Like the experimenters, research participants may have expectations about what they are supposed to do and how they should behave, and these expectations may affect the results of experiments. **Research participant bias** occurs when the behavior of research participants during the experiment is influenced by how they think they are supposed to behave or their expectations about what is happening to them.

research participant bias
In an experiment, the influence of participants' expectations, and of their thoughts on how they should behave, on their behavior.

One example of the power of participant expectations is the placebo effect. The **placebo effect** occurs when participants' expectations, rather than the experimental treatment, produce an outcome. Participants in a drug study might be assigned to an experimental group that receives a pill containing an actual painkiller or to a control group that receives a placebo pill. A **placebo** is a harmless substance that has no physiological effect. This placebo is given to participants in a control group so that they are treated identically to the experimental group except for the active agent—in this case, the painkiller. Giving individuals in the control group a placebo pill allows researchers to determine whether changes in the experimental group are due to the active drug agent and not simply to participants' expectations.

Another way to ensure that neither the experimenter's nor the participants' expectations affect the outcome is to design a **double-blind experiment.** In this design, neither the experimenter administering the treatment nor the participants are aware of which participants are in the experimental group and which are in the control group until the results are calculated. This setup ensures that the experimenter cannot, for example, make subtle gestures signaling who is receiving a drug and who is not. A double-blind study allows researchers to identify the specific effects of the independent variable from the possible effects of the experimenter's and the participants' expectations about it.

Replication   Recall that a key aspect of the scientific method is evaluating conclusions that have been reached in a research study. The process of replication, defined earlier, has a critical role to play in this process. In the last few years, psychologists have become especially concerned about whether results of published studies are, in fact, replicable. When other investigators have tried to reproduce results from many studies they have been unable to produce the same results (Open Science Collaboration, 2015; Shrout & Rodgers, 2018). Studies conducted in fields that often rely on experimental methods have been particularly called into question (Klein & others, 2014). There have been a number of responses to this issue (Pashler & Harris, 2012; Reis & Lee, 2016; Simmons & Simonsohn, 2017). Many changes have been undertaken to ensure and protect the validity of psychological science. Two important principles have emerged to guide researchers. First, scientists should use larger sample sizes to ensure equivalence between groups. They should consider pooling data across labs when a single lab can only collect a small number of participants (for instance in infant research). Second, researchers should be transparent and thorough in the report of methods to allow work to be replicated correctly. One change that has occurred is that researchers are more likely to provide public access to their original data so that others can repeat the statistical analyses used.

Applications of the Three Types of Research

All three types of research that we have considered—descriptive, correlational, and experimental—can be used to address the same research topic (Figure 5). For instance, researchers have been interested in examining the role of intensely positive experiences in human functioning. Abraham Maslow (1971) envisioned the healthiest, happiest people in the world as capable of having intense moments of awe, and he used the descriptive case study approach to examine the role of such "peak experiences" in the lives of individuals who seemed to exemplify the best in human life. Through correlational research, Dan McAdams (2001) probed individuals' descriptions of the most intensely positive experiences of their lives. He found that people who were motivated toward warm interpersonal experiences tended to mention such experiences as the best memories of their lives. Experimental researchers have also investigated this question. In their work, people who were randomly assigned to write about their most intensely positive experiences for a few minutes each day for two or three days experienced enhanced positive mood as well as fewer physical illnesses two months later, compared to individuals in control groups who wrote about unemotional topics (Burton & King, 2004, 2008).

	Descriptive Research			Correlational Research	Experimental Research
Goal	To determine the basic dimensions of a phenomenon.			To determine how variables change together.	To determine whether a causal relationship exists between two variables.
Sample Research Questions	**Observation** How much time are individuals spending each day on Facebook and similar sites? How many people use different kinds of social media?	**Interviews/Surveys** How do people describe their use of social media? Are they accurate? Do people view the social media they use positively or negatively?	**Case Studies** Does the social media page of a particular person (for instance, someone who has committed suicide) reveal important information about the individual?	What is the relationship between the number of hours spent on social media and face-to-face interactions? How does personal page content relate to personality characteristics?	How does going "cold turkey" on social media influence stress levels? If we randomly assign a smiling picture to a personal page, does it produce more friend requests than the identical page with a frowning picture?
Strengths and Weaknesses	The findings would lay the groundwork for future research by establishing the types of questions that ought to be addressed. This work would not tell us, however, about the processes involved or provide generalizable conclusions.			This research would give us information about how variables change together. However, it would not allow us to make causal conclusions.	This research would permit causal conclusions. The potential artificiality of the manipulations might raise concerns about external validity.

FIGURE 5 **Psychology's Research Methods Applied to Studying Social Media Use** Psychologists can apply different methods to study the same phenomenon. The popularity of social media has opened up a host of new research questions for psychologists.

self-quiz

1. A correlation of −.67 indicates
   A. a strong positive relationship.
   B. a strong negative relationship.
   C. a weak positive relationship.
   D. a weak negative relationship.

2. A study on obesity had four groups, each with a different assignment. One group of participants read a brochure about diet and nutrition; another group had a 30-minute nutrition counseling session; a third group read the newspaper; a fourth group watched a video about exercise and fitness. The control group is
   A. the group that had a counseling session.

   B. the group that read the newspaper.
   C. the group that read the brochure.
   D. the group that watched the video.

3. Which of the following statements is *correct?*
   A. Only correlational research allows researchers to determine causality.
   B. Only experimental research allows researchers to determine causality.
   C. Both correlational and experimental research allow researchers to determine causality.
   D. Neither correlational nor experimental research allows researchers to determine causality.

APPLY IT! 4. Jacob wants to study the relationship between falling in love and a person's academic performance. He asks students to fill out a questionnaire in which they answer "true" or "false" to the question, "Did you fall in love this semester?" Then he asks them for their GPA for the semester. Jacob's study is _____ study.
   A. a correlational
   B. an experimental
   C. a sociological
   D. a longitudinal

5 Research Samples and Settings

Among the important decisions to be made about collecting data are whom to choose as the participants and where to the conduct the research. Will the participants be people or animals? Will they be children, adults, or both? Where will the research take place—in a lab or in a natural setting?

The Research Sample

When psychologists conduct a study, they usually want to be able to draw conclusions that will apply to a larger group of people than the participants they actually study. The entire group about which the investigator wants to draw conclusions is the **population.** The subset

population
The entire group about which the researcher wants to draw conclusions.

The research sample might include a particular group, such as all envrionmental activists or all women runners.
(rally) ©M. Stan Reaves/REX/Shutterstock; (runners) ©Grant Falvey/LNP/REX/Shutterstock

sample
The subset of the population chosen by the investigator for study.

of the population chosen by the investigator for study is a **sample.** The researcher might be interested only in a particular group, such as all children who are gifted and talented, all young women who embark on science and math careers, or all gay men. The key is that the sample studied must be representative of the population to which the investigator wants to generalize his or her results. That is, the researcher might study only 100 gifted adolescents, but he or she wants to apply these results to all gifted and talented adolescents.

To mirror the population as closely as possible, the researcher uses a **random sample,** a sample that gives every member of the population an equal chance of being selected. A representative sample would reflect population factors such as age, socioeconomic status, ethnic origin, marital status, geographic location, and religion. A random sample provides much better grounds for generalizing the results to a population than a nonrandom sample, because random selection improves the chances that the sample is representative of the population. A random sample is still a smaller subset of the population but it is more likely to reflect the characteristics of the population.

random sample
A sample that gives every member of the population an equal chance of being selected.

In selecting a sample, researchers must strive to minimize bias, including gender bias. Because psychology is the scientific study of human behavior, it should pertain to *all* humans, and so the participants in psychological studies ought to be representative of humanity as a whole. Early research in the field often included just the male experience—not only because the researchers themselves were often male, but also because the participants too were typically male (Bridges & Etaugh, 2017). For a long time, the human experience studied by psychologists was primarily the male experience.

There also has been a growing realization that psychological research needs to include more people from diverse ethnic groups (Blaine & McClure, 2018). Because a great deal of psychological research involves college student participants, individuals from groups that have not had as many educational opportunities have not been strongly represented in that research. Given the fact that individuals from diverse ethnic groups were excluded from psychological research for so long, we might reasonably conclude that people's real lives are more varied than past research data have indicated.

These issues are important because scientists want to be able to predict *human* behavior, not just non-Latino White male college student behavior. Imagine if policymakers planned their initiatives for a broad range of Americans based on research derived from only a small group of individuals from a particular background. What might the results be? Recent research on the science of happiness around the world has caught the eye of public policymakers, as evidenced in the Psychology in Our World feature.

The Research Setting

All three types of research we examined in the preceding section can take place in different settings. The setting of the research does not determine the type of research it is. Common settings include the research laboratory and natural settings.

The Global Science of Happiness

Between 2005 and 2006, the Gallup Organization collected the first-ever representative sample of Planet Earth, called the Gallup World Poll (GWP) (Diener & others, 2010). GWP

data were collected from 132 nations (accounting for 96 percent of the world's population). Within each country, a representative sample of all adults was collected; the total sample was 136,839 people. Economic prosperity was measured through items about income, buying power, and ownership of modern conveniences. Social prosperity was measured by asking whether respondents had felt respected, had other people they could count on, had a chance to do what they were good at, and felt in control of their life, in the previous day. Finally, respondents indicated their life satisfaction and gave feedback on whether they had had positive emotional experiences (enjoyment, smiling, or laughter) and negative emotional events (worry, sadness, depression, and anger) in the preceding day. These data allowed for an examination of the intriguing question, what factors contribute to happiness levels around the globe?

©Eric Audras/Getty Images

Psychologist Ed Diener and his colleagues (2010; Diener, Tay, & Oishi, 2013; Oishi & Diener, 2014; Tay & Diener, 2011) reported the first results of the GWP. They found that although economic factors predicted greater life satisfaction across nations, positive feelings and low levels of negative feelings were more strongly predicted by social prosperity—factors such as feeling respected and having people to count on (Diener & others, 2010). From the full sample, 89 nations were ranked according to their standing on the different variables collected in the survey. Comparing the ranks of different nations provides interesting clues about the pathways to national happiness. The United States ranked first in income levels but was 26th in positive feelings and 49th in terms of low levels of negative feelings. *Read:* Despite their relative wealth, Americans are not that happy. In contrast, the happiest nation was New Zealand, which ranked 22nd on economic factors. Clearly the wealth of a nation is no guarantee of happiness among its citizens. Costa Rica ranked 4th in positive feelings and 6th in social prosperity but was 41st in economic prosperity. Thus, high levels of positive feelings can exist even in the face of relatively low wealth.

Diener and his colleagues concluded that if nations are interested in fostering well-being among their citizens, focusing on economic variables will not suffice. Attention to variables that represent the social prosperity of citizens will be required to make the world a happier place.

Policymakers have taken notice. In July 2011, the United Nations General Assembly passed a resolution emphasizing the enhancement of the experience of happiness around the world (United Nations, 2011). The resolution stated that

■ The pursuit of happiness is a fundamental and universal human goal.
■ The gross domestic product of a nation does not adequately reflect the happiness and well-being of its citizens.
■ Nations should develop measures of happiness and well-being and use them to guide their national policies.

The authors of the Declaration of Independence recognized the pursuit of happiness as an unalienable human right. In short, the very founders of the United States believed that all people are born with the right to seek out and enjoy happiness. Today, the global science of happiness is dedicated to identifying the routes by which nations can help their citizens achieve this goal.

Because psychological researchers often want to control as many aspects of the situation as possible, they conduct much of their research in a laboratory, a controlled setting with many of the complex factors of the real world, including potential confounds, removed (Tucker-Drob, 2011). Although laboratory research provides a great deal of control, doing research in the laboratory has drawbacks:

- It is almost impossible to conduct research in the lab without the participants knowing they are being studied.

- The laboratory setting is not the real world and therefore can cause the participants to behave unnaturally.

- People who are willing to go to a university laboratory may not be representative of groups from diverse cultural backgrounds.

- Some aspects of the mind and behavior are difficult if not impossible to examine in the laboratory.

Research can also take place in a natural setting. **Naturalistic observation** is observing behavior in a real-world setting. Psychologists conduct naturalistic observations at sporting events, child-care centers, work settings, shopping malls, and other places that people frequent. If you wanted to study the level of civility on your campus for a research project, most likely you would include naturalistic observation of how people treat one another in such gathering places as the cafeteria and the library reading room.

naturalistic observation
The observation of behavior in a real-world setting.

In another example of a natural setting, researchers who use survey methods are increasingly relying on web-based assessments that allow participants to complete the measures using the Internet. These studies might include volunteers who stumble upon a website and decide to take a survey. They might also include individuals who make money by completing surveys online. Researchers have also conducted experiments online. You might wonder if such online experiences are actually similar to real life. Are people really themselves online? Can online experiences be used as substitutes for "real life"? To read about this issue, see the Challenge Your Thinking feature.

The type of research a psychologist conducts, the operational definitions of the variables of interest, and the choice of sample and setting are decisions that ideally are guided by the research question itself. However, sometimes these decisions represent a compromise between the psychologist's key objective (for example, to study a representative sample of Americans) and the available resources (for instance, a sample of 100 college students).

Natural settings and laboratories are common locales for psychological studies. (first) *Jane Goodall, who specializes in animal behavior, has carried out extensive research on chimpanzees in natural settings. Her work has contributed a great deal to our understanding of these intelligent primates.* (second) *Barbara L. Fredrickson, a psychologist at the University of North Carolina, Chapel Hill, whose work investigates topics such as positive emotions and human flourishing, conducts a laboratory study.*
(Goodall) ©Michael Nichols/National Geographic/Getty Images; (Fredrickson) Courtesy of Barbara Fredrickson, University of North Carolina

Are We Truly "Ourselves" Online and Does It Matter?

Participating in social media is a chance for self-expression and a way to share with family and friends, reignite old friendships, and forge new social connections. Facebook can provide a place for people to seek support after a distressing life events such as romantic break-ups (Tran & Joorman, 2015) and health crises (Davis, Anthony, & Pauls, 2015). Certainly, maintaining close social relationships and garnering support during difficult times would be seem to very positive things. Does it matter if these experiences occur online instead of in person? Evidence suggests that it just might. For instance, one study showed that the social sharing and support that occurred on Facebook did not translate to feeling supported in "real" life (Li, Chen, & Popiel, 2015). Indeed, one study of over 1,000 people found that individuals who were randomly assigned to quit Facebook for 1 week showed higher levels of life satisfaction and positive emotions compared to a control group who continued to use Facebook (Tromholt, 2016). Yet, clearly people enjoy engaging in social media and Facebook is wildly popular.

©JGI/Jamie Grill/Blend Images

One important way psychologists have come to understand the relationship between Facebook use and well-being is distinguishing between active and passive Facebook activity. Active usage means engaging in exchanges that invite interactions with others, for example, posting a status update or commenting on a post. Passive usage refers to things like scrolling through one's newsfeed or looking at others' pages, without direct exchanges. Passive usage involves consuming information but not interacting.

To understand why this distinction is important think about the kinds of things people post online. Research shows that people tend to post extremely positive things about themselves and their lives (Hannah & others, 2017). Passively scrolling through those many positive portrayals of other people's lives can foster feelings of envy, inferiority, shame, and anxiety. Passive usage of Facebook is especially likely to take a toll on well-being (Verduyn & others, 2015). In fact, the study of those who quit Facebook found that the benefits of quitting were highest for those who engaged passively and who were prone to feelings of envy (Tromholt, 2016). (Not surprisingly, a particularly distressing type of passive Facebook use is scrolling through the profile of one's ex-boyfriend or girlfriend; Tran & Joorman, 2015).

This research indicates that Facebook and other social media are not that different from other aspects of human life in that their relationship to adjustment depends on how they are used and by whom. Making the most of social media means using these new ways of connecting to engage actively with others. Who we are online may have an important impact on how we feel "in real life."

What Do You Think?

- Is your own use of social media more active or passive, on balance?
- Why do you think people are likely to post about highly positive aspects of their lives?

1. The *entire group* of people about whom a researcher wants to draw conclusions is the
   A. sample.
   B. random sample.
   C. population.
   D. field.

2. When a researcher decides to study a particular group, such as Latino factory workers, the researcher is specifically determining the study's
   A. population.
   B. sample.
   C. research setting.
   D. scope.

3. A drawback of laboratory research is that

A. it is hard to conduct without the participants' knowledge that they are being studied.
B. people who participate in lab studies may not be representative of the diverse world in which we live.
C. the lab setting is unnatural and may thus cause participants to behave unnaturally.
D. all of the above

APPLY IT! 4. Emily, a committed environmentalist, reads a report that among a nationally representative sample, 60 percent of people polled support drilling for oil off the shores of California. The poll includes 1,000 people. Emily scoffs at the results, noting that all of the

people she knows do not support offshore drilling. The poll must be flawed, she insists. How do you evaluate Emily's statement?
   A. Emily is likely to be wrong. A representative sample is more likely to reflect the general population than the small sample of Emily's friends.
   B. Emily is likely to be wrong because 1,000 people is a high number.
   C. Emily is probably right because, as an environmentalist, she is probably more in tune with these issues than any polling organization.
   D. Emily is probably right because even representative polls are usually biased.

6 Conducting Ethical Research

Ethics is an important consideration for all science. This fact came to the fore in the aftermath of World War II, for example, when it became apparent that Nazi doctors had used concentration camp prisoners as unwilling participants in experiments. These atrocities spurred scientists to develop a code of appropriate behavior—a set of principles about the treatment that participants in research have a right to expect. In general, ethical principles of research focus on balancing the rights of the participants with the rights of scientists to ask important research questions.

©Lars A. Niki

The issue of ethics in psychological research may affect you personally if at some point you serve as a participant in a study. In that event, you need to know your rights as a participant and the researchers' responsibilities in ensuring that these rights are safeguarded. Experiences in research can have unforeseen effects on people's lives. Consider, for instance, that many researchers interested in close relationships might ask romantic couples to keep diaries tracking the quality of their interactions (Sherry & others, 2014). Might just paying close attention to this variable influence it? Other researchers have couples come into the lab and discuss a topic that is a source of conflict in that relationship (Campbell & others, 2013). Such procedures are important to measuring how couples handle conflicts. But, could such interactions influence the couple long after the study is over? Researchers have a responsibility to anticipate the personal problems their study might cause and, at least, to inform the participants of the possible fallout.

Ethics comes into play in every psychological study. Even smart, conscientious students sometimes think that members of their church, athletes in the Special Olympics, or residents of the local nursing home where they volunteer present great samples for psychological research. Without proper permission, though, the most well-meaning, kind, and considerate researchers still violate the rights of the participants.

Ethics Guidelines

Various guidelines have been developed to ensure that research is conducted ethically. At the base of all of these guidelines is the notion that a person participating in psychological research should be no worse off coming out of the study than he or she was on the way in.

Today colleges and universities have a review board, typically called the *institutional review board,* or *IRB,* which evaluates the ethical nature of research conducted at their institutions. Proposed research plans must pass the scrutiny of a research ethics committee before the research can be initiated. In addition, the American Psychological Association (APA) has developed ethics guidelines for its members. The APA code of ethics instructs psychologists to protect their participants from mental and physical harm. The participants' best interests need to be kept foremost in the researcher's mind. APA's guidelines address four important issues:

- *Informed consent:* All participants must know what their participation will involve and what risks might develop. For example, participants in a study on dating should be told beforehand that a questionnaire might stimulate thoughts about issues in their relationships that they have not considered. Participants also should be informed that in some instances a discussion of the issues might improve their relationships but that in others it might worsen the relationships and possibly end them. Even after informed consent is given, participants must retain the right to withdraw from the study at any time and for any reason.

- *Confidentiality:* Researchers are responsible for keeping all of the data they gather on individuals completely confidential and, when possible, completely anonymous. Confidential data are not the same as anonymous. When data are confidential, it is possible to link a participant's identity to his or her data.

- *Debriefing:* After the study has been completed, the researchers should inform the participants of its purpose and the methods they used. In most cases, the experimenters also can inform participants in a general manner beforehand about the purpose of the research without leading the participants to behave in a way that they think that the experimenters are expecting. When preliminary information about the study is likely to affect the results, participants must be debriefed after the study's completion.

- *Deception:* This is an ethical issue that psychologists debate extensively. In some circumstances, telling the participants beforehand what the research study is about substantially alters the participants' behavior and invalidates the researcher's data. For example, suppose a psychologist wants to know whether bystanders will report a theft. A mock theft is staged, and the psychologist observes which bystanders report it. Had the psychologist informed the participants beforehand that the study intended to discover the percentage of bystanders who will report a theft, the whole study would have been ruined. Thus, the researcher deceives participants about the purpose of the study, perhaps leading them to believe that it has some other purpose. In all cases of deception, however, the psychologist must ensure that the deception will not harm the participants and that the participants will be told the true nature of the study (will be debriefed) as soon as possible after the study is completed. Note that in studies using deception, participants cannot be fully informed prior to giving consent. This is why participants in studies involving deception should have the option of withdrawing consent after they find out what the study is actually about. As a student of psychology, you will encounter many studies that employ deception. Researchers who employ deception in their studies must be able to justify lying to participants, because doing so is vital to the scientific merit of their work. Psychological researchers take deception seriously and employ it only when no other options would allow them to ask the questions they seek to answer.

The federal government also takes a role in ensuring that research involving human participants is conducted ethically. The Federal Office for Protection from Research Risks is devoted to safeguarding the well-being of participants in research studies. Over the years, the office has dealt with many challenging and controversial issues—among them, informed consent rules for research on psychological disorders, regulations governing research on pregnant women and fetuses, and ethical issues regarding AIDS vaccine research.

Of considerable concern is the ways that the principles of ethical research apply when studies involve *vulnerable populations,* which include children, individuals with psychological disorders, incarcerated individuals, and others who may be especially susceptible to coercion. For example, when children participate in research, parental consent is essential. Children may be asked to agree to participate as well. When prisoners or individuals who are on parole participate in research, it must be clear that their treatment and decisions about their future release or parole will not be influenced by their willingness to participate.

Students who receive extra credit for participating in research might also be considered vulnerable to coercion. They must have an option to receive that same extra credit without agreeing to participate in research.

The Ethics of Research with Animals

For generations, psychologists have used animals in some research. Animal studies have provided a better understanding of and solutions for many human problems (Domjan, 2015). Neal Miller (1985) listed the following areas in which research employing animals has benefited humans:

- Psychotherapy techniques and behavioral medicine
- Rehabilitation of neuromuscular disorders

- Alleviation of the effects of stress and pain
- Drugs to treat anxiety and severe mental illness
- Methods for avoiding drug addiction and relapse
- Treatments to help premature infants gain weight so they can leave the hospital sooner
- Methods used to alleviate memory deficits in old age

Only about 5 percent of APA members use animals in their research. Rats and mice account for 90 percent of all psychological research with animals. It is true that researchers sometimes use procedures with animals that would be unethical with humans, but they are guided by a set of standards for housing, feeding, and maintaining the psychological and physical well-being of their animal subjects. Researchers are required to weigh potential benefits of the research against possible harm to the animal and to avoid inflicting unnecessary pain. Animal abuse is not as common as animal activist groups charge. In short, researchers must follow stringent ethical guidelines, whether animals or humans are the subjects in their studies.

©Rosa Jay/Shutterstock

The Place of Values in Psychological Research

Questions are asked not only about the ethics of psychology but also about its values and its standards for judging what is worthwhile and desirable. Some psychologists argue that psychology should be value-free and morally neutral. From their perspective, the psychologist's role as a scientist is to present facts as objectively as possible. Others believe that because psychologists are human, they cannot possibly be value-free. Indeed, some people go so far as to argue that psychologists should take stands on certain issues. For example, psychological research shows that children reared by gay and lesbian parents are no more likely to be gay than other children and that the children of homosexual partners tend to demonstrate levels of psychological health that are equal to or higher than those of children reared by heterosexual parents (Patterson, 2012, 2014; Patterson & Farr, 2012; Patterson, Riskind, & Tornello, 2014; Patterson & Wainright, 2010). To the extent that some have argued against the rights of gay individuals to adopt children or to retain custody of their biological children, psychologists may have a role to play in the debate about these issues.

self-quiz

1. Providing research participants with information about the purpose of a study at the study's conclusion is called
   A. informed consent.
   B. deception.
   C. debriefing.
   D. confidentiality.

2. The organization that provides ethical guidelines for psychologists is the
   A. American Psychiatric Association.
   B. Institutional Review Board.
   C. American Medical Association.
   D. American Psychological Association.

3. A study could possibly put participants at risk of harm, but the participants are not told about that risk. The ethical standard that has been violated is
   A. debriefing.
   B. informed consent.
   C. deception.
   D. confidentiality.

APPLY IT! 4. Amanda is participating in a psychological study as part of her Intro psychology course. While filling out items on a questionnaire, Amanda finds that some of them embarrass her, and she decides to skip them. As she leaves the study, the experimenter notices these blank questions and asks Amanda to complete them because the research will be ruined without complete data from all participants. Which of the following accurately assesses the ethics of this situation?
   A. Amanda should really complete those questions. What's the big deal?
   B. Amanda is within her rights to leave any question blank if she chooses, and the experimenter has definitely "crossed a line."
   C. Amanda is ethically wrong because she agreed to be in the study, and so she must see it through.
   D. If Amanda read and signed the consent form, she is obligated to do as the experimenter says.

Learning About Psychology Means Learning About You

Throughout your life you have been exposed to a good deal of information about psychological research. In *Experience Psychology* and your introductory psychology class, you will also learn about a multitude of research findings. In this last section, we consider the ways that learning about psychological studies can help you learn about yourself. We start by looking at some guidelines for evaluating psychological research findings that you might encounter in your everyday life.

Encountering Psychology in Everyday Life

Not all psychological information that is presented for public consumption comes from professionals with excellent credentials and reputations at colleges or universities or in applied mental health settings (Stanovich, 2013). Journalists, television reporters, and other media personnel are not usually trained in psychological research. As a result, they often have trouble sorting through the widely varying material they find and making sound decisions about the best information to present to the public. In addition, the media often focus on sensationalistic and dramatic psychological findings to capture public attention. They tend to go beyond what actual research articles and clinical findings really say.

Even when the media present the results of excellent research, they have trouble accurately informing people about the findings and their implications for people's lives. *Experience Psychology* is dedicated to carefully introducing, defining, and elaborating on key concepts and issues, research, and clinical findings. The media, however, do not have the luxury of so much time and space to detail and specify the limitations and qualifications of research. In the end, you have to take responsibility for evaluating media reports on psychological research. To put it another way, you have to consume psychological information critically and wisely. Five guidelines follow.

AVOID OVERGENERALIZING BASED ON LITTLE INFORMATION
Media reports of psychological information often leave out details about the nature of the sample used in a given study. Without information about sample characteristics—such as the number of participants, how many were male or female, or their ethnic representation—it is wise to take research results with a grain of salt. Perhaps most importantly, try to find information about the sample size for any given study. Remember that in an experiment, random assignment will only produce equal groups if the sample was large.

DISTINGUISH BETWEEN GROUP RESULTS AND INDIVIDUAL NEEDS   Just as we cannot generalize from a small group to all people, we also cannot apply conclusions from a group to an individual. When you learn about psychological research through the media, you might be disposed to apply the results to your life. It is important to keep in mind that statistics about a group do not necessarily represent each individual in the group equally well. Imagine, for example, taking a test in a class and being told that the class average was 75 percent, but you got 98 percent. It is unlikely that you would want the instructor to apply the group average to your score.

Sometimes consumers of psychological research can get the wrong idea about whether their experience is "normal" if it does not match group statistics. New parents face this issue all the time. They read about developmental milestones that supposedly characterize an entire age group of children; one such milestone might be that most 2-year-olds are conversing with their parents. However, this group information does not necessarily characterize all children who are developing normally. Albert Einstein did not start talking until he was the ripe old age of 3.

LOOK FOR ANSWERS BEYOND A SINGLE STUDY The media might identify an interesting piece of research and claim that it is something phenomenal with far-reaching implications. Although such pivotal studies do occur, they are rare. It is safer to assume that no single study will provide conclusive answers to an important question, especially answers that apply to all people. In fact, in most psychological domains that prompt many investigations, conflicting results are common. Answers to questions in research usually emerge after many scientists have conducted similar investigations that yield similar conclusions. Remember that you should not take one research study as the absolute, final answer to a problem, no matter how compelling the findings.

AVOID ATTRIBUTING CAUSES WHERE NONE HAVE BEEN FOUND Drawing causal conclusions from correlational studies is one of the most common mistakes the media make. When a true experiment has not been conducted—that is, when participants have not been randomly assigned to treatments or experiences—two variables might have only a noncausal relationship to each other. Remember from the discussion of correlation earlier in the chapter that causal interpretations cannot be made when two or more factors are simply correlated. We cannot say that one causes the other. When you hear about correlational studies, be skeptical of words indicating causation until you know more about the particular research.

CONSIDER THE SOURCE OF PSYCHOLOGICAL INFORMATION Studies conducted by psychologists are not automatically accepted by the rest of the research community. The researchers usually must submit their findings to a journal for review by their colleagues, who make a decision about whether to publish the paper, depending on its scientific merit. This process, called *peer review,* means that research that is published in scholarly journals has survived the scrutiny of experts in a particular area. Although the quality of research and findings is not uniform among all psychology journals, in most cases journals submit the findings to far greater scrutiny than the popular media do (Stanovich, 2013).

Within the media, though, you can usually draw a distinction. The reports of psychological research in respected newspapers such as the *New York Times* and the *Washington Post,* as well as in credible magazines such as *Time* and *Newsweek,* are more trustworthy than reports in tabloids such as the *National Enquirer* and *Star.*

Finally, it is not unusual to read about psychological research online, where bloggers and others might comment on the validity of researchers' findings. When you encounter research-related information on the web, see if you can find the actual study and read it. As helpful as a Google search, a blog, or a Wikipedia entry might be, reading the actual science is crucial to evaluating the conclusions drawn. Whatever the source—serious publication, tabloid, blog, online news outlet, or even academic journal—you are responsible for reading the details behind the reported findings and for analyzing the study's credibility.

> ## *Do It!*
>
> In the next few days, look through several newspapers, magazines, and your favorite online news sources for reports about psychological research. Apply the guidelines for being a wise consumer of information about psychology to these media reports.

Appreciating Psychology as the Science of You

In taking introductory psychology, you have an amazing opportunity. You will learn a great deal about human beings, especially one particular human being: you. Whether the psychological research presented is about emotions and motivation or the structures of the nervous system, it is still essentially about you.

When you think of psychology, you might think first and foremost about the mind and its complex mental processes such as those involved in love, gratitude, hate, and anger. However, psychology has come to recognize more and more that the mind and its operations are intricately connected to the body. As you will see when we examine neuroscience, observations of the brain at work reveal that when mental processes change, so do physical processes. This mind–body link has fascinated philosophers for centuries. Psychology occupies the very spot where the mind and the body meet.

It might be helpful to think concretely about the ways the mind and body can relate to each other even as they are united in the physical reality of a person. Let's say you experience a mental event such as watching a documentary about the dangers of obesity. You decide to embark on a workout regimen for six-pack abdominals. Dedication, goal setting, and self-discipline will be the kinds of mental processes necessary to transform your body. The mind can work on the body, prompting changes to its shape and size.

Similarly, the body can dramatically influence the mind. Consider how fuzzy your thinking is after you stay out too late and how much easier it is to solve life's problems after a good night's sleep. Also think about your outlook on the first day of true recovery from a nagging cold: Everything seems better. Your mood and your work improve. Clearly, physical states such as illness and health influence how we think.

The relationship between the body and mind is illustrated in a major dilemma that countless psychologists have faced: the impact of nature versus nurture. Essentially, psychologists have wondered and debated which of the two is more important to a person—nature (that is, genetic heritage) or nurture (social experiences). The influence of genetics on a variety of psychological characteristics, and the ways that genetic influence can itself be altered by experience, will be addressed in many of the main topics in *Experience Psychology,* from development to personality traits to psychological disorders. You will see that at every turn, your physical and mental self are intertwined in ways you may have never considered.

Throughout *Experience Psychology*, we investigate the ways that all of the various approaches to psychology matter to your life. Psychology is crucially about you, essential to your understanding of your life, your goals, and the ways that you can use the insights of thousands of scientists to make your life healthier and happier.

self-quiz

1. You want to know if getting more exercise will improve your mood. Which research study would be most informative?
   A. A correlational study with a sample of 40 adults.
   B. An experiment that involves randomly assigning 200 students similar to yourself to either a physical activity condition or a control group, and then measuring mood.
   C. A case study of one psychology student's experience with exercise.
   D. A longitudinal study tracking exercise and mood over two years in a sample of 100 grade school children.

2. In a blog post, a scientist describes a recently completed study in which she found that people who were assigned to an exercise group reported 10 times more happiness than those in a control group. She and her colleagues plan to submit the findings for publication. What would a wise reader of science think about this post?
   A. The results are clearly important and represent a major contribution to science.

   B. The results are likely worthless because you cannot believe anything you read in a blog post.
   C. The results are not surprising and are therefore probably true.
   D. The jury is still out on the findings because the research has not gone through peer review.

3. A study reports that height is surprisingly correlated with lifetime income. Specifically, tall people tend to make more money than short people. April is the shortest women in her class and when she reads about the study she becomes upset. What advice would you have for April?
   A. She can still lead a successful life even if she cannot ever make as much money as a tall person.
   B. Correlation does not imply causation and group statistics cannot be assumed to apply to every single case.
   C. Scientists base their conclusions on data. The data show that she is simply very likely to be poor.
   D. Being a critical thinker means accepting whatever the data say.

APPLY IT! 4. Sarah's mother forwards her a chain email warning of an association between drinking orange juice and developing arthritis. Her mom tells her that three of her closest friends are big orange juice fans and they recently developed arthritis. Sarah's mother tells her to stop drinking orange juice and to tell her friends to do the same. Rather than forwarding the email to everyone she knows, Sarah should
   A. gently explain to her mother the importance of considering the source of scientific information.
   B. respectfully tell her mother that even if an association between two variables is found, it does not imply a causal relationship.
   C. kindly ask her mother if the study was published in a scientific journal and if so, which one.
   D. All of the above.

Defining Psychology and Exploring Its Roots

Psychology is the scientific study of human behavior and mental processes. Psychologists approach human behavior as scientists who think critically and who are curious, skeptical, and objective. Psychology emerged as a science from philosophy and physiology. Two founders of the science of psychology are Wilhelm Wundt and William James.

 ## Contemporary Approaches to Psychology

Approaches to psychology include biological, behavioral, psychodynamic, humanistic, cognitive, evolutionary, and sociocultural. All of these perspectives consider important questions about human behavior from different but complementary vantage points.

Psychology's Scientific Method

Psychologists use the scientific method to address research questions. This method involves starting with a theory and then making observations, formulating hypotheses, testing these through empirical research, drawing conclusions, and evaluating these conclusions. The science of psychology is an ongoing conversation among scholars.

 ## Types of Psychological Research

Three types of research commonly used in psychology are descriptive research (finding out about the basic dimensions of some variable), correlational research (finding out if and how two variables change together), and experimental research (determining the causal relationship between variables). In an experiment, the independent variable is manipulated to see if it produces changes in the dependent variable. Experiments involve comparing two groups: the experimental group (the one that receives the treatment or manipulation of the independent variable) and the control group (the comparison group or baseline that is equal to the experimental group in every way except for the independent variable). Experimental research relies on random assignment to ensure that the groups are roughly equivalent before the manipulation of the independent variable.

 ## Research Samples and Settings

Two important decisions that must be made for psychological research are whom to study and where to study them. A sample is the group that participates in a study; the population is the group to which the researcher wishes to generalize the results. A random sample is the best way of ensuring that the sample reflects the population. Research settings include the laboratory as well as real-world, naturalistic contexts. The laboratory allows a great deal of control, but naturalistic settings may give a truer sense of natural behavior.

 ## Conducting Ethical Research

For all kinds of research, ethical treatment of participants is very important. When participants leave a psychological study, they should be no worse off than they were when they entered. Guiding principles for ethical research in psychology include informed consent, confidentiality, debriefing (participants should be fully informed about the purpose of a study once it is over), and explaining fully the use of deception in a study.

 ## Learning About Psychology Means Learning About You

In your everyday life and in introductory psychology, you will be exposed to psychological research findings. In encountering psychological research in the media, you should adopt the attitude of a scientist and critically evaluate the research as presented. In introductory psychology, you should make the most of the experience by applying it to your life. Psychology is, after all, the scientific study of you—your behavior, thoughts, goals, and well-being.

KEY TERMS

behavior
behavioral approach
biological approach
case history
case study
cognitive approach
control group
correlational research
critical thinking
demand characteristics
dependent variable
double-blind experiment

empirical method
evolutionary approach
experiment
experimental group
experimenter bias
external validity
functionalism
humanistic approach
hypothesis
independent variable
internal validity
longitudinal design

mental processes
natural selection
naturalistic observation
neuroscience
operational definition
placebo
placebo effect
population
psychodynamic approach
psychology
random assignment
random sample

replication
research participant bias
sample
science
sociocultural approach
structuralism
theory
third variable problem
validity
variable

ANSWERS TO SELF-QUIZZES

Section 1:   1. A; 2. C; 3. B; 4. B
Section 2:   1. C; 2. D; 3. D; 4. C
Section 3:   1. D; 2. D; 3. B; 4. B

Section 4:   1. B; 2. B; 3. B; 4. A
Section 5:   1. C; 2. B; 3. D; 4. A
Section 6:   1. C; 2. D; 3. B; 4. B

Section 7   1. B; 2. D; 3. B; 4. D

2 The Brain and Behavior

The Empathic Brain

Human beings are the most social creatures on earth. We need each other to survive and living in groups we show each other incredible levels of trust. When we experience difficulties, failures, or profound losses, we turn to each other for support. When we think about the face of our beloved family members or friends expressing concern for our problems, we may not realize that behind and just above those caring faces lies the source of that concern: The brain, an intricate 3-pound organ where all of our actions originate. In fact, research shows that the human brain is a wellspring of empathy. When people see another person suffering, the brains of those observers react automatically as if they themselves are suffering (Haaker, Yi, Petrovic, & Olsson, 2017). You might think of the brain as a kind of computer, but in truth the brain is social organ, one that comes into the world ready to relate to other people (Callaghan & Corbit, 2018; Sliwa & Freiwald, 2017).

Our brains are involved in every aspect of our lives. Every behavior, every thought, is an event in the brain. Imagine: Even as you are reading about the brain, the brain is the engine that is doing the work of reading itself. The brain is also the structure responsible for the research presented here. The brain is at once the object of study and the reason we are able to study it.

1 The Nervous System

The **nervous system** is the body's electrochemical communication circuitry. The field that studies the nervous system is called *neuroscience,* and the people who study it are *neuroscientists.*

One cubic centimeter of brain = 50 million nerve cells. That's about the size of a snack cube of cheese.

The human nervous system is made up of billions of communicating cells, and it is likely the most intricately organized aggregate of matter on the planet. A single cubic centimeter of the human brain consists of well over 50 million nerve cells, each of which communicates with many other nerve cells in information-processing networks that make the most elaborate computer seem primitive.

nervous system The body's electrochemical communication circuitry.

Characteristics of the Nervous System

The brain and nervous system guide our interactions with the world, moving the body and directing our adaptation to our environment. Several extraordinary characteristics allow the nervous system to direct our behavior: complexity, integration, adaptability, and electrochemical transmission.

COMPLEXITY   The human brain and nervous system are enormously complex. The orchestration of all the billions of nerve cells in the brain—to allow you to sing, dance, write, talk, and think—is an awe-inspiring achievement. Right now, your brain is carrying out a multitude of tasks, including seeing, reading, learning, and breathing. Extensive assemblies of nerve cells participate in each of these activities, all at once.

INTEGRATION   The brain is the "great integrator" (Hyman, 2001), meaning that the brain does a wonderful job of pulling information together. Sounds, sights, touch, taste, smells—the brain integrates all of these as we function in the world.

The brain and the nervous system have different levels and many different parts. Brain activity is integrated across these levels through countless interconnections of brain cells and extensive pathways that link different parts of the brain. Each nerve cell can make connections with thousands of others, making an astronomical number of connections. The evidence for these connections is observable, for example, when a loved one takes your hand. How does your brain know, and tell you, what has happened? Bundles of interconnected nerve cells relay information about the sensation in your hand through the nervous system in an orderly fashion, all the way to the areas of the brain involved in recognizing that someone you love is holding your hand. Then the brain might send a reply back and prompt your hand to give him or her a little squeeze.

Adaptation, adaptability, and adapt: Psychologists use these terms when referring to the ability to function in a changing world.

ADAPTABILITY   The world around us is constantly changing. To survive, we must change, or adapt to new conditions. Our brain and nervous system together serve as our agent in adapting to the world. Although nerve cells reside in certain brain regions, they are not fixed, unchanging structures. They have a hereditary, biological foundation, but they are constantly adapting to changes in the body and the environment.

plasticity
The brain's special capacity for change.

The term **plasticity** denotes the brain's special capacity for change. You might believe that thinking is a mental process, not a physical one. Yet thinking *is* a physical event, because your every thought is reflected in physical activity in the brain. Moreover, the brain can be changed by experience. London cab drivers who have developed a familiarity with the city show increases in the size of the brain area thought to be responsible for reading maps (Maguire & others, 2000). Think about that: When you change the way you think, you are literally changing the brain's physical processes and even its shape. Experiences throughout life can have long lasting impact on the brain. For example, studies have shown that individuals who have managerial experience, especially those who supervised a large number of employees, are likely to show less age-related decreases in the size of the hippocampus later in life (Suo & others, 2017). As we will see later, the hippocampus is a brain structure that plays an important role in memory. Your experiences contribute to the wiring or rewiring of your brain (Cirstea & others, 2017; Hoekzema & others, 2017; Maitre & others, 2017; Mooneyham & others, 2017), just as the experiences of those London cab drivers did.

ELECTROCHEMICAL TRANSMISSION The brain and the rest of the nervous system work as an information-processing system, powered by electrical impulses and chemical messengers (Takmakov, 2017). When an impulse travels down a nerve cell, or *neuron,* it does so electrically. When that impulse gets to the end of the line, it communicates with the next neuron using chemicals, as we will consider in detail later in this chapter.

Pathways in the Nervous System

As we interact with and adapt to the world, the brain and the nervous system receive and transmit sensory input (like sounds, smells, and flavors), integrate the information received from the environment, and direct the body's motor activities. Information flows into the brain through input from our senses, and the brain makes sense of that information, pulling it together and giving it meaning. In turn, information moves out of the brain to the rest of the body, directing all of the physical things we do.

*Afferent and efferent are hard to keep straight. It might be helpful to remember that afferent nerves **arrive** at the brain and spinal cord, while efferent nerves **exit** the brain and spinal cord—A for afferent and arrive, and E for efferent and exit.*

afferent nerves
Also called sensory nerves; nerves that carry information about the external environment to the brain and spinal cord via sensory receptors.

efferent nerves
Also called motor nerves; nerves that carry information out of the brain and spinal cord to other areas of the body.

neural networks
Networks of nerve cells that integrate sensory input and motor output.

The nervous system possesses specialized pathways that are adapted for different functions. These pathways are made up of afferent nerves, efferent nerves, and neural networks. **Afferent nerves,** or *sensory nerves*, carry information to the brain and spinal cord. These sensory pathways communicate information about the external environment (for example, seeing a sunrise) and internal body processes (for example, feeling tired or hungry) from sensory receptors to the brain and spinal cord. **Efferent nerves,** or *motor nerves*, carry information out of the brain and spinal cord—that is, they carry the nervous system's output. These motor pathways communicate information from the brain and spinal cord to other areas of the body, including muscles and glands, telling them to get busy. Efferent neurons are called motor neurons because they tell our muscles what to do as we move.

Most information processing occurs through **neural networks.** These are interconnected groups of nerve cells that integrate sensory input and motor output (He, Qian, & Cao, 2017; Senan & others, 2017). For example, as you read your class notes, the input from your eyes is transmitted to

When we touch or gaze at an object, electrical charges and chemical messages pulse through our brain, knitting the cells together into pathways and networks for processing the information.
©Eric Herchaft/SuperStock

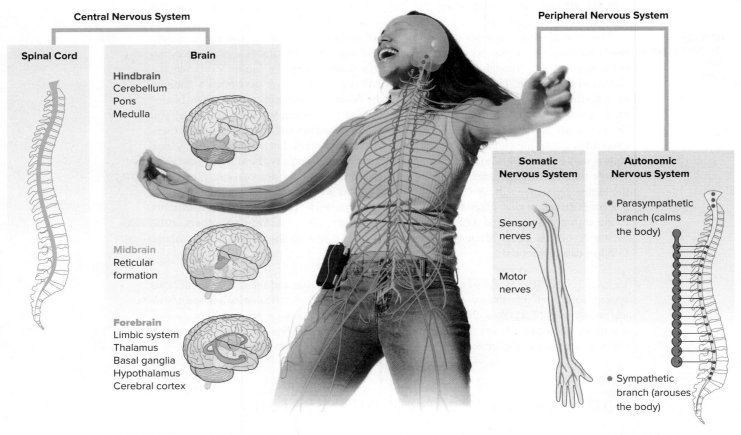

Human Nervous System

Central Nervous System

Peripheral Nervous System

Spinal Cord

Brain

Hindbrain
Cerebellum
Pons
Medulla

Midbrain
Reticular
formation

Forebrain
Limbic system
Thalamus
Basal ganglia
Hypothalamus
Cerebral cortex

**Somatic
Nervous System**

Sensory
nerves

Motor
nerves

**Autonomic
Nervous System**

• Parasympathetic
branch (calms
the body)

• Sympathetic
branch (arouses
the body)

FIGURE 1 **Major Divisions of the Human Nervous System** The nervous system has two main divisions. One is the *central nervous system* (*left*), which comprises the brain and the spinal cord. The nervous system's other main division is the *peripheral nervous system* (*right*), which itself has two parts—the *somatic nervous system,* which controls sensory and motor neurons, and the *autonomic nervous system,* which monitors processes such as breathing, heart rate, and digestion. These complex systems work together to help us successfully navigate the world.
©Photoplay/Media Bakery

your brain and then passed through many neural networks, which translate the characters on the page into neural codes for letters, words, associations, and meanings. Some of the information is stored in the neural networks, and if you read aloud, some is passed on as messages to your lips and tongue. Neural networks make up most of the brain. Working in networks amplifies the brain's computing power.

Divisions of the Nervous System

This truly elegant system is highly ordered and organized for effective function. Figure 1 shows the two primary divisions of the human nervous system: the central nervous system and the peripheral nervous system.

The **central nervous system (CNS)** is the brain and spinal cord. More than 99 percent of all our nerve cells are located in the CNS. The **peripheral nervous system (PNS)** is the network of nerves that connects the brain and spinal cord to other parts of the body. The functions of the peripheral nervous system are to bring information to and from the brain and spinal cord and to carry out the commands of the CNS to execute various muscular and glandular activities.

The peripheral nervous system has two major divisions: the somatic nervous system and the autonomic nervous system. The **somatic nervous system** consists of *sensory nerves* (afferent),

central nervous system (CNS)
The brain and spinal cord.

peripheral nervous system (PNS)
The network of nerves that connects the brain and spinal cord to other parts of the body.

somatic nervous system
The body system consisting of the sensory nerves, whose function is to convey information from the skin and muscles to the central nervous system about conditions such as pain and temperature, and the motor nerves, whose function is to tell muscles what to do.

autonomic nervous system

The body system that takes messages to and from the body's internal organs, monitoring such processes as breathing, heart rate, and digestion.

sympathetic nervous system

The part of the autonomic nervous system that arouses the body to mobilize it for action and thus is involved in the experience of stress.

whose function is to convey information from the skin and muscles to the CNS about conditions such as pain and temperature, and *motor nerves* (efferent), whose function is to tell muscles what to do. The function of the **autonomic nervous system** is to take messages to and from the body's internal organs, monitoring such processes as breathing, heart rate, and digestion. The autonomic nervous system also is divided into two parts. The first part, the **sympathetic nervous system,** arouses the body to mobilize it for action and thus is involved in the experience of stress; the second part, the **parasympathetic nervous system,** calms the body.

Stress is the body's response to **stressors,** which are the circumstances and events that threaten individuals and tax their coping abilities. When we experience stress, our body readies itself to handle the assault of stress; a number of physiological changes take place. You certainly know what stress feels like. Imagine, for example, that you show up for class one morning, and it looks as if everyone else knows that there is a test that day. You hear others talking about how much they have studied, and you nervously ask yourself: "Test? What test?" You start to sweat, and your heart thumps fast in your chest. Sure enough, the instructor shows up with a stack of exams. You are about to be tested on material you have not even thought about, much less studied.

The stress response begins with a fight-or-flight reaction, one of the functions of the sympathetic nervous system. This reaction quickly mobilizes the body's physiological resources to prepare the organism to deal with threats to survival. Clearly, an unexpected exam is not literally a threat to your survival, but the human stress response is such that it can occur in reaction to any threat to personally important motives (Sapolsky, 2004).

When you feel your heart pounding and your hands sweating under stress, those experiences reveal the sympathetic nervous system in action. If you need to run away from a stressor, the sympathetic nervous system sends blood out to your extremities to get you ready to take off.

When we undergo stress, we also experience the release of *corticosteroids,* which are powerful stress hormones (Ives & Bertke, 2017). Corticosteroids in the brain allow us to focus our attention on what needs to be done *now.* For example, in an emergency, people sometimes report feeling strangely calm and doing just what has to be done, whether it is calling 911 or applying pressure to a serious cut. Such experiences reveal the benefits of corticosteroids for humans in times of emergency (Jafari, Kolb, & Mohajerani, 2017). *Acute stress* is the momentary stress that occurs in response to life experiences. When the stressful situation ends, so does acute stress.

However, we are not in a live-or-die situation most of the time when we experience stress. Indeed, we can even "stress ourselves out" just by thinking. *Chronic stress*—that is, stress that goes on continuously—may lead to persistent autonomic nervous system arousal (McKewan, 2017). While the sympathetic nervous system is working to meet the demands of whatever is stressing us out, the parasympathetic nervous system is not getting a chance to do its job of maintenance and repair, of digesting food, or of keeping our organs in good working order. Thus, over time, chronic autonomic nervous system activity can break down the immune system. Chronic stress is clearly best avoided, although this objective is sometimes easier said than done.

Yet the brain, an organ that is itself powerfully affected by chronic stress, can be our ally in preventing such continuous stress. Consider that when you face a challenging situation, you can use the brain's abilities and interpret the experience in a less stressful way. For example, you might approach an upcoming exam or an audition for a play not so much as a stressor but as an opportunity to shine. When we reinterpret potentially stressful situations as challenges rather than threats, we can avoid the experience of stress. Many cognitive therapists believe that changing the way people think about their life opportunities and experiences can help them live less stressfully (Williams & others, 2017). By changing the way we think about potentially stressful events, we can reduce stress. Coming up with ways to consider potential stressors as challenges (not threats) can help to reduce the body's stress response.

At the beginning of this chapter, you learned how changing the way you think can produce physical changes in the brain. In light of this remarkable capacity, it is reasonable to conclude that you can use your brain's powers to change how you look at life experiences—and maybe even deploy the brain as a defense against stress.

Sympathetic, parasympathetic—how to distinguish these? Remember that the sympathetic nervous system feels "sympathy" for you when you're stressed out, and prompts you to take action to address the stressor, and that the parasympathetic nervous system helps you to "rest and digest."

parasympathetic nervous system

The part of the autonomic nervous system that calms the body.

stress

The responses of individuals to environmental stressors.

stressors

Circumstances and events that threaten individuals and tax their coping abilities and that cause physiological changes to ready the body to handle the assault of stress.

self-quiz

1. The characteristics that allow the nervous system to direct behavior are its complexity, integration, electrochemical transmission, and
   A. constancy.
   B. adaptability.
   C. sensitivity.
   D. fight-or-flight response.

2. Neural networks are networks of nerve cells that integrate sensory input and
   A. the fight-or-flight response.
   B. electrochemical transmission.
   C. bodily processes such as heart rate and digestion.
   D. motor output.

3. When you are in danger, the part of the nervous system that is responsible for an increase in your heart rate is the
   A. central nervous system.
   B. peripheral nervous system.
   C. sympathetic nervous system.
   D. parasympathetic nervous system.

APPLY IT! 4. Shannon and Terrell are two college students. Shannon is in a constant state of low-level stress. She spends a lot of time worrying about what might happen, and she gets herself worked up about imagined catastrophes. Terrell is more easygoing, but on his way to class one day he is in a near-miss traffic accident—at the moment he sees the truck coming at him, his body tenses up, his heart races, and he experiences extreme panic. Which answer most accurately identifies the individual who is most likely to catch the cold that is going around their dorm this semester?
   A. Shannon, who is experiencing chronic stress
   B. Terrell, who is experiencing acute stress
   C. Shannon, who is experiencing acute stress
   D. Terrell, who is experiencing chronic stress

2 Neurons

Within each division of the nervous system, much is happening at the cellular level. Nerve cells, chemicals, and electrical impulses work together to transmit information at speeds of up to 330 miles per hour. As a result, information can travel from your brain to your hands (or vice versa) in just milliseconds.

That's fast! Most of us will never experience driving a car that fast. The supersonic rocket car that holds the world record can drive over 700 miles per hour. Its British developers are shooting for over 1,000 miles per hour. Now, the wisdom of driving a car faster than we can think is another story. . .

There are two types of cells in the nervous system: neurons and glial cells. **Neurons** are the nerve cells that handle the information-processing function. The human brain contains about 100 billion neurons. The average neuron is a complex structure with as many as 10,000 physical connections with other cells. Researchers have been especially interested in a special type of neuron called *mirror neurons.* Mirror neurons seem to play a role in imitation and are activated (in primates and humans) when we perform an action but also when we watch someone else perform that same task (Linkovski, Katzin, & Salti, 2017). In addition to imitation, these neurons may play a role in empathy and in our understanding of others.

Glial cells (or glia) provide support, nutritional benefits, and other functions in the nervous system (Kettenmann & Verkhratsky, 2016). Glial cells are the most common cells in the nervous system. In fact, for every neuron there are about 10 glial cells. They have many functions. Glial cells keep neurons running smoothly. These cells are not specialized to process information in the way that neurons are.

You might think of glial cells as the pit crew of the nervous system.

neurons
One of two types of cells in the nervous system; neurons are the nerve cells that handle the information-processing function.

glial cells
The second of two types of cells in the nervous system; glial cells (also called glia) provide support, nutritional benefits, and other functions and keep neurons running smoothly.

Specialized Cell Structure

cell body
The part of the neuron that contains the nucleus, which directs the manufacture of substances that the neuron needs for growth and maintenance.

dendrites
Treelike fibers projecting from a neuron, which receive information and orient it toward the neuron's cell body.

Not all neurons are alike, as they are specialized to handle different information-processing functions. However, all neurons do have some common characteristics. Most neurons are created very early in life, but their shape, size, and connections can change throughout the life span. The way neurons function reflects the major characteristic of the nervous system described at the beginning of the chapter: plasticity. Neurons can and do change.

Every neuron has a cell body, dendrites, and an axon (Figure 2). The **cell body** contains the nucleus, which directs the manufacture of substances that the neuron needs for growth and maintenance. **Dendrites,** treelike fibers projecting from a neuron, receive information and orient it toward the neuron's cell body. Most nerve cells have numerous dendrites, which increase their surface area, allowing each neuron to receive input from many other

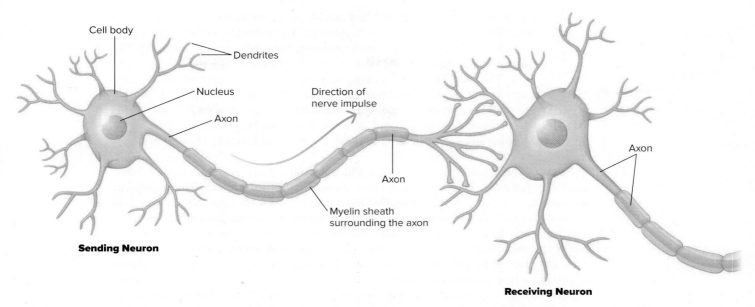

Sending Neuron

Cell body

Dendrites

Nucleus

Axon

Direction of nerve impulse

Axon

Myelin sheath surrounding the axon

Axon

Receiving Neuron

FIGURE 2   **The Neuron** The drawing shows the parts of a neuron and the connection between one neuron and another. Note the cell body, the branching of dendrites, and the axon with a myelin sheath.

axon
The part of the neuron that carries information away from the cell body toward other cells.

neurons. The **axon** is the part of the neuron that carries information away from the cell body toward other cells. Although extremely thin (1/10,000th of an inch—a human hair by comparison is 1/1,000 of an inch), axons can be very long, with many branches. Some extend more than 3 feet—from the top of the brain to the base of the spinal cord.

Covering all surfaces of neurons, including the dendrites and axons, are very thin cellular membranes that are much like the surface of a balloon. The neuronal membranes are semipermeable, meaning that they contain tiny holes, or channels, that allow only certain substances to pass into and out of the neurons.

myelin sheath
A layer of fat cells that encases and insulates most axons.

A **myelin sheath,** consisting of a layer of cells containing fat, encases and insulates most axons. By insulating axons, myelin sheaths speed up transmission of nerve impulses. Glial cells provide myelination (Logan & others, 2017). Numerous disorders are associated with problems in either the creation or the maintenance of this vital insulation. One of them is multiple sclerosis (MS), a degenerative disease of the nervous system in which myelin hardens, disrupting the flow of information through the neurons. Symptoms of MS include blurry and double vision, tingling sensations throughout the body, and general weakness.

©Mark Hunt/Huntstock/Corbis

The myelin sheath developed as the nervous system evolved. As brain size increased, it became necessary for information to travel over longer distances in the nervous system. Axons without myelin sheaths are not very good conductors of electricity. With the insulation of myelin sheaths, axons transmit electrical impulses and convey information much more rapidly (Stange-Marten & others, 2017). We can compare the myelin sheath's development to the evolution of interstate highways as cities grew. Highways keep fast-moving, long-distance traffic from getting snarled by slow local traffic.

The Neural Impulse

To transmit information to other neurons, a neuron sends brief electrical impulses (let's call them "blips") through its axon to the next neuron. As you navigate down this page while you read, hundreds of such impulses will stream down the axons in your arm to tell your muscles when to flex and how quickly. By changing the rate of the signals, or blips, the neuron can vary its message. Those impulses traveling down the axon are electrical. How does a neuron—a living cell—generate electricity? To answer this question, we need to examine the axon.

The axon is a tube encased in a membrane. The membrane has hundreds and thousands of tiny gates in it. These gates are generally closed, but they can open. We call the membrane *semipermeable* because fluids can sometimes flow in and out of these gates. Indeed, there are fluids both inside and outside the axon. Floating in those fluids are electrically charged particles called *ions.*

Some of these ions, notably sodium and potassium, carry positive charges. Negatively charged ions of chlorine and other elements also are present. The membrane surrounding the axon prevents negative and positive ions from randomly flowing into or out of the cell. The neuron creates electrical signals by moving positive and negative ions back and forth through its outer membrane. How does the movement of ions across the membrane occur? Those tiny gates mentioned above, called *ion channels,* open and close to let the ions pass into and out of the cell. Normally when the neuron is *resting,* or not transmitting information, the ion channels are closed, and a slight negative charge is present along the inside of the cell membrane. On the outside of the cell membrane, the charge is positive. Because of the difference in charge, the membrane of the resting neuron is said to be *polarized,* with most negatively charged ions on the inside of the cell and most positively charged ions on the outside. This polarization creates a voltage between the inside and the outside of the axon wall (Figure 3). That voltage, called the neuron's **resting potential,** is between −60 and −75 millivolts. (A millivolt is 1/1,000 of a volt.)

resting potential
The stable, negative charge of an inactive neuron.

For ions, it is true that opposites attract. The negatively charged ions inside the membrane and the positively charged ions outside the membrane will rush to each other if given the chance. Impulses that travel down the neuron do so by opening and closing ion channels, allowing the ions to flow in and out.

A neuron becomes activated when an incoming impulse—a reaction to, say, a pinprick or the sight of someone's face—raises the neuron's voltage, and the sodium gates at the

FIGURE 3 **The Resting Potential** An oscilloscope measures the difference in electrical potential between two electrodes. When one electrode is placed inside an axon at rest and one is placed outside, the electrical potential inside the cell is −70 millivolts (mV) relative to the outside. This potential difference is due to the separation of positive (+) and negative (−) charges along the membrane.

Movement
of impulse →

(a) Action potential generated by an
impulse within a neuron

(b) Movement of sodium (Na⁺) and potassium (K⁺)
ions responsible for the action potential

FIGURE 4 **The Action Potential** An action potential is a brief wave of positive electrical charge that sweeps down the axon as the sodium channels in the axon membrane open and close. (*a*) The action potential causes a change in electrical potential as it moves along the axon. (*b*) The movements of sodium ions (Na⁺) and potassium ions (K⁺) into and out of the axon cause the electrical changes.

base of the axon open briefly. This action allows positively charged sodium ions to flow into the neuron, creating a more positively charged neuron and *depolarizing* the membrane by decreasing the charge difference between the fluids inside and outside the neuron. Then potassium channels open, and positively charged potassium ions move out through the neuron's semipermeable membrane. This outflow returns the neuron to a negative charge. Then the same process occurs as the next group of channels flips open briefly. So it goes all the way down the axon, like a long row of cabinet doors opening and closing in sequence. It is hard to imagine, but this simple system of opening and closing tiny doors is responsible for the fluid movements of a ballet dancer and the flying fingers of a pianist playing a concerto.

The term **action potential** describes the brief wave of positive electrical charge that sweeps down the axon (Figure 4). An action potential lasts only about 1/1,000 of a second, because the sodium channels can stay open for only a very brief time. They quickly close again and become reset for the next action potential. When a neuron sends an action potential, it is commonly said to be "firing."

The action potential abides by the **all-or-nothing principle:** Once the electrical impulse reaches a certain level of intensity, called its *threshold,* it fires and moves all the way down the axon without losing any of its intensity. The impulse traveling down an axon can be compared to the burning fuse of a firecracker. Whether you use a match or blowtorch to light the fuse, once the fuse has been lit, the spark travels quickly and with the same intensity down the fuse.

action potential
The brief wave of positive electrical charge that sweeps down the axon.

all-or-nothing principle
The principle that once the electrical impulse reaches a certain level of intensity (its threshold), it fires and moves all the way down the axon without losing any intensity.

Synapses and Neurotransmitters

The movement of an impulse down an axon may be compared to a crowd's "wave" motion in a stadium. With the wave, there is a problem, however—the aisles. How does the wave get across the aisle? Similarly, neurons do not touch each other directly, and electricity cannot travel over the space between them. Yet somehow neurons manage to communicate. This is where the chemical part of electrochemical transmission comes in. Neurons communicate with each other through chemicals that carry messages across the space. This connection between one neuron and another is one of the

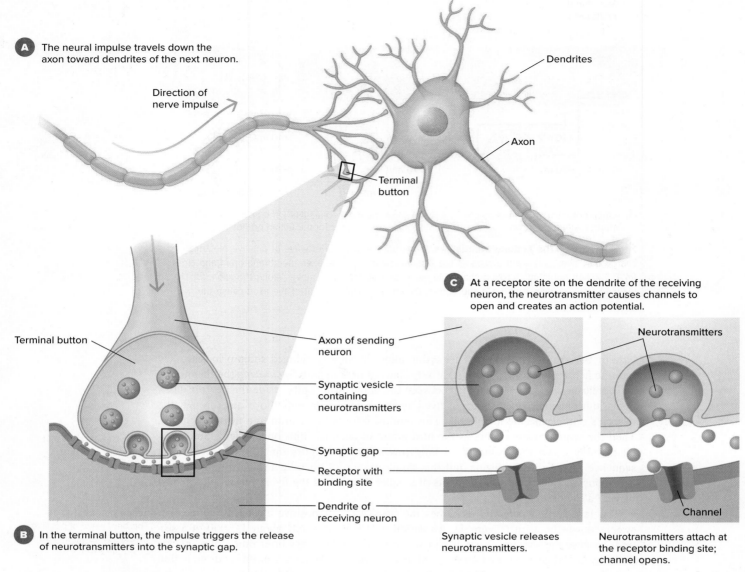

A The neural impulse travels down the axon toward dendrites of the next neuron.

Direction of nerve impulse

Dendrites

Axon

Terminal button

C At a receptor site on the dendrite of the receiving neuron, the neurotransmitter causes channels to open and creates an action potential.

Neurotransmitters

Terminal button

Axon of sending neuron

Synaptic vesicle containing neurotransmitters

Synaptic gap

Receptor with binding site

Dendrite of receiving neuron

B In the terminal button, the impulse triggers the release of neurotransmitters into the synaptic gap.

Synaptic vesicle releases neurotransmitters.

Neurotransmitters attach at the receptor binding site; channel opens.

Channel

FIGURE 5 **How Synapses and Neurotransmitters Work** (*A*) The axon of the *presynaptic* (sending) neuron meets dendrites of the *postsynaptic* (receiving) neuron. (*B*) This is an enlargement of one synapse, showing the synaptic gap between the two neurons, the terminal button, and the synaptic vesicles containing a neurotransmitter. (*C*) This is an enlargement of the receptor site. Note how the neurotransmitter opens the channel on the receptor site, triggering the neuron to fire.

synapses
Tiny spaces between neurons; the gaps between neurons are referred to as synaptic gaps.

neurotransmitters
Chemical substances that are stored in very tiny sacs within the neuron's terminal buttons and involved in transmitting information across a synaptic gap to the next neuron.

most intriguing and highly researched areas of contemporary neuroscience (Badin, Fermani, & Greenfield, 2017). Figure 5 gives an overview of how this connection between neurons takes place.

SYNAPTIC TRANSMISSION   **Synapses** are tiny spaces between neurons; the gap between neurons is referred to as *synaptic gap*. Most synapses lie between the axon of one neuron and the dendrites or cell body of another neuron. Before an impulse can cross the synaptic gap, it must be converted into a chemical signal.

Each axon branches out into numerous fibers that end in structures called *terminal buttons*. Stored in very tiny synaptic vesicles (sacs) within the terminal buttons are chemical substances called **neurotransmitters.** As their name suggests, neurotransmitters transmit, or carry, information across the synaptic gap to the next neuron. When a nerve impulse reaches the terminal button, it triggers the release of neurotransmitter molecules from the synaptic vesicles. The neurotransmitter molecules flood the synaptic gap. Their movements are random, but some of them bump into receptor sites in the next neuron.

The neurotransmitters are like pieces of a puzzle, and the receptor sites on the next neuron are differently shaped spaces. If the shape of the receptor site corresponds to the shape of the neurotransmitter molecule, the neurotransmitter acts like a key to open the receptor site, so that the neuron can receive the signals coming from the previous neuron. After delivering its message, some of the neurotransmitter is used up in the production of energy, and some of it is reabsorbed by the axon that released it to await the next neural impulse. This reabsorption is termed *reuptake*. Essentially, a message in the brain is delivered across the synapse by a neurotransmitter, which pours out of the terminal button just as the message approaches the synapse.

The neurotransmitter-like venom of the black widow spider does its harm by disturbing neurotransmission.
Source: Centers for Disease Control

NEUROCHEMICAL MESSENGERS
There are many different neurotransmitters. Each plays a specific role and functions in a specific pathway. Whereas some neurotransmitters stimulate or excite neurons to fire, others can inhibit neurons from firing (Cash & others, 2017). Some neurotransmitters are both excitatory *and* inhibitory (Li & others, 2017).

As the neurotransmitter moves across the synaptic gap to the receiving neuron, its molecules might spread out, or they might be confined to a small space. The molecules might come in rapid sequence or might be spaced out. The receiving neuron integrates this information before reacting to it.

Neurotransmitters fit into the receptor sites like keys in keyholes. Other substances, such as drugs, can sometimes fit into those receptor sites as well, producing a variety of effects. Similarly, many animal venoms, such as that of the black widow spider, are neurotransmitter-like substances that act by disturbing neurotransmission.

Most neurons secrete only one type of neurotransmitter, but often many different neurons are simultaneously secreting different neurotransmitters into the synaptic gaps of a single neuron. At any given time, a neuron is receiving a mixture of messages from the neurotransmitters. At its receptor sites, the chemical molecules bind to the membrane and do one of two things: They can either excite the neuron, bringing it closer to the threshold at which it will fire, or they can inhibit the neuron from firing. Usually the binding of an excitatory neurotransmitter from one neuron will not be enough to trigger an action potential in the receiving neuron. Triggering an action potential often takes a number of neurons sending excitatory messages simultaneously or fewer neurons sending rapid-fire excitatory messages.

The precise number of neurotransmitters that exist is unknown. Scientists have identified more than 100 neurotransmitters in the brain alone, each with a unique chemical makeup. In organisms ranging from snails to whales, neuroscientists have found the same neurotransmitter molecules that our own brains use. To get a better sense of what neurotransmitters do, let's consider seven that have major effects on behavior.

Acetylcholine *Acetylcholine (ACh)* usually stimulates the firing of neurons and is involved in the action of muscles, learning, and memory (Yoder, Chan, & Taube, 2017). ACh is found throughout the central and peripheral nervous systems. The venom of the black widow spider causes ACh to gush out of the synapses between the spinal cord and skeletal muscles, producing violent spasms.

Individuals with Alzheimer disease, a degenerative brain disorder that involves a decline in memory, have an acetylcholine deficiency (Johannsson & others 2015; Polverino & others, 2017; Sultzer & others, 2017). Some

Botox injections contain botulin, a poison that, by destroying ACh, blocks the recipient's facial muscles from moving. Wrinkles, as well as many genuine facial expressions, are thereby prevented.

medications used to treat the symptoms of Alzheimer disease do so by compensating for the loss of the brain's supply of acetylcholine (Howes, Fang, & Houghton, 2017; Wong & others, 2017).

GABA GABA *(gamma aminobutyric acid)* is found throughout the central nervous system. It is believed to be the neurotransmitter in as many as one-third of the brain's synapses. GABA is important in the brain because it keeps many neurons from firing (Cheng & others, 2017). In this way, it helps to control the precision of the signal being carried from one neuron to the next. Low levels of GABA are linked with anxiety. Antianxiety drugs increase the inhibiting effects of GABA.

You can think of GABA as the brain's brake pedal.

Glutamate *Glutamate* has a key role in exciting many neurons to fire and is especially involved in learning and memory (Matott, Kline, & Hasser, 2017). Too much glutamate can overstimulate the brain and trigger migraine headaches or even seizures. Researchers have recently proposed that glutamate also is a factor in anxiety, depression, schizophrenia, Alzheimer disease, and Parkinson disease (Jasaui & others, 2017; Litim, Morissette, & Di Paolo, 2017; Posporelis & others, 2017). Because of the widespread expression of glutamate in the brain, glutamate receptors have increasingly become the targets of drug treatment for a number of neurological and psychological disorders (Lahti & others, 2017).

Norepinephrine *Norepinephrine* inhibits the firing of neurons in the central nervous system, but it excites the heart muscle, intestines, and urogenital tract. Stress stimulates the release of norepinephrine (Wood & Valentino, 2017; Wong & others, 2012). This neurotransmitter also helps to control alertness. Too little norepinephrine is associated with depression, and too much triggers agitated, manic states. For example, amphetamines and cocaine cause hyperactive, manic states of behavior by rapidly increasing brain levels of norepinephrine (Schmidt & others, 2017).

Recall from the beginning of the chapter that one of the most important characteristics of the brain and nervous system is integration. In the case of neurotransmitters, they may work in teams of two or more. For example, norepinephrine works with acetylcholine to regulate states of sleep and wakefulness.

Dopamine *Dopamine* helps to control voluntary movement and affects sleep, mood, attention, learning, and the ability to recognize rewards in the environment (Schultz, Stauffer, & Lak, 2017; Zald & Treadway, 2017). Dopamine is related to the personality trait of extraversion (being outgoing and gregarious), as we will see when we look at personality. Stimulant drugs such as cocaine and amphetamines produce excitement, alertness, elevated mood, decreased fatigue, and sometimes increased motor activity mainly by activating dopamine receptors (Ashok & others, 2017).

Low levels of dopamine are associated with Parkinson disease, in which physical movements deteriorate (Dirkx & others, 2017; Dunn & others, 2017). Problems regulating dopamine are associated with schizophrenia (Abi-Dargham, 2017), a severe psychological disorder that we will examine when we look at psychological disorders.

FIGURE 6 **Serotonin Pathways** Each of the neurotransmitters in the brain has specific pathways in which it functions. Shown here are the pathways for serotonin.

Serotonin *Serotonin* is involved in the regulation of sleep, mood, attention, and learning. In regulating states of sleep and wakefulness, it teams with acetylcholine and norepinephrine. Serotonin is also a key to maintaining the brain's neuroplasticity, that is, allowing the brain to change with experience (Kraus & others, 2017). Lowered levels of serotonin are associated with depression (Cha & others, 2017). The antidepressant drug Prozac works by slowing down the reuptake of serotonin into terminal buttons, thereby increasing brain levels of serotonin (James & others, 2017). Figure 6 shows the brain pathways for serotonin. There are 15 known types of serotonin receptors in the brain (Hoyer, Hannon, & Martin, 2002; Worth, Holst, & Ponimaskin, 2017) and each type of antidepressant drug has its effects on different receptors.

Endorphins *Endorphins* are natural opiates that mainly stimulate the firing of neurons. Endorphins shield the body from pain and elevate feelings of pleasure. A long-distance runner, a woman giving birth, and a person in shock after a car wreck all have elevated levels of endorphins (Brito, Rasmussen, & Sluka, 2017; Misra & others, 2017; Weinstein & Weinstein, 2014).

As early as the fourth century B.C.E., the Greeks used wild poppies to induce euphoria. More than 2,000 years later, the magical formula behind opium's addictive action was finally discovered. In the early 1970s, scientists found that opium plugs into a sophisticated system of natural opiates that lie deep within the brain's pathways (Pert, 1999; Pert & Snyder, 1973). Morphine (the most important narcotic of opium) mimics the action of endorphins by stimulating receptors in the brain involved with pleasure and pain (Bruehl & others, 2017). This means that morphine, like natural endorphins in the brain, reduces the experience of pain.

Oxytocin *Oxytocin* is a hormone and neurotransmitter that plays an important role in the experience of love and social bonding. A powerful surge of oxytocin is released in mothers who have just given birth, and oxytocin is related to the onset of lactation and breast feeding (Augustine & others, 2017). Oxytocin, however, is not only involved in a mother's ability to provide nourishment for her baby. It is also a factor in the experience of parents who find themselves "in love at first sight" with their newborn (Eldred, 2017).

Although oxytocin release is stimulated by birth and lactation in mothers, might it also be released in fathers? Oxytocin is secreted in males. In one study, oxytocin levels were checked in fathers when their babies were 6 weeks old and when they were 6 months old; when fathers engaged in more stimulating contact with the babies, encouraged the babies' exploration, and directed the babies' attention to objects, the fathers'

Research has linked the hormone oxytocin to bonding between parents and their newborn.
©Vetta/Getty Images

oxytocin levels increased (Feldman & Bakermans-Kranenburg, 2017; Gordon & others, 2010). One study found that when fathers were administered oxytocin, their parenting behavior improved as evidenced in increased positive affect, social gaze, touch, and vocal synchrony when interacting with their infants (Weisman, Zagoory-Sharon, & Feldman, 2014).

Oxytocin is released as part of the sexual orgasm and is thought to play a role in the human tendency to feel pleasure during orgasm and to form emotional bonds with romantic partners (Caruso & others, 2017; Schneiderman & others, 2014). Provocative research has related oxytocin to the way that women respond to stress. According to Shelley Taylor (2001, 2007, 2011a, 2011b, 2014a, 2014b), women under stress do not experience the classic fight-or-flight response—rather, the influx of oxytocin suggests that women may seek bonds with others when under stress. Research supports the idea that oxytocin is associated with this "tend and befriend" stress response in women (Nickels, Kubicki, & Maestripieri, 2017).

DRUGS AND NEUROTRANSMITTERS

Most drugs that influence behavior do so mainly by interfering with the work of neurotransmitters. Drugs can mimic or increase the effects of a neurotransmitter, or they can block those effects. An **agonist** is a drug that mimics or increases a neurotransmitter's effects. For example, the drug morphine mimics the actions of endorphins by stimulating receptors in the brain and spinal cord associated with pleasure and pain. An **antagonist** is a drug that blocks a neurotransmitter's effects. For example, drugs used to treat schizophrenia interfere with the activity of dopamine.

agonist
A drug that mimics or increases a neurotransmitter's effects.

antagonist
A drug that blocks a neurotransmitter's effects.

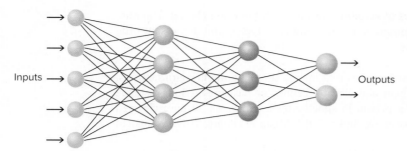

Neural Networks

So far, we have focused mainly on how a single neuron functions and on how a nerve impulse travels from one neuron to another. Now let's look at how large numbers of neurons work together to integrate incoming information and coordinate outgoing information. Figure 7 shows a simplified drawing of a neural network, or pathway. This diagram gives you an idea of how the activity of one neuron is linked with that of many others.

Some neurons have short axons and communicate with other, nearby neurons. Other neurons have long axons and communicate with circuits of neurons some distance away. These neural networks are not static (He, Qian, & Cao, 2017). They can be altered through changes in the strength of synaptic connections. Any piece of information, such as a name, might be embedded in hundreds or even thousands of connections between neurons (Senan & others, 2017; Wickersham & Feinberg, 2012). In this way, human activities such as being attentive, memorizing, and thinking are distributed over a wide range of connected neurons. The strength of these connected neurons determines how well you remember the information.

 There's a big hint here for how to study successfully. When your goal is to remember something, the best way is to build a neural network. That means making connections between the material and other things in your life–experiences, family, everyday habits. Actively engaging with the material will create neural networks to help you remember.

1. The part of the neuron that carries information away from the cell body toward other cells is the
   A. dendrite.
   B. synapse.
   C. nucleus.
   D. axon.

2. The law stating that once the electrical impulse reaches its threshold, it fires and moves down the axon without losing intensity is called
   A. neurotransmission.
   B. the action potential.
   C. the neural impulse.
   D. the all-or-nothing principle.

3. The chemical substances that carry information across the synaptic gap to the next neuron are called
   A. neurotransmitters.
   B. synapses.
   C. endorphins.
   D. hormones.

APPLY IT! 4. Many years ago some researchers found that when people were experiencing stressful, threatening circumstances—in this case, getting a painful electrical shock—they did not "fight" and they did not "flee." Instead, they asked for a friend to sit by them during the shocks. Which of the following helps to explain this "misery loves company" effect?
   A. The participants were all men.
   B. The participants were all women.
   C. The participants had faulty autonomic nervous systems.
   D. The participants had serious psychological disorders.

3 Structures of the Brain and Their Functions

Of course, the human body's extensive networks of neurons are not visible to the naked eye. Fortunately technology is available to help neuroscientists form pictures of the structure and organization of neurons and the larger structures they make up without harming the organism being studied. This section explores techniques that scientists use in brain research and discusses what these tools reveal about the brain's structures and functions. We pay special attention to the cerebral cortex, the region of the brain that is most relevant to the topics in *Experience Psychology*.

How Researchers Study the Brain and Nervous System

Early knowledge of the human brain came mostly from studies of individuals who had suffered brain damage from injury or disease or who had brain surgery to relieve another condition. Modern discoveries have relied largely on technology that enables researchers to "look inside" the brain while it is at work. Let's examine some of these innovative techniques.

BRAIN LESIONING   *Brain lesioning* is an abnormal disruption in the tissue of the brain resulting from injury or disease (Karnath & Rennig, 2017). In a lab setting, neuroscientists produce lesions in laboratory animals to determine the effects on the animal's behavior (Grayson & others, 2017). They create the lesions by surgically removing brain tissue, destroying tissue with a laser, or eliminating tissue by injecting it with a drug (Wang & others, 2017). Examining the person or animal that has the lesion gives the researchers a sense of the function of the part of the brain that has been damaged.

Do you know anyone who has experienced a stroke or brain-damaging head injury? These experiences create lesioned areas in the brain.

ELECTRICAL RECORDING   The *electroencephalograph (EEG)* records the brain's electrical activity. Electrodes placed on the scalp detect brain-wave activity, which is recorded on a chart known as an *electroencephalogram* (Figure 8). This device can assess brain damage, epilepsy (a condition that produces seizures, caused by abnormal electrical surges in the brain), and other problems. In research, it can be used to assess brain activity associated with specific stimuli (Oliver & others, 2017). An advantage of EEG recordings is the electrical activity measured is very rapid and can be measured very precisely so that it is very clear how various stimuli affect the brain.

Paul Ekman, Richard Davidson, and Wallace Friesen (1990) measured EEG activity during emotional experiences provoked by film clips. Individuals in this study watched amusing film clips (such as a puppy playing with flowers, and monkeys taking a bath) as well as clips likely to provoke fear or disgust (a leg amputation and a third-degree burn victim). How does the brain respond to such stimuli? The researchers found that while watching the amusing clips, people tended to exhibit more left than right prefrontal activity, as shown in EEGs. In contrast, when the participants viewed the fear-provoking films, the right prefrontal area was generally more active than the left.

FIGURE 8   An EEG Recording
The electroencephalograph (EEG) is widely used in psychological research.
©annedde/Getty Images

Do these differences generalize to overall differences in feelings of happiness? They just might. Heather Urry and her colleagues (2004) found that individuals who have relatively more left than right prefrontal activity (what is called *prefrontal asymmetry*) tend to rate themselves higher on a number of measures of well-being, including self-acceptance, positive relations with others, purpose in life, and life satisfaction.

Not every recording of brain activity is made with surface electrodes that are attached to the scalp. In *single-unit recording,* which provides information about a single neuron's electrical activity, a thin probe is inserted in or near an individual neuron. The probe transmits the neuron's electrical activity to an amplifier so that researchers can "see" the activity.

BRAIN IMAGING For years, medical practitioners have used X rays to reveal damage inside and outside the body, both in the brain and in other locations. A single X ray of the brain is hard to interpret, however, because it shows only a two-dimensional image of the three-dimensional interior of the brain. An improved technique, *computerized axial tomography* (CAT scan or CT scan), produces a three-dimensional image obtained from X rays of the head that are assembled into a composite image by a computer. The CT scan provides valuable information about the location and extent of damage involving stroke, language disorder, or loss of memory (Königs & others, 2017). The capacity to provide a three-dimensional image of the brain is what makes CT scans superior to single X rays.

Positron-emission tomography (PET scan) is based on metabolic changes in the brain related to activity (Hayama & others, 2016). PET measures the amount of glucose in various areas of the brain and then sends this information to a computer for analysis. Neurons use glucose for energy, so glucose levels vary with the levels of activity throughout the brain. Tracing the amounts of glucose generates a picture of activity levels throughout the brain.

An interesting application of the PET technique is the work of Stephen Kosslyn and colleagues (1996) on mental imagery, the brain's ability to create perceptual states in the absence of external stimuli. For instance, if you were to think of your favorite song right now, you could "hear" it in your mind's ear; or if you reflected on your mother's face, you could probably "see" it in your mind's eye. Research using PET scans has shown that often the same area of the brain—a location called Area 17—is activated when we think of seeing something as when we are actually seeing it. However, Area 17 is not always activated for all of us when we imagine a visual image. Kosslyn and his colleagues asked their participants to visualize a letter in the alphabet and then asked those individuals to answer some yes or no questions about the letter. For instance, a person might be thinking of the letter *C* and have to answer the question "Does it have curvy lines?" The answer would be yes. If the person was thinking of *F*, the answer would be no. The fascinating result of this work was that individuals who showed brain activation on the PET scan in Area 17 while engaged in the visualization task answered the questions faster than those who were not using Area 17.

> So, although human brains are similar to one another in some ways, in other ways, all brains are unique.

Another technique, *magnetic resonance imaging (MRI)*, involves creating a magnetic field around a person's body and using radio waves to construct images of the person's tissues and biochemical activities. The magnetic field of the magnet used to create an MRI image is extremely powerful, many times more powerful than the earth's magnetic field. MRI generates very clear pictures of the brain's interior, does not require injecting the brain with a substance, and (unlike X rays) does not pose a problem of radiation overexposure. Getting an MRI scan involves lying still in a large metal barrel-like tunnel. MRI scans provide an excellent picture of the architecture of the brain and allow us to see if and how experience affects brain structure. For example, a number of studies have shown how training motor skills can affect brain structure (Sale & others, 2017). Consider, for instance, how learning to play the piano or to dance can involve forging new connections in the brain (Alluri & others, 2017; Karpati & others, 2017). In one of the first MRI studies on this topic, Katrin Amunts and colleagues (1997) documented a link between the number of years a person has practiced musical skills (playing the piano, for example) and the size of the brain region that is responsible for controlling hand movements.

Although MRI reveals considerable information about brain structure, it cannot portray brain function. Other techniques, however, can serve as a window on the brain in action. One such method, *functional magnetic resonance imaging,* or *fMRI*, allows scientists literally to see what is happening in the brain while it is working (Figure 9). Like the PET scan, fMRI rests on the idea that mental activity is associated with changes in the brain. While PET is about the use of

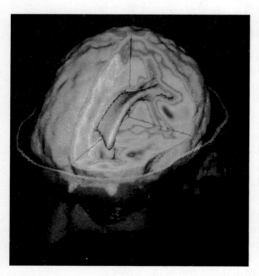

FIGURE 9 **Functional Magnetic Resonance Imaging (fMRI)** Through fMRI, scientists can literally see what areas of the brain are active during a task by monitoring oxygenated blood levels. ©Stegerphoto/Getty Images

glucose as fuel for thinking, fMRI exploits changes in blood oxygen that occur in association with brain activity. When part of the brain is working, oxygenated blood rushes into the area. This oxygen, however, is more than is needed. In a sense, fMRI is based on the fact that thinking is like running sprints. When you run the 100-yard dash, blood rushes to the muscles in your legs, carrying oxygen. Right after you stop, you might feel a tightness in your leg, because the oxygen has not all been used. Similarly, if an area of the brain is hard at work—for example, solving a math problem—the increased activity leads to a surplus of oxygenated blood. This "extra" oxygen allows the brain activity to be imaged.

Getting an fMRI involves reclining in the same large metal barrel as does an MRI, but in the case of fMRI, the person can be doing something—listening to audio signals sent by the researcher through headphones or watching visual images that are presented on a screen mounted overhead. Pictures of the brain are taken, both while the brain is at rest and while it is engaging in an activity such as listening to music, looking at a picture, or making a decision. By comparing the at-rest picture to the active picture, scientists can identify what specific brain activity is associated with the mental experience being studied. fMRI technology is one of the most exciting methodological advances to hit psychology in a long time.

fMRI is also used to study the brain AT REST! It can tell us what the brain is doing, even when it is resting. Such research tells us about what is called the "default network."

Note that saying that fMRI tells us about the brain activity *associated* with a mental experience is a *correlational* statement. Correlations point to the association between variables, not to the potential causal link between them. Although, for example, identifying a picture as a cat may relate to activation in a particular brain area, we do not know if recognizing the cat *caused* the brain activity (Schlinger, 2017).

Sorry, lefties! Most fMRI studies include only right-handed people. As we will see later, handedness can influence brain structure.

Earlier in this chapter, we reviewed how experience can affect the brain. Research using fMRI has tracked the way that spending time in nature can help us and help our brains to cope with stress. To read about this research, see the Intersection.

An additional method for studying brain functioning, and one that *does* allow for causal inferences, is *transcranial magnetic stimulation (TMS)* (He, Fan, & Li, 2017; Kawasaki & others, 2014). TMS is often combined with brain-imaging techniques to establish causal links between brain activity and behavior, to examine neuronal functioning following brain-injuring events such as accidents and strokes, and even to treat some neurological and psychological disorders.

In the TMS procedure, magnetic coils are placed over the person's head and directed at a particular brain area. TMS uses a rapidly changing magnetic field to induce brief electric current pulses in the brain, and these pulses trigger action potentials in neurons (Siebner & others, 2009). Immediately following this burst of action potentials, activity in the targeted brain area is inhibited, causing what is known as a *virtual lesion*. Completely painless, this technique, when used with brain imaging, allows scientists to examine the role of various brain regions. If a brain region is *associated* with a behavior, as demonstrated using fMRI or PET, then the temporary disruption of processing in that area should disrupt that behavior as well. So, for instance, if researchers were doing a study involving the cat recognition example described above, they might use TMS to disrupt the brain area that was associated with cat recognition and see whether the study's participants are temporarily unable to identify a picture of the feline.

It sounds kinda scary, huh? But it's not. TMS is also used to treat some psychological disorders.

How the Brain Is Organized

As a human embryo develops inside its mother's womb, the nervous system begins forming as a long, hollow tube on the embryo's back. At 3 weeks or so after conception, cells making up the tube differentiate into a mass of neurons, most of which then develop into three major regions of the brain: the hindbrain, which is adjacent to the top part of the

Neuroscience and Environmental Psychology: How Does Spending Time in Nature Affect the Brain?

One way that human beings stress themselves out is by ruminating on negative events. Rumination, or brooding, involves prolonged, self-focused, negative thinking. Rumination can involve replaying the same problem or personal mistake over and over.

The remedy for rumination is pretty obvious: Think about something else. But, in order for those other thoughts to truly combat rumination, they must be compelling. Might nature provide an excellent distraction from negative thoughts? Gregory Bratman and his colleagues (2015) conducted a study to explore this very question.

The researchers randomly assigned participants to take a 90-minute walk either in an urban setting or in a natural environment. The dependent variables examined the effects of nature in two ways. First, participants rated how much their thoughts involved rumination, before and after the walk. Second, fMRI was used to measure brain activation in a brain region called the subgenual prefrontal cortex. This area of the brain is active during negative emotional states, such as sadness and stress. The results showed that after the nature walk, participants showed declines in rumination and in activation in the subgenual prefrontal cortex. Among those who walked in the urban setting, no differences were found.

©Colin Anderson/Blend Images LLC

Just as time spent in nature rejuvenates the brain, it might also lay a foundation for environmental engagement (Lambert & others, 2016). Another study showed that individuals who spent time in nature not only showed lower activation in the brain's fear centers, they were more likely to endorse more pro-environmental attitudes. Finally, we often stress out because we feel like we lack the time to do all that needs to be done. Interestingly, research shows when we spend time in nature, time itself appears to slow down (Davydenko & Peetz, 2017). Perhaps after a nature walk, we can breathe a sigh of relief, knowing that we will be able to finish all of those commitments.

The brain can also benefit from spending time in beautiful environments, even if these are created. The new field of neuroarchitecture is concerned with understanding how buildings and natural spaces can be designed to promote human functioning (Coburn, Vartanian, & Chatterjee, 2017).

Our brains are marvelously adaptable, but we might want to bear in mind the environments within which our brains evolved. Taking your brain back to nature may be just the remedy for whatever is on your mind.

\\ Where have you taken your brain lately?

---

spinal cord; the midbrain, which rises above the hindbrain; and the forebrain, which is the uppermost region of the brain (Figure 10).

hindbrain
Located at the skull's rear, the lowest portion of the brain, consisting of the medulla, cerebellum, and pons.

HINDBRAIN   The **hindbrain,** located at the skull's rear, is the lowest portion of the brain. The three main parts of the hindbrain are the medulla, cerebellum, and pons. Figure 11 locates these structures.

The *medulla* begins where the spinal cord enters the skull. This structure controls many vital functions, such as breathing and heart rate. It also regulates our reflexes.

The *cerebellum* extends from the rear of the hindbrain, just above the medulla. It consists of two rounded structures thought to play important roles in motor coordination (Tedesco & others, 2017). Leg and arm movements are coordinated by the cerebellum, for example. When we play golf, practice the piano, or learn a new dance, the cerebellum is hard at work. If another portion of the brain commands us to write the number 7, it is the cerebellum that integrates the muscular activities required to do so. Damage to the cerebellum impairs the performance of coordinated movements. When this damage occurs, people's movements become awkward and jerky. Extensive damage to the cerebellum makes it impossible even to stand up.

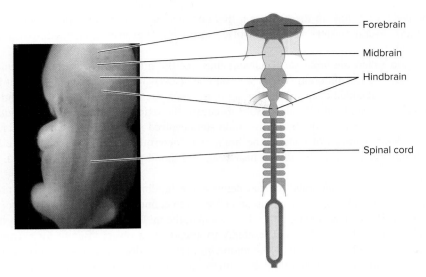

FIGURE 10
Embryological Development of the Nervous System The photograph shows the primitive tubular appearance of the nervous system at 6 weeks in the human embryo. The drawing shows the major brain regions and spinal cord as they appear early in the development of a human embryo.
©Petit Format/Science Source

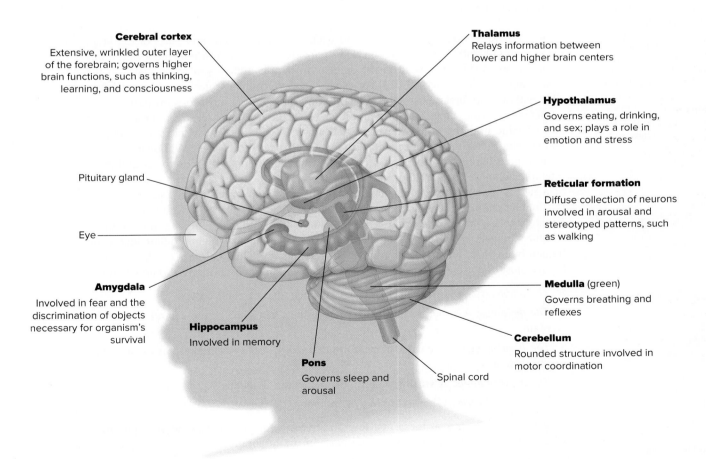

FIGURE 11 **Structure and Regions in the Human Brain** To get a feel for where these structures are in your own brain, use the eye (pictured on the left of the figure) as a landmark. Note that structures such as the thalamus, hypothalamus, amygdala, pituitary gland, pons, and reticular formation reside deep within the brain.

The *pons* is a bridge in the hindbrain that connects the cerebellum and the brain stem. It contains several clusters of fibers involved in sleep and arousal (Scammell, Arrigoni, & Lipton, 2017).

A region called the **brain stem** includes much of the hindbrain (it does not include the cerebellum) and the midbrain (which we examine below) and gets its name because it looks like a stem. Embedded deep within the brain, the brain stem connects at its lower end with the spinal cord and then extends upward to encase the reticular formation in the midbrain. The most ancient part of the brain, the brain stem evolved more than 500 million years ago (Carter, 1998). Clumps of cells in the brain stem determine alertness and regulate basic survival functions such as breathing, heartbeat, and blood pressure (Yeomans, 2012).

MIDBRAIN

The **midbrain,** located between the hindbrain and forebrain, is an area in which many nerve-fiber systems ascend and descend to connect the higher and lower portions of the brain (Peterson & others, 2017). In particular, the midbrain relays information between the brain and the eyes and ears. The ability to attend to an object visually, for example, is linked to one bundle of neurons in the midbrain. Parkinson disease, a deterioration of movement that produces rigidity and tremors, damages a section near the bottom of the midbrain.

Two systems in the midbrain are of special interest. One is the **reticular formation** (see Figure 11), a diffuse collection of neurons involved in stereotyped patterns of behavior such as walking, sleeping, and turning to attend to a sudden noise. The other system consists of small groups of neurons that use the neurotransmitters serotonin, dopamine, and norepinephrine. Although these groups contain relatively few cells, they send their axons to a remarkable variety of brain regions, an operation that perhaps explains their involvement in complex, integrative functions.

FOREBRAIN

You try to understand what all of these terms and parts of the brain mean. You talk with friends and plan a party for this weekend. You remember that it has been 6 months since you went to the dentist. You are confident you will do well on the next exam in this course. All of these experiences and millions more would not be possible without the **forebrain,** the brain's largest division and its most forward part.

Before we explore the structures and function of the forebrain, let's stop for a moment and examine how the brain evolved. The brains of the earliest vertebrates were smaller and simpler than those of later animals. Genetic changes during the evolutionary process were responsible for the development of more complex brains with more parts and more interconnections (Brooker & others, 2015; Simon, 2015). Figure 12 compares the brains of a rat, cat, chimpanzee, and human. In both the chimpanzee's brain and (especially) the human's brain, the hindbrain and midbrain structures are covered by a forebrain structure called the *cerebral cortex.* The human hindbrain and midbrain are similar to those of other animals, so it is the relative size of the forebrain that mainly differentiates the human brain from the brains of animals such as rats, cats, and chimps. The human forebrain's most important structures are listed below with brief descriptions of their locations.

- *The limbic system:* A network of structures under the cerebral cortex.
- *The thalamus:* A structure that sits on top of the brain stem, in the central core of the brain.
- *The basal ganglia:* A cluster of neurons that sits below the cerebral cortex and atop the thalamus.
- *The hypothalamus:* A small structure just below the thalamus.
- *The cerebral cortex:* The outer layer of the brain.

We will take a look at these first four structures before we embark on an exploration of the last. Remember that these are all parts of the forebrain.

Limbic System

The **limbic system,** a loosely connected network of structures under the cerebral cortex, is important in both memory and emotion (LeDoux, 2012). Its two principal structures are the amygdala and the hippocampus (see Figure 11).

---

brain stem
The stemlike brain area that includes much of the hindbrain (excluding the cerebellum) and the midbrain; connects with the spinal cord at its lower end and then extends upward to encase the reticular formation in the midbrain.

midbrain
Located between the hindbrain and forebrain, an area in which many nerve-fiber systems ascend and descend to connect the higher and lower portions of the brain; in particular, the midbrain relays information between the brain and the eyes and ears.

reticular formation
A system in the midbrain comprising a diffuse collection of neurons involved in stereotyped patterns of behavior such as walking, sleeping, and turning to attend to a sudden noise.

forebrain
The brain's largest division and its most forward part.

limbic system
A set of subcortical brain structures central to emotion, memory, and reward processing.

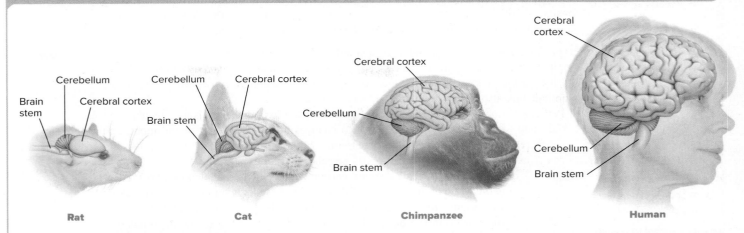

FIGURE 12   **The Brain in Different Species** This figure compares the brain of a rat, a cat, a chimpanzee, and a human being. As you examine the illustrations, remember that each organism's brain is adapted to meet different environmental challenges.
> **What structures are similar across the species?** > **Why do you think there are some common features, and what does this commonality tell us about these brain structures?** > **Why don't rats have a large cerebral cortex?** > **How might life be different for a rat or a cat with a human brain?**

amygdala
An almond-shaped structure within the base of the temporal lobe that is involved in the discrimination of objects that are necessary for the organism's survival, such as appropriate food, mates, and social rivals.

The **amygdala** is an almond-shaped structure located inside the brain toward the base. In fact, there is an amygdala on each side of the brain. The amygdala is involved in the discrimination of objects that are necessary for the organism's survival, such as appropriate food, mates, and social rivals. Neurons in the amygdala often fire selectively at the sight of such stimuli, and lesions in the amygdala can cause animals to engage in inappropriate behavior such as attempting to eat, fight, or even mate with an object like a chair. In *Experience Psychology,* you will encounter the amygdala whenever we investigate intense emotions such as fear and rage (Nicholson & others, 2017). The amygdala also is involved in emotional awareness and expression through its many connections with a variety of brain areas (Morawetz, Alexandrowicz, & Heekeren, 2017).

Our amygdala responds automatically to stimuli—to cute puppies, scary dogs, and attractive potential romantic partners—without our ever noticing.

The **hippocampus** has a special role in the storage of memories. Individuals who suffer extensive hippocampal damage cannot retain any new conscious memories after the damage. It is fairly certain, though, that memories are not stored "in" the limbic system. Instead, the limbic system seems to determine what parts of the information passing through the cortex should be "printed" into durable, lasting neural traces in the cortex.

hippocampus
The structure in the limbic system that has a special role in the storage of memories.

thalamus
The forebrain structure that sits at the top of the brain stem in the brain's central core and serves as an important relay station.

Thalamus   The **thalamus** is a forebrain structure that sits at the top of the brain stem in the central core of the brain (see Figure 11). It serves as an essential relay station, functioning much like a server in a computer network. That is, an important function of the thalamus is to sort information and send it to the appropriate places in the forebrain for further integration and interpretation (Stafford & Huberman, 2017). For example, one area of the thalamus receives information from the cerebellum and projects it to the motor area of the cerebral cortex (Dirkx & others, 2017). Indeed, most neural input to the cerebral cortex goes through the thalamus. Whereas one area of the thalamus works to orient information from the sense receptors (hearing, seeing, and so on), another region seems to be involved in sleep and wakefulness, having ties with the reticular formation.

Basal Ganglia   Above the thalamus and under the cerebral cortex lie large clusters, or *ganglia,* of neurons called **basal ganglia.** The basal ganglia work with the cerebellum and the cerebral cortex to control and coordinate voluntary movements. Basal ganglia enable

basal ganglia
Large neuron clusters located above the thalamus and under the cerebral cortex that work with the cerebellum and the cerebral cortex to control and coordinate voluntary movements.

people to engage in habitual behaviors such as riding a bicycle and typing a text message. Individuals with damage to basal ganglia suffer from either unwanted movement, such as constant writhing or jerking of limbs, or too little movement, as in the slow and deliberate movements of people with Parkinson disease (Zhai & others, 2018).

Hypothalamus   The **hypothalamus,** a small forebrain structure just below the thalamus, monitors three pleasurable activities—eating, drinking, and sex—as well as emotion, stress, and reward (see Figure 11 for the location of the hypothalamus). As we will see later, the hypothalamus also helps direct the endocrine system.

Perhaps the best way to describe the function of the hypothalamus is as a regulator of the body's internal state. It is sensitive to changes in the blood and neural input, and it responds by influencing the secretion of hormones and neural outputs. For example, if the temperature of circulating blood near the hypothalamus is increased by just 1 or 2 degrees, certain cells in the hypothalamus start increasing their rate of firing. As a result, a chain of events is set in motion. Increased circulation through the skin and sweat glands occurs immediately to release this heat from the body. The cooled blood circulating to the hypothalamus slows down the activity of some of the neurons there, stopping the process when the temperature is just right—37.1 degrees Celsius (98.6 degrees Fahrenheit). These temperature-sensitive neurons function like a finely tuned thermostat in maintaining the body in a balanced state.

The hypothalamus also is involved in emotional states, playing an important role as an integrative location for handling stress. Much of this integration is accomplished through the hypothalamus's action on the pituitary gland, an important endocrine gland located just below it.

If certain areas of the hypothalamus are electrically stimulated, a feeling of pleasure results. In a classic experiment, James Olds and Peter Milner (1954) implanted an electrode in the hypothalamus of a rat's brain. When the rat ran to a corner of an enclosed area, a mild electric current was delivered to its hypothalamus. The researchers thought the electric current would cause the rat to avoid the corner. Much to their surprise, the rat kept returning to the corner. Olds and Milner believed they had discovered a pleasure center in the hypothalamus. Olds (1958) conducted further experiments and found that rats would press bars until they dropped over from exhaustion just to continue to receive a mild electric shock to their hypothalamus. One rat pressed a bar more than 2,000 times an hour for a period of 24 hours to receive the stimulation to its hypothalamus (Figure 13). Today researchers agree that the hypothalamus is involved in pleasurable feelings but that other areas of the brain, such as the limbic system and a bundle of fibers in the forebrain, are also important in the link between the brain and pleasure.

The Olds studies have implications for drug addiction. The rat pressed the bar mainly because this action produced a positive, rewarding effect (pleasure), not because it wanted to avoid or escape a negative effect (pain). Cocaine users talk about the drug's ability to heighten pleasure in food, sex, and a variety of activities, highlighting the reward aspects of the drug. We will look into the effects of drugs on the brain's reward centers when we talk about consciousness and learning.

Pleasure center receptors can become inactive after the use of drugs such as Ecstasy and methamphetamine. The damaging effects of these drugs on the brain's reward system are what seduce individuals into a hopeless pursuit of the same feelings they had during their first high–but they will never feel that high again.

FIGURE 13   Results of the Experiment on the Role of the Hypothalamus in Pleasure The graphed results for one rat show that it pressed the bar more than 2,000 times an hour for a period of 24 hours to receive stimulation to its hypothalamus.
©Digital Vision Ltd./SuperStock

The Cerebral Cortex

cerebral cortex
Part of the fore-brain, the outer layer of the brain, responsible for the most complex mental functions, such as thinking and planning.

neocortex
The outermost part of the cerebral cortex, making up 80 percent of the human brain's cortex.

The **cerebral cortex** is part of the forebrain and is the most recently developed part of the brain in the evolutionary scheme. The word *cortex* means "bark" (as in the bark of a tree) in Latin, and the cerebral cortex is in fact the outer layer of the brain. It is in the cerebral cortex that the most complex mental functions, such as thinking and planning, take place.

The **neocortex** (or "new bark") is the outermost part of the cerebral cortex. In humans, this area makes up 80 percent of the cortex (compared with just 30 to 40 percent in most other mammals). The size of the neocortex in mammals is strongly related to the size of the social group in which the organisms live. Some scientists theorize that this part of the human brain, which is responsible for high-level thinking, evolved so that we could understand one another (Dunbar & Schultz, 2007).

The neural tissue that makes up the cerebral cortex covers the lower portions of the brain like a sheet that is laid over the brain's surface. In humans the cerebral cortex is greatly convoluted with lots of grooves and bulges, and these considerably enlarge its surface area (compared with a brain with a smooth surface). The cerebral cortex is highly connected with other parts of the brain. Millions of axons connect the neurons of the cerebral cortex with those located elsewhere in the brain.

FIGURE 14   **The Human Brain's Hemispheres** The two halves (hemispheres) of the human brain can be seen clearly in this photograph.
©A. Glauberman/Science Source

LOBES   The wrinkled surface of the cerebral cortex is divided into two halves called *hemispheres* (Figure 14). Each hemisphere is subdivided into four regions, or *lobes*—occipital, temporal, frontal, and parietal (Figure 15).

occipital lobes
Structures located at the back of the head that respond to visual stimuli.

The **occipital lobes,** located at the back of the head, respond to visual stimuli. Connections among various areas of the occipital lobes allow for the processing of information about such aspects of visual stimuli as their color, shape, and motion. A person can have perfectly functioning eyes, but the eyes only detect and transport information. That information must be interpreted in the occipital lobes for the viewer to "see it." A stroke or a wound in an occipital lobe can cause blindness or wipe out a portion of the person's visual field.

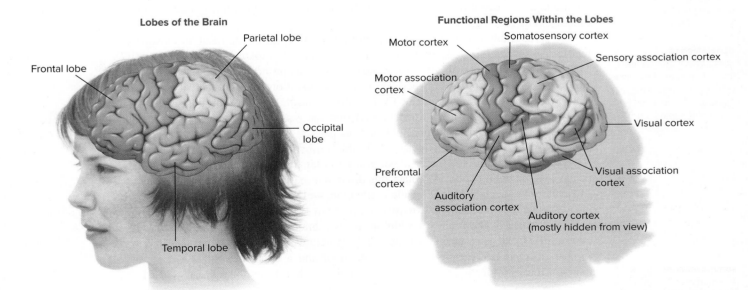

FIGURE 15   **The Cerebral Cortex's Lobes and Association Areas** The cerebral cortex (*left*) is roughly divided into four lobes: occipital, temporal, frontal, and parietal. The cerebral cortex (*right*) also consists of the motor cortex and somatosensory cortex. Further, the cerebral cortex includes association areas, such as the visual association cortex, auditory association cortex, and sensory association cortex.

A computerized reconstruction of Phineas T. Gage's accident, based on measurements taken of his skull.
©Patrick Landmann/Science Source

The **temporal lobes,** the part of the cerebral cortex just above the ears, are involved in hearing, language processing, and memory. The temporal lobes have a number of connections to the limbic system. For this reason, people with damage to the temporal lobes cannot file experiences into long-term memory.

The **frontal lobes,** the portion of the cerebral cortex behind the forehead, are involved in personality, intelligence, and the control of voluntary muscles. A fascinating case study illustrates how damage to the frontal lobes can significantly alter personality. Phineas T. Gage, a 25-year-old foreman who worked for the Rutland and Burlington Railroad, was the victim of a terrible accident in 1848. Phineas and several co-workers were using blasting powder to construct a roadbed. The crew drilled holes in the rock and gravel, poured in the blasting powder, and then tamped down the powder with an iron rod. While Phineas was still tamping it down, the powder exploded, driving the iron rod up through the left side of his face and out through the top of his head. Although the wound in his skull healed in a matter of weeks, Phineas had become a different person. Previously he had been a mild-mannered, hardworking, emotionally calm individual, well liked by all who knew him. Afterward he was obstinate, moody, irresponsible, selfish, and incapable of participating in any planned activities. Damage to the frontal lobe area of his brain had dramatically altered Phineas's personality.

Without intact frontal lobes, humans are emotionally shallow, distract-ible, listless, and so insensitive to social contexts that they may belch with abandon at dinner parties. Individuals with frontal lobe damage become so distracted by irrelevant stimuli that they often cannot carry out some basic directions. In one such case, an individual, when asked to light a candle, struck a match correctly, but instead of light-ing the candle, he put it in his mouth and acted as if he were smoking it (Luria, 1973).

The frontal lobes of humans are especially large when compared with those of other animals. For example, the frontal cortex of rats barely exists; in cats, it occupies a paltry 3.5 percent of the cerebral cortex; in chimpanzees, 17 percent; and in humans, approxi-mately 30 percent.

An important part of the frontal lobes is the **prefrontal cortex,** which is at the front of the motor cortex (see Figure 15) and is involved in higher cognitive functions such as planning, reasoning, and self-control (Miller & Cummings, 2017). The prefrontal cortex functions as an executive control system. It plays a role in monitoring and organizing thinking (Duverne & Koechlin, 2017).

The **parietal lobes,** located at the top and toward the rear of the head, are involved in registering spatial location, attention, and motor control (Sokolowski & others, 2017). Thus, the parietal lobes are at work when you are judging how far you have to throw a ball to get it to someone else, when you shift your attention from one activity to another (turn your attention away from the TV to a noise outside), and as you continue to read. The brilliant physicist Albert Einstein said that his reasoning often was best when he imagined objects in space. It turns out that his parietal lobes were 15 percent larger than average (Witelson, Kigar, & Harvey, 1999; Shi & others, 2017).

A word of caution is in order about going too far in localizing function within a particular lobe or brain region. Although this discussion has attributed specific functions to a particular lobe (such as spatial location, attention, and motor control in the parietal lobe), integration and connection are extensive between any two or more lobes and between lobes and other parts of the brain. In addition, no two brains are exactly alike (Vanderwal & others, 2017). We generalize about the brain's structures and functions, but it is important to bear in mind that people's brains are different and a brain area might not serve the function that is typically associated with it in all people (O'Connor & others, 2017).

SOMATOSENSORY CORTEX AND MOTOR CORTEX Two other important regions of the cerebral cortex are the somatosensory cortex and the motor cor-tex (see Figure 15). The **somatosensory cortex** processes information about body sensations.

temporal lobes
Structures in the cerebral cortex that are located just above the ears and are involved in hearing, language processing, and memory.

frontal lobes
The portion of the cerebral cortex be-hind the forehead, involved in person-ality, intelligence, and the control of voluntary muscles.

prefrontal cortex
An important part of the frontal lobes that is involved in higher cognitive functions such as planning, reasoning, and self-control.

parietal lobes
Structures at the top and toward the rear of the head that are involved in register-ing spatial location, attention, and motor control.

somatosensory cortex
A region in the cerebral cortex that processes infor-mation about body sensa-tions, located at the front of the parietal lobes.

motor cortex
A region in the cerebral cortex, located just behind the frontal lobes, that processes information about voluntary movement.

It is located at the front of the parietal lobes. The **motor cortex,** at the rear of the frontal lobes, processes information about voluntary movement.

The map in Figure 16 shows which parts of the somatosensory and motor cortexes are associated with different parts of the body. It is based on research done by Wilder Penfield (1947), a neurosurgeon at the Montreal Neurological Institute. Penfield worked with patients who had severe epilepsy, and he often performed surgery to remove portions of the epileptic patients' brains. However, he was concerned that removing a portion of the brain might impair some of the individuals' functions. Penfield's solution was to map the cortex during surgery by stimulating different cortical areas and observing the responses of the patients, who were given a local anesthetic so they would remain awake during the operation. He found that when he stimulated certain somatosensory and motor areas of the brain, patients reported feeling different sensations, or different parts of a patient's body moved. For both somatosensory and motor areas, there is a point-to-point relation between a part of the body and a location on the cerebral cortex. In Figure 16, the face and hands are given proportionately more space than other body parts because the face and hands are capable of finer perceptions and movements than are other body areas and therefore need more cerebral cortex representation.

Penfield's technique has influence to this day. Specifically, during brain surgery, patients are often awake. The brain cannot feel pain, so keeping patients awake allows surgeons to ask about what they are feeling, hearing, and seeing, to be sure that the surgery does not damage brain areas that are crucial for consciousness, speech, and other important functions.

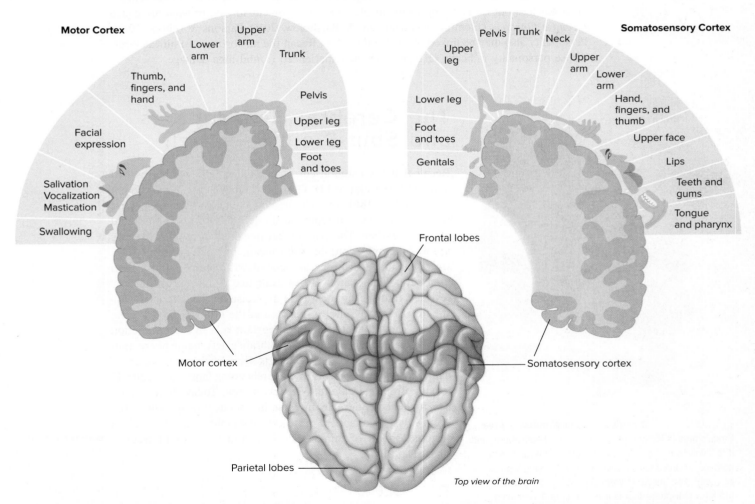

FIGURE 16 **Disproportionate Representation of Body Parts in the Motor and Somatosensory Areas of the Cortex** The amount of cortex allotted to a body part is not proportionate to the body part's size. Instead, the brain has more space for body parts that require precision and control. Thus, the thumb, fingers, and hand require more brain tissue than does the arm.

The point-to-point mapping of somatosensory fields onto the cortex's surface is the basis of our orderly and accurate perception of the world (Chen & others, 2011). When something touches your lip, for example, your brain knows what body part has been touched because the nerve pathways from your lip are the only pathways that project to the lip region of the somatosensory cortex.

ASSOCIATION CORTEX   Embedded in the brain's lobes, the association cortex makes up 75 percent of the cerebral cortex (see Figure 15). **Association cortex** (sometimes called *association areas*) refers to regions of the cerebral cortex that integrate sensory and motor information. The highest intellectual functions, such as thinking and problem solving, occur in association cortex. There are association areas throughout the brain, and each sensory system has its own association area in the cerebral cortex.

Interestingly, damage to a specific part of the association cortex often does not result in a specific loss of function. With the exception of language areas (which are localized), loss of function seems to depend more on the extent of damage to the association cortex than on the specific location of the damage. By observing brain-damaged individuals and using a mapping technique, scientists have found that the association cortex is involved in linguistic and perceptual functioning.

The largest portion of the association cortex is located in the frontal lobes, directly under the forehead. Damage to this area does not lead to somatosensory or motor loss but rather to problems in planning and problem solving or what are called *executive functions* (Fleming, Heintzelman, & Bartholow, 2016; Parsons & others, 2017). Personality also may be linked to the frontal lobes. Recall the misfortune of Phineas Gage, whose personality radically changed after he experienced frontal lobe damage.

The term association cortex applies to cortical material that is not somatosensory or motor cortex, but is NOT filler space!

association cortex
Sometimes called association areas, the region of the cerebral cortex that is the site of the highest intellectual functions, such as thinking and problem solving.

The Cerebral Hemispheres and Split-Brain Research

Broca's area

Wernicke's area

FIGURE 17   Broca's Area and Wernicke's Area
Broca's area is located in the brain's left hemisphere, and it is involved in the control of speech. Individuals with damage to Broca's area have problems saying words correctly. Also shown is Wernicke's area, the portion of the left hemisphere that is involved in understanding language. Individuals with damage to this area cannot comprehend words; they hear the words but do not know what they mean.

Recall that the cerebral cortex is divided into two halves—left and right (see Figure 14). Do these hemispheres have different functions? In 1861, French surgeon Paul Broca saw a patient who had received an injury to the left side of his brain about 30 years earlier. The patient became known as Tan because *tan* was the only word he could speak. Tan suffered from *aphasia*, a language disorder associated with brain damage. Tan died several days after Broca evaluated him, and an autopsy revealed that the injury was to a precise area of the left hemisphere. Today we refer to this area of the brain as *Broca's area*, and we know that it plays an important role in the production of speech. Another area of the brain's left hemisphere that significantly figures in language is *Wernicke's area*, which, if damaged, causes problems in comprehending language. Figure 17 locates Broca's area and Wernicke's area. Today there continues to be considerable interest in the degree to which the brain's left hemisphere or right hemisphere is involved in various aspects of thinking, feeling, and behavior (Trivedi & Bhargava, 2017).

THE ROLE OF THE CORPUS CALLOSUM   For many years, scientists speculated that the **corpus callosum,** the large bundle of axons connecting the brain's two hemispheres, has something to do with relaying information between the two

corpus callosum
The large bundle of axons that connects the brain's two hemispheres, responsible for relaying information between the two sides.

sides (Figure 18). Roger Sperry (1974) confirmed this in an experiment in which he cut the corpus callosum in cats. He also severed certain nerves leading from the eyes to the brain. After the operation, Sperry trained the cats to solve a series of visual problems with one eye blindfolded. After a cat learned the task—say, with only its left eye uncovered—its other eye was blindfolded, and the animal was tested again. The "split-brain" cat behaved as if it had never learned the task. It seems that the memory was stored only in the left hemisphere, which could no longer directly communicate with the right hemisphere.

Further evidence of the corpus callosum's function has come from studies of patients with severe, even life-threatening, forms of epilepsy. Epilepsy is caused by electrical "brainstorms" that flash uncontrollably across the corpus callosum. In one famous case, neurosurgeons severed the corpus callosum of an epileptic patient, now known as W. J., in a final attempt to reduce his unbearable seizures. Sperry (1968) examined W. J. and found that the corpus callosum functions the same in humans as in animals—cutting the corpus callosum seemed to leave the patient with "two separate minds" that learned and operated independently.

FIGURE 18   Corpus Callosum
The corpus callosum is a thick band of about 80 million axons that connects the brain cells in one hemisphere to those in the other. In healthy brains, the two sides engage in a continuous flow of information via this neural bridge.

As it turns out, the right hemisphere receives information only from the left side of the body, and the left hemisphere receives information only from the right side of the body. When you hold an object in your left hand, for example, only the right hemisphere of your brain detects the object. When you hold an object in your right hand, only the left hemisphere of the brain detects it (Figure 19). In individuals with a normally functioning corpus callosum, both hemispheres receive this information eventually, as it travels between the hemispheres through the corpus callosum. In fact, although we might have two minds, we usually use them in tandem.

You can appreciate how well and how rapidly the corpus callosum integrates your experience by thinking about the challenge of doing two things at once. Recall, for example, when you were a kid and you tried to tap your head and rub your stomach at the same time. Even with two separate hands controlled by two separate hemispheres, such dual activity is very difficult.

Figure 19 is tricky. Notice that, unlike the hand, each eye is actually split in half, so that half of the information that each eye sees goes to a different hemisphere. The information on the same side of the eye as the nose crosses over, and the information that is on the outside of each eye stays put.

HEMISPHERIC DIFFERENCES IN FUNCTIONING   In people with intact brains, specialization of function, or what is sometimes called *lateralization,* occurs in some areas. Researchers have uncovered evidence for hemispheric differences in function by sending different information to each ear. Remember, the left hemisphere gets its information (first) from the right ear, and the right hemisphere hears what is going on (first) in the left ear. This research has shown that the brain tends to divide its functioning into one hemisphere or the other as follows:

- *Left hemisphere:* The most extensive research on the brain's two hemispheres has focused on language. Speech and grammar are localized to the left hemisphere (Tussis & others, 2017). Although it is a common misconception that *all* language processing occurs in the left hemisphere, much language processing and production does come from this hemisphere (Regal & others, 2017). For example, in reading, the left hemisphere comprehends syntax (rules for combining words into phrases and sentences)

Left visual field

Fixation point

Right visual field

FIGURE 19 **Information Pathways from the Eyes to the Brain** Each of our eyes receives sensory input from both our left and our right field of vision. Information from the left half of our visual field goes to the brain's right hemisphere (which is responsible for simple comprehension), and information from the right half of our visual field goes to the brain's left hemisphere (the brain's main language center, which controls speech and writing). The input received in either hemisphere passes quickly to the other hemisphere across the corpus callosum. When the corpus callosum is severed, however, this transmission of information cannot occur.
©Nukul Chanada/Shutterstock

Optic nerve

Speech

R

L

Writing

Main language center

Simple comprehension

Visual half field R

Visual half field L

Corpus callosum severed

and grammar, but the right hemisphere does not. The left hemisphere is also keenly involved in singing the words of a song.

■ *Right hemisphere:* The right hemisphere dominates in processing nonverbal information such as spatial perception, visual recognition, and emotion (Carter & others, 2017; Gamond & others, 2017). For example, one part of the right hemisphere, the fusiform face area in the right hemisphere, is mainly at work when we process information about people's faces (Kanwisher, 2006; Schalk & others, 2018).

The right hemisphere is expert at recognizing faces. Researchers have asked people to watch images on a computer screen and to press a button when they see a face. Even right-handed people are much faster at this task when they use their left hand because the information goes directly from the right hemisphere to the hand that hemisphere controls.

■ The right hemisphere also may be more involved than the left hemisphere in processing information about emotions, both when we express emotions ourselves and when we recognize others' emotions (Schirmer & Adolphs, 2017). People are more likely to remember emotion words if they hear them in the left ear. Much of our sense of humor resides in the right hemisphere (Kovarski & others, 2017; Marinkovic & others, 2011). In fact, if you want to be sure that someone laughs at your joke, tell it to the person's left ear.

■ The right hemisphere is also adept at interpreting story meanings and voice intonations (Tang, Hamilton, & Chang, 2017). Further, the right hemisphere excels at picking up a song melody. Importantly, though, it is difficult to learn exactly what the right hemisphere can do, because it cannot just tell us. We have to come up with a way for the right hemisphere to communicate what it knows. The right hemisphere certainly has some verbal abilities, for instance, because people with split brains can draw (with their left hand) pictures of words that have been spoken to them (in the left ear).

Could this be why women, even right-handed women (but not men), automatically carry a baby in the left hand?

Because differences in the functioning of the brain's two hemispheres are known to exist, people commonly use the phrases *left-brained* (meaning logical and rational) and *right-brained* (meaning creative or artistic) as a way of categorizing themselves and others. Such generalizations have no scientific basis, and that is a good thing. We have both hemispheres because we use them both. Regardless of how much fun it might be to label ourselves "right-brained" or "left-brained," we are fortunate to be whole-brained,

The brain's left hemisphere is intricately involved in speech and language, and so it plays a role when we recall song lyrics. The fusiform face area of the brain's right hemisphere is dominant when we process information about people's faces.
(first) ©Image Source/Getty Images; (second) ©Comstock Images/Getty Images

period. The reality is that most day-to-day activities involve a complex interplay between the brain's two hemispheres. Furthermore, of course, our brains can adapt to changes, such as injuries, and each hemisphere can adapt by taking on other functions (Hope & others, 2017).

Integration of Function in the Brain

How do all of the regions of the brain cooperate to produce the wondrous complexity of thought and behavior that characterizes humans? Neuroscience still does not have answers to questions such as how the brain solves a murder mystery or composes a poem or an essay. Even so, we can get a sense of integrative brain function by using a real-world scenario, such as the act of escaping from a burning building.

Imagine that you are sitting at your computer, writing an email, when a fire breaks out behind you. The sound of crackling flames is relayed from your ear through the thalamus, to the auditory cortex, and on to the auditory association cortex. At each stage, the stimulus is processed to extract information, and at some stage, probably at the association cortex level, the sounds are finally matched with something like a neural memory representing sounds of fires you have heard previously. The association "fire" sets new machinery in motion. Your attention (guided in part by the reticular formation) shifts to the auditory signal being held in your association cortex and on to your auditory association cortex, and simultaneously (again guided by reticular systems) your head turns toward the noise. Now your visual association cortex reports in: "Objects matching flames are present." In other regions of the association cortex, the visual and auditory reports are synthesized ("We have things that look and sound like fire"), and neural associations representing potential actions ("flee") are activated. However, firing the neurons that code the plan to flee will not get you out of the chair. The basal ganglia must become engaged, and from there the commands will arise to set the brain stem, motor cortex, and cerebellum to the task of transporting you out of the room. All of this happens in mere seconds.

Which part of your brain did you use to escape? Virtually all systems had a role. By the way, you would probably remember this event because your limbic circuitry would likely have started memory formation when the association "fire" was triggered. The next time the sounds of crackling flames reach your auditory association cortex, the associations triggered would include this most recent escape. In sum, considerable integration of function takes place in the brain (Strother & others, 2017). All of the parts of the nervous system work together as a team to keep you safe and sound.

Could Neuroscience Help Identify the Right Brain for the Job?

Organizations seek to hire individuals who have the right skills for every position. Many employers use various tests that assess personality, cognitive ability, and other relevant skills to make hiring decisions. However, such tests can be inaccurate if people can fake characteristics they think an employer is looking for, reporting themselves as more motivated or reliable than they actually are. In addition, consider that hiring decisions can be biased by what applicants look like, their gender, race/ethnicity, age, and so forth. Is there a solution?

©Phovoir/Shutterstock

Of course, the abilities and characteristics that employers hope to identify are products of brain processes. Consider some of the associations we have reviewed in this chapter. The prefrontal cortex is associated with planning and engaging in self-control. Might someone with a relatively well-developed prefrontal cortex be well suited to an occupation requiring hard work and a great deal of planning? The amygdalae are related to recognizing survival-relevant cues in the environment. Could someone with larger or more active amygdalae be a good bet for the position of air traffic controller? Might someone with greater brain volume in those areas associated with understanding other people be well-suited to positions as therapists or journalists?

Measuring actual brain processes in order to select employees may never be common. However, using such measures, employers might be able to assess job applicants for the very specific abilities required for an occupation.

What Do You Think?

- Do you think it would be ethical to use brain scans to make hiring decisions? Would such decisions be more or less fair than current practices?
- How does your understanding of brain plasticity relate to this issue?

---

1. Four ways that researchers study the brain and the nervous system are electrical recording, imaging, staining, and
   A. biopsy.
   B. lesioning.
   C. lobotomy.
   D. neurosurgery.

2. The brain's three major regions are the hindbrain, the midbrain, and the
   A. brain stem.
   B. reticular formation.

   C. forebrain.
   D. temporal lobes.

3. The most recently developed level of the human brain is the
   A. midbrain.
   B. forebrain.
   C. reticular formation.
   D. brain stem.

APPLY IT! 4. Because Miles suffers from extreme seizures, a surgeon severs his corpus callosum. Using a special technique, researchers present a picture of a flower to Miles's right brain and a picture of a bumblebee to Miles's left brain. When Miles is asked to say out loud what he sees, he is likely to answer
   A. "A flower."
   B. "I don't know."
   C. "A bee."
   D. There is no way to know.

---

4 The Endocrine System

endocrine system
The body system consisting of a set of glands that regulate the activities of certain organs by releasing their chemical products into the bloodstream.

The **endocrine system** consists of a set of glands that regulate the activities of certain organs by releasing their chemical products into the bloodstream. **Glands** are organs or tissues in the body that create chemicals that control many bodily functions. Neuroscientists have discovered that the nervous system and endocrine system are intricately interconnected. They know that the brain's hypothalamus connects the nervous system and the endocrine system and that the two systems work together to control the body's

glands
Organs or tissues in the body that create chemicals that control many bodily functions.

activities. Yet the endocrine system differs significantly from the nervous system in a variety of ways. For one thing, the parts of the endocrine system are not all connected in the way that the parts of the nervous system are. For another thing, the endocrine system works more slowly than the nervous system, because the chemicals released by the endocrine glands are transported through the circulatory system, in the blood. The heart does a mind-boggling job of pumping blood through the body, but blood moves far more slowly than neural impulses do.

The chemical messengers produced by the endocrine glands are called **hormones.** The bloodstream carries hormones to all parts of the body, and the membrane of every cell has receptors for one or more hormones.

The endocrine glands consist of the pituitary gland, the thyroid and parathyroid glands, the adrenal glands, the pancreas, the ovaries in women, and the testes in men (Figure 20). In much the same way that the brain's control of muscular activity is constantly monitored and altered to suit the information received by the nervous system, the action of the endocrine glands is continuously monitored and changed by nervous, hormonal, and chemical signals (Jessen & others, 2017). Recall from earlier in the chapter that the autonomic nervous system regulates processes such as respiration, heart rate, and digestion. The autonomic nervous system acts on the endocrine glands to produce a number of important physiological reactions to strong emotions, such as rage and fear.

hormones
Chemical messengers that are produced by the endocrine glands and carried by the bloodstream to all parts of the body.

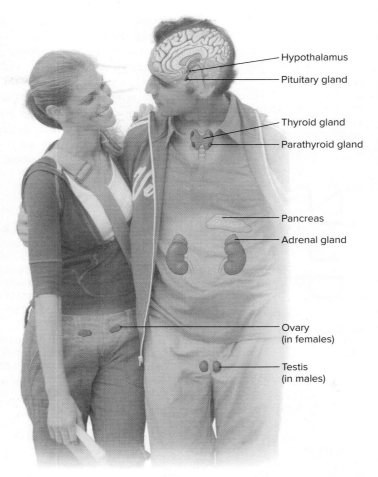

FIGURE 20   **The Major Endocrine Glands** The pituitary gland releases hormones that regulate the hormone secretions of the other glands. The pituitary gland is regulated by the hypothalamus.
©Laurence Mouton/Getty Images

pituitary gland
A pea-sized gland just beneath the hypothalamus that controls growth and regulates other glands.

adrenal glands
Glands at the top of each kidney that are responsible for regulating moods, energy level, and the ability to cope with stress.

pancreas
A dual-purpose gland under the stomach that performs both digestive and endocrine functions.

The **pituitary gland,** a pea-sized gland just beneath the hypothalamus, controls growth and regulates other glands (Figure 21). The anterior (front) part of the pituitary is known as the *master gland* because almost all of its hormones direct the activity of target glands elsewhere. In turn, the anterior pituitary gland is controlled by the hypothalamus.

The **adrenal glands,** located at the top of each kidney, regulate mood, energy level, and the ability to cope with stress. Each adrenal gland secretes epinephrine (also called *adrenaline*) and norepinephrine (also called *noradrenaline*). Unlike most hormones, epinephrine and norepinephrine act quickly. Epinephrine helps a person get ready for an emergency by acting on smooth muscles, the heart, stomach, intestines, and sweat glands. In addition, epinephrine stimulates the reticular formation, which in turn arouses the sympathetic nervous system, and this system subsequently excites the adrenal glands to produce more epinephrine. Norepinephrine also alerts the individual to emergency situations by interacting with the pituitary gland and the liver. You may remember that norepinephrine functions as a neurotransmitter when it is released by neurons. In the adrenal glands, norepinephrine is released as a hormone. In both instances, norepinephrine conveys information—in the first case, to neurons; in the second case, to glands.

The **pancreas,** located under the stomach, is a dual-purpose gland that performs both digestive and endocrine functions. The part of the pancreas that

FIGURE 21

The Pituitary Gland The pituitary gland, which hangs by a short stalk from the hypothalamus, regulates the hormone production of many of the body's endocrine glands. Here it is enlarged 30 times.
©MedicalRF.com

serves endocrine functions produces a number of hormones, including insulin. This part of the pancreas, the islets of Langerhans, turns out hormones like a little factory. Insulin is an essential hormone that controls glucose (blood sugar) levels in the body and is related to metabolism, body weight, and obesity.

The **ovaries,** located in the pelvis on either sides of the uterus in women, and **testes,** located in the scrotum in men, are the sex-related endocrine glands that produce hormones related to sexual development and reproduction. These glands and the hormones they produce play important roles in developing sexual characteristics such as breasts in women and a beard in men. They are also involved in other characteristics and behaviors, as you will see as you learn more about psychology.

ovaries
Sex-related endocrine glands that produce hormones involved in women's sexual development and reproduction.

testes
Sex-related endocrine glands in the scrotum that produce hormones involved in men's sexual development and reproduction.

self-quiz

1. The endocrine glands produce chemicals called
   A. hormones.
   B. neurotransmitters.
   C. endocrine secretions.
   D. bile.

2. The endocrine glands include all of the following except the
   A. pituitary.
   B. pancreas.
   C. liver.
   D. thyroid.

3. The adrenal glands regulate energy level, the ability to deal with stress, and
   A. appetite.
   B. digestion.
   C. motor coordination.
   D. mood.

APPLY IT! 4. Diabetes, a common disorder worldwide, involves problems in the body's regulation of glucose, or blood sugar. This disorder is often treated by diet, but sometimes individuals with diabetes must inject themselves with insulin. The endocrine system gland that is involved in diabetes is the
   A. pituitary.
   B. ovaries.
   C. pancreas.
   D. adrenal.

5 Brain Damage, Plasticity, and Repair

Recall from earlier in this chapter that plasticity is an example of the brain's remarkable adaptability. Neuroscientists have studied plasticity, especially following brain damage, and have charted the brain's ability to repair itself (Cheng, 2017). Brain damage can produce horrific effects, including paralysis, sensory loss, memory loss, and personality deterioration. When such damage occurs, can the brain recover some or all of its functions? Recovery from brain damage varies considerably, depending on the age of the individual, the extent of the damage, and the characteristics of the person (Haller & others, 2017; Jackson & others, 2017).

The Brain's Plasticity and Capacity for Repair

For much of the twentieth century, it was generally concluded that the younger children are, the better their recovery will be from a traumatic brain injury. However, age alone is often not a good indicator of the brain's ability to recover from a traumatic injury (Maxwell, 2012; Mayer, Quinn, & Master, 2017). Although the young child's brain has more plasticity than an older child's, because of its immaturity it also is more vulnerable to insults (Anderson & others, 2009). Thus, assessing outcomes of brain insults based on age alone can be misleading. A research review concluded that children's outcomes following injury to their brain depend on factors related to the injury (nature, severity, and timing of insult), physical factors (age, cognitive capacity, and genetic makeup), and environmental influences (intervention and quality of rehabilitation, family functioning, and social status) (Gomez-Nicola & Perry, 2014). Regarding age, in general, a more severe insult is more damaging to the young child's brain than the older child's brain (Anderson & others, 2005).

A significant factor in recovery is whether some or all of the neurons in an affected area are just damaged or are completely destroyed (Huang & Chang, 2009). If the neurons have not been destroyed, brain function often becomes restored over time as the brain repairs itself.

There are three ways that such repair might take place:

1. *Collateral sprouting,* in which the axons of some healthy neurons adjacent to damaged cells grow new branches (Arkadir, Bergman, & Fahn, 2014; Cobianchi, de Cruz, & Navarro, 2014).

2. *Substitution of function,* in which the damaged region's function is taken over by another area or areas of the brain.

3. *Neurogenesis,* the process by which new neurons are generated. Researchers have found that neurogenesis occurs in mammals such as mice. It is now accepted that neurogenesis can occur in humans (Goritz & Frisén, 2012; Sailor, Schinder, & Lledo, 2017). However, to date, the presence of new neurons has been documented only in the hippocampus, which is involved in memory (Paul, Chaker, & Doetsch, 2017; Xu & others, 2013). Neurogenesis in other mammals has been found in the olfactory bulb (involved in the sense of smell), but few if any of such cells are newly formed in adult humans (Bergman & others, 2012). Researchers are exploring how the grafting of neural stem cells to various regions of the brain, such as the hypothalamus, might increase neurogenesis (Sailor, Schinder, & Lledo, 2017). If researchers can discover how new neurons are generated, possibly the information can be used to fight degenerative diseases of the brain such as Alzheimer disease and Parkinson disease.

Brain Tissue Implants

The brain naturally recovers some functions that are lost following damage, but not all. Recent research has generated excitement about *brain grafts*—implants of healthy tissue into damaged brains (Tornero & others, 2017). The potential success of brain grafts is much better when brain tissue from the fetal stage (an early stage in prenatal development) is used (Monni & others, 2014; Southwell & others, 2014). The neurons of the fetus are still growing and have a much higher probability of making connections with other neurons than do the neurons of adults. In a number of studies, researchers have damaged part of an adult rat's brain, waited until the animal recovered as much as possible by itself, and assessed its behavioral deficits. Then they take the corresponding area of a fetal rat's brain and transplant it into the damaged brain of the adult rat. In these studies, the rats that receive the brain transplants demonstrate considerable behavioral recovery (Tajiri & others, 2014; Tang & others, 2014).

Might such brain grafts be successful with humans suffering from brain damage? Research suggests that they might, but finding donors is a problem (Glaw & others, 2009). Aborted fetuses are a possibility, but using them as a source of graft tissue raises ethical issues. Another type of treatment has been attempted with individuals who have Parkinson disease. Parkinson disease impairs coordinated movement to the point that just walking across a room can be a major ordeal. Fetal dopamine cells are transplanted into the basal ganglia of the individual with Parkinson disease in an effort to improve motor performance. Results for such studies have been limited but encouraging (Björklund & Lindvall, 2017).

The human body contains more than 220 different types of cells, but **stem cells** are unique because they are primitive cells that have the capacity to develop into most types of human cells. Stem cells were first harvested from embryos by researchers at the

stem cells
Unique primitive cells that have the capacity to develop into most types of human cells.

Protecting the Athlete's Brain

In his first two games as a professional American football player, Jahvid Best scored a remarkable 5 touchdowns for the Detroit Lions. His NFL career seemed to be on a fast track to greatness. However, he suffered a concussion during a preseason game the following year. This injury was only one of multiple serious head injuries leading to concussions he had experienced as a football player in high school and college (Laird, 2016). And this one ended his football career. Best was puzzled by the gravity of the situation: How could his life be upended by experiences he could not even remember happening?

A concussion or mild traumatic brain injury (MTBI) is a head injury that leads to temporary loss of brain function (Finkel & others, 2017; Khurana & Kaye, 2012). Symptoms include headache, dizziness, nausea, unequal pupil size, and lack of memory for events surrounding the trauma. Importantly, these symptoms may not be immediately apparent, and contrary to common belief, concussions do not necessarily lead to a lack of consciousness.

©John Mersits/CSM/REX/Shutterstock

MTBIs are an increasing concern among health professionals who work with athletes at every level. Among high school athletes, MTBIs are thought to make up at least 15 percent of sports injuries (Hollis & others, 2014; Wallace & others, 2017). Although concussions can occur in any sport, head injuries are a special concern for youth football players, because of the risk of tackles. A review of deaths among high school football players, spanning 2010 to 2014, found that 24 deaths occurred due to catastrophic brain and spinal cord injuries (Kucera & others, 2017).

Treatment for concussion involves rest and careful monitoring (Wallace & others, 2017). The brain requires time to recover from injury. When the brain has not had time to recover from a concussion, a second injury can cause rapid swelling of the brain, leading to brain stem failure and eventual coma or death (Cobb & Battin, 2004).

Of course, for a concussion to be treated properly, someone must first notice that it has occurred and then must respond appropriately. This responsibility ought not to fall on the injured athlete. Indeed, an individual suffering from a concussion may not recognize his or her own injury, because the trauma has damaged the very organ that would provide the person with insight on the injury.

Psychologists know that motivation can influence perception (Balcetis & Dunning, 2010). Our motives can shape what we see and how we interpret that evidence. Teams, individual players, and their fans want to win, and having star players on the field is seen as crucial to victory. In this context, a coach might reason that an injured player is well enough to return to the field because he or she "seems" normal. And the player, even if suffering from a powerful headache, might choose not to complain because he or she is so motivated to win, to show team loyalty, and to avoid appearing weak.

The dangers of not accurately diagnosing and treating concussions are great. In a recent study, researchers examined 111 brains that were donated by former NFL players (Mez & others, 2017). Among these individuals, all but 1 showed signs of a condition called chronic traumatic encephalopathy (or CTE). CTE is a degenerative condition of the brain that is caused by repeated injuries. Symptoms of CTE include difficulty thinking, memory loss, depression, and suicidal thoughts.

Fortunately for Jahvid Best, the end of his football career was not the end of his life as an athlete. He ran in the 2016 Olympics as a member of the San Lucia National track team (Laird, 2016). He was ultimately defeated by Usain Bolt, but the experience was one he will never forget.

University of Wisconsin, Madison, and Johns Hopkins University in 1998. Because of their amazing plasticity, stem cells might potentially replace damaged cells in the human body, including cells involved in spinal cord injury and brain damage.

Typically, researchers have harvested the stem cells from frozen embryos left over from in vitro fertilization procedures. In these procedures, a number of eggs, or ova, are collected from a woman's ovaries in order to be fertilized in a lab (rather than in the woman's body). In successful in vitro fertilization, the ova are brought together with sperm, producing human embryos. Because the procedure is difficult and delicate, doctors typically fertilize a large number of eggs with the hope that some will survive when implanted in the woman's uterus. In the typical procedure, there are leftover embryos. These embryos are in the *blastocyst* stage, which occurs five days after conception. At this stage the embryo has not yet attached to the uterus. The blastocyst has no brain, no central nervous system, and no mouth—it is an undifferentiated ball of cells.

 Do you support or oppose stem cell research? Why?

Supporters of stem cell technology emphasize that using these cells for research and treatment might relieve a great deal of human suffering. Opponents of abortion disapprove of the use of stem cells in research or treatment on the grounds that the embryos die when the stem cells are removed. (In fact, leftover embryos are likely to be destroyed in any case.) In 2009, President Barack Obama removed restrictions on stem cell research.

self-quiz

1. Repair of the damaged brain might take place by all of the following *except*
   A. substitution of function.
   B. psychotherapy.
   C. collateral sprouting.
   D. neurogenesis.

2. The process by which the axons of healthy neurons adjacent to damaged cells grow new branches is called
   A. substitution of function.
   B. neurogenesis.
   C. collateral sprouting.
   D. dendritic branching.

3. The primitive cells that have the capacity to develop into most types of human cells are called
   A. stem cells.
   B. blastocysts.
   C. collateral cells.
   D. neurogenetic cells.

APPLY IT! 4. Taylor is injured in a serious car accident, suffering head injuries. After the accident, Taylor, who used to be talkative, seems to be unable to speak. Which of the following would best predict that Taylor is likely to regain the ability to talk?
   A. Taylor is male.
   B. Taylor is under 5 years old.
   C. Taylor is over the age of 21.
   D. Taylor is female.

6 Genetics and Behavior

In addition to the brain and nervous system, other aspects of our physiology also have consequences for psychological processes. Genes are one important contributor to these processes. The particular influences of nature (genetic endowment) and of nurture (experience) on psychological characteristics have long fascinated psychologists. Here we begin by examining the central agent of nature: our genetic heritage.

Chromosomes, Genes, and DNA

genes
The units of hereditary information, consisting of short segments of chromosomes composed of DNA.

Within the human body are literally trillions of cells. The nucleus of each human cell contains 46 **chromosomes,** threadlike structures that come in 23 pairs, one member of each pair originating from each parent. Chromosomes contain the remarkable substance **deoxyribonucleic acid (DNA),** a complex molecule that carries genetic information. **Genes,** the units of hereditary information, are short segments of chromosomes composed of DNA. What do genes do? Their main function is to manufacture the proteins that are necessary for maintaining life.

chromosomes
In the human cell, threadlike structures that come in 23 pairs, one member of each pair originating from each parent, and that contain DNA.

deoxyribonucleic acid (DNA)
A complex molecule in the cell's chromosomes that carries genetic information.

FIGURE 22 **Cells, Chromosomes, Genes, and DNA** (*Left*) The body contains trillions of cells, which are the basic structural units of life. Each cell contains a central structure, the nucleus. (*Middle*) Chromosomes and genes are located in the nucleus of the cell. Chromosomes are made up of threadlike structures composed mainly of DNA molecules. (*Right*) A gene is a segment of DNA that contains the hereditary code. The structure of DNA resembles a spiral ladder.

It is not the case that each gene is translated into one and only one protein; moreover, a gene does not act independently. Indeed, rather than being a group of independent genes, the human genome (*genome* refers to an organism's complete genetic material) consists of many genes that collaborate both with one another and with nongenetic factors inside and outside the body (Moore, 2013). The cellular machinery mixes, matches, and links small pieces of DNA to reproduce the genes, and that machinery is influenced by what is going on around it. Figure 22 illustrates the relationship among cells, chromosomes, genes, and DNA.

An international research program called the Human Genome Project is dedicated to documenting the human genome. Initially, it was thought that humans have approximately 100,000 genes. However, more recently, the number of human genes has been revised substantially downward to approximately 20,500 (Ensembl Human, 2010; Lopez & others, 2017). When the genes from one parent combine at conception with the same number of genes from the other parent, the number of possibilities is staggering. Although scientists are still a long way from unraveling all the mysteries of the way genes work, some aspects of this process are well understood, starting with the fact that multiple genes interact to give rise to observable characteristics.

The Study of Genetics

Historically speaking, genetics is a relatively young science. Its origins go back to the mid-nineteenth century, when an Austrian monk named Gregor Mendel studied heredity in generations of pea plants. By cross-breeding plants with different characteristics and noting the characteristics of the offspring, Mendel discovered predictable patterns of heredity and laid the foundation for modern genetics.

©Danny Smythe/Shutterstock

Mendel noticed that some genes seem to be more likely than others to show up in the physical characteristics of an organism. In some gene pairs, one gene is dominant over the other. If one gene of a pair is dominant and one is recessive, according to the **dominant-recessive genes principle,** the dominant gene overrides the recessive gene. A recessive gene exerts its influence only if both genes of a pair are recessive. If you inherit a recessive gene from only one parent, you may never know you carry the gene. In the world of dominant-recessive genes, brown eyes, farsightedness, and dimples rule over blue eyes, nearsightedness, and freckles. If you inherit a recessive gene for a trait from both of your parents, you will show the trait. That is why two brown-eyed parents can have a blue-eyed child: Each parent would have a dominant gene for brown eyes and a recessive gene for blue eyes. Because dominant genes override recessive genes, the parents have brown eyes. However, the child can inherit a recessive gene for blue eyes from each parent. With no dominant gene to override them, the recessive genes make the child's eyes blue.

dominant-recessive genes principle
The principle that if one gene of a pair is dominant and one is recessive, the dominant gene overrides the recessive gene. A recessive gene exerts its influence only if both genes of a pair are recessive.

> # Do It!
> Search the web for information about a happiness gene. How would you evaluate research on such a gene given what you have read so far in *Experience Psychology?* What (if anything) would the existence of such a gene mean for your ability to find happiness in your life?

Unlike eye color, complex human characteristics such as personality and intelligence are likely influenced by many different genes. Scientists use the term *polygenic inheritance* to describe the influences of multiple genes on behavior. The term *gene-gene interaction* is used to describe the ways two or more genes combine to influence characteristics, behavior, diseases, and development (Power, Parkhill, & de Oliveira, 2017).

Today researchers continue to apply Mendel's methods, as well as modern technology, in their quest to expand knowledge about genetics. This section discusses three ways to study genetics: molecular genetics, selective breeding, and behavior genetics.

MOLECULAR GENETICS   The field of *molecular genetics* involves the manipulation of genes using technology to determine their effect on behavior. Researchers who study molecular genetics are trying to discover the specific locations on genes that determine an individual's susceptibility to many diseases and other aspects of health and well-being.

SELECTIVE BREEDING   *Selective breeding* is a genetic method in which organisms are chosen for reproduction based on how much of a particular trait they display. Mendel developed this technique in his studies of pea plants. A more recent example involving behavior is the classic selective breeding study conducted by Robert Tryon (1940). He chose to study maze-running ability in rats. After he trained a large number of rats to run a complex maze, he then mated the rats that were the best at maze running ("maze bright") with each other and the ones that were the worst ("maze dull") with each other. He continued this process with 21 generations of rats. After several generations, the maze-bright rats significantly outperformed the maze-dull rats.

Psychologists have learned a lot from studying rats in mazes.

Selective breeding studies have demonstrated that genes are an important influence on behavior, but that does not mean that experience is unimportant. For example, in another study, maze-bright and maze-dull rats were reared in one of two environments: (1) an impoverished environment that consisted of a barren wire-mesh group cage or (2) an enriched environment that contained tunnels, ramps, visual displays, and other stimulating objects (Cooper & Zubek, 1958). When they reached maturity, only the maze-dull rats that had been reared in an impoverished environment made more maze-learning errors than the maze-bright rats.

GENOME-WIDE ASSOCIATION METHOD   Completion of the Human Genome Project has led to use of the *genome-wide association method* to identify genetic variations linked to a particular disease, such as cancer, cardiovascular disease, or Alzheimer disease (National Human Genome Research Institute, 2012; Zillikens & others, 2017). To conduct a genome-wide association study, researchers obtain DNA from individuals who have the disease under study and from those who do not. Then, each participant's complete set of DNA, or genome, is scanned on machines to determine markers of genetic variation. If certain genetic variations occur more frequently in people who have the disease, the variations point to the region in the human genome where the disease-causing problem exists.

Genes that are close to one another in our DNA are more likely to be inherited together. This link between genes is used in what is called *linkage analysis*. This analysis may help identify the location of certain genes by referring to those genes whose position is already known. This strategy is often used to search for genes associated with risk for a disease. Gene linkage studies are now being conducted on a wide variety of disorders and health issues. A key challenge with genome wide association and linkage studies is that results from these do not consistently replicate. That means that one study might produce a set of conclusions that other studies do not find. As such, it is important for researchers to combine information from many of these studies to insure conclusions are reproducible (Wang & others, 2017).

BEHAVIOR GENETICS   *Behavior genetics* is the study of the degree and nature of heredity's influence on behavior. Behavior genetics is less invasive than molecular genetics and selective breeding. Using methods such as the *twin study,* behavior geneticists examine the extent to which individuals are shaped by their heredity and their environmental experiences (McGue, Rustichini, & Iacono, 2017). In the most common type of twin study, researchers compare the behavioral similarity of identical twins with the behavioral similarity of fraternal twins. Identical twins develop from a single fertilized egg that splits into two genetically identical embryos, each of which becomes a person. Fraternal twins develop from separate eggs and separate sperm, and so they are genetically no more similar than nontwin siblings. They may even be of different sexes.

By comparing groups of identical and fraternal twins, behavior geneticists capitalize on the fact that identical twins are more similar genetically than are fraternal twins. In one twin study, researchers compared 7,000 pairs of Finnish identical and fraternal twins with respect to the personality traits of extraversion (which, as we have seen, means being outgoing) and neuroticism (being psychologically unstable) (Rose & others, 1988). The identical twins were much more alike than the fraternal twins on both of these personality traits, and this result suggests that genes influence both traits.

One problem with twin studies is that adults might stress the similarities of identical twin children more than those of fraternal twins, and identical twins might perceive themselves as a "set" and play together more than fraternal twins do. If so, observed similarities in identical twins might be more strongly influenced by environmental factors than usually thought.

In another type of twin study, researchers evaluate identical twins who have been reared in separate environments. If their behavior is similar, the assumption is that heredity has played an important role in shaping their behavior. This strategy is the basis for the Minnesota Study of Twins Reared Apart, directed by Thomas Bouchard and his colleagues (1996). They bring identical twins who have been reared apart to Minneapolis from all over the world to study their behavior. They ask thousands of questions about their family, childhood, interests, and values. Detailed medical histories are obtained, including information about diet, smoking, and exercise habits.

One pair of twins in the Minnesota study, Jim Springer and Jim Lewis, were separated at 4 weeks of age and did not see each other again until they were 39 years old. They had an uncanny number of similarities, even though they had lived apart for decades. For example, they both worked as part-time deputy sheriffs, had vacationed in Florida, had owned Chevrolets, had dogs named Toy, and had married and divorced women named Betty. Both liked math but not spelling. Both were good at mechanical drawing. Both put on 10 pounds at about the same time in their lives, and both started suffering headaches at 18 years of age. They did have a few differences. For example, one expressed himself better orally, and the other was more proficient at writing. One parted his hair over his forehead; the other wore his hair slicked back with sideburns.

Critics argue that some of the separated twins in the Minnesota study had been together several months prior to their adoption, that some had been reunited prior to testing (in certain cases, for a number of years), that adoption agencies often put identical twins in similar homes, and that even strangers are likely to have some coincidental similarities (Joseph, 2006). To think critically about this issue, see the Psychological Inquiry.

Genes and the Environment

So far, we have talked a lot about genes, and you are probably getting the picture that genes are a powerful force in an organism. The role of genetics in some characteristics may seem obvious; for instance, how tall you are depends to a large degree on how tall your parents are. However, imagine a person growing up in a severely impoverished environment—with poor nutrition, inadequate shelter, little or no medical care, and a mother who had received no prenatal care. This individual may have genes that call for the height of an NBA or a WNBA center, but without environmental support for this genetic capacity, he or she may never reach that genetically programmed height. Thus, the relationship between an individual's genes and the actual person we see before us is not a perfect one-to-one correspondence. Even for a characteristic such as height, genes do not fully determine where a person will stand on this variable. We need to account for the role of nurture, or environmental factors, in the actual characteristics we see in the fully grown person.

If the environment matters for an apparently simple characteristic such as height, imagine the role it might play in complex characteristics such as being outgoing or intelligent. For these psychological characteristics, genes are, again, not directly reflected in the characteristics of the person. Indeed, genes cannot tell us exactly what a person will be like. Genes are simply related to some of the characteristics we see in a person.

To account for this gap between genes and actual observable characteristics, scientists distinguish between a genotype and a phenotype. A **genotype** is a person's genetic heritage, his or her actual genetic material. A **phenotype** is the individual's observable characteristics. The relationship between a genotype and phenotype is not always obvious. Recall that some genetic characteristics are dominant and others are recessive. Seeing that a person has brown eyes (his or her phenotype) tells us nothing about whether the person might also have a gene for blue eyes (his or her genotype) hiding out as well. The phenotype is influenced by the genotype but also by environmental factors.

The term *phenotype* applies to both physical and psychological characteristics. Consider a trait such as extraversion, the tendency to be outgoing and sociable. Even if we knew the exact genetic recipe for extraversion, we still could not perfectly predict a person's level of (phenotypic) extraversion from his or her genes, because at least some of this trait comes from the person's experience. We will revisit the concepts of genotype and phenotype throughout *Experience Psychology.* How does the process from genotype to phenotype work? It's very complex, but at a very basic level in a cell, DNA information is transcribed to RNA (ribonucleic acid), which in turn is translated into amino acids that will become proteins. Once assembled, proteins become capable of producing characteristics in the phenotype.

Whether a gene is "turned on"—working to assemble proteins—is also a matter of collaboration. The activity of genes *(genetic expression)* is affected by their environment. For example, hormones that circulate in the blood make their way into the cell where they can

Identical Twins. We've all heard stories about identical twins who were separated at birth. When these twins meet up in adulthood, people often find the similarities between them to be uncanny. Are these similarities evidence of the extraordinary power of genes? Let's take a closer look.
©Kenneth Sponsler/Getty Images

> Imagine that you did not see the photo of twins above and were simply asked how similar two people of the same gender, ethnicity, appearance, and age might be. > How might even very different environments respond to these individuals similarly? > How many people of this same gender, age, and ethnicity might enjoy similar hobbies? Have similar jobs? > What does this Psychological Inquiry tell you about the power of vivid and unusual cases in the conclusions we reach?

genotype
An individual's genetic heritage; his or her actual genetic material.

phenotype
An individual's observable characteristics.

Environmental influences can affect things like hair color. Just because Mom has dark brown hair doesn't mean she's genetically a brunette! Only her hairdresser knows for sure.

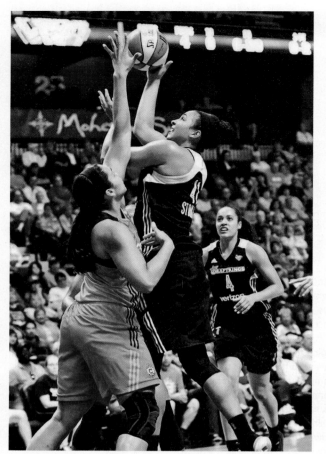

Our height depends significantly on the genes we inherit. However, even if we have genes that call for the stature of a basketball center, we may not reach that genetically programmed height if we lack good nutrition, adequate shelter, and medical care.
©Ron Waite/CSM/REX/Shutterstock

turn genes on and off. The flow of hormones, too, can be affected by environmental conditions, such as light, day length, nutrition, and behavior. Factors such as stress, radiation, and temperature can influence gene expression (Mangino & others, 2017).

Studies are exploring how interactions between heredity and environment influence development, including interactions that involve specific DNA sequences (Davies & Cicchetti, 2014). These studies are concerned with how individuals with the same genetic characteristics can, because of environmental factors, differ from one another in important ways. For instance, research has found that variations in dopamine-related genes interact with supportive or unsupportive family environments to influence children's aggressive behavior (Bakermans-Kranenburg & van IJzendoorn, 2011). Children with a particular genetic characteristic were more likely to behave aggressively if their parents were harsh and insensitive. This type of research concerns **gene × environment (G × E) interaction**—the interaction of a specific measured variation in DNA and a specific measured aspect of the environment. G × E interactions can be tricky to understand. They simply tell us that just because two people share genetic similarities, they are still likely to be different. Even when a gene has a strong relationship to a particular phenotypic characteristic, that characteristic may not show itself in a person if the person's experiences do not lead the gene to express itself. You may know someone with a family history of a particular condition, such as alcoholism. A family history might suggest genetics is involved. Yet, that person may or may not develop the condition if he or she never drinks or does not encounter experiences that promote drinking.

The biological foundations of psychology are in evidence across the entire nervous system, including the brain, the intricately working neurotransmitters, the endocrine system, and the genes. These physical realities of the body work in amazing concert to produce behaviors, thoughts, and feelings. The activities you do each day, from large to small, are all signs of the spectacular success of this physical system. Your mastery of the material in this chapter is but one reflection of the extraordinary capabilities of this biological feat.

gene × environment (g × e) interaction The interaction of a specific measured variation in DNA and a specific measured aspect of the environment.

self-quiz

1. The threadlike structures that are present in the cell nucleus and contain genes and DNA are called
   A. genomes.
   B. polygenic markers.
   C. chromosomes.
   D. stem cells.

2. Researchers study genetics through all of the following methods *except*
   A. twin studies.
   B. selective breeding.
   C. environmental impact studies.
   D. molecular genetics.

3. The individual's *observable* characteristics, influenced by both genetic and environmental factors, are called the
   A. genome.
   B. genotype.
   C. phenotype.
   D. prototype.

APPLY IT! 4. Sarah and Jack both have brown hair. When their son Trent is born, he has bright red hair. Family and friends start making jokes about any male friends of Sarah's who have red hair. Should Jack be worried that he is not Trent's father?
   A. Jack should not be worried because brown hair color is part of the phenotype, not necessarily Sarah's and Jack's genotypes.
   B. Jack should not be worried because Trent's hair color is part of his genotype, not necessarily his phenotype.
   C. Jack should be worried because there is no way for two brunettes to have a baby with red hair. Sarah's been up to no good.
   D. Jack should be worried because Trent's phenotype should match his parents' exactly.

The Nervous System

The nervous system is the body's electrochemical communication circuitry. Four important characteristics of the brain and nervous system are complexity, integration, adaptability, and electrochemical transmission. The brain's special ability to adapt and change is called plasticity.

Decision making in the nervous system occurs in specialized pathways of nerve cells. Three of these pathways involve sensory input, motor output, and neural networks.

The nervous system is divided into two main parts: central (CNS) and peripheral (PNS). The CNS consists of the brain and spinal cord. The PNS has two major divisions: somatic and autonomic. The autonomic nervous system consists of two main divisions: sympathetic and parasympathetic. In particular, the sympathetic nervous system is involved in the experience of stress.

 ## Neurons

Neurons are cells that specialize in processing information. They make up the communication network of the nervous system. The three main parts of the neuron are the cell body, dendrite (receiving part), and axon (sending part). A myelin sheath encases and insulates most axons and speeds up transmission of neural impulses.

A neuron sends information along its axon in the form of brief electric impulses. Resting potential is the stable, slightly negative charge of an inactive neuron. The brief wave of electrical charge that sweeps down the axon, called the action potential, is an all-or-nothing response. The synapse is the space between neurons. At the synapse, neurotransmitters are released from the sending neuron, and some of these attach to receptor sites on the receiving neuron, where they stimulate another electrical impulse. Neurotransmitters include acetylcholine, GABA, glutamate, norepinephrine, dopamine, serotonin, oxytocin, and endorphins. Neural networks are clusters of neurons that are interconnected to process information.

Structures of the Brain and Their Functions

Techniques used to study the brain include brain lesioning, electrical recording, and brain imaging. These methods have revealed much about the brain's major divisions—hindbrain, midbrain, and forebrain.

The cerebral cortex makes up most of the outer layer of the brain, and it is here that higher mental functions such as thinking and planning take place. The wrinkled surface of the cerebral cortex is divided into hemispheres, each with four lobes: occipital, temporal, frontal, and parietal. There is considerable integration and connection among the brain's lobes.

The brain has two hemispheres. Two areas in the left hemisphere that involve specific language functions are Broca's area (speech) and

Wernicke's area (language comprehension). The corpus callosum is a large bundle of fibers that connects the two hemispheres. Research suggests that the left brain is more dominant in processing verbal information (such as language) and the right brain in processing nonverbal information (such as spatial perception, visual recognition, faces, and emotion). Nonetheless, in a person whose corpus callosum is intact, both hemispheres of the cerebral cortex are involved in most complex human functioning.

 ## The Endocrine System

The endocrine glands release hormones directly into the bloodstream for distribution throughout the body. The pituitary gland is the master endocrine gland. The adrenal glands play important roles in mood, energy level, and ability to cope with stress. Other parts of the endocrine system include the pancreas, which produces insulin, and the ovaries and testes, which produce sex hormones.

 ## Brain Damage, Plasticity, and Repair

The human brain has considerable plasticity, although this plasticity is greater in young children than later in development. Three ways in which a damaged brain might repair itself are collateral sprouting, substitution of function, and neurogenesis. Brain grafts are implants of healthy tissue into damaged brains. Brain grafts are more successful when fetal tissue is used. Stem cell research may allow for new treatments for damaged nervous systems.

 ## Genetics and Behavior

Chromosomes are threadlike structures that occur in 23 pairs, with one member of each pair coming from each parent. Chromosomes contain the genetic substance deoxyribonucleic acid (DNA). Genes, the units of hereditary information, are short segments of chromosomes composed of DNA. According to the dominant-recessive genes principle, if one gene of a pair is dominant and one is recessive, the dominant gene overrides the recessive gene.

Two important concepts in the study of genetics are the genotype and phenotype. The genotype is an individual's actual genetic material. The phenotype is the observable characteristics—both physical and psychological—of the person.

Four methods of studying heredity's influence are molecular genetics, selective breeding, genome-wide association studies, and behavior genetics. Two methods used by behavior geneticists are twin studies and adoption studies. Both genes and environment play a role in determining the phenotype of an individual. Even for characteristics in which genes play a large role (such as height and eye color), the environment also is a factor. Gene × environment (G × E) interactions mean that people with the same gene may still differ from each other because of experience.

KEY TERMS

action potential
adrenal glands
afferent nerves
agonist
all-or-nothing principle
amygdala
antagonist
association cortex
autonomic nervous system
axon
basal ganglia
brain stem
cell body
central nervous system (CNS)
cerebral cortex
chromosomes
corpus callosum

dendrites
deoxyribonucleic acid (DNA)
dominant-recessive genes
   principle
efferent nerves
endocrine system
forebrain
frontal lobes
gene × environment (G × E)
   interaction
genes
genotype
glands
glial cells
hindbrain
hippocampus
hormones

hypothalamus
limbic system
midbrain
motor cortex
myelin sheath
neocortex
nervous system
neural networks
neurons
neurotransmitters
occipital lobes
ovaries
pancreas
parasympathetic nervous system
parietal lobes
peripheral nervous
   system (PNS)

phenotype
pituitary gland
plasticity
prefrontal cortex
resting potential
reticular formation
somatic nervous system
somatosensory cortex
stem cells
stress
stressors
sympathetic nervous system
synapses
temporal lobes
testes
thalamus

ANSWERS TO SELF-QUIZZES

Section 1:   1. B; 2. D; 3. C; 4. A
Section 2:   1. D; 2. D; 3. A; 4. B

Section 3:   1. B; 2. C; 3. B; 4. C
Section 4:   1. A; 2. C; 3. D; 4. C

Section 5:   1. B; 2. C; 3. A; 4. B
Section 6:   1. C; 2. C; 3. C; 4. A

3 Sensation and Perception

Those potato chips sound delicious!

Any child knows the essentials of sensation. We see with our eyes, hear with our ears, smell with our noses, and taste with our tongues. What could be simpler? Expert chefs often warn, "We taste with our eyes first," meaning that the way food looks can influence how it tastes to us. Could this warning be literally true? Is it possible that what food looks like (or sounds like) influences how it tastes? Psychologist Charles Spence has conducted numerous studies on the ways our senses combine to produce experience (Piqueras-Fiszman & Spence, 2015). Among other things, his work shows how the color of a mug can influence how coffee tastes—for instance, a white mug can lead to bitter coffee (Twilley, 2015). In addition, the way food sounds can influence its flavor. In one study, participants wore headphones while they munched Pringles potato chips (Zampini & Spence, 2004). Crunching sounds were picked up by a microphone and were fed into the headphones. Here's the catch: The sounds were manipulated by the experimenters so that they sounded louder and higher pitched for some participants. Although the chips were identical, as all Pringles are, those who heard the loud, high-pitched crunches reported the chips as tasting fresher. Another study showed the quality of music heard while eating affected the taste of chocolate: The smoother the music, the creamier and sweeter chocolate tasted (Reinoso Carvalho & others, 2017). These amusing studies have an important lesson about the way we experience the world. What we see, hear, smell, and taste is all that we know of reality in our everyday lives (Brunetti & others, 2017). Our reality is the product of our senses combining in fascinating ways.

©Billie Weiss/Boston Red Sox/Getty Images

This chapter explores sensation and perception, the processes by which we engage with the external world. We first examine vision and then probe hearing, the skin senses, taste, smell, and the kinesthetic and vestibular senses. Without the senses, we would be isolated from the world around us; we would live in dark silence—and in a tasteless, colorless, feelingless void.

1 How We Sense and Perceive the World

Sensation and perception researchers represent a broad range of specialties, including *ophthalmology,* the study of the eye's structure, function, and diseases; *audiology,* the science concerned with hearing; *neurology,* the scientific study of the nervous system; and many others. Understanding sensation and perception requires comprehending the physical properties of the objects of our perception—light, sound, the texture of material things, and so on. The psychological approach to these processes involves understanding the physical structures and functions of the sense organs, as well as the brain's conversion of the information from these organs into experience.

The Processes and Purposes of Sensation and Perception

sensation
The process of receiving stimulus energies from the external environment and transforming those energies into neural energy.

Our world is alive with stimuli—all the objects and events that surround us. A stimulus can be anything that we detect in the world. Sensation and perception are the processes that allow us to detect and understand these various stimuli. We do not actually experience these stimuli directly; rather, our senses allow us to get information about aspects of our environment, and we then take that information and form a perception of the world. **Sensation** is the process of receiving stimulus energies from the external environment and transforming those energies into neural energy. Physical energy such as light, sound, and heat is detected by specialized receptor cells in the sense organs—eyes, ears, skin, nose, and tongue. When the receptor cells register a stimulus, the energy is converted into an electrochemical impulse or action potential that relays information about the stimulus through the nervous system to the brain (Copeland & others, 2017). Recall that an action potential is the brief wave of electrical charge that sweeps down the axon of a neuron for possible transmission to another neuron. When it reaches the brain, the information travels to the appropriate area of the cerebral cortex (Andric, Davis, & Hasson, 2017; Heeger, 2017).

The brain gives meaning to sensation through perception. **Perception** is the process of organizing and interpreting sensory information so that it makes sense. Receptor cells in our eyes record—that is, sense—a sleek silver object in the sky, but they do not "see" a jet plane. So, sensation is about the biological processing that occurs between our sensory systems and the environment, while perception is our experience of those processes in action. Sensation is the biological

perception
The process of organizing and interpreting sensory information so that it makes sense.

Through sensation we take in information from the world; through perception we identify meaningful patterns in that information. Thus sensation and perception work hand in hand when we enjoy a hug and the sweet fragrance of a flower.
©Purestock/SuperStock

If you've ever begged someone to try your favorite food only to have the person give you a shrug and 'meh,' that's the difference between sensation and perception. Both tongues had the same experience. But perception is subjective.

process of the person encountering stimuli. Perception is the brain providing meaning to those encounters.

BOTTOM-UP AND TOP-DOWN PROCESSING

Psychologists distinguish between bottom-up and top-down processing in sensation and perception (Self & others, 2017). In **bottom-up processing,** sensory receptors register information about the external environment and send it up to the brain for interpretation (Klapper & others, 2014; Pattamadilok & others, 2017; Watanabe & Aust, 2017). Bottom-up processing means taking in information and trying to make sense of it. Bottom-up processing begins with the external world. In contrast, **top-down processing** starts with cognitive processing in the brain. In top-down processing we begin with some sense of what is happening (the product of our experiences) and apply that framework to incoming information from the world. Top-down processing is reflected when our expectations affect what we (or think we) see, hear, or feel (Huffman, Rajsic, & Pratt, 2017; Lyngs & others, 2016 ; Rajsic, Taylor, & Pratt, 2017).

One way to understand the difference between bottom-up and top-down processing is to think about how you experience a song you have never heard before versus that same song when you have heard it many times (Figure 1). The first time you hear the song, you listen carefully to get a "feel" for it. That is bottom-up processing: taking the incoming information of the music and relying on that external experience. Now, once you have a good feel for the song, you listen to it in a different way. You have expectations and know what comes next. That is top-down processing. You might even sing along with the song when it comes on the radio or at a club. Be careful, though, because top-down expectations are not always accurate, and you might find yourself singing to a remix that differs from what you are used to.

Top-down processing can happen even in the absence of any stimulus at all. You can experience top-down processing by "listening" to your favorite song in your head. As you "hear" the song in your mind's ear, you are engaged in a perceptual experience produced by top-down processing.

Bottom-up and top-down processing work together in sensation and perception to allow us to function accurately and efficiently (Hartcher-O'Brien, Soto-Faraco, & Adam, 2017). By themselves our ears provide only incoming information about sound in the environment. Only when we consider both what the ears hear (bottom-up processing) and what the brain interprets (top-down

bottom-up processing The operation in sensation and perception in which sensory receptors register information about the external environment and send it up to the brain for interpretation.

top-down processing The operation in sensation and perception, launched by cognitive processing at the brain's higher levels, that allows the organism to sense what is happening and to apply that framework to information from the world.

Eating strawberries, cherries, and red popsicles, little kids often get the idea that red = sweet . . . then they get a taste of red beets! It's always a fun moment when bottom-up experience collides with top-down expectations.

FIGURE 1 Top-Down and Bottom-Up Processes in Perception When you listen to a song for the first time, bottom-up processing allows you to get a feel for the tune. Once you know the song well, you can create a perceptual experience in your mind's ear, by "playing" it in your head. That's top-down processing.

processing) can we fully understand how we perceive sounds in our world. In everyday life, the two processes of sensation and perception are essentially inseparable. For this reason, most psychologists consider sensation and perception as a unified information-processing system.

Top-down expectations can influence what we think we see or hear (Lyngs & others, 2016). For example, in a series of studies, researchers ask people to find a toothbrush in a picture of a bathroom. Participants had no trouble picking out a (regular sized) toothbrush on the counter in front of the sink. However, what they did not seem to notice was a gigantic toothbrush, nearly as big as the counter itself, just behind the sink (Eckstein & others, 2017). In fact, people missed giant objects 13 percent more often than much smaller, but regularly sized objects. The explanation for this difference is that we look for objects based on our expectations for what they should look like, including size.

When the objects of our perception are other people, such expectations can include stereotypes, or our expectations for a person's behavior because of their membership in a particular group. If you hold a stereotype of police as helpful you might be more likely to see a policeman's neutral face as smiling. Similarly, stereotypes we hold can influence our ability to accurately perceive a broad range of other people, sometimes with important consequences. To read about the influence of stereotypes on perception, see the Challenge Your Thinking.

THE PURPOSES OF SENSATION AND PERCEPTION

Why do we perceive the world? From an evolutionary perspective, the purpose of sensation and perception is adaptation that improves a species' chances for survival (Kaiser & Haselhuhn, 2017; Melin & others, 2017; Troscianko & others, 2017). An organism must be able to sense and respond quickly and accurately to events in the immediate environment, such as the approach of a predator, the presence of prey, and the appearance of a potential mate. Not surprisingly, therefore, most animals—from goldfish to gorillas to humans—have eyes and ears, as well as sensitivities to touch and chemicals (smell and taste). Furthermore, a close comparison of sensory systems in animals reveals that each species is exquisitely adapted to the habitat in which it evolved. Animals that are primarily predators generally have their eyes at the front of their faces so that they can perceive their prey accurately. In contrast, animals that are more likely to be someone else's lunch have their eyes on either side of their heads, giving them a wide view of their surroundings at all times.

Dogs can smell better than humans. But that's because dogs need to and humans don't.

Sensory Receptors and the Brain

*There is that word again, afferent. Remember that **afferent** = arrives at the brain.*

All sensation begins with sensory receptors. **Sensory receptors** are specialized cells that detect stimulus information and transmit it to sensory (afferent) nerves and the brain. Sensory receptors are the openings through which the brain and nervous system experience the world. Figure 2 shows the human sensory receptors for vision, hearing, touch, smell, and taste.

sensory receptors
Specialized cells that detect stimulus information and transmit it to sensory (afferent) nerves and the brain.

Most predatory animals have eyes at the front of the face; most animals that are prey have eyes on the side of their head. Through these adaptations, predators perceive their prey accurately, and prey gain a measure of safety from their panoramic view of their environment.
(owl) ©Michael Cummings/Getty Images; (rabbit) ©Vetta/Getty Images

Why Does a Cell Phone Look Like a Gun?

A cell phone. Car keys. A driver's license. A billfold. A bottle of water. A toy gun in a toy aisle.

What all of these mundane objects have in common is that they have all, in various tragic cases, been mistaken for a gun by a police officer who has opened fire on the men holding them. In all of these cases, the police officers were cleared of wrongdoing. Juries and judges concluded that they had made terrible but honest mistakes. Such cases have incited critical attention, including the recent controversy about professional football players kneeling during the national anthem. Could it be a coincidence that the unarmed dead men were all African Americans? What role did race play in these mistakes?

Inspired by such cases, social psychologists have examined how ethnicity might influence the misperception of harmless objects as weapons (Rivers, 2017). In these studies, participants are told that they will see two pictures on a computer screen (Payne, 2006). Their job is to decide, as quickly and accurately as possible, whether the second picture is a gun or a tool. The first picture—always a picture of an African American man or a White man—cues the participants that the judgment is coming. Studies show that, after seeing an African American man's face, participants are quicker to recognize guns accurately in the second picture. In addition, when responses are hurried, participants are more likely to mistakenly view tools as guns when the tools are shown after a picture of an African American man (Rivers, 2017).

How can we understand such results? Social psychologists suggest that when what we perceive is ambiguous, stereotypes can fill in the gaps (Correll & others, 2015). Essentially, this means that the faces of African American men are acting as top-down cues, that facilitate access to stereotypical information indicating the person is dangerous. Perhaps most disturbing, a recent set of studies showed that even when Black male faces were those of children as young as 5 years old, participants were quicker to recognize weapons (Todd, Thiem, & Neel, 2016). Even the faces of children led participants to misperceive harmless objects as weapons.

Could such stereotype-driven top-down processing help us understand shootings of unarmed Black men? Research suggests that it might (Spencer, Charbonneau, & Glaser, 2016). For instance, some studies have participants play a video game in which they must decide whether to shoot or not shoot a potential suspect who is holding either a gun or a harmless object. In these studies, both African American and White participants have been found to decide to shoot more quickly at an armed African American man and to decide not to shoot more quickly at an unarmed White man (Correll & others, 2011). Because African Americans and Whites were equally disposed to react in these ways, the researchers concluded that personal prejudice cannot explain the tendency to let ethnicity guide the decision to shoot or not shoot a suspect. Instead, the explanation may lie in the automatic application of stereotypes (Todd & others, 2016).

(mobile) ©REDPIXEL.PL/Shutterstock; (wallet) ©Ensuper/Shutterstock; (gun) ©photo one/ Shutterstock

The mistakes police have made in shooting unarmed men and boys may be innocent, but they are not inevitable. Individuals who live in a society that does not view ethnic minority individuals as dangerous, aggressive, or likely to be criminals might be less inclined to misperceive a wallet, car keys, or cell phone as a weapon.

What Do You Think?

■ How might this research be used to prevent future tragic mistakes?

■ How does this research influence your views of police use of deadly force?

FIGURE 2 **Human Senses: Organs, Energy Stimuli, and Sensory Receptors** The receptor cells for each sense are specialized to receive particular types of energy stimuli.
(eye) ©Barbara Penoyar/Getty Images; (ear) ©iStockphoto/Getty Images; (skin) ©McGraw-Hill Education/Jill Braaten, photographer; (nose) ©S. Olsson/PhotoAlto; (tongue) ©Glow Images/Superstock

	Vision	Hearing	Touch	Smell	Taste
Sensory Receptor Cells					
Type of Energy Reception	Photoreception: detection of light, perceived as sight	Mechano-reception: detection of vibration, perceived as hearing	Mechano-reception: detection of pressure, perceived as touch	Chemoreception: detection of chemical stimuli, perceived as smell	Chemoreception: detection of chemical stimuli, perceived as taste
Sense Organ	Eyes	Ears	Skin	Nose	Tongue

The frequency of firing communicates intensity for all of our sensory neurons. A loud noise leads to more frequent pulses too. And a very painful jab from a needle leads to more frequent pulses communicating, OUCH!

Figure 3 depicts the flow of information from the environment to the brain. Sensory receptors take in information from the environment, creating local electrical currents. These currents are graded; that means they are sensitive to the intensity of stimulation, such as the difference between a dim and a bright light. These receptors trigger action potentials in sensory neurons, which carry that information to the central nervous system. Because sensory neurons (like all neurons) follow the all-or-nothing principle, the intensity of the stimulus cannot be communicated to the brain by changing the strength of the action potential. Instead, the receptor varies the *frequency* of action potentials sent to the brain. So, if a stimulus is very intense, like the bright sun on a hot day, the neuron will fire more frequently (but with the same strength) to let the brain know that the light is indeed very, very bright.

Other than frequency, the action potentials of all sensory nerves are alike. This sameness raises an intriguing question: How can an animal distinguish among sight, sound, odor, taste, and touch? The answer is that sensory receptors are selective and have different neural pathways. They are specialized to absorb a particular type of energy—light energy, sound vibrations, or chemical energy, for example—and convert it into an action potential.

Sensation involves detecting and transmitting information about different kinds of energy. The sense organs and sensory receptors fall into several main classes based on the type of energy that is transmitted. The functions of these classes include

- *Photoreception:* detection of light, perceived as sight
- *Mechanoreception:* detection of pressure, vibration, and movement, perceived as touch, hearing, and equilibrium
- *Chemoreception:* detection of chemical stimuli, perceived as smell and taste

Each of these processes belongs to a particular class of receptors and brain processes. There are rare cases, however, in which the senses can become confused. The term *synaesthesia* describes an experience in which one sense (say, sight) induces an experience in another sense (say, hearing) (Newell & Mitchell, 2016; Teichmann, Nieuwenstein, & Rich, 2017). An individual might "see" music or "taste" a color, for example. One woman was able to taste sounds, so that a piece of music might taste like tuna fish (Beeli, Esslen, & Jancke, 2005). Neuroscientists are exploring the neurological bases of synaesthesia,

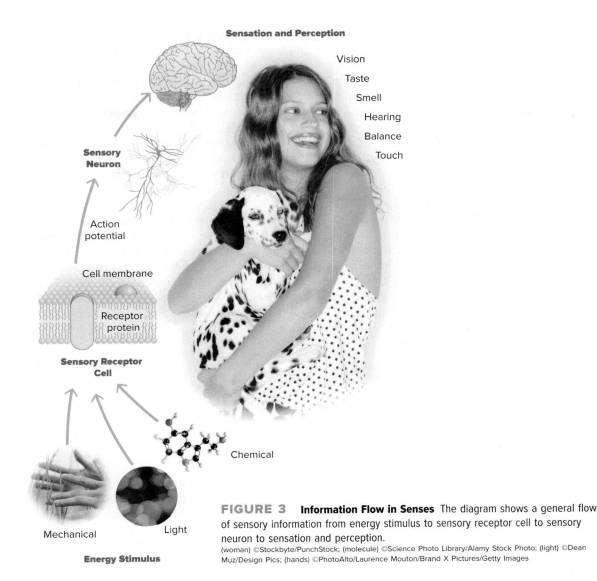

Sensation and Perception

Vision
Taste
Smell
Hearing
Balance
Touch

Sensory Neuron

Action potential

Cell membrane

Receptor protein

Sensory Receptor Cell

Chemical

Mechanical

Light

Energy Stimulus

FIGURE 3 **Information Flow in Senses** The diagram shows a general flow of sensory information from energy stimulus to sensory receptor cell to sensory neuron to sensation and perception.
(woman) ©Stockbyte/PunchStock; (molecule) ©Science Photo Library/Alamy Stock Photo; (light) ©Dean Muz/Design Pics; (hands) ©PhotoAlto/Laurence Mouton/Brand X Pictures/Getty Images

especially in the connections between the various sensory regions of the cerebral cortex (van Leeuwen & others, 2016). For example, one fMRI study identified the parietal cortex, an area of the brain associated with integrating sensory experiences, as the key auditory-visual location in the brain for individuals with synaesthesia who experienced music as color (Neufeld & others, 2012). Another study found, in a blind participant, that "seeing" sounds as color involved activity in the occipital lobe, the brain area responsible for vision (Yong, Hseih, & Milea, 2017).

In the brain, nearly all sensory signals pass through the thalamus, the brain's relay station. From the thalamus, the signals go to the sensory areas of the cerebral cortex, where they are modified and spread throughout a vast network of neurons.

Certain areas of the cerebral cortex are specialized to handle different sensory functions. Visual information is processed mainly in the occipital lobes; hearing, in the temporal lobes; and pain, touch, and temperature, in the parietal lobes. Keep in mind, however, that the interactions and pathways of sensory information are complex, and the brain often must coordinate extensive information and interpret it.

Occipital = the back of the brain; temporal = on the sides; parietal = on the top. (You're welcome!)

An important part of perception is interpreting the sensory messages. Many top-down factors determine this meaning, including signals from different parts of the brain, prior learning, the person's goals, and his or her degree of arousal. Moving in the opposite direction, bottom-up signals from a sensory area may help other parts of the brain maintain arousal, form an image of where the body is in space, or regulate movement.

The principles we have surveyed so far apply to all of the senses. We've seen that the senses are about detecting different energies and that all have specialized receptor cells and areas of the brain that serve their functions. You have probably heard about a "sixth sense"—*extrasensory perception,* or *ESP.* ESP means that a person can detect information from the world without receiving concrete sensory input. Examples of ESP include *telepathy* (the ability to read another person's mind) and *precognition* (the ability to sense future events). The vast majority of psychologists reject the idea that people can foretell the future or read each other's minds (Cameron, 2016; Moulton & Kosslyn, 2008; Wiseman & Watt, 2006).

Think about something like precognition in the ways we have considered sensation and perception. Sensation involves detecting energy from the environment. If ESP exists, consider this: Which afferent neurons send psychic messages from the future to the brain, and what sort of energy conveys these messages? Believers in ESP have not produced answers to these important questions. The success of gambling casinos, daily experiences with surprise, and scientific evidence (Barušs & Rabier, 2014; Rabeyron, 2014) converge to tell us that human beings cannot feel the future. Perhaps we are fine with just the five senses we have.

Thresholds

Any sensory system must be able to detect varying degrees of energy. This energy can take the form of light, sound, chemical, or mechanical stimulation. How much of a stimulus is necessary for you to see, hear, taste, smell, or feel something? What is the lowest possible amount of stimulation that will still be detected?

ABSOLUTE THRESHOLD   One way to think about the lowest limits of perception is to assume that there is an **absolute threshold,** or minimum amount of stimulus energy that a person can detect. In other words, the absolute threshold is the dimmest light, the faintest sound, or the softest touch a person can still see, hear, or feel. When the energy of a stimulus falls below this absolute threshold, we cannot detect its presence; when the energy of the stimulus rises above the absolute threshold, we can detect the stimulus (Heil, Matysiak, & Neubauer, 2017; Tinsley & others, 2016). As an example, find a clock that ticks; put it on a table and walk far enough away that you no longer hear it. Then gradually move toward the clock. At some point, you will begin to hear it ticking. Hold your position and notice that occasionally the ticking fades, and you may have to move forward to reach the threshold; at other times, it may become loud, and you can move backward.

In this experiment, if you measure your absolute threshold several times, you likely will record several different distances for detecting the stimulus. For example, the first time you try it, you might hear the ticking at 25 feet from the clock. However, you probably will not hear it every time at 25 feet. Maybe you hear it only 38 percent of the time at this distance, but you hear it 50 percent of the time at 20 feet away and 65 percent of the time at 15 feet. People have different thresholds. Some have better hearing than others, and some have better vision. Figure 4 shows one person's measured

absolute threshold The minimum amount of stimulus energy that a person can detect.

FIGURE 4   **Measuring Absolute Threshold** Absolute threshold is the minimum amount of energy we can detect. To measure absolute threshold, psychologists have arbitrarily decided to use the criterion of detecting the stimulus 50 percent of the time. In this graph, the person's absolute threshold for detecting the ticking clock is at a distance of 20 feet.
©Wavebreakmedia Ltd/Wavebreak Media/Getty Images

FIGURE 5 **Approximate Absolute Thresholds for Five Senses** These thresholds show the amazing power of our senses to detect even very slight variations in the environment.
©Stockdisc

Vision A candle flame at 30 miles on a dark, clear night

Hearing A ticking clock at 20 feet under quiet conditions

Smell One drop of perfume diffused throughout three rooms

Taste A teaspoon of sugar in 2 gallons of water

Touch The wing of a fly falling on your neck from a distance of 1 centimeter

absolute threshold for detecting a clock's ticking sound. Psychologists have arbitrarily decided that absolute threshold is the point at which the individual detects the stimulus 50 percent of the time—in this case, 20 feet away. Using the same clock, another person might have a measured absolute threshold of 26 feet, and yet another, 18 feet. Figure 5 lists the approximate absolute thresholds of five senses.

Under ideal circumstances, our senses have very low absolute thresholds, so we can be remarkably good at detecting small amounts of stimulus energy. You might be surprised to learn that the human eye can see a candle flame at 30 miles on a dark, clear night. However, our environment seldom gives us ideal conditions with which to detect stimuli. If the night were cloudy or the air smoky, for example, you would have to be much closer to see the candle flame. In addition, other lights on the horizon—car or house lights—would hinder your ability to detect the candle's flicker. **Noise** is the term given to irrelevant and competing stimuli—not just sounds but any distracting stimuli for our senses (Nesti & others, 2014; Zhao & others, 2017). When we are in a noisy environment, it is difficult to detect accurately specific stimuli.

noise
Irrelevant and competing stimuli—not only sounds but also any distracting stimuli for the senses.

DIFFERENCE THRESHOLD   In addition to studying how much energy is required for a stimulus to be detected, psychologists investigate the degree of difference that must exist between two stimuli before the difference is detected. This is the **difference threshold,** or just noticeable difference. An artist might detect the difference between two similar shades of color. A fashion designer might notice a difference in the texture of two fabrics. How different must the colors and textures be for someone to say, "These are different"? Like the absolute threshold, the difference threshold is the smallest difference in stimulation required to discriminate one stimulus from another 50 percent of the time.

difference threshold
The degree of difference that must exist between two stimuli before the difference is detected.

Difference thresholds increase as a stimulus becomes stronger. That means that at very low levels of stimulation, small changes can be detected, but at very high levels, small changes are less noticeable. When music is playing softly, you may notice when your roommate increases the volume by even a small amount. If, however, he or she turns the volume up an equal amount when the music is playing very loudly, you may not notice. **Weber's law,** discovered by German physiologist E. H. Weber more than 150 years ago, is the principle that two stimuli must differ by a constant proportion to be perceived as different. For example, we add 1 candle to 20 candles and notice a difference in the brightness of the candles; we add 1 candle to 120 candles and do not notice a difference, but we would notice the difference if we added 6 candles to 120 candles. Weber's law generally holds true (Heath & others, 2017).

Weber's law
The principle that two stimuli must differ by a constant minimum percentage (rather than a constant amount) to be perceived as different.

Note that 1:20 = 6:120.

SUBLIMINAL PERCEPTION   Can sensations that occur below our absolute threshold affect us without our being aware of them? **Subliminal perception** refers to the detection of information below the level of conscious awareness. In 1957, James Vicary, an advertising executive, announced that he was able to increase popcorn and soft drink sales by secretly flashing the words "EAT POPCORN" and "DRINK COKE" on a movie screen in a local theater (Weir, 1984). Vicary's claims were a hoax, but people have

Subliminal perception
The detection of information below the level of conscious awareness.

©Burke/Triolo/Brand X Pictures

continued to wonder whether behavior can be influenced by stimuli that are presented so quickly that we cannot perceive them.

Studies have shown that the brain (Chiesa & others, 2017; Khalighinejad, & others, 2017) and cardiovscular system (van der Ploeg & others, 2017a, 2017b) respond to information that is presented outside of awareness. In addition, such stimuli can affect behavior (Andersson & others, 2017; Sand & Nillson, 2017). For example, a recent study examined how erotic images would affect people's self-disclosure to a member of a the opposite sex (Birnbaum & others, 2017). Heterosexual participants (college students) were told that the study concerned behavior in the modern dating scene. They were told that they would be interacting through instant messages with a member of the opposite sex. Before the online interaction, participants were asked to complete a number of questions on a computer about their likes and dislikes. Unbeknownst to the participants when they were answering these questions, they were also being primed. Participants were randomly assigned to be exposed to erotic primes (the experimental group) or images of fish (the control group). As they completed the questionnaire, the experimental group were exposed to erotic images for 30 milliseconds (that's 1/100 of a second). In the control group, they were exposed to pictures of fish for the same amount of time. After the priming, participants were asked to send a message about a personally meaningful experience to their partner. The results showed that participants exposed to the erotic images disclosed more deeply to their partner. They were more likely to share more personal, inner-most experiences (Birnbaum & others, 2017). You will learn more about priming in the memory discussion.

Results like those described above can give priming a magical quality. However, it is important to keep in mind that subliminally presented information is registering on some level. Moreover, some have argued that even though primes are presented rapidly, some people may still detect them, consciously (Sand & Nilsson, 2016). Perhaps even more importantly, presenting information so that it can be consciously processed can have stronger effects on behavior than subliminal presentation (Aoyama & others, 2017).

The notion that stimuli we do not consciously perceive can influence our behavior challenges the usefulness of the idea of thresholds (Rouder & Morey, 2009). If stimuli that fall below the threshold can have an impact on us, you may be wondering, what do thresholds really tell us? Further, you might have noticed that the definition of absolute threshold is not that absolute. It refers to the intensity of stimulation detected *50 percent of the time*. How can something absolute change from one trial to the next?

If, for example, you tried the ticking clock experiment described earlier, you might have found yourself making judgment calls. Sometimes you felt very sure you could hear the clock, but other times you were uncertain and probably took a guess. Sometimes you guessed right, and other times you were mistaken. Now, imagine that someone offered to pay you $50 for every correct answer you gave—would the presence of that incentive change your judgments? Alternatively, what if you were charged $50 for every time you said you heard the clock and it was not ticking? In fact, perception is often about making such judgment calls.

An alternative approach to the question of whether a stimulus is detected would emphasize that saying (or not saying) "Yes, I hear that ticking" is actually a *decision (*Hozo & others, 2017). This approach is called signal detection theory. **Signal detection theory** focuses on decision making about stimuli under conditions of uncertainty. In signal detection theory, detection of sensory stimuli depends on a variety of factors besides the physical intensity of the stimulus and the sensory abilities of the observer (Winer & Snodgrass, 2015). These factors include individual and contextual variations, such as fatigue, expectations, and the urgency of the moment. Figure 6 shows how signal detection works.

signal detection theory
An approach to perception that focuses on decision making about stimuli in the presence of uncertainty.

Perceiving Sensory Stimuli

As we just saw, the perception of stimuli is influenced by more than the characteristics of the environmental stimuli themselves. Two important factors in perceiving sensory stimuli are attention and perceptual set.

ATTENTION

The world holds a lot of information to perceive. At this moment you are perceiving the letters and words that make up this sentence. Now gaze around you and fix your eyes on something other than what you are reading. Afterward, curl up the toes on your right foot. In each of these circumstances, you engaged in **selective attention,** which involves focusing on a specific aspect of experience while ignoring others (Scocchia & others, 2014; Sridharan, Schwarz, & Knudsen, 2014). A familiar example of selective attention is the ability to focus on one voice among many in a crowded airline terminal or noisy restaurant. Psychologists call this common occurrence the *cocktail party effect* (Kuyper, 1972; McLachlan & Wilson, 2010).

selective attention
The act of focusing on a specific aspect of experience while ignoring others.

	Observer's Response	
	"Yes, I see the signal."	*"No, I don't see the signal."*
Signal Present	Hit (correct)	Miss (mistake)
Signal Absent	False alarm (mistake)	Correct rejection (correct)

FIGURE 6

Four Outcomes in Signal Detection Signal detection research helps to explain when and how perceptual judgments are correct or mistaken.

Not only is attention selective, but it also is *shiftable*. For example, you might be paying close attention to your instructor's lecture, but if the person next to you starts texting a friend, you might look to see what is going on over there. The fact that we can attend selectively to one stimulus and shift readily to another indicates that we must be monitoring many things at once.

Certain features of stimuli cause people to attend to them. *Novel stimuli* (those that are new, different, or unusual) often attract our attention. If a Ferrari convertible whizzes by, you are more likely to notice it than you would a Ford. Size, color, and movement also influence our attention. Objects that are large, vividly colored, or moving are more likely to grab our attention than objects that are small, dull-colored, or stationary.

Sometimes even very interesting stimuli can be missed if our attention is otherwise occupied (Hyman, Sarb, & Wise-Swanson, 2014). *Inattentional blindness* refers to the failure to detect unexpected events when attention is engaged by a task (Calvillo & Jackson, 2014). When we are working intently on something, such as finding a seat in a packed movie theater, we might not even see an unusual stimulus, such as a friend waving to us in the crowd. Research conducted by Daniel Simons and Christopher Chabris (1999) provides a remarkable example of inattentional blindness. In that study, participants were asked to watch a video of two teams playing basketball. The participants were instructed to closely count the number of passes thrown by each team. During the video, a small woman dressed in a gorilla suit walked through the action, clearly visible for 5 seconds. Surprisingly, over half of the participants (who were apparently deeply engaged in the counting task) never noticed the gorilla. Inattentional blindness is more likely to occur when a task is difficult (Macdonald & Lavie, 2008) and when the distracting stimulus is very different from stimuli that are relevant to the task at hand (White & Aimola Davies, 2008; Wiemer, Gerdes, & Pauli, 2012). Interestingly, when people are primed with the goal to detect and the monitoring task is only moderately difficult, they are more likely to notice the gorilla (Légal & others, 2017).

©Vstock LLC/Getty Images

This research on inattentional blindness suggests the dangers of multitasking when one of the tasks is driving. Engaging in a task such as talking on a cell phone or sending text messages can so occupy attention that little is left over for the important task of piloting a motor vehicle. Research revealed that individuals who text-message while they drive face 23 times the risk of a crash or near-crash compared to nondistracted drivers (Blanco & others, 2009; Hanowski & others, 2009). In this research, cameras continuously observed drivers for more than 6 million miles of driving. Texting drew the drivers' eyes away from the road long enough for the vehicle to travel the length of a football field at 55 miles an hour. The statistics are sobering. In the U.S., more than 8 people are killed

The age group most likely to be using a cell phone while driving is 16- to 24-year-olds.

every day due to distracted drivers and at any given daylight moment an estimated 660,000 drivers are using cellphones or other electronic devices (FCC, 2017).

Research shows that culture influences which stimuli we attend to as we perceive the world (Senzaki, Masuda, & Ishii, 2014). Individuals from Western cultures are more likely to attend to objects in the foreground of scenes (or *focal objects*), while East Asians looking at the same scenes are more likely to notice aspects of the context. For example, in one study (Masuda & Nisbett, 2001), American and Japanese participants were shown video clips of underwater scenes. When asked to describe what they had seen, the Americans were more likely to talk about the colorful fish swimming around, and Japanese participants were more likely to talk about the locations of objects and aspects of the setting. Such differences have led psychologists to conclude that Westerners take a more analytical orientation, while Asians are more likely to see the big picture. Culture also influences the kinds of stimuli that are missed in inattentional blindness. Research on *change blindness* (the tendency to miss changes that have occurred in a scene) shows that when objects in the foreground change, Americans are more likely to notice, while Japanese are more likely to notice when changes occur in the context (Masuda & Nisbett, 2006).

What might explain these cultural differences in attention? One possibility may be differences in the environments that individuals in these cultures typically encounter (Senzaki, Masuda, & Ishii, 2014). In a series of studies, Yuri Miyamoto and her colleagues (Miyamoto, Nisbett, & Masuda, 2006) found through photographic comparisons that Japanese hotels and schools had more detail and were more complex than American hotels and schools. Japanese individuals, then, may develop the tendency to look at the whole picture because navigating their world requires such attention. Interestingly, in another study, Miyamoto and her colleagues had American and Japanese participants watch brief video clips of American or Japanese scenes (Miyamoto, Nisbett, & Masuda, 2006). They found that American and Japanese participants alike noticed changes in focal objects in American scenes but noticed changes in the context in Japanese scenes. This research suggests that while the mechanics of sensation are the same for human beings, the experience of perception can be shaped by the physical environment in which each person lives.

PERCEPTUAL SET   Cover the playing cards on the right in the illustration and look at the playing cards on the left. As quickly as you can, count how many aces of spades you see. Then cover the cards on the left and count the number of aces of spades among the cards on the right.

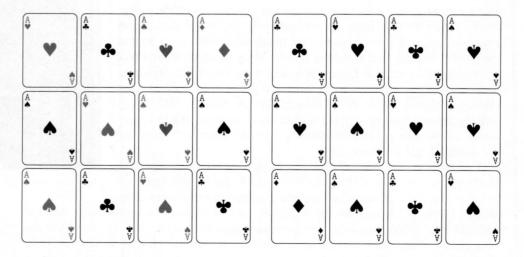

Most people report that they see two or three aces of spades in the set of cards on the left. However, if you look closely, you will see that there are five. Two of the aces of spades are black and three are red. When people look at the set of cards on the right, they are more likely to count five aces of spades. Why do we perceive the two sets of cards differently? We expect the ace of spades to be black because it is always black in a regular deck of cards. We do not expect red spades, so we skip right over the red ones: Expectations influence perceptions.

Psychologists refer to a predisposition or readiness to perceive something in a particular way as a **perceptual set.** Perceptual sets act as "psychological" filters in processing information about the environment (Fei-Fei & others, 2007). Perceptual sets reflect top-down influences on perception. Interestingly, young children are more accurate at the task involving the ace of spades than adults are. Why? Because they have not built up the perceptual set that the ace of spades is black.

perceptual set
A predisposition or readiness to perceive something in a particular way.

Sensory Adaptation

Turning out the lights in your bedroom at night, you stumble across the room to your bed, blind to the objects around you. Gradually the objects reappear and become clearer. The ability of the visual system to adjust to a darkened room is an example of **sensory adaptation**—a change in the responsiveness of the sensory system based on the average level of surrounding stimulation (Hilchey, Klein, & Satel, 2014; Iglesias, 2012).

You have experienced sensory adaptation countless times in your life. You adjust to the water in an initially "freezing" swimming pool. You turn on your windshield wipers while driving, and shortly you are unaware of their rhythmic sweeping back and forth. When you first enter a room, you might be bothered by the hum of the air conditioner, but after a while you get used to it. All of these experiences represent sensory adaptation.

In the example of adapting to the dark, when you turn out the lights, everything is black. Conversely, when you step out into the bright sunshine after spending time in a dark basement, light floods your eyes and everything appears light. These momentary blips in sensation arise because adaptation takes time.

sensory adaptation
A change in the responsiveness of the sensory system based on the average level of surrounding stimulation.

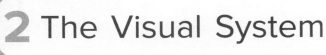

self-quiz

1. Every day, you see, hear, smell, taste, and feel stimuli from the outside world. Collecting data about that world is the function of _____, and interpreting the data collected is the function of _____.
   A. the brain; the spinal cord
   B. the spinal cord; the brain
   C. sensation; perception
   D. perception; sensation

2. The main classes into which the sense organs and sensory receptors fall include all of the following *except*
   A. chemoreception.
   B. electroreception.
   C. photoreception.
   D. mechanoreception.

3. An architect is designing apartments and wants them to be soundproof. She asks a psychologist what the smallest amount of sound is that can be heard. Her question is most related to
   A. the absolute threshold.
   B. the difference threshold.
   C. Weber's law.
   D. the sensory receptors.

APPLY IT! 4. Trina, a first-year college student, goes home at Thanksgiving break after being away from home (for the first time) for three months. She feels as if she has changed a lot, but her parents still treat her like a kid in high school. At Thanksgiving dinner she confronts them, bursting out, "Stop top-down processing me!" Her parents think Trina has lost her mind. Which of the following explains her outburst?
   A. Trina feels that her parents are judging her sophisticated college ways too harshly.
   B. Trina probably ate too much turkey.
   C. Trina feels that her parents have spent too much time analyzing her behavior.
   D. Trina believes that her parents are letting their preconceived ideas of who she is prevent them from seeing her as the person she has become.

2 The Visual System

When Michael May of Davis, California, was 3 years old, an accident left him visually impaired, with only the ability to perceive the difference between night and day. He lived a rich, full life, marrying and having children, founding a successful company, and becoming an expert skier. Twenty-five years passed before doctors transplanted stem cells into May's right eye, a new procedure that gave him partial sight (Bach, 2015; Kurson, 2007). May can now see; his right eye is functional and allows him to detect color and negotiate the world without the use of a cane or reliance on his seeing-eye dog. His visual experience remains unusual, however: He sees the world as if it is an abstract painting. He can catch a ball thrown to him by his sons, but he cannot recognize his wife's face. His brain has to work at interpreting the new information that his right eye is providing. May's experience highlights the intimate connection between the brain and the sense organs in producing perception. Vision is a remarkable process that involves the brain's interpretation of the visual information sent from the eyes. We now explore the physical foundations of the visual system and the processes involved in the perception of visual stimuli.

The Visual Stimulus and the Eye

Our ability to detect visual stimuli depends on the sensitivity of our eyes to differences in light.

LIGHT   *Light* is a form of electromagnetic energy that can be described in terms of wavelengths. Light travels through space in waves. The *wavelength* of light is the distance from the peak of one wave to the peak of the next. Wavelengths of visible light range from about 400 to 700 nanometers (a nanometer is 1 billionth of a meter and is abbreviated nm). The wavelength of light that is reflected from a stimulus determines its hue or color.

Outside the range of visible light are longer radio and infrared radiation waves and shorter ultraviolet and X rays (Figure 7). These other forms of electromagnetic energy continually bombard us, but we do not see them.

FIGURE 7   **The Electromagnetic Spectrum and Visible Light** (*top*) Visible light is only a narrow band in the electromagnetic spectrum. Visible light wavelengths range from about 400 to 700 nanometers. X rays are much shorter, radio waves much longer. (*bottom*) The two graphs show how waves vary in length between successive peaks. Shorter wavelengths are higher in frequency, as reflected in blue colors; longer wavelengths are lower in frequency, as reflected in red colors.

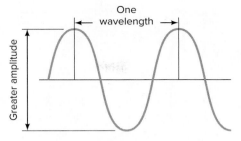

Light waves of greater amplitude make up brighter light.

One wavelength

Greater amplitude

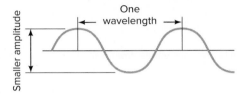

Light waves of smaller amplitude make up dimmer light.

One wavelength

Smaller amplitude

FIGURE 8 **Light Waves of Varying Amplitude** The top graph might suggest a spotlight on a concert stage; the bottom, a candlelit dinner.

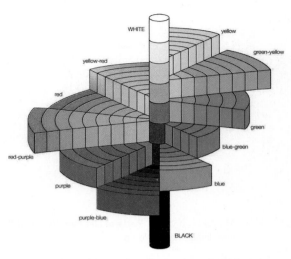

WHITE
yellow
green-yellow
yellow-red
red
green
red-purple
blue-green
purple
blue
purple-blue
BLACK

FIGURE 9 **A Color Tree Showing Color's Three Dimensions: Hue, Saturation, and Brightness** Hue is represented around the color tree—saturation horizontally and brightness vertically.
©Universal Images Group Editorial/Getty Images

We can also describe waves of light in terms of their height, or *amplitude,* which determines the brightness of the stimulus. Finally, the *purity* of the wavelengths—whether they are all the same or a mix of waves—determines the perceived *saturation,* or richness, of a visual stimulus (Figure 8). The color tree shown in Figure 9 can help you to understand saturation. White light is a combination of color wavelengths that is perceived as colorless, like sunlight. Very pure colors have no white light in them. They are located on the outside of the color tree. Notice how, the closer we get to the center of the color tree, the more white light has been added to the single wavelength of a particular color. In other words, the deep colors at the edge fade into pastel colors toward the center.

THE STRUCTURE OF THE EYE   The eye, like a camera, is constructed to get the best possible picture of the world. An accurate picture is in focus, is not too dark or too light, and has good contrast between the dark and light parts. Each of several structures in the eye plays an important role in this process.

If you look closely at your eyes in the mirror, you will notice three parts—the sclera, iris, and pupil (Figure 10). The *sclera* is the white, outer part of the eye that helps to maintain the shape of the eye and to protect it from injury. The *iris* is the colored part of the eye, which might be light blue in one individual and dark brown in another. The *pupil,* which appears black, is the opening in the center of the iris. The iris contains muscles that control the size of the pupil, and hence regulates the amount of light that enters the eye. To get a good picture of the world, the eye needs to be able to adjust the amount of light that enters. In this sense, the pupil acts like the aperture of a camera, opening to let in more light when it is needed and closing to let in less light when there is too much.

If you have ever had your pupils dilated for an eye exam, your doctor has basically opened the pupil up to get a good look at your eye!

Two structures bring the image into focus, the cornea and the lens. The *cornea* is the first structure to encounter the world. It is a clear membrane at the very front of the eye. The *lens* is a transparent and somewhat flexible, disk-like structure filled with a gelatin-like material. Light hits the cornea and then the lens. The function of both of these structures is to bend the light falling on the surface of the eye just enough to focus it at the back. The curved surface of the cornea does most of this bending, while the lens fine-tunes

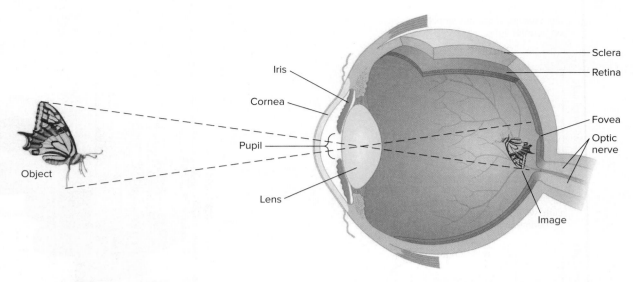

Iris

Cornea

Pupil

Object

Lens

Sclera

Retina

Fovea

Optic nerve

Image

FIGURE 10 **Parts of the Eye** Note that the image of the butterfly on the retina is upside down. The brain allows us to see the image right side up.

things. When you are looking at faraway objects, the lens has a relatively flat shape because the light reaching the eye from faraway objects is parallel and the bending power of the cornea is sufficient to keep things in focus. However, the light reaching the eye from objects that are close is more scattered, so more bending of the light is required to achieve focus.

Without this ability of the lens to change its curvature, the eye would have a tough time focusing on close objects such as reading material. As we get older, the lens loses flexibility and hence its ability to change from its normal flattened shape to the rounder shape needed to bring close objects into focus. That is why many people with normal vision throughout their young adult lives require reading glasses as they age.

The parts of the eye we have considered so far work together to give us the sharpest picture of the world. This effort would be useless, however, without a vehicle for recording the images the eyes take of the world—in essence, the film of the camera. Photographic film is made of a material that responds to light. At the back of the eye is the eye's "film," the multilayered **retina,** which is the light-sensitive surface that records electromagnetic energy and converts it to neural impulses for processing in the brain. The analogy between the retina and film goes only so far, however. The retina is amazingly complex and elegantly designed. It is in fact the primary mechanism of sight. Even after decades of intense study, the full marvel of this structure is far from understood (Franke & Baden, 2017; Walsh & Hitchcock, 2017).

The human retina has approximately 126 million receptor cells. They turn the electromagnetic energy of light into a form of energy that the nervous system can process. There are two kinds of visual receptor cells: rods and cones. Rods and cones differ both in how they respond to light and in their patterns of distribution on the surface of the retina. **Rods** are the receptors in the retina that are sensitive to light, but they are not very useful for color vision. Rods function well under low illumination; they are hard at work at night. Humans have about 120 million rods. **Cones** are the receptors that we use for color perception. Like rods, cones are light-sensitive. However, they require a larger amount of light to respond than the rods do, so they operate best in daylight or under high illumination. There are about 6 million cone cells in human eyes. Figure 11 shows what rods and cones look like.

Rod

Cone

FIGURE 11 **Rods and Cones** In real life, rods and cones look somewhat like stumps and corncobs. To get a sense of how well the cones in the fovea work, try reading out of the corner of your eye. It is difficult because the fovea doesn't get to do the reading for you. Keep in mind that the visual information in the retina that is closest to the nose crosses over, and the visual information on the outer side of the retina stays on that side of the brain.
©Omikron/Science Source

retina
The multilayered light-sensitive surface in the eye that records electromagnetic energy and converts it to neural impulses for processing in the brain.

rods
The receptor cells in the retina that are sensitive to light but not very useful for color vision.

cones
The receptor cells in the retina that allow for color perception.

FIGURE 12 **Direction of Light in the Retina** After light passes through the cornea, pupil, and lens, it falls on the retina. Three layers of specialized cells in the retina convert the image into a neural signal that can be transmitted to the brain. First, light triggers a reaction in the rods and cones at the back of the retina, transducing light energy into electrochemical neural impulses. The neural impulses activate the bipolar cells, which in turn activate the ganglion cells. Then light information is transmitted to the optic nerve, which conveys it to the brain. The arrows indicate the sequence in which light information moves in the retina.

Light
Blind spot
Light
Rod
Cone
Optic nerve
Ganglion cells
Bipolar cells
Rod and cone layer
Retina
Optic nerve

The most important part of the retina is the *fovea,* a tiny area in the center of the retina at which vision is at its best (see Figure 10). The fovea contains only cones and is vital to many visual tasks. Rods are found almost everywhere on the retina except in the fovea.

Figure 12 shows how the rods and cones at the back of the retina convert light into electrochemical impulses. The signal is transmitted to the *bipolar cells* and then moves on to another layer of specialized cells called *ganglion cells* (Steketee & others, 2014). The axons of the ganglion cells make up the **optic nerve,** which carries the visual information to the brain for further processing. Figure 13 summarizes the characteristics of rods and cones.

One place on the retina contains neither rods nor cones. This area, the *blind spot,* is the area on the retina where the optic nerve leaves the eye on its way to the brain (see Figure 12). We cannot see anything that reaches only this part of the retina. To prove to yourself that you have a blind spot, look at Figure 14. Once you have seen the yellow pepper disappear, you have probably noticed it took a while to succeed at this task. Now shut one eye and look around. You see a perfectly continuous picture of the world around you; there is no blind spot. This is a great example of top-down processing and a demonstration of the constructive aspect of perception. Your brain fills in the gap for you (the one that ought to be left by your blind spot) with some pretty good guesses about what must be in that spot, like a creative artist painting in the blind spot.

If you want to see a very faint star, you should gaze slightly away from it, to allow your rods to do their work.

optic nerve
The structure at the back of the eye, made up of axons of the ganglion cells, that carries visual information to the brain for further processing.

Interestingly, squid (and other cephalopods) do not have blind spots because unlike us, their optic nerves do not block the visual field.

Do It!

If you'd like to explore your blind spot more, search for "blind spot demonstrations" online.

Visual Processing in the Brain

The eyes are just the beginning of visual perception. The next step occurs when neural impulses generated in the retina are dispatched to the brain for analysis and integration (Kaiser & Haselhuhn, 2017).

The optic nerve leaves the eye, carrying information about light toward the brain. Light travels in a straight line; therefore, stimuli in the left visual field are registered in the right half of the retina in both eyes, and stimuli in the

What's on the 'nose' side of the retina crosses over.

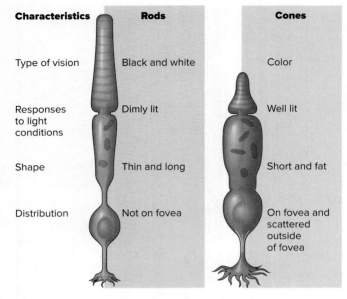

Characteristics	Rods	Cones
Type of vision	Black and white	Color
Responses to light conditions	Dimly lit	Well lit
Shape	Thin and long	Short and fat
Distribution	Not on fovea	On fovea and scattered outside of fovea

FIGURE 13 **Characteristics of Rods and Cones** Rods and cones differ in shape, location, and function.

FIGURE 14 **The Eye's Blind Spot** There is a normal blind spot in your eye, a small area where the optic nerve leads to the brain. To find your blind spot, hold this image at arm's length, cover your left eye, and stare at the red pepper on the left with your right eye. Move the image slowly toward you until the yellow pepper disappears. To find the blind spot in your left eye, cover your right eye, stare at the yellow pepper, and adjust the distance until the red pepper disappears.
©David Tietz/Editorial Image LLC

right visual field are registered in the left half of the retina in both eyes (Figure 15). In the brain, at a point called the *optic chiasm,* the optic nerve fibers divide, and approximately half of the nerve fibers cross over the midline of the brain. As a result, the visual information originating in the right halves of the two retinas is transmitted to the right side of the occipital lobe in the cerebral cortex, and the visual information coming from the left halves of the retinas is transmitted to the left side of the occipital lobe. These crossings mean that what we see in the left side of our visual field is registered in the right side of the brain, and what we see in the right visual field is registered in the left side of the brain (see Figure 15). Then this information is processed and combined into a recognizable object or scene in the visual cortex.

visual cortex
Located in the occipital lobe, the part of the cerebral cortex involved in vision.

THE VISUAL CORTEX   The **visual cortex,** located in the occipital lobe at the back of the brain, is the part of the cerebral cortex involved in vision. Most visual information travels to the primary visual cortex, where it is processed, before moving to other visual areas for further analysis (Takemura & others, 2017; van Gerven, 2017).

An important aspect of visual information processing is the specialization of neurons. Like the cells in the retina, many cells in the primary visual cortex are highly specialized (Angelucci & others, 2017). **Feature detectors** are neurons in the brain's visual system that respond to particular features of a stimulus. These detectors pick up the edges, shapes, colors, and contours of stimuli. David Hubel and Torsten Wiesel (1963) won a Nobel Prize for their research on feature detectors. By recording the activity of a single neuron in a cat while it looked at patterns that varied in size, shape, color, and movement, the researchers found that the visual cortex has neurons that are individually sensitive to different types of lines and angles. One neuron might show a sudden burst of activity when stimulated by lines of a particular angle; another neuron might fire only when moving stimuli appear; yet another neuron might be stimulated when the object in the visual field has a combination of certain angles, sizes, and shapes.

feature detectors
Neurons in the brain's visual system that respond to particular features of a stimulus.

Hubel and Wiesel also noted that when deprived of certain types of visual stimulation early on, kittens lost the ability to perceive these patterns. This finding suggested that there might be a critical period in visual development and that the brain requires stimulation in its efforts to delegate its resources to different perceptual tasks. The brain "learns" to perceive through experience. This explains Michael May's unusual experience, described at the beginning of our examination of the visual system. Once deprived of stimulation, the brain will redistribute its resources to other tasks.

PARALLEL PROCESSING   Sensory information travels quickly through the brain because of **parallel processing,** the simultaneous distribution of information across different neural pathways (Buetti & others, 2016; Cutter, Drieghe, & Liversedge, 2017). A sensory system designed to process information about sensory qualities one at a time (such as processing first the shapes of images, then their colors, then their movements, and finally their locations) would be too slow to keep us current with a rapidly changing world. To function, we need to "see" all of these characteristics at once, which is parallel processing. There is some evidence suggesting that parallel processing also occurs for sensations of touch and hearing (van Polanen, Bergmann Tiest, & Kappers, 2014).

BINDING   Some neurons respond to color, others to shape, and still others to movement; but note that all of these neurons are involved in responding to a given stimulus—for instance, a toddler running toward you. How does the brain know that these physical features, communicated by different neurons, all belong to the same object of perception? The answer is, binding.

One of the most exciting topics in visual perception, **binding** is the bringing together and integration of what is processed by different neural pathways or cells (Rappaport & others, 2016; Zhang & others, 2014). When you see a toddler running toward you, you see the whole cute little person. You perceive a running child, not all the bits and pieces. Through binding, you can integrate information about the toddler's body shape, smile, and movement into a complete image in the cerebral cortex. How binding occurs is a puzzle that fascinates neuroscientists (Dupin, Hayward, & Wexler, 2017; Howe & Ferguson, 2015). Researchers have found that all the neurons throughout pathways that are activated by a visual object pulse together at the same frequency (Engel & Singer, 2001). Within the vast network of cells in the cerebral cortex, this set of neurons appears to *bind* together all the features of the objects into a unified perception (Velik, 2012).

Color Vision

Imagine how dull the world would be without color. Art museums are filled with paintings that are remarkable for their use of color, and flowers would lose much of their beauty if we could not see their rich hues. The process of color perception starts in the retina, the eyes' film. Interestingly, theories about how the retina processes color were developed long before methods existed to study the anatomical and neurophysiological

FIGURE 15   **Visual Pathways to and through the Brain**
Light from each side of the visual field falls on the opposite side of each eye's retina. Visual information then travels along the optic nerve to the optic chiasm, where most of the visual information crosses over to the other side of the brain. From there visual information goes to the occipital lobe at the rear of the brain. All these crossings mean that what we see in the left side of our visual field (here, the shorter, dark-haired woman) is registered in the right side of our brain, and what we see in the right visual field (the taller, blonde woman) is registered in the left side of our brain.
©RubberBall Productions/Getty Images

bases of color perception. Instead, psychologists made some extraordinarily accurate guesses about how color vision occurs in the retina by observing how people see. The two main theories proposed were the trichromatic theory and opponent-process theory. Both turned out to be correct.

The **trichromatic theory,** proposed by Thomas Young in 1802 and extended by Hermann von Helmholtz in 1852, states that color perception is produced by three types of cone receptors in the retina that are particularly sensitive to different but overlapping ranges of wavelengths. The theory is based on experiments showing that a person with normal vision can match any color in the spectrum by combining three other wavelengths. Young and Helmholtz reasoned that if the combination of any three wavelengths of different intensities is indistinguishable from any single pure wavelength, the visual system must base its perception of color on the relative responses of three receptor systems—cones sensitive to red, blue, and green.

The study of defective color vision, or *color blindness* (Figure 16), provides further support for the trichromatic theory. Complete color blindness is rare; most color-blind people, the vast majority of whom are men, can see some colors but not others. The nature of color blindness depends on which of the three kinds of cones is inoperative. The three cone systems are green, red, and blue. In the most common form of color blindness, the green cone system malfunctions in some way, rendering green indistinguishable from certain combinations of blue and red.

In 1878, the German physiologist Ewald Hering observed that some colors cannot exist together, whereas others can. For example, it is easy to imagine a greenish blue but nearly impossible to imagine a reddish green. Hering also noticed that trichromatic theory could not adequately explain afterimages. *Afterimages* are sensations that remain after a stimulus is removed (Figure 17 gives you a chance to experience an afterimage). Color afterimages are common and involve particular pairs of colors. If you look at red long enough, eventually a green afterimage will appear. If you look at yellow long enough, eventually a blue afterimage will appear. These associations between viewing a particular color (yellow) and then experiencing an afterimage of another color (blue) cannot be explained by trichromatic theory.

Hering's observations led him to propose that there were not three types of color receptor cones (as proposed by trichromatic theory) but four, organized into complementary pairs: red-green and blue-yellow. Hering's view, **opponent-process theory,** states that cells in the visual system respond to red-green and blue-yellow colors; a given cell might be excited by red and inhibited by green, whereas another cell might be excited by yellow and inhibited by blue. Opponent process theory does indeed explain afterimages. If you stare at red, for instance, your red-green system seems to "tire," and when you look away, it rebounds and gives you a green afterimage. Try it out and you will see that the opponent-process theory does an excellent job of explaining afterimages.

If the trichromatic theory of color perception is valid, and we do in fact have three kinds of cone receptors like those predicted by Young and Helmholtz, then how can the

trichromatic theory
Theory stating that color perception is produced by three types of cone receptors in the retina that are particularly sensitive to different, but overlapping, ranges of wavelengths.

opponent-process theory
Theory stating that cells in the visual system respond to complementary pairs of red-green and blue-yellow colors; a given cell might be excited by red and inhibited by green, whereas another cell might be excited by yellow and inhibited by blue.

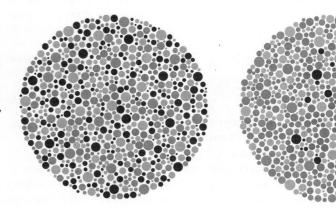

FIGURE 16 **Examples of Stimuli Used to Test for Color Blindness** People with normal vision see the number 8 in the left circle and the number 5 in the right circle. People with red-green color blindness may see just the 8, just the 5, or neither. A complete color-blindness assessment involves the use of 15 stimuli.
©Alexander Kaludov/123RF

FIGURE 17 **Negative Afterimage—Complementary Colors** If you gaze steadily at the dot in the colored panel on the left for a few moments, then shift your gaze to the gray box on the right, you will see the original hues' complementary colors. The blue appears as yellow, the red as green, the green as red, and the yellow as blue. This pairing of colors has to do with the fact that color receptors in the eye are apparently sensitive as pairs: When one color is turned off (when you stop staring at the panel), the other color in the receptor is briefly turned on. The afterimage effect is especially noticeable with bright colors.

opponent-process theory also be accurate? The answer is that the red, blue, and green cones in the retina are connected to retinal ganglion cells in such a way that the three-color code is immediately translated into the opponent-process code (Figure 18). For example, a green cone might inhibit and a red cone might excite a particular ganglion cell. Thus, both the trichromatic and opponent-process theories are correct—the eye and the brain use both methods to code colors.

Perceiving Shape, Depth, Motion, and Constancy

Perceiving visual stimuli means organizing and interpreting the fragments of information that the eye sends to the visual cortex. Information about the dimensions of what we are seeing is critical to this process and critical to our capacity to navigate the world (Kaiser & Haselhuhn, 2017). Among these dimensions are shape, depth, motion, and constancy.

SHAPE   Think about the visible world and its shapes—buildings against the sky, boats on the horizon, the letters on this page. We see

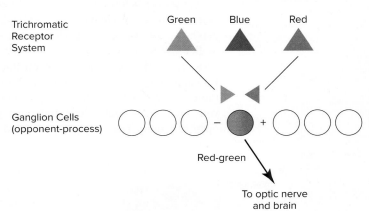

FIGURE 18 **Trichromatic and Opponent-Process Theories: Transmission of Color Information in the Retina** Cones responsive to green, blue, or red light form a trichromatic receptor system in the retina. As information is transmitted to the retina's ganglion cells, opponent-process cells are activated. As shown here, a retinal ganglion cell is inhibited by a green cone (−) and excited by a red cone (+), producing red-green color information.

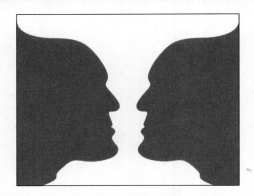

FIGURE 19 **Reversible Figure-Ground Pattern** Do you see the silhouette of a goblet or a pair of faces in profile? Use this figure to think again about bottom-up and top-down processes.
> What processes did you use the first moment you looked at the picture—top-down or bottom-up? > Now try to see the opposite image (if you saw a goblet, look for the faces; if you saw the faces, look for the goblet). Is this top-down or bottom-up processing? > Ask some friends what they see first in this image. What do they report? > What do you think accounts for the differences?

these shapes because they are marked off from the rest of what we see by *contour,* a location at which a sudden change of brightness occurs (Chambaud, Martin, & Barraza, 2014; Erlikhman & Kellman, 2016). Now think about the letters on this page. As you read, you see letters, which are shapes or figures, in a white field or background. The **figure-ground relationship** is the principle by which we organize the perceptual field into stimuli that stand out (*figure*) and those that are left over (*background,* or *ground*). Generally this principle works well for us, but some figure-ground relationships are highly ambiguous, and it may be difficult to tell what is figure and what is ground. Figure 19 shows a well-known ambiguous figure-ground relationship. As you look at this illustration, your perception is likely to shift from seeing two faces to seeing a single goblet.

figure-ground relationship
The principle by which we organize the perceptual field into stimuli that stand out (figure) and those that are left over (ground).

The figure-ground relationship is a gestalt principle (Figure 20 shows others). *Gestalt* is German for "configuration" or "form," and **gestalt psychology** is a school of thought that probes how people naturally organize their perceptions according to certain patterns. One of gestalt psychology's main principles is that the whole is different from the sum of its parts. For example, when you watch a movie, the motion you see in the film cannot be found in the film itself; if you examine the film, you see only separate frames. When you watch the film, the frames move past a light source at a rate of many per second, and you perceive a whole that is very different from the separate frames that are the film's parts. Similarly, thousands of tiny pixels make up an image (whole) on a computer screen.

gestalt psychology
A school of thought interested in how people naturally organize their perceptions according to certain patterns.

DEPTH PERCEPTION Images appear on our retinas in two-dimensional form, yet remarkably we see a three-dimensional world. **Depth perception** is the ability to perceive objects three-dimensionally. Look around you. You do not see your surroundings as flat. You see some objects farther away, some closer. Some objects overlap each other. The scene and objects that you are looking at have depth. How do you see depth? To perceive a world of depth, we use two kinds of information, or cues—binocular and monocular.

depth perception
The ability to perceive objects three-dimensionally.

Because we have two eyes, we get two views of the world, one from each eye. **Binocular cues** are depth cues that depend on the combination of the images in the left and right eyes and on the way the two eyes work together. The pictures are slightly different because the eyes are in slightly different positions. Try holding your hand about 10 inches from your face. Alternately close and open your left and right eyes so that only one eye is open at a time. The image of your hand will appear to jump back and forth, because the

binocular cues
Depth cues that depend on the combination of the images in the left and right eyes and on the way the two eyes work together.

(a)   (b)   (c)

FIGURE 20 **Gestalt Principles of Closure, Proximity, and Similarity** (*a*) *Closure:* When we see disconnected or incomplete figures, we fill in the spaces and see them as complete figures. (*b*) *Proximity:* When we see objects that are near each other, they tend to be seen as a unit. You are likely to perceive the grouping as four columns of four squares, not one set of 16 squares. (*c*) *Similarity:* When we see objects that are similar to each other, they tend to be seen as a unit. Here, you are likely to see vertical columns of circles and squares in the left box but horizontal rows of circles and squares in the right box.

image is in a slightly different place on the left and right retinas. The *disparity*, or difference, between the images in the two eyes is the binocular cue the brain uses to determine the depth, or distance, of an object. The combination of the two images in the brain, and the disparity between them in the eyes, give us information about the three-dimensionality of the world (Georgeson & others, 2016). Thus, the disparity between the images presented by our two eyes contributes to our capacity to see a world in 3D. Glasses that are used to see films in 3D capitalize on the fact that our brain will do a great job of "making sense" of disparate images.

3-D glasses use disparity as well—they present different images to each eye.

Convergence is another binocular cue to depth and distance. When we use our two eyes to look at something, they are focused on the same object. If the object is near us, our eyes converge, or move together, almost crossing. If the object is farther away, we can focus on it without pulling our eyes together. The muscle movements involved in convergence provide information about how far away or how deep something is.

In addition to using binocular cues to get an idea of objects' depth, we rely on a number of **monocular cues,** available from the image in one eye, either right or left. Monocular cues are powerful, and under normal circumstances they can provide a compelling impression of depth. Try closing one eye—your perception of the world still retains many of its three-dimensional qualities. Examples of monocular cues are

convergence
A binocular cue to depth and distance in which the muscle movements in an individual's two eyes provide information about how deep and/or far away something is.

monocular cues
Powerful depth cues available from the image in one eye, either the right or the left.

1. *Familiar size and relative size:* This cue to the depth and distance of objects is based on what we have learned from experience about the standard sizes of objects. We know how large oranges tend to be, so we can tell something about how far away an orange is likely to be by the size of its image on the retina. We also use relative sizes to give us information about objects in the world. We know that dogs are smaller than cars, and we can get a sense for how big a dog is if it is standing in front of a car.

2. *Height in the field of view:* All other things being equal, objects positioned higher in a picture are seen as farther away.

3. *Linear perspective:* Objects that are farther away take up less space on the retina. So, things that appear smaller are perceived to be farther away. As Figure 21 shows, as an object recedes into the distance, parallel lines in the scene appear to converge. If you were drawing a picture of a hill covered with trees, you would likely draw the trees at the front of the picture taller than those farther away, high on the hill. Objects in the horizon appear smaller than those that are closer.

4. *Overlap:* We perceive an object that partially conceals or overlaps another object as closer.

FIGURE 21   An Artist's Use of the Monocular Cue of Linear Perspective
Courtesy National Gallery of Art

FIGURE 22 **Texture Gradient** The gradients of texture create an impression of depth on a flat surface.

5. *Shading:* This cue involves changes in perception due to the position of the light and the position of the viewer. Consider an egg under a desk lamp. If you walk around the desk, you will see different shading patterns on the egg.

6. *Texture gradient:* Texture becomes denser and finer the farther away it is from the viewer (Figure 22).

Depth perception is a remarkably complex adaptation. Individuals with only one functioning eye cannot see depth in the way that those with two eyes can. Other disorders of the eye can also lead to a lack of depth perception. The late Oliver Sacks (2006) described the case of Susan Barry, who had been born with crossed eyes. The operation to correct her eyes left her cosmetically normal, but she was unable to perceive depth throughout her life. As an adult, she became determined to see depth. With a doctor's aid, she found special glasses and performed eye muscle exercises to improve her chances of perceiving in three dimensions. It was a difficult and long process, but one day she noticed things starting to "stick out" at her—as you might when watching a film in 3-D. Although Barry had successfully adapted to life in a flat visual world, she had come to realize that relying on monocular cues was not the same as experiencing the rich visual world of binocular vision. She described flowers as suddenly appearing "inflated." She noted how "ordinary things looked extraordinary" as she saw the leaves of a tree, an empty chair, and her office door projecting out from the background. For the first time, she had a sense of being inside the world she was viewing.

MOTION PERCEPTION Motion perception plays an important role in the lives of many species (Clarke, Longtin, & Maler, 2014; Niehorster & Li, 2017; Qadri, Asen, & Cook, 2014). Indeed, for some animals, motion perception is critical for survival. Both predators and their prey depend on being able to detect motion quickly (Aptekar & Frye, 2013). Frogs and some other simple vertebrates may not even see an object unless it is moving. For example, if a dead fly is dangled motionlessly in front of a frog, the frog cannot sense its winged meal. The bug-detecting cells in the frog's retinas are wired only to sense movement.

Whereas the retinas of frogs can detect movement, the retinas of humans and other primates cannot. In humans and other primates, the brain takes over the job of analyzing motion through highly specialized pathways.

How do humans perceive movement? First, we have neurons that are specialized to detect motion. Second, feedback from our body tells us whether we are moving or whether someone or some object is moving; for example, you move your eye muscles as you watch a ball coming toward you. Third, the environment we see is rich in cues that give us information about movement (Kaiser & Haselhuhn, 2017). For example, when we run, our surroundings appear to be moving.

apparent movement
The perception that a stationary object is moving.

Psychologists are interested in both real movement and **apparent movement,** which occurs when we perceive a stationary object as moving. You can experience apparent movement at IMAX movie theaters. In watching a film of a climb of Mount Everest, you may find yourself feeling breathless as your visual field floods with startling images. In theaters without seats, viewers of these films are often warned to hold the handrail because perceived movement is so realistic that they might fall.

perceptual constancy
The recognition that objects are constant and unchanging even though sensory input about them is changing.

PERCEPTUAL CONSTANCY Retinal images change constantly. Yet even though the stimuli that fall on our retinas change as we move closer to or farther away from objects, or as we look at objects from different orientations and in light or dark settings, our perception of them remains stable. **Perceptual constancy** is the recognition that objects are constant and unchanging even though sensory input about them is changing.

We experience three types of perceptual constancy—size constancy, shape constancy, and color constancy—as follows:

■ *Size constancy* is the recognition that an object remains the same size even though the retinal image of the object changes (Figure 23). Experiment is important to size perception. No matter how far away you are from your car, you know how large it is.

- *Shape constancy* is the recognition that an object retains the same shape even though its orientation to you changes. Look around. You probably see objects of various shapes—chairs and tables, for example. If you walk around the room, you will view these objects from different sides and angles. Even though the retinal image of the object changes as you walk, you still perceive the objects as having the same shape (Figure 24).

- *Color constancy* is the recognition that an object retains the same color even though different amounts of light fall on it. For example, if you are reaching for a green Granny Smith apple, it looks green to you whether you are having it for lunch, in the bright noon sun, or as an evening snack in the pale pink of sunset.

Perceptual constancy tells us about the crucial role of interpretation in perception: We interpret sensation. That is, we perceive objects as having particular characteristics regardless of the retinal image detected by our eyes. Images may flow across the retina, but experiences are made sensible through perception. The many cues we use to visually perceive the real world can lead to *optical illusions* when they are taken out of that real-world context, as you can experience for yourself in Figure 25. Optical illusions involve "tricking" the eye by using cues that work very well in real life vision to create perceptions that do not reflect reality.

As you look over these illusions, consider that culture can influence the extent to which people experience these illusions. In cultures where two-dimensional images, such as drawings on a piece of paper, are not typically used, geometrical illusions are less likely to lead to errors (Segall, Campbell, & Herskovits, 1966).

FIGURE 23 **Size Constancy** Even though our retinal images of the hot air balloons vary, we still realize the balloons are approximately the same size. This illustrates the principle of size constancy.
©Steve Allen/Getty Images

FIGURE 24 **Shape Constancy** The various projected images from an opening door are quite different, yet you perceive a rectangular door.

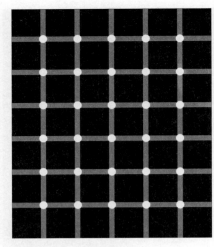

Blinking Effect Illusion
Stare at the white circles and notice the intermittent blinking effect. Your eyes make the static figure seem dynamic, attempting to fill in the white circle intersections with the black of the background.

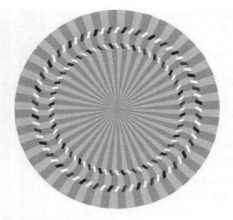

Rotational Illusion
The two rings appear to rotate in different directions when we approach or move away from this figure while fixing our eyes on the center.

Ponzo Illusion
The top line looks much longer than the bottom, but they are the same length.

FIGURE 25   Perceptual Illusions
These illusions show how adaptive perceptual cues can lead to errors when taken out of context. They are definitely fun, but keep in mind that these illusions are based on processes that are quite adaptive in real life. Remember, not everyone sees these illusions. In cultures where exposure to two-dimensional representations is not common, individuals are less fooled by geometric illusions.

Pattern Recognition
Although the diagram contains no actual triangles, your brain "sees" two overlapping triangles. The explanation is that the notched circles and angled lines merely suggest gaps in which complete objects should be. The brain fills in the missing information.

Induction Illusion
The yellow patches are identical, but they look different and seem to take on the characteristics of their surroundings when they appear against different-color backgrounds.

self-quiz

1. When we refer to the hue of a light wave, we are referring to what we perceive as
   A. intensity.
   B. radiation.
   C. brightness.
   D. color.

2. To read this question, you are looking at it. After the light passes into your eyes, the incoming light waves are recorded by receptor cells located in the
   A. retina.
   B. cornea.
   C. blind spot.
   D. optic chiasm.

3. If you are in a well-lighted room, your rods are being used _____ and cones are being used _____.
   A. infrequently; frequently
   B. infrequently; infrequently

C. frequently; infrequently
D. frequently; frequently

APPLY IT! 4. Sondra was driving in the country one afternoon. There was not much traffic on the long, straight road, though Sondra noticed a man walking along the roadside some distance away. Suddenly, as she approached the person, he drifted toward the middle of the road, and Sondra, with screeching brakes, was shocked to realize she had nearly hit a child. Fortunately, the child was not harmed. It had become clear to Sondra that what had seemed like a man some distance away was actually a child who was much closer than she realized. What explains this situation?
   A. Sondra's occipital lobe must be damaged.

   B. Because objects that are smaller on the retina are typically farther away, Sondra was fooled by relative size.
   C. Because objects in the mirror are closer than they appear, Sondra was not able to detect the just-noticeable difference.
   D. Because objects that are smaller on the retina are typically closer than they appear, Sondra was fooled by shape constancy.

3 The Auditory System

Just as light provides us with information about the environment, so does sound. Sounds tell us about the presence of a person behind us, the approach of an oncoming car, the force of the wind, and the mischief of a 2-year-old. Perhaps most important, sounds allow us to communicate through language and song.

The Nature of Sound and How We Experience It

©Daxiao Productions/Shutterstock

At a fireworks display, you may feel the loud boom of the explosion in your chest. At a concert, you might have sensed that the air around you was vibrating. Bass instruments are especially effective at creating mechanical pulsations, even causing the floor to vibrate. When the bass is played loudly, we can sense air molecules being pushed forward in waves from the speaker. How does sound generate these sensations?

Sound waves are vibrations in the air that are processed by the *auditory* (hearing) system. Remember that light waves are much like the waves in the ocean moving toward the beach. Sound waves are similar. Sound waves also vary in length. Wavelength determines the sound wave's *frequency,* that is, the number of cycles (full wavelengths) that pass through a point in a given time interval. *Pitch* is the perceptual experience of the frequency of a sound, whether it is high like a whistle or low like a bass horn. We perceive high-frequency sounds as having a high pitch, and low-frequency sounds as having a low pitch. A soprano voice sounds high-pitched; a bass voice sounds low-pitched. As with the wavelengths of light, human sensitivity is limited to a range of sound frequencies. It is common knowledge that dogs, for example, can hear higher frequencies than humans can.

Sound waves vary not only in frequency but also, like light waves, in amplitude. A sound wave's *amplitude,* measured in decibels (dB), is the amount of pressure the sound wave produces relative to a standard. The typical standard, 0 decibels, is the weakest sound the human ear can detect. *Loudness* is the perception of the sound wave's amplitude. In general, the higher the amplitude of the sound wave, or the higher the decibel level, the louder we perceive the sound to be. Thus, in terms of amplitude, the air is pressing more forcibly against you and your ears during loud sounds and more gently during quiet sounds.

So far we have been describing a single sound wave with just one frequency. A single sound wave is similar to the single wavelength of pure colored light, discussed in the context of color matching. Most sounds, including those of speech and music, are complex sounds, those in which numerous frequencies of sound blend together. *Timbre* is the tone saturation, or the perceptual quality, of a sound. Timbre is responsible for the perceptual difference between a trumpet and a trombone playing the same note and for the quality differences we hear in human voices. Figure 26 illustrates the physical differences in sound waves that produce the various qualities of sounds.

Morgan Freeman and James Earl Jones do a lot of voice-over work because their voices have marvelously rich timbres!

Structures and Functions of the Ear

What happens to sound waves once they reach your ear? How do various structures of the ear transform sound waves into signals that the brain will recognize as sound? Functionally the ear is analogous to the eye. The ear serves the purpose of transmitting a

Physical Dimension	Perceptual Dimension	Form of Sound Waves
Amplitude (intensity)	Loudness	Loud / Soft
Frequency	Pitch	Low / High
Complex sounds	Timbre	(Form of sound wave from a clarinet)

FIGURE 26 **Physical Difference in Sound Waves and the Qualities of Sound They Produce** Here we can see how the input of sound stimuli requires our ears and brain to attend to varying characteristics of the rich sensory information that is sound.

high-fidelity version of sounds in the world to the brain for analysis and interpretation. Just as an image needs to be in focus and sufficiently bright for the brain to interpret it, a sound needs to be transmitted in a way that preserves information about its location, its frequency (which helps us distinguish the voice of a child from that of an adult), and its timbre (which allows us to identify the voice of a friend on the telephone). The ear is divided into three parts: outer ear, middle ear, and inner ear (Figure 27).

OUTER EAR   The **outer ear** consists of the pinna and the external auditory canal. The funnel-shaped *pinna* (plural, *pinnae*) is the outer, visible part of the ear. (Elephants

outer ear
The outermost part of the ear, consisting of the pinna and the external auditory canal.

FIGURE 27 **The Outer, Middle, and Inner Ear** On entering the outer ear, sound waves travel through the auditory canal, where they generate vibrations in the eardrum. These vibrations are transferred via the hammer, anvil, and stirrup to the fluid-filled cochlea in the inner ear. There the mechanical vibrations are converted into an electrochemical signal that the brain will recognize as sound.

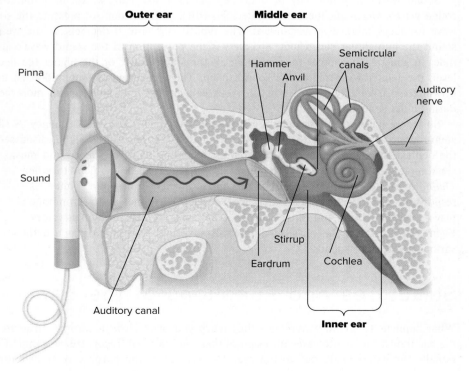

have very large pinnae.) The pinna collects sounds and channels them into the interior of the ear. The pinnae of many animals, such as cats, are movable and serve a more important role in sound localization than do the pinnae of humans. Cats turn their ears in the direction of a faint and interesting sound.

MIDDLE EAR   After passing the pinna, sound waves move through the auditory canal to the middle ear. The **middle ear** channels and amplifies the sound through the eardrum, hammer, anvil, and stirrup to the inner ear. The *eardrum,* or *tympanic membrane,* separates the outer ear from the middle ear and vibrates in response to sound. The eardrum is the first structure that sound touches in the middle ear. The *hammer, anvil,* and *stirrup* are an intricately connected chain of very small bones. When they vibrate, they transmit sound waves to the fluid-filled inner ear (Oxenham, 2018). The muscles that operate these tiny bones take the vibration of the eardrum and transmit it to the *oval window,* the opening of the inner ear.

middle ear
The part of the ear that channels and amplifies sound through the eardrum, hammer, anvil, and stirrup to the inner ear.

If you are a swimmer, you know that sound travels far more easily in air than in water. Sound waves entering the ear travel in air until they reach the inner ear. At the border between the middle and the inner ear—which, as we will see below, is a border between air and fluid—sound meets the same kind of resistance as do shouts directed at an underwater swimmer when the shouts hit the surface of the water. To compensate, the muscles of the middle ear can maneuver the hammer, anvil, and stirrup to amplify the sound waves. Importantly, these muscles, if necessary, can also work to decrease the intensity of sound waves, to protect the inner ear.

*The hammer, anvil, and stirrup are also called the **ossicles**. These are the tiniest bones in the human body.*

INNER EAR   The function of the **inner ear,** which includes the oval window, cochlea, and basilar membrane, is to convert sound waves into neural impulses and send them on to the brain (Sohmer, 2014). The stirrup is connected to the *oval window.* The oval window is a membrane-covered opening that leads from the middle ear to the inner ear. The oval window transmits sound waves to the cochlea. The *cochlea* is a tubular, fluid-filled structure that is coiled up like a snail (Figure 28). The *basilar membrane* lines the inner wall of the cochlea and runs its entire length. It is narrow and rigid at the base of the cochlea but widens and becomes more flexible at the top. The variation in width and flexibility allows different areas of the basilar membrane to vibrate more intensely when exposed to different sound frequencies (Oxenham, 2018; Verberne & others, 2017). For example, the high-pitched tinkle of a little bell stimulates the narrow region of the basilar membrane at the base of the cochlea, whereas the low-pitched tones of a tugboat whistle stimulate the wide end.

inner ear
The part of the ear that includes the oval window, cochlea, and basilar membrane and whose function is to convert sound waves into neural impulses and send them to the brain.

In humans and other mammals, hair cells line the basilar membrane (see Figure 28). These *hair cells* are the sensory receptors of the ear. They are called hair cells because of the tufts of fine bristles, or *cilia,* that sprout from the top of them. The movement of the hair cells against the *tectorial membrane,* a jellylike flap above them, generates resulting impulses that the brain interprets as sound (Sellon, Ghaffari, & Freeman, 2017). Hair cells are so delicate that exposure to loud noise can destroy them, leading to deafness or difficulties in hearing. Once lost, hair cells cannot regenerate. However, researchers are seeking to develop ways to regenerate these crucial aspects of hearing including through the use of stem cells (Franco & Malgrange, 2017).

Cochlear implants are devices that were specifically developed to replace damaged hair cells. A *cochlear implant*—a small electronic device that is surgically implanted in the ear and head—allows deaf or profoundly hard-of-hearing individuals to detect sound (Moberly & others, 2017; Reidy & others, 2017). Cochlear implants are not hearing aids. A hearing aid amplifies sound so a person can hear it. A cochlear implant does not amplify sound. Rather, it works by using electronic impulses to directly stimulate whatever working auditory nerves the recipient has in his or her cochlea. In the United States, approximately 58,000 adults and 38,000 children have had cochlear implants (National Institute on Deafness and Other Communication Disorders, 2014).

FIGURE 28 **The Cochlea** The cochlea is a spiral structure consisting of fluid-filled canals. When the stirrup vibrates against the oval window, the fluid in the canals vibrates. Vibrations along portions of the basilar membrane correspond to different sound frequencies. The vibrations exert pressure on the hair cells (between the basilar and tectorial membranes); the hair cells in turn push against the tectorial membrane, and this pressure bends the hairs. This triggers an action potential in the auditory nerve.

Theories of Hearing

One of the auditory system's mysteries is how the inner ear registers the frequency of sound. Two theories aim to explain this mystery: place theory and frequency theory.

Place theory states that each frequency produces vibrations at a particular place on the basilar membrane. Georg von Békésy (1960) studied the effects of vibration applied at the oval window on the basilar membrane of human cadavers. Through a microscope, he saw that this stimulation produced a traveling wave on the basilar membrane. A traveling wave is like the ripples that appear in a pond when you throw in a stone. However, because the cochlea is a long tube, the ripples can travel in only one direction, from the oval window at one end of the cochlea to the far tip of the cochlea. High-frequency vibrations create traveling waves that maximally displace, or move, the area of the basilar membrane next to the oval window; low-frequency vibrations maximally displace areas of the membrane closer to the tip of the cochlea.

Place theory adequately explains high-frequency sounds but not low-frequency sounds. A high-frequency sound, like the screech of a referee's whistle or the piercing high note of an opera diva, stimulates a precise area on the basilar membrane, just as the theory suggests. However, a low-frequency sound, like the tone of a tuba or the croak of a bullfrog, causes a large part of the basilar membrane to be displaced, making it hard to identify an exact location that is associated with hearing this kind of sound. Looking only at the movement of the basilar membrane, you would get the impression that humans are probably not very good at hearing low-frequency sounds, and yet we are. Therefore, some other factors must be at play in low-frequency hearing.

Békésy won a Nobel Prize in 1961 for his research on the basilar membrane.

place theory
Theory on how the inner ear registers the frequency of sound, stating that each frequency produces vibrations at a particular spot on the basilar membrane.

Frequency theory gets at these other influences by stating that the perception of a sound's frequency depends on how often the auditory nerve fires. Higher-frequency sounds cause the auditory nerve to fire more often than do lower-frequency sounds. One limitation of frequency theory, however, is that a single neuron has a maximum firing rate of about 1,000 times per second. Therefore, frequency theory does not apply to tones with frequencies that would require a neuron to fire more rapidly.

To deal with this limitation of frequency theory, researchers developed the **volley principle,** which states that a cluster of nerve cells can fire neural impulses in rapid succession, producing a volley of impulses. Individual neurons cannot fire faster than 1,000 times per second, but if the neurons team up and alternate their neural firing, they can attain a combined frequency above that rate. To get a sense for how the volley principle works, imagine a troop of soldiers who are all armed with guns that can fire only one round at a time and that take time to reload. If all the soldiers fire at the same time, the frequency of firing is limited and cannot go any faster than it takes to reload those guns. If, however, the soldiers are coordinated as a group and fire at different times, some of them can fire while others are reloading, leading to a greater frequency of firing. Frequency theory better explains the perception of sounds below 1,000 times per second, whereas a combination of frequency theory and place theory is needed to account for sounds above 1,000 times per second.

frequency theory
Theory on how the inner ear registers the frequency of sound, stating that the perception of a sound's frequency depends on how often the auditory nerve fires.

volley principle
Principle addressing limitations of the frequency theory of hearing, stating that a cluster of nerve cells can fire neural impulses in rapid succession, producing a volley of impulses.

 Phew! Two theories and a principle just to explain how we hear.

Auditory Processing in the Brain

As we considered in the discussion of the visual system, once our receptors pick up energy from the environment, that energy must be transmitted to the brain for processing and interpretation. We saw that in the retina, the responses of the rod and cone receptors feed into ganglion cells and leave the eye via the optic nerve. In the auditory system, information about sound moves from the hair cells of the inner ear to the **auditory nerve,** which carries neural impulses to the brain's auditory areas. Remember that it is the movement of the hair cells that transforms the physical stimulation of sound waves into the action potential of neural impulses (Oxenham, 2018).

auditory nerve
The nerve structure that receives information about sound from the hair cells of the inner ear and carries these neural impulses to the brain's auditory areas.

Auditory information moves up the auditory pathway via electrochemical transmission in a more complex manner than does visual information in the visual pathway. Many synapses occur in the ascending auditory pathway, with most fibers crossing over the midline between the hemispheres of the cerebral cortex, although some proceed directly to the hemisphere on the same side as the ear of reception (Lewald & Getzmann, 2011; Stange-Marten & others, 2017). This means that most of the auditory information from the left ear goes to the right side of the brain, but some also goes to the left side of the brain. The auditory nerve extends from the cochlea to the brain stem, with some fibers crossing over the midline. The cortical destination of most of these fibers is the temporal lobes of the brain, beneath the temples of the head. As in the case of visual information, researchers have found that features are extracted from auditory information and transmitted along parallel pathways in the brain (Recanzone & Sutter, 2008).

Localizing Sound

When we hear a fire engine's siren or a dog's bark, how do we know where the sound is coming from? The basilar membrane gives us information about the frequency, pitch, and complexity of a sound, but it does not tell us where a sound is located.

Earlier in the chapter we saw that because our two eyes see slightly different images, we can determine how near or far away an object is. Similarly, having two ears helps us to localize a sound because each receives somewhat different stimuli from the sound source. A sound coming from the left has to travel different distances to the two ears, so if a barking dog is to your

Do It!

Imagine hearing impossible sounds, nonexistent words, or three voices where only two exist. Welcome to the world of auditory illusions. In Figure 25 you tried out some visual illusions. Did you know that there are auditory illusions as well? Search the web for "auditory illusions" and try some out. They can be truly amazing and baffling! Keep in mind, just as you did when looking at the optical illusions, that these illusions emerge as a function of capacities that work very well in the "real world."

FIGURE 29

The Sound Shadow The sound shadow is caused by the listener's head, which forms a barrier that reduces the sound's intensity. Here the sound is to the person's left, so the sound shadow will reduce the intensity of the sound that reaches the right ear.

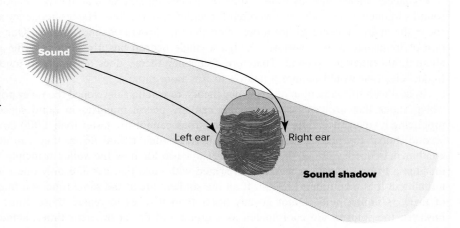

Sound

Left ear   Right ear

Sound shadow

left, your left ear receives the sound sooner than your right ear. Also, your left ear will receive a slightly more intense sound than your right ear in this case. The sound reaching one ear is more intense than the sound reaching the other ear for two reasons: (1) It has traveled less distance, and (2) the other ear is in what is called the *sound shadow* of the listener's head, which provides a barrier that reduces the sound's intensity (Figure 29). Blind individuals use the sound shadow to orient themselves. Compared to other animals, the human capacity to locate sounds is characterized by high levels of precision (Stange-Marten & others, 2017).

Thus, differences in both the *timing* of the sound and the *intensity* of the sound help you to localize a sound (Stange-Marten & others, 2017). You often have difficulty localizing a sound that is coming from a source directly in front of you because it reaches both ears simultaneously. The same is true for sounds directly above your head or directly behind you, because the disparities that provide information about location are not present. So, we are able to localize sounds because we have two ears on the opposite sides of our head. This anatomical setup allows us to use time and intensity to know where a sound is coming from.

self-quiz

1. Your mother's and sister's voices have the same pitch and loudness, but you can tell them apart on the telephone. This is due to the perceptual quality, or _____, of their voices.
   A. timbre
   B. wavelength
   C. frequency
   D. amplitude

2. The major function of the hammer, anvil, and stirrup of the middle ear is
   A. to soften the tone of incoming stimuli for appropriate processing.
   B. to stir cochlear fluid so that bone conduction hearing can occur.
   C. to amplify vibrations and pass them on to the inner ear.

   D. to clean the external auditory canal of any potential wax buildup.

3. The bones of the middle ear are set into motion by vibrations of the
   A. cochlea.
   B. eardrum.
   C. saccule.
   D. basilar membrane.

APPLY IT! 4. Conservative radio personality Rush Limbaugh experienced sudden hearing loss in 2001, after which he received a cochlear implant. He has described his ability to listen to music as dependent on what he heard before becoming deaf. If he had heard a song prior to becoming deaf, he could hear it, but if it was a new song, he could not

make sense of it. Which of the following explains Limbaugh's experience?
   A. He is no longer able to listen to music from a top-down perspective.
   B. He is able to engage in top-down listening, but not bottom-up listening.
   C. He is likely to have experienced damage to the temporal lobes.
   D. He is not able to experience any auditory sensation.

4 Other Senses

Beyond vision and hearing, the body has other sensory systems. These include the skin senses and the chemical senses (smell and taste), as well as the kinesthetic and vestibular senses (systems that allow us to stay upright and to coordinate our movements).

The Skin Senses

You know when a friend has a fever by putting your hand to her head; you know how to find your way to the light switch in a darkened room by groping along the wall; and you know whether a pair of shoes is too tight by the way the shoes touch different parts of your feet when you walk. Many of us think of our skin as a canvas rather than a sense. We color it with cosmetics, dyes, and tattoos. In fact, the skin is our largest sensory system, draped over the body with receptors for touch, temperature, and pain. These three kinds of receptors form the *cutaneous senses*.

TOUCH   Touch is one of the senses that we most often take for granted, yet our ability to respond to touch is astounding. What do we detect when we feel "touch"? What kind of energy does our sense of touch pick up from our external environment? In vision we detect light energy. In hearing we detect the vibrations of air or sound waves pressing against our eardrums. In touch we detect mechanical energy, or pressure against the skin. The lifting of a single hair causes pressure on the skin around the hair shaft. This tiny bit of mechanical pressure at the base of the hair is sufficient for us to feel the touch of a pencil point. More commonly we detect the mechanical energy of the pressure of a car seat against our buttocks or of a pencil in our hand. Is this energy so different from the kind of energy we detect in vision or hearing? Sometimes the only difference is one of intensity—the sound of a rock band playing softly is an auditory stimulus, but at the high volumes that make a concert hall reverberate, this auditory stimulus is also felt as mechanical energy pressing against our skin.

Your ability to find a nickel in your pocket without looking is a truly amazing feat of touch. Not even the most sophisticated robot can do it.

How does information about touch travel from the skin through the nervous system? Sensory fibers arising from receptors in the skin enter the spinal cord. From there the information travels to the brain stem, where most fibers from each side of the body cross over to the opposite side of the brain. Next the information about touch moves on to the thalamus, which serves as a relay station. The thalamus then projects the map of the body's surface onto the somatosensory areas of the parietal lobes in the cerebral cortex (Hirata & Castro-Alamancos, 2010; Sereno, 2017).

Just as the visual system is more sensitive to images on the fovea than to images in the peripheral retina, our sensitivity to touch is not equally good across all areas of the skin. Human toolmakers need excellent touch discrimination in their hands, but they require much less touch discrimination in other parts of the body, such as the torso and legs. The brain devotes more space to analyzing touch signals coming from the hands than from the legs.

TEMPERATURE   We not only can feel the warmth of a comforting hand on our hand, we also can feel the warmth or coolness of a room. We must be able to detect temperature in order to maintain our body temperature. **Thermoreceptors,** sensory nerve endings under the skin, respond to temperature changes at or near the skin and provide input to keep the body's temperature at 98.6 degrees Fahrenheit. There are two types of thermoreceptors: warm and cold. Warm thermoreceptors respond to the warming of the skin, and cold thermoreceptors respond to the cooling of the skin. When warm and cold receptors that are close to each other in the skin are stimulated simultaneously, we experience the sensation of hotness. Figure 30 illustrates this "hot" experience.

The sense of touch is one of the ways we connect with each other. Patting a friend on the shoulder during a difficult time or giving someone a much needed hug are just two of the ways interpersonal touch communicates our feelings. Individuals with mirror-touch synaesthesia experience the sense of touch in an extreme and sometimes troubling way. To read about this fascinating condition, see the Intersection.

PAIN   **Pain** is the sensation that warns us of damage to the body. When contact with the skin takes the form of a sharp pinch, our sensation of mechanical pressure changes from touch to pain. When a pot handle is so hot that it burns our hand, our sensation

thermoreceptors
Sensory nerve endings under the skin that respond to changes in temperature at or near the skin and provide input to keep the body's temperature at 98.6 degrees Fahrenheit.

pain
The sensation that warns an individual of damage to the body.

Warm water   Cold water

FIGURE 30
A "Hot" Experience
When two pipes, one containing cold water and the other warm water, are braided together, a person touching the pipes feels a sensation of "hot." The perceived heat coming from the pipes is so intense that the individual cannot touch them for longer than a couple of seconds.

Sensation and Social Psychology: Why Do Some People Literally Feel What Others Feel?

The human capacity for empathy, the ability to feel what others are feeling, lies at the heart of compassion and caring. For some people with a rare condition called mirror-touch synaesthesia (MTS), the feeling of empathy takes on a very different character. MTS means that a person experiences tactile sensations when the person sees someone else being touched. One of the distinctive features of MTS is the specificity of the experience: Seeing someone else getting a flu shot, a woman with MTS might feel (literally) the needle prick on her own arm. For individuals with MTS, the phrase "I feel your pain" is taken to a completely different level (Martin, Cleghorn, & Ward, 2017).

What explains the phenomenon of MTS? It seems to involve processes at two separate levels—the brain and sensory systems but also the way people think, socially. One theory of MTS relies on the mirror-neuron system for touch (Ward & Banissy, 2015). Recall that when we see another person being touched, our own mirror neurons activate, simulating the other person's experience. A brain-imaging study showed that, among those with MTS, the mirror system is more active in response to seeing another person experience touch (Holle, Banissy, & Ward, 2013). One of the most fascinating aspects of MTS is its social nature. For instance, in the brain-imaging study noted above, individuals with and without MTS were compared as they watched someone touch three different targets: another person's face, a

© PeopleImages/Getty Images

dummy, and an object. The groups only differed when the target of touch was another person's face (Holle, Banissy, & Ward, 2013). This result suggests that MTS is not simply about perceiving touch but is, in some ways, about confusing the self and others. Individuals with MTS seem to experience what another person is experiencing, suggesting that people with MTS cannot disregard what another person is feeling or doing (Cioffi, Banissy, & Moore, 2016).

The role of mirror neurons in MTS is still controversial but research on this unusual experience may help us understand sensation and perception more generally (Linkovski, Katzin, & Salti, 2017).

Imagine having such direct access to other people's feelings. We might think that such a situation would solve a host of problems, removing misunderstandings almost completely. What would it be like to say "I know how you feel" and really mean it? At the same time, individuals with MTS may find the unrelenting bombardment of other people's feelings to be exhausting and difficult. For some, MTS means automatically feeling what another person is experiencing and never knowing if your feelings are really your own (Martin, Cleghorne, & Ward, 2017).

\\ **What would it be like to feel another person's feelings, literally?**

Do It!

If you'd like to learn more about mirror-touch synaesthesia, check out the Entanglement episode of the *Invisibilia* Podcast. www.npr.org/podcasts/510307/Invisibilia

of temperature becomes one of pain. Intense stimulation of any one of the senses can produce pain—too much light, very loud sounds, or too many habanero peppers, for example. Our ability to sense pain is vital for our survival as a species. It functions as a quick-acting messenger that tells the brain's motor systems that they must act fast to minimize or eliminate damage.

Pain receptors are dispersed widely throughout the body—in the skin, in the sheath tissue surrounding muscles, in internal organs, and in the membranes around bone. Although all pain receptors are anatomically similar, they differ in the type of physical stimuli to which they most readily react, with some responding to pressure, others to heat, and others to both. Many pain receptors are chemically sensitive and respond to a range of pain-producing substances.

Pain receptors have a much higher threshold for firing than receptors for temperature and touch (Cassels & Barde, 2017). Pain receptors react mainly to physical stimuli that distort them or to chemical stimuli that irritate them into action. Inflamed joints or sore, torn muscles produce *prostaglandins,* fatty acids that stimulate the receptors and cause the experience of pain. Drugs such as aspirin likely reduce the feeling of pain by reducing prostaglandin production.

Two different neural pathways transmit pain messages to the brain: a fast pathway and a slow pathway (Boddice, 2017). In the *fast pathway,* fibers connect directly with the thalamus and then to the motor and sensory areas of the cerebral cortex. This pathway transmits information about sharp, localized pain, as when you cut your skin. The fast pathway may serve as a warning system, providing immediate information about an injury—it takes less than a second for the information in this pathway to reach the cerebral cortex. In the *slow pathway,* pain information travels through the limbic system, a detour that delays the arrival of information at the cerebral cortex by seconds. The unpleasant, nagging pain that characterizes the slow pathway may function to remind the brain that an injury has occurred and that we need to restrict normal activity and monitor the pain (Ranebo & others, 2017).

Many neuroscientists believe that the brain actually generates the experience of pain. There is evidence that turning pain signals on and off is a chemical process that probably involves *endorphins.* Recall that endorphins are neurotransmitters that function as natural opiates in producing pleasure and pain (Coutaux, 2017). Endorphins are believed to be released mainly in the synapses of the slow pathway.

Perception of pain is complex and often varies from one person to the next (Fillingim, 2017). Some people rarely feel pain; others seem to be in great pain if they experience a minor bump or bruise. When people experience the same potentially pain-causing injury, some may find it to be relatively mild while others are made quite miserable. A person's pain thresholds can also change with age (Lautenbacher & others, 2017). To some degree, these individual variations may be physiological. A person who experiences considerable pain even with a minor injury may have a neurotransmitter system that is deficient in endorphin production. However, perception of pain goes beyond physiology. Although it is true that all sensations are affected by factors such as motivation, expectation, and other related decision factors, the perception of pain is especially susceptible to these factors. For example, when people experience high levels of work stress, their pain threshold tends to be lower (Hven, Frost, & Bonde, 2017).

Studies have shown that women experience more clinical pain and suffer more pain-related distress than men (Bartley & Fillingim, 2016; Carpenter & Patil, 2017; Mansfield & others, 2016). However, this difference is not consistently found and men and women are very similar in pain perception, intensity, and types of pain experienced (Racine & others, 2012a, 2012b). An important factor to consider in the realm of gender differences in pain is the role of cultural expectations (Berke & others, 2017). Men may be more likely than women to respond physiologically to pain while women may be more likely to report openly about their experiences of pain (Etherton, Lawson, & Graham, 2014).

Cultural and ethnic contexts influence the degree to which an individual experiences or reports pain (Kim & others, 2017). Compared to Americans and Europeans, Japanese consider expressing physical pain to be inappropriate and report lower levels of pain (Feng & others, 2017; Onishi & others, 2017). Of course, pain can mean different things to different people. For example, one pain researcher described a ritual performed in India in which a chosen person travels from town to town delivering blessings to the children and the crops while suspended from metal hooks embedded in his back (Melzack, 1973). The individual apparently reports no sensation of pain and appears to be in ecstasy.

The Chemical Senses

The information processed through our senses comes in many diverse forms: electromagnetic energy in vision, sound waves in hearing, and mechanical pressure and temperature in the skin senses. The two senses we now consider, smell and taste, are responsible for processing chemicals in our environment. Through smell, we detect airborne chemicals, and through taste we detect chemicals that have been dissolved in saliva. Smell and taste are frequently stimulated simultaneously. We notice the strong links between the two senses when a nasty cold with lots of nasal congestion takes the pleasure out of eating. Our favorite foods become "tasteless" without their characteristic smells. Despite this link, taste and smell are two distinct systems.

TASTE Think of your favorite food. Why do you like it? Imagine that food without its flavor. The thought of giving up a favorite taste, such as chocolate, can be depressing. Indeed, eating food we love is a major source of pleasure.

How does taste happen? To get at this question, try this. Take a drink of milk and allow it to coat your tongue. Then go to a mirror, stick out your tongue, and look carefully at its surface. You should be able to see rounded bumps above the surface. Those bumps, called **papillae,** contain *taste buds,* the receptors for taste. Your tongue houses about 10,000 taste buds, which are replaced about every two weeks. As people age, however, this replacement process is not quite as efficient, and an older individual may have just 5,000 working taste buds at any given moment. As with all of the other sensory systems we have studied, the information picked up by these taste receptors is transmitted to the brain for analysis and, when necessary, for a response (spitting something out, for example).

The taste fibers leading from a taste bud to the brain often respond strongly to a range of chemicals spanning multiple taste elements, such as salty and sour. The brain processes these somewhat ambiguous incoming signals and integrates them into a perception of taste (Iannilli & others, 2012). So although people often categorize taste sensations along the four dimensions of sweet, bitter, salty, and sour, our tasting ability goes far beyond these. Researchers and chefs have been exploring a taste called *umami* (Maruyama & others, 2006; Satoh-Kuriwada & others, 2014). *Umami* is the Japanese word for "delicious" or "yummy." The taste of umami, one that Asian cooks have long recognized, is the flavor of L-glutamate. What is that taste? Umami is a savory flavor that is present in many seafoods as well as soy sauce, parmesan and mozzarella cheese, anchovies, mushrooms, and hearty meat broths.

Culture certainly influences the experience of taste. Any American who has watched the Japanese version of the TV series *Iron Chef* quickly notices that some people enjoy the flavor of sea urchin, while others just do not get the appeal. In some cultures, food that is so spicy as to be practically inedible for the outsider may be viewed as quite delicious or umami. The culture in which we live can influence the foods we are exposed to as well as our sense of what tastes good. In some cultures, very spicy food is introduced slowly into children's diets so that they can learn what is delicious at an early age.

SMELL Why do we have a sense of smell? One way to appreciate the importance of smell is to think about animals with a more sophisticated sense of smell than our own. A dog, for example, can use smell to find its way back from a long stroll, to distinguish friend from foe, and even (with practice) to detect illegal drugs concealed in a suitcase. In fact, dogs can detect odors in concentrations 100 times lower than those detectable by humans. Given the nasal feats of the average dog, we might be tempted to believe that the sense of smell has outlived its usefulness in humans.

Some people have more papillae than others. A "supertaster" is someone who has as many as 40 papillae in a 6 mm area of the tongue (about the size of a pencil eraser). Supertasters can taste substances that others cannot and thus are valuable to the food and wine industries.

Studying complex tastes like umami is surprisingly important to understanding the nature of human consciousness. These tastes are subjective—the experience goes beyond the simple sensations to a complex experience that is more than the sum of its parts.

papillae
Rounded bumps above the tongue's surface that contain the taste buds, the receptors for taste.

©norikko/Shutterstock

Why Salt Is the Salt of the Earth

Many people, including those with high blood pressure or diabetes and older adults, should keep their salt intake relatively low. That can be hard to do because—as the ingredients list on the labels of most foods reveals—salt is everywhere. A recent study of supertasters might give us a clue as to why salt seems so important to good flavor.

Supertasters have a highly sensitive palate and can detect flavors other folks cannot. Given their heightened taste sensitivity, we might expect supertasters to use less salt than others. One study found just the opposite. Supertasters in fact were more likely to add salt to their food than others (Hayes & Keast, 2011). Why might this be the case? One of the researchers, John E. Hayes, suggests that because supertasters are so sensitive to a wide range of flavors (including the bitterness of some foods), they need more salt to counteract those flavors.

The explanation is that salt does not just make foods salty—it changes how humans experience a whole host of flavors. Have you ever noticed that recipes for even sweet foods like cakes and cookies include a pinch of salt? Chefs know that salt does more than add a salty flavor, and sometimes it seems that everything tastes better with a sprinkle of salt.

©Tom Grill/Getty Images

What do humans use smell for? For one thing, humans need the sense of smell to decide what to eat. We can distinguish rotten food from fresh food and remember (all too well) which foods have made us ill in the past. The smell of a food that has previously made us sick is often by itself enough to make us feel nauseated. For another thing, although tracking is a function of smell that we often associate only with animals, humans are competent odor trackers. We can follow the odor of gas to a leak, the smell of smoke to a fire, and the aroma of a hot apple pie to a windowsill.

What physical equipment do we use to process odor information? Just as the eyes scan the visual field for objects of interest, the nose is an active instrument. We actively sniff when we are trying to track down the source of a fire or an unfamiliar chemical odor. The **olfactory epithelium** lining the roof of the nasal cavity contains a sheet of receptor cells for smell (Figure 31), so sniffing maximizes the chances of detecting an odor. The receptor cells are covered with millions of minute, hairlike antennae that project through the mucus in the top of the nasal cavity and make contact with air on its way to the throat and lungs (Lapid & others, 2011). Interestingly, unlike the neurons of most sensory systems, the neurons in the olfactory epithelium tend to replace themselves after injury (Vukovic & others, 2009).

olfactory epithelium
The lining of the roof of the nasal cavity, containing a sheet of receptor cells for smell.

What is the neural pathway for information about smell? The answer to this question reveals an important difference between the sense of smell and other senses. All other sensory pathways pass through the thalamus but the pathway for smell does not. In smell, the neural pathway goes straight to the olfactory areas in the temporal lobes. Then it projects to various brain regions, especially the limbic system, which is involved in emotion and memory (Huart, Collet, & Rombaux, 2009; Stankewitz & May, 2011). Unlike the other senses, smells take a superhighway to emotion and memory, a phenomenon we will consider in more detail when those topics are discussed.

Olfactory bulb

Olfactory nerve

Bone

Olfactory chemicals

Nasal passage

Receptor cells located in the olfactory epithelium of the upper nasal passage

Olfactory bulb

Nasal passage

FIGURE 31

The Olfactory Sense Airborne molecules of an odor reach tiny receptor cells in the roof of the nasal cavity. The receptor cells form a mucus-covered membrane called the olfactory epithelium. Then the olfactory nerve carries information about the odor to the brain for further processing.
©Tara McDermott

Smell might have a role to play in the chemistry of interpersonal attraction. From an evolutionary perspective, the goal of human mating is to find someone with whom to produce the healthiest offspring (Buss, 2012). Mates with differing sets of genes (known as the *major histocompatibility complex,* or *MHC*) produce healthier offspring with the broadest immune systems (Mueller, 2010). How do we find these people, short of taking a blood test? Martie Haselton (2006) has conducted studies on interpersonal attraction using the "smelly T-shirt" paradigm. In this research, men are asked to wear a T-shirt to bed every day for a week without washing it. After they have been thoroughly imbued with a male's personal scent, the T-shirts are presented to women to smell and rate for attractiveness. Women reliably rate men whose MHCs are different from their own as more attractive, on the basis of the aroma of the T-shirts. Thus, although the eyes may be the window to the soul, the nose might be the gateway to love. Interestingly, researchers have not found these effects for women who are taking contraceptives that alter their hormonal cycles.

The kinesthetic and vestibular senses play an essential role in a baseball pitcher's windup and delivery.
©Digital Vision/Getty Images

The Kinesthetic and Vestibular Senses

You know the difference between walking and running and between lying down and sitting up. To perform even the simplest act of motor coordination, such as reaching out to take a book off a shelf or getting up out of a chair, the brain must constantly receive and coordinate information from every part of the body.

kinesthetic senses
Senses that provide information about movement, posture, and orientation.

vestibular sense
Sense that provides information about balance and movement.

Your body has two kinds of senses that give you information about your movement and orientation in space, as well as help you to maintain balance. The **kinesthetic senses** provide information about movement, posture, and orientation. The **vestibular sense** provides information about balance and movement.

No specific organ contains the kinesthetic senses. Instead, they are embedded in muscle fibers and joints. As we stretch and move, these receptors signal the state of the muscle. *Kinesthesia,* the name for the kinesthetic senses, is a sense that you often do not even notice until it is gone. Try walking when your leg is "asleep" or smiling (never mind talking) when you have just come from a dentist's office and are still under the effects of Novocain.

We can appreciate the sophistication of kinesthesis when we think about it in terms of memory. Even a mediocre typist can bang out 20 words per minute—but how many of us could write down the order of the letters on a keyboard without looking? Typing is a skill that relies on very coordinated sensitivity to the orientation, position, and movements of our fingers. We say that our fingers "remember" the positions of the keys. Likewise, the complicated movements a pitcher uses to throw a baseball cannot be written down or communicated easily using language. They involve nearly every muscle and joint in the body. Most information about the kinesthetic senses is transmitted from the joints and muscles along the same pathways to the brain as information about touch.

You may not think about the kinesthetic senses as senses at all. But these senses are important to our ability to navigate in the world and know where our body is and what it is doing at any given moment.

The vestibular sense tells us whether our head (and hence usually our body) is tilted, moving, slowing down, or speeding up. It works in concert with the kinesthetic senses to coordinate our *proprioceptive feedback,* which is information about the position of our limbs and body parts in relation to other body parts. Consider the combination of sensory abilities involved in the motion of a hockey player skating down the ice, cradling the puck, and pushing it forward with the hockey stick. The hockey player is responding simultaneously to a multitude of sensations, including those produced by the slickness of the ice, the position of the puck, the speed and momentum of the forward progression, and the requirements of the play to turn and to track the other players on the ice.

semicircular canals
Three fluid-filled circular tubes in the inner ear containing the sensory receptors that detect head motion caused when an individual tilts or moves the head and/or the body.

The **semicircular canals** of the inner ear contain the sensory receptors that detect head motion caused when we tilt or move our heads and/or bodies (Figure 32). These canals consist of three fluid-filled, circular tubes that lie in the three planes of the body—right-left, front-back, and up-down. We can picture these as three intersecting hula hoops. As you move your head, the fluid of the semicircular canals flows in different directions and at different speeds (depending on the force of the head movement). Our perception of head movement and position is determined by the movements of these receptor cells (Yoder & Taube, 2014). This ingenious system of using the motion of fluid in tubes to sense head position is similar to the auditory system of the inner ear. However, the fluid movement in the cochlea results from the pressure sound exerts on the oval window, whereas the movements in the semicircular canals reflect physical movements of the head and body. Vestibular sacs in the semicircular canals contain hair cells embedded in a gelatin-like mass. Just as the hair cells in the cochlea trigger hearing impulses in the brain, the hair cells in the semicircular canals transmit information about balance and movement.

The brain pathways for the vestibular sense show the interesting nature of this sense and the importance of structures used for hearing for our sense of balance. Impulses from the vestibular sense begin in the auditory nerve, which contains both the cochlear nerve (with information about sound) and the vestibular nerve (which has information about balance and movement). Most of the axons of the vestibular nerve connect with the medulla, although some go directly

FIGURE 32
The Semicircular Canals and the Vestibular Sense
The semicircular canals provide feedback to the gymnast's brain as her head and body tilt in different directions. Any angle of head rotation is registered by hair cells in one or more semicircular canals in both ears. (*inset*) The semicircular canals.
(gymnast) ©Dominique Douieb/Getty Images; (inner ear) ©MedicalRF.com/Getty Images

Do It!

If you have a few minutes and a strong stomach, give your vestibular system a workout. Spin around quickly and repeatedly for a minute. You can do it in a swivel chair or standing in the center of a room (be careful of sharp edges). When you stop, you will feel dizzy. Here's what's happening. The fluid in the semicircular canals moves rather slowly and changes direction very slowly. When we spin for a while, the fluid eventually catches up with our rate of motion and starts moving in the same direction. When we stop moving, however, the slow-moving fluid keeps on moving. It tells the hair cells in the vestibular canals (which in turn tell the brain) "We are still spinning"—and we feel as if we are.

to the cerebellum. There also appear to be vestibular projections to the temporal cortex, but research has not fully charted their specific pathways.

Information from the sense of vision supplements the combination of kinesthetic and vestibular senses. This principle causes a motorist to slam on the brakes in his tiny sports car when the big truck next to him starts to move forward. When everything in our visual field appears to be moving, it is generally because we are moving.

Throughout this chapter we have viewed sensation and perception as our connections to the world. Sensation builds a bridge between the objects in our environment and the creative interpreter that is our brain. Through perception, our sensations become meaningful and our mental life engages with the environment. Sensation and perception allow us to survive in that environment but also to experience the world in all its vibrancy. Sue Barry, the woman who achieved the ability to perceive depth only after a long, arduous effort, described her encounter with nature on a snowy day. "I felt myself within the snow fall, among the snowflakes . . . . I was overcome with a sense of joy. A snow fall can be quite beautiful—especially when you see it for the first time" (quoted in Sacks, 2006, p. 73). Also, recall Michael May, who was able to see after 25 years of blindness. One night, with his seeing-eye dog Josh at his side, he decided to go look at the sky. Lying on the grass in a field, he opened his eyes. He thought he was "seeing stars"—in the metaphorical sense. He thought that the thousands of white lights in the sky could not really be real, but they were. As he remarked in his vision diary: "How sweet it is" (May, 2003; Stein, 2003).

self-quiz

1. Taste buds are bunched together in
   A. taste cells.
   B. the papillae.
   C. salivary glands.
   D. the olfactory epithelium.

2. _____ is/are involved in the sense of smell.
   A. The papillae
   B. The olfactory epithelium
   C. The thalamus
   D. The pinnae

3. The inner-ear structures that contain the sensory receptors that detect

head motion, as when we move our head and/or body, are the
   A. stirrups.
   B. semicircular canals.
   C. hammer.
   D. cochlea.

APPLY IT! 4. Sean loves anchovy, mushroom, and double-cheese pizza on a whole-wheat crust from his hometown pizzeria. He brings a pie back from home to give his roommate Danny a chance to taste it. Sean is stunned by Danny's reaction to the pizza: "Dude! Epic fail!"

(in other words, he hates it). What does this example demonstrate?
   A. Danny may not have the taste receptors for umami.
   B. Although Sean and Danny have similar tongue anatomy, perception is still a subjective process. Sean is apparently a big umami fan, but Danny is not.
   C. Danny may have a disorder of the olfactory epithelium.
   D. Danny is engaged in top-down processing.

SUMMARY

① How We Sense and Perceive the World

Sensation is the process of receiving stimulus energies from the environment. Perception is the process of organizing and interpreting sensory information to give it meaning. Perceiving the world involves both bottom-up and top-down processing. All sensation begins with sensory receptors, specialized cells that detect and transmit information about a stimulus to sensory neurons and the brain. Sensory receptors are selective and have different neural pathways.

Psychologists have explored the limits of our abilities to detect stimuli. Absolute threshold refers to the minimum amount of energy that people can detect. The difference threshold, or just noticeable difference,

is the smallest difference in stimulation required to discriminate one stimulus from another 50 percent of the time.

Perception is influenced by attention, beliefs, and expectations. Sensory adaptation is a change in the responsiveness of the sensory system based on the average level of surrounding stimulation, essentially the ways that our senses start to ignore a particular stimulus once it is around long enough.

② The Visual System

Light is the stimulus that is sensed by the visual system. Light can be described in terms of wavelengths. Three characteristics of light waves determine our experience: wavelength (hue), amplitude (brightness), and purity (saturation).

In sensation, light passes through the cornea and lens to the retina, the light-sensitive surface in the back of the eye that houses light receptors called rods (which function in low illumination) and cones (which react to color). The fovea of the retina contains only cones and sharpens detail in an image. The optic nerve transmits neural impulses to the brain. There it diverges at the optic chiasm, so that what we see in the left visual field is registered in the right side of the brain and vice versa. In the occipital lobes of the cerebral cortex, the information is integrated.

The trichromatic theory of color perception holds that three types of color receptors in the retina allow us to perceive three colors (green, red, and blue). The opponent-process theory states that cells in the visual system respond to red-green and blue-yellow colors. Both theories are probably correct—the eye and the brain use both methods to code colors.

Shape perception is the ability to distinguish objects from their background. Depth perception is the ability to perceive objects three-dimensionally and depends on binocular (two-eyes) cues and monocular (one-eye) cues. Motion perception by humans depends on specialized neurons, feedback from the body, and environmental cues. Perceptual constancy is the recognition that objects are stable despite changes in the way we see them.

The Auditory System

Sounds, or sound waves, are vibrations in the air that are processed by the auditory system. These waves vary in important ways that influence what we hear. Pitch (how high or low in tone a sound is) is the perceptual interpretation of wavelength frequency. Amplitude of wavelengths, measured in decibels, is perceived as loudness. Complex sounds involve a blending of frequencies. Timbre is the tone saturation, or perceptual quality, of a sound.

The outer ear consists of the pinna and external auditory canal and acts to funnel sound to the middle ear. In the middle ear, the eardrum, hammer, anvil, and stirrup vibrate in response to sound and transfer the vibrations to the inner ear. Important parts of the fluid-filled inner ear are the oval window, cochlea, and basilar membrane. The movement of hair cells between the basilar membrane and the tectorial membrane generates nerve impulses.

Place theory states that each frequency produces vibrations at a particular spot on the basilar membrane. Place theory adequately explains high-frequency sounds but not low-frequency sounds. Frequency theory holds that the perception of a sound's frequency depends on how often the auditory nerve fires. The volley principle states that a cluster of neurons can fire impulses in rapid succession, producing a volley of impulses.

Information about sound moves from the hair cells to the auditory nerve, which carries information to the brain's auditory areas. The cortical destination of most fibers is the temporal lobes of the cerebral cortex. Localizing sound involves both the timing of the sound and the intensity of the sound arriving at each ear.

Other Senses

The skin senses include touch, temperature, and pain. Touch is the detection of mechanical energy, or pressure, against the skin. Touch information travels through the spinal cord, brain stem, and thalamus and on to the somatosensory areas of the parietal lobes. Thermoreceptors under the skin respond to increases and decreases in temperature. Pain is the sensation that warns us about damage to our bodies.

The chemical senses of taste and smell enable us to detect and process chemicals in the environment. Papillae are bumps on the tongue that contain taste buds, the receptors for taste. The olfactory epithelium contains a sheet of receptor cells for smell in the roof of the nose.

The kinesthetic senses provide information about movement, posture, and orientation. The vestibular sense gives us information about balance and movement. Receptors for the kinesthetic senses are embedded in muscle fibers and joints. The semicircular canals in the inner ear contain the sensory receptors that detect head motion.

KEY TERMS

absolute threshold	frequency theory	papillae	sensory receptors
apparent movement	gestalt psychology	parallel processing	signal detection theory
auditory nerve	inner ear	perception	subliminal perception
binding	kinesthetic senses	perceptual constancy	thermoreceptors
binocular cues	middle ear	perceptual set	top-down processing
bottom-up processing	monocular cues	place theory	trichromatic theory
cones	noise	retina	vestibular sense
convergence	olfactory epithelium	rods	visual cortex
depth perception	opponent-process theory	selective attention	volley principle
difference threshold	optic nerve	semicircular canals	Weber's law
feature detectors	outer ear	sensation	
figure-ground relationship	pain	sensory adaptation	

ANSWERS TO SELF-QUIZZES

Section 1: 1. C; 2. B; 3. A; 4. D
Section 2: 1. D; 2. A; 3. A; 4. B

Section 3: 1. A; 2. C; 3. B; 4. B

Section 4: 1. B; 2. B; 3. B; 4. B

4 States of Consciousness

When the Human Mind Is a Buried Treasure

The daily life of Erik Ramsey would seem to be the stuff of nightmares. In 1999, at age 16, he was horribly injured in a car accident. A blood clot in his brain stem caused a stroke, leaving Erik with a rare and permanent condition called *locked-in syndrome* (Foer, 2008). Erik cannot move or speak. He can feel an itch on his face but cannot reach up and scratch it. The only muscles over which he has any control are those that allow him to move his eyes. Erik uses his eye movements to communicate, answering yes (by looking up) or no (by looking down). Asked if he ever wished he had not survived his accident, Erik looked down. For all the limitations in his life, Erik has one important thing left: his mind.

Researchers are working tirelessly to develop computer–brain interfaces that might allow Erik and others like him to communicate using the ability to think. The interfaces use the brain's electrical signals to communicate through a speech synthesizer, to transform thoughts into words. The interfaces can involve wearing an EEG cap that detects brain activity or having electrodes implanted in the brain (Enger, 2016). Computer–brain interfaces are not simply the stuff of science fiction. They serve the important purpose of liberating locked-in patients from their silent prison.

When Erik became too ill to continue participating in research, one of his doctors, neurologist Phil Kennedy, took the extraordinary step of having implants placed in his own brain (Enger, 2016). This drastic and controversial step allowed Kennedy to refine his methods, using a patient with the ability to speak. It was a risky move and, ironically, Kennedy almost lost his own ability to speak. (The electrodes have since been removed.) Why would anyone take such a risk? Why would a scientist risk his brain to move this research forward? He and other scientists working on this problem are devoted to this task because a conscious mind, locked in a body however limited, is still a person very much worth reaching. Such is the power of consciousness.

In this chapter, we review various states of consciousness, explore the world of sleep and dreams, and consider three topics related to altered states of consciousness—psychoactive drugs, hypnosis, and meditation.

1 The Nature of Consciousness

Consciousness is a crucial part of human experience (Blackmore, 2017; Dennett, 2017). Our conscious awareness represents that private inner mind where we think, feel, plan, wish, pray, imagine, and quietly relive experiences. Consider that if we did not have private thoughts and feelings, we could not tell a lie.

In the late nineteenth and early twentieth centuries, psychology pioneer William James (1950) described the mind as a **stream of consciousness,** a continuous flow of changing sensations, images, thoughts, and feelings. The content of our awareness changes from moment to moment. Information moves rapidly in and out of consciousness. Our minds can race from one topic to the next—from the person approaching us to our physical state today to the café where we will have lunch to our strategy for the test tomorrow.

William James thought of just about everything psychologists currently study. Who knows what he might have accomplished with the neuroscience tools we have today?

In his description of the stream of consciousness, James included aspects of our awareness that he described as on the "fringe" of the stream of consciousness. This fringe includes all of the thoughts and feelings that we have *about* our thoughts. We are aware not only of those things that take center stage in our mental life, those shiny fish in the stream of consciousness, but also of all the thoughts and feelings that surround those fish.

Today, psychologists use the term *metacognition* to describe the processes by which we think about thinking (Faivre & others, 2017; O'Leary & Sloutsky, 2017). This term includes our awareness of the fringe elements of the conscious stream. When we read a text, for instance, the difficulty or ease with which we comprehend what is written can influence how we feel about what we read. When written text is easy to read, we are more likely to think that what we are reading is true and accurate (Reber & Greifeneder, 2017).

The metacognitive experience of ease can impact our thought processes in surprising ways. Consider the two items below, taken from a questionnaire that measures the experience of meaning in life (Steger & others, 2006). The top one is printed in a difficult-to-read font, the bottom one in a clear, easy-to-read font:

I HAvE found *a* really *significant* **meaning in** my life.

I have found a really significant meaning in my life.

One study found that participants rated their meaning in life to be lower when the scale used the difficult-to-read font (Trent, Lavelock, & King, 2013). Other research has shown that when young people experienced metacognitive difficulty in thinking about their life goals, they were less likely to believe they could reach those goals (Fisher & Oyserman, 2017; Oyserman, Elmore, & Smith, 2012). The logic behind such results is that while thinking about his or her life goals, the person might reason, "If it is this hard for me to even imagine myself pursuing these goals, they must not be very possible."

During much of the twentieth century, psychologists focused less on the study of mental processes and more on the study of observable behavior. More recently, the study of consciousness has regained widespread respectability in psychology. Indeed, scientists from many different fields are interested in consciousness (Dehaene, Lau, & Kouider, 2017; Friedman & Jack, 2017; Hassabis & others, 2017).

stream of consciousness Term used by William James to describe the mind as a continuous flow of changing sensations, images, thoughts, and feelings.

Defining Consciousness

consciousness
An individual's awareness of external events and internal sensations under a condition of arousal, including awareness of the self and thoughts about one's experiences.

We can define consciousness in terms of its two parts: awareness and arousal. **Consciousness** is an individual's awareness of external events and internal sensations under a condition of arousal.

Awareness includes awareness of the self and thoughts about one's experiences. Consider that on an autumn afternoon, when you see a beautiful tree, vibrant with color, you are not simply perceiving the colors; you are also *aware* that you are seeing them. Having awareness means that our sensory experiences are more than the sum of their parts (Orpwood, 2017).

Arousal, the second part of consciousness, is the physiological state of being engaged with the environment. Thus, a sleeping person is not conscious in the same way that he or she would be while awake.

Consciousness and the Brain

There has been a dramatic increase in theoretical and research interest in determining more specifically how the brain functions to produce consciousness (Feinberg & Mallatt, 2016). The two aspects of consciousness—awareness and arousal—are associated with different parts of the brain (Metzger & others, 2017).

Notice the word associated. Keep in mind that studies showing links between the brain and neural activity are generally correlational studies.

The awareness aspect of consciousness refers to a feeling that we have about our experiences. This feeling is associated with many parts of the brain working in synchrony (Babiloni & others, 2016). It appears that the subjective feeling of awareness occurs in what has been termed a *global brain workspace* that involves various brain areas working in parallel (Dehaene & Changeux, 2011; Michel, 2017). These locations include the front-most part of the brain—the prefrontal cortex—as well as the *anterior cingulate* (an area associated with acts of will) and the *association areas* (Fu & others, 2017; Mashour & Hudetz, 2017). This wide-reaching brain workspace is an assembly of neurons that are thought to work in cooperation to produce the subjective sense of consciousness. Areas of the prefrontal cortex appear to be especially involved in the ways that awareness goes beyond the input of sensory information. For instance, these areas of the brain are active when we taste complex flavors, such as umami, and track the subjective pleasure that accompanies rewarding experiences (Kringelbach, 2005). According to the brain workspace approach to consciousness, the widespread availability of information broadcast throughout the brain is what we experience as conscious awareness (Michel, 2017). Scientists continue to probe the precise neural correlates of consciousness.

Although awareness is linked to many different brain areas working together, arousal is more specific. In the brain, arousal is by the **reticular activating system,** a network of structures including the brain stem, medulla, and thalamus (Krone & others, 2017). Even with a perfectly functioning frontal cortex, a person with damage to these brain areas can remain unconscious. Arousal refers to the ways that awareness is regulated: If we are in danger, we might need to be on "high alert," but if we are in a safe environment with no immediate demands, we can relax, and our arousal may be quite low.

reticular activating system
A network of structures including the brain stem, medulla, and thalamus that determine arousal, one aspect of consciousness.

Theory of Mind

You might think of consciousness as the mind, that part of yourself that contains your private thoughts and feelings. It might seem obvious that other people have private thoughts and feelings as well, but the human ability to recognize the subjective experience of another is a true developmental accomplishment.

©Creatas/Getty Images Plus/Getty Images

theory of mind
Individuals' understanding that they and others think, feel, perceive, and have private experiences.

Developmental psychologists who study children's ideas about mental states use the phrase **theory of mind** to refer to individuals' understanding that they and others think, feel, perceive, and have private experiences (Schneider, Slaughter, & Dux, 2017; Verela, Thompson, & Rosch, 2017).

Developmental psychologists have used a procedure called the *false belief task* to examine children's theory of mind (Rubio-Fernández, Jara-Ettinger, & Gibson, 2017). In one version of the false belief task, the child is asked to consider the following situation (Wellman & Woolley, 1990). Anna is a little girl who has some chocolate that she decides to save for later. She puts it in a blue cupboard and goes outside to play. While Anna is gone, her mother moves the chocolate to the red cupboard. When Anna comes back in, where will she look for her chocolate? Three-year-olds give the wrong answer—they assume that Anna will look in the red cupboard because they know (even though Anna does not) that Anna's mom moved the chocolate to the red one. Four-year-olds answer correctly—they recognize that Anna does not know everything they do and that she will believe the chocolate is where she left it (Wellman & Woolley, 1990). Success at the false belief task is associated with academic achievement (Cavadel & Frye, 2017) and social competence (Lecce & others, 2017). Children who perform the false belief task well are better liked by their peers, in part because they are more likely to behave kindly (Ball, Smetana, & Sturge-Apple, 2017).

Theory of mind is essential to many valuable social capacities, such as empathy and sympathy (Preckel, Kanske, & Singer, 2018). Simon Baron-Cohen (1995, 2008, 2011) is an expert on autism, a disorder that affects communication and social interaction. He has proposed that the emergence of theory of mind is so central to human functioning that evolution would not leave it to chance. Baron-Cohen suggests that we are born with a brain mechanism that is ready to develop a theory of mind. This theory of mind mechanism (TOMM) accounts for the fact that nearly all children over the age of 4 pass the false belief task. Baron-Cohen has proposed that autistic individuals lack the TOMM, a condition that would explain their unique social deficits (Warrier & others, 2017).

Have you ever had a conversation with someone who didn't seem to notice you were really not into it? That person was showing a theory of mind deficit.

Levels of Awareness

The flow of sensations, images, thoughts, and feelings that William James spoke of can occur at different levels of awareness. Although we might think of consciousness as either present or not, there are in fact shades of awareness, observed in comatose patients as well as in everyday life. Here we consider five levels of awareness: higher-level consciousness, lower-level consciousness, altered states of consciousness, subconscious awareness, and no awareness (Figure 1).

HIGHER-LEVEL CONSCIOUSNESS

controlled processes
The most alert states of human consciousness, during which individuals actively focus their efforts toward a goal.

In **controlled processes,** the most alert states of human consciousness, individuals actively focus their efforts toward a goal (Hommel, 2017). For example, observe a classmate as he struggles to master the unfamiliar buttons on his new smartphone. He does not hear you humming or notice the intriguing shadow on the wall. His state of focused awareness illustrates the idea of controlled processes. Controlled processes require selective attention: the ability to concentrate on a specific aspect of experience while ignoring others (Cushing, Gazzaley, & Morsella, 2017). A key aspect of controlled processing is executive function. **Executive function** refers to higher-order, complex cognitive processes, including thinking, planning, and problem solving. These cognitive processes are linked to the functioning of the brain's prefrontal cortex (Friedman & Miyake, 2017). Executive function is the person's capacity to harness consciousness, to focus in on specific thoughts while ignoring others. Because controlled processes demand attention and effort, they are slower than automatic processes. Often, after we have practiced an activity a great deal, we no longer have to think about it while doing it. It becomes automatic and faster.

executive function
Higher-order, complex cognitive processes, including thinking, planning, and problem solving.

LOWER-LEVEL CONSCIOUSNESS

Beneath the level of controlled processes are other levels of conscious awareness. Lower levels of awareness include automatic processes and daydreaming.

Level of Awareness	Description	Examples
Higher-Level Consciousness	Involves controlled processing, in which individuals actively focus their efforts on attaining a goal; the most alert state of consciousness	Doing a math or science problem; preparing for a debate; taking an at-bat in a baseball game
Lower-Level Consciousness	Includes automatic processing that requires little attention, as well as daydreaming	Punching in a number on a cell phone; typing on a keyboard when one is an expert; gazing at a sunset
Altered States of Consciousness	Can be produced by drugs, trauma, fatigue, possibly hypnosis, and sensory deprivation	Feeling the effects of having taken alcohol or psychedelic drugs; undergoing hypnosis to quit smoking or lose weight
Subconscious Awareness	Can occur when people are awake, as well as when they are sleeping and dreaming	Sleeping and dreaming
No Awareness	Freud's belief that some unconscious thoughts are too laden with anxiety and other negative emotions for consciousness to admit them	Having unconscious thoughts; being knocked out by a blow or anesthetized

FIGURE 1

Levels of Awareness Each level of awareness has its time and place in human life.

Automatic Processes A few weeks after acquiring his smartphone, your classmate flips it open and sends a text message in the middle of a conversation with you. He does not have to concentrate on the keys and hardly seems aware of the device in his hand as he continues to talk to you while finishing his lunch. Using his phone has reached the point of automatic processing.

automatic processes
States of consciousness that require little attention and do not interfere with other ongoing activities.

Automatic processes are states of consciousness that require little attention and do not interfere with other ongoing activities. Automatic processes require less conscious effort than controlled processes (Schneider, Slaughter, & Dux, 2017). When we are awake, our automatic behaviors occur at a lower level of awareness than controlled processes, but they are still conscious behaviors. Your classmate pushed the right buttons, so at some level he apparently was aware of what he was doing. This kind of automatic behavior suggests that we can be aware of stimuli on some level without paying attention to them.

Daydreaming Another state of consciousness that involves a low level of conscious effort is *daydreaming,* which lies between active consciousness and dreaming while asleep. It is a little like dreaming while we are awake (Domhoff, 2017; Perogamvros & others, 2017). Daydreams usually begin spontaneously when we are doing something that requires less than our full attention.

Mind wandering is probably the most obvious type of daydreaming (Baldwin & others, 2017; Kane & others, 2017). We regularly take brief side trips into our own private kingdoms of imagery and memory while reading, listening, or working. When we daydream, we drift into a world of fantasy. We perhaps imagine ourselves on a date, at a party, on television, in a faraway place, or at another time in our life. Sometimes our daydreams are about everyday events such as paying the rent, going to the dentist, and meeting with somebody at school or work.

In the brain, mind wandering is related to the activity of a broad set of regions in the brain, called the *default mode network*. This array of connections

One of the most interesting things about mind wandering is that we often don't realize when it happens. We just fall into it. Hey! Are you paying attention?

Are There Benefits to Mind Wandering?

Have you ever had the experience of sitting in lecture, taking careful notes, only to suddenly realize you had stopped paying attention and the page in front of you is blank? Your mind wandered off, leaving you with no information on the last few minutes of lecture. Moreover, because you are feeling embarrassed about not paying attention, you may feel awkward about raising your hand to ask a question. Instead, you may be holding your breath, hoping you are not called on. Experiences like that certainly demonstrate the downside of mind wandering. It is likely no surprise that mind wandering can interfere with learning (Franklin & others, 2016; Pachai & others, 2016). Nevertheless, sometimes almost everyone experiences mind wandering. The fact that mind wandering is common suggests that it must have some benefits for human beings. What might those benefits be?

Research has probed a number of potential functions of mind wandering. For example, after being shown a complex problem, people who have engaged in mind wandering are more likely to have an "aha!" experience, solving problems through sudden insight (compared to those engaged in careful analysis, Zedelius & Schooler, 2015). In addition, although mind wandering is off-task in the present moment, it can play a role in future thinking. Daydreams can remind us of important things ahead. When our mind wanders, it often wanders to the future (Karapanagiotidis & others, 2017; Smallwood &

©Gary Conner/Getty Images

Schooler, 2015). As you daydream while ironing a shirt or walking to the store, you may make plans, solve a problem, or come up with a creative idea.

Another important function of mind wandering is regulating boredom (Pachai & others, 2016). Sometimes a bit of mental "goofing off" is just what a person needs to reengage with an important task. Mind wandering can refresh the mind and give us the chance to come at problems in a new way. Building breaks into lectures, reading, and other tasks that require attention can help students learn.

Mind wandering can be annoying but it is not always a problem. Importantly, some scholars suggest that mind wandering, rather than being an exception to the rule of human attention, is a natural part of our cognitive lives (Thomson, Besner, & Smilek, 2015). This means that instructors, authors, and others, ought not take too personally when a student, reader, or friend has to be nudged back to attention.

What Do You Think?

- What other uses do you believe mind wandering might have in your life?
- What are strategies you might use to reduce mind wandering in your course work?

works together to process information that is not about receiving information from the outside world (Golchert & others, 2017).

People are more likely to experience mind wandering when they are engaged in a task that involves prolonged attention, especially when the person might experience boredom. For example, students in a long lecture may find their minds wandering off to topics that have no relevance to the course material (Pachai & others, 2016). Unfortunately, mind wandering during lectures leads to poorer course performance (Wammes & others, 2016). In the workplace, careful and consistent attention is often required for excellent performance and mind wandering at work can impede performance (Dane, 2017). Finally, although it is experienced as occurring without effort, the wandering mind does use cognitive resources (Gyurkovics, Balota, & Jackson, 2017). For these reasons, we might wonder why mind wandering occurs at all. Does it have benefits? To grapple with this question, see the Challenge Your Thinking.

ALTERED STATES OF CONSCIOUSNESS *Altered states of consciousness* or *awareness* are mental states that are noticeably different from normal awareness. Altered states of

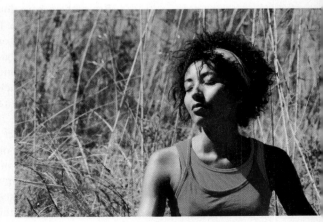
©Picturenet/Getty Images

consciousness can range from losing one's sense of self-consciousness to hallucinating. Such states can be produced by drugs, trauma, fever, fatigue, sensory deprivation, meditation, and possibly hypnosis (Cavanna & others, 2017). Drug use can also induce altered states of consciousness, as we will consider later.

SUBCONSCIOUS AWARENESS   A great deal of brain activity occurs beneath the level of conscious awareness. Psychologists are increasingly interested in the subconscious processing of information, which can take place while we are awake or asleep (Hurme & others, 2017; Railo & others, 2014).

Waking Subconscious Awareness   When we are awake, processes are going on just below the surface of our awareness. For example, while we are grappling with a problem, the solution may pop into our head. Such insights can occur when a subconscious connection between ideas is so strong that it rises into awareness.

Incubation refers to the subconscious processing that leads to a solution to a problem after a break from conscious thought about the problem. Clearly, during incubation, information is being processed even if we are unaware of that processing. Interestingly, successful incubation requires that we first expend effort thinking carefully about the problem (Pachai & others, 2016; Gonzalez-Vallejo & others, 2008).

Evidence that we are not always aware of our brain's processing of information comes from studies of individuals with certain neurological disorders. In one case, a woman who suffered neurological damage was unable to describe or report the shape or size of objects in her visual field, although she was capable of describing other physical perceptions that she had (Milner & Goodale, 1995). Nonetheless, when she reached for an object, she could accurately adjust the size of her grip to allow her to grasp the object. Thus, she did possess some subconscious knowledge of the size and shape of objects, even though she had no awareness of this knowledge.

Subconscious information processing can occur simultaneously in a distributed manner along many parallel tracks. (Recall the discussion of parallel processing of visual information.) For example, when you look at a dog running down the street, you are consciously aware of the event but not of the subconscious processing of the object's identity (a dog), its color (black), and its movement (fast). In contrast, conscious processing occurs in sequence and is slower than much subconscious processing. Note that the various levels of awareness often work together. You might rely on controlled processing when memorizing material for class, but later, the answers on a test just pop into your head as a result of automatic or subconscious processing.

Subconscious Awareness During Sleep and Dreams   When we sleep and dream, our level of awareness is lower than when we daydream, but sleep and dreams are not best regarded as the absence of consciousness (Domhoff, 2017). Rather, they are low levels of consciousness.

Researchers have found that when people are asleep, they remain aware of external stimuli to some degree. In sleep laboratories, when people are clearly asleep (as determined by physiological monitoring devices), they are able to respond to faint tones by pressing a handheld button (Ogilvie & Wilkinson, 1988). In one study, the presentation of pure auditory tones to sleeping individuals activated auditory processing regions of the brain, whereas participants' names activated language areas, the amygdala, and the prefrontal cortex (Stickgold, 2001). We return to the topics of sleep and dreams in the next section.

NO AWARENESS   The term *unconscious* generally applies to someone who has been knocked out by a blow or anesthetized, or who has fallen into a deep, prolonged unconscious state (Lopez-Rolon & others, 2017). However, Sigmund Freud (1917) used the term *unconscious* in a very different way: **Unconscious thought,** said Freud, is a reservoir of unacceptable wishes, feelings, and thoughts that are beyond conscious awareness. In other words, Freud's interpretation viewed the unconscious as a storehouse for vile thoughts and impulses. He believed that some aspects of our experience remain unconscious for good reason, as if we

unconscious thought
According to Freud, a reservoir of unacceptable wishes, feelings, and thoughts that are beyond conscious awareness.

are better off not knowing about them. For example, from Freud's perspective, the human mind is full of disturbing impulses such as a desire to have sex with our parents.

Although Freud's interpretation remains controversial, psychologists now widely accept that unconscious processes do exist. Contemporary researchers acknowledge that many mental processes (thoughts, emotions, goals, and perceptions) can occur outside of awareness (Nava & others, 2016; Rothkirch & Hesselmann, 2017; Shimizu, Lee, & Uleman, 2017).

self-quiz

1. The term *metacognition* refers to
   A. the study of cognitive research.
   B. thinking about thought processes.
   C. cognition that is subliminal.
   D. stream of consciousness thinking.

2. All of the following are examples of automatic processes *except*
   A. a student solving a math problem.
   B. a runner jogging.
   C. a person talking to a friend.
   D. a taxi driver operating a car.

3. Sleep and dreams are most accurately viewed as
   A. the absence of consciousness.
   B. intermittent consciousness.
   C. low levels of consciousness.
   D. high levels of consciousness.

APPLY IT! 4. Xavier is a student in Intro Psych. He has attended every class and taken detailed notes. Before the first exam, he studies and takes practice tests. On the morning of the test, however, he feels suddenly blank. Xavier takes a deep breath and starts answering each question one by one, taking guesses on many questions. The next week, Xavier is thrilled to learn that he got a 100 percent on the exam. He later tells a friend, "I just took guesses and still got a perfect score. Next time I should not even bother studying!" Which of the following is true of Xavier's plan?
   A. It is a good idea, since a lot of psychology is just common sense.
   B. It is a bad idea. Xavier's grade shows that controlled and subconscious processes work together. Controlled processes helped him learn the material so that he was able to take good guesses.
   C. Xavier's plan is not a good idea, because his subconscious helped him on this test, but such processing cannot be counted on to work all the time.
   D. Xavier's plan is a good one. His experience demonstrates that controlled processes are generally not helpful in academic work.

2 Sleep and Dreams

sleep
A natural state of rest for the body and mind that involves the reversible loss of consciousness.

You already know that sleep involves a decrease in body movement and (typically) closed eyes. What is sleep, more precisely? We can define **sleep** as a natural state of rest for the body and mind that involves the reversible loss of consciousness. Sleep must be important, because it takes up about one-third of our lifetime, more than anything else we do. *Why* is sleep so crucial? Before tackling this question, let's first see how sleep is linked to our internal biological rhythms.

 How, where, and with whom we sleep are all influenced by culture. In the United States, infants typically sleep alone, and parents are discouraged from sleeping with their infants. In other countries, such **cosleeping** is an accepted practice. Some cultures encourage a family bed where everyone sleeps together.

Biological Rhythms and Sleep

biological rhythms
Periodic physiological fluctuations in the body, such as the rise and fall of hormones and accelerated/ decelerated cycles of brain activity, that can influence behavior.

Biological rhythms are periodic physiological fluctuations in the body. We are unaware of most biological rhythms, such as the rise and fall of hormones and accelerated and decelerated cycles of brain activity, but they can influence our behavior. These rhythms are controlled by biological clocks, which include annual or seasonal cycles such as the migration of birds and the hibernation of bears, and 24-hour cycles such as the sleep/wake cycle and temperature changes in the human body. Let's further explore the body's 24-hour cycles.

circadian rhythms
Daily behavioral or physiological cycles that involve the sleep/wake cycle, body temperature, blood pressure, and blood sugar level.

CIRCADIAN RHYTHMS **Circadian rhythms** are daily behavioral or physiological cycles. Daily circadian rhythms involve the sleep/wake cycle, body temperature, blood pressure, and blood sugar level (Burman, 2017). For example, body temperature fluctuates about 3 degrees Fahrenheit in a 24-hour day, peaking in the afternoon and reaching its lowest point between 2 A.M. and 5 A.M.

Researchers have discovered that the body monitors the change from day to night by means of the **suprachiasmatic nucleus (SCN),** a small brain structure that uses input from the retina to synchronize its own rhythm with the daily cycle of light and dark (Brancaccio & others, 2017; Van Erum, Van Dam, & De Deyn, 2017). Output from the SCN allows the hypothalamus to regulate daily rhythms such

suprachiasmatic nucleus (SCN)
A small brain structure that uses input from the retina to synchronize its own rhythm with the daily cycle of light and dark; the body's way of monitoring the change from day to night.

Circadian means conforming to a 24-hour cycle. It means DAILY.

Cerebral cortex

Hypothalamus

Suprachiasmatic
nucleus (SCN)

Reticular
formation

FIGURE 2

Suprachiasmatic Nucleus

The suprachiasmatic nucleus (SCN) plays an important role in keeping our biological clock running on time. The SCN is located in the hypothalamus. It receives information from the retina about light, which is the external stimulus that synchronizes the SCN. Output from the SCN is distributed to the rest of the hypothalamus and to the reticular formation.
©Image Source/Alamy Stock Photo

as temperature and hunger and the reticular formation to regulate daily rhythms of sleep and wakefulness (Figure 2). Although a number of biological clocks seem to be involved in regulating circadian rhythms, researchers have found that the SCN is the most important (Han & others, 2012).

Many individuals who are totally blind experience lifelong sleeping problems because their retinas cannot detect light. These people have a kind of permanent jet lag and periodic insomnia because their circadian rhythms often do not follow a 24-hour cycle (da Silva & others, 2017).

DESYNCHRONIZING THE BIOLOGICAL CLOCK Biological clocks can become *desynchronized,* or thrown off their regular schedules. Among the circumstances of life that can introduce irregularities into our sleep are jet travel, changing work shifts, and *insomnia* (the inability to sleep). What effects might such irregularities have on circadian rhythms?

If you fly from Los Angeles to New York and then go to bed at 11 P.M. eastern time, you may have trouble falling asleep because your body is still on west coast time. Even if you sleep for 8 hours that night, you may have a hard time waking up at 7 A.M. eastern time, because your body thinks it is 4 A.M. If you stay in New York for several days, your body will adjust to this new schedule.

The jet lag you experience when you fly from Los Angeles to New York occurs because your body time is out of phase, or synchronization, with clock time (Malhotra, 2017). Jet lag is the result of two or more body rhythms being out of sync. You usually go to bed when your body temperature begins to drop, but in your new location, you might be trying to go to sleep when it is rising. In the morning, your adrenal glands release large doses of the hormone cortisol to help you wake up. In your new geographic time zone, the glands may be releasing this chemical just as you are getting ready for bed at night.

Circadian rhythms may also become desynchronized when shift workers change their work hours (Anjum & others, 2017). Shift-work problems most often affect night-shift workers who never fully adjust to sleeping in the daytime after their work shifts. Such workers may fall asleep at work and are at increased risk for heart disease and gastrointestinal disorders (Choi & others, 2014; Knutsson, 2017).

RESETTING THE BIOLOGICAL CLOCK
If your biological clock for sleeping and waking becomes desynchronized, how can you reset it?

Changing to a night-shift job can desynchronize our biological clocks and affect our circadian rhythms and performance.
©ERproductions Ltd/Blend Images/Corbis

With regard to jet lag, if you take a transoceanic flight and arrive at your destination during the day, it is a good idea to spend as much time outside in the daylight as possible. Bright light during the day, especially in the morning, increases wakefulness, whereas bright light at night delays sleep (Gooley, 2017; Paul & others, 2011).

Why would melatonin be particularly helpful for eastward but not westward travel?

Researchers are studying melatonin, a hormone that increases at night in humans, for its possible effects in reducing jet lag (Iggena, Winter, & Steiner, 2017; Pfeffer, Korf, & Wicht, 2017). Studies have shown that a small dosage of melatonin can reduce jet lag by advancing the circadian clock—an effect that makes it useful for eastward but not westward jet lag (Trivedi & Kumar, 2014).

Why Do We Need Sleep?

All animals require sleep. Furthermore, the human body regulates sleep, as it does eating and drinking, and this fact suggests that sleep may be just as essential for survival. Yet why we need sleep remains a bit of a mystery.

THEORIES ON THE NEED FOR SLEEP A variety of theories have been proposed for the need for sleep (Nicholas, Jordan, & Trinder, 2017). First, from an evolutionary perspective, sleep may have developed because animals needed to protect themselves at night. The idea is that it makes sense for animals to be inactive when it is dark, because nocturnal inactivity helps them to avoid both becoming other animals' prey and injuring themselves due to poor visibility.

A second possibility is that sleep is a way to conserve energy. Spending a large chunk of any day sleeping allows animals to conserve their calories, especially when food is scarce (Siegel, 2005). For some animals, moreover, the search for food and water is easier and safer when the sun is up. When it is dark, it is adaptive for these animals to save their energy. Animals that are likely to serve as someone else's food sleep the least of all. Figure 3 illustrates the average amount of sleep per day of various animals.

A third explanation for the need for sleep is that sleep is restorative (Donatelle, 2015; Fattinger & others, 2017). Scientists have proposed that sleep restores, replenishes, and rebuilds the brain and body, which the day's waking activities can wear out. This idea fits with the feeling of being tired before we go to sleep and restored when we wake up. In support of the theory of a restorative function of sleep, many of the body's cells show increased production and reduced breakdown of proteins during deep sleep (Picchioni & others, 2014). Protein molecules are the building blocks needed for cell growth and for repair of damage from factors such as stress. In one study short sleep duration was associated with higher T-cell and lower NK-cell activity, indicating higher stress levels and lower immune system functioning (Borniger, Cisse, & Nelson, 2017; Fondell & others, 2011).

A final explanation for the need for sleep centers on the role of sleep in brain plasticity (Frank, 2017; Gerashchenko, Pasumarthi, & Kilduff, 2017). Recall that the plasticity of the brain refers to its capacity to change in response to experience. Sleep has been recognized as playing an important role in the ways that experiences influence the brain. For example, neuroscientists recently have argued that sleep enhances synaptic connections between neurons (Grønli, Soulé, & Bramham, 2014; Raven & others, 2017). The lack of sleep leads to weaker connections in the brain (Poh & Chee, 2017), so the brain possesses a less clear representation of new learning. Findings such as these suggest an important role for sleep in the consolidation of memories (Batterink & Paller, 2017). Sleep is vital to the consolidation of memory, whether memory for specific information, for skills, or for emotional experiences (Latchoumane & others, 2017). One possible explanation is that

Hours of Sleep per 24-Hour Period

Animal	Hours
Bat	19.9
Armadillo	18.5
Cat	14.5
Fox	9.8
Rhesus monkey	9.6
Rabbit	8.4
Human	8.0
Cow	3.9
Sheep	3.8
Horse	2.9

FIGURE 3 **From Bats to Horses: The Wide Range of Sleep in Animals** We might feel envious of bats, which sleep nearly 20 hours a day, and more than a little in awe of horses, still running on just under 3 hours of rest.
(bat) ©Ewen Charlton/Getty Images; (horse); ©Fuse/Getty Images

©UpperCut Images/SuperStock

during sleep the cerebral cortex is free to conduct activities that strengthen memory associations, so that memories formed during recent waking hours can be integrated into long-term memory storage. Lost sleep often results in lost memories (Ratcliff & Van Dongen, 2017).

So, if you are thinking about studying all night for your next test, you might want to think again. Sleep can enhance your memory. In one study, participants who had studied word lists the day before performed better in a recall test for those words if they had had a good night's sleep before the test (Racsmány, Conway, & Demeter, 2010). Participants who were tested prior to sleep did not perform as well. Not only can sleep improve your memory, but just losing a few hours of sleep can have negative effects on many cognitive processes, including attention, language, reasoning, and decision making.

THE EFFECTS OF CHRONIC SLEEP DEPRIVATION

Experts recommend that adults get 7 to 9 hours of sleep a night (National Sleep Foundation, 2017). Lack of sleep is stressful and has an impact on the body and the brain. When deprived of sleep, people also have trouble paying attention to tasks and solving problems. Sleep deprivation decreases brain activity in the thalamus and the prefrontal cortex (Krause & others, 2017) and leads to reduced complexity of brain activity (Grant & others, 2018). The tired brain must compensate by using different pathways or alternative neural networks when thinking (Koenis & others, 2011).

Although sleep is unquestionably key to optimal physical and mental performance, we have only to look around us (or into a mirror) to notice that many people do not get sufficient sleep. In a national survey of more than 1,500 U.S. adults conducted by the National Sleep Foundation (2011), 43 percent of 19- to 64-year-olds reported that they rarely or ever get a good night's sleep on weeknights. Sixty percent said that they experience a sleep problem every night or almost every night, such as waking during the night, waking too early, or feeling tired when they wake up in the morning. A majority stated that they get slightly less than 7 hours of sleep a night on weeknights, and 15 percent indicated that they sleep less than 6 hours a night.

Why do Americans get too little sleep? Pressures at work and school, family responsibilities, and social obligations often lead to long hours of wakefulness and irregular sleep/wake schedules. Not having enough hours to do all that we want or need to do in a day, we cheat on our sleep. As a result we may suffer from a "sleep debt," an accumulated level of exhaustion.

Stages of Wakefulness and Sleep

Have you ever been awakened from your sleep and been totally disoriented? Have you ever awakened in the middle of a dream and suddenly gone right back into the dream as if it were a movie running just under the surface of your consciousness? These two circumstances reflect two distinct stages in the sleep cycle.

Stages of sleep correspond to massive electrophysiological changes that occur throughout the brain as the fast, irregular, and low-amplitude electrical activity of wakefulness is replaced by the slow, regular, high-amplitude waves of deep sleep. Using the electroencephalography (EEG) to monitor the brain's electrical activity, scientists have identified four stages of sleep.

The following stages (of wakefulness and sleep) are defined by both the brain's activity and muscle tone. The stages are named by letters and numbers that represent what is going on at that stage, including whether the person is awake or asleep and whether he or she is experiencing rapid eye movement (REM). Non-REM sleep is characterized by a lack of rapid eye movement and little dreaming, as described below.

STAGE W   The "W" here stands for "wake." During this satge, when people are awake, their EEG patterns exhibit two types of waves: beta and alpha. *Beta waves* reflect concentration and alertness. These waves are the highest in frequency and lowest in amplitude. This means that the waves go up and down a great deal, but they do not have very high peaks or very low ebbs. They also are more *desynchronous* than other waves, meaning they do not form a very consistent pattern. Inconsistent patterning makes sense given the extensive variation in sensory input and activities we experience when we are awake.

When we are relaxed but still awake, our brain waves slow down, increase in amplitude, and become more *synchronous,* or regular. These waves, associated with relaxation or drowsiness, are called *alpha waves.*

STAGE N1 (NON-REM1) SLEEP   When people are just falling asleep, they enter the first stage of non-REM sleep. The "N" stands for "non-REM" meaning that rapid eye movements do not occur during these stages. Stage N1 is characterized by drowsy sleep. In this stage, the person may experience sudden muscle movements called *myoclonic jerks*. If you watch someone in your class fighting to stay awake, you might notice his or her head jerking upward. This reaction demonstrates that this first stage of sleep often involves the feeling of falling. EEGs of individuals in stage N1 sleep are characterized by *theta* waves, which are even slower in frequency and greater in amplitude than alpha waves. The difference between being relaxed and being in stage N1 sleep is gradual. Figure 4 shows the EEG pattern of stage N1 sleep, along with the EEG patterns for the other stages of wakefulness and sleep.

Watch people in your classes fight to stay awake–you'll see their heads jerk up. This first stage of sleep often involves the feeling of falling.

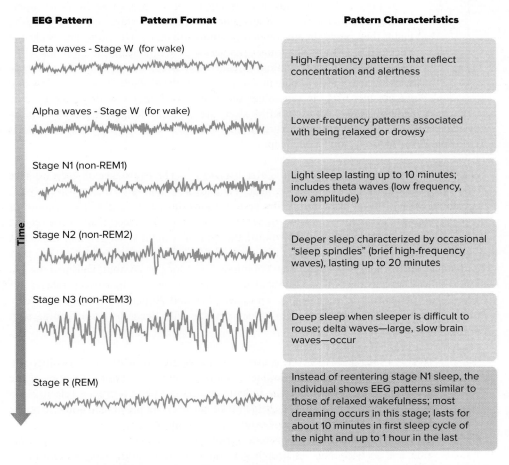

EEG Pattern	Pattern Characteristics
Beta waves - Stage W (for wake)	High-frequency patterns that reflect concentration and alertness
Alpha waves - Stage W (for wake)	Lower-frequency patterns associated with being relaxed or drowsy
Stage N1 (non-REM1)	Light sleep lasting up to 10 minutes; includes theta waves (low frequency, low amplitude)
Stage N2 (non-REM2)	Deeper sleep characterized by occasional "sleep spindles" (brief high-frequency waves), lasting up to 20 minutes
Stage N3 (non-REM3)	Deep sleep when sleeper is difficult to rouse; delta waves—large, slow brain waves—occur
Stage R (REM)	Instead of reentering stage N1 sleep, the individual shows EEG patterns similar to those of relaxed wakefulness; most dreaming occurs in this stage; lasts for about 10 minutes in first sleep cycle of the night and up to 1 hour in the last

FIGURE 4   Characteristics and Formats of EEG Recordings During Stages of Wakefulness and Sleep Even while you are sleeping, your brain is busy. No wonder you sometimes wake up feeling tired.

STAGE N2 (NON-REM2) SLEEP

In stage N2 sleep, muscle activity decreases, and the person is no longer consciously aware of the environment. Theta waves continue but are interspersed with a defining characteristic of stage N2 sleep: sleep spindles. These involve a sudden increase in high-frequency wave bursts (Blume & others, 2017). Stages N1 and N2 are both relatively light stages of sleep, and if people awaken during one of these stages, they often report not having been asleep at all.

STAGE N3 (NON-REM3) SLEEP

Stage N3 sleep is characterized by delta waves, the slowest and highest-amplitude brain waves during sleep. *Delta sleep* is our deepest sleep, the time when our brain waves are least like our brain waves while we are awake. Delta sleep is also called *slow-wave sleep*. This is also the stage when bedwetting (in children), sleepwalking, and sleep talking occur. When awakened during this stage, people usually are confused and disoriented.

FIGURE 5 **REM Sleep** During REM sleep, your eyes move rapidly, as if following the images moving in your dreams.
©Allan Hobson/Science Source

STAGE R (REM) SLEEP

After going through stages N1 to N3, sleepers drift up through the sleep stages toward wakefulness. Instead of reentering stage N1, however, they enter stage R, a different form of sleep called REM (rapid eye movement) sleep. REM sleep is an active stage of sleep during which the most vivid dreaming occurs (Koike & others, 2017; Reinoso-Suárez & others, 2018). The EEG pattern for REM sleep shows fast waves similar to those of relaxed wakefulness, and the sleeper's eyeballs move up and down and from left to right (Figure 5). Interestingly, REM sleep is characterized by theta waves in the hippocampus, which are also present during waking activity (Koike & others, 2017; Vijayan & others, 2017).

A person who is awakened during REM sleep is more likely to report having dreamed than when awakened at any other stage. Even people who claim they rarely dream frequently report dreaming when they are awakened during REM sleep. The longer the period of REM sleep, the more likely the person will report dreaming. Dreams also occur during slow-wave or non-REM sleep, but the frequency of dreams in these stages is relatively low and we are less likely to remember these dreams. Reports of dreaming by individuals awakened from REM sleep are typically longer, more vivid, more physically active, more emotionally charged, and less related to waking life than reports by those awakened from non-REM sleep.

SLEEP CYCLING THROUGH THE NIGHT

The five stages of sleep we have considered make up a normal cycle of sleep. As shown in Figure 6, one of these cycles lasts about 90 to 100 minutes and recurs several times during the night. The amount of deep sleep (stage N3) is much greater in the first half of a night's sleep than in the second half. Most stage R sleep takes place toward the end of a night's sleep, when the REM stage becomes progressively longer. The night's first REM stage might last for only 10 minutes, but the final REM stage might continue for as long as an hour. During a normal night of sleep, individuals will spend about 60 percent of sleep in light sleep (stages N1 and N2), 20 percent in delta or deep sleep (stage N3), and 20 percent in stage R (Webb, 2000). So, you can think of your night's sleep starting with deep sleep and ending with the big show of the night's REM.

SLEEP AND THE BRAIN

The five sleep stages are associated with distinct patterns of neurotransmitter activity initiated in the reticular formation, the core of the brain stem. In all vertebrates, the reticular formation plays a crucial role in sleep and arousal (Vanini & others, 2014) (see Figure 2). As previously noted, damage to the reticular formation can result in coma and death.

Three important neurotransmitters involved in sleep are serotonin, norepinephrine, and acetylcholine. As sleep begins, the levels of neurotransmitters sent to the forebrain from the reticular formation start dropping, and they continue to fall until they reach their lowest levels during the deepest sleep stage—stage N3. Stage R sleep

Remember these three neurotransmitters? Serotonin plays a role in regulating our emotions; norepinephrine regulates arousal; and acetylcholine is involved in muscle movements. AND they help you sleep!

is initiated by a rise in acetylcholine, which activates the cerebral cortex while the rest of the brain remains relatively inactive. REM sleep ends when there is a rise in serotonin and norepinephrine, which increases the level of forebrain activity nearly to the awakened state (El-Sheikh, 2013; Lushington & others, 2014; Miller & O'Callaghan, 2006). You are most likely to wake up just after a REM period. If you do not wake up then, the level of the neurotransmitters falls again, and you enter another sleep cycle.

In addition to the three neurotransmitters reviewed above, GABA, the brain's break pedal also plays a role in sleep (Luppi, Peyron, & Fort, 2017). In particular, GABA receptors appear to help regulate the process of sleep.

We have already reviewed the many negative consequences of sleep deprivation. As noted above, when the brain is sleep deprived.... of course the brain is involved in all that we do and so it is not surprising that sleep deprivation affects the brain and its functioning. Recent research has been able to show, for the first time, how sleep deprivation affects the brain at the level of neurons. To read about this work, see the Intersection.

FIGURE 6 **Cycling Through a Night's Sleep** During a night's sleep, we go through several cycles. Depth of sleep decreases, and REM sleep (shown in green) increases as the night progresses. In this graph, the person is depicted as awakening at about 5 A.M. and then going back to sleep for another hour.

> **How many sleep cycles are presented?** > **How many times does the sleeper wake up?** > **Trace the rise and fall of the neurotransmitters acetylcholine, serotonin, and norepinephrine in the sleep cycle depicted. Has this sleeper achieved a good night's rest? Why or why not?**

Sleep Throughout the Life Span

Getting sufficient sleep is important at every period in human life. Figure 7 shows how total sleep time and time spent in each type of sleep vary over the human life span.

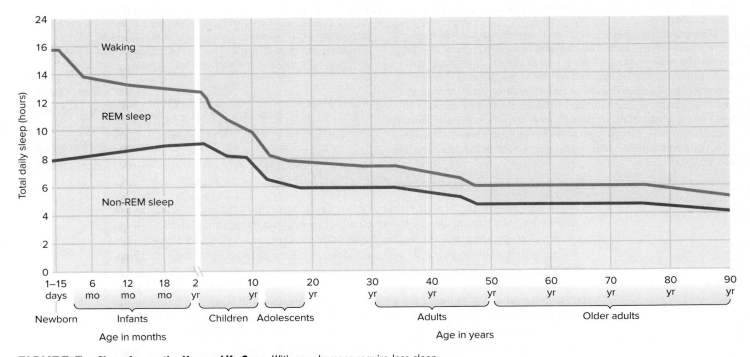

FIGURE 7 **Sleep Across the Human Life Span** With age, humans require less sleep.

Source: Roff Warg, H. P., Muzio, J. N., & Dement, W. C. (1966, 29 April). Ontogenetic development of human dream-sleep cycle. *Science 152*, 604–619 (Figure 1, p. 608). http://www.sciencemag.org/content/152/3722/604.extract

Sleep and Neuroscience: Does Sleep Deprivation Affect Neurons?

Maybe you've been there: Following an (unwise) all-nighter of studying for an important exam you find that the answers you are sure you know just simply do not come to mind. Perhaps your mind goes blank or you simply find yourself unable to recall information that you memorized just hours or even minutes before. You might even feel like your brain is just not working. In a sense, a recent study shows, you are right.

The study examined how sleep deprivation affects the functioning of specific neurons in the brain (Nir & others, 2017). Volunteers who were having continuous single neuron recordings of hundreds of neurons in their brains for medical reasons took part in the study. In addition, and also for medical reasons, some of them were asked to stay awake an entire night before the study. Participants completed a simple task: indicating, as quickly as possible, whether an image presented for a fraction of a second was a face (or not), all while the functioning of single neurons in their brains were monitored.

©Radius Images/Getty Images Plus

Not surprisingly, participants who had not slept performed more poorly on the task: They were slower to complete the judgments and their judgments were less accurate. The longer the task continued, the worse their performance became. The researchers looked specifically at neuronal firing just before and just after the participants made mistakes. What they found was fascinating: Just before these cognitive lapses, individual neurons in the brain were themselves slower to respond and their spike of activity was weaker. After sleep deprivation, even our neurons are sluggish.

This study also demonstrated the battle that unfolds in the brain when a person is striving mightily to complete a task while also needing sleep. The time a person spends awake is related to something scientists call "sleep pressure." Interestingly, sleep pressure is reflected in theta waves in the brain (Bernardi & others, 2015). This means that a person completing a task while sleep deprived is in a very difficult position: The brain has "sort of" gone to sleep (Vyazovsky & others, 2011), even as the person is struggling to complete a task (and stay awake). Not surprisingly, the emergence of theta waves is associated with poor performance on motor and cognitive tasks during wakefulness (Chellappa, Morris, & Scheer, 2017; Devita & others, 2017) and theta waves were especially strong just prior to mistakes (Nir & others, 2017).

Consider that in this study, the task was a very simple one, just recognizing that a face was a face. The researchers suggest that visual recognition itself may slow down as a result of sleep deprivation (Nir & others, 2017). Consider what that might mean the next time you consider staying up all night studying prior to a multiple choice test. You just might not recognize the correct answer right in front of you—the one you totally know you knew.

\\ If you have not had time to study for a test, would it make more sense to lose sleep to study or get a good night's rest? Why?

Sleep may benefit physical growth and brain development in infants and children. For example, deep sleep coincides with the release of growth hormone in children. Children are more likely to sleep well when they avoid caffeine, experience a regular bedtime routine, are read to before going to bed, and do not have a television in their bedroom (Mindell & others, 2009).

As children age, their sleep patterns change. Many adolescents stay up later at night and sleep longer in the morning than they did when they were children, and these shifting sleep patterns may influence their academic work. During adolescence, the brain, especially the cerebral cortex, is continuing to develop, and the adolescent's need for sleep may be linked to this brain development (Zhang & others, 2017).

Studies of adolescent sleep patterns show that, if given the opportunity, adolescents will sleep about 9 and half hours a night (Carskadon, 2006, 2011a, 2011b; Crowley &

Carskadon, 2010; Tarokh & Carskadon, 2010). Most, however, get considerably less than 9 hours of sleep, especially during the week. This shortfall creates a sleep debt that adolescents often attempt to make up on the weekend.

The reason for this adolescent sleep pattern appears to be a delay in the nightly release of the sleep-inducing hormone melatonin. Melatonin is secreted at about 9:30 P.M. in younger adolescents and approximately an hour later in older adolescents. A number of communities have recognized that adolescents require more sleep and have instituted later start times for school, to good effect (Watson & others, 2017). When middle- and high-school students start their days a bit later, health and grades benefit.

Do sleep patterns change in emerging adulthood (18–25 years of age)? Research indicates that they do (Galambos, Howard, & Maggs, 2011). In one study, the weekday bedtimes and rise times of first-year college students were approximately 1 hour 15 minutes later than those of high school seniors (Lund & others, 2010). However, the first-year college students had later bedtimes and rise times than third- and fourth-year college students, indicating that at about 20–22 years of age, a reverse in the timing of bedtimes and rise times occurs.

Sleep patterns also change as people age through the middle-adult (40s and 50s) and late-adult (60s and older) years (Malhotra & Desai, 2010; Nakamura & others, 2011; Schwarz & others, 2017). Many adults in these age spans go to bed earlier at night and wake up earlier in the morning than they did in their younger years. As well, beginning in the 40s, individuals report that they are less likely to sleep through the entire night than when they were younger. Middle-aged adults also spend less time in deep sleep than they did before their middle years.

One study found that changes in sleep duration across five years in middle age were linked to cognitive abilities such as problem solving and memory (Ferrie & others, 2011). In this study, a decrease from 6, 7, or 8 hours of sleep and an increase from 7 or 8 hours were related to lower scores on most cognitive assessments. In late adulthood, approximately 50 percent of older adults complain of having difficulty sleeping (Neikrug & Ancoli-Israel, 2010). Poor sleep and daytime sleepiness are associated with earlier death (Beydoun & others, 2017).

Sleep and Disease

Sleep plays a role in a large number of health problems, diseases, and disorders. For example, stroke and asthma attacks are more common during the night and in the early morning, probably because of changes in hormones, heart rate, and other characteristics associated with sleep (Teodorescu & others, 2006). Sleeplessness is also associated with obesity, diabetes, and heart disease (Mokhlesi & others, 2017).

Neurons that control sleep interact closely with the immune system (Imeri & Opp, 2009). As anyone who has had the flu knows, infectious diseases make us sleepy. The probable reason is that chemicals called cytokines, produced by the body's cells while we are fighting an infection, are powerfully sleep-inducing (Besedovsky, Lange, & Born, 2012; Davis & Raizen, 2017). Sleep may help the body conserve energy and other resources it needs to overcome infection. Sleeplessness is also associated with less effective immune system functioning (Suzuki & others, 2017; Wilder-Smith & others, 2013).

Sleep problems afflict most people who have psychological disorders, including those with depression (Cho & others, 2017). Individuals with depression often awaken in the early hours of the morning and cannot get back to sleep, and they often spend less time in delta wave or deep sleep than do individuals who are not depressed.

©Brian Hagiwara/Getty Images

Sleep problems are common in many other disorders as well, including Alzheimer disease, stroke, cancer, and so forth. In some cases, however, these problems may be due not to the disease itself but to the drugs used to treat the disease.

Sleep Disorders

Many individuals suffer from undiagnosed and untreated sleep disorders that leave them struggling through the day, feeling unmotivated and exhausted (Klingman, Jungquist, & Perlis, 2017). Some of the major sleep problems are insomnia, sleepwalking and sleep talking, nightmares and night terrors, narcolepsy, and sleep apnea.

INSOMNIA   A common sleep problem is *insomnia,* the inability to sleep. Insomnia can involve a problem in falling asleep, waking up during the night, or waking up too early. Between 3 and 5 adults suffer from insomnia (Li & others, 2017). Insomnia is more common among women and older adults, as well as individuals who are thin, stressed, or depressed (Sateia & others, 2017).

For short-term insomnia, most physicians prescribe sleeping pills. However, most sleeping pills stop working after several weeks of nightly use, and their long-term use can interfere with good sleep.

In many cases, mild insomnia often can be reduced by simply practicing good sleep habits. Here are a few tips:

- Always go to bed at the same time, even on weekends.
- Sleep in a dark, quiet place.
- Use your bed only for sleeping, not other tasks.
- Take a hot bath before bed.

In more serious cases, researchers are experimenting with light therapy, melatonin supplements, and other ways to alter circadian cycles (Neubauer, 2014; van Maanen & others, 2016). Behavioral changes (such as avoiding naps and setting an alarm in the morning) can help insomniacs increase their sleep time and awaken less frequently in the night.

SLEEPWALKING AND SLEEP TALKING   *Somnambulism* is the formal term for sleepwalking, which occurs during the deepest stages of sleep (Gedam, Patil, & Shivji, 2018). Somnambulism takes place during stages 3 and 4, usually early in the night, when a person is unlikely to be dreaming. So, it is not the case that people who are sleepwalking are acting out their dreams.

The specific causes of sleepwalking have not been identified, but it is more likely to occur when individuals are sleep deprived or have been drinking alcohol. There is nothing abnormal about sleepwalking, and despite superstition, it is safe to awaken sleepwalkers. In fact, they probably should be awakened, as they may harm themselves wandering around in the dark.

Another quirky night behavior is sleep talking, or *somniloquy.* If you interrogate sleep talkers, can you find out what they did, for instance, last Thursday night? Probably not. Although sleep talkers will converse with you and make fairly coherent statements, they are soundly asleep. Thus, even if a sleep talker mumbles a response to your question, do not count on its accuracy.

There is some evidence of an even rarer sleep behavior—sleep eating. Ambien is a widely prescribed sleep medication for insomnia. Some Ambien users began to notice odd things upon waking up from a much-needed good night's sleep, such as candy wrappers strewn around the room, crumbs in the bed, and food missing from the refrigerator. One woman gained 100 pounds without changing her awake eating or exercise habits. How could this be? Sleep eating is a noted side effect of this sleep aid (Wong & others, 2017).

The phenomenon of sleep eating illustrates that even when we feel fast asleep, we may be "half-awake"—and capable of putting together some unusual late-night snacks, including buttered cigarettes, salt sandwiches, and raw bacon. The maker of Ambien has noted this unusual side effect on the label of the drug. Even more alarming than sleep eating is sleep driving. Sleep experts agree that sleep driving while taking Ambien is rare and extreme but plausible.

For individuals who are battling persistent insomnia, a drug that provides a good night's rest may be worth the risk of these unusual side effects. Furthermore, no one should abruptly stop taking any medication without consulting a physician.

NIGHTMARES AND NIGHT TERRORS

A *nightmare* is a frightening dream that awakens a dreamer from REM sleep (Germain, 2012). The nightmare's content invariably involves danger—the dreamer is chased, robbed, or thrown off a cliff. Nightmares are common. Most of us have had them, especially as young children. Nightmares peak at 3 to 6 years of age and then decline, although the average college student experiences four to eight nightmares a year (Hartmann, 1993). Reported increases in nightmares or worsening nightmares are often associated with an increase in life stressors such as the loss of a relative or a job and conflicts with others.

A *night terror* features sudden arousal from sleep and intense fear. Night terrors are accompanied by a number of physiological reactions, such as rapid heart rate and breathing, loud screams, heavy perspiration, and movement (Gedam, Patil, & Shivji, 2017). Night terrors, which peak at 5 to 7 years of age, are less common than nightmares, and unlike nightmares, they occur during slow-wave, non-REM sleep.

NARCOLEPSY

The disorder *narcolepsy* involves the sudden, overpowering urge to sleep (Antelmi & others, 2017; Dauvilliers & others, 2018). The urge is so uncontrollable that the person may fall asleep while talking or standing up. People with narcolepsy immediately enter REM sleep rather than progressing through the typical sleep stages (Siegel, 2011). Individuals with narcolepsy are often very tired during the day. Narcolepsy can be triggered by extreme emotional reactions, such as surprise, laughter, excitement, and anger. The disorder appears to involve problems with the hypothalamus and amygdala (Brabec & others, 2011).

SLEEP APNEA

Sleep apnea is a sleep disorder in which individuals stop breathing because the windpipe fails to open or because brain processes involved in respiration fail to work properly. People with sleep apnea experience numerous brief awakenings during the night so that they can breathe better, although they usually are not aware of their awakened state. During the day, these people may feel sleepy because they were deprived of sleep at night. A common sign of sleep apnea is loud snoring, punctuated by silence (the apnea).

> **Do It!**
>
> Keep a sleep journal for several nights. Compare your sleep patterns with those described in the text. Do you have a sleep debt? If so, which stages of sleep are you most likely missing? Does a good night's sleep affect your behavior? Keep a record of your mood and energy levels after a short night's sleep and then after you have had at least 8 hours of sleep in one night. What changes do you notice, and how do they compare with the changes predicted by research on sleep deprivation described in the chapter?

Sleep apnea affects between 9 and 38 percent of the population and is more common in men than women (Senaratna & others, 2017). The disorder is most common among infants and adults over the age of 65. Sleep apnea also occurs more frequently among obese individuals, men, and individuals with large necks and recessed chins. Untreated sleep apnea can cause high blood pressure and stroke (Ho & Brass, 2011; Parati, Lombardi, & Narkiewicz, 2007). In addition, the daytime sleepiness caused by sleep apnea can result in accidents, lost productivity, and relationship problems (Devita & others, 2017; Hartenbaum & others, 2006). Sleep apnea is commonly treated by weight-loss programs, side sleeping, propping the head on a pillow, or wearing a device (called a CPAP, for *continuous positive airway pressure*) that sends pressurized air through a mask that prevents the airway from collapsing.

Sleep apnea may also be a factor in *sudden infant death syndrome (SIDS)*, the unexpected sleep-related death of an infant less than 1 year old. SIDS is typically confirmed with an autopsy that reveals no specific cause of death (Chowdhury & others, 2017;

Shapiro-Mendoza & others, 2014). It is common for infants to have short pauses in their breathing during sleep, but for some infants frequent sleep apnea may be a sign of problems in regulating arousal (Rognum & others, 2014). There is evidence that infants who die of SIDS in fact experience multiple episodes of sleep apnea in the days before the fatal event (Kahn & others, 1992). One possible explanation for SIDS is an abnormality in the brain stem areas involving the neurotransmitter serotonin, which is responsible for arousal (Kinney, 2009). Such an abnormality may lead to sleep apnea, which in turn might worsen the brain stem damage, ultimately leading to death.

Dreams

Have you ever dreamed that you left your long-term romantic partner for a former lover? If so, did you tell your partner about that dream? Probably not. However, you would have likely wondered about the dream's meaning, and if so you would not be alone. Since the dawn of language, human beings have attributed great meaning to dreams. As early as 5000 B.C.E., Babylonians recorded and interpreted their dreams on clay tablets. Egyptians built temples in honor of Serapis, the god of dreams. Dreams are described at length in more than 70 passages in the Bible. Psychologists have also examined this fascinating topic.

Sigmund Freud put great stock in dreams as a key to our unconscious minds. He believed that dreams (even nightmares) symbolize unconscious wishes and that analysis of dream symbols could uncover our hidden desires. Freud distinguished between a dream's manifest content and its latent content. **Manifest content** is the dream's surface content, which contains dream symbols that disguise the dream's true meaning; **latent content** is the dream's hidden content, its unconscious—and true—meaning. For example, if a person had a dream about riding on a train and talking with a friend, the train ride would be the dream's manifest content. Freud thought that this manifest content expresses a wish in disguised form. To get to the latent or true meaning of the dream, the person would have to analyze the dream images. In our example, the dreamer would be asked to think of all the things that come to mind when the person thinks of a train, the friend, and so forth. By following these associations to the objects in the manifest content, the latent content of the dream could be brought to light. Artists have sometimes incorporated the symbolic world of dreaming in their work (Figure 8).

manifest content
According to Freud, the surface content of a dream, containing dream symbols that disguise the dream's true meaning.

latent content
According to Freud, a dream's hidden content; its unconscious and true meaning.

FIGURE 8 **Artist's Portrayal of a Dream**
©Timothy Banks

More recently, psychologists have approached dreams not as expressions of unconscious wishes but as mental events that come from various sources. Research has revealed a great deal about the nature of dreams (Domhoff, 2017). A common misconception is that dreams are typically bizarre or strange, but many studies of thousands of dreams, collected from individuals in sleep labs and sleeping at home, have shown that dreams generally are not especially strange. Instead, research shows that dreams are often very similar to waking life (Domhoff, 2017; Schwartz, 2010).

Although some aspects of dreams are unusual, dreams often are no more bizarre than a typical fairy tale, TV show episode, or movie plot. Dreams do generally contain more negative emotion than everyday life; and certainly some unlikely characters, including dead people, sometimes show up in dreams.

There is also no evidence that dreams provide opportunities for problem solving or advice on handling life's difficulties. We may dream about a problem we are dealing with, but we typically find the solution while we are awake and thinking about the dream, not during the dream itself (Domhoff, 2017). There is also no evidence that people who remember their dreams are better off than those who do not (Blagrove & Akehurst, 2000).

So, if the typical dream involves doing ordinary things, what are dreams? The most prominent theories that attempt to explain dreams are cognitive theory and activation-synthesis theory.

Why might we believe dreams are stranger than they really are? Which type of dreams are we more likely to remember? Why?

COGNITIVE THEORY OF DREAMING

The **cognitive theory of dreaming** proposes that we can understand dreaming by applying the same cognitive concepts we use in studying the waking mind. The theory rests on the idea that dreams are essentially subconscious cognitive processing. Dreaming involves information processing and memory. Indeed, thinking during dreams appears to be very similar to thinking in waking life (Domhoff, 2017).

In the cognitive theory of dreaming, there is little or no search for the hidden, symbolic content of dreams that Freud sought. Instead, dreams are viewed as dramatizations of general life concerns that are similar to relaxed daydreams. Even very unusual aspects of dreams—such as odd activities, strange images, and sudden scene shifts—can be understood as metaphorically related to a person's preoccupations while awake (Domhoff, 2017; Zadra & Domhoff, 2010). The cognitive theory also ties the brain activity that occurs during dreams to the activity that occurs during waking life. Earlier we discussed the *default mode network* that refers to a collection of neurons that are active during mind wandering and daydreaming. This network also appears to be active during dreams while we sleep, essentially whenever we are not focused on a task. Research suggests that dreaming during sleep may also emerge from the activity of this network (Perogamvros & others, 2017).

The cognitive theory of dreaming strongly argues that dreams should be viewed as a kind of mental simulation that is very similar in content to our everyday waking thoughts (Aru & Bachmann, 2014; Voss & others, 2014). The same themes that occupy us in our waking life occupy our dreams. That is why this perspective has sometimes been called the *continuity hypothesis* because it emphasizes the link between dreaming and waking thought. This perspective on dreams contrasts with activation-synthesis theory of dreams.

cognitive theory of dreaming
Theory proposing that one can understand dreaming by applying the same cognitive concepts used in studying the waking mind.

activation-synthesis theory
Theory that dreaming occurs when the cerebral cortex synthesizes neural signals generated from activity in the lower part of the brain and that dreams result from the brain's attempts to find logic in random brain activity that occurs during sleep.

ACTIVATION-SYNTHESIS THEORY

According to **activation-synthesis theory,** dreaming occurs when the cerebral cortex synthesizes neural signals generated from activity in the lower part of the brain. Dreams result from the brain's attempts to find logic in random brain activity that occurs during sleep (Hobson, 1999; Hobson & Voss, 2011).

When we are awake and alert, our conscious experience tends to be driven by *external* stimuli—all those things we see, hear, and respond to. During sleep, according to activation-synthesis theory, conscious experience is driven by internally generated stimuli that have no apparent behavioral consequence. A key source of such internal stimulation is spontaneous neural activity in the brain stem (Hobson, 2000). Some of the neural activity that produces dreams comes from external sensory experiences. If a fire truck with sirens blaring drives past your house, you might find yourself dreaming about an emergency. Many of us have had the experience of incorporating the sound of our alarm clock going off in an early morning dream.

You may have noticed how internal states influence your dreams if you have ever been very thirsty while sleeping, and you dream that you get a glass of water.

Supporters of activation-synthesis theory have suggested that neural networks in other areas of the forebrain play a significant role in dreaming (Hobson, Pace-Schott, & Stickgold, 2000). Specifically, they believe that the same regions of the forebrain that are involved in certain waking behaviors also function in particular aspects

©Rubberball/Alamy Stock Photo

of dreaming (Lu & others, 2006). As levels of neurotransmitters rise and fall during the stages of sleep, some neural networks are activated and others shut down. Random neural firing in various areas of the brain leads to dreams that are the brain's attempts to make sense of the activity. So, firing in the primary motor and sensory areas of the forebrain might be reflected in a dream of running and feeling wind on your face. From the activation-synthesis perspective, our nervous system is cycling through various activities, and our consciousness is simply along for the ride (Hobson, 2000, 2004). Dreams are merely a flashy sideshow, not the main event (Hooper & Teresi, 1993). Indeed, one activation-synthesis theorist has referred to dreams as so much "cognitive trash" (Hobson, 2002, p. 23).

Like all dream theories, activation-synthesis theory has its critics. A key criticism is that damage to the brain stem does not necessarily reduce dreaming, suggesting that this area of the brain is not the only starting point for dreaming. Furthermore, life experiences stimulate and shape dreaming more than activation-synthesis theory acknowledges (Domhoff, 2017; Malcolm-Smith & others, 2008).

self-quiz

1. The brain structure that is responsible for the synchronization of circadian rhythm is the
   A. cerebral cortex.
   B. hypothalamus.
   C. reticular formation.
   D. suprachiasmatic nucleus.

2. Immediately entering REM sleep is a symptom of
   A. sleep apnea.
   B. narcolepsy.
   C. night terrors.
   D. somnambulism.

3. The brain waves that are active when we are awake and focused are
   A. alpha waves.
   B. beta waves.
   C. delta waves.
   D. theta waves.

APPLY IT! 4. Bobby and Jill have a friendly competition going in their psychology class. Both have spent several hours studying for the final exam over the last few weeks of school. The night before the final, Bobby declares that he is going to pull an all-nighter, adding 12 full hours to his study time compared to Jill. Altogether, Jill studies 23 hours for the exam, while Bobby studies 35 hours. All other things being equal, who is likely to do better on the exam and why?
   A. Bobby will do better because he studied much more than Jill did.
   B. Jill will do better because she studied a great deal and has the benefit of a good night's sleep, allowing her memory for course material to consolidate.
   C. Bobby will do better because even though he missed some hours of sleep, his memories will be fresher than Jill's.
   D. Jill will do better because Bobby is probably overprepared—35 hours is too long to study anything.

3 Psychoactive Drugs

One way that people seek to alter their own consciousness is through the use of psychoactive drugs. In fact, illicit drug use is a global problem. According to the United Nations Office on Drugs and Crime (UNODC), more than 246 million people worldwide use drugs each year (UNODC, 2017). Drug consumption among youth is a special concern because of its links to problems such as unsafe sex, sexually transmitted infections, unplanned pregnancy, depression, school-related difficulties, and death. The use of drugs among U.S. secondary school students declined in the 1980s but began to increase in the early 1990s (Johnston & others, 2016). Then in the late 1990s and early 2000s, the proportion of secondary school students reporting the use of any illicit drug again declined (Johnston & others, 2016).

Drug use by U.S. high school seniors since 1975 and by U.S. eighth- and tenth-graders since 1991 has been tracked in a national survey called *Monitoring the Future* (Johnston & others, 2016). Figure 9 shows the trends for these groups from 2008 to 2014. Although recent declines in drug use are encouraging, the United States still has one of the highest rates of adolescent drug use of any industrialized nation.

Uses of Psychoactive Drugs

psychoactive drugs
Drugs that act on the nervous system to alter consciousness, modify perception, and change moods.

Psychoactive drugs act on the nervous system to alter consciousness, modify perceptions, and change moods. Some people use psychoactive drugs as a way to deal with life's difficulties. Drinking, smoking, and taking drugs reduce tension, relieve boredom and

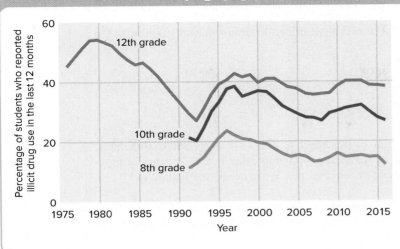

FIGURE 9 **Trends in Drug Use by U.S. Eighth-, Tenth-, and Twelfth-Grade Students** This graph shows the percentage of U.S. eighth-, tenth-, and twelfth-grade students who reported having taken an illicit drug in the last 12 months from 1991 to 2016 (for eighth- and tenth-graders) and from 1975 to 2016 (for twelfth-graders) (Johnston & others, 2016).
Source: Johnston, L. D., O'Malley, P. M., Bachman, J. G., & Schulenberg, J. E. (2013). Monitoring the Future national results on drug use: 2012 Overview, Key Findings on Adolescent Drug Use. Ann Arbor: Institute for Social Research, The University of Michigan.

> Note that data were not collected from eighth- and tenth-graders until 1991. Why do you think these groups were added?
> After the mid-1990s, all age groups show a similar pattern of decline in drug use. Why might this pattern have occurred in all three groups? > What are the implications of using self-reports from children and adolescents in this research? Do you think each group would be similarly likely to be honest, to overreport, or to underreport their drug use?

fatigue, and help people to escape from the harsh realities of life. Some people use drugs because they are curious about their effects.

The use of psychoactive drugs, whether it is to cope with problems or just for fun, can carry a high price tag. These include losing track of one's responsibilities, problems in the workplace and in relationships, drug dependence, and increased risk for serious, sometimes fatal diseases. For example, drinking alcohol may initially help people relax and forget about their worries. If, however, they turn more and more to alcohol to escape reality, they may develop a dependence that can destroy relationships, careers, and their bodies.

Continued use of psychoactive drugs leads to **tolerance,** the need to take increasing amounts of a drug to get the same effect. For example, the first time someone takes 5 milligrams of the tranquilizer Valium, the person feels very relaxed. However, after taking the pill every day for six months, the individual may need to consume twice as much to achieve the same calming effect.

Continuing drug use can also result in **physical dependence,** the physiological need

tolerance
The need to take increasing amounts of a drug to get the same effect.

physical dependence
The physiological need for a drug that causes unpleasant withdrawal symptoms such as physical pain and a craving for the drug when it is discontinued.

psychological dependence
The strong desire to repeat the use of a drug for emotional reasons, such as a feeling of well-being and reduction of stress.

addiction
A physical or a psychological dependence, or both, on a drug.

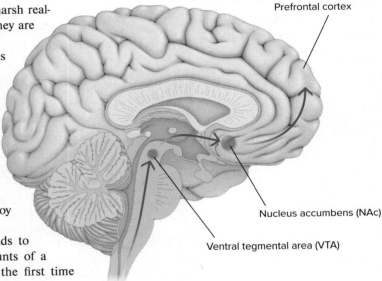

FIGURE 10 **The Brain's Reward Pathway for Psychoactive Drugs** The ventral tegmental area (VTA) and nucleus accumbens (NAc) are important locations in the reward pathway for psychoactive drugs. Information travels from the VTA to the NAc and then up to the prefrontal cortex. The VTA is located in the midbrain just above the pons, and the NAc is located in the forebrain just beneath the prefrontal cortex.
Source: National Institute of Drug Abuse (2001). *Teaching Packet for Psychoactive Drugs.* Washington, DC: National Institute of Drug Abuse, Slide 9.

for a drug that causes unpleasant withdrawal symptoms such as physical pain and a craving for the drug when it is discontinued. **Psychological dependence** is the strong desire to repeat the use of a drug for emotional reasons, such as a feeling of well-being and reduction of stress. **Addiction** refers to a physical or psychological dependence, or both, on the drug. Addiction means that the person's body requires a drug to avoid withdrawal symptoms. **Substance use disorder** is a psychological disorder in which a person's use of a psychoactive drug affects their health, and abilities to work and engage in social relationships.

How does the brain become addicted? Psychoactive drugs increase dopamine levels in the brain's reward pathways (Liujtens & others, 2017). This reward pathway is located in the ventral tegmental area (VTA) and nucleus accumbens (NAc) (Figure 10). Only the

substance use disorder
A psychological disorder in which a person's use of psychoactive drugs (such as alcohol or opiates) affects their health, and abilities to work and engage in social relationships

Ventral tegmental area and *nucleus accumbens* are mouthfuls, but these areas of the brain are vital to the experience of pleasure. Remember these structures; they will come up again and again.

©Henryk Sadura/Alamy Stock Photo

limbic and prefrontal areas of the brain are directly activated by dopamine, which comes from the VTA. Although different drugs have different mechanisms of action, each drug increases the activity of the reward pathway by increasing dopamine transmission. The neurotransmitter dopamine plays a vital role in the experience of rewards.

Types of Psychoactive Drugs

Three main categories of psychoactive drugs are depressants, stimulants, and hallucinogens. All have the potential to cause health or behavior problems or both. To evaluate whether you abuse drugs, see Figure 11.

DEPRESSANTS

Depressants are psychoactive drugs that slow down mental and physical activity. Among the most widely used depressants are alcohol, barbiturates, tranquilizers, and opiates.

depressants
Psychoactive drugs that slow down mental and physical activity.

Alcohol   Alcohol is a powerful drug. It acts on the body primarily as a depressant and slows down the brain's activities. This effect might seem surprising, as people who tend to be inhibited may begin to talk, dance, and socialize after a few drinks. However, people "loosen up" after a few drinks because the brain areas involved in inhibition and judgment slow down. As

Respond "yes" or "no" to the following statements:

Yes	No	
☐	☐	I have gotten into problems because of using drugs.
☐	☐	Using alcohol or other drugs has made my college life unhappy at times.
☐	☐	Drinking alcohol or taking other drugs has been a factor in my losing a job.
☐	☐	Drinking alcohol or taking other drugs has interfered with my studying for exams.
☐	☐	Drinking alcohol or taking drugs has jeopardized my academic performance.
☐	☐	My ambition is not as strong since I've been drinking a lot or taking drugs.
☐	☐	Drinking or taking drugs has caused me to have difficulty sleeping.
☐	☐	I have felt remorse after drinking or taking drugs.
☐	☐	I crave a drink or other drugs at a definite time of the day.
☐	☐	I want a drink or other drug in the morning.
☐	☐	I have had a complete or partial loss of memory as a result of drinking or using other drugs.
☐	☐	Drinking or using other drugs is affecting my reputation.
☐	☐	I have been in the hospital or another institution because of my drinking or taking drugs.

College students who responded yes to items similar to these on the Rutgers Collegiate Abuse Screening Test were more likely to be substance abusers than those who answered no. If you responded yes to just 1 of the 13 items on this screening test, consider going to your college health or counseling center for further screening.

FIGURE 11 **Do You Abuse Drugs?** Take this short quiz to see if your use of drugs and alcohol might be a cause for concern.

Vision is blurred
Speech is impaired
Sensation and perceptions are diminished
Inhibitions, judgment, and intellectual functions are impaired

Motor coordination and reflexes are impaired; balance is disturbed

Blood flow to the skin increases, causing loss of body heat, flushing, and sweating

Heart rate and blood pressure increase

Liver breaks down 0.5–1 ounce of alcohol hourly

Alcohol flows into the stomach and small intestine; excess alcohol in the stomach causes vomiting

Urine output increases in kidneys; more urine passes from the body than is typical

FIGURE 12 **The Physiological and Behavioral Effects of Alcohol** Alcohol has a powerful impact throughout the body. Its effects touch everything from the operation of the nervous, circulatory, and digestive systems to sensation, perception, motor coordination, and intellectual functioning.
(photo) ©George Doyle/Stockbyte/Getty Images

people drink more, their inhibitions decrease even further, and their judgment becomes increasingly impaired. Activities that require intellectual functioning and motor skills, such as driving, become harder to perform. Eventually the drinker falls asleep. With extreme intoxication, the person may lapse into a coma and die. Figure 12 illustrates alcohol's main effects on the body.

The effects of alcohol vary from person to person. Factors in this variation are body weight, the amount of alcohol consumed, individual differences in the way the body metabolizes alcohol, and the presence or absence of tolerance. Men and women differ in terms of the intoxicating effects of alcohol. Because of differences in body fat as well as stomach enzymes, women are likely to be more strongly affected by alcohol than men.

How does alcohol affect the brain? Like other psychoactive drugs, alcohol goes to the VTA and the NAc (Ji & others, 2017). Alcohol also increases the concentration of the neurotransmitter gamma aminobutyric acid (GABA), which is widely distributed in many brain areas, including the cerebral cortex, cerebellum, hippocampus, amygdala, and nucleus accumbens (Blum & others, 2017; Trudell & others, 2014). Researchers believe that the frontal cortex holds a memory of the pleasure involved in prior alcohol use and contributes to continued drinking. Alcohol consumption affects areas of the frontal cortex involved in judgment and impulse control (Bouchard, Brown, & Nadeau, 2012).

After caffeine, alcohol is the most widely used drug in the United States. Over 87 percent of U.S. adults report having drunk an alcoholic beverage at some point in their lives (SAMHSA, 2014). The common use of alcohol is related to other serious problems, including death and injury from driving while drinking. Research has also found a link between alcohol and violence and aggression (Littleton, 2014). More than 60 percent of homicides involve alcohol use by the offender or the victim, and 65 percent of aggressive sexual acts against women are associated with alcohol consumption by the offender.

Sometimes friends think someone who is dangerously drunk just needs to "sleep it off." Drinking to the point of passing out is a symptom of alcohol poisoning. Call 911.

This explains how getting the next drink can become more important than anything else in the person's life.

The Troubles Frequent Binge Drinkers Create . . .

For Themselves[1]

Percent of those surveyed who admitted having had the problem

Missed class	61
Forgot where they were or what they did	54
Engaged in unplanned sex	41
Got hurt	23
Had unprotected sex	22
Damaged property	22
Got into trouble with campus or local police	11
Had five or more alcohol-related problems in school year	47

[1] Frequent binge drinkers were defined as those who had at least four or five drinks at one time on at least three occasions in the previous two weeks.

For Others[2]

Percent of those surveyed who had been affected by drinkers

Had study or sleep interrupted	68
Had to care for drunken student	54
Were insulted or humiliated	34
Experienced unwanted sexual advances	26
Had serious argument	20
Had property damaged	15
Were pushed or assaulted	13
Had at least one of the above problems	87

[2] These figures are from colleges where at least 50 percent of students are binge drinkers.

FIGURE 13 Consequences of Binge Drinking Binge drinking has wide-ranging negative consequences.
(photo) ©George Doyle/Stockbyte/Getty Images. (text) Source: Health and Behavioral Consequences of Binge Drinking in College: A National Survey of Students at 140 Campuses. *Journal of the American Medical Association, vol. 272.*

A special concern is the high rate of alcohol use by U.S. secondary school and college students. However, in the Monitoring the Future survey, the percentage of U.S. high school seniors who reported consuming alcohol in the last 30 days dropped from 72 percent in 1980 to 38.3 percent in 2016. Still, 2 in 5 alcohol users binge drink, defined as drinking more than 5 drinks in a row at one sitting, and binge drinking can be especially problematic, leading to dangerous levels of alcohol.

Binge drinking often increases during the first two years of college and peaks at 21 to 22 years of age (Johnston & others, 2016). Also, as Figure 13 shows, it can take its toll on students (Littlefield & Sher, 2010). In a national survey of drinking patterns on college campuses, almost half of the binge drinkers reported problems such as missed classes, injuries, trouble with police, and unprotected sex (Wechsler & others, 2000, 2002). Binge-drinking college students were 11 times more likely to fall behind in school, 10 times more likely to drive after drinking, and twice as likely to have unprotected sex as college students who did not binge drink. Many emerging adults, however, decrease their alcohol use as they assume adult responsibilities such as a permanent job, marriage or cohabitation, and parenthood (Chen & Jacobson, 2012).

alcoholism
Disorder that involves long-term, repeated, uncontrolled, compulsive, and excessive use of alcoholic beverages and that impairs the drinker's health and social relationships.

Alcoholism is a disorder that involves long-term, repeated, uncontrolled, compulsive, and excessive use of alcoholic beverages and that impairs the drinker's health and social relationships. Approximately 18 million people in the United States are alcoholics (MedlinePlus, 2014). A longitudinal study linked early onset of drinking to later alcohol problems (Hingson, Heeren, & Winter, 2006). Individuals who began drinking alcohol before 14 years of age were more likely to become alcohol dependent than their counterparts who began drinking alcohol at 21 years of age or older.

One in nine individuals who drink continues down the path to alcoholism. Those who do are disproportionately related to alcoholics; family studies consistently find a high frequency of alcoholism in the close biological relatives of alcoholics (Chartier, Thomas, & Kendler, 2017; Savage & others, 2017). A possible explanation is that the brains of people genetically predisposed to alcoholism may be unable to produce adequate dopamine, the neurotransmitter that can make us feel pleasure (Landgren & others, 2011). For these individuals, alcohol may increase dopamine concentration and resulting pleasure to the point where it leads to addiction (Ji & others, 2017; Meyer, Meshul, & Phillips, 2009).

Like other psychological characteristics, though, alcoholism is not all about nature: Nurture matters too. Indeed, research shows that experience plays a role in alcoholism (Kendler, Gardner, & Dick, 2011). Many alcoholics do not have close relatives who are alcoholics (Duncan & others, 2006), a finding that points to environmental influences.

What does it take to stop alcoholism? About one-third of alcoholics recover whether they are in a treatment program or not. This finding came from a long-term study of 700 individuals (Vaillant, 2003). George Vaillant followed the participants for over 60 years, and he formulated the so-called one-third rule for alcoholism: By age 65, one-third are dead or in terrible shape; one-third are still trying to beat their addiction; and one-third are abstinent or drinking only socially. Vaillant found that recovery from alcoholism was predicted by (1) having a strong negative experience with drinking, such as a serious medical emergency; (2) finding a substitute dependency, such as meditation, exercise, or overeating (which has its own adverse health effects); (3) developing new, positive relationships; and (4) joining a support group such as Alcoholics Anonymous.

barbiturates
Depressant drugs, such as Nembutal and Seconal, that decrease central nervous system activity.

Barbiturates **Barbiturates,** such as Nembutal and Seconal, are depressant drugs that decrease central nervous system activity. These types of drugs are likely to make a person feel groggy. Physicians once widely prescribed barbiturates as sleep aids. In heavy dosages, they can lead to impaired memory and decision making. When combined with alcohol (for example, sleeping pills taken after a night of binge drinking), barbiturates can be lethal. Heavy doses of barbiturates by themselves can cause death. For this reason, barbiturates are the drug most often used in suicide attempts. Abrupt withdrawal can produce seizures. Because of the addictive potential and relative ease of toxic overdose, barbiturates have largely been replaced by tranquilizers in the treatment of insomnia.

Handy Survival Tips: Never share prescription drugs. Never take someone else's prescription drugs. Never mix prescription drugs with alcohol.

Tranquilizers **Tranquilizers,** such as Valium and Xanax, are depressant drugs that reduce anxiety and induce relaxation. In small doses tranquilizers can induce a feeling of calm; higher doses can lead to drowsiness and confusion. Tolerance for tranquilizers can develop within a few weeks of usage, and these drugs are addictive. Widely prescribed in the United States to calm anxious individuals, tranquilizers can produce withdrawal symptoms when use is stopped. Prescription tranquilizers were part of the lethal cocktail of drugs that, in 2008, ended the life of actor Heath Ledger, who played the Joker in the Batman film *The Dark Knight*.

tranquilizers
Depressant drugs, such as Valium and Xanax, that reduce anxiety and induce relaxation.

Opioids **Opioids** are a class of drugs that act on the brain's endorphin receptors. These include opium and its natural derivatives (sometimes called *opiates*) as well as chemicals that do not occur naturally but that have been created to mimic the activity of opium. These drugs (also called narcotics) depress activity in the central nervous system and eliminate pain.

Opioids are used as powerful painkillers. The most common drugs derived from opium—morphine and heroin—affect synapses in the brain that use endorphins as their neurotransmitter. When they bind to the brain's opioid receptors, they drive up the production of dopamine, producing feelings of pleasure (NIDA, 2016). When these drugs leave the brain, the affected synapses become understimulated. For several hours after taking an opiate, the person feels euphoric and pain-free and has an increased appetite for food and sex. Opioids are highly addictive, and users experience craving and painful withdrawal when the drug becomes unavailable.

The risk of death from overdose from opioids is very high. Remember, these drugs work by attaching to receptors for endorphins. Such receptors are present in the brain

opioids
A class of drugs that act on the brain's endorphin receptors. These include opium and its natural derivatives (sometimes called opiates) as well as chemicals that do not occur naturally but that have been created to mimic the activity of opium. These drugs (also called narcotics) depress activity in the central nervous system and eliminate pain.

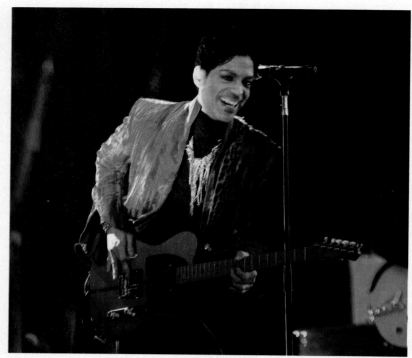
Sadly, Prince Rogers Nelson died in April, 2016, from an accidental overdose of the opioid fentanyl. The artist was known for his dedication to clean living and it is likely he was taking the drug to relieve pain caused by years of performing.
©Northfoto/Shutterstock

stem, the region that controls breathing. Thus, if someone takes too much of an opioid (or an opioid mixed with another drug such as alcohol) they may stop breathing (NIDA, 2016). Naloxone, a drug used to treat opioid overdose, can restore normal breathing. Currently, opioid overdoses in the U.S. represent a national crisis. In 2016, an estimated 64,000 people died from opioid overdose, outnumbering those killed in car accidents by more than 20,000 (NIDA, 2017). A person does not have to be addicted to opioids to die of an overdose of these powerful drugs.

Many people who abuse opioids first encountered them as (legal) prescription pain killers. *Fentanyl* is a fast-acting opioid prescription pain killer that has been implicated in numerous overdoses, including the death of music legend, Prince, in 2016. Fentanyl is estimated to be 50 to 100 times more powerful than morphine (NIDA, 2016).

In 2016, prescription opioids accounted for more deaths than heroin and cocaine combined (NIDA, 2017). The availability of prescription opioids is a public health emergency. Because these drugs are prescribed, people may not realize how powerful and dangerous they are. One healthcare expert cautioned, "Prescription pain pills are similar to having heroin in the medicine cabinet" (Hazelden Betty Ford Foundation, 2015). Even children who live in households where adults have prescription drugs are at risk for overdose (Turkewitz, 2017). Importantly, a recent study showed that a dose of nonopioid medications (such as Tylenol or Motrim) was just as effective as a dose of opioids in treating acute pain in an emergency room (Chang & others, 2017).

Often when a person experiences an overdose, it falls to family and friends to respond. The symptoms of an opioid overdose are (WHO, 2014)

- pinpoint pupils
- unconsciousness
- slowed breathing.

If you think someone has experienced an overdose, immediately call 911 to get help. Bringing pill bottles to the hospital can help professionals know what to do.

STIMULANTS

Stimulants are psychoactive drugs that increase the central nervous system's activity. The most widely used stimulants are caffeine, nicotine, amphetamines, and cocaine.

stimulants Psychoactive drugs, including caffeine, nicotine, amphetamines, and cocaine, that increase the central nervous system's activity.

Caffeine Often overlooked as a drug, caffeine is the world's most widely used psychoactive drug. Caffeine is a stimulant and a natural component of the plants that are the sources of coffee, tea, and cola drinks. Caffeine also is present in chocolate, in many nonprescription medications, and in energy drinks such as Red Bull. People often perceive the stimulating effects of caffeine as beneficial for boosting energy and alertness, but some experience unpleasant side effects.

Caffeinism refers to overindulgence in caffeine. It is characterized by mood changes, anxiety, and sleep disruption. Caffeinism often develops in people who drink five or more cups of coffee (at least 500 milligrams) each day. Common

©C Squared Studios/
Photodisc/Getty Images

Responding to the Opioid Crisis

There is not a group in the United States that has not been affected by the Opioid Crisis. The number of adults aged 24 or younger who died from opioid overdose doubled from 2005 to 2015 (Spencer, 2017). College students are not immune. A survey found that a third of young adults reported opioids to be easy to get and 16 percent reported using prescription drugs not prescribed for them at some point in their lives (Hazelden Betty Ford Foundation, 2015). Student athletes may be particularly at risk as they are likely to receive opioids to treat injuries. Fortunately, communities are taking action to reduce the use and abuse of opioids.

©Robert Dupuis/iStock/Getty Images Plus

Colleges and universities have begun to develop living groups around issues related to drug addiction. These include sober, drug-free housing and specialized living groups for students in recovery (Spencer, 2017). In these living groups, students can pursue the difficult path of recovery surrounded by others on the same path who understand how difficult it can be.

Policy makers, recognizing that addiction is a disease not a crime, have begun to devise innovative ways to treat those addicted to opioids to prevent overdose deaths. Judge Craig Hannah of Buffalo, NY (himself a recovering addict), instituted a special Opiate Crisis Intervention Court (Helmore, 2017). Offenders who report themselves as opioid users are offered the chance to enter a treatment program. Those who accept the offer can look forward to a personal relationship with the judge, as he serves as support on the long road to recovery. It is Judge Hannah's goal to reduce overdose deaths by breaking addiction's hold on people's lives.

---

symptoms are insomnia, irritability, headaches, ringing ears, dry mouth, increased blood pressure, and digestive problems (Uddin & others, 2017).

Caffeine affects the brain's pleasure centers, so it is not surprising that it is difficult to kick the caffeine habit. When individuals who regularly consume caffeinated beverages remove caffeine from their diet, they typically experience headaches, lethargy, apathy, and concentration difficulties. These symptoms of withdrawal are usually mild and subside after several days.

Nicotine   Nicotine is the main psychoactive ingredient in all forms of smoking and smokeless tobacco. Even with all the publicity given to the enormous health risks posed by tobacco, we sometimes overlook the highly addictive nature of nicotine. Nicotine stimulates the brain's reward centers by raising dopamine levels. Behavioral effects of nicotine include improved attention and alertness, reduced anger and anxiety, and pain relief. Figure 14 shows the main effects of nicotine on the body.

Tolerance develops for nicotine both in the long run and on a daily basis, so that cigarettes smoked later in the day have less effect than those smoked earlier. Withdrawal from nicotine often quickly produces strong, unpleasant symptoms such as irritability, craving,

Do It!

Go on a caffeine hunt. Check out the ingredient lists on your favorite beverages, snacks, and painkillers. Which of these contain caffeine? You might be surprised by how much caffeine you consume every day without even knowing it.

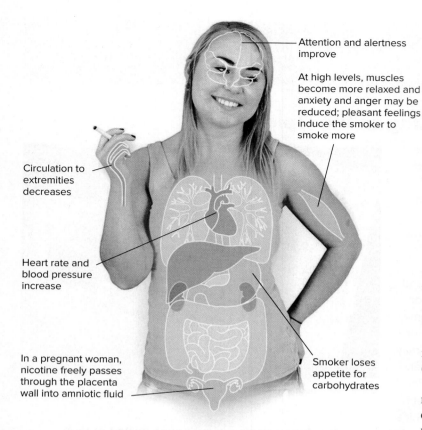

- Attention and alertness improve

- At high levels, muscles become more relaxed and anxiety and anger may be reduced; pleasant feelings induce the smoker to smoke more

- Circulation to extremities decreases

- Heart rate and blood pressure increase

- In a pregnant woman, nicotine freely passes through the placenta wall into amniotic fluid

- Smoker loses appetite for carbohydrates

FIGURE 14 **The Physiological and Behavioral Effects of Nicotine**
Smoking has many physiological and behavioral effects. Highly addictive, nicotine delivers pleasant feelings that make the smoker smoke more, but tobacco consumption poses very serious health risks to the individual.
©Tara McDermott

FIGURE 15 **Trends in Cigarette Smoking by U.S. Secondary School Students** Fortunately, cigarette smoking by U.S. high school students is on the decline.
(photo) ©Photoplay/Flying Colours Ltd/Media Bakery

inability to focus, sleep disturbance, and increased appetite. Withdrawal symptoms can persist for months or longer.

Tobacco poses a grave threat to public health. According to the Centers for Disease Control and Prevention (2017), tobacco is involved in nearly one in every five deaths in the United States, more than the total number killed by AIDS, alcohol, motor vehicles, homicide, illegal drugs, and suicide combined. Smoking is related to cancer not only of the lungs but of many different bodily organs.

Cigarette smoking is decreasing among both adolescents and college students. Figure 15 shows this decline as detected in the Monitoring the Future survey (Johnston & others, 2016). Cigarette smoking peaked in 1996 and 1997 and then decreased as much as 50 percent from 1998 to 2016 (Figure 15).

The drop in cigarette use by U.S. youth may have several sources, including higher cigarette prices, less tobacco advertising reaching adolescents, more antismoking advertisements, and more negative publicity about the tobacco industry than before. Increasingly, adolescents report perceiving cigarette smoking as dangerous, disapprove of it, are less accepting of being around smokers, and prefer to date nonsmokers (Johnston & others, 2016). With respect to college students and young adults, smoking has shown a smaller decline than adolescent and adult smoking.

In sum, cigarette smoking appears to be generally on the decline. Most smokers recognize the serious health risks of smoking and wish they could quit.

Amphetamines *Amphetamines,* or "uppers," are stimulant drugs that people use to boost energy, stay awake, or lose weight. Often prescribed in the form of diet pills, these drugs increase the release of dopamine, which enhances the user's activity level and pleasurable feelings.

Perhaps the most insidious illicit drug for contemporary society is crystal methamphetamine, or crystal meth. Smoked, injected, or swallowed, crystal meth (also called "crank" or "tina") is a synthetic stimulant that causes a powerful feeling of euphoria, particularly the first time it is ingested. Meth is made using household products such as battery acid, cold medicine, drain cleaner, and kitty litter, and its effects have been devastating, notably in rural areas of the United States.

Seriously, don't try it—not even once.

Crystal meth releases enormous amounts of dopamine in the brain, producing intense feelings of pleasure. The drug is highly addictive. The extreme high of crystal meth leads to a severe "come down" experience that is associated with strong cravings. Crystal meth also damages dopamine receptors, so that a person can be chasing a high his or her brain can no longer produce. Because an individual's very first experience with crystal meth can lead to ruinous consequences, the Drug Enforcement Agency has started a website, designed by and targeted at teenagers, www.justthinktwice.com, to share the hard facts of the horrific effects of this and other illicit substances.

Cocaine Cocaine is an illegal drug that comes from the coca plant, native to Bolivia and Peru. Cocaine is either snorted or injected in the form of crystals or powder. Used this way, cocaine floods the bloodstream rapidly, producing a rush of euphoric feelings that lasts for about 15 to 30 minutes. Because the rush depletes the brain's supply of the neurotransmitters dopamine, serotonin, and norepinephrine, an agitated, depressed mood usually follows as the drug's effects decline (Ashok & others, 2017). Figure 16 shows how cocaine affects dopamine levels in the brain.

Crack is a potent form of cocaine, consisting of chips of pure cocaine that are usually smoked. Scientists believe that crack is one of the most addictive substances known. Treatment of cocaine addiction is difficult. Cocaine's addictive properties are so strong that, six months after treatment, more than 50 percent of abusers return to the drug, a statistic that highlights the importance of prevention.

MDMA (Ecstasy) MDMA—called Ecstasy, X, or XTC—is an illegal synthetic drug with both stimulant and hallucinogenic properties. MDMA leads to feelings of warmth, pleasure, and alertness. People have called Ecstasy an "empathogen" because under its influence, users tend to feel warm bonds with others. MDMA produces its effects by releasing serotonin, dopamine, and norepinephrine. The effects of the drug on serotonin are particularly problematic. MDMA depletes the brain of this important neurotransmitter,

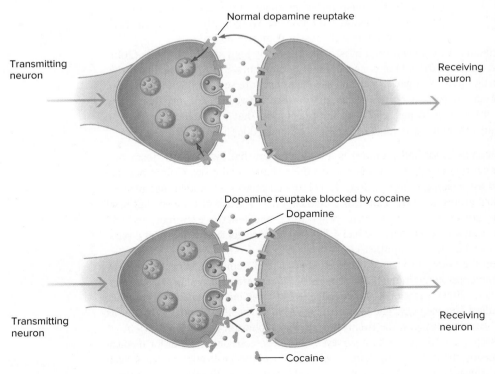

FIGURE 16 **Cocaine and Neurotransmitters** Cocaine concentrates in areas of the brain that are rich in dopamine synapses such as the ventral tegmental area (VTA) and the nucleus accumbens (NAc). (*Top*) What happens in normal reuptake. The transmitting neuron releases dopamine, which stimulates the receiving neuron by binding to its receptor sites. After binding occurs, dopamine is carried back into the transmitting neuron for later release. (*Bottom*) What happens when cocaine is present in the synapse. Cocaine binds to the uptake pumps and prevents them from removing dopamine from the synapse. The result is that more dopamine collects in the synapse, and more dopamine receptors are activated.

©Brand X Pictures/PunchStock

producing lingering feelings of listlessness that often continue for days after use (National Institute on Drug Abuse, 2009).

MDMA impairs memory and cognitive processing. Heavy users of Ecstasy show cognitive deficits that persist even two years after they begin to abstain (Rogers & others, 2009). Because MDMA destroys axons that release serotonin, repeated use might lead to susceptibility to depression (Cadoni & others, 2017; Cowan, Roberts, & Joers, 2008). Other researchers have examined whether MDMA might be useful to help individuals with psychological disorders open up to therapy (Wagner & others, 2017).

HALLUCINOGENS

Hallucinogens are psychoactive drugs that modify a person's perceptual experiences and produce visual images that are not real. Hallucinogens are also called *psychedelic* (from the Greek meaning "mind-revealing") drugs. Marijuana has a mild hallucinogenic effect; LSD, a stronger one.

hallucinogens
Psychoactive drugs that modify a person's perceptual experiences and produce visual images that are not real.

Marijuana

Marijuana is the dried leaves and flowers of the hemp plant *Cannabis sativa,* which originated in Central Asia but is now grown in most parts of the world. The plant's dried resin is known as *hashish.* The active ingredient in marijuana is THC (delta-9-tetrahydrocannabinol). Unlike other psychoactive drugs, THC does not affect a specific neurotransmitter. Rather, marijuana disrupts the membranes of neurons and affects the functioning of a variety of neurotransmitters and hormones. Here we classify marijuana as a mild hallucinogen, although it has diverse effects.

The physical effects of marijuana include increased pulse rate and blood pressure, reddening of the eyes, coughing, and dry mouth. Psychological effects include a mixture of excitatory, depressive, and mildly hallucinatory characteristics. Marijuana can trigger spontaneous unrelated ideas; distorted perceptions of time and place; increased sensitivity to sounds, tastes, smells, and colors; and erratic verbal behavior. The drug can also impair attention and memory. Further, when used daily in large amounts, marijuana can alter sperm count and change hormonal cycles (Olooto, 2017). In addition, pregnant women should avoid using marijuana. Research indicates a number of negative birth outcomes for the offspring of mothers who used marijuana during pregnancy (Volkow, Compton, & Wargo, 2017), including birth defects and later problems in cognitive ability.

Medical marijuana is now legal in about half the United States.
©Wiktor Szymanowicz/REX/Shutterstock

A large number of states in the United States have legalized medical marijuana, and some have legalized it for recreational use among adults. What do you think about these trends?

Marijuana is the illegal drug most widely used by high school students (Johnston & others, 2016). One concern about adolescents' use of marijuana is that the drug might be a gateway to the use of other more serious illicit substances. Although there is a correlational relationship between using marijuana and using other illicit drugs, evidence for the notion that marijuana use leads to the use of other drugs is mixed (Tarter & others, 2006).

LSD

LSD (lysergic acid diethylamide) is a hallucinogen that even in low doses produces striking perceptual changes. Objects change their shapes and glow. Colors become kaleidoscopic and astonishing images unfold. LSD-induced images are sometimes pleasurable and sometimes grotesque. LSD can also influence a user's sense of time so that brief glances at objects are experienced as deep, penetrating, and lengthy examinations, and minutes turn into hours or even days. A bad LSD trip can trigger extreme anxiety, paranoia, and suicidal or homicidal impulses.

LSD's effects on the body can include dizziness, nausea, and tremors. LSD acts primarily on the neurotransmitter serotonin in the brain, though it also can affect dopamine (Halberstadt, 2017; Preller & others, 2017). Emotional and cognitive effects may include rapid mood swings and impaired attention and memory. The use of LSD peaked in the 1960s and 1970s, and its consumption has been decreasing in the twenty-first century (Johnston & others, 2016).

Some of the psychoactive drugs we have surveyed have been considered useful for medical purposes. Consequently, there is ongoing public controversy over the legalization of drugs, such as marijuana, for medical purposes. The debate over medical marijuana illustrates the conflicts that can erupt over the possibility of an illicit drug's legalization. In the late 1970s, it became apparent that marijuana could be used as a treatment for glaucoma (a condition of abnormally high fluid pressure within the eyeball) because cannabis reduces pressure in the eye (American Academy of Ophthalmology, 2003). More recently, researchers have recognized marijuana as a potential treatment for diseases such as AIDS and cancer, as well as for the unpleasant side effects of treating these illnesses (Walsh & others, 2013). For individuals dealing with such challenges, "medical marijuana" may promote appetite, calm anxiety, and stimulate well-being (Joy, Watson, & Benson, 1999). Medical marijuana is now legal in 29 states and the District of Columbia. Figure 17 summarizes the effects of a variety of other psychoactive drugs.

Drug Classification	Medical Uses	Short-Term Effects	Overdose Effects	Health Risks	Risk of Physical/ Psychological Dependence
Depressants					
Alcohol	Pain relief	Relaxation, depressed brain activity, slowed behavior, reduced inhibitions	Disorientation, loss of consciousness, even death at high blood-alcohol levels	Accidents, brain damage, liver disease, heart disease, ulcers, birth defects	Physical: moderate Psychological: moderate
Barbiturates	Sleeping pill	Relaxation, sleep	Breathing difficulty, coma, possible death	Accidents, coma, possible death	Physical and psychological: moderate to high
Tranquilizers	Anxiety reduction	Relaxation, slowed behavior	Breathing difficulty, coma, possible death	Accidents, coma, possible death	Physical: low to moderate Psychological: moderate to high
Opiates (narcotics)	Pain relief	Euphoric feelings, drowsiness, nausea	Convulsions, coma, possible death	Accidents, infectious diseases such as AIDS	Physical: high Psychological: moderate to high
Stimulants					
Amphetamines	Weight control	Increased alertness, excitability; decreased fatigue, irritability	Extreme irritability, feelings of persecution, convulsions	Insomnia, hypertension, malnutrition, possible death	Physical: possible Psychological: moderate to high
Cocaine	Local anesthetic	Increased alertness, excitability, euphoric feelings; decreased fatigue, irritability	Extreme irritability, feelings of persecution, convulsions, cardiac arrest, possible death	Insomnia, hypertension, malnutrition, possible death	Physical: possible Psychological: moderate (oral) to very high (injected or smoked)
MDMA (Ecstasy)	None	Mild amphetamine and hallucinogenic effects; high body temperature and dehydration; sense of well-being and social connectedness	Brain damage, especially memory and thinking	Cardiovascular problems; death	Physical: possible Psychological: moderate
Caffeine	None	Alertness and sense of well-being followed by fatigue	Nervousness, anxiety, disturbed sleep	Possible cardiovascular problems	Physical: moderate Psychological: moderate
Nicotine	None	Stimulation, stress reduction, followed by fatigue, anger	Nervousness, disturbed sleep	Cancer and cardio-vascular disease	Physical: high Psychological: high
Hallucinogens					
LSD	None	Strong hallucinations, distorted time perception	Severe mental disturbance, loss of contact with reality	Accidents	Physical: none Psychological: low
Marijuana*	Treatment of the eye disorder glaucoma	Euphoric feelings, relaxation, mild hallucinations, time distortion, attention and memory impairment	Fatigue, disoriented behavior	Accidents, respiratory disease	Physical: very low Psychological: moderate

*Classifying marijuana is difficult because of its diverse effects.

FIGURE 17 **Categories of Psychoactive Drugs: Depressants, Stimulants, and Hallucinogens** Note that these various drugs have different effects and negative consequences. Marijuana has diverse effects but is typically considered a mild hallucinogen.

1. The most widely consumed drug in the world as a whole is
   A. nicotine.
   B. marijuana.
   C. cocaine.
   D. caffeine.

2. Roger used to feel the effect of one or two alcoholic drinks; he now needs four or five to feel the same effect. Roger is experiencing
   A. physical dependence.
   B. psychological dependence.
   C. withdrawal symptoms.
   D. tolerance.

3. Of the following drugs, the one that is *not* a depressant is
   A. nicotine.
   B. alcohol.
   C. barbiturates.
   D. opiates.

APPLY IT! 4. In high school Kareem was a star student, and drinking alcohol did not fit with his academic ambitions. In college, he started drinking and eventually drank heavily every weekend. He has a lot of trouble making it to his Monday classes, and his grades have dropped from mostly *A*'s to mainly *C*'s, but otherwise he feels he is doing pretty well. A friend asks him about his drinking, and Kareem declares, "I will definitely stop drinking once I am out of college. Besides, no one in my family has ever been an alcoholic, so I am not at risk." Which of the statements below is an accurate assessment of Kareem's belief?
   A. Kareem is probably not at risk for alcoholism, but he might be putting himself at risk for alcohol-related problems, such as drunk driving.
   B. Kareem is at risk for alcohol-related problems only if he also drives while drinking.
   C. Kareem is clearly already suffering from alcohol-related problems. Despite his lack of family history, his alcohol use could put him at risk for dependence. Furthermore, if Kareem is binge drinking, he is risking death by alcohol poisoning.
   D. Kareem appears to have his alcohol use under control and accurately states his lack of risk—he has no family history of alcoholism, and he did not start drinking until he was college-age.

4 Hypnosis

Fifty-three-year-old Shelley Thomas entered a London hospital for a 30-minute pelvic surgery. Before the operation, with her hypnotherapist guiding her, Shelley counted backward from 100 and entered a hypnotic trance. Her surgery was performed with no anesthesia (Song, 2006); rather, Shelley relied on hypnosis to harness her mind's powers to overcome pain.

You may have seen a hypnotist on TV or in a nightclub, putting a person into a trance and then perhaps making him or her act like a chicken or pretend to be a contestant on *The Voice* or enact some similarly strange behavior. When we observe someone in such a trance, we might be convinced that hypnosis involves a powerful manipulation of another person's consciousness. What is hypnosis, really? The answer to this question is itself the source of some debate.

Some psychologists think of hypnosis as an altered state of consciousness, while others believe that it is simply a product of more mundane processes such as focused attention and expectation (Kirsch, 2017). In fact, both views are reasonable, and we may define **hypnosis** as an altered state of consciousness or as a psychological state of altered attention and expectation in which the individual is unusually receptive to suggestions (Heap, 2017). People have used basic hypnotic techniques since the beginning of recorded history, in association with religious ceremonies, magic, and the supernatural (Bartolucci & Lombardo, 2017; Klocek, 2017).

Today, psychology and medicine recognize hypnosis as a legitimate process, although researchers still have much to learn about how it works. In addition, there is continuing debate about whether hypnosis truly is an altered state of consciousness (Lynn, Maxwell, & Green, 2017).

hypnosis
An altered state of consciousness or a psychological state of altered attention and expectation in which the individual is unusually receptive to suggestions.

The Nature of Hypnosis

When Shelley Thomas was in a hypnotic trance, what exactly was happening in her brain and mind? Patterns of brain activity during the hypnotic state suggest that hypnosis produces a state of consciousness similar to other states of consciousness. For example, individuals in a hypnotic state,

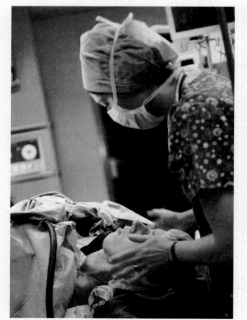

Hypnosis has made its way into some operating rooms as an alternative to traditional anesthesia.
©Virginia Mayo/AP Images

when monitored by an EEG, display a predominance of alpha and beta waves, characteristic of persons in a relaxed waking state (Williams & Gruzelier, 2001). In a brain-imaging study, widespread areas of the cerebral cortex—including the occipital lobes, parietal lobes, sensorimotor cortex, and prefrontal cortex—were activated when individuals were in a hypnotic state (Faymonville, Boly, & Laureys, 2006; Parris, 2017). A similar activation pattern is found in individuals in a nonhypnotic waking state who are engaging in mental imagery. How does the hypnotist lead people into this state of relaxation and imagery?

THE FOUR STEPS IN HYPNOSIS   Hypnosis involves four steps. The hypnotist

1. Minimizes distractions and makes the person to be hypnotized comfortable.

2. Tells the person to concentrate on something specific, such as an imagined scene or the ticking of a watch.

3. Informs the person what to expect in the hypnotic state, such as relaxation or a pleasant floating sensation.

4. Suggests certain events or feelings he or she knows will occur or observes occurring, such as "Your eyes are getting tired." When the suggested effects occur, the person interprets them as being caused by the hypnotist's suggestions and accepts them as an indication that something is happening. This increase in the person's expectations that the hypnotist will make things happen in the future makes the person even more suggestible.

INDIVIDUAL VARIATIONS IN HYPNOSIS   Some people are more easily hypnotized than others, and some are more strongly influenced by hypnotic suggestions. *Hypnotizability* refers to the extent to which a person's responses *are changed* when he or she is hypnotized (Katonai & others, 2017; Milling & others, 2010; Raz & others, 2010). There is no easy way to know if a person is hypnotizable without first trying to hypnotize the individual. If you have the capacity to immerse yourself deeply in an imaginative activity—listening to a favorite piece of music or reading a novel, for example—you might be a likely candidate (Spiegel, 2010). Still, the relationship between the ability to become completely absorbed in an experience and hypnotizability is weak (Nash, 2001).

Explaining Hypnosis

How does hypnosis have its effects? Contemporary theorists disagree as to whether hypnosis is a divided state of consciousness or simply a learned social behavior.

A DIVIDED STATE OF CONSCIOUSNESS   Ernest Hilgard (1977, 1992), in his **divided consciousness view of hypnosis,** proposed that hypnosis involves a special state of consciousness in which consciousness is split into separate components. One component follows the hypnotist's commands, while another component acts as a "hidden observer." Hilgard thought that the "hidden observer" explained why people who are hypnotized will not commit acts that would violate their code of ethics.

Hilgard placed one hand of hypnotized individuals in a bucket of ice-cold water and told them that they would not feel pain but that a part of their mind—a hidden part that would be aware of what was going on—could signal any true pain by pressing a key with the hand that was not submerged (Figure 18). The individuals under hypnosis reported afterward that they had not experienced any pain; yet while their hand had been submerged in the ice-cold water, they had pressed the key with their nonsubmerged hand, and they had pressed it more frequently the longer their hand was in the cold water. Hilgard thus concluded that in

divided consciousness view of hypnosis
Hilgard's view that hypnosis involves a splitting of consciousness into two separate components, one following the hypnotist's commands and the other acting as a "hidden observer."

FIGURE 18   Hilgard's Divided Consciousness Experiment Ernest Hilgard tests a participant in the study in which he had individuals place one arm in ice-cold water.
©Stanford News Service

hypnosis, consciousness has a hidden part that stays in contact with reality and feels pain while another part of consciousness feels no pain.

Critics of Hilgard's view suggest that the hidden observer simply demonstrates that the hypnotized person is not in an altered state of consciousness at all. From this perspective, the hidden observer is simply the person himself or herself, having been given permission to admit to the pain that he or she was always feeling (Green & others, 2005). This argument is part of the social cognitive behavior view of hypnosis.

social cognitive behavior view of hypnosis
The perspective that hypnosis is a normal state in which the hypnotized person behaves the way he or she believes that a hypnotized person should behave.

SOCIAL COGNITIVE BEHAVIOR   Some experts are skeptical that hypnosis is an altered state of consciousness (Chaves, 2000; Lynn & Green, 2011). In the **social cognitive behavior view of hypnosis,** hypnosis is a normal state in which the hypnotized person behaves the way he or she believes that a hypnotized person should behave. The social cognitive perspective frames the important questions about hypnosis around cognitive factors—the attitudes, expectations, and beliefs of good hypnotic participants—and around the powerful social context in which hypnosis occurs (Accardi & others, 2013; Lynn, Maxwell, & Green, 2017). Individuals being hypnotized surrender their responsibility to the hypnotist and follow the hypnotist's suggestions; and they have expectations about what hypnosis is supposed to be like.

Experts have continued to debate whether hypnosis is indeed an altered state of consciousness (Kihlstrom, 2005) or simply a reaction to a special social situation (Lynn & Green, 2011). Although there may be no consensus about what hypnosis is, health professionals have begun to apply this powerful technique to a number of problems.

Uses of Hypnosis

As psychologists' interest in studying consciousness has grown, hypnosis has emerged as a useful tool (Beebe, 2014; Flor, 2014). Some researchers employ hypnosis in a way similar to transcranial magnetic stimulation, to dampen brain processes experimentally (Cox & Bryant, 2008). Combining hypnosis with brain imaging allows researchers to understand both the effects of hypnosis itself and the brain's functioning (Oakley & Halligan, 2011).

Beyond its role in basic research, hypnosis has been applied to a variety of problems. In the United States, practitioners of hypnosis use the technique to treat alcoholism, somnambulism, depression, suicidal tendencies, post-traumatic stress disorder, migraines, overeating, diabetes, and smoking (Alladin, 2014; Entwistle & others, 2014; Hasan & others, 2014). Whether hypnosis actually works for these diverse problems remains debatable (Brown, 2007). Individuals in hypnosis-based treatment programs rarely achieve dramatic results unless they are already motivated to change. Hypnosis is most effective when combined with psychotherapy.

A long history of research and practice has clearly demonstrated that hypnosis can reduce the experience of pain (Jensen & Patterson, 2014; Syrjala & others, 2014). A fascinating study examined the pain perceptions of hypnotized individuals, with the goal of changing their pain threshold. In this study, the brain of each participant was monitored while each received painful electrical shocks (rated 8 or higher on a 1 to 10 pain scale) (Schulz-Stübner & others, 2004). Those who were hypnotized to find the shocks less painful did rate them as lower in pain (giving them a 3 or less). Furthermore, the brain-scanning results were most interesting: The subcortical brain areas (the brain stem and midbrain) of the hypnotized patients responded the same as those of the patients who were not hypnotized, a finding suggesting that these brain structures recognized the painful stimulation. However, the sensory cortex was not activated in the hypnotized patients, an indication that although they sensed pain on some level, they were never conscious of it. In essence, the "ouch" signal never made it to awareness. If a patient is allergic to anesthesia or it is ill-advised for other reasons (the patient has a history of addiction), hypnosis may be a viable alternative. Research shows that it can be effective in pain management for dental and oral surgeries (Montenegro & others, 2017). It has also been shown to assist with cancer symptoms for those at the end of life (Montgomery & others, 2017).

In summary, although the nature of hypnosis remains a mystery, evidence is increasing that hypnosis can play a role in a variety of health contexts, and it can influence the brain in fascinating ways (Jensen & Patterson, 2014). For psychologists, part of the ambiguity about the definition of hypnosis arises from the fact that it has been studied in specific social contexts, involving a hypnotist. It is also possible, however, to experience altered states of consciousness without these special circumstances, as we next consider.

self-quiz

1. The type of brain waves that hypnotized people display include
   A. alpha waves.
   B. delta waves.
   C. gamma waves.
   D. theta waves.

2. The divided consciousness theory of hypnosis receives support from evidence that
   A. hypnosis can block sensory input.
   B. hypnosis can affect voluntary, but not involuntary, behaviors.
   C. hypnotized people often seem to play the role of "good hypnotic subjects."
   D. hypnotized people can be aware of pain sensation without experiencing emotional distress.

3. Hypnosis treatments tend to work best when they are accompanied by

   A. daily meditation.
   B. physical exercise.
   C. yoga.
   D. psychotherapy.

APPLY IT! 4. Ryan and his friends attend a show by the Great Chorizo, a hypnotist. Chorizo asks for volunteers to be hypnotized, and he picks the first five people who raise their hands. He puts the five people into a trance, and within minutes he has them lying on stage sizzling like slices of bacon in a frying pan. When it is all over, one of Ryan's friends remarks that Chorizo must have amazing powers: "That guy could make a person do anything!" Ryan, who has been working on his critical thinking and the psychology of hypnosis, wisely notes which of the following about Chorizo's act?

   A. As long as Chorizo followed the steps of hypnosis described in this text, he probably does have amazing powers of suggestion.
   B. Ryan would need to see Chorizo's training and qualifications prior to rendering judgment.
   C. Chorizo selected the first five volunteers, and these individuals may have been especially motivated, suggestible, and likely to believe in the effects of hypnosis. There is no way to gauge whether Chorizo could have influence over anyone else.
   D. Hypnotizability is similar for all people, so if Chorizo was able to get five people to act like frying bacon, he could probably do just about anything.

5 Meditation

Hypnosis involves a powerful social context, but harnessing the power of consciousness is also possible without the aid of a hypnotist—through meditation. **Meditation** involves attaining a peaceful state of mind in which thoughts are not occupied by worry; the meditator is mindfully present to his or her thoughts and feelings but is not consumed by them. Let's look at how meditation can enhance well-being and examine more closely what it is.

There are many types of meditative practice (Goyal & others, 2014; Kok, Waugh, & Fredrickson, 2013). They share at least two characteristics: focused attention and open monitoring. *Focused attention* means bringing one's awareness to one's inner life and attending to one's thoughts. It means being psychologically present as one thinks. *Open monitoring* refers to the capacity to observe one's thoughts as they happen without getting preoccupied by them; that is, through open monitoring, the person is able to reflect without becoming attached to a particular thought or idea. Research shows that experienced meditators show a pattern of brain activity that is different from both effortful engagement in thought and sleep or drowsiness (Hinterberger & others, 2014).

meditation
The attainment of a peaceful state of mind in which thoughts are not occupied by worry; the meditator is mindfully present to his or her thoughts and feelings but is not consumed by them.

Mindfulness Meditation

Melissa Munroe, a Canadian woman diagnosed with Hodgkin lymphoma (a cancer of the immune system), was tormented by excruciating pain. Seeking ways to cope with the agony, Munroe enrolled in a meditation program. She was skeptical at first. "What I didn't realize," she said, "is that if people have ever found themselves taking a walk in the country-side or in the forest or on a nice pleasant autumn day . . . and find themselves in a contemplative state, that's a form of meditation." Munroe worked hard to use meditation

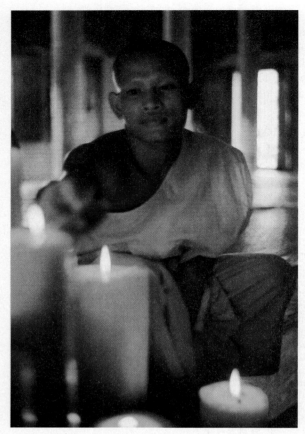
Among those practicing meditation are Zen monks who explore the Buddha-nature at the center of their being.
©Erin Koran

to control her pain. Interestingly, the way she harnessed the power of her mind to overcome pain was by concentrating her thoughts on the pain—not trying to avoid it.

Using *mindfulness meditation,* a technique practiced by yoga enthusiasts and Buddhist monks, Munroe focused on her pain. By doing so, she was able to isolate the pain from her emotional response to it and to her cancer diagnosis. She grew to see her physical discomfort as bearable. Munroe's success shows that contrary to what a nonmeditator might think, meditation is not about avoiding one's thoughts. Indeed, the effort involved in avoidance steers the person away from the contemplative state. Munroe described her thoughts as like people striding by her on the street, walking in the other direction; she explained, "They come closer and closer, then they pass you by." Her sentiment reflects the open monitoring that is common to many forms of meditation.

Jon Kabat-Zinn (2006, 2009) has pioneered using meditation techniques in medical settings. Research by Kabat-Zinn and colleagues has demonstrated the beneficial effects of mindfulness meditation for a variety of conditions, including depression, panic attacks, and anxiety (Miller, Fletcher, & Kabat-Zinn, 1995), chronic pain (Kabat-Zinn, Lipworth, & Burney, 1985), and stress and the skin condition psoriasis (Kabat-Zinn & others, 1998). Many of these effects have also been shown to be long-lasting (Crane & others, 2017).

Richard Davidson and colleagues (including Jon Kabat-Zinn) have studied the brain and immune system changes that might underlie the health and wellness effects of meditation (Davidson & others, 2003; Ferrarelli & others, 2013; Kabat-Zinn & Davidson, 2012). They performed MRIs on the brains of individuals who were in a standard eight-week meditation-training program. After the training program and as compared to a control group, those in the meditation program reported reduced anxiety and fewer negative emotions. Furthermore, brain scans revealed that these individuals showed increased activation in the left hemisphere. Such activation is associated with happiness. In addition, the meditators had a better immune system response to a flu vaccine (Davidson & others, 2003). These results suggest that our conscious minds may have a role to play in enhancing our psychological and physical health (Davidson & Begley, 2012; Kabat-Zinn & Davidson, 2012; Kaliman & others, 2014).

Lovingkindness Meditation

Another popular form of meditation is called *lovingkindness* meditation. The goal of this meditative practice is the development of loving acceptance of oneself and others. Lovingkindness fosters feelings of warmth, friendliness, compassion, and appreciative joy. At its highest level, the person experiences a sense of equanimity, or a feeling of openness to his or her thoughts and feelings without becoming preoccupied with them (Kok, Waugh, & Fredrickson, 2013). In lovingkindness meditation, the meditator begins by developing warm accepting feelings toward himself or herself. Then, the person moves to meditate about a very close other, such as a family member the person loves and respects. Over time, lovingkindness meditation widens to include an ever-broadening circle of people.

Research shows that lovingkindness meditation leads to heightened feelings of social connection, positive emotions (Fredrickson & others, 2008), and better coping with stress (Fredrickson & others, 2003). People who engage in lovingkindness meditation enjoy personal benefits. Might this type of contemplative practice also possess payoffs for the social world? Some research suggests that this form of meditation may help to combat prejudice—that is, unjustified negative views toward an individual based on his or her membership in a group. Research has begun to support the idea that mindfulness practices can help reduce prejudice (Kang, Gray, & Dovidio, 2014; Price-Blackshear & others, 2017).

The Meditative State of Mind

What actually is the meditative state of mind? As a physiological state, meditation shows qualities of sleep and wakefulness yet is distinct from both (Hinterberger & others, 2014). You may have experienced a state called *hypnagogic reverie*—an overwhelming feeling of wellness right before you fall asleep, the sense that everything is going to work out. Meditation has been compared to this relaxed sense that all is well (Friedman, Myers, & Benson, 1998).

In a study of Zen meditators, researchers examined what happens when people switch from their normal waking state to a meditative state (Ritskes & others, 2003). Using fMRI, the experimenters got images of the brain before and after the participants entered the meditative state. They found that the switch to meditation involved initial increases in activation in the basal ganglia and prefrontal cortex (the now familiar area that is often activated during consciousness). However, and interestingly, they also found that these initial activations led to decreases in the anterior cingulate, a brain area that is thought to be associated with acts of will. These results provide a picture of the physical events of the brain that are connected with the somewhat paradoxical state of meditation—controlling one's thoughts in order to let go of the need to control.

Getting Started with Meditation

Would you like to experience the meditative state? If so, you can probably reach that state by following some simple instructions:

- Find a quiet place and a comfortable chair.
- Sit upright in the chair, rest your chin comfortably on your chest, and place your arms in your lap. Close your eyes.
- Now focus on your breathing. Every time you inhale and every time you exhale, pay attention to the sensations of air flowing through your body, the feeling of your lungs filling and emptying.
- After you have focused on several breaths, begin to repeat silently to yourself a single word every time you breathe out. You can make a word up, use the word *one,* or try a word associated with an emotion you want to produce, such as *trust, love, patience, happy*, or *lovingkindness*. Experiment with several different words to see which one works for you.
- If you find that thoughts are intruding and you are no longer attending to your breathing, refocus on your breathing and say your chosen word each time you exhale.

After you have practiced this exercise for 10 to 15 minutes, twice a day, every day for two weeks, you will be ready for a shortened version. If you notice that you are experiencing stressful thoughts or circumstances, simply meditate, on the spot, for several minutes. If you are in public, you do not have to close your eyes; just fix your gaze on a nearby object, attend to your breathing, and say your word silently every time you exhale.

Meditation is an age-old practice. Without explicitly mentioning meditation, some religions advocate related practices such as daily prayer and peaceful introspection. Whether the practice involves praying over rosary beads, chanting before a Buddhist shrine, or taking a moment to commune with nature, a contemplative state clearly has broad appeal and conveys many benefits (Kabat-Zinn & Davidson, 2012; Sharma, Gupta, & Bijlani, 2008). Current research on the contemplative state suggests that there are good reasons why human beings have been harnessing its beneficial powers for centuries.

1. A pre-sleep state of calmness and wellness, with an accompanying feeling of optimism, is called
   A. a trance.
   B. a hypnagogic reverie.
   C. meditation.
   D. mindfulness.

2. Which of the following is *true* about mindfulness meditation?
   A. It involves clearing the mind of all thoughts.
   B. It has not been demonstrated to be effective in pain management.
   C. It increases activation of the right hemisphere of the brain.
   D. It focuses thoughts on specific bodily sensations.

3. In terms of physiology, meditation shows characteristics of
   A. sleep and wakefulness.
   B. sleep and hypnosis.
   C. sleep and hallucinations.
   D. sleep and daydreaming.

APPLY IT! 4. Patricia enjoys walking by a river next to her apartment building nearly every day. As she walks, she loses track of time and just thinks quietly about her life and experiences, letting her thoughts come and go without concern. Sometimes she stops to gaze at the river and enjoys its quiet glistening. After her walks, she always feels refreshed and ready for life's next challenges. One day a friend sees her while walking and says, "Oops, I didn't mean to interrupt your meditation." Patricia says, "Oh I'm not meditating, I'm just taking a walk." Is Patricia right?
   A. Patricia is right. If she does not think she is meditating, then she cannot be meditating.
   B. Patricia is right because she is not sitting down, and she is not repeating a word over and over.
   C. Patricia is not correct. She may not know it, but she is engaged in a contemplative state.
   D. Patricia is not correct. She is meditating because she is in a hypnotic state.

SUMMARY

① The Nature of Consciousness

Consciousness is the awareness of external events and internal sensations, including awareness of the self and thoughts about experiences. Most experts agree that consciousness is likely distributed across the brain. The association areas and prefrontal lobes are believed to play important roles in consciousness.

William James described the mind as a stream of consciousness. Consciousness occurs at different levels of awareness that include higher-level awareness (controlled processes and selective attention), lower-level awareness (automatic processes and daydreaming), altered states of consciousness (produced by drugs, trauma, fatigue, and other factors), subconscious awareness (waking subconscious awareness, sleep, and dreams), and no awareness (unconscious thought).

② Sleep and Dreams

Sleep is a natural state of rest for the body and mind that involves the reversible loss of consciousness. The biological rhythm that regulates the daily sleep/wake cycle is the circadian rhythm. The part of the brain that keeps our biological clocks synchronized is the suprachiasmatic nucleus, a small structure in the hypothalamus that registers light. Such things as jet travel and work shifts can desynchronize biological clocks. Some strategies are available for resetting the biological clock.

We need sleep for physical restoration, adaptation, growth, and memory. Research studies increasingly reveal that people do not function optimally when they are sleep-deprived.

Stages of sleep correspond to massive electrophysiological changes that occur in the brain and that can be assessed by an EEG. The human sleep cycle is defined by stages. In Stage W, the person is awake. In the non-REM stages (stages N1 to N3), the person does not experience rapid eye-movement but moves from light sleep to deep sleep. Stage N3 is the deepest sleep. Most dreaming occurs during stage R or REM sleep. A sleep cycle of five stages lasts about 90 to 100 minutes and recurs several times during the night. The REM stage lasts longer toward the end of a night's sleep.

The sleep stages are associated with distinct patterns of neurotransmitter activity. Levels of the neurotransmitters serotonin, norepinephrine, and acetylcholine decrease as the sleep cycle progresses from stage N1 to N3. Stage R, REM sleep, begins when the reticular formation raises the level of acetylcholine.

Sleep plays a role in a large number of diseases and disorders. Neurons that control sleep interact closely with the immune system, and when our bodies are fighting infection our cells produce a substance that makes us sleepy. Individuals with depression often have sleep problems.

Many people in the United States suffer from chronic, long-term sleep disorders that can impair normal daily functioning. These include insomnia, sleepwalking and sleep talking, nightmares and night terrors, narcolepsy, and sleep apnea.

Contrary to popular belief, most dreams are not bizarre or strange. Freud thought that dreams express unconscious wishes in disguise. The cognitive theory of dreaming attempts to explain dreaming in terms of the same cognitive concepts that are used in studying the waking mind. According to activation-synthesis theory, dreaming occurs when the cerebral cortex synthesizes neural signals emanating from activity in the lower part of the brain. In this view, the rising level of acetylcholine during REM sleep plays a role in neural activity in the brain stem that the cerebral cortex tries to make sense of.

③ Psychoactive Drugs

Psychoactive drugs act on the nervous system to alter states of consciousness, modify perceptions, and change moods. Humans are attracted to these types of drugs because they ease adaptation to change.

Addictive drugs activate the brain's reward system by increasing dopamine concentration. The reward pathway involves the ventral tegmental area (VTA) and nucleus accumbens (NAc). The abuse of psychoactive drugs can lead to tolerance, psychological and physical dependence, and addiction—a pattern of behavior characterized by a preoccupation with using a drug and securing its supply.

Depressants slow down mental and physical activity. Among the most widely used depressants are alcohol, barbiturates, tranquilizers, and opioids.

After caffeine, alcohol is the most widely used drug in the United States. The high rate of alcohol abuse by high school and college students is especially alarming. Alcoholism is a disorder that involves long-term, repeated, uncontrolled, compulsive, and excessive use of alcoholic beverages that impairs the drinker's health and work and social relationships.

Stimulants increase the central nervous system's activity and include caffeine, nicotine, amphetamines, cocaine, and MDMA (Ecstasy). Hallucinogens modify a person's perceptual experiences and produce visual images that are not real. Marijuana has a mild hallucinogenic effect; LSD has a strong one.

 ## Hypnosis

Hypnosis is a psychological state or possibly altered attention and awareness in which the individual is unusually receptive to suggestions. The hypnotic state is different from a sleep state, as confirmed by EEG recordings. Inducing hypnosis involves four basic steps, beginning with minimizing distractions and making the person feel comfortable and ending with the hypnotist's suggesting certain events or feelings that he or she knows will occur or observes occurring.

There are substantial individual variations in people's susceptibility to hypnosis. People in a hypnotic state are unlikely to do anything that violates their morals or that involves a real danger.

Two theories have been proposed to explain hypnosis. In Hilgard's divided consciousness view, hypnosis involves a divided state of consciousness, a splitting of consciousness into separate components.

One component follows the hypnotist's commands; the other acts as a hidden observer. In the social cognitive behavior view, hypnotized individuals behave the way they believe hypnotized individuals are expected to behave.

 ## Meditation

Meditation refers to a state of quiet reflection. Meditation has benefits for a wide range of psychological and physical illnesses. Meditation can also benefit the body's immune system. Research using fMRI suggests that meditation allows an individual to control his or her thoughts in order to "let go" of the need to control.

Mindfulness meditation is a powerful tool for managing life's problems. How we think about our lives and experiences plays a role in determining whether we feel stressed and worried or challenged and excited about life. Seeking times of quiet contemplation can have a positive impact on our abilities to cope with life's ups and downs. The goal of lovingkindness meditation is the development of loving acceptance of oneself and others. This type of meditation fosters feelings of warmth, friendliness, compassion, and appreciative joy.

KEY TERMS

activation-synthesis theory
addiction
alcoholism
automatic processes
barbiturates
biological rhythms
circadian rhythms
cognitive theory of dreaming
consciousness

controlled processes
depressants
divided consciousness view of hypnosis
executive function
hallucinogens
hypnosis
latent content
manifest content

meditation
opiates
physical dependence
psychoactive drugs
psychological dependence
REM sleep
sleep
social cognitive behavior view of hypnosis

stimulants
stream of consciousness
substance use disorder
suprachiasmatic nucleus (SCN)
theory of mind
tolerance
tranquilizers
unconscious thought

ANSWERS TO SELF-QUIZZES

Section 1:   1. B; 2. A; 3. C; 4. B
Section 2:   1. D; 2. B; 3. B; 4. B

Section 3:   1. D; 2. D; 3. A; 4. C
Section 4:   1. A; 2. D; 3. D; 4. C

Section 5:   1. B; 2. D; 3. A; 4. C

5 Learning

Frida: Labrador and Life Saver

n the Fall of 2017, a powerful earthquake hit the state of Oaxaca, Mexico, killing nearly 300 people. As rescuers rushed to the scene, one stood out. She was wearing goggles, a harness, and 2 pairs of boots. When photos hit the media, she became a much beloved hero: Frida, the 7-year-old labrador retriever (Castillo, 2017). There is no doubting that Frida looked adorable but, like other rescue dogs, she was a trained professional. A member of the Mexican Navy's canine unit, in the days following the earthquake she assisted in the rescue of over a dozen people, including several children trapped in a collapsed school. Working with humans and other dogs, Frida has assisted in numerous disaster rescues.

The sight of dogs working to rescue people in the aftermath of a disaster is a common one. We admire their courage and ability but may not always appreciate the grueling process that brought them to these skills. Rescue dogs must demonstrate mastery of numerous difficult tasks, including staying focused even when not on leash and performing search and rescue even without their regular trainers. These dogs must prove that they will perform their duties even when the rewards they receive are little more than a hasty pat on the head from a rescue worker. Rescue dogs are trained professionals. You might wonder how they are able to perform the complex acts required to rescue those in need. The answer can be found in the techniques identified and honed in the psychology of learning, our focus in this chapter.

This chapter begins by defining learning and sketching out its main types—associative learning and observational learning. We then turn to two types of associative learning—classical conditioning and operant conditioning—followed by a close look at observational learning. We next explore the role of cognitive processes in learning, before finally considering biological, cultural, and psychological constraints on learning. As you read, ask yourself about your own beliefs concerning learning. If a dog can learn to enter dangerous areas to search for human survivors surely the human potential for learning has barely been tapped.

1 Types of Learning

Learning anything new involves change. Once you learned the alphabet, it did not leave you; it became part of a "new you" who had been changed through the process of learning. Similarly, once you learn how to drive a car, you do not have to go through the process again at a later time. If you ever try out for the X-Games, you may break a few bones along the way, but at some point you probably will learn a trick or two through the experience, changing from a novice to an enthusiast who can at least stay on top of a skateboard.

By way of experience, too, you may have learned that you have to study to do well on a test, that there usually is an opening act at a rock concert, and that a field goal in U.S. football adds 3 points to the score. Putting these pieces together, we arrive at a definition of **learning:** a systematic, relatively permanent change in behavior that occurs through experience.

learning
A systematic, relatively permanent change in behavior that occurs through experience.

If someone were to ask you what you learned in class today, you might mention new ideas you heard about, lists you memorized, or concepts you mastered. However, how would you define learning if you could not refer to unobservable mental processes? You might follow the lead of behavioral psychologists. **Behaviorism** is a theory of learning that focuses on observable behaviors. From the behaviorist perspective, understanding the causes of behavior requires looking at the environmental factors that produce them. Behaviorists view internal states like thinking, wishing, and hoping as behaviors that are caused by external factors as well. Psychologists who examine learning from a behavioral perspective define learning as relatively stable, observable changes in behavior. The behavioral approach has emphasized general laws that guide behavior change and make sense of some of the puzzling aspects of human life.

 Learning is RELATIVELY permanent—sometimes we forget what we've learned. Also, learning involves EXPERIENCE. Changes in behavior that result from physical maturation would not be considered learning.

behaviorism
A theory of learning that focuses solely on observable behaviors, discounting the importance of such mental activity as thinking, wishing, and hoping.

Behaviorism maintains that the principles of learning are the same whether we are talking about animals or humans. Because of the influence of behaviorism, psychologists' understanding of learning started with studies of rats, cats, pigeons, and even raccoons. A century of research on learning in animals and in humans suggests that many of the principles generated initially in research on animals also apply to humans (Domjan, 2015).

In this chapter we look at two types of learning: associative learning and observational learning. **Associative learning** occurs when we make a connection, or an association, between two events. *Conditioning* is the process of learning these associations. There are two types of conditioning: classical and operant, both of which have been studied by behaviorists.

associative learning
Learning that occurs when an organism makes a connection, or an association, between two events.

In *classical conditioning,* organisms learn the association between two stimuli. As a result of this association, organisms learn to anticipate events. For example, lightning is associated with thunder and regularly precedes it. Thus, when we see lightning, we anticipate that we will hear

This is going to sound very abstract right now. Hang on—once we get to the details, it will make sense.

Classical Conditioning

Operant Conditioning

Stimulus 1
Doctor's office

Stimulus 2
Shot

Behavior

Consequences

FIGURE 1 **Associative Learning: Comparing Classical and Operant Conditioning** (*left*) In this example of classical conditioning, a child associates a doctor's office (stimulus 1) with getting a painful injection (stimulus 2). (*right*) In this example of operant conditioning, performing well in a swimming competition (behavior) becomes associated with getting awards (consequences).

(doctor office) ©Image Source/Jupiterimages; (shot) ©Amble Design; (swimmer) ©Ryan McVay/Getty Images; (medalist) ©MJTH/Shutterstock

thunder soon afterward. Fans of horror films know the power of classical conditioning. Watching a terrifying film, we know that when the camera focuses on a character, but leaves the frame open to show what is behind that person, something terrible is about to happen.

In *operant conditioning,* organisms learn the association between a behavior and a consequence, such as a reward. As a result of this association, organisms learn to increase behaviors that are followed by rewards and to decrease behaviors that are followed by punishment. For example, children are likely to repeat their good manners if their parents reward them with candy after they have shown good manners. Also, if children's bad manners are followed by scolding words and harsh glances by parents, the children are less likely to repeat the bad manners. Figure 1 compares classical and operant conditioning.

Much of learning, however, is not a result of direct consequences but rather of exposure to models performing a behavior or skill. For instance, as you watch someone shoot baskets, you get a sense of how it is done. The learning that takes place when a person observes and imitates another's behavior is called **observational learning.** Observational learning is a common way that people learn in educational and other settings. Observational learning is different from the associative learning described by behaviorism because it relies on mental processes: The learner has to pay attention, remember, and reproduce what the model did. Observational learning is especially important to human beings. In fact, watching other people is another way in which human infants acquire skills.

observational learning
Learning that occurs through observing and imitating another's behavior.

Have you ever noticed that humans' eyes differ from other animals' eyes because the 'whites' can be seen? It might be that this characteristic allows humans to model one another closely—because we can see what the model is looking at.

Human infants differ from baby monkeys in their strong reliance on imitation (Marshall & Meltzoff, 2014). After watching an adult model perform a task, a baby monkey will figure out its own way to do it, but a human infant will do exactly what the model did. Imitation may be the human baby's way to solve the huge problem it faces: to learn the vast amount of cultural knowledge that is part of human life. Many of our behaviors are rather arbitrary. Why do we clap to show approval or wave "hello" or "bye-bye"? The human infant has a lot to learn and may be well served to follow the old adage "When in Rome, do as the Romans do."

Learning applies to many areas of acquiring new behaviors, skills, and knowledge. Our focus in this chapter is on the two types of associative learning—classical conditioning and operant conditioning—and on observational learning.

1. Any situation that involves learning
   A. requires some relatively perma-
      nent change to occur.
   B. requires a great deal of effort.
   C. involves conscious determination.
   D. is relatively automatic.

2. A cat that associates the sound of a
   can opener with being fed has
   learned through
   A. behaviorism.
   B. operant conditioning.
   C. classical conditioning.
   D. observational learning.

3. Which one of the following statements is *true* about learning?
   A. Learning can be accomplished
      only by higher-level species, such
      as mammals.

B. Learning is not permanent.
C. Learning occurs through
   experience.
D. Learning processes in humans are
   distinct from learning processes in
   animals.

APPLY IT! 4. After seeing dogs
catching Frisbees in the park, Lionel decides that he wants to teach his dog Ivan
to do it too. He takes Ivan to the park
and sits with him, making sure that he
watches the other dogs successfully
catching Frisbees. What technique is
Lionel using on Ivan, and what are the
chances for success?
   A. He is using associative learning,
      and his chances for success are

very good, because dogs and
humans both learn this way.
B. He is using operant conditioning,
   and his chances for success are
   very good, because dogs and
   humans both learn this way.
C. He is using observational learning,
   and his chances for success are
   pretty bad, because dogs are not
   as likely as people to learn in this
   way.
D. He is using classical conditioning,
   and his chances for success are
   pretty bad, because dogs are
   much less likely than people to
   learn in this way.

2 Classical Conditioning

Early one morning, Bob is in the shower. While he showers, his wife enters the bathroom and flushes the toilet. Scalding hot water bursts down on Bob, causing him to yell in pain. The next day, Bob is back for his morning shower, and once again his wife enters the bathroom and flushes the toilet. Panicked by the sound of the toilet flushing, Bob yelps in fear and jumps out of the shower stream. Bob's panic at the sound of the toilet illustrates the learning process of **classical conditioning,** in which a neutral stimulus (the sound of a toilet flushing) becomes associated with a meaningful stimulus (the pain of scalding hot water) and acquires the capacity to elicit a similar response (panic).

classical conditioning
Learning process in which a neutral stimulus becomes associated with an innately meaningful stimulus and acquires the capacity to elicit a similar response.

Pavlov's Studies

Even before beginning this course, you might have heard about Pavlov's dogs. The Russian physiologist Ivan Pavlov's work is very well known. Still, it is easy to take its true significance for granted. Importantly, Pavlov demonstrated that neutral aspects of the environment can attain the capacity to evoke responses through pairing with other stimuli and that bodily processes can be influenced by environmental cues.

In the early 1900s, Pavlov was interested in the way the body digests food. In his experiments, he routinely placed meat powder in a dog's mouth, causing the dog to salivate. By accident, Pavlov noticed that the meat powder was not the only stimulus that caused the dog to salivate. The dog salivated in response to a number of stimuli associated with the food, such as the sight of the food dish, the sight of the individual who brought the food into the room, and the sound of the door closing when the food arrived. Pavlov recognized that the dog's association of these sights and sounds with the food was an important type of learning, which came to be called *classical conditioning.*

Pavlov wanted to know why the dog salivated in reaction to various sights and sounds before eating the meat powder. He observed that the dog's behavior included both unlearned and learned components. The unlearned part of classical conditioning is based on the fact that some stimuli automatically produce certain responses apart from any prior learning; in other words, they are innate (inborn). *Reflexes* are such automatic stimulus–response connections. They include salivation in response to food,

Pavlov (the white-bearded gentleman in the center) is shown demonstrating the nature of classical conditioning to students at the Military Medical Academy in Russia.
©Universal Images Group/Getty Images

unconditioned stimulus (US)
A stimulus that produces a response without prior learning.

conditioned stimulus (CS)
A previously neutral stimulus that eventually elicits a conditioned response after being paired with the unconditioned stimulus.

Note that the association between food and salivating is natural (unlearned), while the association between a bell and salivating is learned.

nausea in response to spoiled food, shivering in response to low temperature, coughing in response to throat congestion, pupil constriction in response to light, and withdrawal in response to pain. An **unconditioned stimulus (US)** is a stimulus that produces a response without prior learning; food was the US in Pavlov's experiments. An **unconditioned response (UR)** is an unlearned reaction that is automatically elicited by the US. Unconditioned responses are involuntary; they happen in response to a stimulus without conscious effort. In Pavlov's experiment, salivating in response to food was the UR.

In classical conditioning, a **conditioned stimulus (CS)** is a previously neutral stimulus that eventually elicits a conditioned response after being paired with the unconditioned stimulus. The **conditioned response (CR)** is the learned response to the conditioned stimulus that occurs after CS–US pairing (Pavlov, 1927). Sometimes conditioned responses are quite similar to unconditioned responses, but typically they are not as strong.

In studying a dog's response to various stimuli associated with meat powder, Pavlov rang a bell before giving meat powder to the dog. Until then, ringing the bell did not have a particular effect on the dog, except perhaps to wake the dog from a nap. The bell was a neutral stimulus. However, the dog began to associate the sound of the bell with the food and salivated when it heard the bell. The bell had become a conditioned (learned) stimulus (CS), and salivation was now a conditioned response (CR). In the case of Bob's interrupted shower, the sound of the toilet flushing was the CS, and panicking was the CR after the scalding water (US) and the flushing sound (CS) were paired. Figure 2 summarizes how classical conditioning works, identifying each step in Pavlov's procedure.

Research has shown that salivation can be used as a conditioned response not only in dogs and humans but also in, of all things, cockroaches. In one study, researchers paired the smell of peppermint (the CS, which was applied to the cockroaches' antennae) with sugary water (the US) (Watanabe & Mizunami, 2007). Cockroaches naturally salivate (the UR) in response to sugary foods, and after repeated pairings between the peppermint smell and sugary water, the cockroaches salivated in response to the peppermint scent (the CR). Collecting and measuring the cockroach saliva, the researchers found that the cockroaches had slobbered over that scent for two minutes.

unconditioned response (UR)
An unlearned reaction that is automatically elicited by the unconditioned stimulus.

conditioned response (CR)
The learned response to the conditioned stimulus that occurs after a conditioned stimulus–unconditioned stimulus pairing.

Awesome addition to any résumé: Cockroach Saliva Technician.

FIGURE 2 **Pavlov's Classical Conditioning** In one experiment, Pavlov presented a neutral stimulus (bell) just before an unconditioned stimulus (food). The neutral stimulus became a conditioned stimulus by being paired with the unconditioned stimulus. Subsequently, the conditioned stimulus (bell) by itself was able to elicit the dog's salivation.

ACQUISITION Whether it is human beings, dogs, or cockroaches, the first part of classical conditioning is called acquisition. **Acquisition** is the initial learning of the connection between the US and CS when these two stimuli are paired (as with the peppermint scent and the sugary water). During acquisition, the CS is repeatedly presented followed by the US. Eventually, the CS will produce a response. Note that classical conditioning is a type of learning that occurs without awareness or effort, based on the presentation of two stimuli together. For this pairing to work, however, two important factors must be present: contiguity and contingency.

Contiguity simply means that the CS and US are presented very close together in time—even a mere fraction of a second (Kirkpatrick & Balsam, 2016). In Pavlov's work, if the bell had rung 20 minutes before the presentation of the food, the dog probably would not have associated the bell with the food. However, pairing the CS and US close together in time is not all that is needed for conditioning to occur.

Contingency means that the CS must not only precede the US closely in time; it must also serve as a reliable indicator that the US is on its way (Rescorla, 1966, 1988, 2009). To get a sense of the importance of contingency, imagine that the dog in Pavlov's experiment is exposed to a ringing bell at random times all day long. Whenever the dog receives food, the delivery of the food always immediately follows a bell ring. However, in this situation, the dog will not associate the bell with the food, because the bell is not a reliable signal that food is coming: It rings a lot when no food is on the way. Whereas contiguity refers to the fact that the CS and US occur close together in time, contingency refers to the information value of the CS relative to the US. When contingency is present, the CS provides a systematic signal that the US is on its way.

acquisition
The initial learning of the connection between the unconditioned stimulus and the conditioned stimulus when these two stimuli are paired.

So, contiguity means the CS and US are close in time. Contingency means the CS is reliably and specifically paired with the US.

GENERALIZATION AND DISCRIMINATION

Pavlov found that the dog salivated in response not only to the bell tone but also to other sounds, such as a whistle. These sounds had not been paired with the unconditioned stimulus of the food. Pavlov discovered that the more similar the noise was to the original sound of the bell, the stronger was the dog's salivary flow.

Generalization in classical conditioning is the tendency of a new stimulus that is similar to the original conditioned stimulus to elicit a response that is similar to the conditioned response (Harris, Andrew, & Livesey, 2012; Lissek & others, 2014). Generalization has value in preventing learning from being tied to specific stimuli. For example, once you learn the association between a given CS (say, flashing police lights behind your car) and a particular US (the dread associated with being pulled over), you do not have to learn it all over again when a similar stimulus presents itself (a never-before seen police car with its siren moaning as it cruises directly behind your car). In classical conditioning, this is called stimulus generalization. If you become nervous at the sight of a car that looks like a police car (but is not one), that would also qualify as stimulus generalization.

Stimulus generalization is not always beneficial. For example, the cat that generalizes from a harmless minnow to a dangerous piranha has a major problem; therefore, it is important to also discriminate among stimuli. **Discrimination** in classical conditioning is the process of learning to respond to certain stimuli and not others (Schreurs & others, 2013). To produce discrimination, Pavlov gave food to the dog only after ringing the bell and not after other sounds. In this way, the dog learned to distinguish between the bell and other sounds.

EXTINCTION AND SPONTANEOUS RECOVERY

After conditioning the dog to salivate at the sound of a bell, Pavlov rang the bell repeatedly in a single session and did not give the dog any food. Eventually the dog stopped salivating. This result is **extinction,** which in classical conditioning is the weakening of the conditioned response when the unconditioned stimulus is absent (Bouton & Todd, 2014). Without continued association with the US, the CS loses its power to produce the CR.

Extinction is not always the end of a conditioned response (Goode, Holloway-Erickson, & Maren, 2017). The day after Pavlov extinguished the conditioned salivation to the sound of a bell, he took the dog to the laboratory and rang the bell but still did not give the dog any meat powder. The dog salivated, indicating that an extinguished response can spontaneously recur. **Spontaneous recovery** is the process in classical conditioning by which a conditioned response can recur after a time delay, without further conditioning (Goode, Holloway-Erickson, & Maren, 2017; Franssen & others, 2017). Consider an example of spontaneous recovery you may have experienced: You thought that you had forgotten about (extinguished) an ex-girlfriend or boyfriend, but then you found yourself in a particular context (perhaps the restaurant where you always dined together), and you suddenly got a mental image of your ex, accompanied by an emotional reaction to him or her from the past (spontaneous recovery).

Figure 3 shows the sequence of acquisition, extinction, and spontaneous recovery. Spontaneous recovery can occur several times, but as long as the conditioned stimulus is presented alone (that is, without the unconditioned stimulus), spontaneous recovery becomes weaker and eventually ceases.

generalization (classical conditioning)
The tendency of a new stimulus that is similar to the original conditioned stimulus to elicit a response that is similar to the conditioned response.

discrimination
An unjustified negative or harmful action toward a member of a group simply because the person belongs to that group.

extinction (classical conditioning)
The weakening of the conditioned response when the unconditioned stimulus is absent.

spontaneous recovery
The process in classical conditioning by which a conditioned response can recur after a time delay, without further conditioning.

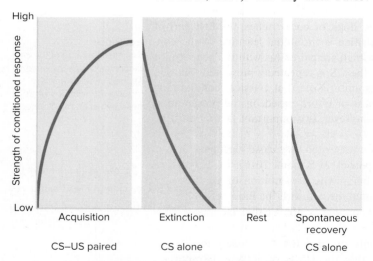

FIGURE 3 **The Strength of a Classically Conditioned Response During Acquisition, Extinction, and Spontaneous Recovery** During acquisition, the conditioned stimulus and unconditioned stimulus are associated. As the graph shows, when this association occurs, the strength of the conditioned response increases. During extinction, the conditioned stimulus is presented alone, and as can be seen, the result is a decrease in the conditioned response. After a rest period, spontaneous recovery appears, although the strength of the conditioned response is not nearly as great at this point as it was after a number of CS–US pairings. When the CS is presented alone again, after spontaneous recovery, the response is extinguished rapidly.

Classical Conditioning in Humans

Classical conditioning has a great deal of survival value for human beings (Powell & Honey, 2013). Here we review examples of classical conditioning at work in human life.

Watson and Rayner conditioned 11-month-old Albert to fear a white rat by pairing the rat with a loud noise. When little Albert was later presented with other stimuli similar to the rat, such as the rabbit shown here with Albert, he was afraid of them too. This study illustrates stimulus generalization in classical conditioning.
©Professor Benjamin Harris, University of New Hampshire

EXPLAINING FEARS   Classical conditioning provides an explanation of fears (Haesen & others, 2017; Waters & others, 2014). John B. Watson (who coined the term *behaviorism*) and Rosalie Rayner (1920) demonstrated classical conditioning's role in the development of fears with an infant named Albert.

First, they showed Albert a white laboratory rat to see if he was afraid of it. He was not (so the rat was a neutral stimulus or *CS*). As Albert played with the rat, the researchers sounded a loud noise behind his head (the noise was then the *US*). The noise caused little Albert to cry (the *UR*). After only seven pairings of the loud noise with the white rat, Albert began to fear the rat even when the noise was not sounded (the *CR*). Albert's fear was generalized to a rabbit, a dog, and a sealskin coat.

Today, Watson and Rayner's (1920) study would violate the ethical guidelines of the American Psychological Association. In any case, Watson correctly concluded that we learn many of our fears through classical conditioning. We might develop fear of the dentist because of a painful experience, fear of driving after having been in a car crash, and fear of dogs after having been bitten by one.

If we can learn fears through classical conditioning, we also can possibly unlearn them through that process (Garcia, 2017; Gujjar & others, 2017). In fact, classical conditioning is incorporated into therapies for treating phobias.

BREAKING HABITS   Psychologists have applied classical conditioning to helping individuals unlearn certain feelings and behaviors (Bulganin, Bach, & Wittmann, 2014). For example, **counterconditioning** is a classical conditioning procedure for changing the relationship between a conditioned stimulus and its conditioned response. Counterconditioning can be used to break the association between certain stimuli (such as a drug of abuse) and positive feelings (Goltseker, Bolotin, & Barak, 2017).

Aversive conditioning is a form of treatment that involves repeated pairings of a stimulus with a very unpleasant stimulus. Electric shocks and nausea-inducing substances are examples of noxious stimuli that are used in aversive conditioning (Kaag & others, 2016). In a treatment to reduce drinking, for example, every time a person drinks an alcoholic beverage, he or she also consumes a mixture that induces nausea. In classical conditioning terminology, the alcoholic beverage is the conditioned stimulus, and the nausea-inducing agent is the unconditioned stimulus. Through a repeated pairing of alcohol with the nausea-inducing agent, alcohol becomes the conditioned stimulus that elicits nausea, the conditioned response. As a consequence, alcohol no longer is associated with something pleasant but rather something highly unpleasant. Antabuse, a drug treatment for alcoholism since the late 1940s, is based on this association (Ullman, 1952). When someone takes this drug, ingesting even the smallest amount of alcohol will make the person quite ill, even if the exposure to the alcohol is through mouthwash or cologne. Antabuse continues to be used in the treatment of alcoholism today (Mutschler & others, 2016; Stein & others, 2017).

Classical conditioning is likely to be at work whenever we engage in mindless, habitual behavior (Wood & Rünger, 2016). Cues in the environment serve as conditioned stimuli, evoking feelings and behaviors without thought. These associations become implicit "if-then" connections: If you are sitting in front of your laptop, then you check your e-mail. These automatic associations can function for good (for instance, you get up every morning and

Poor Albert, right? But anyway, let's bring meaning to his suffering by learning something from it:

US = The loud noise blast

CS = Rat

UR = Crying (in response to the loud blast)

CR = Crying (in response to the rat)

counterconditioning
A classical conditioning procedure for changing the relationship between a conditioned stimulus and its conditioned response.

aversive conditioning
A form of treatment that consists of repeated pairings of a stimulus with a very unpleasant stimulus.

go for a run without even thinking) or ill (you walk into the kitchen and open the fridge for a snack without even thinking).

Let's consider an imaginary Pavlov's dog, called Bill. After years of service in Pavlov's lab, Bill is taken in by a caring family. Now, Bill is not kept in a state of hunger but is allowed to eat whenever he wants. But Bill's family might notice that he runs to his dish, salivating, and seems to want to eat whenever the doorbell rings—even if he is not hungry. Why? Because Bill has acquired an association in which ringing bells evoke food-related behaviors. Bill, our imaginary dog, eats when he is not hungry because of a learned association. Could such a link help explain overeating and obesity in humans? The principles of classical conditioning have been used to combat overweight and obesity in humans by targeting such links (Goldschmidt & others, 2017). To read about this work, see the Intersection.

CLASSICAL CONDITIONING AND THE PLACEBO EFFECT The *placebo effect* is the effect of a substance (such as a pill taken orally) or procedure (such as using a syringe to inject a fluid) that researchers use as a control to identify the actual effects of a treatment. Placebo effects are observable changes (such as a drop in pain) that cannot be explained by the effects of an actual treatment. The principles of classical conditioning help to explain some of these effects (Babel & others, 2017; Geuter, Koban, & Wager, 2017). In this case, the pill or syringe serves as a CS, and the actual drug is the US. After the experience of pain relief following the consumption of a drug, for instance, the pill or syringe might lead to a CR of lowered pain even in the absence of actual painkiller. The strongest evidence for the role of classical conditioning on placebo effects comes from research on the immune system and the endocrine system.

CLASSICAL CONDITIONING AND THE IMMUNE AND ENDOCRINE SYSTEMS Even the human body's internal organ systems can be classically conditioned. The immune system is the body's natural defense against disease. Robert Ader and Nicholas Cohen have conducted a number of studies that reveal that classical conditioning can produce *immunosuppression,* a decrease in the production of antibodies, which can lower a person's ability to fight disease (Ader, 2000; Ader & Cohen, 1975, 2000).

The initial discovery of the link between classical conditioning and immunosuppression came as a surprise. In studying classical conditioning, Ader (1974) was examining how long a conditioned response would last in some laboratory rats. He paired a conditioned stimulus (saccharin solution) with an unconditioned stimulus, a drug called Cytoxan, which induces nausea. Afterward, while giving the rats saccharin-laced water without the accompanying Cytoxan, Ader watched to see how long it would take the rats to forget the association between the two.

Unexpectedly, in the second month of the study, the rats developed a disease and began to die off. In analyzing this unforeseen result, Ader looked into the properties of the nausea-inducing drug he had used. He discovered that one of its side effects was immunosuppression. It turned out that the rats had been classically conditioned to associate sweet water not only with nausea but also with the shutdown of the immune system. The sweet water apparently had become a conditioned stimulus for immunosuppression. So, Ader found that immunosuppression can occur as a result of classical conditioning.

Researchers have found that conditioned immune responses also occur in humans (Tekampe & others, 2017; Tong & others, 2014). For example, in one study, patients with multiple sclerosis were given a flavored drink prior to receiving a drug that suppressed the immune system. After this pairing, the flavored drink by itself lowered immune functioning, similarly to the drug (Giang & others, 1996).

Similar results have been found for the endocrine system (Tekampe & others, 2017). The endocrine system is a loosely organized set of glands that produce and circulate hormones. Research has shown that placebo pills can influence the secretion of hormones if patients had previous experiences with pills containing actual drugs that affected hormone secretion (Benedetti & others, 2003). Studies have revealed that the sympathetic nervous system (the part of the autonomic nervous systems that responds to stress) plays an important role in the learned associations

This is pretty wild. Your body is learning things without your even noticing it.

Learning and Health Psychology: Can Classical Conditioning Help Combat Obesity?

The rates of overweight and obesity in the United States are a public health crisis. A key variable that helps explain the problems of overweight and obesity is that many people eat when they are not hungry. Eating in the absence of hunger (or EAH) plays a role in weight gain. For example, children who eat when they are not hungry are more likely to be overweight as adolescents (Balantekin, Birch, & Savage, 2017). Interestingly, EAH is thought to be caused by reactions to food cues. The term *food cues* refers to the conditioned stimuli that are part of the eating experience, including the sight and smell of tasty food (Goldschmidt & others, 2017). The conditioned response to these cues includes a desire to eat, salivation, and other bodily changes associated with preparing to eat. Essentially, when people look at and smell tasty food, the body automatically prepares to eat. Using the principles of classical conditioning, is it possible to extinguish the link between food cues and eating, thereby reducing EAH? Now, the link between the sight and smell of a freshly baked chocolate chip cookie and eating that cookie might seem so strong that it might be next to impossible to extinguish. Can we separate food cues from eating? Research shows that we can.

In one study (Schyns & others, 2016), overweight women were randomly assigned to one of two conditions. Women in the experimental condition were exposed to the sights and smells of tasty food. These women sat at a table topped with a variety of delicious and decadent foods: chocolate mousse, whipped cream, strawberry mousse, custard, and chocolate cake. They were encouraged to look at the desserts, smell them, and fully imagine themselves eating them—but no tasting allowed. After 80 minutes of fantasizing about eating these desserts, the women were told to throw the desserts in the trash. In the control group, participants were read standard information about body satisfaction and healthy weight for the same amount of time. Next, all participants were required to eat two sandwiches to ensure that no participants were hungry. Finally, the dependent variables were measured. A key dependent variable was EAH, operationalized by a phony "taste test." Participants were presented with the desserts and were told to taste each one and make ratings. They could eat

©Africa Studio/Shutterstock

as much as they wished, and the amount eaten was measured. Recall that because they had just eaten the sandwiches, none of the participants could be hungry, and so the amount of the desserts they ate is a measure of EAH. The results? The experimental group, the women who threw the desserts away, ate less than those in the control condition. In addition, compared to controls, those in the experimental group expressed less agreement with the belief that if tasty food is in front of them, then they must eat it. In short, staring at, smelling, and fantasizing about eating tasty food, but then not eating it, began the process of severing the link between those sights, smells, and thoughts and eating.

Pavlov's original discovery of classical conditioning occurred in the context of food and eating. We should not be surprised, then, that classical conditioning holds a great deal of promise in developing interventions to combat overeating.

\\ **How much is your eating guided by food cues?**

---

between conditioned stimuli and immune and endocrine functioning (Geuter, Koban, & Wager, 2017; Saurer & others, 2008).

TASTE AVERSION LEARNING   Consider this scenario. Mike goes out for sushi with some friends and eats tekka maki (tuna roll), his favorite dish. He then proceeds to a jazz concert. Several hours later, he becomes very ill with stomach pains and nausea. A few weeks later, he tries to eat tekka maki again but cannot stand it. Importantly, Mike does not experience an aversion to jazz, even though he attended the jazz concert that night before getting sick. Mike's experience exemplifies *taste aversion:* a special kind of classical conditioning involving the learned association between a particular taste and nausea

The U.S. Fish and Wildlife Service is trying out taste aversion as a tool to prevent Mexican gray wolves from preying on cattle. To instill taste aversion for beef, the agency is deploying bait made of beef and cowhide but that also contains odorless and flavorless substances that induce nausea (Bryan, 2012). The hope is that wolves that are sickened by the bait will no longer prey on cattle and might even rear their pups to enjoy alternative meals.
©Nagel Photography

Remember, in taste aversion, the taste or flavor is the CS; the agent that made the person sick (it could be a roller-coaster ride or salmonella, for example) is the US; nausea or vomiting is the UR; and taste aversion is the CR.

These results show discrimination in classical conditioning—the kids developed aversions **only** to the specific scapegoat flavors.

habituation
Decreased responsiveness to a stimulus after repeated presentations.

(Davis & Riley, 2010; Garcia & Koelling, 1966; Kwok & Boakes, 2012; Lin, Arthurs, & Reilly, 2014; Scott, 2011).

Taste aversion is special because it typically requires only one pairing of a neutral stimulus (a taste) with the unconditioned response of nausea to seal that connection, often for a very long time. As we consider later, it is highly adaptive to learn taste aversion in only one trial. Consider what would happen if an animal required multiple pairings of a taste with poison. It would likely not survive the acquisition phase. It is notable, though, that taste aversion can occur even if the taste experience had nothing to do with getting sick—perhaps, in Mike's case, he was simply coming down with a stomach bug. Taste aversion can even occur when a person has been sickened by a completely separate event, such as being spun around in a chair (Klosterhalfen & others, 2000). Although taste aversion is often considered an exception to the rules of learning, Michael Domjan (2015) has suggested that this form of learning demonstrates how classical conditioning works in the natural world, where associations matter to survival.

Across species, aversions like taste aversion can be learned based on the way animals select their food. Humans pick our food based on its flavor. As such, it makes sense that we would learn aversions to flavors. In other animals, aversions might be learned based on the scent, color, or other aspects of food (Ward-Fear & others, 2017).

Taste aversion learning is especially important in the context of the traditional treatment of some cancers. Radiation and chemotherapy for cancer often produce nausea in patients, with the result that individuals sometimes develop strong aversions to foods they ingest prior to treatment (Holmes, 1993; Jacobsen & others, 1993). Consequently, they may experience a general tendency to be turned off by food, a situation that can lead to nutritional deficits (Mahmoud & others, 2011).

Researchers have used classical conditioning principles to combat these taste aversions, especially in children, for whom antinausea medication is often ineffective (Skolin & others, 2006) and for whom aversion to protein-rich food is particularly problematic (Ikeda & others, 2006). Early studies demonstrated that giving children a "scapegoat" conditioned stimulus prior to chemotherapy would help limit the taste aversion to only one flavor (Broberg & Bernstein, 1987). For example, children might be given a particular flavor of Lifesaver candy or ice cream before receiving treatment. For these children, the nausea would be more strongly associated with the Lifesaver or the ice cream flavor than with the foods they needed to eat for good nutrition. Fortunately, contemporary cancer treatments may be less likely to cause nausea and treatments for nausea itself have been developed.

DRUG HABITUATION Over time, a person might develop a tolerance for a psychoactive drug and need a higher and higher dose of the substance to get the same effect. Classical conditioning helps to explain **habituation,** which refers to the decreased responsiveness to a stimulus after repeated presentations. A mind-altering drug is an unconditioned stimulus (US): It naturally produces a response in the person's body. This unconditioned stimulus is often paired systematically with a previously neutral stimulus (CS). For instance, the physical appearance of the drug in a pill or syringe, and the room where the person takes the drugs, are conditioned stimuli that are paired with the US of the drug. These repeated pairings should produce a conditioned response, and they do—but it is different from those we have considered so far.

The conditioned response to a drug can be the body's way of *preparing* for the effects of a drug (Everitt & Robbins, 2016). In this case, the body braces itself for the drug effects

Marketing Between the Lines

Classical conditioning is the foundation for many of the commercials bombarding us daily. (Appropriately, when John Watson left the field of psychology, he went on to advertising.) Think about it: Advertising involves creating an association between a product and

©Consumer Trends/Alamy Stock Photo

pleasant feelings (buy that Caffè Misto grande and be happy). Watching TV, you can see how advertisers cunningly apply classical conditioning principles to consumers by showing ads that pair something pleasant (a US) with a product (a CS) in hopes that you, the viewer, will experience those positive feelings toward the product (CR). You might have seen that talking baby (US) trying to get viewers to sign up and buy stocks through E*TRADE (CS). Advertisers continue to exploit classical conditioning principles—for instance, through the technique of product placement, or what is known as *embedded marketing.*

This is how embedded marketing works. Viewing a TV show or movie, you notice that a character is drinking a particular brand of soft drink or eating a particular type of cereal. By placing their products in the context of a show or movie you like, advertisers are hoping that your positive feelings

about the show, movie plot, or a character (the UR) carry over to their product (the CS). Sure, it may seem like a long shot—but all they need to do is enhance the chances that, say, navigating through a car dealership or a grocery store, you will feel attracted to their product. Consider Sheldon from *Big Bang Theory* freaking out after handling a snake and shrieking, "Purell! Purell! Purell!" and the characters on *Modern Family* using iPads. Embedded marketing is also in evidence in many films. In the recent James Bond film, *Casino Royale*, 007 wore an Omega watch. Beats speakers were displayed prominently in a *Transformers* movie. And if you catch a rerun of the syndicated comedy *The Office*, you might recognize that Jim classically conditioned Dwight Schrute with breath mints, modeling Pavlov's work, as you can check out on YouTube (search for *The Office*, Pavlov's Theory). This pop culture moment explicitly demonstrated classical conditioning while also using classical conditioning in product placement for those curiously strong mints, Altoids.

with a conditioned response (CR) that is the opposite of the unconditioned response (UR). For instance, if the drug (the US) leads to an increase in heart rate (the UR), the CR might be a drop in heart rate. The CS—the previously neutral stimulus—serves as a warning that the drug is coming, and the CR in this case is the body's compensation for the drug's effects (Figure 4). In this situation the conditioned response works to decrease the effects of the unconditioned stimulus, making the drug experience less intense. Some drug users try to prevent habituation by varying the physical location of where they take the drug.

This aspect of drug use can play a role in deaths caused by drug overdoses. How might classical conditioning be involved? A user typically takes a drug in a particular setting, such as a bathroom, and acquires a conditioned response to this location (Siegel, 2016). Because of classical conditioning, as soon as the drug user walks into the bathroom, his

FIGURE 4 **Drug Habituation** Classical conditioning is involved in drug habituation. As a result of conditioning, the drug user needs to take more of the drug to get the same effect as before the conditioning. Moreover, if the user takes the drug without the usual conditioned stimulus or stimuli—represented in the middle panel by the bathroom and the drug tablets—overdosing is likely.

(pills): ©Thinkstock/Jupiterimages; (glass): ©Olga Miltsova/Shutterstock; (woman): ©Rick Gomez/Corbis

US | CS | CR

The psychoactive drug is an unconditioned stimulus (US) because it naturally produces a response in a person's body.

Appearance of the drug tablets and the room where the person takes the drug are conditioned stimuli (CS) that are paired with the drug (US).

The body prepares to receive the drug in the room. Repeated pairings of the US and CS have produced a conditioned response (CR).

or her body begins to prepare for and anticipate the drug dose in order to lessen the effect of the drug. However, if the user takes the drug in a location other than the usual one, such as at a rock concert, the drug's effect is greater because no conditioned responses have built up in the new setting, and therefore the body is not prepared for the drug. In cases in which heroin causes death, researchers often have found that the individuals took the drug under unusual circumstances, at a different time, or in a different place relative to the context in which they usually took the drug. In these cases, with no CS signal, the body is unprepared for (and tragically overwhelmed by) the drug's effects. This process can explain why at times, individuals die of an "overdose" when, in fact, the dose of the drug they have ingested would not have typically led to death (Siegel, 2016).

self-quiz

1. Pavlov's dog salivates each time it hears a bell. Now, after several trials of salivating to the bell and *not* receiving any food, the dog stops salivating. The explanation is that
   A. the dog realizes that the bell is not food.
   B. extinction has occurred.
   C. the contingency loop has been disrupted.
   D. spontaneous recovery has not been triggered.

2. A young boy goes to the zoo for the first time with his father and sister. While he is looking at a bird display, his sister sneaks up on him and startles him. He becomes very frightened, and now when he sees birds outside or on TV, he cries. The unconditioned response is
   A. fear.
   B. birds.

   C. having someone sneak up and scare him
   D. going to the zoo.

3. A dog has learned to associate a small blue light coming on with being fed. Now, however, when a small light of any color comes on, the dog salivates. The reason is
   A. extinction.
   B. discrimination.
   C. counterconditioning.
   D. generalization.

APPLY IT! 4. Jake, a college student, goes out to eat with friends at a local Mexican restaurant and orders his favorite food, bean and cheese tamales. Jake and his friends are all dressed in fraternity T-shirts, and they spend the night talking about an upcoming charity event. When he gets home, Jake feels horribly ill and vomits through the night. Later he

finds out that a lot of people in his frat also were sick and that apparently everyone had picked up a stomach bug.
   Consider this as an example of classical conditioning. Based on the description of Jake's experience and your knowledge of classical conditioning, which of the following would you predict to happen in the future?
   A. Jake will probably feel pretty sick the next time he puts on his frat T-shirt.
   B. Jake will probably feel pretty sick the next time someone offers him tamales.
   C. Jake will probably feel pretty sick at the charity event.
   D. Jake should have no trouble eating tamales in the future, because he learned that a stomach bug, not the tamales, made him sick.

3 Operant Conditioning

Recall from early in the chapter that classical conditioning and operant conditioning are forms of associative learning, which involves learning that two events are connected. In classical conditioning, organisms learn the association between two stimuli (US and CS). Classical conditioning is a form of *respondent behavior,* behavior that occurs in automatic response to a stimulus such as a nausea-producing drug, and later to a conditioned stimulus such as sweet water that was paired with the drug.

Classical conditioning explains how neutral stimuli become associated with unlearned, *involuntary* responses. Classical conditioning is not as effective, however, in explaining *voluntary* behaviors such as a student's studying hard for a test, a gambler's playing slot machines in Las Vegas, or a dog's searching for and finding his owner's lost cell phone. Operant conditioning is usually much better than classical conditioning at explaining such voluntary behaviors.

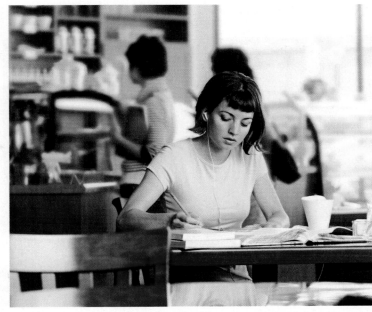

©Juice Images Limited/Alamy Stock Photo

Defining Operant Conditioning

operant conditioning or instrumental conditioning
A form of associative learning in which the consequences of a behavior change the probability of the behavior's occurrence.

Operant conditioning (or **instrumental conditioning**) is a form of associative learning in which the consequences of a behavior change the probability of the behavior's occurrence. The American psychologist B. F. Skinner (1938) developed the concept of operant conditioning. Skinner chose the term *operant* to describe the behavior of the organism. According to Skinner, an operant behavior occurs spontaneously, and the consequences that follow such a behavior determine whether it will be repeated.

Imagine, for example, that you spontaneously decide to take a different route while driving to campus one day. You are more likely to repeat that route on another day if you have a pleasant experience—for instance, arriving at school faster or finding a great new coffee place to try—than if you have a lousy experience such as getting stuck in traffic. In either case, the consequences of your spontaneous act influence whether that behavior happens again.

Recall that *contingency* is an important aspect of classical conditioning in which the occurrence of one stimulus can be predicted from the presence of another one. Contingency also plays a key role in operant conditioning. For example, when a rat pushes a lever (behavior) that delivers food, the delivery of food (consequence) is contingent on that behavior. This principle of contingency helps explain why passersby should never praise, pet, or feed a service dog while he is working (at least without asking first). Providing rewards during such times might interfere with the dog's training.

People sometimes confuse "operant" and "classical" conditioning. Remember that operant conditioning is about what comes AFTER a behavior. Classical conditioning is really about what comes BEFORE an unconditioned stimulus.

Thorndike's Law of Effect

Although Skinner emerged as the primary figure in operant conditioning, the experiments of E. L. Thorndike (1898) established the power of consequences in determining voluntary behavior. At about the same time that Pavlov was conducting classical conditioning experiments with salivating dogs, Thorndike, an American psychologist, was studying cats in puzzle boxes. Thorndike put a hungry cat inside a box and placed a piece of fish outside. To escape from the box and obtain the food, the cat had to learn to open the latch inside the box. At first the cat made a number of ineffective responses. It clawed or bit at the bars and thrust its paw through the openings. Eventually the cat accidentally stepped on the lever that released the door bolt. When the cat returned to the box, it went through the

The law of effect lays the foundation for operant conditioning. What happens AFTER a given behavior determines whether the behavior will be repeated. In 1898? You go, Thorndike!

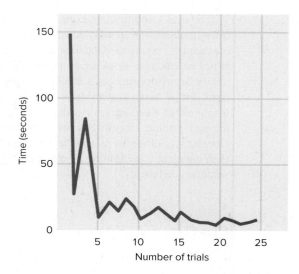

FIGURE 5 **Thorndike's Puzzle Box and the Law of Effect** (*left*) A box typical of the puzzle boxes Thorndike used in his experiments with cats to study the law of effect. Stepping on the treadle released the door bolt; a weight attached to the door then pulled the door open and allowed the cat to escape. After accidentally pressing the treadle as it tried to get to the food, the cat learned to press the treadle when it wanted to escape the box. (*right*) One cat's learning curve over 24 separate trials. Notice that the cat escaped much more quickly after about five trials. It had learned the consequences of its behavior.

law of effect

Thorndike's law stating that behaviors followed by positive outcomes are strengthened and that behaviors followed by negative outcomes are weakened.

same random activity until it stepped on the lever once more. On subsequent trials, the cat made fewer and fewer random movements until finally it immediately stepped on the lever to open the door (Figure 5). Thorndike's resulting **law of effect** states that behaviors followed by satisfying outcomes are strengthened and that behaviors followed by frustrating outcomes are weakened (Domjan, 2016).

The law of effect is important because it presents the basic idea that the consequences of a behavior influence the likelihood of that behavior's recurrence. Quite simply, a behavior can be followed by something good or something bad, and the probability of a behavior's being repeated depends on these outcomes. As we now explore, Skinner's operant conditioning model expands on this idea.

FIGURE 6 **Skinner's Pigeon-Guided Missile** Skinner wanted to help the military during World War II by using pigeons' tracking behavior. A gold electrode covered the tip of the pigeons' beaks. Contact with the screen on which the image of the target was projected sent a signal informing the missile's control mechanism of the target's location. A few grains of food occasionally given to the pigeons maintained their tracking behavior.

Skinner's Approach to Operant Conditioning

Skinner believed that the mechanisms of learning are the same for all species. This conviction led him to study animals in the hope that he could discover the components of learning with organisms simpler than humans, including pigeons. During World War II, Skinner trained pigeons to pilot missiles. Although top navy officials just could not accept pigeons piloting their missiles in a war, Skinner congratulated himself on the degree of control he was able to exercise over the pigeons (Figure 6).

Skinner and other behaviorists made every effort to study organisms under precisely controlled conditions so that they could examine the connection between the operant behavior and the specific consequences in minute detail. One of Skinner's creations in the 1930s to control experimental conditions was the operant conditioning chamber, sometimes called a Skinner box

FIGURE 7 **Skinner's Operant Conditioning Chamber** B. F. Skinner conducts an operant conditioning study in his behavioral laboratory. The rat being studied is in an operant conditioning chamber, sometimes referred to as a Skinner box.
©Nina Leen/Time & Life Pictures/Getty Images

(Figure 7). A device in the box delivered food pellets into a tray at random. After a rat became accustomed to the box, Skinner installed a lever and observed the rat's behavior. As the hungry rat explored the box, it occasionally pressed the lever, and a food pellet was dispensed. Soon the rat learned that the consequences of pressing the lever were positive: It would be fed. Skinner achieved further control by sound-proofing the box to ensure that the experimenter was the only influence on the organism. In many of the experiments, the responses were mechanically recorded, and the food (the consequence) was dispensed automatically. These precautions aimed to prevent human error.

Shaping

Imagine trying to teach even a really smart dog how to do the laundry. The challenge might seem insurmountable, as it is quite unlikely that a dog will spontaneously start putting the clothes in the washing machine. You could wait a very long time for such a feat to happen. It is possible, however, to train a dog or another animal to perform highly complex tasks through the process of shaping.

These human errors might have included cheering the rat on or rewarding him just because the experimenter felt bad for the hungry little guy.

Shaping refers to rewarding successive approximations of a desired behavior (Abramson, Dinges, & Wells, 2016; Francis & Kanold, 2017). For example, shaping can be used to train a rat to press a bar to obtain food. When a rat is first placed in the conditioning box, it rarely presses the bar. Thus, the experimenter may start off by giving the rat a food pellet if it is in the same half of the cage as the bar. Then the experimenter might reward the rat's behavior only when it is within 2 inches of the bar, then only when it touches the bar, and finally only when it presses the bar.

shaping
Rewarding successive approximations of a desired behavior.

Returning to the service dog, rather than waiting for the dog spontaneously to put the clothes in the washing machine, we might reward the dog for carrying the clothes to the laundry room and for bringing them closer and closer to the washing machine. Finally, we might reward the dog only when it gets the clothes inside the washer. Indeed, trainers use this type of shaping technique extensively in teaching animals to perform tricks. A dolphin that jumps through a hoop held high above the water has been trained to perform this behavior through shaping.

Operant conditioning relies on the notion that a behavior is likely to be repeated if it is followed by a reward. A reasonable question is, what makes a reinforcer rewarding? Research examining this question tracks how positive events following a behavior are related to activation of dopamine receptors in the brain (Eaton, Libey, & Fetz, 2016; Steidl & others, 2017).

Principles of Reinforcement

reinforcement
The process by which a stimulus or an event (a reinforcer) following a particular behavior increases the probability that the behavior will happen again.

We noted earlier that a behavior can be followed by something good or something bad. *Reinforcement* refers to those good things that follow a behavior. **Reinforcement** is the process by which a stimulus or event (a *reinforcer*) following a particular behavior increases the probability that the behavior will happen again. Such consequences of a behavior fall into two types, called *positive reinforcement* and *negative reinforcement*. Both types of consequences increase the frequency of a behavior.

Although Thorndike talked about "satisfying" outcomes strengthening behaviors, Skinner took the need for satisfying states out of the equation. For Skinner, if a stimulus increased a behavior, it was reinforcing—no need to talk about how the animal feels.

Through operant conditioning, animal trainers can coax some amazing behaviors from their star performers.
©FilipSinger/EPA-EFE/REX/Shutterstock

POSITIVE AND NEGATIVE REINFORCEMENT

In **positive reinforcement,** the frequency of a behavior increases because it is followed by the presentation of something that increases the likelihood the behavior will be repeated. For example, if someone you meet smiles at you after you say, "Hello, how are you?" and you keep talking, the smile has reinforced your talking. The same principle of positive reinforcement is at work when you teach a dog to "shake hands" by giving it a piece of food when it lifts its paw.

In contrast, in **negative reinforcement** the frequency of a behavior increases because it is followed by the *removal* of something. For example, if your father nagged you to clean out the garage and kept nagging until you cleaned out the garage, your response (cleaning out the garage) removed the unpleasant stimulus (your dad's nagging). Taking an aspirin when you have a headache works the same way: A reduction of pain reinforces the act of taking an aspirin. Similarly, if your laptop is making an irritating buzzing sound, you might give it a good smack on the side, and if the buzzing stops, you are more likely to smack the set again if the buzzing resumes. Ending the buzzing sound rewards the laptop smacking. Even though it is labeled "negative," this kind of reinforcement is about increasing the likelihood that a behavior will be repeated.

Notice that both positive and negative reinforcement involve rewarding behavior—but they do so in different ways. Positive reinforcement means following a behavior with the addition of something, and negative reinforcement means following a behavior with the removal of something. Remember that in this case, "positive" and "negative" have nothing to do with "good" and "bad." Rather, they refer to processes in which something is given (positive reinforcement) or removed (negative reinforcement). Whether it is positive or negative, reinforcement is about increasing a behavior. Figure 8 provides further examples to illustrate the distinction between positive and negative reinforcement.

A special kind of response to negative reinforcement is avoidance learning. **Avoidance learning** occurs when the organism learns that by making a particular response, a negative stimulus can be altogether avoided. For instance, a student who receives one bad grade might thereafter always study hard in order to avoid the negative outcome of bad grades in the future. Even when the bad grade is no longer present, the pattern of behavior sticks. Avoidance learning is very powerful in the sense that the behavior is maintained even in the absence of any aversive stimulus. For example, animals that have been trained to avoid a negative stimulus, such as an electrical shock, by jumping into a safe area may always thereafter gravitate toward the safe area, even when the risk of shock is no longer present.

Experience with unavoidable negative stimuli can lead to a particular deficit in avoidance learning called **learned helplessness,** in which the organism, exposed to uncontrollable aversive stimuli, learns that it has no control over negative outcomes (Reznik & others, 2017). Learned helplessness was first identified by Martin Seligman and his colleagues (Altenor, Volpicelli, & Seligman, 1979; Hannum, Rosellini, & Seligman, 1976), who found that dogs that were first exposed to inescapable shocks were later unable to learn to avoid those shocks, even when they could avoid them (Seligman & Maier, 1967). This inability to learn to escape was persistent: The dogs would suffer painful shocks hours, days, and even weeks later and never attempt to escape. Exposure to unavoidable negative circumstances may also set the

Do It!

Positive reinforcement and negative reinforcement can be difficult concepts to grasp. The real-world examples and accompanying practice exercises on the following website should help to clarify the distinction for you: http://psych.athabascau.ca/html/prtut/

Yes, dog lovers, many have questioned the ethics of this research. What do you think?

positive reinforcement The presentation of a stimulus following a given behavior in order to increase the frequency of that behavior.

negative reinforcement The removal of a stimulus following a given behavior in order to increase the frequency of that behavior.

avoidance learning An organism's learning that it can altogether avoid a negative stimulus by making a particular response.

learned helplessness Through experience with unavoidable aversive stimuli, an organism learns that it has no control over negative outcomes.

Positive Reinforcement

Behavior	Rewarding Stimulus Provided	Future Behavior
You turn in homework on time.	Teacher praises your performance.	You increasingly turn in homework on time.
You wax your skis.	The skis go faster.	You wax your skis the next time you go skiing.
You randomly press a button on the dashboard of a friend's car.	Great music begins to play.	You deliberately press the button again the next time you get into the car.

Negative Reinforcement

Behavior	Stimulus Removed	Future Behavior
You turn in homework on time.	Teacher stops criticizing late homework.	You increasingly turn in homework on time.
You wax your skis.	People stop zooming by you on the slope.	You wax your skis the next time you go skiing.
You randomly press a button on the dashboard of a friend's car.	An annoying song shuts off.	You deliberately press the button again the next time the annoying song is on.

FIGURE 8 **Positive and Negative Reinforcement** Positive reinforcers involve adding something (generally something rewarding). Negative reinforcers involve taking away something (generally something aversive).

stage for humans' inability to learn avoidance, such as with the experience of depression and despair (Kim & others, 2016). Learned helplessness has aided psychologists in understanding a variety of perplexing issues, such as why some victims of domestic violence fail to flee their terrible situation and why some students respond to failure at school by giving up trying.

TYPES OF REINFORCERS   Psychologists classify positive reinforcers as primary or secondary based on whether the rewarding quality of the consequence is innate or learned. A **primary reinforcer** is innately satisfying; that is, a primary reinforcer does not require any learning on the organism's part to make it pleasurable. Food, water, and sexual satisfaction are primary reinforcers. A **secondary reinforcer,** on the other hand, acquires its positive value through an organism's experience; a secondary reinforcer is a learned or conditioned reinforcer. We encounter hundreds of secondary reinforcers in our lives, such as getting an *A* on a test and a paycheck for a job. Although we might think of these as quite positive outcomes, they are not innately positive. We learn through experience that *A*'s and paychecks are good. Secondary reinforcers can be used in a system called a token economy. In a *token economy,* behaviors are rewarded with tokens (such as poker chips or stars on a chart) that can be exchanged later for desired rewards (such as candy or money).

secondary reinforcer
A reinforcer that acquires its positive value through an organism's experience; a secondary reinforcer is a learned or conditioned reinforcer.

primary reinforcer
A reinforcer that is innately satisfying; one that does not take any learning on the organism's part to make it pleasurable.

Parents who are potty-training toddlers often use token economies.

FIGURE 9 **Stimulus Generalization** In the experiment by Norman Guttman and Harry Kalish (1956), pigeons initially pecked a disk of a particular color (in this graph, a color with a wavelength of 550 nm) after they had been reinforced for this wavelength. Subsequently, when the pigeons were presented disks of colors with varying wavelengths, they were likelier to peck those that were similar to the original disk.

SOURCE: Guttman, N., & Kalish, H. I. (1956).

🐚 *If you are accustomed to using your fingers to stretch out text or an image on your smartphone or tablet, you might find yourself trying to do the same thing with a computer monitor and looking foolish. That's a lack of discrimination.*

schedules of reinforcement
Specific patterns that determine when a behavior will be reinforced.

GENERALIZATION, DISCRIMINATION, AND EXTINCTION
Generalization, discrimination, and extinction are important not only in classical conditioning. They also are key principles in operant conditioning.

Generalization In operant conditioning, **generalization** means performing a reinforced behavior in a different situation. For example, in one study pigeons were reinforced for pecking at a disk of a particular color (Guttman & Kalish, 1956). To assess stimulus generalization, researchers presented the pigeons with disks of varying colors. As Figure 9 shows, the pigeons were most likely to peck at disks closest in color to the original. When a student who gets excellent grades in a calculus class by studying the course material every night starts to study psychology and history every night as well, generalization is at work. So, you can think of generalization as exhibiting learning that occurred in one setting in a variety of other similar settings.

Discrimination In operant conditioning, **discrimination** means responding appropriately to stimuli that signal that a behavior will or will not be reinforced (Trask, Thrailkill, & Bouton, 2017). For example, you go to a restaurant that has a "University Student Discount" sign in the front window, and you enthusiastically flash your student ID with the expectation of getting the reward of a reduced-price meal. Without the sign, showing your ID might get you only a puzzled look, not cheap food.

The principle of discrimination helps to explain how a service dog "knows" when he is working. Typically, the dog wears a training harness while on duty but not at other times. Thus, when a service dog is wearing its harness, it is important to treat him like the professional that he is. Similarly, an important aspect of the training of service dogs is the need for selective disobedience. Selective disobedience means that in addition to obeying commands from his human partner, the service dog must at times override such commands if the context provides cues that obedience is not the appropriate response. So, if a guide dog is standing at the corner with his visually impaired human, and the human commands him to move forward, the dog might refuse if he sees the "Don't Walk" sign flashing. Stimuli in the environment serve as cues, informing the organism if a particular reinforcement contingency is in effect.

Extinction In operant conditioning, **extinction** occurs when a behavior is no longer reinforced and decreases in frequency (Orellana Barrera & others, 2017). If, for example, a soda machine that you frequently use starts "eating" your coins without dispensing soda, you quickly stop inserting more coins. Several weeks later, you might try to use the machine again, hoping that it has been fixed. Such behavior illustrates spontaneous recovery in operant conditioning.

SCHEDULES OF REINFORCEMENT
Most of the examples of reinforcement we have considered so far involve *continuous reinforcement,* in which a behavior is reinforced every time it occurs. When continuous reinforcement takes place, organisms learn rapidly. However, when reinforcement stops, extinction takes place quickly. A variety of conditioning procedures have been developed that are particularly resistant to extinction. These involve *partial reinforcement,* in which a reinforcer follows a behavior only a portion of the time. Partial reinforcement characterizes most life experiences. For instance, a golfer does not win every tournament she enters; a chess whiz does not win every match he plays; a student does not get a pat on the back each time she solves a problem.

Schedules of reinforcement are specific patterns that determine when a behavior will be reinforced (DeLeon & others, 2014; Schifani & others, 2017). There are four main

generalization (operant conditioning)
Performing a reinforced behavior in a different situation.

discrimination (operant conditioning)
Responding appropriately to stimuli that signal that a behavior will or will not be reinforced.

extinction (operant conditioning)
Decreases in the frequency of a behavior when the behavior is no longer reinforced.

schedules of partial reinforcement: fixed ratio, variable ratio, fixed interval, and variable interval. With respect to these, *ratio schedules* involve the number of behaviors that must be performed prior to reward, and *interval schedules* refer to the amount of time that must pass before a behavior is rewarded. In a fixed schedule, the number of behaviors or the amount of time is always the same. In a variable schedule, the required number of behaviors or the amount of time that must pass changes and is unpredictable from the perspective of the learner. Let's look concretely at how each of these schedules of reinforcement influences behavior.

Slot machines are on a variable-ratio schedule of reinforcement.
©Massimofusaro/Shutterstock

A *fixed-ratio schedule* reinforces a behavior after a set number of behaviors. For example, if you are playing the slot machines in Atlantic City and if the machines are on a fixed-ratio schedule, you might get $5 back every 20th time you put money in the machine. It would not take long to figure out that if you watched someone else play the machine 18 or 19 times, not get any money back, and then walk away, you should step up, insert your coin, and get back $5. The business world often uses fixed-ratio schedules to increase production. For instance, a factory might require a line worker to produce a certain number of items in order to get paid a particular amount.

Of course, if the reward schedule for a slot machine were that easy to figure out, casinos would not be so successful. What makes gambling so tantalizing is the unpredictability of wins (and losses). Slot machines are on a *variable-ratio schedule,* a system in which behaviors are rewarded an average number of times but on an unpredictable basis. For example, a slot machine might pay off at an average of every 20th time, but the gambler does not know when this payoff will be. The slot machine might pay off twice in a row and then not again until after 58 coins have been inserted. This averages out to a reward for every 20 behavioral acts, but *when* the reward will be given is unpredictable. Variable-ratio schedules produce high, steady rates of behavior that are more resistant to extinction than the other three schedules. Note that to the player, the payoff might seem to depend on the time that has elapsed, but time is not the determining factor. Rather, on ratio schedules, the factor that determines reinforcement is the number of responses emitted. On variable-ratio schedules, that number keeps changing.

Whereas ratio schedules of reinforcement are based on the *number* of behaviors that occur, interval reinforcement schedules are determined by the *time elapsed* since the last behavior was rewarded. A *fixed-interval schedule* reinforces the first behavior after a fixed amount of time has passed. If you take a class that has four scheduled exams, you might procrastinate most of the semester and cram just before each test. Fixed-interval schedules of reinforcement are also responsible for the fact that pets seem to be able to "tell time," eagerly sidling up to their food dish at 5 P.M. in anticipation of dinner. On a fixed-interval schedule, the rate of a behavior increases rapidly as the time approaches when the behavior likely will be reinforced. For example, a government official who is running for reelection may intensify her campaign activities as Election Day draws near.

A *variable-interval* schedule is a timetable in which a behavior is reinforced after a variable amount of time has elapsed. Pop quizzes occur on a variable-interval schedule. So does fishing—you do not know if the fish will bite in the next minute, in a half hour, in an hour, or ever. Because it is difficult to predict when a reward will come, behavior is slow and consistent on a variable-interval schedule.

This is why pop quizzes lead to more consistent levels of studying compared to the cramming that might be seen with scheduled exams.

To sharpen your sense of the differences between fixed- and variable-interval schedules, consider the following example. Penelope and Edith both design slot machines for their sorority's charity casino night. Penelope puts her slot machine on a variable-interval schedule of reinforcement; Edith puts hers on a fixed-interval schedule of reinforcement. On average, both machines will deliver a reward every 20 minutes. Whose slot machine is likely to make the most money for the sorority charity? Edith's machine is likely to lead to long lines just before the 20-minute mark, but people will be unlikely to play on it at

FIGURE 10 **Schedules of Reinforcement and Different Patterns of Responding** In this figure, each hash mark indicates the delivery of reinforcement. Notice on the fixed-ratio schedule the dropoff in responding after each response; on the variable-ratio schedule the high, steady rate of responding; on the fixed-interval schedule the immediate dropoff in responding after reinforcement, and the increase in responding just before reinforcement (resulting in a scalloped curve); and on the variable-interval schedule the slow, steady rate of responding.
> Which schedule of reinforcement represents the "most bang for the buck"? That is, which is associated with the most responses for the least amount of reinforcement? > Which schedule would be best if you have very little time for training? > Which schedule of reinforcement is most common in your life?

other times. In contrast, Penelope's is more likely to entice continuous play, because the players never know when they might hit a jackpot. The magic of variable schedules of reinforcement is that the learner can never be sure exactly when the reward is coming. Figure 10 shows how the different schedules of reinforcement result in different rates of responding.

PUNISHMENT We began this section by noting that behaviors can be followed by something good or something bad. So far, we have explored only the good things—reinforcers that are meant to increase behaviors. Sometimes, however, the goal is to decrease a behavior, and in such cases the behavior might be followed by something unpleasant. **Punishment** is a consequence that *decreases* the likelihood that a behavior will occur. For instance, a child plays with a matchbox and gets burned when she lights one of the matches; the child consequently is less likely to play with matches in the future. As another example, a student interrupts the instructor, and the instructor scolds the student. This consequence—the teacher's verbal reprimand—makes the student less likely to interrupt in the future. In punishment, a response decreases because of its unpleasant consequences. The key difference between a punisher and a reinforcer is that punishing consequences reduce a behavior; reinforcing consequences increase a behavior.

punishment A consequence that decreases the likelihood that a behavior will occur.

The terms *positive* and *negative* apply to punishment in the same way they apply to reinforcement. "*Positive*" means adding something, and "*negative*" means taking something away. So, in **positive punishment**, a behavior *decreases* when it is followed by the presentation of a stimulus. Examples of positive punishment include spanking a misbehaving child and scolding a spouse who forgot to call when she was running late at the office; the coach who makes his team run wind sprints after a lackadaisical practice is also using positive punishment.

In **negative punishment** a behavior *decreases* when a stimulus is removed. Negative punishment means taking away something pleasant to reduce a behavior. Time-out is a form of negative punishment in which a child is removed from a positive reinforcer, such as his or her toys. Getting grounded is also a form of negative punishment as it involves taking a teenager away from the fun things in his life. Figure 11 compares positive reinforcement, negative reinforcement, positive punishment, and negative punishment. These concepts can be tricky, so be sure to take a moment to review Figure 11.

Punishment is sometimes confused with negative reinforcement. (Any kind of) reinforcement increases the behavior it follows. Punishment decreases the behavior it follows.

positive punishment The presentation of a stimulus following a given behavior in order to decrease the frequency of that behavior.

negative punishment The removal of a stimulus following a given behavior in order to decrease the frequency of that behavior.

TIMING AND THE CONSEQUENCES OF BEHAVIOR In operant conditioning, learning is more efficient when the interval between a behavior and its consequence is a few seconds rather than minutes or hours, especially in nonhuman (or primate) animals. For a rat, for example, if a food reward is delayed for more than 30 seconds after the rat presses a bar, the food is virtually ineffective as reinforcement. Similarly, if one wants to train a cat to stop scratching the furniture, immediately squirting the cat with water when it starts scratching will be more effective than waiting until the cat has

Positive Reinforcement

| **Behavior:** You turn in your work project on time. | → | Manager praises you for turning in your project on time. | → | **Effect on behavior:** You turn in your next project on time. |

Negative Reinforcement

| **Behavior:** You take aspirin for a headache. | → | Your headache goes away. | → | **Effect on behavior:** You take aspirin again the next time you have a headache. |

Positive Punishment

| **Behavior:** You don't replace the tires on the family car when your parent asks you to. | → | Your parent is angry at you for not replacing the tires. | → | **Effect on behavior:** You stop dawdling and replace the tires to avoid your parent's anger. |

Negative Punishment

| **Behavior:** Your younger sister comes home two hours after curfew. | → | Your sister is grounded for two weeks. | → | **Effect on behavior:** Your sister doesn't come home late the next time she's allowed to go out with friends. |

FIGURE 11 **Positive Reinforcement, Negative Reinforcement, Positive Punishment, and Negative Punishment** The fine distinctions here can sometimes be confusing. With respect to reinforcement, note that both types of reinforcement are intended to increase behavior, either by presenting a stimulus (in positive reinforcement) or by taking away a stimulus (in negative reinforcement). Punishment is meant to decrease a behavior either by presenting something (in positive punishment) or by taking away something (in negative punishment). The words *positive* and *negative* mean the same things in both cases.

scratched for few minutes. Unlike rats and cats, though, humans have the ability to respond to delayed reinforcers. Let's take a look at how humans respond to immediate versus delayed reinforcement and punishment.

Immediate versus Delayed Reinforcement and Punishment Sometimes important life decisions involve whether to seek and enjoy a small, immediate reinforcer or to wait for a delayed but more highly valued reinforcer. **Delay of gratification** means putting off the pleasure of an immediate reward in order to gain a more valuable reward later. For example, let's say you have a job that pays you weekly. Each week, you could take the pleasure of your paycheck and spend it on clothes, concert tickets, or eating out. Doing so, you might spend all the money earned in one week. Alternatively, you might decide to delay the pleasure of that paycheck, save your money up so that months down the line you can enjoy a bigger reward: a car. In life, we often have the choice between immediate pleasures (for example, going out with friends on a Friday night) and delayed rewards (for example, getting into professional school or getting a great job based on your academic accomplishments).

Timing can also effect human responses to punishing consequences. Not studying at the beginning of a semester can lead to poor grades much later. Fortunately, humans have the capacity to notice that this early behavior contributed to the negative outcome. We can often avoid negative outcomes by imagining them in advance and behaving accordingly.

Many daily behaviors revolve around both rewards and punishments that are immediate and delayed. We might put off going to the dentist to avoid a small punisher (such as the discomfort that comes with getting a cavity

delay of gratification
Putting off the pleasure of an immediate reward in order to gain a larger, later reward.

©Rubberball/Getty Images

DO NOT SKIP FIGURE 11! GO BACK!!! These terms are easy to confuse. It is worth your time to review these terms. Trust me!

filled). However, this procrastination might contribute to greater pain later (such as the pain of having a tooth pulled). Sometimes life is about enduring a little pain now to avoid a lot of pain later.

Consider the following question: How does receiving immediate small reinforcement versus delayed strong punishment affect human behavior? For instance, should Dave eat the cupcake in front of him (an immediate small pleasure) or risk the possible negative consequences that might occur down the line (delayed punishers)? One reason that obesity is such a major health problem is that eating is a behavior with immediate positive consequences—food tastes great and quickly provides a pleasurable, satisfied feeling. Although the potential delayed consequences of overeating are negative (obesity and other possible health risks), the immediate consequences are difficult to override. When the delayed consequences of behavior are punishing and the immediate consequences are reinforcing, the immediate consequences usually win, even when the immediate consequences are minor reinforcers and the delayed consequences are major punishers.

Smoking and drinking follow a similar pattern. The immediate consequences of smoking are reinforcing for most smokers—the powerful combination of positive reinforcement (enhanced attention, energy boost) and negative reinforcement (tension relief, removal of craving). The primarily long-term effects of smoking are punishing and include shortness of breath, a chronic sore throat and/or coughing, chronic obstructive pulmonary disease (COPD), heart disease, and cancer. Likewise, the immediate pleasurable consequences of drinking override the delayed consequences of a hangover or even alcoholism and liver disease.

Now think about the following situations. Why are some of us so reluctant to take up a new sport, try a new dance step, run for office on campus or in local government, or do almost anything different? One reason is that learning new skills often involves minor punishing consequences, such as initially looking and feeling stupid, not knowing what to do, and having to put up with sarcastic comments from others. In these circumstances, reinforcing consequences are often delayed. For example, it may take a long time to become a good enough golfer or a good enough dancer to enjoy these activities, but persevering through the rough patches just might be worth it.

Applied Behavior Analysis

Although behavioral approaches have been criticized for ignoring mental processes and focusing only on observable behavior, these approaches do provide an optimistic perspective for individuals interested in changing their behaviors. That is, rather than concentrating on factors such as the type of person you are, behavioral approaches imply that you can modify even longstanding habits by changing the reward contingencies that maintain those habits (Schlinger, 2017).

One real-world application of operant conditioning principles to promote better functioning is applied behavior analysis. **Applied behavior analysis** (also called **behavior modification**) is the use of operant conditioning principles to change human behavior. In applied behavior analysis, the rewards and punishers that exist in a particular setting are carefully analyzed and manipulated to change behaviors. Applied behavior analysis seeks to identify the rewards that might be maintaining unwanted behaviors and to enhance the rewards of more appropriate behaviors. From this perspective, we can understand all human behavior as being influenced by rewards and punishments. If we can figure out what rewards and punishers are controlling a person's behavior, we can change them—and eventually change the behavior itself.

A manager who rewards staff members with a half day off if they meet a particular work goal is employing applied behavior analysis. So are a therapist and a client when they establish clear consequences of the client's behavior in order to reinforce more adaptive actions and discourage less adaptive ones. A teacher who notices that a troublesome student seems to enjoy the attention he receives—even when that attention is scolding—

applied behavior analysis or behavior modification
The use of operant conditioning principles to change human behavior.

might use applied behavior analysis by changing her responses to the child's behavior, ignoring it instead. These examples show how attending to the consequences of behavior can be used to improve performance in settings such as a workplace and a classroom. Advocates of applied behavior analysis believe that many emotional and behavioral problems stem from inadequate or inappropriate consequences (Schlinger, 2017).

Applied behavior analysis has been effective in a wide range of situations. Practitioners have used it, for example, to train autistic individuals (Zane & others, 2014), children and adolescents with psychological problems (Martin & Pear, 2014), and residents of mental health facilities (Phillips & Mudford, 2008); to instruct individuals in effective parenting (Ahmann, 2014); to enhance environmentally conscious behaviors such as recycling and not littering (Geller, 2002); to get people to wear seatbelts (Streff & Geller, 1986); and to promote workplace safety (Geller, 2006). Applied behavior analysis can help people improve their self-control in many aspects of mental and physical health.

©Phoenixns/Shutterstock

 Note that the teacher-student example involves negative punishment.

self-quiz

1. A mother takes away her son's favorite toy when he misbehaves. Her action is an example of
   A. positive reinforcement.
   B. negative reinforcement.
   C. positive punishment.
   D. negative punishment.

2. The schedule of reinforcement that results in the greatest increase in behavior is
   A. fixed ratio.
   B. variable ratio.
   C. fixed interval.
   D. variable interval.

3. Kelley is scolded each time she teases her little brother. Her mother notices that the frequency of teasing has decreased. Scolding Kelley is an effective
   A. negative reinforcer.
   B. negative punisher.
   C. conditioner.
   D. positive punisher.

APPLY IT! 4. Kevin's girlfriend is very moody, and he never knows what to expect from her. When she is in a good mood, he feels as if he is in heaven, but when she is in a bad mood, she makes him crazy. His friends all think that he should dump her, but Kevin finds that he just cannot break it off. Kevin's girlfriend has him on a _____ schedule of reinforcement.
   A. variable
   B. fixed
   C. continuous
   D. nonexistent

4 Observational Learning

Would it make sense to teach a 15-year-old boy how to drive with either classical conditioning or operant conditioning procedures? Driving a car is a voluntary behavior, so classical conditioning would not apply. In terms of operant conditioning, we could ask him to try to drive down the road and then reward his positive behaviors. Not many of us would want to be on the road, though, when he makes mistakes. Albert Bandura (2010, 2011, 2012) pointed out that if we learned only in such a trial-and-error fashion, learning would be exceedingly tedious and at times hazardous. Instead, Bandura says, many complex behaviors are the result of exposure to competent models. By observing other people, we can acquire knowledge, skills, rules, strategies, beliefs, and attitudes.

Observational learning occurs when a person observes and imitates someone else's behavior.
©Peter Muller/Cultura/Corbis

Bandura's *observational learning,* also called *imitation* or *modeling,* is learning that occurs when a person observes and imitates behavior. The capacity to learn by observation eliminates trial-and-error learning. Often observational learning takes less time than operant conditioning. A famous example of observational learning is the Bobo doll study (Bandura, Ross, & Ross, 1961), in which children who had watched an aggressive adult model punch the doll were more likely to behave aggressively when left alone than were children who had observed a nonaggressive model.

To learn from someone else's actions is different from the types of learning we have discussed so far. If you want to become a great basketball player, watching an NBA game might be a good start. But you have to watch it in a particular way, paying close attention and seeing what sorts of behaviors lead to the best outcomes. Indeed, there are four main processes that are crucial to observational learning: attention, retention, motor reproduction, and reinforcement (Bandura, 1986). Let's review each of these.

In observational learning, the first process that must occur is *attention.* To reproduce a model's actions, you must attend to what the model is saying or doing. You might not hear what a friend says if the stereo is blaring, and you might miss your instructor's analysis of a problem if you are admiring someone sitting in the next row. As a further example, imagine that you decide to take a class to improve your drawing skills. To succeed, you need to attend to the instructor's words and hand movements. Characteristics of the model can influence attention to the model. Warm, powerful, atypical people, for example, command more attention than do cold, weak, typical people.

Retention is the second process required for observational learning to occur. To reproduce a model's actions, you must remember the information and keep it in memory so that you can retrieve it later. A simple verbal description, or a vivid image of what the model did, assists retention. In the example of taking a class to sharpen your drawing ability, you will need to remember what the instructor said and did in modeling good drawing skills.

Motor reproduction, a third element of observational learning, is the process of imitating the model's actions. People might pay attention to a model and encode what they have seen, but limitations in motor development might make it difficult for them to reproduce the model's action. Thirteen-year-olds might see a professional basketball player do a reverse two-handed dunk but be unable to reproduce the pro's play. Similarly, in your drawing class, if you lack fine motor reproduction skills, you might be unable to follow the instructor's example.

Reinforcement is a final component of observational learning. In this case, the question is whether the model's behavior is followed by a consequence. Seeing a model attain a reward for an activity increases the chances that an observer will repeat the behavior—a process called *vicarious reinforcement.* So, if a basketball player is more likely to make the basket when his or her feet are appropriately planted, then that is a behavior that a budding player is more likely to seek to repeat. On the other hand, seeing the model punished makes the observer less likely to repeat the behavior—a process called *vicarious punishment.* If an observer sees that shooting the basket off balance leads to missed shots, that behavior is less likely to be repeated.

In sum, when an observer attends to a model, retains that information in memory, is able to reproduce the models actions, and sees the model receive reinforcement, that observer has a good chance of learning to do what the model does.

To appreciate the steps of observational learning, consider a recent experience of 10-year-old Michigan native, Jacob O'Connor. By modeling behavior, Jacob saved his

FIGURE 12 Bandura's Model of Observational Learning In terms of Bandura's model, if you are learning to ski, you need to attend to the instructor's words and demonstrations. You need to remember what the instructor did and his or her tips for avoiding disasters. You also need the motor abilities to reproduce what the instructor has shown you. Praise from the instructor after you have completed a few moves on the slopes should improve your motivation to continue skiing.

2-year-old brother, Dylan, from drowning (Shapiro, 2017). Jacob happened upon Dylan floating face down in their grandmother's swimming pool. Jacob remembered seeing Dwayne "The Rock" Johnson in the movie *San Andreas*. In the film, Johnson saves his daughter from drowning by performing chest compressions. With just that as his training, Jacob modeled the behavior and saved his brother's life. Note that Jacob paid attention to the disaster film to learn this skill. He *remembered it* when the time was right. He also *saw the behavior lead to a positive outcome*: The Rock saved his daughter's life in the movie. And, of course, he was able to *reproduce the action*s that led to the positive outcome.

Observational learning has been studied in a variety of contexts. Researchers have explored observational learning, for example, as a means by which non human primates learn from one another (Anderson, Kuroshima, & Fujita, 2017). They have also studied it as a process by which people learn whether stimuli are likely to be painful (Yakunchikov & others, 2017) and as a tool individuals use to make economic decisions (Wang & Yu, 2017). Researchers are also interested in comparing learning from experience, learning through observation, and direct instruction (Glogger-Frey, Gaus, & Renkl, 2017).

Observational learning can be an important factor in the functioning of role models in inspiring people and changing their perceptions. Whether a model is similar to us can influence that model's effectiveness in modifying our behavior. The shortage of role models for women and minorities in science and engineering has often been suggested as a reason for the lack of women and minorities in these fields. After the election of Barack Obama as president of the United States, many commentators noted that, for the first time, African American children could see concretely that they might also attain the nation's highest office someday. You may have seen the photo of 5-year-old Jacob Philadelphia feeling President Obama's hair, to see if it was just like his (Calmes, 2012).

Figure 12 summarizes Bandura's model of observational learning.

Do It!

Having positive role models and mentors you can observe can be a significant factor in your learning and success. Make a list of your most important role models and mentors. Next to each, briefly describe how they have influenced you. What would your *ideal* role model or mentor be like?

self-quiz

1. Another name for observational learning is
   A. replication.
   B. modeling.
   C. trial-and-error learning.
   D. visualization.

2. According to Bandura, _____ occurs first in observational learning.
   A. motor reproduction
   B. retention
   C. attention
   D. reinforcement

3. A friend shows you how to do a card trick. However, you forget the second step in the trick and are thus unable to replicate the card trick. There has been a failure in
   A. motor reproduction.
   B. retention.
   C. attention.
   D. reinforcement.

APPLY IT! 4. Shawna is a 15-year-old high school girl whose mother is a highly paid accountant. Shawna's mom works long hours, often complains about her workplace and how much she hates her boss, and seems tired most of the time. When she is asked what she might do when she grows up, Shawna says she does not think she wants to pursue a career in accounting. Her mother is shocked and cannot understand why Shawna would not want to follow in her footsteps. Which of the following is the most likely explanation for this situation?
   A. Shawna has not observed her mother being reinforced for her behavior. She has only experienced vicarious punishment.
   B. Shawna is not aware that her mother is an accountant.
   C. Shawna is too different from her mother for her mother to be an effective role model.
   D. Shawna has not been paying attention to her mother.

5 Cognitive Factors in Learning

In learning about learning, we have looked at cognitive processes only as they apply in observational learning. Skinner's operant conditioning and Pavlov's classical conditioning focus on the environment and observable behavior, not what is going on in the head of the learner. Many contemporary psychologists, including some behaviorists, recognize the importance of cognition and believe that learning involves more than environment–behavior connections (Bandura, 2012; Bjork, Dunlosky, & Kornell, 2013). A good starting place for considering cognitive influences in learning is the work of E. C. Tolman.

Purposive Behavior

E. C. Tolman (1932) emphasized the *purposiveness* of behavior—the idea that much of behavior is goal-directed. Tolman believed that it is necessary to study entire behavioral sequences in order to understand why people engage in particular actions. For example, high school students whose goal is to attend a leading college or university study hard in their classes. If we focused only on their studying, we would miss the purpose of their behavior. The students do not always study hard because they have been reinforced for studying in the past. Rather, studying is a means to intermediate goals (learning, high grades) that in turn improve their likelihood of getting into the college or university of their choice.

We can see Tolman's legacy today in the extensive interest in the role of goal setting in human behavior (Martin & Elliott, 2016). Researchers are especially curious about how people self-regulate and self-monitor their behavior to reach a goal (Vohs & Baumeister, 2016).

©Royalty-Free/Corbis

EXPECTANCY LEARNING AND INFORMATION   In studying the purposiveness of behavior, Tolman went beyond the stimuli and responses of Pavlov and Skinner to focus on cognitive mechanisms. Tolman said that when classical conditioning and operant conditioning occur, the organism acquires certain expectations. In classical conditioning, the young boy fears the rabbit because he expects it will hurt him. In operant conditioning, a woman works hard all week because she expects a paycheck on Friday. So, according to this line of reasoning, when we learn through conditioning, we are not only acquiring associations but expectations about the world. Expectancies are acquired from people's experiences with their environment. Expectancies influence a variety of human experiences. We set the goals we do because we believe that we can reach them. Research supports an important role for expectancies in classical conditioning (Taylor & others, 2017; Weidemann & others, 2016).

Recall the research presented in the Intersection earlier in this chapter. Overweight women were less likely to eat when they were not hungry if they had thrown delicious desserts in the trash (Schyns & others, 2016). At least one reason why throwing the desserts away caused them to eat less is that the manipulation defied their expectancies: They expected to be eating those desserts, not throwing them away.

Expectancies also play a role in the placebo effect. Many painkillers have been shown to be more effective in reducing pain when patients can see the intravenous injection sites than when they cannot (Price, Finniss, & Benedetti, 2008). If patients can see that they are getting a drug, they can harness their own expectations for pain reduction.

Tolman (1932) emphasized that the information value of the conditioned stimulus is important as a signal or an expectation that an unconditioned stimulus will follow. Anticipating contemporary thinking, Tolman believed that the information that the CS provides is the key to understanding classical conditioning. One contemporary

©Vasiliy Koval/Shutterstock

view of classical conditioning describes an organism as an information seeker, using logical and perceptual relations among events, along with preconceptions, to form a representation of the world (Rescorla, 2003, 2005, 2009).

A classic experiment conducted by Leon Kamin (1968) illustrates the importance of an organism's history and the information provided by a conditioned stimulus in classical conditioning. Kamin conditioned a rat by repeatedly pairing a tone (CS) and a shock (US) until the tone alone produced fear (conditioned response). Then he continued to pair the tone with the shock, but he turned on a light (a second CS) each time the tone sounded. Even though he repeatedly paired the light (CS) and the shock (US), the rat showed no conditioning to the light (the light by itself produced no CR). Conditioning to the light was blocked, almost as if the rat had not paid attention. The rat apparently used the tone as a signal to predict that a shock would be coming; information about the light's pairing with the shock was redundant with the information already learned about the tone's pairing with the shock. In this experiment, conditioning was governed not by the contiguity of the CS and US but instead by the rat's history and the information it received. Contemporary classical conditioning researchers are further exploring the role of information in an organism's learning (Hermans & others, 2014; Rescorla & Wagner, 2009).

LATENT LEARNING   Experiments on latent learning provide other evidence to support the role of cognition in learning. **Latent learning (or implicit learning)** is unreinforced learning that is not immediately reflected in behavior. Latent learning is sometimes called incidental learning because it "just happens" as a result of experience. It happens even without reinforcement. In one study, researchers put two groups of hungry rats in a maze and required them to find their way from a starting point to an end point (Tolman & Honzik, 1930). The first group found food (a reinforcer) at the end point; the second group found nothing there. In the operant conditioning view, the first group should learn the maze better than the second group, which is exactly what happened. However, when the researchers subsequently took some of the rats from the nonreinforced group and gave them food at the end point of the maze, they quickly began to run the maze as effectively as the reinforced group. The nonreinforced rats apparently had learned a great deal about the maze as they roamed around and explored it. However, their learning was latent, stored cognitively in their memories but not yet expressed behaviorally. When these rats were given a good reason (reinforcement with food) to run the maze speedily, they called on their latent learning to help them reach the end of the maze more quickly.

Outside a laboratory, latent learning is evident when you walk around a new setting to get "the lay of the land." The first time you visited your college campus, you may have wandered about without a specific destination in mind. Exploring the environment made you better prepared when the time came to find that 8 A.M. class.

latent learning or implicit learning
Unreinforced learning that is not immediately reflected in behavior.

Insight Learning

Like E. C. Tolman, the German gestalt psychologist Wolfgang Köhler believed that cognitive factors play a significant role in learning. Köhler spent four months in the Canary Islands during World War I observing the behavior of apes. There he conducted two fascinating experiments—the stick problem and the box problem. Although these two experiments are basically the same, the solutions to the problems are different. In both situations, the ape discovers that it cannot reach an alluring piece of fruit, either because the fruit is too high or because it is outside of the ape's cage and beyond reach. To solve the stick problem, the ape has to insert a small stick inside a larger stick to reach the fruit. To master the box problem, the ape must stack several boxes to reach the fruit (Figure 13).

FIGURE 13 **Insight Learning** Sultan, one of Wolfgang Köhler's brightest chimps, is faced with the problem of reaching a cluster of bananas overhead. He solves the problem by stacking boxes on top of one another to reach the bananas. Köhler called this type of problem solving "insight learning."
(all): ©3LH/SuperStock

According to Köhler (1925), solving these problems does not involve trial and error or simple connections between stimuli and responses. Rather, when the ape realizes that its customary actions are not going to help it get the fruit, it often sits for a period of time and appears to ponder how to solve the problem. Then it quickly rises, as if it has had a flash of insight, piles the boxes on top of one another, and gets the fruit. **Insight learning** is a form of problem solving in which the organism develops a sudden insight into or understanding of a problem's solution.

The idea that insight learning is essentially different from learning through trial and error or through conditioning has always been controversial (Spence, 1938). Insight learning appears to entail both gradual and sudden processes, and understanding how these lead to problem solving continues to fascinate psychologists. In one study, researchers observed orangutans trying to figure out a way to get a tempting peanut out of a clear plastic tube (Mendes, Hanus, & Call, 2007). The primates wandered about their enclosures, experimenting with various strategies. Typically, they paused for a moment before finally landing on a solution: Little by little they filled the tube with water that they transferred by mouth from their water dishes to the tube. Once the peanut floated to the top, the clever orangutans had their snack. More recent research shows that chimps can solve the floating peanut task through observational learning (Tennie, Call, & Tomasello, 2010).

Insight learning requires thinking "outside the box," setting aside previous expectations and assumptions. One way that insight learning can be enhanced in human beings is through multicultural experiences (Leung & others, 2008). Correlational studies have shown that time spent living abroad is associated with higher insight learning performance among MBA students (Maddux & Galinsky, 2007). Furthermore, experimental studies have demonstrated that exposure to other cultures can influence insight learning. In one study, U.S. college students were randomly assigned to view one of two slide shows—one about Chinese and U.S. cultures and the other about a control topic. Those who saw the multicultural slide show scored higher on measures of creativity and insight, and these changes persisted for a week (Leung & others, 2008). Being exposed to other cultures and other ways of thinking can be a key way to enhance insight and creativity, and a person does not have to travel to enjoy the learning benefits of multicultural experience.

What makes insight learning unique is that "Aha!" moment—but that moment often comes after some trial and error during which many of the "wrong" answers have been thoroughly dismissed.

insight learning
A form of problem solving in which the organism develops a sudden insight into or understanding of a problem's solution.

1. E. C. Tolman emphasized the *purposiveness* of behavior—the idea that much of behavior is oriented toward the achievement of
   A. immortality.
   B. altruism.
   C. goals.
   D. self-esteem.

2. When the answer to a problem just pops into your head, you have experienced
   A. latent learning.
   B. insight learning.
   C. implicit learning.
   D. expectancy learning.

3. A type of learning that does *not* involve trial and error is
   A. insight learning
   B. latent learning.
   C. expectancy learning.
   D. implicit learning.

APPLY IT! 4. Derek is rehearsing his lines and songs for an upcoming production of *Grease*. He is playing the lead role of Danny Zucco. His friend Maria helps him practice his lines and learn the words to his songs. Maria is not in the play and wouldn't even think of appearing onstage. On opening night, Maria is in the audience, and halfway through "Summer Lovin'" people sitting around her are complaining because she is singing along. She also has been saying all of Danny's lines under her breath. What is the explanation?
   A. Maria is demonstrating the power of latent learning.
   B. Maria is demonstrating insight learning.
   C. Maria is showing purposive behavior.
   D. Maria secretly dreams of playing Danny Zucco in an all-female version of *Grease* someday.

6 Biological, Cultural, and Psychological Factors in Learning

Albert Einstein had many special talents. He combined enormous creativity with keen analytic ability to develop some of the twentieth century's most important insights into the nature of matter and the universe. Genes obviously endowed Einstein with extraordinary intellectual skills that enabled him to think and reason on a very high plane, but cultural factors also contributed to his genius. Einstein received an excellent, rigorous European education, and later in the United States he experienced the freedom and support believed to be important in creative exploration. Would Einstein have been able to develop his skills fully and to make such brilliant insights if he had grown up in a less advantageous environment? It is unlikely. Clearly, both biological and cultural factors contribute to learning.

Biological Constraints

Humans cannot breathe under water, fish cannot ski, and cows cannot solve math problems. The structure of an organism's body permits certain kinds of learning and inhibits others. For example, chimpanzees cannot learn to speak English because they lack the necessary vocal equipment.

Dogs who are trained for various tasks can sometimes illustrate the limits of learning principles. You may have heard of Lulu the black lab who made headlines when the U.S. Drug Enforcement Agency tweeted her photo to the world along with the news that she had flunked out of "sniffer dog" training (Chorney, 2017). Lulu simply was not interested in sniffing out illegal drugs on clothes or in luggage or other containers. Fortunately, Lulu was adopted by one of her trainers and currently lives in a happy home where tasks are more to her liking. This case shows that even in the same breed of dogs, some may be able to quickly learn to complete tasks while other are not.

INSTINCTIVE DRIFT   Keller and Marion Breland (1961), students of B. F. Skinner, used operant conditioning to train animals to perform at fairs and conventions and in television advertisements. They applied Skinner's techniques to teach pigs to cart large wooden nickels to a piggy bank and deposit them. They also trained raccoons to pick up

FIGURE 14 **Instinctive Drift** This raccoon's skill in using its hands made it an excellent basketball player, but because of instinctive drift, the raccoon had a much more difficult time dropping coins in a tray.

© Keystone-France/ Hulton Archive/Getty Images

a coin and place it in a metal tray. Although the pigs and raccoons, as well as chickens and other animals, performed most of the tasks well (raccoons became adept basketball players, for example—see Figure 14), some of the animals began acting strangely. Instead of picking up the large wooden nickels and carrying them to the piggy bank, the pigs dropped the nickels on the ground, shoved them with their snouts, tossed them in the air, and then repeated these actions. The raccoons began to hold on to their coins rather than dropping them into the metal tray. When two coins were introduced, the raccoons rubbed them together in a miserly fashion. Somehow these behaviors overwhelmed the strength of the reinforcement. This example of biological influences on learning illustrates **instinctive drift,** the tendency of animals to revert to instinctive behavior that interferes with learning.

Why were the pigs and the raccoons misbehaving? The pigs were rooting, an instinct that is used to uncover edible roots. The raccoons were engaging in an instinctive food-washing response. Their instinctive drift interfered with learning.

instinctive drift
The tendency of animals to revert to instinctive behavior that interferes with learning.

PREPAREDNESS   Some animals learn readily in one situation but have difficulty learning in slightly different circumstances (Garcia & Koelling, 1966, 2009). The difficulty might result not from some aspect of the learning situation but from the organism's biological predisposition (Seligman, 1970). **Preparedness** is the species-specific biological predisposition to learn in certain ways but not others.

preparedness
The species-specific biological predisposition to learn in certain ways but not others.

Much of the evidence for preparedness comes from research on taste aversion (Garcia, 1989; Garcia & Koelling, 2009). Recall that taste aversion involves a single trial of learning the association between a particular taste and nausea. Rats that experience low levels of radiation after eating show a strong aversion to the food they were eating when the radiation made them ill. This aversion can last for as long as 32 days. Such long-term effects cannot be accounted for by classical conditioning, which would argue that a single pairing of the conditioned and unconditioned stimuli would not last that long (Garcia, Ervin, & Koelling, 1966). Taste aversion learning occurs in animals, including humans, that choose their food based on taste and smell. Other species are prepared to learn rapid associations between, for instance, colors of foods and illness.

Another example of preparedness comes from research on conditioning humans and monkeys to associate snakes with fear. Susan Mineka and Arne Ohman (2002; Ohman & Mineka, 2003) have investigated the fascinating natural power of snakes to evoke fear in many mammals. Many monkeys and humans fear snakes, and both monkeys and humans are very quick to learn the association between snakes and fear. In classical conditioning studies, when pictures of snakes (CS) are paired with electrical shocks (US), the snakes are likely to quickly and strongly evoke fear (the CR). Interestingly, pairing pictures of, say, flowers (CS) with electrical shocks produces much weaker associations (Mineka & Ohman, 2002; Ohman & Soares, 1998). Even more significantly, pictures of snakes can serve as conditioned stimuli for fearful responses, even when the pictures are presented so rapidly that they cannot be consciously perceived (Ohman & Mineka, 2001).

The link between snakes and fear has been demonstrated not only in classical conditioning paradigms. Monkeys that have been raised in the lab and that have never seen a snake rapidly learn to fear snakes, even entirely by observational learning. Lab monkeys that see a video of a monkey expressing fear toward a snake learn to be afraid of snakes faster than monkeys seeing the same fear video spliced so that the feared object is a rabbit, a flower, or a mushroom (Ohman & Mineka, 2003).

Mineka and Ohman (2002) suggest that these results demonstrate preparedness among mammals to associate snakes with fear and aversive stimuli. They argue that this association is related to the amygdala (the part of the limbic system that is linked to emotion) and is difficult to modify. These researchers theorize that this preparedness for fear of snakes has emerged out of the threat that reptiles likely posed to our evolutionary ancestors.

Cultural Influences

Traditionally, interest in the cultural context of human learning has been limited, partly because the organisms in those contexts typically were animals. The question arises, how might culture influence human learning? Most psychologists agree that the principles of classical conditioning, operant conditioning, and observational learning are universal and are powerful learning processes in every culture. However, culture can influence the degree to which these learning processes are used (Kempe, Lycett, & Mesoudi, 2014; Matsumoto & Juang, 2013).

In addition, culture can determine the content of learning (Meyer, 2014; Verguts & Chen, 2017). We cannot learn about something we do not experience. The 4-year-old who grows up among the Bushmen of the Kalahari Desert is unlikely to learn about taking baths and eating with a knife and fork. Similarly, a child growing up in Chicago is unlikely to be skilled at tracking animals and finding water-bearing roots in the desert. Learning often requires practice, and certain behaviors are practiced more often in some cultures than in others. In Bali, many children are skilled dancers by the age of 6, whereas Norwegian children are much more likely to be good skiers and skaters by that age.

On the Indonesian island of Bali, young children learn traditional dances, whereas in Norway children commonly learn to ski early in life. As cultures vary, so does the content of learning.
(Bali) ©J.W.Alker; (Norway) ©Lasse Bolstad/Alamy Stock Photo

> **Think of some activities you learned at an early age; how are they related to the culture in which you grew up?** > **What sorts of basic knowledge did these experiences allow you to acquire?** > **How might such early experiences relate to your current learning?** > **How did the adults in your life respond to success or failure, and how has that shaped your experience of learning?**

Psychological Constraints

Are there psychological constraints on learning? For animals, the answer is probably no. For humans, the answer may well be yes. This section opened with the claim that fish cannot ski. The truth of this statement is clear. Biological circumstances make it impossible. If we put biological considerations aside, we might ask ourselves about times in our lives when we feel like a fish trying to ski—when we feel that we just do not have what it takes to learn a skill or master a task. Some people believe that humans have particular learning styles that make it easier for them to learn in some ways but not others. To read about this possibility, see Challenge Your Thinking.

Do Learning Styles Matter to Learning?

earning styles refers to the idea that people differ in terms of the method of instruction that will be most effective for them. You may have heard, for example, that someone can be a *visual learner* (he or she learns by seeing), an *aural learner* (the person learns by listening), or a *kinesthetic learner* (the individual learns through hands-on experience).

The notion that people have different learning styles is extremely popular. Educational psychology textbooks, as well as many school districts, instruct teachers to take such differences into account in the classroom. The argument that teachers should tailor their methods to fit students' learning styles suggests a specific scientific hypothesis: that individuals will *learn better* when instructions are targeted to their particular learning style. What is the evidence for the prediction that tailoring instruction to students' learning styles improves learning?

You may be surprised to learn that a preponderance of research evidence shows that learning styles *do not* matter to learning (An & Carr, 2017). Although children and adults report consistent preferences for particular learning styles, there is *no evidence* that tailoring instructional methods to "visual," "aural," or "kinesthetic" learners produces better learning (Pashler & others, 2008). Interestingly, learning styles do predict the kind of materials participants prefer and attend to, the match between a person's learning style and the mode of instruction is unrelated to learning (Koć-Januchta & others, 2017; Massa & Mayer, 2006).

Why then do people believe that being taught in a way that matches their learning style produces better learning? As we have reviewed the many processes underlying learning, you may have noticed that many of these occur outside of awareness. Through classical conditioning, for example, we can learn associations without even noticing it. People may be unaware of their own learning. Research shows that when material is presented in a way that matches a person's learning style, they are likely to *feel like* they have learned more (Knoll & others, 2017). However, performance on an actual test shows those subjective feelings are misleading: No differences emerged in actual learning.

©Hero Images/Getty Images

The notion of learning styles is appealing at least in part because it reflects something we know to be true: People learn differently. However, the different ways humans learn do not seem to be well captured by learning styles (An & Carr, 2017). The effectiveness of particular methods of teaching may depend more on the material to be covered, a student's prior knowledge, varying abilities, motivation, and other factors. Coming at any topic from many different angles may improve student learning. Teachers may reach more students more effectively when they try different ways of approaching material—for instance, coming up with a hands-on tool to demonstrate a problem—but that is just good instruction, not instruction that is tailored to particular styles. Our senses work together to connect us to the external world. The brain and our sensory organs are not specialized to learn in specific ways.

Is there any harm in our trying to find out our preferred learning style? Perhaps, if the outcome constrains learning—if we assume, for example, that our personal learning style tells us what we cannot do or should not try. Sometimes the most meaningful learning experiences are those that push us outside our comfort zone. Teachers and topics that challenge us to put in extra effort, to see the world and ourselves in different ways, may be the key to meaningful learning. Sometimes the easiest path is not the one most likely to lead to life-changing learning.

What Do You Think?

- Do you think that you have a particular learning style? If so, how does it influence your learning?
- Even if evidence supported the effectiveness of tailoring teaching methods to specific types of learning styles, how would we implement a program based on these ideas?

Carol Dweck (2012, 2017) uses the term *mindset* to describe the way our beliefs about ability dictate what goals we set for ourselves, what we think we *can* learn, and ultimately what we *do* learn. Individuals have one of two mindsets: a *fixed mindset,* in which they believe that their qualities are carved in stone and cannot change; or a *growth mindset,* in which they believe their qualities can change and improve through their effort. These two mindsets have implications for the meaning of failure. From a fixed mindset, failure means lack of ability. From a growth mindset, however, failure tells the person what he or she still needs to learn. Your mindset influences whether you will be optimistic or pessimistic, what your goals will be, how hard you will strive to reach those goals, and how successful you are in college and after.

Dweck (2017) studied first-year pre-med majors taking their first chemistry class in college. Students with a growth mindset got higher grades than those with a fixed mindset. Even when they did not do well on a test, the growth-mindset students bounced back on the next test. Fixed-mindset students typically read and reread the text and class notes or tried to memorize everything verbatim. The fixed-mindset students who did poorly on tests concluded that chemistry and maybe pre-med were not for them. By contrast, growth-mindset students took charge of their motivation and learning, searching for themes and principles in the course and going over mistakes until they understood why they made them. According to Dweck, the key to their success was that they were studying to learn, not just to get a good grade.

Following are some effective strategies for developing a growth mindset (Dweck, 2017):

- *Understand that your intelligence and thinking skills are not fixed but can change.* Even if you are extremely bright, with effort you can increase your intelligence.

- *Become passionate about learning and stretch your mind in challenging situations.* It is easy to withdraw into a fixed mindset when the going gets tough; but as you bump up against obstacles, keep growing, work harder, stay the course, and improve your strategies; you will become a more successful person.

- *Think about the growth mindsets of people you admire.* Possibly you have a hero, someone who has achieved something extraordinary. You may have thought his or her accomplishments came easy because the person is so talented. However, find out more about this person and how he or she works and thinks. You likely will discover that much hard work and effort over a long period of time were responsible for this individual's achievements.

- *Begin now.* If you have a fixed mindset, commit to changing now. Think about when, where, and how you will begin using your new growth mindset.

Dweck's work challenges us to consider the limits we place on our own learning. When we think of the relative absence of women and minorities in math and science professions, we might consider the messages these groups have received about whether they have what it takes to succeed in these domains. Our beliefs about ability profoundly influence what we try to learn. As any 7-year-old with a growth mindset would tell you, you never know what you can do until you try.

self-quiz

1. When a pig's rooting behavior interferes with its learning, the phenomenon is an example of
   A. preparedness.
   B. learned helplessness.
   C. a taste aversion.
   D. instinctive drift.

2. Mineka and Ohman suggest that humans' preparedness for fear of snakes emerged because of
   A. cultural myths.
   B. the religious symbolism of snakes.

   C. the danger that snakes and other reptiles posed to earlier humans.
   D. the limitations of human learning.

3. Believing that studying hard will result in a good grade in a course is an example of
   A. a growth insight.
   B. a growth mindset.
   C. preparedness.
   D. a fixed mindset.

APPLY IT! 4. Frances is a dog person who has just adopted her first-ever cat.

Given her experience in housebreaking her pet dogs, Frances is shocked that her new kitty, Tolman, uses the litter box the very first day and never has an accident in the house. Frances thinks that Tolman must be a genius cat. Tolman's amazing ability demonstrates
   A. psychological constraints on learning.
   B. biological preparedness.
   C. cultural constraints on learning.
   D. that dog people are not very bright.

Types of Learning

Learning is a systematic, relatively permanent change in behavior that occurs through experience. Associative learning involves learning by making a connection between two events. Observational learning is learning by watching what other people do.

Conditioning is the process by which associative learning occurs. In classical conditioning, organisms learn the association between two stimuli. In operant conditioning, they learn the association between behavior and a consequence.

 ## Classical Conditioning

Classical conditioning occurs when a neutral stimulus becomes associated with a meaningful stimulus and comes to elicit a similar response. Pavlov discovered that an organism learns the association between an unconditioned stimulus (US) and a conditioned stimulus (CS). The US automatically produces the unconditioned response (UR). After conditioning (CS–US pairing), the CS elicits the conditioned response (CR) by itself. Acquisition in classical conditioning is the initial linking of stimuli and responses, which involves a neutral stimulus being associated with the US so that the CS comes to elicit the CR. Two important aspects of acquisition are contiguity and contingency.

Generalization in classical conditioning is the tendency of a new stimulus that is similar to the original conditioned stimulus to elicit a response that is similar to the conditioned response. Discrimination is the process of learning to respond to certain stimuli and not to others. Extinction is the weakening of the CR in the absence of the US. Spontaneous recovery is the recurrence of a CR after a time delay without further conditioning.

In humans, classical conditioning has been applied to explaining and eliminating fears, breaking habits, combating taste aversion, and understanding such different experiences as pleasant emotions and drug habituation.

 ## Operant Conditioning

Operant conditioning is a form of learning in which the consequences of behavior produce changes in the probability of the behavior's occurrence. Skinner described the behavior of the organism as operant: The behavior operates on the environment, and the environment in turn operates on the organism. Whereas classical conditioning involves respondent behavior, operant conditioning involves operant behavior. In most instances, operant conditioning is better at explaining voluntary behavior than is classical conditioning.

Thorndike's law of effect states that behaviors followed by positive outcomes are strengthened, whereas behaviors followed by negative outcomes are weakened. Skinner built on this idea to develop the notion of operant conditioning.

Shaping is the process of rewarding approximations of desired behavior in order to shorten the learning process. Principles of reinforcement include the distinction between positive reinforcement (the frequency of a behavior increases because it is followed by a rewarding stimulus) and negative reinforcement (the frequency of behavior increases because it is followed by the removal of an aversive stimulus). Positive reinforcement

can be classified as primary reinforcement (using reinforcers that are innately satisfying) and secondary reinforcement (using reinforcers that acquire positive value through experience). Reinforcement can also be continuous (a behavior is reinforced every time) or partial (a behavior is reinforced only a portion of the time). Schedules of reinforcement—fixed ratio, variable ratio, fixed interval, and variable interval—determine when a behavior will be reinforced.

Operant conditioning involves generalization (giving the same response to similar stimuli), discrimination (responding to stimuli that signal that a behavior will or will not be reinforced), and extinction (a decreasing tendency to perform a previously reinforced behavior when reinforcement is stopped).

Punishment is a consequence that decreases the likelihood that a behavior will occur. In positive punishment, a behavior decreases when it is followed by a (typically unpleasant) stimulus. In negative punishment, a behavior decreases when a positive stimulus is removed from it.

Applied behavior analysis involves the application of operant conditioning principles to a variety of real-life behaviors.

 ## Observational Learning

Observational learning occurs when a person observes and imitates someone else's behavior. Bandura identified four main processes in observational learning: attention, retention, motor reproduction, and reinforcement.

 ## Cognitive Factors in Learning

Tolman emphasized the purposiveness of behavior. Purposiveness refers to Tolman's belief that much of behavior is goal-directed. In studying purposiveness, Tolman went beyond stimuli and responses to discuss cognitive mechanisms. Tolman believed that expectancies, acquired through experiences with the environment, are an important cognitive mechanism in learning.

Köhler developed the concept of insight learning, a form of problem solving in which the organism develops a sudden insight into or understanding of a problem's solution.

 ## Biological, Cultural, and Psychological Factors in Learning

Biological constraints restrict what an organism can learn from experience. These constraints include instinctive drift (the tendency of animals to revert to instinctive behavior that interferes with learned behavior), preparedness (the species-specific biological predisposition to learn in certain ways but not in others), and taste aversion (the biological predisposition to avoid foods that have caused sickness in the past).

Although most psychologists agree that the principles of classical conditioning, operant conditioning, and observational learning are universal, cultural customs can influence the degree to which these learning processes are used. Culture also often determines the content of learning.

In addition, what we learn is determined in part by what we believe we can learn. Dweck emphasizes that individuals benefit enormously from having a growth mindset rather than a fixed mindset.

KEY TERMS

acquisition

applied behavior analysis or behavior modification

associative learning

aversive conditioning

avoidance learning

behaviorism

classical conditioning

conditioned response (CR)

conditioned stimulus (CS)

counterconditioning

delay of gratification

discrimination (classical conditioning)

discrimination (operant conditioning)

extinction (classical conditioning)

extinction (operant conditioning)

generalization (classical conditioning)

generalization (operant conditioning)

habituation

insight learning

instinctive drift

latent learning or implicit learning

law of effect

learned helplessness

learning

negative punishment

negative reinforcement

observational learning

operant conditioning or instrumental conditioning

positive punishment

positive reinforcement

preparedness

primary reinforcer

punishment

reinforcement

schedules of reinforcement

secondary reinforcer

shaping

spontaneous recovery

unconditioned response (UR)

unconditioned stimulus (US)

ANSWERS TO SELF-QUIZZES

Section 1:   1. A; 2. C; 3. C; 4. C
Section 2:   1. B; 2. A; 3. D; 4. B

Section 3:   1. D; 2. B; 3. D; 4. A
Section 4:   1. B; 2. C; 3. B; 4. A

Section 5:   1. C; 2. B; 3. A; 4. A
Section 6:   1. D; 2. C; 3. B; 4. B

6 Memory

The Ubiquitous Selfie, Memory, and Meaning

We have all seen people stretching out their arms to take a picture of themselves with their smartphones. Whether it is standing on the edge of the Grand Canyon, attending a World Series game, or just taking a walk in the park, people want to capture a moment of me-ness, a portrait of the self in whatever context. In fact, it is estimated that millennials (individuals between the ages of 18 and 34) will take over 25,000 selfies in their lifetime (Glum, 2015). It is estimated that over 1 million selfies are taken each day (Bennett, 2014). These photos are mementos of the past—of the places we have visited, the people we have met, and the people we once were. Every selfie is a reflection of a moment of the self, as it once was.

Human beings naturally tend to collect concrete evidence to support their memories—not just pictures but souvenirs: a T-shirt, a coffee mug, or a postcard. The preciousness of this material evidence of where we have been, with whom, and what we did reveals two important truths about memory: First, there are some things we want to remember forever, and, second, we are not sure that memory itself will suffice.

Certainly, memory provides crucial support for many mundane activities—for example, it allows us to know what we were looking for when we opened the fridge, where we left our running shoes, and when we need to mail Aunt Lucy's birthday card. But our memories are also precious because they represent a lasting imprint of our experiences, moments from the past that give our lives meaning.

There are few moments when your life is not steeped in memory. Memory is at work with each step you take, each thought you think, and each word you speak. Through memory, you weave the past into the present. In this chapter, we explore the key processes of memory, including how information gets into memory and how it is stored, retrieved, and sometimes forgotten. We also probe what the science of memory reveals about the best way to study and retain course material, as well as how memory processes can enrich our lives.

1 The Nature of Memory

The stars are shining and the moon is full. A beautiful evening is coming to a close. You look at your significant other and think, "I'll never forget this night." How is it possible that in fact you never will forget it? Years from now, you might tell your children about that one special night so many years ago, even if you had not thought about it in the years since. How does one perfect night become a part of your enduring life memories?

memory
The retention of information or experience over time as the result of three key processes: encoding, storage, and retrieval.

Psychologists define **memory** as the retention of information or experience over time. Memory occurs through three important processes: encoding, storage, and retrieval. Memory requires taking in information (encoding the sights and sounds of that night), storing it or representing it (retaining it in some mental storehouse), and then retrieving it for a later purpose (recalling it when someone asks, "So, how did you two end up together?"). In the next three sections, we focus on these phases of memory: encoding, storage, and retrieval (Figure 1).

Except for the annoying moments when your memory fails or the upsetting situation where someone you know experiences memory loss, you most likely do not consider how much everything you do and say depends on the smooth operation of your memory systems. Think about asking someone for his or her phone number when you have no pencil, paper, or cell phone handy. You must attend to what the person tells you and rehearse the digits in your head until you can store them someplace permanently. Then, when the time comes to record the numbers, say, in your phone, you have to retrieve the identity of the person and the reason you got that phone number to begin with. Was it to ask the person out or to borrow notes for your psychology class? Human memory systems are truly remarkable considering how much information we put into memory and how much we must retrieve to perform life's activities.

You might think of your memories as clearly "yours," but memories are also a way we share who we are with others. They have a role to play in our bonds with others and our sense of identity. To read about the social consequences of memory, see the Intersection.

Encoding
Getting information into memory

Storage
Retaining information over time

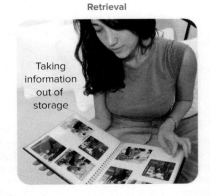

Retrieval
Taking information out of storage

FIGURE 1 **Processing Information in Memory** As you read about the many aspects of memory in this chapter, think about the organization of memory in terms of these three main activities.
(camera): ©Garret Bautista/iStock/Getty Images; (box): ©Grata Victoria/iStock/Getty Images; (woman): ©McGraw-Hill Education/Gary He, photographer

Cognitive Psychology and Developmental Psychology: How Does Reminiscing Affect Our Relationships and Our Development?

Have you ever had one of those experiences in which you looked at your friends and said, "Well, at least this will make a great story!" Stories of shared life experiences provide profound connections between people. Of course, these stories are memories that we share with others. Reminiscing refers to the enjoyable sharing of personal memories with others. What is the function of reminiscing in our lives? Sometimes we reminisce with those who were present at the event, allowing all to relive the experience. Sometimes we reminisce with new acquaintances, as a way to share part of ourselves with them. These examples demonstrate the role of reminiscing in deepening our bonds with others and creating our identity (Fivush, Booker, & Graci, 2017).

Interestingly, research shows that children learn a great deal from reminiscences. Children who reminisce with their parents show a host of developmental benefits, including better memory and emotional skills (Salmon & Reese, 2016). When parents share memories with their children, they are sharing part of themselves and providing a sense of how a person creates a life story (Reese, 2013). The capacity to reminisce in early childhood is linked to enhanced shared thinking, a crucial part of working with others

©India Picture/Shutterstock

(Neale & Pino-Pasternak, 2017). When parents talk about their remembered emotional experiences with their children, the children become more emotionally adept themselves and also more self-accepting (Harris & others, 2017). When mothers reminisce to bond with their children in a way that is child-centered, children are more likely to feel more socially accepted (Kulkofsky, Behrens, & Battin, 2015). When parents and adolescents engage in shared memories they feel closer (Beike & others, 2017).

Of course, reminiscing requires that we have experiences to talk about. Research shows that gifts of experiences (like concert tickets or special meals) lead to greater bonding than material gifts (Chan & Mogilner, 2017). Think about it: Experiences are more likely to become memories, expanding our sense of self, enriching our life stories, and providing us with more meaning to share with others.

\\ When was the last time you reminisced with someone? With whom did you share your memory and why?

2 Memory Encoding

The first step in memory is **encoding,** the process by which information gets into memory storage. When you are listening to a lecture, watching a play, reading a book, or talking with a friend, you are encoding information into memory. Some information gets into memory virtually automatically, whereas encoding other information takes effort. Let's examine some of the encoding processes that require effort. These include attention, deep processing, elaboration, and the use of mental imagery.

encoding
The first step in memory; the process by which information gets into memory storage.

Attention

To begin the process of memory encoding, we have to pay attention to information (Weeks & Hasher, 2017). *Selective attention* involves focusing on a specific aspect of experience while ignoring others. Attention is selective because the brain's resources are limited—they cannot attend to everything. These limitations mean that we have to attend selectively to some things in our environment and ignore others (Dudukovic & Kuhl, 2017; Moene, Miller, & Lloyd, 2017). So, on that special night with your romantic partner, you never noticed the bus that roared by or the people whom you passed as you strolled along the street. Those details did not make it into your enduring memory.

In addition to selective attention, psychologists have described two other ways that attention may be allocated: divided attention and sustained attention. **Divided attention** involves concentrating on more than one activity at the same time. If you are listening to music or the television while you are reading this chapter, you are dividing your attention. **Sustained attention** (also called *vigilance*) is the ability to maintain attention to a selected stimulus for a prolonged period of time (Jangraw & others, 2018; Wang & others, 2014). For example, paying close attention to your notes while studying for an exam is a good application of sustained attention. **Executive attention** involves action planning, allocating attention to goals, error detection and compensation, monitoring progress on tasks, and dealing with novel or difficult circumstances. Thus, executive attention involves directing attention to engage in higher-level cognitive functioning.

How many times a day do you find yourself multitasking like this individual?
©Eternity in an Instant/Lifesized/Getty Images

divided attention
Concentrating on more than one activity at the same time.

sustained attention
The ability to maintain attention to a selected stimulus for a prolonged period of time.

executive attention
The ability to plan action, allocate attention to goals, detect errors and compensate for them, monitor progress on tasks, and deal with novel or difficult circumstances.

Not paying attention can be especially detrimental to encoding. *Multitasking,* which in some cases involves dividing attention not just between two activities but among three or more, may be the ultimate in divided attention (Finley, Benjamin, & McCarley, 2014; Uncapher & others, 2017). It is not unusual for high school and college students simultaneously to divide their attention among homework, instant messaging, web surfing, and looking at an iTunes playlist. Multitaskers are often very confident in their multitasking skills (Pattillo, 2010). However, one study revealed that heavy media multitaskers performed worse on a test of task-switching ability, apparently because of their decreased ability to filter out interference from the irrelevant task (Ophir, Nass, & Wagner, 2009). Such research indicates that trying to listen to a lecture in class while texting or playing a game on your cell phone (or checking out social media on your lap top) is likely to impede your ability to pay adequate attention to the lecture. Divided attention decreases encoding. We remember information better when we devote our attention to it.

Remember that the next time you sit down to study in front of the TV or a computer.

Levels of Processing

Another factor that influences memory is whether we engage with information superficially or really get into it. Fergus Craik and Robert Lockhart (1972) first suggested that

FIGURE 2
Depth of Processing
According to the levels of
processing principle, deeper
processing of stimuli
produces better memory of
them.

	Level of Processing	Process	Examples
Depth of Processing (arrow pointing down)	**Shallow**	Physical and perceptual features are analyzed.	The lines, angles, and contour that make up the physical appearance of an object, such as a car, are detected.
	Intermediate	Stimulus is recognized and labeled.	The object is recognized as a car.
	Deep	Semantic, meaningful, symbolic characteristics are used.	Associations connected with *car* are brought to mind—you think about the Porsche or Ferrari you hope to buy or the fun you and friends had on spring break when you drove a car to the beach.

levels of processing
A continuum of memory processing from shallow to intermediate to deep, with deeper processing producing better memory.

encoding can be influenced by levels of processing. The term **levels of processing** refers to a continuum from shallow to intermediate to deep, with deeper processing producing better memory.

Imagine that you are asked to memorize a list of words, including the word *mom*. Shallow processing includes noting the physical features of a stimulus, such as the shapes of the letters in the word *mom*. Intermediate processing involves giving the stimulus a label, as in reading the word *mom*. The deepest level of processing entails thinking about the meaning of a stimulus—for instance, thinking about the meaning of the word *mom* and about your own mother, her face, and her special qualities.

The more deeply we process, the better the memory (Howes, 2006; Rose & Craik, 2012). For example, researchers have found that if we encode something meaningful about a face and make associations with it, we are more likely to remember the face (Harris & Kay, 1995). The restaurant server who strives to remember the face of the customer and to imagine her eating the food she has ordered is using deep processing (Figure 2).

Elaboration

elaboration
The formation of a number of different connections around a stimulus at a given level of memory encoding.

Effective encoding of a memory depends on more than just depth of processing. Within deep processing, the more extensive the processing, the better the memory (Dudukovic & Kuhl, 2017). **Elaboration** refers to the formation of a number of different connections around a stimulus at any given level of memory encoding. Elaboration is like creating a huge spider web of links between some new information and everything one already knows, and it can occur at any level of processing. In the case of the word *mom,* a person can elaborate on mom even at a shallow level—for example, by thinking of the shapes of the letters and how they relate to the shapes of other letters, say, how an *m* looks like two *n*'s. At a deep level of processing, a person might focus on what a mother is or might think about various mothers he or she knows, images of mothers in art, and portrayals of mothers on television and in film. Generally speaking, the more elaborate the processing, the better memory will be. Deep, elaborate processing is a powerful way to remember.

When you engage in elaborate, deep processing, you are setting the stage for later remembering by leaving lots of paths to follow when you need to recall the material. Who knows which of these cues will help you remember, but you'll have lots of possibilities.

For example, rather than trying to memorize the definition of memory, you would do better to weave a complex spider web around the concept of memory by coming up with a real-world example of how information enters your mind, how it is stored, and how you can retrieve it. Thinking of concrete examples of a concept is a good way to understand it. *Self-reference*—relating material to your own experience—is another effective way to elaborate on information, drawing mental links between aspects of your own life and new information (Hunt & Ellis, 2004) (Figure 3).

The process of elaboration is evident in the physical activity of the brain. Neuroscience research has shown a link between elaboration during encoding and brain activity (Kaneda, Shigemune, & Tsukiura, 2017). In one study, researchers placed individuals in magnetic resonance imaging (MRI) machines and flashed one word every 2 seconds on a screen inside (Wagner & others, 1998). Initially, the individuals simply noted whether the words were in uppercase or lowercase letters. As the study progressed, they were asked to determine whether each word meant something concrete, such as chair or book, or abstract, such as love or democracy. The participants showed more neural activity in the left frontal lobe of the brain during the concrete/abstract task than they did when they were asked merely to state whether the words were in uppercase or lowercase letters. Further, they demonstrated better memory in the concrete/abstract task. The researchers concluded that greater elaboration of information is linked with neural activity, especially in the brain's left frontal lobe, and with improved memory.

FIGURE 3 **Memory Improves When Self-Reference Is Used** In one study, researchers asked participants to remember lists of words according to the words' physical, acoustic (sound), semantic (meaning), or self-referent characteristics. As the figure illustrates, when individuals generated self-references for the words, they remembered them better.

As noted above, laptops and tablets interfere with learning because they distract attention (Ravizza, Uitvlugt, & Fenn, 2017). Yet, even when digital devices are used only for notes (not surfing the web, checking social media, or live tweeting an introductory psychology lecture), pen and paper outperform laptops in student memory for material. Why would this be the case? To answer that question, see the Challenge Your Thinking.

Imagery

One of the most powerful ways to make memories distinctive is to use mental imagery (Keogh & Pearson, 2017). Mental imagery entails visualizing material that we want to remember in ways that create a lasting portrait. Imagery functions as a powerful encoding tool for all of us, certainly including the world champions of memory listed in Figure 4.

Memorization of...	Record Holder	Country	Year	Record
Written numbers in 1 minute, no errors	Gunther Karsten	Germany	2007	102 numbers
Random words in 15 minutes*	Simon Reinhard	Germany	2010	300 words
Speed to recall a single deck of 52 shuffled playing cards, no errors	Simon Reinhard	Germany	2011	21.19 seconds
Historic dates in 5 minutes	Johannes Mallow	Germany	2011	132 dates
Abstract images in 15 minutes	Johannes Mallow	Germany	2013	492 images

FIGURE 4

World Champions of Memory For memorization wizards such as these world record holders, imagery is a powerful encoding tool.

SOURCE: The International World Record Breakers' Club

*Participants view random words in columns of 25 words. Scoring is tabulated by column: one point for each word. One mistake reduces the score for that column by half, and the second mistake reduces the score for that column to zero.

Challenge YOUR THINKING

Why Is the Pen Mightier Than the Keyboard?

Class notes are a vital tool for doing well in college. Anyone who has missed a day of lecture knows how important it is to get someone's notes to prepare for exams. Notes provide "external storage" for course material: They allow us to retain information that has not been committed to memory (yet).

Research shows that typed (versus handwritten) lecture notes often better reflect, exactly what was in a lecture, word for word. However, there are negative effects of laptop internet use during class (Ravizza, Uitvlugt, & Feen, 2017). For example, in a series of studies, students were randomly assigned to take notes on laptops or with a pen and notebook while watching various presentations. Across all studies, compared to handwritten notes, typing on a laptop produced more notes and notes that showed more overlap with exactly what presenters had said (Mueller & Oppenheimer, 2014). Yet, importantly, in those same studies, students using laptops performed more poorly on memory tests, especially when the tests involved understanding the concepts presented. Why might this be the case?

To answer this question, we need to think about another way note taking influences memory—namely, through depth of processing during encoding. Taking notes can be an opportunity for deeply processing course material, and this is where handwritten notes are superior to typed notes.

Here's why: Because students can type so much faster than they can write, they are more likely to simply type verbatim, that is, word for word, what the instructor says (Mueller & Oppenheimer, 2014), which is an activity that requires little thought. Students who simply transcribe lectures are basically "court reporters" for a class. In contrast, because writing notes by hand is slower, students must make decisions: What should be written down and what should not? What words will summarize a point as quickly

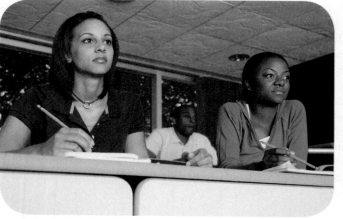

©James Woodson/Photodisc/Getty Images

as possible? How can an idea be described so that it will be understandable later?

Handwritten notes, then, are more likely to represent active engagement with the material during encoding. Handwritten notes reflect an effort to put course information in "one's own words." That is deep processing. Even though typed notes are more likely to be verbatim transcripts of lectures, they are also less likely to represent deep processing.

Now, you might be thinking that because they are more accurate reflections of lectures, laptop notes would be best for studying. A final study showed that this was not the case. In that study, students were given laptops or notebooks to take notes on lectures about bats, bread, vaccines, and respiration. One week later, they were permitted to study their notes for 10 minutes before answering difficult questions about the lectures. The results? Only those who took notes by hand benefited from studying (Mueller & Oppenheimer, 2014).

This research tells us that learning involves more than time spent studying. Attending class, paying attention to an instructor's presentation, and actively and deeply engaging with course material—not just when we study but when we first encounter the material—is vital to creating long-lasting memories.

What Do You Think?

- How will this research affect your approach to your courses?
- Students with disabilities sometimes require laptops for note-taking. How might this research affect the way they take notes?

Consider, for instance, Rajveer Meena, who, in 2015, recited the digits of pi to the first 70,000 decimal places. Think about memorizing a list of 70,000 numbers. How would you go about it? One way would be to use mental imagery to create a kind of visual mental walk through the digits. To memorize the first 8 digits of pi (3.1415926), one might say, "3 is a chubby fellow who walks with a cane (1), up to a take-out window (4), and orders 15 hamburgers. The cook (9), who has very large biceps (2), slips on his way to deliver the burgers (6)."

Mental imagery comes in handy in everyday life. Think about a restaurant server. After reciting your rather complicated order to a server, you notice that he is not writing anything down. Waiting patiently through your friends' orders, you wonder, "How can he possibly remember all this?" When the meal arrives, however, everything is exactly right. Waiters seem to commit remarkable acts of memory routinely. How do they do it? Asked to share his secrets, a college student who moonlights in food service explained: "I always try to remember the person's face and imagine him eating the food he's ordered."

Classic studies by Allan Paivio (1971, 1986, 2007) have documented how imagery can improve memory. Paivio argues that memory is stored in one of two ways: as a verbal code (a word or a label) or an image code. Paivio thinks that the image code, which is highly detailed and distinctive, produces better memory than the verbal code. His *dual-code hypothesis* claims that memory for pictures is better than memory for words because pictures—at least those that can be named—are stored as both image codes and verbal codes (Paivio & Sadoski, 2011; Welcome & others, 2011). Thus, when we use imagery to remember, we have two potential avenues by which we can retrieve information.

 Easy, right? Remembering a picture means remembering two things: the image AND the word that goes with it.

©Ryan McVay/Getty Images

self-quiz

1. Shane is studying for a vocabulary test. When he studies the word *braggart,* he thinks of how his friend Bill acts whenever Bill wins a tennis match. Shane is processing this word at a(n)
   A. shallow level.
   B. intermediate level.
   C. deep level.
   D. personal level.

2. The extensiveness of processing information at a given level is called
   A. scope of processing.
   B. depth of processing.
   C. span of memory.
   D. elaboration.

3. One of the most effective ways to make our memories distinctive is to use mental
   A. cues.
   B. rehearsal.
   C. imagery.
   D. concentration.

APPLY IT! 4. Linus and Polly are arguing over the best way to study for an upcoming psychology exam. Polly tries to tell Linus that the best way to remember things is to use flashcards, but Linus, an astrophysics major, spends a lot of time jotting down the connections between his psychology class and concepts from astrophysics. Polly warns him,

"You are wasting your time. You're just going to get confused." What do you think of Polly's warning?
   A. Linus should listen to Polly. There truly is one best way to remember things.
   B. Polly should back off. Linus is elaborating on the material at a deep level, and this approach will probably pay off on the exam.
   C. Linus is likely to get confused when the exam has no astrophysics questions.
   D. Polly will do better because flashcards require shallow processing.

3 Memory Storage

The quality of encoding does not alone determine the quality of memory. A memory also needs to be stored properly after it is encoded. **Storage** encompasses how information is retained over time and how it is represented in memory.

We remember some information for less than a second, some for half a minute, and some for minutes, hours, years, or even a lifetime. Richard Atkinson and Richard Shiffrin (1968) formulated an early popular theory of memory that acknowledged the varying life span of memories (Figure 5). The **Atkinson-Shiffrin theory** states that memory storage involves three separate systems:

- Sensory memory: time frames of a fraction of a second to several seconds
- Short-term memory: time frames up to 30 seconds
- Long-term memory: time frames up to a lifetime

storage
The retention of information over time and how this information is represented in memory.

Atkinson-Shiffrin theory
Theory stating that memory storage involves three separate systems: sensory memory, short-term memory, and long-term memory.

FIGURE 5 **Atkinson and Shiffrin's Theory of Memory** In this model, sensory input goes into sensory memory. Through the process of attention, information moves into short-term memory, where it remains for 30 seconds or less unless it is rehearsed. When the information goes into long-term memory storage, it can be retrieved over a lifetime.

As you read about these three memory storage systems, you will find that time frame is not the only thing that makes them different from one another. Each type of memory also operates in a distinctive way and has a special purpose.

Sensory Memory

sensory memory
Memory system that involves holding information from the world in its original sensory form for only an instant, not much longer than the brief time it is exposed to the visual, auditory, and other senses.

Sensory memory holds information from the world in its original sensory form for only an instant, not much longer than the brief time it is exposed to the visual, auditory, and other senses. Sensory memory is very rich and detailed, but we lose the information in it quickly unless we use certain strategies that transfer it into short-term or long-term memory.

Think about the sights and sounds you encounter as you walk to class on a typical morning. Literally thousands of stimuli come into your field of vision and hearing—cracks in the sidewalk, chirping birds, a noisy motorcycle, the blue sky, faces and voices of hundreds of people. You do not process all of these stimuli, but you do process a number of them. In general, you process many more stimuli at the sensory level than you consciously notice. Sensory memory retains this information from your senses, including a large portion of what you think you ignore. However, sensory memory does not retain the information very long.

Echoic memory (from the word *echo*) refers to auditory sensory memory, which is retained for up to several seconds. Imagine standing in an elevator with a friend who suddenly asks, "What was that song?" about the piped-in tune that just ended. If your friend asks his question quickly enough, you just might have a trace of the song left in your sensory registers.

©SIMONKR/Getty Images

Type of Sensory Register

Auditory   Visual

Up to several seconds   About ¼ second

FIGURE 6 **Auditory and Visual Sensory Memory** If you hear this bird's call while walking through the woods, your auditory sensory memory holds the information for several seconds. If you see the bird, your visual sensory memory holds the information for only about ¼ of a second.

(bird) ©Steve Byland/123RF; (ear) ©Geoff du Feu/Alamy Stock Photo; (eye) ©ColorBlind Images/Blend Images LLC

Iconic memory (from the word *icon,* which means "image") refers to visual sensory memory, which is retained only for about ¼ of a second (Figure 6). Visual sensory memory is responsible for our ability to "write" in the air using a sparkler on the Fourth of July—the residual iconic memory is what makes a moving point of light appear to be a line. The sensory memory for other senses, such as smell and touch, has received little attention in research studies.

The first scientific research on sensory memory focused on iconic memory. Remember that iconic memory is that part of sensory memory that includes images. In George Sperling's (1960) classic study, participants viewed patterns of stimuli such as those in Figure 7. As you look at the letters, you have no trouble recognizing them. However, Sperling flashed the letters on a screen for very brief intervals, about $1/20$ of a second. Afterward, the participants could report only four or five letters. With such a short exposure, reporting all nine letters was impossible.

Some participants in Sperling's study reported feeling that for an instant, they could see all nine letters within a briefly flashed pattern. They ran into trouble when they tried to name all the letters they had initially seen. One hypothesis to explain this experience is that all nine letters were initially processed as far as the iconic sensory memory level. This is why all nine letters were seen. However, forgetting from iconic memory occurred so rapidly that the participants did not have time to transfer all the letters to short-term memory, where they could be named.

Sperling reasoned that if all nine letters are actually processed in sensory memory, they should all be available for a brief time. To test this possibility, Sperling sounded a low, medium, or high tone just after a pattern of letters was shown. The participants were told that the tone was a signal to report only the letters from the bottom, middle, or top row. Under these conditions, the participants performed much better, and this outcome suggests a brief memory for most or all of the letters in the display. Sperling showed that an entire array of information is briefly present in iconic memory. To experience this phenomenon, glance at this page for just a second. All of the letters are present in your sensory memory for an instant, creating a mental image that momentarily exists in its entirety.

FIGURE 7

Sperling's Sensory Memory Experiment This array of stimuli is similar to those flashed for about $1/20$ of a second to the participants in Sperling's study.

Sperling's solution is truly remarkable. He realized that by giving the participants the signal, he could help them to scan their mental image quickly so that they could find specific pieces of the information that it contained in various places. Their ability to do so demonstrates that all the material was actually there. Fantastic!

Short-Term Memory

short-term memory
Limited-capacity memory system in which information is usually retained for only as long as 30 seconds unless strategies are used to retain it longer.

Much information goes no further than the stage of auditory and visual sensory memory. We retain this information for only a brief instant. However, some information, especially that to which we pay attention, proceeds into short-term memory. **Short-term memory** is a limited-capacity memory system in which information is usually retained for only as long as 30 seconds unless we use strategies to retain it longer. Compared with sensory memory, short-term memory is limited in capacity, but it can store information for a longer time.

George Miller (1956) examined the limited capacity of short-term memory in the classic paper "The Magical Number Seven, Plus or Minus Two." Miller pointed out that on many tasks individuals are limited in how much information they can keep track of without external aids. Usually the limit is in the range of 7 ± 2 items. The most widely cited example of this phenomenon involves *memory span,* the number of digits an individual can report back in order after a single presentation of them. Most college students can remember eight or nine digits

What are some important numbers in your life? Do they follow the 7 ± 2 rule?

without making errors (think about how easy it is to recall a phone number). Longer lists pose problems because they exceed short-term memory capacity. If you rely on simple short-term memory to retain longer lists, you probably will make errors.

CHUNKING AND REHEARSAL   Two ways to improve short-term memory are chunking and rehearsal. *Chunking* involves grouping or "packing" information that exceeds the 7 ± 2 memory span into higher-order units that can be remembered as single units. Chunking works by making large amounts of information more manageable (Akyürek & others, 2017; Yamaguchi & others, 2017).

To get a sense of chunking, consider this word list: *hot, city, book, forget, tomorrow,* and *smile.* Hold these words in memory for a moment; then write them down. If you recalled the words, you succeeded in holding 30 letters, grouped into six chunks, in memory. Now hold the following list in memory and then write it down:

O   LDH   ARO   LDAN   DYO   UNGB   EN

How did you do? Do not feel bad if you did poorly. This string of letters is very difficult to remember, even though it is arranged in chunks. The problem is that the chunks lack meaning. If you re-chunk the letters to form the meaningful words "Old Harold and Young Ben," they become much easier to remember.

Another way to improve short-term memory involves *rehearsal*: the conscious repetition of information (Camos, Lagner, & Loaiza, 2017; Lindeman, Zengel, & Skowronski, 2017). Information stored in short-term memory lasts half a minute or less without rehearsal. However, if rehearsal is not interrupted, information can be retained indefinitely. Rehearsal is often verbal, giving the impression of an inner voice, but it can also be visual or spatial, giving the impression of a private inner eye (Darling, Allen, & Havelka, 2017; Ginsberg & others, 2017).

Rehearsal works best when we must briefly remember a list of numbers or items such as entrées from a dinner menu. When we need to remember information for longer periods of time, as when we are studying for a test coming up next week or even an hour from now, other strategies usually work better. A main reason rehearsal does not work well for retaining information over the long term is that rehearsal often involves just mechanically repeating information, without imparting meaning to it. The fact that, over the long term, we remember information best when we add meaning to it demonstrates the importance of deep, elaborate processing.

Though useful, Atkinson and Shiffrin's theory of the three time-linked memory systems fails to capture the dynamic way short-term memory functions (Baddeley, 2008, 2012). Short-term memory is not just about storing information; it is about attending to information, manipulating it, and using it to solve problems (Cowan & others, 2011a, 2011b; Loaiza & others, 2014). How can we understand these processes? The concept of working memory is one way psychologists have addressed this question.

working memory
A combination of components, including short-term memory and attention, that allow individuals to hold information temporarily as they perform cognitive tasks; a kind of mental workbench on which the brain manipulates and assembles information to guide understanding, decision making, and problem solving.

WORKING MEMORY   **Working memory** refers to a combination of components, including short-term memory and attention, that allow us to hold information temporarily as we perform cognitive tasks (Cowan, 2008, 2017; Cowan & others, 2012). Working memory is not the same thing as short-term memory. For instance, a person can hold a list of words in short-term memory by rehearsing them over and over. A measure of short-term memory capacity, then, might simply involve counting how many words in the list the person can remember. Working memory capacity is separable from short-term memory capacity. We cannot be rehearsing information while we are working on solving a problem. This may be why measures of short-term memory capacity are not strongly related to cognitive aptitudes, such as intelligence, while working memory capacity is (Cowan, 2008). Because short-term memory capacity can rely on rehearsal, 7 ± 2 chunks are generally manageable. However, in working memory, if the chunks are relatively complex, most young adults can remember only 4 ± 1, that is, three to five chunks (Cowan, 2010). Working memory is not a passive storehouse with shelves to store information until it moves to long-term memory, but rather it is an active memory system.

Working memory can be thought of as a mental blackboard, a place where we can imagine and visualize. In this sense, working memory is the context for conscious thought (Bronfman & others, 2014). Anthropologists, archaeologists, and psychologists have been interested in understanding how working memory evolved. For example, prehistoric tools (Haidle, 2010) and works of art (Wynn, Coolidge, & Bright, 2009) reveal how early humans thought. Consider the *Lion Man,* an ivory sculpture archaeologists found in a cave in Germany. The 28-cm figurine, with the head of a lion and the body of a man, is believed to have been created 32,000 years ago (Balter, 2010). This ancient work of art must have been the product of an individual who had the capacity to see two things and, in working memory, ask something like, "What would they look like if I combined them?" Some commentators have suggested that working memory lays the foundation for creative culture (Haidle, 2010). Working memory has been proposed as a key difference between Neanderthal and *Homo sapiens* (Wynn & Coolidge, 2010).

Working memory has served as a helpful framework for addressing practical problems outside the laboratory. For example, advances in understanding working memory have allowed researchers to identify students at risk for academic underachievement and to improve their memory (Carretti & others, 2014; Rennie, Beebe-Frankenberger, & Swanson, 2014). Working memory also has been beneficial in the early detection of Alzheimer disease and other cognitive problems (Charlesworth & others, 2014; Price & others, 2017).

Working memory is a kind of mental workbench on which the brain manipulates and assembles information to help us understand, make decisions, and solve problems. If, say, all of the information on the hard drive of your computer is like long-term memory, then working memory is comparable to what you have open and active at any given moment. Working memory has a limited capacity, and, to take the computer metaphor further, the capacity of the working memory is like RAM.

How does working memory work? British psychologist Alan Baddeley (1993, 1998, 2003, 2008, 2012, 2013) has proposed an influential model of working memory featuring a three-part system that allows us to hold information temporarily as we perform cognitive tasks.

Figure 8 shows Baddeley's view of the three components of working memory. The three components are the *central executive,* the *phonological loop,* and the *visuo-spatial sketchpad.* Think of them as a boss (the central executive) who has two assistants (the phonological loop and the visuo-spatial sketchpad) to help do the work. Be sure to examine Figure 8 carefully.

1. The *phonological loop* is specialized to briefly store speech-based information about the sounds of language. The phonological loop contains two separate components: an acoustic code (the sounds we heard), which decays in a few seconds, and rehearsal, which allows us to repeat the words in the phonological store.

2. The *visuo-spatial sketchpad* stores visual and spatial information, including visual imagery. As in the case of the phonological loop, the

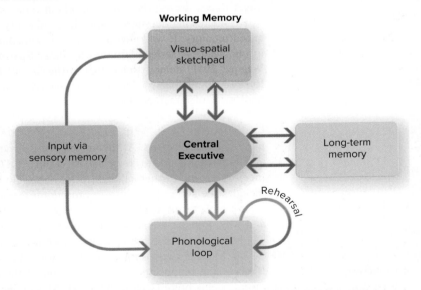

FIGURE 8 **Baddeley's View of Working Memory** In Baddeley's working memory model, working memory consists of three main components: the phonological loop, the visuo-spatial sketchpad, and the central executive. The phonological loop and the visuo-spatial sketchpad serve as assistants, helping the central executive do its work. Input from sensory memory goes to the phonological loop, where information about speech is stored and rehearsal takes place, and to the visuo-spatial sketchpad, where visual and spatial information, including imagery, is stored. Working memory is a limited capacity system, and information is stored there only briefly. Working memory interacts with long-term memory, drawing information from long-term memory and transmitting information to long-term memory for longer storage.

Think about it! Working memory is, in some ways, the very essence of consciousness—your ability to quietly think to yourself in the private little workshop in your head.

capacity of the visuo-spatial sketchpad is limited. If we try to put too many items in the visuo-spatial sketchpad, we cannot represent them accurately enough to retrieve them successfully. The phonological loop and the visuo-spatial sketchpad function independently. We can rehearse numbers in the phonological loop while making spatial arrangements of letters in the visuo-spatial sketchpad.

3. The *central executive* integrates information not only from the phonological loop and the visuo-spatial sketchpad but also from long-term memory. In Baddeley's (2008, 2012) view, the central executive plays important roles in attention, planning, and organizing. The central executive acts like a supervisor who monitors which information deserves our attention and which we should ignore. It also selects which strategies to use to process information and solve problems (Allen, Baddeley, & Hitch, 2014; Hu & others, 2014). Like the phonological loop and the visuo-spatial sketchpad, the central executive has a limited capacity. If working memory is like the files you have open on your computer, the central executive is you. You pull up information you need, close out other things, and so forth.

Though it is compelling, Baddeley's notion of working memory is merely a conceptual model describing processes in memory. Neuroscientists have only just begun to search for brain areas and activity that might be responsible for these processes (Bray, 2017).

Long-Term Memory

long-term memory
A relatively permanent type of memory that stores huge amounts of information for a long time.

Long-term memory is a relatively permanent type of memory that stores huge amounts of information for a long time. The capacity of long-term memory is staggering. John von Neumann (1958), a distinguished mathematician, put the size at 2.8×10^{20} (280 quintillion) bits, which in practical terms means that our storage capacity is virtually unlimited. Von Neumann assumed that we never forget anything; but even considering that we do forget things, we can hold several billion times more information than a large computer.

An interesting question is how the availability of information on the Internet has influenced memory. If we know we can look something up on the web, why bother storing it in our head? A series of studies by Betsy Sparrow and her colleagues (Sparrow, Liu, & Wegner, 2011) demonstrated that in the face of difficult memory tasks, people are likely to think immediately of looking to the computer for the answer rather than doing the hard work of remembering.

COMPONENTS OF LONG-TERM MEMORY   Long-term memory is complex, as Figure 9 shows. At the top level, it is divided into substructures of explicit memory and implicit memory (Heyselaar & others, 2017; Moskovitch & others, 2016). Explicit memory can be further subdivided into episodic and semantic memory. Implicit memory includes the systems involved in procedural memory, classical conditioning, and priming.

In simple terms, explicit memory has to do with remembering who, what, where, when, and why; implicit memory has to do with remembering how. To explore the distinction, let's look at the case of a person known as H. M. Afflicted with severe epilepsy, H. M. underwent surgery in 1953, when he was 27 years old, that involved removing the hippocampus and a portion of the temporal lobes of both hemispheres in his brain (Carey, 2009). H. M.'s epilepsy improved, but something devastating happened to his memory. Most dramatically, he developed an inability to form new memories that outlive working memory. H. M.'s memory time frame was only a few minutes at most, so he lived, until his death in 2008, in a perpetual present and could not remember past events (explicit memory). In contrast, his memory of how to do things (implicit memory) was less affected. For example, he could learn new physical tasks, even though he had no memory of how or when he learned them.

H. M. spent most of his life in the present moment. His legacy to cognitive science is unforgettable. When he died, many of the psychologists who had studied his case felt as if they had lost a friend–even if a friend who had never been able to remember them.

H. M.'s situation demonstrates a distinction between explicit memory, which was dramatically impaired in his case, and implicit memory, which in his case was less

FIGURE 9 Systems of Long-Term Memory Long-term memory stores huge amounts of information for long periods of time, much like a computer's hard drive. The hierarchy in the figure shows the division of long-term memory at the top level into explicit memory and implicit memory. Explicit memory can be further divided into episodic and semantic memory; implicit memory includes procedural memory, priming, and classical conditioning.

influenced by his surgery. Let's explore the subsystems of explicit and implicit memory more thoroughly.

explicit memory or declarative memory
The conscious recollection of information, such as specific facts or events and, at least in humans, information that can be verbally communicated.

Explicit Memory **Explicit memory (declarative memory)** is the conscious recollection of information, such as specific facts and events and, at least in humans, information that can be verbally communicated (Tulving, 1989, 2000). Examples of using explicit, or declarative, memory include recounting the events in a movie you have seen and recalling which politicians are in the president's cabinet.

How long does explicit memory last? Explicit memory includes things you are learning in your classes even now. Will this information stay with you? Research by Harry Bahrick has examined this question. Ohio Wesleyan University, where Bahrick is a professor of psychology, is a small (about 1,800 students) liberal arts school that boasts very loyal alumni who faithfully return to campus for reunions and other events. Bahrick (1984) took advantage of this situation to conduct an ingenious study on the retention of course material over time. He gave vocabulary tests to individuals who had taken Spanish in college as well as to a control group of college students who had not taken Spanish in college. The individuals chosen for the study had used Spanish very little since their college courses. Some individuals were tested at the end of an academic year (just after having taken their Spanish courses), but others were tested years after graduation—as many as 50 years later. When Bahrick assessed how much the participants had forgotten, he found a striking pattern (Figure 10): Forgetting tended to occur in the first three years after taking the classes and then leveled off, so that adults maintained considerable knowledge of Spanish vocabulary words up to 50 years later.

Bahrick (1984) assessed not only how long ago the adults had studied Spanish but also how well they did in Spanish during college. Those who had earned an *A* in their courses 50 years earlier remembered more Spanish than adults who had gotten a *C* grade when taking Spanish only one year earlier. Thus, how well students initially learned the material was even more important than how long ago they had studied it. Bahrick (2000) calls information that is retained for such a long time "permastore" content. Permastore memory represents that portion of original learning that appears destined to be with the person

What course material do you think you will never forget?

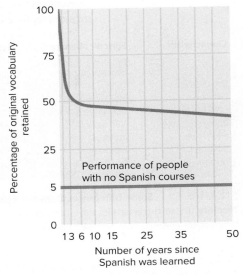

FIGURE 10 Memory for Spanish as a Function of Age Since Spanish Was Learned An initial steep drop over about a three-year period in remembering the vocabulary learned in Spanish classes occurred. However, there was little dropoff in memory for Spanish vocabulary from three years after taking Spanish classes to 50 years after taking them. Even 50 years after taking Spanish classes, individuals still remembered almost 50 percent of the vocabulary.
SOURCE: Bahrick, Harry P. Journal of Experimental Psychology: General, 113(1), Mar 1984, 1-29.

virtually forever, even without rehearsal. In addition to focusing on course material, Bahrick and colleagues (1974) probed adults' memories for the faces and names of their high school classmates. Thirty-five years after graduation, the participants visually recognized 90 percent of the portraits of their high school classmates, with name recognition being almost as high. These results held up even in relatively large classes (the average class size in the study was 294).

Canadian cognitive psychologist Endel Tulving (1972, 1989, 2000) has been the foremost advocate of distinguishing between two subtypes of explicit memory: episodic and semantic. **Episodic memory** is the retention of information about the where, when, and what of life's happenings—how we remember life's episodes. Episodic memory is autobiographical. For example, episodic memory includes the details of where you were when your younger brother or sister was born, what happened on your first date, and what you ate for breakfast this morning.

Semantic memory is a person's knowledge about the world. It includes one's areas of expertise, general knowledge of the sort learned in school, and everyday knowledge about the meanings of words, famous individuals, important places, and common things. For example, semantic memory is involved in a person's knowledge of chess, of geometry, and of who the Dalai Lama, LeBron James, and Lady Gaga are. An important aspect of semantic memory is that it appears to be independent of an individual's personal identity with the past. You can access a fact—such as the detail that Lima is the capital of Peru—and not have the foggiest notion of when and where you learned it.

The difference between episodic and semantic memory is also demonstrated in certain cases of amnesia (memory loss) (Moscovitch, 2013). A person with amnesia might forget entirely who she is—her name, family, career, and all other vital information about herself—yet still be able to talk, know what words mean, and have general knowledge about the world, such as what day it is or who currently holds the office of U.S. president (Rosenbaum & others, 2005). In such cases, episodic memory is impaired, but semantic memory is functioning.

Your recollection of your first day on campus is an episodic memory. If you take a history class, your memory of the information you need to know for a test involves semantic memory.

episodic memory
The retention of information about the where, when, and what of life's happenings—that is, how individuals remember life's episodes.

semantic memory
A person's knowledge about the world.

Characteristic	Episodic Memory	Semantic Memory
Units	Events, episodes	Facts, ideas, concept
Organization	Time	Concepts
Emotion	More important	Less important
Retrieval process	Deliberate (effortful)	Automatic
Retrieval report	"I remember"	"I know"
Education	Irrelevant	Relevant
Intelligence	Irrelevant	Relevant
Legal testimony	Admissable in court	Inadmissable in court

FIGURE 11 Some Differences Between Episodic and Semantic Memory These characteristics have been proposed as the main ways to differentiate episodic from semantic memory.

Figure 11 summarizes some aspects of the episodic/semantic distinction. The differences that are listed are controversial. One criticism is that many cases of explicit, or declarative, memory are neither purely episodic nor purely semantic but fall in a gray area in between. Consider your memory for what you studied last night. You probably added knowledge to your semantic memory—that was, after all, the reason you were studying. You probably remember where you were studying, as well as about when you started and when you stopped. You probably also can remember some minor occurrences, such as a burst of loud laughter from the room next door or the coffee you spilled on the desk.

Is episodic or semantic memory involved here? Tulving (1983, 2000) argues that semantic and episodic systems often work together in forming new memories. In such cases, the memory that ultimately forms might consist of an autobiographical episode and semantic information.

Implicit (Nondeclarative) Memory
In addition to explicit memory, there is a type of long-term memory that is related to non-consciously remembering skills and sensory perceptions rather than consciously remembering facts. **Implicit memory (nondeclarative memory)** is memory in which behavior is affected by prior experience without a conscious recollection of that experience. Implicit memory comes into play, for example, in the skills of playing tennis and snowboarding, as well as in the physical act of text messaging. Another example of

This is also why you might find yourself knowing the words to a song you hate. You've heard it so many times that you've memorized it without even wanting to.

implicit memory or nondeclarative memory
Memory in which behavior is affected by prior experience without a conscious recollection of that experience.

implicit memory is the repetition in your mind of a song you heard playing in the supermarket, even though you had not noticed that song playing.

Three subsystems of implicit memory are procedural memory, classical conditioning, and priming. All of these subsystems refer to memories that you are not aware of but that influence behavior (Slotnick & Schacter, 2006).

procedural memory
Memory for skills.

Procedural memory is a type of implicit memory process that involves memory for skills (Doll, Shohamy, & Daw, 2014). For example, assuming that you are an expert typist, when you type a paper you are not conscious of where the keys are for the various letters; somehow, your well-learned, nonconscious skill of typing allows you to hit the right keys. Similarly, once you have learned to drive a car, you remember how to go about it: You do not have to remember consciously how to drive the car as you put the key in the ignition, turn the steering wheel, depress the gas pedal, and step on the brake pedal.

To grasp the difference between explicit and procedural memory, imagine trying to describe in words how to tie a shoe—a procedure you can easily perform—without having a shoe around.

Another type of implicit memory involves classical conditioning, a form of learning. Recall that classical conditioning involves the automatic learning of associations between stimuli, so that one stimulus comes to evoke the same response as the other. Classically conditioned associations involve nonconscious, implicit memory. So, without realizing it, you might start to like the person who sits next to you in your favorite class, because she is around while you are feeling good.

Thanks to implicit memory, we can perform a learned skill, such as playing tennis, without thinking about it consciously.
©Design Pics/Darren Greenwood

priming
The activation of information that people already have in storage to help them remember new information better and faster.

Priming is the activation of information that people already have in storage to help them remember new information better and faster (Lerner & Shriki, 2014; McNamara, 2013). In a common demonstration of priming, individuals study a list of words (such as *hope, walk,* and *cake*). Then they are given a standard recognition task to assess explicit memory. They must select all of the words that appeared in the list—for example, "Did you see the word *hope?* Did you see the word *form?*" Then participants perform a stem-completion task, which assesses implicit memory. In this task, they view a list of incomplete words (for example, *ho__, wa__, ca__*), called word stems, and must fill in the blanks with whatever word comes to mind. The results show that individuals more often fill in the blanks with the previously studied words than would be expected if they were filling in the blanks randomly. For example, they are more likely to complete the stem *ho__* with *hope* than with *hole*. This result occurs even when individuals do not recognize the words on the earlier recognition task. Because priming takes place even when explicit memory for previous information is not required, it is assumed to be an involuntary and unconscious process (Mele, Mattiassi, & Urgesi, 2014). Priming occurs when something in the environment evokes a response in memory—such as the activation of a particular concept.

Yeah baby! Classical conditioning is back! Yes, this automatic associative learning involves memory!

HOW MEMORY IS ORGANIZED Explaining the forms of long-term memory does not address the question of how the different types of memory are organized for storage. The word *organized* is important: Memories are not haphazardly stored but instead are carefully sorted.

Here is a demonstration. Recall the 12 months of the year as quickly as you can. How long did it take you? What was the order of your recall? Chances are, you listed them within a few seconds in chronological order (January, February, March, and so on). Now try to remember the months in alphabetical order. How long did it take you? Did you make any errors? It should be obvious that your memory for the months of the year is organized in a particular way. Indeed, one of memory's most distinctive features is its organization.

Researchers have found that if people are encouraged to organize material simply, their memories of the material improve even if they receive no warning that their memories

©Goran Bogicevic/Shutterstock

will be tested (Mandler, 1980). Psychologists have developed a variety of theories of how long-term memory is organized. Let's consider two of these more closely: schemas and connectionist networks.

Schemas

You and a friend have taken a long drive to a new town where neither of you has ever been before. You stop at the local diner, have a seat, and look over the menu. You have never been in this diner before, but you know exactly what is going to happen. Why? Because you have a schema for what happens in a restaurant. When we store information in memory, we often fit it into the collection of information that already exists, as you do even in a new experience with a diner. A **schema** is a preexisting mental concept or framework that helps people to organize and interpret information (Gilboa & Marlatte, 2017). Schemas from prior encounters with the environment influence the way we handle information—how we encode it, what inferences we make about it, and how we retrieve it.

Schemas can also be at work when we recall information. Schema theory holds that long-term memory is not very exact. We seldom find precisely the memory that we want, or at least not all of what we want; hence, we have to reconstruct the rest. Our schemas support the reconstruction process, helping us fill in gaps between our fragmented memories.

We have schemas for lots of situations and experiences—for scenes and spatial layouts (a beach, a bathroom), as well as for common events (playing football, writing a term paper). A **script** is a schema for an event (Schank & Abelson, 1977). Scripts often have information about physical features, people, and typical occurrences. This kind of information is helpful when people need to figure out what is happening around them. For example, if you are enjoying your after-dinner coffee in an upscale restaurant and a man in a tuxedo comes over and puts a piece of paper on the table, your script tells you that the man probably is a waiter who has just given you the check. Scripts help to organize our storage of memories about events.

Connectionist Networks

Schema theory has little or nothing to say about the role of the physical brain in memory. Thus, a new theory based on brain research has generated a wave of excitement among psychologists. **Connectionism, or parallel distributed processing (PDP),** is the theory that memory is stored throughout the brain in connections among neurons, several of which may work together to process a single memory (McClelland, 2011). Recall the concept of neural networks and the idea of parallel sensory processing pathways. These concepts also apply to memory.

In the connectionist view, memories are not large knowledge structures (as in schema theories). Instead, memories are more like electrical impulses, organized only to the extent that neurons, the connections among them, and their activity are organized (Xiao & others, 2017; Yaffe & others, 2017). Any piece of knowledge—such as your dog's name—is embedded in the strengths of hundreds or thousands of connections among neurons and is not limited to a single location.

How does the connectionist process work? A neural activity involving memory, such as remembering your dog's name, is spread across a number of areas of the cerebral cortex. The locations of neural activity, called *nodes,* are interconnected. When a node reaches a critical level of activation, it can affect another node across synapses. We know that the human cerebral cortex contains millions of neurons that are richly interconnected through hundreds of millions of synapses. Because of these synaptic connections, the activity of one neuron can be influenced by many other neurons. Owing to these simple reactions, the connectionist view argues that changes in the strength of synaptic connections are the fundamental bases of memory (McClelland & others, 2010). From the connectionist network perspective, memories are organized sets of neurons that

script
A schema for an event, often containing information about physical features, people, and typical occurrences.

schema
A preexisting mental concept or framework that helps people to organize and interpret information. Schemas from prior encounters with the environment influence the way individuals encode, make inferences about, and retrieve information.

connectionism
Also called parallel distributed processing (PDP), the theory that memory is stored throughout the brain in connections among neurons, several of which may work together to process a single memory.

This is why elaboration in encoding is so helpful. It is laying down all these pathways in your brain that light up when you try to remember.

are routinely activated together. The process by which these interconnected networks are formed is called *consolidation*. When neurons continually fire together in these interconnected ways, a memory forms; even though a memory may feel like "one thing," such as one fact or one story, it is represented in multiple connected paths in the brain.

Part of the appeal of the connectionist view is that it is consistent with what we know about brain function and allows psychologists to simulate human memory studies using computers (Marcus, 2001). Connectionist approaches also help to explain how priming a concept (winning a race) can influence behavior (getting more donations). Furthermore, insights from this connectionist view support brain research undertaken to determine where memories are stored in the brain (McClelland, 2011; McClelland & Rumelhart, 2009), another fascinating and complex topic.

Indeed, so far we have examined the many ways cognitive psychologists think about how information is stored. The question remains, where? Although memory may seem to be a mysterious phenomenon, it, like all psychological processes, must occur in a physical place: the brain.

HOW MEMORIES ARE STORED Karl Lashley (1950) spent a lifetime looking for a location in the brain in which memories are stored. He trained rats to discover the correct pathway in a maze and then cut out various portions of the animals' brains and retested their memory of the maze pathway. Experiments with thousands of rats showed that the loss of various cortical areas did not affect rats' ability to remember the pathway, leading Lashley to conclude that memories are not stored in a specific location in the brain. Other researchers, continuing Lashley's quest, agreed that memory storage is diffuse, but they developed additional insights. Canadian psychologist Donald Hebb (1949, 1980) suggested that assemblies of cells, distributed over large areas of the cerebral cortex, work together to represent information, just as the connectionist network perspective would predict.

Neurons and Memory Modern neuroscience supports the idea that memories are composed of specific sets or circuits of neurons. Brain researcher Larry Squire, for example, says that most memories are probably clustered in groups of about 1,000 neurons (1990, 2007). At the same time, single neurons are also at work in memory (Braun & others, 2012; Squire, 2007). Researchers who measure the electrical activity of single cells have found that some respond to faces and others to eye or hair color, for example. Still, in order for you to recognize your Uncle Harry, individual neurons that provide information about hair color, size, and other characteristics must act together.

Yes, it is kind of weird, but although you may experience a memory as "one thing"–a story or a fact–it is actually represented not in one place in the brain but in many interconnected processes.

Researchers also believe that brain chemicals may be the ink with which memories are written. Recall that neurotransmitters are the chemicals that allow neurons to communicate across the synapse. These chemicals play a crucial role in forging the connections that represent memory.

Ironically, some of the answers to complex questions about the neural mechanics of memory come from studies on a very simple experimental animal—the inelegant sea slug. Eric Kandel and James Schwartz (1982) chose this large snail-without-a-shell because of the simple architecture of its nervous system, which consists of only about 10,000 neurons. (You might recall that the human brain has about 100 billion neurons.)

The sea slug is hardly a quick learner or an animal with a good memory, but it is equipped with a reliable reflex. When anything touches the gill on its back, it quickly withdraws it. First the researchers accustomed the sea slug to having its gill prodded. After a while, the animal ignored the prod and stopped withdrawing

©Carson Ganci/Design Pics

its gill. Next the researchers applied an electric shock to its tail when they touched the gill. After many rounds of the shock-accompanied prod, the sea slug violently withdrew its gill at the slightest touch. The researchers found that the sea slug remembered this message for hours or even weeks. They also determined that shocking the sea slug's gill releases the neurotransmitter serotonin at the synapses of its nervous system, and this chemical release basically provides a reminder that the gill was shocked. This "memory" informs the nerve cell to send out chemical commands to retract the gill the next time it is touched. If nature builds complexity out of simplicity, then the mechanism used by the sea slug may work in the human brain as well.

Researchers have proposed the concept of *long-term potentiation* to explain how memory functions at the neuron level. In line with connectionist theory, this concept states that if two neurons are activated at the same time, the connection between them—and thus the memory—may be strengthened (Nabavi & others, 2014; Palmeri & others, 2017). Long-term potentiation has been demonstrated experimentally by administering a drug that increases the flow of information from one neuron to another across the synapse, raising the possibility of someday improving memory through drugs that increase neural connections (Prieto & others, 2017; Zorumski & Izumi, 2012).

Imagine that what we experience as memory is actually a collection of well-worn pathways in our brain.

In sum then, memory is *not* a place in the brain. It is best understood as a series of connections. These connections become well-worn paths in our brains but they are active processes, not locations. In fact, research shows that similar neurons area activated in the brain when we encode *and* when we retrieve a memory (Kragel & others, 2017). So when the brain remembers it recreates the neural activity that encoded the information.

Brain Structures and Memory Functions   No specific brain structure is "where" memories are. However, structures do play a role in the processes of memory. Many different parts of the brain and nervous system are involved in the rich, complex process that is memory. Although there is no one memory center in the brain, researchers have demonstrated that specific brain structures are involved in particular aspects of memory.

Figure 12 shows the location of brain structures active in different types of long-term memory. Note that implicit memory and explicit memory appear to involve different locations in the brain.

- *Explicit memory:* Neuroscientists have found that the hippocampus, the temporal lobes in the cerebral cortex, and other areas of the limbic system play a role in explicit memory. In many aspects of explicit memory, information is transmitted from the hippocampus to the frontal lobes, which are involved in both *retrospective* (remembering things from the past) and *prospective* (remembering things we need to do in the future) memory (McDaniel & Einstein, 2007). The left frontal lobe is especially active when we encode new information into memory; the right frontal lobe is more active when we subsequently retrieve it (Babiloni & others, 2006). In addition, the amygdala, which is part of the limbic system, is involved in emotional memories (Xu & others, 2014).

- *Implicit memory:* The cerebellum (the structure at the back and toward the bottom of the brain) is active in the implicit memory required to perform skills (Pliatsikas, Johnstone, & Marinis, 2014). Various areas of the cerebral cortex, such as the temporal lobes and hippocampus, function in priming (Kim, 2011).

Neuroscientists studying memory have benefited greatly from the use of MRI scans, which allow the tracking of neural activity during cognitive tasks (Luo & others, 2014). In one study, participants viewed color photographs of indoor and outdoor scenes while in an MRI machine (Brewer & others, 1998). The experimenters told them that they would receive a memory test about the scenes. After the MRI scans, the participants were asked which pictures they remembered well, vaguely, or not at all. The researchers compared their memories with the brain scans and found that the greater the activation in both prefrontal lobes and a particular region of the hippocampus during viewing, the better the participants remembered the scenes.

FIGURE 12 **Structures of the Brain Involved in Different Aspects of Long-Term Memory** Note that explicit memory and implicit memory appear to involve different locations in the brain.

Frontal lobes
(episodic memory)

Amygdala
(emotional memories)

Temporal lobes
(explicit memory, priming)

Hippocampus
(explicit memory, priming)

Cerebellum
(implicit memory)

self-quiz

1. You tell your friends about the great time you had at the local Six Flags amusement park. Most of the information that you have forgotten about this experience was most likely processed in your
   A. personal memory.
   B. short-term memory.
   C. long-term memory.
   D. sensory memory.

2. Short-term memory has a _____ capacity than sensory memory and a _____ duration.
   A. more limited; longer
   B. less limited; longer
   C. larger; shorter
   D. more limited; shorter

3. According to the connectionist network view of memory, memories are _____, and according to the schema theory of memory, memories are _____.
   A. abstract concepts; large knowledge structures
   B. neural connections; large knowledge structures
   C. parallel concepts; electrical impulses
   D. concurrent concepts; nodes of information

APPLY IT! 4. Before an exam, Professor Sweetheart tells the class how brilliant they are. She tells the students that she has seen them learning the concepts in class and feels confident that everyone can remember the material. In contrast, Professor Meanie tells her class that she realizes they have been bored most of the time, probably cannot remember most of the material, and that she does not expect much from this group of uninspired pupils. Although the material is the same and the tests are the same, Professor Sweetheart's students perform better on the test. What basic memory process might explain this difference?
   A. The professors are classically conditioning the students in their classes.
   B. The professors are priming different behavior, so that concepts related to learning and brilliance are more available to Professor Sweetheart's students.
   C. The professors are influencing the semantic memory of the students.
   D. The professors are influencing the episodic memory of the students.

4 Memory Retrieval

Remember that unforgettable night of shining stars with your romantic partner? Let's say the evening has indeed been encoded deeply and elaborately in your memory. Through the years you have thought about the night a great deal and told your best friends about it. The story of that night has become part of the longer story of your life with your significant other. Fifty years later, your grandson asks, "How did you two end up together?" You share that story you have been saving for just such a question. What are the retrieval processes that allow you to do so?

Retrieval takes place when information that was retained in memory comes out of storage. You might think of long-term memory as a library. You retrieve information in a fashion similar to the process you use to locate and check out a book in an actual library.

retrieval
The memory process that occurs when information that was retained in memory comes out of storage.

To retrieve something from your mental data bank, you search your store of memory to find the relevant information. Retrieval means you take information out of storage.

The efficiency with which you retrieve information from memory is impressive. It usually takes only a moment to search through a vast storehouse to find the information you want. When were you born? What was the name of your first date? Who developed the first psychology laboratory? You can, of course, answer all of these questions instantly. Retrieval of memory is a complex and sometimes imperfect process (Geib & others, 2017).

Before examining ways that retrieval may fall short, let's look at some basic concepts and variables that are known to affect the likelihood that information will be accurately encoded, stored, and ultimately retrieved. As we will see, retrieval depends heavily on the circumstances under which a memory was encoded and the way it was retained (Dudukovic & Kuhl, 2017).

Serial Position Effect

The **serial position effect** is the tendency to recall the items at the beginning and end of a list more readily than those in the middle. If you are a reality TV fan, you might notice that you always seem to remember the first person to get voted off and the last few survivors. All those people in the middle, however, are a blur. The *primacy effect* refers to better recall for items at the beginning of a list; the *recency effect* refers to better recall for items at the end. Together with the relatively low recall of items from the middle of the list, this pattern makes up the serial position effect (Laming, 2010). See Figure 13 for a typical serial position effect that shows a weaker primacy effect and a stronger recency effect.

serial position effect
The tendency to recall the items at the beginning and end of a list more readily than those in the middle.

Psychologists explain these effects using principles of encoding. With respect to the primacy effect, the first few items in the list are easily remembered because they are rehearsed more or because they receive more elaborative processing than do words later in the list (Atkinson & Shiffrin, 1968; Craik & Tulving, 1975). Working memory is relatively empty when the items enter, so there is little competition for rehearsal time. Moreover, because the items get more rehearsal, they stay in working memory longer and are more likely to be encoded successfully into long-term memory. In contrast, many items from the middle of the list drop out of working memory before being encoded into long-term memory.

As for the recency effect, the last several items are remembered for different reasons. First, when these items are recalled, they might still be in working memory. Second, even if these items are not in working memory, the fact that they were just encountered makes them easier to recall. Interestingly, both primacy and recency can influence how we feel about stimuli as well. In one study, wine tasters were more likely to prefer the first wine they sipped, an outcome demonstrating primacy (Mantonakis & others, 2009). In another study, participants felt that the best was saved for last when they evaluated paintings and *American Idol* audition tapes, an outcome demonstrating recency (Li & Epley, 2009).

PSYCHOLOGICAL INQUIRY

FIGURE 13 **The Serial Position Effect** When a person is asked to memorize a list of words, the words memorized last usually are recalled best, those at the beginning next best, and those in the middle least efficiently.

SOURCE: Murdock, Jr., B. B. *Human Memory: Theory and Data.* Potomac, MD: Lawrence Erlbaum Associates, 1974.

> What is the probability that the item presented in the 15th position will be remembered? > Which is stronger—primacy or recency? Why? > Using the information in the graph, if it is the end of a semester and you are studying for finals, which information would it be best to brush up on, and why?

Ever tried speed dating? How did the serial position effect influence the person you liked the best?

Retrieval Cues and the Retrieval Task

Two other factors are involved in retrieval: the nature of the cues that can prompt your memory and the retrieval task that you set for yourself. We consider each in turn.

If effective cues for what you are trying to remember do not seem to be available, you need to create them—a process that takes place in working memory. For example, if you have a block about remembering a new friend's name, you might go through the alphabet, generating names that begin with each letter. If you manage to stumble across the right name, you will probably recognize it.

We can learn to generate retrieval cues. One good strategy is to use different subcategories as retrieval cues. For example, write down the names of as many of your classmates from middle or junior high school as you can remember. When you run out of names, think about the activities you were involved in during those school years, such as math class, student council, lunch, drill team, and so on. Does this set of cues help you to remember more of your classmates?

Although cues help, your success in retrieving information also depends on the retrieval task you set for yourself. For instance, if you are simply trying to decide whether something seems familiar, retrieval is probably a snap. Let's say that you see a short, dark-haired woman walking toward you. You quickly decide that she is someone who shops at the same supermarket as you do. However, remembering her name or a precise detail, such as when you met her, can be harder. Such distinctions have implications for police investigations: A witness might be certain she has previously seen a face, yet she might have a hard time deciding whether it was at the scene of the crime or in a mug shot.

RECALL AND RECOGNITION   The presence or absence of good cues and the retrieval task required are factors in an important memory distinction: recall versus recognition. *Recall* is a memory task in which the individual has to retrieve previously learned information, as on essay tests. *Recognition* is a memory task in which the individual only has to identify (recognize) learned items, as on multiple-choice tests. Recall tests such as essay tests have poor retrieval cues. You are told to try to recall a certain class of information ("Discuss the factors that caused World War I"). In recognition tests such as multiple-choice tests, you merely judge whether a stimulus is familiar (such as that Archduke Franz Ferdinand was assassinated in 1914).

Some people say they are better at essay tests, and some prefer multiple choice. Which type of person are you? From a memory perspective, multiple-choice tests should be easier—they rely on recognition.

You probably have heard some people say that they never forget a face. However, recognizing a face is far simpler than recalling a face "from scratch," as law enforcement officers know. In some cases, police bring in an artist to draw a suspect's face from witnesses' descriptions (Figure 14). Recalling faces is difficult, and artists' sketches of suspects are frequently not detailed or accurate enough to result in apprehension.

ENCODING SPECIFICITY   Another consideration in understanding retrieval is the *encoding specificity principle,* which states that information present at the time of encoding or learning tends to be effective as a retrieval cue (Unsworth, Brewer, & Spillers, 2011). For example, you know your instructors when they are in the classroom setting—you see them there all the time. If, however, you run into one of them in an unexpected setting and in more casual attire, such as at the gym in workout clothes, the person's name might escape you. Your memory might fail because the cues you encoded are not available for use.

CONTEXT AT ENCODING AND RETRIEVAL   An important consequence of encoding specificity is that a change in context between encoding and retrieval can cause memory to fail (Boywitt & Meiser, 2012; Smith & Handy, 2014). In many instances, people remember better when they attempt to recall information in the same context in which they learned it—a process referred to as *context-dependent memory.* This better recollection is believed to occur because people have encoded features of the context in which

FIGURE 14 **Remembering Faces** (*first*) The FBI artist's sketch of Ted Kaczynski. Kaczynski, also known as the Unabomber, is a serial killer who conducted a sequence of mail bombings targeting universities and airlines beginning in the late 1970s. (*second*) A photograph of Kaczynski. The FBI widely circulated the artist's sketch, which was based on bits and pieces of observations people had made of the infamous Unabomber, in the hope that someone would recognize him. Would you have been able to recognize Kaczynski from the artist's sketch? Probably not. Although most people say they are good at remembering faces, they usually are not as good as they think they are.
(first): ©ho/AP Images; (second): ©AP Images

they learned the information along with the actual information. Such features can later act as retrieval cues (Eich, 2007).

In one study, scuba divers learned information on land and under water (Godden & Baddeley, 1975). Later they were asked to recall the information when they were either on land or under water. The divers' recall was much better when the encoding and retrieval contexts were the same (both on land or both under water).

Special Cases of Retrieval

We began this discussion by likening memory retrieval to looking for and finding a book in the library. However, the process of retrieving information from long-term memory is

©Purestock/SuperStock

not as precise as the library analogy suggests. When we search through our long-term memory storehouse, we do not always find the exact "book" we want—or we might find the book but discover that several pages are missing. We have to fill in these gaps somehow.

Our memories are affected by a number of things, including the pattern of facts we remember, schemas and scripts, the situations we associate with memories, and the personal or emotional context. Certainly, everyone has had the experience of remembering a shared situation with a particular individual, only to have the person remind us, "Oh, that wasn't me!" Such moments provide convincing evidence that memory may well be best understood as "reconstructive." This subjective quality of memory certainly has implications for important day-to-day procedures such as eyewitness testimony.

While the factors that we have discussed so far relate to the retrieval of generic information, various kinds of special memory retrieval also have generated a great deal of research. These memories have special significance because of their relevance to the self, to their emotional or traumatic character, or because they show unusually high levels of apparent accuracy (Piolino & others, 2006). Researchers in cognitive psychology have debated whether these memories rely on processes that are different from those already described or are simply extreme cases of typical memory processes (Lane & Schooler, 2004; Schooler & Eich, 2000). We now turn to these special cases of memory.

RETRIEVAL OF AUTOBIOGRAPHICAL MEMORIES

autobiographical memory
A special form of episodic memory, consisting of a person's recollections of his or her life experiences.

Autobiographical memory, a special form of episodic memory, is a person's recollections of his or her life experiences (Bluck, 2017; Habermas & Köber, 2014). An intriguing discovery about autobiographical memory is the *reminiscence bump,* the effect that adults remember more events from the second and third decades of life than from other decades (Bohn, Koppel, & Harris, 2017). This reminiscence bump may occur because these are the times in our life when we have many novel experiences or because it is during our teens and 20s that we are forging a sense of identity (Rathbone, O'Connor, & Moulin, 2017). Generally, the very first few years of life are not characterized by many autobiographical memories.

Autobiographical memories are complex and seem to contain unending strings of stories and snapshots, but researchers have found that they can be categorized (Marsh & Roediger, 2013). For example, based on their research, Martin Conway and David Rubin (1993) sketched a structure of autobiographical memory that has three levels (Figure 15). The most abstract level consists of *life time periods;* for example, you might remember something about your life in high school. The middle level in the hierarchy is made up of *general events,* such as a trip you took with your friends after you graduated from high school. The most concrete level in the hierarchy is composed of *event-specific knowledge;* for example, from your postgraduation trip, you might remember the exhilarating experience you had the first time you jet-skied. When people tell their life stories, all three levels of information are usually present and intertwined.

Most autobiographical memories include some reality and some myth. Personality psychologist Dan McAdams (2001, 2006) argues that autobiographical memories are less about facts and more about meanings. They provide a reconstructed, embellished telling of the past that connects the past to the present.

RETRIEVAL OF EMOTIONAL MEMORIES

When we remember our life experiences, the memories are often wrapped in emotion. Emotion affects the encoding and storage of memories and thus shapes the details that are retrieved. The role that emotion plays in memory is of considerable interest to contemporary researchers and has echoes in public life.

flashbulb memory
The memory of emotionally significant events that people often recall with more accuracy and vivid imagery than everyday events.

Flashbulb memory is the memory of emotionally significant events that people often recall with more accuracy and vivid imagery than everyday events (Luminet & Curci, 2018). Many adults can remember, for example, where they were when they first heard of the terrorist attacks on the United States on September 11, 2001. An intriguing dimension of flashbulb memories is that several decades later, people often remember where they were and what was going on in their lives at the time of such an emotionally charged event. These memories seem to be part of an adaptive system that fixes in memory the details that accompany important events so that they can be interpreted at a later time.

Level	Label	Description
Level 1	Life time periods	Long segments of time measured in years and even decades
Level 2	General events	Extended composite episodes measured in days, weeks, or months
Level 3	Event-specific knowledge	Individual episodes measured in seconds, minutes, or hours

FIGURE 15 **The Three-Level Hierarchical Structure of Autobiographical Memory** When people relate their life stories, all three levels of information are typically present and intertwined.

Many people have flashbulb memories of where they were and what they were doing when terrorists attacked the World Trade Center towers in New York City on September 11, 2001.
©Flickr Open/Robert J Fisch/Getty Images

Most people express confidence about the accuracy of their flashbulb memories. However, flashbulb memories probably are not as accurately etched in our brain as we think. One way to gauge the accuracy of flashbulb memories is to probe how consistent the details of these memories remain over time. Research on memories of the 9/11 terrorist attacks shows that the accuracy of memory was predicted by people's physical proximity to the event; for instance, the memories of individuals in New York were more accurate than the recollections of those in Hawaii (Pezdek, 2003). In another study, Canadian students' memories for 9/11 were tested one week following the tragedy; they were tested again six months after the attacks. At six months after the events, students were better at remembering details about their own experience of hearing about the event than they were at recalling details of the event itself (Smith, Bibi, & Sheard, 2003). These findings reflect our subjective experience of flashbulb memories. We might say, "I will never forget where I was when I heard about [some important event]." Such a statement supports research showing that we may be more likely to remember our personal experiences of an event rather than the details of the event itself.

Still, on the whole, flashbulb memories do seem more durable and accurate than memories of day-to-day happenings (Demiray & Freund, 2014). One possible explanation is that flashbulb memories are quite likely to be rehearsed in the days following the event. However, it is not just the discussion and rehearsal of information that make flashbulb memories so long-lasting. The emotions triggered by flashbulb events also figure in their durability. Although we have focused on negative news events as typical of flashbulb memories, such memories can also occur for positive events. An individual's wedding day and the birth of a child are events that may become milestones in personal history and are always remembered.

MEMORY FOR TRAUMATIC EVENTS In 1890, the American psychologist and philosopher William James said that an experience can be so emotionally arousing that it almost leaves a scar on the brain. Personal traumas are candidates for such emotionally stirring experiences.

Some psychologists argue that memories of emotionally traumatic events are accurately retained, possibly forever, in considerable detail (Langer, 1991). There is good evidence that memory for traumatic events is usually more accurate than memory for ordinary events (Boals & Rubin, 2011; Rubin, 2011; Schooler & Eich, 2000). Consider the traumatic experience of some children who were kidnapped at gunpoint on a school bus in Chowchilla, California, in 1976 and then buried underground for 16 hours before escaping. The children had the classic signs of traumatic memory: detailed and vivid recollections.

However, when a child psychiatrist interviewed the children four to five years after the chilling episode, she noted striking errors and distortions in the memories of half of them (Terr, 1988). How can a traumatic memory be so vivid and detailed yet at the same time have inaccuracies? A number of factors can be involved. Some children might have made perceptual errors while encoding information because the episode was so shocking. Others might have distorted the information and recalled the episode as being less traumatic than it was in order to reduce their anxiety about it. Other children, in discussing the terrifying event with others, might have incorporated bits and pieces of these people's recollections of what happened.

A long-held belief is that memories of real-life traumas are more accurate and longer-lasting than memories of everyday events. Stress-related hormones likely play a role in memories that involve personal trauma. The release of stress-related hormones, signaled by the amygdala and regulated by the hippocampus (see Figure 12), likely accounts for some of the extraordinary durability and vividness of traumatic memories (Bucherelli & others, 2006; Goosens, 2011). However, an increasing number of studies are challenging the belief that memory for traumatic events is highly accurate or even long-lasting. One view is that in traumatic circumstances—such as combat trauma—our brains develop "gist" memories that allow us to avoid future dangers but may not include the necessary detail and precision required by the judicial system (Morgan & Southwick, 2014).

REPRESSED MEMORIES   Can an individual forget, and later recover, memories of traumatic events? A great deal of debate surrounds this question (Bruck & Ceci, 2012, 2013; Lamb & others, 2015). *Repression* is a defense mechanism by which a person is so traumatized by an event that he or she forgets it and then forgets the act of forgetting. According to psychodynamic theory, repression's main function is to protect the individual from threatening information.

The prevalence of repression is hotly contested. Most studies of traumatic memory indicate that a traumatic life event such as childhood sexual abuse is very likely to be remembered. However, there is at least some evidence that childhood sexual abuse may not be remembered. Linda Williams and her colleagues have conducted a number of investigations of memories of childhood abuse (Banyard & Williams, 2007; Liang, Williams, & Siegel, 2006; Williams, 2003, 2004). One study involved 129 women for whom hospital emergency room records indicated a childhood abuse experience (Williams, 1995). Seventeen years after the abuse incident, the researchers contacted the women and asked (among other things) whether they had ever been the victim of childhood sexual abuse. Of the 129 women, most reported remembering and never having forgotten the experience. Ten percent of the participants reported having forgotten about the abuse at least for some portion of their lives.

If it does exist, repression can be considered a special case of **motivated forgetting,** which occurs when individuals forget something because it is so painful or anxiety laden that remembering it is intolerable. This type of forgetting may be a consequence of the emotional trauma experienced by victims of rape or physical abuse, war veterans, and survivors of earthquakes, plane crashes, and other terrifying events. These emotional traumas may haunt people for many years unless they can put the details out of mind. Even when people have not experienced trauma, they may use motivated forgetting to protect themselves from memories of painful, stressful, or otherwise unpleasant circumstances (Anderson & Hanslmayr, 2014; Shu, Gino, & Bazerman, 2011).

Cognitive psychologist Jonathan Schooler suggested that recovered memories are better termed *discovered memories* because, regardless of their accuracy, individuals do experience them as real (Geraerts & others, 2009; Schooler, 2002). Schooler and his colleagues (1997) investigated a number of cases of discovered memories of abuse, in which they

motivated forgetting
Forgetting that occurs when something is so painful or anxiety-laden that remembering it is intolerable.

sought independent corroboration by others. They were able to identify actual cases in which the perpetrator or some third party could verify a discovered memory. For example, Frank Fitzpatrick forgot abuse at the hands of a Catholic priest, but his report of the abuse, years later, was corroborated by witnesses who had also been abused (*Commonwealth of Massachusetts v. Porter,* 1993). The existence of such cases suggests that it is inappropriate to reject all claims by adults that they were victims of long-forgotten childhood sexual abuse.

How do psychologists consider these cases? Generally, there is consensus on a few key issues (Knapp & VandeCreek, 2000). First, all agree that child sexual abuse is an important and egregious problem that historically has not been acknowledged. Second, psychologists widely believe that most individuals who were sexually abused as children remember all or part of what happened to them and that these continuous memories are likely to be accurate. Third, there is broad agreement that it is possible for someone who was abused to forget those memories for a long time, and it is also possible to construct memories that are false but that feel very real to an individual. Finally, it is highly difficult to separate accurate from inaccurate memories, especially if methods such as hypnosis have been used in the "recovery" of memories.

Do It!

Cognitive psychologist Sam Sommers blogged about his experiences as an expert witness in an armed robbery case. He used his expertise on eyewitness memory in the case. Check out his account by googling "Sam Sommers eyewitness."

Do It!

To test your ability to be a good eyewitness, visit one of the following websites:

> www.pbs.org/wgbh/pages/ frontline/shows/dna/
>
> https://public.psych.iastate.edu/ glwells/theeyewitnesstest.html

Did this exercise change your opinion of the accuracy of eyewitness testimony? Explain.

EYEWITNESS TESTIMONY   By now, you should realize that memory is not a perfect reflection of reality. Understanding the distortions of memory is particularly important when people are called on to report what they saw or heard in relation to a crime. Eyewitness testimonies, like other sorts of memories, may contain errors, and faulty memory in criminal matters has especially serious consequences (Bruck & Ceci, 2012, 2013; Lamb & others, 2015). When eyewitness testimony is inaccurate, the wrong person might go to jail or even be put to death, or the perpetrator of the crime might not be prosecuted. It is important to note, however, that witnessing a crime is often traumatic for the individual, and so this type of memory typically fits in the larger category of memory for highly emotional events.

Much of the interest in eyewitness testimony focuses on distortion, bias, and inaccuracy in memory (Frenda, Nichols, & Loftus, 2011). One reason for distortion is that memory fades. In one study, people were able to identify pictures with 100 percent accuracy after a 2-hour time lapse. However, four months later they achieved an accuracy of only 57 percent; chance alone accounts for 50 percent accuracy (Shepard, 1967).

Unlike a video, memory can be altered by new information (Simons & Chabris, 2011). In one study, researchers showed students a film of an automobile accident and then asked them how fast the white sports car was going when it passed a barn (Loftus, 1975). Although there was no barn in the film, 17 percent of the students mentioned the barn in their answer.

Bias is also a factor in faulty memory (Brigham & others, 2007). Studies have shown that people of one ethnic group are less likely to recognize individual differences among people of another ethnic group (Behrman & Davey, 2001); Latino eyewitnesses, for example, may have trouble distinguishing among several Asian suspects. In one relevant experiment, a mugging was shown on a television news program (Loftus, 1993). Immediately after, a lineup of six suspects was broadcast, and viewers were asked to phone in and identify which one of the six individuals they thought had committed the robbery. Of the 2,000 callers, more than 1,800 identified the wrong person, and even though the robber was a non-Latino White male, one-third of the viewers identified an African American or a Latino suspect as the criminal. Importantly, too, witness confidence is not necessarily a good indicator of accuracy of eyewitness accounts. One study showed that women's accounts were more accurate than men's but that men expressed greater confidence in their memories (Areh, 2011).

PSYCHOLOGY IN OUR WORLD

Using Psychological Research to Improve Police Lineups

In his book *Convicting the Innocent,* law professor Brandon Garrett (2011) traced the first 250 cases in the United States in which a convicted individual was exonerated—proved to be not guilty—by DNA evidence. Of those cases, 190 (or *76 percent*) involved mistaken eyewitness identification of the accused. Every year, more than 75,000 individuals are asked to identify suspects, and experts estimate that these identifications are wrong one-third of the time (The Week Staff, 2011).

©Cleveland PD/REX/Shutterstock

To reduce the chances that innocent individuals will be accused of crimes, law enforcement officials are applying psychological research findings to improve the way they conduct criminal lineups. In such lineups, a witness views a group of individuals in real time or looks at photos of individuals, one of whom is the suspect. The witness is asked to identify the perpetrator of the crime if he or she is among those shown. Psychological research has influenced these procedures in two ways.

First, based on the suspicion that even very subtle bias can influence witness judgments, *double-blind* procedures have been adopted by many jurisdictions (Brewer & Wells, 2011). Recall that in a double-blind study, neither the participants nor the experimenter knows what condition the participants are in, to reduce the effects of bias on the results. The city of Dallas, for example, uses a double-blind approach to police lineups. A specific unit conducts all lineups, and no one involved in administering the lineup has any knowledge of the case or of which individual is suspected of the crime (Goode & Schwartz, 2011).

Another procedure supported by research is the use of sequential rather than simultaneous presentation of individuals or photographs in a lineup. Showing individuals or their photos in a lineup one at a time (sequentially) rather than all at once (simultaneously) is less likely to lead to false identifications (Steblay, Dysart, & Wells, 2011). The reason for the difference is that when presented with a set of suspects simultaneously, victims tend to choose the person who looks the most like their memory of the perpetrator. Studies show that when the actual perpetrator in a simulated crime is removed from a simultaneous lineup, people will pick the "filler person"—an individual who is not suspected of the crime and is simply filling up the lineup—who most closely resembles the perpetrator (Wells, 1993).

A recent large-scale field study, headed by Gary Wells (Wells, Steblay, & Dysart, 2011), examined the effectiveness of double-blind sequential and simultaneous lineups in four different jurisdictions in the United States in actual criminal investigations. The results showed that sequential presentation of photo lineups led to fewer mistaken identifications than did simultaneous presentation. Wells and colleagues concluded that double-blind sequential lineups are a promising avenue for improving the accuracy of eyewitness identification.

CSI and other TV crime dramas might give the impression that DNA evidence is widely available to protect innocent people from false accusations. However, researchers estimate that fewer than 5 percent of legal cases involving eyewitness identifications include biological evidence to potentially exonerate mistakenly identified convicts (Wells, Steblay, & Dysart, 2011). So, for many crimes, eyewitness identification remains an important piece of evidence—and improving the validity of these identifications is thus a crucial goal.

Hundreds of individuals have been harmed by witnesses who have made a mistake (Frenda, Nichols, & Loftus, 2011). One estimate indicates that each year approximately 7,500 people in the United States are arrested for and wrongly convicted of serious crimes (Huff, 2002).

More recently, researchers have suggested that eyewitness accounts can be more accurate if the witness closes his or her eyes. Why might that help?

Faulty memory is not just about accusing the wrong person. Understandably, given the circumstances, witnesses can be mistaken about many aspects of a crime. For many mass shootings, early reports from eyewitnesses indicate multiple shooters were involved in an attack. Yet, in the end, the killings are attributable to a single gunmen, perhaps because the frightened witnesses could not fathom a single person being responsible for so many gunshots.

©Marie P. Marzi/AP Images

Faulty memories complicated the search for the perpetrators in the sniper attacks that killed 10 people in the Washington, DC, area in 2002. Police released photos of the type of white truck or van that witnesses said they saw fleeing some of the crime scenes (right). In the end, however, the suspects were driving a blue car when law enforcement officials apprehended them (above).
©WJZ-TV/AP Images

self-quiz

1. The tendency to remember the items at the beginning and end of a list more easily than the items in the middle is the
   A. bookends effect.
   B. serial cues effect.
   C. serial position effect.
   D. endpoints effect.

2. Carrie prides herself on "never forgetting a face," although she frequently cannot put the correct name with a specific face. Carrie is really saying that she
   A. is better at recognition than at recall.
   B. is better at recall than at recognition.
   C. is better at memory retrieval than at memory reconstruction.

D. is better at memory reconstruction than at memory recall.

3. Faulty memory can occur due to
   A. bias.
   B. receipt of new information.
   C. distortion.
   D. all of the above

APPLY IT! 4. Andrew is getting ready for a group interview for a job he really wants. The group session will take place at the beginning of the day, followed by individual interviews. When the manager who is conducting the interviews calls Andrew, he tells him that because he has not talked to any of the other candidates yet, Andrew can decide when he would like his individual interview to be.

There are five candidates. Which position should Andrew take?
   A. Andrew should go third because that way he will be right in the middle, and the interviewer will not be too nervous or too tired.
   B. Andrew should go either first or last, to be the candidate most likely to be remembered.
   C. Andrew should probably go second so that he will not be sitting around feeling nervous for too long—and besides, asking to go first might seem pushy.
   D. It will not matter, so Andrew should just pick a spot randomly.

5 Forgetting

Human memory has its imperfections, as we have all experienced. It is not unusual for two people to argue about whether something did or did not happen, each supremely confident that his or her memory is accurate and the other person's is faulty. We all have had the frustrating experience of trying to remember the name of some person or some place but not quite being able to retrieve it. Missed appointments, misplaced keys, the failure to recall the name of a familiar face, and inability to recall your password for Internet access are everyday examples of forgetting. Why do we forget?

One of psychology's pioneers, Hermann Ebbinghaus (1850–1909), was the first person to conduct scientific research on forgetting. In 1885, he made up and memorized a list of 13 nonsense syllables and then assessed how many of them he could remember as time passed. (Nonsense syllables are meaningless combinations of letters that are unlikely to have been learned already, such as *zeq, xid, lek,* and *riy.*) Even just an hour later, Ebbinghaus could recall only a few of the nonsense syllables he had memorized. Figure 16 shows Ebbinghaus's learning curve for nonsense syllables. Based on his research, Ebbinghaus concluded that most forgetting takes place soon after we learn something.

If we forget so quickly, why put effort into learning something? Fortunately, researchers have demonstrated that forgetting is not as extensive as Ebbinghaus envisioned (Hsieh & others, 2009). Ebbinghaus studied meaningless nonsense syllables. When we memorize more meaningful material—such as poetry, history, or the content of this text—forgetting is neither so rapid nor so extensive. Following are some of the factors that influence how well we can retrieve information from long-term memory.

 Never forget: Ebbinghaus was the first to study forgetting.

Hermann Ebbinghaus (1850–1909)
Ebbinghaus was the first psychologist to conduct scientific research on forgetting.
©Bettmann/Getty Images

Encoding Failure

Sometimes when people say they have forgotten something, they have not really forgotten it; rather, they never encoded the information in the first place. Encoding failure occurs when the information was never entered into long-term memory.

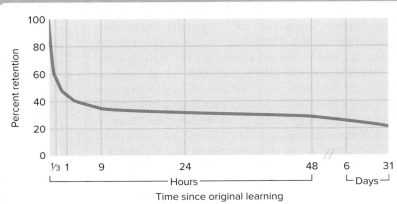

PSYCHOLOGICAL INQUIRY

FIGURE 16   Ebbinghaus's Forgetting Curve This figure illustrates Ebbinghaus's conclusion about forgetting.
> **When is information most likely to be forgotten?** > **What might explain differences in the slope of this curve for different individuals and different material?** > **Based on this graph, when is the best time to study new material to prevent it from being forgotten?**

FIGURE 17

Which Is a Real U.S. Penny?
In the original experiment, participants viewed 15 versions of pennies; only one version was an actual U.S. penny. This figure shows only 7 of the 15 versions, and as you likely can tell, the task is still very difficult. Why?

©David A. Tietz/Editorial Image, LLC

(a) (b) (c) (d)

(e) (f) (g)

As an example of encoding failure, think about what the U.S. penny looks like. In one study, researchers showed 15 versions of the penny to participants and asked them which one was correct (Nickerson & Adams, 1979). Look at the pennies in Figure 17 and see whether you can tell which is the real penny. Most people do not do well on this task. Unless you are a coin collector, you probably have not encoded a lot of specific details about pennies. You may have encoded just enough information to distinguish them from other coins (pennies are copper-colored, dimes and nickels are silver-colored; pennies fall between the sizes of dimes and quarters). The correct answer? Penny c is the right one.

The penny exercise illustrates that we encode and enter into long-term memory only a small portion of our life experiences. In a sense, then, encoding failures really are not cases of forgetting; they are cases of not remembering.

Retrieval Failure

Problems in retrieving information from memory are clearly examples of forgetting. Psychologists have theorized that the causes of retrieval failure include problems with the information in storage, the effects of time, personal reasons for remembering or forgetting, and the condition of the brain (Davis & Zhong, 2017; Öztekin & Badre, 2011).

INTERFERENCE *Interference* is one reason that people forget (Arnett & Wagers, 2017). According to **interference theory,** people forget not because memories are lost from storage but because other information gets in the way of what they want to remember.

There are two kinds of interference: proactive and retroactive. **Proactive interference** occurs when material that was learned earlier disrupts the recall of material learned later (Yi & Friedman, 2011). Remember that *pro-* means "forward in time." For example, suppose you had a good friend 10 years ago named Prudence and that last night you met someone named Patience. You might find yourself calling your new friend Prudence because the old information (Prudence) interferes with retrieval of new information (Patience). **Retroactive interference** occurs when material learned later disrupts the retrieval of information learned earlier. Remember that *retro-* means "backward in time." Suppose you have lately become friends with Ralph. In sending a note to your old friend Raul, you might mistakenly address it to Ralph because the new information (Ralph) interferes with the old information (Raul). Figure 18 depicts another example of proactive and retroactive interference.

Proactive and retroactive interference might both be explained as problems with retrieval cues. The reason the name Prudence interferes with the name Patience and

interference theory
The theory that people forget not because memories are lost from storage but because other information gets in the way of what they want to remember.

proactive interference
Situation in which material that was learned earlier disrupts the recall of material that was learned later.

retroactive interference
Situation in which material that was learned later disrupts the retrieval of information that was learned earlier.

Proactive Interference

Old information interferes with new information

| Study for biology test | Study for psychology test | Take psychology test |

Time →

Retroactive Interference

New information interferes with old information

| Study for psychology test | Study for biology test | Take psychology test |

Time →

FIGURE 18
Proactive and Retroactive Interference *Pro-* means "forward"; in proactive interference, old information has a forward influence by getting in the way of new material learned. *Retro-* means "backward"; in retroactive interference, new information has a backward influence by getting in the way of material learned earlier.

the name Ralph interferes with the name Raul might be that the cue you are using to remember the one name does not distinguish between the two memories. For example, if the cue you are using is "my good friend," it might evoke both names. The result might be retrieval of the wrong name or a kind of blocking in which each name interferes with the other and neither comes to mind. Retrieval cues (such as "friend" in our example) can become overloaded, and when that happens we are likely to forget or to retrieve incorrectly.

These are tricky. PRO-active means what you learned BEFORE interferes with later material; RETRO-active means what you learn now interferes with earlier material.

DECAY   Another possible reason for forgetting is the passage of time. According to **decay theory,** when we learn something new, a neurochemical memory trace forms, but over time this trace disintegrates. Decay theory suggests that the passage of time always increases forgetting.

decay theory
Theory stating that when an individual learns something new, a neurochemical memory trace forms, but over time this trace disintegrates; suggests that the passage of time always increases forgetting.

Memories often do fade with the passage of time, but decay alone cannot explain forgetting. For example, under the right retrieval conditions, we can recover memories that we seem to have forgotten. You might have forgotten the face or name of someone in your high school class, for instance, but when you return to the setting where you knew the person, you might remember. Similarly, you may not have thought about someone from your past for a very long time, but when the person friends you on Facebook, you may remember a lot of prior experiences with him or her.

Many things we think we have forgotten are just waiting for the right cues to pop into our lives.

TIP-OF-THE-TONGUE PHENOMENON   We are all familiar with the retrieval glitch called **tip-of-the-tongue (TOT) phenomenon**—a type of "effortful retrieval" that occurs when we are confident that we know something but cannot quite pull it out of memory (Schwartz, 2011). In a TOT state we usually can successfully retrieve characteristics of the word, such as the first letter and the number of syllables, but not the word itself. The TOT phenomenon arises when we can retrieve some of the desired information but not all of it (Gollan & others, 2014; Resnik & others, 2014).

tip-of-the-tongue (TOT) phenomenon
A type of effortful retrieval associated with a person's feeling that he or she knows something (say, a word or a name) but cannot quite pull it out of memory.

The TOT phenomenon demonstrates that we do not store all of the information about a particular topic or experience in one way. If you have ever struggled to think of a specific word, you probably came up with various words that mean the same thing as the word you were looking for, but you still had a nagging feeling that none was quite right. Sometimes you might find the solution in an unexpected way. For example, imagine that you are doing a crossword puzzle with the clue "colorful scarf" for a seven-letter word. You have a feeling you know this word. If you have not thought of the answer yet, say the following word aloud: *bandage.* If you were experiencing the TOT phenomenon when doing the crossword, thinking of *bandage* might have helped you come up with the correct answer, *bandana.* Although the meaning of *bandage* is unrelated to that of *bandana,* the fact that these words start with the same sounds (and therefore are linked in verbal memory) can lead you to the word *bandana* (Abrams & Rodriguez, 2005).

PROSPECTIVE MEMORY: REMEMBERING (OR FORGETTING) WHEN TO DO SOMETHING

The main focus of this chapter has been on **retrospective memory,** which is remembering the past. **Prospective memory** involves remembering information about doing something in the future; it includes memory for intentions (Smith, Hunt, & Murray, 2017). Prospective memory includes both timing (when we have to do something) and content (what we have to do).

We can make a distinction between time-based and event-based prospective memory. *Time-based prospective memory* is our intention to engage in a given behavior after a specified amount of time has gone by, such as an intention to make a phone call to someone in one hour. In *event-based prospective memory,* we engage in the intended behavior when some external event or cue elicits it, as when we give a message to a roommate upon seeing her. The cues available in event-based prospective memory make it more effective than time-based prospective memory (McDaniel & Einstein, 2007).

Some failures in prospective memory are referred to as *absentmindedness.* We are more absentminded when we become preoccupied with something else, are distracted by something, or are under a lot of time pressure. Absentmindedness often involves a breakdown between attention and memory storage (Schacter, 2001). Fortunately, research has shown that our goals are encoded into memory along with the features of situations that would allow us to pursue them. Our memories, then, prepare us to recognize when a situation presents an opportunity to achieve those goals.

Researchers also have found that older adults perform worse on prospective memory tasks than younger adults do, but typically these findings are true only for artificial lab tasks (Smith, Horn, & Bayen, 2012; Zollig & others, 2012). In real life, older adults generally perform as well as younger adults in terms of prospective memory (Rendell & Craik, 2000). Generally, prospective memory failure (forgetting to do something) occurs when retrieval is a conscious, effortful (rather than automatic) process (Henry & others, 2004).

Amnesia Recall the case of H. M. in the discussion of explicit and implicit memory. In H. M.'s surgery, the part of his brain that was responsible for laying down new memories was damaged beyond repair. The result was **amnesia,** the loss of memory. H. M. suffered from **anterograde amnesia,** a memory disorder that affects the retention of new information and events (*antero-* indicates amnesia that moves forward in time) (Levine & others, 2009). What he learned before the surgery (and thus before the onset of amnesia) was not affected. For example, H. M. could identify his friends, recall their names, and even tell stories about them—*if* he had known them before the surgery. People who met H. M. after the surgery remained strangers, even if they spent thousands of hours with him. H. M.'s postsurgical experiences were rarely encoded in his long-term memory.

Amnesia also occurs in a form known as **retrograde amnesia,** which involves memory loss for a segment of the past but not for new events (*retro-* indicates amnesia that moves back in time) (Abbate & others, 2012). Retrograde amnesia is much more common than anterograde amnesia and frequently occurs when the brain is assaulted by an electrical shock or a physical blow such as a head injury to a football player. In contrast to anterograde amnesia, in retrograde amnesia the forgotten information is old—it occurred prior to the event that caused the amnesia—and the ability to acquire new memories is not affected. Sometimes individuals have both anterograde and retrograde amnesia.

retrospective memory
Remembering information from the past.

prospective memory
Remembering information about doing something in the future; includes memory for intentions.

©Siede Preis/Stockbyte/Getty Images

amnesia
The loss of memory.

anterograde amnesia
A memory disorder that affects the retention of new information and events.

retrograde amnesia
Memory loss for a segment of the past but not for new events.

1. The term for the failure of information to enter into long-term memory is
   A. rehearsal failure.
   B. encoding failure.
   C. proactive interference.
   D. retroactive interference.

2. Marco, a college freshman, is sure that he knows the name of his old Little League coach, but he cannot quite pull the name out of his memory. Marco is experiencing
   A. anterograde amnesia.
   B. retrograde amnesia.
   C. associative interference.
   D. tip-of-the-tongue phenomenon.

3. Retrospective memory involves remembering information about doing something in the _____, and prospective memory involves remembering information about doing something in the _____.
   A. past; present
   B. past; future
   C. present; future
   D. present; past

APPLY IT! 4. Carlos, who is fluent in Spanish, is planning a trip to Paris and decides to take a course in French. On Carlos's first French vocabulary quiz, his instructor notes that he has mixed up a lot of Spanish words with French words. Carlos cannot understand why, because he has always excelled at learning languages. What is happening to Carlos?

A. Carlos is experiencing retroactive interference. His knowledge of Spanish is interfering with learning the new French words.
B. Carlos is experiencing proactive interference. His knowledge of Spanish is interfering with learning the new French words.
C. Carlos is experiencing anterograde amnesia. He seems unable to learn new words.
D. Carlos has hit his limit on languages. He should stick to Spanish and visit Barcelona instead.

6 Tips from the Science of Memory— for Studying and for Life

How can you apply your new knowledge of memory processes to improving your academic performance—and your life? No matter what model of memory you use, you can sharpen your memory by thinking deeply about the "material" of life and connecting the information to other things you know. Perhaps the one most well-connected node or most elaborate schema to which you can relate something is the self—what you know and think about yourself. To make something meaningful and to secure its place in memory, you must make it matter to yourself.

If you think about memory as a physical event in the brain, you can see that memorizing material is like training a muscle. Repeated recruitment of sets of neurons creates the connection you want to have available not only at exam time but throughout life.

Organizing, Encoding, Rehearsing, and Retrieving Course Content

ORGANIZE   Before you engage the powerful process of memory, the first step in improving your academic performance is to make sure that the information you are studying is accurate and well organized. Just organizing material can lead to better memory.

Tips for Organizing

- Review your course notes routinely and catch potential errors and ambiguities early. There is no sense in memorizing inaccurate or incomplete information.

- Organize the material in a way that will allow you to commit it to memory effectively. Arrange information, rework material, and give it a structure that will help you to remember it.

- Experiment with different organizational techniques. One approach is to use a hierarchy such as an outline. You might create analogies (such as the earlier comparison of retrieval from long-term memory to finding a book in the library) that take advantage of your preexisting schemas.

ENCODE   Once you ensure that the material to be remembered is accurate and well organized, it is time to memorize. Although some types of information are encoded automatically, academic learning usually requires considerable effort.

Tips for Encoding

- Pay attention. Remember that staying focused on one thing is crucial. In other words, avoid divided attention.

- Process information at an appropriate level. Think about the material meaningfully and process it deeply.

- Elaborate on the points to be remembered. Make associations to your life and to other aspects of the material you want to remember.

- Use imagery. Devising images to help you remember (such as the mental picture of a computer screen to help you recall the concept of working memory) allows you to "double-encode" the information.

- Understand that encoding is not simply something that you should do before a test. Rather, encode early and often. During class, while reading, or in discussing issues, take advantage of opportunities to create associations to your course material. Once you have your notes for a lecture, rehearse that information right away.

REHEARSE   While learning material initially, relate it to your life and attend to examples that help you do so. After class, rehearse the course material over time to solidify it in memory.

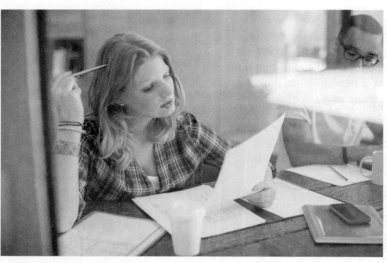
©Caiaimage/Glow Images

Tips for Rehearsing

- Rewrite, type, or retype your notes. Some students find this exercise a good form of rehearsal.

- Talk to people about what you have learned and how it is important to real life in order to reinforce memory. You are more likely to remember information over the long term if you understand it and relate it to your world than if you mechanically rehearse and memorize it. Rehearsal works well for information in short-term memory, but when you need to encode, store, and then retrieve information from long-term memory, it is much less efficient. Thus, for most information, understand it, give it meaning, elaborate on it, and personalize it.

- Test yourself. It is not enough to look at your notes and think, "Oh, yes, I know this." Sometimes recognition instills a false sense of knowing. If you look at a definition, and it seems so familiar that you are certain you know it, challenge yourself. What happens when you close the book and try to reconstruct the definition? Check your personal definition with the technical one in the book. How did you do?

- While reading and studying, ask yourself questions such as "What is the meaning of what I just read?" "Why is this important?" and "What is an example of the concept I just read about?" When you make a concerted effort to ask yourself questions about what you have read or about an activity in class, you expand the number of associations you make with the information you will need to retrieve later.

- Treat your brain kindly. If you are genuinely seeking to improve your memory performance, keep in mind that the brain is a physical organ. Perhaps the best way to promote effective memory storage is to make sure that your brain is able to function at maximum capacity. That means resting it, nourishing it by eating well, and keeping it free of mind-altering substances.

RETRIEVE   So, you have studied not just hard but deeply, elaborating on important concepts and committing lists to memory. You have slept well and eaten a nutritious breakfast, and now it is exam time. How can you best retrieve the essential information?

Tips for Retrieving

- Use retrieval cues. Sit in the same seat where you learned the material. Remember that the exam is full of questions about topics that you have thoughtfully encoded. Some of the questions on the test might help jog your memory for the answers to others.

- Sit comfortably, take a deep breath, and stay calm. Bolster your confidence by recalling that research on long-term memory has shown that material that has been committed to memory is there for a very long time—even among those who may experience a moment of panic when the test is handed out.

Memory is clearly crucial for learning and academic success, but memory serves far more functions. It is the fundamental ingredient of our life stories, as we next consider.

Autobiographical Memory and the Life Story

Autobiographical memory may be one of the most important aspects of human life (Unsworth, Spillers, & Brewer, 2012). For instance, one of the many functions that autobiographical memory serves is to allow us to learn from our experiences (Pillemer, 1998). In autobiographical memory, we store the lessons we have learned from life. These memories become a resource to which we can turn when faced with life's difficulties.

Autobiographical memory also allows us to understand ourselves and provides us with a source of identity. In his studies of self-defining autobiographical memories, Jefferson Singer and his colleagues maintain that these internalized stories of personal experience serve as signs of the meaning we have created out of our life events and give our lives coherence (Baddeley & Singer, 2008, 2010; Singer & Blagov, 2004; Singer & Conway, 2008, 2011). According to Dan McAdams (2006, 2009, 2011a, 2011b), autobiographical memories form the core of our personal identity. A number of studies have shown that the stories we tell about our lives have important implications. For instance, McAdams and his colleagues have demonstrated that individuals who describe important life experiences that go from bad to better (*redemptive stories*) are more *generative*—that is, they are the kind of people who make a contribution to future generations, people who leave a legacy that will outlive them (Bauer, McAdams, & Sakaeda, 2005). These individuals are also better adjusted than those whose self-defining memories go from good to bad (labeled *contamination stories*). Clearly, the construction and reconstruction of autobiographical memory may reveal important aspects of how individuals function, grow, and discover meaning in their lives (King & Hicks, 2006).

Our memories are an intimate way to share a part of ourselves with others, as a grandfather does with his grandchild.
©Glow Asia/AP Images

A final function of autobiographical memory, and perhaps its most vital aspect, is its role in social bonding (Alea & Bluck, 2003; Bluck 2017; Bruce, 1989; Nelson, 1993). Our memories are a valuable way to share a part of ourselves with others. Sharing personal experience is a way to foster intimacy, create bonds, and deepen existing ties. When we know a person's most cherished autobiographical memory, we know that he or she is no longer just an acquaintance but clearly a friend. To the extent that social bonds are necessary for survival, it makes sense that human beings can remember and share those memories with one another and that sharing our memories is a key pathway for sharing ourselves.

Keeping Memory Sharp

As a process rooted in the brain, memory is also an indicator of brain functioning. Preserving memory is of vital importance as we age. A strong message from research on aging and memory is that, as for many things in life, the phrase "Use it or lose it" applies to memory.

Consider the case of Richard Wetherill, a retired lecturer and an uncommonly good chess player (Melton, 2005). Wetherill was so skilled that he was able to think eight moves ahead in a chess match. At one point, he noticed that he was having trouble playing chess—he could think only five moves ahead. He was sure that something was seriously wrong with him, despite his wife's assurances that she noticed no changes. A battery of cognitive tests revealed no abnormalities, and a brain scan was similarly reassuring. Two years later, Wetherill was dead, and the autopsy showed a brain ravaged by Alzheimer disease, a progressive, irreversible brain disorder that is characterized by gradual deterioration of memory, reasoning, language, and eventually physical functioning. Brain damage of this sort should indicate a person who was incapable of coherent thought. Wetherill's symptoms, however, had been limited to a small decline in his skill at playing chess.

Wetherill's case is surprising but also typical. Individuals who lead active intellectual lives seem to be protected against the mental decline generally associated with age. Indeed, research has shown that individuals who are educated, have high IQs, and remain mentally engaged in complex tasks tend to cope better with a variety of assaults to the brain, including Alzheimer disease, stroke, head injury, and even poisoning with

©Tetra Images/Alamy Stock Photo

neurotoxins (Melton, 2005). Some research has suggested that an active mental life leads to the accumulation of a "cognitive store"—an emergency stash of mental capacity that allows individuals to avoid the negative effects of harm to the brain.

Yaakov Stern found that among a group of individuals with Alzheimer disease who appeared to be equal in terms of their outward symptoms, those who were more educated were suffering from much worse brain damage, yet they were functioning at a level similar to others with relatively less damage (Stern & others, 1992). Stern and his colleagues (2004) have also shown that intellectual pursuits such as playing chess and reading reduce the severity of Alzheimer symptoms. More recent research showed that while maintaining an active mental life can reduce the speed of cognitive decline associated with Alzheimer disease, it can also be related to more rapid decline once a person is diagnosed (Wilson & others, 2010).

Apparently, a lifetime of mental activity and engagement produces this cognitive reserve that allows the brain to maintain its ability to recruit new neural networks that compensate for damage. These brains are better able to adopt a backup plan to maintain the individual's level of functioning (Andel & others, 2005). The clear message from these studies is the importance of building up a cognitive reserve by staying mentally active throughout life. In addition to educational achievement, remaining physically and cognitively active also seems to play a role in maintaining a sharp mind (Erickson, Miller, & Roecklein, 2012; Park & Bischof, 2011). Modern conveniences can sometimes work against the goal of keeping the brain active. Individuals who rely on a GPS device to get around, for instance, may fail to exercise the hippocampus, a very important area for combating age-related cognitive decline (Bohbot & others, 2011).

Before we leave the science of memory, let's consider the role of memory in shaping meaningful experiences in daily life. Think of the most meaningful event of your life. Clearly, that event is one that you remember, among all the things you have experienced in your life. We all have certain particularly vivid autobiographical memories that stand out as indicators of meaning, such as those studied by Jefferson Singer that we reviewed above. In fact, however, everyday life is filled with potentially remarkable moments—a beautiful sunrise, a delicious meal prepared just for you, an unexpected telephone call from an old friend. Experiencing everyday life in its richness requires us to be attentive and engaged. Sometimes the daily chores and hassles of life lead us to feel that we are just going through the motions. This sort of mindless living may be a way to survive, but it is unlikely to be a way to thrive.

The processes of attention and encoding that we have explored in this chapter suggest that actively engaging in life—investing ourselves in the events of the day (Cantor & Sanderson, 1999)—is the way we can be assured that our life stories are rich and nuanced. That way, when someone asks, "So, tell me about yourself," we have a story to tell.

self-quiz

1. To improve your performance in your courses, you must make sure the information you are studying is
   A. well organized.
   B. accurate.
   C. complete.
   D. all of the above

2. One way to improve the accuracy and efficiency of retrieval is through the use of
   A. retrieval cues.
   B. encoding cues.
   C. storage cues.
   D. none of the above

3. Factors associated with keeping a sharp mind as we age include all of the following *except*

A. educational attainment.
B. being physically active.
C. engaging in comfortable, easy tasks.
D. having a high IQ.

 APPLY IT! 4. Albert is a retiree in his mid-60s. His wife, who is the same age, likes to read the latest novels and attend poetry readings. She also works the daily crossword puzzle in *The New York Times* and is taking a language class. Albert thinks that she is wasting her time and that retirement should be a time of kicking back. They both worked hard in school and had great careers, so what more does she want, Albert protests. Which of the

following might be good advice for Albert's wife?
A. She should tell Albert that all of this mental activity is likely to keep her mind sharp and that he should join her in some of her pursuits.
B. She should probably relax more. After all, at her age, how much more can she really learn?
C. She should leave Albert alone; he is taking retirement seriously.
D. She should continue in her activities, but they will not have any impact on her later memory ability.

SUMMARY

1 The Nature of Memory

Memory is the retention of information over time. The three processes involved in memory are encoding (getting information into storage), storage (retaining information over time), and retrieval (taking information out of storage).

2 Memory Encoding

Encoding requires attention, but the attention must be selective. Memory is negatively influenced by divided attention.

According to the theory of levels of processing, information is processed on a continuum from shallow (sensory or physical features are encoded) to intermediate (labels are attached to stimuli) to deep (the meanings of stimuli and their associations with other stimuli are processed). Deeper processing produces better memory. Elaboration, the extensiveness of processing at any given level of memory encoding, improves memory. Using imagery, or mental pictures, as a context for information can improve memory.

Memory Storage

The Atkinson-Shiffrin theory describes memory as a three-stage process: sensory memory, short-term memory, and long-term memory.

Sensory memory holds perceptions of the world for only an instant. Visual sensory memory (iconic memory) retains information for about ¼ of a second; auditory sensory memory (echoic memory) preserves information for several seconds.

Short-term memory is a limited-capacity memory system in which information is usually retained for as long as 30 seconds. Short-term memory's limitation is 7 ± 2 bits of information. Chunking and rehearsal can benefit short-term memory. Working memory involves a combination of short-term memory and attention that allow us to hold information temporarily as we perform cognitive tasks. Baddeley's model of working memory has three components: a central executive and two assistants (phonological loop and visuo-spatial sketchpad).

Long-term memory is a relatively permanent type of memory that holds huge amounts of information for a long time. Long-term memory has two main subtypes: explicit and implicit memory. Explicit memory is the conscious recollection of information, such as specific facts or events. Implicit memory affects behavior through prior experiences that are not consciously recollected. Explicit memory has two dimensions. One dimension includes episodic memory and semantic memory. The other dimension includes retrospective memory and prospective memory. Implicit memory is multidimensional too and includes systems for procedural memory, priming, and classical conditioning.

Memory Retrieval

The serial position effect is the tendency to recall items at the beginning and the end of a list better than the middle items. The primacy effect is the tendency to recall items at the beginning of the list better than the middle items. The recency effect is the tendency to remember the items at the end of a list better than the middle items.

Retrieval is easier when effective cues are present. Another factor in effective retrieval is the nature of the retrieval task. Simple recognition of previously remembered information in the presence of cues is generally easier than recall of the information. According to the encoding specificity principle, information present at the time of encoding or learning tends to be effective as a retrieval cue, a process referred to as context-dependent memory.

Retrieval also benefits from priming, which activates particular connections or associations in memory. The tip-of-the-tongue phenomenon occurs when we cannot quite pull something out of memory. Five special cases of retrieval are autobiographical memory, emotional memory, memory for trauma, repressed memory, and eyewitness testimony.

Autobiographical memory is a person's recollections of his or her life experiences. Autobiographical memory has three levels: life time periods,

general events, and event-specific knowledge. Biographies of the self connect the past and the present to form our identity. Emotional memories may be especially vivid and enduring. Particularly significant emotional memories, or flashbulb memories, capture emotionally profound events that people often recall accurately and vividly.

Memory for personal trauma also is usually more accurate than memory for ordinary events, but it too is subject to distortion and inaccuracy. People tend to remember the core information about a personal trauma but might distort some of the details. Personal trauma can cause individuals to repress emotionally laden information so that it is not accessible to consciousness.

Repression means forgetting a particularly troubling experience because it would be too upsetting to remember it. Eyewitness testimony may contain errors due to memory decay or bias.

Forgetting

Encoding failure is forgetting information that was never entered into long-term memory. Retrieval failure can occur for at least four reasons.

First, interference theory stresses that we forget not because memories are lost from storage but because other information gets in the way of what we want to remember. Interference can be proactive (as occurs when material learned earlier disrupts the recall of material learned later) or retroactive (as occurs when material learned later disrupts the retrieval of information learned earlier).

Second, decay theory states that when we learn something new, a neurochemical memory trace forms, but over time this chemical trail disintegrates.

The third reason for retrieval failure is that motivated forgetting occurs when we want to forget something. It is common when a memory becomes painful or anxiety-laden, as in the case of emotional traumas such as rape and physical abuse.

Finally, amnesia, the physiologically based loss of memory, can be anterograde, affecting the retention of new information or events; retrograde, affecting memories of the past but not memories of new events; or a combination of both.

Tips from the Science of Memory—for Studying and for Life

Effective encoding strategies when studying include paying attention and minimizing distraction, understanding the material rather than relying on rote memorization, asking yourself questions, and taking good notes. Research on memory suggests that the best way to remember course material is to relate it to many different aspects of your life.

Autobiographical memories, particularly self-defining memories, play a significant role in identity and social relationships. Our self-defining memories provide a unique source of identity, and sharing those memories with others plays a role in social bonding.

Taking on challenging cognitive tasks throughout life can stave off the effects of age on memory and lessen the effects of Alzheimer disease.

Engaging in everyday life means living memorably. Mindfulness to life events provides a rich reservoir of experiences upon which to build a storehouse of autobiographical memory.

KEY TERMS

amnesia

anterograde amnesia

Atkinson-Shiffrin theory

autobiographical memory

connectionism or parallel distributed processing (PDP)

decay theory

divided attention

elaboration

encoding

episodic memory

explicit memory or declarative memory

flashbulb memory

implicit memory or nondeclarative memory

interference theory

levels of processing

long-term memory

memory

motivated forgetting

priming

proactive interference

procedural memory

prospective memory

retrieval

retroactive interference

retrograde amnesia

retrospective memory

schema

script

semantic memory

sensory memory

serial position effect

short-term memory

storage

sustained attention

tip-of-the-tongue (TOT) phenomenon

working memory

ANSWERS TO SELF-QUIZZES

Section 1:   1. D; 2. B; 3. A; 4. A
Section 2:   1. C; 2. D; 3. C; 4. B

Section 3:   1. D; 2. A; 3. B; 4. B
Section 4:   1. C; 2. A; 3. D; 4. B

Section 5:   1. B; 2. D; 3. B; 4. B
Section 6:   1. D; 2. A; 3. C; 4. A

7 Thinking, Intelligence, and Language

The Value of a Really Good Idea

The modern world is filled with amazing things. New technologies arise, seemingly daily, making life easier, more efficient, or more interesting. Have you ever noticed that sometimes the hottest new thing solves a problem that you never even realized you had? Sometimes a really good idea starts with just noticing a problem that many people face, and being the first person to recognize that there is a better way—a solution.

Having a really good idea is typically the beginning of a long journey. But a recent great idea concerned making a long journey much shorter. Inventor, engineer, and business magnate Elon Musk recently proposed a new very fast train, using technology called *hyperloop*, that would allow passengers to travel the 354-mile journey from Los Angeles to San Francisco in half an hour (Langridge & Betters, 2017). Musk has offered a similar proposal that would cut the time to travel from New York City to Washington, D.C., to 29 minutes. The hyperloop technology is aimed at reducing friction, catapulting the train at speeds of over 700 miles per hour. Passengers (and freight) could ride in pressurized capsules that travel inside tubes. The development of Hyperloop-1, marketed as selling not transportation but time, itself, sounds impossible, like the flying cars of science fiction. Yet, it is underway.

How would someone come up with such an idea? Of course, it would seem to take a great deal of intelligence, problem-solving ability, expertise, and creativity. However, consider as well that the original idea of this technology was first introduced in 1972 (Langridge & Betters, 2017). The fact that this remarkable innovation is only now being implemented tells us that solving a problem takes more than just a good idea. It requires means, motivation, and the ability to solve all the little problems that come with transforming a great idea into reality.

Cognitive psychology is the study of mental processes. This chapter investigates the basic cognitive processes of thinking, problem solving, reasoning, and decision making. We first define cognition and look at the cognitive revolution that led to new thinking about the workings of the human mind. We then review capacities associated with superior problem solving: critical thinking, creativity, and perhaps most important, intelligence. We conclude by surveying the unique contributions of language to mental processes.

1 The Cognitive Revolution in Psychology

Cognitive psychologists study **cognition**—the way in which information is processed and manipulated in remembering, thinking, and knowing. Cognitive psychology is a relatively young field, scarcely more than a half-century old. Let's begin by tracing its history.

After the first decade of the twentieth century, behaviorism dominated the thinking of experimental psychologists. Behaviorists such as B. F. Skinner argued that the human mind is a black box best left to philosophers, and they considered observable behavior to be psychologists' proper focus. The behaviorist perspective had little use for the mental processes occurring in that dark place between your ears.

In the 1950s psychologists' views began to change. The advent of computers provided a new way to think about the workings of the human mind. If we could "see" what computers were doing internally, maybe we could use our observations to study human mental processes, scientists reasoned. Indeed, computer science was a key motivator in the birth of the study of human cognition. The first modern computer, developed by mathematician John von Neumann in the late 1940s, showed that machines could perform logical operations. In the 1950s, researchers speculated that computers might model some mental operations, and they believed that such modeling might shed light on how the human mind works (Mandler, 2007; Marcus, 2001).

Cognitive psychologists often use the computer as an analogy to help explain the relationship between cognition and the brain (Presti, 2016). They describe the physical brain as the computer's hardware and cognition as its software. Herbert Simon (1969) was among the pioneers in comparing the human mind to computer processing systems. In this analogy, the sensory and perceptual systems provide an "input channel," similar to the way data are entered into the

cognition
The way in which information is processed and manipulated in remembering, thinking, and knowing.

Mathematician John von Neumann (1903–1957) pioneered in the early development of computers. The fact that his computer could perform logical operations led researchers to imagine that computers might model some mental processes and that such modeling might shed light on how the human mind functions.
Source: U.S. Department of Energy

Human

Input

↓

Brain, mind, cognition (memory, problem solving, reasoning, consciousness)

↓

Output

Computers

Input

↓

Hardware and software (memory, operations)

↓

Output

FIGURE 1

Computers and Human Cognition An analogy is sometimes drawn between human cognition and the way computers work. The physical brain is analogous to a computer's hardware, and cognition is analogous to a computer's software.

(photo): ©Creatas/PictureQuest

artificial intelligence (AI)
A scientific field that focuses on creating machines capable of performing activities that require intelligence when they are done by people.

In 2017, Facebook shutdown an AI engine after it was discovered that two "chatbots" were talking to each other in a language they created that was unknown to humans!

computer (Figure 1). As input (information) comes into the mind, mental processes, or operations, act on it, just as the computer's software acts on the data. The transformed input generates information that remains in memory much in the way a computer stores what it has worked on. Finally, the information is retrieved from memory and "printed out" or "displayed" (so to speak) as an observable response.

Computers provide a logical and concrete, but oversimplified, model of the mind's processing of information. Inanimate computers and human brains function quite differently in some respects. For example, most computers receive information from a human who has already coded the information and removed much of its ambiguity. In contrast, each brain neuron can respond to ambiguous information transmitted through sensory receptors such as the eyes and ears.

Computers can do some things better than humans. For example, they can perform complex numerical calculations much faster and more accurately than humans could ever hope to (Liu & others, 2012). Computers can also apply and follow rules more consistently and with fewer errors than humans and can represent complex mathematical patterns better than humans. Recent research has shown that computers might be better than humans at cooperating to win a game (Snow, 2017).

Of course, the human mind is aware of itself; the computer is not. No computer is likely to approach the richness of human consciousness (Ashrafian, 2014; Reggia, 2013; Thill, Padó, & Ziemke, 2014). Still, researchers have made enormous advances in the "human" areas like facial recognition (Zhang & others, 2016).

Certainly the computer's role in cognitive psychology continues to increase. An entire scientific field called **artificial intelligence (AI)** focuses on creating machines capable of performing activities that require intelligence when they are done by people. AI is especially helpful in tasks requiring speed, persistence, and a vast memory (Goel & Davies, 2011). AI systems also assist in diagnosing medical illnesses and prescribing treatment, examining equipment failures, evaluating loan applicants, and advising students about which courses to take (Oliva & others, 2014; Pecina & others, 2014). An AI system called *Deepstack* recently defeated numerous

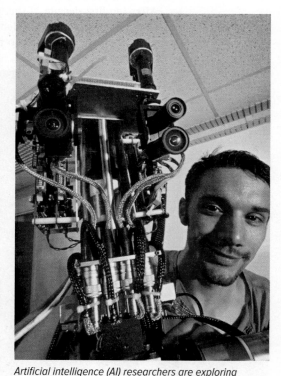

Artificial intelligence (AI) researchers are exploring frontiers that were once the context for sci-fi movie plots. Cog is a human-form robot built by the Humanoid Robotics Group at the Massachusetts Institute of Technology. The sensors and structures in Cog's AI system model human sensory and motor activity as well as perception. Cog's creators have sought to achieve humanlike functioning and interactions with people—both of which, they hope, will lead to new, humanlike learning experiences for the robot. Think about it: How might research findings from experiments such as Cog be applied to real-world situations?
©Volker Steger/Peter Arnold Inc./Getty Images

professional poker players (Moravčík & others, 2017). Recently, NASA allowed the Mars lander computer to take on a role previously reserved for humans: Choosing which materials should be collected for close examination with great success (Francis & others, 2017). Computer scientists and engineers continue to develop computers that more closely approximate human thinking (Borghi & Cangelosi, 2014; Maniadakis & Trahanias, 2014). A survey of over 350 AI experts showed that most believed robots will outperform humans in just about everything by 2060 (Revell, 2017).

Cognitive robotics is a field of study that seeks to endow a robot with intelligent behavior so it can function in the world much like humans do (Carlson & others, 2014; Conti & others, 2016; Law & others, 2014). Thus, efforts are being made to provide robots with processing equipment that will let them perceive, attend, memorize, learn, reason, and make decisions (Broz & others, 2014; Paglieri & others, 2014). Cognitive psychologists, neuroscientists, computer scientists, and engineers are all involved in the fascinating, rapidly growing field of cognitive robotics. A fascinating challenge faced by those seeking to model robots after humans is the *uncanny valley* (Ho & McDorman, 2017). The uncanny valley refers to the fact that robots that represent very close facsimiles of humans sometimes evoke revulsion in people. Something about these robots feels not quite right to human observers.

By the late 1950s the cognitive revolution was in full swing. The term *cognitive psychology* became a label for approaches that sought to explain observable behavior by investigating mental processes and structures that could not be directly observed (Ashcraft & Radvansky, 2014; Goldstein, 2015). We now build on concepts introduced in the memory chapter by exploring thinking, problem solving, and decision making.

Have you noticed that intelligent computers on TV and in the movies almost always turn out to be evil? Why do you think fictional treatments of AI often portray smart computers as scary?

©Javier Larrea/age fotostock

If you were creeped out by the "dead eyes" of animated characters in the movie Polar Express or the just-not-right quality of the humans in Monsters vs. Aliens, you've experienced the uncanny valley.

2 Thinking

When you save a computer file, you might hear a sound from inside or see a processing icon, and you know the computer is processing the work you have just done. Unlike a computer, the brain does not make noise to let us know it is working. Rather, the brain's processing is the silent operation of thinking. **Thinking** involves manipulating information mentally by forming concepts, solving problems, making decisions, and reflecting in a

thinking
The process of manipulating information mentally by forming concepts, solving problems, making decisions, and reflecting critically or creatively.

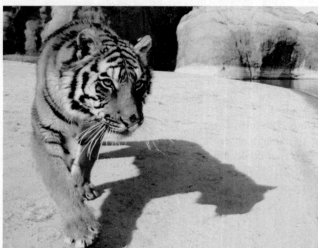

Although it has a ducklike bill and lays eggs, the platypus is nevertheless a mammal like the tiger, as platypus females produce milk with which they feed their young. The prototypical birdlike characteristics of the platypus can lead us to think mistakenly that the platypus is a bird. Its atypical properties place the platypus on the extreme of the concept mammal.

(platypus): ©John Carnemolla/Getty Images; (tiger): ©John Giustina/Getty Images

critical or creative manner. Let's explore the nature of concepts—the components of thinking—and investigate the cognitive processes of problem solving, reasoning, and decision making.

Concepts

A fundamental aspect of thinking is the notion of concepts. **Concepts** are mental categories that are used to group objects, events, and characteristics. Creating categories is one way we make sense of information in the world. We know that apples and oranges are both fruits. We know that poodles and collies are both dogs and that cockroaches and ladybugs are both insects. These items differ from one another in various ways, and yet we recognize that they belong together because we have concepts for fruits, dogs, and insects. Concepts are important for four reasons:

- First, **concepts allow us to generalize**. If we did not have concepts, each object and event in our world would be unique and brand new to us each time we encountered it.

- Second, **concepts allow us to associate experiences and objects**. Basketball, ice hockey, and track are sports. The concept *sport* gives us a way to compare these activities.

- Third, **concepts aid memory, making it more efficient so that we do not have to reinvent the wheel each time we come across a piece of information**. Imagine having to think about how to sit in a chair every time we find ourselves in front of one.

- Fourth, **concepts provide clues about how to react to a particular object or experience**. Perhaps you have had the experience of trying an exotic new cuisine and feeling puzzled as you consider the contents of your plate. If a friend tells you reassuringly, "That's food!" you know that given the concept *food,* it is okay to dig in.

concept
A mental category that is used to group objects, events, and characteristics.

prototype model
A model emphasizing that when people evaluate whether a given item reflects a certain concept, they compare the item with the most typical item(s) in that category and look for a "family resemblance" with that item's properties.

One way that psychologists explain the structure of concepts is the prototype model. The **prototype model** emphasizes that when people evaluate whether a given item reflects a certain concept, they compare the item with the most typical item(s) in that category and look for a "family resemblance" with that item's properties. Birds generally fly and sing, so we know that robins and sparrows are both birds. We recognize exceptions to these properties, however—we know that a penguin is still a bird even though it does not fly or sing. The prototype model maintains that people use characteristic properties to create a representation of the average or ideal member—the prototype—for each concept. Comparing individual cases to our mental prototypes may be a good way to decide quickly whether something (or someone) fits a particular category.

Prototypes come in handy, but they can be misleading when applied to people, as we will see.

Do It!

You are a member of the concept human. Do a quick search online for "uncanny valley examples." It will make your skin crawl. What is it about these "not-quite-human" examples that is so disconcerting to you as a member of the concept human?

Problem Solving

Concepts tell us *what* we think about but not *why* we think. *Why* do we bother to engage in the mental effort of thinking? Consider Levi Hutchins, an ambitious young clockmaker who, in 1787, invented the alarm clock. *Why* did he go to the trouble? He had a specific goal—he wanted to get up before sunrise every morning—yet he faced a dilemma in accomplishing that goal. A problem exists when a person has a goal with no clear way to achieve it. **Problem solving** means finding an appropriate way to attain a goal when the goal is not readily available (Vernon, Hocking, & Tyler, 2016). Problem solving entails following several steps, overcoming mental obstacles, and developing expertise.

FOLLOWING THE STEPS IN PROBLEM SOLVING Psychological research points to four steps in the problem-solving process.

1. Find and Frame Problems

Recognizing a problem is the first step toward a solution (Vernon, Hocking, & Tyler, 2016). Finding and framing problems involves asking questions in creative ways and "seeing" what others do not.

The ability to recognize and frame a problem is difficult to learn but it can be learned. For example, brain storming in a group may be a great way to generate and define problems. Many real-world problems are ill defined or vague and have no clear-cut solutions. Inventors are visionaries who see problems that everyone else is content to live with. Recognizing problems involves being aware of and open to experiences (two mental habits we will examine later). It also means listening carefully to that voice in your head that occasionally sighs, "There must be a better way."

2. Develop Good Problem-Solving Strategies

Once we find a problem and clearly define it, we need to develop strategies for solving it. Among the effective strategies are subgoals, algorithms, and heuristics.

Subgoals are intermediate goals or intermediate problems to solve that put us in a better position for reaching the final goal or solution. Imagine that you are writing a paper for a psychology class. What are some subgoaling strategies for approaching this task? One might be locating the right books and research journals on your chosen topic. At the same time that you are searching for the right publications, you will likely benefit from establishing some subgoals within your time frame for completing the project. If the paper is due in two months, you might set a subgoal of a first draft of the paper two weeks before it is due, another subgoal of completing your reading for the paper one month before it is due, and still another subgoal of starting your library research tomorrow. Notice that in establishing the subgoals for meeting the deadline, we worked backward. Working backward in establishing subgoals is a good strategy. You first create the subgoal that is closest to the final goal and then work backward to the subgoal that is closest to the beginning of the problem-solving effort.

Algorithms are strategies that guarantee a solution to a problem. Algorithms come in different forms, such as formulas, instructions, and the testing of all possible solutions. We use algorithms in cooking (by following a recipe) and driving (by following directions to an address). Compared to humans, computers can more efficiently apply algorithms (Jin, Hamiez, & Hao, 2017).

©Mellenthin/face to fa/Allrightimages/age fotostock

For a human, an algorithmic strategy might take a long time to solve a simple problem. Staring at a rack of letters during a game of Scrabble, for example, you might find yourself moving the tiles around and trying all possible combinations to make a high-scoring word. Instead of using an algorithm to solve your Scrabble problem, however, you might rely on some rules of thumb about words and language.

Heuristics are such shortcut strategies or guidelines that suggest a solution to a problem but do not guarantee an answer (Shan & Yang, 2017). In your Scrabble game, you know

We will come back to heuristics. Keep in mind that they are cognitive shortcuts.

that if you have a Q, you are going to need a U. If you have an X and a T, the T is probably not going to come right before the X. In this situation, heuristics allow you to be more efficient than algorithms would. In the real world, we are more likely to solve the types of problems we face by heuristics than by algorithms. Heuristics help us to narrow down the possible solutions and to find one that works.

3. Evaluate Solutions   Once we think we have solved a problem, we will not know how effective our solution is until we find out if it works. It helps to have in mind a clear criterion for the effectiveness of the solution. For example, what will your criterion be for judging the effectiveness of your solution to the psychology assignment, your psychology paper? Will you judge your solution to be effective if you simply complete the paper? If you get an *A*? If the instructor says that it is one of the best papers a student ever turned in on the topic?

4. Rethink and Redefine Problems and Solutions over Time   An important final step in problem solving is to rethink and redefine problems continually (Vernon, Hocking, & Tyler, 2016). Good problem solvers tend to be more motivated than the average person to improve on their past performances and to make original contributions. Can we make the computer faster and more powerful? Can we make the iPhone even more distracting?

AN OBSTACLE TO PROBLEM SOLVING: BECOMING FIXATED   A key ingredient of being a good problem solver is to acknowledge that one does not know everything—that one's strategies and conclusions are always open to revision. Optimal problem solving may require a certain amount of humility, or the ability to admit that one is not perfect and that there may be better ways than one's tried and true methods to solve life's problems. Sometimes to solve a problem we must forget what we think we know (Gómez-Ariza & others, 2017). It is easy to fall into the trap of becoming fixated on a particular strategy for solving a problem.

One way to avoid getting stuck in the process of problem solving is to set the goal of finding at least two solutions to a problem. That way you don't stop at your first solution!

Fixation involves using a prior strategy and failing to look at a problem from a fresh, new perspective. **Functional fixedness** occurs when individuals fail to solve a problem because they are fixated on a thing's usual functions. If you have ever used a shoe to hammer a nail, you have overcome functional fixedness to solve a problem.

An example of a problem that requires overcoming functional fixedness is the Maier string problem, depicted in Figure 2 (Maier, 1931). The problem is to figure out how to tie two strings together when you must stand in one spot and cannot reach both at the same time. It seems as though you are stuck. However, there is a pair of pliers on a table. Can you solve the problem?

The solution is to use the pliers as a weight, tying them to the end of one string (Figure 3). Swing this string back and forth like a pendulum and grasp the stationary string. Your past experience with pliers and your fixation on their usual function makes this a difficult problem to solve. To do so, you need to find an unusual use for the pliers—in this case, as a weight to create a pendulum.

Multicultural experiences are one way to increase insight and creativity.

Effective problem solving often necessitates trying something new, or *thinking outside the box*—that is, exploring novel ways of approaching tasks and challenges and finding solutions. This might require admitting that one's past strategies were not ideal or do not readily translate to a particular situation. Students who are used to succeeding in high school by cramming for tests and relying on parental pressure to get homework done may find that in college these strategies are no longer viable ways to succeed. To explore how fixation might play a role in your own problem solving, see Figure 4.

fixation
Using a prior strategy and failing to look at a problem from a fresh new perspective.

functional fixedness
Failing to solve a problem as a result of fixation on a thing's usual functions.

Reasoning and Decision Making

In addition to forming concepts and solving problems, thinking includes the higher-order mental processes of reasoning and decision making. These activities require rich connections

FIGURE 2
Maier String Problem How can you tie the two strings together if you cannot reach them both at the same time?

FIGURE 3
Solution to the Maier String Problem Use the pliers as a weight to create a pendulum motion that brings the second string closer.

The Candle Problem
How would you mount a candle on a wall so that it won't drip wax on a table or a floor while it is burning?

The Nine-Dot Problem
Take out a piece of paper and copy the arrangement of dots shown below. Without lifting your pencil, connect the dots using only four straight lines.

The Six-Matchstick Problem
Arrange six matchsticks of equal length to make four equilateral triangles, the sides of which are one matchstick long.

FIGURE 4 **Examples of How Fixation Impedes Problem Solving** These tasks help psychologists measure creative problem solving. *Solutions to the problems are presented at the end of the chapter.*

among neurons and the ability to apply judgment. The end result of this type of thinking is an evaluation, a conclusion, or a decision.

reasoning
The mental activity of transforming information to reach conclusions.

inductive reasoning
Reasoning from specific observations to make generalizations.

REASONING   **Reasoning** is the mental activity of transforming information to reach conclusions. Reasoning is involved in problem solving and decision making. It is also a skill closely tied to critical thinking (Brase, 2014; Newman, Gibb, & Thompson, 2017). Reasoning can be either inductive or deductive (Figure 5).

Inductive reasoning involves reasoning from specific observations to make generalizations (Liang & others, 2014; McAbee, Landis, & Burke, 2017). Inductive reasoning is an important way that we form beliefs about the world. For instance, having turned on your cell phone many times without having it explode, you have every reason to believe that it will not explode the next time you turn it on. From your prior experiences with the phone, you form the

Sour milk notwithstanding, strong inductive reasoning is generally based on many observations. A woman who decides that all men are rats after two bad boyfriends is overgeneralizing.

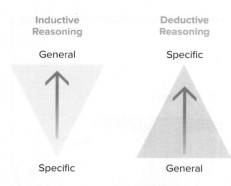

Inductive
Reasoning

Deductive
Reasoning

General

Specific

Specific

General

FIGURE 5 **Inductive and Deductive Reasoning** (*left*) The triangle represents inductive reasoning—going from specific to general. (*right*) The triangle represents deductive reasoning—going from general to specific.

general belief that it is not likely to become a dangerous object. Or, imagine taking a sip of milk from a container and finding that it tastes sour. Inductive reasoning is at work when you throw out the whole container even though you haven't tasted every drop.

Inductive reasoning is responsible for a great deal of scientific knowledge. We know, for instance, that men and women are genetically different, with women having two X chromosomes and men having an X and a Y chromosome, although no one has actually tested every single human being's chromosomes to verify this generalization. Psychological research is often inductive. Whenever psychologists study a sample in order to make generalizations about a population from which the sample is drawn, that is inductive reasoning (McAbee, Landis, & Burke, 2017). Note that this involves going from a few observations to generalizing about a larger group.

In contrast, **deductive reasoning** is reasoning from a general case that we know to be true to a specific instance (Cole, 2016). Using deductive reasoning, we draw conclusions based on facts (Malaia, Tommerdahl, & McKee, 2014). For example, we might start with the general premise that all Texans love the Dallas Cowboys. Thus, if John is a Texan, we logically might surmise that John loves the Dallas Cowboys. Notice, however, that the logic of this deductive reasoning requires that the first statement be true; if all Texans do not love the Cowboys, John just might be a Philadelphia Eagles fan.

deductive reasoning Reasoning from a general case that is known to be true to a specific instance.

When psychologists and other scientists use theories to make predictions and then evaluate their predictions by making further observations, deductive reasoning is at work. When psychologists develop a hypothesis from a theory, they are using a form of deductive reasoning, because the hypothesis is a specific, logical extension of the general theory. If the theory is true, then the hypothesis will be true as well.

DECISION MAKING Think of all the decisions, large and small, that you have to make in life. Should you major in biology, psychology, or business? Should you go to graduate school right after college or get a job first? Should you establish yourself in a career before settling down to have a family? Do you want fries with that? **Decision making** involves evaluating alternatives and choosing among them (LeBoeuf & Shafir, 2012).

Keeping inductive and deductive reasoning straight can be a challenge. Remember that deduction is what a detective does: Collecting up evidence to draw a conclusion.

decision making The mental activity of evaluating alternatives and choosing among them.

Reasoning uses established rules to draw conclusions. In contrast, in decision making, such rules are not established, and we may not know the consequences of the decisions (Abadie, Waroquier, & Terrier, 2017; Newman, Gibb, & Thompson, 2017). Some of the information might be missing, and we might not trust all of the information we have. Making decisions means weighing information and coming to some conclusion that we feel will maximize our outcome: Yes, we will be able to see the movie from this row in the theater; no, we will not run that red light to get to class on time.

TWO TYPES OF REASONING AND DECISION MAKING Many psychologists divide reasoning and decision making into two levels—one that is automatic (often referred to as *Type 1* or *system 1*) and one that is controlled (often called *Type 2* or *system 2*) (Evans, 2012; Stanovich, 2012). The automatic system involves processing that is rapid, heuristic, and intuitive; it entails following one's hunches or gut feelings about a particular decision or problem (Halberstadt, 2010; Markovits, Brisson, & de Chantal, 2017). Intuitive judgment means knowing that something feels right even if the reason why is unknown (Topolinski & Strack, 2009). In contrast, the controlled system is slower, effortful, and analytical. It involves conscious reflection about an issue. This is the kind of thinking that might be required to solve a difficult math problem, for example.

Although conscious effortful thinking is invaluable for solving many problems, research has shown that intuitive processing may also have an important role to play in decision making (Calabretta, Gemser, & Wijnberg, 2017; Li & others, 2016; Ward & King, 2017;

Zolo, Pellegrini, & Ciappei, 2016). Sometimes, compared to effortful reflection, intuitive decision making can be less biased and more efficient in decision making (Schooler, Ohlsson, & Brooks, 1993). For example, in one study (Halberstadt & Catty, 2008) participants were told that their job was to rate the popularity of particular songs. Participants listened to brief snippets of the songs. Half of the participants were asked to first reflect on the reasons a specific song might be popular. The other half simply rendered their judgments intuitively, without much thought. Those who intuitively judged the songs were actually more accurate in their popularity ratings, because they based these ratings on how familiar the song was to them. Basing judgments on the feeling of familiarity was a good idea in this case, as popular songs are likely to be familiar to everyone. Those who analyzed their reasons were less accurate because thinking about reasons disrupted this natural association.

The popular media sometimes portray intuitive hunches as sort of magical. However, these gut feelings do not emerge out of thin air. Rather, they are the product of automatic processes (Halberstadt, 2010); of learned associations (Kahneman & Klein, 2009; Unkelbach, 2007); and of implicit memory (Cheng & Huang, 2011). Your gut feelings about the right answer on a test are certainly more likely to be accurate if you have put in the requisite hours of conscious effortful study.

What determines which system of reasoning we use? The type of problem to be solved may dictate the type of processing used. If a problem is difficult, we might harness system 2 processing. For less taxing decisions, we might go with system 1, following our immediate gut feeling. One factor that influences processing style is mood. A negative mood (feeling sad or worried) fosters more analytical, effortful cognitive processing (Moberly & Watkins, 2009). In contrast, a positive mood (feeling happy or cheerful) facilitates more rapid processing, promoting the use of heuristics and viewing the big picture. A positive mood may provide a signal that all is well and that we can safely go with our intuitive hunches for the task at hand (Clore & Palmer, 2009).

It is important to keep in mind that system 1 processes are as rapid as they are because they often rely on heuristics. The use of heuristics can lead to mistakes when these rules of thumb are applied inappropriately (Kahneman & Klein, 2009), as we now consider.

Biases and Heuristics   Additional fruitful subjects of decision-making research are the biases and heuristics (rules of thumb) that affect the quality of decisions. In many cases, our decision-making strategies are well adapted to deal with a variety of problems (Nisbett & Ross, 1980). Heuristics, for example, are intuitive and efficient ways of solving problems and making decisions; they are often at work when we make a decision by following a gut feeling. However, heuristics and gut feelings can lead to mistakes. Here we look at a few biases and heuristic errors, summarized in Figure 6.

One of the most powerful biases in human decision making is loss aversion. **Loss aversion** refers to the tendency to strongly prefer to avoid losses compared to acquiring gains. We dislike the prospect of losing something we have more than we enjoy the prospect of gaining something new, even when the prospect of a gain outweighs the loss (Kahneman & Tversky, 1984). Imagine that you have a *B+* in a class with an optional, but likely very challenging, final exam. If you do well on the final, you could nudge your grade to an *A−*. But if you do poorly, your *B+* could plummet to a *C*. Would you risk what you already have for the chance to get a better grade?

loss aversion
The tendency to strongly prefer to avoid losses compared to attempting to acquire gains.

Loss aversion has been demonstrated in many different contexts and samples (Canessa & others, 2017; Novemsky & Kahneman, 2005; Wang, Rieger, & Hens, 2017). Indeed, so much research has been done concerning the way that human beings weigh losses more than gains that scholars have been able to estimate that losses appear to be two times more powerful than gains (Vohs & Luce, 2010).

Loss aversion helps to explain a variety of phenomena in psychology and economics. For example, the *endowment effect* means that people ascribe greater value to things they already own, compared to objects owned by someone else. In one study (Kahneman, Knetsch, & Thaler, 1990), some participants were shown a mug and were asked how much they would be willing to

Can you see how loss aversion explains the endowment sunk cost? The idea is that once we own something it becomes one of the many things we would hate to lose!

Loss Aversion	Confirmation Bias	Base Rate Neglect	Hindsight Bias	Representativeness Heuristic	Availability Heuristic
Description Tendency to weigh potential losses more heavily than potential gains **Example:** An investor decides not to buy stock in a new company even though the chances of financial gain outweigh the chances of financial loss.	**Description** Tendency to search for and use information that supports rather than refutes one's ideas **Example:** A politician accepts news that supports his views and dismisses evidence that runs counter to these views.	**Description** Tendency to ignore information about general principles in favor of very specific but vivid information **Example:** You read a favorable expert report on a TV you are intending to buy, but you decide not to buy it when a friend tells you about a bad experience with that model.	**Description** Tendency to report falsely, after the fact, that one accurately predicted an outcome **Example:** You read about the results of a particular psychological study and say, "I always knew that," though in fact you have little knowledge about the issues examined in the study.	**Description** Tendency to make judgments about group membership based on physical appearances or one's stereotype of a group rather than available base rate information **Example:** The victim of a holdup, you view police photos of possible perpetrators. The suspects look very similar to you, but you choose the individual whose hair and clothing look dirtiest and most disheveled.	**Description** Prediction about the probability of an event based on the ease of recalling or imagining similar events **Example:** A girl from an extended family in which no family member ever attended college tells her mother that she wants to be a doctor. Her mother cannot imagine her daughter in such a career and suggests that she become a home healthcare aide.

FIGURE 6 **Decision-Making Problems: Biases and Heuristics** Biases and heuristics (rules of thumb) affect the quality of many of the decisions we make.
(first) ©Digital Vision/SuperStock; (second) ©stevecoleimages/Getty Images

pay for it. Other participants were actually given the mug to keep and then were asked how much they would be willing to sell it for. In both groups the mugs were identical—simple coffee mugs with the university insignia on them. However, those who owned the mug believed it was worth $3 more than those who just looked it over. Somehow, just by owning it, it became more valuable.

Loss aversion also explains why sometimes it is so hard to cut our losses when we are in a losing battle. The *sunk cost fallacy* refers to the fact that people are reluctant to give up on a venture because of past investment. If we were perfectly rational we would make decisions based only on current circumstances, maximizing the benefits and minimizing costs. However, past investment biases our judgments. Economically, sunk cost fallacy means "throwing good money after bad."

Imagine that you have just suffered through two years of training to become an accountant. What you have discovered is that you neither enjoy accounting nor are you good at it. The courses have been a struggle and you have just managed to pass. Should you stick with it? If you were making a decision rationally based on current circumstances alone, you might decide to change course and switch majors. However, doing so would also mean recognizing that the last two years have been "wasted." You have sunk a lot of resources into something you no longer even want. But sunk costs may spur you to stick it out, or even try harder. Sunk costs reflect loss aversion in that we dread the thought of losing the effort, time, and money we have already put into a venture if we give up.

Confirmation bias is the tendency to search for and use information that supports our ideas rather than refutes them (Mercier, 2017). Confirmation bias is also sometimes called "Myside bias" because it is all about collecting up evidence that our views are correct. Our decisions can also become further biased

Confirmation bias is one way to understand the polarization in U.S. politics. People get their news from different sources that agree with their previous views. And on social media they limit themselves to information that agrees with them.

confirmation bias
The tendency to search for and use information that supports one's ideas rather than refutes them.

because we tend to seek out and listen to people whose views confirm our own while we avoid those with dissenting views. It is easy to detect the confirmation bias in the way that many people think. Consider politicians. They often accept news that supports their views and dismiss evidence that runs counter to those views. Avoiding confirmation bias means applying the same rigorous analysis to both sides of an argument.

Hindsight bias is our tendency to report falsely, after the fact, that we accurately predicted an outcome (Van Boekel, Varma, & Varma, 2017). It is sometimes referred to as the "I knew it all along effect." With this type of bias, people tend to view events that have happened as more predictable than they were, and to represent themselves as being more accurate in their predictions than they actually were. Although the hindsight bias might sound self-serving in the sense that it means remembering ourselves as having known more than we really did know, cognitive psychologists recognize that this bias may be based on new learning and on updating our knowledge about the world (Nestler, Blank, & Egloff, 2010; Pezzo, 2011). One reason for hindsight bias is that actual events are more vivid in our minds than all those things that failed to happen, an effect called the availability heuristic.

hindsight bias
The tendency to report falsely, after the fact, that one has accurately predicted an outcome.

The **availability heuristic** refers to a prediction about the probability of an event based on the ease of recalling or imagining similar events (Taylor & others, 2017). For example, have you ever experienced a sudden fear of flying after hearing about an airplane crash? Shocking events such as plane crashes stick in our minds, making such disasters seem common. The chance of dying in a plane crash in a given year, however, is tiny (1 in 400,000) compared to the chance of dying in a car accident (1 in 6,500). Because car accidents are less newsworthy, they are less likely to catch our attention and remain in our awareness. The availability heuristic can reinforce generalizations about others in daily life (Chou & Edge, 2012). Imagine, for instance, that Elvedina, a Mexican American girl, tells her mother that she wants to be a doctor. Her mother, who has never seen a Latina doctor, finds it hard to conceive of her daughter's pursuing such a career and might suggest that she try nursing instead.

availability heuristic
A prediction about the probability of an event based on the ease of recalling or imagining similar events.

Also reflective of the impact of vivid cases on decision making is **base rate neglect,** the tendency to ignore information about general principles in favor of very specific but vivid information (Pennycook & Thompson, 2017). Let's say that as a prospective car buyer, you read *Consumer Reports* and find that a panel of experts rates a particular vehicle exceptionally well. You might still be swayed in your purchasing decision, however, if a friend tells you about her bad experiences with that car. Similarly, imagine being told that the average exam score for a test in your psychology class was 75 percent. If you were asked to guess a random student's score, 75 percent would be a good answer—the mean tells us the central tendency of any distribution. Yet if the student provided just a little bit of information, such as how many hours he or she studied, you might give too much weight to that specific information, losing sight of the valuable base rate information you have in the class mean.

base rate neglect
The tendency to ignore information about general principles in favor of very specific but vivid information.

To experience another heuristic in action, consider the following example. Your psychology professor tells you she has assembled 100 men in the hallway outside your classroom. The group consists of 5 librarians and 95 members of the Hells Angels motorcycle club. She is going to randomly select one man to enter the room, and you can win $100 if you accurately guess whether he is a librarian or a Hells Angel. The man stands before you. He is in his 50s, with short graying hair, and he wears thick glasses, a button-down white shirt, a bow tie, neatly pressed slacks, and loafers. Is he a librarian or a Hells Angel? If you guessed librarian, you have fallen victim to the representativeness heuristic.

*Gut instincts can be powerful. Imagine ignoring your hunch that the man was a librarian, and yet it turned out that he **was** a librarian (despite the odds). How hard would you kick yourself then?*

The **representativeness heuristic** is the tendency to make judgments about group membership based on physical appearances or the match between a person and one's stereotype of a group rather than on available base rate information (Nilsson, Juslin, & Olsson, 2008). Essentially, a stereotype is the use of concepts to make generalizations about a group of people. In the example just described, the base rate information tells you that 95 times out of 100, the man in your class is likely to be a Hells Angel. The best approach to winning the $100 might be simply to shut your eyes and guess Hells Angel, no matter what the man looks like.

representativeness heuristic
The tendency to make judgments about group membership based on physical appearances or the match between a person and one's stereotype of a group rather than on available base rate information.

Help Wanted: Critical and Creative Thinkers

©Rawpixel.com/Shutterstock

It is hard to imagine any occupation where critical thinking and creativity would not be useful abilities. The best places to work often are characterized as flexible, diverse, learning-oriented, and open in communication.

Google, the Internet company, is often selected as one of the best places to work (Gillet, 2016). Google gets about 2 million job applicants a year. What do Google managers look for in potential employees? They seek to hire creative, brainy, and hardworking people who work well in a context that is relatively free of structure.

In both hiring decisions and the day-to-day workflow, many organizations seek creativity and thinking outside the box. Some organizations even hire consultants to help promote creative and critical thinking in managers and employees. Being a great problem solver involves not only know-how and motivation but also the capacity to meet every challenge with an open mind.

The representativeness heuristic can be particularly damaging in the context of social judgments. Consider a scenario where a particular engineering corporation seeks to hire a new chief executive officer (CEO). Lori, a top-notch candidate with an undergraduate engineering degree and an MBA from an outstanding business school, applies. If there are few women in upper management at the firm, the company's board of directors might inaccurately view Lori as not fitting their view of the prototypical CEO—and miss the chance to hire an exceptional candidate.

Note that the company's directors are using a prototype model for the category CEO—and making a mistake.

Thus, heuristics help us make decisions rapidly. To solve problems accurately and make the best decisions, however, we must sometimes override these shortcuts and think more deeply, critically, and creatively.

Thinking Critically and Creatively

Problem solving and decision making are basic cognitive processes that we use multiple times each day. Certain strategies lead to better solutions and choices than others, and some people are especially good at these cognitive exercises. In this section we examine two skills associated with superior problem solving: critical thinking and creativity.

CRITICAL THINKING Critical thinking means thinking reflectively and productively and evaluating the evidence. Scientists are critical thinkers. Critical thinkers grasp the deeper meaning of ideas, question assumptions, and decide for themselves what to believe or do (Cargas, Williams, & Rosenberg, 2017; Fong & others, 2017). Critical thinking requires maintaining a sense of humility about what we know (and what we do not know). It means being motivated to see past the obvious.

Critical thinking is vital to effective problem solving. Colleges and universities are increasingly striving to instill critical thinking in students (Fong & others, 2017). A problem in elementary and high schools is that high stakes testing may move teachers to concentrate on getting students to give a single correct answer in an imitative way rather than on encouraging new ideas (Foote, 2012). Further, many people are inclined naturally to stay on the surface of problems rather than to stretch their minds. The cultivation of two mental habits is essential to critical thinking: mindfulness and open-mindedness.

Mindfulness means being alert and mentally present for one's everyday activities. The mindful person maintains an active awareness of the circumstances of his or her life. According to Ellen Langer (1997, 2000, 2005; Bercovitz & others, 2017), mindfulness is a key to critical thinking. Langer distinguishes mindful behavior from mindless behaviors—automatic activities we perform without thought.

> **mindfulness**
> The state of being alert and mentally present for one's everyday activities.

In a classic study, Langer found that people (as many as 90 percent) would mindlessly give up their place in line for a copy machine when someone asked, "Can I go first? I need to make copies" as compared to when the same person simply said, "Can I go first?" (just 60 percent) (Langer, Blank, & Chanowitz, 1978). For the mindless persons in the study, even a completely meaningless justification—after all, everyone in line was there to make copies—was reason enough to step aside. A mindless person engages in automatic behavior without careful thinking. In contrast, a mindful person is engaged with the environment, responding in a thoughtful way to various experiences.

Open-mindedness means being receptive to other ways of looking at things. People often do not even know that there is another side to an issue or evidence contrary to what they believe. Simple openness to other viewpoints can help to keep individuals from jumping to conclusions. As Socrates once said, knowing what it is you do not know is the first step to true wisdom.

> **open-mindedness**
> The state of being receptive to other ways of looking at things.

Being mindful and maintaining an open mind may be more difficult than the alternative of going through life on automatic pilot. Critical thinking is valuable, however, because it allows us to make better predictions about the future, to evaluate situations objectively, and to effect appropriate changes. In some sense, critical thinking requires courage. When we expose ourselves to a broad range of perspectives, we risk finding out that our assumptions might be wrong. When we engage our critical minds, we may discover problems, but we are also more likely to have opportunities to make positive changes.

> **creativity**
> The ability to think about something in novel and unusual ways and to devise unconventional solutions to problems.

CREATIVE THINKING In addition to thinking critically, coming up with the best solution to a problem may involve thinking creatively. The word *creative* can apply to an activity or a person, and creativity as a process may be open even to people who do not think of themselves as creative. When we talk about **creativity** as a characteristic of a person, we are referring to the ability to think about something in novel and unusual ways and to devise unconventional solutions to problems.

> **divergent thinking**
> Thinking that produces many solutions to the same problem.

We can look at the thinking of creative people in terms of divergent and convergent thinking. **Divergent thinking** produces many solutions to the same problem. **Convergent thinking** produces the single best solution to a problem. Creative thinkers do both types of thinking (An, Song, & Carr, 2016). Divergent thinking occurs during *brainstorming,* which occurs when a group of people openly throw out a range of possible solutions to a problem, even some that might seem crazy. Having a lot of possible solutions, however, still requires that they come up with the solution that is best. That is where convergent thinking comes in. Convergent thinking means taking all of those possibilities and finding the right one for the job. Convergent thinking is best when a problem has only one right answer.

> **convergent thinking**
> Thinking that produces the single best solution to a problem.

Individuals who think creatively also show the following characteristics (Perkins, 1984).

- *Flexibility and playful thinking:* Creative thinkers are flexible and play with problems. This trait gives rise to the paradox that although creativity takes hard work, the work goes more smoothly if it is taken

Do It!

To get a sense of the roles of divergent and convergent thinking in creativity, try the following exercise. First take 10 minutes and jot down all of the uses that you can think of for a cardboard box. Don't hold back—include every possibility that comes to mind. That list represents divergent thinking. Now look the list over. Which of the possible uses are most unusual or most likely to be worthwhile? That's convergent thinking.

lightly. In a way, humor greases the wheels of creativity (Goleman, Kaufman, & Ray, 1993). When you are joking around, you are more likely to consider any possibility and to ignore the inner censor who can condemn your ideas as off base.

- *Inner motivation:* Creative people often are motivated by the joy of creating. They tend to be less inspired than less creative people by grades, money, or favorable feedback from others. Thus, creative people are motivated more internally than externally (Hennessey, 2011).

- *Willingness to face risk:* Creative people make more mistakes than their less imaginative counterparts because they come up with more ideas and more possibilities. They win some; they lose some. Creative thinkers know that being wrong is not a failure—it simply means that they have discovered that one possible solution does not work.

- *Objective evaluation of work:* Most creative thinkers strive to evaluate their work objectively. They may use established criteria to make judgments or rely on the judgments of respected, trusted others. In this manner, they can determine whether further creative thinking will improve their work.

self-quiz

1. An example of a concept is
   A. a basketball.
   B. a daisy.
   C. a vegetable.
   D. an eagle.

2. Deductive reasoning starts at _____ and goes to _____.
   A. the general; the specific
   B. the specific; the general
   C. fixation; function
   D. function; fixation

3. All of the following are characteristic of creative thinkers *except*
   A. inner motivation.
   B. functional fixedness.
   C. objectivity.
   D. risk taking.

APPLY IT! 4. The students in an architecture class are given the assignment to design a new student center for their campus. They have one week to submit their first drafts. Jenny and David, two students in the class, spend the first day very differently. Jenny quickly decides on what her building will look like and starts designing it. David spends the first day doodling and devises 20 different styles he might use, including a Gothic version, a spaceship design, a blueprint with a garden growing on top, and another plan that looks like a giant elephant (the school's mascot).

When Jenny sees David's sketches, she scoffs, "You're wasting your time. We have only a week for the first draft!" On the second day, David selects his best effort and works on that one until he finishes it. Which of the following is true of these strategies?
   A. Jenny is effectively using divergent thinking in her strategy.
   B. David should be using heuristics given the limited time for the project.
   C. Jenny is criticizing David for engaging in deductive reasoning.
   D. David is using divergent thinking first and will get to convergent thinking later, while Jenny has engaged only in convergent thinking.

3 Intelligence

Like the term *creative,* the word *intelligent* can apply to a behavior or a person. We might say that someone who decides to quit smoking has made an intelligent choice. When we apply the word to a person, however, defining intelligent can be trickier.

Cultures vary in the ways they define intelligence (Ang, van Dyne, & Tan, 2011; Zhang & Sternberg, 2012). Most European Americans think of intelligence in terms of reasoning and thinking skills, but people in Kenya consider responsible participation in family and social life an integral part of intelligence. An intelligent person in Uganda is someone who knows what to do and follows through with appropriate action. Intelligence to the Iatmul people of Papua New Guinea involves the ability to remember the names of 10,000 to 20,000 clans. The residents of the widely dispersed Caroline Islands incorporate the talent of navigating by the stars into their definition of intelligence (Figure 7). Some cultures do not even have a word that refers to intelligence as most Westerners think of it. For instance, Mandarin Chinese has words for specific abilities, such as wisdom, but not one single word that means, essentially, being smart (Yang & Sternberg, 1997a, 1997b).

FIGURE 7 **Iatmul and Caroline Island Intelligence** The intelligence of the Iatmul people of Papua New Guinea involves the ability to remember the names of many clans. On the 680 Caroline Islands in the Pacific Ocean east of the Philippines, the intelligence of the inhabitants includes the ability to navigate by the stars.

(Iatmul) ©National Geographic Creative/Alamy Stock Photo; (Caroline): ©Angelo Giampiccolo/Shutterstock

In the United States, we generally define **intelligence** as an all-purpose ability to do well on cognitive tasks, to solve problems, and to learn from experience. The idea that intelligence captures a common general ability that is reflected in performance on various cognitive tests was introduced by Charles Spearman (1904). Spearman noted that schoolchildren who did well in math also did well in reading, and he came up with the idea that intelligence is a general ability, which he called *g*. This view of intelligence suggests that general intelligence underlies performance in a variety of areas, whether it is mathematics, verbal ability, or abstract reasoning. Spearman's *g* essentially assumes that the intelligent person is a jack-of-all-cognitive trades.

intelligence
All-purpose ability to do well on cognitive tasks, to solve problems, and to learn from experience.

Measuring Intelligence

Psychologists measure intelligence using tests that produce a score known as the person's *intelligence quotient (IQ)*. To understand how IQ is derived and what it means, let's first examine the criteria for a good intelligence test: validity, reliability, and standardization.

In the realm of testing, **validity** refers to the extent to which a test measures what it is intended to measure. If a test is supposed to measure intelligence, then it should measure intelligence, not some other characteristic, such as anxiety. One of the most important indicators of validity is the degree to which it predicts an individual's performance when that performance is assessed by other measures, or *criteria,* of the attribute (Neukrug & Fawcett, 2015). For example, a psychologist might validate an intelligence test by asking employers of the individuals who took the test how intelligent they are at work. The employers' perceptions would be a criterion for measuring intelligence. When the scores on a measure relate to important outcomes (such as employers' evaluations), we say the test has high *criterion validity.*

validity
The soundness of the conclusions that a researcher draws from an experiment. In the realm of testing, the extent to which a test measures what it is intended to measure.

Test validity means that a scale measures what it says it measures. In experiments, validity refers to the soundness of the conclusions that a researcher draws from an experiment.

Reliability is the extent to which a test yields a consistent, reproducible measure of performance. That is, a reliable test is one that produces the same score over time and repeated testing. Reliability and validity are related. If a test is valid, then it must be reliable, but a reliable test need not be valid. People can respond consistently on a test, but the test might not be measuring what it purports to measure.

reliability
The extent to which a test yields a consistent, reproducible measure of performance.

Good intelligence tests are not only reliable and valid but also standardized (Neukrug & Fawcett, 2015). **Standardization** involves developing uniform procedures for administering

standardization
The development of uniform procedures for administering and scoring a test, and the creation of norms (performance standards) for the test.

Validity

Does the test measure what it purports to measure?

Reliability

Is test performance consistent?

Standardization

Are uniform procedures for administering and scoring the test used?

FIGURE 8

Test Construction and Evaluation Tests are a tool for measuring important abilities such as intelligence. Good tests show high reliability and validity and are standardized so that people's scores can be compared.

intelligence quotient (IQ)
An individual's mental age divided by chronological age multiplied by 100.

and scoring a test, as well as creating norms, or performance standards, for the test. Increasingly such testing is done on computers. Uniform testing procedures require that the testing environment be as similar as possible for all individuals. Norms are created by giving the test to a large group of individuals representative of the population for whom the test is intended. Norms tell us which scores are considered high, low, or average. Many tests of intelligence are designed for individuals from diverse groups. So that the tests are applicable to such different groups, many of them have norms for individuals of different ages, socioeconomic statuses, and ethnic groups (Urbina, 2011). Figure 8 summarizes the criteria for test construction and evaluation.

IQ TESTS In 1904, the French Ministry of Education asked psychologist Alfred Binet to devise a method that would determine which students did not learn effectively from regular classroom instruction. School officials wanted to reduce overcrowding by placing such students in special schools. Binet and his student Theophile Simon developed an intelligence test to meet this request. The test consisted of 30 items ranging from the ability to touch one's nose or ear on command to the ability to draw designs from memory and to define abstract concepts. Binet's test is now known as the Stanford-Binet and it is still widely used.

Alfred Binet (1857–1911) *Binet constructed the first intelligence test after being asked to create a measure to determine which children would benefit from instruction in France's schools.*
Source: National Library of Medicine/NIH

To measure intelligence, Binet came up with the idea of comparing a person's mental abilities to the mental abilities that are typical for a particular age group.

Binet developed the concept of **mental age (MA),** which is an individual's level of mental development relative to that of others. Binet reasoned that a child of very low mental ability would perform like a normal child of a younger age. To think about a person's level of intelligence, then, we might compare the person's mental age (MA) to his or her *chronological age (CA),* or age from birth. A very bright child has an MA considerably above CA; a less bright child has an MA considerably below CA.

mental age (MA)
An individual's level of mental development relative to that of others.

The German psychologist William Stern devised the term **intelligence quotient (IQ)** in 1912. IQ consists of an individual's mental age divided by chronological age multiplied by 100:

$$IQ = (MA/CA) \times 100$$

Note that the meaning of the IQ score is essentially the relationship of a person's mental age to his or her chronological age. If mental age is the same as chronological age, then the individual's IQ is 100 (average); if mental age is above chronological age, the IQ is more than 100 (above average); if mental age is below chronological age, the IQ is less than 100 (below average). For example, a 6-year-old child with a mental age of 8 has an IQ of 133, whereas a 6-year-old child with a mental age of 5 has an IQ of 83.

In childhood, mental age increases as the child ages, but once he or she reaches about age 16, the concept of mental age loses its meaning. That is why many experts today prefer to examine IQ scores in terms of how unusual a person's score is when compared to the scores of other adults. For this purpose, researchers and testers use standardized norms that they have identified in the many people who have been tested.

Another measure of intelligence is the Wechsler scales, developed by David Wechsler (1939). There are three versions of the scale. For those ages 16 and older, the Wechsler Adult Intelligence Scale (the WAIS) includes items such as vocabulary, working memory capacity, math problems, and the ability to complete jigsaw puzzles. For children between the ages of 6 and 16, the Wechsler Intelligence Scale for Children (the WISC) includes vocabulary and comprehension but also has tasks such as putting together blocks to fit a particular pattern. Finally, a version developed for children as young as 2½ is the Wechsler Pre-School and Primary Scale of Intelligence (the WPPSI, pronounced "whipsy"). On this measure, children are asked, for instance, to point to a picture that depicts a word the examiner says, to complete a block design, and to answer basic knowledge questions. If you have taken an IQ test, chances are it was one of the Wechsler scales. It is currently the most popular measure of intelligence. In addition to summary scores for general IQ, the Wechsler scales include scores for areas such as verbal comprehension, perceptual reasoning, working memory, and processing speed.

Both the Stanford-Binet and the Wechsler scales provide measures of Spearman's *g*. Both of these measures of intelligence have a long history of research demonstrating their reliability, and they both feature standardized administration procedures and norms. Finally, they predict results that we would expect, including academic performance and a variety of life outcomes, including lower risk for psychological disorders (Wraw & others, 2016) and economic and career success (Bergman & others, 2014; Spengler & others, 2015).

Intelligence shares a strong relationship with physical health and longevity (Anstey, Mack, & von Sanden, 2006; Gottfredson & Deary, 2004; Schaefer & others, 2016). Research especially supports the idea that declines in cognitive abilities over time predict risk of mortality (Aichele, Rabbitt, & Ghisletta, 2015). Are there specific cognitive abilities that are likely to predict longer, healthier lives? To read about research on this topic, see the Intersection.

Over the years, IQ tests like the Stanford-Binet and Wechsler scales have been given to thousands of children and adults of different ages selected at random from different parts of the United States. When the scores for many people are examined, these approximate a normal distribution (Figure 9). A **normal distribution** is a symmetrical, bell-shaped curve, with a majority of the scores falling in the middle of the possible range and few scores appearing toward the extremes of the range.

normal distribution
A symmetrical, bell-shaped curve, with a majority of test scores (or other data) falling in the middle of the possible range and few scores (or other data points) appearing toward the extremes.

CULTURAL BIAS IN TESTING   Many early intelligence tests were culturally biased, favoring people who were from urban rather than rural environments, of middle rather than low socioeconomic status, and non-Latino White rather than African American (Provenzo, 2002). For example, a question on an early test asked what one should do if one finds a 3-year-old child in the street. The correct answer was "call the police." However, children from inner-city families who perceive the police as scary are unlikely to choose this answer. Similarly, children from rural areas might not choose this answer if there is no police force nearby. Such questions clearly do not measure the knowledge necessary to adapt to one's environment or to be "intelligent" in an inner-city or a rural neighborhood (Scarr, 1984). In addition, members of minority groups may not speak English or may speak nonstandard English. Consequently, they may be at a disadvantage in trying to understand verbal questions that are framed in standard English, even if the content of the test is appropriate (Cathers-Shiffman & Thompson, 2007).

PSYCHOLOGICAL INQUIRY

FIGURE 9   The Normal Curve and Stanford-Binet IQ Scores The distribution of IQ scores approximates a normal curve. Remember that the area under the curve represents the number of people who obtain a given score. >**Does most of the population fall in the low, middle, or high range of scores? How do you know?** >**If someone scored 132 on the test, how many people scored below that person's score?** >**Intelligence follows a normal distribution, meaning it produces this bell curve. What other human characteristics might have the same distribution?**

Cognitive and Health Psychology: Does Thinking Fast Relate to Living Longer?

The types of skills that should be included in assessments of intelligence has been the topic of controversy since the beginnings of intelligence testing. One aspect of cognitive ability that is not included in either the Stanford-Binet or the Wechsler scales is processing speed. *Processing speed* refers to the time it takes a person to render quick decisions. For example, given a sheet of paper with a matrix of letters on it, how quickly can a person find the letter "w"? Or, when shown two letter strings, like "sico" and "milk," and asked to choose which one is a word, how long does it take the person to pick "milk"? The idea that processing speed ought to be included as a part of cognitive ability has been around for a long time (Thurstone, 1938). You might be thinking of all the ways that making fast decisions might lead to bad decisions. But being able to quickly respond to these kinds of simple tasks with accuracy might just be a strong predictor of longevity (Salthouse, 1993). Let's take a look at the science.

Recently, researchers (Aichele, Rabbitt, & Ghisletta, 2016) studied cognitive processing in a 29-year longitudinal study in the United Kingdom. More than 6,000 people took part. Most of them were in their 40's or 50's when the study began. The researchers measured not only processing speed but also a host of other variables relevant to mortality risk, including gender, smoking, prescription drug use, general intelligence, and so on. This work is notable because the outcome of interest was whether or not people died during the 29 years of the study, an important outcome indeed. The results? The faster people responded to questions like those noted above the less likely folks were to die. How strong was the association between processing speed and mortality risk? It was not as strong as the association found for smoking but was stronger than that for illness frequency, prescription medications, and leisure activity (Aichele, Rabbitt, & Ghisletta, 2016).

Why would processing speed share a strong relationship with longevity? There are a few possible reasons. First, processing speed can be measured with more precision than many other variables. Second, this single cognitive ability may represent many levels of functioning for the person. So, changes in processing speed can reflect changes in cognitive ability, physical ability, and

©Inti St Clair/Blend Images LLC

other psychological factors. Although the fact that processing speed does not represent a "pure" measure of a single characteristic may seem to muddy the waters, it may actually be a strength for practitioners interested in using psychological measures to assess risk for death: One measure that captures a host of important variables. Processing speed measures can also be tailored to specific languages and cultures with relative ease.

Interestingly, alongside processing speed, another variable that strongly predicted risk for death was people's subjective feelings of their own health. Even controlling for more objective indicators of health and illness, a person's rating of whether they felt well was a strong predictor of survival (Aichele, Rabbitt, & Ghisletta, 2016). A finding that highlights, again, the potential usefulness of measures that capture untold underlying processes in predicting health and longevity.

\\ **Why do you think cognitive ability is related to health and longevity?**

---

culture-fair tests
Intelligence tests that are intended to be culturally unbiased.

Researchers have sought to develop tests that accurately reflect a person's intelligence, regardless of cultural background. **Culture-fair tests** are intelligence tests that are intended to be culturally unbiased. One type of culture-fair test includes questions that are familiar to people from all socioeconomic and ethnic backgrounds. A second type contains no verbal questions. Figure 10 shows a question similar to ones found in the Raven Progressive Matrices Test. Even though tests such as the Raven Progressive Matrices are designed to be culture-fair, people with more education still score higher than do those with less education.

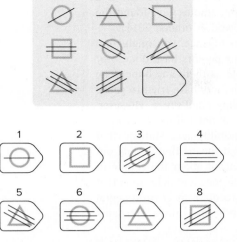

FIGURE 10 Sample Item from the Raven Progressive Matrices Test For this item, the respondent must choose which of the numbered figures would come next in the order. Why is number 6 the right answer?

Source: Raven's Progressive Matrices (Advanced Progressive Matrices), 1998.

Why is it so hard to create culture-fair tests? Just as the definition of intelligence may vary by culture, most tests of intelligence reflect what is important to the dominant culture. If tests have time limits, the test will be biased against groups not concerned with time. If languages differ, the same words might have different meanings for different language groups. Even pictures can produce bias, because some cultures have less experience with drawings and photographs (Anastasi & Urbina, 1996). Because of such difficulties, Robert Sternberg (2012; Zhang & Sternberg, 2012) concludes that there are no culture-fair tests, only culture-reduced tests.

Moreover, within the same culture, different groups can have different attitudes, values, and motivation, and these variations can affect their performance on intelligence tests (Ang & van Dyne, 2009; Sternberg, 2012). Questions about railroads, furnaces, seasons of the year, distances between cities, and so on can be biased against groups who have less experience than others with these contexts. One explanation for the effects of education on IQ test scores is that education (and other environmental factors) may influence intelligence, a possibility to which we now turn.

Do It!

Try out a culture-fair IQ test for yourself. Go to http://psychologytoday.tests.psychtests.com/take_test.php?idRegTest=3202. Once you have checked it out, do a web search for intelligence tests and see if you get the same results when you take different tests. Do the websites provide information about the reliability and validity of the tests?

Genetic and Environmental Influences on Intelligence

There is no doubt that genes influence intelligence (Esposito, Grigorenko, & Sternberg, 2012; Hanscombe & others, 2012). One research review concluded that there may be more than 1,000 genes that affect intelligence, each possibly having a small influence on an individual's intelligence (Davies & others, 2011). Instead of identifying "intelligence" genes, researchers have worked to identify a set of genetic characteristics (called *alleles*) that predict educational attainment. Some people have only a few of these, some have more than that, and some have a great deal. Not surprisingly, this set of genetic characteristics that predicts educational attainment is related to intelligence scores (Chabris & others, 2015; Domingue & others, 2015). A recent study showed that the amount of these alleles people have predicts numerous important outcomes over the lifespan, from reading ability in childhood to retirement planning in adulthood (Belsky & others, 2016).

©FatCamera/Getty Images

heritability
The proportion of observable differences in a group that can be explained by differences in the genes of the group's members.

Some researchers use a statistic called heritability to describe the extent to which the observable differences among people in a group can be explained by the genetic differences of the group's members. **Heritability** is the proportion of observable differences in a group that can be explained by differences in the genes of the group's members. For intelligence, that means that heritability tells us how much of the differences we observe in intelligence is attributable to differences in genes. Because heritability is a proportion, the highest degree of heritability is 100 percent. Twin studies have found the heritability of intelligence to be as high as 75 percent (Trzaskowski & others, 2014).

As you consider this discussion of genetic influences on intelligence, you might find yourself reflecting on some of the less than brilliant things your parents have done over the years, and you may be feeling discouraged. If IQ is heritable, is there any hope? The heritability statistic has certainly been one way that some researchers have tried to gauge the influence of genetics on psychological characteristics including intelligence. However, it is important to understand this statistic for what it can and cannot tell us about intelligence or any characteristic. First and most important, heritability is a statistic that provides information about a group, not a single individual. That means that finding out that heritability for intelligence is 75 percent tells us nothing at all about the source of an individual person's intelligence. We cannot dissect your intelligence and determine that you got 75 percent of it from your parents' genes and 25 percent from environmental experiences that you have had with your parents, teachers, friends, and others. Heritability has no meaning when applied to a single case.

Also, heritability estimates can change over time and across different groups (Nisbett & others, 2012; Turkheimer & others, 2003). If a group of individuals lives in the same advantageous setting (with good nutrition, supportive parents, excellent schools, stable neighborhoods, and plenty of opportunities), heritability estimates for intelligence might be quite high, as this optimal environment allows genetic characteristics to flourish to their highest potential. However, if a group of individuals lives in a highly variable environment (with some individuals experiencing rich, nurturing environments full of opportunity and others experiencing less supportive contexts), genetic characteristics may be less predictive of differences in intelligence in that group, relative to environmental factors.

Even if the heritability of a characteristic is very high, the environment still matters. Take height, for example. More than 90 percent of the variation in height is explained by genetic variation. Humans continue to get taller and taller, however, and this trend demonstrates that environmental factors such as nutrition have an impact. Similarly, in the case of intelligence, researchers widely agree that for most people, modifications in environment can change their IQ scores considerably (Esposito, Grigorenko, & Sternberg, 2012; Nisbett & others, 2012). Enriching an environment can improve children's achievement in school and support their development of crucial workplace skills. Children from impoverished socioeconomic backgrounds who are adopted into more economically advantaged families often have IQs that are higher than those of their biological parents (Sternberg, Grigorenko, & Kidd, 2005).

Indeed, research provides strong support for the conclusion that childhood experiences can profoundly affect IQ. The Database of Raising Intelligence is a continuously updated collection of research on the effects of various interventions on children's intelligence, ranging from infancy to age 5. John Protzko, Joshua Aronson, and Clancy Blair (2013) published the results of an analysis of over 74 interventions involving more than 37,000 children. All of the studies included were experiments, meaning that participants were randomly assigned to receive the intervention and then IQs (the dependent variable) were compared to those in the control groups. The analysis provided strong evidence for four environmental interventions that affect childhood IQ (Protzko, Aronson, & Blair, 2013):

- *Dietary supplements* One type of dietary supplement that has been found to positively influence childhood IQ is long-chain polyunsaturated fatty acids, commonly referred to as Omega-3 fatty acids. These acids are found in breast milk, fish oil, salmon, walnuts, spinach, and avocados. When pregnant women, nursing mothers, and infants received 1,000 milligram supplements of Omega-3 fatty acids, the supplements led to a more than 3.5 point increase in IQ points.

- *Educational interventions* Research shows that early childhood education can improve the IQ of economically disadvantaged young children: Early educational interventions, especially those that involved training on complex tasks, led to an increase in IQ of more than 4 points.

- *Interactive reading* Interactive reading means that parents ask open-ended questions, encourage the child to read, and engage with the child actively about what they are reading together. Interactive reading raised a child's IQ by over 6 points, and this was especially true if the interventions occurred at younger ages.

- *Preschool* Sending a child to preschool increased IQ by more than 4 points (Protzko, Aronson, & Blair, 2013). Socioeconomic status played an important role in these results. For economically disadvantaged children, those whose parents might not have been able to afford preschool except for the studies in which they were enrolled, attending preschool raised IQs by as much as 7 points. Preschool curricula including a language-development component were especially effective. The researchers note that the effects of preschool may not be maintained if children are not continually exposed to complex cognitive challenges in their environments as they move to grade school.

One effect of the environment on intelligence is evident in rapidly increasing IQ test scores around the world, a phenomenon called the *Flynn effect* (Flynn, 1999, 2006, 2011, 2013). Scores on these tests have been rising so fast that a high percentage of people regarded as having average intelligence at the turn of the twentieth century would be regarded as having below average intelligence today (Figure 11). Because the increase has taken place in a relatively short period of time, it cannot be due to heredity but rather may be due to rising levels of education attained by a much greater percentage of the world's population or to other environmental factors, such as the explosion of information to which people are now exposed. A recent meta-analysis suggested that the Flynn effect is stronger in adults than children and may be declining in recent years (Pietschnig & Voracek, 2015).

Environmental influences are complex (Maholmes, 2014; Raver, Roy, & Pressler, 2015). Growing up with all the advantages does not guarantee success. Children from wealthy families may have easy access to excellent schools, books, tutors, and travel, but they may take such

Do It!

Many different intelligence tests are available online, such as at www.iqtest.com/. Give this one a try and then do a web search for intelligence tests and see if you get the same results when you take a different test. Do the websites tell you how reliable the tests are? Do they provide information on standardization or validity? If your scores on the two tests are very different, what might account for this variation?

PSYCHOLOGICAL INQUIRY

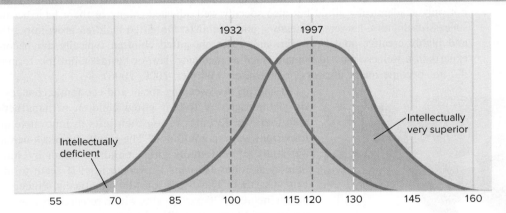

FIGURE 11 **The Increase in IQ Scores from 1932 to 1997** As measured by the Stanford-Binet intelligence test, American children seem to be getting smarter. Scores of a group tested in 1932 fell along a bell-shaped curve, with half below 100 and half above. Note that if children's scores from 1997 were plotted on this same scale, the average would be 120.
SOURCE: Winerman, L. Monitor, March 2013, 44(1), 30.

> How would average children from 1932 compare to children from the more recent sample? Would they still be "average"? > Note the far ends (or tails) of the 1932 curve. How would these children be considered by the standards of the more recent scores? > More recently, it's been reported that the average IQ rose by nearly 30 points from 1932 to 2012. Can you draw the curve for 2012 on this graph?

opportunities for granted and not be motivated to learn and to achieve. Alternatively, poor or disadvantaged children may be highly motivated and successful. Caregivers who themselves lacked educational opportunities may instill a strong sense of the value of learning and achievement in their children. Oprah Winfrey, the offspring of an unwed teenage couple, was reared in the inner city by her grandmother, who instilled in her a love of reading and a strong belief that she had the ability to do great things.

Let's return to the idea that the word *intelligent* describes not only people but also behaviors. Mastering skills, thinking about life actively, and making life decisions thoughtfully are intelligent behaviors that people can engage in regardless of the numerical intelligence quotient on their permanent record. Intelligent behavior is always an option, no matter one's IQ score. Our beliefs about cognitive ability, specifically whether it is fixed or changeable, have important implications for the goals we set for learning new skills (Dweck, 2006, 2013). We never know what we might accomplish if we try, and no one is doomed because of a number, no matter how powerful that number may seem.

Extremes of Intelligence

Intelligence, then, appears to emerge from a combination of genetic heritage and environmental factors. As we have seen, scores on IQ tests generally conform to the bell-shaped normal curve. We now examine the implications of falling on either tail of that curve.

gifted
Possessing high intelligence (an IQ of 130 or higher) and/or superior talent in a particular area.

GIFTEDNESS   There are people whose abilities and accomplishments outshine those of others—the *A+* student, the star athlete, the natural musician. People who are **gifted** have high intelligence (an IQ of 130 or higher) and/or superior talent in a particular area. Individuals who are highly gifted are typically not gifted in many domains, and research on giftedness is increasingly focused on domain-specific developmental trajectories (Kell & Lubinski, 2014; Sternberg & Bridges, 2014; Thagard, 2014).

Lewis Terman (1925) conducted a study of 1,500 children whose Stanford-Binet IQs averaged 150, a score that placed them in the top 1 percent. A popular myth is that gifted children are maladjusted, but Terman found that his participants (the "Termites") were not only academically gifted but also socially well adjusted. Many of them later became successful doctors, lawyers, professors, and scientists. Do gifted children grow into gifted and highly creative adults? In Terman's research, gifted children typically did become experts in a well-established domain, such as medicine, law, or business; but the Termites did not become major creators or innovators (Winner, 2000, 2006).

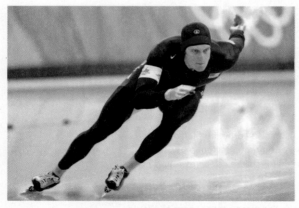
Olympic speed-skating gold medalist Joey Cheek well illustrates giftedness. Beyond his accomplishments on the ice, he studied economics and Chinese at Princeton University and is cofounder of Team Darfur, an organization dedicated to raising awareness of human rights abuses in Sudan.
©Kalle Parkkinen/REX/Shutterstock

In light of the sweeping social and economic changes of the digital age, are today's gifted children perhaps better able than the Termites to use their gifts in innovative and important ways in adulthood? The results from a longitudinal study of profoundly gifted children begun by Julian Stanley at Johns Hopkins University in 1971 seem to indicate just that. The Study of Mathematically Precocious Youth includes 320 participants whom researchers recruited before age 13 based on IQ scores, with the group's average IQ estimated at 180. This group is said to represent the top 1 in 10,000 IQ scores (Lubinski & others, 2001). Following up on these individuals in their 20s, David Lubinski and his colleagues (2006) found that these strikingly gifted young people were doing remarkable things. At age 23, they were pursuing doctoral degrees at a rate 50 times higher than the average. Some reported achievements such as receiving creative writing awards, creating original art and music, publishing in scholarly journals, and developing commercially viable software and video games. Thus, unlike the Termites, this group has been extraordinarily creative and innovative (Wai, Lubinski, & Benbow, 2005).

Like intelligence itself, giftedness is likely a product of both heredity and environment (Duggan & Friedman, 2014; Johnson & Bouchard, 2014). Experts who study giftedness point out that gifted individuals recall showing signs of high ability in a particular area at a very young age, prior to or at the beginning of formal training (Howe & others, 1995). This result suggests the importance of innate ability in giftedness. However, researchers also have found that the individuals who enjoy world-class status in the arts, mathematics, science, and sports all report strong family support and years of training and practice (Bloom, 1985). Deliberate practice is an important characteristic of individuals who become experts in a particular domain (Grigorenko & others, 2009).

Meeting the needs of gifted students in the classroom can be challenging. When students are not sufficiently challenged in their regular classes alternatives might include attending advanced classes in their domain of exceptional ability, as did Bill Gates, who took college math classes at 13, and famed cellist Yo-Yo Ma, who graduated from high school at 15 and then attended the Juilliard School of Music.

One important factor in gifted education is identifying children as gifted. Although many standardized tests are used to screen all children for IQ, parents or teachers may also nominate students as likely candidates for gifted instruction. Once these children are tested and identified as gifted, they are invited to enroll into such programs. This means that, for some students, qualifying for gifted instruction involves someone else's *social perception*. Being recognized as possibly gifted depends on an adult noticing that a child might be highly intelligent. Social perception can be influenced by stereotypes. Stereotypes are generalizations about individuals based on their group membership. Stereotypes do not take into account all the variability that group members likely possess. The notion that stereotypes about gifted children exist and that these stereotypes affect who is included in gifted programs is suggested by the fact that certain groups—such as African Americans and Latino Americans, those for whom English is a second language, and those with physical and learning disabilities—are underrepresented in U.S. gifted programs (Carman, 2011). Importantly, contrary to stereotypes that the gifted are poorly adjusted (Preckel & others, 2015), gifted children are not terribly different from their average-ability classmates in terms of personality and social characteristics (Wilson, 2015). Gifted students are likely to be more emotionally stable and less worrying than their average-ability counterparts (Ziedner & Shani-Zinovoch, 2011).

A serious U.S. public policy question is how to allocate resources: Should we be enhancing the experience of gifted students or bringing everyone up to a standard level? What's your opinion? How much money would you be willing to pay in taxes to accomplish both goals?

INTELLECTUAL DISABILITY

intellectual disability
A condition of limited mental ability in which an individual has a low IQ, usually below 70 on a traditional intelligence test, and has difficulty adapting to everyday life.

INTELLECTUAL DISABILITY Just as some individuals are at the high extreme of intelligence, others are at the lower end. **Intellectual disability** is a condition of limited mental ability in which an individual has low cognitive abilities and has difficulty adapting to everyday life. In the United States, about 5 million people fit this definition of intellectual disability. Although in the past specific IQ score cut-offs might be given for the diagnosis of a person as intellectually disabled, current standards are more flexible. A person with an IQ of around 70 who has difficult managing the challenges of life would likely be described as intellectually disabled (McNicholas & others, 2017).

It is a relatively new idea to think about intellectual disability as involving functional impairment rather than a low IQ test score. This change represents progress in understanding the role of adaptive behaviors in determining who requires additional supports and who does not. Note that a low IQ score in the context of a person who, say, holds down a job and has warm relationships with other people, would not indicate adaptive problems. It is not unusual to find clear *functional* differences between two people who have the same low IQ. For example, looking at two individuals with a similarly low IQ, we might find that one of them is married, employed, and involved in the community while the other requires constant supervision in an institution. Such differences

Individuals with Down syndrome may excel in sensitivity toward others. The possibility that other strengths or intelligences coexist with cognitive ability (or disability) has led some psychologists to propose the need for expanding the concept of intelligence.
©Monkey Business Images/Getty Images

in social competence have led psychologists to include deficits in adaptive behavior in their definition of intellectual disability (McNicholas & others, 2017).

Intellectual disability may have an organic cause, or it may be cultural and social in origin (McNicholas & others, 2017). *Organic intellectual disability* is caused by a genetic disorder or brain damage; *organic* refers to the tissues or organs of the body, so there is some physical damage in organic retardation. Down syndrome, one form of organic intellectual disability, occurs when an extra chromosome is present in the individual's genetic makeup. Most people who suffer from organic retardation have an IQ between 0 and 50.

Cultural-familial intellectual disability is a mental deficit with no evidence of organic brain damage. Individuals with this type of disability have an IQ between 55 and 70. Psychologists suspect that such mental deficits result at least in part from growing up in a below-average intellectual environment. As adults these individuals usually go unnoticed, perhaps because adult settings do not tax their cognitive skills as much. It may also be that the intelligence of such individuals increases as they move toward adulthood.

There are several classifications of intellectual disability (Hodapp & others, 2011). In one classification system, disability ranges from mild, to moderate, to severe or profound, according to the person's IQ (Heward, 2013). The large majority of individuals diagnosed with intellectual disability fall in the mild category. Many U.S. states and school systems still use this type of system (McNicholas & others, 2017). However, these categories, based on IQ ranges, are not perfect predictors of functioning. As noted above, it is not unusual to find clear *functional* differences between two people who have the same low IQ. For example, looking at two individuals with a similarly low IQ, we might find that one of them is married, employed, and involved in the community while the other requires constant supervision in an institution. Such differences in social competence have led psychologists to include deficits in adaptive behavior in their definition of intellectual disability.

The American Association on Intellectual and Developmental Disabilities (2010) has developed an assessment that examines a person's level of adaptive behavior in three life domains:

- *Conceptual skills:* For example, literacy and understanding of numbers, money, and time.
- *Social skills:* For example, interpersonal skills, responsibility, self-esteem, and ability to follow rules and obey.
- *Practical skills:* For example, activities of daily living such as personal care, occupational skills, health care, travel/transportation, and use of the telephone.

Assessment of capacities in these areas can be used to determine the amount of care the person requires for daily living, not as a function of IQ but of the person's ability to negotiate life's challenges.

Individuals with Down syndrome may never accomplish the academic feats of those who are gifted. However, they may be capable of building close, warm relations with others; inspiring loved ones; and bringing smiles into an otherwise gloomy day (Van Riper, 2007). Individuals with Down syndrome moreover might possess different kinds of intelligence, even if they are low on general cognitive ability. The possibility that other intelligences exist alongside cognitive ability (or disability) has inspired some psychologists to suggest that we need more than one concept of intelligence.

Theories of Multiple Intelligences

Is it more appropriate to think of an individual's intelligence as a general ability or, rather, as a number of specific abilities? Traditionally, most psychologists have viewed intelligence as a general, all-purpose problem-solving ability that, as we have seen, is sometimes referred to as *g*. Others have proposed that we think about different kinds of intelligence,

In the U.S. "Rosa's Law," passed in 2010, removed the offensive terms "mentally retarded" and "mental retardation" from all federal communications.

such as *emotional intelligence,* the ability to perceive emotions in ourselves and others accurately (Fiori & others, 2014). Robert Sternberg and Howard Gardner have developed influential theories presenting the viewpoint that there are *multiple intelligences.*

STERNBERG'S TRIARCHIC THEORY AND GARDNER'S MULTIPLE INTELLIGENCES

Robert J. Sternberg (1986, 2004, 2008, 2011, 2012, 2013a, 2013b, 2014a, 2014b) developed the **triarchic theory of intelligence,** which says that intelligence comes in multiple (specifically, three) forms:

triarchic theory of intelligence
Sternberg's theory that intelligence comes in three forms: analytical, creative, and practical.

Analytical intelligence: The ability to analyze, judge, evaluate, compare, and contrast.

Creative intelligence: The ability to create, design, invent, originate, and imagine.

Practical intelligence: The ability to use, apply, implement, and put ideas into practice.

Howard Gardner (1983, 1993, 2002) suggests there are nine types of intelligence, or "frames of mind." These are described here, with examples of the types of vocations in which they are reflected as strengths (Campbell, Campbell, & Dickinson, 2004):

©LightField Studios/Shutterstock

Verbal: The ability to think in words and use language to express meaning. Occupations: author, journalist, speaker.

Mathematical: The ability to carry out mathematical operations. Occupations: scientist, engineer, accountant.

Spatial: The ability to think three-dimensionally. Occupations: architect, artist, sailor.

Bodily-kinesthetic: The ability to manipulate objects and to be physically adept. Occupations: surgeon, craftsperson, dancer, athlete.

Musical: The ability to be sensitive to pitch, melody, rhythm, and tone. Occupations: composer, musician.

Interpersonal: The ability to understand and interact effectively with others. Occupations: teacher, mental health professional.

Intrapersonal: The ability to understand oneself. Occupations: theologian, psychologist.

Naturalist: The ability to observe patterns in nature and understand natural and human-made systems. Occupations: farmer, botanist, ecologist, landscaper.

Existentialist: The ability to grapple with the big questions of human existence, such as the meaning of life and death, with special sensitivity to issues of spirituality. Gardner has not identified an occupation for existential intelligence, but one career path would likely be philosopher.

According to Gardner, everyone has all of these intelligences to varying degrees. As a result, we prefer to learn and process information in different ways. We learn best when we can do so in a way that uses our stronger intelligences.

Do you know people some might call "book smart" and others who are "people smart"? What kinds of intelligence do they show?

EVALUATING THE APPROACHES OF MULTIPLE INTELLIGENCES

Sternberg's and Gardner's approaches have stimulated teachers to think broadly about what makes up children's competencies. They have motivated educators to develop programs that instruct students in multiple domains. These theories have also contributed to interest in assessing intelligence and classroom learning in innovative ways, such as by evaluating student portfolios (Woolfolk, 2015).

Doubts about multiple intelligences persist, however. A number of psychologists think that the proponents of multiple intelligences have taken the concept of specific intelligences too far (Reeve & Charles, 2008). Some critics argue that a research base to support the three intelligences of Sternberg or the nine intelligences of Gardner has not yet emerged. People who excel at one type of intellectual task are likely to excel in others (Brody, 2007). Thus, individuals who do well at memorizing lists of digits are also likely to be good at solving verbal problems and spatial layout problems. Other critics ask, if musical skill, for example, reflects a distinct type of intelligence, why not also label the skills of outstanding chess players, prizefighters, painters, and poets as types of intelligence? In sum, controversy still characterizes whether it is more accurate to conceptualize intelligence as a general ability, specific abilities, or both (M. K. Gardner, 2014; Irwing & others, 2012; Trzaskowski & others, 2014).

Our examination of cognitive abilities has highlighted how individuals differ in the quality of their thinking and how thoughts may differ from one another. Some thoughts reflect critical thinking, creativity, or intelligence. Other thoughts are perhaps less inspired. One thing thoughts have in common is that they often involve language. Even when we talk to ourselves, we do so with words. The central role of language in cognitive activity is the topic to which we now turn.

self-quiz

1. The reproducibility of a test's result is known as
   A. criterion validity.
   B. validity.
   C. standardization.
   D. reliability.

2. A 10-year-old child has a mental age of 8. The child's IQ is
   A. 60.
   B. 80.
   C. 100.
   D. 125.

3. According to twin studies, what percent of differences in intelligence among people is due to genetic differences?
   A. 35 percent
   B. 50 percent
   C. 75 percent
   D. 90 percent

APPLY IT! 4. Shortly after Joshua's birth, his parents found that he had a genetic condition that causes mental retardation. They worried about their son's future. Which of the following most accurately relates to Joshua's future?
   A. Genes are not the sole cause of intelligence, and providing Joshua with a rich and stimulating environment will make the most of his genetic endowment. Furthermore, although Joshua may never excel in cognitive ability, there are likely other realms of life in which he can be successful.
   B. Because intelligence is strongly heritable, providing a rich environment to Joshua is unlikely to have any impact on his eventual intelligence and ability.
   C. Genes cause 75 percent of Joshua's intelligence, so environmental factors can influence only 25 percent of his cognitive abilities.
   D. Genes have nothing to do with intelligence, so Joshua's parents have no need to worry.

4 Language

language
A form of communication—whether spoken, written, or signed—that is based on a system of symbols.

Language is a form of communication, whether spoken, written, or signed, that is based on a system of symbols. We need language to speak with others, listen to others, read, and write. Language is not just how we speak to others but how we talk to ourselves. Consider an occasion, for example, when you have experienced the feeling of a guilty conscience, of having done something you should not have. The little voice in your head that clamors, "You shouldn't have done that! Why did you do it?" speaks to you in your mother tongue. In this section we first examine the fundamental characteristics of language and then trace the links between language and cognition.

The Basic Properties of Language

All human languages have **infinite generativity,** the ability to produce an endless number of meaningful sentences. This superb flexibility comes from five basic rule systems:

- **Phonology:** a language's sound system. Language is made up of basic sounds, or *phonemes*. Phonological rules ensure that certain sound sequences occur (for example, *sp, ba,* and *ar*) and others do not (for example, *zx* and *qp*) (Vihman, 2014). A good example of a phoneme in the English language is /k/, the sound represented by the letter *k* in the word *ski* and by the letter *c* in the word *cat*. Although the /k/ sound is slightly different in these two words, the /k/ sound is described as a single phoneme in English.

- **Morphology:** a language's rules for word formation. Every word in the English language is made up of one or more morphemes. A *morpheme* is the smallest unit of language that carries meaning. Some words consist of a single morpheme—for example, *help*. Others are made up of more than one; for example, *helper* has two morphemes, *help + er*. The morpheme *-er* means "one who"—in this case, "one who helps." As you can see, not all morphemes are words; for example, *pre-, -tion,* and *-ing* are morphemes. Just as the rules that govern phonemes ensure that certain sound sequences occur, the rules that govern morphemes ensure that certain strings of sounds occur in particular sequences (Croft, 2012).

- **Syntax:** a language's rules for combining words to form acceptable phrases and sentences (Dixon, 2012). If someone says, "John kissed Emily" or "Emily was kissed by John," you know who did the kissing and who was kissed in each case because you share that person's understanding of sentence structure. You also understand that the sentence "You didn't stay, did you?" is a grammatical sentence but that "You didn't stay, didn't you?" is unacceptable.

- **Semantics:** the meaning of words and sentences in a particular language. Every word has a unique set of semantic features (Parish-Morris, Golinkoff, & Hirsh-Pasek, 2013). *Girl* and *woman,* for example, share many semantic features (for instance, both signify female human beings), but they differ semantically in regard to age. Words have semantic restrictions on how they can be used in sentences. The sentence "The bicycle talked the boy into buying a candy bar" is syntactically correct but semantically incorrect. The sentence violates our semantic knowledge that bicycles do not talk.

- **Pragmatics:** the useful character of language and the ability of language to communicate even more meaning than is said (Al-Wer, 2012). The pragmatic aspect of language allows us to use words to get the things we want. If you ever find yourself in a country in which you know only a little of the language, you will certainly take advantage of pragmatics. Wandering the streets of, say, Madrid, you might approach a stranger and ask, simply, "Autobus?" (the Spanish word for *bus*). You know that given your inflection and perhaps your desperate facial expression, the person will understand that you are looking for the bus stop.

With this basic understanding of language in place, we can examine the connections between language and cognition.

infinite generativity
The ability of language to produce an endless number of meaningful sentences.

phonology
A language's sound system.

morphology
A language's rules for word formation.

syntax
A language's rules for combining words to form acceptable phrases and sentences.

semantics
The meaning of words and sentences in a particular language.

pragmatics
The useful character of language and the ability of language to communicate even more meaning than is verbalized.

Language and Cognition

Language is a vast system of symbols capable of expressing most thoughts. Language is the vehicle for communicating most of our thoughts to one another. Although we do not always think in words, our thinking would be greatly impoverished without words. Moreover, the development of thinking and talking is strongly intertwined in children (Kidd & Arciuli, 2016; Perszyk & Waxman, 2018) and late adolescents and young adults (Kievit & others, 2017).

The connection between language and thought has been of considerable interest to psychologists. Some have even argued that we cannot think without language. This proposition has produced heated controversy. Is thought dependent on language, or is language dependent on thought?

THE ROLE OF LANGUAGE IN COGNITION

Recall that memory is stored not only in the form of sounds and images but also in words. Language helps us think, make inferences, tackle difficult decisions, and solve problems. Language is a tool for representing ideas.

Today, most psychologists would accept these points. However, linguist Benjamin Whorf (1956) went a step further: He argued that language determines the way we think, a view that has been called the *linguistic relativity hypothesis*. Whorf and his student Edward Sapir were specialists in Native American languages, and they were fascinated by the possibility that people might perceive the world differently as the result of the different languages they speak. The Inuit people in Alaska, for instance, have a dozen or more words to describe the various textures, colors, and physical states of snow. In contrast, English has relatively few words to describe snow, and thus, according to Whorf's view, English speakers cannot see the different kinds of snow because they have no words for them.

Think of all the words we have for coffee drinks. What might this say about our society?

Whorf's bold claim appealed to many scholars. Some even tried to apply Whorf's view to sex differences in color perception. Asked to describe the colors of two sweaters, a woman might say, "One is mauve and the other is magenta," while a man might say, "They're both pink." Whorf's view of the influence of language on perceptual ability might suggest that women are able to see more colors than men simply because they have a richer color vocabulary (Hepting & Solle, 1973). It turns out, however, that men can learn to discriminate among the various hues that women use, and this outcome suggests that Whorf's view is not quite accurate.

Indeed, critics of Whorf's ideas say that words merely reflect, rather than cause, the way we think. The Inuits' adaptability and livelihood in Alaska depend on their capacity to recognize various conditions of snow and ice. A skier or snowboarder who is not Inuit might also know numerous words for snow, far more than the average person, and a person who does not know the words for the different types of snow might still be able to perceive these differences.

Whorf's view is that our cultural experiences with a particular concept shape a catalog of names that can be either rich or poor. Consider how rich your mental library of names for a camel might be if you had extensive experience with camels in a desert world, and how poor your mental library of names for snow might be if you lived in a tropical world of palm trees and parrots. Despite its intriguing appeal, Whorf's view is controversial, and many psychologists do not believe it plays a pivotal role in shaping thought.
(Berber): ©eAlisa/Shutterstock; (Inuit): ©bikeriderlondon/Shutterstock

Interestingly, research has shown that Whorf might have been accurate for information that is presented to the left hemisphere of the brain. That is, when colors were presented in the right visual field (and therefore went to the left brain), having names for the colors enhanced perception of and discrimination between those colors (Gilbert & others, 2006).

Although the strongest form of Whorf's hypothesis—that language determines perception—seems doubtful, research has continued to demonstrate the influence of language on how we think, even about something as fundamental as our own personalities. For example, in a series of studies, researchers interviewed bilingual individuals (that is, people who fluently speak two languages, in this case Spanish and English) (Ramirez-Esparza & others, 2006). Each person rated his or her own personality characteristics, once in Spanish and once in English. Across all studies, and regardless of whether the individuals lived in a Spanish-speaking or an English-speaking country, respondents reported themselves as more outgoing, nicer, and more responsible when responding to the survey in English.

A final area of research demonstrating the link between language and thinking concerns the positive association between being fluent in more than one language and cognitive abilities, sometimes called the "bilingual advantage." Some research has shown that bilingual individuals show superior performance on some cognitive ability measures of cognitive control, especially with regard to shifting one's attention from one frame of reference to another (Ong & others, 2017; Stasenko, Matt, & Gollan, 2017). However, the evidence is mixed (Ross & Melinger, 2017). Moreover, the link between language and cognitive abilities is likely a two-way street: Training in cognitive control can have benefits for language processing (Hussey & Novick, 2012).

THE ROLE OF COGNITION IN LANGUAGE   Clearly, then, language can influence cognition. Researchers also study the possibility that cognition is an important foundation for language (Jackendoff, 2012).

One feature of human language that separates it from animal communication is the capacity to talk about objects that are not currently present (Hockett, 1960). A study comparing 12-month-old infants (who had not yet begun to talk) to chimpanzees suggests that this cognitive skill may underlie eventual language (Liszkowski & others, 2009). In this study, infants were more likely to communicate their desire for a toy by pointing to the place where the toy *used to be*. For many infants, this was the first thing they did to get their point across to another person who was present. In contrast, chimpanzees rarely pointed to where their desired object (food) had been, except as they desperately started pointing all over the place. So, even before they can talk, humans are communicating with others about what they want. Sometimes that communication demonstrates an appreciation of shared knowledge even about objects that are no longer present.

Consider how this research connects to theory of mind. Why would infants point to a place where an object used to be if they didn't know that something was going on in the head of a person with them? Why would we talk to one another at all if we didn't know that other people have a subjective awareness?

If language is a reflection of cognition in general, we would expect to find a close link between language ability and general intellectual ability. In particular, we would expect to find that problems in cognition are paralleled by problems in language. We would anticipate, for example, that general intellectual disability is accompanied by lowered language abilities. It is often but not always the case that individuals with intellectual disability have reduced language proficiency. For instance, individuals with Williams syndrome, a genetic disorder that affects about 1 in 20,000 births, tend to show extraordinary verbal, social, and musical abilities while having an extremely low IQ and difficulty with motor tasks and numbers. Williams syndrome demonstrates that intellectual disability is not always accompanied by poor language skills.

Consider as well individuals who have learning disabilities related to reading. **Dyslexia** is a learning disability characterized by difficulty with learning to read fluently and with accurate comprehension, despite normal intelligence. Individuals with dyslexia may have difficulty learning to decipher the meaning of letters on a page and may take longer to read than those who do not have the disorder. Clearly, even in its definition, dyslexia can occur in individuals with a range of IQs, and research shows that it is indeed independent of cognitive ability more generally (Ferrer & others, 2010; Toffalini, Pezzuti, & Cornoldi,

dyslexia
A learning disability characterized by difficulty with learning to read fluently and with accurate comprehension, despite normal intelligence.

2017; van Viersen & others, 2016). Many extraordinarily gifted individuals have had dyslexia, including the late Steve Jobs, founder of Apple. Research on dyslexia may be a key to understanding the differences between language and cognition.

In summary, although thought influences language and language influences thought, there is increasing evidence that language and thought are not part of a single system. Instead, they seem to have evolved as separate but related components of the mind.

Biological and Environmental Influences on Language

Everyone who uses language in some way "knows" its rules and has the ability to create an infinite number of words and sentences. Is this knowledge the product of biology, or is language learned and influenced by experiences in the environment?

BIOLOGICAL INFLUENCES   Scientists believe that humans acquired language about 100,000 years ago. In evolutionary time, then, language is a very recent human ability. However, a number of experts believe that biological evolution that occurred long before language emerged undeniably shaped humans into linguistic creatures (Chomsky, 1975). The brain, nervous system, and vocal apparatus of our predecessors changed over hundreds of thousands of years. Physically equipped to do so, *Homo sapiens* went beyond grunting and shrieking to develop abstract speech. This sophisticated language ability gave humans an enormous edge over other animals and increased their chances of survival (Pinker, 1994).

Noam Chomsky (b. 1928) *MIT linguist Noam Chomsky was one of the early architects of the view that children's language development cannot be explained by environmental input. In Chomsky's view, language has strong biological underpinnings, with children biologically prewired to learn language at a certain time and in a certain way.*
©Tracey Nearmy/Epa/REX/Shutterstock

Language Universals   American linguist Noam Chomsky (1975) has argued that humans come into the world biologically prewired to learn language at a certain time and in a certain way. According to Chomsky and many other language experts, the strongest evidence for language's biological basis is the fact that children all over the world reach language milestones at about the same time and in about the same order, despite vast variations in the language input they receive from their environments. For example, in some cultures adults never talk to infants under 1 year of age, yet these infants still acquire language.

In Chomsky's view, children cannot possibly learn the full rules and structure of languages by only imitating what they hear. Rather, nature must provide children with a biological, prewired, universal grammar, allowing them to understand the basic rules of all languages and to apply these rules to the speech they hear. They learn language without an awareness of its underlying logic. Think about it: The terms we used above to define the characteristics of language—*phonology, morphology, semantics,* and so forth—may be new to you, but on some level you have mastered these principles. This mastery is demonstrated by your reading of this book, writing a paper for class, and talking with a friend. Like all other humans, you are engaged in the use of a rule-based language system even without knowing that you know those rules.

Language and the Brain   There is strong evidence to back up experts who believe language has a biological foundation. Neuroscience research has shown that the brain contains particular regions that are predisposed to language use (Diaz, Rizio, & Zhuang, 2016; Griffiths & others, 2013; Tando & others, 2014). Language processing, such as speech and grammar, mainly occurs in the brain's left hemisphere. Recall the importance of Broca's area, which contributes to speech production, and Wernicke's area, which is involved in language comprehension. Using brain-imaging techniques, researchers have found that when an infant is about 9 months old, the part of the brain that stores and indexes many kinds of memory becomes fully functional (Bauer, 2013). This is also the time at which infants appear to be able to attach meaning to words, for instance to look at the ball if someone says "ball"—a development suggesting links among language, cognition, and the development of the brain.

ENVIRONMENTAL INFLUENCES   Decades ago, behaviorists opposed Chomsky's hypothesis and argued that language represents nothing more than chains of responses acquired through reinforcement (Skinner, 1957). A baby happens to babble "ma-ma"; mama rewards the baby with hugs and smiles; the baby says "mama" more and more. Bit by bit, said the behaviorists, the baby's language is built up. According to behaviorists, language is a complex learned skill, much like playing the piano or dancing.

Such a view of language development is simply not tenable, however, given the rapid way children learn language, as well as the lack of evidence that social environments carefully reinforce language skills (Brown, 1973). This is not to say the environment has no role in language development. Many language experts argue that a child's experiences, the particular language to be learned, and the context in which learning takes place can strongly influence language acquisition (Beaty & Pratt, 2015; Berko Gleason & Ratner, 2013; Senechal & Lefevre, 2014).

Think about how often parents "reinforce" children for saying the wrong thing: They laugh and smile when toddlers mispronounce words or use the wrong word altogether. Like calling boots "boops!" Too cute. But kids grow out of these habits eventually...

Cases of children who have lacked exposure to language provide evidence for the important role of the environment in language development. Such children rarely speak normally. However, in such cases the children are often exposed to abuse and so it is unclear whether their difficulties reflect that abuse or lack of exposure to language, specifically (Rymer, 1993).

A recent case of a woman who was exposed to language for the first time at age 32 provides an excellent case in point. The woman, called "Chelsea," grew up in a rural community in a large and loving family (Curtiss, 2014). Likely due to prenatal exposure to a virus, she was born with hearing disabilities. She did not receive an accurate diagnosis of partial deafness until the age of 32 when she was fitted with her first hearing aids. With those hearing aids, Chelsea's hearing was in the normal range. Scans of Chelsea's brain reveal that it is in the normal range and her IQ falls between 77 and 89.

After 32 years in silence, Chelsea was exposed, for the first time, to the sounds of language. For three decades, Chelsea has received training both for spoken and sign language. Through the years, Chelsea has shown the ability to acquire and use a range of words. Her vocabulary and understanding of the meaning of words is remarkable, though her performance on standardized tests does not always reflect the abilities she shows in everyday life. In contrast, she has never acquired a sense of grammar. Verbal acts you likely never think about, such as putting a subject before a verb in a sentence, have escaped her. For example, in response to a picture of a boy riding a bike, Chelsea said, "Riding ride bike ride boy ride" (Curtiss, 2014, p. 124).

A remarkable aspect of this case is that in the context of these language deficits, Chelsea's math abilities are normal. She has a sense of number meanings and is able to keep a checkbook and do her own shopping. She can use her watch to tell time. Thus, this case offers two important conclusions. First, Chelsea's language deficits support the idea of a "critical period" for language development, a special time in a child's life (usually the preschool years) during which language must develop or it never will. Second, the fact that Chelsea's mathematical ability appears to have been spared such deficits supports the idea (reviewed above) that, though connected, language and cognition are separable (Curtiss, 2014).

Whether the case of Chelsea confirms the idea of a critical period, her experiences and those of others who lack exposure to language in early childhood certainly support the idea that the environment is crucial for the development of language.

Clearly, most humans do not learn language in a social vacuum. From infancy, most children are exposed to a great deal of language. And infants' attention to the conversations going on with them and around them predicts language development (Vouloumanos

FIGURE 12 **The Power of Smile and Touch** Research has shown that when mothers immediately smiled and touched their 8-month-old infants after they had babbled, the infants subsequently made more complex speechlike sounds than when mothers responded randomly to their infants.
©Camille Tokerud/Photographer's Choice/Getty Images

& Curtin, 2014). The support and involvement of caregivers and teachers greatly facilitate a child's language learning (Hirsh-Pasek & Golinkoff, 2014). For example, one study showed that when mothers immediately smiled and touched their 8-month-old infants after they had babbled, the infants subsequently made more complex speechlike sounds than when mothers responded to their infants in a random manner (Goldstein, King, & West, 2003) (Figure 12).

Research findings about environmental influences on language learning complicate the understanding of its foundations. In the real world of language learning, children appear to be neither exclusively biologically programmed linguists nor exclusively socially driven language experts (Ratner, 1993). We have to look at how biology and environment interact when children learn language. That is, children are biologically prepared to learn language but benefit enormously from being immersed in a competent language environment from an early age (Hoff, 2014; Tomasello, 2014).

One environmental factor that has been shown to predict language development is socioeconomic status. Compared to children from affluent families, children from poorer economic backgrounds show lower levels of language skills, including vocabulary and understanding of syntax and grammar (Perkins, Finegood, & Swain, 2013). Socioeconomic differences translate into language development differences as early as 18 months of age (Fernald, Marchman, & Weisleder, 2013).

In a highly influential study conducted in the 1980s, researchers examined the association between language environments and socioeconomic status (Hart & Risley, 1995; Risley & Hart, 2006). The study involved 42 families that included an infant between 7 and 9 months old. The families represented four different socioeconomic backgrounds: Upper class/affluent, middle class, lower class, and finally, financial poor who received financial support (welfare). Each family was visited for one hour a month until the infants were 3 years old. During the visit, the researcher simply sat quietly and taped the interactions, producing over 1,300 hours of taped conversation (Singhal, 2017). The study found that, by three years of age, all of the children developed normally in terms of learning to talk and acquiring the basic rules of English and a fundamental vocabulary. However, the researchers found large differences in the sheer amount of language to which the children were exposed and in the level of the children's language development. For example, in a typical hour, the affluent parents spent a great deal more time talking to their children and exposing them to varied vocabulary in the process. Indeed, extrapolating from their findings, the researchers estimated that by 4 years of age, the average child from the poorer family group would been exposed to *30 million* fewer words than the average child from the affluent family group (Hart & Risley, 1995; Risley & Hart, 2006). Following some of the children into third grade, the researchers found that their language deficits at 3 years continued into grade school (Hart & Risley, 1995). This study gave rise to the idea that filling the 30 million word gap might improve the lives of children from poorer families (Hindman, Wasik, & Snell, 2016; Singhal, 2017). Might we be able to foster better language skills by changing the way impoverished parents interact with their children? As is often the case when science is brought to bear on social policy, the answer to that question is complex. To take a closer look at this controversy and the study that started it all, see the Challenge Your Thinking.

Can Reducing the "Word Gap" Lead to Better Outcomes for Disadvantaged Children?

Research showing a 30 million word gap between children from wealthy vs. poorer families (Hart & Risley, 1995) has inspired communities to implement interventions targeting this gap (Singhal, 2017). Parent-infant interactions are taped and then used to teach parents skills to improve language development. These skills include talking to children directly, incorporating a wider range of unusual words in interactions (such as "gaze" and "view" rather than simply "look"), and reading in an active way that involves defining new words and asking and answering questions (Weisleder & Fernald, 2013). These may seem like relatively harmless tips for language development (Greenwood & others, 2017; Hindman, Wasik, & Snell, 2016). But is it that simple? Advocates of such interventions would say that, although it may not be simple, it is at least a clear way to potentially make a difference in the lives of children from low income families (Singhal, 2017).

©spass/Shutterstock

The application of the "30 million word gap" finding to real life has been criticized methodologically and conceptually. First, although the amount of conversation collected was large, the sample itself was not. Indeed, the entire "welfare" group contained just 6 families, all of them African American. The affluent group contained 13 families, only one of whom was African American. Should such small (and ethnically unbalanced) samples lead to strong conclusions? Second, as you know, correlation does not imply causation. Because the number of words included in conversations was related to children's language development does not imply that word-exposure causes development. Similarly, the fact that language deficits at age 3 correlated with grade school performance does not imply that these deficits cause that performance. Both of these associations might be due to the host of differences between families and especially the wide-ranging effects of poverty, including access to healthcare, education, and nutrition. Third, it is possible that families differed in their responses to the presence of the researcher during the visits. Poor families might be more guarded in the presence of a stranger and may have felt less comfortable talking while being watched. This criticism suggests that the conversations drawn from the poor families might be biased.

In addition to methodological weaknesses, critics have noted that designing interventions to get poor people to behave more like wealthy people imposes values, suggesting that there is only one right way to parent, teach, and speak (Blum & Riley, 2014). Targeting the word gap risks stigmatizing the poor and labeling their families "language deficient" (Anders & others, 2016). In addition, focusing on the word gap may underestimate the stress that is involved in living in poverty. Indeed, critics argue, why not combat poverty directly rather than focusing on the word gap?

Language development is a crucial part of academic success. Finding ways to promote language development in children is a valuable goal. Considering how we can meet this goal highlights the fact that language is not only a means of communications but also the way we transmit culture and values and how we think about and define our own identities (Anders & others, 2016).

What Do You Think?

- Do you think interventions targeting the word gap are a good idea? Why or why not?
- Why do you think a study with such a small sample has had such impact?

Language Development over the Life Span

Most individuals develop a clear understanding of their language's structure, as well as a large vocabulary, during childhood. Most adults in the United States have acquired a vocabulary of nearly 50,000 words. Researchers have taken a great interest in the process by which these aspects of language develop. Their many studies have provided an understanding of the milestones of language development (Figure 13).

Language researchers are fascinated by babies' speech even before the little ones say their first words (Goldin-Meadow, 2014a, 2014b). *Babbling*—endlessly repeating sounds and syllables, such as *bababa* and *dadada*—begins at the age of about 4 to 6 months and is

0–6 Months	Cooing. Discrimination of vowels. Babbling present by 6 months.
6–12 Months	Babbling expands to include sounds of spoken language. Gestures used to communicate about objects. First words spoken 10–13 months.
12–18 Months	Understands 50+ words on average.
18–24 Months	Vocabulary increases to an average of 200 words. Two-word combinations.
2 Years	Vocabulary rapidly increases. Correct use of plurals. Use of past tense. Use of some prepositions.
3–4 Years	Mean length of utterances increases to 3–4 morphemes in a sentence. Use of yes and no questions, wh- questions. Use of negatives and imperatives. Increased awareness of pragmatics.
5–6 Years	Vocabulary reaches an average of about 10,000 words. Coordination of simple sentences.
6–8 Years	Vocabulary continues to increase rapidly. More skilled use of syntactical rules. Conversational skills improve.
9–11 Years	Word definitions include synonyms. Conversational strategies continue to improve.
11–14 Years	Vocabulary increases with addition of more abstract words. Understanding of complex grammar forms. Increased understanding of function a word plays in a sentence. Understands metaphor and satire.
15–20 Years	Understands adult literary works.

Note: This list is meant not to be exhaustive but rather to highlight some of the main language milestones. Also keep in mind that there is a great deal of variation in the ages at which children can reach these milestones and still be considered within the normal range of language development.

FIGURE 13

Language Milestones All children are different and acquire language at varying rates, but these milestones provide a general sense of how language emerges in human life.

FIGURE 14

From Universal Linguist to Language-Specific Listener A baby is shown in Patricia Kuhl's research laboratory. In this research, babies listen to recorded voices that repeat syllables. When the sounds of the syllables change, the babies quickly learn to look at the bear. Using this technique, Kuhl has demonstrated that babies are universal linguists until about 6 months of age but in the next 6 months become language-specific listeners.

(both): ©2003 University of Washington, Institute for Learning and Brain Sciences (I-LABS)

determined by biological readiness, not by the amount of reinforcement or the ability to hear (Stoel-Gammon & Menn, 2013). Even deaf babies babble for a time (Lenneberg, Rebelsky, & Nichols, 1965). Babbling probably allows babies to exercise their vocal cords and helps develop the ability to articulate different sounds.

Patricia Kuhl's research reveals that long before they begin to learn words, infants can sort through a number of spoken sounds in search of the ones that have meaning (1993, 2012, Ramírez-Esparza, García-Sierra, & Kuhl, 2014). Kuhl argues that from birth to about 6 months of age, children are "universal linguists" who are capable of distinguishing each of the sounds that make up human speech. By about 6 months of age, they have started to specialize in the speech sounds (or phonology) of their native language (Figure 14).

A child's first words, uttered at the age of 10 to 13 months, name important people ("dada"), familiar animals ("kitty"), vehicles ("car"), toys ("ball"), food ("milk"), body parts ("eye"), clothes ("hat"), household items ("clock"), and greetings ("bye"). These were babies' first words a century ago, and they are babies' first words still (Bloom, 2004).

By the time children reach the age of 18 to 24 months, they usually utter two-word statements. They quickly grasp the importance of expressing concepts and the role that language plays in communicating with others (Owens, 2015). To convey meaning in two-word statements, the child relies heavily on gesture, tone, and context. Although these two-word sentences omit many parts of speech, they are remarkably effective in conveying many messages. When a toddler demands, "Pet doggie!" parents know he means, "May I please pet the doggie?" Very young children learn that language is a good way to get what they want, suggesting that they grasp another aspect of language—its pragmatics.

Although childhood is an important time for language learning, we continue to learn language (new words, new skills) throughout life. For many years, it was claimed that if individuals did not learn a second language prior to puberty, they would never reach native-language learners' levels in the second language (Johnson & Newport, 1991). However, research indicates a more complex conclusion: Sensitive periods likely vary across different language systems (Thomas & Johnson, 2008). Thus, for late second-language learners, such as adolescents and adults, new vocabulary is easier to learn than new sounds and new grammar (Neville, 2006). For example, children's ability to pronounce words with a native-like accent in a second language typically decreases with age, with an especially sharp drop occurring after about 10 to 12 years of age. In addition, there is great variability in the capacity to learn a second (or third) language in adulthood (Qi & others, 2017).

For adults, learning a new language requires a special kind of cognitive exercise. As we have seen, a great deal of language learning in infancy and childhood involves recognizing the sounds that are part of one's native tongue. This process also entails learning to ignore sounds that are not important to one's first language. For instance, in Japanese, the phonemes /l/ and /r/ are not distinguished from each other, so that, for a Japanese adult, the word *lion* is not distinguishable from the name *Ryan*. Research suggests that mastering a new language in adulthood may involve overriding such learned habits and learning to listen to sounds that one previously ignored. Indeed, adults can learn to hear and discriminate sounds that are part of a new language, and this learning can contribute to speech fluency and language skill (Evans & Iverson, 2007; Saito, 2017).

Around the world, young children learn to speak in two-word utterances at 18 to 24 months of age.
©Anita van Zyl/age fotostock

The Candle Problem

The solution requires a unique perception of the function of the box in which the matches came. It can become a candleholder when tacked to the wall.

The Nine-Dot Problem

Most people have difficulty with this problem because they try to draw the lines within the boundaries of the dots. Notice that by extending the lines beyond the dots, the problem can be solved.

The Six-Matchstick Problem

Nothing in the instructions said that the solution had to be two-dimensional.

Solutions to problems from Figure 4.

Thus, learning a new language in adulthood involves cognitively stretching ourselves away from our assumptions. Such a process might play a role in enhancing not only our language skills but also our cognitive ability generally. Some research has shown that cognitive training using challenging tasks can increase ability (Jaeggi & others, 2008) and foster changes in the brain (Colom & others, 2016). However, the overall benefits of engaging in cognitive challenges for cognitive ability are controversial (Au & others, 2016; Melby-Lervåg & Hulme, 2016; Melby-Lervåg, Redick, & Hulme, 2016). Nevertheless, applying and stretching our abilities to think and problem solve certainly cannot hurt as we take on the many challenges of the modern world.

self-quiz

1. The rules of language are known as _____, whereas the meaning of language is known as _____.
   A. phonology; morphology
   B. morphology; phonology
   C. semantics; syntax
   D. syntax; semantics

2. Noam Chomsky's view of language acquisition centers on
   A. environmental factors.
   B. biological factors.
   C. social factors.
   D. person-specific factors.

3. Williams syndrome demonstrates that
   A. mental retardation always leads to language deficits.
   B. extraordinary language ability can exist even in a person with mental retardation.
   C. without high intelligence, verbal ability is always low.
   D. mental retardation never leads to language deficits.

APPLY IT! 4. Susan and her husband Terence adopted a baby boy from another country. Their son is 4 months old, and they are worried because they are not sure he was exposed to a lot of talking before they adopted him. What advice would you give these nervous new parents?
   A. They should be worried. They should bombard their new son with words and reward any indication of talking throughout his childhood.
   B. They do not have to worry. In some cultures children are rarely talked to, but all kids (except in extreme cases) learn to talk. They should enjoy talking with and reading to their new little guy but also feel confident that he will certainly acquire language.
   C. They should be worried, especially because their child is a boy.
   D. We simply cannot know what the future holds for their son, because language is mostly genetic anyway.

SUMMARY

1 The Cognitive Revolution in Psychology

Cognition is the way in which information is processed and manipulated in remembering, thinking, and knowing. The advent of the computer in the mid-twentieth century spurred a cognitive revolution in which psychologists took on the challenge of understanding human information processing. Artificial intelligence (AI), the science of creating machines capable of performing activities that require intelligence when they are done by people, is a byproduct of the cognitive revolution.

2 Thinking

Concepts are mental categories used to group objects, events, and characteristics. Concepts help us to generalize; they improve our memories; and they keep us from having to learn new things with every new instance or example of a concept. The prototype model suggests that members of a concept vary in terms of their similarity to the most typical item.

Problem solving is an attempt to find a way to attain a goal when the goal is not readily available. The four steps in problem solving are to (1) find and frame the problem, (2) develop good problem-solving strategies, (3) evaluate solutions, and (4) rethink and redefine problems and solutions over time. Among effective strategies for solving problems are sub-goals (the intermediate goals and problems that put you in a better position to reach your goal), algorithms (strategies that guarantee a solution), and heuristics (shortcuts that suggest, but do not guarantee, a solution to a problem).

Reasoning is the mental activity of transforming information to reach conclusions. Inductive reasoning is reasoning from the specific to the general. Deductive reasoning is reasoning from the general to the specific. Decision making involves evaluating alternatives and making choices among them. Biases and heuristics that may lead to problematic decision-making include loss aversion, confirmation bias, base rate neglect, hindsight bias, the availability heuristic, and the representativeness heuristic.

Critical thinking and creativity improve problem solving. Critical thinking involves thinking productively, evaluating the evidence, being mindful, and keeping an open mind. Creativity is the ability to think in novel and unusual ways and to come up with unconventional solutions. Creative thinkers are flexible and playful, self-motivated, willing to face risk, and objective in evaluating their work.

3 Intelligence

Intelligence consists of the ability to solve problems and to adapt to and learn from everyday experiences. Traditionally, intelligence has been measured by tests designed to compare people's performance on cognitive tasks.

A good test of intelligence meets three criteria: validity, reliability, and standardization. Validity is the extent to which a test measures what it is intended to measure. Reliability is how consistently an individual performs on a test. Standardization focuses on uniform procedures for administering and scoring a test and establishing norms.

Binet developed the first intelligence test. Individuals from age 2 through adulthood take the current Stanford-Binet test (so called because the revisions were completed at Stanford University). Some intelligence tests are unfair to individuals from different cultures. Culture-fair tests are intelligence tests that are intended to be culturally unbiased.

Genes are clearly involved in intelligence. The proportion of differences in intelligence that is explained by genetic variation (or heritability) is substantial. Environmental influences on intelligence have also been demonstrated. The fact that intelligence test scores have risen considerably around the world in recent decades—called the Flynn effect—supports the role of environment in intelligence.

At the extreme ends of intelligence are giftedness and intellectual disability. People who are gifted have high intelligence (IQ of 130 or higher) and/or superior talent for a particular domain. Research has shown that individuals who are gifted are likely to make important and creative contributions. Intellectual disability is a condition of limited mental ability in which the individual has low cognitive ability (for instance an IQ below 70); has difficulty adapting to everyday life; and has an onset of these characteristics during childhood. Intellectual disability can have an organic cause (called organic intellectual disability) or can be social and cultural in origin (called cultural-familial intellectual disability).

Instead of focusing on intelligence as a single, broad cognitive ability, some psychologists have broken intelligence up into a variety of areas of life skills. Sternberg's triarchic theory states there are three main types of intelligence: analytical, creative, and practical. Gardner identifies nine types of intelligence, involving skills that are verbal, mathematical, spatial, bodily-kinesthetic, musical, interpersonal, intrapersonal, naturalist, and existential. The multiple-intelligences approaches have broadened the definition of intelligence and motivated educators to develop programs that instruct students in different domains. Critics maintain that multiple-intelligences theories include factors that really are not part of intelligence, such as musical skills. Critics also say that there is not enough research to support the concept of multiple intelligences.

Language

Language is a form of communication that is based on a system of symbols. All human languages have common aspects, including infinite generativity and organizational rules about structure. Any language has five characteristics: phonology, the sound system of a language; morphology, the rules for combining morphemes, which are meaningful strings of sounds that contain no smaller meaningful parts; syntax, the ways words are combined to form acceptable phrases and sentences; semantics, the meaning of words and sentences; and pragmatics, the uses of language.

Although language and thought influence each other, there is increasing evidence that they evolved as separate, modular, biologically prepared components of the mind. Evolution shaped humans into linguistic creatures. Chomsky said that humans are biologically prewired to learn language at a certain time and in a certain way. In addition, there is strong evidence that particular regions in the left hemisphere of the brain are predisposed to be used for language. Experience is also crucial to language development. It is important for children to interact with language-skilled people. Children are biologically prepared to learn language but benefit enormously from being in a competent language environment from early in development.

Although we often think of language, thinking, and intelligence as fixed when we are adults, research shows that we can continue to master skills and even increase intelligence by engaging in challenging mental tasks.

KEY TERMS

algorithms
artificial intelligence (AI)
availability heuristic
base rate neglect
cognition
concept
confirmation bias
convergent thinking
creativity
culture-fair tests
decision making
deductive reasoning

divergent thinking
dyslexia
fixation
functional fixedness
gifted
heritability
heuristics
hindsight bias
inductive reasoning
infinite generativity
intellectual disability
intelligence

intelligence quotient (IQ)
language
loss aversion
mental age (MA)
mindfulness
morphology
normal distribution
open-mindedness
phonology
pragmatics
problem solving
prototype model

reasoning
reliability
representativeness heuristic
semantics
standardization
subgoals
syntax
thinking
triarchic theory of
    intelligence
validity

ANSWERS TO SELF-QUIZZES

Section 1: 1. D; 2. C; 3. D; 4. C
Section 2: 1. C; 2. A; 3. B; 4. D

Section 3: 1. D; 2. B; 3. C; 4. A

Section 4: 1. D; 2. B; 3. B; 4. B

8 Human Development

The You You Used to Be

Take a moment to consider your life in its entirety. On the day you were born, you were a bundle of mystery. Today you might seem like a completely different person—certainly, you are taller and likely have more hair. As you think of all the experiences you have had throughout your life, ask yourself how these have led to the person you are now. To be sure, some characteristics fall by the wayside as we mature, but others are still there, as sure as the freckles from first grade still pepper your arms. What were you like in kindergarten? A shy child or an outgoing little tike? One study found that more socially skilled kindergartners (as rated by their teachers) were, 20 years later, more highly educated and likely to be employed than their less skilled counterparts (Jones, Greenberg, & Crowley, 2015). Children whose mothers worked outside the home are likely to differ from others as adults: Girls whose mothers worked are more likely to be employed themselves and boys whose mothers worked are more likely to have wives who work (Cain Miller, 2015). Such findings demonstrate how, in some ways, our journey from infancy to adulthood can seem like a straight line: A plot without many twists and turns. What such findings do not capture are all the ways we differ in our paths and the active ways we can alter the line of development.

At one time we were all infants and children. Some of the characteristics and experiences that shaped our lives in those earliest days continue to influence us (Nave & others, 2017). Some just happened and others we made happen. As adults, we continue to grow and change and create a future toward which to strive. We can also reach out to change the futures of others. Developmental psychologists probe the process of growth and change throughout the lifespan.

Developmental psychologists are interested in all the ways a person grows and changes throughout life, from its beginning to its inevitable end. We start by defining human development and examining central issues in developmental psychology. In the heart of the chapter, we look at the processes and outcomes of development in three broad domains of life: physical, cognitive, and socioemotional. We then explore the links among these developmental areas by probing gender development, followed by a survey of moral development and death, dying, and grieving. The chapter closes with a look at the positive ways individuals can shape their development in adulthood.

1 Exploring Human Development

Development refers to the pattern of continuity and change in human capabilities that occurs throughout the course of life. Most development involves growth, although it also includes decline (for example, physical abilities may decline with age). Let's begin our consideration of human development by addressing several key questions and issues that are especially relevant to understanding how human beings grow and change through the life span.

development
The pattern of continuity and change in human capabilities that occurs throughout life, involving both growth and decline.

Research Methods in Developmental Psychology

Human development is about changes that occur with age. Sometimes this research involves looking at how people of various ages differ on characteristics. To know what age-related differences mean, however, we must consider the kind of research presented.

In **cross-sectional designs,** a number of people are assessed at one point in time. Age differences can then be noted. By examining how the ages of these individuals relate to the characteristics measured, researchers can find out whether younger individuals differ from older ones. Age differences, however, are not the same as developmental change.

cross-sectional design
A research design in which a group of people are assessed on a psychological variable at one point in time.

 Remember, cross-sectional designs involve measuring characteristics at one and only one time point. Longitudinal designs involve measuring the same characteristics in the same people multiple times.

One problem in cross-sectional studies is cohort effects. *Cohort effects* are differences between individuals that stem not necessarily from their ages but from the historical and social time period in which they were born and developed (Kennison & others, 2017). For instance, individuals who were born in the 1940s might be less likely to have attended college than those born in the 1990s. Differences observed between these groups might be due not to their age but rather to these differing experiences. Consider your own cohort. How might experiences that are unique to your age group lead you and your peers to be different from other generations?

In order to draw more definitive conclusions about human development, researchers must use a different kind of research design. A **longitudinal study** assesses the same participants multiple times over a lengthy period. A longitudinal study can find out not only whether age groups differ but also whether the same individuals change with respect to a particular characteristic as they age. Strong statements about developmental changes in psychological characteristics require longitudinal designs. Using these and other methods, human development researchers have grappled with big questions that are relevant to all of psychology, as we consider next.

longitudinal design
A special kind of systematic observation, used by correlational researchers, that involves obtaining measures of the variables of interest in multiple waves over time.

How Do Nature and Nurture Influence Development?

Developmental psychologists are interested in understanding how nature and nurture contribute to development. **Nature** refers to a person's biological inheritance, especially his or her genes. **Nurture** refers to the individual's environmental and social experiences. Understanding development requires that we take into account the contributions of both genes (nature) and the environment (nurture).

Recall that a *genotype* is the individual's genetic heritage—the actual genetic material. We also examined the idea of a *phenotype* (the person's observable characteristics). The phenotype shows the contributions of both nature (genetic heritage) and nurture (environment). Whether and how the genotype is expressed in the phenotype may depend on the environment. For example, a person might be born with the genes to be the next LeBron James but without the necessary environmental factors such as good nutrition, sound medical care, access to a basketball court, and superb coaching, that potential might never be reached.

Consider the genetic condition called phenylketonuria (PKU). Caused by two recessive genes, PKU results in an inability to metabolize the amino acid phenylalanine. Decades ago, it was thought that the genotype for PKU led to a specific phenotype, namely, irreversible brain damage, intellectual disability, and seizures. However, experts now know that as long as individuals with the genotype for PKU stick to a diet that is very low in phenylalanine, these characteristics in the phenotype can be avoided (Bernstein & others, 2017). These environmental precautions can change the phenotype associated with this genotype.

The PKU example tells us that a person's observable characteristics (phenotype) might not reflect his or her genetic heritage (genotype) very precisely because of the particular experiences the person has had.

Instead, for each genotype, a *range* of phenotypes may be expressed, depending on environmental experiences. The person whom we see before us emerges out of an interplay of genetic and environmental experiences. Development is the product of nature, nurture, and the complex interaction of the two (Meaney, 2017).

Although it might be easy to think of genes as the blueprint for a person, development is not a process that follows a genetic master plan (Turkheimer, 2011). In fact, it is difficult to tell a simple story about how development occurs. One way that scientists and philosophers think about complex processes such as development is through the concept of emergent properties. An *emergent property* is a big entity (like a person) that is a consequence of the interaction of multiple lower-level factors (Gottlieb, 2007; Nalepka & others, 2017). Development is about the complex interactions of genes and experience that build the whole person.

> *What factors in your childhood environment influenced your expression of your gifts and abilities?*

> *A flock of birds flying in formation illustrates an emergent property. The birds may appear to be following a leader, but they aren't. Instead, each individual bird is following its own local rules. What you see as a flock of birds is in fact a collection of individual birds, each one 'doing its own thing' but creating the formation (the emergent property) you recognize as a flock.*

nature
An individual's biological inheritance, especially his or her genes.

nurture
An individual's environmental and social experiences.

Do Early Experiences Rule Us for Life?

The PKU example above suggests the power of early experience (nurture) in human development. A key question in developmental psychology is the extent to which childhood experiences determine aspects of later life. Some research shows that unless infants experience warm, nurturing caregiving in the first year or so of life, they will not develop to their full potential (Boldt, Kochanska, & Jonas, 2017; Phillips & Lowenstein, 2011). Other studies demonstrate the power of later experience in influencing development in adulthood (Antonucci, Ajrouch, & Birditt, 2014; Kjellström & Stålne, 2017). Life-span developmentalists stress that experiences throughout life contribute to development (Dunlop, Bannon, & McAdams, 2017; Park & others, 2014). Both early and later experience make significant contributions to development, so no one is doomed to be a total prisoner of his or her childhood.

Human development is complex because it is the product of several processes. The hormonal changes of puberty, a baby's playing with blocks and an older couple's embrace reflect physical, cognitive, and socioemotional processes, respectively.
(teen shaving) ©Arina Habich/Alamy Stock Photo; (baby) ©JGI/Tom Grill/Blend Images/Getty Images; (couple) ©moodboard/Corbis

A key concept in understanding the role of negative early experiences in later development is resilience. **Resilience** refers to a person's ability to recover from or adapt to difficult times. Resilience means that despite encountering adversity, a person shows signs of positive functioning (Labella & Masten, 2018; Taylor & Conger, 2017). Resilience can involve factors that compensate for difficulties, buffering the individual from the effects of these hardships. Moderate difficulties early in life can be strengthening experiences that lay the groundwork for effective future coping (Ager, 2013; Dooley & others, 2017; Seery, Holman, & Silver, 2010). Although often studied as an aspect of childhood (Masten, 2014) and adolescence (Montgomery, 2010), resilience can also characterize development in adulthood and old age (Bradley & Hojjat, 2017; Kuchel, 2017).

resilience
A person's ability to recover from or adapt to difficult times.

Nature, Nurture, and You

Because you cannot pick your genes or your parents, it would seem as if you are stuck with the genes and environment you got at birth. However, the truth is that you have a vital role to play throughout development. As an active developer, you take the raw ingredients of nature and nurture and make them into the person you are (Turkheimer, 2011). Active developers, then, *interact* with their own genes and environment to produce the persons they become. In this sense, the developer him or herself can be a powerful force in their own development.

Indeed, some psychologists believe that people can develop beyond what their genetic inheritance and environment give them. They argue that a key aspect of development involves seeking optimal experiences in life (Halfon & Forrest, 2018). History is filled with examples of people who go beyond what life has given them to achieve extraordinary things. Such individuals author a unique developmental path, sometimes transforming apparent weaknesses into real strengths.

In individuals' efforts to experience life in optimal ways, they develop *life themes* that involve activities, social relationships, and life goals (Frensch, Pratt, & Norris, 2007;

Rathunde, 2010; Schofield, Larsson & Ward, 2017). Some people are more successful at constructing optimal life experiences than others. Among the public figures who have succeeded are Martin Luther King, Jr., Mother Teresa, Nelson Mandela, Bill and Melinda Gates, and Oprah Winfrey. These individuals looked for and found meaningful life themes as they developed. Their lives were not restricted to biological survival or to settling for their particular life situations.

Three Domains of Development

The pattern of development is complex because it is the product of several processes in three domains of life—physical, cognitive, and socioemotional:

1. *Physical processes* involve changes in an individual's biological nature. Genes inherited from parents, the hormonal changes of puberty and menopause, and changes throughout life in the brain, height and weight, and motor skills all reflect the developmental role of biological processes. Physical development is often termed *maturation* because it involves an unfolding of biological processes.

2. *Cognitive processes* involve changes in an individual's thought, intelligence, and language. It refers to a host of skills, such as learning to read, engaging in problem solving, and mastering calculus. Observing a colorful mobile as it swings above a crib, constructing a sentence about the future, imagining oneself as a contestant on *The Voice* or as president of the United States, memorizing a new telephone number—these activities reflect the role of cognitive processes in development.

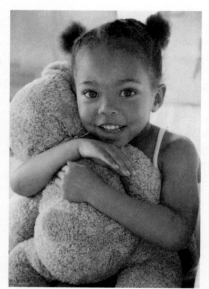

3. *Socioemotional processes* involve changes in an individual's relationships with other people, changes in emotions, and changes in personality. An infant's smile in response to her mother's touch, a girl's development of assertiveness, an adolescent's joy at the senior prom, a young man's aggressiveness in sport, and an older couple's affection for each other all reflect the role of socioemotional processes.

©Fancy Collection/SuperStock

Throughout this chapter we will trace these developmental processes along the broad periods of the life span, namely:

- *Childhood,* the period from infancy (birth to 24 months) through childhood (up to about age 10).

- *Adolescence,* the period beginning around ages 10 to 12 and spanning the transition from childhood to adulthood.

- *Adulthood,* the period that is generally separated into early (the 20s and 30s), middle (the 40s through the mid-60s), and late (mid-60s and beyond).

After tracing changes in physical, cognitive, and socioemotional development across the life span, we will turn to topics that demonstrate how strongly intertwined these processes are, including gender and moral development as well as death and dying. Think of Hannah, an infant whose parents place a teddy bear in her crib. As an infant she might simply look at the teddy bear when her parents jiggle it in front of her. Over time, she not only can see the teddy bear but also can reach for it. She might even remember that the teddy bear exists and might cry for it when it is not with her. As a toddler, when she carries it around, she is demonstrating her physical abilities to do so, as well as her capacity to use the teddy bear as a source of comfort. As an adolescent, Hannah might no longer sleep with her teddy, but she might give him a place of honor on a shelf. As you read this chapter's separate sections on physical, cognitive, and socioemotional development, remember that you are studying the development of an integrated human being in whom body, mind, emotion, and social relationships are interdependent.

1. The late Diana, Princess of Wales, devoted a considerable effort to eliminating land mines. Her work illustrates
   A. a life theme.
   B. a genotype.
   C. a physical process.
   D. a phenotype.

2. Development can be best described as
   A. due entirely to nature.
   B. due entirely to nurture.
   C. the product of the interaction of nature and nurture.
   D. none of the above

3. An example of an optimal experience is
   A. cooking food to eat.
   B. getting a great buy on those boots you wanted.
   C. volunteering time to teach adults to read.
   D. competing with others.

APPLY IT! 4. Sonja and Pete are engineers who met during college. They share a love of mathematics and science and have successful engineering careers. When their daughter Gabriella is born, they decorate her room with numbers and spend a great deal of time counting objects and talking about math with her. In her school years, Gabriella is particularly gifted in mathematics. Gabriella does not become an engineer, but she does have a career as a terrific math teacher. Which statement is most accurate in describing Gabriella?

A. Her math ability is a direct result of her genetic heritage.
B. Her math ability is a direct result of her environmental experiences.
C. The fact that she became a teacher instead of an engineer shows that neither genetics nor environment matters that much to development.
D. Gabriella's development shows the influence of genetics, environment, their interaction, and Gabriella's capacity to forge a life theme that is meaningful to her.

2 Physical Development

In this section, we trace the ways that individuals grow and change *physically,* starting with *prenatal* ("before birth") physical development. Then we consider the physical changes associated with childhood, adolescence, and the phases of adulthood. Throughout, we consider the ways the brain changes in each developmental period.

Prenatal Physical Development

Prenatal development is a time of astonishing change, beginning with conception. Conception occurs when a single sperm cell from the male merges with the female's ovum (egg) to produce a zygote, a single cell with 23 chromosomes from the biological mother and 23 from the biological father.

THE COURSE OF PRENATAL DEVELOPMENT Development from zygote to fetus is divided into three periods:

1. *Germinal period—weeks 1 and 2:* The germinal period begins with conception. After 1 week and many cell divisions, the zygote is made up of 100 to 150 cells. By the end of 2 weeks, the mass of cells has attached to the uterine wall. It is in the period that the fertilized egg is called a zygote.

2. *Embryonic period—weeks 3 through 8:* At this point, the zygote has become an embryo. The rate of cell differentiation intensifies, support systems for the cells develop, and the beginnings of organs appear (Figure 1a). In the third week, the neural tube, which eventually becomes the spinal cord, starts to take shape. Within the first 28 days after conception, the neural tube is formed and closes, encased inside the embryo. Problems in neural tube development can lead to birth defects such as spina bifida, in which the spinal cord is not completely enclosed by the spinal column, or severe underdevelopment of the brain. Folic acid, a B vitamin found in orange juice and leafy green vegetables, greatly reduces the chances of neural tube defects. By the end of the embryonic period, the heart begins to beat, the arms and legs become more differentiated, the face starts to form, and the intestinal tract appears (Figure 1b).

 Note that 28 days is before most women even know they are pregnant. That's why doctors recommend that all women who might become pregnant take folic acid supplements (about 400 micrograms a day) to prevent neural tube defects.

(a)

(b)

(c)

FIGURE 1 From Embryo to Fetus (*a*) At about 4 weeks, an embryo is about 0.2 inch (less than 1 centimeter) long. The head, eyes, and ears begin to show; the head and neck are half the length of the body. (*b*) At 8 weeks, the developing individual is about 1.6 inches (4 centimeters) long and has reached the end of its embryonic phase. It has become a fetus. Everything that will be found in the fully developed human being has now begun to form. The fetal stage is a period of growth and perfection of detail. The heart has been beating for a month, and the muscles have just begun their first exercises. (*c*) At 4½ months, the fetus is just over 7 inches (about 18 centimeters) long. If the thumb comes close to the mouth, the head may turn, and the lips and tongue begin their sucking motions—a reflex for survival.

(a) ©Dr G. Moscoso/Science Source; (b) ©Anatomical Travelogue/Science Source; (c) ©Nestle/Petit Format/Science Source

3. *Fetal period—months 2 through 9:* At 2 months, the fetus is the size of a kidney bean and has already started to move around. At 4 months, the fetus is 5 inches long and weighs about 5 ounces (Figure 1c). At 6 months, the fetus has grown to a pound and a half. The last three months of pregnancy are the time when organ functioning increases, and the fetus puts on considerable weight and size, adding baby fat. The average newborn is about 19 inches long and weighs about 7 pounds.

Until about 70 years ago, people were unaware of the role that maternal diet and behavior might play for the developing fetus. Although it floats in a comfortable, well-protected womb, the fetus is not immune to the larger environment surrounding the mother. Indeed, sometimes prenatal development is disrupted by environmental insults.

A reality check for pregnant women who continue to smoke to alleviate stress: Imagine a baby puffing on a lit cigarette. A pregnant woman who smokes is smoking for two.

THREATS TO THE FETUS A *teratogen* is any agent that causes a birth defect. Teratogens include chemical substances ingested by the mother (such as nicotine, if the mother smokes, or alcohol, if she drinks) and certain illnesses (such as rubella, or German measles). Substances that are ingested by the mother can lead to serious birth defects (Flamier, Singh, & Rasmussen, 2017). Heroin is an example of a teratogen. Babies born to heroin users are at risk for many problems, including premature birth, low birth weight, physical defects, breathing problems, and death.

Fetal alcohol spectrum disorders (FASD) are a cluster of abnormalities and problems that appear in babies whose mothers drank alcohol during pregnancy (Schwartz & others, 2017). These abnormalities include a small head; facial characteristics such as wide-spaced eyes, a flattened nose, and an underdeveloped upper lip; defects in the limbs and heart; and below-average intelligence. The U.S. Surgeon General recommends that no alcohol should be consumed during pregnancy. The best advice is for a woman who is pregnant or thinking of becoming pregnant to avoid alcohol.

The effects of teratogens depend on the timing of exposure. The body part or organ system that is developing when the fetus encounters the teratogen is most vulnerable. Genetic characteristics may buffer or worsen the effects of a teratogen. Perhaps most importantly, the environment children experience *after birth* can influence the ultimate effects of prenatal insults.

Preterm infants (those born prior to 37 weeks after conception) and low birth weight infants may be at risk for developmental difficulties. Many preterm and low birth-weight infants are healthy, but as a group they have more health and developmental problems than do typical birth-weight infants (Emberson & others, 2017; Peyton & others, 2017).

The number and severity of these problems increase when infants are born very early and as their birth weight decreases. Survival rates for infants who are born very early and very small have risen, but with this improved survival rate has come increased rates of severe brain damage (McNicholas & others, 2014).

However, postnatal experience plays a crucial role in determining the ultimate effects of preterm birth. For example, infant massage and kangaroo care, in which the newborn is held upright against the parent's bare chest, much as a baby kangaroo is carried by its mother, can improve developmental outcomes for preterm and low birth-weight infants and may have benefits for parents as well (McClure, 2017).

Physical Development in Infancy and Childhood

Human infants are among the world's most helpless neonates. One reason for that helplessness is that we are born not quite finished. From an evolutionary perspective, what sets humans apart from other animals is our enormous brain. Getting that big brain out of the relatively small birth canal is a challenge that nature has met by sending human babies out of the womb before the brain has fully developed. The first months and years of life allow the developing human (and his or her environment) to put the finishing touches on that important organ.

REFLEXES   Newborns come into the world equipped with several genetically wired reflexes that are crucial for survival. Babies are born with the ability to suck and swallow. If they are dropped in water, they will naturally hold their breath, contract their throats to keep water out, and move their arms and legs to stay afloat at least briefly. Some reflexes persist throughout life—coughing, blinking, and yawning, for example. Others, such as automatically grasping something that touches the fingers, disappear in the months following birth as infants develop voluntary control over many behaviors. Figure 2 shows some examples of infant reflexes.

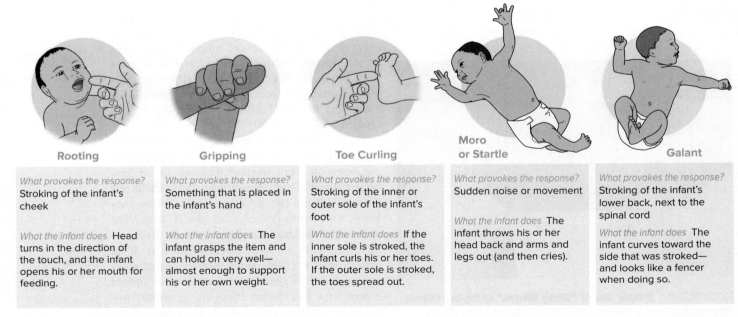

Rooting

What provokes the response? Stroking of the infant's cheek

What the infant does Head turns in the direction of the touch, and the infant opens his or her mouth for feeding.

Gripping

What provokes the response? Something that is placed in the infant's hand

What the infant does The infant grasps the item and can hold on very well—almost enough to support his or her own weight.

Toe Curling

What provokes the response? Stroking of the inner or outer sole of the infant's foot

What the infant does If the inner sole is stroked, the infant curls his or her toes. If the outer sole is stroked, the toes spread out.

Moro or Startle

What provokes the response? Sudden noise or movement

What the infant does The infant throws his or her head back and arms and legs out (and then cries).

Galant

What provokes the response? Stroking of the infant's lower back, next to the spinal cord

What the infant does The infant curves toward the side that was stroked—and looks like a fencer when doing so.

FIGURE 2   Some Infant Reflexes Infants are born with a number of reflexes to get them through life, and they are incredibly cute when they perform them. These reflexes disappear as infants mature.

MOTOR AND PERCEPTUAL SKILLS   Relative to the rest of the body, a newborn's head is gigantic, and it flops around uncontrollably. Within 12 months, the infant becomes capable of sitting upright, standing, stooping, climbing, and often walking. During the second year, growth decelerates, but rapid gains occur in such activities as running and climbing.

Motor skills and perceptual skills are coupled and depend on each other. To reach for something, the infant must be able to see it. Babies are continually coordinating their movements with information they perceive through their senses to learn how to maintain their balance, reach for objects in space, and move across various surfaces and terrains (Adolph & Robinson, 2015; Müller, Valentini, & Bandeira, 2017). Consider what happens when a baby sees a fun toy across the room. Because she can see it, she is motivated to get it. She must perceive the current state of her body and learn how to use her limbs to get to the goal. In turn, action educates perception. For example, watching an object while holding and touching it helps infants to learn about its texture, size, and hardness. Moving from place to place in the environment teaches babies how objects and people look from different perspectives and whether surfaces will support their weight. Demonstrating the profound connections across levels of development, motor skills in infancy predict intelligence measured at age 4 (Heineman & others, 2017).

Infants are energetic developers. When infants are motivated to do something, they may create a new motor behavior, such as reaching out to grab a new toy or mommy's earrings. That new behavior is the result of many converging factors: the developing nervous system, the body's physical properties and its movement possibilities, the goal the infant is motivated to reach, and environmental support for the skill (Kretch, Franchak, & Adolph, 2014). Research using EEG shows that the 10-week-old infant brain responds differently to seeing people moving if the babies have engaged in reflex walking while being held (Reid, Kaduk, & Lunn, 2018).

Researchers used to think that motor milestones (such as sitting up, crawling, and walking) unfolded as part of a genetic plan. Psychologists now recognize that motor development is not the consequence of nature or nurture alone (da Silva & others, 2017).

Environmental experiences play a role in motor development. In one study, 3-month-old infants participated in play sessions wearing "sticky mittens"—mittens with palms that stick to the edges of toys and allow the infants to pick up the toys (Needham, Barrett, & Peterman, 2002, p. 279) (Figure 3). Infants who participated in sessions with the mittens grasped and manipulated objects earlier in their development than a control group of infants who did not receive the "mitten" experience. The experienced infants looked at the objects longer, swatted at them, and were more likely to put the objects in their mouths. The sticky mittens exercise is especially effective if the parents encourage the child while they use the mittens (Needham & others, 2017).

Psychologists face a daunting challenge in studying infant perception. Infants cannot talk, so how can scientists learn whether they can see or hear certain things? Psychologists who study infants rely on what infants can do to understand what they know. One thing infants can do is look. The **preferential looking** technique involves giving an infant a choice of what object to look at. If an infant shows a reliable preference for one stimulus (say, a picture of a face) over another (a scrambled picture of a face) when these are repeatedly presented in differing locations, we can infer that the infant can tell the two images apart (Dunn & Bremner, 2017; Reynolds & Richards, 2018).

🐚 *Infants' motor skills are limited by gravity. Infants can sometimes do a lot more when weightless. Holding a baby up in a kiddie pool, we can see how the infant can stand and even take some steps quite deftly, without body weight getting in the way.*

©C Squared Studios/Stockbyte/Getty Images

FIGURE 3   Infants' Use of "Sticky Mittens" to Explore Objects Amy Needham and her colleagues (2002) found that "sticky mittens" enhance young infants' object exploration skills.
Courtesy of Amy Needham, Duke University

preferential looking A research technique that involves giving an infant a choice of what object to look at.

At birth   1 month   3 months   15 months

Using this technique on babies even within hours after they are born, researchers have shown that infants prefer to look at faces rather than other objects and to look at attractive faces more than at unattractive ones (Johnson & Hannon, 2015; Lee & others, 2013). Also, researchers have found that as early as 7 days old, infants are already engaged in organized perception of faces and are able to put together sights and sounds. If presented with two faces with mouths moving, infants will watch the face whose mouth matches the sounds they are hearing (Lewkowicz, 2010; Lewkowicz & Hansen-Tift, 2012; Pascalls & Kelly, 2008). At 3 months, infants prefer real faces to scrambled faces and their mother's face to a stranger's (Barrera & Maurer, 1981). Research using brain imaging suggests that infants may know more than even this clever strategy can tell us.

THE BRAIN   As an infant plays, crawls, shakes a rattle, smiles, and frowns, his or her brain is changing dramatically. At birth and in early infancy, the brain's 100 billion neurons have only minimal connections. The infant brain literally is ready and waiting for the experiences that will create these connections. During the first 2 years of life, the dendrites of the neurons branch out, and the neurons become far more interconnected (Figure 4); infancy is a time when the brain is all about making connections. Myelination, the process of encasing axons with fat cells (the myelin sheath), begins prenatally and continues after birth well into adolescence and adulthood (Forbes & Gallo, 2017; Rowley & others, 2017).

During childhood, *synaptic connections* increase dramatically. Recall that a synapse is a gap between neurons that is bridged by chemical neurotransmitters. Nearly twice as many synapses are available as will ever be used (Huttenlocher, 1999). The connections that are made become stronger and will survive; the unused ones will be replaced by other neural pathways or disappear. In the language of neuroscience, these unused connections will be "pruned." Figure 5 illustrates the steep growth and later pruning of synapses during infancy in specific areas of the brain. As you can see, the degree of pruning that occurs is extensive, however it is a precise process. Research has linked problems in the pruning process to later psychological disorders (Neniskyte & Gross, 2017). Note as well that pruning is at least partly based on experience—unused connections are pruned away, demonstrating again, the way that the brain adapts to experience.

Brain-imaging studies show that children's brains also undergo amazing anatomical changes. Repeated brain scans of the same children for up to 4 years show that the amount of brain material in some areas can nearly double within as little as a year, followed by a drastic loss of tissue as unneeded cells are purged and the brain continues to reorganize itself. The overall size of the brain does not change very much, but local patterns within the brain change tremendously. From 3 to 6 years of age, the most rapid growth takes place in the frontal lobe areas, which are involved in planning and organizing new actions

The brain's plasticity makes it different from any other bodily organ. It comes into the world ready for whatever world it might encounter, and the features of that world influence its very structure. Other organs physically grow as we do. But the brain's very essence is attached to the world in which it lives.

FIGURE 5

Synaptic Density in the Human Brain from Infancy to Adulthood The graph shows the dramatic increase and then pruning in synaptic density in three regions of the brain: visual cortex, auditory cortex, and prefrontal cortex. Synaptic density is believed to be an important indication of the extent of connectivity between neurons.

Source: P. R. Huttenlocher and A. S. Dabholkar, "Regional Differences in the Synaptogenesis in the Human Cerebral Cortex," *Journal of Comparative Neurology*, 1997, 387 (2), 167–168.

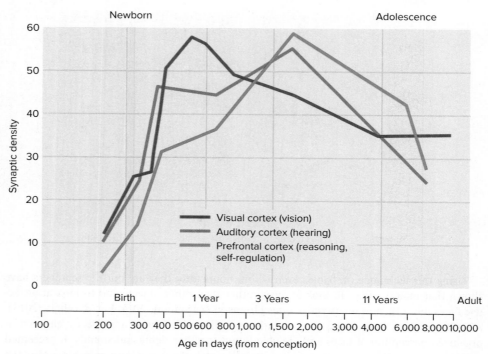

and in maintaining attention to tasks. These brain changes are not simply the result of nature; new experiences in the world also promote brain development (Gallagher & others, 2017; Maitre & others, 2017; Sale, Berardi, & Maffei, 2014). Thus, as in other areas of development, nature and nurture operate together.

Physical Development in Adolescence

Adolescence refers to the developmental period spanning the transition from childhood to adulthood, beginning around 10 to 12 years of age and ending at 18 to 21 years of age. Dramatic physical changes characterize adolescence, especially early adolescence. Among the major physical changes of adolescence are those involving puberty and the brain.

PUBERTY   The signature physical change in adolescence is **puberty,** a period of rapid skeletal and sexual maturation that occurs mainly in early adolescence. In general, we know when an individual is going through puberty, but we have a hard time pinpointing its beginning and its end. Except for *menarche* (girls' first menstrual cycle), no single marker defines it. For boys the first whisker or first nocturnal ejaculation (or wet dream) could mark its appearance, but both may go unnoticed.

puberty
A period of rapid skeletal and sexual maturation that occurs mainly in early adolescence.

The jump in height and weight that characterizes pubertal change occurs about two years earlier for girls than for boys (Figure 6). In the United States today, the average beginning of the growth spurt is 9 years of age for girls and 11 years for boys. The peak of pubertal change occurs at an average age of 11½ for girls and 13½ for boys.

Hormonal changes lie at the core of pubertal development. The concentrations of certain hormones increase dramatically during puberty (Nguyen, Ducharme & Karama, 2017). *Testosterone,* an androgen, is associated in boys with the development of genitals, an increase in height, and voice change. *Estradiol,* an estrogen, is associated in girls with breast, uterine, and skeletal development. Developmental psychologists believe that hormonal changes account for at least some of the

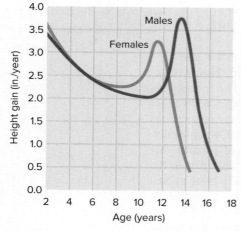

FIGURE 6

Pubertal Growth Spurt On average, the pubertal growth spurt begins and peaks about two years earlier for girls (starts at 9, peaks at 11½) than for boys (starts at 11½, peaks at 13½).

Source: J. M. Tanner et al., in Archives of Diseases in Childhood 41, 1966.

emotional ups and downs of adolescence, but hormones are not alone responsible for adolescent behavior (Cameron & others, 2017).

From our discussion earlier in this chapter, recall that physical and socioemotional development are intertwined. This link is demonstrated in the implications of timing of puberty for socioemotional outcomes. Boys who mature earlier than their peers tend to show more positive socioemotional outcomes, such as being popular with their peers and having higher self-esteem (Cooper & Bidaisee, 2017; de Guzman & Nishina, 2014). In one study, boys who matured early in adolescence were more successful and less likely to drink alcohol or smoke cigarettes than late-maturing boys some 39 years later (Taga, Markey, & Friedman, 2006). In contrast, early maturation predicts girls' vulnerability to a number of problems (Chen, Rothman, & Jaffee, 2017; Hamilton & others, 2014). Early-maturing girls are at risk for smoking, drinking alcohol, depression, and disordered eating (Chen, Rothman, & Jaffee, 2017; Graber, 2013; Harden & Mendle, 2011). Older men may take sexual advantage of these girls.

Recently, experts have noted that children seem to be entering puberty earlier than in previous times. What factors might explain this change?

THE ADOLESCENT BRAIN   Based on experience and hormonal changes, in adolescence, brain changes first occur at the subcortical level in the **limbic system,** which is the seat of emotions and where rewards are experienced. The limbic system matures much earlier than the prefrontal cortex and is almost completely developed by early adolescence (Blakemore & Mills, 2014; Casey, 2015; Herting & Sowell, 2017). The limbic system structure that is especially involved in emotion is the amygdala. Figure 7 shows the locations of the limbic system, amygdala, and prefrontal cortex. These changes in the brain may help to explain why adolescents often display very strong emotions and seek immediate rewards but may not successfully control these passions (Reyna & Zayas, 2014). Because of the relatively slow development of the prefrontal cortex, which continues to mature into early adulthood, adolescents may lack the cognitive skills to control their impulses effectively. This developmental disjunction may account for increased risk taking and other problems in adolescence (Piekarski & others, 2017; Steinberg, 2015a, 2015b).

limbic system
A set of subcortical brain structures central to emotion, memory, and reward processing.

A major question is which comes first—biological changes in the brain or experiences that stimulate these changes? Consider a study in which the brain reactivity of children and adolescents was measured as they were shown images. The results showed that adolescents had stronger brain responses to changes in emotional facial expressions compared to children (Rosen & others, 2017). These results fit with the view that adolescents are more preoccupied with social standing and other people's feelings. Yet, were the results due to biology or to experience? Is it possible that adolescents' brains were so responsive because of exposure to the middle and high school social scene? This correlational study

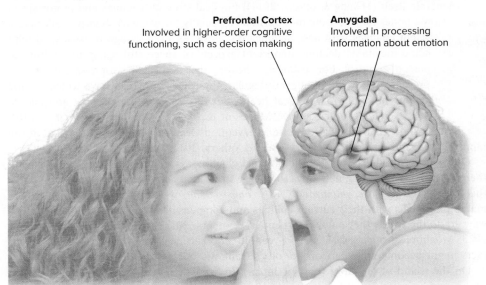

Prefrontal Cortex
Involved in higher-order cognitive functioning, such as decision making

Amygdala
Involved in processing information about emotion

FIGURE 7
Developmental Changes in the Adolescent's Brain
The amygdala, which is responsible for processing information about emotion, matures earlier than the prefrontal cortex, which is responsible for making decisions and other higher-order cognitive functions.
©Brand X Pictures/Stockbyte/Getty Images

cannot answer that question, and once again we encounter the fascinating truth about the brain: It shapes and is shaped by experience.

Physical Development in Adulthood

As in other developmental periods, our bodies change during adulthood. Most of the changes that occur after adolescence involve declines in physical and perceptual abilities, as we now consider.

PHYSICAL CHANGES IN EARLY ADULTHOOD

Most adults reach their peak physical development during their 20s and are the healthiest then. Early adulthood, however, is also the time when many physical skills begin to decline. The downward trend in strength and speed often is noticeable in the 30s. Another realm in which physical changes occur with age is in the ability to perceive the world. Although it may not be noticeable, perceptual decline begins in early adulthood. For instance, starting at about age 18, hearing begins a gradual decline.

PHYSICAL CHANGES IN MIDDLE AND LATE ADULTHOOD

Many physical changes in the 40s or 50s involve changes in appearance. The skin has begun to wrinkle and sag because of the loss of fat and collagen in underlying tissues. Small, localized areas of skin pigmentation produce age spots, especially in areas exposed to sunlight such as the hands and face. Hair becomes thinner and grayer due to a lower replacement rate and a decline in melanin production. Individuals lose height in middle age as a result of bone loss in the vertebrae, and many gain weight (Zheng & others, 2017). Once individuals reach their 40s, age-related changes to their vision usually become apparent, especially difficulty in seeing things up close. The sense of taste can also be affected by age, as taste buds are less likely to be replaced.

For women, entering middle age means that menopause will soon occur. Usually in the late 40s or early 50s, a woman's menstrual periods cease. With menopause comes a dramatic drop in the ovaries' production of estrogen. Estrogen decline produces uncomfortable symptoms in some menopausal women, such as *hot flashes* (sudden, brief flushing of the skin and a feeling of elevated body temperature), nausea, fatigue, and rapid heartbeat. However, menopause overall is not the negative experience for most women it was once thought to be (Brockie & others, 2014; Guérin, & others, 2017).

With age, for both men and women, a variety of bodily systems are likely to show the effects of wear and tear as the body becomes less and less able to repair damage and regenerate itself (Hwang & others, 2014). Physical strength declines and motor speed slows; bones may become more brittle (especially for women). Nearly every bodily system changes with age. Significantly, however, even as age is associated with some inevitable decline, important aspects of successful aging are within the person's control. For instance, a healthy diet and regular exercise can help to prevent or slow these effects. Regular physical activity can have wide-reaching benefits not only for physical health but for cognitive functioning as well (de Souto Barreto & others, 2018; Morrison & Mayer, 2017; Zhu & others, 2016). Studies show that physical exercise interventions lead to increases in the size of the hippocampus and improved memory (Best & others, 2017; Rosano & others, 2017).

How is your current behavior building a foundation for a healthy late adulthood? If your future self could time-travel to visit you, would he or she say "Thanks!"–or instead "What were you thinking?"

One way older adults navigate the physical changes associated with age is by changing their goals and developing new ways to engage in desired activities. Psychologists refer to this process as *selective optimization with compensation,* which means that older adults match their goals with their current abilities and compensate for declines by finding other ways to do the things they enjoy (Carpentieri & others, 2017; Freund, Nikitin, & Riediger, 2013; Moghimi & others, 2017). A 75-year-old who can no longer drive because of cataracts might become an expert on her city's train and bus system, for example.

On the island of Okinawa (part of Japan), individuals live longer than anywhere else in the world, and Okinawa has the world's highest prevalence of *centenarians*—people who live to 100 years or beyond. Examination of Okinawans' lives provides insights into their longevity. Specific factors are diet (they eat nutritious foods such as grains, fish, and vegetables); lifestyle (they are easygoing and experience low stress); community (Okinawans look out for one another and do not isolate or ignore older adults); activity (they lead active lifestyles, and many older adults continue to work); and spirituality (they find a sense of purpose in spiritual matters) (Willcox, Scapagnini, & Willcox, 2014; Willcox & Willcox, 2014). Just as physical changes are interwoven with socioemotional processes in childhood and adolescence, so they are as human beings enter the later stages of life.

Biological Theories of Aging

Of the many proposed biological theories of aging, three especially merit attention: cellular-clock theory, free-radical theory, and hormonal stress theory.

The *cellular-clock theory* is Leonard Hayflick's (1977) view that cells can divide a maximum of about 100 times and that, as we age, our cells become less capable of dividing. Hayflick found that the total number of cell divisions is roughly related to the individual's age. Based on the way cells divide, Hayflick placed the upper limit of the human life span at about 120 years.

People often say life's too short. But imagine living to be 120 years old. At age 70 you would still have 50 years to fill with life.

Scientists have been examining why cells lose their ability to divide (Ding & others, 2014). The answer may lie at the tips of chromosomes. Each time a cell divides, the *telomeres* protecting the ends of chromosomes shorten (Figure 8). After about 100 replications, the telomeres are dramatically reduced, and the cell no longer can divide (Shalev & others, 2013). There is considerable interest in discovering ways to maintain high levels of the telomere-extending enzyme—telomerase—through genetic manipulation of chemical telomerase activators. One factor that has been demonstrated to reduce telomere length is stress (Lucas & others, 2017; Roberts & others, 2017). For example, a recent study showed that adolescents who experienced chaotic family environments with low levels of parental support felt more negative emotion which in turn predicted decreases in telomere length

FIGURE 8 **Telomeres and Aging** The photograph shows telomeres lighting up the tips of chromosomes. The figure illustrates how the telomeres shorten every time a cell divides. Eventually, after about 100 divisions, the telomeres are greatly reduced in length. As a result, the cell can no longer reproduce and it dies.

(photo) ©Los Alamos National Laboratory/Getty Images

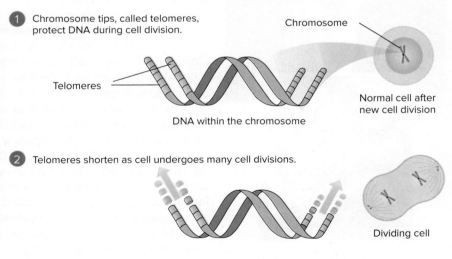

1. Chromosome tips, called telomeres, protect DNA during cell division.

Chromosome

Telomeres

DNA within the chromosome

Normal cell after new cell division

2. Telomeres shorten as cell undergoes many cell divisions.

Dividing cell

3. Ultimately, telomeres become too short, exposing DNA, which becomes damaged, and the cell dies. This is the normal life and death cycle of a cell.

Cell death

(Brody, Yu, & Shalev, 2017). Stress-reducing activities might, then, be expected to enhance telomerase activity. One study showed that individuals who participated in a three-month meditation retreat (which included meditating for 6 hours a day) showed greater telomerase activity relative to a control group (Jacobs & others, 2011).

The *free-radical theory* of aging states that people age because unstable oxygen molecules known as *free radicals* are produced inside their cells. These molecules damage DNA and other cellular structures (Matkarimov & Saparbaev, 2017). The damage done by free radicals may lead to a range of disorders, including cancer and arthritis (Poprac & others, 2017).

Hormonal stress theory argues that aging in the body's hormonal system can lower resistance to stress and increase the likelihood of disease. As individuals age, stress hormones stay in the bloodstream longer. Prolonged, elevated levels of stress hormones are linked to increased risks for many diseases, including cardiovascular disease, cancer, and diabetes (Kim-Fuchs & others, 2014; McEwan, 2017). Recently, the hormonal stress theory of aging has focused on the role of chronic stress in diminishing the functioning of the immune system (Guardino & others, 2017; Mate, Madrid, & De la Fuente, 2014). As we have seen previously, prolonged stress can leave a person vulnerable to disease as the body is not given an opportunity to rest and repair.

Aging and the Brain For decades, scientists believed that no new brain cells are generated past early childhood. However, researchers have recently discovered that adults can grow new brain cells throughout life (Anacker & Hen, 2017; Otteson, 2017), although evidence is limited to the hippocampus and the olfactory bulb (Brus, Keller, & Lévy, 2013; Huart, Rombaux, & Hummel, 2013). Researchers currently are studying factors that might inhibit and promote *neurogenesis* (the term used to describe the generation of new neurons), including various drugs, stress, and exercise (Broad, 2017; Sailor, Schinder, & Lledo, 2017).

Some brain areas shrink more than others with aging. The prefrontal cortex is one area that shrinks, and research has linked this shrinkage to a decrease in working memory and other cognitive activities in older adults (Reichel & others, 2017; Tian & others, 2017). The sensory regions of the brain—such as the primary visual cortex, primary motor cortex, and somatosensory cortex—are less vulnerable to the aging process (Rodrigue & Kennedy, 2011).

Even in late adulthood, the brain has remarkable repair capability (Cai & others, 2014). Stanley Rapaport (1994) compared the brains of younger and older adults when they were engaged in the same tasks. The older adults' brains literally rewired themselves to compensate for losses. If one neuron was not up to the job, neighboring neurons helped to pick up the slack. Rapaport concluded that as brains age, they can shift responsibilities for a given task from one region to another.

Changes in lateralization may provide one type of adaptation in aging adults. *Lateralization* is the specialization of function in one hemisphere of the brain or the other. Using neuroimaging techniques, researchers have found that brain activity in the prefrontal cortex is lateralized less in older adults than in younger adults when they are engaging in cognitive tasks (Cabeza, 2002; van Dinteren & others, 2017). So, younger adults activate only one hemisphere to complete a task well. Older adults can show the same level of performance but reach that goal by using both hemispheres. The decrease in lateralization in older adults might play a compensatory role in the aging brain. That is, using both hemispheres may improve the cognitive functioning of older adults.

Results from the Nun Study support the role of experience in maintaining brain function. Recall that this study involves nearly 700 nuns in a convent in Mankato, Minnesota (Snowdon, 2003, 2007) (Figure 9).

In older adults, the brain hemispheres may work together more often—becoming jacks-of-all-trades to do what each used to do separately.

FIGURE 9 The Brains of the Mankato Nuns Nun Study participant Sister Nicolette Welter remained an active, contributing member of her community until her death in 2014, at age 102. (*inset*) A neuroscientist holds a brain donated by one of the Mankato Nun Study participants.
(Sister Nicolette) ©Scott Takushi/KRT/Newscom; (brain) ©Steve Liss/Time Life Pictures/Getty Images

By examining the nuns' donated brains as well as others, neuroscientists have documented the aging brain's ability to grow and change (Pakhomov & Hemmy, 2014). Even the oldest Mankato nuns lead intellectually challenging lives, and neuroscientists believe that stimulating mental activities increase dendritic branching. Keeping the brain actively engaged in challenging activities can help to slow the effects of age.

In sum, in the physical domain across the life span, we see a dramatic pattern of growth and change in infancy, childhood, and adolescence followed by leveling off and decline in adulthood. How might this progression influence (and be influenced by) the way the developing person thinks about himself or herself and the world? To examine this question, we turn to the cognitive domain of human development.

1. The first two weeks after conception are referred to as the
   A. fetal period.
   B. germinal period.
   C. embryonic period.
   D. zygotic period.

2. Puberty is generally characterized by all of the following *except*
   A. a decrease in concentrations of certain hormones.
   B. a dramatic increase in height and weight.
   C. an increase in idealistic and abstract thinking.
   D. the development of thought.

3. The hormone associated with girls' breast, uterine, and skeletal development during puberty is
   A. testosterone.
   B. estradiol.

C. androgen.
D. norepinephrine.

APPLY IT! 4. Gabriel's grandfather has always been a fitness nut. Even at age 83, he continues to work out, lifting weights, swimming, and taking pride in his physique. After his grandfather beats him in a swimming race, Gabriel rolls his eyes and comments that all this work makes no sense at this point in his grandfather's life. Aside from calling him on his sour grapes, what would you say about Gabriel's viewpoint?
   A. Gabriel is right. All that working out is probably inappropriate and even unhealthy for someone in his 80s.
   B. Gabriel is wrong, because if his grandfather stays active, he can completely avoid all of the

physical changes associated with age.
   C. Gabriel is wrong. His grandfather's hard work might be paying off in a variety of ways, including his physical health and his cognitive and emotional functioning generally.
   D. Gabriel is right, and his grandfather seems to be in denial about the effects of age on physical development.

3 Cognitive Development

Cognitive development refers to how thought, intelligence, and language processes change as people mature. *Cognition* refers to the operation of thinking and also to our cognitive skills and abilities. In this section, you will encounter one of the biggest names in all of psychology, Jean Piaget, who presented a theory of cognitive development that has had lasting impact on the field. We examine Piaget's contributions and also consider more recent research on the relationship between cognitive abilities and age.

Cognitive Development from Childhood into Adulthood

The Swiss developmental psychologist Jean Piaget (1896–1980) traced cognitive development through childhood into adulthood. Let's begin by reviewing Piaget's approach.

PIAGET'S THEORY OF COGNITIVE DEVELOPMENT   In Piaget's view, human beings use schemas to make sense of their experience. A *schema* is a mental concept or framework that organizes information and provides a structure for interpreting it. Schemas are expressed as various behaviors and skills that the child can exercise in relation to objects or situations. For example, sucking is an early, simple schema. Later and more

Jean Piaget (1896–1980) *Piaget, the famous Swiss psychologist, changed the way we think about the development of children's minds.*
©Farrell Grehan/CORBIS/Corbis via Getty Images

complex schemas include licking, blowing, crawling, and hiding. In adulthood, schemas may represent more complex expectations and beliefs about the world.

Piaget (1952) described two processes responsible for how people use and adapt their schemas:

assimilation
An individual's incorporation of new information into existing knowledge.

1. **Assimilation** means that individuals incorporate new information into existing schemas. In assimilation, when faced with a new experience, the person applies old ways of doing things. For infants, this might involve applying the schema of sucking to whatever new object they encounter. For a toddler it might mean calling all animals "doggie." For an adolescent, it might mean using the skills learned while playing video games to drive a car. For an adult, it might mean solving a conflict with a spouse using ways that worked in the past with friends or previous romantic partners.

accommodation
An individual's adjustment of his or her schemas to new information.

2. **Accommodation** means that individuals change their schemas in response to new experience. Rather than using one's old ways of doing things, in accommodation, new experiences lead to changes in existing schemas or even the development of new schemas. For example, after several months of experience, the infant who has been sticking everything in her mouth might begin to accommodate the sucking schema by being more selective with it. The toddler who recognizes that all animals are not "doggies" might learn the words for "cat" or "horse." The adolescent who has typically gone with the flow of social pressure might develop a new way of dealing with peer pressure by standing up for his beliefs. For an adult, accommodation may mean rethinking old strategies for problem solving when a new challenge, such as the loss of a job or the onset of illness, presents itself.

So, we assimilate experiences into schemas and accommodate schemas to experience.

PIAGET'S STAGES OF COGNITIVE DEVELOPMENT According to Piaget, cognitive development occurs in four stages (Figure 10). Each stage involves a way of making sense of the world that is qualitatively different from the way before it.

Sensorimotor Stage	**Preoperational Stage**	**Concrete Operational Stage**	**Formal Operational Stage**
The infant constructs an understanding of the world by coordinating sensory experiences with physical actions. An infant progresses from reflexive, instinctual action at birth to the beginning of symbolic thought toward the end of the stage. A key component of this stage is object permanence.	The child begins to represent the world with words and images. These words and images reflect increased symbolic thinking and go beyond the connection of sensory information and physical action. Thinking is egocentric, meaning the child cannot take another's perspective.	The child can now reason logically about concrete events and classify objects into different sets. Hallmarks of this stage are the capacities to reverse operations and appreciate the concept of conservation.	The adolescent reasons in more abstract, idealistic, and logical ways. A characteristic of this stage is hypothetical-deductive reasoning.
Birth to 2 Years of Age	2 to 7 Years of Age	7 to 11 Years of Age	11 Years of Age Through Adulthood

FIGURE 10 **Piaget's Four Stages of Cognitive Development** Jean Piaget described how human beings, through development, become ever more sophisticated thinkers about the world.

(first) ©Stockbyte/Getty Images; (second) ©BananaStock/PunchStock; (third) ©image100/Corbis; (fourth) ©Purestock/SuperStock

sensorimotor stage
Piaget's first stage of cognitive development, lasting from birth to about 2 years of age, during which infants construct an understanding of the world by coordinating sensory experiences with motor (physical) actions.

object permanence
Piaget's term for the crucial accomplishment of understanding that objects and events continue to exist even when they cannot directly be seen, heard, or touched.

Sensorimotor Stage   Piaget's first stage, the **sensorimotor stage,** lasts from birth to about 2 years of age. In this stage, infants construct an understanding of the world by coordinating sensory experiences (such as seeing and hearing) with motor (physical) actions—hence the term *sensorimotor*. As newborns they have little more than reflexive patterns with which to work. By the end of this stage, 2-year-olds show complex sensorimotor patterns and are beginning to use symbols or words in their thinking.

Object permanence is Piaget's term for the crucial accomplishment of understanding that objects continue to exist even when they cannot directly be seen, heard, or touched. Piaget believed that "out of sight" literally was "out of mind" for very young infants. Piaget studied object permanence by showing an infant an interesting toy and then covering the toy with a blanket. Piaget reasoned that if infants understood that the toy still existed, they would try to uncover it (Figure 11). Piaget thought the development of object permanence continues throughout the sensorimotor period.

Preoperational Stage   Piaget's second stage, the **preoperational stage,** lasts from approximately 2 to 7 years of age. Preoperational thought is more symbolic than sensorimotor thought. In preschool years, children begin to represent their world with words, images, and drawings. Thus, their thoughts begin to exceed simple connections of sensorimotor information and physical action.

The type of symbolic thinking that children are able to accomplish during this stage is limited. They still cannot perform what Piaget called *operations,* by which he meant mental representations that are "reversible." Preoperational children have difficulty understanding that reversing an action may restore the original conditions from which the action began.

A well-known test of whether a child can think "operationally" is to present a child with two identical beakers, A and B, filled with liquid to the same height (Figure 12). Next to them is a third beaker (C). Beaker C is tall and thin, whereas beakers A and B are short and wide. The liquid is poured from B into C, and the child is asked whether

With object permanence, the infant starts thinking about future events, as in 'When will I see Mommy again?' The child can take comfort in the knowledge that Mommy will be back. Object permanence also means getting a first taste of the human capacity for longing—for missing someone who is not there.

preoperational stage
Piaget's second stage of cognitive development, lasting from about 2 to 7 years of age, during which thought is more symbolic than sensorimotor thought.

PSYCHOLOGICAL INQUIRY

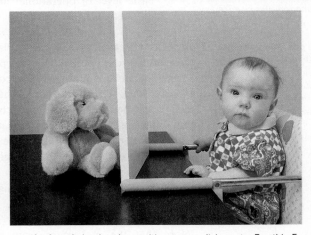

FIGURE 11 **Object Permanence** Piaget regarded object permanence as one of infancy's landmark cognitive accomplishments. For this 5-month-old boy, out of sight is literally out of mind. The infant looks at the toy dog (*left*), but when his view of the toy is blocked (*right*), he does not search for it.
(both) ©D. Goodman/Science Source

> If this boy fails to try to find the toy dog, Piaget assumed that meant he does not know it still exists. What other factors might explain his lack of looking for the toy? > What motor skills are necessary for the little boy to perform this behavior? > What kinds of goals are required for him to seek out the toy?

FIGURE 12   Piaget's Conservation Task

The beaker test determines whether a child can think operationally—that is, can mentally reverse action and understand conservation of the substance. (*a*) Two identical beakers are presented to the child, each containing the same amount of liquid. As the child watches, the experimenter pours the liquid from B into C, which is taller and thinner than A and B. (*b*) The experimenter then asks the child whether beakers A and C have the same amount of liquid. The preoperational child says no. When asked to point to the beaker that has more liquid, the child points to the tall, thin one.

©Marmaduke St. John/Alamy Stock Photo

the amounts in A and C are the same. The 4-year-old child invariably says that the amount of liquid in the tall, thin beaker (C) is greater than that in the short, wide beaker (A). The 8-year-old child consistently says the amounts are the same. The 4-year-old child, a preoperational thinker, cannot mentally reverse the pouring action; that is, she cannot imagine the liquid going back from container C to container B. Piaget said that such a child has not grasped the concept of *conservation,* a belief in the permanence of certain attributes of objects despite superficial changes. When a child has mastered conservation he or she understands the principle of reversibility: That while superficially different, some aspects of objects can be restored when an operation is reversed.

The child's thought in the preoperational stage is egocentric. This does not mean that the child is self-centered or arrogant but that preoperational children cannot put themselves in someone else's shoes. They cannot take another's perspective.

Preoperational thinking is also intuitive. This means that preoperational children make judgments based on gut feelings rather than logic. In reaching a basic level of operational understanding, the child progresses to the third of Piaget's cognitive stages.

Preschoolers aren't trying to make their parents crazy. They may say remarkably cruel things, but they are not able to gauge how their words might make someone else feel.

concrete operational stage
Piaget's third stage of cognitive development, lasting from about 7 to 11 years of age, during which the individual uses operations and replaces intuitive reasoning with logical reasoning in concrete situations.

Concrete Operational Stage   Piaget's **concrete operational stage** (7 to 11 years of age) involves using operations and replacing intuitive reasoning with logical reasoning in concrete situations. Children in the concrete operational stage can successfully complete the beaker task described above. They are able to mentally imagine the operation of reversing the pouring of the liquid back into the wide beaker. Many of the concrete operations identified by Piaget are related to the properties of objects. For instance, when playing with Play-doh, the child in the concrete operational stage realizes that *the amount of Play-doh is not changed by changing its shape.* One important skill at this stage of reasoning is the ability to classify or divide things into different sets or subsets and to consider their interrelations. (You might remember the childhood song that goes, "One of these things is not like the others," which effectively aimed to coax you into concrete operations).

Note that the movement from preoperational to concrete operational thought involves greater sophistication in comparing objects and understanding what characteristics are constant about the objects we see in the world. Concrete operational thought involves operational thinking, classification skills, and logical reasoning in concrete contexts. However, at this stage children are not thinking abstractly or hypothetically. According to Piaget, this kind of abstract, logical reasoning occurs in the fourth, and final, cognitive stage.

Formal Operational Stage Individuals enter the **formal operational stage** of cognitive development at 11 to 15 years of age. This stage continues through the adult years. Formal operational thought is more abstract and logical than concrete operational thought. Most importantly, formal operational thinking includes thinking about things that are not concrete, making predictions, and using logic to come up with hypotheses about the future. Formal operational thought can be directed at thought itself, as the reasoner comes to think about how they think.

Unlike elementary schoolchildren, adolescents can conceive of hypothetical, purely abstract possibilities. This type of thinking is called *idealistic* because it involves comparing how things are to how they might be. Adolescents also think more logically. They begin to think more as a scientist thinks, devising plans to solve problems and systematically testing solutions. Piaget called this type of problem solving *hypothetical-deductive reasoning*. The phrase denotes adolescents' ability to develop hypotheses, or best hunches, about ways to solve a problem such as an algebraic equation. It also denotes their ability to systematically deduce, or come to a conclusion about, the best path for solving the problem. In adolescents and throughout the rest of life, Piaget believed that mature reasoning would be characterized by this capacity to hypothesize, reflect, and use logic to reach conclusions. In contrast, before adolescence, children are more likely to solve problems by trial and error.

In summary, over the course of Piaget's four developmental stages, a person progresses from sensorimotor cognition to abstract, idealistic, and logical thought. Piaget based his stages on careful observation of children's behavior, but there is always room to evaluate theory and research. Let's consider the current thinking about Piaget's theory of cognitive development.

EVALUATING AND EXPANDING ON PIAGET'S THEORY Piaget opened up a new way of looking at how children's minds develop. We owe him for a long list of concepts that have enduring power and fascination, including schemas, assimilation, accommodation, cognitive stages, object permanence, egocentrism, and conservation. We owe Piaget for the currently accepted view of children as active, constructive thinkers who play a role in their own development. Nevertheless, just as other psychological theories have been criticized and amended, so have Piaget's.

The key challenge of the nature versus nurture debate is understanding what infants bring with them into the world (nature) and what they learn from experience (nurture). Piaget's approach emphasized the experiences that infants have with the world and how those experiences shape infant cognitive development. However, in the past several decades, many studies on infant development using sophisticated experimental techniques have challenged Piaget's view of sensorimotor development (Brooks & Meltzoff, 2014; Johnson & Hannon, 2015), as we now consider.

An Alternative View: The Nativist Approach Nativist approaches to infant cognitive development suggest that infants bring a great deal more with them into the world than Piaget realized. For example, object permanence develops earlier than Piaget thought. Research by Renée Baillargeon and her colleagues (2004, 2014; Baillargeon, Scott, & Bian, 2016) shows that infants as young as 3 to 4 months expect objects to be *substantial* (in the sense that other objects cannot move through them) and *permanent* (in the sense that they continue to exist even when they are hidden).

Another example of a nativist theorist is Elizabeth Spelke (Huang & Spelke, 2014; Spelke, 2011; Spelke, Bernier, & Snedeker, 2013). She endorses a **core knowledge approach**, which states that infants are born with domain-specific knowledge systems. Among these knowledge systems are those involving space, number sense, object permanence, and language (which we will discuss later in this chapter). Strongly influenced by evolution, the core knowledge domains are theorized to be "prewired" to allow infants to make sense of their world (Coubart & others, 2014). After all, Spelke asks, how could infants possibly grasp the complex world in which they live if they did not begin life equipped with core sets of knowledge? In this approach, core knowledge forms a foundation around which

formal operational stage
Piaget's fourth stage of cognitive development, which begins at 11 to 15 years of age and continues through the adult years; it features thinking about things that are not concrete, making predictions, and using logic to come up with hypotheses about the future.

core knowledge approach
A perspective on infant cognitive development that holds that babies are born with domain-specific knowledge systems.

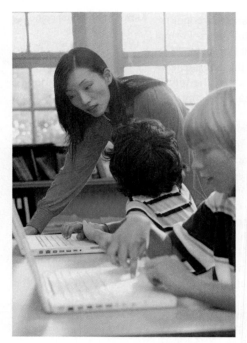

©Deborah Jaffe/Corbis

more mature cognitive functioning and learning develop. The core knowledge perspective argues that Piaget greatly underestimated the cognitive abilities of young infants (Liu & Spelke, 2017; Liu & others, 2017).

A major criticism of the nativist approach is that these scholars focus too much on what happens inside the infant's head apart from the rich social environments in which babies live (Nelson, 2013). Critics point out that even young infants have already accumulated hundreds, and in some cases thousands, of hours of experience in grasping what the world is about, which gives considerable room for the environment's role in the development of infant cognition (Highfield, 2008).

Whether infants bring this knowledge with them into the world, as the nativists believe, or it is acquired through early experience, many researchers conclude that young infants are far more competent than Piaget thought (Baillargeon, Scott, & Bian, 2016; Johnson & Hannon, 2015). Such findings have led many developmental psychologists to assert that we must expand our appreciation for the perceptual and cognitive tools that are available to infants with very little experience (Baillargeon, Scott, & Bian, 2016; Scott & Baillargeon, 2013; Spelke, Bernier, & Snedeker, 2013).

Vygotsky: Cognitive Development in Cultural Context

Piaget did not think that culture and education play important roles in cognitive development. For Piaget, the child's active interaction with the physical world was all that was needed for cognitive development. The Russian psychologist Lev Vygotsky (1962) took a different approach, recognizing that cognitive development is an interpersonal process that happens in a cultural context. Vygotsky emphasized not only the importance of social interaction for learning and developing but also the wider cultural context. For him, talking about development outside that context makes no sense.

Vygotsky thought of children as apprentice thinkers who develop as they interact in dialogue with more knowledgeable others, such as parents and teachers. Vygotsky believed that these expert thinkers spur cognitive development by interacting with a child in a way that is just above the level of sophistication the child has mastered. In effect, these interactions provide *scaffolding* that allows the child's cognitive abilities to be built higher and higher.

Teachers and parents, in other words, provide a framework for thinking that is always just at a level the child can strive to attain. Furthermore, in Vygotsky's view, the goal of cognitive development is to learn the skills that will allow the individual to be competent in his or her particular culture. These expert thinkers are not simply guiding a child into a level of cognitive sophistication, but also, along the way, sharing with the child important aspects of culture, such as language and customs. For Vygotsky, a child is not simply learning to think about the world—he or she is learning to think about *his or her own world*.

Scaffolding is a way of learning that we use throughout life. Whenever we interact with someone who has more expertise, we have a new scaffold to climb.

Information Processing Approach

The information-processing theory of development focuses on basic cognitive processes such as attention, memory, and problem solving (Barrouillet, 2015). For instance, from this perspective, researchers examine how the development of working memory (the mental workspace used for problem solving) relates to other aspects of children's development (Freeman & others, 2017; Gray & others, 2017). Children who have better working memory are more advanced in reading comprehension, math skills, and problem solving than their counterparts with less effective working memory (Friedman & others, 2017; Peng & others, 2016). One study found that students with low working memory were at higher risk of dropping out of high school, even accounting for socioeconomic status and IQ (Fitzpatrick & others, 2015).

Another important aspect of cognitive development is **executive function**. Executive function refers to complex cognitive processes, including thinking, planning, and problem

executive function
Higher-order, complex cognitive processes, including thinking, planning, and problem solving.

solving. For children to be successful in school, they must be able to sit still, wait in line, and so forth. These simple tasks require self-control and the capacity to inhibit one's automatic responses. It is not surprising then that executive function during the preschool years is linked to school readiness (Pellicano & others, 2017). Executive function also predicts the development of social cognitive abilities, including theory of mind: the understanding that other people experience private knowledge and mental states (Devine & others, 2016).

Parents and teachers play important roles in the development of executive function. Parents who model executive function and self-control can serve as scaffolds for these skills (Mazursky-Horowitz & others, 2017). A variety of activities increase children's executive function, such as training to improve working memory (Kirk & others, 2017; Sasser & others, 2017), aerobic exercise (Ishihara & others, 2017), and mindfulness training (Mak & others, 2017). Sometimes very specific cognitive activities, ones that require children to stretch the way they think, can influence executive function. For example, 5-year-olds who were instructed to complete an executive function measure as if they were someone else (for example, Batman) performed better than children without these special instructions (White & others, 2017).

The information processing approach differs from Piaget's classic perspective in that it does not look for qualitative differences across the lifespan. Instead, it examines how people think, using common processes, at every phase of life. From this perspective, we can ask whether children think like adults do for many different topics. Adults might engage in wishful thinking when they are about to take on a difficulty goal: Will that person we find very attractive accept our offer of a date? Will the paper we just handed in earn an A? When we think about questions like these, we might hear a quiet "yes" that tells us to go for it. Do children engage in wishful thinking? To read about research on this question, see the Intersection.

Revisionist Views of Adolescent and Adult Cognition

Researchers have also expanded on Piaget's view of adolescent cognition. In addition to advancing into Piaget's stage of formal operational thinking, another characteristic of adolescent thinking, especially in early adolescence, is *egocentrism*. Adolescent egocentrism involves the belief that others are as preoccupied with the adolescent as he or she is, that one is unique, and that one is invincible (meaning unable to be harmed). Egocentrism at this developmental period is revealed, for example, when an adolescent perceives others to be noticing and watching her or him more than is the case. Think of the teenage boy who cannot be seen at the mall unless his hair is "just so." For him, everyone in the world will be watching when he makes his entrance. Posting pictures on social media that keep one's followers abreast of the minutiae of one's life might also express adolescent egocentrism. The sense of invincibility is the most dangerous aspect of adolescent egocentrism. This belief may lead to behaviors such as drag racing, drug use, and unsafe sex (Aalsma, Lapsley, & Flannery, 2006).

At every age we put our own special stamp on egocentrism. Have you ever noticed that each of your instructors seems to think that his or her class is the only one you're taking?

Piaget underestimated infant cognition but he may have overestimated adolescents' and adults' cognitive achievements. Formal operational thought does not emerge as consistently and universally in early adolescence as Piaget envisioned (Kuhn, 2008), and many adolescents and adults do not reason as logically as Piaget proposed. It may be that even in adulthood, we do not use logical reasoning to make decisions but rather to justify decisions that are the product of the intuitive hunches that characterize cognition in childhood (Mercier & Sperber, 2011).

Finally, developmental psychologists interested in cognition have noted that cognitive changes can occur *after* Piaget's formal operations stage. For Piaget, formal operational thought is the highest level of thinking, and he argued that no new qualitative changes in cognition take place in adulthood. Developmental psychologists, however, in expanding their focus to the entire life span, have tracked the ways that cognitive skills might change throughout adulthood.

Developmental Psychology and Cognitive Psychology: Do Children Engage in Wishful Thinking?

With her eyes shut tight, a 3-year-old makes a wish and blows out her birthday candles. For children, wishing has magical properties: Just making a wish can make it come true (Schneider, 1998).

When children make judgments, do they let their wishes color their thinking? This is a difficult question to answer through research. When predicting outcomes, children often rely on the effort heuristic. This heuristic means that the likelihood of getting what you want is determined by how hard you work (Stipek & Mac Iver, 1989). This heuristic (which is, of course, often true), might lead children to overestimate their performance on tasks, simply because they imagine themselves working very hard. A very clever study examined the question of childhood wishful thinking while avoiding this overestimation problem. Let's take a closer look at the study.

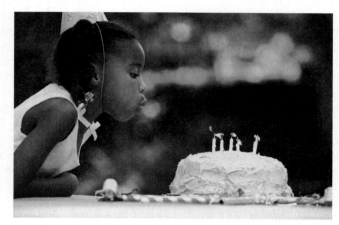

©Terry Vine/ Blend Images/Getty Images

Preschoolers (ages 3 to 5), who participated one at a time, were shown four very fun little toys (such as colorful balloons and magnetic letters) by an experimenter (Bernard, Clément, & Mercier, 2016). The toys were placed in two plastic eggs: three toys in one egg and one in the other. The eggs were closed up. The experimenter then put the eggs in a box, gave them a good shake, and announced that he would close his eyes and pull one egg out. The child's task was to guess whether that egg contained three toys or just one toy. Notice that this task involves no effort at all, just guessing.

The experimenter repeated this procedure over eight trials. For half of the trials, the child was told that the eggs and toys would eventually be put away for another child. For the other half of the

trials, the child was told that he or she could keep whatever toys were found. The key question is whether the children's guesses depended on whether they got to keep the toys. Wishful thinking would be revealed if children guessed that the egg contained three toys more often when they got to keep the toys.

Results showed plenty of wishful thinking: Among the 3- and 4-year-olds especially, the guesses were about 50–50 when the children knew they would not get to keep the toys but were higher (as high as 75 percent) when they knew they would get to keep the toys. Interestingly, 5-year-olds did not share this overly optimistic view. Instead, they showed a naive theory of randomness, assuming that overall the three-toy egg should be found half the time (Bernard, Clément, & Mercier, 2016).

These results suggest that even young children's predictions about the future are colored by what they hope will happen. Wishful thinking seems to be a characteristic of very basic cognitive processes.

Clearly, wishful thinking continues, in varied ways, into adulthood. Of course, wishful thinking can be problematic when it prevents a person from facing challenges head on. Nevertheless, it is interesting to think about how such thinking might be adaptive, for children and adults, allowing us to maintain a sense of optimism about what might be just around the corner.

\\ Even young children's predictions about the future are colored by what they hope will happen. Are yours?

Cognitive Processes in Adulthood

Recall that for Piaget, each stage of cognitive development entails a way of thinking that is *qualitatively different* from the stage before. From Piaget's perspective, meaningful cognitive development ceases after the individual reaches the formal operational stage. Subsequent research has examined not qualitative differences in thinking over time, but the ebb and flow of cognitive abilities as a function of age. What kind of cognitive changes occur in adults?

COGNITION IN EARLY ADULTHOOD Some experts on cognitive development argue that the typical idealism of Piaget's formal operational stage is replaced in young adulthood by more realistic, pragmatic thinking (Labouvie-Vief, 1986). Gisela Labouvie-Vief (2006) proposed that the increasing complexity of cultures in the past century has generated a greater need for reflective, more complex thinking that takes into account the changing nature of knowledge and the kinds of challenges contemporary thinkers face. She emphasizes that key aspects of cognitive development for young adults include deciding on a particular worldview or philosophy of life, recognizing that the worldview is subjective, and understanding that diverse worldviews should be acknowledged. In her perspective, only some individuals attain the highest level of thinking.

COGNITION IN MIDDLE ADULTHOOD
What happens to cognitive skills in middle adulthood? Although some cross-sectional studies indicate that middle adulthood is a time of cognitive decline, longitudinal evidence presents a different picture. K. Warner Schaie is conducting an extensive longitudinal study measuring a host of different intellectual abilities in adults repeatedly, starting in 1956 (Schaie, 1994, 2007, 2010, 2012). The highest level of functioning for four of the six intellectual abilities occurred in middle adulthood (Schaie, 2010, 2012). Only two of the six abilities declined in middle age. Based on the longitudinal data he has collected so far, Schaie concluded that middle adulthood is the period when many people reach their peak for a range of intellectual skills.

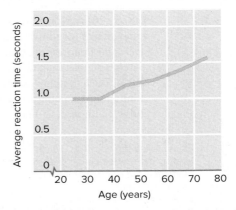

FIGURE 13 **The Relationship between Age and Reaction Time** In one study, the average reaction time slowed in the 40s, and this decline accelerated in the 60s and 70s (Salthouse, 1994). The task used to assess reaction time required individuals to match numbers with symbols on a computer screen.

Source: Salthouse, T. A. (1994). The nature of the influence of speed on adult age differences in cognition. *Developmental Psychology*, 30 (2), 240–259.

> **When is processing fastest? Slowest?** > **When does speed of processing start to slow down?** > **This was a cross-sectional study performed in 1994 using a computerized task. How might cohort effects explain the differences observed?** > **How would a longitudinal study examine this same question?**

COGNITION IN LATE ADULTHOOD
Many contemporary psychologists conclude that some dimensions of intelligence decline in late adulthood, whereas others are maintained or may even increase (Anderson & Craik, 2017; Dixon & others, 2013). One of the most consistent findings is that when the speed of processing information is involved, older adults do not perform as well as their younger counterparts (Figure 13). This decline in speed of processing is apparent in middle-aged adults and becomes more pronounced in older adults (Salthouse, 2012, 2017).

In general, older adults perform more poorly than younger adults in most, but not all, aspects of memory (Brockmole & Logie, 2013). In the area of memory involving knowledge of the world (for instance, the capital of Peru), older adults usually take longer than younger adults to remember the information, but they often are able to retrieve it (Kuo & others, 2014). In the important area of memory in which individuals manipulate and assemble information to solve problems and make decisions, decline occurs in older adults as well (Peich, Husain, & Bays, 2013).

Some aspects of cognition might improve with age. One such area is **wisdom,** expert knowledge about the practical aspects of life (Ferrari & Westrate, 2013; Staudinger & Gluck, 2011). Wisdom may increase with age because of the buildup of life experiences, but individual variations characterize people throughout their lives (Grossman & others, 2010). Thus, not every older person has wisdom, and some young people are wise beyond their years.

Some factors can lessen the decline in cognitive ability among older adults. Training these adults to use specific strategies can enhance their memory, and there is increasing evidence that physical fitness sharpens the thinking skills of

wisdom
Expert knowledge about the practical aspects of life.

In younger individuals wisdom may come at a cost. They might gain wisdom from living through difficult life experiences.

older adults (de Frias & Dixon, 2014; Mayas & others, 2014). When older adults continue to increase their engagement in cognitive and physical activities, they are better able to maintain their cognitive functioning in late adulthood (Park & others, 2014; Rebok & others, 2014). Some software-based cognitive training games have been found to improve older adults' cognitive function (Hertzog & others, 2009; Nouchi & others, 2013). However, and importantly, training does not consistently generalize to other tasks or cognitive outcomes not targeted by the intervention (Guye & von Bastian, 2017; Souders & others, 2017). Indeed, many experts conclude that older adults are less able to adapt than younger adults and thus are limited in how much they can improve their cognitive skills (Finch, 2009; Salthouse, 2012).

1. Of the following activities, which are healthy older adults most likely to perform more poorly compared to younger adults?
   A. Reciting facts about the Civil War.
   B. Reacting as fast as possible to a word presented on a computer screen.
   C. Remember how to perform tasks like tying a shoe.
   D. Remembering the lyrics to a song they know well.

2. Most cognitive skills reach their peak during _____, and most show decline during _____
   A. early adulthood; middle adulthood.
   B. middle adulthood; late adulthood.
   C. adolescence; early adulthood.
   D. adolescence; middle adulthood.

3. Vygotsky stressed that cognitive development is an interpersonal process that happens in a _____ context.
   A. historical
   B. physical
   C. cultural
   D. positive

APPLY IT! 4. Tyrone is babysitting his younger cousins, who are ages 3, 4, and 9. For lunch, each child will be drinking apple juice, which they all love. Tyrone has only three serving cups—one that is short and wide, and two that are tall and thin. Although Tyrone pours the same amount of juice into all the cups, the younger kids fuss and fight over who gets stuck with the short, wide cup. The 9-year-old shrugs and takes the wide cup. Tyrone later proclaims, "Those other two kids are really spoiled brats! Thank goodness the oldest is not so selfish." Which of the following best applies to Tyrone's conclusion?
   A. Tyrone is right—young kids are more likely to be spoiled and whiny.
   B. Tyrone does not understand that the younger kids do not recognize that the amount of juice in the cups is the same. The 9-year-old is not being unselfish; he or she knows the amounts are the same.
   C. The 9-year-old probably does not understand that the wider cup contains the same amount of juice as the other two.
   D. Tyrone probably got an *A* in Developmental Psychology.

4 Socioemotional Development

How do our social and emotional lives change through childhood and adulthood? Recall that *socioemotional processes* involve changes in an individual's social relationships, emotional life, and personal qualities.

Socioemotional Development in Infancy

When we observe the newborns behind the window of a hospital nursery, one thing is clear: Humans differ from one another in terms of their emotional demeanor from the very beginnings of life. Some are easygoing, and some are prone to distress. Furthermore, in the earliest days of life, infants encounter a social network that will play an important role as they develop a sense of self and world. To begin exploring the socioemotional aspects of development, we focus first on the ingredients of emotional and social processes that are present very early in life—infant temperament and attachment (Groh & others, 2017).

temperament
An individual's behavioral style and characteristic way of responding.

TEMPERAMENT **Temperament** refers to an individual's behavioral style and characteristic ways of responding. For infants, temperament centers on their emotionality and ways of reacting to stimuli in the environment. Does the infant look with interest at a new toy, or shy away? Is he or she easily soothed after an upset? Answers to these questions provide information about infant temperament.

There are a number of ways to think about infant temperament. For example, psychiatrists Stella Chess and Alexander Thomas (1977) identified three basic types of temperament in children:

1. The *easy child* generally is in a positive mood, quickly establishes regular routines in infancy, and easily adapts to new experiences.

2. The *difficult child* tends to be fussy and to cry frequently and engages in irregular daily routines.

3. The *slow-to-warm-up child* has a low activity level, tends to withdraw from new situations, and is very cautious in the face of new experiences.

Other researchers have suggested that we should think about infants as being high or low on different dimensions, such as *effortful control* or *self-regulation* (controlling arousal and not being easily agitated), *inhibition* (being shy and showing distress in an unfamiliar situation), and *negative affectivity* (tending to be frustrated or sad) (Kagan, 2013). Regardless of what the precise aspects of temperament might be, the emotional characteristics that a child brings into the world serve as a foundation for later personality (Goodvin, Thompson, & Winer, 2016; Putnam & Gartstein, 2017) and the child's earliest social bonds might set the stage for later social relationships (Groh & others, 2017; Thompson, 2015a).

Culture can influence the meaning of a difficult child. In cultures where women are expected to spend all of their time and energy catering to their children, a "difficult" child might be just the ticket.

ATTACHMENT   Infants need warm social interaction to survive and develop. A classic study by Harry Harlow (1958) demonstrated the essential importance of warm contact. Harlow separated infant monkeys from their mothers at birth and placed them in cages in which they had access to two artificial "mothers." One of the mothers was a physically cold wire mother; the other was a warm, fuzzy cloth mother (the "contact comfort" mother). Each mother could be outfitted with a feeding mechanism. Half of the infant monkeys were fed by the wire mother, half by the cloth mother. The infant monkeys nestled close to the cloth mother and spent little time on the wire one, even if it was the wire mother that gave them milk (Figure 14). When afraid, the infant monkeys ran to the comfy mom. This study clearly demonstrates that what the researchers described as "contact comfort," not feeding, is crucial to the attachment of an infant to its caregiver.

Infant attachment is the close emotional bond between an infant and his or her caregiver. British psychiatrist John Bowlby (1969, 1989) theorized that the infant and the

As skeptical scientists, psychologists needed Harlow to demonstrate that even if the warm, snuggly mother didn't provide food, she was still a source of comfort.

infant attachment
The close emotional bond between an infant and its caregiver.

Fed on cloth mother
Fed on wire mother

Hours per day spent with cloth mother

Hours per day spent with wire mother

Mean hours per day

Days of age

1–5   6–10   11–15   16–20   21–25

FIGURE 14
Contact Time with Wire and Cloth Surrogate Mothers
Regardless of whether the infant monkeys were fed by a wire or a cloth mother, they overwhelmingly preferred to spend contact time with the cloth mother.
©Science Source

mother instinctively form an attachment, just like other animals. In Bowlby's view, the newborn comes into the world equipped to stimulate the caregiver to respond; it cries, clings, smiles, and coos. Bowlby thought that our early relationships with our caregiver are internalized and serve as our schemas for our sense of self and the social world. From Bowlby's perspective, infant experiences set the stage for future relationships, including our romantic relationships as adults. Many developmental psychologists concur that attachment during the first year provides an important foundation for later development (Sroufe, Coffino, & Carlson, 2010).

Mary Ainsworth devised a way to measure children's attachment, called the *strange situation test* (Ainsworth, 1979; Ainsworth & others, 1978). In this procedure, caregivers leave infants alone with a stranger and then return. Responses of children to this situation are used to classify their attachment style. Ainsworth used the term **secure attachment** to describe how infants use the caregiver, usually the mother, as a secure base from which to explore the environment. In the strange situation, the secure infant is upset when the mother leaves but calms down and appears happy to see her when she returns. Infants who are securely attached are more likely to have mothers who are consistent, responsive, and accepting, and who express affection toward them than are infants who are insecurely attached (Leerkes & others, 2017). The securely attached infant moves freely away from the mother but also keeps tabs on her by periodically glancing at her. An insecurely attached infant, in contrast, avoids the mother or is ambivalent toward her. In the strange situation, such an infant might not even notice the mother has gone (sometimes called *avoidant* or *dismissive attachment style*) or conversely might respond with intense distress, only to rage at the mother when she returns (sometimes called *anxious* or *preoccupied attachment style*) (Brownell & others, 2015).

One criticism of attachment theory is that it does not adequately account for cultural variations (Mistry, Contreras, & Dutta, 2013). For example, in some cultures infants show strong attachment to many people, not just to their primary caregiver (Rothbaum & others, 2000, 2007). Infants in agricultural societies tend to form attachments to older siblings who are assigned a major responsibility for younger siblings' care.

Another critique of attachment theory is that it may not account for temperamental differences among infants that might color the attachment relationship (Kagan, 2013). A recent research review demonstrated that although attachment and temperament are linked they are also separable phenomena (Groh & others, 2017). Caregivers and infants likely share genetic characteristics, and it might be that the attachment relationship is really a product of these shared genes. Despite such criticisms there is ample evidence that secure attachment is important to development (Powell & others, 2014; Thompson, 2015a, 2015b; Thompson, Meyer, & McGinley, 2014).

Equipped with the key basic ingredients of temperament and attachment, how does a human being develop in the socioemotional domain? This question was addressed by Erik Erikson, who devised a theory of what he called psychosocial development. Erikson's theory has powerfully guided thinking about how human beings' social and emotional capacities develop throughout the entire life span.

Erikson's Theory of Socioemotional Development

Take a thorough look at Figure 15. The details of Erikson's perspective are important. Think about your own life—what were you doing during these stages?

The life-span development theory of the influential psychologist Erik Erikson (1902–1994), who trained as a psychoanalyst under Sigmund Freud, proposed eight psychosocial stages of development from infancy through late adulthood. In calling the stages *psychosocial*, Erikson meant to emphasize how a person's psychological life is embedded in and shaped by social relationships and challenges faced by the developing person. Figure 15 illustrates all of Erikson's eight stages.

Trust versus Mistrust

Developmental period: Infancy (Birth to 1½ years)

Characteristics: A sense of trust requires a feeling of physical comfort and minimal amount of fear about the future. Infants' basic needs are met by responsive, sensitive caregivers.

Autonomy versus Shame and Doubt

Developmental period: Toddlerhood (1½ to 3 years)

Characteristics: After gaining trust in their caregivers, infants start to discover that they have a will of their own. They assert their sense of autonomy, or independence. They realize their will. If infants are restrained too much or punished too harshly, they are likely to develop a sense of shame and doubt.

Initiative versus Guilt

Developmental period: Early childhood (preschool years, ages 3–5)

Characteristics: As preschool children encounter a widening social world, they are challenged more and need to develop more purposeful behavior to cope with these challenges. Children are now asked to assume more responsibility. Uncomfortable guilt feelings may arise, though, if the children are irresponsible and are made to feel too anxious.

Industry versus Inferiority

Developmental period: Middle and late childhood (elementary school years, 6 years–puberty)

Characteristics: At no other time are children more enthusiastic than at the end of early childhood's period of expansive imagination. As children move into the elementary school years, they direct their energy toward mastering knowledge and intellectual skills. The danger at this stage involves feeling incompetent and unproductive.

Identity versus Identity Confusion

Developmental period: Adolescence (10–20 years)

Characteristics: Individuals are faced with finding out who they are, what they are all about, and where they are going in life. An important dimension is the exploration of alternative solutions to roles. Career exploration is important.

Intimacy versus Isolation

Developmental period: Early adulthood (20s, 30s)

Characteristics: Individuals face the developmental task of forming intimate relationships with others. Erikson described intimacy as finding oneself yet losing oneself in another person.

Generativity versus Stagnation

Developmental period: Middle adulthood (40s, 50s)

Characteristics: A chief concern is to assist the younger generation in developing and leading useful lives.

Integrity versus Despair

Developmental period: Late adulthood (60s–)

Characteristics: Individuals look back and evaluate what they have done with their lives. The retrospective glances can be either positive (integrity) or negative (despair).

FIGURE 15 **Erikson's Eight Stages of Psychosocial Development** Erikson changed the way psychologists think about development by tracing the process of growth over the entire life span.

(first) ©Tari Faris/Getty Images; (second) ©Stock 4B RF/Getty Images; (third) ©Ariel Skelley/DigitalVision/Getty Images; (fourth) ©Ariel Skelley/Blend Images LLC; (fifth) ©Cohen/Ostrow/Photodisc/Getty Images; (sixth) ©Blue Moon Stock/ Alamy Stock Photo; (seventh) ©McGraw-Hill Education/Ken Karp, photographer; (eighth) ©Ryan McVay/Photodisc/Getty Images

Erik Erikson (1902–1994) *Erikson generated one of the most important developmental theories of the twentieth century.*
©Ted Streshinsky/CORBIS/Corbis via Getty Images

From Erikson's (1968) perspective, each stage represents the developmental task that the individual must master at a particular place in the life span. According to Erikson, these developmental tasks are represented by two possible outcomes, such as trust versus mistrust (Erikson's first stage). If an infant's physical and emotional needs are well taken care of, he or she will experience an enduring sense of trust in others. If, however, these needs are frustrated, the person might carry concerns about trust throughout life, with bits of this unfinished business being reflected in the rest of the stages. Erikson described each stage as a turning point with two opposing possible outcomes—one, greater personal competence; the other, greater weakness and vulnerability. Using Erikson's eight stages as a guide, let's consider the ways humans develop in terms of their capacities for interpersonal relationships and emotional well-being.

SOCIOEMOTIONAL DEVELOPMENT IN CHILDHOOD: FROM TRUST TO INDUSTRY The first four of Erikson's eight stages apply to childhood. Each stage is linked with the activities associated with human life at each age:

■ *Trust versus mistrust:* Infancy (birth to 1½ years) is concerned with establishing trust in the social world. At this stage, the helpless infant depends on caregivers to establish a sense that the world is a predictable and friendly place. Without a sense of trust, the child lacks a firm foundation for social relationships.

■ *Autonomy versus shame and guilt:* During toddlerhood (1½ to 3 years), children, many of whom are going through toilet training, experience the beginnings of self-control. When these young children have the opportunity to experience control over their own behaviors, they develop the capacity for independence and confidence. This is the time when young children begin to say "no!" and assert themselves in interactions with others.

■ *Initiative versus guilt:* In early childhood (ages 3 to 5), preschoolers experience what it is like to forge their own interests and friendships and to take on responsibilities. If you have ever spent time with a 3-year-old, you know how often the child wants to help with whatever an adult is doing. When they experience a sense of taking on responsibility, preschoolers develop initiative. Otherwise, according to Erikson, they may feel guilty or anxious.

■ *Industry versus inferiority:* During middle and late childhood (6 years to puberty), children enter school and gain competence in academic skills. Just as the label *industry* would suggest, children find that this is the time to get to work, learn, achieve, and learn to enjoy learning.

From Erikson's perspective, then, children should grow toward greater levels of autonomy and self-confidence as they progress from infancy to school age and beyond. Is there a particular parenting style that is most likely to lead to these sorts of outcomes? Let's find out.

Parenting and Childhood Socioemotional Development Researchers have tried to identify styles of parenting associated with positive developmental outcomes (Smetana, 2017). Diana Baumrind (1991, 1993) described four basic styles of interaction between parents and their children:

authoritarian parenting
A restrictive, punitive parenting style in which the parent exhorts the child to follow the parent's directions and to value hard work and effort.

authoritative parenting
A parenting style that encourages the child to be independent but that still places limits and controls on behavior.

1. **Authoritarian parenting** is a strict punitive style. The authoritarian parent firmly limits and controls the child with little verbal exchange. In a difference of opinion about how to do something, for example, the authoritarian parent might say, "You do it my way or else." Children of authoritarian parents sometimes lack social skills, show poor initiative, and compare themselves with others.

2. **Authoritative parenting** encourages the child to be independent but still places limits and controls on behavior. This parenting style

This is tricky: **Authoritarian** *and* **authoritative** *sound very similar, but they are very different!*

is more collaborative. Extensive verbal give-and-take is allowed, and parents are warm and nurturing toward the child. An authoritative father might put his arm around the child in a comforting way and say, "You know you should not have done that; let's talk about how you can handle the situation better next time." Children of authoritative parents tend to be socially competent, self-reliant, and socially responsible.

3. **Neglectful parenting** is distinguished by a lack of parental involvement in the child's life. Children of neglectful parents might develop a sense that other aspects of the parents' lives are more important than they are. Children whose parents are neglectful tend to be less competent socially, to handle independence poorly, and (especially) to show poor self-control.

4. **Permissive parenting** places few limits on the child's behavior. A permissive parent lets the child do what he or she wants. Some parents deliberately rear their children this way because they believe that the combination of warm involvement and few limits will produce a creative, confident child. However, children with very permissive parents typically rate poorly in social competence. They often fail to learn respect for others, expect to get their own way, and have difficulty controlling their behavior. Recall that socioemotional development means becoming increasingly adept at controlling and regulating one's emotions and behaviors. Children may require structure from their caregivers to acquire these skills.

The Cultural Context of Parenting   Culture influences the effects of parenting on children, especially authoritarian parenting. In one study, mothers from four collectivistic cultures (Iran, India, Egypt, and Pakistan) described themselves as authoritarian but did not express negative attitudes about their children, and the children did not show negative outcomes (Rudy & Grusec, 2006). A large scale cross-cultural meta-analysis found that across cultures and nations, some aspects of authoritative parenting are associated with positive child outcomes and some aspects of authoritarian parenting are associated with negative outcomes (Pinquart & Kauser, 2018). The researchers concluded that, across the globe, parents should be encouraged to adopt the authoritative style.

SOCIOEOMOTIONAL DEVELOPMENT IN ADOLESCENCE: THE EMERGENCE OF IDENTITY
Erikson (1968) viewed the key challenge of adolescence as identity versus identity confusion. In seeking an *identity,* adolescents must find out who they are, what they are all about, and where they are going in life. Adolescents are confronted with many new roles and adult statuses—from the vocational to the romantic. If they do not adequately explore their identities during this stage, they emerge confused about who they are. Adolescents who spend this time in their lives exploring alternatives can reach some resolution of the identity crisis and emerge with a new sense of self. Those who do not successfully resolve the crisis become confused, suffering what Erikson calls *identity confusion*. This confusion is expressed in one of two ways: Either individuals withdraw, isolating themselves from peers and family, or they lose themselves in the crowd.

Marcia's Theory of Identity Status   Building on Erikson's ideas, James Marcia proposed the concept of *identity status* to describe an adolescent's position in the development of an identity (Kroger, Martinussen, & Marcia, 2010; Marcia, 1980, 2002). Marcia described two dimensions, exploration and commitment. *Exploration* refers to a person's investigating various options for a career and for personal values. *Commitment* involves deciding which identity path to follow and personally investing in attaining that identity. Various combinations of exploration and commitment give rise to one of four identity statuses, according to Marcia (Figure 16):

- *Identity diffusion:* The adolescent has neither explored nor committed to an identity. Adolescents experiencing identity diffusion have not confronted the crisis of identity or are so overwhelmed by the challenge of answering the question "Who am I?" that

	Has the person made a commitment?	
	Yes	No
Has the person explored meaningful alternatives regarding some identity question? **Yes**	Identity achievement	Identity moratorium
NO	Identity foreclosure	Identity diffusion

FIGURE 16

Marcia's Four Statuses of Identity Who are you? When you think of how you have come to identify yourself, which of these four statuses does your answer best represent?

they have withdrawn. Eventually, as they engage in life, these adolescents will begin the process of thinking about what matters (and what does not) and enter into the stage of exploration called *moratorium*.

- *Identity moratorium:* The adolescent is actively exploring and trying on new roles but has not committed to a particular identity. For example, consider an adolescent who passionately throws himself into a variety of internship opportunities to see what different jobs might be like.

- *Identity foreclosure:* The adolescent has committed to a particular identity but has done so without actually exploring his or her options. An example is a girl who decides to pursue accounting as a major in college because everyone in her family is an accountant.

- *Identity achievement:* After exploring the options and committing to an identity, the adolescent emerges with a sense of his or her own values and principles, a sense of the kind of person he or she wishes to be, and goal commitments that provide his or her life with a feeling of purpose.

Let's consider an example to illustrate Marcia's theory. Four teenagers, Mary, Tyron, Jennifer, and Hank, attend a summer camp for future engineers. Because they are all at the same camp, we might think they all identify with the idea of becoming an engineer. But they may differ in how much they have explored their identities or committed to this identity. For example, last summer, Mary attended a camp for future medical professionals; the following school year she interned at a law firm. She is still exploring her options. She has not committed to being an engineer and is therefore in *identity moratorium*. In contrast, Tyron has also deeply considered many different careers, imagining himself as a news reporter, a surgeon, and an engineer. He has shadowed different professionals in their jobs. Ultimately, he is excited about an engineering career. Tyron would be in *identity achievement*. The key difference between moratorium and achievement is that in moratorium the person is still exploring. Now, neither Jennifer nor Hank has explored their options. Jennifer wants to be an engineer because her parents are engineers. She never really considered alternative paths. Jennifer occupies *identity foreclosure*. Finally, Hank is attending the camp because his parents are hoping it sparks an interest in him to start thinking about the future. Hank has neither explored nor committed to an identity and is therefore in *identity diffusion*. Note that Jennifer and Hank are similarly lacking in exploration but Jennifer is highly committed to the engineer identity.

Ethnic Identity within a Larger Culture Developing an identity in adolescence can be especially challenging for individuals from ethnic minority groups (Brittian Loyd & Williams, 2017; González & others, 2017; White & others, 2017; Yoon & others, 2017). As they mature, many adolescents become acutely aware of the evaluation of their ethnic group by the majority culture. In addition, an increasing number of minority adolescents face the challenge of *biculturalism*—identifying in some ways with their ethnic minority group and in other ways with the majority culture (Basilio & others, 2014; Knight & others, 2014).

For ethnic minority youth, feeling both a positive attachment to their minority group and an attachment to the larger culture is related to more positive academic and emotional outcomes (Rivas-Drake & others, 2014; Williams & others, 2014). Although it might seem that being a member of an ethnic minority would make life more stressful, having a strong ethnic identity can buffer adolescents from the effects of discrimination (Douglass & Umaña-Taylor, 2017). For both minority and majority adolescents, developing a positive identity is an important life theme (Azmitia, Syed, & Radmacher, 2013; Schwartz, Vignoles, Brown, & Zagefka, 2014). In addition to ethnic identity, adolescence can be a time when other aspects of one's identity come to the fore, such as sexual orientation or gender identity

(Eisenberg & others, 2017). Sexual and gender minority youth may face high levels of bullying and other social challenges (Earnshaw & others, 2017). For these individuals developing a positive view of sexual orientation or gender minority identity also predicts better outcomes (Hall, 2017) as does an accepting, supportive family, school, and community environment (Bouris & Hill, 2017; Romijnders & others, 2017).

Parents and Peers Parents and peers can help the adolescent answer the central questions of identity, "Who am I, and who do I hope to become?" To help adolescents reach their full potential, a key parental role is to be an effective manager—one who locates information, makes contacts, helps to structure offsprings' choices, and provides guidance. By assuming this managerial role, parents help adolescents to avoid pitfalls and to work their way through the decisions they face (Van Petegem & others, 2017; Wang & others, 2014; Yap & others, 2014).

For parents to play an active role in the development of their sons and daughters, they have to know what is going on in their adolescent's life. Research on adolescents' management of their parents' access to information, especially disclosing or concealing strategies about their activities, shows that adolescents are more willing to disclose information to parents when parents ask teenagers questions and when the parent–child relationship is characterized by a high level of trust and acceptance (McElvaney, Greene, & Hogan, 2014; Smetana, 2011a, 2011b).

During adolescence, individuals spend more time with peers than they did in childhood. Peer influences can be positive or negative. A significant aspect of positive peer relations is having one or more close friends. Adolescents can learn to be skilled and sensitive partners in intimate relationships by forging close friendships with peers (Hoorn, Crone, & Liejenhorst, 2017). However, some friends can negatively impact adolescents' development (Ray & others, 2017). Hanging out with delinquent peers in adolescence can be a strong predictor of substance abuse, delinquent behavior, and depression (Pinquart, 2017).

If you could travel back in time and visit your adolescent self, what would you tell him or her?

For Erikson, once the issues of identity have been resolved, the young adult turns to the important domain of intimate relationships. However, contemporary scholars note that many young people seem to be putting off the kinds of commitments to marriage, family, and career that we associate with adult life. Jeffrey Arnett (2006, 2007, 2010, 2012) introduced the concept of emerging adulthood to describe this transitional period that is partly an extended adolescence and partly a phase of experimenting with adult roles. If you are a traditional-age college student, you are at this point in the life span. Let's briefly examine socioemotional development in this life stage.

SOCIOEMOTIONAL DEVELOPMENT IN EMERGING ADULTHOOD

emerging adulthood
The transitional period from adolescence to adulthood, spanning approximately 18 to 25 years of age.

Emerging adulthood is the transitional period from adolescence to adulthood (Arnett, 2006, 2007, 2012, 2014; Arnett & Fischel, 2013). The age range for emerging adulthood is approximately 18 to 25 years of age. Experimentation and exploration characterize the emerging adult. Many emerging adults are still investigating their career path, their identity, and the kinds of close relationships they will have.

Jeffrey Arnett (2006, 2010) identified five main features of emerging adulthood:

Some people enter adulthood earlier than others. Some marry, start a family, and take up full-time employment right out of high school. Do you think these individuals experience "emerging adulthood"?

- *Identity exploration, especially in love and work:* Emerging adulthood is the time of significant changes in identity for many individuals.
- *Instability:* Residential changes peak during emerging adulthood, a time during which there also is often instability in love, work, and education.
- *Self-focus:* Emerging adults "are self-focused in the sense that they have little in the way of social obligations, little in the way of duties and commitments to others, which leaves them with a great deal of autonomy in running their own lives" (Arnett, 2006, p. 10).

- *Feeling "in between":* Many emerging adults consider themselves neither adolescents nor full-fledged adults.

- *The age of possibilities, a time when individuals have an opportunity to transform their lives:* Arnett (2006) describes two ways in which emerging adulthood is the age of possibilities: (1) Many emerging adults are optimistic about their future, and (2) for emerging adults who have experienced difficult times while growing up, emerging adulthood presents an opportunity to guide their lives in a more positive direction.

Emerging adults have more choices—and more control over those choices—in their daily life. The choices they make with regard to their life goals have implications for their later well-being (Hill & others, 2011), suggesting that this time of life sets the stage for later development. Eventually, though perhaps later than previous generations, emerging adults adopt the mantle of adulthood. According to Erikson, the early part of adulthood is occupied with the experience of loving, intimate relationships.

SOCIOEMOTIONAL DEVELOPMENT IN EARLY ADULTHOOD: INTIMACY VERSUS ISOLATION

The sixth of Erikson's (1968) eight stages, *intimacy versus isolation,* refers to the challenge of forming intimate relationships with others or becoming socially isolated. Erikson describes intimacy as both finding oneself and losing oneself in another. If the young adult develops healthy friendships and an intimate relationship with a partner, intimacy will likely be achieved. One key way that young adults achieve intimacy is through long-term relationships with a romantic partner, often including marriage.

Marriage and Families

A striking change in social attitudes in recent decades has been the decreased stigma attached to individuals who do not maintain what were long-considered conventional families. Adults today choose many different ways of living and form many types of families. They live alone, live with a partner, marry or divorce. Contemporary families are sometimes blends of families from previous relationships. Sometimes the couples that head households are the same sex.

©Purestock/SuperStock

Cohabitation refers to living together in a sexual relationship without being married, and there has been a dramatic increase in the number of cohabiting U.S. couples since 1970. The trend shows no sign of letting up. In 2016, 18 million Americans were cohabiting with a partner compared to just 7.5 million in 2010 (U.S. Census Bureau, 2017a). Interestingly, cohabitation appears to be especially on the rise among divorced Americans aged 50 and older, who saw a 75 percent increase in cohabitation rates.

With regard to marriage, contemporary women are waiting much longer to marry. For example, in 1980, the average age for a first marriage in the United States was 24.7 for men and 22.0 for women, but in 2017, the average age for a first marriage in the United States had climbed to 29.5 years for men and 27.4 years for women (U.S. Census Bureau, 2017b).

What makes a successful marriage? John Gottman has been studying married couples' lives since the early 1970s. He interviews couples, films them interacting with each other, and even measures their heart rate and blood pressure during their interactions (Gottman, Swanson, & Swanson, 2002; Madhyastha, Hamaker, & Gottman, 2011). He also checks back with the couples every year to see how their marriages are faring. He and his colleagues continue to follow married heterosexual couples, as well as same-sex partners, to try to understand what makes relationships successful. Gottman (2006) has found these four principles at work in successful marriages:

1. *Nurturing fondness and admiration:* Partners sing each other's praises. When couples put a positive spin on their talk with and about each other, the marriage tends to work.

2. *Turning toward each other as friends:* Partners see each other as friends and turn toward each other for support in times of stress and difficulty.

3. *Giving up some power:* Bad marriages often involve one partner who is a powermonger. This is more common in husbands, but some wives have the problem as well.

4. *Solving conflicts together:* Couples work to solve problems, regulate their emotion during times of conflict, and compromise to accommodate each other.

SOCIOEMOTIONAL DEVELOPMENT IN MIDDLE ADULTHOOD: GENERATIVITY VERSUS STAGNATION

Erikson's seventh stage, *generativity versus stagnation,* occurs in middle adulthood. Generativity means creating something of value that will benefit future generations. A generative person feels that he or she has left a lasting legacy and helped the next generation in important ways. This feeling that one has made a lasting and memorable contribution to the world is related to higher levels of psychological well-being (Ko & others, 2016; Serrat & others, 2017). The feeling of having done nothing of value for future generations is stagnation. Although Erikson did not think that parenting alone was a guarantee of generativity, he did believe that parenting could be a way to experience this important developmental accomplishment. Midlife adults can also experience generativity through mentoring, volunteering, and political activism.

SOCIOEMOTIONAL DEVELOPMENT AND AGING: INTEGRITY VERSUS DESPAIR

From Erikson's perspective, the person who has entered life's later years is engaged in looking back—evaluating his or her life, seeking meaning, and coming to terms with death. Erikson called this eighth and final stage *integrity versus despair.* If the individual experiences life as a meaningful and coherent whole, he or she faces the later years with a strong sense of meaning and low fear of death. In the absence of integrity, the older adult is filled with despair and fear (Westerhof, Bohlmeijer, & McAdams, 2017). Current research on socioemotional development and aging reveals that Erikson was correct in his view that meaning is a central concern for older adults. However, he may have overlooked that this meaning derives not necessarily from the past but also from the present.

In terms of social relationships, older adults become more selective about their social networks. At the same time, older adults report higher levels of happiness than their younger counterparts (Carstensen & others, 2011; Stanley & Isaacowitz, 2011). Laura Carstensen developed *socioemotional selectivity theory* to explain the narrowing of social contacts and the increase in positive emotion that occur with age (Carstensen, 2006; Carstensen & others, 2011; English & Carstensen, 2014). The theory states that because they recognize their limited time on earth, older adults tend to be selective in their social interactions, striving to maximize positive and meaningful experiences. Although younger adults may gain a sense of meaning in life from long-term goals, older adults derive meaning from satisfying relationships and activities in the *present.* Unlike younger adults, who may be preoccupied with the future, older adults may embrace the present moment with increasing vitality (Hicks & others, 2012; Kotter-Grühn & Smith, 2011; Lachman & others, 2008). Socioemotional selectivity theory posits that it is not age itself but rather limited time that leads adults to focus on the present. Young adults who are asked to imagine having limited time show the same pattern of maximizing positive meaning in the present.

Just as physical changes can influence socioemotional experience, socioemotional factors can influence physical health. In one study, adults who had expressed positive attitudes about aging some 20 years previously, lived, on average, 7.5 years longer than those with more negative attitudes about aging (Levy & others, 2002). An important factor in the link between attitudes and longevity was a person's belief that life is full, hopeful, and worthwhile.

If you were about to take a yearlong trip, how, and with whom, would you choose to spend your last two weeks at home?

EVALUATING ERIKSON'S THEORY

Using Erikson's framework, we have followed the active developer from the early accomplishment of trust in the social world through to his or her capacity to experience a strong sense of meaning in a life well lived. Erikson's perspective has a number of strengths. He was the first to emphasize that development is a lifelong process and does not stop with childhood. He also developed important ideas about the central themes that often occupy human life at various ages. However, Erikson's conclusions have had their critics. First, Erikson mainly practiced case study research and based his ideas on the lives of single individuals not large scale studies of representative samples. Second, because Erikson tried to capture each stage with a single theme (such as intimacy vs. isolation), Erikson left out other important developmental tasks that might occur in various stages. For example, Erikson said that the main task for young adults is to resolve the conflict between intimacy and isolation. However, another significant developmental task in early adulthood involves careers and work. Erikson's approach did not anticipate the kind of identity exploration that currently continues to occur in emerging adulthood. Despite these criticisms, Erikson is a giant in developmental psychology.

1. All of the following are examples of generativity *except*
   A. teaching the English language to recent U.S. immigrants.
   B. successfully investing one's earnings and enjoying a satisfying retirement.
   C. volunteering at a homeless shelter.
   D. acting as a scout leader.

2. Recent studies on socioemotional development and aging indicate that
   A. older adults put a great deal of stock in life's meaning.
   B. older adults may be more selective in their social interactions than younger adults.
   C. older adults are happier than their younger counterparts.
   D. all of the above

3. With regard to ethnic identity, psychological research indicates that
   A. adolescents who downplay the importance of their ethnic identity do better in school.

   B. adolescents use their ethnic identity to avoid developmental tasks.
   C. adolescents who have a strong ethnic identity are better able to cope with stress.
   D. adolescents from different racial groups face the same challenges to their ethnic identity.

APPLY IT! 4. Rosemary's Grandpa Jack is 80 years old and wears a hearing aid and glasses, and he has always been very active. He and Rosemary's grandmother spend a great deal of time with their children and grandchildren, and both laugh a lot and seem genuinely to enjoy life. Grandpa Jack recently resigned his position as a member of the local senior citizen's council. He tells Rosemary that the council had become a hassle. Rosemary wonders whether this decision is normal and reasonable or whether her granddad is feeling depressed. Based on your reading of this example and this chapter, should Rosemary be worried?
   A. Rosemary should be worried because it appears that Grandpa Jack is withdrawing from opportunities for generativity.
   B. Rosemary should be worried because Grandpa Jack should stay involved in community activities given that such involvement is related to being happier and healthier.
   C. Rosemary should probably not be worried. Grandpa Jack just sounds as if he is going through what most people do when they are faced with limited time: maximizing meaningful social contacts.
   D. Rosemary should not be worried because Grandpa Jack has completed Erikson's stages, and it makes sense that he is probably preparing for death by withdrawing from the world.

5 Gender Development

gender
The social and psychological aspects of being female or male.

gender identity
A person's inner concept of themselves in relation to the ideas of being male, female, both, or neither.

sexual orientation
The direction of an individual's erotic interests, today viewed as a continuum from exclusive male–female relations to exclusive same-sex relations.

So far, we have explored development across the human life span in the physical, cognitive, and socioemotional domains. In this section, we examine an important aspect of the human experience—gender development—that illustrates the links across the various domains of development. Understanding the development of gender requires attention to all three life domains—physical (or biological), cognitive, and socioemotional.

Gender refers to the social and psychological aspects of being male or female. The development of gender is a complex process that includes biological, cognitive, and socioemotional factors. Gender is not simply biological sex. Gender is a person's understanding of the meaning of gender in their life, their gender identity and gender expression. **Gender identity** is a person's inner concept of themselves in relation to the ideas of being male, female, both, or neither (Krieger, 2017). Gender identity can be the same or different from the sex one is assigned at birth and can be thought of as a continuum from female to male. Gender identity is distinct from **sexual orientation** (which we will review in the Personality Chapter). It is also separable from *gender expression,* the ways people present themselves through their appearance, including hairstyle, clothing choices, voice, and behavior.

Human Identities and the Changing Gender Landscape

Contemporary society has witnessed the emergence of many gender identities. Many of these identities have a long history in human experience but have only recently entered the mainstream conversation. In some ways, the science of gender has scarcely been able to keep up with the gender statuses people now occupy—*Facebook* currently offers more than 50 gender options for its user profiles. Let's review two of these, transgender and non-binary identities.

Transgender refers to experiencing one's psychological gender (and gender expression) as different from one's biological or "natal" (meaning "at birth") sex. It's opposite is "cisgender," which refers to individuals who experience a match among their experienced, expressed, and natal gender. Over 1 million Americans identify as transgender (Peachman,

©GotoCuisinette/iStock/Getty

2017), and increasingly these individuals include youth (Krieger, 2017). For example, by the age of 4, Ellie Ford (whose natal sex was male) demonstrated to her parents in many ways that she was a girl. At a princess themed birthday party, she told her mother, "Mom, I'm not a boy; I'm a girl in my heart and mind" (Peachman, 2017). Youth who identify as transgender have more options than in the past. Medications to delay puberty can provide a "time-out" from sexual development, preventing the permanent bodily changes spurred by puberty (Liebowitz & de Vries, 2016). Gender-affirming surgery is a treatment pursued by some adults, but many transgender individuals do not desire surgery (Bockting & others, 2016). Some opt for hormone treatment only or no treatment. For some individuals, being transgender means living according to the belief that a person can be a man who happens to have a vagina or a woman who has a penis—as an individual who occupies a different but valid gender territory.

Non-binary gender identities include identification as a blend of both male and female or as neither male nor female. Individuals who identify as non-binary may refer to themselves with various labels including *genderqueer, genderfluid, transmasculine or transfeminine,* or *third gender* (Krieger, 2017). It is not uncommon for non-binary individuals to choose gender neutral names and to choose, explicitly, the pronouns by which they prefer to be called ("they" and "them"). These changes can be difficult for friends and family to accommodate but they are expressions of the person's innermost self. To be *mis-gendered* can be quite hurtful (Frohard-Dourlent & others, 2017).

The changing gender landscape has inspired many different reactions, ranging from warm acceptance to outrage (Peachman, 2017). However, controversies over restrooms should not cloud the fact that people who are different from typical are no less valuable. Learning new ways to understand the experience of others can be challenging but it is important keep in mind that for many people, labels like "transgender" or "non-binary" reflect life-changing discoveries: A name for a feeling and longing that before had no description.

Biology and Gender Development

Humans typically have 46 chromosomes arranged in pairs. The 23rd pair may have an X-shape (made by two X chromosomes) or it may look like an upside down Y (one X and one Y chromosome). The XX pair produces a female and the XY pair produces a male.

In the first few weeks after conception, male and female embryos look alike. When the Y chromosome triggers the secretion of *androgens,* the main class of male sex hormones, male sex organs start to differentiate from female sex organs. Low androgen levels in a female embryo allow for the typical development of female sex organs.

This is why biological males are more likely to show characteristics like color blindness that are linked to the X chromosome. Biological females have a backup X chromosome.

Research on very young infants suggests the roles of genes and prenatal hormones in producing differences between the sexes (Hines, 2013). For example, one study examined 1-day-old male and female infants. The infants were shown two stimuli: a human face and a mobile made from a picture of that face (Connellan & others, 2000). The researchers found that the baby girls spent more time looking at the human face, while the baby boys were more interested in the mobile. Research on infants from 3 to 8 months of age found that boys spent more time looking at typical boy toys, including trucks, and girls spent more time looking at typical girl toys, such as dolls (Alexander, Wilcox, & Woods, 2009). Small but consistent differences in infant toy preferences have been reported in a number of studies (Todd & others, 2018). More recent research has shown that these gender-based preferences in the first year of life predict such preferences by the age of 4 (Lauer, Ilksoy, & Lourenco, 2018). Such differences are thought to be biologically, not socially, based because very young infants have not yet had social experiences that might influence gender development. In addition, similar differences have been reported in nonhuman primates (Lonsford, 2017). Biological differences, though, do not tell the whole story of gender development.

Cognitive Aspects of Gender Development

Recall from Piaget's theory that a schema is a mental framework that organizes and guides an individual's thoughts. A *gender schema* is a mental framework for understanding what it means to be male or female in one's culture. Through experience, children learn that gender is an important organizing principle in social life, and they come to recognize that boys and girls, and men and women, are different in ways that matter. This gender schema then serves as a cognitive framework by which children interpret further experiences related to gender.

Because of where they are in cognitive development, very young children may believe that a person's sex can change depending on superficial features. They may reason that girls have long hair, and so if that hair is cut short, a girl becomes a boy.

How do gender schemas develop? Theorists suggest that children acquire these schemas through learning in the social world (Bandura & Bussey, 2004). Such learning occurs through processes, including reinforcement and punishment, observational learning, and modeling (Bandura & Bussey, 2004).

In subtle ways, children may be rewarded (or punished) for behavior depending on whether the behavior conforms to expectations for their sex. The child's social environment responds to behaviors in various ways, coloring his or her perception of their appropriateness. A girl might learn that pretending to be a

Children learn about gender differences through experience—by observing the activities and behavior of others.
©LightField Studios/Shutterstock

professional football player is not a way to please her parents. A boy might pick up on his mother's subtle frown when he announces that he wants to try on her high-heeled shoes. Interestingly research has shown that the small gender difference in toy preferences grows with age and is most stark when children are being observed in a lab (rather than playing at home) (Todd & others, 2018). Such results suggest the pressure children feel as they age to conform to gender norms especially when they feel they are being watched.

According to Albert Bandura (1986), modeling is an especially potent mechanism for transmitting values. Children gain information about gender from models of each sex. Who goes to work every day? Who does the housekeeping? When children see their parents and other adults engaging in gender-related behavior (and as they observe whether and how these behaviors are reinforced), they learn about how men and women behave.

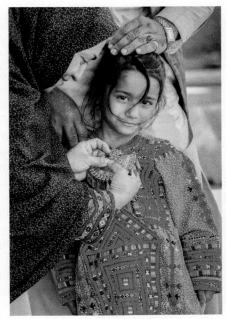

In Iran, legal and cultural beliefs about women's and men's respective roles in the family and society have roots in religious tradition. Despite some change, traditional gender roles widely persist in the Islamic republic.
©Delbars/Shutterstock

Socioemotional Experience and Gender Development

Social experiences clearly influence gender development. After all, behaviors are rewarded or punished by other people in the child's world (Liben, Bigler, & Hilliard, 2014). In addition to parents, peers also play an important role in gender development. Especially between the ages of 6 and 11, peer groups often segregate into boy groups and girl groups (Maccoby, 2002). Peers are stricter than most parents in rewarding behavior that conforms to gender rules and in punishing behavior that violates those rules. For example, children can be punitive toward boys who engage in behaviors that are not typically boyish (Wallien & others, 2010). As children grow up, they adopt **gender roles,** which involve expectations for how females and males should think, act, and feel (Eagly, 2009, 2012). These gender roles represent beliefs about appropriate behavior for the sexes.

Again we see how cognitive development matters. At this age, kids are in Piaget's concrete operations stage, associated with putting things (and people) in categories.

gender roles
Roles that reflect the individual's expectations for how females and males should think, act, and feel.

Culture plays a vital role in the content of gender roles (Koenig & others, 2011; Mistry, Contreras, & Dutta, 2013). Some cultures emphasize that children should be reared to adopt traditional gender roles. Parents in these cultures bring up boys to be powerful, aggressive, and independent and girls to be sensitive to others, good at relationships, and less assertive. Other cultures emphasize rearing boys and girls to be more similar—raising boys to be just as caring toward others as girls and raising girls to be just as assertive as boys. Iran and China are two countries in which traditional gender roles continue to dominate, but the United States has moved toward more diversity in gender roles.

While acknowledging biological differences between males and females, many psychologists believe that social and cultural factors have a much stronger influence on eventual gender identity (Bandura & Bussey, 2004; Eagly & Wood, 2011, 2012). From this perspective, differences in men's and women's career and life choices can be explained by differences in the availability of role models and beliefs about self-efficacy and personal control in these roles. Janet Shibley Hyde (2005, 2007, 2014), an expert on the psychology of gender, has periodically reviewed studies of gender differences in a wide range of characteristics. She has found that where differences do emerge, they are quite small. Overall, Hyde has found strong support for what she calls the **gender similarities hypothesis**—the idea that men and women (and boys and girls) are much more similar than they are different (Hyde, 2005, 2007, 2014).

The gender differences we see in terms of pursuing math and science careers are not about differences in ability. Rather, they appear to be about the kinds of beliefs, expectations, and role models males and females have about these careers.

gender similarities hypothesis
Hyde's proposition that men and women (and boys and girls) are much more similar than they are different.

Nature and Nurture Revisited: The John/Joan Case

Although it seems clear that gender emerges as a function of a variety of intermingling processes, some have debated whether one of these processes is more important than the others. John Money, a well-known sex researcher, believed strongly that socialization was the main determinant of gender. In the 1960s, a case presented itself that gave Money the opportunity to test this theory. In 1965 twin boys were born, and a few months after birth, one twin's penis was destroyed during circumcision. Money persuaded the boy's parents to allow him to surgically transform the injured male genitals into female genitals and to agree to treat the child as a girl. The former boy was reared as a girl and, according to Money, essentially became a girl (Money & Tucker, 1975). The John/Joan case became famous as an example of nurture's triumph over nature. For many years, this case was used as evidence for the amazing flexibility of gender.

Milton Diamond, a biologist and strong critic of Money's theory, followed up on Money's most famous case (Diamond & Sigmundson, 1997). Diamond found that over time, "Joan" became less and less interested in being a girl and eventually refused to continue the process of feminization that Money had devised. We now know that "Joan" was really David Reimer, whose biography, *As Nature Made Him,* written by John Colapinto (2000), revealed the difficulties of his life as a boy, then a girl, then a boy, and finally a man. David struggled with traumatic gender-related life experiences and depression, eventually committing suicide in 2004. The John/Joan case of gender development illuminates the complex ways in which the physical, cognitive, and socioemotional domains of development intersect and influence one another.

Though David's story seems to indicate that biological factors powerfully guide gender development, remember that it is difficult to make generalizations based on a single case study. Other similar cases have had more positive outcomes.

self-quiz

1. Among other factors, the development of gender involves
   A. personality factors.
   B. cognitive factors.
   C. sensory factors.
   D. all of the above

2. The term for a cognitive framework for understanding what it means to be male or female in a given culture is
   A. gender role.
   B. gender identity.
   C. gender diversity.
   D. gender schema.

3. Childhood peer groups
   A. are not concerned with rewarding and punishing gender-related behavior in members of the group.
   B. play a key role in a person's gender development.

   C. typically are mixed, including both males and females.
   D. none of the above

APPLY IT! 4. When Jerry announces he's planning to major in mechanical engineering, his proud parents are not surprised. They tell their friends, "We *knew* he was destined to be interested in mechanical things. Even as a tiny infant he loved mechanical toys and never gave his stuffed animals a second look! He's always been our little engineer." What does research on the psychology of gender development have to say about Jerry's parents' conclusion?
   A. Jerry may have always been their little engineer, but their comments to friends suggest that Jerry was not very different from most baby boys.

   B. Jerry's parents' observations are supported by research showing that very early interest in mechanical toys predicts later career decisions in both males and females.
   C. Jerry's parents' observations cannot be true, because very young infants cannot tell the difference between mechanical toys and stuffed animals.
   D. Jerry's parents are probably biased by cultural beliefs, and so they remember his behavior in infancy fitting their preexisting beliefs about gender roles.

6 Moral Development

Moral development involves changes that occur with age in people's thoughts, feelings, and behaviors regarding the principles and values that guide them as they interact with others (Walker, 2014a, 2014b). Much research on moral reasoning and thinking has revolved around Lawrence Kohlberg's theory of moral development.

Kohlberg's Theory

Kohlberg (1958) began his study of moral thinking by asking children, adolescents, and adults questions about a series of stories. One of the stories goes something like this. A man, Heinz, whose wife is dying of cancer, knows about a drug that might save her life. He approaches the pharmacist who has the drug, but the pharmacist refuses to give it to him without being paid a very high price. Heinz is unable to scrape together the money and decides to steal the drug.

Lawrence Kohlberg (1927–1987)
Kohlberg created a provocative theory of moral development. In his view, "Moral development consists of a sequence of qualitative changes in the way an individual thinks."
©Lee Lockwood/The LIFE Images Collection/Getty Images

After reading the story, the interviewee was asked questions about the moral dilemma. Should Heinz have stolen the drug? Kohlberg was less interested in the answer to this question than he was to the response to the next one: Why? Based on the reasons people gave for their answers, Kohlberg (1986) evaluated their level of moral development. Kohlberg's stages of moral development consisted of three broad levels, which include

How would you answer Kohlberg's question?

1. *Preconventional:* The individual's moral reasoning is based primarily on the consequences of a behavior and on punishments and rewards from the external world. Reasoning is guided by not wanting Heinz to go to jail or by concern for the pharmacist's profits. A child who reasons that he should not steal the drug because someone might get mad would occupy this stage.

2. *Conventional:* The individual abides by standards learned from parents or society's laws. At this level the person might reason that Heinz should act in accord with expectations or his role as a good husband or should follow the law no matter what. Here, someone who reasoned that Heinz should not steal the drug because stealing is against the law would occupy this stage.

3. *Postconventional:* The individual recognizes alternative moral courses, explores the options, and then develops an increasingly personal moral code. At this level, the person might reason that Heinz's wife's life is more important than a law. When a person is able to think deeply and reason beyond consequences or external codes (such as laws), that person is reasoning at the postconventional level.

Kohlberg studied with Piaget and his approach to moral reasoning emphasized the ability to think in sophisticated ways. For Kohlberg, a sense of justice was at the heart of moral reasoning, which he believed laid the foundation for moral behavior.

Critics of Kohlberg

A criticism of Kohlberg is that his view does not adequately reflect concern for other people and social bonds (Ball & others, 2017; Killen & Smetana, 2014). Kohlberg's theory is called a *justice perspective* because it emphasizes the rights of the individual as the key to sound moral reasoning. In contrast, the *care perspective*, which is at the core of Carol Gilligan's (1982) approach to moral development, views people in terms of their connectedness with others and stresses interpersonal communication, relationships, and concern for others. From Gilligan's perspective this weakness in Kohlberg's approach explains why, using his measures, women generally score lower than men on moral development.

Similarly, Kohlberg neglected the influence of culture on morality. Because of its central role in how we relate to each other, culture influences the ways

Carol Gilligan (b. 1936) *Gilligan argues that Kohlberg's approach does not give adequate attention to relationships. In Gilligan's view, "Many girls seem to fear, most of all, being alone—without friends, family, and relationships."*
©Frazer Harrison/Getty Images

individuals navigate moral dilemmas (Gibbs, 2014). Current research on moral judgment shows that moral decisions are influenced by many different cultural values; it is not limited to care versus justice (Graham & others, 2011; Rai & Fiske, 2011). For instance, modern moral psychologists include not only care and justice but liberty, loyalty, and purity as important dimensions of moral reasoning.

You might have noticed a particular limitation of Kohlberg's emphasis on cognitive reasoning—that a person can know the right thing to do and yet might act in an immoral way (Hardy & Carlo, 2011). Contemporary research on moral development focuses on behavior that reflects moral goodness and on the socioemotional factors associated with this behavior.

Moral Development in a Socioemotional Context

prosocial behavior
Behavior that is intended to benefit other people.

Researchers interested in moral development have increasingly focused on the factors that predict **prosocial behavior,** behavior that is intended to benefit other people (Dovidio & others, 2017). Research has examined how attachment (Gross & others, 2017), cognitive abilities (O'Toole, Monks, & Tsermentseli, 2017), and brain reactivity (Decety, Meidenbauer, & Cowell, 2017) predict acts of kindness in children. Warm, empathic parenting is associated with children's prosocial behavior (Michalik & others, 2007), while rejecting and harsh parenting is linked to lower prosocial behavior and moral disengagement (Hyde, Shaw, & Moilanen, 2010). Childhood characteristics are important because longitudinal research shows that kind, moral children are more likely to be kind, moral adults (Eisenberg & Spinrad, 2014).

Other modern research on moral development has focused on when a child first shows signs of possessing a conscience (Scrimgeour, Mariotti, & Blandon, 2017). Having a conscience means hearing that voice in our head that tells us that something is morally good or bad. What sorts of experiences give rise to this inner voice? Researchers have examined the conversations toddlers have with their mothers to identify features of those interactions associated with moral development. Clear and elaborate parent–child interactions that are rich with emotional content and that include shared positive emotion foster conscience development (Laible & Karahuta, 2014).

You have likely heard the phrase, "Children can be cruel." This statement is often made after children have been unkind to a classmate or have said something inappropriate and hurtful (without, perhaps, being aware of its hurtfulness). Yet, anyone who has spent time with a 3-year-old knows that "Can I help?" is often the first thing out of a child's mouth when a project is underway, whether it is baking cookies or cleaning the house (Pettygrove & others, 2013). Helping emerges early in human life. In a recent study, 18- and 30-month-olds were given 2 chances to help an adult in need. The majority of 18-month-olds and nearly all of the 30-month-olds helped on at least one task (Waugh & Brownell, 2017). A large body of evidence supports the idea that in the first 2 years of life, children experience empathy for people in need, begin to understand the principle of fairness, and show the ability to behave prosocially (Hammond & others, 2017; Newton, Thompson, & Goodman, 2016; Sommerville & others, 2013; Warneken & Tomasello, 2007).

Prosociality, engaging in behaviors aimed at improving the well-being of another, is sometimes considered a defining aspect of humanity because, unlike other animals, people extend kindness and trust not only to kin but to strangers (Warneken, 2015, 2018). How can we make sense of the extreme prosociality of human beings? Let's consider this issue from the perspective of developmental psychology. Must children be taught to be kind? Or is it possible they show kindness very early, even without the strong influence of parents and others? To read about research probing these questions, check out the Challenge Your Thinking.

Are Children Natural Helpers?

To understand the nature of human prosociality, developmental psychologists have probed the earliest signs of moral understanding in very young infants. Because infants cannot simply report on their feelings and opinions, these studies employ two main strategies, preferential looking (and reaching) (Van de Vondervoort & Hamlin, 2016) and psychophysiological measures (Miller & Hastings, 2016).

Consider research testing whether 3-month-old infants distinguish between kind and unkind actors. In these studies, researchers show very young infants some version of a puppet show. In the show, a little puppet tries to climb a steep hill. On to the scene come two other puppets. One of them (the hinderer) stands at the top of the hill and prevents the little one from making progress. The other (the helper) gives the little puppet help up the hill. Using this set up, studies have shown that infants avoid

(both) ©Dave King/Getty Images;

looking at the hinderer and when they are able to reach, show a preference for the helper (Hamlin & Wynn, 2011; Hamlin, Wynn, & Bloom, 2007, 2010; Scola & others, 2015). A variation on this paradigm showed 8-month-old infants a version of the puppet show in which the helper and hinderer were unsuccessful in their intentions. They tried to help (or hinder) but failed. Those 8-month-olds still showed a preference for the (unsuccessful) helper, demonstrating some grasp of good (and bad) intentions (Hamlin, 2013). Even very young infants appear to have a grasp of what it means to be nice (versus mean) (Van de Vondervoort & others, 2018; Van de Vondervoort & Hamlin, 2016).

Studies using psychophysiological measures have examined how infant brains respond to viewing prosocial acts. Studies of 6-month-old infants have shown that when babies witness a prosocial action, areas in the brain associated with social perception as well as pointing and looking, are activated (Gredebäck & others, 2015) and that brain activity predicted preferences for the helpers (Cowell & Decety, 2015).

Combined with evidence that toddlers are likely to spontaneously help even without being asked (Warneken, 2013, 2016) and do so even if no one will know they have helped (Hepach & others, 2017), some scholars view this research as indicating that human infants come into the world equipped to live in a cooperative society (Warneken, 2015, 2018). Consider that in the environments in which humans evolved children would have had to lend a hand for families to survive. Humans are such supremely social creatures, it makes sense that we have evolved to start out our lives ready to help.

What Do You Think?

- How might socialization affect infants' prosociality as they develop?
- Do you think human nature is essentially selfless or selfish? Why?

1. In Kohlberg's preconventional stage, moral reasoning centers on
   A. parental standards and established laws.
   B. personal moral standards.
   C. a behavior's consequences, as well as rewards and punishments from the external world.
   D. loyalty to other people.

2. Moral behavior is influenced by all of the following *except*
   A. early attachments.
   B. culture.
   C. parenting.
   D. the senses.

3. Efforts that are geared to helping others are referred to as
   A. the care perspective.
   B. prosocial behavior.
   C. the justice perspective.
   D. socioemotional behavior.

APPLY IT! 4. Chris and Amanda are parents to 3-year-old Emma, who is always getting into trouble in preschool. She says mean things, snatches toys from other children, and engages in a lot of mischief. Her parents want to instill a strong sense of conscience in their little troublemaker. Which of the following strategies is best supported by the research you read about above?
   A. The parents should punish Emma for her mischief swiftly and without a word of discussion. Trying to reason with a 3-year-old is a mistake.
   B. The parents should reward Emma consistently for good behavior and ignore her misdeeds. She is probably just trying to get attention.
   C. The parents should engage Emma in conversations about her behaviors, praising her for her good deeds and talking about the feelings that others might have when she gets in trouble. They should try to be clear and not focus only on the bad things she does.
   D. The parents should do nothing. Age 3 is too young to worry about these issues, and Emma will not understand what they are talking about until she is much older.

7 Death, Dying, and Grieving

Everything that lives will eventually die. This is, and always has been, the reality for living organisms. Because human beings possess the capacity for consciousness, we are aware of our own mortality. Our ability to imagine ourselves in the future makes the reality of our own eventual demise inescapable. Researchers from a variety of perspectives have examined the ways that the awareness of death influences our thoughts, feelings, and behaviors.

Fireworks displays are thrilling rituals that make us feel like valued and invested participants in the larger culture.
©Photo by Young Yun/Moment/Getty Images

Terror Management Theory: A Cultural Shield against Mortality

In the 1970s anthropologist Ernest Becker (1971) drew together theory and research from the social sciences to devise a grand theory of human life and culture. According to Becker, the human capacity for awareness that we will someday die creates the potential for overwhelming terror. Yet somehow we go about life without being preoccupied by the terrifying reality of death. Why is this so?

Becker proposed that as our capacity for self-awareness evolved, so did the human ability to create and invest in culture. Culture provides the customary beliefs, practices, religious rules, and social order for humans living together. Becker asserted that being part of a larger culture shields us from the terror of our own mortality. He maintained that by investing in our cultural worldview (our beliefs, routine practices, and standards for conduct), we are able to enjoy a sense of immortality. Culture provides both religious ideas about life after death and a context for accomplishments that will outlive us. As long as we feel that we are valued members of a culture, this status will buffer us against our fears of personal death.

Social psychologists Jeffrey Greenberg, Sheldon Solomon, and Tom Pyszczynski applied Becker's ideas in empirical research. They named their approach *terror management theory (TMT)* (Solomon, Greenberg, & Pyszczynski, 1991). A multitude of studies have explored terror management theory (Arndt & Goldenberg, 2017; Burke, Martens, & Faucher, 2010). This research shows that when reminded of their own death, people will endorse cultural beliefs more strongly (Arrowood & others, 2017), reject individuals who violate those beliefs (Leippe, Bergold, & Eisenstadt, 2017), and seek to maintain or enhance their self-esteem (Pyszczynski & others, 2004). Terror management studies support Becker's idea that cultural beliefs act as a buffer against the ultimate reality of our inevitable demise. Studies on the theory suggest that reminders of death can serve not only to promote defensive processes but also to spur people's creativity and motivation toward personal growth (Vail & others, 2012). Interestingly, research shows that compared to younger adults, older adults are less likely to strongly defend their cultural worldview after contemplating their own death (Maxfield & others, 2012), perhaps because they have come to accept that death is a fact of life.

Although terror management research tells us a great deal about how individuals cope with the reality of death in the abstract, it has yet to explore the process of dying itself. Even if one invests in a culture and in so doing establishes a sense of symbolic immortality, the reality of death remains. For aged or gravely ill persons, that reality can be experienced with particular vividness. How do individuals react when their own death is near?

Kübler-Ross's Stages of Dying

Elisabeth Kübler-Ross pioneered psychology's interest in the process of dying in her seminal book *On Death and Dying* (1969). Focusing on terminally ill individuals, Kübler-Ross identified five progressive stages of coping with death:

1. *Denial:* The person rejects the reality of impending death. He or she may express thoughts such as "I feel fine—this cannot be true."

2. *Anger:* Once the reality of death sets in, the individual feels angry and asks, "Why me?" The unfairness of the situation may be especially upsetting.

3. *Bargaining:* The individual may bargain with God, with doctors, or within his or her own head: "If I can just have a little more time, I'll do anything."

4. *Depression:* The person feels profound sadness and may begin to give up on life: "What's the point of doing anything?"

5. *Acceptance:* The person comes to terms with the difficult reality of his or her own death. A realization sets in that "it will be okay."

©Photodisc/SuperStock

Kübler-Ross eventually applied her stages of dying to a variety of life experiences, such as grieving for a loved one or mourning the loss of a job. Her book was important because it called on psychologists to confront the difficult problem of death. Still, her work has been criticized, and recent research has called into question a number of her ideas, such as the notion that everyone goes through these stages in the order she envisioned. One danger in the presentation of stages of dying is that it seems to represent a "right" way to die or the "best" way to grieve. Clearly, just as infants differ from one another from birth, so do individuals who face the end of life.

Bonanno's Theory of Grieving

Losing a loved one is certainly likely to be stressful. Research by George Bonanno and his colleagues has tracked individuals who have experienced bereavement, such as the loss of a spouse, over time (Bonanno, 2004, 2005; Bonanno, Westphal, & Mancini, 2011; Maccallum, Malgaroli, & Bonanno, 2017). That research has identified four different patterns of grief:

1. *Resilience:* Resilient individuals experience immediate grief over their loss but only for a brief time and return quickly to their previous levels of functioning. Such individuals do not experience a profound disruption of life, despite having gone through a staggering loss.

2. *Recovery:* In the recovery pattern, the individual experiences profound sadness and grief that dissipates more slowly. The individual will ultimately return to previous levels of functioning, but as a much slower and more gradual unfolding over time.

3. *Chronic dysfunction:* In this case, a traumatic grief experience leads to a long-term disruption of functioning in important life domains. Chronically dysfunctional individuals may ultimately be at risk for psychological disorders such as depression.

4. *Delayed grief or trauma:* Some individuals do not experience the sadness or distress evoked by a loss immediately following that loss. Instead, these intense feelings may come over the person weeks or even months later.

You might think that resilient individuals represent the lucky few. But Bonanno has found that resilience is actually the most common pattern.

Carving Meaning Out of the Reality of Death

Death is a difficult concept to contemplate. Consider, though, that the reality of death is one of the things that makes life so precious. Reminders of death can increase individuals' perception that life is meaningful and satisfying (King, Hicks, & Abdelkhalik, 2009). Furthermore, knowing that our loved ones will eventually die makes our commitments to our social relationships all the more heroic.

Indeed, the reality of death makes our commitment to life more meaningful. In the next section we will revisit that commitment, an important factor in development itself.

1. Studies on terror management theory indicate that when reminded of their own death, people
   A. lose interest in maintaining or building their self-esteem.
   B. endorse cultural beliefs more strongly.
   C. become less creative.
   D. reject the mainstream thinking of their culture.

2. Kübler-Ross's proposed stages of coping with death include all of the following *except*
   A. feeling angry.
   B. making amends to others.
   C. denying that death will come.
   D. accepting death.

3. In Bonanno's theory of grieving, the pattern in which the individual grieves for only a brief time and quickly resumes normal functioning is called
   A. recovery.
   B. rehabilitation.
   C. resilience.
   D. resolution.

APPLY IT! 4. When Lionel, Tawnya's beloved husband of 20 years, dies of a sudden heart attack, Tawnya is grief stricken. But just a few weeks later, she returns to work and is back to her routine, caring for her teenage sons. Considering her loss, she seems to be doing surprisingly well. Tawnya starts to wonder if there is something wrong with her. She loved Lionel deeply and remembers how, when her own father died, her mother seemed to be devastated for a long time. Tawnya confesses her feelings to a friend. According to research on grieving, which of the following would be the friend's best response?
   A. "Just work through your grief, and maybe join a support group so you can open up more. You need to get in touch with your feelings!"
   B. "So maybe your relationship with Lionel wasn't so great after all."
   C. "There are lots of ways to grieve. Your experience isn't unusual. Maybe it's your way of bouncing back. Talk about your loss if you wish, but don't assume there's something wrong."
   D. "You're holding in your emotions. You're going to get an ulcer or cancer if you keep this up. Let your feelings out!"

8 Active Development as a Lifelong Process

When you think about developmental psychology, child development may still be the first thing that pops into mind. However, development is in fact a lifelong process: You remain on this very day in the midst of your development, wherever you are in the adult life span. Further, as an active developer, you blaze your own developmental trail. Where will you carve that path as you go through life? How might you "grow yourself"?

One way that adults develop is through coping with life's difficulties. To understand how, let's revisit Piaget's ideas of assimilation and accommodation in childhood cognitive development and see how they apply to adult development (Block, 1982).

All of us have experiences that we might regret. But even these experiences can have meaning to the extent that they contribute to who we are now.

Recall that in assimilation, existing cognitive structures are used to make sense out of the current environment. Assimilation allows a person to enjoy a feeling of meaning because current experiences fit into his or her preexisting schemas (King & Hicks, 2007). However, life does not always conform to one's expectations. When experience conflicts with existing schemas, it is necessary to modify current ways of thinking. Accommodation is the process whereby existing schemas are modified or new structures are developed. Accommodation helps individuals to change so that they can make sense of life's previously incomprehensible events. For example, when people encounter a negative life circumstance such as an illness or a loss, they have the opportunity to change—to develop and to mature (Blackie & others, 2017; Jayawickreme & Blackie, 2016; Jayawickreme, Brocato, & Blackie, 2017; LoSavio & others, 2011). Indeed, research suggests that those who are faced with difficulties in life are more likely to come to a rich, complex view of themselves and the world when they are able to acknowledge, with mindfulness, the ways these experiences have changed them (King & Hicks, 2007).

©Petar Paunchev/Shutterstock

Earlier, you had the opportunity to complete the Satisfaction with Life Scale. An item on that scale was, "If I could live my life over I would change almost nothing." One way to think about maturity is to revisit that item and consider the experiences you have had in your trip in the time machine of development. The mature person, dedicated to life while also acknowledging potentially negative experiences, may be the person who is able to give that item a high rating, valuing his or her life "warts and all" (King & Hicks, 2007).

Development involves change, so development in adulthood may mean maintaining an openness to changing and to being changed by experience. Consider someone who has spent much of his or her early adult life pursuing wealth and career success but then turns to more selfless pursuits in middle age. To contribute to the well-being of the next generation, the individual devotes energy and resources to helping others—say, by volunteering for a charity or working with young people.

These motivations are demonstrated by numerous individuals who use their successes for the betterment of the world. Actor George Clooney, for example, has dedicated himself to a variety of humanitarian causes. Clooney cofounded the organization Not On Our Watch to end the genocide in Sudan as well as to stop atrocities elsewhere. However, one need not be middle-aged to attend to the motivations to make the world a better place. For instance, Facebook founder Mark Zuckerberg donated $100 million to public schools in Newark, New Jersey.

Development, then, is an ongoing process we experience throughout life as we encounter opportunities to grow, change, and make a mark in the world, however grandly or humbly. Each period of life sets the stage for the next. But at each of these we might revise the script, rewriting the next chapters of our lives.

SUMMARY

Exploring Human Development

Development is the pattern of change in human capabilities that begins at birth and continues throughout the life span. Both nature (biological inheritance) and nurture (environmental experience) influence development extensively. However, people are not at the mercy of either their genes or their environment when they actively construct optimal experiences. Resilience refers to the capacity of individuals to thrive during difficulties at every stage of development. Development is characterized along three interrelated levels—physical, cognitive, and socioemotional aspects of experience.

Physical Development

Prenatal development progresses through the germinal, embryonic, and fetal periods. Certain drugs, such as alcohol, can have an adverse effect on the fetus. Preterm birth is another potential problem, but its effects

may depend on experiences after birth. The infant's physical development is dramatic in the first year, and a number of motor milestones are reached in infancy. Extensive changes in the brain, including denser connections between synapses, take place in infancy and childhood.

Puberty is a period of rapid skeletal and sexual maturation that occurs mainly in early adolescence. Hormonal changes lie at the core of pubertal development. Most adults reach their peak physical performance during their 20s and are healthiest then. However, physical skills begin to decline during the 30s. Even in late adulthood, the brain has remarkable repair capacity and plasticity.

Cognitive Development

Jean Piaget introduced a theory of cognitive development. From his view, children use schemas to actively construct their world, either assimilating new information into existing schemas or adjusting schemas to accommodate it. Piaget identified four stages of cognitive development: the sensorimotor stage, the preoperational stage, the concrete operational stage, and the formal operational stage. According to Piaget, cognitive development in adolescence is characterized by the appearance of formal operational thought, the final stage in his theory. This stage involves abstract, idealistic, and logical thought.

Piaget argued that no new cognitive changes occur in adulthood. However, some psychologists have proposed that the idealistic thinking of adolescents is replaced by the more realistic, pragmatic thinking of young adults. Longitudinal research on intelligence shows that many cognitive skills peak in middle age. Overall, older adults do not do as well on memory and other cognitive tasks and are slower to process information than younger adults. However, older adults may have greater wisdom than younger adults.

 ## Socioemotional Development

In infancy, among the key basic ingredients of socioemotional development are temperament—the child's overall emotional demeanor—and attachment. Erik Erikson proposed an influential theory of eight psychosocial stages that characterize socioemotional development from infancy to late adulthood. In each stage, the individual seeks to resolve a particular socioemotional conflict. The childhood stages involve a movement from trust to industry. Adolescents experience Erikson's fifth stage, identity versus identity confusion.

Marcia proposed four statuses of identity based on crisis and commitment. Psychologists refer to the period between adolescence and adulthood as emerging adulthood. This period is characterized by the exploration of identity through work and relationships, instability, and self-focus.

Erikson's three stages of socioemotional development in adulthood are intimacy versus isolation (early adulthood), generativity versus stagnation (middle adulthood), and integrity versus despair (late adulthood). Researchers have found that remaining active increases the likelihood that older adults will be happier and healthier. They also have found that older adults often reduce their general social affiliations. Older adults are motivated to spend more time with close friends and family members.

 ## Gender Development

Gender development involves physical (biological), cognitive, and socioemotional processes. Biological factors in gender development include sex chromosomes and hormones. Cognitive factors include gender schemas and gender roles, with the latter being strongly influenced by culture. Socioemotional aspects of gender include parental and peer responses to gender-related behavior. With regard to gender differences, research indicates that men and women are more similar than different.

 ## Moral Development

Moral development encompasses both cognitive and socioemotional processes. Kohlberg proposed a cognitive-developmental theory of moral development with three levels (preconventional, conventional, and postconventional). More recent research, such as Carol Gilligan's, has focused on the development of prosocial behavior and the influence of socioemotional factors in putting moral reasoning into action.

 ## Death, Dying, and Grieving

Understanding the physical reality of death requires consideration of its socioemotional features. Terror management theory research has shown that awareness of death leads to investment in cultural worldviews. Elisabeth Kübler-Ross proposed a stage model of confronting death, in which the dying individual progresses from denial to acceptance. George Bonanno has shown that grief unfolds in four patterns—resilience, recovery, chronic dysfunction, and delayed grief. Awareness of death can render life more meaningful and satisfying.

 ## Active Development as a Lifelong Process

Development is an ongoing process that is influenced by the active developer at every point in the life span. In adulthood, development can be especially shaped by the ways individuals confront significant life events. Coping with stressful experiences and being open to change can be catalysts for adult development.

KEY TERMS

accommodation	executive function	nature	resilience
assimilation	formal operational stage	neglectful parenting	secure attachment
authoritarian parenting	gender	nurture	sensorimotor stage
authoritative parenting	gender identity	object permanence	sexual orientation
concrete operational stage	gender roles	permissive parenting	temperament
core knowledge approach	gender similarities hypothesis	preferential looking	wisdom
cross-sectional design	infant attachment	preoperational stage	
development	limbic system	prosocial behavior	
emerging adulthood	longitudinal study	puberty	

ANSWERS TO SELF-QUIZZES

Section 1: 1. A; 2. C; 3. C; 4. D
Section 2: 1. B; 2. A; 3. B; 4. C
Section 3: 1. B; 2. B; 3. C; 4. B

Section 4: 1. B; 2. D; 3. C; 4. C
Section 5: 1. B; 2. D; 3. B; 4. A
Section 6: 1. C; 2. D; 3. B; 4. C

Section 7: 1. B; 2. B; 3. C; 4. C

9 Motivation and Emotion

What Would You Do If You Won the Lottery?

I n August 2017, Mavis Wanczyk, a 53-year-old hospital worker in Chicopee, MA, won the largest single lottery jackpot in history when her winning Powerball ticket brought her a $759 million windfall. That very day, she quit her job (Zorthian, 2017). You might be surprised to learn that Mavis's decision is unusual among lottery winners. One study of lottery winners found that only 12 percent quit their jobs (Furaker & Hedenus, 2009). In fact, more than 60 percent of lottery winners make very few changes to their lives (Arvey, Harpaz, & Liao, 2004). Given the financial freedom to do whatever they like, many people choose to keep doing what they are doing. Think about the wealthiest people in the world. Facebook founder Mark Zuckerberg, at age 33, is worth over $71 billion. Even if he spent $100,000 per day, he would have to live *1,959 years* to spend it all. Yet, he continues to work. Why do people work even when they do not "have to" to make money? Clearly, work must mean more to us than simply a way to meet economic needs. Whenever we ask the question why, we are asking about motivation. Why do any of us do the big and small things we do in our everyday lives? This is the question we will be grappling with in this chapter. In addition, we will be considering emotions: The feelings that tell us how we are doing in attaining the things we want.

The terms *motivation* and *emotion* come from the Latin word *movere,* which means "to move." Motivation and emotion are the "go" of human life, providing the steam that propels us to overcome obstacles and to accomplish the great and little things we do every day. Our emotions often define for us what we really want: We feel joy or sorrow depending on how events influence our most cherished life dreams.

1 Theories of Motivation

motivation
The force that moves people to behave, think, and feel the way they do.

Motivation is the force that moves people to behave, think, and feel the way they do. Motivated behavior is energized, directed, and sustained. Psychologists have proposed a variety of theories about why organisms are motivated to do what they do. In this section we explore some of the main theoretical approaches to motivation.

The Evolutionary Approach

In the early history of psychology, the evolutionary approach emphasized the role of instincts in motivation. *Ethology*—the study of animal behavior—also has described motivation from an evolutionary perspective. Studying the natural behavior of animals allows scientists to identify instincts.

instinct
An innate (unlearned) biological pattern of behavior that is assumed to be universal throughout a species.

An **instinct** is an innate (unlearned) biological pattern of behavior that is assumed to be universal throughout a species. Generally, an instinct is set in motion by a "sign stimulus"—something in the environment that turns on a fixed pattern of behavior. Instincts may explain a great deal of nonhuman animal behavior. In addition, some human behavior is instinctive. For example, let's consider infant reflexes. Babies do not have to learn to suck; they instinctively do it when something is placed in their mouth. So, for infants, an object touching the lips is a sign stimulus. After infancy, though, it is hard to think of specific behaviors that all human beings engage in when presented with a particular stimulus.

 You might think that some stimuli provide a strong case for instinctive responses. Doesn't everyone respond to chocolate with the behavior of eating? Not so fast—some people don't even like chocolate!

According to evolutionary psychologists, the motivations for sex, aggression, achievement, and other behaviors are rooted in our evolutionary past (Lewis & others, 2017), and we can understand similarities among members of the human species through these shared evolutionary roots. Because evolutionary approaches emphasize the passing on of one's genes, these theories focus on domains of life that are especially relevant to reproduction. Evolutionary approaches focus on how members of a species are the same as each other and seek to establish principles that apply to everyone in the same way, similar to instincts in animals. However, in general human beings are so different from each other and human behavior is so complex that explaining human motivation on the basis of species-specific instinct is inappropriate. Indeed, it would hardly

Human newborns display behavioral reflexes such as holding on to a rope so that they can be lifted. In our evolutionary past, this gripping reflex appeared in primates, allowing an infant to cling to its mother's hair while she moved about.
©Bettmann/Getty Images

seem adaptive for humans to have a fixed action pattern that is invariably set in motion by a particular signal in the environment. To understand human behavior, psychologists have developed a variety of other approaches, as we now consider.

Drive Reduction Theory

Another way to think about motivation is through the constructs of need and drive. A **need** is a physical or biological deprivation that energizes the drive to eliminate or reduce the deprivation. A **drive** is an aroused state that occurs because of a physiological need. You can think of a drive as a psychological itch that requires scratching. Generally, psychologists think of needs as underlying our drives. You may have a need for water; the drive that accompanies that need is your feeling of being thirsty. Usually but not always, needs and drives are closely associated. For example, when your body needs food, your hunger drive will probably be aroused. An hour after you have eaten a hamburger, your body might still need essential nutrients (thus you need food), but your hunger drive might have subsided.

need
A deprivation that energizes the drive to eliminate or reduce the deprivation.

drive
An aroused state that occurs because of a physiological need.

The following example should reinforce that drive pertains to a psychological state whereas need involves a physiological state, and that drives do not always follow from needs. If you are deprived of oxygen because of a gas leak, you may feel lightheaded but may not realize that your condition is the result of a gas leak that is creating a need for air. Because you do not perceive it, your need for air fails to create a drive for oxygen that might lead you to open a window. Moreover, drives sometimes seem to come out of nowhere. Imagine, for instance, having eaten a fine meal and feeling full to the point of not wanting another single bite—until the waiter wheels over the dessert cart. Suddenly you feel ready to tackle the double chocolate oblivion, despite your lack of hunger.

This is why scents are added to gas—so that it can be smelled—and also why we need carbon monoxide detectors, because we cannot tell when we need oxygen!

Drive reduction theory explains that as a drive becomes stronger, we are motivated to reduce it. The goal of drive reduction is **homeostasis,** the body's tendency to maintain an equilibrium, or steady state. Literally hundreds of biological states in our bodies must be maintained within a certain range: temperature, blood sugar level, potassium and sodium levels, oxygenation, and so on. When you dive into an icy swimming pool, your body uses energy to maintain its normal temperature. When you walk out of an air-conditioned room into the heat of a summer day, your body releases excess heat by sweating. These physiological changes occur automatically to keep your body in an optimal state of functioning.

homeostasis
The body's tendency to maintain an equilibrium, or steady state.

Drive reduction theory does not provide a comprehensive framework for understanding motivation. Think about all your own favorite courses or leisure activities. Many of these probably involve hard work. In fact, many of them increase rather than reduce drives. Many things that people choose to do involve increasing (not decreasing) tensions—for example, taking a challenging course in school, raising a family, and working at a difficult job. Human motivation cannot be entirely explained by drive reduction because we seem motivated to increase (not decrease) many drives.

Optimum Arousal Theory

When psychologists talk about arousal, they are generally referring to a person's feelings of being alert and engaged. When we are very excited, our arousal levels are high. When we are bored, they are low. You have probably noticed that motivation influences arousal levels. Sometimes you can want something (for example, to do well on a test) so much that you feel "overmotivated" and anxious. On the other hand, you might be so unmotivated for a task (such as doing dishes) that you can hardly force yourself to complete it.

Early in the twentieth century, two psychologists described how arousal can influence performance. According to their formulation, now known as the **Yerkes-Dodson law,** performance is best under conditions of moderate arousal rather than either low or high arousal. At the low end of arousal, you may be too lethargic to perform tasks well; at the high end, you may not be able to concentrate. Think about how aroused you were the last time you took a test. If your arousal was too high, you might have felt too nervous to concentrate, and your performance likely suffered. If it was too low, you may not have worked fast enough to finish the test. Also think about performance in sports. Being too aroused usually harms athletes' performance; a thumping heart and rapid breathing have accompanied many golfers' missed putts. However, if athletes' arousal is too low, they may not concentrate well on the task at hand.

Overlearning is a crucial part of the training regimen by which the elite Navy SEALS prepare for missions, such as the 2011 raid on Osama bin Laden's compound in Pakistan and the al Qaeda leader's eventual death.
Source: U.S. Navy

PSYCHOLOGICAL INQUIRY

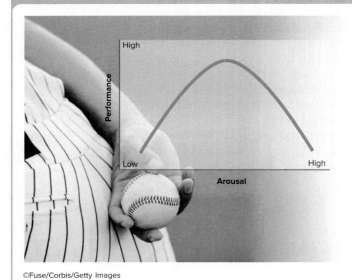

©Fuse/Corbis/Getty Images

Obeying the (Yerkes–Dodson) Law

The graph displays the relationship between arousal (shown on the X, or horizontal, axis) and performance (shown on the Y, or vertical, axis). Note that the curve is an inverted U.

Using the figure as a reference, answer the questions below:

1. What was your arousal level the last time you took an exam? If you were very nervous, your arousal level would be considered high. If you were excited and engaged but not too worried, your level would be in the medium range. If you were feeling sluggish, your arousal level would be low.

2. How did you actually do on that test? Plot your performance on the graph. Does it fit with the Yerkes–Dodson prediction?

3. Now think about performance in sports or the arts. Imagine your favorite athlete, musician, or actor. How might that person feel when he or she is on the spot, trying to sink a winning free throw, strike out the last batter, or impress an audience? How might arousal influence performance in those cases?

4. In many professions, individuals are forced to perform under conditions of very high arousal. These include EMTs, lifeguards, and emergency room staff. (Name some others.) How might such individuals train themselves to perform even under conditions of extreme arousal?

The relationship between arousal and performance is one reason that individuals who have to perform well under stressful conditions (such as EMTs, lifeguards, and marines) are trained to *overlearn* important procedures so that they do not require much thought. With this extra learning, when these individuals are under conditions of high arousal, they can rely on automatic pilot to do what needs to be done.

1. The force that moves people to behave, think, and feel the way they do is
   A. emotion.
   B. instinct.
   C. need.
   D. motivation.

2. Natalie will be taking an exam today. According to the Yerkes-Dodson law, the condition that will allow Natalie to score highest on the exam is
   A. no anxiety.
   B. moderate anxiety.
   C. high anxiety.
   D. high relaxation.

3. Which of the following statements is correct?
   A. Instincts have little to do with animal behavior.
   B. Instincts are learned patterns of behavior.
   C. Instincts direct most aspects of human behavior.
   D. Instincts are innate and biological.

APPLY IT! 4. Jared is a star player on his school's basketball team. In a crucial game, the score is tied with just a few seconds left on the clock, and Jared finds himself at the free-throw line preparing to shoot the winning baskets. The opponents' coach calls a time-out to "ice" Jared's nerves. Finally, as Jared steps up to the line, the rival team's students scream and jump around in an attempt to psych Jared out. His heart racing, Jared sinks both baskets, and his team wins. Which of the following is most likely true of this situation?
   A. The opposing team's coach and student fans know that low arousal leads to poor performance.
   B. Jared has practiced free throws so many times that he can land them even when he is highly aroused.
   C. Jared is showing the effects of very high arousal on performance.
   D. Jared is generally a sluggish person, and his performance is helped by his low levels of arousal.

2 Hunger and Sex

Some of the influence of motivation in our lives is tied to physiological needs. Two behaviors that are central to the survival of our species are eating and sex. In this section we examine the motivational processes underlying these behaviors.

The Biology of Hunger

You know you are hungry when your stomach growls and you feel those familiar hunger pangs. What role do such signals play in hunger?

GASTRIC SIGNALS   In 1912, Walter Cannon and A. L. Washburn conducted an experiment that revealed a close association between stomach contractions and hunger (Figure 1). As part of the procedure, a partially inflated balloon was passed through a tube inserted in Washburn's mouth and pushed down into his stomach. A machine that measures air pressure was connected to the balloon to monitor Washburn's stomach contractions. Every time Washburn reported hunger pangs, his stomach was also contracting. Sure enough, a growling stomach needs food. The stomach tells the brain not only

FIGURE 1   **Cannon and Washburn's Classic Experiment on Hunger** In this experiment, the researchers demonstrated that stomach contractions, which were detected by the stomach balloon, accompany a person's hunger feelings, which were indicated by pressing the key. Line A in the chart records increases and decreases in the volume of the balloon in the participant's stomach. Line B records the passage of time. Line C records the participant's manual signals of feelings of hunger. Line D records a reading from the belt around the participant's waist to detect movements of the abdominal wall and ensure that such movements are not the cause of changes in stomach volume.

FIGURE 2 **Leptin and Obesity** The obese mouse on the left is untreated; the one on the right has been given injections of leptin.
©The Rockefeller University/AP Images

how full it is but also how much nutrient is present, which is why rich food stops hunger faster than the same amount of water. The hormone cholecystokinin (CCK) helps start the digestion of food, travels to the brain through the bloodstream, and signals us to stop eating (Mhalhal & others, 2017). Hunger involves a lot more than an empty stomach, however.

BLOOD CHEMISTRY   Three key chemical substances play a role in hunger, eating, and satiety (the state of feeling full): glucose, insulin, and leptin.

Glucose (blood sugar) is an important factor in hunger, probably because the brain critically depends on sugar for energy. One set of sugar receptors, located in the brain itself, triggers hunger when sugar levels fall too low. Another set of sugar receptors is in the liver, which stores excess sugar and releases it into the blood when needed. The sugar receptors in the liver signal the brain when its sugar supply falls, and this signal also can make you hungry.

The hormone *insulin* also plays a role in glucose control (Abraham & others, 2014; Zahn & others, 2016). When we eat complex carbohydrates such as bread and pasta, insulin levels go up and fall off gradually. When we consume simple sugars such as candy, insulin levels rise and then fall sharply—the all-too-familiar "sugar low" (Rodin, 1984). Blood glucose levels are affected by complex carbohydrates and simple sugars in similar ways, so we are more likely to eat within the next several hours after eating simple sugars than after eating complex carbohydrates.

The chemical substance *leptin* (from the Greek word *leptos,* meaning "thin"), released by fat cells, decreases food intake and increases energy expenditure or metabolism (DePaoli, 2014; Liu & others, 2017). Leptin's functions were discovered in a strain of genetically obese mice, called *ob mice* (Pelleymounter & others, 1995). Because of a genetic mutation, the fat cells of ob mice cannot produce leptin. The ob mouse has a low metabolism, overeats, and gets extremely fat. Leptin appears to act as an anti-obesity hormone (Mele & others, 2016; Tutone & others, 2014). If ob mice are given daily injections of leptin, their metabolic rate increases, and they become more active, eat less, and lose weight. Figure 2 shows an untreated ob mouse and an ob mouse that has received injections of leptin.

In humans, leptin concentrations have been linked with weight, body fat, and weight loss in response to dieting (Matheny & others, 2014). Problems in regulating leptin have been implicated in both obesity and depression (Milaneschi, & others, 2017).

BRAIN PROCESSES   The hypothalamus plays a central role in regulating important body functions, including hunger. More specifically, activity in two areas of the hypothalamus regulates hunger. The *lateral hypothalamus* (*lateral* means "on the outer parts") is involved in stimulating eating. When an electrical current is passed through this area in a well-fed animal, the animal begins to eat. If this part of the hypothalamus is destroyed, even a starving animal will show no interest in food. The *ventromedial hypothalamus* (*ventromedial* means "on the inner locations") is involved in reducing hunger and restricting eating. When this area of an animal's brain is stimulated, the animal stops eating. When the area is destroyed, the animal eats profusely and quickly becomes obese.

This can be tricky. These locations play opposite roles in hunger. Remember LATERAL means on the outside (like going out to eat when you are hungry). VENTROMEDIAL means on the inside (like staying in because you are not hungry).

Although the lateral and ventromedial hypothalamuses both influence hunger, there is much more to the brain's role in determining hunger than these on/off centers in the hypothalamus. Neurotransmitters (the chemical messengers that convey information from neuron to neuron) and neural circuits (clusters of neurons that often involve different parts of the brain) also function in hunger. Leptin influences eating by inhibiting the production of a neurotransmitter in the hypothalamus that induces eating. The neurotransmitter serotonin is partly responsible for the satiating effect of CCK, and serotonin antagonists have been used to treat obesity in humans (Voigt & Fink, 2015). A recent study showed that a drug that increased circulating serotonin led to healthier food choices (Vlaev & others, 2017).

Obesity

Given that the brain and body are elegantly wired to regulate eating behavior, why do so many people in the United States overeat and suffer the effects of overeating? Among developed nations, more than half of adults and 1 in 6 children are overweight or obese (OECD, 2017). Adult obesity rates are highest in the United States and Mexico and are lowest in Japan and South Korea (OECD, 2017). Being overweight or obese increases one's risk for a variety of health problems, including cardiovascular disease, type 2 diabetes, some cancers, sleep problems, including sleep apnea (when the person stops breathing during sleep (Hovick & Bigsby, 2016; Lynch, Elmore, & Kotecki, 2015; Mahmuda, Akhter, & Nath, 2017; Tabung & others, 2017; Zhang & others, 2017). Overweight and obesity are global health problems.

 The World Health Organization coined the term **globesity** to refer to the worldwide problem of obesity.

Why so many people overeat to the point of obesity is a motivational puzzle, because it involves eating when one is not in need of nutrition. As is the case with much behavior, in eating, biological, cognitive, and sociocultural factors interact in diverse ways in different individuals, making it difficult to point to a specific cause (Monnereau & others, 2017).

THE BIOLOGY OF OBESITY

Obesity clearly has a genetic component. After the discovery of the ob gene in mice, researchers found a similar gene in humans. Some individuals do inherit a tendency to be overweight (Wiemerslage & others, 2016; Zhou & others, 2015). Only 10 percent of children who do not have obese parents become obese themselves, whereas 40 percent of children who have one obese parent become obese, and 70 percent of children who have two obese parents become obese. Identical human twins have similar weights, even when they are reared apart (Maes, Neal, & Eaves, 1997).

©Comstock/Jupiter Images

set point
The weight maintained when the individual makes no effort to gain or lose weight.

Another factor in weight is **set point,** the weight maintained when the individual makes no effort to gain or lose weight. Set point is determined in part by the amount of stored fat in the body (Berthoud, Münzberg, & Morrison, 2017). Fat is stored in *adipose cells,* or fat cells (Furukawa & others, 2017). When these cells are filled, you do not get hungry. When people gain weight—because of genetic predisposition, childhood eating patterns, or adult overeating—their fat-cell number increases, and they might not be able to get rid of extra ones. A normal-weight individual has 10 to 20 billion fat cells. An obese individual can have up to 100 billion fat cells (Fried, 2008). Consequently, an obese individual has to eat more to feel satisfied.

PSYCHOLOGICAL FACTORS IN HUNGER AND OBESITY

Psychologists used to think that obesity stemmed from factors such as unhappiness and external food cues. These ideas make some sense; drowning one's sorrows in chocolate or eating some cookies just because they are there seems common enough to explain overeating. However, a number of factors are more important than emotional state and external stimuli (Rodin, 1984). For example, social context can affect how much people eat. Research has shown that women may select smaller portions and eat less (especially when eating with men) in order to appear more feminine. Conversely men may eat larger portions to appear more masculine (Cavazza, Guidetti, & Butera, 2017).

From an evolutionary view, human taste preferences developed at a time when reliable food sources were scarce. Our earliest ancestors needed a lot of calories to survive in challenging circumstances. They likely developed a preference for sweet and fatty foods. Today many people still have a taste for such foods, though today's sweet and fatty foods provide far more calories than we need with far less nutritional value. Learned associations of food with a particular time and place are characteristic of many organisms, including humans (Maxwell & others, 2017). If it is noon, we eat lunch; in a movie theater, we eat popcorn.

Beyond these factors, subtle cues can influence how much people consume. Growing portion sizes have been implicated in the alarming rates of obesity in the United States (Steenhuis & Poelman, 2017). Not surprisingly, a key predictor of portion size is liking of the food (Spence & others, 2016). If we like pizza, we may see a typical portion as 3 slices, not just 1 (Labbe & others, 2017).

It is puzzling, though, that portion sizes should matter. After all, a person does not have to eat all of the food presented to him or her. Why do people eat an entire portion of food when just a bit of it might have led to the same feeling of fullness? Of course, parents often teach their children to "finish what's on your plate" (Potter & others, 2017). Many people rely not on a feeling of fullness but rather the sight of an empty plate or bowl as the cue to stop eating (Hinton & others, 2013). Increasingly, cleaning one's plate has involved eating more and more food: Since 1900 the diameter of the average plate has increased from about 9½ inches to nearly a foot (Marteau, 2015).

Relying on something like a clean plate to indicate that one should stop eating is a sign of eating mindlessly, "on automatic pilot." Mindless eating can involve eating until one has finished a portion (no matter how large) or not paying attention to the sheer amount one has consumed (Kristeller & Epel, 2014; Steenhuis & Poelman, 2017). One factor in mindless eating is the appearance of food (Reinders & others, 2017). A recent series of studies examined how people perceive the size of food portions when these are presented either stacked vertically or spread out (Szocs & Lefebvre, 2017). It appears that diners use the surface area of food on a plate as a guide to how much food the plate contains. This means that looking at equal amounts of, say, mashed potatoes on two plates, the one that is shaped like a tower may look like less food than the one presented in a flat mound (Szocs & Lefebvre, 2017). In these studies, participants appeared to be using the visual surface area of food as a *heuristic* to estimate portion size.

Remember this study the next time you eat Pringles. Definitely unstack them to eat less!

How might we reduce mindless eating? One step that has been taken by policy-makers and restaurants is to provide information about the calories and fat in various dishes on menus. To read about the effects of such information on eating, see the Psychology in Our World.

Dieting is a continuing obsession in the United States. However, even if we are trying to lose weight, we must eat to survive. For our species to survive, we also have to have sex. Like hunger, sex has a strong physiological basis, as well as cognitive and sociocultural components.

The Biology of Sex

Given the central role of sexual behavior in reproduction, understanding the processes that underlie sexual behavior in all animals, including humans, is a vital goal for science (Woodson, Neimeyer, & Bergan, 2017). What brain areas are involved in sex? What role do hormones play in sexual motivation? What is the nature of the human sexual response pattern? This section answers these central questions about the biology of sex.

What's on the Menu and Why It Matters

Looking at a menu, it can be hard to know exactly how much calories each item contains. Some foods may look and sound healthy but be high in calories. On its own, lettuce is very low in calories. But a dinner-sized Caesar salad with chicken, dressing, cheese, and croutons can contain nearly 600 calories, which is about the same as two McDonald's cheeseburgers. In 2015, the U.S. Food and Drug Administration implemented a rule requiring chain restaurants to include caloric information on their menus. Can such information change diners' preferences? Research shows that it can (Birch, Savage, & Fisher, 2015; Cioffi & others, 2015; Haws & Liu, 2016). When diners are given information about the caloric content of food, they are more likely to think about it, remember it, and choose food with fewer calories (Hammond & others, 2015).

In addition to providing calorie information, many restaurants are providing a choice of full or smaller portions. One study showed that when half-portions were priced at half the amount of full portions, people were more likely to choose the lower calorie, smaller portion (Haws & Liu, 2016). Another series of studies showed that the rationale behind "Happy Meals," in which a meal comes with a small nonfood gift, can also be applied to adults. In those studies, adults were more likely to order a smaller portion of their selection if it came with a free gift, such as a chance to win frequent flyer miles or a small amount of money (Reimann, Bechara, & MacInnis, 2015).

These studies show how psychological research can inform policy. They may also inspire some motivated restaurateur to devise some delicious adult-style happy meals.

©Olga Nayashkova/Shutterstock

THE HYPOTHALAMUS, CEREBRAL CORTEX, AND LIMBIC SYSTEM

Motivation for sexual behavior is centered in the hypothalamus (Micevych & Meisel, 2017; Petrulis, 2013). However, like many other areas of motivation, brain functioning related to sex radiates outward to connect with a wide range of other brain areas in both the limbic system and the cerebral cortex (Bell & others, 2013).

Researchers have shown the importance of the hypothalamus in sexual activity by electrically stimulating or surgically removing it. Electrical stimulation of certain hypothalamic areas increases sexual behavior while surgical removal of some hypothalamic areas inhibits sexual behavior. Electrical stimulation of the hypothalamus in a male can lead to as many as 20 ejaculations in an hour. The limbic system, which runs through the hypothalamus, also seems to be involved in sexual behavior. Its electrical stimulation can produce penile erection in males and orgasm in females.

Temporal lobe damage in male cats has been shown to impair the animals' ability to select an appropriate partner. The tomcats with temporal lobe damage try to copulate with everything in sight, including teddy bears, chairs—and even researchers! In humans, the temporal lobes of the neocortex (located on the sides of the brain) play an important role in moderating sexual arousal and directing it to an appropriate goal object (Carroll, 2013).

The brain tissues that produce sexual feelings and behaviors are activated by various neurotransmitters in conjunction with sex hormones. Like scratching an itch, sexual motivation also is characterized by a basic urge-reward-relief cycle. That means that we become sexually aroused, feel a strong urge to engage in sexual behavior, engage in that behavior, and then experience a rewarding sensation, followed by feelings of calm relief. The motivation for sex is generated by excitatory neurotransmitters (Hull & Dominguez, 2006). The intense reward of orgasm is caused by a massive rush of dopamine, and the deep feeling of relaxation that follows is linked with the hormone oxytocin (Behnia & others, 2014).

One substance that is known to decrease testosterone is black licorice. Some researchers have participants eat black licorice as a way to manipulate testosterone levels.

SEX HORMONES   The two main classes of sex hormones are estrogens and androgens. **Estrogens,** the class of sex hormones that predominate in females, are produced mainly by the ovaries. **Androgens,** such as testosterone, the class of sex hormones that predominate in males, are produced by the testes in males and by the adrenal glands in both males and females. For men, higher androgen levels are associated with sexual motivation and orgasm frequency (Shea, Wongt, & Chen, 2014). Research suggests that increasing testosterone in women increases sex drive and the frequency of satisfying sexual experiences (Braunstein, 2007; Davis, 2013), although it may carry a heightened risk for breast cancer.

estrogens
The class of sex hormones that predominate in females, produced mainly by the ovaries.

androgens
The class of sex hormones that predominate in males, produced by the testes in males and by the adrenal glands in both males and females.

THE HUMAN SEXUAL RESPONSE PATTERN   What physiological changes do humans experience during sexual activity? To answer this question, William Masters and Virginia Johnson (1966) carefully observed and measured the physiological responses of 382 female and 312 male volunteers as they masturbated or had sexual intercourse. Masters and Johnson identified a **human sexual response pattern** consisting of four phases: excitement, plateau, orgasm, and resolution.

human sexual response pattern
According to Masters and Johnson, the characteristic sequence of physiological changes that humans experience during sexual activity, consisting of four phases: excitement, plateau, orgasm, and resolution.

The *excitement phase* begins the process of erotic responsiveness. It lasts from several minutes to several hours, depending on the nature of the sex play involved. Engorgement of blood vessels and increased blood flow in genital areas and muscle tension characterize the excitement phase. The most obvious signs of response in this phase are the beginnings of lubrication of the vagina and partial erection of the penis.

The second phase of the human sexual response, the *plateau phase,* is a continuation and heightening of the arousal begun in the excitement phase. The increases in breathing, pulse rate, and blood pressure that occurred during the excitement phase become more intense, penile erection and vaginal lubrication are more complete, and orgasm is closer.

©Eric Audras/ONOKYO/Getty Images

The third phase of the human sexual response cycle is *orgasm,* which involves an explosive discharge of neuromuscular tension and an intensely pleasurable feeling. How long does orgasm last? Some individuals sense that time is standing still when it takes place, but in fact orgasm lasts for only about 3 to 15 seconds.

Following orgasm, the individual enters the *resolution phase,* in which blood vessels return to their normal state. A sex difference in this phase is that females may be stimulated to orgasm again without delay. Males enter a refractory period during which they cannot have another orgasm.

Cognitive and Sensory/Perceptual Factors in Sexuality

From experience, we know that our cognitive world plays an important role in sexuality. We might be sexually attracted to someone but understand that we must inhibit our sexual urges until the relationship has time to develop. We have the cognitive capacity to think about the importance of respecting our partners and not taking sexual advantage of someone. We also have the cognitive capacity to generate sexual images—to become sexually aroused just by thinking about erotic images or our romantic partners (Stanton, Campbell, & Loving, 2014).

Sexual motivation is influenced by *sexual scripts,* stereotyped patterns of expectancies for how people should behave sexually (Ross & Coleman, 2011; Sakaluk & others, 2014). We carry these scripts with us in our memories. Women and men can have different sexual scripts, and these may be influenced by media portrayals (Seabrook & others, 2017). Traditional ideas about women and men suggest that women are more likely than men to link sexual intercourse with love. In contrast, men are more likely to emphasize sexual conquest. Research suggests that these differences do continue to persist (Masters & others, 2013). Some sexual scripts involve a double standard, such as, for example, judging that it is okay for male but not female adolescents to have sex or for women to bear the blame if they become pregnant. Sexual scripts have also been implicated when young women feel that they are being coerced into sexual behavior (French & Neville, 2017).

Coercion has no place in sexual intimacy.

Cognitive interpretation of sexual activity also involves our perceptions of the individual with whom we are having sex and his or her perceptions of us (Alvarez & Garcia-Marques, 2011; Cornelius & Kershaw, 2017). We imbue our sexual acts with perceptual questions, such as is she loyal to me and what will our future relationship be like? Amid the wash of hormones in sexual activity is the cognitive ability to control, reason about, and try to make sense of the activity.

Sensation and perception are also involved in sexual behavior. The sensory system of touch usually predominates during sexual intimacy, but vision also plays a powerful role for some individuals. In general, women are more aroused by touch; men, by what they see.

Cultural Factors in Sexuality

The influence of culture on sexuality was demonstrated dramatically in a classic analysis by John Messenger (1971) of the people living on the small island of Inis Beag off the coast of Ireland. They knew nothing about tongue kissing or hand stimulation of the penis, and they detested nudity. For both females and males, premarital sex was out of the question. Men avoided most sexual experiences because they believed that sexual intercourse reduced their energy level and was bad for their health. Under these repressive conditions, sexual intercourse occurred only at night, taking place as quickly as possible. As you might suspect, female orgasm was rare in this culture (Messenger, 1971).

In contrast, around the same time that Messenger was studying the people of Inis Beag, Donald Marshall (1971) was studying the Mangaian culture in the South Pacific. In Mangaia, young boys were taught about masturbation and encouraged to engage in it as much as they liked. At age 13, the boys underwent a ritual, initiating them into sexual manhood. First, their elders instructed them about sexual strategies, including how to aid their female partner in having orgasms. Two weeks later, the boy had intercourse with an experienced woman who helped him hold back from ejaculation until she experienced orgasm with him. By the end of adolescence, Mangaians had sex nearly every day. Mangaian women reported a high frequency of orgasm.

One way that societies teach youth about sex and sexuality is through formal education. Although many topics associated with sex and sexuality spur controversy, most people concerned with sex education share two relatively uncontroversial goals: to encourage the very young to delay sexual activity and to reduce teen pregnancy and sexually transmitted infections. When adolescents delay having sexual intercourse until after middle school they are more likely to use condoms and are likely to have fewer different sex partners, reducing the risk for unintended pregnancies and sexual transmitted infections (Lerner & Hawkins, 2016). As such, devising ways to encourage youth to delay sexual behavior is an important goal for all who care about their welfare. As we will see, though, achieving this uncontroversial goal can be controversial.

What are some aspects of your own culture that influence your sexual behavior?

SEX EDUCATION   Generally, sex education programs can be divided into two types. First, *comprehensive* sex education involves providing students with comprehensive knowledge about sexual behavior, birth control, and the use of condoms in protecting against sexually transmitted infections, while encouraging them to delay sexual activity and practice abstinence. Another form of sex education is the *abstinence-only* approach (or abstinence-only-until-marriage). Abstinence-only educational programs emphasize that sexual behavior outside of marriage is harmful to individuals of any age. Instructors can present contraceptives and condoms only in terms of their failure rates. Abstinence-only sex education promotes the notion that abstinence is the only effective way to avoid pregnancy and sexually transmitted infections. Be aware that the first assumption of abstinence-only sex education, that sexual behavior outside of marriage is harmful, has not been supported by research (Santelli & others, 2017).

Which approach to sex education most effectively delays sexual activity and prevents teen pregnancy? Comprehensive sex education programs achieve these goals at far greater rates than abstinence only programs (Beh, 2015; Jaramillo & others, 2017; Kohler, Manhart, & Lafferty, 2008). Students exposed to abstinence-only programs do not delay initiation of sexual behavior, are not likely to use protection when they do have sex, and are at risk for sexually transmitted infections and unplanned pregnancy (Santelli & others, 2017). Importantly, providing youth with comprehensive sex education does not make them more likely to have sex (Kirby, 2008). In 2010, the United States Congress cut funding for some abstinence-only programs and funded comprehensive sex education programs. However, states within the U.S. vary in terms of the ways that sex education is implemented and what information is shared (Santelli & others, 2017).

Americans still have difficulty talking openly about sexual behavior, leading some to worry that pornography has replaced serious sex education and open communication.

Teen births in the U.S. have been declining. In 2014, the number of teen births in the U.S. was 24.2 per 1000 female teenagers, a drop of over 50 percent from 1990 (Office of Adolescent Health, 2016). Those births represent nearly a quarter of a million babies born to teen mothers. Teen birth rates have continued to decline, hitting an all-time low of 20.3 births per 1000 teenagers in 2016 (Hamilton & others, 2017). The reasons for these declines are difficult to identify. Evidence indicates that teens are delaying first intercourse and using birth control (Linbergh, Santelli, & Desai, 2016; Sedgh & others, 2015).

Even in the context of these improvements in teen pregnancy rates, it is important to bear in mind that the U.S. teen pregnancy rate is still much higher than other developed nations. In addition, there are important ethnic differences in teen birth rates, with Latina American teens having twice as high a birth rate as White/European Americans (Office of Adolescent Health, 2016).

Sexual Behavior and Orientation

In the United States, varying sexual behaviors and attitudes reflect the country's diverse multicultural population, and Americans collectively fall somewhere in the middle of a continuum going from repressive to liberal. We are more conservative in our sexual habits than was once thought. However, we are somewhat more open-minded regarding sexual orientation than a century ago.

In this discussion, we first define sexual behavior and examine the frequencies of different sexual practices while noting the difficulties associated with doing research in these areas. We then turn to the factors that play a role in determining sexual orientation.

DEFINING SEXUAL BEHAVIOR   What constitutes sexual behavior—what we commonly refer to as "sex"? Most people might answer that question with "vaginal intercourse," but what about other sexual behaviors, such as anal sex and oral sex? If someone has engaged in these practices, is he or she still a "virgin"? If your significant other reported to you that he or she had recently engaged in oral sex with another person, would you consider that sexual infidelity? What if he or she spent an hour sexting an attractive friend? These are the kinds of questions that come up in trying to define sexual behavior (McBride & others, 2017; Sewell, McGarrity, & Strassberg, 2017).

One possibility is to define sex as activities that are involved in reproduction and fertilization. By this interpretation, many gay men and women are virgins, as are adolescents who engage exclusively in, say, oral sex. Further, from this point of view, too, masturbation would not be a sexual behavior.

Another approach is to define sexual behavior by the arousal and sexual responses that occur when the behavior is performed. Though broader, this definition still might leave out individuals who themselves might say that they are engaged in sexual behavior. For instance, if a person is unable to experience sexual arousal but performs oral sex on a partner, has that person engaged in sexual behavior? Alternatively, we might broaden the definition a great deal and define sexual behaviors to include behaviors that are specific to each individual and that are pleasurable in a particular way—one that is unusually intimate and personal.

Confusion over what counts as sex can lead to potentially risky behavior. For example, oral sex has become relatively common during the teen years, with 33 percent of girls and 38 percent of boys between the ages of 15 and 17 reporting having engaged in oral sex (Copen, Chandra, & Martinez, 2012). For many adolescents, oral sex appears to be a recreational activity, and because many individuals under age 20 do not view the practice as sex, they believe that it is a safe alternative to intercourse (Halpern & Haydon, 2012).

RESEARCH ON SEXUAL BEHAVIOR   When people in the United States engage in sexual behavior, what do they do, and how often? Alfred Kinsey and his colleagues conducted the earliest research on this topic in 1948. Kinsey is widely recognized as a pioneer who brought scientific attention to sexual behavior. He was interested in studying sex objectively, without concern about guilt or shame. He collected data wherever he could find it, interviewing anyone willing to discuss the intimate details of his or her sex life.

The *Kinsey Reports,* published in two volumes, presented his findings for men (Kinsey, Pomeroy, & Martin, 1948) and women (Kinsey, Martin, & Pomeroy, 1953). Among the data that shocked his readers were Kinsey's estimates of the frequency of bisexuality in men (nearly 12 percent) and women (7 percent) and his estimate that at least 50 percent of married men had been sexually unfaithful. Although acknowledged for initiating the scientific study of sexual behavior, Kinsey's work was limited by the lack of representative samples.

Remember the importance of having a representative sample. Kinsey's research included only those who were willing to talk about their sex lives—a biased sample.

More recent surveys have provided a more nuanced picture of sexual behavior. For example, a national study of sexual behavior in the United States among adults 25 to 44 years of age found that 98 percent of the women and 97 percent of the men said that they had ever engaged in vaginal intercourse (Chandra & others, 2011). Also in this study, 89 percent of the women and 90 percent of the men reported that they ever had oral sex with an opposite-sex partner, and 36 percent of the women and 44 percent of the men stated that they ever had anal sex with an opposite-sex partner. A recent study of a sample of 278 newlyweds found that within a 2-week period, couples had sex an average of 3 to 4 times (Meltzer & McNulty, 2016).

A study comprising a representative sample of nearly 3,000 Swedes examined the frequency of different sexual behaviors in the previous month (Brody & Costa, 2009). The results showed that on average, men reported having vaginal intercourse 5 times and masturbating 4.5 times in the previous month. On average, women reported having vaginal intercourse about 5 times but masturbated less than 2 times during the previous month. For both men and women, oral sex occurred approximately 2 times and anal sex less than once (Brody & Costa, 2009).

Additional interesting information about the frequency of sexual behavior comes from a survey given to large samples of adults in the U.S. Starting in 1989, the survey asked participants about how many times they had had sex in the past year. Results spanning the years 1989 until 2014, including over 26,000 people, showed that overall sexual frequency has declined over the years (Twenge, Sherman, & Wells, 2017). For instance, between 1989 and 1994, respondents estimated that they had had sex approximately 60 times in the past year. In comparison, from 2010 to 2014, that number had dropped to about 54 times. Interestingly, this drop appears to exist because current younger generations are especially having less sex. Holding age constant, those born in the 1930s reported having sex about 6 times more often per year than those born in the 1990s. Another interesting trend from these data is a difference that has emerged in the effects of marriage on sexual frequency. Prior to 2003, married (or partnered) adults reported having more sex than the unmarried (or unpartnered). However, that difference disappeared in 2003 and by 2014, unmarried (or unpartnered) individuals reported having more sex than married (or partnered) people (Twenge, Sherman, & Wells, 2017).

Does sexual frequency matter to couples and individuals? For couples in a relationship, it is important to keep in mind that sexual intimacy exists in the context of a larger relationship, but sexual satisfaction does matter to relationship satisfaction (Schoenfeld & others, 2017). Sexual intimacy can create a deep bond between partners (McNulty, Wenner, & Fisher, 2016). A study of "sexual afterglow" in newlywed couples showed that having sex led to enhanced sexual satisfaction for 48 hours afterward (Meltzer & others, 2017). The stronger the couples' sexual afterglow, the more satisfied they were in their marriages over time. Sexual quality of life has been shown to decline with age, but older couples tend to focus more on the quality rather than quantity of sex with their partners (Forbes, Eaton, & Krueger, 2017). With regard to individual well-being, results have shown that sexual frequency does predict higher well-being but only up to a point. The frequency of sexual behavior is positively associated with psychological well-being but having sex once a week appears to be the amount at which this relationship levels off so that having sex more than once a week fails to increase well-being (Muise, Schimmack, & Impett, 2016). In this sense, sexual behavior appears to share a similar pattern with financial resources. For both sexual frequency and income, these variables are positively related to well-being but that relationship levels off once a particular point is met.

Gender Differences in Sexual Attitudes and Behavior   Differences between the sexes in sexual attitudes and sexual behaviors are areas on which a good deal of research has focused. However, many of the relevant studies have relied on self-reports of sexual behaviors, so the observed differences may have more to do with contrasting societal expectations for the two sexes than with actual differences in behavior. A meta-analysis revealed that for the following factors, stronger sex differences in sexuality were found: Men engaged in more masturbation, viewed more pornography, reported engaging in more casual sex, and had more permissive attitudes about casual sex than did women (Petersen & Hyde, 2010). Research has called into question many of the established differences between males and females in the domain of sexual behavior. For example, in a classic study, Russell Clark and Elaine Hatfield (1989) sent five men and five women experimenters to a college campus with a mission. They were to approach members of the opposite sex whom they found quite attractive and say, "I have been noticing you around campus. I find you very attractive." Then they were to ask one of three questions:

■ "Would you like to go out with me?"
■ "Would you like to go to my apartment with me?"
■ "Would you like to go to bed with me?"

The independent variables were the sex of the person approached and the type of question asked. The dependent variable was whether that person said yes or no to the question. There was no difference between men and women in their answers to the "going out" question—about half of each sex said yes. However, large sex differences emerged for the other two questions. Nearly 70 percent of men said yes to the "apartment" question, while most women said no. For the "bed" question, 75 percent of the men said yes, but *none* of the women did. For many years, this study was recognized as supporting the predictions that men are more interested in casual sex than are women and that women are choosier than men.

Can you identify a confound in the study design? Recall that a confound is a variable, other than the independent variable, that systematically differs across groups and that

338 // CHAPTER 9 // Motivation and Emotion

might explain differences between them on the dependent measure. Think about it—women were always approached *by men*, and men were always approached *by women*. Isn't it possible that the sex of the person doing the asking might have influenced whether those who were approached said yes to the proposal?

In a series of studies, Terri Conley (2011) showed that the proposer's characteristics influence whether the approached person accepts or rejects a proposal for casual sex. For instance, Conley found that both men and women rated a male stranger as potentially more dangerous than a female stranger. Would women be so choosy if they were approached by a familiar person rather than a stranger? Conley discovered that women were more likely to report that they would say yes to casual sex if it was offered by a familiar person, such as an attractive friend, or by a celebrity, such as Johnny Depp.

Other established gender differences in sexuality have also begun to fall by the wayside (Conley & others, 2011; Peterson & Hyde, 2011). For instance, men often report having more sex partners than women do. In a study using a fake lie detector test (called the *bogus pipeline*), however, this difference disappeared when men and women thought that the researchers could tell if they were lying (Alexander & Fisher, 2003).

This difference has always been puzzling, right? I mean, who were those men having sex with?

Do men at least *think about* having sex more often than women do? In another study, undergraduate participants kept tallies of how many times they thought about sex, food, and sleep for a week (Fisher, Moore, & Pittenger, 2012). Men did report thinking about sex more than women did. However, men also thought about food and sleep more than their female counterparts did. The researchers concluded that men may be more focused than women on their own physical needs.

Compared to men, women tend to show more changes in their sexual patterns and sexual desires over their lifetime (Baumeister, 2000; Diamond, Dickenson, & Blair, 2017; Kanazawa, 2017). Women are more likely than men, for instance, to have had sexual experiences with same- and opposite-sex partners, even if they identify themselves strongly as heterosexual or lesbian (Santtila & others, 2008). In contrast, male sexual interest may be more limited to particular targets of attraction (Chivers, 2017; Chivers & Brotto, 2017). One study compared the sexual arousal of heterosexual women, lesbian women, heterosexual men, and homosexual men while they watched erotic films of various sexual acts featuring male and female actors or bonobo apes. The films included scenes of sexual activity between same- and opposite-sex human partners and between opposite-sex bonobos, and scenes of men and women masturbating alone or engaging in aerobic exercise while naked. Sexual arousal was measured physiologically by monitoring the sex organs of men and women for indicators of arousal. Both heterosexual women and lesbian women were aroused by all of the films showing sexual activity (including those featuring the bonobos). However, gay men were aroused only by the films that included men, and heterosexual men were aroused only by the films that included women (Chivers, Seto, & Blanchard, 2007).

sexual orientation
The direction of an individual's erotic interests, today viewed as a continuum from exclusive male–female relations to exclusive same-sex relations.

SEXUAL ORIENTATION
Sex is clearly an important and powerful motivation. As such it makes sense to think about the direction of a person's sexual feelings. An individual's **sexual orientation** refers to the direction of his or her erotic interests. A person who identifies himself or herself as heterosexual is generally sexually attracted to members of the opposite sex. Someone who identifies himself or herself as homosexual is generally sexually attracted to members of the same sex.

Today, sexual orientation is commonly viewed as occurring along two dimensions. Those refer to how much a person is sexually attracted to members of the opposite sex and how much a person is attracted to members of the same sex. A person who experiences sexual interest in members of both sexes might self-identify as *bisexual,* meaning that they are sexually attracted to people of both sexes. In addition, a person who experiences low (or no) sexual interest in anyone might self-identify as *asexual* (Brotto & Yule, 2017), although whether asexuality ought to be

An individual's sexual orientation is most likely determined by a combination of genetic, hormonal, and perhaps psychological factors.
©Jakob Helbig/Getty Images

Homosexual behavior has been observed in nearly 1,500 species of animals, including rats, nonhuman primates, ostriches, goats, guppies, dolphins, and fruit flies (Bagemihl, 1999; Sommer and Vasey, 2006).

considered sexual orientation in its own right is still debated among scientists (Chasin, 2017; Cranney, 2017).

Despite the widespread use of labels such as "homosexual," "gay," "lesbian," "bisexual," or "asexual" some researchers argue that they are misleading. Because a person's erotic attractions may be fluid, these commentators say, references to a construct such as a fixed sexual orientation ignores the potential flexibility of human sexual attraction and behavior (Diamond & Savin-Williams, 2015; Kanazawa, 2017).

It is difficult to know precisely how many gays, lesbians, and bisexuals there are in the world, partly because fears of discrimination may prevent individuals from answering honestly on surveys. Estimates of the frequency of homosexuality range from 2 percent to 10 percent of the population and are typically higher for men than women (Zietsch & others, 2008). A recent Gallup poll found that 4.1 percent of Americans identified as LGBT (that is, lesbian, gay, bisexual, or transgender; Gates, 2017). That percentage would indicate that there are 10 million people who are LGBT, just less than the population of the state of Michigan. The number of millennials (those born between 1980 and 1998) identifying as LGBT was 7.3 percent (Gates, 2017).

Research shows that gay and lesbian individuals are similar to their heterosexual counterparts in many ways (L. M. Diamond, 2013a, 2013b; Savin-Williams, 2015).

Essentially, gay men are quite similar to heterosexual men, and lesbians are quite similar to heterosexual women.

Regardless of their sexual orientation, all people have similar physiological responses during sexual arousal and seem to be aroused by the same types of tactile stimulation. Investigators typically find no differences among lesbians, gays, bisexuals, and heterosexuals in a wide range of attitudes, behaviors, and psychological adjustment (Allen & Diamond, 2012). An important aspect of sexual minority well-being is coping with prejudice and discrimination (Riggle & others, 2017).

What explains a person's sexual orientation? Speculation about this question has been extensive. Scientists have learned about factors that *do not* predict sexual orientation. First, being reared by a gay parent does not increase the chances of being gay (Farr & Patterson, 2013; Patterson & Farr, 2014). In fact, the vast majority of gay individuals have heterosexual parents. Nor does a particular parenting style relate to the emergence of homosexuality (Bell, Weinberg, & Hammersmith, 1981). Think about it for a moment: Any theory of sexual orientation must be able to explain not only homosexuality but also *heterosexuality* (Breedlove, 2017). Why is it that the majority of people feel sexually attracted to the opposite sex and never question that feeling? Given the many different ways in which parents interact with their children and the fact that the vast majority of people are heterosexual, it seems unlikely that the emergence of heterosexuality is explained by particular parenting strategies. The fact that most homosexual and bisexual individuals have heterosexual parents contradicts the influence of observational learning or modeling in the development of sexual orientation. Further, same-sex sexual experience or experimentation in childhood does not predict eventual adult homosexuality (Bailey, 2003; Bogaert, 2000).

Researchers have examined a number of biological factors that might contribute to sexual attraction to the same sex. For example, research shows that genes play a role in sexual orientation. Twin studies have been used to estimate the heritability of sexual orientation. Heritability is a statistic that indicates the extent to which observed differences in a given characteristic can be explained based on differences in genes. A study of nearly 4,000 twins in Sweden demonstrated that the heritability of same-sex sexual behavior was about 35 percent in men and 19 percent in women (Langstrom & others, 2010). These heritability estimates suggest that although genes play a role in sexual orientation, genes are not as strong an influence as they are for other characteristics, such as intelligence. Researchers are investigating the molecular genetics of male homosexuality (Sanders & others, 2015). In addition to genes, researchers have found that, for women in particular, same sex attraction may be rooted, at least in part, in prenatal exposure to androgens (male hormones) (Balthazart & Court, 2017; Breedlove, 2017).

Genetic explanations for homosexuality present a puzzle for evolutionary psychologists. How can a characteristic that decreases a person's likelihood of reproducing be passed down genetically (Chaladze, 2016)? One possibility is that some of the same genes that contribute to homosexuality may also lead to reproductive success for heterosexual individuals who possess them (Iemmola & Ciani, 2009). Research has examined twin pairs in which one twin is heterosexual and the other homosexual (Zietsch & others, 2008). Heterosexual twins of homosexual individuals are likely to possess attractive qualities (such as, for men, being caring and gentle; and for women, being assertive and sexually open) and to have more sex partners than heterosexual individuals with heterosexual twins (Zietsch & others, 2008).

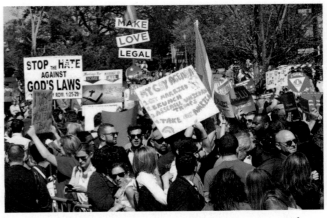

Although same-sex marriage can be a contentious issue, support for marriage equality hit an all-time high of 60 percent in the United States in 2015.
©Patsy Lynch/REX/Shutterstock

Clearly, much remains to be explained about the determination of sexual orientation. Similar to many other psychological characteristics, an individual's sexual orientation most likely depends on a combination of genetic, hormonal, and perhaps psychological factors. No one factor alone causes sexual orientation and the relative weight of each factor can vary between men and women and one individual to the next (Balthazart & Court, 2017).

Whether heterosexual, homosexual, or bisexual, a person cannot be talked out of his or her sexual orientation. Homosexuality is present in all cultures, regardless of whether a culture is accepting or intolerant. Research tells us that whether one is homosexual, heterosexual, or bisexual, sexual orientation is not a choice but an integral part of the functioning human being and his or her sense of self (Breedlove, 2017).

Available evidence suggests that gay and lesbian households exist in 99 percent of counties throughout the United States, and approximately one in four of these households includes children (O'Barr, 2006). Children reared by gay men and lesbian women tend to be as well adjusted as those from heterosexual households, are no more likely to be homosexual themselves, and are no less likely to be accepted by their peers (Farr & Patterson, 2013; Oakley, Farr, & Scherer, 2017; Patterson, 2013, 2014; Patterson & Farr, 2014; Sumontha, Farr, & Patterson, 2017).

Research suggests that gay parents are likely to prioritize diversity in their parenting and emphasize with children the importance of respecting all kinds of families (Oakley, Farr, & Scherer, 2017). One study compared the incidence of coparenting (the support that parents give each other in raising a child) in adoptive heterosexual, lesbian, and gay couples with preschool-aged children (Farr & Patterson, 2013). Both self-reports and observations indicated that lesbian and gay couples shared child care more than heterosexual couples did, with lesbian couples being the most supportive of each other and gay couples the least supportive of each other in parenting. Another study revealed more positive parenting in adoptive gay father families and fewer child externalizing problems in these families than in heterosexual families (Golombok & others, 2014).

In the United States, same-sex marriage and gay parenting have generated controversy, especially in political election years. The current legal status of same sex marriage fits with the scientific consensus that marriage equality for same-sex couples supports their well-being and the well-being of their children (American Psychological Association, 2004).

1. Obesity
   A. does not have a genetic component.
   B. is linked to good health.
   C. is associated with the body's set point.
   D. has most recently decreased in the United States.

2. The brain structure(s) *primarily* involved in motivation for sexual behavior is(are) the
   A. hypothalamus.
   B. temporal lobes.
   C. hippocampus.
   D. medulla.

3. Research indicates that one factor that can predict a person's sexual orientation is

   A. the parenting style with which he or she grew up.
   B. having a homosexual parent.
   C. having a heterosexual parent.
   D. genetic background.

APPLY IT! 4. A small town's school board is considering what type of sex education program to adopt for the high school. A number of individuals have expressed concern that giving students information about contraception will send the message that it is okay to engage in sexual activity. Which of the following reflects the research relevant to this issue?
   A. Students who are given information about contraception generally

have sex earlier and more frequently than individuals who are not given this information.
   B. Students who are given abstinence-only education are least likely to engage in sex at all.
   C. Sex education in schools has shown no relationship to adolescent sexual activity.
   D. Students who are given comprehensive information about contraception are less likely to become pregnant during adolescence and are not more likely to engage in sexual activity.

3 Beyond Hunger and Sex: Motivation in Everyday Life

Food and sex are crucial to human survival. Surviving is not all we do, however. Think about the wide range of human actions and achievements reported in the news—everything from a man's donation of his kidney to the rise of a woman who grew up in poverty to be the CEO of a major corporation. Such behavior is not easily explained by motivational approaches that focus on physiological needs. Today psychologists appreciate the role of the goals that people set for themselves in motivation. In this section, we explore the ways that psychologists explain the processes underlying everyday human behavior.

Maslow's Hierarchy of Human Needs

hierarchy of needs
Maslow's theory that human needs must be satisfied in the following sequence: physiological needs, safety, love and belongingness, esteem, and self-actualization.

Humanistic theorist Abraham Maslow (1954, 1971) proposed a **hierarchy of needs** (Figure 3) that must be satisfied in the following sequence: physiological needs, safety, love and belongingness, esteem, and self-actualization. The strongest needs are at the base of the hierarchy (physiological), and the weakest are at the top (self-actualization). According to this hierarchy, people are motivated to satisfy their need for food first and to satisfy their need for safety before their need for love. If we think of our needs as calls for action, hunger and safety needs shout loudly, while the need for self-actualization beckons with a whisper. Maslow asserted that each lower need in the hierarchy comes from a deficiency, such as being hungry, afraid, or lonely, and that we see the higher-level needs in a person who is relatively sated in these basic needs. Such an individual can turn his or her attention to the fulfillment of a higher calling, achieving a sense of meaning by contributing something of lasting value to the world.

 Maslow later added self-transcendence as a need even higher than self-actualization. Self-transcendence involves a level of experience that is beyond the self, including spirituality, compassion, and morality. What other needs do you think Maslow left out of his original hierarchy?

Self-actualization, the highest and most elusive of Maslow's needs, is the motivation to develop one's full potential as a human being. According to Maslow, self-actualization is possible only after the other needs in the hierarchy are met. Maslow cautions that most people stop moving up the hierarchy after they have developed a high level of esteem and thus do not become self-actualized.

The idea that human motives are hierarchically arranged is appealing; however, Maslow's ordering of the needs is debatable. Some people, for example, might seek greatness in a career to achieve self-esteem while putting on hold their needs for love and belongingness. Certainly history is full of examples of individuals

self-actualization
The motivation to develop one's full potential as a human being—the highest and most elusive of Maslow's proposed needs.

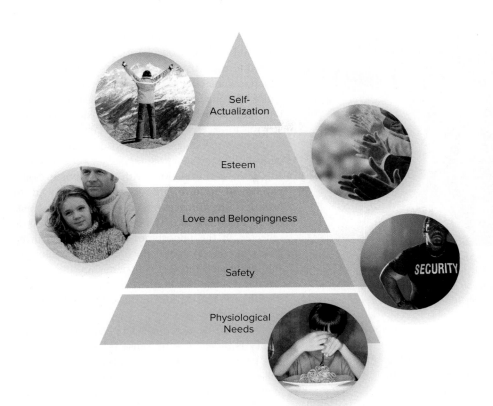

FIGURE 3
Maslow's Hierarchy of Needs Abraham Maslow developed the hierarchy of human needs to show that we have to satisfy basic physiological needs before we can satisfy other, higher needs.

(mountain) ©photogl/iStock/Getty Images; (clapping) ©Brand X Pictures/ PunchStock; (father and daughter) ©Digital Vision; (security) ©Brand X Pictures; (eating) ©Brooke Fasani/ Corbis

who, in the most difficult circumstances, were still able to perform acts of kindness that seem to come from higher-level needs. Research demonstrates that poor individuals are more likely than wealthy individuals to give generously to others (Kraus & others, 2012; Piff & others, 2010).

Perhaps Maslow's greatest contribution to our understanding of motivation is that he asked the key question about motivation for modern people: How can we explain what humans do, once their bellies are full? That is, how do we explain the "why" of human behavior when survival is not the most pressing need? This is the kind of questioning that inspired self-determination theory.

Self-Determination Theory

Building from Maslow's humanistic approach, Richard Ryan and Edward Deci (2017) have developed a theory of motivation that emphasizes particular kinds of needs as factors in optimal human functioning. Their **self-determination theory** asserts that there are three basic organismic needs: competence, relatedness, and autonomy. These psychological needs are innate and exist in every person. They are basic to human growth and functioning, just as water, soil, and sunshine are necessary for plant growth. This metaphor is especially apt, because once we plant a seed, all it requires to thrive and grow is a supportive environment. Similarly, self-determination theory holds that all of us have the capacity for growth and fulfillment in us, ready to emerge if our basic needs are met.

From the perspective of self-determination theory, these organismic needs do not arise from deficits. Self-determination theory is not a drive reduction theory. Like Maslow, Deci and Ryan argue that these needs concern personal growth, not the filling of deficiencies (Deci & Ryan, 2000, 2012; Ryan & Deci, 2017). Let's examine each of these needs in depth.

The first organismic need described by self-determination theory, *competence*, is met when we feel that we are able to bring about desired outcomes. Competence motivation involves *self-efficacy* (the belief that you have the competence to accomplish a given goal

self-determination theory Deci and Ryan's theory asserting that all humans have three basic, innate organismic needs: competence, relatedness, and autonomy.

Paralympics competitors command powerful self-determination. Paralympic sprinting and long-jump medalist Kelly Cartwright says, "To advance in life you need to believe in yourself and you need to set goals for yourself. Push yourself, because you can achieve anything in life if you put your mind to it" (Paralympic Movement, 2012).
©A. Ricardo/Shutterstock

or task) and *mastery* (the sense that you can gain skills and overcome obstacles). Competence is also related to expectancies for success. One domain in which competence needs may be met is in the realm of achievement. Some individuals are highly motivated to succeed and spend considerable effort striving to excel.

The second organismic need described by self-determination theory is *relatedness*—the need to engage in warm relations with other people. Some psychologists have proposed that the need to belong is the strongest human motivator (Baumeister & Leary, 2000). The need for relatedness is reflected in the importance of parents' nurturing children's development, the intimate moments of sharing private thoughts in friendship, the uncomfortable feelings we have when we are lonely, and the powerful attraction we have for someone else when we are in love.

The third need proposed by self-determination theory is *autonomy*—the sense that we are in control of our own life. Autonomy is not just being independent and self-reliant; it is a key aspect of feeling that one's behavior is self-motivated and emerging from genuine interest (Sheldon & others, 2017). Of course, many of the behaviors we engage in may feel like things we are forced to do, but a sense of autonomy is strongly related to well-being (Sheldon & others, 2005). Teachers, bosses, parents, and caregivers can increase the well-being of students, employees, offspring, and partners when they support the person's sense of autonomy (Hobson & Maxwell, 2017; Nie & others, 2015; Niemiec & Coulson, 2017; Uysal, Ascigil, & Turunc, 2017; van der Kaap-Deeder & others, 2017).

Research on the role of motivation in well-being supports the idea that progress on goals that serve the three organismic needs is strongly related to well-being (Koletzko, Herrmann, & Brandstätter, 2015; Sheldon & Elliot, 1998). Further, valuing more extrinsic qualities—such as money, prestige, and physical appearance—over these organismic concerns is associated with lowered well-being, lowered self-actualization, and physical illness (Kasser & Ryan, 1996; Kasser & others, 2004). Self-determination theory maintains that when we are engaged in intrinsically motivated behavior that meets our needs for competence, relatedness, and autonomy, we are likely to experience personal growth and optimal well-being (Ryan & Deci, 2017).

From the perspective of self-determination theory, an essential aspect of healthy functioning is actively engaging in behaviors that are self-directed. Human beings engage in many behaviors that easily fit into this ideal. But, the appeal of some of the things we spend a great deal of time doing are not as easily explained by self-determination theory. Consider how much time you spend watching TV (or TV shows on a device). The average American spends about 30 hours a week watching television shows (Bureau of Labor Statistics, 2017). Although younger Americans watch less television on televisions, they still spend substantial time watching TV shows, especially binge watching (spending at least 5 hours watching a particular show) (Deloitte, 2016). Whether watching on a smartphone or laptop or television set, watching television shows is certainly passive. It involves simply watching and enjoying. Compared to other leisure activities like playing sports, working out, reading, or even playing video games, watching TV seems unlikely to involve engaging actively with an activity. Can we place the behavior of watching television in the context of optimal human functioning? To see how, check out the Challenge Your Thinking.

Like any theory, self-determination theory has ignited some controversies. One important issue is the extent to which the three needs are universal. Cultures vary in how strongly they promote the needs for competence, relatedness, and autonomy. Many Western cultures—among them, the United States, Canada, and western European countries—are

Can Watching TV Shows Contribute to Optimal Well-Being?

If it is Sunday night, it is a good bet that many Americans are anxiously awaiting the latest episode of *Game of Thrones*. The popularity of shows like *Game of Thrones, Stranger Things,* and the *Walking Dead* attests to the appeal of television dramas for everyday people. Can the science of motivation explain what makes these dramas so popular? A recent series of studies applied self-determination theory to try to identify the qualities of TV dramas that make them especially appealing (Adachi & others, 2017). The researchers surmised that popular shows may be appealing because they are more likely to present themes that bring about need-related experiences. So by engaging even passively with TV dramas, we may have an opportunity to engage our intrinsic needs and vicariously learn and even grow from what we've seen.

In one study, participants were randomly assigned to watch one of two TV dramas, either the very successful *Jessica Jones* or the considerably less successful *Killer Women*. Afterward, participants rated the extent to which each show possessed characteristics that might be associated with intrinsic needs. These characteristics included intellectual stimulation, meaningful or virtuous messages, novelty and surprise, and identification with the protagonist. The main dependent measures were whether participants were intrinsically interested in watching the show again and whether they would recommend it to another

©Hill Street Studios/Getty Images

person. The results showed that the more popular show was more likely to possess characteristics that appeal to intrinsic needs. In addition, and most importantly, these features predicted interest in watching the show again and being willing to recommend it to a friend (Adachi & others, 2017).

In thinking about these results you might be thinking about shows like *Breaking Bad,* in which the characters are not virtuous people, at all. These researchers suggest that even when characters are not "good people" we can connect with them and grapple with the moral issues that plague them. Certainly humanity has been compelled by drama since the beginning of our species. These results suggest that whether it is Sophocles, Shakespeare, or George R.R. Martin, and whether we are gathered at a theater or huddled around a screen, we are engaged with dramas that pull at our central human motivations.

What Do You Think?

- Do you have a favorite TV drama? What makes it so appealing?
- Do you think people watch comedies for the same reasons as drama? Why or why not?

---

termed *individualistic* because they emphasize individual achievement, independence, and self-reliance. In contrast, many Eastern cultures—such as China, Japan, and Korea—are called *collectivistic* because they stress affiliation, cooperation, and interdependence (Triandis, 2000). However, cross-cultural evidence suggests that the needs emphasized by self-determination theory are valued in both Western and Eastern cultures and similarly associated with well-being (Yu, Levesque-Bristol, & Maeda, 2017).

Self-determination theory maintains that one of the most important aspects of healthy motivation is the sense that we do the things we do because we have freely chosen to do them. When our behaviors follow from the needs for competence, autonomy, and relatedness, we experience intrinsic motivation. When our behavior serves needs for other values, such as prestige, money, or approval, our behavior is extrinsically motivated (Deci, 2013; Deci & Ryan, 1994, 2012; Ryan & Deci, 2000, 2001, 2009). We examine this important distinction between intrinsic and extrinsic motivation next.

Intrinsic versus Extrinsic Motivation

One way psychologists understand the "why" of our goals is by distinguishing between intrinsic and extrinsic motivation. **Intrinsic motivation** is based on internal factors such as organismic needs (competence, relatedness, and autonomy), as well as curiosity, challenge,

intrinsic motivation
Motivation based on internal factors such as organismic needs (competence, relatedness, and autonomy), as well as curiosity, challenge, and fun.

extrinsic motivation
Motivation that involves external incentives such as rewards and punishments.

and fun. When we are intrinsically motivated, we explore, investigate, and master because doing so is enjoyable. **Extrinsic motivation** involves external incentives such as rewards and punishments. When we are extrinsically motivated, we engage in a behavior for some external payoff or to avoid an external punishment. Some students study hard because they are internally motivated to put forth considerable effort and achieve high quality in their work (intrinsic motivation). Other students study hard because they want to make good grades or avoid parental disapproval (extrinsic motivation).

If someone is producing shoddy work, seems bored, or has a negative attitude, offering an external incentive may improve motivation. There are times, though, when external rewards can diminish intrinsic motivation. The problem with using a reward as an incentive is that individuals may perceive that the reward rather than their own motivation caused their achievement behavior. Indeed, research comparisons often reveal that people whose motivation is intrinsic show more interest, excitement, and confidence in what they are doing than those whose motivation is extrinsic. Intrinsic motivation often results in improved performance, persistence, creativity, and self-esteem (Ryan & Deci, 2013). A recent study tested the associations between intrinsic and extrinsic motivation and supervisor ratings, work commitment, burnout, and work-family conflict, among employees in various industries (Kuvaas & others, 2017). The results showed that intrinsic motivation predicted higher evaluations and commitment and lower burnout and work-family conflict. In contrast, extrinsic motivation was negatively related (or unrelated) to positive work outcomes.

Of course, many very successful individuals are both intrinsically motivated (they have high personal standards of achievement and emphasize personal effort) and extrinsically motivated (they are strongly competitive). Elite athletes such as Olympic team members, as well as individuals who are highly successful in the business world, may be motivated by both intrinsic and extrinsic rewards. Indeed, many of us might think of the ideal occupation as one in which we get paid well (an extrinsic reward) for doing the very thing we love to do (intrinsic motivation).

The very term *intrinsic motivation* suggests that some activities are their own reward. If such is the case, we might expect that the brain would process intrinsically motivated activities as if they were rewards. Does it? To find out, see the Intersection.

Self-Regulation: The Successful Pursuit of Goals

Today many psychologists approach motivation by asking about goals and values and seeking to understand how these motivational forces shape behavior. Psychologists have referred to goals by various names, including *personal projects, best possible selves, life tasks,* and *personal strivings* (King, 2008). All of these terms reflect the goals a person is trying to accomplish in everyday life. Self-generated goals can range from trivial matters (such as letting a bad haircut grow out) to life tasks (such as becoming a good parent).

self-regulation
The process by which an organism effortfully controls its behavior in order to pursue important objectives.

Goal approaches to motivation include **self-regulation,** the process by which an individual effortfully controls behavior in order to pursue important objectives (Cole & others, 2017). A key aspect of self-regulation is getting feedback about how we are doing in our goal pursuits (Lee, 2016). Our daily mood has been proposed as a way that we may receive this feedback—that is, we feel good or bad depending on how we are doing in the areas of life we value. Note that the role of mood in self-regulation means that we cannot be happy all the time. To pursue our goals effectively, we have to be open to the bad news that might occasionally come our way.

Putting our personal goals into action is a potentially complex process that involves setting goals, planning for their implementation, and monitoring our progress. Individuals' success improves when they set goals that are specific and moderately challenging

Motivation and Neuroscience: Can We See Intrinsic Motivation in the Brain?

A great deal of research in neuroscience has examined how the brain processes rewards. That is, researchers have been interested in seeing how the brain responds when the person might receive, say, a $5 reward or win a contest. Research has shown that such rewards are associated with activation in the striatum (Haber & Knutson, 2010). The striatum is considered to be responsible for integrating reward-related information. Yet note that these circumstances are not simply rewarding, they are *extrinsically* rewarding. How does the brain process intrinsically rewarding activities? To find out, researchers (Lee & Reeve, 2017) used fMRI to monitor brain activity while participants completed a task that was intrinsically interesting or not.

How did the researchers operationalize intrinsic interest? For the intrinsically interesting task, participants were asked questions that were likely to inspire curiosity. These included "What book is most likely to be shoplifted?" and "Which animal can shed up to 30,000 teeth in its lifetime?" In the control condition the questions were not interesting, including "What is the capital of

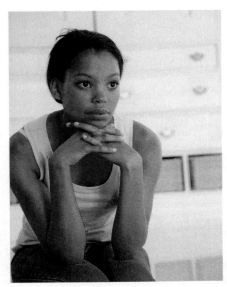
©Fancy Collection/SuperStock

France?" and "What country has the highest population?"

After confirming that participants did find the intrinsically interesting question more interesting, they compared the brains of participants in each condition. They found that, as expected, the striatum, the hub of reward processing, was more activated in the interesting group than in the uninteresting group (Lee & Reeve, 2017). These results are important because they show that the brain responds to stimuli that are just plain interesting as if they are rewards. Of course, psychologists who study intrinsic motivation would assert, that is, in fact, what they are.

By the way, the answer to those curious questions above? *The Bible* and sharks. If you could not stop thinking about those questions, what do you think your striatum was doing?

\\ **What are some activities you find intrinsically rewarding?**

(Bandura, 1997; Schunk, 2012). A fuzzy, nonspecific goal is "I want to be successful." A concrete, specific goal is "I want to have a 3.5 average at the end of the semester." You can set both long-term and short-term goals. When you set long-term goals, such as "I want to be a clinical psychologist," make sure that you also create short-term goals as steps along the way, such as "I want to get an *A* on my next psychology test." Make commitments in manageable chunks. Planning how to reach a goal and monitoring progress toward the goal are critical aspects of achievement. Monitoring goal progress leads to higher achievement (Harkin & others, 2016).

Even as we keep our nose to the grindstone in pursuing short-term goals, it is also important to have a sense of the big picture. Dedication to a long-term dream or personal mission can enhance the experience of purpose in life. While short-term goals can provide a sense of accomplishment, attaching these goals to a future dream can allow individuals to experience a sense of meaning and to maintain their efforts in the face of short-term failure (Houser-Marko & Sheldon, 2008). Recent research showed that thinking about the big picture of goal pursuit can also facilitate the accomplishment of smaller goals. In the studies, participants were asked to imagine that they had completed a goal. They were to imagine success in all its glory and then to plan backwards, from attainment to the subgoals themselves. This strategy led to better goal success (Jooyoung, Lu, & Hedgcock, 2017).

self-quiz

1. Rank-order the following needs according to Maslow's hierarchy: hunger, self-esteem, social relationships, safety.
   A. Social relationships must be fulfilled first, followed by hunger, safety, and finally self-esteem.
   B. Self-esteem must be fulfilled first, followed by social relationships, safety, and hunger.
   C. Hunger must be fulfilled first, followed by safety, social relationships, and finally self-esteem.
   D. Safety must be fulfilled first, followed by hunger, social relationships, and finally self-esteem.

2. Self-efficacy is most related to which need from self-determination theory?
   A. autonomy.
   B. relatedness.
   C. competence.
   D. self-actualization.

3. Of the following, the individual who will likely perform best is someone with
   A. high extrinsic motivation.
   B. low extrinsic motivation.
   C. high intrinsic motivation.
   D. low intrinsic motivation.

APPLY IT! 4. Kim cannot wait to play with her new Xbox. Unfortunately, she has an exam tomorrow and needs to study instead of trying out her new game. Which strategy should help Kim do well on the exam?
   A. Kim should put the new game cartridge up on her bookshelf as a reminder that she can have fun soon if she studies.
   B. Kim should allow herself to look the game over and maybe even play a little before settling down to study.
   C. Kim should put the game away where she cannot even see it or think about it. She will then be able to study without distraction.
   D. Kim should play with the game for as long as she likes, to get it out of her system.

4 Emotion

Octavia Spencer displayed a range of emotions, from surprise to joy to gratitude, when she won the Academy Award for Best Supporting Actress for the film The Help in 2012.
©Jim Smeal/BEI/REX/Shutterstock

As the concept of self-regulation implies, motivation and emotion are closely linked. We can feel happy or sad depending on how events influence the likelihood of our getting the things we want in life. Sometimes our emotions take us by surprise and give us a reality check about what we really want. We might think, for example, that we have lost interest in our romantic partner until that person initiates a breakup. Suddenly, we realize how much he or she really means to us. Anyone who has watched an awards show on television surely knows the link between motivation and emotion. Strolling in on the red carpet, the celebrities stress how honored they are to be nominated; but behind the Hollywood smiles is the longing to win. When the announcement is made, "And the Oscar goes to . . .," the cameras zoom in to catch a glimpse of real emotion: the winner's face lighting up with joy and, of course, the moment of disappointment for the others.

Emotions are certainly complex. The body, the mind, and the face play key roles in emotion, although psychologists debate which of these components is most significant in emotion and how they mix to produce emotional experiences (Fiacconi, Dekraker, & Köhler, 2015; Kayser, 2017; Khan, Schmidt, & Chen, 2017). For our purposes, **emotion** is feeling, or *affect,* that can involve physiological arousal (such as a fast heartbeat), conscious experience (thinking about being in love with someone), and behavioral expression (a smile or grimace).

emotion
Feeling, or affect, that can involve physiological arousal (such as a fast heartbeat), conscious experience (thinking about being in love with someone), and behavioral expression (a smile or grimace).

Biological Factors in Emotion

A friend whom you have been counseling about a life problem calls you to say, "We need to talk." As the time of your friend's visit approaches, you get nervous. What could be going on? You feel burdened—you have a lot of work to do, and you do not have time for a talk session. You also worry that she might be angry or disappointed about something you have done. When she arrives with a gift-wrapped package and a big smile, your nerves give way to relief. She announces, "I wanted to give you this present to say thanks for all your help over the last few weeks." Your heart warms, and you feel a strong sense of your enduring bond with her. As you moved

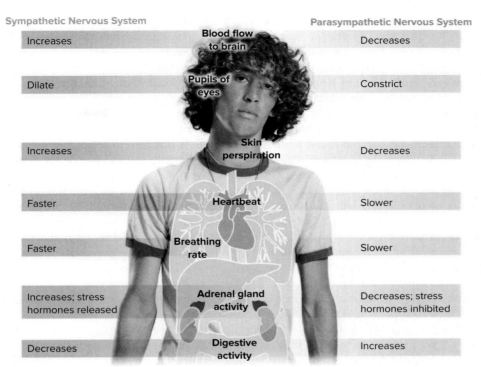

Sympathetic Nervous System		Parasympathetic Nervous System
Increases	Blood flow to brain	Decreases
Dilate	Pupils of eyes	Constrict
Increases	Skin perspiration	Decreases
Faster	Heartbeat	Slower
Faster	Breathing rate	Slower
Increases; stress hormones released	Adrenal gland activity	Decreases; stress hormones inhibited
Decreases	Digestive activity	Increases

FIGURE 4

The Autonomic Nervous System and Its Role in Arousing and Calming the Body The two parts of the autonomic nervous system work in different ways. The sympathetic nervous system arouses the body in reaction to a stressor, evoking the fight-or-flight response. In contrast, the parasympathetic nervous system calms the body, promoting relaxation and healing. Remember, the latter system functions to "rest and digest."

©James Woodson/Getty Images

through the emotions of worry, relief, and joy, your body changed. Indeed, the body is a crucial part of our emotional experience.

AROUSAL   Recall that the *autonomic nervous system (ANS)* takes messages to and from the body's internal organs, monitoring such processes as breathing, heart rate, and digestion. The ANS is divided into the sympathetic and the parasympathetic nervous systems (Figure 4). The *sympathetic nervous system (SNS)* is involved in the body's arousal; it is responsible for a rapid reaction to a stressor, sometimes referred to as the fight-or-flight response. The SNS immediately causes an increase in blood pressure, a faster heart rate, more rapid breathing for greater oxygen intake, and more efficient blood flow to the brain and major muscle groups. All of these changes prepare us for action. At the same time, the body stops digesting food, because it is not necessary for immediate action (which could explain why just before an exam, students usually are not hungry).

The *parasympathetic nervous system (PNS)* calms the body. Whereas the sympathetic nervous system prepares the individual for fighting or running away, the parasympathetic nervous system promotes relaxation and healing. When the PNS is activated, heart rate and blood pressure drop, stomach activity and food digestion increase, and breathing slows.

The sympathetic and parasympathetic nervous systems evolved to improve the human species' likelihood for survival, but it does not take a life-threatening situation to activate them. Emotions such as anger and fear are associated with elevated SNS activity as exemplified in heightened blood pressure and heart rate. States of happiness and contentment also activate the SNS to a lesser extent.

Remember:
Sympathetic = "fight or flight"
Parasympathetic = "rest and digest"

MEASURING AROUSAL   Because arousal includes a physiological response, researchers have been intrigued by how to measure it accurately. One aspect of emotional arousal is *skin conductance level (SCL)* response, a rise in the skin's electrical conductivity when sweat gland activity increases. A sweaty palm conducts electricity better than a dry palm, and this difference provides the basis for SCL, which produces an index of arousal that has been used in many studies of emotion.

Another measure of arousal is the **polygraph** or lie detector, a machine examiners use to try to determine whether someone is lying. The polygraph monitors changes in the body—heart rate, breathing, and SCL—thought to be influenced by emotional states.

In a typical polygraph test, the examiner asks the individual a number of neutral questions and several key, less neutral questions. If the individual's heart rate, breathing, and SCL responses increase substantially when the key questions are asked, the individual is assumed to be lying (Palmatier & Rovner, 2014; Schenk & others, 2014).

How accurate is the lie detector? Although it measures the degree of arousal to a series of questions, no one has found a unique physiological response to telling lies (Lykken, 1987, 2001; Seymour & others, 2000). Heart rate and breathing can increase for reasons other than lying, and this effect can make it difficult to interpret the physiological indicators of arousal. Accurately identifying truth or deception is linked with the skill of both the examiner and the individual being examined. Body movements and the presence of certain drugs in the person's system can interfere with the polygraph's accuracy. Sometimes the mere presence of the polygraph and the individual's belief that it is accurate in detecting deception trigger a confession of guilt. Police may use the polygraph in this way to get a suspect to confess (Gannon & others, 2014). However, in too many instances it has been misused and misrepresented. Experts argue that the polygraph errs just under 50 percent of the time, especially as it cannot distinguish between such feelings as anxiety and guilt (Iacono & Lykken, 1997).

If a test confuses anxiety and guilt, how can it distinguish between a nervous person and a liar?

The Employee Polygraph Protection Act of 1988 restricts polygraph testing outside government agencies, and most courts do not accept the results of lie detectors. However, some psychologists defend the polygraph's use, saying that polygraph results are as sound as other admissible forms of evidence, such as hair fiber analysis (Grubin & Madsen, 2006). The majority of psychologists, though, argue against the polygraph's use because of its inability to tell who is lying and who is not (Iacono & Lykken, 1997; Lykken, 1998; Saxe & Ben-Shakhur, 1999; Steinbrook, 1992).

PHYSIOLOGICAL THEORIES OF EMOTION

Imagine that you are on a picnic in the country. Suddenly, a bull runs across the field toward you. Why are you afraid? Common sense tells you that you are trembling and fleeing from the bull because you are afraid, but William James (1950) and Carl Lange (1922) said emotion works in the opposite way. According to the **James-Lange theory,** emotion results from physiological states triggered by stimuli in the environment. Essentially, the theory proposes that after the initial perception of a stimulus, the experience of the emotion results from the perception of one's own physiological changes (changes in heart rate, breathing, and sweating patterns, for example). In the case of the charging bull, you see the bull approaching and you run away. Your aroused body then sends sensory messages to your brain, at which point emotion is perceived. You do not run away because you are afraid; rather, you are afraid because you are running away.

©Digital Vision/Punchstock

Remember for James-Lange: Bodily responses comes first, then we feel an emotion; for Cannon-Bard, these two things happen at the same time

James-Lange theory
The theory that emotion results from physiological states triggered by stimuli in the environment.

Walter Cannon (1927) presented an alternative physiologically based theory of emotion. To understand it, imagine the bull and the picnic once again. Seeing the bull approaching causes your brain's thalamus simultaneously to (1) stimulate your autonomic nervous system to produce the physiological changes involved in emotion (increased heart rate, rapid breathing) and (2) send messages to your cerebral cortex, where the experience of emotion is perceived. Philip Bard (1934) supported this analysis, and the theory became known as the **Cannon-Bard theory**—the proposition that emotion and physiological reactions occur simultaneously. In the Cannon-Bard theory, the body plays a less important role than in the James-Lange theory.

Cannon-Bard theory
The proposition that emotion and physiological reactions occur simultaneously.

NEURAL CIRCUITS AND NEUROTRANSMITTERS

Contemporary researchers are keenly interested in identifying the neurotransmitters and neural circuitry involved in emotions. For example, dopamine and endorphins are linked to positive emotions (Burgdorf, Panksepp, & Moskal, 2014). Norepinephrine functions in regulating arousal and anxiety (Jones, Chase, & Fournier, 2016). Low levels of serotonin are linked to anger and aggression (da Cunha-Bang & others, 2017) and the persistence of negative moods (van Roekel & others, 2017).

With regard to brain structures that play a role in emotion, a great deal of research concerns the amygdalae, the almond-shaped structures in the limbic system (Frank & others, 2014; Wang & others, 2014). The amygdalae house circuits that are activated when we encounter important, survival-relevant stimuli in the environment. The limbic system, including the amygdalae, is involved in the experience of positive emotions (Vrticka & others, 2014). However, most research has focused on the important role of the amygdalae in the experience of negative emotion, particularly fear.

Research by Joseph LeDoux and his colleagues (LeDoux, 1996, 2002, 2008, 2012, 2013, 2014; LeDoux & Pine, 2016) has documented the central role of the amygdalae in fear. When the amygdalae determine that danger is present, they shift into high gear, marshaling the brain's resources in an effort to protect the organism from harm. This fear system evolved to detect and respond to predators and other types of natural dangers that threaten survival or territory.

The brain circuitry that involves the emotion of fear can follow two pathways: a direct pathway from the thalamus to the amygdala or an indirect pathway from the thalamus through the sensory cortex to the amygdala (Figure 5). The direct pathway does not convey detailed information about the stimulus, but it has the advantage of speed—and speed clearly is an important characteristic of information for an organism facing a threat to its survival. The indirect pathway carries nerve impulses from the sensory organs (eyes and ears, for example) to the thalamus (recall that the thalamus is a relay station for incoming sensory stimuli); from the thalamus, the nerve impulses travel to the sensory cortex, which then sends appropriate signals to the amygdala.

Recall that the amygdalae are linked with emotional memories. LeDoux and his colleagues say that the amygdalae hardly ever forget (Debiec & LeDoux, 2006; Duvarci, Nader, & LeDoux, 2008; LeDoux, 2001, 2008, 2012, 2013, 2014). This quality is useful, because once we learn that something is dangerous, we do not have to relearn it. However, we pay a penalty for this ability. Many people carry fears and anxieties around with them that they would like to get rid of but cannot seem to shake. We will look at such fears when we explore phobias. Part of the reason fears are so difficult to change is that the

The amygdala's ability to respond quickly to threatening stimuli is adaptive. Think about early humans, facing a world filled with threatening predators. Members of our species who had to encounter a hungry tiger more than once before learning to avoid it probably didn't survive to reproduce. So, we have our great-great-great-great-great-great-great grandparents to thank for our amygdala.

FIGURE 5

Direct and Indirect Brain Pathways in the Emotion of Fear Information about fear can follow two pathways in the brain when an individual sees a snake. The direct pathway (*broken arrow*) conveys information rapidly from the thalamus to the amygdala. The indirect pathway (*solid arrows*) transmits information more slowly from the thalamus to the sensory cortex (here, the visual cortex) and then to the amygdala.

(snake) ©IT Stock/PunchStock; (women) ©pathdoc/Shutterstock

Visual thalamus

Visual cortex

Amygdala

amygdalae are well connected to the cerebral cortex, in which thinking and decision making primarily occur (Pina & Cunningham, 2017). The amygdala is in a much better position to influence the cerebral cortex than the other way around, because it sends more connections to the cerebral cortex than it gets back. This may explain why it is so hard to control our emotions, and why, once fear is learned, it is so hard to erase.

Researchers are also finding that the cerebral hemispheres may be involved in understanding emotion. Richard Davidson and his colleagues have shown that the cerebral hemispheres work differently in positive and negative emotions (Davidson, 2000; Davidson & Begley, 2012; Davidson & others, 2003; Light & others, 2009, 2011; Reuter-Lorenz & Davidson, 1981; Urry & others, 2004). Research suggests that people who show relatively more left than right prefrontal activation tend to be happier.

Cognitive Factors in Emotion

Does emotion depend on the tides of the mind? Are we happy only when we think we are happy? Cognitive theories of emotion center on the premise that emotion always has a cognitive component (Frijda, 2007; Langeslag & Surti, 2017; Tong, 2015; Tong & Jia 2017). Thinking is said to be responsible for feelings of love and hate, joy and sadness. While cognitive theorists do recognize the role of the brain and body in emotion, they give cognitive processes the main credit for these responses.

two-factor theory of emotion
Schachter and Singer's theory that emotion is determined by two factors: physiological arousal and cognitive labeling.

THE TWO-FACTOR THEORY OF EMOTION   In the **two-factor theory of emotion** developed by Stanley Schachter and Jerome Singer (1962), emotion is determined by two factors: physiological arousal and cognitive labeling. Schachter and Singer argued that we look to the external world for an explanation of why we are aroused. We interpret external cues and label the emotion. For example, if you feel good after someone has made a pleasant comment to you, you might label the emotion "happy." If you feel bad after you have done something wrong, you may label the feeling "guilty."

To test their theory of emotion, Schachter and Singer (1962) injected volunteer participants with epinephrine, a drug that produces high arousal. After participants received the drug, they observed someone else behave in either a euphoric way (shooting papers at a wastebasket) or an angry way (stomping out of the room). As predicted, the euphoric and angry behavior influenced the participants' cognitive interpretation of their own arousal. When they were with a happy person, they rated themselves as happy; when they were with an angry person, they said they were angry. This effect occurred, however, only when the participants were not told about the true effects of the injection. When they were told that the drug would increase their heart rate and make them jittery, they had no reason to attribute their own arousal to the other person. This pattern of results supports the two-factor theory because the emotions of the partner were only used as an explanation when the effects of the injection were ambiguous.

In general, research supports the belief that misinterpreted arousal intensifies emotional experiences (Leventhal & Tomarken, 1986). Imagine that you are late for class on an important exam day. You sprint across campus, arriving just in time for the test. As you look over the questions, your heart is racing, your breathing is fast, and you feel sweaty. Are you nervous about the test or just recovering from your run to the classroom? The two-factor theory suggests that you just might mistake your bodily sensations as indications that you are scared of the test.

THE PRIMACY DEBATE: COGNITION OR EMOTION?   Which comes first, thinking or feeling? Fans of vintage episodes of TV's *Star Trek* may recognize this theme from the frequent arguments between Mr. Spock, the logical Vulcan, and Bones, the emotional doctor on the *Enterprise*. In the 1980s and 1990s, two eminent psychologists, Richard Lazarus (1922–2002) and Robert Zajonc (1923–2008) (whose name sounds like the word *science*), debated the question of which is central, cognition or emotion.

Lazarus (1991) argued for the primacy of thinking—he believed cognitive activity to be a precondition for emotion. Lazarus said that we cognitively appraise ourselves and our social circumstances. These appraisals—which include values, goals, commitments, beliefs, and expectations—determine our emotions. People may feel happy because they have a deep religious commitment, angry because they did not get the raise they anticipated, or fearful because they expect to fail an exam. Zajonc (1984) disagreed with Lazarus. Emotions are primary, he said, and our thoughts are a result of them. Zajonc famously argued that "preferences need no inferences," meaning that the way we feel about something on a "gut level" requires no thought.

Which of the two psychologists was right? Both were likely correct. Lazarus talked mainly about a cluster of related events that occur over a period of time, whereas Zajonc described single events or a simple preference for one stimulus over another. Lazarus was concerned with love over the course of months and years, a sense of value to the community, and plans for retirement; Zajonc spoke about a car accident, an encounter with a snake, and a preference for ice cream rather than spinach.

Some of our emotional reactions are virtually instantaneous and probably do not involve cognitive appraisal, such as shrieking upon detecting a snake. Other emotional circumstances, especially long-term feelings such as a depressed mood or anger toward a friend, are more likely to involve cognitive appraisal. Indeed, the direct and indirect brain pathways described earlier support the idea that some of our emotional reactions do not involve deliberate thinking, whereas others do (LeDoux, 2001, 2012).

Behavioral Factors in Emotion

Remember that our definition of emotion includes not only physiological and cognitive components but also a behavioral component. The behavioral component can be verbal or nonverbal. Verbally, a person might show love for someone by professing it in words or might display anger by saying nasty things. Nonverbally, a person might smile, frown, show a fearful expression, look down, or slouch.

The most interest in the behavioral dimension of emotion has focused on the nonverbal behavior of facial expressions (Saneiro & others, 2014; Wilhelm & others, 2014). Emotion researchers have been intrigued by people's ability to detect emotion from a person's facial expression (Matsumoto & Hwang, 2014; Nelson & Russell, 2014). In a typical research study, participants, when shown photographs like those in Figure 6, are usually able to identify six emotions: happiness, anger, sadness, surprise, disgust, and fear (Ekman & O'Sullivan, 1991).

Might our facial expressions not only reflect our emotions but also influence them? According to the **facial feedback hypothesis,** facial expressions can influence emotions as well as reflect them (Dzokoto & others, 2014). In this view, facial muscles send signals to the brain that help us to recognize the emotion we are experiencing (Lee & others, 2013). For example, we feel happier when we smile and sadder when we frown.

Support for the facial feedback hypothesis comes from an experiment by Paul Ekman and his colleagues (1983). In this study, professional actors moved their facial muscles in very precise ways, such as raising their eyebrows and pulling them together, raising their upper eyelids, and stretching their lips horizontally back to their ears (you might want to try this yourself). They were asked to hold their expression for 10 seconds, during which time the researchers measured their heart rate and body temperature. When the actors moved facial muscles in the ways described, they showed a rise in heart rate and a steady body temperature—physiological reactions that characterize fear. When they made an angry facial expression (with a penetrating stare, brows drawn together and downward, and lips pressed together or opened and pushed forward), their heart rate and body temperature both increased. The facial feedback hypothesis provides support for the James-Lange

facial feedback hypothesis
The idea that facial expressions can influence emotions as well as reflect them.

This description fits with Stanislavski's "method acting," which suggests that to feel a particular emotion, an actor should imitate the behavior of someone feeling that emotion.

Consider what this might mean for someone who is forced to wear a smile at work all the time, such as a flight attendant or waiter.

FIGURE 6 **Recognizing Emotions in Facial Expressions** Look at the six photographs and determine the emotion reflected in each of the faces.

(first) ©Ioannis Pantzi/Shutterstock; (second) ©Monkey Business Images/Getty Images; (third) ©Marcos Mesa Sam Wordley/Shutterstock; (fourth) ©Mix and Match Studio/Shutterstock; (fifth) ©Ranta Images/Shutterstock; (sixth) ©Masterfile

> First, without reading ahead, label each picture with the emotion you think it shows. > Second, match the pictures to each of the following emotions: anger, happiness, surprise, disgust, sadness, and fear. > Okay, the right answers for that second exercise are (top) happiness, anger, sadness; (bottom) surprise, disgust, fear. How does this analysis change your views of the universal quality of facial expressions of emotion?

theory of emotion discussed earlier—namely, that emotional experiences can be generated by changes in and awareness of our own bodily states.

Sociocultural Factors in Emotion

Are the facial expressions that are associated with different emotions largely innate, or do they vary across cultures? Are there gender variations in emotion? Answering these questions requires a look at research findings on sociocultural influences in emotions.

CULTURE AND THE EXPRESSION OF EMOTION
In *The Expression of the Emotions in Man and Animals,* Charles Darwin stated that the facial expressions of human beings are innate, not learned; are the same in all cultures around the world; and have evolved from the emotions of animals (Darwin, 1872/1965). Today psychologists still believe that emotions, including facial expressions of emotion, have strong biological ties (Peleg & others, 2006). For example, children who are blind from birth and have never observed the smile or frown on another person's face smile or frown in the same way that children with normal vision do. If emotions and facial expressions that go with them are unlearned, then they should be the same the world over. Is that in fact the case?

Extensive research has examined the universality of facial expressions and the ability of people from different cultures accurately to label the emotion that lies behind facial expressions. Paul Ekman's careful observations reveal that the many faces of emotion do not differ significantly from one culture to another (Ekman, 1980, 1996, 2003). For example,

Ekman and his colleague (Ekman & Friesen, 1969) photographed people expressing emotions such as happiness, fear, surprise, disgust, and grief. When they showed the photographs to people from the United States, Chile, Japan, Brazil, and Borneo (an Indonesian island in the western Pacific), the participants, across the various cultures, recognized the emotions the faces were meant to show (Ekman & Friesen, 1969). Another study focused on the way the Fore tribe, an isolated Stone Age culture in New Guinea, matched descriptions of emotions with facial expressions (Ekman & Friesen, 1971). Before Ekman's visit, most of the Fore had never seen a Caucasian face. Ekman's team showed them photographs of people's faces expressing emotions such as fear, happiness, anger, and surprise. Then they read stories about people in emotional situations and asked the Fore to pick out the face that matched the story. The Fore were able to match the descriptions of emotions with the facial expressions in the photographs. Figure 7 shows the similarity of facial expressions of emotions by many different people.

Whereas facial expressions of basic emotions appear to be universal, display rules for emotion vary (Fischer, 2006; Fok & others, 2008). **Display rules** are sociocultural standards that determine when, where, and how emotions should be expressed (Hudson & Jacques, 2014; Zhu, Ho, & Bonanno, 2013). For example, although happiness is a universally expressed emotion, when, where, and how people display it may vary from one culture to another. The same is true for other emotions, such as fear, sadness, and anger. Members of the Utku culture in Alaska, for example, discourage anger by cultivating acceptance and by dissociating themselves from any display of anger. If an unexpected snowstorm hampers a trip, the Utku do not express frustration but accept the storm and build an igloo. The importance of display rules is especially evident when we evaluate the emotional expression of another. Does that grieving husband on a morning talk show seem appropriately distraught over his wife's murder? Or might he be a suspect?

Like facial expressions, some other nonverbal signals appear to be universal indicators of certain emotions. For example, regardless of where they live, when people are depressed,

display rules
Sociocultural standards that determine when, where, and how emotions should be expressed.

Display rules can also be seen as you watch sporting events. Think about the difference between the subdued crowd at Wimbledon versus the raucous U.S. Open.

their emotional state shows not only in their sad facial expressions but also in their slow body movements, downturned heads, and slumped posture. Many nonverbal signals of emotion, though, vary from one culture to another. For example, male-to-male kissing is commonplace in Yemen but uncommon in the United States. The "thumbs up" sign, which in most cultures means either that everything is okay or that one wants to hitch a ride, is an insult in Greece, similar to a raised third finger in the United States—a cultural difference to keep in mind if you find yourself backpacking through Greece.

GENDER INFLUENCES   You probably know the stereotype about gender and emotion: She is emotional; he is not. This stereotype is a powerful and pervasive image across cultures (Brescoll, 2016). However, researchers have found that men and women are often more alike in the way they experience emotion than the stereotype would lead us to believe (Carothers & Reis, 2013).

Women and men often use the same facial expressions, adopt the same language, and describe their emotional experiences similarly when they keep diaries about their experiences. For many emotional experiences, researchers do not find gender differences (Hyde, 2014). Where differences do emerge, they suggest that women report more feelings of sadness and anxiety than men do, and men report more anger and irritability than women do (Schirmer, 2013).

To understand these differences, we must consider the contexts in which emotions are experienced and expressed (Brannon, 1999; Brody, 1999; Shields, 1991). Women may be judged harshly for expressions of anger, and men might be evaluated as "weak" if they express worry or sadness. Both women and men are certainly aware of the stereotypes for their emotional behavior (Blakemore, Berenbaum, & Liben, 2009; Schirmer, 2013). Gender differences in emotion are much more tied to social context than to biological sex (Derntl & others, 2012).

Classifying Emotions

There are more than 200 words for emotions in the English language, indicating their complexity and variety. Not surprisingly, psychologists have created ways to classify emotions—to summarize these many emotions along various dimensions, including their valence and arousal.

VALENCE   The *valence* of an emotion refers to whether it feels pleasant or unpleasant. You probably are not surprised to know that happiness, joy, pleasure, and contentment are positively valenced emotions. In contrast, sadness, anger, worry, and feeling upset are negatively valenced emotions. Research has shown that emotions tend to go together based on their valence, so that if someone is sad, he or she is also likely to be angry or worried, and if a person is happy, he or she is also likely to be feeling confident, joyful, and content (Watson, 2001).

We can classify many emotional states on the basis of valence. Indeed, according to some experts in emotion (Watson, 2001), there are two broad dimensions of emotional experience: negative affect and positive affect. **Negative affect** refers to emotions such as anger, guilt, and sadness. **Positive affect** refers to emotions such as joy, happiness, and interest. Although it seems essential to consider the valence of emotions as a way to classify them, valence does not fully capture all that we need to know about emotional states. The joy a person experiences at the birth of a child and the mild high at finding a $5 bill are both positive states, but they clearly differ in important ways.

AROUSAL LEVEL   The *arousal level* of an emotion is the degree to which the emotion is reflected in an individual's being active, engaged, or excited versus being more passive, relatively disengaged, or calm. Positive and negative emotions can be high or low in arousal. Ecstasy and excitement are examples of high-arousal positive emotions, whereas

negative affect
Negative emotions such as anger, guilt, and sadness.

positive affect
Pleasant emotions such as joy, happiness, and interest.

contentment and tranquility are low-arousal positive emotions. Examples of high-arousal negative emotions are rage, fury, and panic, while irritation and boredom represent low-arousal negative emotions.

Valence and arousal level are independent dimensions that together describe a vast number of emotional states. Using these dimensions, we can effectively create a wheel of mood states (Figure 8). The illustration shows what psychologists call a *circumplex model* of mood (Posner, Russell, & Peterson, 2005). A circumplex is a type of graph that creates a circle from two independent dimensions. Using the two dimensions of valence and arousal level, we can arrange emotional states in an organized fashion (Valenza & others, 2014).

Adaptive Functions of Emotions

In considering the functions of emotions, it is fairly easy to come up with a good reason for us to have emotions such as fear and anger. Negative emotions carry direct and immediate adaptive benefits in situations that threaten survival. Negative emotions indicate clearly that something is wrong and that we must take action. Positive emotions do not signal a problem. So, what is the adaptive function of positive emotions?

Confronting this question, Barbara Fredrickson proposed the **broaden-and-build model** of positive emotion (Fredrickson, 1998, 2013; Fredrickson & Siegel, 2017). She argues that the function of positive emotions lies in their effects on our attention and our ability to build resources. The broaden-and-build model begins with the influence of positive emotions on cognitive processing.

Positive moods, such as contentment and humor, have been shown to broaden our attentional focus; they allow us to see the forest for the trees. As a result, when in a good mood, we may be more disposed to think outside the box—to see unusual possibilities that escaped us before. In addition, a good mood, Fredrickson says, gives us a chance to build resources—to make friends, to exercise to promote our health, to branch out in new ways. These activities allow us to build up strengths that we can use when we encounter life's difficulties (Kok, Catalino, & Fredrickson, 2008). For example, joy broadens people by creating the urge to play, push the limits, and be creative. Interest broadens people by creating the motivation to explore, absorb new information and experiences, and expand the self (Csikszentmihalyi, 1990; Ryan & Deci, 2000). Positive emotions facilitate "approach" behavior (Otake & others, 2006; Watson, 2001), meaning that when we are feeling good, we are more likely to go after the rewards we want and to face our problems head on.

Positive emotions might play an important role in the ability of resilient individuals to cope successfully with life's challenges. Resilience refers to the ability to bounce back from negative experiences, to be flexible and adaptable when things are not going well. Resilient individuals might be thought of as tall trees that have the ability to bend but do not break in response to strong winds. In contrast, people who

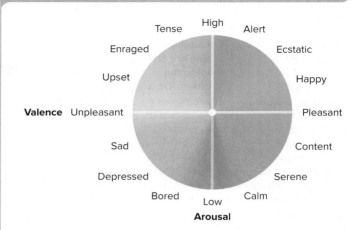

FIGURE 8   A Circumplex Model of Mood Using the dimensions of valence and arousal, this wheel-like figure shows a variety of emotional states. > Find "upset" and "sad" on the circumplex. According to the circumplex, these emotions differ primarily on the dimension of arousal. Which is higher on arousal? Do you agree with the placement of these emotions? Explain. > According to the circumplex, which emotion is the exact opposite of "serene"? > Where would you place the following emotions: embarrassed, proud, worried, angry?

©Kelly Redinger/Design Pics

Do It!

Recall that some psychologists believe that the ability to identify and regulate one's emotions is a kind of intelligence. Emotionally intelligent people are also thought to be better at reading the emotional expressions of others. Do a web search for *emotional intelligence tests* and take some online quizzes, or just try this one at http://greatergood.berkeley.edu/ei_quiz/. Do you think you are emotionally intelligent? Does your performance on the test seem to reflect your actual experience? What is your opinion of the test you tried? Is there information on the site for its validity and reliability?

lack resilience might be characterized as more brittle—more likely to snap or break in the face of adversity (Block & Kremen, 1996).

Resilient individuals are zestful, optimistic, and energetic in their approach to life (Block & Kremen, 1996). They cultivate positive emotion through the use of humor (Segerstrom, 2006). Michelle Tugade, Barbara Fredrickson, and Lisa Feldman Barrett (2004) found that the superior coping of resilient individuals came from their ability to use positive emotions to spring back from negative emotional experiences. Using measures of cardiovascular activity, the researchers discovered that resilient individuals were better able to regulate their responses to stressful situations (for instance, being told they were about to give an important speech) by strategically experiencing positive emotion.

Resilient individuals seem to show a kind of emotional wisdom; they capitalize on the power of positive emotions to reverse the stress of negative feelings. This skill has been demonstrated in response to a specific stressful event: the terrorist attacks of September 11, 2001. In one study, resilient individuals were found to be less likely to fall prey to depression after 9/11, and this capacity to flourish in the face of the crisis was a result of their attention to positive emotions (Fredrickson & others, 2003).

self-quiz

1. The James-Lange theory of emotion states that
   A. emotion happens first, followed by physiological reactions.
   B. physiological reactions happen first, followed by emotion.
   C. physiological reactions and emotion happen simultaneously.
   D. the body plays a minimal role in emotion.

2. In the case of fearful stimuli, *indirect* neural pathways go first to the thalamus and
   A. then to the hypothalamus, followed by the amygdala.
   B. then to the sensory cortex, followed by the amygdala.
   C. then to the hippocampus.
   D. then to the hypothalamus, followed by the sensory cortex, and finally the hippocampus.

3. The facial feedback hypothesis is consistent with the theory of emotion known as
   A. the James-Lange theory.
   B. the Cannon-Bard theory.
   C. direct theory.
   D. indirect theory.

APPLY IT! 4. Seymour is talking to his friend about his sadness over his recent breakup with his girlfriend. His girlfriend cheated on him, but Seymour was willing to forgive her. She was not interested, though, and broke things off. As Seymour talks, his friend notices that Seymour is clenching his teeth, making fists, and generally getting angry. The friend says, "You know, you sound more angry than sad." Why might Seymour have confused anger and sadness?
   A. Sadness and anger are similar in terms of their arousal level.
   B. Seymour's friend is probably wrong given that sadness produces the same facial expression as anger.
   C. Because he is a man, Seymour probably does not understand emotion very well.
   D. Sadness and anger have the same valence, so someone who is feeling sad is likely to also feel angry. Seymour is probably feeling both of these negative emotions.

5 Motivation and Emotion: The Pursuit of Happiness

Motivation is about what people want, and a quick scan of the best-seller list or the self-help section of any bookstore would seem to indicate that one thing people want very much is to be happy or happier. Can people get happier? Let's consider the evidence.

Biological Factors in Happiness

As we have seen, the brain is certainly at work in the experience of positive emotions. Genes also play a role. For instance, research on the heritability of well-being has tended to show that a substantial proportion of well-being differences among people can be explained by genetic differences. The heritability estimates for happiness range from 50 to 80 percent (Lykken, 1999). Remember that heritability is a statistic that describes characteristics of a group, that heritability estimates can vary across groups and over time, and that even highly heritable characteristics can be influenced by experience. Thus, a person is not necessarily doomed to an unhappy life, even if the person knows that he or she has particularly miserable parents.

Recall the concept of *set point* in our discussion of weight. There may also be a happiness set point, a person's general level of happiness when the individual is not trying to increase happiness (Sheldon & Lyubomirsky, 2007, 2012). Like our weight, our happiness levels may fluctuate around this set point (Dijkhuizen & colleagues, 2017). In trying to increase happiness, we must consider the role of this powerful starting spot that is likely the result of genetic factors and personal dispositions.

Given these potential biological limitations, other factors also complicate the pursuit of happiness, including the hedonic treadmill and the dangers of striving for happiness itself.

Obstacles in the Pursuit of Happiness

The first key challenge individuals encounter in trying to increase their happiness is the hedonic (meaning "related to pleasure") treadmill (Brickman & Campbell, 1971; Fredrick & Loewenstein, 1999). The term *hedonic treadmill* captures the idea that any aspect of life that enhances one's positive feelings is likely to do so for only a short time, because individuals generally adapt rapidly to any life change that would presumably influence their happiness. Winning the lottery, moving into a dream home, or falling in love may lead to temporary gains in the experience of joy, but eventually people go back to their baseline (Schkade & Kahneman, 1998). That is, what is first experienced as a life-changing improvement fades to a routine. How can individuals increase their happiness if such pleasure enhancers quickly lose their power? Clearly, happiness is not about shopping at the right stores, because new possessions will likely lead to only a momentary burst of pleasure, gradually giving way to the set point.

A second obstacle in the goal of enhancing happiness is that pursuing happiness for its own sake is rarely a good way to get happy or happier. When happiness is the goal, the pursuit is likely to backfire (Schooler, Ariely, & Loewenstein, 2003). Indeed, those who explicitly link the pursuit of their everyday goals to happiness fare quite poorly (McIntosh, Harlow, & Martin, 1995).

In light of this difficult path, how can we enhance our happiness without having any new capacity for joy become ho-hum? How might we achieve happiness without pursuing it in and of itself?

Happiness Activities and Goal Striving

Sonja Lyubomirsky and her colleagues have proposed a promising approach to enhancing happiness (Lyubomirsky, 2008, 2011, 2013; Sheldon & Lyubomirsky, 2007; Sin & Lyubomirsky, 2009). They suggest that intentional activities like being physically active, expressing kindness, showing gratitude, being optimistic, dwelling less on negative experiences, and engaging in positive self-reflection all enhance positive affect (Kruse & others, 2014; Lyubomirsky & others, 2011a, 2011b; Sheldon & Lyubomirsky, 2007). Behaving altruistically—habitually helping others, especially through acts of service—is another powerful happiness booster, according to Lyubomirsky (2008, 2013).

©Diane Collins and Jordan Hollender/Getty Images

©SW Productions/Getty Images

One technique for practicing positive self-reflection is to keep a gratitude journal. Studies by Robert Emmons and Michael McCullough (2004) have demonstrated the ways that being grateful can enhance happiness and psychological well-being. In one study, individuals kept a diary in which they counted their blessings every day. Those who did so were better off than others on various measures of well-being. Although some individuals seem to be naturally more grateful than others, experimental evidence indicates that even people who are not naturally grateful can benefit from counting their blessings (Emmons & McCullough, 2003; McCullough, Emmons, & Tsang, 2002).

Another potentially useful approach to amplifying happiness is to commit to the pursuit of personally meaningful goals. Pause and write down the things you are trying to accomplish in your everyday behavior. You might identify goals such as "to get better grades" and "to be a good friend (or partner or parent)." Working toward such everyday goals relates strongly to subjective well-being (Brunstein, 1993; Sheldon, 2002). Goal pursuit provides the glue that meaningfully relates a chain of life events, endowing life with beginnings, middles, and ends (King, 2008).

The scientific literature on goal investment offers a variety of ideas about the types of goals that are likely to enhance happiness. To optimize the happiness payoffs of goal pursuit, one ought to set goals that are important and personally valuable and that reflect the intrinsic needs of relatedness, competence, and autonomy (Sheldon, 2002). These goals also should be moderately challenging and should share an instrumental relationship with each other so that the pursuit of one goal facilitates the accomplishment of another (Emmons & King, 1988).

With regard to the hedonic treadmill, goal pursuit has a tremendous advantage over many other ways of trying to enhance happiness. Goals change and are changed by life experience. As a result, goal pursuit may be less susceptible to the hedonic treadmill over time. Goals accentuate the positive but do not necessarily eliminate the negative. When we fail to reach our goals, we may experience momentary increases in unhappiness (Pomerantz, Saxon, & Oishi, 2000), which can be a very good thing. Because goals can make us happy and unhappy, they keep life emotionally interesting, and their influence on happiness does not wear off over time.

Overall, goal pursuit may lead to a happier life. Goals keep the positive possible and interesting. The conclusion to be drawn from the evidence, assuming that you want to enhance your happiness, is to strive mightily for the goals that you value. You may fail now and then, but missing the mark will only make your successes all the sweeter. Even in the pursuit of happiness, it is important to keep in mind that positive and negative emotions are both adaptive and that the best life is one that is emotionally rich.

self-quiz

1. Studies have demonstrated that variance in well-being is
   A. quite heritable.
   B. surprisingly unpredictable.
   C. extreme.
   D. dependent on the cultural context.

2. Similarly to our body weight, our personal happiness levels may fluctuate around
   A. our popularity.
   B. our stress levels.
   C. a set point.
   D. the seasons of the year.

3. Researchers have discovered that one way for individuals to engage in positive self-reflection and experience meaning in life is to

   A. write down what they are thankful for in a diary.
   B. pursue the hedonic treadmill.
   C. practice transience.
   D. refresh their coping skills.

APPLY IT! 4. Bonita works at a small advertising agency. She is committed to her work goals and always gives her all when she has a task to perform. She is deeply disappointed when a potential client decides to go with another firm after Bonita put a whole week into her presentation. A coworker notices Bonita's distress and says, "You know, you only feel so bad because you care too much. You should be like me. I don't care about anything, and I'm never disappointed."

What does the psychology of happiness tell us about this situation?
   A. Although Bonita feels disappointed now, her overall approach will likely lead to greater happiness in the long term.
   B. Bonita's colleague is right on. Bonita should disengage from her goals, and then she will never be disappointed.
   C. Bonita's colleague will probably be happier than Bonita in the long term and will likely have a greater sense of purpose in life.
   D. Bonita's happiness depends more on her genetic makeup than on any particular life experience.

SUMMARY

Theories of Motivation

Motivated behavior is energized, directed, and sustained. Early evolutionary theorists considered motivation to be based on instinct—the innate biological pattern of behavior.

A drive is an aroused state that occurs because of a physiological need or deprivation. Drive reduction theory was proposed as an explanation of motivation, with the goal of drive reduction being homeostasis: the body's tendency to maintain equilibrium.

Optimum arousal theory focuses on the Yerkes-Dodson law, which states that performance is best under conditions of moderate rather than low or high arousal. Moderate arousal often serves us best, but there are times when low or high arousal is linked with better performance.

Hunger and Sex

Stomach signals are one factor in hunger. Glucose (blood sugar) and insulin both play an important role in hunger. Glucose is needed for the brain to function, and low levels of glucose increase hunger. Insulin can cause a rise in hunger.

Leptin, a protein secreted by fat cells, decreases food intake and increases energy expenditure. The hypothalamus plays an important role in regulating hunger. The lateral hypothalamus is involved in stimulating eating; the ventromedial hypothalamus, in restricting eating.

Obesity is a serious problem in the United States. Heredity, basal metabolism, set point, and fat cells are biological factors involved in obesity. Time and place affect eating. Our early ancestors ate fruits to satisfy nutritional needs, but today we fill up on the empty calories in sweets.

Motivation for sexual behavior involves the hypothalamus. The role of sex hormones in human sexual behavior, especially in women, is not clear. Masters and Johnson mapped out the human sexual response pattern, which consists of four physiological phases: excitement, plateau, orgasm, and resolution.

Thoughts and images are central in the sexual lives of humans. Sexual scripts influence sexual behavior, as do sensory/perceptual factors. Females tend to be more sexually aroused by touch; males, by visual stimulation.

Sexual values vary across cultures. These values influence sexual behavior.

Describing sexual practices in the United States has been challenging due to the difficulty of surveying a representative sample of the population. Research suggests that Americans have sex less often than they did in the past. Sex education has sometimes been a controversial issue, but research shows that nations with comprehensive sex education have far lower rates of teen pregnancy and sexually transmitted infections than does the United States.

Sexual orientation refers to the direction of a person's erotic attraction. Sexual orientation—heterosexual, homosexual, or bisexual—is most likely determined by a combination of genetic, hormonal, cognitive, and environmental factors. Based on scientific evidence, the APA supports marriage equality for gay people. Research shows that children reared by gay parents are not more likely to be gay and are similar in adjustment to their peers.

Beyond Hunger and Sex: Motivation in Everyday Life

According to Maslow's hierarchy of needs, our main needs are satisfied in this sequence: physiological needs, safety, love and belongingness, esteem, and self-actualization. Maslow gave the most attention to self-actualization: the motivation to develop to one's full potential.

Self-determination theory states that intrinsic motivation occurs when individuals are engaged in the pursuit of organismic needs that are innate and universal. These needs include competence, relatedness, and autonomy. Intrinsic motivation is based on internal factors. Extrinsic motivation is based on external factors, such as rewards and punishments.

Self-regulation involves setting goals, monitoring progress, and making adjustments in behavior to attain desired outcomes. Research suggests that setting short-term goals is a good strategy for reaching a long-term goal.

Emotion

Emotion is feeling, or affect, that has three components: physiological arousal, conscious experience, and behavioral expression. The biology of emotion focuses on physiological arousal involving the autonomic nervous system and its two subsystems. Skin conductance level and the polygraph have been used to measure emotional arousal.

The James-Lange theory states that emotion results from physiological states triggered by environmental stimuli: Emotion follows physiological reactions. The Cannon-Bard theory states that emotion and physiological reactions occur simultaneously. Contemporary biological views of emotion increasingly highlight neural circuitry and neurotransmitters. LeDoux has charted the neural circuitry of fear, which focuses on the amygdala and consists of two pathways, one direct and the other indirect. It is likely that positive and negative emotions use different neural circuitry and neurotransmitters.

Schachter and Singer's two-factor theory states that emotion is the result of both physiological arousal and cognitive labeling. Lazarus believed that cognition always directs emotion, but Zajonc argued that emotion directs cognition. Both probably were right.

Research on the behavioral component of emotion focuses on facial expressions. The facial feedback hypothesis states that facial expressions can influence emotions, as well as reflect them.

Most psychologists believe that facial expressions of basic emotions are the same across cultures. However, display rules, which involve nonverbal signals of body movement, posture, and gesture, vary across cultures.

Emotions can be classified based on valence (pleasant or unpleasant) and arousal (high or low). Using the dimensions of valence and arousal, emotions can be arranged in a circle, or circumplex model.

Positive emotions likely play an important role in well-being by broadening our focus and allowing us to build resources. Resilience is an individual's capacity to thrive even during difficult times. Research has shown that one way resilient individuals thrive is by experiencing positive emotions.

⑤ Motivation and Emotion: The Pursuit of Happiness

Happiness is heritable, and there is reason to consider each person as having a happiness set point. Still, many people would like to increase their level of happiness. One obstacle to changing happiness is the hedonic treadmill: the idea that we quickly adapt to changes that might enhance happiness. Another obstacle is that pursuing happiness for its own sake often backfires.

Ways to enhance happiness include engaging in physical activity, helping others, positively self-reflecting, and experiencing meaning (such as by keeping a gratitude journal). Another way to enhance happiness is to pursue personally valued goals passionately.

KEY TERMS

androgens	extrinsic motivation	James-Lange theory	self-determination theory
broaden-and-build model	facial feedback hypothesis	motivation	self-regulation
Cannon-Bard theory	hierarchy of needs	need	set point
display rules	homeostasis	negative affect	sexual orientation
drive	human sexual response pattern	polygraph	two-factor theory of emotion
emotion	instinct	positive affect	Yerkes-Dodson law
estrogens	intrinsic motivation	self-actualization	

ANSWERS TO SELF-QUIZZES

Section 1:   1. D; 2. B; 3. D; 4. B
Section 2:   1. C; 2. A; 3. D; 4. D

Section 3:   1. C; 2. C; 3. C; 4. C
Section 4:   1. B; 2. B; 3. A; 4. D

Section 5:   1. A; 2. C; 3. A; 4. A

10 Personality

"So much time has passed but it hasn't changed a thing"

Thanks to social media, keeping track of long-lost friends is easier than it used to be. Looking at Facebook or Instagram posts from someone you haven't seen since first grade, you probably still recognize something that makes the person familiar—still, the friend you had from long ago. Friendships are like that.

Brian Kelly (age 70) and Edward Costello (age 68) were best friends growing up in Belfast in Northern Ireland. They were extremely close but in the 1970s they each moved away, starting their lives and families in separate places. They had no contact for 43 years but they were part of each other's life stories. Brian's children had listened to many tales of their father's teenaged adventures with his best friend, Ed. The joy of those memories was touched with sadness at having lost track of his pal. Forty-three years later, after much digging, the friends were reunited (Molloy & Murphy, 2016). As Brian's children watched, they two men hugged and immediately picked up talking, joking, and whispering. "They were . . . best . . . friends and although so much time has passed, it hasn't changed a thing," Brian's daughter observed.

How is it possible to feel that way, after over four decades? Surely, for Brian and Ed, many things had changed. But something about each of them remained the same. There is something about each person that makes that person who he or she is—that makes the person recognizable to those who "knew them when"—whether from the first day of school, at summer camp, or in college. Age and life experiences can change us, but something about us endures. That "something" is personality, the focus of this chapter.

In this chapter, we survey classic theories of personality from the major psychological perspectives. We also review contemporary research on personality. The chapter concludes with a look at personality assessment.

1 Psychodynamic Perspectives

personality
A pattern of enduring, distinctive thoughts, emotions, and behaviors that characterize the way an individual adapts to the world.

psychodynamic perspectives
Theoretical views emphasizing that personality is primarily unconscious (beyond awareness).

 If we knew the dark truth of our existence, we might do something as desperate as the tragic Greek hero Oedipus, who unwittingly murdered his father and married his mother–and then gouged out his own eyes.

Personality is a pattern of enduring, distinctive thoughts, emotions, and behaviors that characterize the way an individual adapts to the world. Psychologists have approached these enduring characteristics in a variety of ways, focusing on different aspects of the person.

Psychodynamic perspectives on personality emphasize that personality is primarily unconscious (that is, beyond awareness). According to this viewpoint, those enduring patterns that make up personality are largely unavailable to our conscious awareness, and they powerfully shape our behaviors in ways that we cannot consciously comprehend. Psychodynamic theorists use the word *unconscious* differently from how other psychologists might use the term. From the psychodynamic perspective, aspects of our personality are unconscious because they must be; this lack of awareness is motivated. These mysterious, unconscious forces are simply too frightening to be part of our conscious awareness. Compared to other approaches to personality, psychodynamic approaches put the greatest emphasis on unconscious processes.

Psychodynamic theorists believe that behavior is only a surface characteristic and that to truly understand someone's personality, we have to explore the symbolic meanings of that behavior and the deep inner workings of the mind (Cratsley, 2016; Wachtel, 2017). Psychodynamic theorists also stress the role of early childhood experience in adult personality. From this vantage point, the adult is a reflection of those childhood experiences that shape our earliest conceptions of ourselves and others. These characteristics were sketched by the architect of psychoanalytic theory, Sigmund Freud.

Freud's Psychoanalytic Theory

Sigmund Freud (1856–1939)
Freud's theories have strongly influenced how people in Western cultures view themselves and the world.
©Universal History Archive/UIG/REX/Shutterstock

Sigmund Freud, one of the most influential thinkers of the twentieth century, was born in Freiberg, Moravia, today part of the Czech Republic, in 1856 and died in London at the age of 83. Freud spent most of his life in Vienna, but he left the city near the end of his career to escape the Holocaust. In his lifetime Freud was a celebrated figure. He was a charming and charismatic figure (Anderson, 2017).

For Freud, the sexual drive was the most important motivator of all human activity. However, Freud did not define the word *sex* as you might think. He felt that sex was anything that provided organ pleasure. Anything pleasurable was sex, to Freud. As we will see, Freud thought that the human sexual drive was the main determinant of personality development, and he felt that psychological disorders, dreams, and all human behavior represent the conflict between this unconscious sexual drive and the demands of civilized human society.

So, if you hear someone describe the joys of eating a decadent dessert like double-chocolate fudge cake as "better than sex," remember that in Freud's view, eating that cake is sex.

Freud developed *psychoanalysis,* his approach to personality, through his work with patients suffering from hysteria. *Hysteria* refers to physical symptoms that have no physical cause. For instance, a person might be unable to see, even with perfectly healthy eyes, or unable to walk, despite having no physical injury.

In Freud's day (the Victorian era, a time marked by strict rules regarding sexual relations), many young women suffered from physical problems that could not be explained by actual physical illness. In his practice, Freud spent many long hours listening to these women talk about their symptoms. Freud came to understand that the hysterical symptoms stemmed from unconscious psychological conflicts. These conflicts centered on experiences in which the person's drive for pleasure was thwarted by the social pressures of Victorian society. Furthermore, the particular symptoms were symbolically related to these underlying conflicts. One of Freud's patients, Fraulein Elisabeth Von R., suffered from horrible leg pains that prevented her from standing or walking. The fact that Fraulein Elisabeth could not walk was no accident. Through analysis, Freud discovered that Fraulein Elisabeth had had a number of experiences in which she wanted nothing more than to take a walk but had been prevented from doing so by her duty to her ill father.

*We call it a **Freudian** slip when someone makes a mistake in speech or action that seems to express unconscious wishes—such as a typo spelling "Freud" as "Fraud."*

Freud came to use hysterical symptoms as his metaphor for understanding dreams, slips of the tongue, and all human behavior. Everything we do, he said, has a multitude of unconscious causes.

Drawing from his work in analyzing patients, as well as himself, Freud developed his model of the human personality. He described personality as like an iceberg, existing mostly below the level of awareness, just as the massive part of an iceberg lies beneath the surface of the water. Figure 1 illustrates this analogy and depicts the extensiveness of the unconscious part of our mind, in Freud's view.

id
The part of the person that Freud called the "it," consisting of unconscious drives; the individual's reservoir of sexual energy.

ego
The Freudian structure of personality that deals with the demands of reality.

superego
The Freudian structure of personality that serves as the harsh internal judge of the individual's behavior; what is often referred to as *conscience.*

STRUCTURES OF PERSONALITY   The three parts of the iceberg in Figure 1 reflect the three structures of personality that Freud described. Freud (1917) called these structures the id, the ego, and the superego. You can get a better feel for these Latin labels by considering their English translations: The id is literally the "it," the ego is the "I," and the superego is the "above-I."

The **id** consists of unconscious drives and is the individual's reservoir of sexual energy. This "it" is a pool of amoral and often vile urges pressing for expression. In Freud's view, the id has no contact with reality. The id works according to the *pleasure principle,* the Freudian concept that the id always seeks pleasure.

The world would be dangerous and scary, however, if personalities were all id. As young children mature, they learn that they cannot slug other children in the face, that they have to use the toilet instead of diapers, and that they must negotiate with others to get the things they want. As children experience the constraints of reality, a new element of personality is formed—the **ego,** the Freudian structure of personality that deals with the demands of reality. Indeed, according to Freud, the ego abides by the *reality principle.* That is, it tries to bring the individual pleasure within the norms of society. The ego helps us to test reality, to see how far we can go without getting into trouble and hurting ourselves. Whereas the id is completely unconscious, the ego is partly conscious. It houses our higher mental functions—reasoning, problem solving, and decision making, for example.

So, remember:
ID = pleasure principle
EGO = reality principle

One of Freud's most famous essays, "The Ego and the Id," was titled "Das Ich und Das Ess" in German, meaning "The I and the It."

The id and ego do not consider whether something is right or wrong. Rather, the **superego** is the harsh internal judge of our behavior. The superego is

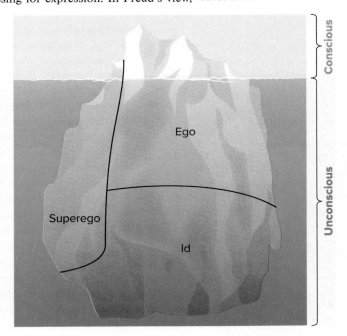

FIGURE 1   **The Conscious and Unconscious Mind: The Iceberg Analogy** The iceberg analogy illustrates how much of the mind is unconscious in Freud's theory. The conscious mind is the part of the iceberg above water; the unconscious mind, the part below water. Notice that the id is totally unconscious, whereas the ego and the superego can operate at either the conscious or the unconscious level.

reflected in what we often call *conscience* and evaluates the morality of our behavior. Like the id, the superego does not consider reality; it considers only whether the id's impulses can be satisfied in acceptable moral terms.

The ego acts as a mediator between the conflicting demands of the id and the superego, as well as the real world. Your ego might say, for example, "I will have sex only in a committed relationship and always practice safe sex." Your id, however, screams, "Sex! Now!" and your superego commands, "Sex? Don't even think about it."

DEFENSE MECHANISMS   The conflicts that erupt among the demands of the id, the superego, and reality create a great deal of anxiety for the ego. The ego has strategies for dealing with this anxiety, called defense mechanisms. **Defense mechanisms** are tactics the ego uses to reduce anxiety by unconsciously distorting reality. Freud's daughter Anna introduced and developed many different kinds of defense mechanisms (Wachtel, 2017).

defense mechanisms
Tactics the ego uses to reduce anxiety by unconsciously distorting reality.

The most primitive defense mechanism is *denial,* in which the ego simply refuses to acknowledge anxiety-producing realities. In denial, for instance, a man might refuse to accept his diagnosis of cancer. Other defense mechanisms are more complex. For example, imagine that Jason's id is demanding to express an unconscious desire to have sex with his mother. Clearly, acting on this impulse would not please the superego or society at large. If he became aware of this impulse, Jason might recoil in horror. Instead, Jason's ego might use the defense mechanism of displacement, and he might develop a relationship with a girlfriend who looks and acts like his mother. *Displacement* means directing unacceptable impulses at a less threatening target. Through displacement, the ego allows Jason to express his id impulse in a way that will not land him in trouble. Of course, Jason's friends might chuckle at the resemblance between his mother and his girlfriend, but you can bet that Jason will never notice.

Displacement provides the foundation for another defense mechanism, sublimation. *Sublimation* is a special form of displacement in which the person expresses an unconscious wish in a socially valued way, such as a boxer who sublimates his aggressive drive in the ring. Similarly, a woman might sublimate her desires to cut into people by becoming a surgeon.

Another defense mechanism is *projection.* In projection, we see in others those impulses that we most fear or despise in ourselves. For instance, our negative attitudes toward individuals who are different from us may express our unconscious beliefs about ourselves. Projection has been used to explain prejudice.

Anna Freud (1895–1982) *The youngest of Sigmund Freud's six children, Anna Freud not only did influential work on defense mechanisms but also pioneered in the theory and practice of child psychoanalysis.*
©Mary Evans/Sigmund Freud Copyrights/
The Image Works

Reaction formation is a defense mechanism in which a person's conscious experience is exactly the opposite of their true unconscious desires. Reaction formation helps to explain hypocrisy and why it is that so many people who rail against the immorality of contemporary society are themselves revealed to be engaged in the very activities they publicly condemned.

Repression is the most powerful and pervasive defense mechanism. Repression pushes unacceptable id impulses back into the unconscious mind. Repression is the foundation for all of the psychological defense mechanisms, whose goal is to repress threatening impulses, that is, to push them out of awareness. Freud said, for example, that our early childhood experiences, many of which he believed were sexually laden, are too threatening for us to deal with consciously, so we reduce the anxiety of childhood conflict through repression.

Two final points about defense mechanisms are important. First, defense mechanisms are unconscious; we are not aware that we are calling on them. Second, when used in moderation or on a temporary basis, defense mechanisms are not necessarily unhealthy. Indeed, defense mechanisms that help to relieve anxiety over particular experiences may help people cope (Cramer, 2015; Porcerelli & others, 2017). For example, the defense mechanism of *denial* can help a person cope upon first getting the news that his or her death is impending, and the defense mechanism of *sublimation* involves transforming unconscious impulses into activities that actually benefit society. Note that the defense mechanism of sublimation means that even the very best things that human beings accomplish—a beautiful work of art, an amazing act of kindness—are still explained by unconscious sexual drives and defenses (Kim, Zeppenfeld, & Cohen, 2013).

PSYCHOSEXUAL STAGES OF PERSONALITY DEVELOPMENT

Freud believed that human beings go through universal stages of personality development and that at each developmental stage we experience sexual pleasure in one part of the body more than in others. Each stage is named for the location of sexual pleasure at that stage. *Erogenous zones* are parts of the body that have especially strong pleasure-giving qualities at particular stages of development. Freud thought that our adult personality is determined by the way we resolve conflicts between these early sources of pleasure—the mouth, the anus, and then the genitals—and the demands of reality.

©Corbis/VCG/Getty Images

- *Oral stage (first 18 months):* The infant's pleasure centers on the mouth. Chewing, sucking, and biting are the chief sources of pleasure that reduce tension in the infant.

- *Anal stage (18 to 36 months):* During a time when most children are experiencing toilet training, the child's greatest pleasure involves the anus and urethra and their functions. Freud recognized that there is pleasure in "going" and "holding it" as well as in the experience of control over one's parents in deciding when to do either.

- *Phallic stage (3 to 6 years):* The name of Freud's third stage comes from the Latin word *phallus,* which means "penis." Pleasure focuses on the genitals as the child discovers that self-stimulation is enjoyable.

In Freud's view, the phallic stage has a special importance in personality development because it triggers the Oedipus complex. This name comes from the Greek tragedy, mentioned earlier, in which Oedipus kills his father and marries his mother. The **Oedipus complex** is the boy's intense desire to replace his father and enjoy the affections of his mother. Eventually, the boy recognizes that his father might punish him for these incestuous wishes, specifically by cutting off the boy's penis. *Castration anxiety* refers to the boy's intense fear of being mutilated by his father. To reduce this conflict, the boy identifies with his father, adopting the male gender role. The intense castration anxiety is repressed into the unconscious and serves as the foundation for the development of the superego.

Oedipus complex
According to Freud, a boy's intense desire to replace his father and enjoy the affections of his mother.

The superego wields a lot of power-it is essentially the internalized castrating father.

Freud recognized that there were differences between boys and girls in the phallic stage. Because a girl does not have a penis, she cannot experience castration anxiety, Freud reasoned. Instead, she compares herself to boys and realizes that she is missing something—a penis. Without experiencing the powerful force of castration anxiety, a girl cannot develop a superego in the same sense that boys do. Given this inability, Freud concluded, women were morally inferior to men, and this inferiority explained their place as second-class citizens in Victorian society. Freud believed that girls experience "castration completed," resulting in *penis envy*—the intense desire to obtain a penis by eventually marrying and bearing a son.

*In Freud's view, **anatomy is destiny.** By this he meant that anatomy (whether a person has a penis or not) determines whether he or she will develop a superego.*

While noting that his views ran counter to the early feminist thinkers of his time, Freud stood firm that the sexes are not equal in every way. He considered women to be somewhat childlike in their development and thought it was good that fathers, and eventually husbands, should guide them through life. He asserted that the only hope for women's moral development was education.

- *Latency period (6 years to puberty):* This phase is not a developmental stage but rather a kind of psychic time-out. After the drama of the phallic stage, the child sets aside all interest in sexuality. Although we now consider these years extremely important to development, Freud felt that this was a time in which no psychosexual development occurred.

- *Genital stage (adolescence and adulthood):* The genital stage is the time of sexual reawakening, a point when the source of sexual pleasure shifts to someone outside the family.

FIGURE 2

Defense Mechanisms and Freudian Stages If a person is fixated at a psychosexual stage, the fixation can color his or her personality in many ways, including the defense mechanisms the person might use to cope with anxiety.

Stage	Adult Extensions (Fixations)	Sublimations	Reaction Formations
Oral	Smoking, eating, kissing, oral hygiene, drinking, chewing gum	Seeking knowledge, humor, wit, sarcasm, being a food or wine expert	Speech purist, food faddist, prohibitionist, dislike of milk
Anal	Notable interest in one's bowel movements, love of bathroom humor, extreme messiness	Interest in painting or sculpture, being overly giving, great interest in statistics	Extreme disgust with feces, fear of dirt, prudishness, irritability
Phallic	Heavy reliance on masturbation, flirtatiousness, expressions of virility	Interest in poetry, love of love, interest in acting, striving for success	Puritanical attitude toward sex, excessive modesty

Freud believed that in adulthood the individual becomes capable of the two hallmarks of maturity: love and work. However, Freud felt that human beings are inevitably subject to intense conflict, reasoning that everyone, no matter how healthy or well adjusted, still has an id pressing for expression. Adulthood, even in the best of circumstances, still involves reliving the unconscious conflicts of childhood.

Freud argued that the individual may become stuck in any of these developmental stages if he or she is underindulged or overindulged at a given stage. For example, a parent might stop breast- or bottle-feeding the child too early, be too strict in toilet training, punish the child for masturbating, or smother the child with too much attention. When a child is over or under-indulged at a stage, he or she may experience fixation. *Fixation* occurs when a particular psychosexual stage colors an individual's adult personality. For instance, an *anal retentive* person (someone who is obsessively neat and organized) is fixated at the anal stage. The idea of fixation explains how, according to Freud's view, childhood experiences can have an enormous impact on adult personality. Figure 2 illustrates possible links between adult personality characteristics and fixation at the oral, anal, and phallic stages.

Psychodynamic Critics and Revisionists

Because Freud was among the first theorists to explore personality, some of his ideas have needed updating and revision over time, while others have been tossed out altogether (Birkhofer, 2017; Frosch, 2014). In particular, Freud's critics have said that his ideas about sexuality, early experience, social factors, and the unconscious mind were misguided (Adler, 1927; Erikson, 1968; Fromm, 1947; Horney, 1945; Jung, 1917; Kohut, 1977; Rapaport, 1967; Sullivan, 1953). They stress the following points:

- Sexuality is not the pervasive force behind personality that Freud believed it to be (Knight, 2014). Furthermore, the Oedipus complex is not as universal as Freud maintained. Freud's concepts were heavily influenced by the setting in which he lived and worked—turn-of-the-century Vienna, a society that, compared with contemporary society, was sexually repressed and male-dominated.

- The first five years of life are not as powerful in shaping adult personality as Freud thought. Later experiences deserve more attention.

- The ego and conscious thought processes play a more dominant role in our personality than Freud believed; he claimed that we are forever captive to the instinctual, unconscious clutches of the id. In addition, the ego has a separate line of development from the id, so achievement, thinking, and reasoning are not always tied to sexual impulses.

- Sociocultural factors are much more important than Freud believed. In stressing the id's dominance, Freud placed more emphasis on the biological basis of personality. More contemporary psychodynamic scholars have especially emphasized the interpersonal setting of the family and the role of early social relationships in personality development (Barratt, 2017; de Almeida Silva & others, 2016; Tal & Tal, 2017).

A number of dissenters and revisionists to Freud's theory have been influential in the development of psychodynamic theories. Erik Erikson, whose psychosocial stages we examined in relation to human development, is among these. Here we consider three other thinkers—Karen Horney, Carl Jung, and Alfred Adler—who made notable revisions to Freud's approach.

HORNEY'S SOCIOCULTURAL APPROACH

Karen Horney (1885–1952) rejected the classical psychoanalytic concept that anatomy is destiny and cautioned that some of Freud's most popular ideas were only hypotheses. She insisted that these hypotheses be supported with observable data before being accepted as fact. She also argued that sociocultural influences on personality development should be considered (Mitchell, 2014; Vena, 2015).

Consider Freud's concept of penis envy, which attributed some of the behavior of his female patients to their repressed desire to have a penis. Horney pointed out that women might envy the penis not because of some neurotic tendencies but because of the status that society bestows on those who have one. Further, she suggested that both sexes envy the attributes of the other, with men coveting women's reproductive capacities (Horney, 1967).

Horney also believed that the need for security, not for sex, is the prime motive in human existence. Horney reasoned that an individual whose needs for security are met should be able to develop his or her capacities to the fullest extent. Horney (1964) felt that the unhappiness of modern people comes not so much from conflicts over sexual drives as from hating ourselves because we cannot live up to impossible standards. She viewed psychological health as allowing the person to express his or her talents and abilities freely and spontaneously.

Karen Horney (1885–1952)
Horney developed the first feminist criticism of Freud's theory. Horney's view emphasizes women's positive qualities and self-evaluation.
©Bettmann/Getty Images

JUNG'S ANALYTICAL THEORY

Freud's contemporary Carl Jung (1875–1961) shared Freud's interest in the unconscious, but he believed that Freud underplayed the unconscious mind's role in personality. In fact, Jung believed that the roots of personality go back to the dawn of human existence. The **collective unconscious** is Jung's name for the impersonal, deepest layer of the unconscious mind, shared by all human beings because of their common ancestral past. In Jung's theory, the experiences of a common past have made a deep, permanent impression on the human mind (Christian, 2017; Greco & Deutsch, 2017).

Jung posited that the collective unconscious contains **archetypes,** emotionally laden ideas and images that have rich and symbolic meaning for all people. Jung concluded that these archetypes emerge in art, literature, religion, and dreams (Bassil-Morozow, 2015; Cwik, 2017; Moreman, 2014). Exploring archetypes was an important step in self-development. Archetypes are essentially predispositions to respond to the environment in particular ways.

Jung used the terms *anima* and *animus* to identify two common archetypes. He believed each of us has a passive feminine side—the anima—and an assertive masculine side—the animus. Another archetype, the *persona,* represents the public mask that we all wear during social interactions. Jung believed that the persona is an essential archetype because it allows us always to keep some secret part of ourselves hidden from others.

Many students find Jung's approach to personality to be odd and unexpected. Yet, many have also encountered a contemporary measure of personality that was inspired by Jung's approach. To read about the Myers-Briggs Type Indicator, see the Psychology in Our World.

ADLER'S INDIVIDUAL PSYCHOLOGY

Alfred Adler (1870–1937) was one of Freud's earliest followers, but his approach to personality was drastically different from Freud's. In Adler's **individual psychology,** people are motivated by purposes and goals—thus, perfection, not pleasure, is their key

collective unconscious
Jung's term for the impersonal, deepest layer of the unconscious mind, shared by all human beings because of their common ancestral past.

archetypes
Jung's term for emotionally laden ideas and images in the collective unconscious that have rich and symbolic meaning for all people.

individual psychology
Adler's view that people are motivated by purposes and goals and that perfection, not pleasure, is thus the key motivator in human life.

Carl Jung (1875–1961) *Swiss psychoanalytic theorist Carl Jung developed the concepts of the collective unconscious and archetypes.*
©ANL/REX/Shutterstock

What's Your Type?

Personality assessment is enormously useful in business settings. Strangely enough, one of the most popular assessment tools for personnel decisions is the Myers-Briggs Type Indicator (MBTI) developed in the 1940s by the mother–daughter team of Katherine Briggs and Isabel Briggs Myers (Briggs & Myers, 1998), neither of whom was trained in psychology or assessment (Saunders, 1991).

Based on a book by Carl Jung (1977), the Myers-Briggs questionnaire provides people with feedback on their personality "type" based on four dimensions:

1. Extraversion (basing one's actions on outward conditions) versus introversion (being more introspective)

2. Sensing (relying on what can be sensed about reality) versus intuiting (relying on gut feelings and unconscious processes)

3. Thinking (relying on logic) versus feeling (relying on emotion)

4. Judgment (using thinking and feeling) versus perception (using sensing and intuiting)

These MBTI dimensions are used to create categories that are labeled with letters; for example, an extraverted person who relies on sensation, thinking, and judgment would be called an ESTJ.

The MBTI has become so popular that people in some organizations introduce themselves as an INTJ or an INSP in the same way that people might exchange their astrological signs. Unfortunately, as in the case of astrology, strong evidence for the actual value of the MBTI types for personnel selection and job performance is weak at best (Hunsley & others, 2015; Pittenger, 2005). In fact, the MBTI is neither reliable (people get different scores with repeated testing) nor valid (it does not predict what it should). For example, there is no evidence that particular MBTI types are better suited to particular occupations (Bjork & Druckman, 1991; Gardner & Martinko, 1996).

Given this lack of empirical support, why does MBTI remain popular? Some practitioners have found it to be useful in their own work (Fornacieri & Lund Dean, 2013; McCaulley, 2000), whether or not they are aware of the lack of scientific evidence for the types. The MBTI has been well marketed, and those who pay for the scale and its training may be motivated to find evidence in their own lives to support the notion that it works. Many students are stunned to learn that this measure originates in the theory of Carl Jung.

It can be fun to learn about our personalities and to be given these letter labels. When we read that an *INTJ* is someone who is "introspective and likely to sometimes argue a point just for the sake of argument," we might think, "They really figured me out." However, this description could be true of virtually anyone, as is the case for most astrological profiles. The tendency to see ourselves in such vague descriptions is called the Barnum effect, after P. T. Barnum, the famous showman. The wily Barnum—simply by dispensing vague, general descriptions that would likely be true of anyone—convinced people that he could read minds.

©Amir Ridhwan/Shutterstock

The popularity of the Myers-Briggs letter typology attests to the power of marketing, the persistence of confirmation bias (the tendency to use information that supports our ideas rather than refutes them), and the Barnum effect. Most troubling to personality psychologists is that although other psychological measures may not be as exciting and mysterious as those four letters, they are more likely to provide reliable and valid information about job performance. Moreover, valid personality feedback can be obtained for considerably less than the MBTI price tag of $49.95!

motivator. Adler argued that people have the ability to take their genetic inheritance and their environmental experiences and act upon them creatively to become the person they want to be.

Adler thought that everyone strives for superiority by seeking to adapt, improve, and master the environment (Del Corso, Rehfuss, & Galvin, 2011). Striving for superiority is our response to the uncomfortable feelings of inferiority that we experience as infants and young children when we interact with bigger, more powerful people. *Compensation* is Adler's term for the individual's attempt to overcome imagined or real inferiorities or weaknesses by developing one's own abilities. Adler believed that compensation is normal, and he said that we often make up for a weakness in one ability by excelling in a different ability. For example, a person of small stature and limited physical abilities (like Adler himself) might compensate by excelling in academics. In addition to striving for superiority, Adler believed that each person possesses a natural impulse toward warm relationships with other people. Adler called this the *social interest* (Clark, 2016).

Adler believed that birth order could influence how successfully a person would strive for superiority. He viewed firstborn children to be particularly vulnerable given that they begin life as the center of attention but then are knocked off their pedestal by their siblings. Adler in fact believed that the firstborn are more likely to suffer from psychological disorders and to engage in criminal behavior. Youngest children, however, also are potentially in trouble because they are most likely to be spoiled. The healthiest birth order? According to Adler, those (including Adler himself) who are middle-born are in an especially advantageous situation because they have older siblings as built-in inspiration for superiority striving. Importantly, though, Adler did not believe that anyone was doomed by birth order. Rather, sensitive parents could help children in any position in the family to negotiate their needs for superiority.

Many students (but especially middle children) find Adler's approach to the effects of birth order on personality to be fascinating. Adler only theorized about birth order; he did not conduct empirical research to investigate whether birth order affects personality—either as he proposed or in any other way. To read about this topic, see the Challenge Your Thinking.

©william87/iStock/Getty Images

Evaluating the Psychodynamic Perspectives

Although psychodynamic theories have diverged from Freud's original psychoanalytic version, they share some core principles:

- Personality is determined both by current experiences and, as the original psychoanalytic theory proposed, by early life experiences.

- Personality can be better understood by examining it developmentally—as a series of stages that unfold with the individual's physical, cognitive, and socioemotional development.

Does Birth Order Matter to Personality?

Alfred Adler's ideas about birth order strike a chord with many people. You might have some beliefs about this issue yourself. Ask yourself, what is the typical firstborn, middle, or youngest child like? Common beliefs about birth order include that firstborns are natural leaders; "babies of the family" are indulged; middle children are neglected (like Jan Brady). Chances are, if you have siblings (and even if you do not), you have some hypotheses about the way birth order relates to personality. Do these naive theories have a kernel of truth? The answer to that question might surprise you. Let's take a look at the data.

Impressive contemporary research examining the relationship between birth order and personality characteristics has included very large samples: nearly 400,000 U.S. teenagers (Damian & Roberts, 2015a) as well as over 5,000 U.S. adults, nearly 5,000 British adults, and over 10,000 German teens and adults (Rohrer, Egloff, & Schmukle, 2015). For each sample, participants completed measures of personality characteristics. Information was collected about birth order, family size, socioeconomic status, and other potential "third variables." In addition, the studies compared individuals across different families (for example, comparing all firstborns to all secondborns) as well as within families (comparing siblings to each other).

Because the research used very large samples, included a host of potential confounds, and employed the most sophisticated analytical tools, the investigators were very well positioned to find links between birth order and

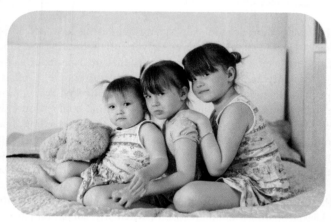
©Natalia Lebedinskaia/Shutterstock

personality, if those links existed. The results? For all of the samples, the relationship between birth order and personality was, essentially, zero. Birth order was unrelated to personality characteristics. For example, firstborns were not more likely to have leadership characteristics nor were they more responsible (Damian & Roberts, 2015a; Rohrer, Egloff, & Schmukle, 2015). The lack of associations held as well across genders: Whether older brothers or sisters were compared to younger brothers and sisters, no systematic differences in personality characteristics were found.

The results were very clear-cut, yet the intuition that birth order matters to personality seems to persist. In fact, some researchers refer to the idea that birth order predicts personality as "zombie theory," one that should die but somehow simply won't (Damian & Roberts, 2015b). Perhaps the biggest mystery of all is why the idea that personality is linked to birth order is so compelling.

What Do You Think?

- Are you convinced that birth order bears no relationship to personality? Why or why not?
- Where do your beliefs about personality and birth order originate?

- We mentally transform our experiences, giving them meaning that shapes our personality.
- The mind is not all consciousness; unconscious motives lie behind some of our puzzling behavior.
- The individual's inner world often conflicts with the outer demands of reality, creating anxiety that is not easy to resolve.
- Personality and adjustment—not just the experimental laboratory topics of sensation, perception, and learning—are rightful and important topics of psychological inquiry.

Psychodynamic perspectives have come under fire for a variety of reasons. Some critics say that psychodynamic theorists overemphasize the influence of early family experiences on personality and do not acknowledge that people retain the capacity for change and adaptation throughout life. Some psychologists believe moreover that Freud and Jung put too much faith in the unconscious mind's ability to control behavior. Others object that Freud placed too much importance on sexuality in explaining personality.

Some have argued, too, that psychoanalysis is not a theory that researchers can test through empirical studies. However, numerous empirical studies on concepts such as defense mechanisms and the unconscious have proved this criticism to be unfounded (Cohen, Kim, & Hudson, 2017; Porcerelli & others, 2017). At the same time, another version of this argument may be accurate. Although it is certainly possible to test hypotheses derived from psychoanalytic theory through research, the question remains whether psychoanalytically oriented individuals who believe strongly in Freud's ideas would be open to research results that call for serious changes in the theory.

In light of these criticisms, it may be hard to appreciate why Freud continues to have an impact on psychology. Keep in mind that Freud made a number of important contributions, including being the first to propose that childhood is crucial to later functioning, that development might be understood in terms of stages, and that unconscious processes might play a significant role in human life.

self-quiz

1. According to Freud, our conscience is a reflection of the
   A. ego.
   B. collective unconscious.
   C. id.
   D. superego.

2. All of the following are examples of defense mechanisms *except*
   A. sublimation.
   B. repression.
   C. latency.
   D. displacement.

3. A theorist who focused on archetypes is
   A. Karen Horney.
   B. Sigmund Freud.
   C. Alfred Adler.
   D. Carl Jung.

APPLY IT! 4. Simone and her older sister have an intense sibling rivalry. Simone has tried to best her sister in schoolwork, fashion sense, and sporting achievements. Simone's sister complains that Simone needs to get a life of her own. What would Alfred Adler say about Simone's behavior?
   A. Simone is engaging in the defense mechanism of displacement, striving to conquer her sister when it is really her mother she wishes to defeat.
   B. Simone is expressing her animus archetype by engaging in masculine-style competition.
   C. Simone is expressing superiority striving by trying to overcome her sister—a healthy way for middle children to pursue superiority.
   D. Simone lacks a sense of basic trust in the world, and her parents must have been neglectful of her.

2 Humanistic Perspectives

Humanistic perspectives stress a person's capacity for personal growth and positive human qualities. Humanistic psychologists believe that we all have the ability to control our lives and to achieve what we desire (Robbins, 2016; Schneider, Pierson, & Bugental, 2015; Starcher & Allen, 2016; Wong, 2017).

humanistic perspectives
Theoretical views stressing a person's capacity for personal growth and positive human qualities.

Humanistic perspectives contrast with both psychodynamic perspectives and behaviorism. Humanistic theorists sought to move beyond Freudian psychoanalysis and behaviorism to a theory that might capture the rich and potentially positive aspects of human nature.

Maslow's Approach

A leading architect of the humanistic movement was Abraham Maslow (1908–1970), who is also known for developing a hierarchy of needs to explain motivation. Maslow believed that we can learn the most about human personality by focusing on the very best examples of human beings—self-actualizers.

Recall that at the top of Maslow's (1954, 1971) hierarchy was the need for self-actualization. Self-actualization is the motivation to develop one's full potential as a human being. Maslow described self-actualizers as spontaneous, creative, and possessive of a childlike capacity for awe. According to Maslow, a person at this optimal level of existence would be tolerant of others, have a gentle sense of humor, and be likely to pursue the greater good. Self-actualizers also maintain a capacity for "peak experiences," or breathtaking moments of spiritual insight. As examples of self-actualized individuals, Maslow included

Pablo Casals (cellist), Albert Einstein (physicist), Ralph Waldo Emerson (writer), William James (psychologist), Thomas Jefferson (politician), Eleanor Roosevelt (humanitarian, diplomat), and Albert Schweitzer (humanitarian).

Created nearly 50 years ago, Maslow's list of self-actualizers is clearly biased. Maslow focused on highly successful individuals he thought represented the best of the human species. Because Maslow concentrated on people who were successful in a particular historical context, his self-actualizers were limited to those who had opportunities for success in that context. Maslow thus named considerably more men than women, and most of the individuals were from Western cultures and of European ancestry. Today, we might add to Maslow's list individuals such as Nobel Peace Prize winners the Dalai Lama (Tenzin Gyatso), Tibetan spiritual and political leader; and Malala Yousafzai, the Pakistani girl who survived an assassination attempt in 2012 and at age 17 became the youngest person ever to receive the coveted prize for her activism for access to education.

Rogers's Approach

The other key figure in the development of humanistic psychology, Carl Rogers (1902–1987), began his career as a psychotherapist struggling to understand the unhappiness of the individuals he encountered in therapy. Rogers's groundbreaking work established the foundations for more contemporary studies of personal growth and self-determination.

Yes, another Carl. But Rogers and Jung are quite different in their approaches.

In the knotted, anxious verbal stream of his clients, Rogers (1961) noted the things that seemed to be keeping them from reaching their full potential. Based on his clinical observations, Rogers devised his own approach to personality. Rogers believed that we are all born with the raw ingredients of a fulfilling life. We simply need the right conditions to thrive. Just as a sunflower seed, once planted in rich soil and given water and sunshine, will grow into a strong and healthy flower, all humans will flourish in the appropriate environment.

Carl Rogers (1902–1987) *Rogers was a pioneer in the development of the humanistic perspective.*
©Michael Rougier/The LIFE Picture Collection/Getty Images

This analogy is particularly apt and reveals the differences between Rogers's view of human nature and Freud's. A sunflower seed does not have to be shaped away from its dark natural tendencies by social constraints, nor does it have to reach a difficult compromise between its vile true impulses and reality. Instead, given the appropriate environment, it will grow into a beautiful flower. Rogers believed that, similarly, each person is born with natural capacities for growth and fulfillment. We are also endowed with an innate sense—a gut feeling—that allows us to evaluate whether an experience is good or bad for us. Finally, we are all born with a need for positive regard from others. We need to be loved, liked, or accepted by people around us. As children interacting with our parents, we learn early on to value the feeling that they value us, and we gain a sense of valuing ourselves.

EXPLAINING UNHAPPINESS If we have innate tendencies toward growth and fulfillment, why are so many people so unhappy? The problem arises when our need for positive regard from others is not

©Thorsten Indra/Alamy Stock Photo

met *unconditionally*. **Unconditional positive regard** is Rogers's term for being accepted, valued, and treated positively regardless of one's behavior. Unfortunately, others often value us only when we behave in particular ways that meet what Rogers called conditions of worth. **Conditions of worth** are the standards we must live up to in order to receive positive regard from others. For instance, parents might give their son positive regard only when he achieves in school, succeeds on the soccer field, or chooses a profession that they themselves value. According to Rogers, as we grow up, people who are central to our lives condition us to move away from our genuine feelings, to earn their love by pursuing those goals that they value, even if those goals do not reflect our deepest wishes.

Rogers's theory includes the idea that we develop a *self-concept,* our conscious representation of who we are and who we wish to become, during childhood. Optimally, this self-concept reflects our genuine, innate desires, but it also can be influenced by conditions of worth. Conditions of worth can become part of who we think we ought to be. As a result, we can become alienated from our genuine feelings and strive to actualize a self that is not who we were meant to be. A person who dedicates himself or herself to such goals might be very successful by outward appearances but might feel utterly unfulfilled. Such an individual might be able to check off all the important boxes in life's to-do lists, and to do all that he or she is "supposed to do," but never feel truly happy.

PROMOTING OPTIMAL FUNCTIONING   To remedy this situation, Rogers believed that the person must reconnect with his or her true feelings and desires. He proposed that to achieve this reconnection, the individual must experience a relationship that includes three essential qualities: unconditional positive regard, as defined above; empathy; and genuineness.

First, Rogers said that regardless of what they do, people need unconditional positive regard. Although an individual might lack unconditional positive regard in childhood, he or she can experience this unconditional acceptance from others later, in friendships and/or romantic relationships or during sessions with a therapist. Even when a person's behavior is inappropriate, obnoxious, or unacceptable, he or she still needs the respect, comfort, and love of others.

According to Rogers, anyone can help another person thrive, by offering that person unconditional positive regard and empathy, and by being yourself—who you really are—with that person.

Second, Rogers said that individuals can become more fulfilled by interacting with people who are empathic toward them. Empathy involves being a sensitive listener and understanding another's true feelings.

Finally, genuineness is a requirement in the individual's path to becoming fully functioning. Being genuine means being open with one's feelings and dropping all pretenses and facades. The importance that Rogers placed on the therapist's acting genuinely in the therapeutic relationship demonstrates his strong belief in the positive character of human nature. For Rogers, we can help others simply by being present for them as the authentic individuals we are.

In sum, Rogers's approach to therapy involved allowing the person to value him or herself, to overcome conditions of worth, and to begin to live spontaneously and authentically. This optimal outcome is provided by interacting with the person with unconditional positive regard (instead of conditions of worth), accurate empathy, and genuineness.

Evaluating the Humanistic Perspectives

The humanistic perspectives emphasize that the way we perceive ourselves and the world is an essential element of personality. Humanistic psychologists also stress that we need to consider the whole person and the positive bent of human nature. Their emphasis on conscious experience has given us the view that personality contains a well of potential that can be developed to its fullest.

©Image Source

Some critics believe that humanistic psychologists are too optimistic about human nature and that they overestimate people's freedom and rationality. Others say that the humanists may promote excessive self-love and narcissism by encouraging people to think so positively about themselves. Still others argue that humanistic approaches do not hold individuals accountable for their behaviors, if all negative human behavior is seen as emerging out of negative situations.

Self-determination theory demonstrates the way that psychologists have tested humanistic ideas that might appear too abstract and difficult to test (Adachi & others, 2017; Lumb, Beaudry, & Blanchard, 2017; Poile, 2017). That research, on the ways that following our innate needs for competence, autonomy, and relatedness is crucial for well-being, bears witness to the enduring impact of humanistic perspectives on contemporary personality psychology. Rogers's approach to psychotherapy continues to have influence on practice as well (Miller & Moyers, 2017).

self-quiz

1. In Maslow's theory, the motivation to develop one's full potential as a human being is called
   A. self-satisfaction.
   B. self-actualization.
   C. self-sufficiency.
   D. self-determination.

2. Rogers proposed that in order to become fulfilled, the individual requires all of the following *except*
   A. unconditional positive regard.
   B. genuineness.
   C. self-actualization.
   D. empathy.

3. A child who consistently strives for an *A* in math and science in order to secure the affection of her parents is trying to establish

   A. unconditional positive regard.
   B. conditions of worth.
   C. self-actualization.
   D. empathy.

APPLY IT! 4. Phoebe and Joey, parents to little Jennifer, believe that because so many things in life involve hard work, it is important for Jennifer to earn the good things that happen to her. They make it clear to Jennifer that one of the things she must earn is their approval, and they tell her that they love her only when she does well in school and behaves according to their standards. They are certain that this training will instill in Jennifer the importance of working hard and valuing the good things she gets in life. What would Carl Rogers say about Phoebe and Joey's parenting style?
   A. They are on the right track, as all children need strict limits and must learn discipline.
   B. What they are doing is fine but will have little influence on Jennifer, because genes matter most to personality.
   C. They are likely to be creating a fixation in Jennifer, and she will spend a lifetime working out her unconscious conflicts.
   D. They are setting Jennifer up to value herself only when she meets certain standards and would be better advised to love her unconditionally.

3 Trait Perspectives

If you are setting up a friend on a blind date, you are likely to describe the person in terms of his or her traits, or lasting personality characteristics. Trait perspectives on personality have been the dominant approach for nearly four decades.

Trait Theories

trait theories
Theoretical views stressing that personality consists of broad, enduring dispositions (traits) that tend to lead to characteristic responses.

According to **trait theories,** personality consists of broad, enduring dispositions (traits) that tend to lead to characteristic responses. In other words, we can describe people in terms of the ways they behave, such as whether they are outgoing, friendly, private, or hostile. People who have a strong tendency to behave in certain ways are referred to as "high" on the traits; those with a weak tendency to behave in these ways are "low" on the traits. Although trait theorists differ about which traits make up personality, they agree that traits are the fundamental building blocks of personality (Ion & others, 2017; Kawamoto, Van der Linden, & Dunkel, 2017; Lipnevich & others, 2017).

Gordon Allport (1897–1967), sometimes referred to as the father of American personality psychology, was particularly bothered by the negative view of humanity that psychoanalysis portrayed. He rejected the notion that the unconscious was central to an understanding of personality. He further believed that to understand healthy people, we must focus on their lives in the present, not on their childhood experiences.

Allport believed that personality psychology should be concerned with understanding healthy, well-adjusted individuals. He described such persons as showing a positive but objective sense of self and others, interest in issues beyond their own experience, a sense of humor, common sense, and a unifying philosophy of life—typically but not always provided by religious faith (Allport, 1961). Allport dedicated himself to the idea that psychology should have relevance to social issues facing contemporary society, and his scholarship has influenced not only personality psychology but also the psychology of religion and prejudice.

In defining personality, Allport (1961) stressed each person's uniqueness and capacity to adapt to the environment. For Allport, the crucial unit for understanding personality is the trait. He defined traits as mental structures that make different situations the same for the person. For Allport, traits are structures inside a person that cause behavior to be similar even in different situations. For instance, if Carly is sociable, she is likely to behave in an outgoing, happy fashion whether she is at a party or in a group study session. Allport's definition implies that behavior should be consistent across different situations.

We get a sense of the down-to-earth quality of Allport's approach to personality by looking at his study of traits. In the late 1930s, Allport and his colleague H. S. Odbert (1936) sat down with two big unabridged dictionaries and pulled out all the words that could be used to describe a person—a method called the *lexical approach*. This approach reflects the idea that if a trait is important to people in real life, it ought to be represented in the natural language people use to talk about one another. Furthermore, the more important a trait is, the more likely it is that it should be represented by a single word. Allport and Odbert started with 18,000 words and gradually pared down that list to 4,500.

It's called 'lexical' because a lexicon is a dictionary or vocabulary. These researchers are generally starting with the words we use to describe other people.

As you can appreciate, 4,500 traits make for a very long questionnaire. Imagine that you are asked to rate a person, Ignacio, on some traits. You use a scale from 1 to 5, with 1 meaning "not at all" and 5 meaning "very much." If you give Ignacio a 5 on "outgoing," what do you think you might give him on "shy"? Clearly, we may not need 4,500 traits to summarize the way we describe personality. Still, how might we whittle down these descriptors further without losing something important?

With advances in statistical methods and the advent of computers, the lexical approach became considerably less unwieldy. Researchers could analyze responses to the words to look for underlying structures that might account for their overlap. Specifically, a statistical procedure called *factor analysis* allowed researchers to identify which traits go together in terms of how they are rated. Factor analysis tells us what items on a scale people are responding to as if they mean the same thing. For example, if Ignacio got a 5 on "outgoing," he probably would get a 5 on "talkative" and a 1 or 2 on "shy." If Sarah is high on "hardworking," she is probably also going to be high on "reliable." Factor analysis helps a scientist identify the dimensions, or factors, that explain this kind of overlap among item ratings. One important characteristic of factor analysis is that it relies on the scientist to interpret the meaning of the factors, and the researcher must make some decisions about how many factors are enough to explain the data.

©Fuse/Getty Images

In 1963, W. T. Norman reanalyzed the Allport and Odbert traits and concluded that only five factors were needed to summarize these traits. Norman's research set the stage for the dominant approach in personality psychology today: the five-factor model (Digman, 1990).

The Five-Factor Model of Personality

Pick a friend and jot down 10 of that person's most notable personality traits. Did you perhaps list "reserved" or "a good leader"? "Responsible" or "unreliable"? "Sweet," "kind," or "friendly"? Maybe even "creative"? Researchers in personality psychology have found that there are essentially five broad personality dimensions that are represented in the natural language; these dimensions also summarize the various ways psychologists have studied traits (Allik & others, 2017; Costa & McCrae, 2010, 2013; De Roover & others, 2017; Gorbaniuk & others, 2017).

The **big five factors of personality**—the broad traits that are thought to describe the main dimensions of personality—are neuroticism (which refers to the tendency to worry and experience negative emotions), extroversion, openness to experience, agreeableness, and conscientiousness. Although personality psychologists typically refer to the traits as N, E, O, A, and C on the basis of the order in which they emerge in a factor analysis, if you create an anagram from these first letters of the trait names, you get the word *OCEAN*. Figure 3 more fully defines the big five traits.

Each of the big five traits has been the topic of extensive research. The following sampling of research findings on each trait sheds light on the interesting work that the five-factor model has inspired:

- *Neuroticism* is related to feeling negative emotion more often than positive emotion in one's daily life and to experiencing more lingering negative states (Tackett & Lahey, 2017). Neuroticism has been shown as well to relate to more health complaints (Kööts Ausmees & others, 2016), risk for cognitive decline with age (Terracciano & others, 2017), and higher incidence of nightmares (Randler, Schredl, & Göritz, 2017). A longitudinal study of older adults showed that neuroticism predicted greater risk of diagnoses with a number of physical illnesses, including high blood pressure, heart disease, and arthritis (Weston, Hill, & Jackson, 2015) during the 4 years of the study. One reason for the links between neuroticism and ill health may be that neuroticism is associated with a more sedentary lifestyle, including spending more time sitting (Allen, Walter, & McDermott, 2017).

- Individuals high in *extraversion* are more likely than others to engage in social activities (Emmons & Diener, 1986; Wilt & Revelle, 2017), experience gratitude (McCullough, Emmons, & Tsang, 2002), and show a strong sense of meaning in life (King & others, 2006). In addition, extraverts are more forgiving (Thompson & others, 2005). Extraversion predicts spending more time texting (Schroeder & Sims, 2017). One study found that extraverted salespeople sold more cars, especially if they were also good at picking up interpersonal cues (Blickle, Wendel, & Ferris, 2010). Extraverted CEOs are better

big five factors of personality The five broad traits that are thought to describe the main dimensions of personality: openness to experience, conscientiousness, extraversion, agreeableness, and neuroticism (emotional instability).

FIGURE 3

The Big Five Factors of Personality Each of the broad supertraits encompasses more narrow traits and characteristics. Use the acronym *OCEAN* to remember the big five personality factors (openness, conscientiousness, extraversion, agreeableness, and neuroticism).

Openness to Experience
Imaginative and interested in cognitively engaging with abstract ideas as well as perceptions, nature, and the arts. Someone high in openness enjoys thinking about issues from all sides and is not interested in conventional ways of doing things.

Conscientiousness
Reliable, hard-working, and dependable. Someone high in conscientiousness is disciplined, goal-directed, and organized.

Extraversion
Outgoing, sociable, and lively. A person high in extraversion is not shy and tends to be enthusiastic with others.

Agreeableness
Kind, nice, and trusting. A person high in agreeableness is likely to be gentle and helpful to others.

Neuroticism
A worrier, anxious, and insecure. Someone who is high on neuroticism is likely to be stressed out by negative events and is prone to experiencing distress. Neuroticism is sometimes labeled by its opposite end. Those low in neuroticism are high in emotional stability.

able to get their managers to feel like members to "buy in" to a team vision and in turn, their firms are more productive (Araujo-Cabrera & others, 2017).

- *Openness to experience* is related to liberal values, open-mindedness, tolerance (Sutin, 2017), and creativity (Madrid & Patterson, 2016). Openness to experience is viewed as having two components: Intellect and Openness. Intellect refers to engaging cognitively with abstract ideas and reasoning (DeYoung, 2015). Openness refers to engaging cognitively with perceptions, fantasies, and emotions (Taylor, Mckay, & Kaufman, 2017). Each of these facets relates to different kinds of creativity: Intellect predicts greater scientific creativity; Openness predicts greater artistic creativity (Kaufman & others, 2016). Openness to experience is also associated with superior cognitive functioning, achievement, and IQ across the life span (Briley, Domiteaux, & Tucker-Drob, 2014). Those high in openness to experience are more likely to daydream (Eldredge, 2016), to dress distinctively (Naumann & others, 2009), to pursue entrepreneurial goals (for instance, starting their own business), and to experience success in those pursuits (Zhao, Seibert, & Lumpkin, 2010). In a study in a work context, openness to experience predicts upward job mobility and getting promotions, in turn, predicted increases in openness to experience (Nieß & Zacher, 2015). Openness to experience has also been linked to better health, including lower risk of high blood pressure, stroke, and diabetes (Weston, Hill, & Jackson, 2015). Moreover, one meta-analysis found that higher levels of openness to experience were linked to living longer (Ferguson & Bibby, 2012). Openness to experience is the one trait of the Big 5 that predicts higher capacity to produce humorous jokes (Nusbaum, Silvia, & Beaty, 2017).

- *Agreeableness* is related to generosity and altruism (Graziano & Tobin, 2017), to reports of religious faith (Haber, Koenig, & Jacob, 2011), and to more satisfying romantic relationships (Donnellan, Larsen-Rife, & Conger, 2005). Agreeable people have more positive attitudes toward organ donation and are more likely to register to donate (Hill, 2016). There are also links between agreeableness and viewing other people positively (Wood, Harms, & Vazire, 2010). In online dating profiles, agreeable individuals are less likely than people who score low on this trait to lie about themselves (Hall & others, 2010). Agreeableness is negatively related to traditional and cyberbullying (van Geel & others, 2017). Agreeableness is associated with lower experience of stress while coping with difficult times (Morgan & others, 2017).

Do It!

You are probably getting curious to know where you stand on the big five factors of personality. This website will give you a chance to find out: http://www.personalitytest.org.uk/

- *Conscientiousness* is a key predictor of positive outcomes in a variety of life domains (Jackson & Roberts, 2017). A meta-analysis found that conscientiousness, but not the other big five factors, was linked to college students' grade point averages (McAbee & Oswald, 2013); conscientiousness has also been linked to better work performance (Brown & others, 2011). Conscientiousness predicts better-quality friendships (Jensen-Campbell & Malcolm, 2007), higher levels of religious faith (Saroglou, 2010), and a forgiving attitude (Balliet, 2010). Conscientiousness is associated as well with dressing neatly, especially in the case of men (Naumann & others, 2009) and, like openness, is related to entrepreneurial success (Zhao, Seibert, & Lumpkin, 2010). Low levels of conscientiousness are linked to higher levels of criminal behavior (Wiebe, 2004), substance abuse (Walton & Roberts, 2004), and pathological gambling (Hwang & others, 2012). Conscientiousness shares a stronger relationship to longevity than do the other four factors (Hill & others, 2011). Conscientiousness predicts lower risk of cognitive decline with age (Terracciano & others, 2017) as well as lower risk of high blood pressure, stroke, and arthritis (Weston, Hill, & Jackson, 2015). One reason that conscientiousness is associated with good health is its positive association with healthy behaviors (Allen, Walter, & McDermott, 2017). Conscientiousness is the trait that captures people's strong desire to achieve. A recent study showed that after doing poorly on important standardized tests (such as the GRE, MCAT, or LSAT), conscientiousness predicted taking the test again (Barron & others, 2017).

Keep in mind that because the five factors are theoretically independent of one another, a person can be any combination of them. Do you know a neurotic extravert or an agreeable introvert?

In many ways, the role of personality traits in our life depends on the situations in which we find ourselves (Moskowitz & Fournier, 2014). Personality traits can be strengths or weaknesses, depending on the types of situations we encounter and the kinds of situations we seek out for ourselves (Block, 2010; King & Trent, 2012). Even a trait like agreeableness may be a liability when the situation calls for confrontational behavior. For instance, a woman whose marriage is breaking up might wish for a divorce lawyer who treats her kindly but might prefer one who is less than agreeable at the bargaining table. Eminent psychologist Lee Cronbach (1957, p. 679) once said, "If for each environment there is a best organism, for every organism there must be a best environment." If our personalities are not particularly well suited to a situation, we can change that situation or create one that fits better (King & Trent, 2012).

A great context for thinking about the fit between a person and a situation is time of day. Are you the kind of person who tries to schedule your day so none of your classes meet before 10 A.M.? Or do you try to have all your classes finished by 10 A.M.? To read about the psychology of morningness and eveningness see the Intersection.

CROSS-CULTURAL STUDIES ON THE BIG FIVE

Some research on the big five factors addresses the extent to which the factors appear in personality profiles in different cultures (Farahani & others, 2016; Kjell & others, 2013; Kwan & Hermann, 2014; Lingjaerde, Føreland, & Engvik, 2001). The question is, do the big five show up in the assessment of personality in cultures around the world? Some research suggests that they do (Kajonius & Giolla, 2017): A version of the five factors appears in diverse languages, including Chinese, English, Japanese, Finnish, and Polish (Lovik & others, 2017; Paunonen & others, 1992; Zhou & others, 2009). Still, there have been some contexts in which the five factors do not appear to be represented in the natural language. Among the big five, the factors most likely to emerge across cultures and languages are extraversion, agreeableness, and conscientiousness, with neuroticism and openness to experience being more likely to emerge only in English-speaking samples (De Raad & others, 2010).

THE STUDY OF TRAITS IN ANIMALS

A growing area of research in trait psychology concerns identifying and studying traits in animals (Weiss, 2017). For example, researchers have found evidence for at least some of the big five personality traits in animals, including domestic dogs (Gosling, 2008; Gosling, Kwan, & John, 2003) and hyenas (Gosling & John, 1999). In addition, studies have turned up evidence for general personality traits (such as overall boldness) in a range of animals including wild vervet monkeys (Blaszczyk, 2017), guinea pigs (Brust & Guenther, 2017), sea lions (Ciardelli & others, 2017), black rats (Žampachová & others, 2017), mink (Lehmkuhl Noer & others, 2016), and reptiles (Siviter & others, 2017). Research has even shown consistent individual differences in the behavior of *hoverflies* (called *flower flies* in the U.S.) (Odermatt, Frommen, & Menz, 2017).

Research on animal personality is important to the field of personality psychology because it allows researchers to study factors like early socialization and genetic heritage, in participants for whom such issues are much easier to control and measure (Adams & others, 2015; Siviter & others, 2017), compared to humans. In addition, comparing the personalities of different groups of nonhuman primates (for instance monkeys vs. Great Apes, our closest cousins) provides a window into the evolution of human personality characteristics (Weiss, 2017).

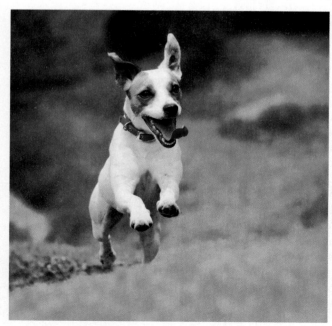

©Ammit Jack/Shutterstock

Personality and Sleep Science: Are You a Morning Person or an Evening Person and Does It Matter?

Consider the following questions:

■ In order to feel at your very best, what time would you get up in the morning, if you had complete control over your plans for the day?

■ Imagine you have an important test that is likely be mentally exhausting. You must be at your very best. You can start the test at any time during a day. It is completely up to you. What time would you choose to start the exam?

Items like these are used to measure *circadian preference,* a person's optimal time to wake up easily and when they feel most alert. Put simply, circadian preference tells us how much someone is a morning person (sometimes called a lark) or an evening person (sometimes called an owl). We may label ourselves morning and evening people but circadian preferences, like other psychological characteristics, fit the normal curve so very few people are actually extremes of either morningness or eveningness. A recent meta-analysis showed that circadian preferences are related to the Big 5 traits. Conscientiousness is associated with morningness, and openness to experience and extraversion are linked to eveningness (Lipnevich & others, 2017). But circadian preferences are not simply the same thing as the Big 5.

Does the degree to which one is a morning or evening person matter? Research suggests that, although the associations are not large, fortune favors the larks of the world. Not only is morningness associated with higher life satisfaction and lower levels of distress, but switching to a lark-like schedule leads to higher levels of happiness (Hasler, Buysse, & Germain, 2016). Morning people are likely to be more active during the day and less likely to be depressed, to smoke, and to be bothered by daytime sleepiness (Suh & others, 2017). Interestingly, eveningness shares a small positive correlation with intelligence, yet morningness (which is unrelated to cognitive ability) is associated with better academic outcomes (Diaz-Morales & Escribano, 2013; Preckel & others, 2013).

How can we make sense of these differences? It turns out that much of the lark-advantage is explained by sleep quality. Quite simply, larks get better sleep and are more well-rested (Bakotic, Radosevic-Vidacek, & Koscec Bjelajac, 2017). It is easy to see how this sleep advantage would translate into many benefits in well-being, health, and occupational outcomes.

Consider the fit that exists between larks and the social world. School and work start times are often in the morning. Imagine a lark and an owl showing up to take an exam for an early morning class: One is bright eyed and ready. The other is feeling jet-lagged. Imagine how a lark might feel starting the day at noon or doing their most important work at 10 P.M.

Interestingly, self-reports of circadian preference are intended to tap into what is called the chronotype. Technically, the chronotype

©Aila Images/Shutterstock

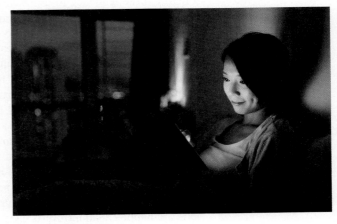

©leungchopan/Shutterstock

refers not just to a person's subjective feelings but behavioral and biological patterns that regulate wakefulness, including hormonal changes, the sleep cycle, and body temperature. A puzzle in this research is that studies have yet to show consistent positive relationships between self-reports of circadian preferences and more direct, objective measures of chronotype (Putilov, 2017). That means that some people may believe they are owls when they are physically larks.

\\ How might owls create better situations for themselves?

NEUROTICISM, EXTRAVERSION, AND WELL-BEING You have probably noticed that some people seem to go through life having fun, while others appear to feel distress at even the slightest problem. You might think that most happiness can be explained by the events that happen to us—of course, you reason, a person is going to be happy if she is doing well in school and has a loving romantic partner, but unhappy if she is doing poorly and has just experienced a painful breakup. In fact, research has shown that life events explain relatively little about a person's overall well-being.

On average, some people appear to be happier than others. Among the most consistent findings in personality research is the strong relationship between personality traits and well-being (Cosentino & Solano, 2017; Womick & King, 2018). Specifically, extraversion is related to higher levels of well-being, and neuroticism is strongly related to lower levels of well-being (Gale & others, 2013; Soto, 2014; Wieder-Huszla & others, 2014). These links between extraversion and higher levels of well-being, and between neuroticism and lower levels of well-being, are consistent and have even been found in orangutans (Weiss, King, & Perkins, 2006). What explains these connections?

Traits, Mood, and Subjective Well-Being

To begin, let's define subjective well-being as psychologists do. **Subjective well-being** is a person's assessment of his or her own level of positive affect relative to negative affect, and the individual's evaluation of his or her life in general (Diener, 2000; Diener & Lucas, 2014). When psychologists measure subjective well-being, they often focus on a person's positive and negative moods and life satisfaction.

Remember you completed the Satisfaction with Life Scale in the chapter "The Science of Psychology."

subjective well-being A person's assessment of his or her own level of positive affect relative to negative affect, and an evaluation of his or her life in general.

This definition of subjective well-being provides a clue as to why the traits of neuroticism and extraversion might be so strongly related to one's level of well-being. Neuroticism is the tendency to experience negative emotion. Neurotic individuals experience more negative mood than others, and their moods are more changeable. In contrast, extraversion is more strongly tied to positive mood. In fact, positive mood is recognized as the core of extraversion (Hermes & others, 2011). To the extent that neurotic individuals are more prone to negative emotion, it would seem that this trait might take a toll on overall well-being. Interestingly, however, research has shown that neurotics can be happy—especially if they are also extraverted (Hotard & others, 1989). Extraversion is strongly related to well-being, even for those high on neuroticism. Why might this be the case?

An early theory about the relationship between extraversion and high levels of well-being was that extraverts engage in behaviors that are themselves related to higher well-being and positive mood, such as socializing with others. Thus, the thinking went, maybe extraverts are happier because they choose to spend more time with other people. Despite the logic of this explanation, research has shown that extraverts are happier than introverts even when they are alone (Lucas & Baird, 2004). A study of Facebook users showed that extraversion predicted happiness, regardless of how many "friends" people had (Lönnqvist & Itkonen, 2014).

In fact, research has supported the conclusion that extraverts are simply happier regardless of what they are doing or with whom they are doing it. Understanding this association between extraversion and happiness continues to motivate research in personality psychology (Smillie, 2013; Wacker, 2017; Weiss & others, 2016).

A recent series of studies highlighted one reason extraverts feel happier than introverts: Compared to introverts, extraverts are more likely to feel that they are making a positive contribution to the world (Sun & others, 2017).

Traits and States

If you are neurotic or an introvert—or even a neurotic introvert—you may be feeling your mood deflating like a helium-filled balloon in a heat wave. If personality is stable, what good is it to find out that your personality might make you miserable?

One way to think about these issues is to focus on the difference between *traits* and *states* (Geiser & others, 2017). As we have seen, traits are enduring characteristics—they represent the way you generally are. In contrast, states (such as positive and negative moods) are briefer experiences. Having a trait, such as neuroticism, that predisposes

©Ingram Publishing/SuperStock

you to feelings of worry (a state) does not mean that your overall well-being must suffer. Instead, recognizing that you tend to be neurotic may be an important step in noting when your negative moods are potentially being fed by traits and are not necessarily the result of objective events. Finding out that you have a personality style associated with lowered levels of happiness should not lead you to conclude that you are doomed. Rather, this information can allow you to take steps to improve your life, to foster good habits, and to make the most of your unique qualities. Indeed, increasingly, personality research has begun to examine the ways that behaving out of character—that is, doing things that may not match with one's traits—may lead to boosts in mood and well-being (Sun & others, 2017).

Evaluating the Trait Perspective

Studying people in terms of their personality traits has practical value. Identifying a person's traits allows us to know that individual better. Using traits, psychologists have learned a great deal about the connections between personality and our health, ways of thinking, career success, and relations with others.

The trait approach has been faulted, however, for missing the importance of situational factors in personality and behavior (Kammrath & Scholer, 2013; Moskowitz & Fournier, 2014). For example, a person might say that she is introverted when meeting new people but very outgoing when with family and friends. Further, some have criticized the trait perspective for painting an individual's personality with very broad strokes. Traits can tell us much about someone whom we have never met but reveal little about the nuances of each individual's personality.

self-quiz

1. All of the following are among the big five factors of personality *except*
   A. openness to experience.
   B. altruism.
   C. conscientiousness.
   D. extraversion.

2. A researcher is doing a study from the lexical approach to identify the dimensions of personality in the natural language of people whose tribe was only recently discovered. Which of the following traits are most likely to be uncovered?
   A. extraversion
   B. agreeableness
   C. conscientiousness
   D. all of the above

3. The personality factor that is most linked with a higher IQ is

   A. neuroticism.
   B. conscientiousness.
   C. agreeableness.
   D. openness to experience.

APPLY IT! 4. Sigmund, a high-achieving psychoanalyst, always sees his patients in a timely manner and completes his written work ahead of the deadline. A brilliant public speaker, he is often surrounded by enthusiastic admirers, and he enjoys being the center of attention. He has some pretty wild, abstract ideas and has developed a complex theory to explain all of human behavior. He is an unconventional thinker, to say the least. He does not respond well to criticism and reacts poorly to even slight disapproval. Which

of the following best describes Sigmund's personality?
   A. low conscientiousness, high extraversion, low neuroticism, high openness to experience
   B. high conscientiousness, high extraversion, high openness to experience, high neuroticism
   C. high conscientiousness, low extraversion, low openness to experience, low neuroticism
   D. low conscientiousness, high extraversion, low openness to experience, high neuroticism

4 Social Cognitive Perspectives

Social cognitive perspectives on personality emphasize conscious awareness, beliefs, expectations, and goals. While incorporating principles from behaviorism, social cognitive psychologists explore the person's ability to reason; to think about the past, present, and future; and to reflect on the self. They emphasize the person's individual interpretation of situations and thus focus on the uniqueness of each person by examining how behavior is tailored to the diversity of situations in which people find themselves.

Social cognitive theorists are not interested in broad traits. Rather, they investigate how more specific factors, such as beliefs, relate to behavior and performance. In this section

social cognitive perspectives
Theoretical views emphasizing conscious awareness, beliefs, expectations, and goals.

Albert Bandura (b. 1925) *Bandura's practical, problem-solving social cognitive approach has made a lasting mark on personality theory and therapy.*
©Cheriss May/NurPhoto/Getty Images

we consider the two social cognitive approaches, developed respectively by Albert Bandura and Walter Mischel.

Bandura's Social Cognitive Theory

B. F. Skinner, whose work we examined in the "Learning" chapter, believed that there is no such thing as "personality"; rather, he emphasized behavior and felt that internal mental states were irrelevant to psychology. Albert Bandura (1986, 2001, 2007, 2011a, 2011b) found Skinner's approach to be far too simplistic for understanding human functioning. Bandura took the basic tenets of behaviorism and added recognition of the role of mental processes in determining behavior. While Skinner saw behavior as caused by the situation, Bandura pointed out that the person can cause situations, and sometimes the very definition of the situation itself depends on the person's beliefs about it. For example, is that upcoming exam an opportunity to show your stuff or a threat to your ability to achieve your goals? The test is the same either way, but your unique take on it can influence a host of behaviors (studying hard, worrying, and so on).

Bandura's social cognitive theory states that behavior, environment, and person/cognitive factors are all important in understanding personality. Bandura coined the term *reciprocal determinism* to describe the way behavior, environment, and person/cognitive factors interact to create personality (Figure 4). The environment can determine a person's behavior, and the person can act to change the environment. Similarly, person/cognitive factors can both influence behavior and be influenced by behavior. From Bandura's perspective, then, behavior is a product of a variety of forces, some of which come from the situation and some of which the person brings to the situation. In turn, how we behave can influence both the situation and ourselves. We now review the important processes and variables Bandura used to understand personality.

PSYCHOLOGICAL INQUIRY

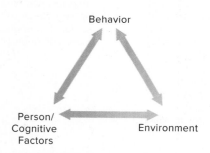

FIGURE 4 **Bandura's Social Cognitive Theory** Bandura's social cognitive theory emphasizes the reciprocal influences of behavior, environment, and person/cognitive factors. Notice that from Bandura's perspective, all of those arrows are double-headed, meaning that causation goes in both directions. Consider the following events and experiences. Describe how factors from each of the three points on the triangle spur changes in the other two and how those influences might come back again.

> **A Behavior: You study hard and get an A on your Intro Psych exam.** > **An Environment: Your Intro Psych instructor provides lecture notes online and does a thorough review for each exam.** > **A Person/Cognitive Factor: You feel very confident about your ability to do well in Intro Psych.**

OBSERVATIONAL LEARNING

Recall Bandura's belief that observational learning is a key aspect of how we learn. Through observational learning, we form ideas about the behavior of others and then possibly adopt this behavior ourselves. For example, a young boy might observe his father's aggressive outbursts and hostile exchanges with other people; when the boy is with his peers, he might interact in a highly aggressive way, showing the same characteristics as his father's behavior. Social cognitive theorists believe that we acquire a wide range of behaviors, thoughts, and feelings through observing others' behavior and that these observations strongly shape our personalities (Bandura, 2010).

In addition to emphasizing the important role of observation and learning, Bandura's social cognitive approach emphasizes characteristics that can influence behavior. These are not broad traits but rather "smaller" more specific beliefs that a person might have about a specific task or situation. Two of the most important beliefs are personal control and self-efficacy.

PERSONAL CONTROL

Personal control refers to the degree to which a person believes he or she is in charge of the outcomes of behaviors. Psychologists commonly describe a sense of behavioral control as coming from inside the person (an *internal locus of control*) or outside the person (an *external locus of control*). When we feel that we ourselves are controlling our choices and behaviors, the locus of control is internal, but when other influences are controlling them, the locus of control is external.

©Vitalii Nesterchuk/Shutterstock

Consider the question of whether you will perform well on your next test. With an internal locus of control, you believe that you are in command of your choices and behaviors, and your answer will depend on what you can realistically do (for example, study hard or attend a special review session). From the perspective of an external locus of control, however, you might say that you cannot predict how things will go because so many factors influence performance, such as whether the test is difficult and if the exam room is too hot or too cold.

Feeling a strong sense of personal control is vital to many aspects of performance, well-being, and physical health (Bandura, 2011b; Lachman, Teshale, & Agrigoroaei, 2015; Sheppes & Gross, 2015; Turiano & others, 2014).

SELF-EFFICACY

self-efficacy
The belief that one can master a situation and produce positive change.

Self-efficacy is the belief that one has the competence to accomplish a given goal or task. Bandura and others have shown that self-efficacy is related to a number of positive developments in people's lives, including solving problems, becoming more sociable, initiating and maintaining a diet or an exercise program, and quitting smoking (Bandura, 2011b; Schunk, 2012). Self-efficacy influences whether people even try to develop healthy habits, as well as how much effort they expend in coping with stress, how long they persist in the face of obstacles, and how much stress and pain they experience (Mailey & McAuley, 2014; Samuelson & others, 2017; Zhaoyang, Martire, & Sliwinski, 2017). Self-efficacy is also linked with successful job interviewing, job performance, and achievement in a creative profession (Beeftink & others, 2012; Tay, Ang, & Van Dyne, 2006). We will return to the topics of personal control and self-efficacy in the context of making healthy changes in behavior in the chapter on health psychology.

Self-efficacy means having a can-do attitude.

Mischel's Contributions

Like Albert Bandura, Walter Mischel is a social cognitive psychologist who has explored how personality influences behavior. Mischel has left his mark on the field of personality in two notable ways. First, his critique of the idea of consistency in behavior ignited a flurry of controversy. Second, he has proposed the CAPS model, a new way of thinking about personality.

MISCHEL'S CRITIQUE OF CONSISTENCY

Whether we are talking about unconscious sexual conflicts, traits, or motives, all of the approaches we have considered so far maintain that these various personality characteristics are an enduring influence on behavior. This shared assumption was attacked in 1968 with the publication of Walter Mischel's *Personality and Assessment,* a book that nearly ended the psychological study of personality.

To understand Mischel's argument, recall Gordon Allport's definition of a trait as a characteristic that ought to make different situations equivalent for a given person. This quality of traits suggests that a person should behave consistently in different situations—in other words, the individual should exhibit

Mischel's critique nearly ended the field of personality psychology! Remember—he said there was no such thing as cross-situational consistency in behavior...

cross-situational consistency. For example, an outgoing person should act highly sociably whether she is at a party or in the library. However, Mischel looked at the research compiled on trait prediction of behavior and found it to be lacking. He concluded that there was no evidence for cross-situational consistency in behavior—and thus no evidence for the existence of personality as it had been previously assumed to exist.

Rather than understanding personality as consisting of broad, internal traits that make for consistent behavior across situations, Mischel said that personality often changes according to a given situation. Mischel asserted that behavior is discriminative—that is, a person looks at each situation and responds accordingly. Mischel's view is called *situationism,* the idea that personality and behavior often vary considerably from one context to another.

Personality psychologists responded to Mischel's situationist attack in a variety of ways (Donnellan, Lucas, & Fleeson, 2009; Funder, 2009; Hogan, 2009). Researchers showed that it is not a matter of *whether* personality predicts behavior, but *when and how* it does so, often in combination with situational factors. The research findings were that

- The narrower and more limited a trait is, the more likely it will predict behavior.

- Some people are consistent on some traits, and other people are consistent on other traits.

- Personality traits exert a stronger influence on an individual's behavior when situational influences are less powerful. A very powerful situation is one that contains many clear cues about how a person is supposed to behave. For example, even a highly talkative person typically sits quietly during a class lecture. In weaker situations, however, such as during his or her leisure time, the person may spend most of the time talking.

Keep in mind as well that people are not randomly assigned to situations in real life. We select the situations we are in. This means that even if situations determine behavior, traits play a role in determining which situations people choose—such as going to a party or staying home to study (Emmons & Diener, 1986).

Let's pause and consider what it means to be consistent. You might believe that being consistent is part of being a genuine, honest person and that tailoring behavior to different situations means being fake. On the other hand, consider that someone who never changes his or her behavior to fit a situation might be unpleasant—a "drag" to have around. Think for example about someone who cannot put aside his competitive drive even when playing checkers with a 4-year-old. Clearly, adaptive behavior might involve sometimes being consistent and sometimes tailoring behavior to the situation.

©Image Source/Getty Images

Over time, Mischel has developed an approach to personality that he feels is better suited to capturing the nuances of the relationship between the individual and situations in producing behavior. Imagine trying to study personality without using traits or broad motives. What would you focus on? Mischel's answer to this dilemma is his CAPS theory.

CAPS THEORY
Mischel's theory of personality is centered in his work on *delay of gratification*—putting off a pleasurable experience in the interest of some larger but later reward. Mischel and his colleagues examined how children managed to delay gratification (Mischel, Cantor, & Feldman, 1996; Mischel & Moore, 1980; Mischel & Ayduk, 2011). They placed children in a specific difficult situation—being alone in a room with a tempting cookie in their reach. The children were told that if they wanted to at any time, they could ring a bell and eat the cookie. Otherwise, they could wait until the experimenter returned, and then they would get two cookies. The children were then left alone to face this self-control dilemma. In truth, the experimenter was not coming back. The researchers were interested in measuring how long the children could wait before giving in to temptation and eating the cookie.

©Comstock/Stockbyte/Getty Images

The children responded in various ways. Some kids sat dead still, focused on the tempting cookie. Some smelled the cookie. Others turned away, sang songs, picked their noses, or did anything but pay attention to the cookie. How did the children who were able to resist temptation do it? Mischel and colleagues found that the kids who distracted themselves from the cookie by focusing on "cool thoughts" (non-cookie-related things) were better able to delay gratification. In contrast, children who remained focused on the cookie and all its delightful qualities—what Mischel called "hot thoughts"—ate the cookie sooner (Metcalfe & Mischel, 1999). This work demonstrates that avoiding these hot issues might be a good way to see a long-term plan through to completion.

How does this work relate to personality? Mischel and his colleagues continued to study those children for many years. They found that the amount of time the children were able to delay gratification predicted their academic performance in high school and college (Mischel, 2004) and even their self-regulation skills in their 40s (Casey & others, 2011). These results indicate remarkable coherence in personality over time. Note that self-regulation in a child is very different from what it involves in adulthood. Mischel's idea is that even though the behaviors are quite different, they make sense as an expression of a personality characteristic.

Mischel's revised approach to personality is concerned with just such *coherence* in the pattern of behavior over time, not with consistency across differing situations. That is, Mischel and his colleagues have studied how behaviors in very different situations have a coherent pattern, such as a child's waiting to eat the cookie versus that same individual's (as a grown college student) deciding to stay home and study instead of going out to party. Might individual differences in delay of gratification in early childhood be linked to developmental outcomes in adulthood? In one study, using the delay of gratification task just described, longer delay of gratification at 4 years of age was linked to a lower body mass index (BMI) three decades later (Schlam & others, 2013).

In keeping with the social cognitive emphasis on the person's cognitive abilities and mental states, Mischel conceptualizes personality as a set of interconnected **cognitive affective processing systems (CAPS)** (Kross, Mischel, & Shoda, 2010; Mischel, 2004, 2009; Mischel & Ayduk, 2011; Mischel & Shoda, 1999; Orom & Cervone, 2009). According to CAPS theory, our thoughts and emotions about ourselves and the world affect our behavior and become linked in ways that matter to behavior. Personal control and self-efficacy are connections of sorts that a person has made among situations, beliefs, and behaviors. Imagine someone—let's call him Raoul—who is excited by the challenge of a new assignment given by his boss. Raoul may think about all the possible strategies to complete the project and get down to work immediately. Yet this go-getter may respond differently to other challenges, depending on who gives the assignment, what it is, or whether he feels he can do a good job.

CAPS is concerned with how personality works, not with what it is (Mischel & Ayduk, 2011; Shoda & Mischel, 2006). From the CAPS perspective, it makes no sense to ask a person "How extraverted are you?" because the answer is always, "It depends." A person may be outgoing in one situation (on the first day of class) and not another (right before an exam), and this unique pattern of flexibility is what personality is all about.

Not surprisingly, CAPS theory focuses on how people behave in different situations and how they uniquely interpret situational features. From this perspective, knowing that Crystal is an extravert tells us little about how she will behave in a group discussion in her psychology class. We need to know about Crystal's beliefs and goals in the discussion. For example, does she want to impress the instructor? Is she a psychology major? Are several members of the class good friends of hers? We also need to know about her personal understanding of the situation itself: Is this an opportunity to shine, or is she thinking about her test for the next class? Research using the CAPS approach generally involves observing individuals behaving in a variety of contexts in order to identify the patterns of associations that exist among beliefs, emotions, and behavior for each individual person across different situations.

These studies have become known as the **Marshmallow Studies**. *But the reward was often a cookie or a pretzel. Just FYI!*

Mischel focused on **coherence**, *or whether behaviors make sense across different situations—not whether they are the very same behavior.*

cognitive affective processing systems (CAPS) Mischel's theoretical model for describing that individuals' thoughts and emotions about themselves and the world affect their behavior and become linked in ways that matter to that behavior.

Is your own behavior mostly consistent across different situations?

Evaluating the Social Cognitive Perspectives

Social cognitive theory focuses on the interactions of individuals with their environments. The social cognitive approach has fostered a scientific climate for understanding personality that highlights the observation of behavior. Social cognitive theory emphasizes the influence of cognitive processes in explaining personality and suggests that people have the ability to control their environment.

Critics of the social cognitive perspective have suggested a number of weaknesses in this approach. These are noted below:

- The social cognitive approach is too concerned with change and situational influences on personality. It does not fully account for the enduring qualities of personality.

- Social cognitive theory ignores the role biology plays in personality.

- In its attempt to incorporate both the situation and the person into its view of personality, social cognitive psychology tends to lead to very specific predictions for each person in any given situation, making generalizations impossible.

1. The following are components of Bandura's social cognitive theory *except*
   A. self-efficacy.
   B. unconscious motivations.
   C. personal control.
   D. observational learning.

2. According to Mischel's 1968 book, behavior is determined by
   A. traits.
   B. biology.
   C. situations and the person's perceptions of them.
   D. unconscious motives.

3. The cognitive affective processing systems (CAPS) approach is centrally concerned with

   A. how personality works in different situations.
   B. how genetic inheritance affects personality.
   C. what biological factors influence personality.
   D. what personality is.

APPLY IT! 4. Omri thinks of himself as an extravert, but he rarely speaks up in his classes. He is especially quiet when he meets new people, especially authority figures such as a new boss. What would Mischel say about Omri's behavior?
   A. Omri is not really an extravert at all; he just does not understand that.

   B. Omri is being discriminative in his behavior. He is probably extraverted in some situations and introverted in others, and that should not be surprising.
   C. Omri is probably fixated at the phallic stage of development.
   D. Omri was not given enough unconditional positive regard in his childhood.

5 Biological Perspectives

The notion that physiological processes influence personality has been around since ancient times. Around 400 B.C.E., Hippocrates, the father of medicine, described human beings as having one of four basic personalities based on levels of particular bodily fluids (called *humours*). For Hippocrates, a "sanguine" personality was a happy, optimistic individual who happened to have an abundance of blood. A "choleric" person was quick-tempered with too much yellow bile. A "phlegmatic" personality referred to a placid, sluggish individual with too much phlegm (mucus), and a "melancholic" pessimist had too much black bile.

Although Hippocrates's ideas about bodily fluids have fallen by the wayside, personality psychologists have long acknowledged that personality involves the brain and biological processes, although they often have assumed the processes to exist rather than actually studying them. Freud's psychosexual stages bear witness to his strong belief in the connection between the mind (personality) and the body. Allport defined traits as "neuropsychic" structures and personality as a "psychophysical" system. More recently, advances in method and theory have led to fascinating research on the role of biological processes in personality.

Theories Linking Personality and the Brain

The brain is clearly important in personality, as in other psychological phenomena. Recall the case of Phineas Gage. One of the key effects of Gage's horrific accident was that it changed his personality. He went from being gentle, kind, and reliable to being angry, hostile, and untrustworthy. More generally, any consistent pattern of behavior, thought, and feeling must be reflected in patterns in the brain (Allen & DeYoung, 2017). Research has begun to probe this idea but "personality neuroscience" is still a new endeavor (Abram & DeYoung, 2017). Before describing specific findings from research studies, let's review two theoretical approaches to the biology of personality. These theories, one by Hans Eysenck and the other by Jeffrey Gray, have garnered the most interest.

EYSENCK'S RETICULAR ACTIVATION SYSTEM THEORY

British psychologist Hans Eysenck (1967) was among the first to describe the role of a particular brain system in personality. He developed an approach to extraversion/introversion based on the *reticular activation system* (RAS).

Recall that the reticular formation is located in the brain stem and plays a role in wakefulness or arousal. The RAS is the name given to the reticular formation and its connections. Eysenck posited that all of us share an optimal arousal level, a level at which we feel comfortably engaged with the world. However, Eysenck proposed, the RAS of extraverts and introverts differs with respect to the baseline level of arousal. You know that an extravert tends to be outgoing, sociable, and dominant and that an introvert is quieter and more reserved and passive. According to Eysenck, these outward differences in behavior reflect different arousal regulation strategies (Figure 5). Extraverts wake up in the morning under-aroused, *below* the optimal level, whereas introverts start out *above* the optimal level.

If *you* were feeling under-engaged with life, what might you do? You might listen to loud music or hang out with friends—in other words, behave like an extravert. If, on the other hand, you were feeling over-aroused or too stimulated, what would you do? You might spend time alone, keep distractions to a minimum, maybe sit quietly and read a book—in other words, you might act like an introvert.

Thus, from Eysenck's perspective, we can understand the traits of extraversion/introversion as characteristic patterns of behavior that aim to regulate arousal around our baseline. Research has not shown that extraverts and introverts differ in terms of baseline arousal but, rather, that introverts may be more sensitive to arousing stimuli (Mitchell & Kumari, 2016).

GRAY'S REINFORCEMENT SENSITIVITY THEORY

Building from Eysenck's work, Jeffrey Gray proposed a neuropsychology of personality, called **reinforcement sensitivity theory,** that has been the subject of much research (Allen & DeYoung, 2017;

reinforcement sensitivity theory
A theory proposed by Jeffrey Gray identifying two biological systems linked to learning associations between behaviors and rewards or punishers. The behavioral activation system is sensitive to learning about rewards. The behavioral inhibition system is sensitive to learning about punishers.

Introversion	Personality Characteristics	Extraversion
Quiet, reserved, passive	Personality Characteristics	Outgoing, social, dominant
Above optimal level	Level of Arousal	Below optimal level
Keeping distractions to a minimum	Typical Activities	Seeking out distractions
Being alone		Spending time with friends
Reading quietly		Listening to loud music

FIGURE 5

Eysenck's Reticular Activation System Theory Eysenck viewed introversion and extraversion as characteristic behavioral patterns that aim to regulate arousal around the individual's baseline level.

(left) ©drbimages/E+/Getty Images; (right) ©Stockbyte/Getty Images

Behavioral Activation System

Sensitive to
Environmental reward

Behavior
Seek positive
consequences/rewards

Character of Emotion
Positive

Personality Trait
Extraversion

Behavioral Inhibition System

Sensitive to
Environmental punishment

Behavior
Avoid negative
consequences/punishments

Character of Emotion
Negative

Personality Trait
Neuroticism

FIGURE 6

Gray's Reinforcement Sensitivity Theory Gray theorized that two neurological systems, the BAS and the BIS, explain differences in an organism's attention to environmental rewards and punishments, and in this way shape personality.

(top): ©Matthias G. Ziegler/Shutterstock; (bottom): ©xubingruo/Getty Images

Gray, 1987; Gray & McNaughton, 2000; Smillie & others, 2012). On the basis of animal learning principles, Gray posited that two neurological systems—the *behavioral activation system (BAS)* and the *behavioral inhibition system (BIS)*— could be viewed as underlying personality, as Figure 6 shows.

According to Gray, these systems explain differences in an organism's attention to rewards and punishers in the environment. An organism sensitive to rewards is more likely to learn associations between behaviors and rewards and therefore to show a characteristic pattern of seeking out rewarding opportunities. In contrast, an organism with a heightened sensitivity to punishers in the environment is more likely to learn associations between behaviors and negative consequences. Such an organism shows a characteristic pattern of avoiding such consequences.

In Gray's theory, the BAS is sensitive to rewards in the environment, predisposes one to feelings of positive emotion, and underlies the trait of extraversion (Quilty & others, 2014). In contrast, the BIS is sensitive to punishments and is involved in avoidance learning; it predisposes the individual to feelings of fear and underlies the trait of neuroticism (Thake & Zelenski, 2013). Psychologists often measure the BAS and BIS in humans by using questionnaires that assess a person's attention to rewarding or punishing outcomes (Choi, Tsuji, & Watanuki, 2017).

To summarize, Gray's approach described two systems, one for activation and one for inhibition. Those high in behavioral activation should learn associations between behaviors and rewards more quickly. Such people should also experience more positive emotion. In contrast, those high in behavioral inhibition should learn associations between behavior and punisher more rapidly and experience more negative mood.

Gray's conceptual model of reinforcement sensitivity proposed interacting brain systems as primarily responsible for the behavioral manifestations of the BAS and BIS. Research has provided some evidence for the biological underpinnings of these systems, as we will see below.

THE BRAIN AND NEUROTRANSMITTERS Research has demonstrated links between brain areas and neurotransmitters, on the one hand, and personality traits, on the other, which fit Gray's model. Here we review evidence for the two most studied traits, extraversion and neuroticism, and then consider the evidence for the other five factors.

Extraversion and the Neuroscience of Reward Gray viewed extraversion as being especially sensitive to rewards in the environment. As such, we might expect that volume and activity in the brain's reward centers (for instance, the ventral tegmental area and the nucleus accumbens) would be associated with extraversion, a hypothesis that has received some support (Allen & DeYoung, 2017). For example one study showed that extraversion predicted greater activity in the nucleus accumbens while participants waited to receive a $5 reward (Wu & others, 2014).

A key neurotransmitter in the process of reward learning is dopamine. Recall that dopamine is a "feel good" neurotransmitter vital to learning that certain behaviors are rewarding and to sending the message "Do it again!" Research has shown that dopamine is also a factor in BAS or extraversion (Depue & Fu, 2013; DeYoung, 2013; Munafo & others, 2008; Wacker & others, 2012). Scholars have suggested that early encounters with warm caregivers and positive life experiences can promote the growth of dopamine-producing cells and receptors. These early experiences can make the brain especially sensitive to rewards, setting the neurochemical stage for extraversion (Depue & Collins, 1999).

Neuroticism and Avoiding Punishment Research has also found associations between neuroticism and particular brain structures and neurotransmitters. From Gray's perspective, neuroticism is concerned with avoiding negative outcomes and feeling anxiety.

Recall that the amygdalae are parts of the limbic system that are especially active in response to emotionally evocative or survival-relevant stimuli. Studies have shown that neuroticism is related to more persistent activation in the amygdalae in response to aversive or disturbing stimuli (Schuyler & others, 2014). In addition, neuroticism is associated with fewer connections between these emotion-related brain structures and those areas of the brain (such as the prefrontal cortex) that help in regulating emotion (Allen & DeYoung, 2017).

Neuroticism has also been consistently related to the neurotransmitter serotonin (Brummett & others, 2008; Middeldorp & others, 2007). Low levels of serotonin are linked to negative moods and emotions. Neuroticism is especially related to a certain serotonin transporter gene and to the binding of serotonin in the thalamus (Gonda & others, 2009; Harro & others, 2009; Vinberg & others, 2010). Individuals who have less circulating serotonin are prone to negative mood; giving them drugs that inhibit the reuptake of serotonin tends to decrease negative mood and enhance feelings of sociability (Hart & Ksir, 2015). Serotonin is also implicated in aggressive behavior (Qiu & others, 2014), as well as in depression (Pierz & Thase, 2014).

A final link between biological processes and neuroticism is the hypothalamic-pituitary-adrenal (HPA) axis. The HPA represents the body's stress regulation system. Neuroticism is associated with poorer regulation of the HPA and more chronic stress (Abram & DeYoung, 2017; Allen & DeYoung, 2017).

Other Traits Although most research has concerned the more emotional traits of extraversion and neuroticism, some personality neuroscience studies have examined the other three traits of the Big 5. Findings are generally mixed but some recent work is suggestive of how personality and behavior may be shaped by (and shape) neural processes. These studies also call our attention to the fact that traits may overlap in their neural correlates. For example, openness to experience, that trait that is most about curiosity and interest has been associated with dopamine and serotonin (Allen & DeYoung, 2017). Agreeableness has been linked to greater neural connections in areas responsible for thinking about other people and to neurotransmitters including oxytocin and serotonin (Perry, Mankuta, & Shamay-Tsoory, 2015). Finally, conscientiousness has been found to relate to greater brain volume in areas that are thought to play a role in controlling attention and impulses and planning (DeYoung, 2015).

The Brain and Traits Finding associations between brain activity or neurotransmitters and personality does not tell us, however, about the potential *causal pathways* between these variables. Consider that behavior and experience can influence brain processes and therefore determine brain activity. The link between neuroticism and serotonin provides a telling example. Although neuroticism has been related to the serotonin transporter gene, research demonstrates that individuals with this genetic marker are not inevitably likely to be worriers. For such individuals, the levels of well-being or distress they experience may depend mostly on their environment. For example, if a person has this gene and experiences a warm, supportive environment, he or she is at *lower* risk for depression and distress (Eley & others, 2004; Vinberg & others, 2010; Way & Gurbaxani, 2008). In short, biological processes take place within a larger social context, and how these processes express themselves may depend on that social world.

Personality and Behavioral Genetics

Behavioral genetics is the study of the inherited underpinnings of behavioral characteristics. A great deal of research in behavioral genetics has involved twin studies, and the hub of this work is, appropriately, the University of Minnesota, Twin Cities.

Twin study findings demonstrate that genetic factors explain a substantial amount of the observed differences in each of the big five traits. Heritability estimates for the five factors are about 50 percent (Bouchard & Loehlin, 2001; Mõttus & others, 2017; South & Krueger, 2008). Remember that to do these studies, researchers compare identical

behavioral genetics
The study of the inherited underpinnings of behavioral characteristics.

twins, who share 100 percent of their genes, with fraternal twins, who share just 50 percent. All of the participants complete questionnaires measuring their traits. Then the researchers see if the identical twins are more similar to each other than the fraternal twins. One potential explanation for the strong relationship between personality characteristics and well-being is that the same genetic factors may play a role in traits such as extraversion, neuroticism, and well-being (Caprara & others, 2009; Liu & others, 2017; Weiss & others, 2016).

The heritability statistic describes a group, not an individual, and heritability does not mean that traits are set in stone. Understanding the role of genetic factors in personality is enormously complex. Research on non-twin samples often suggests much lower heritability, for reasons that are not well understood (DeYoung & Clark, 2012). Furthermore, because genes and environment are often intertwined, it is very difficult to tease apart whether, and how, genes or experience explains enduring patterns of behavior (South & others, 2014). For instance, a child who is genetically predisposed to disruptive behavior may often end up in a time-out or involved in arguments with parents or teachers. When that child emerges as an adult with a "fighting spirit" or lots of "spunk," are those adult traits the product of genes, experiences, or both?

Finally, most traits are probably influenced by multiple genes. Genome-wide association studies, seeking to identify the specific combinations of genetic characteristics that are linked to individual traits, have produced results that often have failed to replicate (Genetics of Personality Consortium, 2015; Kim & others, 2015; Qiu, Martin, & Blache, 2017; van den Berg & others, 2016).

Evaluating the Biological Perspectives

Research that explores the biological aspects of personality is likely to remain a key avenue of research. This work ties the field of personality to animal learning models, advances in brain imaging, developmental psychology, and evolutionary theory (Gartstein & others, 2016; Walker, Jackson, & Frost, 2017; Weiss, 2017). However, a few cautions are necessary in thinking about biological variables and their place in personality.

As we considered above, biology can be the effect, not the cause, of personality. To be sure that you grasp this idea, first remember that personality is the individual's characteristic pattern of behavior, thoughts, and feelings. Then recall from previous chapters that behavior, thoughts, and feelings are physical events in the body and brain. If traits predispose individuals to particular, consistent behaviors, thoughts, and emotional responses, traits may play a role in forging particular habitually used pathways in the brain. To the extent that personality represents a person's characteristic pattern of thought, feeling, and behavior, personality may not only be influenced by the brain—it may also play a role in the brain's very structure and functions.

self-quiz

1. Eysenck suggested that introversion and extraversion are influenced by the brain's
   A. amygdala.
   B. reticular activation system.
   C. thalamus.
   D. prefrontal cortex.

2. Gray's reward sensitivity theory of personality suggests that extraversion and neuroticism can be understood as two neurological systems linked to _____ in the individual's environment.
   A. stability and consistency
   B. stability and change

C. rewards and punishments
D. opportunities for growth

3. A technique commonly used by researchers in the specialized field known as behavioral genetics is
   A. priming studies.
   B. naturalistic observation.
   C. genetic experiments.
   D. twin studies.

APPLY IT! 4. Dorian's parents are both very outgoing, while Dorian is quiet and reserved. Her parents often embarrass her in public with their loud voices and crazy antics. When Dorian learns

that extraversion is 50 percent heritable, she starts to wonder if she will eventually become as irritating as her parents. What is your advice for Dorian?
   A. She should start getting used to the idea of being an extravert—she's doomed.
   B. She has nothing to worry about, because heritability is only about twins.
   C. She should remember that heritability is a statistic that applies only to a group, not to a single case.
   D. She should be glad, because as an extravert she is likely to be happier.

6 Personality Assessment

One of the great contributions of personality psychology to the science of psychology is its development of rigorous methods for measuring mental processes. Psychologists use a number of scientifically developed methods to evaluate personality. They assess personality for different reasons, from clinical evaluation to career counseling and job selection.

Self-Report Tests

The most commonly used method of measuring personality characteristics is the **self-report test,** which directly asks people whether specific items describe their personality traits. Self-report personality tests include items such as

> I am easily embarrassed.
>
> I love to go to parties.
>
> I like to watch cartoons on TV.

Respondents choose from a limited number of answers (yes or no, true or false, agree or disagree).

One problem with self-report tests is a factor called *social desirability.* To grasp the idea of social desirability, imagine answering the item "I am lazy at times." This statement is probably true for everyone, but would you feel comfortable admitting it? When motivated by social desirability, individuals say what they think the researcher wants to hear or what they think will make them look better. One way to measure the influence of social desirability is to give individuals a questionnaire that is designed to tap into this tendency. Such a scale typically contains many universally true but threatening items ("I like to gossip at times," "I have never said anything intentionally to hurt someone's feelings"). If scores on a trait measure correlate with this measure of social desirability, we know that the test takers were probably not being straightforward with respect to the trait measure. That is, if a person answers one questionnaire in a socially desirable fashion, he or she is probably answering all the questionnaires that way.

Another way to get around social desirability is to design scales so that it is virtually impossible for the respondent to know what the researcher is trying to measure. One means of accomplishing this goal is to use an **empirically keyed test,** a type of self-report test that is created by first identifying two groups that are known to be different. The researcher would give these two groups a large number of questionnaire items and then see which items show the biggest differences between the groups. Those items would then become part of the scale to measure the group difference. For instance, a researcher might want to develop a test that distinguishes between individuals with a history of substance abuse and those with no such history. The researcher might generate a long list of true/false items that ask about a variety of different topics but that do not even mention substance abuse. These numerous questions are presented to the members of the two groups, and on the basis of the responses, the researcher can then select the items that best discriminate between the members of the differing groups (Segal & Coolidge, 2004).

Note that an empirically keyed test avoids the issue of social desirability because the items that distinguish between the two groups are not related in any obvious way to the actual purpose of the test. For instance, those without a substance abuse history might typically respond "true" to the item "I enjoy taking long walks," while those with a history of substance abuse might respond "false"; but this item does not mention substance use, and there is no clear reason why it should distinguish between these groups.

Indeed, an important consideration with respect to empirically keyed tests is that researchers often do not know why a given test item distinguishes between two groups.

self-report test
Also called an objective test or an inventory, a method of measuring personality characteristics that directly asks people whether specific items describe their personality traits.

empirically keyed test
A type of self-report test that presents many questionnaire items to two groups that are known to be different in some central way.

An empirically keyed test can have items that seem to have nothing to do with the variable of interest.

Imagine, for example, that an empirically keyed test of achievement motivation includes an item such as "I prefer to watch sports on TV instead of romantic movies." A researcher might find that this item does a good job of distinguishing between higher-paid versus lower-paid managers in a work setting. However, does an item such as this example measure achievement motivation or, instead, simply the respondents' gender?

MMPI   The **Minnesota Multiphasic Personality Inventory (MMPI)** is the most widely used and researched empirically keyed self-report personality test. The MMPI was initially constructed in the 1940s to assess "abnormal" personality tendencies. The current version of the inventory, the MMPI-2, is the most extensively used measure in the United States and around the world to assess personality and predict outcomes (Butcher, 2010; Butcher & others, 2011; Graham, 2012). The scale features 567 items and provides information on a variety of personality characteristics. The MMPI also includes a variety of items meant to assess whether the respondent is lying or trying to make a good impression.

Some of the MMPI-2 scales measure characteristics associated with psychological disorders, such as depression and schizophrenia. Other scales include masculinity/femininity and introversion.

Minnesota Multiphasic Personality Inventory (MMPI) The most widely used and researched empirically keyed self-report personality test.

The MMPI is not only used by clinical psychologists to assess mental health (Williams & Lally, 2017; Greene, 2011). It is also a tool for hiring decisions (Caillouet & others, 2010), and in forensic settings it is used for assessing criminal risk (Bow, Flens, & Gould, 2010).

Published in 2008, the MMPI-2-RF is a more streamlined version with 338 items; it has completely different clinical scales than the MMPI-2. For example, while the MMPI-2 has scales for depression, paranoia, hypochondriasis, and social introversion, the MMPI-2-RF does not have these scales but does have scales for low positive emotions, antisocial behavior, dysfunctional negative emotions, and demoralization. Still, many practitioners continue to use the MMPI-2 (Williams & Lally, 2017).

ASSESSMENT OF THE BIG FIVE FACTORS   Paul Costa and Robert McCrae (2010) constructed the *Neuroticism Extraversion Openness Personality Inventory–3* (or *NEO-PI-3,* for short), a self-report test geared to assessing the five-factor model: openness, conscientiousness, extraversion, agreeableness, and neuroticism (emotional instability). The test also evaluates six subdimensions that make up the five main factors (Costa & others, 2014; McCrae, Harwood, & Kelly, 2011). Other measures of the big five traits have relied on the lexical approach and offer the advantage of being available without a fee.

Unlike empirically keyed tests, measures of the big five generally contain items that are straightforward; for instance, the trait "talkative" might show up on an extraversion scale. These items have what psychologists call **face validity.** A test item has face validity if it seems on the surface to fit the trait in question. Measures of personality traits include items that are both positive and negative for each trait. For example, to measure agreeableness, we might ask people to rate themselves on traits like "nice" and "kind" but also "hostile" and "selfish." Such items allow scientists to measure the full range of a trait and avoid a response bias called *yea saying* (that is, having a person simply saying yes to whatever is asked).

For example, an item measuring neuroticism that is very face valid would be "I am a worrier."

face validity The extent to which a test item appears to fit the particular trait it is measuring.

A key challenge for researchers who use self-report tests is ensuring the accuracy of participants' responses (Griffith & Converse, 2011; Ziegler, MacCann, & Roberts, 2011). One way that researchers gauge the truthfulness or accuracy of responses in self-reports is by having an individual who knows the test taker well provide ratings of that person (Anusic & others, 2009). If the test taker's and the acquaintance's ratings agree, the researchers might put more faith in the self-reports than they otherwise would.

It is likely you would be able to give a reasonably good assessment of your own levels of traits such as neuroticism and extraversion. What about the more mysterious aspects of yourself and others? If you are like most people, you view psychological assessments as tools to find out things you do not already know about yourself. For that objective, psychologists might turn to projective tests.

Projective Tests

A **projective test** presents individuals with an ambiguous stimulus and asks them to describe it or to tell a story about it—to project their own meaning onto the stimulus. This method assumes that the ambiguity of the stimulus allows individuals to interpret it based on their feelings, desires, needs, and attitudes. The test is especially designed to elicit the individual's unconscious feelings and conflicts, providing an assessment that goes deeper than the surface of personality. Projective tests attempt to get inside the mind to discover how the test taker really feels and thinks; they aim to go beyond the way the individual overtly presents himself or herself. Projective tests are theoretically aligned with the psychodynamic perspectives on personality, which give more weight to the unconscious than do other perspectives. Projective techniques also require content analysis. The examiner must code the responses for the underlying motivations revealed in the story.

FIGURE 7

Type of Stimulus Used in the Rorschach Inkblot Test What do you see in this figure? Do you see two green seahorses? Or a pair of blue spiders? A psychologist who relies on the Rorschach test would examine your responses to find out who you are.
©MadamSaffa/Shutterstock

THE RORSCHACH INKBLOT TEST

A famous projective test is the **Rorschach inkblot test,** developed in 1921 by the Swiss psychiatrist Hermann Rorschach. The test consists of 10 cards, half in black-and-white and half in color, which the individual views one at a time (Figure 7). The test taker is asked to describe what he or she sees in each of the inkblots. The individual may say, for example, "I see two fairies having a tea party" or "This is a picture of the female reproductive organs." These responses are scored based on indications of various underlying psychological characteristics (Hubbard & Hegarty, 2016; Schwartz, 2014; Searls, 2017).

Rorschach scores may predict some psychological outcomes but not others (Mihura & others, 2013). Many researchers are skeptical about the Rorschach (Garb & others, 2001; Hunsley & Bailey, 2001; Weiner, 2004). They have criticized the test's reliability and validity. If the Rorschach were reliable, two different scorers would agree on the personality characteristics of the individual being tested. If the Rorschach were valid, it would predict behavior outside of the testing situation; it would predict, for example, whether an individual will attempt suicide, become severely depressed, cope successfully with stress, or get along well with others. Conclusions based on research evidence suggest that the Rorschach does not meet these criteria of reliability and validity (Lilienfeld, Wood, & Garb, 2000). Thus, many psychologists have serious reservations about the Rorschach's use in diagnosis and clinical practice.

Although still administered in clinical circles (Campos & others, 2014), the Rorschach is not commonly used in personality research. However, the projective method itself remains a tool for studying personality, especially in the form of the Thematic Apperception Test (TAT).

THE THEMATIC APPERCEPTION TEST

The **Thematic Apperception Test (TAT),** developed by Henry Murray and Christiana Morgan in the 1930s, is designed to elicit stories that reveal a person's unconscious motivations.

Henry Murray (1893–1988) was a personality psychologist who put great stock in the the role of the unconscious in human behavior. His approach to personality was colored by his interest in the theories of Freud and Jung (Anderson, 2017). Murray believed that people are unaware of their motives. We can see the process of getting to our goals but have no access to why we are doing what we are doing. Because our motives are outside awareness, we cannot simply ask a person what they want. To access unconscious motivations, along with Christiana Morgan, Murray developed the TAT.

The TAT consists of a series of pictures like the one in Figure 8, each on an individual card or slide. The TAT test taker is asked to tell a story about each of the pictures, including events leading up to the situation described, the characters' thoughts and feelings, and the way the situation turns out. The tester assumes that the person projects his or her own unconscious feelings and thoughts into the story (Hibbard & others, 2010; Stein & others, 2014). In addition to being administered as a projective test in clinical practice, the TAT is used in research on people's need for achievement, affiliation, power, intimacy, and a variety of other needs (Brunstein & Maier, 2005; Campos & others, 2014); unconscious defense mechanisms (Cramer, 2008a; Cramer & Jones, 2007); and cognitive styles (Woike, 2008). In contrast to the Rorschach, TAT measures have shown high interrater reliability and validity (Woike, 2001).

Murray posited 22 different unconscious needs to explain behavior. The three needs that have been the focus of most current research are the need for achievement (an enduring concern for attaining excellence and overcoming obstacles), for affiliation (an enduring concern for establishing and maintaining interpersonal connections), and for power (an enduring concern for having impact on the social world).

The scoring that is applied to TAT stories has been applied to other written texts as well. For example, David Winter (2005) analyzed the motives revealed in inaugural addresses of U.S. presidents. He found that certain needs evidenced in these speeches corresponded to later events during the person's presidency. For instance, presidents who scored high on need for achievement, such as Jimmy Carter, were less successful during their terms. Note that the need for achievement is about striving for personal excellence and may have little to do with playing politics, negotiating interpersonal relationships, or delegating responsibility. Presidents who scored high on need for power tended to be judged as more successful (John F. Kennedy, Ronald Reagan), and presidents whose addresses included a great deal of warm, interpersonal imagery (suggesting a high need for affiliation) tended to experience scandal during their presidencies (Richard M. Nixon).

Current research uses the same rationale as that proposed by Morgan and Murray to measure unconscious motives. In these studies, the measure is sometimes referred to as the *picture story exercise* and the pictures used are more contemporary. In addition, researchers have tried to create computerized scoring schemes to aid in content analyses.

Other Assessment Methods

Self-report questionnaires and projective techniques are just two of the multitude of assessment methods developed and used by personality psychologists. Personality psychologists might also measure behavior directly, by observing a person either live or in a video. In addition, cognitive assessments have become more common in personality psychology, as researchers probe such topics as the relationship between personality and processes of attention and memory. Many personality psychologists incorporate friend or peer ratings of individuals' traits or other characteristics. Personality psychologists also employ a host of psychophysiological measures, such as heart rate and skin conductance. Increasingly, personality psychologists are incorporating brain imaging as well.

Whether personality assessments are being used by clinical psychologists, psychological researchers, or other practitioners, the choice of assessment instrument depends on the researcher's theoretical perspective. Figure 9 lists which methods are associated with each perspective, summarizes each approach and its major assumptions, and gives a sample research question for each. Personality psychology is a diverse field, unified by a shared interest in understanding people—all of us.

Approach	Summary	Assumptions	Typical Methods	Sample Research Question
Psychodynamic	Personality is characterized by unconscious processes. Childhood experiences are of great importance to adult personality.	The most important aspects of personality are unconscious.	Case studies, projective techniques.	How do unconscious conflicts lead to dysfunctional behavior?
Humanistic	Personality evolves out of the person's innate, organismic motives to grow and actualize the self. These healthy tendencies can be undermined by social pressure.	Human nature is basically good. By getting in touch with who we are and what we really want, we can lead happier, healthier lives.	Questionnaires, interviews, observation.	Can situations be changed to support individuals' organismic values and enhance their well-being?
Trait	Personality is characterized by five general traits that are represented in the natural language that people use to describe themselves and others.	Traits are relatively stable over time. Traits predict behavior.	Questionnaires, observer reports.	Are the five factors universal across cultures?
Social Cognitive	Personality is the pattern of coherence that characterizes a person's interactions with the situations he or she encounters in life. The individual's beliefs and expectations, rather than global traits, are the central variables of interest.	Behavior is best understood as changing across situations. To understand personality, we must understand what each situation means for a given person.	Multiple observations over different situations; video-recorded behaviors rated by coders; questionnaires.	When and why do individuals respond to challenging tasks with fear versus excitement?
Biological	Personality characteristics reflect underlying biological processes such as those carried out by the brain, neurotransmitters, and genes. Differences in behaviors, thoughts, and feelings depend on these processes.	Biological differences among individuals can explain differences in their personalities.	Brain imagining, twin studies, molecular genetic studies.	Do genes explain individual differences in extraversion?

FIGURE 9 **Approaches to Personality Psychology** This figure summarizes the broad approaches to personality described in this chapter. Many researchers in personality do not stick with just one approach but apply the various theories and methods that are most relevant to their research questions. > **What is one question you have that is relevant to personality psychology? How would each approach address that question?** > **Which approach do you think is most likely to have an impact on the future of personality psychology?** > **How might the popularity of social media and access to online studies influence the various approaches to personality?**

self-quiz

1. An empirically keyed test is one that
   A. has right and wrong answers.
   B. discriminates between different groups.
   C. has face validity.
   D. has both easy and difficult questions.

2. A problem with self-report tests, and one that researchers try to overcome, is the issue of
   A. social desirability.
   B. memory lapse.
   C. participant bias.
   D. scorer bias.

3. The assessment technique that asks participants to tell a story about the stimuli they see is the

   A. Rorschach inkblot test.
   B. Minnesota Multiphasic Personality Inventory (MMPI).
   C. NEO-P-I.
   D. Thematic Apperception Test (TAT).

APPLY IT! 4. Hank applies for a job as a ticket taker at a movie theater. After his interview, he is asked to complete a set of questionnaires. That night, he brags to friends, "They had me answer all these questions about whether I would ever steal from work, gossip about people, or sneak into a movie without paying. I just lied about everything! They'll never know. The job is mine." One of Hank's friends has taken Intro Psych and has news for Hank.

Which of the following best captures what he will say?
   A. Good job, Hank. They have no way of knowing you lied. Good luck with the job!
   B. Hank, if you lied on all the questions to make yourself look good, they will be able to detect it. It's called social desirability, and you fell for it.
   C. Hank, unless the measures involved telling stories, your lies will never be revealed.
   D. Hank, you will probably get the job, but your future employer sounds naive. Didn't they know you could just lie on those tests?

Psychodynamic Perspectives

Freud developed psychoanalysis through his work with patients suffering from hysterical symptoms (physical symptoms with no physical cause). Freud viewed these symptoms as representing conflicts between sexual drive and duty. Freud believed that most personality—which, in his theory, includes components he called the id, ego, and superego—is unconscious. The ego uses various defense mechanisms, Freud said, to reduce anxiety.

A number of theorists criticized and revised Freud's approach. Horney said that the need for security, not sex or aggression, is our most important need. Jung developed the concept of the collective unconscious, a storehouse of archetypes. Adler's individual psychology stresses that people are striving toward perfection.

Weaknesses of the psychodynamic perspectives include overreliance on reports from the past and overemphasis of the unconscious mind. Strengths of psychodynamic approaches include recognizing the importance of childhood, conceptualizing development through stages, and calling attention to the role of unconscious processes in behavior.

 Humanistic Perspectives

Humanistic perspectives stress a person's capacity for personal growth and positive human qualities. Maslow developed the concept of a hierarchy of needs, with self-actualization being the highest human need. In Rogers's approach, each of us is born with a tendency toward growth, a sense of what is good and bad for us, and a need for unconditional positive regard. Because we are often denied unconditional positive regard, we may become alienated from our innate growth tendencies. In order to reconnect with these innate tendencies, Rogers felt, a person required a relationship that included unconditional positive regard, empathy, and genuineness.

The humanistic perspectives promote the positive capacities of human beings. The weaknesses of the approach are a tendency to be too optimistic and an inclination to downplay personal responsibility.

 Trait Perspectives

Trait theories emphasize that personality consists of traits—broad, enduring dispositions that lead to characteristic responses. Allport stated that traits should produce consistent behavior in different situations, and he used the lexical approach to personality traits, which involves using all the words in the natural language that could describe a person as a basis for understanding the traits of personality.

The current dominant perspective in personality psychology is the five-factor model. The big five traits include openness, conscientiousness, extraversion, agreeableness, and neuroticism. Extraversion is related to enhanced well-being, and neuroticism is linked to lowered well-being.

Studying people in terms of their traits has value. However, trait approaches are criticized for focusing on broad dimensions and not attending to each person's uniqueness.

 Social Cognitive Perspectives

Social cognitive theory states that behavior, environment, and person/cognitive factors are important in understanding personality. In Bandura's view, these factors reciprocally interact.

Two key concepts in social cognitive theory are self-efficacy and personal control. Self-efficacy is the belief that one can master a situation and produce positive outcomes. Personal control refers to individuals' beliefs about whether the outcomes of their actions depend on their own internal acts or on external events.

In 1968, Mischel's controversial book *Personality and Assessment* stressed that people do not behave consistently across different situations but rather tailor their behavior to suit particular situations. Personality psychologists countered that personality does predict behavior for some people some of the time. Very specific personality characteristics predict behavior better than very general ones, and personality characteristics are more likely to predict behavior in weak versus strong situations.

Mischel developed a revised approach to personality centered on a cognitive affective processing system (CAPS). According to CAPS, personality is best understood as a person's habitual emotional and cognitive reactions to specific situations.

A particular strength of social cognitive theory is its focus on cognitive processes. However, social cognitive approaches have not given adequate attention to enduring individual differences, to biological factors, and to personality as a whole.

 Biological Perspectives

Eysenck suggested that the brain's reticular activation system (RAS) plays a role in introversion/extraversion. He thought of these traits as the outward manifestations of arousal regulation. Gray developed a reinforcement sensitivity theory of personality, suggesting that extraversion and neuroticism can be understood as two neurological systems that respond to rewards (the behavioral activation system, or BAS) and punishments (the behavioral inhibition system, or BIS) in the environment.

Dopamine is associated with behavioral approach (extraversion), and serotonin with behavioral avoidance (neuroticism). Behavioral genetics studies have shown that the heritability of personality traits is about 50 percent. Studies of biological processes in personality are valuable but can overestimate the causal role of biological factors.

 Personality Assessment

Self-report tests assess personality by asking participants about their preferences and behaviors. One problem in self-report research is the tendency for individuals to respond in socially desirable ways. Empirically keyed tests avoid social desirability problems by using items that distinguish between groups even if we do not know why the items do so.

The most popular test for assessing the big five traits is the NEO-PI-R, which uses self-report items to measure each of the traits. The Minnesota Multiphasic Personality Inventory (MMPI) is the most widely used empirically keyed personality test.

Projective tests, designed to assess unconscious aspects of personality, present individuals with an ambiguous stimulus, such as an inkblot or a picture, and ask them to tell a story about it. Projective tests are based on the assumption that individuals will project their personalities onto these stimuli. The Thematic Apperception Test (TAT) is a projective test that has been used in personality research. Other assessment methods include behavioral observation, obtaining peer reports, and psychophysiological and neuropsychological measures.

KEY TERMS

archetypes

behavioral genetics

big five factors of personality

cognitive affective processing
  systems (CAPS)

collective unconscious

conditions of worth

defense mechanisms

ego

empirically keyed test

face validity

humanistic perspectives

id

individual psychology

Minnesota Multiphasic Personality
  Inventory (MMPI)

Oedipus complex

personality

projective test

psychodynamic perspectives

reinforcement sensitivity theory

Rorschach inkblot test

self-efficacy

self-report test

social cognitive perspectives

subjective well-being

superego

Thematic Apperception Test
  (TAT)

trait theories

unconditional positive regard

ANSWERS TO SELF-QUIZZES

Section 1:   1. D; 2. C; 3. D; 4. C
Section 2:   1. B; 2. C; 3. B; 4. D

Section 3:   1. B; 2. D; 3. D; 4. B
Section 4:   1. B; 2. C; 3. A; 4. B

Section 5:   1. B; 2. C; 3. D; 4. C
Section 6:   1. B; 2. A; 3. D; 4. B

11

Social Psychology

Can one hour change a life?

D o I belong here? Do I have what it takes to succeed? The way new college students answer these questions can have important implications for their college experience, their academic success, and whether they graduate (Adelman & others, 2017; Jury & others, 2017). Coming to college can be especially challenging for first-generation college students (those whose parents never attended college). These students can experience a mix of emotions—from excitement and pride to homesickness and worry (Fisher, O'Donnell, & Oyserman, 2017). Many universities have instituted orientation programs to ease the transition for such students. At one school, new students listened for an hour as seniors shared stories about coming to college and learning how to be successful. In this "difference-education" program, the stories highlighted students' diverse backgrounds and how these experiences influenced their college life, both as weaknesses and as strengths. Sounds inspiring, but can something as minor as an hour in an orientation program really have an impact on how students adjust to college over the long haul?

A team of psychologists decided to answer this question. Two years after this orientation experience, the researchers recruited students who had taken part in the difference-education experience as well as students who had participated in an orientation program about the transition to college but that did not highlight diverse backgrounds (Stephens & others, 2015). The students came to the lab and were asked to complete a series of stressful tasks, including giving a speech about themselves and completing standardized tests. Their bodily responses to the stressful tasks were measured, and the results of the study were striking: Even two years later, participants who had received the difference-education orientation were more likely to talk about their own diverse backgrounds as strengths in their speeches. In addition, first-generation students who had received difference education were more physiologically balanced during the stressful tasks. These results speak to the enduring power of a simple experience to help students recognize that they do have what it takes to succeed in college.

Our expectations for others and ourselves, our identities, roles, and group memberships can influence us in profound ways throughout our lives. Our answers to the question, "Do I belong here?" guide us in and out of social situations everyday. All of the factors that influence our answers are of central interest to social psychology.

1 Defining Social Psychology

Human beings are an extremely social species. We need one another to survive. Our thoughts and emotions are often about the people we care about. Our goals often include interpersonal relationships, our families, friends, and romantic partners. The social groups we belong to provide a sense of identity. Our actions are often directed toward (or in response to) another person.

Think about it. Even if you are the world's biggest loner . . . Did you make your own clothes? Shoes? Toothbrush? People need people.

social psychology
The study of how people think about, influence, and relate to other people.

The fundamental social nature of human existence is the focus of social psychology. **Social psychology** is the scientific study of how people think about, influence, and relate to other people. Social psychologists study how a person's thoughts, feelings, and behaviors are influenced by the actual (or imagined) presence of others. Social psychology places many topics from other areas of psychology—including neuroscience, perception, cognition, learning, motivation, and emotion—into a social context.

Social psychology is similar to *sociology*, the study of human societies, organizations, and institutions. Although both sociology and social psychology examine human social behavior, sociologists focus on the group level. In contrast, social psychologists are interested in how individuals influence groups and how groups influence individuals. Unlike sociologists, social psychologists often concentrate on the immediate social situation to understand what causes people to behave as they do. For example, a social psychologist might be interested in studying how the presence of just one other person might influence your behavior.

Features of Social Psychology

Social psychology shares many characteristics with other areas of psychology but it is distinctive in at least two central ways, its connection to real life and its reliance on experimental methods. We review each of these features next.

SOCIAL PSYCHOLOGY IS CONNECTED TO REAL LIFE
Since its earliest days, social psychology has been inspired by real-life events. For example, the emergence of social psychology, as a field, can be traced back to the years after the U.S. Civil War (Morawski & Bayer, 2013). Imagine what the country was like then—with the nation recovering from a bloody conflict that nearly ended the union and with people who were once slaves living among former slave owners. How might these individuals come to live together in harmony and equality? There were many problems to be solved and people began to consider that the new science of psychology might help solve them. Similarly, after World War II, social psychology experienced extraordinary growth as scientists dedicated themselves to understanding the events that led to the war, the rise of the Nazis, and the Holocaust. During the civil rights movement in the United States, social psychologists were interested in studying all of the ways that changing situational factors might alter a person's life for the better (Stangor, 2016). Today, racism and prejudice remain central research topics in social psychology.

Social psychologists not only take inspiration from real-life events, but their research has important implications for many aspects of everyday life. Social psychological research includes topics like leadership, organizational behavior, marketing, and persuasion.

©Chris Schmidt/E+/Getty Images

SOCIAL PSYCHOLOGICAL RESEARCH IS (OFTEN) EXPERIMENTAL

Although some social psychological research is correlational in nature, more often than not social psychologists use experimental methods. This means that social psychologists are likely to manipulate an independent variable, for example, an aspect of the social context, to draw causal conclusions about its effects on some outcome (the dependent variable).

AN EXAMPLE: THE BYSTANDER EFFECT

To put these characteristics together, let's review a classic study to give you a taste of social psychology. In 1964, a young woman named Kitty Genovese was brutally murdered in New York City. She was attacked at about 3 A.M. in a courtyard surrounded by apartment buildings. It took the slayer approximately 30 minutes to kill Genovese. Thirty-eight neighbors watched the gory scene from their windows and heard Genovese's screams. Media reports declared that no one helped or called the police. Those reports turned out to be erroneous (Manning, Levine, & Collins, 2007). Nevertheless, inspired by this case, social psychologists John Darley and Bibb Latané (1968) surmised that people might have been less likely to help simply because there were other people present. These scientists devised a number of studies to examine when the presence of others would lead individuals to be less likely to help a person in distress.

The studies involved staging various emergencies. For example, there might be a woman in the hallway in distress, or smoke might begin to slowly fill the room from a vent. The independent variable was whether the participant was alone or with other people. The dependent measure was whether people acted to respond to the emergency (or how long it took them to do so).

The studies showed that when alone, a person was likely to take action about 75 percent of the time, but when another bystander was present, the figure dropped to 50 percent (Darley & Latané, 1968). These results demonstrate the **bystander effect,** the tendency of an individual to be less likely to help in an emergency when other people are present. What explains the bystander effect? One factor might be that people looked to others for cues about how to behave. Another is deindividuation, a process in which anonymous individuals lose a sense of personal responsibility, a topic we will return to later.

The bystander effect is still in evidence. You have probably seen photos of a person in distress or danger, tweeted and re-tweeted without any indication that someone helped.

bystander effect The tendency of an individual who observes an emergency to be less likely to help when other people are present than when the observer is alone.

The discovery of the bystander effect demonstrates how social psychology often works. Darley and Latané noticed an important event in the social world. They developed a hypothesis about the variables that might have led to the event. Then, they sought to test their hypothesis experimentally.

2 Social Cognition

Social cognition explores how people select, interpret, remember, and use social information (Forgas, Fiedler, & Sedikides, 2012; Judd & Park, 2017). Essentially, it is the way that individuals think in social situations (Rivers, Calanchini, & Sherman, 2016; Stroessner & Sherman, 2015). Increasingly, social cognitive psychologists have begun to include brain imaging techniques to their research to help identify where social cognitive processes occur.

social cognition
The area of social psychology exploring how people select, interpret, remember, and use social information.

Some experts have argued that social cognition—thinking about other people—is more fundamental than thinking about anything else.

Person Perception

person perception
The processes by which an individual uses social stimuli to form impressions of others.

Person perception refers to the processes by which we form impressions of others (Hehman & others, 2017). When we first meet someone, typically the new acquaintance quickly makes an impression on us. First impressions happen very quickly. In one study, just a 100-millisecond exposure to unfamiliar faces was sufficient for individuals to form an impression (Todorov, 2017). First impressions can be powerful. Another study showed that impressions that students formed of instructors after very brief exposure at the beginning of a course predicted eventual teaching evaluations and student performance (although quality of instruction still mattered to student learning) (Samudra & others, 2016). Another study showed that less experienced nurses expressed greater willingness to care for individuals whose faces appeared more trustworthy (Mattorozzi & others, 2016).

Are first impressions accurate? Research suggests that they can be. Based on photographs or very brief interactions or video clips, people are able to accurately discern a person's romantic interest in them (Place & others, 2012), propensity for violence (Stillman, Maner, & Baumeister, 2010), leadership (Tskhay, Zhu, & Rule, 2017), and sexual orientation (Stern & others, 2013). In addition, a large body of evidence suggests that even in cases where two people are only slightly acquainted, ratings of personality traits can be surprisingly accurate, in adults (Carney, Colvin, & Hall, 2007) and children (Tackett & others, 2016). The first 90 seconds may be all that is needed to predict what a person is likely to do in the rest of a social interaction (Murphy & others, 2015).

How does the brain make a first impression? Research shows that the dorsomedial prefrontal cortex (or dmPFC, the area of the brain just above your forehead) is involved in first impression formation (Ferrari & others, 2016a). For example, studies using transcranial magnetic stimulation show that when processing in the dmPFC is disrupted, people are slower to render judgments of a person's traits (Ferrari & others, 2016b). The dmPFC is thought to play a role in our sense of self as well as in our judgments of others.

What is it about people that gives away so much information so quickly? People reveal themselves in many ways, including body language, emotional expressions, styles of dress, and hairstyle (Martinez & others, 2016; Olivola & Todorov, 2017; Zwebner & others, 2017). A recent study showed that people watching brief clips (or static photographs) of a basketball game could tell who was winning (and who was trailing) even when the faces of the players was hidden (Furley & Schweizer, 2016).

The face is a very important social cue (Olivola & Todorov, 2017; Todorov, 2017). An early analysis by Alexander Todorov and his colleagues (2005) demonstrated the power of the face. These researchers asked people to rate the competence of individuals from photographs of their faces. The faces were of candidates in U.S. House and Senate elections from 2000 to 2004. Respondents' ratings accurately predicted the outcome for about *70 percent* of the elections. The faces of candidates are especially likely

The face is a powerful social cue.
©Hybrid Images/Cultura/Getty Images

Some places have begun to include a photograph of candidates on the election ballots. What do you think of this idea?

to influence voters if the voters have little information about the election (Lev-On & Waismel-Manor, 2016).

Other aspects of faces can also have important implications for social perception, as we now consider.

PHYSICAL ATTRACTIVENESS

Physical attractiveness is a powerful social cue (Schein, Trujillo, & Langlois, 2017). Judith Langlois and her colleagues found that even 3- to 6 month-old infants showed a preference for looking at attractive faces versus unattractive faces, as rated by adults (Hoss & Langlois, 2003; Ramsey & others, 2004). This attractiveness bias is visited upon infants as well. Compared to when they view attractive babies, adults show subtle signs of negative emotion in their facial expressions when they look at pictures of unattractive babies (Schein & Langlois, 2015).

You might be asking, what makes a face attractive? Social psychologists have examined this question as well. *People* magazine's "50 Most Beautiful People" issue might lead you to conclude that attractiveness is about being exceptional in some physical way. Consider Beyoncé's radiant smile or Ryan Gosling's icy blue eyes. It turns out, though, that very attractive faces are actually *average*. Using computer technology that allowed them to average together digital photographs of a large group of individuals of varying attractiveness, Langlois and her colleagues (1994) created composite faces. A large sample of college students then rated the individual faces and the composites. The results showed that individual faces were less attractive than faces that were created by averaging 8, 16, or 32 other faces. "Averageness" (along with symmetry and youthfulness) is a key aspect of facial attractiveness. In fact, research suggests that average faces are, literally, "easy on the eyes." A study using EEG showed that average and attractive faces are more quickly processed and identified as human faces by the brain (Trujillo, Jankowitsch, & Langlois, 2014). Attractive faces are more rapidly processed and this easy processing in turn leads to more pleasant mood (Schein, Trujillo, & Langlois, 2017).

> **Do It!**
>
> Check out this website to see how the averaging of faces works: www.faceresearch.org/demos/average. Pick some faces you consider unattractive. What happens when you average them together? If you have a digital photograph of yourself and some friends, see what happens when you average those faces. Do you agree that average faces are more attractive than any single face?

In addition, attractive individuals are generally assumed to have a variety of positive characteristics, including being better adjusted, socially skilled, friendly, likable, extraverted, and apt to achieve superior job performance (Langlois & others, 2000). These positive expectations for physically attractive individuals have been referred to as the "beautiful is good" stereotype.

A **stereotype** is a generalization about a group's characteristics that does not consider any variations from one individual to another. Stereotypes are a natural extension of the limits on human cognitive processing and our reliance on concepts in cognitive processing (Carpenter & others, 2017; Fiske & Tablante, 2014). We save time and effort by lumping people into groups. Unfortunately, in doing so we miss the unique characteristics of each member of those groups.

stereotype
A generalization about a group's characteristics that does not consider any variations from one individual to another.

Is there any truth to the "beautiful is good" stereotype? Attractive people may indeed possess a number of positive characteristics (Langlois & others, 2000). A recent longitudinal study showed that greater facial attractiveness at age 9 predicted higher psychological well-being and lowered depression at age 60 (Datta Gupta, Etcoff, & Jaeger, 2016). Another longitudinal study showed that, in combination with cognitive ability and self-control, physical attractiveness in adolescence predicted greater education level which in turn predicted higher income in adulthood (Converse & others, 2016). Does that mean that attractiveness is naturally related to, for example, being happier or enjoying career success? Not necessarily.

One way that stereotypes can influence individuals is **self-fulfilling prophecy.** In a self-fulfilling prophecy, social expectations cause individuals to act in ways that make their expectations come true. Robert Rosenthal and Lenore Jacobsen conducted a classic self-fulfilling prophecy study in 1968. They told grade-school teachers that five students were "late bloomers"—that these students had high levels of ability that would likely shine forth over time. In reality, the students had been selected randomly. Nonetheless, a year later,

self-fulfilling prophecy
Social expectations that cause an individual to act in such a way that the expectations are realized.

teachers' expectations for the "late bloomers" were reflected in student performance—the academic performance of these five was beyond that of other students. Self-fulfilling prophecy effects show the potential power of stereotypes and other sources of expectations on human behavior.

How do you think the teachers influenced the late bloomers? What kind of behaviors led to the kids' enhanced performance?

More recent research continues to support the idea that expectations can serve as self-fulfilling prophecies (Willard & Madon, 2016). For example, among older adults, expectations about whether growing old involves loneliness (Pickhartova, Bowling, & Victor, 2016) predict actual experiences of loneliness. Another study of nearly 5000 adults showed that negative attitudes about aging predicted slower walking speed two years later (Robertson & others, 2015). Finally, when people meet someone online, expectations can have a large effect on the quality of their interactions (Clark & Green, 2017).

Let's apply self-fulfilling prophecy to physically attractive individuals. If we expect attractive people to have positive characteristics, we treat them differently from others. Remember, even attractive babies are more likely to be met with smiling faces compared with unattractive babies (Schein & Langlois, 2015). Studies have shown that social perceivers are likely to give attractive people better treatment. For example, in one study participants were able to punish or reward others whom they had observed playing a game with a partner (Putz & others, 2016). The results showed that when they cheated, attractive players were punished less than unattractive players. When they behaved prosocially (cooperating with the other player) attractive players were rewarded more than unattractive players. Over the course of a lifetime, positive treatment from others may help to produce the confirmation of positive expectations for attractive people.

We all have many attributes or social cues that serve as information for social perceivers. One such social cue is our names. Names often provide an array of information about people, including gender, age, social class, and ethnicity. Names have been shown to be powerful cues in some instances. For example, a study of scientists showed that when an applicant for a research assistant position in a lab had a male name, the applicant was more likely to be offered a position (and higher salary) than when identical qualifications were offered by an applicant with a female name (Moss-Racusin & others, 2012).

Names are interesting social cues because, of course, babies often are named prior to being born. Yet, people do associate particular characteristics with certain names. For example, one study showed that, in the United States, the name Katherine implies that the woman is likely to be more competent (Mehrabian, 2001). Is it possible that these expectations for Katherines will lead them to be more competent? The idea of self-fulfilling prophecy would suggest that they just might.

A recent set of studies brings together a number of the concepts we have discussed so far, including person perception, facial appearance, stereotypes and self-fulfilling prophecy. This work has found a surprising answer to the question, Do we look like our names? To read about it, see the Challenge Your Thinking.

The "what is beautiful is good" stereotype suggests that positive expectations can influence subsequent behavior. Could stereotypes that carry negative expectations combine with self-fulfilling prophecy effects as well? Research shows that the answer to that question is, unfortunately, yes. In fact, stereotypes not only influence our views of others but also sometimes influence the feelings and performance of individuals in stereotyped groups (Grand, 2017).

stereotype threat
An individual's fast-acting, self-fulfilling fear of being judged based on a negative stereotype about his or her group.

Stereotype threat is an individual's fast-acting, self-fulfilling fear of being judged based on a negative stereotype about his or her group (Griffin & Hu, 2015; Schmader, Hall, & Croft, 2014). A person who experiences stereotype threat is well aware of stereotypical expectations for him or her as a member of the group. In stereotype-relevant situations, the individual experiences anxiety about living "down" to expectations and consequently underperforms (Grand, 2017). Stereotype threat is experienced by members of many groups, including those in ethnic minority groups, girls and women, individuals who are members of sexual minority groups, the elderly, individuals with low socioeconomic status, individuals with a disability, and those who are addicts in recovery (Aronson &

Stereotype threat affects performance on math tests by women compared to men and on tests of "natural athletic ability" by non-Latino White American men. If there is a negative stereotype about a group, members of that group will likely worry about "living down" to those expectations.

Do We Look Like Our Names?

Have you ever met someone and thought, "Even if I didn't already know your name is Bob, I would have thought you were a Bob"? Sometimes people just seem to fit their names. What is it that makes "Bob" Bob-like? How can a baby named Bob grow into an adult who seems high in "Bob-ness"? A program of studies examined these questions (Zwebner & others, 2017). The rationale behind this research was that, first, we have social expectations or stereotypes associated with how people with particular names should look. Then, those stereotypes become self-fulfilling prophecies such that people start to conform to the appearance associated with their names. The researchers suggested that there at least two ways a person might start looking like their name. First, there are aspects of appearance that we can control, such as style of dress and hair. A person might use these avenues to start to look like their names. Second, habitual facial expressions can, over time, affect facial appearance even when the person's face is at rest. In these ways, "Marys" and "Lauras" and "Aprils" and "Bobs" might all come to look like their names. So, if Matthew lives in a culture that expects "Matthews" to be studious, he might spend a lot of time reading, wear glasses, and a serious expression.

To test their idea, which they called the "face-name matching hypothesis," the researchers (Zwebner & others, 2017) first tested whether people could pick out the actual name of a person from a picture, in a multiple choice test. The results showed that people were better than chance at picking the right name for each face. This effect held only within culture (where people would share the same expectations) and only for people who use their real name (not a nickname).

©Tiffany Bryant/Shutterstock

Of course, human perceivers might be biased by all kinds of variables. If the face-name matching effect is real, it should be the product of objective differences between faces of people with different names. In some ways, all Bobs or Joses or Sarahs, should "look alike." To test this possibility, the researchers used a computer to create an algorithm that could accurately match faces (from photos) with their real names, using a database of over 90,000 pictures from social media. Once the computer had learned to make these distinctions, it was tested on a new set of faces. The results? The computer picked the right name for faces with accuracy well above chance. What aspects of the face was the computer attending to? Analyses revealed that the computer rendered its judgments using information around the eyes and mouth—those places where we often show our emotions (Zwebner & others, 2017).

These fascinating studies demonstrate the interplay between expectations and reality, and the ways that social cues over which we have little control can have implications for how others view us and who we become.

What Do You Think?

- Do you look like your name? Do friends who share your name look like you?

- What factors besides facial expressions might account for the face-name effect?

---

others, 2013; Cadaret & others, 2017; Jordano & Touron, 2017; von Hippel & others, 2017). Stereotype threat can interfere with the performance of people who find themselves engaged in a setting in which they feel they do not belong. For example, stereotype threat has been implicated in the shortage of men in stereotypically feminine roles such as grade school teachers (Kalokerinos & others, 2017).

Stereotype threat is activated when aspects of a situation remind people that expectations for them are low. Claude Steele and Eliot Aronson (1995, 2004) have shown that when a test is presented to African American and non-Latino White American students who have first simply checked a box indicating their ethnicity, African Americans do not perform as well. In situations where ethnicity was not made salient, no differences in performance emerged. Even children have an awareness that when someone tries to do something that does not fit with stereotypes, the person is likely to be anxious (Wegmann, 2017).

Maybe it is time to put questions about gender and race/ethnicity at the end of these tests!

Stereotype threat has been implicated in the problems that educators have getting boys interested in reading (Pansu & others, 2016). Recent evidence has shown that stereotype threat not only interferes when people are in a performance situation but also as they are learning. Women in science and math contexts performed more poorly because stereotype threat robbed them of their attention during training (Grand, 2017).

Of course, once you get to know a person, you have a lot more information than simply physical appearance or stereotypes with which to form an opinion of him or her. The process by which we come to understand the causes of others' behavior is called *attribution,* another important process in social cognition.

Attribution

As we navigate the social world, we need to gather information about the people we encounter. Is he trustworthy? Will she be friendly? We often answer these questions by observing a person's actions and drawing inferences about the type of person he or she is likely to be. Making inferences means taking the information we have and coming up with a good guess about who someone is and what they are likely to do in the future (Fishman & Husman, 2017; Livengood, Sytsma, & Rose, 2017; Todorov & others, 2015). The results of those inferences are our attributions. Attributions are explanations of the causes of behavior. The way we explain the behaviors of other people can affect our beliefs about them and how we feel about them (Hillebrandt & Barclay, 2017; Ruybal & Siegel, 2017).

Attribution theory identifies the important dimensions at work in attributions. It states that people are motivated to discover the underlying causes of behavior in order to make sense of that behavior (Heider, 1958; Kelley, 1973; Weiner, 2006). Attributions vary along three dimensions (Jones, 1998):

attribution theory
The view that people are motivated to discover the underlying causes of behavior as part of their effort to make sense of the behavior.

1. *Internal and external causes:* Internal attributions include causes inside and specific to the person, such as his or her traits and abilities. External attributions include causes outside the person, such as situational factors. Did Beth get an *A* on the test because she is smart or because the test was easy?

2. *Stable and unstable causes:* Is the cause relatively enduring and permanent, or is it temporary? Did Aaron blow up at his girlfriend because he is a hostile guy or because he was in a bad mood that day?

3. *Controllable and uncontrollable causes:* We perceive that we have power over some causes (for instance, by preparing delicious food for a picnic) but not others (rain on picnic day).

ATTRIBUTIONAL ERRORS AND BIASES

In attribution theory, the person who produces the behavior is called the *actor.* The person who offers a causal explanation of the actor's behavior is called the *observer.* Actors often explain their own behavior in terms of external (or situational) causes. In contrast, observers frequently explain the actor's behavior in terms of internal causes (such as personality traits). When observers make attributions about behaviors, they often overestimate the importance of internal traits and underestimate the importance of external situations when they seek explanations of another person's behavior (Gilbert & Malone, 1995; Jones & Harris, 1967; Wang & others, 2017) (Figure 1). This mistake is called the **fundamental attribution error.** Ann might explain that she honked her car horn at someone who was slow to move when the light turned green because she was in a hurry to get to the hospital to see her ill father, but the driver she honked at might think she was just rude.

fundamental attribution error
Observers' overestimation of the importance of internal traits and underestimation of the importance of external situations when they seek explanations of another person's behavior.

Just how fundamental is the fundamental attribution error? Cross-cultural studies show that this error is more common among Westerners. Those from more collectivistic cultures are more likely to look to the situation to explain the behavior of others (Imada, 2012; Morris & Peng, 1994; Rips, 2011).

A brain imaging study showed that activity in the brain in an area associated with thinking about other people's mental states (the medial

Observer Tends to give internal, trait explanations of actor's behavior

"She's late with her report because she can't concentrate on her own responsibilities."

Actor Tends to give external, situational explanations of own behavior

"I'm late with my report because other people keep asking me to help them with their projects."

FIGURE 1 **The Fundamental Attribution Error** In this situation, the supervisor is the observer, and the employee is the actor.

(with glasses) ©Kris Timken/Blend Images LLC; (without glasses) ©John Dowland/Getty Images

PFC) was related to a higher tendency to commit the fundamental attribution error (Moran, Jolly, & Mitchell, 2014). Such results support the idea that this error occurs because people focus on trying to understand an actor's mental states. In this process, the potential influence of the situation may be missed. Indeed, the fundamental attribution error can be reduced by taking the perspective of others as we try to explain their behavior (Hooper & others, 2015). When we put ourselves in the other person's shoes, we might be able to see through his or her eyes, reducing the fundamental attribution error.

It's challenging to remember how much the situation can influence behavior. Try avoiding this attributional error for just one day: When you see someone do something, think about the situational factors that might cause that person's behavior.

Just as we make attributions about the behavior of others, we also make attributions about our own actions. **Self-serving bias** refers to the tendency to take credit for one's own successes and to deny responsibility for one's own failures (Alston & others, 2013; Lee-Bates & others, 2017). Think about taking a psychology exam. If you do well, you are likely to take credit for that success ("I knew that stuff")—that is, to make internal attributions. If you do poorly, however, you are more likely to blame situational factors ("The test was too hard")—that is, to make external attributions.

self-serving bias The tendency to take credit for one's successes and to deny responsibility for one's failures.

HEURISTICS IN SOCIAL INFORMATION PROCESSING
Just as heuristics are useful in general information processing, they can play a role in *social* information processing (Capraro, Jordan, & Rand, 2014; Rand, 2016). Heuristics can be helpful tools for navigating the complex social landscape, but they can lead to mistakes.

Stereotypes are a type of heuristic in that they allow us to make quick judgments using very little information. Relying on stereotypes can lead to serious errors in social information processing. For example, having never encountered an Asian American point guard, many college basketball coaches failed to appreciate the skills of Jeremy Lin. Lin simply did not fit the stereotype of a great point guard, and stereotypes of Asian Americans did not suggest that his abilities would be well suited to success on the court. Could an Asian American fulfill the leadership role of point guard on an elite basketball team? Lin had a stellar career at Harvard University; but it was not until 2012 that he captured the attention of NBA fans everywhere during a streak of amazing games for the New York Knicks, shattering stereotypes along the way. He now plays for the Brooklyn Nets.

One common heuristic is the false consensus effect. Ask yourself: "How many students at my school support the death penalty?" Your answer is likely to depend on whether you support the death penalty. The **false consensus effect** is the overestimation of the degree to which everybody else thinks or acts the way we do. Interestingly, research has shown that activity in the brain's reward areas is associated with greater levels of false consensus bias (Welborn & others, 2017), suggesting that it feels good to conclude that others share our views. The false consensus effect shows that we sometimes use ourselves as our best guess about the social world, suggesting the special place of the self in social information processing.

In the false consensus effect, we are using our SELVES as a heuristic!

false consensus effect Observers' overestimation of the degree to which everybody else thinks or acts the way they do.

The Self as a Social Object and Social Comparison

We process social information not only to understand other people but also to understand ourselves. A great deal of research in social cognition revolves around "the self," our mental representation of who we are and what we are like. The self is different from other social objects because we know so much more about ourselves than we do about others. The self is special as well because we value ourselves. One of the most important self-related variables is *self-esteem,* the degree to which we have positive or negative feelings about ourselves (Kernis, 2013). In general, research has shown that it is good to feel good about oneself (Iancu, Bodner, & Ben-Zion, 2014; Solomon, 2013).

Some have argued that self-esteem is a bad thing. Typically such arguments focus on unrealistically high or unstable self-esteem.

Individuals with high self-esteem often possess a variety of **positive illusions**—rosy views of themselves that are often a bit better than reality (Biggane, Allen, & Albert, 2016;

positive illusions Favorable views of the self that are not necessarily rooted in reality.

Molouki & Pronin, 2014). Indeed, research shows that many of us think of ourselves as "above average" on many valued characteristics, including how trustworthy, objective, and capable we are (Howell & Ratliff, 2017; Sedikides & others, 2014). Holding positive illusions is linked to psychological health and academic achievement (Chung, Schriber, & Robins, 2016; Taylor, 2011, 2013, 2014; Taylor & Sherman, 2008). Nevertheless, self-esteem can become problematic if a person's self-views change a great deal from one moment to the next and if it is blown out of proportion (Geukes & others, 2017).

©Blue Jean Images/Getty Images

Have you ever felt a sense of accomplishment about getting a *B* on a test, only to feel deflated when you found out that your friend in the class got an *A*? Comparing ourselves to other people is one way we come to understand our own behavior. **Social comparison** is the process by which we evaluate our thoughts, feelings, behaviors, and abilities in relation to others. Social comparison tells us what our distinctive characteristics are and aids us in building an identity.

social comparison
The process by which individuals evaluate their thoughts, feelings, behaviors, and abilities in relation to others.

Over 60 years ago, Leon Festinger (1954) proposed a theory of social comparison positing that when individuals lack an objective way to evaluate their opinions and abilities, they compare themselves with others. Furthermore, to get an accurate view, people are most likely to compare themselves with others who are similar to themselves. Extended and modified over the years, Festinger's social comparison theory continues to provide an important rationale for how individuals come to know themselves (Lev-Ari, Baumgarten-Katz, & Zohar, 2014; Neugebauer, Ray, & Sassenberg, 2016; Schneider & Valet, 2017).

Attitudes

attitudes
An individual's opinions and beliefs about people, objects, and ideas—how the person feels about the world.

Attitudes are our opinions and beliefs about people, objects, and ideas—how we feel about the world. Social psychologists are interested in many questions about attitudes, including how attitudes relate to behavior and whether and how attitudes can change (Petty & Briñol, 2015).

ATTITUDES AND BEHAVIOR
It might seem obvious that attitudes should lead to behavior. Attitudes do predict behavior, but only *sometimes*. Specifically, attitudes are likely to guide behavior under the following conditions (Briñol & Petty, 2012; Schröder & Wolf, 2017):

- **When the person's attitudes are strong** (Ajzen, 2001): The stronger an attitude toward a particular topic, the more likely a person will act on it. Attitudes tend to be especially strong about issues we believe are morally important. Just labeling a topic moral can increase the strength of attitudes about it (Luttrell & others, 2016).

- **When the person shows a strong awareness of his or her attitudes and when the person rehearses and practices them** (Fazio & Olsen, 2007; Fazio & others, 1982): For example, a person who has been asked to give a speech about the benefits of recycling is more likely to recycle than is an individual with the same attitude about recycling who has not put the idea into words or defined it in public.

- **When the person has a vested interest:** People are more likely to act on attitudes when the issue at stake will affect them personally. For example, a classic study examined whether students would show up for a rally protesting a change that would raise the legal drinking age from 18 to 21 (Sivacek & Crano, 1982). Although students in general were against the change, those in the critical age group (from 18 to 20) were more likely to turn out to protest.

Beyond being places to connect and keep up with others, social media sites like Facebook and Twitter are forums for comparing how we measure up to other people.
©JGI/Jamie Grill/Getty Images

What are your attitudes about social issues such as the death penalty, gun ownership, and climate change? How do these views influence your behavior?

BEHAVIOR AND ATTITUDES Not only do attitudes influence behavior, but behavior can influence attitudes. And changes in behavior can precede changes in attitudes. Social psychologists offer two main explanations of why behavior influences attitudes: cognitive dissonance theory and self-perception theory.

Cognitive Dissonance Theory

Cognitive dissonance, another concept introduced by Festinger (1957), is the psychological discomfort (*dissonance*) caused by two inconsistent thoughts. According to the theory, we feel uneasy when we notice an inconsistency between what we believe and what we do. In a classic study, Festinger and J. Merrill Carlsmith (1959) asked college students to engage in a series of very boring tasks, such as sorting spools into trays. These participants were later asked to persuade another student (who was in fact a confederate) to participate in the study by telling him that the task was actually interesting and enjoyable. Half of the participants were randomly assigned to be paid $1 for telling this white lie, and the other half received $20. Afterward, all of the participants rated how interesting and enjoyable the task really was.

Those who were paid only $1 to tell the lie rated the task as more enjoyable than those who were paid $20. Festinger and Carlsmith reasoned that those paid $20 to tell the lie could attribute their behavior to the high value of the money they received. On the other hand, those who were paid $1 experienced cognitive dissonance: "How could I *lie* for just $1? If I said I liked the task, I must have really liked it." The inconsistency between what they *did* (tell a lie) and what they *were paid for it* (just $1) moved these individuals to change their attitudes about the task. Those who were paid $20 were unlikely to experience dissonance. Only those underpaid for lying would be expected to change their attitudes about the task.

When attitudes and behavior conflict, we can reduce cognitive dissonance in one of two ways: change our behavior to fit our attitudes or change our attitudes to fit our behavior. In the classic study above, participants changed their attitudes about the task to match their behavior. If you have a positive attitude about recycling but pitched a soda can in the trash, for example, you might feel dissonance ("Wait, I believe in recycling, yet I just pitched that can") and relieve that dissonance by rationalizing ("Recycling is not really *that* important"). Through cognitive dissonance, your behavior changed your attitude.

Effort justification is one type of dissonance reduction. It refers to rationalizing the amount of effort we put into getting something by increasing its value. Effort justification explains strong feelings of loyalty toward a group based on the effort it takes to gain admission into that group. Working hard to get into an organization (such as a Greek society or the Marines) or a profession (such as medicine or law) can change our attitudes about it. According to cognitive dissonance theory, individuals in these situations are likely to think, "If it's this tough to get into, it must be worth it."

What happens in the brain as people experience cognitive dissonance? An *f*MRI study induced dissonance by having people reflect about a variety of decisions and behaviors that likely conflicted with their values. That study showed that dissonance was associated with activity in areas of the brain involved in integrating emotion and cognition, as well as empathy (anterior cingulate cortex and the insula) (de Vries, Byrne, & Kehoe, 2015).

Social psychologists continue to develop Festinger's approach to cognitive dissonance (Hinojosa & others, 2017). Cognitive dissonance can help explain diverse important phenomena such as when a victim of partner violence must decide whether to leave or stay in the relationship (Nicholson & Lutz, 2017), how people make decisions about unpleasant medical screenings (Ent & Gerend, 2016), or when and how people use tax write-offs for charitable giving (Kim & Bay, 2017).

Self-Perception Theory

Self-perception theory is Daryl Bem's (1967) take on how behavior influences attitudes. According to self-perception theory, individuals make inferences about their attitudes by observing their behavior. That is, behaviors can cause attitudes, because when we are questioned about our attitudes, we think back on our behaviors for information. If someone asked about

Remember, random assignment is used to make sure that groups are equal in every way except for the independent variable—which in this study was how much the participants were paid for the lie. The rating of enjoyment was the dependent variable.

Remember, a confederate is a person who is in cahoots with the experimenter.

If you have ever played devil's advocate in an argument (arguing a point just for the sake of argument), you might have found yourself realizing that maybe you do hold the views you have pretended to advocate. That's self-perception theory at work.

cognitive dissonance
An individual's psychological discomfort (dissonance) caused by two inconsistent thoughts.

self-perception theory
Bem's theory on how behaviors influence attitudes, stating that individuals make inferences about their attitudes by perceiving their behavior.

your attitude toward sushi, you might think, "Well, I rarely eat it, so I must not like it." Your behavior has led you to recognize something about yourself that you had not noticed before. According to Bem, we are especially likely to look to our behavior to determine our attitudes when those attitudes are unclear.

Figure 2 compares cognitive dissonance theory and self-perception theory. Both theories have merit in explaining the connection between attitudes and behavior, and these opposing views bring to light the complexity that may exist in this connection. Another route to attitude change is persuasion.

Persuasion

Persuasion involves trying to change someone's attitude—and often behavior as well (Briñol & others, 2017; Petty & Briñol, 2015). Teachers, lawyers, and sales representatives study techniques that will help them sway their audiences (children, juries, and buyers). Perhaps the most skilled persuaders of all are advertisers, who combine a full array of techniques to sell everything from cornflakes to carpets to cars.

Think about the last advertisement you saw. Who presented the message? What did the message say? How was the message presented? Every act of persuasion is multifaceted. How do these many different aspects relate to attitude change? You might think that if a persuasive argument is based on sound logic, it should win the day. But the quality of an argument is only one aspect of persuasion.

Festinger Cognitive Dissonance Theory

We are motivated toward consistency between attitudes and behavior and away from inconsistency.

Example: "I hate my job. I need to develop a better attitude toward it or else quit."

Bem Self-Perception Theory

We make inferences about our attitudes by perceiving and examining our behavior and the context in which it occurs, which might involve inducements to behave in certain ways.

Example: "I am spending all of my time thinking about how much I hate my job. I really must not like it."

FIGURE 2 **Two Theories of the Connections between Attitudes and Behavior** Although we often think of attitudes as causing behavior, behavior can change attitudes, through either dissonance reduction or self-perception.
©Photodisc/Getty Images

After all, advertisers spend huge amounts of money for celebrity endorsements. If an argument is good, why would it matter if LeBron James delivers it?

elaboration likelihood model Theory identifying two ways to persuade: a central route and a peripheral route.

TECHNIQUES OF PERSUASION The **elaboration likelihood model** identifies two pathways of persuasion: a central route and a peripheral route (Petty & Cacioppo, 1986; Teeny, Briñol, & Petty, 2017). The *central route* works by engaging the audience thoughtfully with a sound, logical argument. The *peripheral route* involves factors such as the attractiveness of the person giving the message or the emotional power of an appeal. The peripheral route is effective when people are not paying close attention or lack the time or energy to think about the message. As you might guess, television advertisers often use the peripheral route to persuasion on the assumption that during the commercials you are probably not paying full attention to the screen. However, the central route is more persuasive when people have the ability and the motivation to pay attention.

Attitudes that are changed using the central route are more likely to persist than attitudes that are changed using the peripheral route.

RESISTING PERSUASION One of the ways people resist persuasion is through counter-arguing. This means that as they are

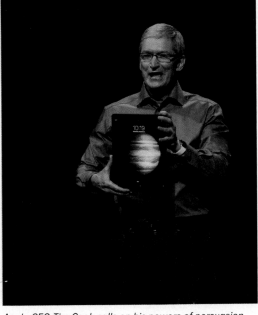

Apple CEO Tim Cook calls on his powers of persuasion whenever Apple introduces a new product.
©Monica Davey/Epa/REX/Shutterstock

PSYCHOLOGY IN OUR WORLD

Making the Sale!

Sooner or later, nearly everyone will be in a position of selling someone something. Social psychologists have studied ways in which social psychological principles influence whether a salesperson makes that sale (Cialdini, 1993, 2016). The effectiveness of these strategies continues to be borne out in research (Cantarero, Gamian-Wilk, & Dolinski, 2017; Guéguen & others, 2016).

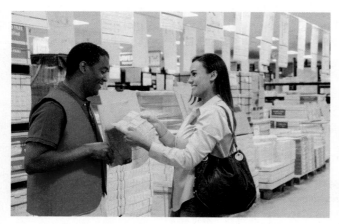

©Ariel Skelley/Blend Images

One strategy is called the *foot-in-the-door* technique (Freedman & Fraser, 1966). The foot-in-the-door strategy involves making a smaller request ("Would you be interested in a three-month trial subscription to a magazine?") at the beginning, saving the biggest demand ("How about a full year?") for last. The foot-in-the-door strategy works because complying with the smaller request sets the stage for the person to maintain consistency between their prior behavior and the next one (and avoid dissonance).

A different strategy is called the *door-in-the-face* technique (Cialdini & others, 1975). The door-in-the-face technique involves making the biggest pitch first ("Would you be interested in a full-year subscription?"), which the customer probably will reject, and then making a smaller "concessionary" demand ("Okay, then, how about a three-month trial?"). This technique relies on the fact that the customer feels a sense of obligation: You let him off the hook with that big request; maybe he should be nice and take the smaller offer.

As the foot-in-the-door technique attests, cognitive dissonance can be a powerful sales tool. Sometimes the harder we work to buy something, the more we want it. After all, did you buy that strange lamp on eBay—or did you *win* it?

---

exposed to a message, they defend against the information by mentally generating arguments against it. Students who binge drink, for instance, have been shown to be most likely to counter-argue against public service announcements on the dangers of binge drinking (Zhou & Shapiro, 2017). Making messages self-relevant can help to short circuit the tendency to counter-argue.

Of course, sometimes, we are interested in helping people avoid persuasion. After all, advertisers, salespeople, and politicians work hard to persuade us sometimes with little concern for whether their products and policies might actually help us. Social psychologists are interested in identifying ways people can effectively resist persuasion (Hornsey & Fielding, 2017). One way to resist persuasion is through *inoculation* (Banas & Richards, 2017; McGuire, 2003; McGuire & Papageorgis, 1961). Just as administering a vaccine inoculates individuals from a virus by introducing a weakened or dead version of that virus to the immune system, giving people a weak version of a persuasive message and allowing them time to argue against it can help individuals avoid persuasion.

YOU ARE HEREBY INOCULATED! College students are preyed upon by credit card companies!

"Inoculation" helps college students resist plagiarism (Compton & Pfau, 2008) as well as credit card marketing appeals (Compton & Pfau, 2004). When individuals are warned that they are going to be hit with persuasive appeals and are given arguments to help them resist these pitches, they are able to do so.

3 Social Behavior

We do not just think socially; we also behave in social ways. Two particular behaviors that have interested psychologists represent the extremes of human social activity: altruism and aggression.

Altruism

Over 100,000 adults and children await lifesaving kidney or liver transplants each year. A staggering 4,500 people will die awaiting a transplant (Donate Life, 2017). Recently, people have begun to offer their own kidneys or parts of their livers to save the lives of individuals in need. In 2015, 6,000 transplants were made possible by living donors (Donate Life, 2017). These individuals are sometimes family members but they can also be strangers. Such extraordinary acts of selfless giving are inspiring but also sometimes puzzling (Carney, 2017).

altruism
Giving to another person with the ultimate goal of benefiting that person, even if it incurs a cost to oneself.

egoism
Giving to another person to ensure reciprocity; to gain self-esteem; to present oneself as powerful, competent, or caring; or to avoid social and self-censure for failing to live up to society's expectations.

In everyday life, we witness and perform "random acts of kindness"—maybe adding a quarter to someone's expired parking meter or giving up our seat on a bus to someone in need. All of these acts are *prosocial behaviors*—they all involve helping another person (Eisenberg, Eggum, & Spinrad, 2015; Schroeder & Graziano, 2015; Toumbourou, 2016). Such acts of kindness bear the markings of altruism. **Altruism** means giving aid to another person with the ultimate goal of benefiting that person, even if it incurs a cost to oneself. Are acts of kindness truly altruistic?

Psychologists debate whether human behavior is ever truly altruistic. Altruistic motives contrast with selfish or egoistic motives (Cialdini, 1991; Hawley, 2014; Hirschberger, 2015). **Egoism** means helping another person for personal gain, such as to feel good, or avoid guilt. Kindness might also serve selfish purposes by ensuring *reciprocity*, meaning that we help another person to increase the chances that the person will return the favor.

An example of animal altruism—a baboon plucking bugs from another baboon. Most acts of animal altruism involve kin.
©karenfoleyphotography/Shutterstock

Altruism has presented a puzzle for evolutionary psychologists (van Doorn & Taborsky, 2012). How can a behavior that rewards others, and not oneself, be adaptive? Evolutionary theorists note that helping is especially likely to occur among family members, because helping a relative also means promoting the survival of the family's genes (Buss, 2015). Evolutionary theorists believe that reciprocity in relationships with nonfamily members is essentially the mistaken application of a heuristic that made sense in human evolutionary history—to engage in selfless acts of kindness to one's own family (Chuang & Wu, 2017; Kavashan & others, 2017; Nowak, Page, & Sigmund, 2000).

Acts of kindness seem to have a powerful payoff for those who do them. Helping others strongly and consistently leads to increased positive mood (Omoto & Snyder, 1995; Schaller & Cialdini, 1988; Stukas, Snyder, & Clary, 2015; Toumbourou, 2016; Snippe & others, 2017). Prosocial spending, or spending money on others rather than oneself, is linked to greater well-being, potentially universally (Aknin & others, 2013). Engaging in volunteer work enhances volunteers' sense of being a good person and their health (Piliavin & Siegl, 2015). A meta-analysis showed that older adults who engaged in volunteering had a lower mortality risk than those who did not (Okun, Yeung, & Brown, 2013).

What was the last altruistic act you committed? What led to your behavior? How did you feel afterward?

Does the fact that behaving prosocially leads to feelings of pleasure mean that such behavior is always selfish? Feelings of pleasure are linked with adaptive behaviors—those things we need to do to survive and reproduce. Might it be that the strong link between pleasure and kindness demonstrates that engaging in prosocial behavior is an important adaptation for humans who are so dependent on one another for survival?

Setting aside the question of whether such acts are altruistic, in this section we review biological, psychological, and sociocultural factors that predict prosocial behavior. As you read, consider whether you think altruism is a problem to be solved or a natural aspect of human life.

BIOLOGICAL FACTORS IN PROSOCIAL BEHAVIOR   Genetic factors explain between 30 and 53 percent of the differences we see in the tendency to engage in kind acts (Fortuna & Knafo, 2014). These genetic factors, in turn, are related to neurotransmitters in the brain (Christ, Carlo, & Stoltenberg, 2016). High levels of serotonin are associated with prosocial behavior (Crockett, 2009). Dopamine receptors in the brain are also associated with prosocial behavior (Knafo, Israel, & Ebstein, 2011). Finally, the neurohormone oxytocin, which plays a role in social bonding, is associated with enhanced prosocial behavior (De Dreu, 2014; Ratner & Way, 2013).

In terms of brain structures, research suggests that when we feel compassion for another person, areas of the midbrain associated with the perception of pain are likely to be active (Simon-Thomas & others, 2012). These same areas are associated with nurturing parental behaviors, suggesting that neural factors associated with the parent–child relationship are involved in kindness toward others.

PSYCHOLOGICAL FACTORS IN PROSOCIAL BEHAVIOR   Among the psychological factors that play a role in prosocial behavior are empathy, personality, and mood.

empathy
A feeling of oneness with the emotional state of another person.

Empathy   **Empathy** is a person's feeling of oneness with the emotional state of another. When we feel empathy for someone, we feel what that person is feeling. Empathy allows us to put ourselves in another person's shoes (Davis, 2015). We can feel empathy even for those we do not particularly like, as was demonstrated when Yankee fans delighted in the playing of "Sweet Caroline" (a tradition of their arch rivals, the Boston Red Sox), following the bombing of the Boston Marathon in 2013. When we are feeling empathy for someone else's plight, we are moved to action—not to make ourselves feel better but out of genuine concern for the other person (Batson, 2002, 2006, 2012; Batson, Lishner, & Stocks, 2015).

Personality   Agreeableness is the personality trait most strongly associated with prosocial behaviors (Caprara & others, 2010; Graziano & Habashi, 2015; Habashi, Graziano,

& Hoover, 2016). The association between agreeableness and brain structures helps to illuminate its role in acts of kindness. Agreeableness is related to greater volume in the posterior cingulate cortex (DeYoung & others, 2010), a brain area associated with understanding other people's beliefs and with empathy (Hubbard & others, 2016; Saxe & Powell, 2006).

Mood   Our mood can determine whether or not we engage in kind behaviors. Happy people are more likely than unhappy people to help others (Snippe & others, 2017; Snyder & Lopez, 2007). Indeed, a study in which participants reported their mood and acts of kindness multiple times during a day over several days showed that positive mood predicted more kind acts, which, in turn, led to even more positive mood (Snippe & others, 2017). Does it then follow that being in a bad mood makes people less helpful? Not necessarily, because adults (especially) generally understand that doing good for another person can be a mood booster. When people are in a bad mood, they might be likely to help if they think that doing so will improve their mood.

SOCIOCULTURAL FACTORS IN PROSOCIAL BEHAVIOR   Three sociocultural factors that influence prosocial behavior are socioeconomic status, gender, and the media.

Socioeconomic Status   Although they have less, those of lower socioeconomic status tend to be more likely to help than those who have more (Piff & others, 2010). Compared to more wealthy individuals, those from poorer backgrounds tend be more attuned to the suffering of others (Stellar & others, 2012). It may be that relative wealth promotes a focus on maintaining one's standing in the world to the detriment of reaching out to help those in need (Kraus & others, 2012). Wealthier individuals are more likely to engage in public giving while less well-off individuals are more likely to give privately (Kraus & Callaghan, 2016).

Gender   Given the role of empathy in helping, we might think that women should be more likely to help than men. After all, stereotypes tell us that women are more empathic than men. However, as in most domains, it is useful to think about gender in context (Biernat & Deaux, 2012). Compared to men, women are more likely to experience an immediate impulse to behave prosocially toward a person in need (Rand & others, 2016). Women are more likely than men to act on these impulses to help when the context involves existing interpersonal relationships or nurturing, such as volunteering time to help a child with a personal problem (Diekman & Clark, 2015; Eagly, 2009). Men, on the other hand, are more likely to help in situations in which a perceived danger is present (for instance, picking up a hitchhiker) and in which they feel competent to help (as in assisting someone with a flat tire) (Eagly & Crowley, 1986).

Media   Media—including music, TV, film, and video games—can influence prosocial behavior. Listening to music with prosocial lyrics can promote kindness (Greitemeyer, 2009). Watching television shows with positive content predicts prosocial behavior (Hearold, 1986). Playing prosocial video games enhances prosocial thoughts (Greitemeyer & Osswald, 2011) and acts of kindness in children and adolescents (Harrington & O'Connell, 2016). When videogames include prosocial content, the players are more likely to behave prosocially during the game (Jin & Li, 2017). A series of studies showed that participants who played a video game such as Lemmings, in which the player

The Samburu people of Kenya are very spiritual, believing in and praying daily to the god Ngai. In addition to the factors discussed here, the presence of established religions within a culture is related to prosocial behaviors.
©Eric Lafforgue/Gamma-Rapho via Getty Images

tries to save the hapless creatures from a variety of disasters, were more likely than those who played either a neutral or a violent game to help an experimenter pick up a cup of spilled pencils and to intervene when a confederate posing as the experimenter's ex-boyfriend came in and began to harass her (Greitemeyer & Osswald, 2010).

Some evolutionary scientists have suggested that altruism, especially when it is directed at the members of one's own group, may coexist with hostile actions toward others outside one's group (Arrow, 2007). A soldier may perform selfless acts of altruism for his or her country, but for a person on the other side of the conflict, that behavior is harmful. Thus, altruism within a group may be linked to aggression. Perhaps the greatest puzzle is that a species capable of incredible acts of kindness can also perpetrate horrifying acts of violence.

Aggression

aggression
Social behavior whose objective is to harm someone, either physically or verbally.

Aggression refers to social behavior whose objective is to harm someone, either physically or verbally. Aggression is common in humans and nonhuman animals. From an evolutionary standpoint, it would appear that it was adaptive for early humans to have the ability to fight. What factors explain aggressive behavior? Psychologists have investigated biological, psychological, and sociocultural factors.

BIOLOGICAL INFLUENCES IN AGGRESSION Researchers who approach aggression from a biological viewpoint examine the influence of genetics and neurobiological factors.

©Eric Isselee/Shutterstock

Genes The role of genes in aggression is most easily seen in nonhuman animals and in the process of selective breeding. After a number of breedings among only aggressive animals and among only docile animals, vicious and timid strains of animals emerge. The vicious strains attack nearly anything in sight; the timid strains rarely fight, even when attacked. The genetic basis for aggression is less clear in humans and may depend on the type of aggression studied (Quayyum & others, 2015; Veroude & others, 2016). Specifically, twin studies show that unprovoked physical aggression may be more influenced by genes, but more reactive aggression may be more susceptible to environmental effects.

Neurobiological Factors Although humans do not have a specific aggression center in the brain, aggressive behavior often results when areas such as the limbic system are stimulated by electric currents (Bartholow, 2018). The frontal lobes of the brain—the areas most involved in executive functions such as planning and self-control—have also been implicated in aggression. Research has examined the brains of individuals who have committed the ultimate act of violence: murder (Nordstrom & others, 2011). The results indicate that murderers may differ from others in deficits in the functioning of these areas of the brain.

Behavior can influence hormone levels. So, higher testosterone may be an effect of aggressive behavior, not its cause.

Neurotransmitters—particularly, lower levels of serotonin—have been linked to aggressive behavior (Allely & others, 2014; Bartholow, 2018), although the association is quite small (Duke & others, 2013).

Hormones are another biological factor that may play a role in aggression. The hormone that is typically implicated in aggressive behavior is testosterone. Research on rats and other animals has shown that testosterone relates to aggression (Cunningham & McGinnis, 2007), but results with humans have been less consistent (van Bokhoven & others, 2006).

PSYCHOLOGICAL INFLUENCES ON AGGRESSION Psychological influences on aggression include personality characteristics, frustrating circumstances, and cognitive and learning factors.

Personality   Low levels of agreeableness are associated with more aggressive behavior (Muris, Meesters, & Timmermans, 2013). In addition, individuals whose personalities predispose them to feeling callous and cold toward others are more likely to engage in aggression (Paulhus & Jones, 2017). In addition, a constellation of traits including low agreeableness, low conscientiousness, and high levels of neuroticism is associated with aggression (Settles & others, 2012). A meta-analysis showed that individuals who are high on hostility and irritability are more likely to behave aggressively, whether provoked or not (Bettencourt & others, 2006).

Frustrating and Aversive Circumstances   Many years ago, John Dollard and his colleagues (1939) proposed that *frustration,* the blocking of an individual's attempts to reach a goal, triggers aggression. The *frustration-aggression hypothesis* states that frustration always leads to aggression. When people feel frustrated and like their goals are being thwarted, they are more likely to behave aggressively (Przybylski & others, 2014).

Psychologists later recognized that, besides frustration, a broad range of aversive experiences can cause aggression. They include physical pain, personal insults, crowding, and unpleasant events. Aversive circumstances also include factors in the physical environment, such as the weather. Murder, rape, and assault increase when temperatures are the highest, as well as in the hottest years and the hottest cities (Anderson & Bushman, 2002; Lynott & others, 2017).

Cognitive Determinants   Aspects of the environment may prime us to behave aggressively (Zheng & Zhang, 2016). Priming involves making something salient to a person, even without the person's awareness. So, anything that makes us think aggressive thoughts could be associated with heightened aggression. Research by Leonard Berkowitz and others has shown that the mere presence of a weapon (such as a gun) may prime hostile thoughts and produce aggression (Anderson, Benjamin, & Bartholow, 1998; Berkowitz, 1993; Berkowitz & LePage, 1996). The tendency for the presence of firearms to enhance aggression is known as the *weapons effect*. In support of Berkowitz's ideas, a well-known study found that individuals who lived in a household with a gun were 2.7 times more likely to be murdered than those dwelling in a household without a gun (Kellerman & others, 1993).

This is a correlational study. What are some third variables that might explain the association between gun ownership and murder?

Observational Learning   Social cognitive theorists believe that individuals learn aggression through reinforcement and observational learning (Bandura, 2011). Observing others engage in aggressive actions can evoke aggression. One of the strongest predictors of aggression is witnessing aggression in one's own family (Ferguson & others, 2008). Watching television provides a ready opportunity to observe aggression in our culture, which we consider further in the discussion below on media violence.

SOCIOCULTURAL INFLUENCES ON AGGRESSION

Aggression and violence are more common in some cultures than others (Macfarlan & others, 2014). In this section, we review sociocultural influences on aggression including the "culture of honor," gender, and media influences.

The Culture of Honor   Dov Cohen has examined how cultural norms about masculine pride and family honor may foster aggressive behavior (Cohen, 2001; Vandello & Cohen, 2004, 2008; Vandello & others, 2009). In *cultures of honor*, a man's reputation is thought to be an essential aspect of his economic survival. Such cultures see insults to a man's honor as diminishing his reputation and view violence

©metinkiyak/iStock/Getty Images

Cognitive dissonance could lead to even greater valuing of one's personal honor. That honor would have to be really important for a person to harm a family member.

as a way to compensate for that loss. In these cultures, family pride might lead to so-called honor killings in which, for example, a female rape victim is slain by her male family members so that they, in turn, are not "contaminated" by the rape.

Cohen has examined how, in the United States, southerners are more likely than northerners to be aggressive when honor is at stake. In one study, Cohen and his colleagues (1996) had men who were from either the North or the South take part in an experiment that required them to walk down a hallway. A member of the study passed all the men, bumping against them and quietly calling them a derogatory name. The southerners were more likely than the northerners to think their masculine reputation was threatened, to become physiologically aroused by the insult, and to engage in actual aggressive or dominant acts. In contrast, the northerners were less likely to perceive a random insult as "fightin' words."

Gender
Are men or women more aggressive? The answer depends on the particular *type* of aggression we are talking about. **Overt aggression** refers to physically or verbally harming another person directly. Boys and men tend to be higher in overt aggression than girls and women. As children, boys are more likely than girls to get in fights in which they are physically aggressive toward one another (Bukowski, Brendgen, & Vitaro, 2007). As adolescents, males are more likely to join gangs and to commit violent acts (Dodge, Coie, & Lynam, 2006). As adults, men are more likely than women to be chronically hostile and to commit violent crimes (White & Frabutt, 2006). Of the murders committed in 2015, within the group in which gender of perpetrator could be identified, 89 percent were committed by men (FBI, 2016).

overt aggression
Physical or verbal behavior that directly harms another person.

Men were also the victims of these crimes, 70 percent of the time.

Women's smaller physical size may be one reason they are less likely to engage in overt aggression. To understand aggressive tendencies in girls and women, researchers have focused instead on **relational aggression,** behavior that is meant to harm the social standing of another person through activities such as gossiping and spreading rumors (Kawabata, Tseng, & Crick, 2014; Mathieson, Klimes-Dougan, & Crick, 2014; Leaper, 2015).

relational aggression
Behavior that is meant to harm the social standing of another person.

Relational aggression differs from overt aggression in that it requires that the aggressor have a considerable level of social and cognitive skill. To be relationally aggressive, an individual must have a good understanding of social circumstances and be motivated to plant rumors that are likely to damage the intended party. Relational aggression is more subtle than overt aggression, and the relationally aggressive individual may not seem to be aggressive to others, as the aggressive acts typically are committed secretly.

©Bananastock/age fotostock

It is not clear that girls are more relationally aggressive than boys, but research consistently shows that relational aggression constitutes a greater percentage of girls' overall aggression than it does for boys (Underwood, 2011). One research review revealed that girls engage in more relational aggression than boys in adolescence but not in childhood (Smith, Rose, & Schwartz-Mette, 2010). Relational aggression is complex and research suggests that girls who show relational aggression toward others are themselves likely to be the victims of relational aggression particularly if they are unpopular (Ferguson, Zimmer-Gembeck, & Duffy, 2016).

Although relational aggression does not lead to the physical injury that might result from overt aggression, it can be extremely painful nevertheless. Phoebe Prince, a 15-year-old who had recently moved from Ireland to the United States with her family, became the target of unrelenting rumors and harassment from a group of popular girls at her high school after she had a brief relationship with a popular senior boy. Prince became so distraught that she hanged herself after school one day. Even after her suicide, the girls who had harassed her posted rumors about her on the Facebook page that was set up as a memorial (Cullen, 2010).

©PeopleImages/E+/Getty Images

Media Images of violence pervade the U.S. popular media: newscasts, television shows, sports broadcasts, movies, video games, Internet videos, and song lyrics. Do portrayals of violence lead to aggression?

Although some critics reject the conclusion that TV violence causes aggression (Savage & Yancey, 2008), many scholars insist that TV violence can prompt aggressive or antisocial behavior in children (Brown & Tierney, 2011; Bushman & Huesmann, 2012; Comstock, 2012). Of course, television violence is not the only cause of aggression in children or adults. Like all social behaviors, aggression has multiple determinants (Matos, Ferreira, & Haase, 2012).

As we discussed earlier, research shows that prosocial video games foster prosocial behavior. Do violent video games foster aggression? Correlational studies demonstrate an association between playing violent video games and a number of negative outcomes. A meta-analysis concluded that children and adolescents who play violent video games extensively are more aggressive, less sensitive to real-life violence, and more likely to engage in delinquent acts than their counterparts who spend less time playing the games or do not play them at all (Anderson & others, 2010). However, the effects of exposure to video game violence on aggressive behavior is likely to be small (Hilgard, Englehardt, & Rouder, 2017).

Again, correlation does not imply causation. Critics of research showing a link between violent video games and aggression stress that many studies have not consistently measured important and possibly influential third variables, such as family violence, in predicting both video game use and aggression (Ferguson & Kilburn, 2010; Ferguson, 2015; Hilgard & others, 2015). To conclude that violent video games lead to aggression, experiments are required. Experimental evidence shows that playing violent video games, especially those that are highly realistic, can lead to more aggressive thoughts and behaviors in children and adults (DeWall, Anderson, & Bushman, 2013; Gentile & others, 2014; Hollingdale & Greitemeyer, 2014). Importantly, the optimal safeguards against experimental bias have not always been applied in such research. That means, researchers have not necessarily examined potential confounds in the studies. The violence present in a video game may not be the "active ingredient" that leads to aggression. For example, a series of studies showed games that were experienced as frustrating and difficult were more likely to lead to aggression, even if the games had no violent content (Przybylski & others, 2014).

Critics of the conclusion that violent video game exposure leads to aggression have pointed out that acts of aggression studied in the laboratory are not generalizable to real-world criminal violence (Ritter & Elsea, 2005; Savage, 2008; Savage & Yancey, 2008). Operationalizing aggression in the laboratory is challenging. Researchers might provide participants the opportunity to "aggress" against another, for instance, by subjecting the individual to a blast of loud noise, dispensing a mild electrical shock, or administering a large dose of Tabasco to swallow. Whether these operational definitions of aggression are applicable to real-life violence is a matter of much debate (Savage & Yancey, 2008).

There is no question that the potential link between video game violence and aggressive behavior is contentious. Scholars can look at the same data and interpret it in very different ways (Boxer & others, 2015; Ferguson, 2015). When you encounter research on this controversial topic, be sure to examine the specific aspects of the studies described.

Increasingly, researchers who study the effects of video games are gamers themselves. How do you think this fact might change the way the research is designed and the conclusions drawn?

self-quiz

1. Egoism is in evidence when
   A. a mother physically protects her children from the ravages of a tornado at risk to her own life.
   B. a person donates bone marrow to a complete stranger.
   C. a coffee shop customer pays for the latte of the stranger in line behind him.
   D. a speaker compliments his staff's achievements in order to make himself look good.

2. Research on the relationship between socioeconomic status and prosocial behavior shows that on average
   A. the poor give more than the rich.
   B. the rich give more than the poor.
   C. there is no association between socioeconomic status and prosocial behavior.

D. the extremely rich are most likely to give.

3. With respect to male and female aggression,
   A. males engage in more overt aggression than females.
   B. females engage in more overt aggression than males.
   C. males engage in more relational aggression than females.
   D. both sexes engage about equally in overt and relational aggression.

APPLY IT! 4. While driving, Nate sees an elderly man struggling to change a flat tire. Nate stops and helps the man and then continues to his girlfriend's house. When Nate tells his girlfriend about his act of kindness, she says, "I would never have done that."

Nate suggests that he just must be nicer than she is. Considering the social psychology of helping, is Nate right?
   A. Nate is right because men are generally more helpful then women.
   B. Nate is right because he engaged in a selfless act of altruism.
   C. Nate is not right because his girlfriend may not have felt safe stopping to help someone on a country road at night.
   D. Nate is not right because he probably got a lot of praise from his girlfriend, rendering his act selfish.

4 Close Relationships

Along with good health and happiness, close relationships figure prominently in most people's notions of a good life. Every day we see commercials lauding the ability of various online matchmaking sites to link us up with the love of our life. Online dating services are expected to represent a $3 billion industry in 2017 (Dating Sites Reviews, 2017).

Because close romantic relationships are so crucial for most of us, it is no wonder that social psychologists are interested in studying this vital part of human existence. A vast literature has accumulated in social psychology, examining attraction, love, and intimacy.

Attraction

At the beginning of this chapter, we considered one key factor in interpersonal attraction, namely, physical attractiveness. Research on interpersonal attraction has illuminated a variety of other factors that play a role in the process of becoming attracted to someone.

PROXIMITY, ACQUAINTANCE, AND SIMILARITY   Even in the age of Internet dating, it is very unlikely that you are going to become attracted to someone without meeting the person. Proximity, or physical closeness, is a strong predictor of attraction. You are more likely to become attracted to an individual you pass in the hall every day than someone you rarely see. One potential mechanism for the role of proximity in attraction is the mere exposure effect (Zajonc, 1968, 2001). The **mere exposure effect** means that the more we encounter someone or something (a person, a word, an image), the more likely we are to start liking the person or thing even if we do not realize we have seen it before.

mere exposure effect
The phenomenon that the more individuals encounter someone or something, the more probable it is that they will start liking the person or thing even if they do not realize they have seen it before.

We are not only more likely to be attracted to people whom we have seen before, but also more likely to like someone if we are led to believe we will be meeting that person. Let's say you are sitting in a room and an experimenter tells you there are two strangers next door, one of whom you will be meeting and the other not. Research shows that you are likely to begin to like the first person, in anticipation of your interaction (Insko & Wilson, 1977). In addition, if you find out that someone whom you do not yet know already likes you, that is a sure sign that you will find yourself attracted to that person.

Similarity also plays an important role in attraction (Singh, Chen, & Wegener, 2014). We have all heard that opposites attract, but what is true of magnets is not typically true of human beings. We like to associate with people who are similar to us (Berscheid, 2000). Our friends and lovers are much more like us than unlike us: We share with them similar attitudes, behavior patterns, taste in clothes, intelligence, personality, other friends, values, lifestyle, and physical attractiveness.

Potential matchmakers, take note: If you want to pair up two friends in a romantic relationship, tell each of them how much the other liked his or her social media feed.

EVOLUTIONARY APPROACHES TO ATTRACTION   Evolutionary psychologists focus on gender differences in the variables that account for attraction (Buss, 2015). Evolutionary psychologists argue that women and men have faced different pressures in the course of human evolution (Geary, 2006). They stress that the different statuses of the sexes in terms of reproduction are the key to understanding how this evolution took place (Buss, 2015).

From the perspective of evolutionary psychology, the goal for both men and women is to produce children. For men, this evolutionary task is complicated by the fact that in the human species, paternity is somewhat more mysterious than motherhood. To be sure that a woman is not already pregnant with another man's child, evolutionary psychologists say, men should be more strongly attracted to younger women. Youth is also likely to indicate a woman's fertility. For women, the task of producing offspring is an innately difficult one. Although a man might focus on quantity of sexual partners, a woman must focus on quality and search for a mate who will invest his resources in her and her offspring.

Personal ads show evidence of these evolutionary differences. When men place ads seeking women, they typically look for youth and beauty (a potential proxy for health and fertility) and offer tangible resources—for example, by describing themselves as a "professional who owns a home" (Buss, 2015). When women place ads seeking men, they are more likely to offer youth and beauty and to seek resources. The personal ads of gay men and lesbians offer an intriguing context for consideration. In general, research has shown that gay men seek youth and beauty, whereas lesbians seek personal qualities such as stability and a sense of humor. Evolutionary thinkers suggest that such results provide evidence for strong sex-linked adaptive patterns.

Critics of evolutionary psychology theory argue that humans have the decision-making ability to change their gender behavior and thus are not locked into their evolutionary past. They cite extensive cross-cultural variation in gender behavior and mate preference as proof that social experience affects gender behavior (Matlin, 2012). For example, Alice Eagly's (2010, 2012) *social role view of gender* asserts that social, not evolutionary, experiences have led to differences in gender behavior. The social role approach acknowledges the biological differences between men and women but stresses the ways these differences are played out in a range of cultures and societal contexts. In Eagly's view, as women adapted to roles with less power and less status in society, they showed more cooperative, less dominant profiles than men. Thus, the social hierarchy and division of labor are important causes of gender differences in power, assertiveness, and nurturing behavior (Eagly & Antonakis, 2014; Eagly, Gartzia, & Carli, 2014). Indeed, in cultures that view the sexes more equally, women appear to be less likely to prefer mates with economic resources (Kasser & Sharma, 1999).

Love

Some relationships deepen to friendship and perhaps even to love. Social psychologists have long puzzled over exactly what love is (Berscheid, 2006, 2010; Sternberg, 2013). One way to think about love is to consider the types of love that characterize different human relationships—for instance, friendships versus romantic relationships (Hendrick & Hendrick, 2009; Rawlins & Russell, 2013). Here we consider two types of love: romantic love and affectionate love.

As love matures, romantic love tends to evolve into affectionate love.
©Ronnie Kaufman/Blend Images LLC

Poets, playwrights, and musicians through the ages have celebrated the fiery passion of romantic love—and lamented the searing pain when it fails. Think about songs and books that hit the top of the charts. Chances are, they are about romantic love. **Romantic love, or passionate love,** is love with strong components of sexuality and infatuation, and it often predominates in the early part of a love relationship (Hendrick & Hendrick, 2006). This is the kind of sexually charged feeling we usually mean when we talk about being "in love" (Berscheid, 1988).

Love is more than just passion, however. **Affectionate love, or companionate love,** is the type of love that occurs when an individual has a deep, caring affection for another person and desires to have that person near. There is a growing belief that the early stages of love have more romantic ingredients and that, as love matures, passion tends to give way to affection (Berscheid & Regan, 2005).

romantic love or passionate love
Love with strong components of sexuality and infatuation, often predominant in the early part of a love relationship.

affectionate love or companionate love
Love that occurs when an individual has a deep, caring affection for another person and desires to have that person near.

Models of Close Relationships

A key question that is posed in the social psychology of close relationships is what it takes for couples for stay together for the long haul (Finkel, Simpson, & Eastwick, 2017). You have probably heard that the divorce rate in the U.S. is 50 percent, meaning half of marriages will end in divorce. This statistic is misleading, however, because individuals who have multiple marriages are more likely than others to get divorced. The divorce rate in the U.S. has been steadily declining and the actual percentage of first marriages that are likely to end in divorce is closer to 30 or 40 percent (Abrams, 2016). Scientists who study close relationships have suggested that today's marriages are different from marriages of the past. Couples are less likely to think of marriage as a means to economic and personal stability and more likely to consider the role of marriage in personal fulfillment and personal growth (Finkel & others, 2015). Here we review two of the approaches to close relationships that represent an older way of conceptualizing marriage (social exchange theory) and a more contemporary approach (the investment model).

SOCIAL EXCHANGE THEORY The social exchange approach to close relationships focuses on the costs and benefits of one's romantic partner. **Social exchange theory** is based on the idea of social relationships as involving an exchange of goods, the objective of which is to minimize costs and maximize benefits. From this perspective, the most important predictor of relationship success is *equity*—that is, having both partners feel that each is doing his or her "fair share." Essentially, social exchange theory asserts that we keep a mental balance sheet, tallying the pluses and minuses associated with our romantic partner—what we put in ("I paid for our last date") and what we get out ("He brought me flowers").

social exchange theory
The view of social relationships as involving an exchange of goods, the objective of which is to minimize costs and maximize benefits.

As relationships progress, however, equity may no longer apply. Happily married couples are less likely to keep track of "what I get versus what I give," and they avoid thinking about the costs and benefits of their relationships (Clark & Chrisman, 1994).

🐚 Think of long-term couples you know in which one partner remains committed even when the benefits are hard to see, as when a person's romantic partner is gravely ill for a long time.

THE INVESTMENT MODEL Another way to think about long-term romantic relationships is to focus on the underlying factors that characterize stable, happy relationships compared to others. The **investment model** examines the ways that commitment, investment, and the availability of attractive alternative partners predict satisfaction and stability in relationships (Rusbult, Agnew, & Arriaga, 2012; Segal & Fraley, 2016). From this perspective, long-term relationships are likely to continue when both partners are committed to the

investment model
A model of long-term relationships that examines the ways that commitment, investment, and the availability of attractive alternative partners predict satisfaction and stability in relationships.

relationship and have invested a great deal in it—and when there are few tempting alternatives (other attractive partners) around.

Commitment to the relationship is especially important and predicts a willingness to sacrifice for a romantic partner. In one study, individuals were given a chance to climb up and down a short staircase, over and over, so that their partner would not have to do so. Those who were more committed to their partner worked harder to climb up and down repeatedly, to spare their loved one the burden (Van Lange & others, 1997).

self-quiz

1. With regard to happy relationships, social exchange theory tells us that
   A. we are happiest when we are giving in a relationship.
   B. we are happiest when we are receiving in a relationship.
   C. we are happiest when there is a balance between giving and receiving in a relationship.
   D. equity is important to happiness only in long-lasting relationships.

2. The role of similarity in attraction would predict
   A. that opposites attract.
   B. that relationships with more give and take are best.
   C. that we are attracted to people who are similar to us.
   D. that romantic love is more important than affectionate love.

3. Affectionate love is more common _____, whereas romantic love is more common _____.
   A. in men; in women
   B. in women; in men
   C. early in a relationship; later in a relationship
   D. later in a relationship; early in a relationship

APPLY IT! 4. Daniel and Alexa have been dating for two years. Alexa meets a new guy during spring break and cheats on Daniel. When she tells Daniel about it, he is crushed but forgives her. He reasons that because the two of them have worked together on their relationship for two years, it makes no sense to throw it all away based on one mistake. Which theory would predict that Daniel is likely to cheat on Alexa in the future?
   A. the investment model
   B. social exchange theory
   C. evolutionary theory
   D. theory of affectionate love

5 Social Influence and Group Processes

Social psychologists are interested in understanding how the presence of other people pushes us toward some actions (and away from others). Here we consider two types of social influence—conformity and obedience—and then how the mere presence of others can influence a person's behavior. Finally, we consider how the groups to which we belong influence how we treat others.

Conformity and Obedience

Research on conformity and obedience started in earnest after World War II. Psychologists sought answers to the disturbing question of how ordinary people could be influenced to commit the sort of atrocities inflicted on Jewish people and other minorities during the Holocaust. A central question is, how extensively will people change their behavior to coincide with what others are doing or dictating?

conformity
A change in a person's behavior to coincide more closely with a group standard.

CONFORMITY **Conformity** is a change in a person's behavior to coincide more closely with a group standard. Conformity takes many forms and affects many aspects of people's lives, in negative and positive ways. Conformity is at work, for example, when a person comes to college and starts to drink alcohol heavily at parties, even though he or she might have never been a drinker before. Conformity is also involved when we obey the rules and regulations that allow society to run smoothly. Consider how chaotic it would be if people did not conform to social norms such as stopping at a red light and not punching others in the face. Conformity can also be a powerful way to increase group cohesion. Even something as simple as marching in step together or singing a song with a group can lead to enhanced cooperation among group members (Wiltermuth &

 Think you are a nonconformist? To feel the pressure of conformity, the next time you get on an elevator with other people, DO NOT TURN AROUND to face the door.

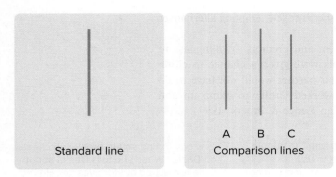

FIGURE 3 **Asch's Conformity Experiment** The figures show the stimulus materials for the Asch conformity experiment on group influence.

Heath, 2009). Interestingly, research suggests that reciprocity (that is, feeling that people are bonded by mutual helping) is a stronger source of group cooperation than conformity (Romano & Bailliet, 2017).

Asch's Experiment Put yourself in this situation: You are taken into a room where you see five other people seated along a table. A person in a white lab coat enters the room and announces that you are about to participate in an experiment on perceptual accuracy. The group is shown two cards—the first having only a single vertical line on it and the second having three vertical lines of varying length. You are told that the task is to determine which of the three lines on the second card is the same length as the line on the first card. You look at the cards and think, "What a snap. It's so obvious which is the same" (Figure 3).

What you do not know is that the other people in the room are confederates working with the experimenter. On the first several trials, everyone agrees about which line matches the standard. Then on the fourth trial, each of the others picks the same incorrect line. As the last person to make a choice, you have the dilemma of responding as your eyes tell you or conforming to what the others before you said. How would you answer? Solomon Asch conducted this classic experiment on conformity in 1951. Asch instructed the confederates to give incorrect responses on 12 of 18 trials. To his surprise, Asch (1951) found that the volunteer participants conformed to the incorrect answers 35 percent of the time. Subsequent research has supported the notion that the pressure to conform is strong (Fein & others, 1993; Malakh-Pines & Maslach, 2002)—but why do people go along with the group even when faced with clear-cut information such as the lines in the Asch experiment?

Two main factors contribute to conformity: informational social influence and normative social influence. **Informational social influence** refers to the influence other people have on us because we want to be right. Members of the groups may know something we don't. So, we follow the group to be right. In contrast, **normative social influence** is the influence others have on us because we want them to like us. Whether the group is a gang or members of a profession such as medicine, if a particular group is important to us, we might adopt a clothing style that people in the group wear or use the same slang words, and we might assume a certain set of attitudes that characterizes the group's members.

informational social influence
The influence other people have on us because we want to be right.

normative social influence
The influence other people have on us because we want them to like us.

Conformity and the Brain Conformity is a powerful social force, but why is it so important to us to fit in with a group? Research in social psychology and neuroscience has provided an interesting answer. Research suggests that our brains may actually "feel better" when we fit in.

An fMRI study examined what happens in the brain when people find out that their opinions conflict with those of others (Klucharev & others, 2009). Women were asked to rate a variety of female faces for attractiveness, and their brains were scanned while they received feedback about whether their ratings agreed with those of the other group members. When participants were told that their ratings differed from the group's ratings, they showed enhanced activation in the brain area typically associated with monitoring for errors. In other words, the brain responded to judgments that differed from the group judgments as if they were *mistakes*. Furthermore, when the women's ratings were different from the group's ratings, women experienced less activation in the brain's reward centers. The more women's brains responded to being different as an error (and not rewarding), the more they conformed when given a chance to re-rate the faces. These results suggest that, for humans, conformity is rewarding.

Do you think the brain could learn to like being different?

Conformity and Culture Individualistic cultures value individuality, individual accomplishments, differences, and uniqueness. Collectivistic cultures value the group and group harmony. It is not surprising, then, that collectivism has been associated with greater levels of conformity. A research review, summarizing 133 experiments following Asch's design, found that individualism within cultures was negatively correlated with conformity (Bond & Smith, 1996).

OBEDIENCE   **Obedience** is behavior that complies with the explicit demands of an individual in authority. We are obedient when an authority figure demands that we do something, and we do it. Obedient behavior sometimes can be distressingly cruel. Millions of people throughout history have obeyed commands to commit terrible acts all in the name of "just following orders." How can we come to understand the tendency to obey?

obedience
Behavior that complies with the explicit demands of the individual in authority.

Milgram's Experiment   A classic series of experiments by Stanley Milgram (1965, 1974) demonstrated the profound power of obedience. Imagine that, as part of a psychology experiment on the effects of punishment on memory, you are asked to deliver a series of electric shocks to another person. Your role is to be the "teacher" and to punish the mistakes made by the "learner." Each time the learner makes a mistake, you are to increase the intensity of the shock.

You are introduced to the learner, a nice 50-year-old man who mumbles something about having a heart condition. Strapped to a chair in the next room, he communicates with you through an intercom. The apparatus in front of you has 30 switches, ranging from 15 volts (slight) to 450 volts (marked as beyond dangerous, "XXX").

As the trials proceed, the learner quickly runs into trouble and is unable to give the correct answers. As you increase the intensity of the shock, the learner says that he is in pain. At 150 volts, he demands to have the experiment stopped. At 180 volts, he cries out that he cannot stand it anymore. At 300 volts, he yells about his heart condition and pleads to be released. If you hesitate in shocking the learner, the experimenter tells you, "You must go on; the experiment requires that you continue."

Milgram's studies became the subject of a 1970s TV movie called The Tenth Level. *The film starred William Shatner as Stephen Turner—a character based on Stanley Milgram.*

Eventually the learner stops responding altogether, and the experimenter tells you that not responding is the same as a wrong answer. The learner is unresponsive. He might be injured or even dead. Would you keep going? Do you think most people would? As shown in Figure 4, when Milgram conducted this study, the majority of the teachers obeyed the experimenter: Almost two-thirds delivered the full 450 volts. By the way, the 50-year-old man was a confederate and was not being shocked at all. Of course, the teachers were unaware that the learner was only pretending to be shocked.

"You must go on. The experiment requires that you continue." With those simple statements the experimenter was able to calmly command people (as far as they knew) to shock a man to unconsciousness and possibly death. Such is the power of obedience to authority.

Milgram's studies have long been a subject of controversy. Under today's ethical guidelines, it is unlikely that these experiments would have been approved (Griggs & Whitehead, 2015). Nonetheless, we are still learning from Milgram's data. A meta-analysis of his experiments suggested that the critical decision was at the 150-volt level, when the learner first requested that the experiment be halted. At that point, 80 percent of those who were going to stop did

FIGURE 4   Milgram's Obedience Study In Milgram's experiments, the "learner" was strapped into a chair. The experimenter made it look as if a shock generator was being connected to the learner's body through several electrodes. The chart shows the percentage of "teachers" who stopped shocking the learner at each voltage level.

Burger had to exclude participants who had heard of Milgram's studies. In effect, people who had learned the lessons of Milgram's work were not given a chance to show their stuff.

so (Packer, 2008). Individuals who were going to disobey were those who responded to the learner's first request to be set free.

Would Milgram's results apply today? To examine this question, Jerry Burger (2009) set up a study very similar to Milgram's, with a key exception: Burger's participants were never allowed to go higher than 150 volts. At 150 volts, the confederate asked to end the study, and immediately after participants decided whether to continue, the experiment was ended. The results? They are shown in Figure 5. Surprisingly, Burger's participants were only slightly less likely to obey than Milgram's had been.

Burger (2014) suggested that 4 key factors likely explain the tendencies of participants to shock the learner. These include

1. The novelty of the situation. Participants had little idea of how they should or could respond.

2. The normative information provided. This means that participants might have interpreted the experimenter's authority as suggesting how people should behave.

3. The opportunity to deny responsibility. Participants did not have to feel personally responsible for what happened. They could blame the experimenter.

4. The limited time to think about the decision. Participants were not given very much time to think over their response.

The Stanford Prison Experiment Another controversial demonstration of the power of obedience is provided by the famous Stanford prison experiment, conducted by Philip Zimbardo in 1971. This research illustrates the potentially horrific effects of obedience, not only on those who obey but on those who wield authority.

Zimbardo and his students created a simulated prison in the basement of a Stanford University building (Haney, Banks, & Zimbardo, 1973; Zimbardo, 1972, 1973, 2007). Newspaper ads recruited men for a two-week study of prison life for which participants would be paid $15 per day (about $88 per day today). After undergoing screening to ensure they were psychologically healthy, 24 men began the study. Each was assigned to the role of either prisoner or guard.

The prisoners were "arrested" at their homes, booked and fingerprinted at the local police station, and brought to the prison. They were strip-searched and given uncomfortable uniforms of smocks and stocking caps. Prisoners were assigned three to a cell, where they were to spend most of their time, night and day, for the entire study. The guards wore uniforms and mirrored sunglasses (to prevent eye contact with prisoners) and wielded wooden batons.

Zimbardo, who served as the prison superintendent, told the guards that they had all the power in the prison and the prisoners would have none (Zimbardo, 1989). He informed the guards that they would be taking away each prisoner's individuality. Guards were to refer to the prisoners only by their uniforms' identification numbers.

The course of this study surprised even Zimbardo (2007). Things got ugly very quickly. Within the first 36 hours, a prisoner had to be released when he started screaming, cursing,

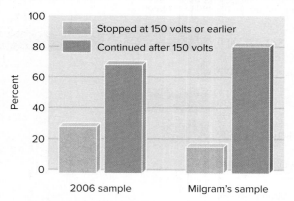

PSYCHOLOGICAL INQUIRY

FIGURE 5 **Obedience Now and Then** This figure shows, side by side, the results of Burger's (2009) study and the results of one of Milgram's studies. The vertical, or Y, axis shows the percent of individuals who stopped or continued after the learner's first expression of a desire to end the study.
SOURCE: Berger, J. "Replicating Milgram: Would people still obey today?" *American Psychology, 64,* 1-11, 2009. American Psychological Association

> Comparing the two sets of results, does the similarity surprise you? Why or why not? > If you had been a "teacher" in either of these studies, what would you have done? How does learning about Milgram's study influence your response?

and raging uncontrollably. On the second day, a group of prisoners blockaded themselves in their cells. Additional guards were brought in to control the uprising. Some guards attacked prisoners with fire extinguishers while not being watched by the research staff. One-third of the guards behaved in extremely sadistic ways, humiliating and harassing prisoners, forcing them to stand naked, or allowing them to urinate and defecate only in a bucket in their cells. A prisoner who went on a hunger strike was locked in "solitary confinement," essentially a dark closet. The study was cut short after just six days, prompted by a graduate student's concern for participant safety (Zimbardo, Maslach, & Haney, 2000).

Zimbardo concluded that situational factors powerfully affect human behavior. To explain why prisoners did not quit the study, he argued that they had internalized their roles. To explain the guards' cruelty, Zimbardo reasoned that when an authority figure removes personal responsibility, when other people are dehumanized, and when norms support otherwise horrifying behavior, true evil can emerge. The conclusions drawn from this work are similar to those of the Milgram obedience studies: Anyone would do these vile things if put in the same situation, and good people will do evil things to other good people if the situation supports those deeds (Zimbardo, Maslach, & Haney, 2000).

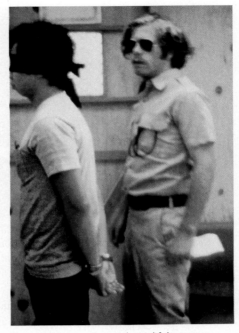

A guard keeps a stern and watchful eye on a prisoner during the Stanford prison experiment.
©Philip G. Zimbardo, Inc.

Like Milgram's studies, the Stanford prison experiment has been criticized on ethical grounds (De Vos, 2010; Fromm, 1973; Savin, 1973). As was the case with Milgram's participants, those in the prison experiment did not express regret and felt the study was worthwhile (Zimbardo, 2007). Perhaps you can see how cognitive dissonance might explain such responses.

Scholars have questioned whether the study provides evidence for Zimbardo's portrayal of human nature as open to evil acts in powerful situations (Haslam & Reicher, 2003). One study suggests that Zimbardo's participants may not have been representative of people in general. Recall that Zimbardo recruited participants with an ad that mentioned "prison life." Thomas Carnahan and Sam McFarland (2007) placed two ads in a newspaper, one that mentioned prison life and one that did not. They found that individuals who answered the first ad differed from those who answered the second: They were higher on characteristics such as aggression and exploitativeness and lower in altruism and empathy. So, the volunteers for Zimbardo's study may have differed from the general public in important ways.

Can you think of a time when you resisted conformity or obedience? Would you have obeyed in Milgram's and/or Zimbardo's experiments?

In addition, interviews with the participants in the study and Zimbardo's own research notes suggest that he may have more actively pushed guard to engage in some of the objectionable behavior (Le Texier, 2018).

Group Influence

In February 2017, Timothy Piazza, a Penn State University sophomore, lost consciousness from a combination of toxic levels of alcohol and injuries he suffered while stumbling around in an intoxicated state. Piazza had pledged the Beta Theta Pi fraternity, and his fraternity brothers had hazed him and his fellow pledges. Security camera footage showed that after Piazza passed out he was checked on by fraternity members, who appeared to slap him and splash water on his face. He died. Hazing is illegal and 18 members of Piazza's fraternity were arrested and charged with various offenses, including 8 young men charged with involuntary manslaughter (Boteler, 2017). Sadly, cases like Piazza's seem to make headlines routinely. In addition to the horrible tragedy of a young person dying senselessly, these cases highlight the puzzle of human group behavior. Consider that it is unlikely that any of the members of Beta Theta Pi would have intentionally harmed Piazza if acting alone. Yet in the context of a group engaging in harmful behavior, these young

The Ku Klux Klan demonstrates a variety of ways that human beings can deindividuate: turning out in groups, acting under cover of darkness, and wearing white hoods to conceal identity.
©Greg Mathieson/REX/Shutterstock

men participated in a cruel and tragic act. Why do individuals who would never perform destructive, even murderous, acts when alone perpetrate them when in a group? This central question has driven research in the social psychology of group influence.

DEINDIVIDUATION   One process that sheds light on the behavior of individuals in groups is **deindividuation,** which occurs when being part of a group reduces personal identity and erodes the sense of personal responsibility (Levine, Cassidy, & Jentzsch, 2010). The effects of deindividuation are visible in the wild street revelry that erupts after a team's victory in the World Series or Super Bowl, as well as in mass civic observances such as big-city Fourth of July celebrations. Deindividuation is apparent not just in the behavior of mobs. The Stanford prison experiment described earlier provides a dramatic example of how social situations and the roles we take on in life can influence deindividuation. One explanation for the effects of deindividuation is that groups give us anonymity. When we are part of a group, we may act in an uninhibited way because we believe that no one will be able to identify us. Of course the anonymity provided by social media, online message boards, and comment sections provides a prime context to observe the effects of deindividuation on human behavior (Coles & West, 2016; Mikal & others, 2016).

deindividuation
The reduction in personal identity and erosion of the sense of personal responsibility when one is part of a group.

SOCIAL CONTAGION   Have you ever noticed that a movie you watched in a crowded theater seemed funnier than it did when you watched the DVD alone at home? People laugh more when others are laughing. Babies cry when other babies are crying. The effects of others on our behavior can take the form of **social contagion,** imitative behavior involving the spread of behavior, emotions, and ideas (Choi, Kensinger, & Rajaram, 2017; Cooper & others, 2014; Hodas & Lerman, 2014). Social contagion effects can be observed in varied phenomena such as social fads, the popularity of dog breeds (Herzog, 2006), the spread of unhealthy behaviors like smoking and drinking among adolescents (Rodgers, 2007), and symptoms of eating disorders among young women (Forman-Hoffman & Cunningham, 2008).

social contagion
Imitative behavior involving the spread of behavior, emotions, and ideas.

Want to observe social contagion? Sit in a quiet but crowded library and start coughing. You will soon notice others coughing. Similarly, imagine that you are walking down the sidewalk, and you come upon a group of people who are all looking up. How likely is it that you can avoid the temptation of looking up to see what is so interesting to them?

GROUP PERFORMANCE   Are two or three heads better than one? Some studies reveal that we do better in groups; others show that we are more productive when we work alone (Paulus, 1989). We can make sense out of these contradictory findings by looking closely at the circumstances in which performance is being analyzed (Nijstad, 2009).

Social Facilitation   If you have ever given a presentation in a class, you might have noticed that you did a much better job standing in front of your classmates than during any of your practice runs. **Social facilitation** occurs when an individual's performance improves because of the presence of others (Herman, 2017; Mendes, 2007). Robert Zajonc (1965) argued that the presence of other individuals arouses us. The arousal produces energy and facilitates our performance in groups. If our arousal is too high, however, we are unable to learn new or difficult tasks efficiently. Social facilitation, then, improves our performance on well-learned tasks. For new or difficult tasks, we might be best advised to work things out on our own before trying them in a group.

social facilitation
Improvement in an individual's performance because of the presence of others.

Social Loafing   Another factor in group performance is the degree to which one's behavior is monitored. **Social loafing** refers to each person's tendency to exert less effort in a group because of reduced accountability for individual effort. The effect of social loafing is lowered group performance (Latané, 1981). The larger the group, the more likely it is that an individual can loaf without detection. Social loafing is less common when group leaders are fair (De Backer & others, 2015).

social loafing
Each person's tendency to exert less effort in a group because of reduced accountability for individual effort.

GROUP DECISION MAKING   Many social decisions take place in groups—juries, teams, families, clubs, school boards, and the U.S. Senate, for example (Fisher, 2017; Sueur, Deneubourg, & Petit, 2012). What happens when people put their minds to the task of making a group decision? How do they decide whether a criminal is guilty, whether one country should attack another country, whether a family should stay home or go on vacation, or whether sex education should be part of a school curriculum? Three aspects of group decision making bear special mention: risky shift and group polarization; groupthink; and majority and minority influence.

Risky Shift and Group Polarization   Imagine that you have a friend, Lisa, who works as an accountant. All her life Lisa has longed to be a writer. In fact, she believes that she has the next great American novel in her head. She just needs time and energy to devote to writing it. Would you advise Lisa to quit her job and go for it? What if you knew beforehand that her chances of success were 50-50? How about 60-40? How much risk would you advise her to take?

risky shift
The tendency for a group decision to be riskier than the average decision made by the individual group members.

Researchers asked participants to consider fictitious dilemmas like this one and asked them how much risk the characters in the dilemmas should take (Stoner, 1961). When the individuals discussed the dilemmas as a group, they were more willing to endorse riskier decisions than when they were queried alone. The so-called **risky shift** is the tendency for a group decision to be riskier than the average decision made by the individual group members (Goethals & Demorest, 1995).

group polarization effect
The solidification and further strengthening of an individual's position as a consequence of a group discussion or interaction.

We do not always make riskier decisions in a group than when alone, however; hundreds of research studies show that being in a group moves us more strongly in the direction of the position we initially held (Moscovici, 1985). The **group polarization effect** is the solidification and further strengthening of an individual's position as a consequence of a group discussion or interaction. Initially held views often become more polarized because of group discussion. Group polarization may occur because, during the discussion, people hear new, more persuasive arguments that strengthen their original position. Group polarization also might arise because of social comparison. We may find that our opinion is not as extreme as others' opinions, and we might be influenced to take a stand at least as strong as the most extreme advocate's position.

groupthink
The impaired group decision making that occurs when making the right decision is less important than maintaining group harmony.

Groupthink   **Groupthink** refers to the impaired group decision making that occurs when making the right decision is less important than maintaining group harmony. Instead of engaging in an open discussion of all the available information, in groupthink, members of a group place the highest value on conformity and unanimity. Members are encouraged to "get with the program," and dissent meets with very strong disapproval.

Groupthink can result in disastrous decisions. Irving Janis (1972) introduced the concept of groupthink to explain a number of enormous decision-making errors throughout history. Such errors include the lack of U.S. preparation for the Japanese bombing of Pearl Harbor during World War II, the escalation of the Vietnam War in the 1960s, the Watergate coverup in 1974, and the *Challenger* space shuttle disaster in 1986. After the terrorist attacks of September 11, 2001, some suggested that groupthink had interfered with the proper implementation of intelligence. Whistleblower Colleen Rowley, a special agent in the Federal Bureau of

Many people were aware that Harvey Weinstein was sexually harassing actresses, but, demonstrating groupthink, those people maintained their silence as part of his organization or the larger Hollywood community.
©Arnold Jerocki/EPA/REX/Shutterstock

The decision in 2011 for the Navy SEALS to conduct a raid on Osama bin Laden's compound and to assassinate him involved an open discussion. Although most of President Obama's advisors hedged their bets, Vice President Biden specifically advised against the raid, while then-CIA Director Leon Panetta explicitly recommended going in (Landler, 2012).

Investigation (FBI), revealed that the FBI power hierarchy had been unresponsive to information that might have helped prevent the attacks.

Symptoms of groupthink include overestimating the power and morality of one's group, close-mindedness and unwillingness to hear all sides of an argument, and pressure for uniformity (Post & Panis, 2011). Groupthink can occur whenever groups value conformity over accuracy.

Groupthink can be prevented if groups avoid isolation, allow the airing of all sides of an argument, have an impartial leader, include outside experts in the debate, and encourage members who are strongly identified with the group to speak out in dissent (Packer, 2009).

Majority and Minority Influence Most groups make decisions by voting, and, even in the absence of groupthink, the majority usually wins. The majority impacts group decision making through both informational influence (they have greater opportunity to share their views) and normative influence (they set group norms). Those who do not go along may be ignored or even given the boot.

Even so, minority opinion holders can make a difference. Because it is outnumbered, the minority cannot win through normative pressure; instead, it must apply informational pressure. If the minority presents its views consistently and confidently, then the majority is more likely to listen to the minority's perspectives. A powerful way that minority opinion holders can exert influence is by winning over former majority members to their points of view.

In crowdsourcing, individuals provide ideas to solve problems, usually through Internet sites. This way of collecting ideas is thought to reduce the kinds of group biases that exist in face-to-face groups. Are online groups more or less likely to exhibit groupthink or minority influence?

Social Identity

Think about the groups of which you are a member—religious and social organizations, your ethnic group, your nationality. When someone asks you to identify yourself, how often do you respond by mentioning these group memberships? How much does it matter to you whether the people you associate with are members of the same groups as you?

social identity
The way individuals define themselves in terms of their group membership.

Social identity refers to the way individuals define themselves in terms of their group membership. In contrast to personal identity, which can be highly individualized, social identity assumes some commonalities with others (Abrams, 2014). A person's social identity might include identifying with a religious group, a country, a social organization, a workplace a political party, a sports team, and many other groups. These diverse forms of social identity reflect the numerous ways people connect to groups and social categories (Hogg, 2012). Social psychologist Kay Deaux (2001) identified five distinct types of social identity: ethnicity and religion, political affiliation, vocations and avocations, personal relationships, and stigmatized groups (Figure 6).

Ethnicity & Religion

Jewish
Asian American
Southern Baptist
West Indian

Relationships

Parent
Mother
Son
Widow

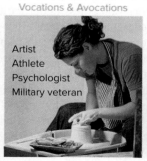

Vocations & Avocations

Artist
Athlete
Psychologist
Military veteran

Political Affiliation

Environmentalist
Feminist
Republican

Stigmatized Identities

Overweight person
Person with AIDS
Homeless person
Alcoholic

FIGURE 6   Types of Social Identity When we identify ourselves, we draw on a host of different characteristics associated with the various social groups to which we belong.

SOURCE: K. Deaux; J. Worell (ed.)Encyclopedia of Women and Gender: Sex, Similarities and Differences and the Impact of Society on Gender (1969). Photos: (ethnicity): ©Rob Melnychuk/Getty Images; (relationships): ©Trinette Reed/Brand X Pictures/Jupiterimages; (vocation): ©Digital Vision/SuperStock; (political): ©moodboard/Corbis; (stigmatized): ©Stockbyte/PunchStock

Ethnic identity and religious identity are central to many individuals' social identity (Cooper, Gonzalez, & Wilson, 2015; Vedder & Phinney, 2014). Ethnic identity can be a source of pride for individuals. In the United States, special events celebrate the rich cultural contributions of many different groups to the society. Such experiences may provide individuals with an important resource in coping with biases they may encounter in life (Crocker, Major, & Steele, 1998). Feeling connected to one's ethnic group may buffer individuals from the stressful effects of injustice (Marks & others, 2015).

What groups define you?

Social psychologist Henry Tajfel (1978), a Holocaust survivor, wanted to explain the extreme violence and prejudice that his religious group (Jews) experienced. Tajfel's **social identity theory** states that social identity is a crucial part of self-image and a valuable source of positive feelings about oneself. To feel good about ourselves, we need to feel good about the groups to which we belong. For this reason, we invariably think of the group to which we belong as an *in-group,* a group that has special value in comparison with other groups, called *out-groups*. To improve our self-image, we continually compare our in-groups with out-groups (Parks, 2007). In the process, we often focus more on the differences between the two groups than on their similarities.

Such groups are referred to as **minimal groups** because group assignment is arbitrary and meaningless.

social identity theory
The view that social identity is a crucial part of self-image and a valuable source of positive feelings about oneself.

Research by Tajfel (1978), along with that by many others who have used his theory, showed how easy it is to lead people to think in terms of "us" and "them." In one experiment, Tajfel had participants look at a screen featuring a huge number of dots and estimate how many dots were displayed. He then assigned the participants to groups based on whether they overestimated or underestimated the number of dots. Once assigned to one of the two groups, the participants were asked to award money to other participants. Invariably, individuals awarded money only to members of their own group. If we favor the members of a group that was formed on such trivial bases, it is no wonder that we show intense in-group favoritism when differences are not so trivial.

As noted in the description of altruism, there may be a thin line between positive feelings and behaviors toward one's own group and hostile feelings and behaviors toward out-groups.

Research in developmental psychology has shown that ingroup favoritism is likely part of human nature, based on the ways that infants respond to seeing members of groups interact (Pun & others, 2017). For example, in a series of studies, 17-month-old infants expected characters they watched to be nicer to ingroup members than to outgroup members (Jin & Baillargeon, 2017). The infants looked longer when ingroup members did not show favoritism to each other. Another series of studies showed that 6- and 8-year-olds showed ingroup favoritism as well when it came to giving nice things to group members (Böhm & Buttelmann, 2017). Interestingly, in none of these studies did children appear to desire to harm outgroups, however.

ethnocentrism
The tendency to favor one's own ethnic group over other groups.

The tendency to favor one's own ethnic group over other groups is called **ethnocentrism.** Ethnocentrism does not simply mean taking pride in one's group; it also involves asserting the group's superiority over other groups. As such, ethnocentrism encourages in-group/out-group, we/they thinking (Dovidio & others, 2012). Consequently, ethnocentrism implies that ethnic out-groups are not simply different; they are worse than one's group. Hence, ethnocentrism may underlie prejudice.

Prejudice

prejudice
An unjustified negative attitude toward an individual based on the individual's membership in a group.

Prejudice is an unjustified negative attitude toward an individual based on the individual's membership in a particular group. The group can be made up of people of a specific ethnicity, sex, age, religion—essentially, people who are different in some way from a prejudiced person (Jost, Gaucher, & Stern, 2014). Prejudice

©Stephen Chung/LNP/REX/Shutterstock

as a worldwide phenomenon can be seen in many eruptions of hatred in human history. In the Balkan Peninsula of eastern Europe, the Serbs' prejudice against Bosnians prompted the Serb policy of "ethnic cleansing." The prejudice of the Hutus against the Tutsis in Rwanda led them to go on a murderous rampage, attacking the Tutsis with machetes. Certainly, current events in the United States serve to remind us that prejudice is still alive and well.

Indeed, a powerful example of destructive prejudice within U.S. society is racial prejudice against African Americans. When Africans were brought to colonial America as slaves, they were considered property and treated inhumanely. In the first half of the twentieth century, most African Americans still lived in the South and remained largely segregated based on skin color; restaurants, movie theaters, and buses had separate areas for Whites and Blacks.

It is useful at this point to note that talking openly about race and ethnicity can be awkward. Even coming up with labels to use to describe different groups of people can be difficult. In the United States, typical labels have changed from Black and White to African American or European American. But even these labels are not without problems. Many times labels are based not on information about the person's origins, but solely on the color of the person's skin. Nelson Mandela, for instance, was not African American. He was African. How do we distinguish between Mandela and F. W. de Klerk, the (White) former South African president who shared the Nobel Peace Prize with Mandela in 1993 for abolishing apartheid?

Many times, when we look at a questionnaire where a person has checked off his or her race, we rely simply on the person's own assessment of group membership. Former President Barack Obama embodies the complex issues of race in America. His mother was European American, his father African, and he labels himself African American. In our discussion here, we will use the terms *Black* and *White* when in a particular study the actual ethnic background of targets of social judgment is not specified. In these instances, the only cue to the person's background, or anything else about that person, is skin color. Skin color can have remarkable effects on how people are treated.

Despite progress over the years, there remain notable racial disparities among Americans, in terms of poverty, employment, education, and healthcare. Research continues to demonstrate the influence of race in U.S. life. In one study, researchers sent out 5,000 résumés in response to 1,200 job ads placed in newspapers in Chicago and Boston. The résumés were identical in qualifications. They differed only in whether the names of the candidates were stereotypically White or Black. "White" names included Meredith, Emily, Brad, and Greg. "Black" names included Tamika, Lakisha, Darnell, and Kareem. The researchers found that even with identical qualifications, the applicants with "White-sounding" names were 50 percent more likely to be called for an interview (Bertrand & Mullainathan, 2004). Similarly a recent study showed that although counseling psychologists were equally likely to call back potential clients regardless of whether their names were Black or White-sounding, the voice mails left for clients with White-sounding names were more likely to include information about services offered (Shin & others, 2016).

Do It!

Want to participate in a social psychological experiment? You can do so online. Hundreds of studies are available at www.socialpsychology.org.

Results such as these are troubling. Keep in mind that responses to "Black"-sounding names might not reflect intentional biases but instead subtle and potentially unconscious racial biases. The potentially unconscious nature of racism in modern life is a challenge for researchers interested in understanding and reducing prejudice.

Because racial prejudice is socially unacceptable, few people today would readily admit to racist or prejudicial views. Today, prejudiced individuals are more likely than before to appear unprejudiced on the surface while nevertheless holding racist views at a deeper level. Indeed, individuals may not be consciously aware of their own racial (or gender or age) biases.

What are your attitudes toward individuals of an ethnic background different from your own? How do these attitudes compare with those of your parents?

To confront this problem, social psychologists examine prejudicial attitudes on two levels—explicit racism and implicit racism. *Explicit racism* is a person's conscious and openly shared attitude, which might be measured using a questionnaire.

Implicit racism refers to attitudes that exist on a deeper, hidden level (Willard, Isaac, & Carney, 2015). Explicit prejudice is thought to relate to behaviors that people control. Implicit prejudice is thought to predict more spontaneous, less self-conscious actions, such as facial expressions and body gestures. Implicit attitudes must be measured with a method that does not require awareness. For example, implicit racism is sometimes measured using the Implicit Associations Test (IAT), a computerized survey that assesses the ease with which a person can associate a Black or White person with good things (for example, flowers) or bad things (for example, misery) (Greenwald & others, 2009; Nosek & Banaji, 2007; Nosek & others, 2014). This test is based on the idea that preexisting biases may make it easier to associate some social stimuli with positive rather than negative items. Although the IAT is widely used, scholars have raised concerns about its validity (Blanton & others, 2015).

If you want to try the IAT, go to: https://implicit.harvard.edu/ implicit/takeatest.html See what you think!

FACTORS IN PREJUDICE   Why do people develop prejudice? Competition between groups, especially when resources are scarce, can contribute to prejudice. For example, competition between immigrants and established low-income members of a society for jobs can lead to prejudice. People may develop negative attitudes about other groups when they feel bad about themselves or their success in life.

How does prejudice develop? Social and developmental psychologists have examined this issue extensively (Costello & Hodson, 2014). As we have seen, infants and children seem to have a sense of ingroup bias. Such bias is likely one factor in prejudice. Another factor is parental attitudes. Parents who hold prejudicial attitudes are more likely to have children who express bias as well, especially if the children identify strongly with their parents (Sinclair, Dunn, & Lowery, 2005). In addition, children who are exposed to information about genetic differences between races, for instance in biology textbooks, are more likely to believe that race differences in intelligence are genetic and are less likely to desire to be friends with children from other groups (Donovan, 2017). Research has also shown that children who encounter many different kinds of people in their lives are less likely to hold prejudicial attitudes (Raabe & Beelman, 2011).

A final factor that might underlie prejudice comes from the limits on our information-processing abilities. Human beings are limited in their capacity for effortful thought, but they face a complex social environment. To simplify the challenge of understanding others' behavior, people use categories or stereotypes. Stereotypes can be a powerful force in developing and maintaining prejudicial attitudes.

STEREOTYPES AND PREJUDICE   Recall that stereotypes are generalizations about a group that deny variations within the group. Researchers have found that we are less likely to detect variations among individuals who belong to "other" groups than among individuals who belong to "our" group. So, we might see the people in our in-group as varied, unique individuals while viewing the members of out-groups as all the same. Thinking that "they all look alike" can be a particular concern in the context of eyewitness identification (Brigham, 1986). At the root of prejudice is a particular kind of stereotype: a generalization about a group that contains negative information that is applied to all members of that group (Wetherell, 2012).

DISCRIMINATION   When prejudicial attitudes are put into action people are treated unfairly. Behaviors that are based on prejudice are discriminatory. **Discrimination** refers to an unjustified negative or harmful action toward a member of a group simply because the person belongs to that group. Discrimination results when negative emotional reactions combine with prejudicial beliefs and are translated into behavior (Foels & Pratto, 2014). Many forms of discrimination are illegal in the U.S. workplace. Since the Civil Rights Act of 1964 (revised in 1991), it has been unlawful to deny someone employment on the basis of gender or ethnicity (Parker, 2006).

discrimination
An unjustified negative or harmful action toward a member of a group simply because the person belongs to that group.

Psychologists in many different areas are interested in understanding the differences that exist between different groups of people especially on physical and psychological health. *Health disparities* refer to often preventable differences in physical functioning (including disease, injury, violence) and psychological functioning (including depression and anxiety) that are experienced by socially disadvantaged groups. For example, in the United States, African Americans have a lower life expectancy (75.3 years) compared with European Americans (79 years) (Kochanek, Murphy, & Xu, 2015). In addition, African Americans aged 18 to 49 are 2 times as likely to die from heart disease compared with European Americans (CDC, 2017). Although statistics like these are improvements over previous years, there remain important differences between African Americans and European Americans. Such health disparities likely spring from many sources such as access to health information, healthcare, nutrition, opportunities for physical activity, and so forth (Abbott & Elliott, 2017; Talamantes & Moreno, 2015).

Evidence supports the idea that racism plays a role in health disparities. For example, a recent study examined the vital statistics for over 31 million infants born in the United States between 2002 and 2012 (Orchard & Price, 2017). Those data showed that Black mothers were 60 percent more likely than White mothers to give birth to low birth weight or preterm infants. More interestingly, the researchers combined the birth data with data collected as part of Project Implicit, which involves collecting implicit and explicit measures of racism from nearly 2 million adults across the U.S. Those data were used to identify counties as high or low in racism. When they combined the birth data with the racism scores, the researchers found that the racial gap in infant birth weight was 14 percent higher in counties characterized by high levels of implicit racism and 22 percent higher in counties characterized by high levels of explicit racism (Orchard & Price, 2017).

Prejudice can contribute to health disparities in other ways as well. Living in an unfair context is stressful (Brown, 2017; Lucas & others, 2017; Major & Townsend, 2012). Such stress might contribute to health disparities, with those who experience prejudice and discrimination showing poorer physical and psychological health. To read about research on the ways experiences with prejudice and discrimination may affect healthy functioning, see the Intersection.

Improving Intergroup Relations

The groups we belong to give us a sense of identity and self-esteem. Yet, at the same time, these feelings may lead to negative views of other groups. Certainly, conflicts among various groups are rampant in the modern world. Human beings have innumerable ways to draw lines dividing themselves based on national borders, religious faith, race, and ethnicity. Martin Luther King, Jr., said, "I have a dream that my four little children will one day live in a nation where they will not be judged by the color of their skin but by the content of their character." How might we attain the world that King envisioned? Social psychologists have strived to identity the factors that might lead to better relationships between different groups (Shelton & Richeson, 2014).

One way might be for people to come to know one another better so that they can get along. However, in daily life many people interact with individuals from other ethnic groups, and this contact does not necessarily lead to tolerance or warm relations. Indeed, researchers have consistently found that contact by itself—attending the same school or working in the same company—does not necessarily improve relations among people of different ethnic backgrounds. So, rather than focusing on contact per se, researchers have examined how *various features* of a contact situation may be optimal for reducing prejudice and promoting intergroup harmony (Stott, Drury, & Reicher, 2012).

Although legal segregation is no longer permitted, **voluntary** segregation continues. Look around your classrooms and dining halls. Do you see students separating themselves by ethnic categories? How does this convention impede intergroup relations, and how might it be broken?

Studies have shown that contact is more effective if the people involved think that they are of equal status, feel that an authority figure sanctions their positive relationships, and believe that friendship might emerge from the interaction (Pettigrew & Tropp, 2006). Another important feature of optimal intergroup contact is *task-oriented cooperation*—working together on a shared goal.

An example of the power of task-oriented cooperation is Muzafer Sherif's Robbers Cave Study. Even before Jeff Probst started handing out color-coded "buffs" on the TV

Social Psychology and Health Psychology: What Is the Physical and Psychological Cost of Prejudice and Discrimination?

When we encounter experiences that challenge our capacities to cope, our bodies react with a stress response. This response involves speeding up the heart and energizing our bodies to take action. Stress hormones are secreted to help us escape whatever the threatening situation might be. The effectiveness of a person's stress response can be assessed by measuring the amount of cortisol, a stress hormone, in the person's saliva (Busse & others, 2017).

Numerous studies show that experiences with prejudice and discrimination can alter the body's stress response, rendering it dysfunctional (Busse & others, 2017; Paradies & others, 2015; Pascoe & Smart-Richman, 2009). Dysfunction in the stress response correlates with higher levels of cardiovascular disease, depression, and anxiety (Busse & others, 2017).

Might success buffer the negative effects of prejudice and discrimination on the body's response to stress? Perhaps once people experience improvements in their socioeconomic status, they might be less likely to respond to prejudice and discrimination in less healthy ways. Let's take a look at a study testing this possibility.

In this study (Townsend & others, 2014), working class and middle class Latina American women were told that they and a partner (a confederate) would be taking part in a mock job interview. The participants would role-play job applicants and the confederate the interviewer. The women were told that if the interviewer decided their performance warranted a job offer, they would receive a chance to win $50. Prior to interacting, the participants were shown a questionnaire completed by the interviewer. Participants were randomly assigned to information that the interviewer was prejudiced or not. After the interview portion, all participants were told that the interviewer had evaluated them negatively and would not offer them the job. Salivary cortisol was measured at

©Getty Images

the very beginning of the study and again at the end, after the women received the negative feedback about their performance in the interview.

The results showed that, compared to the working class women, the middle class women were especially prone to experience less adaptive stress responses following this encounter with prejudice (Townsend & others, 2014). In addition, the middle class women (but not the working class women) had greater difficulty on a cognitively challenging task completed at the end of the study. So, rather than mitigate responses to stress, financial status rendered unfairness all the more stressful.

Other studies have demonstrated similar results for different groups. For example, a study of African American men showed that experiences with prejudice and discrimination were especially strongly related to depression among those of higher socioeconomic status and higher education (Hudson & others, 2012).

In a sense, individuals who experience prejudice and discrimination are placed in a difficult bind. Because they know that expressions of prejudice are socially frowned upon, they may feel that they never really know if those who express low levels of prejudice are genuine or simply saying what is expected. This situation can breed distrust (Major & others, 2016). It can be especially painful to be reminded of the existence of prejudice and discrimination in the context of personal success.

\\ **What factors might help to buffer the effects of prejudice and discrimination on the body's stress response?**

show *Survivor,* Sherif and his colleagues (1961) had the idea of exploring group processes by assigning 11-year-old boys to two competitive groups (the "Rattlers" and the "Eagles") in a summer camp called Robbers Cave.

Sherif, disguised as a janitor so that he could unobtrusively observe the Rattlers and the Eagles, arranged for the two groups to compete in baseball, touch football, and tug-of-war. If you have watched reality television, you have some idea how this experiment went. In short order, relations between the groups got downright ugly. Members of each group expressed negative opinions of members of the other group, and the Rattlers and Eagles became battling factions. What would bring these clashing groups together? Sherif created tasks that required the joint efforts of both groups, such as working together to repair the camp's only water supply and pooling their money to rent a movie. When the groups were required to work cooperatively to solve problems, the Rattlers and Eagles developed more positive relationships. Figure 7 shows how competitive and cooperative activities changed perceptions of the out-group.

Yes, the Robbers Cave is yet another CLASSIC in social psychology!

BREAKING THE PREJUDICE HABIT
Given that much of prejudice in contemporary life is likely to be implicit—meaning that it happens automatically and can occur unconsciously—it is important to ask whether we can change not only explicit attitudes but implicit ones as well. Implicit prejudice rests on automatic associations: You see a person from a different ethnic, racial, or religious group, and stereotypical thoughts pop into your head. In this sense, prejudice is a habitual way of thinking.

Can we short-circuit these automatic connections and reduce implicit prejudice? A study by Patricia Devine and her colleagues (2012) suggests that we can. African American participants were randomly assigned to an experimental group that received an intervention to reduce implicit prejudice or a control group that simply completed the dependent measures. Based on the idea that to change racial attitudes people must be aware of them, the first step was to measure implicit racial prejudice using the IAT and give the participants their scores. These scores can be surprising to many people who feel they are not prejudiced against people of color. Next, participants in the experimental group were trained in various ways to break the prejudice habit. This training to introduce new habits of the mind included noticing stereotypic thoughts about African Americans and replacing them with more individualized information about the person. Participants were also trained to think about individuals who do not fit the stereotype of various outgroups, and they were encouraged to put themselves in the other's position and consider things from that person's perspective. Finally, participants were urged to seek out contact with members of the outgroup. The results showed that, six weeks later, participants who had experienced this intervention did show reductions in implicit bias against African Americans. In addition, these individuals were more likely to express concerns about the problems of discrimination in U.S. society. These results, and those of contact interventions, suggest that even though the problem of racial tension in the United States and across the world may seem insurmountable, it is possible to improve relations among groups.

PSYCHOLOGICAL INQUIRY

FIGURE 7 **Attitudes toward the Out-Group Following Competitive and Cooperative Activities** This graph shows the negative feelings expressed by members of the Eagles and Rattlers toward the other group after a competitive tournament and cooperative activity.

SOURCE: M. Sherif et al., The Robber's Cave Experiment: Intergroup Conflict and Cooperation (1988).

> When did hostility between the groups peak? When did it drop? > In your own life, what examples are there of holding particular attitudes toward a group different from your own? How have your attitudes changed, and what events preceded those changes? > What is up with the Eagles? What are some reasons why they might be more negative about the Rattlers?

1. All of the following are related to deindividuation *except*
   A. doing something as part of a large group.
   B. hearing someone explicitly call your name and express recognition of you.
   C. losing your sense of personal responsibility while taking part in a group activity.
   D. wearing a disguise while taking part in a group activity.

2. Which of the following is the true statement about the difference between conformity and obedience?
   A. Conformity has a stronger influence on behavior than obedience.
   B. Conformity does not involve an explicit command from others.
   C. Conformity happens in small groups, whereas obedience happens in large groups.
   D. Conformity is based on wanting to be right; obedience is based on wanting to be liked.

3. A White woman says she is not racist but avoids sitting near Black individuals. She has
   A. high explicit racism, low implicit racism.
   B. high explicit racism, high implicit racism.
   C. low explicit racism, low implicit racism.
   D. low explicit racism, high implicit racism.

APPLY IT! 4. Will is bothered by the way students segregate themselves in the campus commons, with all the African American students generally eating in one area, the Latinos in another, the Asians in another, and the non-Latino Whites in another. Bill starts the Students Together program to get students to interact more and to promote interethnic harmony. Which of the following strategies is most likely to work, based on the social psychological evidence?
   A. Assign seats in the lunchroom so that students have to sit with members of other ethnic groups.
   B. Identify problems of common interest to students of all groups and initiate ethnically diverse discussion groups aimed at solving those problems.
   C. Post signs in the commons that encourage interethnic contact.
   D. None of the above, because nothing will work.

SUMMARY

 ## Defining Social Psychology

Social psychology is the scientific study of how people think about, influence, and relate to other people. This subfield of psychology is relevant to everyday life, it is broad, and it typically relies on experimental methods. An example of social psychology in action is provided by classic research on the bystander effect: the tendency for an individual who observes an emergency to help less when other people are present than when the observer is alone.

 ## Social Cognition

Social cognition refers to the ways we process social information. The face conveys information to social perceivers, including attractiveness. Self-fulfilling prophecy means that our expectations of others can have a powerful impact on their behavior. Attributions are our thoughts about why people behave as they do and about who or what is responsible for the outcome of events. Attribution theory views people as motivated to discover the causes of behavior as part of their effort to make sense of it. The dimensions used to make sense of the causes of human behavior include internal/external, stable/unstable, and controllable/uncontrollable.

The fundamental attribution error is observers' tendency to overestimate traits and to underestimate situations when they explain an actor's behavior. Self-serving bias means attributing our successes to internal causes and blaming our failures on external causes. Heuristics are used as shortcuts in social information processing. One such heuristic is a stereotype—a generalization about a group's characteristics that does not consider any variations among individuals in the group.

The self is our mental representation of our own characteristics. Self-esteem is important and is related to holding unrealistically positive views of ourselves. Stereotype threat is an individual's fast-acting, self-fulfilling fear of being judged based on a negative stereotype about his or her group. To understand ourselves better, we might engage in social comparison, evaluating ourselves by comparison with others.

Attitudes are our feelings about people, objects, and ideas. We are better able to predict behavior on the basis of attitudes when an individual's attitudes are strong, when the person is aware of his or her attitudes and expresses them often, and when the attitudes are specifically relevant to the behavior. Sometimes changes in behavior precede changes in attitude.

According to cognitive dissonance theory, our strong need for cognitive consistency causes us to change our behavior to fit our attitudes or to change our attitudes to fit our behavior. Self-perception theory stresses the importance of making inferences about attitudes by observing our own behavior, especially when our attitudes are not clear.

 ## Social Behavior

Altruism is an unselfish interest in helping someone else. Reciprocity often is involved in altruism. Individuals who are in a good mood are more helpful. Empathy is also linked to helping.

Women are more likely to help in situations that are not dangerous and involve caregiving. Men are more likely to help in situations that involve danger or in which they feel competent.

One view of the biological basis of aggression is that early in human evolution, the most aggressive individuals were likely to be the survivors. Neurobiological factors involved in aggressive behavior include the neurotransmitter serotonin and the hormone testosterone. Psychological factors in aggression include frustrating and aversive circumstances. Sociocultural factors include cross-cultural variations, the culture of honor, and violence in the media. The question of whether men or women are more aggressive depends on the particular *type* of aggression that is involved.

 ## Close Relationships

We tend to be attracted to people whom we see often, whom we are likely to meet, and who are similar to us. Romantic love (passionate love) includes feelings of infatuation and sexual attraction. Affectionate love (companionate love) is more akin to friendship and includes deep, caring feelings for another.

Social exchange theory states that a relationship is likely to be successful if individuals feel that they get out of the relationship what they put in. The investment model focuses on commitment, investment, and the availability of attractive alternatives in predicting relationship success.

5 Social Influence and Group Processes

Conformity involves a change in behavior to coincide with a group standard. Factors that influence conformity include informational social influence (going along to be right) and normative social influence (going along to be liked).

Obedience is behavior that complies with the explicit demands of an authority. Stanley Milgram conducted landmark research on obedience, demonstrating its power. Another such demonstration is the Stanford prison experiment, illustrating the potential effects of obedience not only on individuals who obey but also on those who exercise authority.

People often change their behaviors when they are in a group. Deindividuation refers to the lack of inhibition and diffusion of responsibility that can occur in groups. Social contagion refers to imitative behaviors involving the spread of behavior, emotions, and ideas. Our performance in groups can be improved through social facilitation and lowered because of social loafing.

Risky shift refers to the tendency for a group decision to be riskier than the average decision made by the individual group members. The group polarization effect is the solidification and further strengthening of a position as a consequence of group discussion or interaction. Groupthink involves impaired decision making and avoidance of realistic appraisal to maintain harmony in the group.

Social identity is the way individuals define themselves in terms of their group membership. Social identity theory states that when individuals are assigned to a group, they invariably think of it as the in-group. Identifying with the group allows the person to have a positive self-image. Ethnocentrism is the tendency to favor one's own ethnic group over others.

Prejudice is an unjustified negative attitude toward an individual based on membership in a group. Prejudice can be based on ethnicity, sex, age, religion, sexual orientation, or any characteristic that makes people different from one another.

Prejudice is also based on stereotypes. The cognitive process of stereotyping can lead to discrimination, an unjustified negative or harmful action toward a member of a group simply because he or she belongs to that group. Discrimination results when negative emotional reactions combine with prejudicial beliefs and are translated into behavior. A key outcome of prejudice and discrimination is health disparities.

An effective strategy for enhancing the effects of intergroup contact is to set up task-oriented cooperation among individuals from different groups. Implicit biases can be targeted by bringing mindful attention to one's thoughts when interacting with people from different backgrounds.

KEY TERMS

affectionate love or companionate love
aggression
altruism
attitudes
attribution theory
bystander effect
cognitive dissonance
conformity
deindividuation
discrimination
egoism

elaboration likelihood model
empathy
ethnocentrism
false consensus effect
fundamental attribution error
group polarization effect
groupthink
informational social influence
investment model
mere exposure effect
normative social influence
obedience

overt aggression
person perception
positive illusions
prejudice
relational aggression
risky shift
romantic love or passionate love
self-fulfilling prophecy
self-perception theory
self-serving bias
social cognition
social comparison

social contagion
social exchange theory
social facilitation
social identity
social identity theory
social loafing
social psychology
stereotype
stereotype threat

ANSWERS TO SELF-QUIZZES

Section 1: 1. B; 2. A; 3. B; 4. C
Section 2: 1. D; 2. A; 3. C; 4. B

Section 3: 1. D; 2. A; 3. A; 4. C
Section 4: 1. C; 2. C; 3. D; 4. A

Section 5: 1. B; 2. B; 3. D; 4. B

12 Psychological Disorders

Making castles from life's stones

Sitting in her office, Erica Crompton (2017), a writer living and working in London, could not help but notice the bars on the windows of the building. The bars were there for security reasons, as is common. However, Erica could not escape the idea that they were part of a conspiracy: She was convinced that she had committed some heinous act she could not remember and the police were spying on her to collect evidence. Someone somewhere was sending her a message that she would soon be behind bars. Walking down the street, every passing police officer was a threat, someone waiting to arrest her. What those working in the office with Erica did not know was that she had schizophrenia, a severe psychological disorder. Erica long hid her diagnosis from others, in fear of being judged negatively. She struggled to keep up appearances from 9 to 5, every day. Now working as a freelance writer and mental health advocate, Erica's message to the world is this: We can take the stones life throws at us and build castles (Crompton, 2017). She views herself, as all of us must, as a work in progress. She has created a life that allows her the flexibility to get regular therapy and maintain her medications.

Individuals with psychological disorders are not so different from the rest of us. They are brothers, sisters, grandparents, uncles, aunts, and parents, classmates, and coworkers: People with life stories to share. Psychological disorders may make their lives more difficult and our relationships with them more challenging, but they cannot take away the humanity that binds them to us.

This chapter explores the meaning of the word *abnormal* as it relates to psychology. We examine various theoretical approaches to understanding abnormal behavior and survey the main psychological disorders. We then briefly review suicide. Finally, we delve into how stigma plays a role in the lives of individuals struggling with psychological disorders, and we consider how even difficult, troubled lives remain valuable and meaningful.

1 Defining and Explaining Abnormal Behavior

What makes behavior "abnormal"? The American Psychiatric Association (2001, 2006, 2013) defines abnormal behavior in medical terms: a mental illness that affects or is manifested in a person's brain and can affect the way the individual thinks, behaves, and interacts with others. Abnormal behavior may also be defined by three criteria that distinguish it from normal behavior: **Abnormal behavior** is deviant, maladaptive, or personally distressful over a relatively long period of time. Only one of these criteria needs to be present for a behavior to be labeled "abnormal," but typically two or all three are present.

abnormal behavior
Behavior that is deviant, maladaptive, or personally distressful over a relatively long period of time.

Three Criteria of Abnormal Behavior

Let's take a close look at what each of the three characteristics of abnormal behavior entails:

Context matters! If the woman who washes her hands three or four times an hour and takes repeated showers works in a sterile lab with toxic chemicals or live viruses, her behavior might be quite adaptive.

1. Abnormal behavior is *deviant.* Abnormal behavior is atypical or statistically unusual. However, Alicia Keys, Tim Howard, and Mark Zuckerberg are atypical in many of their behaviors, and yet we do not categorize them as abnormal. We do often consider atypical behavior abnormal, though, when it deviates from what is acceptable in a culture. A woman who washes her hands three or four times an hour and takes seven showers a day is abnormal because her behavior deviates from cultural norms.

Accomplished individuals such as singer-songwriter Alicia Keys, champion soccer goalkeeper Tim Howard, and Facebook CEO Mark Zuckerberg are atypical but not abnormal. However, when atypical behavior deviates from cultural norms, it often is considered abnormal.
(Alicia Keys) ©David Buchan/REX/Shutterstock; (Tim Howard) ©Tannen Maury/EPA/REX/Shutterstock; (Mark Zuckerberg) ©Miquel Benitez/REX/Shutterstock

2. Abnormal behavior is *maladaptive*. In psychology, the term *maladaptive* means that a behavior or characteristic disrupts the person's ability to lead a satisfying life, interfering with one's ability to function effectively in the world. A man who believes that he can endanger others through his breathing may go to great lengths to isolate himself from people for what he believes is their own good. His belief negatively affects his everyday functioning; thus, his behavior is maladaptive. Behavior that presents a danger to the person or those around him or her is also considered maladaptive (and abnormal).

3. Abnormal behavior is *personally distressful* over a long period of time. The person engaging in the behavior finds it troubling. A woman who secretly makes herself vomit after every meal may never be seen by others as deviant (because they do not know about it), but this pattern of behavior may cause her to feel intense shame, guilt, and despair. A person may not realize they have a psychological disorder but still feel extremely distressed by the effects of the disorder on their life.

*Which of these three qualities—deviation from what is acceptable, maladaptiveness, and personal distress—do you think is **most important** to calling a behavior abnormal? Why?*

Culture, Context, and the Meaning of Abnormal Behavior

Because culture establishes the norms by which people evaluate their own and others' behaviors, culture is at the core of what it means to be normal or abnormal (Bartholomew, 2017; Koelkebeck & others, 2017; O'Connor, 2017). In evaluating behavior as normal or abnormal, culture matters in complex ways. Cultural norms provide guidance about how people should behave and what behavior is healthy or unhealthy. Importantly, however, cultural norms can be mistaken. Consider that smoking cigarettes was once not only judged to be an acceptable habit but also promoted as a healthy way to relax. The point is, definitions of *normal* change as society changes.

Consider, for instance, that a symptom of one of Sigmund Freud's most famous patients, Anna O., was that she was not interested in getting married.

Significant, too, is the fact that cultural norms can be limiting, oppressive, and prejudicial (Potter, 2012). Individuals who fight to change the established social order sometimes face the possibility of being labeled deviant—and even mentally ill. In the late nineteenth and early twentieth centuries, for instance, women in Britain who demonstrated for women's right to vote were widely viewed to be mentally ill. When a person's or a group's behavior challenges social expectations, we must open our minds to the possibility that such actions are in fact an adaptive response to injustice. People may justifiably challenge what everyone thinks is true and may express ideas that seem strange. They should be able to make others feel uncomfortable without being labeled abnormal.

Further, as individuals move from one culture to another, interpretations and evaluations of their behavior must take into account the norms in their culture of origin (Betancourt & others, 2017; Huang & others, 2017; Motti-Stefanidi & Masten, 2017). Historically, people entering the United States from other countries were examined at Ellis Island, and many were judged to be mentally or intellectually impaired simply because of differences in their language and customs.

Cultural variation in what it means to be normal or abnormal makes it very difficult to compare different psychological disorders across different cultures. Many of the diagnostic categories we trace in this chapter primarily reflect Western (and often U.S.) notions of normality, and applying these to other cultures can be misleading and even inappropriate (Kirmayer, Gomez-Carrillo, & Veissière, 2017). Throughout this chapter, we will see how culture influences the experience of psychological disorders.

Do It!

Spend 15 to 20 minutes observing an area with a large number of people, such as a mall, a cafeteria, or a stadium during a game. Identify and make a list of behaviors you would classify as abnormal. How does your list of behaviors compare with the definition of abnormal provided above? What would you change in the list if you were in a different setting, such as a church, a bar, or a library? What does this exercise tell you about the meaning of abnormal?

Theoretical Approaches to Psychological Disorders

What causes people to develop a psychological disorder, that is, to behave in deviant, maladaptive, and personally distressful ways? Theorists have suggested various approaches to this question.

THE BIOLOGICAL APPROACH
The *biological approach* attributes psychological disorders to organic, internal causes. This perspective primarily focuses on the brain, genetic factors, and neurotransmitter functioning as the sources of abnormality.

The biological approach is evident in the **medical model,** which describes psychological disorders as medical diseases with a biological origin. From the perspective of the medical model, abnormalities are called "mental illnesses," the afflicted individuals are "patients," and they are treated by medical doctors. This perspective generally neglects contextual factors, such as the person's social relationships, that may play a role in psychological disorders.

medical model
The view that psychological disorders are medical diseases with a biological origin.

THE PSYCHOLOGICAL APPROACH
The *psychological approach* emphasizes the contributions of experiences, thoughts, emotions, and personality characteristics in explaining psychological disorders. Psychologists might focus, for example, on the influence of childhood experiences, personality traits, learning experiences, or cognitions in the development and course of psychological disorders.

THE SOCIOCULTURAL APPROACH
The *sociocultural approach* emphasizes the social contexts in which a person lives, including gender, ethnicity, socioeconomic status, family relationships, and culture. For instance, poverty is related to rates of psychological disorders (Walker & Druss, 2017). The sociocultural perspective places less emphasis on biological processes such as genetics or brain structures and functions, and more emphasis on how a person with these biological characteristics exists in the larger context and adapts to the world.

The sociocultural perspective stresses the ways that cultures influence the understanding and treatment of psychological disorders. The frequency and intensity of psychological disorders vary and depend on social, economic, technological, and religious aspects of cultures (Matsumoto & Juang, 2016). Some disorders are culture-related, such as *windigo,* a disorder recognized by northern Algonquian Native American groups that involves fear of being bewitched and turned into a cannibal.

Importantly, different cultures may interpret the same pattern of behaviors in different ways. When psychologists look for evidence of the occurrence of a particular disorder in different cultures, they must keep in mind that behaviors considered symptoms of a disorder might not be labeled as illness or dysfunction within a particular cultural context. Cultures might have their own interpretations of these behaviors, so researchers must probe whether locals ever observe these patterns of behavior, even if they are not considered illness (Draguns & Tanaka-Matsumi, 2003). For example, in one study researchers interviewed a variety of individuals in Uganda to see whether dissociative disorders, including dissociative identity disorder (which you might know as multiple personality disorder), existed in that culture (van Duijl, Cardeña, & de Jong, 2005; van Duijl, Kleijn, & de Jong, 2014). They found that while most dissociative disorders were recognizable to Ugandans, the local healers labeled what Westerners consider dissociative identity disorder as spirit possession.

THE BIOPSYCHOSOCIAL MODEL
Abnormal behavior can be influenced by biological factors (such as genes), psychological factors (such as childhood experiences), and sociocultural factors (such as gender). These factors can operate alone, but they often act in combination with one another.

Sometimes this approach is called *biopsychosocial.* From the biopsychosocial perspective, biological, psychological, and social factors are all significant ingredients in producing both normal and abnormal behavior. Furthermore, these ingredients may combine in unique ways, so that one depressed person might differ from another in terms of the key factors associated with the development of the disorder.

Why do we need to consider these multiple factors? As you will see throughout this chapter, generally speaking, there is no one gene or experience that leads inevitably to the development of a psychological disorder. Two people can share the same gene—one develops a disorder but another does not. Similarly, two people might have the same experience, such as childhood neglect, and one might develop a disorder but the other does not. Thus, to understand the development of psychological disorders, we must consider a variety of *interacting* factors from each of the domains of experience.

An important concept that has helped psychologists understand the ways different factors influence the development of psychological disorders is the **vulnerability-stress hypothesis** (also called the **diathesis-stress model**). The vulnerability-stress hypothesis suggests that pre-existing conditions (such as genetic characteristics, personality dispositions, or experiences) may put a person at risk of developing a psychological disorder. This vulnerability in combination with stressful experiences can lead to a psychological disorder. The important bottom line is that the vulnerability-stress hypothesis acknowledges that neither predispositions nor experiences lead directly to the development of a psychological disorder. Rather, they may combine to enhance a person's likelihood of developing a disorder.

vulnerability-stress hypothesis or diathesis-stress model
A theory holding that preexisting conditions (genetic characteristics, personality dispositions, experiences, and so on) put an individual at risk of developing a psychological disorder.

Classifying Abnormal Behavior

To understand, treat, and prevent abnormal behavior, psychiatrists and psychologists have devised systems classifying those behaviors into specific psychological disorders. Classifying psychological disorders provides a common basis for communicating. If one psychologist says that her client is experiencing depression, another psychologist understands that a particular pattern of abnormal behavior has led to this diagnosis. A classification system can also help clinicians predict how likely it is that a particular disorder will occur, which individuals are most susceptible to it, how the disorder progresses, and what the prognosis (or outcome) for treatment is (Morrison, 2017; Wakefield, 2015).

Further, a classification system may benefit the person suffering from psychological symptoms. Having a name for a problem can be a comfort and a signal that treatments are available. On the other hand, officially naming a problem can also have serious negative implications for the person because of the potential for creating *stigma,* a mark of shame that may cause others to avoid or to act negatively toward an individual. We discuss stigma further at the end of this chapter.

THE *DSM* CLASSIFICATION SYSTEM   In 1952, the American Psychiatric Association (APA) published the first major classification of psychological disorders in the United States, the *Diagnostic and Statistical Manual of Mental Disorders.* Its current version, *DSM-5,* was published in 2013. This edition of the *DSM* is the product of a 14-year revision process. *DSM-5* differs in many ways from its predecessors. Throughout the history of the *DSM,* the number of disorders listed has increased dramatically. For example, *DSM-5* includes new diagnoses such as gambling addiction.

The *DSM* is not the only diagnostic system. The World Health Organization devised the *International Classification of Diseases and Related Problems (ICD-10),* which includes a chapter on mental and behavioral disorders. A goal of the authors of *DSM-5* was to bring diagnoses closer to the *ICD-10,* although the two manuals remain different in important ways.

DSM-5
The *Diagnostic and Statistical Manual of Mental Disorders (DSM-5),* 5th ed.; the major classification of psychological disorders in the United States.

CRITIQUES OF THE *DSM*   *DSM-5* has been criticized on a number of grounds. A central criticism that applies to all versions of the *DSM* is that it treats psychological disorders as if they are medical illnesses, taking an overly biological view of disorders that

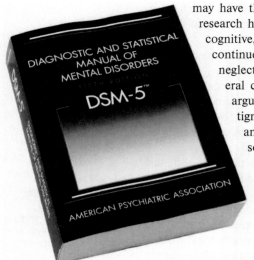

©Studio Works/Alamy Stock Photo

may have their roots in social experience (Blashfield & others, 2014). Even as research has shed light on the complex interaction of genetic, neurobiological, cognitive, social, and environmental factors in psychological disorders, *DSM-5* continues to reflect the medical model (British Psychological Society, 2011), neglecting factors such as poverty, unemployment, and trauma. Another general criticism of the *DSM* is that it focuses strictly on problems. Critics argue that emphasizing *strengths* as well as weaknesses might help to destigmatize psychological disorders. Identifying a person's strengths can be an important step toward maximizing his or her ability to contribute to society (Robbins, Kamens, & Elkins, 2017; Roten, 2007).

Other criticisms of *DSM-5* include the following:

- It relies too much on social norms and subjective judgments.

- Too many new categories of disorders have been added, some of which do not yet have consistent research support and whose inclusion will lead to a significant increase in the number of people being labeled as having a mental disorder.

- Loosened standards for some existing diagnoses will add to the already very high rates of these.

An example of a change that occurred in *DSM-5* that has inspired some controversy is the diagnosis of somatic symptom and related disorders. **Somatic symptom and related disorders** are defined as bodily symptoms that are either very distressing or that interfere with a person's functioning along with excessive thoughts, feelings, and behaviors about those symptoms (Rief & Martin, 2014). In previous versions of the *DSM*, for these symptoms to be classified as a psychological disorder, it was required that the physical symptoms lacked a medical explanation. Now, it is possible for a person to be diagnosed with somatic symptom disorder even if they have an actual physical illness.

Previously, these symptoms were more like hysterical symptoms: Physical problems with no physical cause.

somatic symptom and related disorders
Psychological disorders characterized by bodily symptoms that are either very distressing or that interfere with a person's functioning along with excessive thoughts, feeling, and behaviors about the symptoms.

Final Terms and Cautions

Before we begin reviewing various psychological diagnoses, let's clarify common terms and issues. First, keep in mind that many people with psychological disorders have more than one diagnosis, simultaneously. For example, an adult with a diagnosis of depression may also have an anxiety disorder. The term **comorbidity** means that person has two or more disorders at the same time.

Throughout our review, we will be considering the etiology of the disorders. *Etiology* refers to the causes of disorders. For most disorders there is not one known cause. Instead, researchers have identified risk factors that contribute to a person developing a psychological disorder. **Risk factors** are characteristics, experiences, or exposures that increase the likelihood of a person developing a disorder. Risk factors are correlated with the development of a disorder. Of course, correlation does not imply causation. Many people with a particular risk factor may not ever develop a disorder.

As we review the disorders, we will also briefly touch on common treatments. These treatments, our focus in Chapter 13, are generally divided into two types, psychotherapy and medication. **Psychotherapy** is a nonmedical process that helps individuals with psychological disorders recognize and overcome their problems. Psychotherapies can involve a variety of activities, including talking, providing support, coaching, and specific procedures to relieve maladaptive behavioral patterns. Medications are drugs that are used to treat the symptoms of psychological disorders. These often involve addressing dysregulation of neurotransmitters in the brain.

A final word of caution: It is very common for individuals who are learning about psychological disorders to recognize the symptoms and behaviors of disorders in themselves or in people around them. Keep in mind that only trained professionals can diagnose a psychological disorder.

comorbidity
The simultaneous presence of two or more disorders in one person. The conditions are referred to as "*comorbid*."

risk factor
Characteristics, experiences, or exposures that increase the likelihood that a person will develop a psychological disorder.

psychotherapy
A nonmedical process that helps individuals with psychological disorders recognize and overcome their problems.

self-quiz

1. All of the following are characteristics of abnormal behavior *except*
   A. it is typical.
   B. it causes distress.
   C. it is maladaptive.
   D. it is deviant.

2. The medical model interprets psychological disorders as medical diseases with a/an
   A. environmental origin.
   B. sociocultural origin.
   C. biological origin.
   D. biopsychosocial origin.

3. A central complaint about the *DSM-5* is that it neglects factors such as

   A. inherited tendencies toward particular diseases.
   B. age.
   C. economic and employment status.
   D. all of the above

APPLY IT! 4. Since she was a little girl, 19-year-old Francesca has believed that whenever she walks through a doorway, she must touch the doorframe 12 times and silently count to 12 or else her mother will die. She has never told anyone about this ritual, which she feels is harmless, similar to carrying a lucky charm. Engaging in this private ritual has no effect on her ability to achieve her

goals. Which of the following is true of Francesca's behavior?
   A. Francesca's behavior is abnormal only because it is different from the norm. It is not maladaptive, nor does it cause her distress.
   B. Francesca's behavior fits all three characteristics of abnormal behavior.
   C. Francesca's behavior is maladaptive, because it bothers her.
   D. Francesca's behavior does not fit any of the characteristics of abnormal behavior.

2 Neurodevelopmental Disorders

Neurodevelopmental disorders are in childhood (American Psychiatric Association, 2013) and are traced to genetic differences, atypical brain development, or prenatal exposure to substances that adversely affect development. This class of disorders includes communication disorders (such as language delays), learning disabilities, and intellectual disability (for example, Down Syndrome). In this section, we review two neurodevelopmental disorders in depth—autism spectrum disorder and attention-deficit/hyperactivity disorder.

Not all disorders diagnosed in childhood are considered "neurodevelopmental" disorders. For instance, children can be diagnosed with depression or anxiety disorders and these are not generally considered neurodevelopmental.

Autism Spectrum Disorder

Autism spectrum disorder (ASD) is characterized by two key features.

1. Individuals with ASD show persistent deficits in social communication and social interaction across a variety of settings.

2. Individuals with ASD show restrictive repetitive behaviors, interests, and activities.

Typically diagnosed in childhood, the symptoms of ASD are likely to color the person's behavior throughout life (Clark, Barbaro, & Dissanayake, 2017). For instance, infants may prefer not to be held or cuddled. Children may not develop the ability to speak. Adults may have persistent problems communicating with others. Repetitive behaviors in childhood may include hand flapping and head banging. Children with ASD might become preoccupied by particular stimuli or activities, like repeatedly opening and closing a door. Later in life, restrictive interests might involve an enthusiastic or obsessive interest in a topic, such as trains or American history.

For many years, it was estimated that about 5 children in 1000 had ASD. Recent estimates are much higher, suggesting that ASD affects 1 in 68 8-year-olds

©UrsaHoogle/E+/Getty Images

(Christensen & others, 2016). There are likely many reasons for this increase, including earlier diagnoses with increased attention to early warning signs (Soke & others, 2017). ASD is 2 to 5 times more common in boys than in girls (Ecker & others, 2017). ASD occurs in all ethnic groups and at all levels of socioeconomic status.

ASD is called a *spectrum* because the level of impairment that people with ASD experience is extremely variable (Hassall, 2017; Laurelut & others, 2016; Lerner & others, 2017). At one end of the spectrum, some individuals with ASD may never develop the capacity to speak and have profound difficulties caring for themselves and living independently. At the other end, individuals with ASD may do well in school, experience successful careers, and have enduring relationships with others (Kaboski, McDonnell, & Valentino, 2017). For example, Temple Grandin (2006), an accomplished scientist with ASD, described in her memoir *Thinking in Pictures* how she has had to commit to memory the fact that non-autistic people think in words, not images, and that their facial expressions reveal important information about their feelings.

Previously, high functioning individuals on the autism spectrum might be diagnosed with "Asperger's Syndrome," but because ASD now acknowledges the whole spectrum of functioning this diagnosis is no longer used.

Some individuals with ASD are effective advocates for themselves and contrast their ways of thinking, feeling, and existing in the world to "neurotypicals." For these individuals, ASD is a way of existing in a world of others who differ from them in essential ways. These individuals assert that ASD should be understood as a type of valuable *neurodiversity* (Baron-Cohen, 2017).

To explore the neurodiversity movement check out, http://autisticadvocacy.org/

The process of receiving a diagnosis of ASD often begins when parents and pediatricians notice potential signs of ASD, such as language delays (CDC, 2017; Dow & others, 2017). Despite high levels of awareness, most children with ASD are diagnosed after age 3 and many are not diagnosed until after age 6 (Sheldrick, Maye, & Carter, 2017). One concern is that children of diverse ethnic, racial, and socio-economic backgrounds may not receive the evaluations they need to have access to treatments (Durkin & others, 2017).

Because early intervention strongly predicts better outcomes (Feinberg & others, 2016; Suma & others, 2016), researchers have searched for ways to identify children with ASD prior to the age of 3. Parents of children with ASD often report having suspected a problem much earlier in their lives (Crane & others, 2016; Zablotsky & others, 2017). Still, infants vary greatly in their development and it is likely common for parents of all children to sometimes wonder if their child is developing typically.

In a landmark study, Julie Osterling and Geraldine Dawson (1994) searched for objective evidence of early signs of ASD in an common place: home videos. These researchers collected videos of children's first birthday parties from 22 families. For half, the birthday boy or girl would later be diagnosed with ASD; the others would develop typically. A team of coders, unaware of whether a child would eventually be diagnosed with ASD or not, carefully watched the videos and coded aspects of the child's behavior.

The results? Even at just one year, compared to their typically developing peers, children who would be diagnosed with ASD were less likely to look when someone called their name; to point or show an object to another person; and to look at the face of a person interacting with them (Osterling & Dawson, 1994). This study led to additional research on early warning signs of ASD in infants and toddlers. Results indicate that, compared to typically developing children, very young children who will develop ASD show low levels of joint attention (looking at objects with another person), low levels of attention to other children, less interest in the gaze of another person, and lower sophistication in pretend play (Clifford & Dissanayake, 2008; Wilson & others, 2017).

Focusing on 1st birthday parties is important. Can you think of two reasons why this step is considered a strength of this work?

UNDERSTANDING AUTISM SPECTRUM DISORDER AND ITS ORIGINS

Theoretical approaches to understanding autism seek to explain the symptoms of ASD as responses to central problems in cognition, sensation, or social motivation. Knowing which processes "come first" might help to develop diagnostic evaluations and to specify directions for treatment (Weitlauf & others, 2017).

For example, the *cognitive approach* to ASD emphasizes deficits in theory of mind. Recall from the States of Consciousness chapter that theory of mind refers to our understanding that other people have subjective experiences that may differ from our own. From the cognitive perspective, the child with ASD navigates the social world without this key source of information. Simon Baron-Cohen (1995, 2011) proposed that individuals with ASD are missing this important feature of social development. Support for this approach comes from the fact that individuals with ASD perform less well on theory of mind tasks compared to typically developing children (Farrar, Seung, & Lee, 2017; Rasga, Quelhas, & Byrne, 2017).

In a similar vein, the *social motivation approach* to ASD suggests that individuals with ASD are profoundly less interested in social stimuli compared to typically developing people. This difference affects what an infant attends to, the experiences he or she seeks out, and what he or she learns through experience (Chevallier & others, 2012). Research shows that children with ASD differ from typically developing children in their lack of attention to faces and to the gaze of others during social interactions (Burnside, Wright, & Poulin-Dubois, 2017; Frazier & others, 2017).

Finally, the *sensory processing approach* to ASD focuses on the fact that individuals with ASD process sensory experiences differently from others (Ida-Eto & others, 2017; Maule & others, 2017). Visually, they are more likely to focus on fine details rather than the "big picture." They may be highly sensitive to sounds and tactile sensations. In addition, those with ASD may have problems organizing and integrating their sensory experiences (Robertson & Baron-Cohen, 2017). Imagine that the world was an overwhelming cacophony of stimulation: Painfully bright lights and colors, loud noises, and scratchy clothes. How might you behave? From the sensory processing perspective, overwhelming sensory experiences are the heart of ASD (Bogdashina, 2016).

What causes ASD? This question is quite complex. Currently, there is strong scientific consensus about two things that *do not* cause ASD. First, particular parenting styles do not lead children to develop ASD (Mandy & Lai, 2016). Second, vaccines do not cause ASD (Anjali & others, 2015).

Risk factors for ASD include older parental age and prenatal exposure to some chemicals (Christensen & others, 2013). Maternal infections, such as rubella or "German measles" (Hutton, 2016), during pregnancy are also risk factors for ASD (Spann & others, 2017). Finally, complications before, during, and immediately after birth are associated with higher risk for ASD for the infants later in life (Getahun & others, 2017). By far, the two most important factors in ASD are genes and the brain. We review each of these below.

For a child with ASD, the world may be an overwhelming cacophony of stimulation.
©Stoked/Stockbyte/Media Bakery

Illusory correlation *appears to explain the subjective link between vaccines and ASD—because vaccines are often administered at the same time that communication and social skills are developing.*

Genetic and Brain Differences

Genes play an important role in the development and persistence of ASD (Taylor & others, 2017). Children whose siblings have ASD are at increased risk for the disorder (Wen & others, 2017). Research in molecular genetics has compared the genomes (the entire genetic array) of individuals with ASD to typical individuals. This research has linked many genetic mutations (that is, alterations or changes in the molecules that make up our genes) to the development of ASD (Chaste, Roeder, & Devlin, 2017; Dou & others, 2017). However, within a family, siblings can possess the same genetic mutations and one may develop ASD and the other not (Woodbury-Smith & others, 2017), indicating that genes are not a sole cause of ASD.

How are brain structure and function related to ASD? Research addressing this question has focused on brain areas linked to language and social information processing. For example, a recent study probed the ways that adolescents with ASD process speech compared to typically developing controls. The results showed that while typically developing adolescents showed activity in both the left and right hemisphere as they processed speech, those with ASD processed speech primarily on the left hemisphere only, without involvement of the right hemisphere (Galilee, Stafanidou, & McCleery, 2017). Recall that the right hemisphere, though not the center of language processing, contributes to the understanding of word meanings, connotation, and metaphor.

A large scale post-mortem (that is, after death) study compared the donated brains of 418 individuals with ASD to brains of 509 neurotypical adults. The study found that those with ASD had less white matter connections to areas of the brain involved in facial expressions and processing theory of mind (Cheng & others, 2015). These results fit with the deficits associated with ASD, but it is important to keep in mind that behavior affects the brain. So, it is not possible to know if these differences emerge from genetic differences or from a lifetime of behavior. The idea that the brain continues to change with experience is supported by research showing that brain differences in those with ASD increase with age (Lee, Azmitia, & Whitaker-Azmitia, 2017).

Etiological Diversity Clearly there is no single genetic or brain characteristic that serves as the key factor in the development of ASD. ASD appears to be *etiologically diverse*, meaning that the underlying causes of this disorder might vary from person to person (Betancur, 2011). One way to think about this complexity is to stay mindful of the fact there are only so many ways to be human. A child, no matter his or her genes, will not sprout wings and begin to fly. He or she will stay, always, human. Individuals on the autism spectrum may share symptoms, such as hand flapping, restricted interests, or difficulty in social interactions, for different underlying reasons. These many reasons may produce similar symptoms because those symptoms are within the realm of what human beings do.

Think about the symptoms of ASD. You likely know someone you might describe as having some levels of these characteristics. In fact, research shows that parents and siblings of children with ASD often show "subclinical" levels of traits (meaning the levels of the traits are not extreme or atypical and do not qualify as abnormal) that are associated with autism, like having restricted interests or being less socially engaged (Bora & others, 2017; Ruzich & others, 2017). Considering ASD in this way helps us recognize that individuals with the disorder are not qualitatively different from others, they are not only on the autism spectrum but on the *human* spectrum.

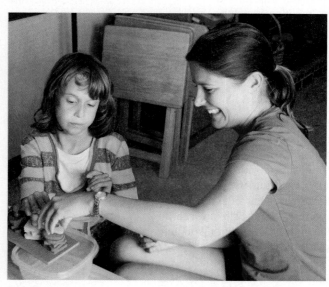
©ktaylorg/E+/Getty Images

TREATMENT   There is no cure for ASD, but treatments can greatly improve the lives of many individuals with the disorder. Intense behavioral approaches, incorporating principles of operant conditioning, are the standard treatment for ASD (Woo & Leon, 2013). Specifically, **applied behavior analysis**, as reviewed in the Learning chapter, has proven effective in treating ASD (Thompson, 2013). How intense is the treatment? Typically, it involves over 20 hours of behavioral intervention per week for 1 to 3 years, using reinforcement, shaping, and discrimination (Thompson, 2013). Researchers continue to integrate innovative methods to applied behavior analysis to treat ASD (Koegel & others, 2017).

In addition to therapy, medications may be used to help alleviate especially troubling symptoms including irritability, tantrums, aggression, or self-harm. The drugs used to treat these symptoms include strong psychiatric medications that are used to treat schizophrenia, an adult disorder we will review later (Brown & others, 2017; Li & others, 2017; Moazen-Zadeh & others, 2017).

applied behavior analysis or behavior modification The use of operant conditioning principles to change human behavior.

Individuals with ASD often have other diagnoses as well. It is not uncommon for children with ASD to receive a dual-diagnosis of ASD and attention-deficit/hyperactivty disorder (Joshi & others, 2017; Reynolds & others, 2017), our next topic.

Attention-Deficit/Hyperactivity Disorder

Attention-deficit/hyperactivity disorder (or ADHD) is a neurodevelopmental disorder characterized by persistent problems in sustaining attention and difficulty engaging in quiet activities for a prolonged period. The disorder is characterized by three main symptoms (APA, 2013):

attention-deficit/ hyperactivity disorder (ADHD)
One of the most common psychological disorders of childhood, in which individuals show one or more of the following: inattention, hyperactivity, and impulsivity.

1. *inattention*: The tendency to wander off tasks, lacking persistence, and difficulty sustaining focus.

2. *hyperactivity*: Excessive activity when it is inappropriate, including excessive fidgeting and restlessness.

3. *impulsivity*: Taking actions without planning or thinking, including inability to delay gratification.

For a diagnosis of ADHD, symptoms must be observed before the age of 12 and must occur across a variety of settings. So, a 5th grader who is fidgety at school but able to sit for periods of time studying or constructing a complex Lego set at home is unlikely to have ADHD. A child with ADHD might have particular problems in regulating excitement or exuberance and show a lack of caution in their behavior.

ADHD occurs in most cultures in about 5% of children (APA, 2013), although there are wide differences across countries in the prevalence of ADHD (Taylor, 2017). Boys are more likely to be diagnosed with ADHD than girls (Fairman, Peckham, & Sclar, 2017). Experts previously thought that most children "grow out" of ADHD, however, around 70 percent of adolescents (Sibley & others, 2012) and adults (Asherson & others, 2010) diagnosed as children continue to experience ADHD symptoms (Zhu & others, 2017).

Children with ADHD can be in danger because they may climb or run into dangerous situations without thinking.

In the U.S., ADHD is one of the most common psychological disorders of childhood, with diagnoses skyrocketing in recent years. In 2012, 11 percent of American children aged 4 to 17 had been diagnosed with ADHD at some point in their lives (CDC, 2017). Rates of diagnosis are higher for White/European American children than other ethnic/ racial groups (Fairman, Peckham, & Sclar, 2017).

High rates of ADHD have prompted some to suggest that psychiatrists, parents, and teachers are labeling normal childhood behavior a psychological disorder (Timimi, 2017; Wakefield, 2016). These scholars argue that many ADHD diagnoses are the product of medicalizing what is simply annoying or typical childhood behavior (Armstrong 2017; Koutsoklenis & Gaitanidis, 2017). Those who endorse this view argue that in the absence of a specific genetic or brain-related explanation, ADHD should not be considered a psychological diagnosis. However, as we will see, most psychological disorders lack such simple explanations. Moreover, left untreated, ADHD is related to serious negative outcomes.

ADHD interferes with schooling and social development (Colomer & others, 2017). Children and adolescents with ADHD are likely to show lower levels of academic performance (Gray & others, 2017; Liu & others, 2017; Sjöwall & others, 2017; Zendarski & others, 2017). Youth with ADHD are likely to have problems in peer relations, especially because of their inability to regulate excitement (Thorell & others, 2017). Adolescents with ADHD more likely to be bullied (Becker & others, 2017). Compared to typically developing peers, youth with ADHD are more likely to engage in delinquent behavior (Patterson, DeGarmo, & Knutson, 2000; Soltis & others, 2017). In college students, ADHD symptoms predict lower quality relationships (McKee, 2017). Adults who were diagnosed with ADHD as children show poorer educational outcomes, relationship difficulties, incarceration, and lower socioeconomic status SES (Faraone & others, 2015;

Owens & others, 2017). Importantly, these many negative outcomes can be prevented by effective treatments (Thapar & Cooper, 2016).

ADHD diagnosis is based on interviewing the child and parents, combined with standard assessments completed by parents and teachers. ADHD symptoms may occur in other disorders (Caplan, 2017; Guzick & others, 2017; Spitzer & others, 2017), and so it is important for children to be carefully assessed. Although overdiagnosis is a concern, some groups, such as children from disadvantaged backgrounds, may have less access to evaluation and high quality treatment (Cummings & others, 2017).

A diagnosis of ADHD requires that symptoms appear in childhood. It is not uncommon for adults diagnosed in childhood to continue to experience symptoms that require treatment. The possibility that an adult might be diagnosed with ADHD without previously having symptoms has been the subject of some controversy. To read about his issue, see the Challenge Your Thinking.

UNDERSTANDING ADHD AND ITS ORIGINS   Risk factors for ADHD include very premature birth (Scott & others, 2017), low birth weight, and prenatal exposure to alcohol (Eilertsen & others, 2017) and smoking (He & others, 2017). Childhood lead exposure (Kim & others, 2018) in combination with factors such as poverty (Perera & others, 2018) is also associated with ADHD. Exposure to some pesticides can, in conjunction with genetic risk, heighten the chances that a child will develop ADHD (Chang & others, 2018). Large scale longitudinal studies show that children who experience more adverse events, such as physical, sexual, or verbal abuse, and neglect, are more likely to be diagnosed with ADHD (Brown & others, 2017; Jimenez & others, 2017).

Genetic differences appear to play a role in ADHD. Twin studies indicate that up to 70 percent of the variance in ADHD is accounted for by genetic variability (Faraone & others, 2005). Genetic studies suggest that ADHD is polygenic, meaning that it is related to the interaction of two or more genes (Doyle & others, 2017). Molecular genetic studies have identified 8–10 specific genetic locations associated with ADHD (Bidwell & others, 2017), including the genes responsible for transporting dopamine and serotonin (Klein & others, 2017). Genetic differences associated with ADHD do not appear to be specific to the disorder and may represent genetic risk for other psychological disorders (Ritter & others, 2017; van Hulzen & others, 2017).

These genetic differences are thought to affect brain development in ways that contribute to ADHD. For example, one hypothesis about the origins of ADHD is the *delayed maturation hypothesis* (Klein & others, 2017). This hypothesis says that individuals with ADHD have brains that develop more slowly than typically developing individuals, especially with regard to the prefrontal cortex (Beare & others, 2017; Shaw & others, 2007), the area of the brain most associated with planning, thinking, and self-control. Research supporting this hypothesis shows that ADHD is associated with reduced cortical thickness (Cherkasova & others, 2017; Newman & others, 2016; Shaw & others, 2007). In addition, individuals with ADHD may have fewer connections between the prefrontal cortex and other brain regions (Beare & others, 2017; Bethlehem & others, 2017).

This research fits well with cognitive approaches to ADHD that emphasize problems in executive function as being the root cause of problems in the lives of those with ADHD (Barkley, 1997; Graham, 2017). Preschoolers who score low on measures of working memory function and capacity to regulate their extreme positive emotions are more likely to show ADHD symptoms in adolescence (Sjöwall & others, 2017). Moreover, it may be that differences in working memory, rather than ADHD, *per se,* which explain lower academic performance among children with the disorder (Simone & others, 2017).

Another neurobiological focus has been the areas of the brain that are responsible for reward learning and seeking out rewarding stimuli. Individuals with ADHD have less brain volume in the brain's reward centers (Hoogman & others, 2017; Hulst & others, 2017). ADHD is also associated with dysregulation in the neurotransmitter dopamine and pathways that carry this important neurotransmitter (Volkow & others, 2011). In addition to dopamine, dysregulation of acetylcholine and melatonin in infancy predict the development of ADHD (Hellmer & Nyström, 2017). Such findings fit with problems that

Can Adults Develop ADHD?

Increasingly adults are seeking treatment for ADHD, especially with stimulant medications, even if they were not diagnosed as children (McGough, 2016). The reasons for this increase are unclear but some scientists have suggested that it is time to consider the reality that "late onset" ADHD may be a legitimate disorder. Some studies have identified adults who appear to be suffering from ADHD who did not experience symptoms during childhood (Agnew-Blais & others, 2016; Caye & others, 2016). Others have countered that these studies have lacked strong measures of childhood symptoms and may represent late-*detection* rather than late onset (Castellanos, 2015; Solanto, 2017).

Can adults develop ADHD without having symptoms in childhood? Recently, a team of researchers realized they might have the answer to this question in an unexpected place: A sample of over 200 individuals who were included as a control group in a longitudinal study of children with ADHD (Sibley & others, 2017).

©Antonio Guillem/Shutterstock

The original study included a sample of children with ADHD and a sample that was recruited to serve as a comparison. Children in the control group were screened to be free of ADHD symptoms at age 10. Both groups were followed until the age of 25. Focusing on the comparison group only, the researchers were able to identify 40 people who appeared to show adult onset ADHD.

A close examination of these 40 cases led to the conclusion that *95 percent* did not fit an ADHD diagnosis. Some of the cases had shown ADHD symptoms in adolescence. A substantial portion were found to have symptoms as a result of substance abuse (for example alcoholism). Many of the cases were experiencing symptoms because of other psychological disorders (such as anxiety). Finally, one person experienced symptoms only in a specific context.

In all, just 2 adults remained who might be considered to have ADHD starting in adulthood (Sibley & others, 2017).

This research shows that although some adult onset cases of ADHD may be valid, careful assessment is important to rule out a host of other factors. You might be wondering why it matters if an adult receives a "false" diagnosis of ADHD. It is important because it contradicts decades of understanding of the disorder, challenging even the potential causes that have been identified in infancy. Moreover, stimulant medications have different effects on the brains of children compared to adults (Schrantee & others, 2016). When an adult who has never been diagnosed with ADHD requests stimulant medications, we must consider the possibility of *malingering*, that is, pretending to have a disorder in order to obtain medication for nonmedical purposes (Leppma & others, 2017). Certainly, the controversy over adult onset ADHD demonstrates the limits of self-diagnosis: It should never be the case that a person is diagnosed with a particular disorder because that disorder is the one with which he or she is most familiar.

What Do You Think?

- Do you think adults with no history of childhood ADHD symptoms should be treated the same as those with a childhood history of the disorder? Why or why not?

- Why do you think many adults are coming forward seeking help for "late onset" ADHD?

---

individuals with ADHD have delaying gratification and regulating reward motivation (Martinelli, Mostofsky, & Rosch, 2017).

TREATMENT Stimulant medication, such as Ritalin or Adderall, is often the first line of treatment for ADHD because these medications often work (Pelham & others, 2017). It may seem surprising that individuals who are too active would be treated with stimulants. These medications work because they increase the amount of circulating dopamine (Schrantree & others, 2016). This increase in dopamine means that the child does not have to engage in activity to experience the pleasure that dopamine evokes.

Giving children medication is always best done with extreme care. Although some have been concerned that children who are given stimulant drugs might be at risk for developing substance abuse problems, research results have been mixed. Indeed, it may be that symptoms of ADHD rather than medical treatment of the disorder predict substance use

©Vgstockstudio/Shutterstock

(Molina & Pelham, 2014). Untreated, ADHD has the capacity to cause a great deal of harm to a child and his or her future.

Children and adults with ADHD can also benefit from non-medical interventions. Often combined with medication, these interventions include many different activities, such as physical exercise (Den Heijer & others, 2017), sports training (Altszuler & others, 2017), meditation (Evans & others, 2017), academic tutoring and training (Tamm & others, 2017), and driving safety (Bruce & others, 2017).

Psychotherapy can be effective in treating ADHD in children whose symptoms do not respond to medication or who are very young (Daley & Dupaul, 2016; Sprich & others, 2016). Psychotherapy has also been found to be effective in treating ADHD in adults (Knouse, Teller, & Brooks, 2017) as well as parents of children with ADHD (Sprich & others, 2016).

self-quiz

1. The dominant approach to treating autism spectrum disorder is
   A. applied behavior analysis.
   B. medication.
   C. psychodynamic therapy.
   D. electroconvulsive therapy.

2. Describing autism spectrum disorder as etiologically diverse means that
   A. the disorder is caused by very specific *de novo* genetic mutations.
   B. scientists have not studied potential causes of autism spectrum disorder.
   C. autism spectrum disorder is the result of the same brain structure differences across all individuals with the disorder.

   D. two people on the autism spectrum can show the same symptoms for different underlying reasons.

3. Which of the following is not considered relevant to ADHD?
   A. The brain's reward centers.
   B. The thickness of the prefrontal cortex.
   C. The volume of the occipital lobe.
   D. The speed with which the brain develops.

APPLY IT! 4. Jeremy is 7 years old and in second grade. He has trouble sitting still in class and often forgets to raise his hand before shouting out the answers to questions. His teacher sug-

gests to his parents that he should be tested for ADHD because his behavior is disrupting her class. Which of the following would be the best argument against Jeremy having ADHD?
   A. At home most evenings, Jeremy spends long hours sitting quietly, in deep concentration, playing chess against his grandfather.
   B. At home, Jeremy is very fidgety and unable to concentrate for very long on any tasks.
   C. There is no history of ADHD in Jeremy's family.
   D. Jeremy is too young to have ADHD.

3 Anxiety and Anxiety-Related Disorders

Think about how you felt before a make-or-break exam or a big presentation—or perhaps as you noticed police lights flashing behind your speeding car. Did you feel jittery and nervous? These are the feelings of normal anxiety—an unpleasant feeling of fear and dread.

anxiety disorders
Disabling (uncontrollable and disruptive) psychological disorders that feature motor tension, hyperactivity, and apprehensive expectations and thoughts.

In contrast, **anxiety disorders** involve fears that are uncontrollable, disproportionate to the actual danger the person might be in, and disruptive of ordinary life. They feature motor tension (jumpiness, trembling), hyperactivity (dizziness, a racing heart), and apprehensive expectations and thoughts. *DSM-5* recognizes 12 types of anxiety disorders. In this section, we survey four common anxiety disorders:

- Generalized anxiety disorder
- Panic disorder
- Specific phobia
- Social anxiety disorder

We will also review a disorder that is not classified as an anxiety disorder but is related to the experience of anxiety:

- Obsessive-compulsive disorder (categorized under Obsessive-compulsive and related disorders)

Generalized Anxiety Disorder

generalized anxiety disorder Psychological disorder marked by persistent anxiety for at least six months, and in which the individual is unable to specify the reasons for the anxiety.

When you are worrying about getting a speeding ticket, you know why you are anxious; there is a specific cause. **Generalized anxiety disorder** is different from such everyday feelings of anxiety in that sufferers experience persistent anxiety for at least six months and are unable to specify the reasons for the anxiety (Ruscio & others, 2017). People with generalized anxiety disorder are nervous most of the time. They may worry about their work, relationships, or health (Goodwin, Yiend, & Hirsche, 2017). That worry can also take a physical toll and cause fatigue, muscle tension, stomach problems, and difficulty sleeping.

What is the etiology of generalized anxiety disorder? Among the biological factors are genetic predisposition, deficiency in the neurotransmitter GABA, and brain differences (particularly in the amgdala; Makovac & others, 2016). A recent brain imaging study showed that for individuals with GAD, the brain responds more strongly to everyday worries (Blair & others, 2017).

Another contributor to GAD are abnormalities in the *respiratory* system (Montgomery & others, 2017). Interestingly, researchers sometimes use respiratory challenge to study GAD. In such studies, healthy volunteers breathe air that is 7.5 percent carbon dioxide (or CO_2). This level of CO_2 induces feelings of threat and anxiety, suggesting the role of the respiratory system in many anxiety disorders (Battaglia, 2017) including GAD (Baldwin & others, 2017).

Psychological and sociocultural risk factors include having harsh (or even impossible) self-standards, overly strict and critical parents, automatic negative thoughts when feeling stressed, and a history of uncontrollable traumas or stressors (such as an abusive parent) (Kelly & Mezuk, 2017). Women are more likely than men to suffer from GAD (Kinney, Boffa, & Amir, 2017). In addition, people who tend to be worriers in general or who are always on the lookout for threats in the environment may be at risk for GAD (Goodwin, Yiend, & Hirsch, 2017).

Treatment for GAD often includes medications that mimic the action of GABA (the brain's brake pedal), such as pregabalin (Lyrica) (Generoso & others, 2017). Psychotherapy can also be effective in reducing GAD, especially if the person with GAD experiences a strong empathic bond to the therapist (Borza, 2017; Constantino & others 2017).

GABA is the neurotransmitter that inhibits neurons from firing—it's like the brain's brake pedal. Problems with GABA are often implicated in anxiety disorders.

Panic Disorder

panic disorder Anxiety disorder in which the individual experiences recurrent, sudden onsets of intense apprehension or terror, often without warning and with no specific cause.

Much like everyone else, you might sometimes have a specific experience that sends you into a panic. For example, you work all night on a paper, only to have your computer crash before you saved your last changes, or you are about to dash across a street just when you see a large truck coming right at you. Your heart races, your hands shake, and you might break into a sweat.

In **panic disorder**, a person experiences recurrent, sudden onsets of intense terror, often without warning and with no specific cause. Panic attacks can produce severe palpitations, extreme shortness of breath, chest pains, trembling, sweating, dizziness, and a feeling of helplessness (Meuret, Kroll, & Ritz, 2017). People with panic disorder may feel that they are having a heart attack or going to die.

During a panic attack, the brain registers fear in the network of the cortico limbic regions (amygdala, hippocampus, and prefrontal) (Canteras & Graeff, 2014; Deckert & others, 2017). Charles Darwin, the scientist who proposed the theory of evolution, suffered from intense panic disorder (Barloon & Noyes, 1997).

What is the etiology of panic disorder? Theories of the origins of panic attack take into account biological, psychological, and sociocultural factors. In terms of biological factors, individuals may have a genetic predisposition to the disorder (Deckert & others, 2017; Jensen & others, 2014). Of particular interest to researchers are genes that direct the action of neurotransmitters such as norepinephrine, GABA and serotonin (Graef, 2017;

A panic attack can be a one-time occurrence. People with panic disorder have recurrent attacks that sometimes cause them to be afraid to even leave their homes, a condition called agoraphobia.

Many experts interpret Edvard Munch's painting *The Scream* as an expression of the terror brought on by a panic attack.
©Mariano Garcia/Alamy Stock Photo

Paul & others, 2014). Another brain chemical, *lactate,* which plays a role in brain metabolism, has been found to be elevated in individuals with panic disorder (Riske & others, 2017). Experimental research has shown that increasing lactate levels can produce panic attacks (Reiman & others, 1989), suggesting that problems in regulating lactate may play a role in panic disorder (Riske & others, 2017). Other research points to the involvement of a wider range of genes and bodily systems, implicating genes involved in hormone regulation (Demiralay & others, 2017) and responses to stress (Wichman & others, 2017). Compared to other anxiety disorders, panic disorder shares a strong relationship with medical illnesses and it may be that these illnesses affect the body's fight or flight system (Meuret, Kroll, & Ritz, 2017).

With respect to psychological influences, learning processes are one factor that has been considered in panic disorder. Classical conditioning research has shown that learned associations between bodily cues of respiration and fear can play a role in panic attacks (Blechert & others, 2013). Interestingly, CO_2 has been found to be a very strong conditioned stimulus for fear, suggesting that humans may be *biologically prepared* to learn an association between high concentrations of CO_2 and fear (Graef, 2017; Spiacci & others, 2018). Thus, some researchers have suggested that at the heart of panic attacks are the learned associations between CO_2 and fear (De Cort & others, 2012; Marin & others, 2017).

In addition, the learning concept of *generalization* may apply to panic attack. Recall that in classical conditioning, generalization means showing a conditioned response (in this case, fear) to conditioned stimuli other than the particular one used in learning. Research shows that individuals who suffer from panic attacks are more likely to display overgeneralization of fear learning (Lange & others, 2017; Lissek & others, 2010). Why might those who suffer from panic attacks be more likely to show stronger and more generalized fear associations? One possibility is that the biological predispositions as well as early experiences with traumatic life events may play a role in setting the stage for such learning (De Venter & others, 2017; Pilecki, Arentoft, & McKay, 2011).

In terms of sociocultural factors, in the United States, women are twice as likely as men to have panic attacks (Li & Graham, 2017). Possible reasons include biological differences in hormones and neurotransmitters (Altemus, 2006; Masdrakis, Papageorgiou, & Markianos, 2017). Compared to men, women are more likely to complain of distressing respiratory experiences during panic attacks (Sheikh, Leskin, & Klein, 2002). Interestingly, one study showed that healthy women are more likely to experience panic-related emotions when exposed to air enriched with CO_2 (Nillni & others, 2012).

Research also suggests that women may cope with anxiety-provoking situations differently than men do, and these differences may explain the gender difference in panic disorder (Lovick, 2014; Viswanath & others, 2012). Panic attack has been observed in a variety of cultures, though there are some cultural differences in the experience of these attacks (Agorastos, Haasen, & Huber, 2012). For instance, in Korea, panic attacks are less likely to include a fear of dying than is the case in other societies (Weissman & others, 1995).

There are a number of effective treatments for panic disorder, including individual (Chambless & others, 2017) and group therapy (Schwartze & others, 2017). Medications that have a tranquilizing effect can also help those suffering with panic disorder (Davies, Nash, & Nutt, 2017).

An earlier explanation of panic attack was called the **suffocation false alarm theory.** Can you see why it was initially proposed?

Whenever you encounter gender differences in this discussion, ask yourself whether men or women might be more likely to report having problems or to seek treatment. Research on psychological disorders is often based on individuals who have reported symptoms or sought help. If men are less likely to report symptoms or seek treatment, the data may underestimate the occurrence of psychological disorders in men.

Specific Phobia

Many people are afraid of spiders and snakes; indeed, thinking about letting a tarantula crawl over one's face is likely to give anyone the willies. It is not uncommon to be afraid

Acrophobia	Fear of high places	Arachnophobia	Fear of spiders	Mysophobia	Fear of dirt
Aerophobia	Fear of flying	Astrapophobia	Fear of lightning	Nyctophobia	Fear of darkness
Ailurophobia	Fear of cats	Cynophobia	Fear of dogs	Ophidiophobia	Fear of nonpoisonous snakes
Algophobia	Fear of pain	Gamophobia	Fear of marriage		
Amaxophobia	Fear of vehicles, driving	Hydrophobia	Fear of water	Thanatophobia	Fear of death
		Melissophobia	Fear of bees	Xenophobia	Fear of strangers

FIGURE 1 **Specific Phobias** This figure features examples of specific phobias—anxiety disorders characterized by irrational and overwhelming fear of a particular object or situation.

of particular objects or specific environments such as extreme heights. For most of us, these fears do not interfere with daily life. A fear becomes a phobia when a situation is so dreaded that an individual goes to almost any length to avoid it. A snake phobia that keeps a city-dweller from leaving his apartment is clearly disproportionate to the actual chances of encountering a snake. **Specific phobia** is a psychological disorder in which an individual has an irrational, overwhelming, persistent fear of a particular object or situation. Specific phobias come in many forms, as shown in Figure 1.

Where do specific phobias come from? Approaches to answering this question typically first acknowledge that fear plays an important role in adaptive behavior. Fear tells us when we are in danger and need to take to action. The importance of this function suggests that fears should be relatively quickly learned, because learning to fear things that will harm us keeps us out of harm's way. Specific phobias, then, might be considered an extreme and unfortunate variant on this adaptive process (Haesen & others, 2017; Muris & Merckelbach, 2012).

Many explanations of specific phobias view these disorders as based on experiences, memories, and learned associations (Mieri & others, 2017; Veale & others, 2013). For example, the individual with a fear of heights perhaps experienced a fall from a high place earlier in life and therefore associates heights with pain (a classical conditioning explanation). Alternatively, he or she may have heard about or watched others who demonstrated terror of high places (an observational learning explanation), as when a little girl develops a fear of heights after sitting next to her terrified mother and observing her clutch the handrails, white-knuckled, as the roller coaster creeps steeply uphill. Not all people who have a specific phobia can easily identify experiences that explain these, so other factors may also be at play. Each specific phobia may have its own neural correlates (Klahn & others, 2017; Peñate & others, 2017) and some people may be especially prone to develop phobias (Burstein & others, 2012; Shihata, McEvoy, & Mullan, 2017).

Just as the theories of the origins of specific phobia rely largely on associative learning, treatment for specific phobias often rely on learning principles. These psychotherapies often use the concept of extinction to remove the link between a feared stimulus (such as a spider) and feelings of intense anxiety (Lange & others, 2017; Matthews & others, 2017). Interestingly, specific phobia is associated with the development of other psychological disorders, suggesting it may be an early sign of vulnerability to a range of disorders (Wardenaar & others, 2017) and an opportunity for early intervention.

specific phobia
Psychological disorder in which an individual has an irrational, overwhelming, persistent fear of a particular object or situation.

Social Anxiety Disorder

Imagine how you might feel just before you first meet the parents of the person you hope to marry. You might feel fearful of committing some awful gaffe, ruining the impression you hope to make on them. Or imagine getting ready to give a big speech before a crowd and suddenly realizing you have forgotten your notes. **Social anxiety disorder** (also called **social phobia**) is an intense fear of being humiliated or embarrassed in social situations like these (Asher, Asnaani, & Aderka, 2017; Gilboa-Schechtman & others, 2017; Leichsenring & Leweke, 2017). Not surprisingly, individuals with social anxiety disorder often avoid social interactions. Singers Carly Simon and Barbra Streisand have dealt with social anxiety disorder.

Where does social anxiety disorder come from? Research supports the role of genetics in the disorder. For example, a large-scale genome-wide association study found significant contribution of specific genetic locations to the disorder (Stein & others, 2017). Interestingly, those same genetic locations were associated with lower levels of the personality trait extraversion. In addition, neural circuitry involving the thalamus, amygdala, and cerebral cortex has been linked to social anxiety disorder (Yang & others, 2017; Damsa, Kosel, & Moussally, 2009). A number of neurotransmitters also may be involved, especially serotonin (Christensen & others, 2010). Social anxiety disorder may involve vulnerabilities, such as genetic characteristics or parenting styles that lay a foundation of risk, combined with learning experiences in a social context (Higa-McMillan & Ebesutani, 2011; Pejic & others, 2013).

Finally, cognitive explanations of the disorder focus on the person's beliefs about the possibility of social failure and automatic negative thoughts that follow from those beliefs (Nordahl & others, 2017). An additional cognitive factor is that attentional bias toward negative information may play a role in the persistence of the disorder (Heeren & others, 2017). As we have seen many times, expectations can color perception and experience. In social anxiety disorder, the person may be constantly looking for indications of social failure and consequently interpret social cues in a negative light. These perceptions then might lead them to avoid social interactions all the more.

Treatment for social anxiety disorder often involves psychotherapy that aims at exposing the person to social stimuli while instilling a calm mindset. Such therapy might even incorporate encountering others in virtual reality rather than in person (Bouchard & others, 2017). Psychotherapy can combat the beliefs, thoughts, and expectations that feed into the disorder (Thurston & others, 2017). Medications used to treat social anxiety disorder include drugs that regulate serotonin (typically used for depression) and drugs that serve to reduce anxiety (Curtiss & others, 2017). Innovative treatments for social anxiety disorder may be on the horizon. For example, administration of oxytocin (the hormone and neurotransmitter related to social bonding) has been shown to relieve social anxiety (Jones & others, 2017) and oxytocin may become a treatment for the disorder. Finally, it may be that individuals with social anxiety disorder will benefit from direct stimulation to the brain that temporarily disrupts the area of the brain involved in attention to threat (Heeren & others, 2017).

In *DSM-5,* generalized anxiety disorder, panic disorder, specific phobia, and social anxiety disorder are all classified as anxiety disorders. Our next topic, obsessive-compulsive disorder is not included under the umbrella of anxiety disorders. Instead, this disorder has its own separate category. Nonetheless, anxiety is relevant to obsessive-compulsive disorder, as we shall see.

Obsessive-Compulsive Disorder

Just before leaving on a long road trip, you find yourself checking to be sure you locked the front door. As you pull away in your car, you are stricken with the thought that you forgot to turn off the coffeemaker. Going to bed the night before an early flight, you check your alarm clock a few times to be sure you will wake up on time. These are examples of normal checking behavior.

In contrast, the disorder known as **obsessive-compulsive disorder (OCD)** features anxiety-provoking thoughts that will not go away and/or urges to perform repetitive, ritualistic behaviors to prevent or produce some future situation. *Obsessions* are recurrent thoughts. *Compulsions* are recurrent behaviors (Amitai & others, 2017). Individuals with OCD dwell on their doubts and repeat their routines sometimes hundreds of times a day. The most common compulsions are excessive checking, cleansing, and counting. Game show host Howie Mandel has coped with OCD, as have soccer star David Beckham, singer-actor Justin Timberlake, and actor Jessica Alba. Obsessive-compulsive symptoms have been found in many cultures, and culture plays a role in the content of obsessive thoughts or compulsive behaviors (Matsunaga & Seedat, 2011).

An individual with OCD might believe that she has to touch the doorway with her left hand whenever she enters a room and count her steps as she walks. If she does not complete this ritual, she may be overcome with a sense of fear that something terrible will happen (Myers & others, 2017).

What is the etiology of obsessive-compulsive disorder? In terms of biological factors, genes are certainly involved (Arnold & others, 2017; Tang & others, 2014). Also, brain-imaging studies have suggested neurological links for OCD (Bokor & Anderson, 2014). One neuroscientific analysis is that the frontal cortex or basal ganglia are so active in OCD that numerous impulses reach the thalamus, generating obsessive thoughts or compulsive actions (Hauser & others, 2017; Rotge & others, 2009). Low levels of the neurotransmitters serotonin, dopamine, and glutamate likely are involved in the brain pathways linked with OCD (Pauls & others, 2014).

In one study, fMRI was used to examine the brain activity of individuals with OCD before and after treatment (Nakao & others, 2005). Following effective treatment, a number of areas in the frontal cortex showed decreased activation. The limbic system appears to be hyperactivated in those with OCD, even when situations have no uncertainty (Stern & others, 2013). Animal research has shown that dysfunction in the circuitry connecting the thalamus to the amygdalae (the brain structures that activate in response to survival relevant stimuli) can produce OCD-like symptoms in rats (Ullrich & others, 2017).

In terms of psychological factors, OCD sometimes occurs during a period of life stress such as that surrounding the birth of a child or a change in occupational or marital status (Brander & others, 2016). In addition, the features of a person's symptoms (such as the type of ritual the person feels compelled to enact) may be predicted by aspects of the person's personality and experience (Vickers & others, 2017). According to the cognitive perspective, what differentiates individuals with OCD from those who do not have it is the ability to turn off negative, intrusive thoughts by ignoring or effectively dismissing them (Bouvard & others, 2017; Leahy, Holland, & McGinn, 2012).

Treatments for OCD may rely on behavioral principles that treat OCD symptoms as learned avoidance. This treatment involves having the person *not* engage in his or her ritual and allowing them to experience the fact that the dreaded outcome never happens. Repeated experience of this sort is thought to help extinguish the fear response (Eilam, 2017; Motivala & others, 2017). Psychotherapies also target the nonrational beliefs and automatic thoughts that occur in the context of OCD, helping the person to gain control of his or her mental life. Finally, medications that help in regulating serotonin can be effective in treating OCD (Walkup & Mohatt, 2017).

obsessive-compulsive disorder (OCD)
Disorder in which the individual has anxiety-provoking thoughts that will not go away and/or urges to perform repetitive, ritualistic behaviors to prevent or produce some future situation.

As long as the person performs the ritual, she never finds out that the terrible outcome doesn't happen. The easing of the anxiety exemplifies **negative reinforcement** (having something bad taken away after performing a behavior).

OCD-Related Disorders

The *DSM-5* includes other disorders that are thought to be related to OCD (Abramowitz & Jacoby, 2015). All of these involve repetitive behavior and often anxiety. Here are some examples:

■ *Hoarding disorder* involves compulsive collecting, poor organization skills, and difficulty discarding things, along with cognitive deficits in information processing speed, problems with decision making, and procrastination (Levy & others, 2017). Individuals with hoarding disorder find it difficult to throw things away and are troubled by the feeling that they might need items like old newspapers at a later time.

- *Excoriation* (or skin picking) refers to the particular compulsion of picking at one's skin, sometimes to the point of injury. Skin picking is more common among women than men and sometimes occurs as a symptom of autism spectrum disorder.

- *Trichotillomania* (hair pulling) entails compulsively pulling at the hair from the scalp, eyebrows, and other body areas. Hair pulling from the scalp can lead to bald patches that the person can go to great lengths to disguise.

- *Body dysmorphic disorder* involves a distressing preoccupation with imagined or slight flaws in one's physical appearance. Individuals with this disorder cannot stop thinking about how they look and repeatedly compare their appearance to others, check themselves in the mirror, and so forth. Body dysmorphic disorder may include maladaptive behaviors such as compulsive exercise and body building and repeated cosmetic surgery and occurs about equally in men and women.

self-quiz

1. Sudden episodes of extreme anxiety or terror that involve symptoms such as heart palpitations, trembling, sweating, and fear of losing control are characteristic of
   A. generalized anxiety disorder.
   B. specific phobia.
   C. obsessive-compulsive disorder.
   D. panic disorder.

2. A person feels that they must tap the door frame 23 times prior to entering a room and if they do not complete this ritual something terrible will happen. This ritual has come to dominate the person's life so they cannot even leave the house in the morning. Which psychological disorder involves these symptoms?
   A. Panic disorder
   B. Generalized anxiety disorder
   C. Obsessive-compulsive disorder
   D. Specific phobia

3. An irrational, overwhelming, persistent fear of a particular object or situation is a defining characteristic of
   A. obsessive-compulsive disorder.
   B. specific phobia.
   C. panic disorder.
   D. generalized anxiety disorder.

APPLY IT! 4. Lately Tina has noticed that her mother appears to be overwhelmed with worry about everything. Her mother has told Tina that she is having trouble sleeping and is experiencing racing thoughts of all the terrible things that might happen at any given moment. Tina's mother is showing signs of
   A. panic disorder.
   B. obsessive-compulsive disorder.
   C. generalized anxiety disorder.
   D. specific phobia.

4 Trauma and Stress-Related Disorders

As we have seen, many psychological disorders involve a combination of factors, including genetic characteristics and experiences. Some psychological disorders, though, are more intimately attached to extremely negative experiences. In this section, we review two types of disorders that involve trauma: post-traumatic stress disorder and dissociative disorders. Traumatic experiences are severe and extremely disturbing. These experiences may involve the threat of death or serious injury or sexual violence, in which a person feels intense fear and helplessness (Schönfeld & Ehlers, 2017). Traumas can involve a single horrific incident or a pattern of negative experiences. Sometimes such experiences are so extreme that they splinter a person's very sense of self.

Post-Traumatic Stress Disorder

post-traumatic stress disorder (PTSD)
Anxiety disorder that develops through exposure to a traumatic event, a severely oppressive situation, cruel abuse, or a natural or unnatural disaster.

If you are ever in even a minor car accident, you may have a nightmare or two about it. You might even find yourself reliving the experience for some time. This normal recovery process takes on a devastating character in **post-traumatic stress disorder (PTSD),** a disorder that develops through exposure to a traumatic event that overwhelms the person's abilities to cope. *DSM-5* has expanded the kinds of experiences that might foster PTSD, recognizing that the disorder can occur not only in individuals who directly experience a trauma but also in those who witness it and those who only *hear* about it (APA, 2013). The symptoms of PTSD vary but include

- Flashbacks in which the individual relives the event. A flashback can make the person lose touch with reality and reenact the event for seconds, hours, or, very rarely, days. A person having a flashback—which can come in the form of images, sounds, smells, and/or feelings—usually believes that the traumatic event is happening all over again.
- Avoiding emotional experiences and avoiding talking about emotions with others.
- Emotional numbness and a reduced ability to feel emotions.
- Excessive arousal, resulting in an exaggerated startle response or an inability to sleep.
- Difficulties with memory and concentration.
- Impulsive behavior.

PTSD can occur in response to a wide variety of extremely disturbing events. Such events can include natural disasters (such as hurricanes or earthquakes), combat and war-related trauma, unnatural disasters (such as car accidents, plane crashes, terrorist attacks, or mass shootings), childhood abuse and victimization, and sexual violence. Health crises are also linked to the development of PTSD (Swartzman & others, 2017). A recent study showed that as many as 1 in 5 adults diagnosed with cancer developed PTSD symptoms within 4 years (Chan & others, 2017). Different traumas can have different consequences for symptoms, such as survivor guilt, lingering feelings of betrayal and powerlessness, or enduring worries about safety (Badour, Resnick, & Kilpatrick, 2017). What traumatic experiences have in common is their capacity to shatter the basic assumptions of life, including beliefs about the fairness of existence and one's place in the world. Traumatic life experiences challenge a person's capacities to cope. PTSD symptoms can follow a trauma immediately or after months or even years (Hiller & others, 2016; Steenkamp & others, 2017). Most individuals who are exposed to a traumatic event experience some of the symptoms in the days and weeks following exposure (National Center for PTSD, 2014).

One type of traumatic event linked to PTSD that is unfortunately common for American college students is sexual victimization (Dworkin & others, 2017; Rosellini & others, 2017). Such traumas can include rape, sexual assault, or sexual harassment. All three of these behaviors can be perpetrated by men and women, and in opposite sex and same sex situations. Rape refers to forced sexual intercourse including both verbal and physical force. Sexual assault refers to a wider range of behaviors including unwanted sexual contacts by a perpetrator on a victim. Sexual assault may or may not include force and includes actions such as grabbing or fondling. Sexual harassment is unwelcome conduct of a sexual nature that offends, humiliates, or intimidates another person. In the workplace and at school, sexual harassment includes unwanted sexual advances, requests for sexual favors, and other verbal or physical conduct of a sexual nature. In recent years, the commonplace nature of these inappropriate and often illegal behaviors has come to light in high profile cases of individuals using positions of power to force others to engage in sexual acts. Compared to women who have not been victims of a violent crime, women who had experienced sexual victimization are approximately 6 times more likely to develop PTSD (Gilmore & others, 2017; Kilpatrick, 2000).

How can survivors of sexual victimization be helped? In addition to treatment for their psychological disorders, sexual assault survivors benefit from

Prior to deployment, U.S. troops receive stress-management training aimed at helping to prevent PTSD and other disorders that might be triggered by the high-stress conditions of war.
©Brian L Wickliffe/REX/Shutterstock

Sexual Victimization on Campus

Sadly, careful estimates suggest that 1 in 5 women will experience sexual assault during their college years (Muehlenhard & others, 2017). Of course, sexual victimization of any kind is unacceptable in any community, but sexual violence experienced by college women is shocking because it occurs in the context of the college experience itself. Coming to college can be a life-changing experience that prepares a person for a bright future. Unfortunately, for many people college can involve life-changing experiences of another sort entirely.

©tommaso79/Shutterstock

In the U.S., Title IX, a law passed in 1972 to guarantee gender equality in education and opportunities, is the law that motivates efforts to combat sexual misconduct on college and university campuses. Title IX states, in part, "No person in the United States shall, on the basis of sex, be excluded from participation in, be denied the benefits of, or be subjected to discrimination under any education program or activity receiving Federal financial assistance" (U.S. Department of Justice, 2015).

You may be wondering how Title IX, with its focus on discrimination, is relevant to the issue of sexual victimization on campus. Sexual victimization is associated with lower grades, decreased academic motivation, and higher rates of dropping out of college (Baker & others, 2016; Banyard & others, 2017). Equal access to education means access to a safe learning environment where everyone is supported to achieve. This means that institutions of higher learning must do all that they can proactively to prevent sexual victimization, to assist victims of sexual misconduct, and make every effort to ensure that the victimization is not repeated.

Many universities have implemented educational campaigns to raise awareness about the serious problem of sexual misconduct on campus. Involving all members of a learning community, including faculty, staff, and administrators, is crucial to the effectiveness of such interventions (Sales & Krause, 2017). College men have a vital role to play in transforming cultures and intervening in situations that appear ripe for misconduct (Hoxmeier, Acock, & Flay, 2017).

Everyone has a right to obtain an education without concern for sexual victimization. Do you know about sexual assault or harassment prevention and victim resources at your school? If not, right now would be a great time to seek out this information. If you or someone you know has been the victim of rape or sexual assault, call 800.656.HOPE (4673) for the Rape, Abuse, Incest National Network (RAINN), for support, information, and to be connected with resources in your area.

· ·

strong social support (Dworkin, Ullman, & others, 2017). Individuals who have access to information and medical and legal help are better able to cope with this trauma. Unfortunately, too often, victims of sexual assault are unaware of the resources available to them (Holland, Rabelo, & Cortina, 2017). For this reason, many colleges and universities have taken steps to better educate their communities about such services and also about the laws surrounding sexual assault and harassment, and their expectations for appropriate behavior. Indeed, an important way to prevent PTSD is to prevent sexual victimization.

What causes PTSD? Clearly, one factor is the traumatic event itself. However, not every individual exposed to the same event develops PTSD (Whitman & others, 2013). There-fore, other factors must influence a person's vulnerability to the disorder. These include a history of previous traumatic events and conditions, such as abuse and psychological disorders (John, Cisler, & Sigel, 2017; Steine & others, 2017), cultural background (Alford, 2016), and genetic predisposition (Stein, 2017). These preexisting conditions make indi-viduals more vulnerable to PTSD when they are combined with stressful events. Thus, PTSD may be best explained by a vulnerability-stress model.

Traumatic life events can profoundly affect the way a person copes with other life events (John, Cisler, & Sigel, 2017). Traumas can alter the delicate balance of neurotransmitters, hormones, and other biological systems, such that PTSD can color the way the body and brain react to stress (Girgenti & others, 2017; Susann & others, 2017). PTSD is associated with decreased volume in the hippocampus, that brain structure most associated with integrating memories (Nelson & Tumpap, 2017).

Clearly, many aspects of PTSD are linked with memory. A classic symptom of PTSD is intrusive memories and flashbacks, involving the feeling that the traumatic life event is happening in the here and now (Brewin, 2014). The "now-ness" of intrusive memories is thought to occur because, in the midst of trauma, people tend to process experience on a perceptual level. That means that the person is not interpreting or making sense of experience but rather encoding it in a direct way. This quality of perceptual processing is thought to explain why traumatic memories are likely to be cued by environmental stim-uli and also why they are so vivid (Brewin, 2014). In a sense, this means that traumatic memories may retain a "rawness" that is unlike other memories. Given these profound links between PTSD and memory, we might ask whether PTSD relates to everyday mem-ory in important ways. To learn about research addressing this issue, see the Intersection.

Treatments for PTSD include psychotherapies using classical conditioning paradigms to break the links between current experiences and deep feelings of trauma (Beidel & others, 2017) as well as therapies aimed at changing beliefs and behavior (Kredlow & others, 2017). In addition, group therapy with other survivors of similar trauma can be helpful (Levi & others, 2017). Among survivors of sexual assault, self-defense training can be an effective way to reinstate a sense of personal control and efficacy (Penciotti & Orcutt, 2017). Finally, medications are also used to help those with PTSD (Golier, Yehuda, & Baker, 2017) often in conjunction with intense psychotherapy.

Dissociative Disorders

Have you ever been on a long car ride and completely lost track of time, so that you could not even remember a stretch of miles along the road? Have you been so caught up in a daydream that you were unaware of the passage of time? These are examples of normal dissociation. *Dissociation* refers to psychological states in which the person feels discon-nected from immediate experience.

At the extreme of dissociation are individuals who persistently feel a sense of discon-nection. **Dissociative disorders** are psychological disorders that involve a sudden loss of memory or change in identity. Under extreme stress or shock, the individual's conscious awareness becomes dissociated (separated or split) from previous memories and thoughts (Stein & others, 2014). Individuals who develop dissociative disorders may have problems putting together different aspects of consciousness, so that experiences at different levels of awareness might be felt as if they are happening to someone else. In *DSM-5,* dissocia-tive disorders are not included as a trauma-related disorder but are placed in close proxim-ity to these to reflect the level of overlap between disorders like PTSD and dissociative disorders (APA, 2013). Indeed, some individuals with PTSD also experience dissociation from experience (Nijenhuis, 2017).

Psychologists believe that dissociation is a way of dealing with extreme stress (Bailey & Brand, 2017; Ensink & others, 2017; Frewen & Lanius, 2014). Through dissociation,

dissociative disorders
Psychological disorders that involve a sudden loss of memory or change in identity due to the dissociation (sepa-ration) of the individual's conscious awareness from previous memories and thoughts.

Clinical Psychology and Cognitive Psychology: How Does PTSD Affect Autobiographical Memory?

Going about your everyday life, you may have memories pop into your head, even when you are not intentionally trying to recall them. The sight of your dog's picture on your desk may remind you of the last time you snuggled with your best fuzzy pal. Smelling a pizza being delivered next door might remind you of your favorite pizza place back home and the last time you sat down to have a delicious slice. Autobiographical memories can visit us mentally without much effort and for many of us such memories are a source of comfort and identity. They remind us of who we are and who we have always been.

Now, think about autobiographical memory in the context of PTSD. For individuals with PTSD, such memories can be extremely negative and triggered by sounds, sights, and smells that remind the person of traumatic experience. People with PTSD might learn to guard against the unintentional recruitment of autobiographical memories in order to shield themselves from the intrusion of trauma. Such individuals may get into the mental habit of avoiding autobiographical memories. Could such a habit affect autobiographical memories, more generally?

A recent study addressed this question (Schönfeld & Ehlers, 2017). All participants had experienced a serious traumatic event within the last 5 years. One group had been diagnosed with PTSD

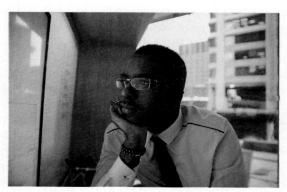
©Hero Images/Media Bakery

and the other group had not. The participants kept a week-long diary of the unintentional autobiographical memories that occurred to them each day. The researchers compared the characteristics of the memories shared by the two groups.

A key finding of this study was that, overall, those with PTSD recorded about half as many unintentional memories compared to those who did not have PTSD. In addition, participants with PTSD recorded fewer memories that were unrelated to the trauma. These results suggest that engaging in the habit of suppressing (or holding back) one's memories may bleed over into other experiences, leaving those with PTSD with impoverished autobiographical experience, in general.

These results demonstrate the powerful bond between PTSD and memory. They show the ways that PTSD can alter memory processes and reshape a person's daily mental life. The steps people take to avoid reminders of a trauma can affect their lives in important ways, draining the "me-ness" that colors ongoing mental life through autobiographical memory.

\\ **Have you ever experienced intrusive memories? What were they like?**

individuals mentally protect their conscious self from the traumatic event. As noted above, dissociative disorders often occur in people who also show signs of PTSD (Choi & others, 2017; Dorahy & van der Hart, 2014). Both psychological disorders are thought to be rooted, in part, in extremely traumatic life events (Elklit, Hyland, & Shevlin, 2014). The notion that dissociative disorders are related to problems in pulling together emotional memories is supported by findings showing lower volume in the hippocampus and amygdala in individuals with dissociative disorders (McDonald & White, 2013; Vermetten & others, 2006). The hippocampus is especially involved in consolidating memory and organizing life experience into a coherent whole (Xu & others, 2014).

Dissociative disorders are perhaps the most controversial of all diagnostic categories, with some psychologists believing that they are often mistakenly diagnosed and others arguing they are underdiagnosed (Freeland & others, 1993; Rydberg, 2017; Sar, Akyuz, & Dogan, 2007). Two kinds of dissociative disorders are dissociative amnesia and dissociative identity disorder.

DISSOCIATIVE AMNESIA Amnesia is the inability to recall important events (Pyszora, Fahy, & Kopelman, 2014). Amnesia can result from a blow to the head that

dissociative amnesia
Dissociative disorder characterized by extreme memory loss that is caused by extensive psychological stress.

produces trauma in the brain. **Dissociative amnesia** is a type of amnesia characterized by extreme memory loss that stems from extensive psychological stress (Bailey & Brand, 2017; Granacher, 2014). People experiencing dissociative amnesia remember everyday tasks like how to hail a cab and use a phone. They forget only aspects of their own identity and autobiographical experiences.

Sometimes individuals suffering from dissociative amnesia will also unexpectedly travel away from home, occasionally even assuming a new identity (Mamarde & others, 2013). For instance, on August 28, 2008, Hannah Upp, a 23-year-old middle school teacher in New York City, disappeared while out for a run (Marx & Didziulis, 2009). She had no wallet, no identification, no cell phone, and no money. Her family, friends, and roommates posted flyers around the city and messages on the Internet. As days went by, they became increasingly concerned that something terrible had happened. Finally, Hannah was found floating face down in the New York harbor on September 16, sunburned and dehydrated but alive. She remembered nothing of her experiences. To her, it felt like she had gone out for a run and 10 minutes later was being pulled from the harbor. To this day, she does not know what event might have led to her dissociative amnesia, nor does she remember how she survived during her two-week disappearance.

At one point during her dissociative amnesia, Hannah was approached by someone who asked if she was the Hannah everyone was looking for, and she answered no.

Dissociative amnesia is believed to be caused by extremely stressful events. Treatment for this disorder is likely to involve psychotherapy that provides the person an opportunity to process their traumatic memories in safe context.

DISSOCIATIVE IDENTITY DISORDER

Dissociative identity disorder (DID), formerly called *multiple personality disorder,* is the most dramatic, least common, and most controversial dissociative disorder. Individuals with this disorder have two or more distinct personalities or identities (Brand, Lowenstein, & Spiegel, 2014). Each identity has its own memories, behaviors, and relationships. One identity dominates at one time, another takes over at another time. Individuals sometimes report that a wall of amnesia separates their different identities (Morton, 2017) however, research suggests that memory does transfer across these identities, even if the person believes it does not (Huntjens & others, 2014; Kong, Allen, & Glisky, 2008). The shift between identities usually occurs under distress (Sar, Akyuz, & Dogan, 2007) but sometimes can also be controlled by the person (Kong, Allen, & Glisky, 2008).

dissociative identity disorder (DID)
Formerly called multiple personality disorder, a dissociative disorder in which the individual has two or more distinct personalities or selves, each with its own memories, behaviors, and relationships.

A famous real-life example of dissociative identity disorder is the "three faces of Eve" case, based on the life of a woman named Chris Sizemore (Thigpen & Cleckley, 1957) (Figure 2). Eve White was the original dominant personality. She had no knowledge of her second personality, Eve Black, although Eve Black had been alternating with Eve White for a number of years. Eve White was bland, quiet, and serious. By contrast, Eve Black was carefree, mischievous, and uninhibited. Eve Black would emerge at the most inappropriate times, leaving Eve White with hangovers, bills, and a reputation in local bars that she could not explain. During treatment, a third personality emerged: Jane. More mature than the other two, Jane seems to have developed as a result of therapy.

The factors that contribute to DID remain something of a mystery. Research links a high rate of extraordinarily severe

FIGURE 2 **The Three Faces of Eve** Chris Sizemore, the subject of the 1950s book and film *The Three Faces of Eve,* is shown here with a work she painted, titled *Three Faces in One.*
©Gerald Martineau/Getty Images

sexual or physical abuse during early childhood to the condition (Cook & others, 2017; Ross & Ness, 2010). Some psychologists believe that a child can cope with intense trauma by dissociating from the experience and developing other alternate selves as protectors. Sexual abuse has occurred in as many as 70 percent or more of DID cases (Foote & others, 2006); however, the majority of individuals who have been sexually abused do not develop DID. The vast majority of individuals with DID are women. A genetic predisposition might also exist, as the disorder tends to run in families (Dell & Eisenhower, 1990).

Until the 1980s, only about 300 cases of dissociative identity disorder had ever been reported (Suinn, 1984). In the past 30 years, hundreds more cases have been diagnosed (Dorahy & others, 2014). Social cognitive approaches point out that diagnoses have tended to increase whenever the popular media present a case, as in the miniseries *Sybil* and the Showtime drama *United States of Tara*. From this perspective, individuals develop multiple identities through social contagion. After exposure to these examples, people may be more likely to view multiple identities as a real condition. Some experts believe, in fact, that dissociative identity disorder is a *social construction*—that it represents a category some people adopt to make sense of their experiences (Spanos, 1996). Rather than being a single person with many conflicting feelings, wishes, and potentially awful experiences, the individual compartmentalizes different aspects of the self into independent identities. In some cases, therapists have been accused of creating alternate personalities. Encountering an individual who appears to have a fragmented sense of self, the therapist may begin to treat each fragment as its own "personality" (Spiegel, 2006).

Cross-cultural comparisons can shed light on whether dissociative identity disorder is primarily a response to traumatic events or the result of a social cognitive factor like social contagion. If dissociation is a response to trauma, individuals with similar levels of traumatic experience should show similar degrees of dissociation, regardless of their exposure to cultural messages about dissociation. In China, the popular media *do not* commonly portray individuals with dissociative disorder, and professional knowledge of the disorder is rare. One study comparing individuals from China and Canada (where dissociative identity disorder is a widely publicized condition) found reports of traumatic experience to be similar across groups and to relate to dissociative experiences similarly as well (Ross & others, 2008), casting some doubt on the notion that dissociative experiences are entirely a product of social contagion.

*Therapists and patients are making **attributions** to understand abnormal behavior.*

Because they are rare, research documenting the effectiveness of treatments for dissociative disorders is limited. A recent study showed that long-term, in-depth, intensive psychotherapy led to improvement in functioning (Myrick & others, 2017). A key concern is that therapists remain objective in treatment and do not evoke multiple identities in the patient.

self-quiz

1. Dissociative identity disorder is associated with unusually high rates of
   A. anxiety.
   B. abuse during early childhood.
   C. depression.
   D. divorce.

2. Which of the following is true for post-traumatic stress disorder?
   A. It always occurs immediately after a trauma.
   B. It typically affects only people who have been in combat.
   C. It is associated with intrusive memories and flashbacks.
   D. It is not possible to treat PTSD.

3. The vulnerability-stress approach helps to account for which of the following?
   A. Among survivors of a mass shooting, only some will develop PTSD.
   B. Individuals with dissociative identity disorder have often heard of others with the disorder.
   C. People in a support group all share symptoms of PTSD.
   D. Dissociative identity disorder is quite uncommon.

APPLY IT! 4. Eddie often loses track of time. He is sometimes late for appointments because he is so engrossed in whatever he is doing. While working on a term paper in the library, he gets so caught up in what he is reading that he is shocked when he looks up and sees that the sun has set and it is night. Which of the following best describes Eddie?
   A. Eddie is showing signs of dissociative identity disorder.
   B. Eddie is showing signs of dissociative memory disorder.
   C. Eddie is showing normal dissociative states.
   D. Eddie is at risk for dissociative amnesia.

5 Disorders Involving Emotion and Mood

Our emotions and moods tell us how we are doing in life. We feel good or bad depending on our progress on important goals, the quality of our relationships, and so on. For some individuals, however, the link between life experiences and emotions is off-kilter. They may feel sad for no reason or a sense of elation in the absence of any great accomplishment. Several psychological disorders involve this kind of dysregulation in a person's emotional life. In this section we examine two such disorders—depressive disorders and bipolar disorders.

Depressive Disorders

depressive disorders
Mood disorders in which the individual suffers from depression—an unrelenting lack of pleasure in life.

Everyone feels blue sometimes. A romantic breakup, the death of a loved one, or a personal failure can cast a dark cloud over life. Sometimes, however, a person might feel unhappy and not know why. **Depressive disorders** are disorders in which the individual suffers from *depression,* an unrelenting lack of pleasure in life. Depressive disorders are common. In 2015, a representative U.S. survey of over 68,000 individuals aged 12 and up found that 6.7 percent of adults and 12.5 percent of adolescents reported at least one depressive episode (that is, depressed mood that interfered with daily living) in the last year (Center for Behavioral Health Statistics and Quality, 2016). Depression often occurs in the context of chronic physical illnesses, such as diabetes, heart disease, or multiple sclerosis (Boeschoten & others, 2017; Rossom & others, 2017).

A variety of cultures recognize depression, and studies have shown that across cultures depression is characterized as involving an absence of joy, low energy, and high levels of sadness (Chang & others, 2017; Chen & others, 2017). Culture may influence the ways individuals describe their experience. For instance, people from Eastern cultures may be less likely to talk about their emotional states, and more likely to describe depressive symptoms in terms of bodily feelings and symptoms, than those from Western cultures (Draguns & Tanaka-Matsumi, 2003). Many successful individuals have been diagnosed with depression. They include musicians Sheryl Crow and Eric Clapton, actors Drew Barrymore, Halle Berry, and Jim Carrey, artist Pablo Picasso, astronaut Buzz Aldrin (the second moon walker), and J. K. Rowling, the author of the *Harry Potter* series.

This painting by Vincent Van Gogh, Portrait of Dr. Gachet, *reflects the extreme melancholy that characterizes the depressive disorders.*
©Art Reserve/Alamy Stock Photo

Major depressive disorder (MDD) involves a significant depressive episode and depressed characteristics, such as lethargy and hopelessness, for at least two weeks. MDD impairs daily functioning, and the National Institute of Mental Health (NIMH) has called it the leading cause of disability in the United States (NIMH, 2016). The symptoms of major depressive disorder may include

major depressive disorder (MDD)
Psychological disorder involving a major depressive episode and depressed characteristics, such as lethargy and hopelessness, for at least two weeks.

- Depressed mood most of the day.
- Reduced interest or pleasure in activities that were once enjoyable.
- Significant weight loss or gain or significant decrease or interest in appetite.
- Trouble sleeping or sleeping too much.
- Fatigue or loss of energy.
- Feeling worthless or guilty in an excessive or inappropriate manner.
- Problems in thinking, concentrating, or making decisions.
- Recurrent thoughts of death and suicide.
- No history of manic episodes (periods of euphoric mood).

Individuals who experience less extreme depressive mood for more than two months may be diagnosed with *persistent depressive disorder.* This disorder includes symptoms such as hopelessness, lack of energy, poor concentration, and sleep problems.

What are the causes of depressive disorders? A variety of biological, psychological, and sociocultural factors have been implicated in their development.

BIOLOGICAL FACTORS   The biological factors implicated in depressive disorders include genes, brain structure and function, and neurotransmitters. Genes may predispose a person to depression but their influence is likely affected by experience (Strachan & others, 2017). That means that genetic characteristics can make a person vulnerable to develop depression. For instance, depression has been linked to particular features of the serotonin transporter gene (Iscan & others, 2017) but these features do not lead directly to depression. Rather, they are associated with depression only if the person's social environment was stressful (Ignácio & others, 2014). In fact, individuals who possess these genetic features are at a *decreased* risk for depression if they experience a warm, positive social environment (Eley & others, 2004).

In addition, specific brain structures are involved in depression. For example, depressed individuals show lower levels of brain activity in a section of the prefrontal cortex that is involved in generating actions (Duman & others, 2012; Ghosal, Hare, & Duman, 2017) and in regions of the brain associated with the perception of rewards in the environment (Gaffrey & others, 2018; Howland, 2012). A depressed person's brain may not recognize opportunities for pleasurable experiences. In addition, brain imaging research shows that when faced with negative stimuli, people with depression are less likely to spontaneously activate those areas of the brain that serve to regulate emotion (Radke & others, 2017). Depression also likely involves problems in neurotransmitter regulation. Individuals with depressive disorder appear to have too few receptors for the neurotransmitters serotonin and norepinephrine (Hamon & Blier, 2013; Rolls, 2017; Kraus & others, 2017).

PSYCHOLOGICAL FACTORS   Psychological explanations of depression draw on behavioral learning theories and cognitive theories. One behavioral view of depression focuses on *learned helplessness,* which involves an individual's feelings of powerlessness after exposure to aversive circumstances over which the person has no control. One theory is that learned helplessness can lead people to become depressed (Seligman, 1975). Learned helplessness interferes with learning and disrupts motivation (Reznik & others, 2017). When individuals cannot control important outcomes in their lives and have no way to avoid negative experiences, they eventually feel helpless and stop trying to change their situations. This helplessness spirals into hopelessness (Haeffel & others, 2017).

Cognitive explanations of depression focus on the thoughts and beliefs that contribute to this sense of hopelessness (Alloy & others, 2017; Beck & Haigh, 2014). Psychiatrist Aaron Beck (1967) proposed that negative thoughts reflect self-defeating beliefs that shape depressed individuals' experiences. These habitual negative thoughts magnify and expand depressed persons' negative experiences (Lam, 2012). For example, a depressed individual might overgeneralize about a minor occurrence—say, turning in a work assignment late—and think that he or she is worthless. A depressed person might view a minor setback such as getting a *D* on a paper as the end of the world. The accumulation of such cognitive distortions can lead to depression (Fazakas-DeHoog, Rnic, & Dozois, 2017; Kiosses & others, 2017).

The way people think can also influence the course of depression. Depressed individuals may ruminate on negative experiences and negative feelings, playing them over and over again in their minds (Klemanksi & others, 2017). This tendency to ruminate is associated with the development of depression as well as other psychological problems such as binge eating and substance abuse (McLaughlin & others, 2014; Tait & others, 2014). In addition, the relationship between rumination and depression may run both ways, as depression can spur a person to adopt a ruminative mindset (Krause & others, 2017).

Another cognitive view of depression focuses on people's attributions—their attempts to explain what caused something to happen (Moore & others, 2016; Rueger

& George, 2017). Depression is thought to be related to a *pessimistic* attributional style. In this style, individuals regularly explain negative events as having internal causes ("It is my fault I failed the exam"), stable causes ("I'm going to fail again and again"), and global causes ("Failing this exam shows that I won't do well in any of my courses"). Pessimistic attributional style means blaming oneself for negative events and expecting the negative events to recur (Abramson, Seligman, & Teasdale, 1978). This pessimistic style can be contrasted with an *optimistic* attributional style, which is essentially its opposite. Optimists make external attributions for bad things that happen ("I did badly on the test because it's hard to know what a professor wants on the first exam"). They also recognize that these causes can change ("I'll do better on the next one") and that they are specific ("It was only one test"). Optimistic attributional style has been related to lowered depression and decreased suicide risk in a variety of samples (Horwitz & others, 2017; Rasmussen & Wingate, 2011; Tindle & others, 2012).

SOCIOCULTURAL FACTORS

Individuals with a low socioeconomic status (SES), especially people living in poverty, are more likely to develop depression than their higher-SES counterparts (Joshi & others, 2017; Wittayanukorn, Qian, & Hansen, 2014). A longitudinal study of adults revealed that depression increased as one's standard of living and employment circumstances worsened (Lorant & others, 2007). Studies have found very high rates of depression in Native American groups, among whom poverty, hopelessness, and alcoholism are widespread (Kisely & others, 2017).

Women are nearly twice as likely as men to develop depression (Hodes & others, 2017; Salk, Hyde, & Abramson, 2017). As Figure 3 shows, this gender difference occurs in many countries (Inaba & others, 2005). It also occurs across many different age groups (Salk, Hyde, & Abramson, 2017). Potential explanations

Another gender difference to consider: Why might men show lower levels of depression than women?

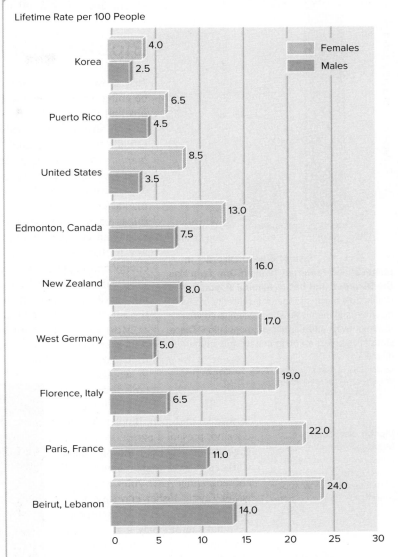

Lifetime Rate per 100 People

FIGURE 3 **Gender Differences in Depression Across Cultures** This graph shows the rates of depression for men and women in nine cultures (Weissman & Olfson, 1995).

SOURCE: Weissman and Olfson, Science 269(779), 1995. *American Association for the Advancement of Science.*

> **Which cultures have the highest and lowest rates of depression? What might account for these differences?** > **Which cultures have the largest gender difference in depression? What might account for these differences?** > **In order to be diagnosed with depression, a person has to seek treatment for the disorder. How might gender and culture influence a person's willingness to get treatment?**

There are numerous effective treatments for depression. These include a variety of psychotherapies that target different aspects of the disorder, including reducing self-defeating beliefs and automatic thoughts, reducing distress, and helping to improve emotion regulation. In addition, medications, especially those aimed at regulating serotonin and norepinephrine are commonly used to treat depression.

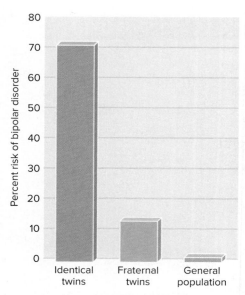

FIGURE 4 **Risk of Bipolar Disorder in Identical and Fraternal Twins if One Twin Has the Disorder, and in the General Population** Notice how much stronger the similarity of bipolar disorder is in identical twins as compared with fraternal twins and the general population. These statistics suggest a strong genetic role in the disorder.

SOURCE: *Annual Review of Neuroscience*, 20, 1997. Annual Reviews. www.annualreviews.org

bipolar disorder
Mood disorder characterized by extreme mood swings that include one or more episodes of mania, an overexcited, unrealistically optimistic state.

of this difference range from differences in biological systems to social structural differences in the treatment of men and women (Hodes & others, 2017; Salk & others, 2016).

Bipolar Disorder

Just as we all have down times, there are times when things seem to be going phenomenally well. For individuals with bipolar disorder, the ups and downs of life take on an extreme and often harmful tone. **Bipolar disorder** is a disorder characterized by extreme mood swings that include one or more episodes of *mania,* an overexcited, unrealistically optimistic state. A manic episode is like the flipside of a depressive episode. The person who experiences mania feels on top of the world. Imagine all the things you might do if you were filled with excitement and confidence, even if those feelings were not rooted in reality. A person has tremendous energy and might sleep very little. You might do many things that you should not. A manic state features an impulsivity that can get the individual in trouble. For example, the sufferer might spend his life savings on a foolish business venture.

Most individuals with bipolar disorder experience multiple cycles of depression interspersed with mania, usually separated by six months to a year. Unlike depressive disorders, which are more likely to occur in women, bipolar disorder is equally common in women and men. Bipolar disorder does not prevent a person from being successful. Award-winning actor Catherine Zeta-Jones, dancer and choreographer Alvin Ailey, and actor-writer Carrie Fisher (Princess Leia) were diagnosed with bipolar disorder.

What factors play a role in the development of bipolar disorder? Genetic influences are stronger predictors of bipolar disorder than of depressive disorders (Charney & others, 2017; Kaminsky & others, 2014). An individual with an identical twin who has bipolar disorder has a 70 percent probability of also having the disorder, and a fraternal twin has a more than 10 percent probability (Figure 4). Researchers continue to explore the specific genetic location of bipolar disorder (McCarthy & others, 2014; Nurnberger & others, 2014).

Other biological processes are also a factor. Like depression, bipolar disorder is associated with differences in brain activity. Figure 5

*There are 2 types of bipolar disorder. In **bipolar I disorder**, people have very extreme manic episodes and may even hallucinate, seeing or hearing things that are not there. **Bipolar II disorder** is less severe, involving a less extreme level of euphoria.*

FIGURE 5 **Brain Metabolism in Mania and Depression** PET scans of an individual with bipolar disorder, who is described as a rapid cycler because of how quickly severe mood changes occurred. (*top and bottom*) The person's brain in a depressed state. (*middle*) A manic state. The PET scans reveal how the brain's energy consumption falls in depression and rises in mania. The red areas in the middle row reflect rapid consumption of glucose.
Courtesy Drs. Lewis Baxter and Michael Phelps, UCLA School of Medicine

shows the metabolic activity in the cerebral cortex of an individual cycling through depressive and manic phases. Notice the decrease in metabolic activity in the brain during depression and the increase in metabolic activity during mania (Baxter & others, 1985). In addition to high levels of norepinephrine and low levels of serotonin, studies link high levels of the neurotransmitter glutamate to bipolar disorder (Kubo & others, 2017; Singh & others, 2010; Sourial-Bassillious & others, 2009).

Bipolar disorder is typically treated with the medication lithium. Lithium is thought to stabilize mood but the precise way that it does so is not fully understood (Miller & others, 2017). Lithium may be combined with other medications to treat depression and other symptoms. In addition, individuals with bipolar can benefit from psychotherapy (Sylvia & others, 2017). Research continues to examine the optimal match between persons and treatments to most effectively relieve the suffering of those with bipolar disorder.

Psychologists and psychiatrists have noted cases of children who appear to suffer from bipolar disorder (Goldstein & others, 2017). A key dilemma in such cases is that treating bipolar disorder in adults involves administering drugs, like lithium, that have not been approved for children's use. The side effects of these drugs could put children's health and development at risk. To address this issue, the *DSM-5* includes a new diagnosis, *disruptive mood dysregulation disorder,* which is considered a depressive disorder in children who show persistent irritability and recurrent episodes of out-of-control behavior (APA, 2013). This decision is not without controversy. As we saw with ADHD, some children who are perceived to be prone to wild mood swings may be simply behaving like children. In addition, it is notable that cases of suspected bipolar disorder in children are far more common in the U.S. than in Europe or Canada (Post & others, 2017).

self-quiz

1. To be diagnosed with bipolar disorder, an individual must experience
   A. a manic episode.
   B. a depressive episode.
   C. a psychotic break.
   D. a suicidal episode.

2. All of the following are a symptom of major depressive disorder except
   A. fatigue.
   B. weight change.
   C. thoughts of death.
   D. periods of euphoria and very high energy.

3. A true statement about genes and depression is that genes
   A. directly cause depression. If you have a particular genetic characteristic you will certainly develop depression.
   B. may produce a vulnerability to depression, meaning that if you have a particular genetic characteristic you might be at risk for depression, depending on your experience.
   C. are unrelated to depression.
   D. are the most important factor in determining whether someone develops depression.

APPLY IT! 4. During his first two college years, Barry has felt "down" most of the time. He has had trouble concentrating and difficulty making decisions. Sometimes he is so overwhelmed with deciding on his major and struggling to focus that he feels hopeless. He has problems with loss of appetite and sleeps a great deal of the time, and in general his energy level is low. Barry has found that things he used to love, like watching sports and playing video games, are just no fun anymore. Which of the following is most likely to be true of Barry?
   A. Barry has an anxiety disorder.
   B. Barry is entering the depressive phase of bipolar disorder.
   C. Barry is likely experiencing depression.
   D. Barry is experiencing the everyday blues that everyone gets from time to time.

6 Eating Disorders

For some people, concerns about weight and body image become a serious, debilitating disorder (Schiff, 2015). For such individuals, the very act of eating is an arena where a variety of complex biological, psychological, and cultural issues are played out, often with tragic consequences.

A number of famous people have coped with eating disorders, including Ashley Judd, Paula Abdul, Mary-Kate Olsen, and Kelly Clarkson. Eating disorders are characterized by extreme disturbances in eating behavior—from eating very, very little to eating a great deal. In this section we examine three eating disorders—anorexia nervosa, bulimia nervosa, and binge-eating disorder.

Disorders of eating can vary across cultures. In Fiji, a disorder known as **macake** involves poor appetite and refusing to eat. Very high levels of social concern meet this refusal, and individuals with macake are strongly motivated to start eating and enjoying food again.

Anorexia Nervosa

Anorexia nervosa is an eating disorder that involves the relentless pursuit of thinness through starvation. Anorexia nervosa is much more common in girls and women than boys and men and affects between 0.5 and 3.7 percent of young women (NIMH, 2016b). The American Psychiatric Association (2013) lists these main characteristics of anorexia nervosa:

- Significantly low body weight compared to what is considered normal for age and height, and refusal to maintain weight at a healthy level.
- An intense fear of gaining weight that does not decrease with weight loss.
- A distorted body image (Stewart & others, 2012). Even when individuals with anorexia nervosa are extremely thin, they never think they are thin enough.

Over time, anorexia nervosa can lead to physical changes, such as the growth of fine hair all over the body, thinning of bones and hair, severe constipation, and low blood pressure (NIMH, 2016b). Dangerous and even life-threatening complications include damage to the heart and thyroid. Anorexia nervosa is said to have the highest mortality rate (about 5.6 percent of individuals with anorexia nervosa die within 10 years of diagnosis) of any psychological disorder (Hoek, 2006; NIMH, 2016b).

Anorexia nervosa typically begins in the teenage years, often following an episode of dieting and some type of life stress (Fitzpatrick, 2012; Solmi & others, 2015). Most individuals with anorexia nervosa are non-Latina White female adolescents or young adults from well-educated middle- and upper-income families (Darcy, 2012; Dodge, 2012). They are often high-achieving perfectionists (Forbush, Heatherton, & Keel, 2007). Obsessive thinking about weight and compulsive exercise are also related to anorexia nervosa (Hildebrandt & others, 2012). Individuals with anorexia nervosa seem to be very controlled in what they are doing. Yet, the disorder itself is a type of impulsivity: It involves engaging in very risky behaviors (Lavender & others, 2017).

Individuals with anorexia nervosa may lack personal distress over their symptoms. Recall that personal distress over one's behavior is just one aspect of the definition of abnormal.

Pop singer Demi Lovato has been open about her struggles with disordered eating. She has shared that many women her in family struggled with bulimia nervosa and anorexia. Lovato has been public about her own experiences in the hopes of raising awareness that recovery from eating disorders is possible.
©Kristina Bumphrey/StarPix/REX/Shutterstock

Bulimia Nervosa

Bulimia nervosa is an eating disorder in which an individual (typically female) consistently follows a binge-and-purge eating pattern. The individual goes on an eating binge and then purges by self-induced vomiting or the use of laxatives. Most people with bulimia nervosa are preoccupied with food, have a strong fear of becoming overweight, and are depressed or anxious (Cuzzolaro, 2014). One recent study found that bulimics have difficulty controlling their emotions (Lavender & others, 2014). Because bulimia nervosa occurs within a normal weight range, the disorder is often difficult to detect. A person with bulimia nervosa usually keeps the disorder a secret and experiences a great deal of self-disgust and shame.

Dentists and dental hygienists are sometimes the first to recognize the signs of bulimia nervosa.

Bulimia nervosa can lead to complications such as a chronic sore throat, kidney problems, dehydration, and gastrointestinal disorders (NIMH, 2014b). The disorder is also related to dental problems, as persistent exposure to the stomach acids in vomit can wear away tooth enamel.

Bulimia nervosa typically begins in late adolescence or early adulthood (Levine, 2002). The disorder affects between 1 and 4 percent of

©Corbis/VCG/Getty Images

young women (NIMH, 2016b). Like those with anorexia nervosa, many young women who develop bulimia nervosa are highly perfectionistic (Lampard & others, 2012). At the same time, they tend to have low levels of self-efficacy (Sysko & others, 2017). In other words, these are young women with very high standards but very low confidence that they can achieve their goals. Impulsivity, negative emotion, and obsessive-compulsive disorder are also related to bulimia (Roncero, Perpina, & Garcia-Soriano, 2011). Bulimia nervosa is associated, too, with a high incidence of sexual and physical abuse in childhood (Lo Sauro & others, 2008). Finally, brain imaging research suggests that women with bulimia nervosa may use binge eating as a way to distract themselves from negative feelings (Collins & others, 2017).

Although much more common in women, bulimia can also affect men. Elton John has described his struggles with this eating disorder.

Anorexia Nervosa and Bulimia Nervosa: Causes and Treatments

What is the etiology (cause) of anorexia nervosa and bulimia nervosa? For many years researchers thought that sociocultural factors, such as media images of very thin women and family pressures, were the central determinants of these disorders (Le Grange & others, 2010). Media images that glorify extreme thinness can indeed influence women's body image, and emphasis on the thin ideal is related to anorexia nervosa and bulimia nervosa (Benowitz-Fredericks & others, 2012). Media images can affect women's concerns about eating (White & others, 2016). However, as powerful as these media messages might be, countless females are exposed to media images of unrealistically thin women, but relatively few develop eating disorders. Many young women embark on diets, but comparatively few of them develop eating disorders.

Eating disorders occur in cultures that do not emphasize the ideal of thinness, although the disorders may differ from Western descriptions. For instance, in Eastern cultures, individuals can show the symptoms of anorexia nervosa, but they lack the fear of getting fat that is common in North Americans with the disorder (Pike, Yamamiya, & Konishi, 2011).

Contemporary researchers have increasingly probed the potential biological underpinnings of these disorders, examining in particular the interplay of social and biological factors. Genes play a substantial role in both anorexia nervosa and bulimia nervosa (Cuesto & others, 2017; Duncan & others, 2017). Indeed, genes influence many psychological characteristics (for example, perfectionism, impulsivity, obsessive-compulsive tendencies, and thinness drive) and behaviors (restrained eating, binge eating, self-induced vomiting) that are associated with anorexia nervosa and bulimia nervosa (Laplana & others, 2014; Tang & others, 2014). These genes are also factors in the regulation of serotonin, and problems in regulating serotonin are related to both anorexia nervosa and bulimia nervosa (Rozenblat & others, 2017).

Even as biological factors play a role in the emergence of eating disorders, eating disorders themselves affect the body, including the brain. While social factors and experiences may play a role in triggering dieting, the physical effects of dieting, bingeing, and purging may change the neural networks that then sustain the disordered pattern, in a kind of vicious cycle (Fuglset & others, 2014; Kaye & others, 2013).

Although anorexia and bulimia nervosa are serious disorders, recovery is possible (Fitzpatrick, 2012; Kuipers & others, 2017). Anorexia nervosa may require hospitalization. The first target of intervention is promoting weight gain, in extreme cases using a feeding tube. A common obstacle in the treatment of anorexia nervosa is that individuals with the disorder deny that anything is wrong. They maintain their belief that thinness and restrictive dieting are correct and not a sign of mental illness (Wilson, Grilo, & Vitousek, 2007). Still, drug therapies and psychotherapy (especially cognitive therapy and family therapy) have been shown to be effective in treating anorexia nervosa, as well as bulimia nervosa (Andries & others, 2014; Bailey & others, 2014; Ciao & others, 2015).

Binge-Eating Disorder

Binge-eating disorder (BED) is characterized by recurrent episodes of consuming large amounts of food during which the person feels a lack of control over eating (APA, 2013). Unlike an individual with bulimia nervosa, someone with BED does not try to purge. Most individuals with BED are overweight or obese (Carrard, Van der Linden, & Golay, 2012).

Individuals with BED often eat quickly, eat a great deal when they are not hungry, and eat until they are uncomfortably full. They frequently eat alone because of embarrassment or guilt, and they feel ashamed and disgusted with themselves after overeating. BED is the most common of all eating disorders—affecting men, women, and ethnic groups within the United States more similarly than anorexia nervosa or bulimia nervosa (Azarbad & others, 2010). An estimated 2 to 5 percent of Americans will suffer from BED in their lifetime (Brownley & others, 2017; NIMH, 2016b).

BED is thought to characterize approximately 8 percent of individuals who are obese. Unlike obese individuals who do not suffer from BED, binge eaters are more likely to place great value on their physical appearance, weight, and body shape (Grilo, Masheb, & White, 2010). The complications of BED are those of obesity more generally, including diabetes, hypertension, and cardiovascular disease.

Binge-Eating Disorder: Causes and Treatments

Researchers are examining the role of biological and psychological factors in BED. Genes play a role (Cuesto & others, 2017) as does dopamine, the neurotransmitter related to reward pathways in the brain (Heal & others, 2017). The fact that binge eating often occurs after stressful events suggests that binge eaters use food to regulate their emotions (Weinbach, Sher, & Bohon, 2018). The areas of the brain and endocrine system that respond to stress are overactive in individuals with BED (Cuesto & others, 2017; Lo Sauro & others, 2008), and this overactivity leads to high levels of circulating cortisol, the hormone most associated with stress. Individuals with BED may be more likely to perceive events as stressful and then seek to manage that stress by binge eating.

Little research has examined the sociocultural factors in BED. One study showed that Mexicans who immigrated to the United States and Mexican Americans were more likely to develop BED than were Mexicans who lived in Mexico, controlling for a variety of factors (Swanson & others, 2012).

Just as treatment for anorexia nervosa first focuses on weight gain, some believe that treatment for BED should first target weight loss (DeAngelis, 2002). Others argue that individuals with BED must be treated for disordered eating per se, and they insist that if the underlying psychological issues are not addressed, weight loss will not be successful or permanent (Hay & others, 2009). Treatments for BED include psychotherapies that address beliefs and cognitions and emotion regulation as well as medications that regulate mood and assist in weight loss (Brownley & others, 2017).

Unlike individuals with anorexia nervosa or bulimia nervosa, most people with binge-eating disorder are overweight or obese.
©Digital Vision/Photodisc/Getty Images

1. The main characteristics of anorexia nervosa include all of the following except
   A. absence of menstrual periods after puberty.
   B. distorted image of one's body.
   C. strong fears of weight gain even as weight loss occurs.
   D. intense and persistent tremors.

2. A person with bulimia nervosa typically
   A. thinks a lot about food.
   B. is considerably underweight.
   C. is a male.
   D. is not overly concerned about gaining weight.

3. The most common of all eating disorders is

A. bulimia nervosa.
B. anorexia nervosa.
C. binge-eating disorder.
D. gastrointestinal disease.

APPLY IT! 4. Nancy is a first-year straight-*A* premed major. Nancy's roommate Luci notices that Nancy has lost a great deal of weight and is extremely thin. Luci observes that Nancy works out a lot, rarely finishes meals, and wears bulky sweaters all the time. Luci also notices that Nancy's arms have fine hairs growing on them, and Nancy has mentioned never getting her period anymore. When Luci asks Nancy about her weight loss, Nancy replies that she is very concerned that she not gain the "freshman 15" and is feeling good about

her ability to keep up with her work and keep off those extra pounds. Which of the following is the most likely explanation for what is going on with Nancy?
   A. Nancy likely has bulimia nervosa.
   B. Despite her lack of personal distress about her symptoms, Nancy likely has anorexia nervosa.
   C. Nancy has binge-eating disorder.
   D. Given Nancy's overall success, it seems unlikely that she is suffering from a psychological disorder.

7 Schizophrenia

schizophrenia
Severe psychological disorder characterized by highly disordered thought processes; individuals suffering from schizophrenia may be referred to as psychotic because they are so far removed from reality.

psychosis
A state in which a person's perceptions and thoughts are fundamentally removed from reality.

Schizophrenia is a severe psychological disorder that is characterized by highly disordered thought processes. These disordered thoughts are referred to as *psychotic*. **Psychosis** refers to a severely impaired psychological condition in which a person's thoughts and emotions are divorced from reality. The world of the person with schizophrenia is deeply frightening and chaotic.

Schizophrenia is usually diagnosed in early adulthood, around age 18 for men and 25 for women. Individuals with schizophrenia may see things that are not there, hear voices inside their heads, and live in a strange world of twisted logic. They may say odd things, show inappropriate emotion, and move their bodies in peculiar ways. Often, they are socially withdrawn and isolated.

It is difficult to imagine the ordeal of people living with schizophrenia, who constitute about half of the patients in psychiatric hospitals. Although schizophrenia is less common than disorders like depression, those with schizophrenia are more likely to require hospitalization. The suicide risk for individuals with schizophrenia is eight times that for the general population (Roy & Pompili, 2016; Pompili & others, 2007). For many with the disorder, controlling it means using powerful medications to combat symptoms. The most common cause of relapse is that individuals stop taking their medication. They might do so because they feel better and believe they no longer need the drugs, they do not realize that their thoughts are disordered, or the side effects of the medications are too unpleasant.

Seeking treatment for schizophrenia takes courage. It requires that individuals accept that their perception of the world—their very sense of reality—is mistaken.

Symptoms of Schizophrenia

Psychologists generally classify the symptoms of schizophrenia as positive symptoms, negative symptoms, and cognitive deficits.

POSITIVE SYMPTOMS The positive symptoms of schizophrenia are marked by a distortion or an excess of normal function. They are "positive" because they reflect something added above and beyond normal behavior. Positive symptoms of schizophrenia include hallucinations, delusions, thought disorders, and disorders of movement.

Hallucinations are sensory experiences that occur in the absence of real stimuli. Hallucinations are usually auditory—the person might complain of hearing voices—or visual,

hallucinations
Sensory experiences that occur in the absence of real stimuli.

and much less commonly they can be experienced as smells or tastes (Bhatia & others, 2009; Galderisi & others, 2014). Culture affects the form hallucinations take, as well as their content and sensory modality—that is, whether the hallucinations are visual, auditory, or manifest as smells or tastes (Bauer & others, 2011). Visual hallucinations involve seeing things that are not there, as in the case of Moe Armstrong. At the age of 21, while serving in Vietnam as a Marine medical corpsman, Armstrong experienced a psychotic break. Dead Vietcong soldiers appeared to talk to him and beg him for help and did not seem to realize that they were dead. Armstrong, now a successful businessman and a sought-after public speaker who holds two master's degrees, relies on medication to keep such experiences at bay (Bonfatti, 2005).

delusions
False, unusual, and sometimes magical beliefs that are not part of an individual's culture.

Delusions are false, unusual, and sometimes magical beliefs that are not part of an individual's culture. A delusional person might think that he is Jesus Christ or Muhammad; another might imagine that her thoughts are being broadcast over the radio. It is crucial to distinguish delusions from cultural ideas such as the religious belief that a person can have divine visions or communicate personally with a deity. Generally, psychology and psychiatry do not treat these ideas as delusional.

For individuals with schizophrenia, delusional beliefs that might seem completely illogical to the outsider are experienced as all too real. At one point in his life, Bill Garrett, a college student diagnosed with schizophrenia, was convinced that a blister on his hand was a sign of gangrene. So strong was his belief that he tried to cut off his hand with a knife, before being stopped by his family (Park, 2009).

Thought disorder refers to the unusual, sometimes bizarre thought processes that are characteristic positive symptoms of schizophrenia (Morgan & others, 2017). The thoughts of persons with schizophrenia can be disorganized and confused. Often individuals with schizophrenia do not make sense when they talk or write. For example, someone with schizophrenia might say, "Well, Rocky, babe, happening, but where, when, up, top, side, over, you know, out of the way, that's it. Sign off." These incoherent, loose word associations, called *word salad,* have no meaning for the listener. The individual might also make up new words (called *neologisms,* Orlov & others, 2017). In addition, a person with schizophrenia can show **referential thinking,** which means giving personal meaning to completely random events (So & others, 2017). For instance, the individual might believe that a traffic light has turned red because he or she is in a hurry.

referential thinking
Ascribing personal meaning to completely random events.

catatonia
State of immobility and unresponsiveness, lasting for long periods of time.

A final type of positive symptom is *disorders of movement.* A person with schizophrenia may show unusual mannerisms, body movements, and facial expressions. The individual may repeat certain motions over and over or, in extreme cases, may become catatonic. **Catatonia** is a state of immobility and unresponsiveness that lasts for long periods of time. Although these symptoms of schizophrenia may lead others to perceive these individuals as strange, individuals with this disorder can lead creative lives (Figure 6).

NEGATIVE SYMPTOMS

Schizophrenia's positive symptoms are characterized by a distortion or an excess of normal functions. In contrast, schizophrenia's negative symptoms reflect the loss or decrease of normal functions. These negative symptoms can include social withdrawal, behavioral deficits, and apparent lack of emotion. One negative symptom is **flat affect,** which means the display of

flat affect
The display of little or no emotion—a common negative symptom of schizophrenia.

FIGURE 6 **People with schizophrenia can be productive and creative.** Artist Adam Raven was diagnosed with schizophrenia and thought he would never paint again. However, with treatment he has become an advocate for the importance of creativity in the lives of those with severe psychological disorders.
©Alex Lentati/Evening Standard/REX/Shutterstock

little or no emotion (Cho & others, 2017; Lepage & others, 2011). Individuals with schizophrenia also may be lacking in the ability to read the emotions of others (Chambon, Baudouin, & Franck, 2006). They may experience a lack of positive emotional experience in daily life and show a deficient ability to plan, initiate, and engage in goal-directed behavior. Importantly, the appearance of the absence of emotion may mask emotional experience, as individuals with schizophrenia report more negative emotion and less positive emotion than those without the disorder in their daily lives (Cho & others, 2017).

Because negative symptoms are not as obviously part of a psychiatric illness, people with schizophrenia may be perceived as lazy and unwilling to better their lives.

COGNITIVE SYMPTOMS   Cognitive symptoms of schizophrenia include difficulty sustaining attention, problems holding information in memory, deficits in the ability to self-reflect, and inability to interpret information and make decisions (Garety & others, 2014; McGregor, Riordan, & Thornton, 2017; Tas & others, 2014). These symptoms may be subtle and are often detected only through neuropsychological tests. Researchers now recognize that to understand schizophrenia's cognitive symptoms fully, measures of these symptoms must be tailored to particular cultural contexts (Ishikawa & others, 2017; Mehta & others, 2011).

Causes of Schizophrenia

A great deal of research has focused on schizophrenia's causes, including biological, psychological, and sociocultural factors involved in the disorder.

BIOLOGICAL FACTORS   Research provides strong support for biological explanations of schizophrenia. Especially compelling is the evidence for a genetic predisposition (Dai & others, 2014; Lu & others, 2017). However, structural brain abnormalities and neurotransmitters also are linked to this severe psychological disorder.

Heredity   Research supports the notion that schizophrenia is at least partially due to genetic factors (Warnica & others, 2014). As genetic similarity to a person with schizophrenia increases, so does a person's risk of developing schizophrenia, as Figure 7 shows (Cardno & Gottesman, 2000). Such data strongly suggest that genetic factors play a role in schizophrenia. Researchers are seeking to pinpoint the chromosomal location of genes involved in susceptibility to schizophrenia (Marshall & others, 2018). Identifying the specific genetic characteristics that enhance vulnerability to a psychotic episode may help in devising early interventions and treatments (Matsumoto & others, 2017).

Structural Brain Abnormalities   Studies have found structural brain abnormalities in people with schizophrenia. Imaging techniques such as MRI scans clearly show enlarged ventricles in the brain (Birur & others, 2017; Rais & others, 2012). Ventricles are fluid-filled spaces, and enlargement of the ventricles indicates the deterioration in other brain tissue. Individuals with schizophrenia also have a small frontal cortex (the area in which thinking, planning, and decision making take place) and show less activity in this area than individuals who do not have schizophrenia (Cotter & others, 2002; Hassan & others, 2017).

Still, the differences between the brains of healthy individuals and those with schizophrenia are small (National Institute of Mental Health, 2014c). Microscopic studies of brain tissue after death reveal small changes in the distribution or characteristics of brain cells in persons with schizophrenia. It appears that many of these changes occurred prenatally, because they are not accompanied by glial cells, which are always present when a brain injury occurs after birth. It may be that problems in prenatal development such as infections (De Picker & others, 2017) predispose a brain to developing schizophrenic symptoms during puberty and young adulthood (Fatemi & Folsom, 2009). One study sought to trace genetic differences to brain structure and function in schizophrenia (Sekar & others, 2016). Recall that part of brain development involves the process of synaptic

FIGURE 7 **Lifetime Risk of Developing Schizophrenia According to Genetic Relatedness** As genetic relatedness to an individual with schizophrenia increases, so does the risk of developing schizophrenia.

SOURCE: Irving Gottesman, 2004

> Which familial relationships have the lowest and highest level of genetic overlap? > What is the difference in genetic overlap between identical twins and non-twin siblings? > What is the difference in risk of schizophrenia between identical twins and non-twin siblings?

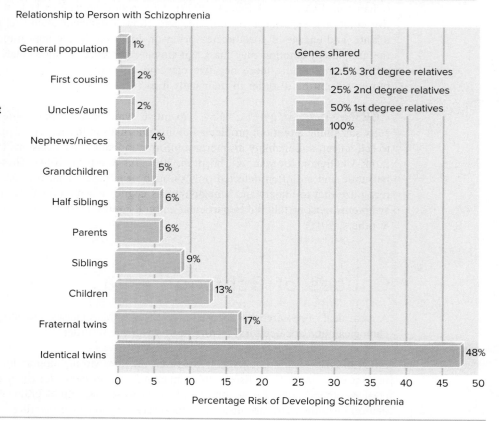

Relationship to Person with Schizophrenia

Genes shared
- 12.5% 3rd degree relatives
- 25% 2nd degree relatives
- 50% 1st degree relatives
- 100%

Relationship	%
General population	1%
First cousins	2%
Uncles/aunts	2%
Nephews/nieces	4%
Grandchildren	5%
Half siblings	6%
Parents	6%
Siblings	9%
Children	13%
Fraternal twins	17%
Identical twins	48%

Percentage Risk of Developing Schizophrenia

pruning. This means that connections that are weak or rarely used are pruned away as the brain matures. This study showed that a specific genetic feature that guides the pruning process was faulty in those with schizophrenia. For these individuals the pruning process was faster or more extensive than in typical development (Sekar & others, 2016). Such results suggest that during late adolescence and early adulthood (when psychotic symptoms often first appear), brain development may be going awry.

Problems in Neurotransmitter Regulation Whether it is the amount of dopamine, its production, or its uptake, there is good evidence that problems regulating the neurotransmitter dopamine play a role in schizophrenia (Duan & others, 2017; Howes & others, 2017). A link between dopamine and psychotic symptoms was first noticed when the drug L-dopa (which increases dopamine levels) was given to individuals as a treatment for Parkinson disease. In addition to relieving Parkinson symptoms, L-dopa caused some to experience psychosis (Janowsky, Addario, & Risch, 1987; Madras, 2013). Further, drugs that reduce psychotic symptoms often block dopamine (van Os & Kapur, 2009).

Previously we have encountered dopamine as the "feel good" neurotransmitter that helps us recognize rewarding stimuli in the environment. How can a neurotransmitter that is associated with good things play a crucial role in schizophrenia?

An early biological explanation for schizophrenia is that it is linked to excess dopamine production. One way to think about the role of dopamine in schizophrenia is to view dopamine as a neurochemical messenger that in effect shouts out, "Hey! This is important!" whenever we encounter opportunities for reward. Imagine what it might be like to be bombarded with such messages about even the smallest details of life (Kapur, 2003). The person's own thoughts might take

Poorly regulated dopamine basically tells the person that everything is important.

Recall that Moe Armstrong experienced his first symptoms during the extremely stressful experience of the Vietnam War.

on such dramatic proportions that they sound like someone else's voice talking inside the person's head. Fleeting ideas such as "It's raining today because I didn't bring my umbrella to work" suddenly seem not silly but true. Shitij Kapur (2003) has suggested that hallucinations, delusions, and referential thinking may be expressions of the individual's attempts to make sense of such extraordinary feelings.

©fStop Images - Vladimir Godnik/Brand X Pictures/Getty Images

PSYCHOLOGICAL FACTORS Psychologists used to explain schizophrenia as rooted in childhood experiences with unresponsive parents. Such explanations have fallen by the wayside. Contemporary theorists do recognize that stress may contribute to the development of this disorder. Experiences are now viewed through the lens of the vulnerability-stress hypothesis, described earlier, suggesting that individuals with schizophrenia may have biological risk factors that interact with experience to produce the disorder.

SOCIOCULTURAL FACTORS Sociocultural background is not considered a *cause* of schizophrenia, but sociocultural factors do appear to affect the *course* of the disorder, or how it progresses. Across cultures, individuals with schizophrenia in developing, nonindustrialized nations tend to have better outcomes than those in developed, industrialized nations (Jablensky, 2000; Myers, 2010). This difference may be due to the fact that in developing nations, family and friends are more accepting and supportive of individuals with schizophrenia. In Western samples, marriage, warm supportive friends (Jablensky & others, 1992; Wiersma & others, 1998), and employment are related to better outcomes for individuals diagnosed with schizophrenia (Rosen & Garety, 2005).

Some experts have called for a focus on preventing schizophrenia by identifying those at risk and then intervening early to reduce the level of disability they experience (Addington & others, 2011; Walder & others, 2012). Early intervention can be important because a strong predictor of relapse (that is, having symptoms again after treatment) is the amount of time a person spends in a psychotic state without treatment (Bora & others, 2017; ten Velden Hegelstad & others, 2012). A large scale study demonstrated that young adults who received intensive team-based treatment including medications, therapy, and occupational, educational, and family support rapidly following a first psychotic episode experienced better quality of life two years later, compared to those receiving only medication and community care (Kane & others, 2015). This rapid, comprehensive treatment was especially effective if the person began treatment very early.

Is there a way to know who might be at risk for schizophrenia? One study showed that among those with a family history of schizophrenia, lower levels of *social* functioning distinguished those who went on to develop schizophrenia (Cornblatt & others, 2012).

Do It!

If you have never met anyone with schizophrenia, why not get to know Moe Armstrong online? Search for clips of one of Moe's many speeches on YouTube.

self-quiz

1. A negative symptom of schizophrenia is
   A. hallucinations.
   B. flat affect.
   C. delusions.
   D. neologisms.

2. Joel believes that he has superhuman powers. He is likely suffering from
   A. hallucinations.
   B. delusions.
   C. negative symptoms.
   D. referential thinking.

3. The biological causes of schizophrenia include

   A. problems with the body's regulation of dopamine.
   B. abnormalities in brain structure such as enlarged ventricles and a small frontal cortex.
   C. genetic predisposition.
   D. All of the above

APPLY IT! 4. During a psychiatric hospital internship, Tara approaches a young man sitting alone in a corner, and they have a short conversation. He asks her if she is with the government, and she tells him that she is not. She asks him a few questions and walks away. She tells her advisor later that what

disturbed her about the conversation was not so much what the young man said, but that she had this feeling that he just was not really there. Tara was noticing the _____ symptoms of schizophrenia.
   A. positive
   B. negative
   C. cognitive
   D. genetic

8 Personality Disorders

personality disorders
Chronic, maladaptive cognitive-behavioral patterns that are thoroughly integrated into an individual's personality.

Imagine that your personality—the very thing about you that makes you *you*—is the core of your life difficulties. That is what happens with **personality disorders,** which are chronic, maladaptive cognitive-behavioral patterns that are thoroughly integrated into an individual's personality. Because they are fully integrated into the person's personality, these disorders can be difficult to treat. Personality disorders are relatively common. In a representative U.S. sample, researchers found that 15 percent had a personality disorder (Grant & others, 2004). Figure 8 reviews the 10 personality disorders included in *DSM-5*.

In this section we survey the two personality disorders that have been the object of most study: antisocial personality disorder and borderline personality disorder. Both are associated with dire consequences. Specifically, antisocial personality disorder is linked to criminal activity and violence; borderline personality disorder, to self-harm and suicide.

Personality Disorder	Description
Paranoid Personality Disorder	Paranoia, suspiciousness, and deep distrust of others. People with this disorder are always on the lookout for danger and the slightest social mistreatment. They may be socially isolated.
Schizoid Personality Disorder	Extreme lack of interest in interpersonal relationships. People with this disorder are emotionally cold and apathetic, and they are generally detached from interpersonal life.
Schizotypal Personality Disorder	Socially isolated and prone to odd thinking. People with this disorder often have elaborate and strange belief systems and attribute unusual meanings to life events and experiences.
Antisocial Personality Disorder	Manipulative, deceitful, and amoral. People with this disorder lack empathy for others, are egocentric, and are willing to use others for their own personal gain.
Borderline Personality Disorder	Emotionally volatile and unstable sense of self. These individuals are prone to mood swings, excessive self-criticism, extreme judgments of others, and are preoccupied with being abandoned.
Histrionic Personality Disorder	Attention-seeking, dramatic, lively, and flirtatious. These individuals are inappropriately seductive in their interactions with others.
Narcissistic Personality Disorder	Self-aggrandizing yet overly dependent on the evaluations of others. People with this disorder view themselves as entitled and better than others. They show deficits in empathy and in understanding the feelings of others.
Avoidant Personality Disorder	Socially inhibited and prone to feelings of inadequacy, anxiety, and shame. These individuals feel inadequate and hold back in social situations. They have unrealistic standards for their own behavior and avoid setting goals, taking personal risks, or pursuing new activities.
Dependent Personality Disorder	Dependent on others for emotional and physical needs. People with this disorder perceive others as powerful and competent and themselves as childlike and helpless.
Obsessive-Compulsive Personality Disorder	Conforming rigidly to rules. These individuals show an excessive attachment to moral codes and are excessively orderly in daily life.

FIGURE 8   The 10 Personality Disorders Included in *DSM-5* Diagnoses of these disorders require that the person be over the age of 18, and all involve pervasive aspects of the person that color cognition, emotion, and behavior. Note that some of the labels are potentially confusing. Schizoid and schizotypal personality disorders are not the same thing as schizophrenia (though schizotypal personality disorder may proceed to schizophrenia). Further, obsessive-compulsive personality disorder is not the same thing as obsessive-compulsive disorder.
SOURCE: American Psychiatric Association, *Diagnostic and Statistical Manual of Mental Disorders*, 5th Ed. 2003

Antisocial Personality Disorder

antisocial personality disorder (ASPD) Psychological disorder characterized by guiltlessness, law-breaking, exploitation of others, irresponsibility, and deceit.

Antisocial personality disorder (ASPD) is a psychological disorder characterized by guiltlessness, law-breaking, exploitation of others, irresponsibility, and deceit. Although they may be superficially charming, individuals with ASPD do not play by the rules, and they often lead a life of crime and violence. ASPD is far more common in men than in women (a 3 to 1 ratio). ASPD is related to criminal behavior, vandalism, substance abuse, and alcoholism (Chun & others, 2017; Goldstein & others, 2017). Those with ASPD are impulsive, meaning they may act without thinking through their decisions, and they typically do not experience remorse or guilt for their harmful actions.

ASPD is characterized by

- Failure to conform to social norms or obey the law.
- Deceitfulness, lying, using aliases, or conning others for personal profit or pleasure.
- Impulsivity.
- Irritability and aggressiveness; getting into physical fights or perpetrating assaults.
- Reckless disregard for the safety of self or others.
- Consistent irresponsibility, inconsistent work behavior; not paying bills.
- Lack of remorse, indifference to the pain of others, or rationalizing; hurting or mistreating another person.

Although ASPD is associated with criminal behavior, not all individuals with ASPD engage in crime, and not all criminals suffer from ASPD. Some individuals with ASPD can have successful careers. There are antisocial physicians, clergy members, lawyers, and just about any other occupation. Still, such individuals tend to be exploitative of others, and they break the rules, even if they are never caught.

A number of factors intertwine to produce ASPD. Research has linked ASPD to low levels of activation in the prefrontal cortex and has related these brain differences to poor decision making and problems in learning (Jiang & others, 2016; Yang & Raine, 2009). Both genetic factors (Rosenström & others, 2017; Garcia & others, 2010) and childhood abuse are associated with ASPD, but there is evidence that genetic differences may distinguish abused children who go on to commit violent acts from those who do not (Caspi & others, 2002; Lynam & others, 2007).

Individuals with ASPD show lower levels of autonomic nervous system arousal and are less stressed than others by aversive circumstances, including punishment (Fung & others, 2005; Raine & Venables, 2017). They have the ability to keep their cool while engaging in deception (Verschuere & others, 2005), suggesting that those with ASPD might be able to fool a polygraph. The underaroused autonomic nervous system may be a key difference between adolescents who become antisocial adults and those whose behavior improves during adulthood (Fagan, Zhang, & Gao, 2017; Raine, Venables, & Williams, 1990). Individuals with ASPD may have difficulty empathizing with other people and show deficits in theory of mind (Newbury-Helps, Feigenbaum, & Fonagy, 2017).

The term *psychopath* is sometimes used to refer to a subgroup of individuals with ASPD (Crego & Widiger, 2014). Psychopaths are remorseless predators who engage in violence to get what they want. Examples of psychopaths include serial killers John Wayne Gacy, who murdered 33 boys and young men, and Ted Bundy, who confessed to murdering at least 30 young women. Psychopaths tend to show less prefrontal activation than normal individuals and to have structural abnormalities in the amygdala, as well as the hippocampus, the brain structure most closely associated with memory (Seara-Cardoso & Viding, 2014; Thijssen & Kiehl, 2017).

John Wayne Gacy (top) *and Ted Bundy* (bottom) *exemplify the subgroup of people with ASPD who are also psychopathic.*
(both) ©Bettmann/Getty Images

Lack of autonomic nervous system activity suggests why individuals with ASPD might be able to fool a polygraph (lie detector).

Their functioning frontal lobes might help successful psychopaths avoid getting caught.

Importantly, these brain differences are most pronounced in "unsuccessful psychopaths"—individuals who have been arrested for their behaviors (Yang & others, 2005). In contrast, "successful psychopaths"—individuals who have engaged in antisocial behavior but have not gotten caught—are more similar to healthy controls in terms of brain structure and function. However, in their behavior, successful psychopaths demonstrate a lack of empathy and a willingness to act immorally; they victimize others to enrich their own lives. Psychopaths show deficiencies in learning about fear and have difficulty processing information related to the distress of others, such as sad or fearful faces (Dolan & Fullam, 2006).

A key challenge in treating individuals with ASPD, including psychopaths, is their ability to con even sophisticated mental health professionals. They may encounter mental health professionals in the context of substance abuse treatment but many never seek therapy, and others end up in prison, where treatment is rarely an option.

Borderline Personality Disorder

borderline personality disorder (BPD)
Psychological disorder characterized by a pervasive pattern of instability in interpersonal relationships, self-image, and emotions, and of marked impulsivity beginning by early adulthood and present in a variety of contexts.

Borderline personality disorder (BPD) is a pervasive pattern of instability in interpersonal relationships, self-image, and emotions, and of marked impulsivity beginning by early adulthood and present in various contexts. Individuals with BPD are insecure, impulsive, and emotional (Wehbe-Alamah & Wolgamott, 2014). BPD is related to self-harming behaviors such as *cutting* (injuring oneself with a sharp object but without suicidal intent) and also to suicide (Goodman & others, 2017; Homan & others, 2017).

At the very core of BPD is profound instability in mood, in sense of self, and in relationships. BPD is characterized by four essential features (Trull & Brown, 2013):

1. Unstable affect

2. Unstable sense of self and identity, including self-destructive impulsive behavior and chronic feelings of emptiness

3. Negative interpersonal relationships that are unstable, intense, and characterized by extreme shifts between idealization and devaluation

4. Self-harm, including recurrent suicidal behavior, gestures, or threats or self-mutilating behavior

Individuals with BPD are prone to wild mood swings and very sensitive to how others treat them. They often feel as if they are riding a nonstop emotional rollercoaster (Selby & others, 2009), and their loved ones may have to work hard to avoid upsetting them. Individuals with BPD tend to see the world in black-and-white terms, a thinking style called *splitting*. For example, they typically view other people as either hated enemies with no positive qualities or as beloved, idealized friends who can do no wrong.

Movie depictions of BPD include Fatal Attraction, Single White Female, and Obsessed. Where these films get it wrong is that they show BPD as leading to more harm to others than to the self.

Borderline personality disorder is far more common in women than men. Women make up 75 percent of those with the disorder (Chun & others, 2017; Oltmanns & Powers, 2012). A renowned expert on BPD, Marsha Linehan revealed that she herself has struggled with the disorder (Carey, 2011).

The potential causes of BPD are likely complex and include biological factors as well as childhood experiences. The role of genes in BPD has been demonstrated in a variety of studies and across cultures (McCarthy & others, 2014). The heritability of BPD is between 30 and 70 percent (Conde & others, 2017; Distel & others, 2008).

Many individuals with borderline personality disorder report experiences of childhood sexual abuse, as well as physical abuse and neglect (Kulacaogula & others, 2017. It is not clear, however, whether abuse is a primary cause of the disorder (Trull & Brown, 2013). Childhood abuse experiences may combine with genetic factors in promoting BPD.

This would be a vulnerability-stress hypothesis explanation for BPD.

Cognitive factors associated with BPD include a tendency to hold a set of irrational beliefs (Leahy, Holland, & McGinn, 2012). These include thinking that one is powerless and innately unacceptable and that other people are dangerous and hostile (Arntz, 2005). Individuals with BPD also display *hypervigilance:* the tendency to be constantly on the alert, looking for threatening information in the environment (Sieswerda & others, 2007).

Up until 30 years ago, experts thought that BPD was untreatable. More recent evidence, however, suggests that many individuals with BPD show improvement over time—as many as 50 percent within two years of starting treatment (Gunderson, 2008). One key aspect of successful treatment appears to be a reduction in social stress, such as that due to leaving an abusive romantic partner or establishing a sense of trust in a therapist (Gunderson & others, 2003). Effective treatment for BPD includes a program of psychotherapies that are brought together to help people with the disorder on many different levels, including behavior, cognition, emotion, and sense of self (Choi-Kain & others, 2017).

To recognize the severe toll of BPD on those suffering from it (and on their families and friends), the U.S. House of Representatives declared May to be National Borderline Personality Disorder Awareness Month.

self-quiz

1. Individuals with ASPD
   A. are incapable of having successful careers.
   B. are typically women.
   C. are typically men.
   D. rarely engage in criminal behavior.

2. People with BPD
   A. pay little attention to how others treat them.
   B. rarely have problems with anger or strong emotion.
   C. tend to have suicidal thoughts or engage in self-harming actions.
   D. tend to have a balanced viewpoint of people and things rather than to see them as all black or all white.

3. All of the following are true of BPD except

   A. BPD can be caused by a combination of nature and nurture—genetic inheritance and childhood experience.
   B. recent research has shown that people with BPD respond positively to treatment.
   C. a common symptom of BPD is impulsive behavior such as binge eating and reckless driving.
   D. BPD is far more common in men than women.

APPLY IT! 4. Your new friend Maureen tells you that she was diagnosed with borderline personality disorder at the age of 23. She feels hopeless when she considers that her mood swings and unstable self-esteem are part of her very personality. Despairing, she asks, "How will I ever change?" Which of the following statements about Maureen's condition is accurate?
   A. Maureen should seek therapy and strive to improve her relationships with others, as BPD is treatable.
   B. Maureen's concerns are realistic, because a personality disorder like BPD is unlikely to change.
   C. Maureen should seek treatment for BPD because there is a high likelihood that she will end up committing a criminal act.
   D. Maureen is right to be concerned, because BPD is most often caused by genetic factors.

9 Suicide

Thinking about suicide is not necessarily abnormal. However, attempting or completing the act of suicide is abnormal. Approximately 90 percent of individuals who die by suicide are estimated to have a diagnosable psychological disorder (National Alliance on Mental Illness, 2013). The most common disorders among individuals who die by suicide are depression and anxiety (Fried & others, 2013). Many individuals who, to the outside eye, seem to be leading successful and fulfilling lives have died as a result of suicide. Examples include comedian-actor Robin Williams, actor Marilyn Monroe, novelist Ernest Hemingway, and grunge music icon Kurt Cobain (who died by suicide after lifelong battles with ADHD and bipolar disorder).

Sadly, suicide has been on the rise in the United States in recent years. In 2014, 42,773 people died by suicide, the highest number since 1986 (Curtin, Warner, & Hedegaard, 2016). That number was less than 30,000 in 1999. In 2014, suicide was the 10th-highest cause of death in the U.S. (American Foundation for Suicide Prevention, 2016). Research indicates that for every completed suicide, 25 attempted suicides occur (American Foundation for Suicide Prevention, 2016). Approximately 4,400 adolescents die by suicide each year (Eaton & others, 2012). Even more shocking, in the United States suicide is the third-leading cause of death among children 10 to 14 years of age. Emerging adults (18 to 25 years of age) have triple the rate of suicide of adolescents (Park & others, 2006). Given these grim statistics, psychologists work with individuals to reduce the frequency

FIGURE 9 **When Someone Is Threatening Suicide** Do not ignore the warning signs if you think someone you know is considering suicide. Talk to a counselor if you are reluctant to say anything to the person yourself.
©Nathan Lau/Design Pics

and intensity of suicidal impulses. Figure 9 provides good advice on what to do and what not to do if you encounter someone you believe is considering suicide.

Why would individuals seek to end their own lives? Biological, psychological, and sociocultural circumstances can be contributing factors.

BIOLOGICAL FACTORS   Genetic factors appear to play a role in suicide, which tends to run in families (Cha & others, 2018; Coon & others, 2013). The Hemingways are one famous family that has been plagued by suicide. Five Hemingways, spread across generations, died by suicide, including the writer Ernest Hemingway and his granddaughter Margaux, a model and actor. Similarly, in 2009, Nicholas Hughes—a successful marine biologist and the son of Sylvia Plath, a poet who died by suicide—tragically hanged himself.

Note that people whose parents died by suicide may be more likely to consider suicide as an option. So, environment matters.

Suicide is correlated with low levels of the neurotransmitter serotonin (Di Narzo & others, 2014). Individuals who attempt suicide and who have low serotonin levels are 10 times more likely to attempt suicide again than are attempters who have high serotonin levels (Courtet & others, 2004). Poor physical health, especially when it is chronic, is another risk factor for suicide (Webb & others, 2012).

PSYCHOLOGICAL FACTORS   Psychological factors that can contribute to suicide risk include psychological disorders and traumatic experiences (Miller & others, 2013; Ramberg & others, 2014). An immediate and highly stressful circumstance—such as the loss of a loved one, losing one's job, flunking out of school, or an unwanted pregnancy—can lead people to wish to end their lives (Kumar & George, 2013; Reeves, McKee, & Stuckler, 2014). In addition, substance abuse is linked with suicide (Kaplan & others, 2014). Finally, a recent longitudinal study showed that individuals who were bullied in adolescence were at higher risk for suicide than those who were not bullied (Foss Sigurdson & others, 2017).

An expert on suicide, Thomas Joiner (2005) has proposed a comprehensive theory of the phenomenon. His *interpersonal theory of suicide* states that suicide involves two factors (Hames, Hagan, & Joiner, 2013; Joiner, 2005; Joiner & Ribeiro, 2011; Smith & others, 2013):

- A desire to die
- The acquired capability for suicide

The desire to die, from this perspective, emerges when a person's social needs are not met. Individuals who feel they do not belong, are chronically lonely, and who perceive themselves to be a burden on others are more likely to experience a desire to die (Hames, Hagan, & Joiner, 2013; Lamis, Ballard, & Patel, 2014).

Even among those with a desire to die, however, a key variable is the person's acquired capability to complete a suicide attempt. For most people, a fear of death and a strong desire to avoid feeling pain prevent us from suicide. Research suggests that one way individuals might overcome these natural motivations is to develop a tolerance for pain through previous experiences of injury (Joiner, Ribeiro, & Silva, 2012). Through past experiences, then, the interpersonal theory asserts that individuals are able to extinguish the fear response.

SOCIOCULTURAL FACTORS

Chronic economic hardship can be a factor in suicide (Kerr & others, 2017). Cultural and ethnic contexts also are related to suicide attempts. In the United States, adolescents' suicide attempts vary across ethnic groups. As Figure 10 illustrates, more than 20 percent of Native American/Alaska Native (NA/AN) female adolescents reported that they had attempted suicide in the previous year, and suicide accounts for almost 20 percent of NA/AN deaths in 15- to 19-year-olds (Goldston & others, 2008). As the figure also shows, African American and non-Latino White

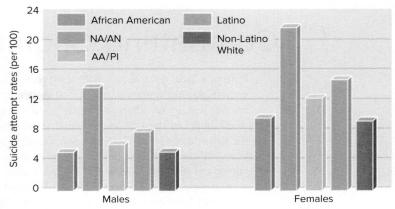

FIGURE 10 Suicide Attempts by U.S. Adolescents from Different Ethnic Groups Note that the data shown are for one-year rates of self-reported suicide attempts. NA/AN = Native Americans/Alaska Native; AA/PI = Asian American/Pacific Islander.
©Ryan McVay/Photodisc/Getty Images

males reported the lowest incidence of suicide attempts. A major risk factor in the high rate of suicide attempts by NA/AN adolescents is their elevated rate of alcohol abuse.

Suicide rates vary worldwide; the lowest rates occur in countries with cultural and religious norms against ending one's own life. According to the World Health Organization (WHO), among the nations with the highest suicide rates are Guyana, South Korea, Sri Lanka, and Lithuania. Among the nations with the lowest rates are Saudi Arabia, Lebanon, Kuwait, and Haiti (WHO, 2015). Of the 171 nations ranked by the WHO, the United States ranks 50th.

Within cultures, economic conditions and ethnic contexts may contribute to suicide risk. Research has also linked suicide to the culture of honor. Recall that in honor cultures, individuals are more likely to interpret insults as fighting words and to defend their personal honor with aggression. One set of studies examined suicide and depression in the United States, comparing geographic regions that are considered to have a culture of honor (for example, the South in the United States) with other areas. Even accounting for a host of other factors, suicide rates were found to be higher in states with a culture of honor (Osterman & Brown, 2011). There are gender differences in suicide. Men are four times more likely to complete suicide than women (Curtin, Warner, & Hedegaard, 2016). According to the CDC, men are more likely to use a firearm while women are more likely to use poison in a suicide attempt.

*Men are less likely than women to **report** being depressed but are **more** likely to **die by** suicide. Clearly, depression in men might be underestimated.*

self-quiz

1. The neurotransmitter that has been linked to suicide is
   A. GABA.
   B. norepinephrine.
   C. serotonin.
   D. oxytocin.

2. The interpersonal theory of suicide suggests that suicide involves two things. First, the desire to die, and second,
   A. a genetic predisposition.
   B. a family history of suicide.
   C. the acquired capability for suicide.
   D. a severe life stressor.

3. In terms of sociocultural factors and suicide, research supports which of the following?

A. Within culture of honor states, suicide is less likely because people are more religious.
B. Individuals of high income levels are particularly at risk for suicide.
C. Women are more likely than men to die by suicide.
D. In the U.S., older White men have a high rate of suicide.

APPLY IT! 4. Jerome is writing a paper on the influence of culture on suicide. He tells you that he is going to focus on how different countries have different suicide rates because culture basically means differences in

country of origin. What is your advice to Jerome?
   A. Jerome is on the right track.
   B. Jerome should consider that within a country there may be cultural differences that play a role in suicide, such as the culture of honor in the southern United States.
   C. Jerome should note that gender does not have a role to play in suicide in most cultures.
   D. Jerome should note that the suicide rate in the United States is the highest in the world.

10 Combatting Stigma

Putting a label on a person with a psychological disorder can make the disorder seem like something that happens only to other people. The truth is that psychological disorders are not just about other people; they are about people, period. In 2015, nearly 20 percent of all adults in the U.S. experienced some psychological disorder in the last year (Center for Behavioral Health Statistics and Quality, 2016). Chances are that you or someone you know will experience a psychological disorder. Figure 11 shows how common many psychological disorders are in the United States.

A classic and controversial study illustrates that labels of psychological disorder can be "sticky"—hard to remove once they are applied to a person. David Rosenhan (1973) recruited eight adults (including a stay-at-home mother, a psychology graduate student, a pediatrician, and some psychiatrists), none with a psychological disorder, to see a psychiatrist at various hospitals. These "pseudo-patients" were instructed to act normally except to complain about hearing voices that said things like "empty" and "thud." All eight expressed an interest in leaving the hospital and behaved cooperatively. Nevertheless, all eight were labeled with schizophrenia and kept in the hospital from 3 to 52 days. None of the mental health professionals they encountered ever questioned the diagnosis that was given to these individuals, and all were discharged with the label "schizophrenia in remission." The label "schizophrenia" had stuck to the pseudo-patients and caused the professionals around them to interpret their quite normal behavior as abnormal. Clearly, once a person has been labeled with a psychological disorder, that label colors how others perceive everything else he or she does.

Labels of psychological disorder carry with them a wide array of implications for the individual. Is the person still able to be a good friend? A good parent? A competent worker? A significant concern for individuals with psychological disorders is the negative attitudes that others might have about people struggling with a psychological disorder (Angermeyer & Schomerus, 2017). Stigma can be a barrier for individuals coping with a psychological disorder, as well as for their families and loved ones (Corrigan & Penn, 2015; Evans-Lacko & others, 2014). Negative attitudes about individuals with psychological disorders are common in many cultures, and cultural norms and values influence these attitudes (Abdullah & Brown, 2011). Fear of stigma can prevent individuals from seeking treatment and from talking about their problems with family and friends.

	Number of U.S. Adults in a Given Year (Millions)	Percentage of U.S. Adults
Anxiety Disorders		
General anxiety disorder	6.8	3.1%
Panic disorder	6.0	2.7%
Specific phobia	19.2	8.7%
PTSD	7.7	3.5%
Major Depressive Disorder	14.8	6.7%
Bipolar Disorder	5.7	2.6%
Schizophrenia	2.4	1.1%

FIGURE 11 The 12-Month Prevalence of the Most Common Psychological Disorders If you add up the numbers in this figure, you will see that the totals are higher than the numbers given in the text. The explanation is that people are frequently diagnosed with more than one psychological disorder. An individual who has both a depressive and an anxiety disorder would be counted in both of those categories.
©Ryan McVay/Photodisc/Getty Images

Consequences of Stigma

The stigma attached to psychological disorders can provoke prejudice and discrimination toward individuals who are struggling with these problems, complicating an already difficult situation. Having a disorder and experiencing the stigma associated with it can also negatively affect one's physical health.

PREJUDICE AND DISCRIMINATION

Labels of psychological disorders can be damaging because they may lead to negative stereotypes, which play a role in prejudice. For example, the label "schizophrenic" often has negative connotations such as "frightening" and "dangerous."

Vivid cases of extremely harmful behavior by individuals with psychological disorders can perpetuate the stereotype that people with such disorders are violent. You have probably heard of such cases. In 2007, Cho Seung-Hui, a college student, murdered 32 students and faculty at Virginia Tech University before killing himself. James Eagan Holmes committed a mass shooting in an Aurora, Colorado, movie theater in July 2012, leaving 12 dead and 58 injured. The following December, Adam Lanza killed his mother and then killed 20 children and 6 adults at Sandy Hook Elementary School in Newtown, Connecticut, before killing himself. In 2018, Nikolas Cruz allegedly murdered 17 people in a Florida high school.

Aside from having committed these notorious acts of violence, these four individuals have something else in common—they were all described as having a history of psychological disorders. For Cho, it was depression and anxiety; for Lanza, it was a type of autism spectrum disorder as well as anxiety, depression, and anorexia. Holmes was reported to suffer from schizophrenia or a personality disorder. Although a specific diagnosis has not been identified, Cruz had a history of mental illness and treatments. Such vivid cases may give the erroneous impression that individuals who suffer from psychological disorders are prone to violence. That impression is called an *illusory correlation*, because it is an illusion. Consider that these young men share other qualities as well. For instance, they were all young men. They are no more representative of people with psychological disorders than they are representative of young men.

Individuals with psychological disorders are often aware of the negative stigma attached to these conditions and may themselves have previously held such negative attitudes. Seeking the assistance they need may involve accepting a stigmatized identity. Even mental health professionals can fall prey to prejudicial attitudes toward those who are coping with psychological disorders (Nordt, Rossler, & Lauber, 2006). Improved knowledge about the neurobiological and genetic processes involved in many psychological disorders appears to be a promising direction for interventions to reduce such prejudice. Research shows that information about the role of genes in these disorders reduces prejudicial attitudes (WonPat-Borja & others, 2012).

Among the most feared aspects of stigma is discrimination, or acting prejudicially toward a person who is a member of a stigmatized group. In the workplace, discrimination against a person with a psychological disorder violates the law. The Americans with Disabilities Act (ADA) of 1990 made it illegal to refuse employment or a promotion to someone with a psychological disorder when the person's condition does not prevent performance of the job's essential functions (Cleveland, Barnes-Farrell, & Ratz, 1997). A person's appearance or behavior may be unusual or irritating, but as long as that individual is able to complete the duties required of a position, employment or promotion cannot be denied.

If a friend discloses to you that they have a psychological disorder, you might wonder how best to behave. One tip is to think about how you would act if the friend told you that they have arthritis or diabetes. You can't "cure" those conditions and you can't "cure" your friend. You do not have to have all the answers but being there to listen and support may be the best way to be a friend.

PHYSICAL HEALTH

Individuals with psychological disorders are more likely to be physically ill and two times more likely to die than their psychologically healthy counterparts (Gittelman, 2008). They are also more likely to be obese, to smoke, to drink excessively, and to lead sedentary lives (Geoffroy, Li, & Power, 2014; Hagger-Johnson & others, 2014; Smith & others, 2014).

You might be thinking that these physical health issues are the least of their worries. If people struggling with schizophrenia want to smoke, why not let them? This type of thinking sells short the capacity of psychological and psychiatric treatments to help those with psychological disorders. Research has shown that health-promotion programs can work well for individuals with a severe psychological disorder (Koenig & Butters, 2014; Mairs & Bradshaw, 2013). When we disregard the potential of physical health interventions for people with psychological disorders to make positive life changes, we reveal our biases.

Overcoming Stigma

How can we combat the stigma of psychological disorders? One obstacle to changing people's attitudes toward individuals with psychological disorders is that mental illness is often "invisible." That is, sometimes a person we know can have a disorder without our being aware. We may be unaware of *many* good lives around us that are being lived under a cloud of psychological disorder, because worries about being stigmatized keep the affected individuals from "coming out." Thus, stigma leads to a catch-22: Positive examples of individuals coping with psychological disorders are often missing from our experience because those who are doing well shun public disclosure of their disorders (Corrigan & Penn, 2015; Jensen & Wadkins, 2007).

A critical step toward eliminating stigma is to resist thinking of people with disorders as completely defined by their condition. Instead, it is vital to recognize that they are still people, who demonstrate considerable strengths both in confronting their disorder and in carrying on despite their problems—and their achievements. By creating a positive environment for people with disorders, we encourage more of them to become confidently "visible" and empower them to be positive role models.

After reading this chapter, you know that many admired individuals have dealt with psychological disorders. Their diagnoses do not detract from their accomplishments. To the contrary, their accomplishments are all the more remarkable in the context of the challenges they have faced.

Do It!

Visit the Schizophrenia Oral History Website, at http://www.schizophreniaoralhistories.com/.

self-quiz

1. The percentage of Americans 18 years of age and older who suffer from a diagnosable psychological disorder in a given year is closest to
   A. 15 percent.
   B. 26 percent.
   C. 40 percent.
   D. 46 percent.

2. The stigma attached to psychological disorders can have implications for
   A. the physical health of an individual with such a disorder.
   B. the psychological well-being of an individual with such a disorder.
   C. other people's attitudes and behaviors toward the individual with such a disorder.
   D. all of the above

3. Labeling psychological disorders can lead to damaging
   A. stereotyping.
   B. discrimination.
   C. prejudice.
   D. all of the above

APPLY IT! 4. Liliana has applied for a job after graduation doing data entry for a polling firm. During her second interview, Liliana asks the human resources manager whether the job's health benefits include prescription drug coverage, as she is on anti-anxiety medication for generalized anxiety disorder. Which of the following statements is most applicable, legally and otherwise, in light of Liliana's request?
   A. The human resources manager should tell the hiring committee to avoid hiring Liliana because she has a psychological disorder.
   B. It is illegal for the firm to deny Liliana employment simply because she has a psychological disorder.
   C. Liliana should not have asked that question, because she will not be hired.
   D. Liliana must be given the job, or the firm could face a lawsuit.

SUMMARY

1 Defining and Explaining Abnormal Behavior

Abnormal behavior is deviant, maladaptive, or personally distressful. Theoretical perspectives on the causes of psychological disorders include biological, psychological, sociocultural, and biopsychosocial approaches.

Biological approaches to disorders describe psychological disorders as diseases with origins in structural, biochemical, and genetic factors. Psychological approaches include the behavioral, social cognitive, and trait perspectives. Sociocultural approaches place emphasis on the larger social context in which a person lives, including marriage, socioeconomic status, ethnicity, gender, and culture. Biopsychosocial approaches view the interactions among biological, psychological, and social factors as significant forces in producing both normal and abnormal behavior.

The classification of disorders provides a shorthand for communication, allows clinicians to make predictions about disorders, and helps them to decide on appropriate treatment. The *Diagnostic and Statistical Manual of Mental Disorders (DSM)* is the classification system clinicians use to diagnose psychological disorders. Some psychologists contend that the *DSM* perpetuates the medical model of psychological disorders, labels everyday problems as psychological disorders, and fails to address strengths.

Neurodevelopmental Disorders

Neurodevelopmental disorders are a class of psychological disorders that are diagnosed in childhood and often traced to atypical brain development, genetic differences, or prenatal exposure to substances that adversely affect development. Autism Spectrum Disorder (ASD) is typically diagnosed in early childhood and involves deficits in communication and social relationships. The level of impairment experienced by people with ASD is variable. ASD is linked to genetics and brain development but no single cause has been identified. Treatments include intense behavioral-oriented therapies as well as medication. Attention-deficit/hyperactivity disorder (ADHD) is characterized by problems maintaining attention, excessive, inappropriate activity, and high levels of impulsivity. ADHD is typically diagnosed in childhood and, left untreated, can have numerous negative consequences for people. Genetic and brain differences, especially in the prefrontal cortex and reward centers, are linked to ADHD. Treatment for ADHD typically involves stimulant medications. Nonmedical treatments such as psychotherapy, often offered in conjunction with medication, can also be effective in treating ADHD.

Anxiety and Anxiety-Related Disorders

Anxiety disorders are characterized by unrealistic and debilitatingly high levels of anxiety. Generalized anxiety disorder involves a high level of anxiety with no specific reason for the anxiety. Panic disorder involves attacks marked by the sudden onset of intense terror.

Specific phobias entail an irrational, overwhelming fear of a particular object, such as snakes, or a situation, such as flying. Social anxiety disorder refers to the intense fear that one will do something embarrassing or humiliating in public. Obsessive-compulsive disorder involves anxiety-provoking thoughts that will not go away (obsession) and/or urges to perform repetitive, ritualistic behaviors to prevent or produce some future situation (compulsion). A variety of experiential, psychological, and genetic factors have been shown to relate to these disorders.

Trauma and Stress-Related Disorders

Some psychological disorders are strongly tied to specific traumatic events. One such disorder, post-traumatic stress disorder (PTSD) includes flashbacks, emotional avoidance, emotional numbing, and excessive arousal. A variety of experiential, psychological, and genetic factors have been shown to relate to PTSD. Dissociative disorders are also linked to traumatic experience. Dissociative amnesia involves memory loss caused by extensive psychological stress. In dissociative identity disorder, formerly called multiple personality disorder, two or more distinct personalities are present in the same individual; this disorder is rare.

Disorders Involving Emotion and Mood

In depressive disorders, the individual experiences a serious depressive episode and depressed characteristics such as lethargy and hopelessness. Biological explanations of depressive disorders focus on heredity, neurophysiological abnormalities, and neurotransmitter deregulation. Psychological explanations include behavioral and cognitive perspectives.

Sociocultural explanations emphasize socioeconomic and ethnic factors, as well as gender.

Bipolar disorder is characterized by extreme mood swings that include one or more episodes of mania (an overexcited, unrealistic, optimistic state). Most individuals with bipolar disorder go through multiple cycles of depression interspersed with mania. Genetic influences are stronger predictors of bipolar disorder than depressive disorder, and biological processes are also a factor in bipolar disorder.

Eating Disorders

Anorexia nervosa is characterized by extreme underweight and starvation. The disorder is related to perfectionism and obsessive-compulsive tendencies. Bulimia nervosa involves a pattern of binge eating followed by purging through self-induced vomiting. In contrast, binge-eating disorder involves binge eating without purging.

Anorexia nervosa and bulimia nervosa are much more common in women than men, but there is no gender difference in binge-eating disorder. Although sociocultural factors were once primary in explaining eating disorders, newer evidence points to the role of biological factors.

Schizophrenia

Schizophrenia is a severe psychological disorder characterized by highly disordered thought processes. Positive symptoms of schizophrenia are behaviors and experiences that are present in individuals with schizophrenia but absent in healthy people; they include hallucinations, delusions, thought disorder, and disorders of movement. Negative symptoms of schizophrenia are behaviors and experiences that are part of healthy human life that are absent for those with this disorder; they include flat affect and an inability to plan or engage in goal-directed behavior.

Biological factors (heredity, structural brain abnormalities, and problems in neurotransmitter regulation, especially dopamine), psychological factors (vulnerability-stress hypothesis or diathesis-stress model), and sociocultural factors may be involved in schizophrenia. Psychological and sociocultural factors are not viewed as stand-alone causes of schizophrenia, but they are related to the course of the disorder.

Personality Disorders

Personality disorders are chronic, maladaptive cognitive-behavioral patterns that are thoroughly integrated into an individual's personality. Two common types are antisocial personality disorder (ASPD) and borderline personality disorder (BPD).

Antisocial personality disorder is characterized by guiltlessness, lawbreaking, exploitation of others, irresponsibility, and deceit. Individuals with this disorder often lead a life of crime and violence. Psychopaths—remorseless predators who engage in violence to get what they want—are a subgroup of individuals with ASPD.

Borderline personality disorder is a pervasive pattern of instability in interpersonal relationships, self-image, and emotions. This disorder is related to self-harming behaviors such as cutting and suicide.

Biological factors for ASPD include genetic, brain, and autonomic nervous system differences. The potential causes of BPD are complex and include biological and cognitive factors as well as childhood experiences.

Suicide

Severe depression and other psychological disorders can lead individuals to want to end their lives. Theorists have proposed biological, psychological, and sociocultural explanations of suicide. The interpersonal theory of suicide suggests that dying by suicide requires the desire to die and the acquired capability to kill oneself.

 ## Combatting Stigma

Stigma can create a significant barrier for people coping with a psychological disorder, as well as for their loved ones. Fear of being labeled can prevent individuals with a disorder from getting treatment and from talking about their problems with family and friends. In addition, the stigma attached to psychological disorders can lead to prejudice and discrimination toward individuals who are struggling with these problems. Having a disorder and experiencing the stigma associated with it can also negatively affect the physical health of such individuals. We can help to combat stigma by acknowledging the strengths and the achievements of individuals coping with psychological disorders.

KEY TERMS

abnormal behavior
anorexia nervosa
antisocial personality disorder (ASPD)
anxiety disorders
attention-deficit/hyperactivity disorder (ADHD)
binge-eating disorder (BED)
bipolar disorder
borderline personality disorder (BPD)

bulimia nervosa
catatonia
comorbidity
delusions
depressive disorders
dissociative amnesia
dissociative disorders
dissociative identity disorder (DID)
DSM-5
flat affect

generalized anxiety disorder
hallucinations
major depressive disorder (MDD)
medical model
obsessive-compulsive disorder (OCD)
panic disorder
personality disorders
post-traumatic stress disorder (PTSD)
psychosis

psychotherapy
referential thinking
risk factors
schizophrenia
social anxiety disorder or social phobia
somatic symptom and related disorders
specific phobia
vulnerability-stress hypothesis or diathesis-stress model

ANSWERS TO SELF-QUIZZES

Section 1: 1. A; 2. C; 3. C; 4. A
Section 2: 1. A; 2. D; 3. C; 4. A
Section 3: 1. D; 2. C; 3. B; 4. C
Section 4: 1. B; 2. C; 3. A; 4. C

Section 5: 1. A; 2. D; 3. B; 4. C
Section 6: 1. D; 2. A; 3. C; 4. B
Section 7: 1. B; 2. B; 3. D; 4. B
Section 8: 1. C; 2. C; 3. D; 4. A

Section 9: 1. C; 2. C; 3. D; 4. B
Section 10: 1. B; 2. D; 3. D; 4. B

13 Therapies

The Immense, Invisible Burden of Secrets

"**W**hy didn't we see it coming?" "How did we not know?" "How did she not know how much we loved her?" Such are the questions that hang in the air for family and friends left behind by suicide. Losing a loved one is never easy, but losing someone to suicide is, perhaps uniquely, devastating. When a loved one commits suicide, it is the abrupt end of conversation: It reveals all that we did not know that was going on behind someone else's eyes.

The first time Jonathan Roth attempted suicide, he begged his family to keep it secret, fearing the stigma of being called "crazy" (Roth, 2016). His family had no idea that their agreement only signaled their agreement with his shame. Five months later, he ended his life. Jonathan's family realized, too late, that there was no more shame in his psychological disorder than in a physical illness. And they realized that he was, secretly, suffering. Suicide reveals secrets. And often, the suicide itself becomes a secret (Levi-Belz, 2016), hidden in vaguely worded obituaries and even fictitious illnesses.

Secret suffering has a particular sting. Holding in a secret prevents us from benefiting from the support of others, from sharing who we really are with others, and from getting a reality check. Like Jonathan, people sometimes feel they must hide psychological disorders and even milder distress. Yet, there is help and hope in unburdening ourselves to individuals who are trained to help.

©Maridav/Shutterstock

The science of psychology has led to the development of various treatments to help relieve psychological suffering. These different forms of therapy are the focus of this chapter. We first consider broad approaches to treating disorders. Then we turn to a consideration of psychotherapy, including effectiveness and the numerous approaches to psychotherapy devised by psychologists. Next we examine biological and sociocultural approaches to therapy.

1 Approaches to Treating Psychological Disorders

To begin our survey of treatments for psychological disorders, we review three broad approaches to the topic—psychological, biological, and sociocultural. All therapies share the goal of relieving the suffering of individuals with psychological disorders, but they differ in their focus and in the types of professionals who are able to deliver them. Let's take a look at each of these broad perspectives on therapy.

The Psychological Approach to Therapy

clinical psychology
An area of psychology that integrates science and theory to prevent and treat psychological disorders.

Clinical psychology is the area of psychology that integrates science and theory to prevent and treat psychological disorders. To treat psychological disorders, clinical psychologists use psychotherapy. **Psychotherapy** is a nonmedical process that helps individuals with psychological disorders recognize and overcome their problems. Psychotherapists employ a number of strategies including talking, interpreting, listening, rewarding, challenging, and modeling.

psychotherapy
A nonmedical process that helps individuals with psychological disorders recognize and overcome their problems.

Psychotherapy is practiced by a variety of mental health professionals, including clinical psychologists, counselors, and social workers. Figure 1 lists the main types of mental health professionals, their degrees, the years of education required, and the nature of their training. Licensing and certification are two ways in which society retains control over psychotherapy practitioners (Carkhuff, 2017). Laws at the state level are used to license or certify such professionals. These laws specify the training individuals must have and provide for some assessment of an applicant's skill through formal examination.

During graduate school, those seeking a PhD in clinical psychology begin to see clients under the supervision of a licensed clinical psychologist. In addition to completing their graduate work, these individuals complete a clinical internship, one year spent providing supervised therapy in an accredited site, to hone their therapeutic skills. Psychotherapy may be given alone or in conjunction with medication. In most states in the United States this privilege is reserved for psychiatrists or other medical doctors.

The Biological Approach to Therapy

biological therapies
Also called *biomedical therapies*, treatments that reduce or eliminate the symptoms of psychological disorders by altering aspects of body functioning.

The biological approach to therapy adopts the medical model, which views psychological disorders as akin to diseases requiring specific treatments, typically medications. Such **biological therapies,** also called *biomedical therapies,* are treatments that reduce or eliminate the symptoms of psychological disorders by altering aspects of body functioning.

Generally speaking, those who administer biological therapies are required to have completed the training to become a medical doctor (that is, an MD). *Psychiatrists* are medical doctors who specialize in treating psychological disorders. In the United States,

Professional Type	Degree	Education Beyond Bachelor's Degree	Nature of Training
Clinical Psychologist	PhD or PsyD	5–7 years	Requires both clinical and research training. Includes a 1-year internship in a psychiatric hospital or mental health facility. Some universities have developed PsyD programs, which have a stronger clinical than research emphasis. The PsyD training program takes as long as the clinical psychology PhD program and also requires the equivalent of a 1-year internship.
Psychiatrist	MD	7–9 years	Four years of medical school, plus an internship and residency in psychiatry, is required. A psychiatry residency involves supervision in therapies, including psychotherapy and biomedical therapy.
Counseling Psychologist	MA, PhD, PsyD, or EdD	3–7 years	Similar to clinical psychologist but with emphasis on counseling and therapy. Some counseling psychologists specialize in vocational counseling. Some counselors complete master's degree training, others PhD or EdD training, in graduate schools of psychology or education.
School Psychologist	MA, PhD, PsyD, or EdD	3–7 years	Training in graduate programs of education or psychology. Emphasis on psychological assessment and counseling practices involving students' school-related problems. Training is at the master's or doctoral level.
Social Worker	MS W/DSW or PhD	2–5 years	Graduate work in a school of social work that includes specialized clinical training in mental health facilities.
Psychiatric Nurse	RN, MA, or PhD	0–5 years	Graduate work in a school of nursing with special emphasis on care of mentally disturbed individuals in hospital settings and mental health facilities.
Occupational Therapist	BS, MA, or PhD	0–5 years	Emphasis on occupational training with focus on physically or psychologically handicapped individuals. Stresses getting individuals back into the mainstream of work.
Pastoral Counselor	None to PhD or DD (Doctor of Divinity)	0–5 years	Requires ministerial background and training in psychology. An internship in a mental health facility as a chaplain is recommended.
Counselor	MA or MEd	2 years	Graduate work in a department of psychology or department of education with specialized training in counseling techniques.

FIGURE 1 Main Types of Mental Health Professionals A wide range of professionals with varying levels of training have taken on the challenge of helping people with psychological disorders.

psychiatrists complete medical school and then spend an additional four years in a psychiatric residency program. During their residency, these individuals continue training in diagnosing disorders, understanding the effects of drug therapies on disorders, and practicing psychotherapy (Schmidt & Foli-Andersen, 2017). For licensing in the United States, these individuals are required to demonstrate proficiency in different approaches to psychotherapy that we will review later in this chapter. As noted above, although psychologists and psychiatrists can both administer psychotherapy, for the most part, only psychiatrists can prescribe medications. When a psychotherapist believes that a client would benefit from medication, he or she might refer that client to a trusted psychiatrist to obtain a prescription.

For a number of years, psychologists have sought to obtain the right to prescribe drug treatments to their clients. As of this writing, the only states that permit psychologists to prescribe drugs are New Mexico and Louisiana. In these states, clinical psychologists complete additional training in medicine to qualify for prescription privileges. Other states have also considered granting psychologists these privileges, often in response to a lack of psychiatrists to treat those with psychological disorders in many areas.

Those who support the idea that psychologists ought to have prescription privileges argue that this change in regulations would make treatment more efficient for those with psychological disorders. In addition, they note that a psychologist's likely first impulse is to treat with psychotherapy, rather than medication, reducing the potential overuse of strong drugs when they are not needed. Those who oppose such a change note that psychoactive drugs are powerful and affect many body systems. They feel that additional training simply cannot replace the level of expertise required to prescribe and monitor these medicines. Further, those with psychological disorders may also have physical illnesses that psychologists would not be trained to diagnose or treat.

What do you think? Should psychologists have prescription privileges? Do they in your state?

The Sociocultural Approach to Therapy

sociocultural therapies
Treatments that acknowledge the relationships, roles, and cultural contexts that characterize an individual's life, often bringing them into the therapeutic context.

In the treatment of psychological disorders, psychological therapies seek to modify emotions, thinking, and behavior, and biological therapies change the body. In contrast, **sociocultural therapies** view the individual as part of a system of relationships that are influenced by social and cultural factors. This approach to therapy involves acknowledging the relationships, roles, and cultural contexts that characterize a person's life and often bring them into the therapeutic context (Becvar & Becvar, 2017; D'Arrigo-Patrick & others, 2017; Feltham, Hanley, & Winter, 2017).

From the sociocultural approach, to help a person suffering, we must recognize the many layers of social connections that exist in the person's life and how these may contribute to not only the development of psychological problems but their treatment as well. The sociocultural approach to therapy recognizes and seeks to intervene within these social connections, recognizing the person as a member of a couple, a family, and a group. Sociocultural approaches acknowledge as well that individual's lives may be shaped in important ways by societal norms, roles, and cultural expectations and beliefs (Aggarwal, 2018).

Sociocultural approaches to therapy may be practiced by trained psychotherapists, social workers, psychiatric social workers (those especially trained to intervene with those with psychological disorders), as well as paraprofessionals. A *paraprofessional* is an individual who has been taught by a professional to provide some mental health services but who does not have formal mental health training (Shechtman & Tutian, 2017). The paraprofessional may have personally had the disorder; for example, a chemical dependency counselor may also be a person recovering from addiction.

self-quiz

1. The area of psychology that integrates science and theory to prevent and treat psychological disorders is called
   A. personality psychology.
   B. social psychology.
   C. clinical psychology.
   D. abnormal psychology.

2. Which of the following occupations requires a medical degree?
   A. psychotherapist
   B. paraprofessional
   C. psychologist
   D. psychiatrist

3. A nonmedical process that helps individuals with psychological disorders recognize and overcome their problems is the definition of
   A. psychiatric treatment.
   B. psychotherapy.
   C. social intervention.
   D. sociological analysis.

APPLY IT! 4. Your friend Susanna tells you that, based on what she's seen on TV, she knows she wants to be a psychiatrist. It is her dream to spend each day interacting with others and through that interaction help them to break free of psychological disorders. Her plan is to major in psychology and then enter a PhD program in clinical psychology. Which of the following is the best advice for Susanna?
   A. Her plan sounds great, but she is not going to be a psychiatrist; she's going to be a psychologist.
   B. Susanna has planned the exact right course for becoming a psychiatrist.
   C. Susanna's plan will qualify her to prescribe drugs but not do therapy.
   D. Susanna will be able to both prescribe drugs and perform psychotherapy.

2 Psychotherapy

Although there are different types of psychotherapy, they all involve a trained professional engaging in an interpersonal relationship with someone who is suffering. Later in this section, we will review the specific types of psychotherapies that have been developed from broad theoretical approaches in psychology. Before we do so, let's consider some general issues that are common to all forms of psychotherapy.

Central Issues in Psychotherapy

Psychotherapy can be a very desirable type of treatment. One study showed that 90 percent of those surveyed report that they would prefer to talk to someone than to take medicines for their problems (Duncan & others, 2010). Still, a person seeking psychotherapy might wonder whether it works, whether some therapies work better than others, what factors influence a therapy's effectiveness, and how forms of therapy differ. In this section, we address these questions.

Psychotherapy works! And without a lot of side effects! Are you surprised by these conclusions?

DOES PSYCHOTHERAPY WORK?   There are many debates in psychology, but the effectiveness of psychotherapy in treating psychological disorders is not one of them. Many studies have been conducted to answer the question, "Does psychotherapy work?" and the answer is a resounding yes (American Psychological Association, 2012). A large body of research and multiple meta-analyses support this conclusion (Beck, 2005; Butler & others, 2006; Clemens, 2010; Duncan & Reese, 2013; Lambert, 2001; Lipsey & Wilson, 1993; Luborsky & others, 2002; Wampold, 2001). Individuals who experience 12 to 14 sessions of psychotherapy are more likely to improve compared to those who receive a placebo treatment or no treatment at all and are likely to maintain these improvements for 2 to 3 years, provided that the treatment they receive is based on sound psychological theory (Lambert, 2013). Figure 2 shows the results of an analysis of treatment outcomes.

People who are contemplating seeing a psychotherapist do not just want to know whether psychotherapy in general is effective, but also which form of psychotherapy is most effective. In some ways, this question pits the different brands of psychotherapy against each other in a kind of horse race. It is important to bear in mind that it is human nature for psychologists to have allegiances or loyalties to the brand of psychotherapy they use and in which they were trained. The results of many studies addressing the "which therapy is the best" question show that, although there is strong research supporting the notion that therapy is effective, no one therapy has been shown to be significantly

PSYCHOLOGICAL INQUIRY

FIGURE 2 **The Effects of Psychotherapy** In a review of studies, more than 70 percent of individuals who saw a therapist improved, whereas less than 40 percent who received a placebo and less than 20 percent who received no treatment improved (Lambert, 2001).
> **Why do you think participants in the "no treatment" group improved?**
> **Do these results allow us to make a causal claim about the effectiveness of therapy? Why or why not? Does one therapy work better than others?**

more effective than the others, overall (Duncan & Reese, 2013; Gelo, Pritz, & Rieken, 2014; Lambert, 2001; Luborsky & others, 2002; Wampold, 2001; Wampold & others, 2017).

Indeed, the answer to the question which type of therapy works best may be, "It depends on the person's diagnosis." That is, some therapies might be more effective than others for particular psychological disorders (Cooper & others, 2017; Palpacuer & others, 2017). Some psychologists believe that therapies should be tailored to particular disorders, and therapists should rely on research evidence when they decide on a course of treatment (Chambless, 2002; Duncan & Reese, 2013). From this perspective, ideally, each disorder would be treated using the particular type of therapy that has been shown by research to work best for that disorder (Christopherson & VanScoyoc, 2013; Chu & Leino, 2017).

Other psychologists argue that targeting particular disorders with specific treatments amounts to taking an overly medical approach (Berg & Slaattelid, 2017; Horvath, 2013; Miller & others, 2013). In medicine, drugs (like antibiotics) are specifically prescribed to treat particular illnesses (like strep throat), but, these critics argue, psychotherapies are not like medicines that target a particular disease. They stress that psychotherapies are best understood as promoting better functioning through common characteristics that lead to benefits. These psychologists are concerned that closely dictating what therapists should do takes away the flexibility that potentially might be vital for improvement.

Relying on empirical research in making treatment decisions is challenging because the evidence is not always clear-cut: For instance, research is not always conducted on appropriate samples (that is, people who are actually diagnosed with particular disorders), or the samples may not be representative of the people clinicians see in practice (Wampold, 2013). A serious problem in relying on empirical evidence to guide treatment decisions is that such evidence is limited or nonexistent for many disorders. Moreover, relying on research to direct decisions leaves the clinician in the dark when research-recommended treatments do not work for a particular client.

A special task force appointed by the president of the American Psychological Association reached a compromise between these two positions. The task force endorsed evidence-based practice. **Evidence-based practice** means that decisions about treatment are made using the best available research and considering the therapist's clinical judgment and client characteristics, culture, and preferences (APA Presidential Task Force on Evidence-Based Practice, 2006; Barlow & others, 2013; Duncan & Reese, 2013; Hofmann & Barlow, 2014). Although evidence-based practice recognizes the importance of scientific evidence, it also permits flexibility for clinicians to consider a broad range of factors in deciding on a course of therapy.

Some people think this compromise is a good one, and others think it is a cop out: After all, as scientists we should be putting our money where our mouth is. What do you think?

evidence-based practice
Integration of the best available research with clinical expertise in the context of client characteristics, culture, and preferences.

FACTORS IN EFFECTIVE PSYCHOTHERAPY Research has also addressed the factors that play an important role in determining the effectiveness of psychotherapy. Here we review three such factors: the therapeutic alliance, the therapist, and the client.

The Therapeutic Alliance The **therapeutic alliance** is the relationship between the therapist and client. When therapists and clients feel they are engaged in a real working relationship characterized by trust, respect, and cooperation, the therapeutic alliance is strong. This alliance is an important element of successful psychotherapy (Laws & others, 2017; Quilty & others, 2017).

therapeutic alliance
The relationship between the therapist and client—an important element of successful psychotherapy.

It is important for therapists to monitor the quality of the relationship with each client (Jacobs & others, 2016; Okun & Kantrowitz, 2015). Clients of therapists who did not assess the quality of the alliance were two times more likely to drop out of therapy (Hubble & Miller, 2004). Among those who completed therapy, clients of therapists who failed to assess their alliance were three to four times more likely to have a negative outcome (Hubble & Miller, 2004).

The Therapist Whether psychotherapy works or not depends more on the particular therapist than on the type of therapy used. Therapists differ in their level of expertise, their deep knowledge about psychological problems, and their treatment (Miller & others, 2013). Therapists with high expertise are those who not only possess a great deal of knowledge but who continue to learn, and monitor client progress, and make changes when necessary.

Research has also shown that the match between a therapist's style and client personality can influence whether therapy is effective. For example, if a client has a strong resistance to changing, a therapist who is more laid back and less directive may have greater success than one who engages directly with the client (Beutler & others, 2012).

The Client   Another major factor in therapeutic outcomes is the person seeking treatment. Indeed, meta-analyses suggest that the quality of the client's participation is the most important determinant of whether therapy is successful (Bohart & Tallman, 2010; McKay, Imel, & Wampold, 2006). Even though individuals often seek therapy due to difficulties and problems in their life, it is their strengths, abilities, skills, and motivation that account for therapeutic success (Fuertes & Nutt Williams, 2017; Jensen, Mortensen, & Lotz, 2014; Lombardi, Button, & Westra, 2014; Wampold & Brown, 2005). One study found that patients' failure to develop increased self-esteem over the course of therapy was the main reason they dropped out of therapy (Kegel & Flückiger, 2014). A review of the extensive evidence on therapeutic efficacy concluded: "The data make abundantly clear that therapy does not make clients work, but rather clients make therapy work" (Hubble & Miller, 2004, p. 347).

The remainder of this section focuses on four main approaches to psychotherapy: psychodynamic, humanistic, behavioral, and cognitive therapy, as well as eclectic approaches to therapy that combine many different techniques.

Psychodynamic Therapies

The **psychodynamic therapies** stress the importance of the unconscious mind, extensive interpretation by the therapist, and the role of early childhood experiences in the development of an individual's problems. The goal of psychodynamic therapies is to help individuals gain insight into the unconscious conflicts that are the source of their problems. Many psychodynamic approaches grew out of Freud's psychoanalytic theory of personality. Today some therapists with a psychodynamic perspective practice Freudian techniques, but others do not (Minges, Solomonov, & Barber, 2017).

PSYCHOANALYSIS   **Psychoanalysis** is Freud's therapeutic technique for analyzing an individual's unconscious thoughts. Freud believed that a person's current problems could be traced to childhood experiences, many of which involved unconscious sexual conflicts. Only through extensive questioning, probing, and analyzing was Freud able to put together the pieces of the client's personality and help the individual become aware of how these early experiences were affecting present behavior. The psychoanalyst's goal is to bring unconscious conflicts into conscious awareness, thus giving the client insight into his or her core problems and freeing the individual from unconscious influences. To reach the shadowy world of the unconscious, psychoanalytic therapists use the therapeutic techniques of free association, interpretation, dream analysis, analysis of transference, and analysis of resistance.

Free association involves encouraging individuals to say aloud whatever comes to mind, no matter how trivial or embarrassing. When Freud detected a person resisting the spontaneous flow of thoughts, he probed further. He believed that the crux of the person's problem probably lurked below this point of resistance. Encouraging people to talk freely, Freud reasoned, would allow their deepest thoughts and feelings to emerge. *Catharsis* is the release of emotional tension a person experiences when reliving an emotionally charged and conflicting experience.

Interpretation plays an important role in psychoanalysis. Interpretation means that the analyst does not take the patient's statements and behavior at face value; rather, to understand

psychodynamic therapies
Treatments that stress the importance of the unconscious mind, extensive interpretation by the therapist, and the role of early childhood experiences in the development of an individual's problems.

psychoanalysis
Freud's therapeutic technique for analyzing an individual's unconscious thoughts.

free association
A psychoanalytic technique that involves encouraging individuals to say aloud whatever comes to mind, no matter how trivial or embarrassing.

interpretation
A psychoanalyst's search for symbolic, hidden meanings in what the client says and does during therapy.

the source of the person's conflicts, the therapist searches for symbolic, hidden meanings in the individual's words and deeds. From time to time, the therapist suggests possible meanings of the person's statements and behavior.

dream analysis
A psychoanalytic technique for interpreting a person's dreams.

Dream analysis is a psychoanalytic technique for interpreting a person's dreams. Psychoanalysts believe that dreams contain information about unconscious thoughts, wishes, and conflicts (Freud, 1899/1911). From this perspective, dreams provide our unconscious with an outlet to express our unconscious wishes, a mental theater in which our deepest and most secret desires can be played out. According to Freud, every dream, even our worst nightmare, contains a hidden, disguised wish. Nightmares might express a wish for punishment, or the sheer horror we feel during the nightmare might itself be the disguise.

Freud distinguished between the dream's manifest content and latent content. *Manifest content* refers to the conscious, remembered aspects of a dream. If you wake up remembering a dream about being back in sixth grade with your teacher scolding you for not turning in your homework, that is the dream's manifest content. *Latent content* refers to the unconscious, hidden aspects that are symbolized by the manifest content. To understand your dream, a psychoanalyst might ask you to free-associate to each of the elements of the manifest content. What comes to your mind when you think of being in sixth grade or of your teacher? According to Freud, the latent meaning of a dream is locked inside the dreamer's unconscious mind. The psychoanalyst's goal is to unlock that secret meaning by having the individual free-associate about the manifest dream elements. The analyst interprets the dream by examining the manifest content for disguised unconscious wishes and needs, especially those that are sexual and aggressive. Dream symbols can mean different things to different dreamers. Freud (1899/1911) recognized that the true meaning of any dream symbol depends on the individual.

The dreamer "knows" what the dream means, but its meaning is locked in the unconscious mind.

Freud believed that transference was an inevitable—and essential—aspect of the analyst–patient relationship. **Transference** is the psychoanalytic term for the client's relating to the analyst in ways that reproduce or relive important relationships in the client's life. A client might interact with an analyst as if the analyst were a parent or lover, for example. Transference can be used therapeutically as a model of how individuals relate to important people in their lives (Herron, 2015).

transference
A client's relating to the psychoanalyst in ways that reproduce or relive important relationships in the client's life.

Resistance is the psychoanalytic term for the client's unconscious defense strategies that prevent the analyst from understanding the person's problems. Resistance occurs because it is painful for the client to bring conflicts into conscious awareness. By resisting analysis, the individual does not have to face

Freud would say that the appearance of resistance means the analyst is getting very close to the truth.

resistance
A client's unconscious defense strategies that prevent the person from gaining insight into his or her psychological problems.

the threatening truths that underlie his or her problems. Showing up late or missing sessions, arguing with the psychoanalyst, and faking free associations are examples of resistance. A major goal of the analyst is to break through this resistance.

CONTEMPORARY PSYCHODYNAMIC THERAPIES Psychodynamic therapy has changed extensively since its beginnings almost a century ago. Nonetheless, many contemporary psychodynamic therapists still probe unconscious thoughts about early childhood experiences to get clues to their clients' current problems, and they try to help individuals gain insight into their emotionally laden, repressed conflicts (Marzillier, 2014; Morris, Javier, & Herron, 2015). However, contemporary psychoanalysts accord more power to the conscious mind and to a person's current relationships, and they generally place less emphasis on sex (Minges, Solomonov, & Barber, 2017). In addition, clients today rarely lie on a couch as they did in Freud's time, or see their therapist several times a week, as was the norm in early psychodynamic therapy. Instead, they sit in a comfortable chair facing the therapist, and weekly appointments are typical.

Some contemporary psychodynamic therapists focus on the self in social contexts, as Heinz Kohut (1977) recommended. In Kohut's view, early social relationships with attachment figures such as parents are critical. As we develop, we internalize those relationships, and they serve as the basis for our sense of self. Kohut (1977) believed that the therapist's job is to replace unhealthy childhood relationships with the healthy relationship the therapist provides. From Kohut's perspective, the therapist needs to interact with the client in empathic and understanding ways. Empathy and understanding are also cornerstones for humanistic therapies, as we next consider.

Humanistic Therapies

The underlying philosophy of humanistic therapies is captured by the metaphor of how an acorn, if provided with appropriate conditions, will grow—pushing naturally toward its actualization as an oak tree (Schneider, 2002). In **humanistic therapies,** people are encouraged toward self-understanding and personal growth. The humanistic therapies are unique in their emphasis on the person's self-healing capacities. In contrast to psychodynamic therapies, humanistic therapies emphasize conscious rather than unconscious thoughts, the present rather than the past, and self-fulfillment rather than illness (House, Kalisch, & Maidman, 2017).

©Brand X Pictures/Stockbyte/Getty Images Plus

humanistic therapies
Treatments that uniquely emphasize people's self-healing capacities and that encourage clients to understand themselves and to grow personally.

Client-centered therapy (also called *Rogerian therapy* or *nondirective therapy*) is a form of humanistic therapy, developed by Carl Rogers, in which the therapist provides a warm, supportive atmosphere to improve the client's self-concept and to encourage the client to gain insight into problems (Rogers, 1961, 1980). The goal of client-centered therapy is to help clients identify and understand their own genuine feelings and become more *congruent*, bringing their actual self closer to their ideal self.

client-centered therapy
Also called *Rogerian therapy* or *nondirective therapy,* a form of humanistic therapy, developed by Rogers, in which the therapist provides a warm, supportive atmosphere to improve the client's self-concept and to encourage the client to gain insight into problems.

One way to achieve this goal is through active listening and **reflective speech,** a technique in which the therapist mirrors the client's own feelings back to the client. For example, as a woman is describing her grief over the traumatic loss of her husband in a drunk-driving accident, the therapist might suggest "You sound angry" to help her identify her feelings.

reflective speech
A technique in which the therapist mirrors the client's own feelings back to the client.

Rogers believed that humans require three essential elements to grow: unconditional positive regard, empathy, and genuineness. These three elements are reflected in his approach to therapy:

- *Unconditional positive regard:* The therapist constantly recognizes the inherent value of the client, providing a context for personal growth and self-acceptance.
- *Empathy:* The therapist strives to put himself or herself in the client's shoes—to feel the emotions the client is feeling.
- *Genuineness:* The therapist is a real person in his or her relationship with the client, sharing feelings and not hiding behind a facade.

If you were a therapist, would you be able to maintain positive regard for a client while also being genuine? Imagine that your client admitted to harming children. Could you successfully offer the person positive regard?

Clinical Psychology and Social Psychology: Can Authentic Interactions Help Those with Social Anxiety?

One way that close relationships enhance our lives is by giving us a chance to express who we really are. We know that we have found a true friend when we have revealed our authentic selves and found someone who (still) loves us. In contrast, when our behavior involves hiding who we really are, it is difficult to feel good about ourselves (Gino, Kouchaki, & Galinsky, 2015) or our relationships (Gordon & Chen, 2016). One of the worst consequences of social anxiety disorder (SAD) is its effect on people's relationships. Those with SAD have fewer friends and report less satisfaction with their social relationships (Alden & Taylor, 2004; Dryman & others, 2016; Levine & others, 2015).

Individuals with SAD, who are terrified of being humiliated in social interactions, engage in what are called *safety behaviors* (Grumet & Fitzpatrick, 2016). Safety behaviors involve protecting oneself from feared outcomes by avoiding self-disclosure and putting up a false front. Such behavior makes sense: If you are extremely afraid of dreaded outcomes, keeping your true self hidden probably seems like a good idea. But note that as a result of their intense fear, those with SAD are robbed of the opportunity to be themselves around others as well as the other benefits that come with authentic self-expression.

A simple but elegant study (Plasencia, Taylor, & Alden, 2016) examined whether reducing safety behaviors would allow those with SAD to be more authentic and to enjoy a social interaction more. Individuals seeking treatment for SAD had a conversation with a member of the opposite sex (who was a confederate of the

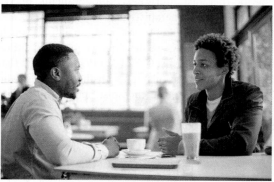

©Resolution Productions/ Blend Images/Getty Images

experimenters). Prior to the interaction, participants were randomly assigned to an experimental group or to a control group. In the experimental group, they were told that during the coming interaction, they should not do anything intended to hide their true feelings or their genuine selves. Even though they might be afraid, they needed to stay in the interaction and not engage in safety behaviors. The control group was told that simply engaging in social interactions for a longer time than usual was important. After the interaction, participants rated the quality of the interaction as well as their level of experienced authenticity.

The results showed that, compared to controls, those in the experimental group used fewer safety behaviors, reported more authenticity, and enjoyed the interaction more. Importantly, these outcomes were all related. The fewer safety behaviors, the more authentic participants felt. In turn, the more authentic they felt, the higher their ratings of interaction quality (Plasencia, Taylor, & Alden, 2016). These results paint a poignant portrait of the prison that SAD can be for those struggling with it. Their anxiety leads to behaviors that keep them separate from others, denying them the warm light of authenticity. But just as Carl Rogers himself might have predicted, being who we truly are in a genuine way with another leads to high quality interactions and perhaps over time, better well-being.

\\ **What safety behaviors do you engage in?**

Do It!

To experience Rogerian therapy firsthand, a quick YouTube search for Carl Rogers and therapy will give you a chance to see his approach in action.

For genuineness to coexist with unconditional positive regard, that regard must be a sincere expression of the therapist's true feelings. The therapist may distinguish between the person's behavior and the person himself or herself. Although the person is acknowledged as a valuable human being, the client's behavior can be evaluated negatively: "You are a good person but your actions are not." Rogers's positive view of humanity extended to his view of therapists. He believed that by being genuine with the client, the therapist could help the client improve.

The idea that authentic interactions are a key to psychotherapeutic healing is at the very heart of humanistic approaches. Individuals with social anxiety disorder experience interpersonal encounters as highly stressful and likely to lead to negative judgments. Can engaging authentic social interactions be helpful to these people? To read about research addressing this question, see the Intersection.

Behavior Therapies

Psychodynamic and humanistic methods are sometimes called *insight therapies* because they encourage self-awareness as the path to psychological health. Behavior therapies take a different approach. Insight and self-awareness are not the keys to helping individuals develop more adaptive behavior patterns, behavior therapists say. Rather, behavior therapists offer action-oriented strategies to help people change their behavior (Levis, 2017). Specifically, **behavior therapies** use principles of learning to reduce or eliminate maladaptive behavior. Behavior therapists say that individuals can become aware of why they are depressed and yet still be depressed. They strive to eliminate the depressed *symptoms* or *behaviors* rather than trying to get individuals to gain insight into, or awareness of, why they are depressed (Miltenberger, 2016).

Although initially based almost exclusively on the learning principles of classical and operant conditioning, behavior therapies have become more diverse (Spiegler & Guevremont, 2016). As social cognitive theory grew in popularity, behavior therapists increasingly included observational learning, cognitive factors, and self-instruction in their treatments (Perry & others, 2017; Spain & others, 2017). Through self-instruction, therapists try to get people to change what they say to themselves.

behavior therapies
Treatments, based on behavioral and social cognitive theories, that use principles of learning to reduce or eliminate maladaptive behavior.

CLASSICAL CONDITIONING TECHNIQUES Various techniques of classical conditioning have been used in treating psychological disorders. For example in the treatment of specific phobias, clinicians have used systematic desensitization. **Systematic desensitization** is a behavior therapy that treats anxiety by teaching the client to associate deep relaxation with increasingly intense anxiety-producing situations.

Figure 3 shows a desensitization hierarchy. *Desensitization* involves exposing someone to a feared situation in a real or an imagined way (McMullen & others, 2017). Desensitization is based on the classical conditioning process of extinction. During extinction, the conditioned stimulus is presented without the unconditioned stimulus, leading to a decreased conditioned response. During systematic desensitization, the person continually maintains a state of relaxation in the face of increasingly anxiety-producing stimuli.

systematic desensitization
A behavior therapy that treats anxiety by teaching the client to associate deep relaxation with increasingly intense anxiety-producing situations.

Another application of classical conditioning to changing behavior is aversive conditioning. Aversive conditioning entails repeated pairings of an undesirable behavior with aversive stimuli to decrease the behavior's positive associations. Through aversive conditioning, people can learn to avoid behaviors such as smoking, overeating, and drinking alcohol. Electric shocks, nausea-inducing substances, and verbal insults are some of the noxious stimuli used in aversive conditioning (Sommer & others, 2006). Figure 4 illustrates how classical conditioning is the backbone of aversive conditioning.

OPERANT CONDITIONING TECHNIQUES The idea behind using operant conditioning as a therapeutic approach is that just as maladaptive behavior patterns are learned, they can be unlearned. Therapy involves conducting a careful analysis of the person's environment to determine the consequences that are associated with problematic behaviors. Specifically, the question to be answered is, "How is the problematic behavior being reinforced?" Especially important is changing the consequences of the person's behavior to ensure that healthy, adaptive replacement behaviors are followed by positive reinforcement.

1 A month before an examination

2 Two weeks before an examination

3 A week before an examination

4 Five days before an examination

5 Four days before an examination

6 Three days before an examination

7 Two days before an examination

8 One day before an examination

9 The night before an examination

10 On the way to the university on the day of an examination

11 Before the unopened doors of the examination room

12 Awaiting distribution of examination papers

13 The examination paper lies facedown before her

14 In the process of answering an examination paper

FIGURE 3   A Desensitization Hierarchy Involving Test Anxiety In this hierarchy, the individual begins with his or her least feared circumstance (a month before the exam) and moves through each of the circumstances until reaching the most feared circumstance (answering the exam questions on test day). At each step, the person replaces fear with deep relaxation and successful visualization.

©Hero Images/Getty Images

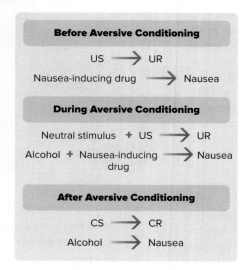

FIGURE 4   Classical Conditioning: The Backbone of Aversive Conditioning This figure shows how classical conditioning can produce a conditioned aversion to alcohol. Recall the abbreviations US (unconditioned stimulus), UR (unconditioned response), CS (conditioned stimulus), and CR (conditioned response).
> What is the conditioned stimulus? > What is the likely effect of alcohol prior to aversion therapy? Is this effect learned or not? > What role, if any, does a person's motivation play in aversive conditioning?

These ideas are used in applied behavior analysis, which involves establishing positive reinforcement connections between behaviors and rewards so that individuals engage in appropriate behavior and extinguish inappropriate behavior. Consider, for example, a man with obsessive-compulsive disorder (OCD) who engages in a compulsive ritual such as checking that he has locked the door of his house 10 times every time he leaves his home. If he does not complete his ritual, he is overcome with anxiety that something dreadful will happen. Note that whenever he completes the ritual, nothing dreadful does happen, and his anxiety is relieved. His compulsion is a behavior that is reinforced by the relief of anxiety and the fact that nothing dreadful happens. Such a ritual, then, could be viewed as avoidance learning. An operant conditioning–based therapy would involve stopping the behavior to extinguish this avoidance. Specifically, allowing the man to experience the lack of catastrophic consequences in the absence of repeatedly checking the lock, as well as training him to relax, might help to eliminate the compulsive rituals. Indeed, behavior therapy is effective in treating OCD (Bonchek, 2009).

It may strike you as unusual that behavioral approaches do not emphasize gaining insight and self-awareness. However, for the very reason that they do not stress these goals, such treatments may be particularly useful in individuals whose cognitive abilities are limited, such as adults with developmental disabilities or children. Applied behavior analysis can be used, for instance, to treat individuals with autism who engage in self-injurious behaviors such as head banging (LeBlanc & Gillis, 2012; Wheeler, Mayton, & Carter, 2015).

 BECAUSE it does not rely on cognitive ability, therapy directed at changing behaviors can be remarkably useful.

As reviewed in the chapter on psychological disorders, applied behavior analysis has proven effective in treating individuals with autism (Thompson, 2013). A research review of 65 studies concluded that early intervention using high-intensity behavior analysis over extended time frames produced improved cognitive and language functioning in children with autism spectrum disorders (Weitlauf & others, 2014).

Cognitive Therapies

cognitive therapies
Treatments emphasizing that cognitions (thoughts) are the main source of psychological problems; therapies that attempt to change the individual's feelings and behaviors by changing cognitions.

Cognitive therapies emphasize that *cognitions,* or thoughts, are the main source of psychological problems, and they attempt to change the individual's feelings and behaviors by changing cognitions. *Cognitive restructuring,* a general concept for changing a pattern of thought that is presumed to be causing maladaptive behavior or emotion, is central to cognitive therapies. Cognitive therapies differ from psychoanalytic therapies by focusing more on overt symptoms than on deep-seated unconscious thoughts, by providing more structure to the individual's thoughts, and by being less concerned about the origin of the problem. Compared with humanistic therapies, cognitive therapies provide more of a framework and more analysis, and they are based on specific cognitive techniques.

FOUNDATIONS OF COGNITIVE THERAPIES
All cognitive therapies involve two basic assumptions: Human beings have control over their feelings, and how

individuals feel about something depends on how they think about it (Beck, 2006; Ellis, 2005). This approach to therapy was introduced by Aaron Beck, whose research and practice laid the foundation for applying cognitive principles to treating psychological disorders. Cognitive therapy involves getting people to recognize the connections between their thoughts and their feelings and helping them use thinking to change their feelings (Beck & Haigh, 2014; Müller-Engelmann & Steil, 2017). *Cognitive restructuring,* a general concept for changing a pattern of thought that is presumed to be causing maladaptive behavior or emotion, is central to cognitive therapies.

When was the last time you were upset? What kinds of thoughts did you have about the situation?

Unfortunately, thoughts that lead to emotions can happen so rapidly that we are not even aware of them. Thus, the first goal of therapy is to bring these automatic thoughts into awareness so that they can be changed. The therapist helps clients to identify their own automatic thoughts and to keep records of their thought content and emotional reactions.

With the therapist's assistance, clients learn to recognize logical errors in their thinking and to challenge the accuracy of these automatic thoughts. Logical errors in thinking can lead individuals to the following erroneous beliefs (Butcher, Hooley, & Mineka, 2013):

Aaron Beck (b. 1921) *Aaron Beck's method stresses that the goal of therapy should be to help people to recognize and eliminate illogical and self-defeating thinking.*
©Clem Murray/Philadelphia Inquirer/MCT/Newscom

- Perceiving the world as harmful while ignoring evidence to the contrary—for example, when a young woman still feels worthless after a friend has just told her how much other people genuinely like her.

- Overgeneralizing on the basis of limited examples—such as a man's seeing himself as worthless because one person stopped dating him.

- Magnifying the importance of undesirable events—such as seeing one failure as the end of the world.

- Engaging in absolutist thinking—such as exaggerating the importance of someone's mildly critical comment and perceiving it as proof of total inadequacy.

Do It!

The Beck Institute for Cognitive Behavior Therapy maintains a website chronicling the latest developments in cognitive therapy and including a variety of videos of Beck himself. Check out the site at www.beckinstitute.org/

Cognitive therapists guide individuals in identifying their irrational and self-defeating thoughts. Then they get clients to challenge these thoughts and to consider more positive ways of thinking. Cognitive therapies all involve the basic assumption that human beings have control over their feelings and that how individuals feel about something depends on how they think about it.

Figure 5 describes some of the most widely used cognitive therapy techniques.

COGNITIVE-BEHAVIOR THERAPY   **Cognitive-behavior therapy (CBT)** is a combination of cognitive therapy, with its emphasis on reducing self-defeating thoughts, and behavior therapy, with its emphasis on changing behavior. In CBT, the therapist takes a directive role, engaging in a dialogue to help the client identify automatic thoughts and the feelings they produce and working with the client to change those thoughts while also focusing on changing behavior (Wright & others, 2017). In CBT, the client may be given homework assignments directed at these behavioral changes.

cognitive-behavior therapy
A therapy that combines cognitive therapy and behavior therapy with the goal of developing the client's self-efficacy.

Self-instructional methods are cognitive-behavior techniques aimed at teaching individuals to modify their own behavior (Watson & Tharp, 2014). Using self-instructional techniques, cognitive-behavior therapists prompt clients to change what they say to themselves. The therapist gives the client examples of constructive statements, known as *reinforcing self-statements,* which the client can repeat in order to take positive steps to cope with stress or meet a goal. The therapist also encourages the client to practice the statements through role playing and strengthens the client's newly acquired skills through reinforcement.

An important aspect of cognitive-behavior therapy is self-efficacy: the belief that one can master a situation and produce positive outcomes (Bandura, 2001, 2009, 2010, 2012). At each step of the therapy process, clients need to bolster their confidence by telling

Cognitive Therapy Technique	Description	Example
Challenge Idiosyncratic Meanings	Explore personal meaning attached to the client's words and ask the client to consider alternatives.	When a client says he will be "devastated" by his spouse leaving, ask just how he would be devastated and ways he could avoid being devastated.
Question the Evidence	Systematically examine the evidence for the client's beliefs or assertions.	When a client says she can't live without her spouse, explore how she lived without the spouse before she was married.
Reattribution	Help the client distribute responsibility for events appropriately.	When a client says that his son's failure in school must be his fault, explore other possibilities, such as the quality of the school.
Examine Options and Alternatives	Help the client generate alternative actions to maladaptive ones.	If a client considers leaving school, explore whether tutoring or going part-time to school are good alternatives.
Decatastrophize	Help the client evaluate whether he is overestimating the nature of a situation.	If a client states that failure in a course means he or she must give up the dream of medical school, question whether this is a necessary conclusion.
Fantasize Consequences	Explore fantasies of a feared situation: if unrealistic, the client may recognize this; if realistic, work on effective coping strategies.	Help a client who fantasizes "falling apart" when asking the boss for a raise to role-play the situation and develop effective skills for making the request.
Examine Advantages and Disadvantages	Examine advantages and disadvantages of an issue, to instill a broader perspective.	If a client says he "was just born depressed and will always be that way," explore the advantages and disadvantages of holding that perspective versus other perspectives.
Turn Adversity to Advantage	Explore ways that difficult situations can be transformed into opportunities.	If a client has just been laid off, explore whether this is an opportunity for her to return to school.
Guided Association	Help the client see connections between different thoughts or ideas.	Draw the connections between a client's anger at his wife for going on a business trip and his fear of being alone.
Scaling	Ask the client to rate her emotions or thoughts on scales to help gain perspective.	If a client says she was overwhelmed by an emotion, ask her to rate her feelings on a scale from 0 (not at all) to 100 (I fell down in a faint).
Thought Stopping	Provide the client with ways of stopping a cascade of negative thoughts.	Teach an anxious client to picture a stop sign or hear a bell when anxious thoughts begin to snowball.
Distraction	Help the client find benign or positive distractions to take attention away from negative thoughts or emotions temporarily.	Have a client count to 200 by 13s when he feels himself becoming anxious.
Labeling of Distortions	Provide labels for specific types of distorted thinking to help the client gain more distance and perspective.	Have a client keep a record of the number of times a day she engages in all-or-nothing thinking—seeing things as all bad or all good.

FIGURE 5 **Cognitive Therapy Techniques** Cognitive therapists develop strategies to help change the way people think.

	Cause of Problem	Therapy Emphasis	Nature of Therapy and Techniques
Psychodynamic Therapies	Client's problems are symptoms of deep-seated, unresolved unconscious conflicts.	Discover underlying unconscious conflicts and work with client to develop insight.	Psychoanalysis, including free association, dream analysis, resistance, and transference: therapist interprets heavily, operant conditioning.
Humanistic Therapies	Client is not functioning at an optimal level of development.	Develop awareness of inherent potential for growth.	Person-centered therapy, including unconditional positive regard, genuineness, accurate empathy, and active listening; self-appreciation emphasized.
Behavior Therapies	Client has learned maladaptive behavior patterns.	Learn adaptive behavior patterns through changes in the environment or cognitive processes.	Observation of behavior and its controlling conditions; specific advice given about what should be done; therapies based on classical conditioning, operant conditioning.
Cognitive Therapies	Client has developed inappropriate thoughts.	Change feelings and behaviors by changing cognitions.	Conversation with client designed to get him or her to change irrational and self-defeating beliefs.

FIGURE 6 **Therapy Comparisons** Different therapies address the same problems in very different ways. Many therapists use the tools that seem right for any given client and his or her problems.

SOURCE: A. Freeman and M. A. Reinecke, "Cognitive Therapy," in A. S. Gurman, ed., Essential Psychotherapies.

themselves messages such as "I'm going to master my problem," "I can do it," "I'm improving," and "I'm getting better." As they gain confidence and engage in adaptive behavior, the successes become intrinsically motivating. Before long, individuals persist (with considerable effort) in their attempts to solve personal problems because of the positive outcomes that were set in motion by self-efficacy.

CBT is the most common form of therapy used today, and it has proved effective in treating a host of disorders. It has been integrated into treatment of anxiety disorders, depression, personality disorders, eating disorders, and, in conjunction with medication, bipolar disorder and schizophrenia. The four psychotherapies—psychodynamic, humanistic, behavior, and cognitive—are compared in Figure 6.

Therapy Integrations

As many as 50 percent of therapists identify themselves as not adhering to one particular method. Rather, they refer to themselves as "integrative" or "eclectic." **Integrative therapy** is a combination of techniques from different therapies based on the therapist's judgment of which particular methods will provide the greatest benefit for the client (Clarkin, 2012; Prochaska & Norcross, 2013). Integrative therapy is characterized by openness to various ways of applying diverse therapies. For example, a therapist might use a behavioral approach to treat an individual with panic disorder and a cognitive approach to treat a client with major depressive disorder.

integrative therapy Using a combination of techniques from different therapies based on the therapist's judgment of which particular methods will provide the greatest benefit for the client.

Because clients present a wide range of problems, it makes sense for therapists to use the best tools in each case rather than to adopt a "one size fits all" program. Sometimes a given psychological disorder is so difficult to treat that it requires the therapist to bring all of his or her tools to bear (Choi-Kain & others, 2017). For example, borderline personality disorder involves emotional instability, impulsivity, and self-harming behaviors. This disorder responds to a therapy called *dialectical behavior therapy*, or *DBT* (Lungu & Linehan, 2017). Like psychodynamic approaches, DBT assumes that early childhood experiences are important to the development of borderline personality disorder. However, DBT employs a variety of techniques, including homework assignments, cognitive interventions, intensive individual therapy, and group sessions involving others with the disorder. Group sessions focus on mindfulness training as well as emotional and interpersonal skills training.

What might the popularity of integrative approaches mean for the training of new therapists?

Seeking Therapy? There Is Probably an App for That

Researchers are developing and studying a broad range of smartphone applications for therapy (Carey, 2012; Parikh & Huniewicz, 2015). Such apps, sometimes called "mHealth," meaning *mobile health-related interventions,* provide immediate feedback aimed at modifying thoughts and behaviors. Therapy apps are meant to be mobile extensions of evidence-based therapies (Lui, Marcus, & Barry, 2017). These apps could mean access to therapy for millions of people—advice and strategies for managing emotions and changing thoughts at the tap of the screen.

©one photo/Shutterstock

Although possibly less portable, *Internet-based treatment* (also referred to as *cybertherapy* or *e-therapy*) involves getting therapeutic help online. A research review of Internet-based treatments concluded that most studies have focused on mood and anxiety disorders (Andersson & Titov, 2014). In comparisons of Internet-based cognitive-behavior therapy and face-to-face cognitive-behavior therapy for depression, equivalent outcomes were found with long-term positive effects still present three years after treatment (Andersson & Hedman, 2013; Andersson & others, 2013).

However, e-therapy websites and mHealth apps are controversial among mental health professionals (Emmelkamp, 2011; Lui, Marcus, & Barry, 2017). For one thing, many of these sites do not include the most basic information about the therapists' qualifications (Norcross & others, 2013). In addition, because cybertherapy occurs at a distance, these sites typically exclude individuals who are having thoughts of suicide. Further, confidentiality, a crucial aspect of the therapeutic relationship, cannot always be guaranteed on a website. On the plus side, though, individuals who are unwilling or unable to seek out face-to-face therapy may be more disposed to get help online, and early studies indicate some success of Internet-based therapies (Andersson & Titov, 2014; Norcross & others, 2013). With regard to therapeutic apps, there is simply not enough research supporting their usefulness in the context of psychological disorders (Lui, Marcus, & Barry, 2017).

E-therapy and therapeutic apps may represent the wave of the future, but for many professionals, human contact is a vital ingredient in psychological healing. Psychiatrist Andrew Garber cautions, "We are built as human beings to figure out our place in the world, to construct a narrative in the context of a relationship that gives meaning to our lives" (Carey, 2012). Technology, in other words, may never replace the power of human conversation.

DBT was developed by Marsha Linehan, a renowned psychologist, who "came out" as suffering from borderline personality disorder herself.

Therapy integrations are conceptually compatible with the biopsychosocial model of abnormal behavior. That is, many therapists believe that abnormal behavior involves biological, psychological, and social factors. Many single-therapy approaches concentrate on one aspect of the person more than others; for example, drug therapies focus on biological factors, and cognitive therapies probe psychological factors. Another integrative method is to combine psychotherapy with drug therapy. Combined cognitive therapy and drug therapy has been effective in treating ADHD, anxiety and depressive disorders, eating disorders, substance abuse disorders (Clarke & others, 2013), and schizophrenia. A mental health team that includes a psychiatrist and a clinical psychologist might conduct this integrative therapy. The use of medication to treat psychological disorders is a type of biological approach to therapy, our next topic.

self-quiz

1. A behavioral therapy technique that is often used for treating specific phobia disorder is
   A. aversive conditioning.
   B. self-instruction.
   C. systematic desensitization.
   D. counterconditioning.

2. The psychotherapy approach that focuses on the ways in which early childhood relationships unconsciously affect current relationships is
   A. client-centered therapy.
   B. psychodynamic therapy.
   C. cognitive therapy.
   D. applied behavior analysis.

3. The therapy that has unconditional positive regard at its core is
   A. psychodynamic therapy.
   B. cognitive therapy.
   C. dialectical behavior therapy.
   D. client-centered therapy.

APPLY IT! 4. Cara has taken a few psychology classes. When she decides to see a therapist for help with her relationship with her mother, she is certain that the therapist will make her lie on a couch and talk about her childhood. When her appointments begin, Cara is surprised that the therapist asks her to just talk about her feelings and offers little feedback. At other times, the therapist talks to Cara about her thoughts and beliefs and gives her homework. On other appointments, the therapist asks Cara about her dreams and childhood. The kind of therapy Cara is getting is
   A. cognitive-behavioral.
   B. humanistic.
   C. psychodynamic.
   D. integrative.

3 Biological Therapies

As mentioned at the beginning of the chapter, *biological therapies* or *biomedical therapies* are treatments that reduce or eliminate the symptoms of psychological disorders by altering aspects of body functioning. Drug therapy is the most common form of biomedical therapy. Electroconvulsive therapy and psychosurgery are much less widely used biomedical therapies.

Drug Therapy

Although people have long used medicines and herbs to alleviate symptoms of emotional distress, it was not until the twentieth century that drug treatments revolutionized mental healthcare. Psychotherapeutic drugs are used mainly in three diagnostic categories: anxiety disorders, mood disorders, and schizophrenia. In this section you will read about the effectiveness of drugs for these various disorders—antianxiety drugs, antidepressant drugs, and antipsychotic drugs.

 Have you ever taken a prescription drug for a psychological problem? As you read, see if that medication is described. Does the description fit with your experience?

antianxiety drugs
Commonly known as tranquilizers, drugs that reduce anxiety by making individuals calmer and less excitable.

ANTIANXIETY DRUGS   **Antianxiety drugs** are commonly known as *tranquilizers*. These drugs reduce anxiety by making individuals calmer and less excitable. Benzodiazepines are the antianxiety drugs that generally offer the greatest relief for anxiety symptoms, though these drugs are potentially addictive. They work by binding to the receptor sites of neurotransmitters that become overactive during anxiety. The most frequently prescribed benzodiazepines include Xanax, Valium, and Librium (Bernardy & others, 2012). A nonbenzodiazepine—buspirone or BuSpar—is commonly used to treat generalized anxiety disorder.

Benzodiazepines are relatively fast-acting, taking effect within hours. Side effects of benzodiazepines include drowsiness, loss of coordination, fatigue, and mental slowing (Fields, 2013). These effects can be hazardous when a person is driving or operating machinery, especially when the individual first starts taking the medication. Benzodiazepines also have been linked to abnormalities in babies born to mothers who took them during pregnancy (Yonkers & others, 2017). Further, the combination of benzodiazepines with alcohol and with other medications can lead to problems such as depression (Dell'osso & Lader, 2012). Antianxiety medications are best used only temporarily for symptomatic relief. Too often, they are overused and can become addictive.

The death of actor Heath Ledger was due to a fatal combination of antianxiety drugs, alcohol, pain killers, and sleeping pills.

ANTIDEPRESSANT DRUGS **Antidepressant drugs** regulate mood. The four main classes of antidepressant drugs are tricyclics, such as Elavil; tetracyclics such as Avanza; monoamine oxidase (MAO) inhibitors, such as Nardil; and selective serotonin reuptake inhibitors, such as Prozac, Paxil, and Zoloft. These antidepressants are all thought to help alleviate depressed mood through their effects on neurotransmitters in the brain. In different ways, they all allow the person's brain to increase or maintain its level of important neurotransmitters (Ingersoll & Rak, 2016). You will notice that many antidepressant drugs influence serotonin. Low levels of this neurotransmitter are associated with negative mood and aggression. Let's take a close look at each of these types of antidepressants.

- *Tricyclics*, so-called because of their three-ringed molecular structure, are believed to work by increasing the level of certain neurotransmitters, especially norepinephrine and serotonin (Taurines & others, 2011). Tricyclics reduce the symptoms of depression in approximately 60 to 70 percent of cases. Tricyclics usually take two to four weeks to improve mood. Adverse side effects may include restlessness, faintness, trembling, sleepiness, and memory difficulties. A meta-analysis of 30 years of studies concluded that the older antidepressant drugs, such as the tricyclics, reduced depression more effectively than the newer antidepressant drugs (Undurraga & Baldessarini, 2012).

- *Tetracyclic antidepressants,* named for their four-ringed structure, are also called *noradrenergic and specific serotonergic antidepressants*, or NaSSAs. These drugs have effects on both norepinephrine and serotonin, enhancing brain levels of these neurotransmitters. *MAO inhibitors* are thought to work by blocking the enzyme monoamine oxidase, which breaks down the neurotransmitters serotonin and norepinephrine in the brain (Undurraga & Baldessarini, 2017). Scientists believe that the blocking action of MAO inhibitors allows these neurotransmitters to stick around and help regulate mood. MAO inhibitors are not as widely used as tricyclics because potentially they are more harmful. MAO inhibitors may be especially risky because of their potential interactions with certain foods and drugs. Cheese and other fermented foods—including alcoholic beverages, such as red wine—can interact with the inhibitors to raise blood pressure and, over time, cause a stroke.

- *Selective serotonin reuptake inhibitors*, or SSRIs, target serotonin and work mainly by interfering only with the reabsorption of serotonin in the brain (Molyneaux & others, 2014). Figure 7 shows how this process is thought to work. The positive effects of serotonin in the synapse may be related to the role of this neurotransmitter in maintaining the brain's adaptability and capacity to change with experience (Kraus & others, 2017). SSRIs are the most commonly prescribed antidepressants, due to their effectiveness in reducing the symptoms of depression with fewer side effects than other antidepressants (Fields, 2013). Nonetheless, they can have side effects, including insomnia, anxiety, headache, and impaired sexual functioning (Rheker & others, 2017) and produce severe withdrawal symptoms if the individual abruptly stops taking them (Cosci, 2017).

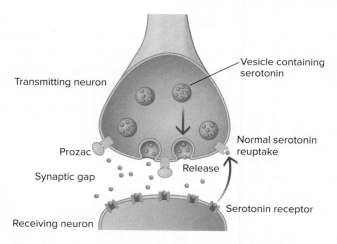

Transmitting neuron

Vesicle containing serotonin

Prozac

Synaptic gap

Release

Normal serotonin reuptake

Serotonin receptor

Receiving neuron

FIGURE 7 How the Antidepressant Prozac Works
Secreted by a transmitting neuron, serotonin moves across the synaptic gap and binds to receptors in a receiving neuron. Excess serotonin in the synaptic gap is normally reabsorbed by the transmitting neuron. The antidepressant Prozac blocks this reuptake of serotonin by the transmitting neuron, however, leaving excess serotonin in the synaptic gap. The excess serotonin is transmitted to the receiving neuron and circulated through the brain. The result is hypothesized to be a reduction of the serotonin deficit found in depressed individuals.

Beyond their usefulness in treating mood disorders, antidepressant drugs are often effective for a number of anxiety disorders, as well as some eating and sleep disorders. Increasingly, antidepressants are prescribed for other common problems, such as chronic pain. Such prescriptions are called "off label" because they involve using a drug for reasons other than those recommended.

Some people experience depression that does not respond to existing antidepressant medications. From the biological approach, this calls for new drugs to be developed. Developing new drugs is a costly affair, often involving many years and millions of dollars (Nutt & Goodwin, 2011). New medications must be tested in special studies called *clinical trials*. In clinical trials, large samples of volunteers are randomly assigned to either an experimental group that receives the new treatment or a control group. The control group may receive no treatment, a different already established medication, or a placebo (that is, a substance that looks identical to the medication but contains no active ingredient). After treatment, levels of depression are measured. From the perspective of a pharmaceutical company, if the experimental group does not show lower depression than the control group, the clinical trial has failed.

It is not surprising that the U.S. Food and Drug Administration requires that new drugs be shown to be better than a placebo (Khan, Khan, & Brown, 2002). What *is* surprising is how difficult it is for drugs to surpass this hurdle: Clinical trials often fail when new antidepressant medications are compared to placebos (Nelson & others, 2013). These failures have led to a decline in new drug development (Khan & others, 2017; Rihmer & others, 2012), leading some experts to warn that the development of new medications is in a state of crisis (Cressey, 2011). At the center of this crisis is the power of the placebo effect and what to do about it. To read more about this topic, see the Challenge Your Thinking feature.

Effexor is also commonly prescribed for depression. It inhibits the reuptake of serotonin and norepinephrine and is thus called a serotonin-norepinephrine reuptake inhibitor, or SNRI (Jasiak & Bostwick, 2014).

MEDICATION FOR BIPOLAR DISORDER **Lithium** is widely used to treat bipolar disorder. Lithium is the lightest of the solid elements in the periodic table of elements. A recent research review concluded that there is good evidence for lithium's efficacy in treating the mania side of bipolar disorder and some, but less robust, evidence for its effectiveness in treating bipolar depression and mixed episodes (Curran & Ravindran, 2014). Continuing research seeks to identify genetic and brain characteristics of people most likely to benefit from lithium (Moreira & others, 2017; Spuhler & others, 2017).

lithium
The lightest of the solid elements in the periodic table of elements, widely used to treat bipolar disorder.

The amount of lithium that circulates in the bloodstream must be carefully monitored because the effective dosage is precariously close to toxic levels. Kidney and thyroid gland complications as well as weight gain can arise as a consequence of lithium therapy (Berk & others, 2017). Lithium is thought to stabilize moods by influencing norepinephrine and serotonin, but the exact mechanism of its effect is unknown (Ago & others, 2012).

If you are a fan of Nirvana or Evanescence or batteries, you know lithium has a variety of uses.

The effectiveness of lithium depends on the person's staying on the medication. Some consumers may be troubled by the association between lithium and weight gain, and others may go off the drug when they are feeling well. Individuals with bipolar disorder may also be treated with other medications as needed for depression or mania. In addition, sometimes those with bipolar are treated with antipsychotic drugs, our next topic.

Antipsychotic Drugs

Antipsychotic drugs are powerful drugs that diminish agitated behavior, reduce tension, decrease hallucinations, improve social behavior, and produce better sleep patterns in individuals who have a severe psychological disorder, especially schizophrenia (Ingersoll & Rak, 2016; Krause & Pogarell, 2017). Before antipsychotic drugs were developed in the 1950s, few, if any, interventions brought relief from the torment of psychotic symptoms.

Neuroleptics are the most extensively used class of antipsychotic drugs (Garver, 2006). When taken in sufficient doses, neuroleptics reduce schizophrenic symptoms (Kane & others, 2014). The most widely accepted explanation for the effectiveness of neuroleptics is their affect on dopamine and dopamine pathways in the brain. A recent study demonstrated that, indeed, antipsychotic medications affect blood flow to areas of the brain that are rich in dopamine and that these medications appear to increase the brain's capacity to process this dopamine, leading to reduced symptoms (Eisenberg & others, 2017).

antipsychotic drugs
Powerful drugs that diminish agitated behavior, reduce tension, decrease hallucinations, improve social behavior, and produce better sleep patterns in individuals with a severe psychological disorder, especially schizophrenia.

Challenge YOUR THINKING

Are Antidepressants Better Than Placebos?

Although the exact contribution of placebo effects to treatment outcomes is a matter of some controversy (Nehama & others, 2014; Rihmer & others, 2012), meta-analyses show that antidepressant drugs are about 20 percent better than placebos in reducing depression (Bridge & others, 2009; Kirsch, 2009; Kirsch & others, 2008; Rihmer & others, 2012). Put another way, about 80 percent of the effect of drugs on depression can be explained by the placebo effect. If placebos can provide 80 percent of their effect, are antidepressants of any real use?

Answering this question requires that we consider not only whether antidepressants work but for whom they might be effective (Mancini & others, 2014; Nelson & others, 2013). For example, it appears that for the most severely depressed, medication is quite a bit more effective than placebo (Fournier & others, 2010). Importantly, often the most severely depressed and suicidal are screened out of clinical trials (Rihmer & others, 2012). So clinical trials may not actually test the value of antidepressants among those for whom they are most needed and potentially most effective. In addition, although 20 percent may seem small, to a person suffering from depression it might be a very valuable 20 percent.

The placebo effect involves a person's beliefs and expectations that a medication will produce relief. As the use of drugs to treat depression has become more common, the placebo effect appears to be growing (Khan & others, 2017; Rutherford & Roose, 2013), creating a catch-22 for those who are striving to create new treatments: The more people come to believe that a treatment will work, the stronger the placebo effect is likely to be.

One approach to this issue suggests that going forward researchers should do all that can be done to reduce the psychological factors that increase a person's belief in a medication (Fava & others, 2017; Khan, Faucett, & Brown, 2014). This idea is based on the notion that removing expectations might rid medication studies of the placebo effect.

©JGI/Jamie Grill/Blend Images LLC

A very different approach suggests that we should harness the power of placebo effects to improve people's lives. Placebo effects are not always temporary: 75 percent of those who improve in response to a placebo remain well over the long term (Khan, Redding, & Brown, 2008). Rather than reacting to placebo response as if it is something to be avoided, why not do whatever we can to boost it, and, in so doing, improve depression (Rutherford & Roose, 2013)? From this perspective, we might identify the key contributors to placebo effects and maximize them to enhance the effectiveness of treatments. One such ingredient appears to be thinking that one is being given a drug. When participants are told they might not be receiving a drug, the effects of medications are reduced (Rutherford & Roose, 2013).

The placebo effect demonstrates the power of belief and expectations even in the context of serious psychological disorders. Interestingly, research comparing psychotherapy to a placebo pill has shown that the placebo effect accounts for a great deal of the effects of psychotherapy as well (Cuijpers & others, 2014; Furukawa & others, 2017). Belief in a treatment can play a role in its effectiveness, no matter what form that treatment takes.

What Do You Think?

- If you were suffering from a psychological disorder, how would you feel if a doctor prescribed a placebo without your knowledge?

- If you were suffering from a physical disorder, how would you feel if a doctor prescribed a placebo without your knowledge?

- Do your answers to those questions differ? Why or why not?

Recall that people with schizophrenia have difficulty regulating the neurotransmitter dopamine, which is associated with the experience of reward.

Neuroleptics do not cure schizophrenia; they treat its symptoms, not its causes. If an individual with schizophrenia stops taking the drug, the symptoms return. Neuroleptic drugs have substantially reduced the length of hospital stays for individuals with schizophrenia. However, when these individuals are able to return to the community (because the drug therapy reduces their symptoms), many have difficulty coping with the demands of society. In the absence of symptoms, many struggle to justify to themselves that they should continue to take the very medications that have reduced their symptoms, particularly because neuroleptic drugs can have severe side effects, including stroke. Drugs that treat disturbed thought by reducing dopamine can also induce a lack of pleasure (Kapur, 2003).

Another potential side effect of neuroleptic drugs is *tardive dyskinesia*, a neurological disorder characterized by involuntary random movements of the facial muscles, tongue, and mouth, as well as extensive twitching of the neck, arms, and legs (Carbon & others, 2017). Up to 20 percent of individuals with schizophrenia who take neuroleptics develop this disorder. As you may recall, movement disorders are a positive symptom of schizophrenia, and tardive dyskinesia can also occur in individuals suffering from psychiatric disorders who have not taken neuroleptic drugs (Chouinard, 2006).

Newer antipsychotic drugs—called *atypical antipsychotic medications*—that were introduced in the 1990s appear to influence dopamine and serotonin. The two most widely used medications in this group, Clozaril (clozapine) and Risperdal (risperidone), show promise for reducing schizophrenia's symptoms without the side effects of neuroleptics (Laffont & others, 2015).

Off-label uses of Risperdal include treating aggressive and self-injurious behavior in children, people with autism, and elderly people with dementia.

Strategies to increase the effectiveness of antipsychotic drugs involve administering small dosages over time rather than a large initial dose, and combining drug therapy with psychotherapy. Along with drug treatment, individuals with schizophrenia may need training in vocational, family, and social skills (Csillag & others, 2016).

Figure 8 lists the drugs used to treat various psychological disorders, their effectiveness, and their side effects. Note that for some anxiety disorders, such as agoraphobia, MAO inhibitors (antidepressant drugs) might be used instead of antianxiety drugs.

Psychological Disorder	Drug	Effectiveness	Side Effects
Everyday Anxiety and Anxiety Disorders			
Everyday Anxiety	Antianxiety drugs; antidepressant drugs	Substantial improvement short term	Antianxiety drugs: less powerful the longer people take them; may be addictive Antidepressant drugs: see below under depressive disorders
Generalized Anxiety Disorder	Antianxiety drugs	Not very effective	Less powerful the longer people take them; may be addictive
Panic Disorder	Antianxiety drugs	About half show improvement	Less powerful the longer people take them; may be addictive
Agoraphobia	Tricyclic drugs and MAO inhibitors	Majority show improvement	Tricyclics: restlessness, fainting, and trembling MAO inhibitors: toxicity
Specific Phobias	Antianxiety drugs	Not very effective	Less powerful the longer people take them; may be addictive
Mood Disorders			
Depressive Disorders	Tricyclic drugs, MAO inhibitors, and SSRI drugs	Majority show moderate improvement	Tricyclics: cardiac problems, mania, confusion, memory loss, fatigue MAO inhibitors: toxicity SSRI drugs: nausea, nervousness, insomnia, and, in a few cases, suicidal thoughts
Bipolar Disorder	Lithium	Large majority show substantial improvement	Toxicity
Schizophrenic Disorders			
Schizophrenia	Neuroleptics; atypical antipsychotic medications	Majority show partial improvement	Neuroleptics: irregular heartbeat, low blood pressure, uncontrolled fidgeting, tardive dyskinesia, and immobility of face Atypical antipsychotic medications: less extensive side effects than with neuroleptics, but can have a toxic effect on white blood cells

FIGURE 8 **Drug Therapy for Psychological Disorders** This figure summarizes the types of drugs used to treat various psychological disorders.

Electroconvulsive Therapy

Electroconvulsive therapy (ECT), commonly called shock therapy, causes a seizure in the brain. ECT is given mainly to treat major depressive disorder.
©Will McIntyre/Science Source

The goal of **electroconvulsive therapy (ECT)**, commonly called *shock therapy*, is to set off a seizure in the brain, much like what happens spontaneously in some forms of epilepsy. The notion of causing a seizure to help cure a psychological disorder has been around since ancient times. Hippocrates, the ancient Greek father of medicine, first noticed that malaria-induced convulsions would sometimes cure individuals who were thought to be insane (Endler, 1988). Following Hippocrates, many other medical doctors noted that head traumas, seizures, and convulsions brought on by fever would sometimes lead to the apparent cure of psychological problems.

In the early twentieth century, doctors induced seizures by insulin overdose and other means and used this procedure primarily to treat schizophrenia. In 1937, Ugo Cerletti, an Italian neurologist specializing in epilepsy, developed the procedure by which seizures could be induced using electrical shock. With colleagues, he developed a fast, efficient means of causing seizures in humans, and ECT gained wide use in psychiatric hospitals (Endler, 1988). Unfortunately, in earlier years, ECT was used indiscriminately, sometimes even to punish patients, as in the book and film *One Flew Over the Cuckoo's Nest*.

Today, doctors use ECT primarily to treat severe depression (Brown & others, 2014), especially among older women (Suri & others, 2015). It is difficult to know how frequently ECT is used because this information has not been routinely collected (Leiknes, Jarosh-von Schweder, & Høie, 2012). Fortunately, the contemporary use of ECT bears little resemblance to its earlier uses. A small electric current lasting for 1 second or less passes through two electrodes placed on the individual's head. The current stimulates a seizure that lasts for approximately a minute. ECT is given mainly to individuals who have not responded to drug therapy or psychotherapy, and its administration involves little discomfort. The patient receives anesthesia and muscle relaxants before the current is applied; this medication allows the individual to sleep through the procedure, minimizes convulsions, and reduces the risk of physical injury (Stripp, Jorgensen, & Olsen, 2017). Increasingly, ECT is applied only to the brain's right side. The individual awakens shortly afterward with no conscious memory of the treatment.

What sets ECT apart from other treatments is the rapid relief it can produce in a person's mood (Medda, Toni, & Perugi, 2014). ECT may be especially effective as a treatment for acute depression in individuals who are at great risk of suicide (Kellner, 2006).

ECT is controversial. Its potential side effects remain a source of debate and contradictory findings (Crowley & others, 2008). These possible effects include memory loss and other cognitive impairments and are generally more severe than drug side effects (Caverzasi & others, 2008). Some individuals treated with ECT report prolonged and profound memory loss (Choi & others, 2011). Side effects are typically lessened if only one side of the brain is stimulated. Despite the potential problems of ECT, some psychiatrists argue that for certain individuals this invasive treatment can have life-enhancing—and even life-saving—benefits (Huuhka & others, 2012). However, and importantly, few studies have examined the long-term benefits of ECT especially comparing it to placebos (Read & Arnold, 2017).

More recently, practitioners are treating some forms of depression, as well as other disorders, by using other brain stimulation therapies, especially deep brain stimulation and transcranial magnetic stimulation (NIMH, 2014; Zhang & others, 2013). In *deep brain stimulation*, doctors surgically implant electrodes in the brain that emit signals to alter the brain's electrical circuitry. Deep brain stimulation was initially developed as a treatment

electroconvulsive therapy (ECT)
Also called *shock therapy*, a treatment, sometimes used for depression, that sets off a seizure in the brain.

for Parkinson disease but now also is being used to treat individuals with treatment-resistant depression and obsessive-compulsive disorder (McIntyre & others, 2015). For instance, deep brain stimulation of the nucleus accumbens (part of the brain's reward pathways) has been effective in treating severe depression (Bais, Figee, & Denys, 2014). *Transcranial magnetic stimulation* uses a magnet rather than electrical current to activate the brain, and it has been approved by the Food and Drug Administration as a treatment for individuals who have not responded to at least one antidepressant medication (Brunelin & others, 2014). Transcranial stimulation appears to have far less wide-reaching impact on the brain than ECT or medications (Chau & others, 2017). Transcranial magnetic stimulation has also been found to be effective in treating the negative symptoms of schizophrenia (Hasan & others, 2017) and shows promise in treating OCD as well (Mantovani & others, 2017). For each disorder, the precise area of the brain to be stimulated is chosen to reflect the problems associated with the disorder.

Psychosurgery

psychosurgery
A biological therapy, with irreversible effects, that involves removal or destruction of brain tissue to improve the individual's adjustment.

Psychosurgery is a biological intervention that involves the removal or permanent destruction of brain tissue to improve the individual's adjustment. The effects of psychosurgery cannot be reversed.

In the 1930s, Portuguese physician Antonio Egas Moniz developed a surgical procedure in which an instrument was inserted into the brain and rotated, severing fibers that connect the frontal lobe and the thalamus. Moniz theorized that by severing the connections between these structures, the surgeon could alleviate the symptoms of severe mental disorders (Soares & others, 2013). In 1949, Moniz received the Nobel Prize for developing the procedure, which he felt should be used with extreme caution and only as a last resort.

In 1939 a former patient shot Moniz, leaving him a paraplegic. Moniz subsequently retired.

After hearing about Moniz's procedure, American neurologist Walter Freeman became the champion of *prefrontal lobotomies* (a term Freeman coined). Freeman developed his own technique, performed using a device similar to an ice pick, in surgeries that lasted mere minutes. A dynamic and charismatic advocate of this procedure, in the 1950s and 60s Freeman traveled the country in a van he called the "lobotomobile," demonstrating the surgery in state-run mental institutions. In his career, Freeman performed over 3,000 lobotomies (Caruso & Sheehan, 2017; El-Hai, 2005). Prefrontal lobotomies were conducted on tens of thousands of patients from the 1930s through the 1960s. These numbers speak not only to Freeman's persuasive charm but also to the desperation many physicians felt in treating institutionalized patients with severe psychological disorders (Lerner, 2005).

Subsequent research called the lobotomy procedure into question (Landis & Erlick, 1950; Mettler, 1952). Many individuals who received lobotomies suffered permanent and profound brain damage (Soares & others, 2013). Ethical concerns arose because, in many instances, giving consent for the lobotomy was a requirement for release from a mental hospital. Like ECT, lobotomies were being used as a form of punishment and control. In the late 1970s new regulations classified the procedure as experimental and established safeguards for patients.

It makes more sense to target the amygdala rather than the frontal lobes, considering the functions of these brain areas.

Fortunately, crude lobotomies are no longer performed, and Freeman's technique is certainly not typical of contemporary psychosurgery. Modern psychosurgery is quite precise and involves making just a small lesion in the amygdala or another part of the limbic system (Fountas & Smith, 2007; Neumaier & others, 2017). Today, only several hundred patients who have severely debilitating conditions undergo psychosurgery each year. Psychosurgery may be performed for OCD, major depression, or bipolar disorder rather than for schizophrenia (Shelton & others, 2010; van Vliet & others, 2013). Just as Moniz originally suggested, the procedure is now used only as a last resort—and with the utmost caution.

1. _____ are used to treat schizophrenia, whereas _____ are used to treat anxiety.
   A. Benzodiazepines; neuroleptics
   B. Neuroleptics; benzodiazepines
   C. MAO inhibitors; tricyclics
   D. Tricyclics; MAO inhibitors

2. Atypical antipsychotic medications work by
   A. increasing the release of presynaptic neurotransmitters.
   B. acting as an antagonist to dopamine.
   C. stopping the reuptake of serotonin.
   D. inhibiting enzymes that break down norepinephrine.

3. A true statement about electroconvulsive therapy is that
   A. it is less effective than medication.
   B. it takes several weeks to see results.
   C. it takes effect more rapidly than medication.
   D. it is painful.

APPLY IT! 4. Serena experienced times when her mood was very negative for prolonged periods. She was deeply troubled by her feelings and lacked a sense of pleasure in life. At other times, she felt on top of the world. Antidepressant medications brought her no relief.

Finally, her psychiatrist prescribed a different drug, which is helping Serena. Not only have her dark moods leveled out, but she is experiencing more stable positive moods. Which of the following is likely true of Serena's experience?
   A. Serena has a depressive disorder, and the drug is an MAO inhibitor.
   B. Serena has an anxiety disorder, and the drug is a benzodiazipene.
   C. Serena has bipolar disorder, and the drug is lithium.
   D. Serena has an eating disorder, and the drug is an SSRI.

4 Sociocultural Approaches and Issues in Treatment

This section focuses on sociocultural approaches to the treatment of psychological disorders. These methods view the individual as part of a system of relationships that are influenced by various social and cultural factors (Feltham, Hanley, & Winter, 2017; Sue & others, 2016). We first review common sociocultural approaches and then survey various cultural perspectives on therapy.

Group Therapy

Individuals who share a psychological problem may benefit from observing others cope with a similar problem. In turn, helping others can improve individuals' feelings of competence and efficacy. The sociocultural approach known as **group therapy** brings together individuals who share a psychological disorder in sessions that are typically led by a mental health professional.

group therapy
A sociocultural approach to the treatment of psychological disorders that brings together individuals who share a particular psychological disorder in sessions that are typically led by a mental health professional.

Advocates of group therapy point out that individual therapy puts the client outside the normal context of the relationships—family, marital, or peer-group relationships, for example—where many psychological problems develop. Yet such relationships may hold the key to successful therapy, these advocates say. By taking the context of important groups into account, group therapy may be more successful than individual therapy.

Group therapy takes many diverse forms—including psychodynamic, humanistic, behavior, and cognitive therapy—plus approaches that do not reflect the major psychotherapeutic perspectives (Corey, 2016). Six features make group therapy an attractive treatment format (Yalom & Leszcz, 2005):

1. *Information:* Individuals receive information about their problems from either the group leader or other group members.
2. *Universality:* Many individuals develop the sense that no one else has frightening and unacceptable impulses. In the group, individuals observe that others suffer and feel anguish as well.
3. *Altruism:* Group members support one another with advice and sympathy and learn that they have something to offer others.

©digitalskillet/Getty Images

4. *Experience of a positive family group:* A therapy group often resembles a family (in family therapy, the group *is* a family), with the leaders representing parents and the other members siblings. In this new family, old wounds may be healed, and new, more positive family ties may be made.

5. *Development of social skills:* Feedback from peers may correct flaws in the individual's interpersonal skills. Self-centered individuals may see that they are self-centered if five other group members inform them about this quality; in one-on-one therapy, the individual might not believe the therapist.

6. *Interpersonal learning:* The group can serve as a training ground for practicing new behaviors and relationships. A hostile person may learn that he or she can get along better with others by behaving less aggressively, for example.

Family and Couples Therapy

Relationships with family members and significant others are certainly an important part of human life. Sometimes these vital relationships can benefit from a helpful outsider. **Family therapy** is group therapy among family members (Becvar & Becvar, 2017; Kottler & Shepard, 2015). **Couples therapy** is group therapy involving married or unmarried couples whose major problem lies within their relationship. These approaches stress that although one person may have psychological symptoms, these symptoms are a function of the family or couple relationship (Hewison, Clulow, & Drake, 2014).

In family therapy, four of the most widely used techniques are

family therapy
Group therapy with family members.

couples therapy
Group therapy involving married or unmarried couples whose major problem lies within their relationship.

1. *Validation:* The therapist expresses an understanding and acceptance of each family member's feelings and beliefs and thus validates the person. The therapist finds something positive to say to each family member.

2. *Reframing:* The therapist helps families reframe problems as family problems, not an individual's problems. A delinquent adolescent boy's problems are reframed in terms of how each family member contributed to the situation. The parents' lack of attention to the boy or marital conflict may be involved, for example.

3. *Structural change:* The family therapist tries to restructure the coalitions in a family. In a mother–son coalition, the therapist might suggest that the father take a stronger disciplinarian role to relieve the mother of some burden. Restructuring might be as simple as suggesting that the parents explore satisfying ways of being together, such as going out once a week for a quiet dinner.

4. *Detriangulation:* In some families, one member is the scapegoat for two other members who are in conflict but pretend not to be. For example, parents of a girl with anorexia nervosa might insist that their marriage is fine but find themselves in subtle conflict over how to handle the child. The therapist tries to disentangle, or detriangulate, this situation by shifting attention away from the child to the conflict between the parents.

Couples therapy proceeds similarly to family therapy. Conflict in marriages and in relationships between unmarried individuals frequently involves poor communication. In some instances, communication has broken down entirely. The therapist tries to improve the communication between the partners and help them understand and solve their problems. Couples therapy addresses diverse problems such as alcohol abuse, jealousy, sexual issues, infidelity, gender roles, two-career families, divorce, remarriage, and the special concerns of blended families (Suddeath, Kerwin, & Dugger, 2017).

Self-Help Support Groups

Self-help support groups are voluntary organizations of individuals who get together on a regular basis to discuss topics of common interest. The self-help support group is conducted by a paraprofessional or a member of the common-interest group. Self-help support groups play a key and valuable role in our nation's mental health (Norcross & others, 2013). A survey in 2002 revealed that for mental health support alone, nearly 7,500 such groups existed in the United States, with more than 1 million members (Goldstrom & others, 2006). In addition to reaching so many people in need of help, these groups are important because they use community resources and are relatively inexpensive. They also serve people who are otherwise less likely to receive help, such as those with a limited education or a low income.

Self-help support groups provide members with a sympathetic audience for social sharing and emotional release. The social support, role modeling, and sharing of concrete strategies for solving problems that unfold in self-help groups add to their effectiveness. A woman who has been raped might not believe a male therapist who tells her that, with time, she will put the pieces of her shattered life back together. The same message from another rape survivor—someone who has had to work through the same feelings of rage, fear, and violation—might be more believable.

There are myriad self-help groups, including groups for cocaine abusers, dieters, victims of child abuse, and people with various medical conditions (heart disease, cancer, diabetes, and so on). Alcoholics Anonymous (AA) is one of the best-known self-help groups. Mental health professionals often recommend AA for clients struggling with alcoholism (Kelly, 2017). Some studies show a positive effect for AA, but others do not (Zemore, 2017). One study found that AA reduced drinking by improving self-efficacy related to not drinking in social contexts, fostering positive changes in social networks, increasing spirituality/religiousness, and reducing negative affect (Kelly & others, 2012).

Harmful group processes like groupthink and social contagion can arise in support groups.

For individuals who tend to cope by seeking information and affiliation with similar peers, self-help support groups can reduce stress and promote adjustment. However, as with any group therapy, there is a possibility that negative emotions will spread through the group, especially if the members face circumstances that deteriorate over time, as terminal cancer patients do. Group leaders who are sensitive to the spread of negative emotions can minimize such effects.

In addition to face-to-face groups, a multitude of online support groups has also emerged (Norcross & others, 2013). Online support groups have promise, but they can have downsides. In the absence of guidance from a trained professional, members may lack the expertise and knowledge to provide optimal advice. The emergence of pro-anorexia (or "pro-ana") sites on Instagram, Tumblr, and the web, which *promote* anorexia, exemplifies the potentially negative side of social media "support" phenomenon (Branley & Covey, 2017).

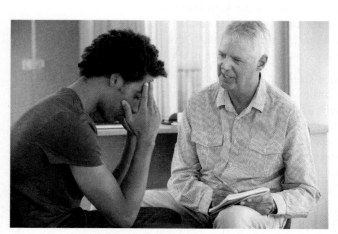

Community mental health includes services such as medical care, one-on-one counseling, self-help support groups, workshops, and supported residences like halfway houses.
©Mark Bowden/Getty Images

Community Mental Health

The community mental health movement was born in the 1960s, when society recognized that locking away individuals with psychological disorders and disabilities was inhumane and inappropriate. The deplorable conditions inside some psychiatric facilities spurred the movement as well. The central idea behind the community mental health movement was that individuals with disorders ought to remain within society and with their families and should receive treatment in community mental health centers. This movement also reflected economic concerns, as it was thought that institutionalizing people was more expensive than treating them in the community at large. Thus, with the passage of the Community Mental Health Act of 1963, large numbers of individuals with psychological disorders were transferred from mental institutions to community-based facilities, a process called *deinstitutionalization*. Although at least partially motivated by a desire to help individuals with psychological disorders more effectively, deinstitutionalization has been implicated in rising rates of homelessness. The success of community mental health services depends on the resources and commitment of the communities in which they occur.

Community mental health involves training teachers, ministers, family physicians, nurses, and others who directly interact with community members to offer lay counseling and workshops on topics such as coping with stress, reducing drug use, and assertiveness training (Lim & others, 2012). Advocates and providers of community mental health believe that the best way to treat a psychological disorder is through prevention (Feinstein, Richter, & Foster, 2012).

Community psychologists move beyond focus on the individual, embedding the person who has a disorder in a larger familial, local, societal, and cultural context. A key goal of community psychology is to empower individuals and groups to enact change in their lives and communities (Society for Community Research and Action, 2017). Community psychologists are dedicated to helping people who are disenfranchised from society, such as those living in poverty, to lead happier, more productive lives (Bond & others, 2017). All community mental health programs may rely on financial support from local, state, and federal governments.

How much would you be willing to pay in taxes to support community mental health programs?

Cultural Perspectives

The psychotherapies discussed earlier in this chapter—psychodynamic, humanistic, behavior, and cognitive—center on the individual. This focus is generally compatible with the needs of people in Western cultures such as the United States, where the emphasis is on the individual rather than the group (family, community, or ethnic group). However, these psychotherapies may not be as effective with people who live in collectivistic cultures that place more importance on the group (Sue & others, 2016). Some psychologists argue that family therapy is likely to be more effective with people in cultures that place a high value on the family, such as Latino and Asian cultures (Guo, 2005). Research shows that adapting or tailoring the therapist relationship to cultural background and to religious/spiritual orientation improves therapy effectiveness (Norcross, 2011).

If you think about psychotherapy as a conversation among people, you can appreciate the profound and intricate ways culture can influence the psychotherapeutic process. Throughout our exploration of psychology, we have noted the ways in which culture is expressed in language, in our modes of talking to one another, and in the things we talk about. Placing the conversation that is psychotherapy within a cultural framework is enormously complex. Cultures may differ, for instance, in terms of how they view the appropriateness of talking with an elder about personal problems or of talking about one's feelings at all (Asnaani & Hofmann, 2012). Cultural issues in therapy include factors such as socioeconomic status, ethnicity, gender, country of origin, current culture, and religious beliefs and traditions (Diller, 2015; Huey & others, 2014).

When therapists engage with clients in a culturally sensitive way, a key goal is to not immediately assume too much about how culture influences the person. Each person must be treated as an individual.

Cross-cultural competence refers both to how skilled a therapist feels about being able to manage cultural issues that might arise in therapy and to how the client perceives the therapist's ability (Watson, Raju, & Soklaridis, 2017). Dominant features of cross-cultural competence are demonstrating respect for cultural beliefs and practices and balancing the goals of a particular therapeutic approach with the goals and values of a culture.

cross-cultural competence
A therapist's assessment of his or her abilities to manage cultural issues in therapy and the client's perception of those abilities.

ETHNICITY Many ethnic minority individuals prefer discussing problems with parents, friends, and relatives rather than mental health professionals (Diller, 2015; Sue & others, 2016). Might therapy progress best, then, when the therapist and the client are from the same ethnic background? Researchers have found that when there is an ethnic match between the therapist and the client and when ethnic-specific services are provided, clients are less likely to drop out of therapy early, and in many cases these clients have better treatment outcomes (Jackson & Greene, 2000). Ethnic-specific services include culturally appropriate greetings and arrangements (for example, serving tea rather than coffee to Chinese American clients), providing flexible hours for treatment, and employing a bicultural/bilingual staff (Nystul, 1999).

 How would you feel receiving treatment from a therapist who differed from you in ethnic background? In gender? In religious faith?

Nonetheless, therapy can be effective when the therapist and client are from different ethnic backgrounds if the therapist has excellent clinical skills and is culturally sensitive (Akhtar, 2006). Culturally skilled psychotherapists have good knowledge of their clients' cultural groups, understand sociopolitical influences on clients, and have competence in working with culturally diverse groups (Austad, 2009).

GENDER One byproduct of changing gender roles for women and men is reevaluation of the goal of psychotherapy (Guerin, 2017). Traditionally, the goal has been autonomy or self-determination for the client. However, autonomy and self-determination are often more central to men than to women, whose lives generally are characterized more by relatedness and connection with others. Thus, some psychologists argue that therapy goals should involve increased attention to relatedness and connection with others, especially for women, or should emphasize both autonomy/self-determination and relatedness/connection to others (Notman & Nadelson, 2002).

Feminist therapists believe that traditional psychotherapy continues to carry considerable gender bias and has not adequately addressed the specific concerns of women. Thus, several alternative, nontraditional therapies have arisen that aim to help clients break free from traditional gender roles and stereotypes. In terms of improving clients' lives, the goals of feminist therapists are no different from those of other therapists. However, feminist therapists believe that women must become alert to the possibility of bias and discrimination in their own lives in order to achieve their mental health goals.

SUMMARY

1 Approaches to Treating Psychological Disorders

Three approaches to treating psychological disorders are psychotherapy, biological therapies, and sociocultural approaches. Psychotherapy is the process that mental health professionals use to help individuals recognize, define, and overcome their disorders and improve their adjustment. Biological treatments involve drugs and other procedures that change the functioning of the body. Sociocultural approaches to treating psychological disorders emphasize that helping a person requires acknowledging the relationships, roles, and cultural contexts that characterize a person's life; these characteristics and features are often brought into the therapeutic context.

2 Psychotherapy

Psychotherapy is the process that mental health professionals use to help individuals recognize, define, and overcome their disorders and improve their adjustment.

In Freudian psychoanalysis, psychological disorders stem from unresolved unconscious conflicts, believed to originate in early family experiences. A therapist's interpretation of free association, dreams, transference, and resistance provides paths for understanding the client's unconscious conflicts. Although psychodynamic therapy has changed, many contemporary psychodynamic therapists still probe the unconscious mind for early family experiences that might provide clues to clients' current problems.

In humanistic therapies, the analyst encourages clients to understand themselves and to grow personally. Client-centered therapy, developed by Rogers, is a type of humanistic therapy that includes active listening, reflective speech, unconditional positive regard, empathy, and genuineness.

Behavior therapies use learning principles to reduce or eliminate maladaptive behavior. They are based on the behavioral and social cognitive theories of personality. Behavior therapies seek to eliminate symptoms or behaviors rather than to help individuals gain insight into their problems.

The two main behavior therapy techniques based on classical conditioning are systematic desensitization and aversive conditioning. In systematic desensitization, individuals with anxiety are treated by helping them to associate deep relaxation with increasingly intense anxiety-producing situations. In aversive conditioning, repeated pairings of the undesirable behavior with aversive stimuli decrease the behavior's pleasant associations.

In operant conditioning approaches to behavior therapy, an analysis of the person's environment determines which factors need modification. Applied behavior analysis is the application of operant conditioning to change behavior. Its main goal is to replace maladaptive behaviors with adaptive ones.

Cognitive therapies emphasize that the individual's cognitions (thoughts) are the root of abnormal behavior. Cognitive therapies attempt to change the person's feelings and behaviors by changing cognitions. The most popular form of therapy is cognitive-behavior therapy, which combines cognitive and behavior therapy techniques and emphasizes self-efficacy and self-instructional methods.

As many as 50 percent of practicing therapists refer to themselves as "integrative" or "eclectic." Integrative therapy combines techniques from different therapies based on the therapist's judgment of which methods will provide the greatest benefit.

 Biological Therapies

Biological approaches to therapy include drugs, electroconvulsive therapy (ECT), and psychosurgery. Psychotherapeutic drugs that treat psychological disorders fall into three main categories: antianxiety drugs, antidepressant drugs, and antipsychotic drugs.

Benzodiazepines are the most commonly used antianxiety drugs. Antidepressant drugs regulate mood; the four main classes are tricyclics, tetracyclics, MAO inhibitors, and SSRI drugs. Lithium is used to treat bipolar disorder. Antipsychotic drugs are administered to treat severe psychological disorders, especially schizophrenia.

Practitioners use electroconvulsive therapy, which triggers a brain seizure, to alleviate severe depression when other interventions have failed. Deep brain stimulation, which applies electrical stimulation in precise brain locations, is also used to treat some forms of depression. Psychosurgery is an irreversible procedure in which brain tissue is destroyed. Though rarely used today, psychosurgery is much more precise now than in the days of prefrontal lobotomies.

 Sociocultural Approaches and Issues in Treatment

Group therapies emphasize that relationships can hold the key to successful therapy. Family therapy is group therapy involving family members. Four widely used family therapy techniques are validation, reframing, structural change, and detriangulation. Couples therapy is group therapy with married or unmarried couples whose major problem is within their relationship.

Self-help support groups are voluntary organizations of individuals who get together on a regular basis to discuss topics of common interest. They are conducted by a paraprofessional or a member of the common-interest group.

The community mental health movement emerged out of the belief that the mental healthcare system was not adequately reaching people in poverty and deinstitutionalized individuals. Empowerment is a common goal of community mental health.

Psychotherapies' traditional focus on the individual may be successful in individualistic cultures, but individual-centered psychotherapies may not work as well in collectivistic cultures. Therapy is often more effective when there is an ethnic match between the therapist and the client, although culturally sensitive therapy can be provided by a therapist from a different ethnic background.

The psychotherapeutic emphasis on autonomy may pose a problem for the many women who value connectedness in relationships. Feminist-based therapies emphasize the importance of raising women's awareness of the influence of traditional gender roles and stereotypes in their lives.

KEY TERMS

antianxiety drugs
antidepressant drugs
antipsychotic drugs
behavior therapies
biological or biomedical therapies
client-centered therapy
clinical psychology
cognitive-behavior therapy (CBT)

cognitive therapies
couples therapy
cross-cultural competence
dream analysis
electroconvulsive therapy (ECT)
evidence-based practice
family therapy
free association

group therapy
humanistic therapies
integrative therapy
interpretation
lithium
psychoanalysis
psychodynamic therapies
psychosurgery

psychotherapy
reflective speech
resistance
sociocultural therapies
systematic desensitization
therapeutic alliance
transference

ANSWERS TO SELF-QUIZZES

Section 1:   1. C; 2. D; 3. B; 4. A
Section 2:   1. C; 2. B; 3. D; 4. D

Section 3:   1. B; 2. B; 3. C; 4. C
Section 4:   1. C; 2. B; 3. B; 4. C

14 Health Psychology

The importance of listening to your body

mportant exams, work hassles, family crises: We all face stressful life events. Now, imagine if the stressful events of your life involved parachuting into hostile territory in the middle of the night to perform a military raid. Scientists study the people who face such extreme stress in order to understand their resilience. How do they bounce back after stressful events that might lead many people to crumble (Reynolds, 2016)? They have discovered one of the secrets of resilience: The ability to listen to one's bodies in a particularly precise way. For this research (Simmons & others, 2012), participants are placed in an MRI scanner while wearing a mask. When the researcher presses a button, the mask begins to close, making it very hard to breathe. The brain scans show that among elite soldiers, the brain areas responsible for monitoring breathing and heart rate becoming very active when the mask begins to close. However, this activity does not escalate or lead to panic. Rather, the brains of resilient individuals dampen the response allowing them to quickly recover. Recent research (Haase & others, 2016) has identified this pattern in every day people who report themselves as resilient and tuned into their own bodies. Among those low in resilience, brain activity was low as the mask began to close. They did not listen to their bodies. During the "breathless moments" they panicked. Sometimes coping effectively with stress and bouncing back means having the capacity to listen to our bodies without overreacting. The experience of stress and its association with our physical health is influenced by contexts, behaviors, motivations, thoughts, and feelings—in other words, by factors at the very heart of the science of psychology.

The focus of this chapter is health psychology, the field devoted to promoting healthy practices and understanding the psychological processes that underlie health and illness. After first defining the field, we examine the ways psychologists explain the process of making healthy life changes and the resources on which individuals can draw to achieve positive change. Next we survey the psychology of stress and coping and consider psychological perspectives on making wise choices in four vital areas: physical activity, diet, the decision to smoke or not to smoke, and safer sex. Fittingly, the chapter closes with a look at psychology's role in shaping a good life.

Health Psychology and Behavioral Medicine

Health psychology emphasizes psychology's role in establishing and maintaining health and preventing and treating illness (Taylor, 2018). Health psychology reflects the belief that lifestyle choices, behaviors, and psychological characteristics can play important roles in health (Schwebel, McClure, & Severson, 2017; Segerstrom, 2017; Sheeran, Klein, & Rothman, 2017; Van Dyck & others, 2017). A related discipline, **behavioral medicine,** is an interdisciplinary field that focuses on developing and integrating behavioral and biomedical knowledge to promote health and reduce illness (Nigg, Jake-Schoffman, & Janke, 2017). The concerns of health psychology and behavioral medicine overlap: Health psychology primarily focuses on behavioral, social, emotional, motivational, and cognitive factors (Harris & others, 2017; Hughes & others, 2016), whereas behavioral medicine centers on behavioral, social, and biomedical factors. Note that what sets health psychology apart from behavioral medicine is its interest in what goes on inside the person's head (emotion, cognition, and motivation).

Related to health psychology and behavioral medicine are the fields of health promotion and public health (Buscemi & others, 2017; Dietz, 2015; Morley & others, 2017; Torrens Armstrong, 2017). *Health promotion* involves helping people change their lifestyle to optimize their health and assisting them in achieving balance in physical, emotional, social, spiritual, and intellectual health and wellness. Health promotion can be a goal of a company's human resources department, as well as state and city health departments, and it is sometimes a specialty for social workers and other members of the helping professions (Johnson, 2017; Morley & others, 2017). *Public health* is concerned with studying health and disease in large populations to guide policymakers (Casteñeda & others, 2015). Public health experts identify public health concerns, set priorities, and design interventions for health promotion. An important goal of public health is to ensure that all populations have access to cost-effective healthcare and health promotion services (Lunde & others, 2017; Torrens Armstrong, 2017).

A job in health promotion or public health can involve creating attention-grabbing public service advertisements and brochures to alert the public to health-related issues. If you have seen one of thetruth.com's antismoking ads on TV (or their hashtag #FinishIT on twitter) or noticed a "Click It or Ticket" sign on a highway, you have a good feel for what health promotion and public health are all about.

health psychology
A subfield of psychology that emphasizes psychology's role in establishing and maintaining health and preventing and treating illness.

behavioral medicine
An interdisciplinary field that focuses on developing and integrating behavioral and biomedical knowledge to promote health and reduce illness; overlaps with and is sometimes indistinguishable from health psychology.

The Biopsychosocial Model

The interests of health psychologists and behavioral medicine researchers are broad. The biopsychosocial model in the context of psychological disorders applies to health psychology as well, because health psychology integrates biological, psychological, and social factors in health (Helgeson & Zajdel, 2017; Marsac & others, 2017).

For example, stress is a focal point of study across the broad field of psychology (Fox & others, 2017; Moberg & others, 2017; Toussaint, Shields, & Slavich, 2016). Study of the brain and behavior, for instance, acknowledges the impact of stress on the autonomic nervous system. Furthermore, an individual's state of consciousness, as well as his or her process of thinking about events in particular ways, can influence the experience of stress. Stressful events also affect our emotions, which are themselves psychological and physical events. Aspects of our personalities, too, may be associated with stress and can influence our health. Finally, social contexts can shape both an individual's experience of stress and his or her ability to cope with it.

Connections between Mind and Body

From the biopsychosocial perspective, the many diverse aspects of each human being are tightly intertwined. Our bodies and minds are deeply connected. After suffering a heart attack, one health psychologist ruefully noted that none of his colleagues in the field had thought to ask him whether heart disease was part of his family history, ignoring the obvious question that a medical doctor would ask first. Although the mind is responsible for much of what happens in the body, it is not the only factor. Even as we consider the many ways that psychological processes contribute to health and disease, we must understand that sometimes illness happens for other reasons—affecting even those who have led healthy lives.

While it might be fascinating to think about how the mind may influence bodily health, it is also important to appreciate that the body may influence the mind as well. Health psychology and behavioral medicine are concerned not only with how psychological states influence health, but also with how health and illness may influence the person's psychological experience, including cognitive abilities, stress, and coping (Helgeson & Zajdel, 2017; Trump & Mendenhall, 2017). A person who is feeling psychologically run-down may not realize that the level of fatigue is the beginning stage of an illness. In turn, being physically healthy can be a source of psychological wellness.

1. Health psychologists believe that a key factor in health are an individual's

   _____.

   A. psychological characteristics
   B. lifestyle
   C. behaviors
   D. all of the above

2. According to the text, health psychology overlaps in significant ways with
   A. philosophy.
   B. behavioral medicine.
   C. neuroscience.
   D. behaviorism.

3. The experience of stress can depend on
   A. one's state of consciousness.
   B. one's personality.
   C. one's social situation.
   D. all of the above

APPLY IT! 4. Anastasia is committed to getting all A's this semester. In her pursuit of academic excellence, she decides to sleep only three hours a night, to drink a lot of coffee, and to stop wasting time at the gym. She studies nearly 12 hours every night. During finals week, Anastasia is so exhausted that she sleeps through one of her exams and fails another because she cannot concentrate. Which of the following best explains what happened?
   A. Anastasia probably didn't study as hard as she claimed.
   B. Anastasia forgot that the body can affect the functioning of the mind.
   C. Anastasia took too many hard classes this semester.
   D. Anastasia set her goals too high.

2 Making Positive Life Changes

One of health psychology's missions is to help individuals identify and implement ways they can effectively change their behaviors for the better. **Health behaviors**—practices that have an impact on physical well-being—include adopting a healthy approach to stress, exercising, eating right, brushing one's teeth, performing breast and testicular exams, not smoking, drinking in moderation (or not at all), and practicing safe sex. Before exploring what health psychologists have learned about the best ways to make healthy behavioral changes, we first focus on the process of change itself.

health behaviors
Practices that have an impact on physical well-being.

Theoretical Models of Change

In many instances, changing behaviors begins by changing attitudes. Psychologists have sought to understand how changing attitudes can lead to behavioral changes.

A number of theoretical models have addressed the factors that likely play roles in effective health behavior changes. The **theory of reasoned action** is one powerful approach to this issue. The theory suggests that effective change requires three important things (Ajzen, 2012a, 2012b; Ajzen & Albarracin, 2007; Ajzen & Fishbein, 1980, 2005):

1. specific intentions about the behavioral change

2. positive attitude about the new behavior

3. belief that one's social group looks upon the new behavior favorably

theory of reasoned action
Theoretical model stating that effective change requires individuals to have specific intentions about their behaviors, as well as positive attitudes about a new behavior, and to perceive that their social group looks positively on the new behavior as well.

If, for example, you smoke and want to quit smoking, you will be more successful if you devise an explicit intention of quitting, feel good about it, and believe that your friends support you. Icek Ajzen (pronounced "I-zen") modified the theory of reasoned action to include the fact that not all of our behaviors are under our control. The **theory of planned behavior** includes the three basic ideas of the theory of reasoned action but adds a fourth: The person's perceptions of control over the outcome (Ajzen, 2002, 2012a, 2012b, 2015).

As we will see later, perceiving that one has control can have important implications for a number of life domains.

theory of planned behavior
Theoretical model that includes the basic ideas of the theory of reasoned action but adds the person's perceptions of control over the outcome.

The theory of reasoned action and its extension, the theory of planned behavior, have accurately predicted whether individuals successfully enact healthy behaviors (Ajzen & Albarracin, 2007; Lin, 2016), including cancer screening (Roncancio, Ward, & Fernandez, 2013), HIV prevention (Jozaghi & Carleton, 2015; Kalichman, 2007), preventing the use and abuse of drugs (Lorenzo-Blanco & others, 2016; Roberto, Shafer, & Marmo, 2014) including prescription stimulants (Gallucci & others, 2015), preventing binge drinking in college students (Case, Sparks, & Pavey, 2016; Elliott & Ainsworth, 2012), increasing exercise (Plotnikoff & others, 2011), changing eating habits (Hackman & Knowlden, 2014; Menozzi & others, 2017), increasing willingness to intervene in dating violence (Casey, Lindhorst, & Storer, 2017; Lemay & others, 2017) and reducing cyberbullying in adolescents (Heirman & Walrave, 2012).

Remember the key difference between the theory of reasoned action and the theory of planned behavior is a sense of control!

The Stages of Change Model

stages of change model
Theoretical model describing a five-step process by which individuals give up bad habits and adopt healthier lifestyles.

The **stages of change model** describes the process by which individuals give up bad habits and adopt healthier lifestyles. The model breaks down behavioral changes into five steps, recognizing that real change does not occur overnight with one monumental decision, even if that night is New Year's Eve (Norcross, Krebs, & Prochaska, 2011; Prochaska, Norcross, & DiClemente, 2013).

Have you made a healthy life change recently? As we go over these stages, ask yourself whether they apply to your experience.

Stage	Description	Example
Precontemplation **1**	Individuals are not yet ready to think about changing and may not be aware that they have a problem that needs to be changed.	Overweight individuals are not aware that they have a weight problem.
Contemplation **2**	Individuals acknowledge that they have a problem but may not yet be ready to change.	Overweight individuals know they have a weight problem but aren't yet sure they want to commit to losing weight.
Preparation/ determination **3**	Individuals are preparing to take action.	Overweight individuals explore options they can pursue in losing weight.
Action/willpower **4**	Individuals commit to making a behavioral change and enact a plan.	Overweight individuals begin a diet and start an exercise program.
Maintenance **5**	Individuals are successful in continuing their behavior change over time.	Overweight individuals are able to stick with their diet and exercise regimens for 6 months.

FIGURE 1 **Stages of Change Model Applied to Losing Weight** The stages of change model has been applied to many different health behaviors, including losing weight.

Rather, change occurs in progressive stages, each characterized by particular issues and challenges (Figure 1). Those stages are

- Precontemplation
- Contemplation
- Preparation/determination
- Action/willpower
- Maintenance

PRECONTEMPLATION   The *precontemplation stage* occurs when individuals are not yet genuinely thinking about changing. They may even be unaware that they have a problem behavior. Individuals who drink to excess but are not aware that their drinking is affecting their work may be in the precontemplation phase. At this stage, raising one's consciousness about the problem is crucial.

A woman who smokes may find her consciousness raised by the experience of becoming pregnant. A man who is stopped for drunk driving may be forced to take a good look at his drinking. Similarly, overweight individuals may not recognize their problem until they see photos of themselves taken at a family reunion or until they learn that an order of a McDonald's Big Mac, large fries, and large chocolate shake amounts to over 2,000 calories, the recommended caloric intake for an adult woman for an entire day.

It is common for individuals in the precontemplation phase to deny that their behavior is a problem and to defend it, claiming that "I don't drink/smoke/eat that much." Overweight individuals may discover that they do eat "that much" when they start keeping track of calories.

CONTEMPLATION   In the *contemplation stage,* individuals acknowledge the problem but may not be ready to commit to change. As the name of the stage suggests, at this point individuals are actively thinking about change. They might reevaluate themselves and the place of this behavior in their life. They understandably may have mixed feelings about giving up a bad habit. For example, how will they deal with missing their friends on a smoke break? Or going out drinking? Or packing a healthy lunch instead of heading to the drive-thru? They may weigh the short-term gains of the harmful behavior against the long-term benefits of changing. Future rewards can be difficult to pursue when immediate pleasures beckon. Sure, it would be nice to be thinner, but losing weight is going to take time, and that hot fudge sundae is right there, looking very delicious.

PREPARATION/DETERMINATION

In the *preparation/determination stage,* individuals are getting ready to take action. At this point, self-belief and especially beliefs about one's ability to "see it through" are very important. A key consideration is whether individuals truly feel they are ready to change.

During the preparation/determination stage, individuals start thinking concretely about how they might take on their new challenge. For example, they explore options for the best ways to quit smoking or drinking or to start an exercise program. Some smokers might consider trying a nicotine patch or participating in a support group for people wanting to quit. Individuals who are seeking to lose weight might think about joining a gym or setting the alarm clock for a 6:00 A.M. run.

ACTION/WILLPOWER

At the *action/willpower stage,* individuals commit to making a real behavioral change and enact an effective plan. An important challenge at this stage is to find ways to support the new, healthy behavior pattern. One approach is to establish reinforcements or rewards for the new behavior. Individuals who have quit smoking might focus on how much better food tastes after they have given up cigarettes. Successful dieters might treat themselves to a shopping trip to buy new, smaller-size clothes. Acknowledging, enjoying, and celebrating accomplishments can motivate consistent behavior.

Another source of support for new behaviors is the individual's social network (Taylor, 2018). Friends, family, and members of a support group can help through their encouraging words and behaviors. Members of a family might all quit smoking at the same time or join the individual in physical activities or healthier eating.

Can you quit smoking if you are spending time with smokers? Can you avoid binge drinking if you regularly go to keg parties?

Finally, individuals may focus on alternative behaviors that replace the unhealthy ones. Instead of bar hopping, they might join a group dedicated to activities not associated with drinking alcohol, such as a dance club or community theater group. In other words, effective change also involves avoiding temptations.

MAINTENANCE

In the *maintenance stage,* individuals successfully avoid temptation and consistently pursue healthy behaviors. They may become skilled at anticipating tempting situations and avoid them or actively prepare for them. If smokers seeking to kick the habit know that they always enjoy a cigarette after a big meal out with friends, they might mentally prepare themselves for that temptation before going out. Successful dieters might post a consciousness-raising photograph on the refrigerator. Individuals who feel like they have control over their decision to make a life change are more likely to make it to the maintenance stage (Vancampfort & others, 2016).

At some point, individuals in maintenance may find that actively fighting the urge to indulge in unhealthy behaviors is no longer necessary. *Transcendence* means that they are no longer

©Stockbyte/Getty Images

consciously engaged in maintaining their healthy lifestyle; rather, the lifestyle has become a part of who they are. They are now nonsmokers, healthy eaters, or committed runners.

RELAPSE   One challenge during the maintenance stage is to avoid **relapse,** a return to former unhealthy patterns. Relapse is a common aspect of change, and it can be discouraging. However, the majority of people who eventually do change do not succeed on the first try. Rather, they try and fail and try again, cycling through the five stages several times before achieving a stable, healthy lifestyle. Consequently, individuals who are experts in changing health behavior consider relapse to be normal (Prochaska & Norcross, 2013).

relapse
A return to former unhealthy patterns.

If you have ever tried to adopt a healthier lifestyle by dieting, starting an exercise program, or quitting smoking, you might know how bad you feel when you experience relapse. One slip, however, does not mean that you are a failure and will never reach your goal. Rather, when a slipup occurs, you have an opportunity to learn, to think about what led to the relapse, and to devise a strategy for preventing it in the future. Successful dieters, for example, do not let one lapse in the doughnut shop ruin the week (Phelan & others, 2003).

Relapse is a normal part of change. What does this principle suggest about recovery from drug addiction?

EVALUATION OF THE STAGES OF CHANGE MODEL   The stages of change model has been applied successfully to a broad range of behaviors. These include cigarette smoking (Gantiva & others, 2015; Luh & others, 2014), exercise (Zhu & others, 2014), healthy food choices (Klöckner, 2017), cancer prevention behaviors (Choi, Chung, & Park, 2013), safe-sex practices (Arden & Armitage, 2008), and substance use and abuse (Harrell & others, 2013). The model has also been used to predict adherence to safe practices at work (Rothmore, Aylward, & Karnon, 2015) and to behavior change in criminal offenders (Yong & others, 2015).

Despite its relevance to a variety of behaviors, the stages of change model is controversial (Brug & others, 2005; Joseph, Breslin, & Skinner, 1999). Some critics have questioned whether the stages are mutually exclusive and whether individuals move from one stage to another in the order proposed (Littrell & Girvin, 2002). A meta-analysis showed that the sequence of stages may vary depending on the specific domain of health change (Rosen, 2000). Critics of the model also point out that it refers more to attitudes that change than to behaviors (West, 2005). On the more positive side, some evidence suggests that the stages of change model does a good job of capturing the ways that individuals make positive life changes (Gantiva & others, 2015; Lippke & others, 2009, 2010). A meta-analysis of 39 studies that encompassed more than 8,000 psychotherapy clients found that the stages of change model was effective in predicting psychotherapy outcomes (Norcross, Krebs, & Prochaska, 2011).

Experts argue that the model can be a tool for therapists who are trying to help clients institute healthy behavior patterns. Sometimes, sharing the model with individuals who are trying to change provides them with a useful language for understanding the change process, for reducing uncertainty, and for developing realistic expectations for the difficult journey (Hodgins, 2005; Schüz & others, 2009; Valesquez & others, 2016).

self-quiz

1. The theoretical model that breaks down behavioral change into five distinct steps is the
   A. theory of planned behavior.
   B. theory of reasoned action.
   C. cognitive theory of change.
   D. stages of change model.

2. When someone who is trying to change a behavior returns to unhealthy patterns, we say that he or she is in a state of
   A. denial.
   B. relapse.
   C. plateau.
   D. maintenance.

3. The stages of change model
   A. is not at all controversial.
   B. applies to a wide variety of behaviors.
   C. does not apply to cigarette smoking.
   D. does not apply to safe-sex practices.

APPLY IT! 4. Malcolm has been trying to quit smoking for two years. During his last attempt, he went three full months without smoking but then had a cigarette after a big fight with his girlfriend. He is feeling hopeless about his chances of quitting. What does the

stages of change model say about Malcolm's situation?
   A. Relapse is a normal part of change. Malcolm might think about why he relapsed and try to move on from there with a new strategy.
   B. Malcolm has blown it and will probably never quit smoking.
   C. Malcolm is stuck in the contemplation phase of change.
   D. Malcolm is unusual in that he had a relapse after three full months. He probably has a particularly strong addiction to cigarettes.

3 Resources for Effective Life Change

Making positive changes to promote health can be very challenging. Fortunately, we all have various psychological, social, and cultural resources at our disposal to help us in the journey to a healthier lifestyle. In this section we consider some of these tools that can help us achieve effective change and, ultimately, a healthier life.

Motivation

Recall that motivation refers to the "why" of behavior. Motivational tools for self-change involve changing for the right reasons. Research shows that motivation is important at every stage in the change process (Serafini, Shipley, & Stewart, 2016). Moreover, change is most effective when you are doing it for you. When people feel that they freely chose their new behaviors, change is more likely to persist (Kushnir & others, 2016; Stice, Shaw, & Marti, 2006).

Self-determination theory distinguishes between intrinsic motivation, doing something because you want to, and extrinsic motivation, doing something for external rewards. Research has shown that creating a context in which people feel more in control, more autonomous, and more competent is associated with enhanced outcomes for a broad array of health behaviors, including controlling diabetes through diet and exercise (Koponen, Simonsen, & Suominen, 2017), quitting smoking (Patten & others, 2016), and getting physically active (Liu & Chung, 2016). Individuals are more likely to succeed in their New Year's resolutions if they approach them with a sense of both self-efficacy and autonomy (Koestner & others, 2006).

©Radius Images/Alamy Stock Photo

implementation intentions
Specific strategies for dealing with the challenges of making a life change.

Planning and goal setting are also crucial to making effective change. Researchers have found that individuals who come up with specific strategies, or **implementation intentions,** for dealing with the challenges of making a life change are more successful than others at navigating change (Armitage & Arden, 2016). "Implement" means put into action. So, implementation intentions are strategies for actually putting our health goals to work. Setting short-term, achievable goals also allows individuals to experience the emotional payoff of small successes along the way to self-change. The novice exerciser who catches a glimpse of his new biceps in the mirror gets a mood boost. These feelings of satisfaction can help to motivate continued effort toward achieving health goals (Harris & others, 2014). Implementation intentions are especially effective if they are tied to a person's identity and sense of self (Kendzierski & others, 2015).

Enjoying the payoffs of our efforts to change also means that we must monitor our goal progress. It is important to get feedback on one's progress in the pursuit of any goal. If an individual finds out that she is falling short, she can try to identify areas that need work. On the other hand, discovering that she is doing well can be a potent motivator for future progress.

Whether the news is good or bad, information is important for making real progress.

Social Relationships

Research has shown, again and again, that social ties are an important, if not the most important, variable in predicting health (Cohen-Mansfield & Perach, 2015; Courtin & Knapp, 2017; Hill & others, 2016; Karantzas & Gillath, 2017; Sbarra, 2015). In a landmark study, social isolation had six times the effect on mortality rates that cigarette smoking had (House, Landis, & Umberson, 1988). Loneliness is linked with impaired physical health (Hawkley & Cacioppo, 2012a, 2012b; Momtaz & others, 2012) and mental health (Jaya & others, 2017). Longitudinal studies show that chronic loneliness predicts dying from a range of causes, over time (Luo & others, 2012; Patterson & Veenstra, 2010). Loneliness is thought to play such a large role in health because it is linked to poorer health behaviors, including lower levels of physical activity, higher levels of stress, and poor sleep (Christiansen, Larsen, & Lasgaard, 2016).

One way that social connections make a difference in our lives is what psychologists call social support (Li, Ji, & Chen, 2014). **Social support** is information and feedback from others indicating that one is loved and cared for, esteemed and valued, and included in a network of communication and mutual obligation. Social support has three types of benefits (Taylor, 2018):

social support
Information and feedback from others indicating that one is loved and cared for, esteemed and valued, and included in a network of communication and mutual obligation.

1. *Tangible assistance:* Family and friends can provide goods and services in stressful circumstances, as when gifts of food are given after the death of a loved one.

2. *Information:* Individuals who extend support can also recommend specific strategies to help the person under stress cope. Friends may notice that a coworker is over-loaded with work and suggest ways of better managing time or delegating tasks.

3. *Emotional support:* Individuals under stress often suffer emotionally and may develop depression, anxiety, or loss of self-esteem. Friends and family can reassure the stressed person that he or she is valuable and loved. Knowing that others care allows a person to manage stress with greater assurance.

Social support can help as a person prepares for a stressful experience, allowing the person to see the event in a less negative light. It can also help after the stressful event, helping the person recover. Research shows that social support can act as a shield, pro-tecting people from negative psychological and physical consequences of difficult or trau-matic events (Cantwell, Muldoon, & Gallagher, 2014). For example, it is not common for symptoms of PTSD to be associated with increases in physical illness symptoms. A study of military personnel who had been deployed to Iran, Iraq, and Afghanistan found that among whose who felt their unit was "like a family," PTSD symptoms were less likely to be associated with physical symptoms (Luciano & McDevitt-Murphy, 2017). Similar results were found for those who experienced high levels of social support from family and friends after returning from combat (Luciano & McDevitt-Murphy, 2017).

Social support is important for children as well (Ciarrochi & others, 2017). A recent study examined the ways that social support buttressed the well-being of 430 children who were orphaned in Rwanda. These children were left orphaned by war and illness and lived in a variety of sometimes very difficult circumstances, including on the street, in orphan-ages, in foster homes, or in child-headed households. Among these children, social support especially from adults was associated with higher psychological well-being and less distress (Caserta, Punamäki, & Pirttilä-Backman, 2017). In fact, the negative association between adult social support and distress was similar to that for having access to three meals a day.

One way that people gain support during difficult times is through *social sharing*—turning to others who act as a sounding board or a willing ear. Individuals who are striving to make healthy life changes might join a group of others who are also struggling with the same issue. Social sharing can also occur in online support groups.

Sometimes sharing our thoughts and feelings does not have to be very social to be helpful. James Pennebaker and his colleagues (Pennebaker, 1997a, 1997b, 2004) have demonstrated that writing about traumatic life events for 20 minutes a day over two or three days is associated with improved health, fewer illnesses, greater immune system function, and superior reactions to vaccines. Although writing about trauma is usually linked to increased distress in the short term, over the long run it brings physical and psychological health benefits (Baddeley & Pennebaker, 2011; Frattaroli, 2006; Pennebaker & Chung, 2007, 2011; Smyth, 1998). Studies have shown that expressive writing can lead to benefits for many different groups (Bryan & Lu, 2016; Greenbaum & Javdani, 2017; Travagin, Margola, & Revenson, 2015). Although typically expressive writing studies have focused on sharing about negative life events and expressing negative feelings (Lee & others, 2016), studies have found health benefits for writing about one's best possible future self (Loveday, Lovell, & Jones, 2017) and intensely positive life experiences (Burton & King, 2004, 2008; King, 2002). If you would like to give this simple intervention a try, see Figure 2.

Getting support from others is important, but *giving* support can also have benefits (Crocker, Canevello, & Brown, 2017). A study of 423 older adult couples who were followed for five years revealed how helping others benefits physical health (Brown & others, 2003). At the beginning of the study, the couples were asked about the extent to which they had given or received emotional or practical help in the past year. Five years later, those who said they had helped others were half as likely to have died. One possible reason for this finding is that helping others may reduce the output of stress hormones, an effect that improves cardiovascular health and strengthens the immune system (Hackett & others, 2012; Hawkley & Cacioppo, 2012a, 2012b).

> Find a quiet place to write.
>
> Pick just one topic to explore through writing.
>
> Dedicate yourself to at least 20 minutes of writing about that topic.
>
> While writing, do not be concerned with grammar or spelling; just let yourself go and write about all of the emotions, thoughts, and feelings associated with the experience you are writing about.
>
> If you feel that writing about something negative is not for you, try writing about your most positive life experiences, about the people you care about, or all the things you feel grateful for in life.

FIGURE 2 **Harnessing the Power of Writing** Try this simple exercise to explore the health benefits of writing.
©Ryan McVay/Getty Images

One way that psychologists study social connections is by examining people's social networks, that is, all the different social ties they have to people in their lives, including family, friends, co-workers and so forth. Having a broad, diverse social network may be especially important during difficult times (Hawkley & Cacioppo, 2012a, 2012b; Taylor, 2018). Some research has linked diverse social networks to longer life (Vogt & others, 1992) but others have found no association between social network size and health outcomes (Julsing & others, 2016; LeRoy & others, 2017).

Religious Faith

Religious faith is strongly related to maintaining a healthy lifestyle and to good health (Fastame, Hitchcott, & Penna, 2017; Krause & Hayward, 2014). Many religions frown on excess and promote moderation. Indeed, weekly religious attendance relates to a host of healthy behaviors, including not smoking, taking vitamins, walking regularly, wearing seat belts, exercising strenuously, sleeping soundly, and drinking moderately or not at all (Haber, Koenig, & Jacob, 2011; Hill & others, 2006; Mellor & Freeborn, 2011). A number of studies have linked religious participation to a longer and healthier life (Campbell, Yoon, & Johnstone, 2009; Krause, 2006; McCullough & Willoughby, 2009).

In addition to promoting healthier behaviors, religious participation may also benefit health through its relationship to social support (Le & others, 2016; Hovey & others, 2014). Belonging to a faith community may give people access to a warm group of others who are available during times of need. This community is there to provide transportation to the doctor, to check in with the individual during hard times, and simply to stand next to the individual during a worship service, as a fellow member of the community. The social connections promoted by religious activity can forestall anxiety and depression and help to prevent isolation and loneliness (Dein, Cook, & Koenig, 2012; Rosmarin, Krumrei, & Andersson, 2009; Ross & others, 2009). For example, a study of African Americans found that church-based social support was protective against depressive symptoms (Chatters & others, 2014).

Religious faith and spirituality more generally may also be important factors in good health because they provide a sense of life meaning and a buffer against the effects of stressful life events (Gutierrez, Park, & Wright, 2017; Hooker, Masters, & Park, 2017; Park, 2012; Sacco & others, 2014). Religious thoughts can play a role in maintaining hope and stimulating motivation for positive life changes. A recent study showed that among a sample of individuals coping with diagnoses of heart failure or cancer, those who were higher in religious faith increased in the sense of meaning in life over time (George & Park, 2017). Belief in the enduring meaningfulness of one's life can help one keep perspective and see life's hassles in the context of the big picture (Park, 2012).

How might these results apply to a person who is not religious?

Personality Characteristics

Personality traits are powerful instruments in the self-change toolbox. Here we survey some of the personality characteristics related to health.

CONSCIENTIOUSNESS
Conscientious individuals are responsible and reliable; they like structure and seeing a task to its completion. Conscientiousness is not the sexiest trait, but it is the most important of the big five traits when it comes to health, healthy living, and longevity (Hill, Nickel, & Roberts, 2014; Turiano & others, 2015). Various studies show that conscientious people tend to do all the things that they are told are good for their health, such as getting regular exercise, eating healthy foods, avoiding drinking and smoking, wearing seat belts, monitoring their blood pressure, and checking smoke detectors (O'Connor & others, 2009; Turiano & others, 2012; Wilson & others, 2016). Research has also shown that conscientious individuals are not as likely to die as their counterparts who are less conscientious (Hill & others, 2011; Roberts, Donnellan, & Hill, 2013).

PERSONAL CONTROL
Another personality characteristic associated with taking the right steps toward a long, healthy life is a sense of personal control, what is referred to as an *internal locus of control* (Taylor, 2018). Feeling in control can reduce stress during difficult times (Lachman, Teshale, & Agrigoroaei, 2015) and can lead to the development of problem-solving strategies to deal with life's challenges. An individual with a good sense of personal control might reason, "If I stop smoking now, I will not develop lung cancer."

A person with a low level of personal control may feel that whatever happens happens—it is meant to be or a matter of (good or bad) luck.

A sense of personal control has been linked to a lower risk for common chronic diseases such as cancer and cardiovascular disease (Sturmer, Hasselbach, & Amelang, 2006). Further, like conscientiousness, a sense of personal control might also help people avoid a risky lifestyle that involves health-compromising behaviors. Consider a study of East German migrants to West Germany who found themselves unemployed (Mittag & Schwarzer, 1993). Individuals in the study often turned to heavy drinking for solace—unless, that is, they had a sense of personal control (as measured by survey items such as "When I'm in trouble, I can rely on my ability to deal with the problem effectively"). Overall, across a wide range of studies, a sense of personal control has been related to emotional well-being, successful coping with a stressful event, healthy behavior change, and good health (Hughes, Berg, & Wiebe, 2012; Sheppes, Suri, & Gross, 2015; Turiano & others, 2014; Zhang & Jang, 2017).

Learned helplessness means believing that one has no control over outcomes in one's life.

SELF-EFFICACY
Recall that self-efficacy is an individual's belief that he or she can master a situation and produce positive outcomes. Self-efficacy affects behavior in many situations, ranging from solving personal problems to going on diets. Self-efficacy influences

whether individuals try to develop healthy habits, how much effort they expend in coping with stress, how long they persist in the face of obstacles, and how much stress they experience (Thompson, & others, 2017).

Research has shown that self-efficacy is related to success in a wide variety of positive life changes. These include achieving weight loss (Nezami & others, 2016), exercising (Strachan & others, 2016), quitting smoking (Berndt & others, 2012; Shadel & others, 2017), reducing substance abuse (Goldsmith & others, 2012), and leading a healthy lifestyle (Axelsson & others, 2012). Self-efficacy is strongly linked to cardiovascular functioning following heart failure; individuals high in self-efficacy not only are less likely to suffer a second hospitalization due to heart failure but also are likely to live longer (Maeda & others, 2012; Sarkar, Ali, & Whooley, 2009). If there is a problem to be fixed, self-efficacy—having a can-do attitude—is related to finding a solution.

How might culture influence the roles of self-efficacy and personal control in health?

Throughout this book, we have examined the placebo effect as a positive response to a treatment that has no medicinal power. The placebo effect results from the individual's belief in the effectiveness of the treatment. Can you really adopt a healthier exercise routine? Maybe or maybe not, but believing that you can allows you to harness the placebo effect. Self-efficacy is the power of belief in yourself.

OPTIMISM   One factor that is often linked to positive functioning and adjustment is optimism. Researchers have found that optimism is associated with taking proactive steps to protect one's health, while pessimism is linked to engaging in health-compromising behaviors (Carver & Scheier, 2014). Martin Seligman (1990) views optimism as a matter of how a person explains the causes of bad events. Optimists identify the causes of bad events as external, unstable, and specific, whereas pessimists identify them as internal, stable, and global. Studies have associated explaining life events optimistically with positive outcomes, including a better quality of life (Carver & Scheier, 2014).

Other researchers define optimism as the expectancy that good things are more likely and that bad things are less likely to occur in the future (Carver & Scheier, 2009, 2014). This view focuses on how people pursue their goals and values. Even when faced with misfortune, optimists keep working to reach their goals, whereas pessimists give up.

Numerous studies reveal that optimists generally function more effectively and are physically and mentally healthier than pessimists (Avvenuti, Baiardini, & Giardini, 2016). For instance, in a sample of men with coronary heart disease, optimists were less likely to experience negative health events over the course of a year (Hevey, McGee, & Horgan, 2014). A recent study revealed that being optimistic and having an optimistic spouse were both associated with better health (Kim, Chopik, & Smith, 2014). Optimism has been linked to more effective immune system functioning and better health (Engberg & others, 2013). And a study of centenarians (people who live to be 100 or more years of age) revealed that those who were in better health had a higher level of optimism than their pessimistic counterparts (Tigani & others, 2012). Optimists are also more likely to seek out potentially threatening health risk information (Taber & others, 2015).

As you think about the traits we have examined—conscientiousness, personal control, self-efficacy, and optimism—and their relationship to good health, an important practical tip to keep in mind is that you can *cultivate* these qualities. Studies show that even conscientiousness, the most stable of these characteristics, can increase, especially in young adulthood. It is important as well to keep in mind that these various resources may relate to each other in important ways. A person with a high level of self-efficacy may be more optimistic about health decisions and challenges (Hajek & Helmut-König, 2017).

It is also possible for these characteristics to lead to unrealistic expectations (Jansen & others, 2017). It is important to always bear in mind that not everything is under a person's control and that includes health outcomes. Research results pointing to the links between various personality characteristics and better health outcomes can sometimes create a burden on individuals who are struggling with illness (Jones & Ruthig, 2015; Ruthig & Holfeld, 2016). To read about this issue, see Challenge Your Thinking.

How Powerful Is the Power of Positive Thinking?

Research demonstrating the role of psychological variables in health, disease, and mortality is extremely appealing because it gives us a sense we have some control over our physical health. Yet as reassuring as such findings might be, these factors are not a psychological recipe for immortality. When scientists find a link between some psychological factor and an important health outcome, the popular media often latch on to the results as if they mean that such factors play a causal role in disease. Such research can sometimes lead to victim blaming: thinking that a person is ill or has died because of a deficit of self-efficacy or optimism.

A compelling case in point is provided by research on "fighting spirit" in combatting breast cancer. In a study published over three decades ago, 69 women were interviewed three months after undergoing surgery for breast cancer (Greer, Morris, & Pettingale, 1979). Based on these interviews, the researchers categorized the women's responses to breast cancer as denial, fighting spirit, quiet resignation, or helplessness. The researchers then followed up on the women five years later to see whether they had experienced a recurrence. The results of the follow-up study showed that women whose responses were characterized by either denial or fighting spirit were less likely to have had a recurrence of cancer. This study led to the conclusion that women with breast cancer should be encouraged to adopt a fighting attitude toward their cancer. The idea that a fighting spirit is important to breast cancer survival continues to hold sway in interventions for women coping with the disease (Coyne & Tennen, 2010).

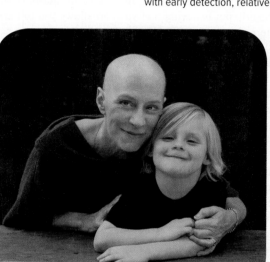
©King Lawrence/Blend Images

Crucially, this finding, based on a single study with a relatively small sample, has not withstood the test of time. Subsequent research, especially studies employing much larger samples, has failed to show any link between adopting a fighting spirit and breast cancer outcomes (Petticrew, Bell, & Hunter, 2002; Phillips & others, 2008; Watson & others, 2005).

Although the reality that a fighting spirit does not improve a woman's chances of beating cancer might seem disappointing, many have welcomed this news. As one expert commented, such findings "may help to remove any continuing feelings of guilt or sense of blame for breast cancer relapse from those women who worry because they cannot always maintain a fighting spirit or a positive attitude" (Dobson, 2005). The widespread belief that adopting a fighting spirit was key to cancer survival imposed a burden on individuals already dealing with a difficult life experience.

Does this conclusion mean that psychosocial variables have no role to play in disease? Certainly not. One study that found no effect of fighting spirit did show that initial helplessness in response to diagnoses was a predictor of poorer outcomes among women with breast cancer (Watson & others, 2005). Knowing that a person feels helpless early on may prompt professionals to provide much needed information about treatment and the potential for long-term recovery. Indeed, among the factors that (happily) complicate this type of research are that many cancers have effective treatments and that, especially with early detection, relatively few individuals die or experience a recurrence.

A recent study of individuals with Stage IV colorectal cancer showed that, although hope and optimism were unrelated to disease progression, depression was (Schofield & others, 2016). Family and friends can provide support that helps a person maintain quality of life without pressuring the person the "be positive" (Hill, 2016). Professionals can also use information about psychological characteristics to build in behavioral supports that might be needed to help a person stick with treatment and optimize her outcomes.

People deal with potentially life-threatening diagnoses in different ways. Dutch swimmer Maarten van der Weijden was diagnosed with leukemia in 2001 at the age of 20 but went on to win Olympic gold in 2008. With respect to his diagnosis, he remarked, "I . . . simply surrendered to the doctors. You always hear those stories that you have to think positively, that you have to fight to survive. This can be a great burden for patients. It has never been proven that you can cure cancer by thinking positively or by fighting" (quoted in Coyne, Tennen, & Ranchor, 2010, p. 40).

What Do You Think?

- In the 1979 study, fighting spirit and denial both were associated with better outcomes. Why do you think people latched on to fighting spirit rather than denial as a key intervention?

- If someone you love were diagnosed with cancer, how would the research reported here influence the support you would provide to that person?

self-quiz

1. All of the following are powerful tools for self-change *except*
   A. ethnic heritage.
   B. religious faith.
   C. personality traits.
   D. motivation.

2. The benefits of social support include all of the following *except*
   A. information.
   B. tangible assistance.
   C. emotional support.
   D. victim blaming.

3. Optimists explain the causes of bad events as
   A. external.
   B. internal.
   C. global.
   D. stable.

APPLY IT! 4. Daniel was recently diagnosed with diabetes. His doctor gave him a new diet to control his condition. Which of the following situations offers the *best* chances that Daniel will stick with the diet?
   A. Daniel loves junk food and does not want to follow the diet, but his mother and aunt, both living with diabetes, are pressuring him to follow the doctor's recommendations.
   B. Daniel has always had trouble following through on doing what is good for him, though he says he wants more structure in his life.
   C. Clark, Daniel's roommate, has a brother with diabetes, and Clark tells Daniel about how his brother has coped and what diet he follows; Clark offers to introduce them.
   D. Daniel has a pessimistic personality and expects things to work out badly.

4 Toward a Healthier Mind (and Body): Controlling Stress

If you could change one thing about your behavior, what would you choose? Would the change perhaps have to do with feeling stressed out much of the time? Maybe you wish you could stop facing every daily challenge with tension. Let's look at the problems that can arise when you feel chronically stressed and the ways you can better manage your stress.

Stress and Its Stages

Stress is the response to environmental stressors, the circumstances and events that threaten individuals and tax their coping abilities. Hans Selye (1974, 1983), the founder of stress research, focused on the body's response to stressors, especially the wear and tear due to the demands placed on the body. After observing patients with different problems—the death of someone close, loss of income, arrest for embezzlement—Selye concluded that any number of environmental events or stimuli would produce the same stress symptoms: loss of appetite, muscular weakness, and decreased interest in the world. Selye realized that whenever people experienced stressors, they experienced a common phenomenon, stress.

Getting married, having a baby, graduating from college—although positive life events, these achievements can be stressful because they are also major life changes.

general adaptation syndrome (GAS) Selye's term for the common effects of stressful demands on the body, consisting of three stages: alarm, resistance, and exhaustion.

General adaptation syndrome (GAS) is Selye's term for the common effects on the body when demands are placed on it (Figure 3). The GAS consists of three stages: alarm, resistance, and exhaustion. Selye's model is especially useful in helping us understand the link between stress and health.

The body's first reaction to a stressor, in the *alarm stage,* is a temporary state of shock during which resistance to illness and stress falls below normal limits. In trying to cope with the initial effects of stress, the body releases hormones that, in a short time, adversely affect the functioning

FIGURE 3 **Selye's General Adaptation Syndrome** The general adaptation syndrome (GAS) describes an individual's response to stress in terms of three stages: (1) alarm, in which the body mobilizes its resources; (2) resistance, in which the body strives mightily to endure the stressor; and (3) exhaustion, in which resistance becomes depleted.

of the immune system, the body's network of natural defenses. During this time the individual is prone to infections from illness and injury.

In the *resistance stage* of Selye's general adaptation syndrome, glands throughout the body manufacture different hormones that protect the individual. Endocrine and sympathetic nervous system activity are not as high as in the alarm stage, although they still are elevated. During the resistance stage, the body's immune system can fight off infection with remarkable efficiency. Similarly, hormones that reduce the inflammation normally associated with injury circulate at high levels.

If the body's all-out effort to combat stress fails and the stress persists, the individual moves into the *exhaustion stage*. At this point, wear and tear takes its toll—the person might collapse in exhaustion, and vulnerability to disease increases. Serious, possibly irreversible damage to the body—such as a heart attack or even death—may occur.

hypothalamic-pituitary-adrenal axis (HPA axis) The complex set of interactions among the hypothalamus, the pituitary gland, and the adrenal glands that regulate various body processes and control reactions to stressful events.

The body system that plays the greatest role in Selye's GAS model is the **hypothalamic-pituitary-adrenal axis (HPA axis)**. The HPA axis is a complex set of interactions among the hypothalamus (part of the brain's limbic system), the pituitary gland (the master gland of the endocrine system), and the adrenal glands (endocrine system glands located on top of each kidney) (Spencer & Deak, 2017). The HPA axis regulates various body processes, including digestion, immune system responses, emotion, and energy expenditure. The axis also controls reactions to stressful events, and these responses will be our focus here.

When the brain detects a threat in the environment, it signals the hypothalamus to release corticotropin-releasing hormone (CRH). In turn, CRH stimulates the pituitary gland to produce another hormone that causes the adrenal glands to release cortisol. Cortisol is itself the "stress hormone" that directs cells to make sugar, fat, and protein available so the body can take quick action. Cortisol also suppresses the immune system.

Recall the difference between acute stress and chronic stress. Acute stress can sometimes be adaptive, and in acute stress cortisol plays an important role in helping us to take the necessary action to avoid dire consequences. Typically, once the body has dealt with a given stressor, our cortisol level returns to normal. However, under chronic stress, the HPA axis can remain activated over the long haul.

The activity of the HPA axis varies from one person to the next. These differences may be explained by genes as well as by particular stressful experiences (Di Iorio & others, 2017; Odeon & others, 2017; Thoma & others, 2017). Research with nonhuman animals and humans has shown that pre- and post-natal stress can influence the development of the HPA axis (Koss & others, 2014; Laurent & others, 2014; Mustoe & others, 2014). When the HPA is chronically active, various systems in the body suffer.

Stress and the Immune System

psychoneuroimmunology A new field of scientific inquiry that explores connections among psychological factors (such as attitudes and emotions), the nervous system, and the immune system.

Chronic stress can have serious implications for the body, in particular the immune system. Interest in links between the immune system and stress spawned the field of **psychoneuroimmunology,** which explores connections among psychological factors (such as attitudes and emotions), the nervous system, and the immune system (Acabchuk & others, 2017; Mracsko & others, 2014; Stowell, Robles, & Kane, 2013).

The immune system and the central nervous system are similar in their modes of receiving, recognizing, and integrating signals from the external environment (Arisi, 2014).

 Recall that the immune system can learn through classical conditioning.

The central nervous system and the immune system both possess "sensory" elements that receive information from the environment and other parts of the body and "motor" elements that carry out an appropriate response. Both systems also rely on chemical mediators for communication. CRH, a key hormone shared by the central nervous system and the immune system, is produced in the hypothalamus, as we saw above, and unites the stress and immune responses.

Stress can profoundly influence the immune system. Acute stressors (sudden, stressful, one-time life events) can produce immunological changes. For example, in relatively healthy HIV-infected individuals, as well as in individuals with cancer, acute stressors are associated with poorer immune system functioning (McIntosh & Rosselli, 2012; Pant & Ramaswamy, 2009). In addition to acute stressors, chronic stressors (long-lasting agents of stress) are associated with an increasing downturn in immune system responsiveness (Acabchuk & others, 2017; Schmidt & others, 2016; Straub, 2014). This effect has been linked to a downturn in immune system functioning in a number of contexts, including worries about living next to a damaged nuclear reactor, failures in close relationships (divorce, separation, and marital distress), depression, loneliness, and burdensome caregiving for a family member with progressive illness (Fagundes & others, 2013; Jaremka & others, 2013a, 2013b, 2014).

Researchers hope to determine the precise links among psychological factors, the brain, and the immune system (Capoccia & others, 2013). Preliminary hypotheses about the interaction that causes vulnerability to disease include:

- Stressful experiences lower the efficiency of immune systems, making individuals more susceptible to disease.
- Stress directly promotes disease-producing processes.
- Stressful experiences may cause the activation of dormant viruses that diminish the individual's ability to cope with disease.

These hypotheses may lead to clues for more successful treatments for some of the most challenging diseases to conquer, AIDS and cancer among them.

Sheldon Cohen and his colleagues have carried out a number of studies on the effects of stress, emotion, and social support on immunity and susceptibility to infectious disease (Cohen & Lemay, 2007; Cohen & others, 2009, 2012; Sneed & others, 2012). In one such study, Cohen and his colleagues (1998) focused on 276 adults who were exposed to viruses and then quarantined for five days. Figure 4 shows the dramatic results. The longer the participants had experienced major stress in their lives before the study, the more likely they were to catch a cold. Cohen concluded that stress-triggered changes in the immune system and hormones might create greater vulnerability to infection. These findings suggest that when we are under stress, we need to take better care of ourselves than usual (Cohen & others, 2009, 2012).

Meditation is a great way to cope with stress and has positive benefits for the immune system.

Stress and Cardiovascular Disease

There is also reason to believe that stress increases an individual's risk for cardiovascular disease (Ellins & others, 2017; Murphy, Cohn, & Loria, 2017). Chronic stress is associated with poor cardiovascular function, high blood pressure, heart disease, and early death (Goodson & others, 2017; Schulz, 2007; Wiernik & others, 2014). Individuals who have had major life changes (such as the death of a spouse and the loss of a job) have a higher incidence of cardiovascular disease and early death (Mostofsky & others, 2012; Taylor, 2018). People in a chronically stressed condition, such as that stemming from work stress or prolonged loneliness, are also more likely to take up smoking, start overeating, and avoid exercising, behaviors linked with cardiovascular disease (Steptoe & Kivimaki, 2012; Zimmerman, 2012).

Just as personality characteristics such as a sense of control or self-efficacy can help buffer an individual against stress, other personality characteristics have been shown to worsen stress, with special significance

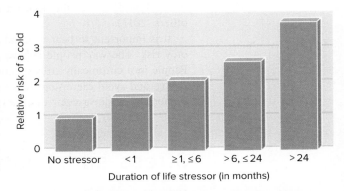

FIGURE 4 **Stress and the Risk of Developing a Cold** In a study by Cohen and others (1998), the longer individuals had a life stressor, the more likely they were to develop a cold. The four-point scale is based on the odds (0 = lower; 4 = higher) of getting a cold.

for cardiovascular illness. In particular, people who are impatient or quick to anger or who display frequent hostility have an increased risk for cardiovascular disease (Espnes & Byrne, 2016).

In the late 1950s, a secretary for two California cardiologists, Meyer Friedman and Ray Rosenman, observed that the chairs in their waiting rooms were tattered and worn, but only on the front edges. The cardiologists had also noticed the impatience of their cardiac patients, who often arrived exactly on time and were in a great hurry to leave. Intrigued by this consistency, they conducted a study of 3,000 healthy men between the ages of 35 and 59 over eight years to find out whether people with certain behavioral characteristics might be prone to heart problems (Friedman & Rosenman, 1974). During the eight years, one group of men had twice as many heart attacks or other forms of heart disease as the other men. Further, autopsies of the men who died revealed that this same group had coronary arteries that were more obstructed than those of the other men.

Friedman and Rosenman described the common personality characteristics of the men who developed coronary disease as the **Type A behavior pattern.** They theorized that a cluster of characteristics—being excessively competitive, hard-driven, impatient, and hostile—is related to the incidence of heart disease. Rosenman and Friedman labeled the behavior of the healthier group, who were typically relaxed and easygoing, the **Type B behavior pattern.**

Further research on the link between Type A behavior and coronary disease indicates that the association is not as strong as Friedman and Rosenman believed (Suls & Swain, 1998; Williams, 2001, 2002). However, researchers have found that certain components of Type A behavior are more precisely linked with coronary risk (Spielberger, 2004). The Type A behavior component most consistently associated with coronary problems is hostility (Appleton & others, 2016; Ohira & others, 2012). People who are hostile outwardly or who turn anger inward are more likely to develop heart disease than their less angry counterparts (Eng & others, 2003; Matthews & others, 2004). Such people have intense physiological reactions to stress: Their hearts race, their breathing quickens, and their muscles tense up. One study found that hostility was a better predictor of coronary heart disease in older men than smoking, drinking, high caloric intake, or high levels of LDL cholesterol (Niaura & others, 2002).

There has been increased interest in the **Type D behavior pattern,** which describes individuals who are generally distressed, frequently experience negative emotions, and are socially inhibited (Ginting & others, 2014; Schoormans & others, 2017). Even after adjustment for depression, Type D individuals face a threefold increased risk of adverse cardiovascular outcomes (Denollet & Conraads, 2011). A meta-analysis also found that Type D persons with cardiovascular disease are at a higher risk for major adverse cardiac events and have a lower health-related quality of life (O'Dell & others, 2011). A recent study of individuals with colorectal cancer demonstrated that it was the negative affect component of the Type D personality that predicted mortality and especially in men (Schoormans & others, 2017).

It is important to bear in mind that the body's internal reactions to stress are not the only risk. The way people behave when they are stressed can contribute to disease risk. People in a chronically stressed condition are more likely to take up smoking, start overeating, and avoid exercising. All of these stress-related behaviors are linked with the development of cardiovascular disease (Appleton & others, 2016).

Stress and Cancer

Given the association of stress with poor health behaviors such as smoking, it is not surprising that stress has also been related to cancer risk (Nezu & others, 2013). Stress sets in motion biological changes involving the autonomic, endocrine, and immune systems. If the immune system is not compromised, it appears to help provide resistance to

Type A behavior pattern
A cluster of characteristics—including being excessively competitive, hard-driven, impatient, and hostile—that is related to a higher incidence of heart disease.

Type B behavior pattern
A cluster of characteristics—including being relaxed and easygoing—that is related to a lower incidence of heart disease.

Students who set high standards sometimes think they are 'Type A' but remember that the key feature of Type A is **hostility!** Type A folks often have explosive tempers.

Type D behavior pattern
A cluster of characteristics—including being generally distressed, having negative emotions, and being socially inhibited—that is related to adverse cardiovascular outcomes.

cancer and slow its progression. Researchers have found, however, that the physiological effects of stress inhibit a number of cellular immune responses (Hayakawa, 2012). Cancer patients show diminished natural killer cell (NK-cell) activity in the blood (Rosental & others, 2012) (Figure 5). Low NK-cell activity is linked with the development of further malignancies, and the length of survival for the cancer patient is related to NK-cell activity (Hegmans & Aerts, 2014; Leung, 2014).

Thus, stress is clearly a factor not only in immune system functioning and cardiovascular health but also in the risk for cancer. In light of these links, understanding the psychological processes by which individuals can effectively handle stressful circumstances is a crucial topic in health psychology (Epel & Lithgow, 2014; Stowell, Robles, & Kane, 2013).

FIGURE 5 **NK Cells and Cancer** Two natural killer (NK) cells (*yellow*) are shown attacking a leukemia cell (*red*). Notice the blisters that the leukemia cell has developed to defend itself. Nonetheless, the NK cells are surrounding the leukemia cell and are about to destroy it.
©Eye of Science/Science Source

Cognitive Appraisal and Coping with Stress

What stresses you out? Stressors can be anything from losing irreplaceable notes from a class, to being yelled at by a friend, to failing a test, to being in a car wreck.

Although everyone's body may respond similarly to stressors, not everyone perceives the same events as stressful. Whether an experience "stresses you out" depends on how you think about that experience (Rogers & Maytan, 2012). For example, you may perceive an upcoming job interview as a threatening obligation, whereas your roommate may perceive it as a challenging opportunity—a chance to shine. You might view a *D* on a paper as a crushing blow; your roommate may view the same grade as an incentive to work harder. To some degree, then, what is stressful depends on how one thinks about events (Gomes & Teixeira, 2014; Kaiseler & others, 2014; Schröder & others, 2012).

Let's face it. Just reading about the negative effects of stress can be stressful.

cognitive appraisal
Individuals' interpretation of the events in their life as harmful, threatening, or challenging and their determination of whether they have the resources to cope effectively with the events.

coping
Managing taxing circumstances, expending effort to solve life's problems, and seeking to master or reduce stress.

STEPS IN COGNITIVE APPRAISAL **Cognitive appraisal** refers to an individual's interpretation of an event as either harmful, threatening, or challenging, and the person's determination of whether he or she has the resources to cope effectively with the event. **Coping** is essentially a kind of problem solving. It involves managing taxing circumstances, expending effort to solve life's problems, and seeking to master or reduce stress.

Richard Lazarus articulated the importance of cognitive appraisal to stress and coping (1993, 2000). In Lazarus's view, people appraise events in two steps: primary appraisal and secondary appraisal. In *primary appraisal,* individuals interpret whether an event involves *harm or loss* that has already occurred, a *threat* of some future danger, or a *challenge* to be overcome. Lazarus believed that perceiving a stressor as a challenge to be overcome rather than as a threat is a good strategy for reducing stress. To understand Lazarus's concept of primary appraisal, consider two students, each with a failing grade in a psychology class at midterm. Sam is almost frozen by the stress of the low grade and looks at the rest of the term as a threatening prospect. In contrast, Pam does not become overwhelmed by the harm already done and the threat of future failures. She sees the low grade as a challenge that she can address and overcome.

In *secondary appraisal,* individuals evaluate their resources and determine how effectively they can be marshaled to cope with the

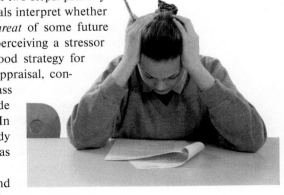

©image100 Ltd./Getty Images

event. This appraisal is secondary because it both comes after primary appraisal and depends on the degree to which the event is appraised as harmful, threatening, or challenging. Sam might have some helpful resources for coping with his low midterm grade, but he views the stressful circumstance as so harmful and threatening that he does not take stock of and use his resources. Pam, in contrast, evaluates the resources she can call on to improve her grade. These include asking the instructor for suggestions about how to improve her studying for the tests, managing time to include more study hours, and consulting with high-achieving classmates.

problem-focused coping
The coping strategy of squarely facing one's troubles and trying to solve them.

emotion-focused coping
The coping strategy that involves responding to the stress that one is feeling—trying to manage one's emotional reaction—rather than focusing on the root problem itself.

TYPES OF COPING   Research has identified two types of coping. **Problem-focused coping** is the cognitive strategy of squarely facing one's troubles and trying to solve them. For example, if you are having trouble with a class, you might go to the campus study skills center and sign up for a program to learn how to study more effectively. Having done so, you have faced your problem and attempted to do something about it. Problem-focused coping might involve coming up with goals and implementation intentions, the problem-solving steps we examined earlier in this chapter.

Emotion-focused coping entails responding to the stress that one is feeling—trying to manage the emotional reaction—rather than confronting the root problem. If you use emotion-focused coping, you might avoid going to a class that is a problem for you. Instead, you might say the class does not matter, deny that you are having difficulty with it, joke about it with your friends, or pray that you will do better.

In some circumstances, emotion-focused coping can be beneficial in dealing with life's problems. Denial is one of the main protective psychological mechanisms for navigating the flood of feelings that occurs when the reality of death or dying becomes too great. For example, one study found that following the death of a loved one, bereaved individuals who directed their attention away from their negative feelings had fewer health problems and were rated as better adjusted by their friends, compared to bereaved individuals who did not use this coping strategy (Coifman & others, 2007). Denial can be used to avoid the destructive impact of shock by postponing the time when one has to deal with stress. In other circumstances, however, emotion-focused coping can be a problem. Denying that the person you dated does not love you anymore when he or she has become engaged to someone else keeps you from getting on with life.

Emotion-focused coping can be adaptive in situations in which there is no solution to a problem, such as grieving over a loved one's death, when in fact it makes sense to focus on feeling better and accepting the present circumstances.

Many individuals successfully use both problem-focused and emotion-focused coping when adjusting to a stressful circumstance. For example, in one study, individuals said they employed both problem-focused and emotion-focused coping strategies in 98 percent of the stressful situations they encounter (Folkman & Lazarus, 1980). Over the long term, though, problem-focused coping usually works best (Pavani & others, 2016; Tuncay & Musabak, 2015).

Strategies for Successful Coping

A stressful circumstance becomes considerably less stressful when a person successfully copes with it. Effective coping is associated with a sense of personal control, a healthy immune system, personal resources, and positive emotions.

Multiple coping strategies often work better than a single strategy, as is true with any problem-solving challenge. People who have experienced a stressful life event or a cluster of difficulties might actively embrace problem solving and consistently take advantage of opportunities for positive experiences, even in the context of the bad times they are going through. Positive emotion can give them a sense of the big picture, help them devise possible solutions, and allow them to make creative connections.

Optimists are not just denying that anything bad can happen. They are actively engaged with reality, even when it contains threatening news.

Optimism can play a strong role in effective coping (Taylor & others, 2012). Lisa Aspinwall has found, for example, that optimistic people are more likely to attend to and remember potentially threatening health-related information than are pessimists (Aspinwall, 1998, 2011; Aspinwall, Leaf, & Leachman, 2009; Aspinwall & Pengchit, 2013). Aspinwall views optimism as a resource that allows individuals to engage constructively with potentially frightening information. Optimists are more likely than others to seek out genetic testing in order to learn about their risk for disease (Aspinwall & others, 2013). Optimists engage with life from a place of strength, so when an optimist finds out, for instance, that a favorite pastime, tanning, is related to an elevated risk of skin cancer, the information is important but not overwhelming. In contrast, pessimists are already living in a bleak world and prefer not to hear more bad news.

Another personality trait that appears to promote thriving during difficult times is hardiness. **Hardiness** is characterized by a sense of commitment rather than alienation, and of control rather than powerlessness, as well as a perception of problems as challenges rather than threats (Maddi & others, 2017). Hardiness is the trait displayed by the basketball player whose team is down by two points with seconds remaining on the clock when he shouts, "Coach! Give me the ball!" Many of us would shrink from such a high-pressure moment.

The links among hardiness, stress, and illness were the focus of the Chicago Stress Project, which studied male business executives 32 to 65 years of age over a five-year period (Kobasa, Maddi, & Kahn, 1982; Maddi, 1998). During the five years, most of the executives experienced stressful events such as divorce, job transfers, a close friend's death, inferior work-performance evaluations, and reporting to an unpleasant boss. Figure 6 shows how hardiness buffered these individuals from stress-related illness (Kobasa & others, 1986).

Other researchers also have found support for the role of hardiness in illness and health and especially coping with difficult times (Abdollahi & others, 2014; Pitts & others, 2016). For instance, a recent study found that mothers of children with cancer were less likely to suffer from traumatic stress symptoms if they were high in hardiness (Stoppelbein, McRae, & Greening, 2017).

Like other psychological characteristics we have reviewed in this chapter, hardiness is related to taking a positive approach to coping. You might start to think that being a positive person and looking on the bright side is always the best for coping. But, certainly, negative events and negative feelings are a fact of life. How might these feelings fit into a healthy life? To read about how psychologists have come to answer this question, see the Intersection.

hardiness
A personality trait characterized by a sense of commitment rather than alienation and of control rather than powerlessness; a perception of problems as challenges rather than threats.

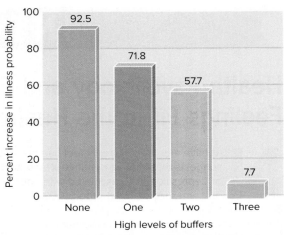

FIGURE 6 Illness in High-Stress Business Executives In one study of high-stress business executives, a low level of all three buffers (hardiness, exercise, and social support) involved a high probability of at least one serious illness in that year. High levels of one, two, and all three buffers decreased the likelihood of at least one serious illness occurring in the year of the study.

Stress Management Programs

"Avoid stress" may be good advice, but life is full of potentially stressful experiences. Sometimes just checking email or answering a phone can be an invitation for stress.

Because many people have difficulty regulating stress, psychologists have developed techniques that individuals can learn (Richardson, 2017). **Stress management programs** teach individuals how to appraise stressful events, develop coping skills, and put these skills to practical use. Some stress management programs teach a range of techniques to handle stress; others focus on a specific technique, such as relaxation or assertiveness training.

Stress management programs are often taught through workshops, which are becoming more common in the workplace (Richardson, 2017; Taylor, 2018). Aware of the high cost in lost productivity due to stress-related disorders, many organizations have become increasingly motivated to help their workers identify and cope with stressful

stress management program
A regimen that teaches individuals how to appraise stressful events, how to develop skills for coping with stress, and how to put these skills into use in everyday life.

Health Psychology and Emotion: How Do Negative Feelings Fit in the Healthy Life?

Negative emotions not only feel bad but some research suggests that chronic negative states, such as hostility or depression, are associated with poor health outcomes (Appleton & others, 2016; Schoormans & others, 2017). Yet, in reality some negative emotions are inevitable. Whether positive or negative, our moods attach us to the events of life and provide feedback about how we are doing on the goals that are important to us. Is there a way to think about sadness, anger, or disappointment, that illuminates the role of these feelings in healthy human functioning? Increasingly, psychologists have become interested in answering this question.

First, research has begun to recognize that that whether emotions are positive or negative may not be the most important aspect of those feelings. People who are able to feel, whether the emotions are positive or negative, are likely better off than those who avoid feeling. For example, one study showed that people who were good at posing facial expressions of both sadness and joy showed better cardiovascular function (Tuck, Adams, & Consedine, 2017). Similarly, a 10-year longitudinal study showed that adults who experienced positive and negative feelings, at the same time, showed better physical health and less age-related decline in physical health (Hershfield & others, 2013). Such findings have led some scholars to conclude that a "healthy mix of emotions" is optimal for healthy aging (Trudel-Fitzgerald & others, 2017).

Another way to approach this topic is to consider the ways people feel about and respond to their own negative feelings. Should negative feelings be avoided at all costs? Or might we see

©sebra/Shutterstock

that they have a role to play in our lives? Some people view negative emotions as valuable experiences (Luong & others, 2016). For these individuals, negative emotions are not related to poorer physical functioning. Rather, among those who value negative feelings, experiencing sadness or anger is not associated with physical symptoms (Luong & others, 2016). Interestingly those who value negative emotions tend to experience less negative emotion, overall (a benefit that is not associated with valuing positive emotion). This finding suggests that the way people think about their negative feelings can be just as important as the feelings themselves.

Indeed, a recent series of studies examined how accepting one's negative feelings related to psychological health (Ford & others, 2017). The studies showed that individuals who practiced acceptance of their negative feelings had better psychological health than those who focused on changing those feelings. Moreover, again, those who accepted their negative feelings were likely to experience less negative emotion overall. This emerging evidence suggests that negative emotions are not always problems to be solved. Rather, they are a natural part of life. When we value those feelings and accept the lesson they convey, we can appreciate their place in our lives.

\\ **If you tend to stress out over negative feelings, how might you approach them differently?**

circumstances. Colleges and universities similarly run stress management programs for students.

Do stress management programs work? A recent study examined whether stressed adults showed improvements after a 3-week stress resort that focused on relaxation and physical exercise (Stier-Jarmer & others, 2016). Participants were randomly assigned to experience the stress management program or a control group. The results showed that those in the stress management group experienced lower stress and less risk of burn out compared to the control group. These benefits persisted up to 6 months.

Coping effectively with stress is essential for physical and mental health. Still, there is a lot more we can do to promote our health. Healthful living—establishing healthy habits and evaluating and changing behaviors that interfere with good health—helps us avoid the damaging effects of stress. Just as the biopsychosocial perspective predicts, healthy changes in one area of life can have benefits that flow to other areas.

1. Selye's term for the pattern of common effects on the body when demands are placed on it is
   A. exhaustion syndrome.
   B. the Type A behavior pattern.
   C. the Type B behavior pattern.
   D. general adaptation syndrome.

2. A personality trait that is characterized by a sense of commitment and control, as well as by a perception of problems as challenges rather than threats, is
   A. self-efficacy.
   B. self-determination.
   C. hardiness.
   D. self-confidence.

3. Dealing with difficult circumstances, expending effort to solve life's problems, and seeking to control or reduce stress are key aspects of
   A. coping.
   B. cognitive appraisal.
   C. primary appraisal.
   D. secondary appraisal.

APPLY IT! 4. In addition to taking a full load of classes, Bonnie works at two part-time jobs and helps her sister care for two toddlers. Bonnie is achievement oriented and strives to get A's in all of her courses. Because of her many commitments, she is often in a hurry and regularly does more than one thing at a time, but she tells people that she enjoys her busy routine. Which answer best assesses whether Bonnie is Type A and at risk for cardiovascular disease?
   A. Bonnie's hurriedness and achievement orientation indicate that she is Type A and probably at risk for cardiovascular disease.
   B. Although Bonnie may experience stress, the lack of hostility mentioned in this description suggests that she is not Type A or at risk for cardiovascular disease.
   C. Bonnie is a "hot reactor" and thus at risk for cardiovascular disease.
   D. Bonnie is Type A, but her enjoyment of life means that she is not at risk for cardiovascular disease.

5 Toward a Healthier Body (and Mind): Behaving as If Your Life Depends upon It

There is no escaping it: Getting stress under control is crucial for a healthy mind and body. It is also important to make wise behavioral choices in four additional life domains where healthy habits can benefit both body and mind. In this section we examine the advantages of becoming physically active, eating right, quitting smoking, and practicing safe sex.

Becoming Physically Active

Imagine that there was a time when, to change a TV channel, people had to get up and walk a few feet to turn a knob. Consider the time when people physically had to go to the library and hunt through card catalogs and shelves to find information rather than going online and googling. As our daily tasks have gotten increasingly easy, we have become less active, and inactivity is a serious health problem (Wuest & Fisette, 2015). A recent report of three nationally representative samples of U.S. adults showed that those who reported themselves as less active than their peers were 71 percent more likely to die during the study period (Zahrt & Crum, 2017).

Any activity that expends physical energy can be part of a healthy lifestyle. It can be as simple as taking the stairs instead of an elevator, walking or biking to class instead of driving, or getting up and dancing instead of sitting at the bar. In addition to its link to longevity, physical activity corresponds with other positive outcomes, including a lower probability of developing cardiovascular disease and cancer (Patnode & others, 2017; Sturgeon & others, 2017), weight loss in overweight individuals (Blais & others, 2017), improved cognitive functioning (Baker & others, 2017; Bott & others, 2107), better academic performance (Cappelen & others, 2017), better emotion regulation (Bernstein & McNally, 2017), positive coping with stress (Cairney & others, 2014), and increased self-esteem and body image (Martin Ginis & others, 2014; Nasstasia & others, 2017), and healthier aging (Morris & others, 2017). Physical exercise also reduces levels of anxiety (Legey & others, 2017) and depression (Poyatos-León, & others, 2017; Uemura & others, 2017; Zanetidou & others, 2017).

FIGURE 7 **The Jogging Hog Experiment**
Jogging hogs reveal the dramatic effects of exercise on health. In one investigation, a group of hogs was trained to run approximately 100 miles per week (Bloor & White, 1983). Then the researchers narrowed the arteries that supplied blood to the hogs' hearts. The hearts of the jogging hogs developed extensive alternate pathways for blood supply, and 42 percent of the threatened heart tissue was salvaged, compared with only 17 percent in a control group of non-jogging hogs.
Courtesy of Colin M. Bloor/UC San Diego Health Sciences

Even a real pig benefits from exercise; Figure 7 shows the positive effects of physical activity in hogs. Being physically active is like investing energy in a wellness bank account: Activity enhances physical well-being and gives us the ability to face life's potential stressors energetically (Donatelle, 2015).

Exercise is one special type of physical activity. **Exercise** formally refers to structured activities whose goal is to improve health. Although exercise designed to strengthen muscles and bones or to improve flexibility is important to fitness, many health experts stress the benefits of **aerobic exercise,** which is sustained activity—jogging, swimming, or cycling, for example—that stimulates heart and lung functioning.

In one study, exercise meant the difference between life and death for middle-aged and older adults (Blair & others, 1989). More than 10,000 men and women were divided into categories of low fitness, medium fitness, and high fitness. Then they were studied over eight years. As shown in Figure 8, sedentary participants (low fitness) were more than twice as likely to die during the study's eight-year time span than those who were moderately fit, and more than three times as likely to die as those who were highly fit. The positive effects of physical fitness occurred for both men and women. Further, another study revealed that adults aged 60 and over who were in the lowest fifth in terms of physical fitness as determined by a treadmill test were four times more likely to die over a 12-year period than their counterparts who were in the top fifth of physical fitness (Sui & others, 2007). This study also showed that older adults who were overweight but physically fit had a lower mortality risk over the 12 years than their normal-weight counterparts who were low in fitness (Sui & others, 2007). In addition, a longitudinal study found that men who exercised regularly at 72 years of age had a 30 percent higher probability of being alive at 90 years of age than their sedentary counterparts (Yates & others, 2008).

exercise
Structured activities whose goal is to improve health.

aerobic exercise
Sustained activity—jogging, swimming, or cycling, for example—that stimulates heart and lung functioning.

Fitness here refers to the body's ability to supply fuel during sustained physical activity.

Make time in your day to exercise. It might mean waking up earlier or forgoing watching TV. The benefits are well worth it.

PSYCHOLOGICAL INQUIRY

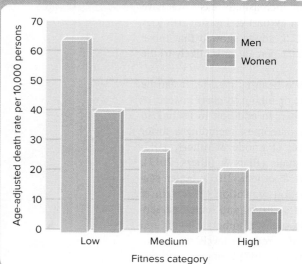

FIGURE 8 **Physical Fitness and Mortality** This graph presents the results of an eight-year longitudinal study of more than 10,000 men and women (Blair & others, 1989). The horizontal, or X, axis shows the participants divided by their levels of fitness as well as their sex. The vertical, or Y, axis shows the death rates.
>**Which groups had the highest and lowest death rates?** >**Comparing the results for men and women, what role does biological sex play in mortality?** >**This is a correlational study, so causation cannot be assumed. What third variables might explain the results?**

Moderate	Vigorous
Walking briskly (3–4 mph)	Walking briskly uphill or with a load
Swimming, moderate effort	Swimming, fast treading crawl
Cycling for pleasure or transportation (≤10 mph)	Cycling, fast or racing (>10 mph)
Racket sports, table tennis	Racket sports, singles tennis, racketball
Conditioning exercise, general calisthenics	Conditioning exercise, stair ergometer, ski machine
Golf, pulling cart or carrying clubs	Golf, practice at driving range
Canoeing, leisurely (2.0–3.9 mph)	Canoeing, rapidly (≥4 mph)
Home care, general cleaning	Moving furniture
Mowing lawn, power mower	Mowing lawn, hand mower
Home repair, painting	Fix-up projects

FIGURE 9 **Moderate and Vigorous Physical Activities** At minimum, adults should strive for 30 minutes of moderate activity each day. That activity can become even more beneficial if we "pump it up" to vigorous.

(leaves) ©Reed Kaestner/Corbis; (dog) ©Stockbyte/PunchStock

Health experts recommend that adults engage in at least 30 minutes of moderate physical activity on most, preferably all, days of the week and that children exercise for 60 minutes daily. Most specialists advise that exercisers raise their heart rate to at least 60 percent of their maximum rate. Only about one-fifth of adults are active at these recommended levels. Figure 9 lists physical activities that qualify as moderate and, for comparison, vigorous. Research suggests that both moderate and intense activities may produce important physical and psychological gains and improve quality of life (Focht, 2012).

One often-welcome payoff for increasing physical activity is weight loss. Frequently, researchers have found that the most effective component of weight-loss programs is regular exercise (Gordon, Chen, & Durstine, 2014; Kuhle & others, 2014). Another way to combat weight problems is through changes in diet.

Eating Right

The biggest health risk facing modern North Americans is being overweight or obese (Ogden & others, 2015; Schiff, 2015a, 2015b). "Overweight" and "obese" are labels for ranges of weight that are greater than what experts consider healthy for an individual's height (CDC, 2014b). In recent years, the percentage of individuals who are overweight or obese has been increasing at an alarming rate. As Figure 10 indicates, the prevalence of being overweight or obese in the United States changed little from 1960 to 1980 (Flegal & others, 2012; Ogden & Carroll, 2010; Ogden & others, 2012). However, from 2009 to 2014, 69 percent of U.S. adults were overweight or obese, with over 36 percent in the obese category (Ogden & others, 2015). Around the world, obesity rates have more than doubled since 1980 (World Health Organization, 2016).

Exercising regularly is one great way to lose weight. Making healthy dietary choices is another (Hendrickson & Rasmussen, 2017; Schiff, 2015a, 2015b). Eating right means selecting sensible, nutritious foods that maximize health and wellness. Despite our seemingly boundless food options, many of us are unhealthy eaters. We take in too much sugar and not enough foods high in vitamins, minerals, and fiber, such as fruits, vegetables, and

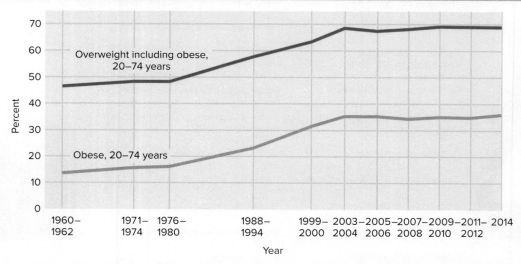

FIGURE 10 **Changes in the Percentage of U.S. Adults 20 to 74 Years of Age Classified as Overweight or Obese, 1960–2014** Being overweight or obese poses the greatest overall health risk for Americans today. In this graph, the vertical, or Y, axis shows the percentage of people considered overweight or obese, and the horizontal, or X, axis shows the years for these values.
> **Thinking of these lines as data points, is time positively or negatively correlated with overweight/obesity? Why?** > **Find the year of your birth on the X axis. How has the body weight of Americans changed during your lifetime?** > **What years show the steepest rise in weight gain? What factors might explain this increase?**

grains. We eat too much fast food and too few well-balanced meals—choices that increase our fat and cholesterol intake, both of which are implicated in long-term health problems (Bertoia & others, 2016; Lynch, Elmore, & Kotecki, 2015).

Healthy eating means incorporating tasty, healthy foods into meals and snacks. Healthy eating is not just about weight loss but also about committing to lifelong healthy food habits. Several health goals can be accomplished through a sound nutritional plan. Not only does a well-balanced diet provide more energy, but it also can lower blood pressure and lessen the risk for cancer (Eguchi & others, 2012). Two studies totaling more than 110,000 U.S. adults found that a high level of red meat consumption was linked to an increased risk of earlier death due to cardiovascular disease and cancer (Pan & others, 2012).

Losing weight and opting for healthier foods can be difficult, especially when you are just starting out. Many weight-loss fads promise weight loss with no effort, no hunger, and no real change in one's food consumption. These promises are unrealistic. Making genuine, enduring changes in eating behavior is hard work—but this does not mean that pessimism is required. Rather, positive expectations and self-efficacy are important because the task at hand is challenging.

The National Weight Control Registry is an ongoing study of people who have lost at least 40 pounds and kept it off for at least two years. Research on these successful dieters gives us important tips on how people who keep the weight off achieve this goal (L. G. Ogden & others, 2012; Raynor & others, 2005). Successful dieters show consistency in what they eat, plan their meals, weigh themselves, and stay active, especially limiting time spent watching TV or other screens (Thomas & others, 2014).

The truth is that keeping weight off is an ongoing process. Moreover, the longer a dieter keeps the weight off, the less likely he or she is to gain it back (McGuire & others, 1999). Further, research suggests that making small changes in the availability of junk food can have an impact on eating and weight (Rozin & others, 2011).

One key practice is eating breakfast, especially whole-grain cereals.

So, just don't buy the junk food! If it is not around, you won't eat it.

Environments That Support Active Lifestyles

French food—featuring delicious cheeses, heavy sauces, and buttery pastries—is one of the richest cuisines on the planet. Yet the obesity rate in France is less than half that of the U.S. (OECD, 2017). Why are Americans so much more likely to be obese than the French? Part of the gap may be due to differences in food portions (Rozin & others, 2003), but another factor is how people get to their food. In the United States grocery shopping typically involves a trip in a car, whereas in France individuals are more likely to walk or ride a bicycle (Ferrières, 2004).

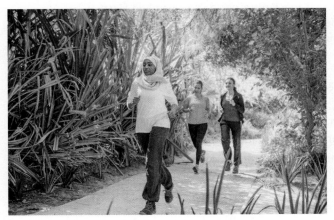

©Naufal MQ/Getty Images

A major obstacle to promoting exercise in the United States is that many U.S. cities are not designed in ways that promote walking or cycling. Advocates for change say that by making life too easy and too accommodating to cars and drivers, urban designers have created an *obesogenic* (obesity-promoting) environment—a context where it is challenging for people to engage in healthy activities (Henderson, 2008; Lydon & others, 2011). Countries such as the Netherlands and Denmark have adopted urban planning strategies that promote walking and biking and discourage car use. In the Netherlands, 60 percent of all journeys taken by people over age 60 are by bicycle (Henderson, 2008).

Environmental contexts that invite physical activity increase activity levels (Mackenbach & others, 2016). For example, one quasi-experimental study examined the effects of changes to the physical environment on activity. The study focused on an urban neighborhood in which a greenway (a biking and walking trail) was retrofitted to connect with pedestrian sidewalks. Researchers counted the number of people outside engaging in physical activity in that neighborhood for a two-hour period at various times over two years. Compared to two other similar neighborhoods, the neighborhood with the trail featured more people walking and biking (Fitzhugh, Bassett, & Evans, 2010). Environmental characteristics that welcome physical activity are also associated with health and wellness. In one study, elderly people who lived near parks, tree-lined streets, and areas for taking walks showed higher longevity over a five-year study period (Takano, Nakamura, & Watanabe, 2002).

Other aspects of city design can influence obesity rates, including access to nutritious foods (Lydon & others, 2011) and the perceived safety of neighborhoods (Eisenstein & others, 2011). By shedding light on how environmental factors influence healthy lifestyles, research on human behavior can meaningfully impact public policy.

Quitting Tobacco Use

Another health-related goal is giving up tobacco, including smoking. Evidence from a number of studies underscores the dangers of exposure to tobacco and being around smokers (American Cancer Society, 2015). For example, smoking is linked to 30 percent of cancer deaths, 21 percent of heart disease deaths, and 82 percent of chronic pulmonary

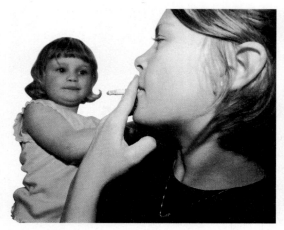

©Image Source/Corbis

disease deaths. Secondhand smoke is implicated in as many as 9,000 lung cancer deaths a year. Children of smokers are at special risk for respiratory and middle-ear diseases (CDC, 2017).

Fewer people smoke today than in the past, and almost half of the living adults who ever smoked have quit. In 2015, 15 percent of all adults in the United States smoked, with men being more likely to smoke than women (CDC, 2016). Although these numbers represent a substantial decline from 40 years ago, when 50 percent of men smoked, 36.5 million American adults still smoke. Exposure to tobacco through chewing or dipping also predicts higher risk of cardiovascular disease, a variety of cancers, and dental problems (American Cancer Society, 2015).

Quitting tobacco use has enormous health benefits. When individuals stop smoking, their risk of fatal lung cancer declines over time. Nicotine addiction makes quitting a challenge. Nicotine, the active drug in tobacco, is a stimulant that increases a person's energy and alertness, a pleasurable and reinforcing experience (Grando, 2014). In addition, nicotine stimulates neurotransmitters that have a calming or pain-reducing effect (Malin, Anderson, & Goyarzu, 2017).

Research confirms that giving up smoking (and other forms of tobacco use) can be difficult, especially in the early days of quitting. There are various ways to quit (Bradizza & others, 2017; Piper & others, 2017), including:

■ *Going cold turkey:* Some individuals succeed by stop using tobacco without making any major lifestyle changes. They decide they are going to quit, and they do.

■ *Using a substitute source of nicotine:* Nicotine gum, the nicotine patch, the nicotine inhaler, and nicotine spray work on the principle of supplying small amounts of nicotine to diminish the intensity of withdrawal.

■ *Seeking therapeutic help:* Some people get professional help to kick the tobacco habit.

No one method for quitting smoking or other tobacco use is foolproof (Piper & others, 2017). Often a combination of approaches is the best strategy. Furthermore, quitting for good typically requires more than one try, as the stages of change model suggests.

Practicing Safe Sex

One certainty in the human experience is that satisfying sexual experiences are part of a happy life. Sexual behavior also has important implications for physical health. We have previously examined research findings on unplanned pregnancy and on educational approaches that can help prevent teen pregnancy. Here we look at another aspect of sexuality: protecting oneself from sexually transmitted infections (STIs). Naturally, by not having sex, individuals can avoid both unplanned pregnancy and STIs. However, even for those whose goal is abstinence, knowledge about preventing unwanted pregnancy and STIs is important, because as the stages of change model suggests, we sometimes fall short of our goals.

PROTECTING AGAINST SEXUALLY TRANSMITTED INFECTIONS

sexually transmitted infection (STI)
An infection that is contracted primarily through sexual activity—vaginal intercourse as well as oral and anal sex.

A **sexually transmitted infection (STI)** is an infection that is contracted primarily through sexual activity—vaginal intercourse as well as oral and anal sex. STIs affect about one of every six adults (CDC, 2016). Some STIs are bacterial in origin, as in the case of gonorrhea and syphilis, and others are caused by viruses, as in the case of genital herpes and HIV. STIs are an important health concern because they can have implications for a person's future fertility, risk of cancer, and life expectancy. The United States has recently seen a rise in rates of bacterial STIs, including syphilis (CDC, 2016).

Acquired immune deficiency syndrome (AIDS) is caused by the sexually transmitted human immunodeficiency virus (HIV), which destroys the body's immune system. In 2014, more than 37,000 new HIV infections were reported in the United States. Improvements in drug therapies have greatly enhanced the chances of a person who is HIV positive living a long life.

The risk for people who have HIV is that they will go on to develop AIDS. Without treatment, such individuals are vulnerable to germs that a normal immune system can destroy. Because of increased education and improved drug therapies, deaths due to AIDS have declined in the United States (CDC, 2017). Even in this era of treatment advances, however, AIDS remains incurable. Many people who are HIV-positive do not know that they have contracted the virus.

All sexually active people are at risk of contracting HIV and other STIs. The only 100 percent safe behavior is abstinence from sex, which many individuals do not view as an option. Sensual activities such as cuddling, massage, and mutual masturbation (without the exchange of bodily fluids) present no risk of developing an STI. Sexual activities that involve penetration, including vaginal or anal intercourse as well as oral sex, are riskier behaviors that can be made less risky with the use of proper protection, including condoms. Individuals who believe they are at risk for HIV infection may also seek prophylactic (that is, preventative) medication, called PrEP.

In your own sexual experience, it may be difficult to gauge the accuracy of a partner's estimates of risk and his or her HIV status. The wisest course is always to protect yourself from infection by using a latex condom. Unfortunately, in young adult relationships, experiences of commitment and trust tend to be negatively related to consistent condom use (Agnew & others, 2017). That is, couples may believe that once they are committed to each other, condoms are no longer necessary. Such a belief may leave both partners vulnerable to STIs.

When correctly used, latex condoms help to block the transmission of many STIs. Condoms are most effective in preventing gonorrhea, syphilis, chlamydia, and AIDS. Consistent condom use also significantly reduces the risk that males will transmit to their female partners the human papilloma virus (HPV), some types of which can cause cervical cancer (Miksis, 2008). Although condoms are less effective against the spread of herpes than against other STIs, consistent condom use reduces the risk of herpes infection for both men and women (Stanaway & others, 2012).

Research has shown that safe-sex programs are especially effective if they include the eroticization of condom use—that is, making condoms part of the sensual experience of foreplay (Scott-Sheldon & Johnson, 2006). Analyses of HIV prevention programs (including over 350 intervention groups and 100 control groups) by Dolores Albarracin and her colleagues have produced important recommendations for the best ways to influence behavior (Albarracin, Durantini, & Earl, 2006; Albarracin & others, 2005, 2008; Durantini & Albarracin, 2009, 2012). The studies have found that fear tactics are relatively less effective and that programs emphasizing active skill building (for example, role playing the use of condoms), self-efficacy, and positive attitudes about condom use are successful with most groups.

acquired immune deficiency syndrome (AIDS)
A sexually transmitted infection, caused by the human immunodeficiency virus (HIV), that destroys the body's immune system.

Anyone who thinks that condom use is inconvenient might well consider which is more convenient–using a condom or contracting gonorrhea or HIV.

1. Regular physical activity and, in particular, exercise are associated with all of the following *except*
   A. weight loss.
   B. increased self-esteem.
   C. less incidence of depression.
   D. premature death in middle-age and older adults.

2. The biggest health risk facing most Americans today is
   A. heart disease.
   B. cancer.
   C. overweight and obesity.
   D. stress.

3. Typically, the *best* approach to quitting smoking is to
   A. go cold turkey.
   B. use a nicotine patch.
   C. use a combination of methods.
   D. get help from a therapist.

APPLY IT! 4. J. C. and Veronica promote student health causes on their college campus. This year, they are targeting wise sexual choices. Which of the following is the most promising strategy for their campaign?
   A. They should focus on fear of disease as a motivator for condom use.
   B. They should focus on promoting non-risky sexual activities, eroticizing condom use, and teaching students skills for effective condom use, reminding students that even if they do not intend to have sex, it is best to be safe.
   C. They should focus only on students who are already engaging in sexual behavior.
   D. They should encourage students, before having sex, simply to ask their partners how many sexual partners they have had.

6 Psychology and Your Good Life

In this discussion of health psychology, we have examined how the mental and physical aspects of your existence intertwine and influence each other. The field of health psychology illustrates how all of the various areas of psychology converge to reveal that interplay.

An experience as deceptively simple as taking in and perceiving a sunset becomes stunningly complex in the context of a human life.
©Dirima/Getty Images

As a human being, you are both a physical entity and a system of mental processes that are themselves reflected in that most complex of physical organs, the brain. At every moment, both body and mind are present and affecting each other. Caring for your brain and mind—the resources that make it possible for you to read this book, study for tests, listen to lectures, fall in love, share with friends, help others, and make a difference in the world—is worthy of being a life mission.

Many pages ago, we defined psychology as the scientific study of behavior and mental processes, broadly meaning the things we do, think, and feel. Reflect for a moment on the psychological dimensions of vision. When we studied the human visual system, we examined the processes by which those amazing sense organs, our eyes, detect color, light, dark, shape, and depth. We probed the ways that the brain takes that information and turns it into perception—how a pattern of colors, shapes, and light come to be perceived as a flower, a fall day, a sunset. Visual systems, we discovered, are generally the same from one person to the next. Thus, you can memorize the different parts of the human eye and know that your understanding is true for just about all the human eyes you will encounter in life.

However, even something as deceptively simple as perceiving a sunset through the sense of vision becomes amazingly complex when we put it in the context of a human life. Is that sunset the first you see while on your honeymoon, or right after a painful romantic breakup, or as a new parent? Placing even the most ordinary moment in the context of a human life renders it extraordinary and fascinating.

This fascination is a primary motivation for the science of psychology itself. Humans have always pondered the mysteries of behavior, thought, and emotion. Why do we do the things we do? How do we think and feel? In this book, we have explored the broad range of topics that have interested psychologists throughout the history of this young science.

Coming to the close of this introduction to psychology allows you to take stock of what psychology has come to mean to you now, as well as to consider what it might mean to you in the future. Whether or not you continue coursework in psychology, this book has highlighted opportunities for your future exploration about yourself and your world. In each of the real-life examples of human experience described in these pages—moments of heroism, weakness, joy, pain, and more—psychology has had a lesson to share with respect to the person that is you. Making the most of what you have learned about psychology means making the most of yourself and your life.

Do It!

Think back to all the topics of this book. Which did you find most interesting? Go to your school's library and locate the journals that are devoted to that subject (you can ask a librarian for help). Browse a recent issue. What specific topics are scientists studying? If a particular study described in this book sounded interesting, you can probably obtain it online. Do a Google "Scholar" search on the authors and take a look at the original article. What did the authors conclude? What did you learn?

Health Psychology and Behavioral Medicine

Health psychology emphasizes biological, psychological, and social factors in human health. Closely aligned with health psychology is behavioral medicine, which combines medical and behavioral knowledge to reduce illness and promote health. These approaches demonstrate the biopsychosocial model by examining the interaction of biological, psychological, and social variables as they relate to health and illness. Stress is an example of a biological, psychological, and social construct.

Health psychology and behavioral medicine bring the relationship of the mind and body to the forefront. These approaches examine the reciprocal mind–body relationship: how the body is influenced by psychological states and how mental life is influenced by physical health.

Making Positive Life Changes

The theory of reasoned action suggests that we can make changes by devising specific intentions for behavioral change. We are more likely to follow through on our intentions if we feel good about the change and if we believe that others around us also support the change. The theory of planned behavior incorporates these factors as well as our perceptions of control over the behavior.

The stages of change model posits that personal change occurs in a series of five steps: precontemplation, contemplation, preparation/determination, action/willpower, and maintenance. Each stage has its own challenges. Relapse is a natural part of the journey toward change.

Resources for Effective Life Change

Motivation is an important part of sustaining behavioral change. Change is more effective when people do it for intrinsic reasons (because they want to) rather than extrinsic reasons (to gain rewards). Implementation intentions are the specific ways individuals plan to institute changes.

Social relationships are strongly associated with health and survival. Social support refers to the aid provided by others to a person in need. Support can take the form of tangible assistance, information, or emotional support. Social support is strongly related to functioning and coping with stress.

Religious faith is associated with enhanced health. One reason for this connection is that religions often frown on excess and promote healthy behavior. In addition, religious participation allows individuals to benefit from a social group, and religion provides a meaning system on which to rely in times of difficulty.

Personality characteristics related to positive health behaviors include conscientiousness, personal control, self-efficacy, and optimism. Conscientious individuals are likely to engage in healthy behaviors and live longer. Personal control is associated with better coping with stress. Self-efficacy is the person's belief in his or her own ability to master a situation and produce positive outcomes. Optimism refers to a particular explanatory style as well as to the inclination to have positive expectations for the future. Studies have shown that both of these types of optimism relate to positive health outcomes.

Toward a Healthier Mind (and Body): Controlling Stress

Stress is the response of individuals when life circumstances threaten them and tax their ability to cope. Selye characterized the stress response with his concept of a general adaptation syndrome (GAS), which has three stages: alarm, resistance, and exhaustion.

Chronic stress takes a toll on the body's natural disease-fighting abilities. Stress is also related to cardiovascular disease and cancer.

To kick the stress habit means remembering that stress is a product of how we think about events in our lives. Taking control of our appraisals allows us to see potentially threatening events as challenges. Hardiness is associated with thriving during stressful times.

The Type A behavior pattern, particularly the hostility component, is associated with stressing out angrily when things are going badly. This hostility leads to poor health outcomes. There is growing interest in the Type D behavior pattern, seen in individuals who experience generalized and frequent distress, negative emotions, and social inhibition; research has associated this pattern with an elevated risk of cardiovascular problems. When a person is unable to manage stress alone, stress management programs provide options for relief.

Toward a Healthier Body (and Mind): Behaving as If Your Life Depends upon It

Exercise has many positive psychological and physical benefits. Tips for increasing one's activity level include starting small by making changes in one's routine to incorporate physical activity and keeping track of progress.

Overweight and obesity pose the greatest health risks to Americans today. They can be largely avoided by eating right, which means selecting nutritious foods and maintaining healthy eating habits for a lifetime, not just while on a diet. A combination of healthy eating and exercise is the best way to achieve weight loss.

Despite widespread knowledge that smoking causes cancer, some people still smoke. Methods of quitting include going cold turkey, using a substitute source of nicotine, and seeking therapy. Quitting for good is difficult and usually takes more than one try. Usually a combination of methods is the best strategy for quitting.

Practicing safe sex is another aspect of health behavior of interest to health psychologists. Condoms help prevent both unwanted pregnancy and the transmission of sexually transmitted infections (STIs). Interventions to promote condom use are most successful when they include making condom use sexy, promoting contraceptive skills and self-efficacy, and encouraging positive attitudes about condoms.

Psychology and Your Good Life

Psychology is all about you. This book has aimed to show the relevance of psychology to your health and wellness and to help you appreciate the many, and deep, connections between this comparatively new science and your life.

KEY TERMS

acquired immune deficiency
   syndrome (AIDS)

aerobic exercise

behavioral medicine

cognitive appraisal

coping

emotion-focused coping

exercise

general adaptation syndrome
   (GAS)

hardiness

health behaviors

health psychology

hypothalamic-pituitary-adrenal axis
   (HPA axis)

implementation intentions

problem-focused coping

psychoneuroimmunology

relapse

sexually transmitted infection
   (STI)

social support

stages of change model

stress management program

theory of planned behavior

theory of reasoned action

Type A behavior pattern

Type B behavior pattern

Type D behavior pattern

ANSWERS TO SELF-QUIZZES

Section 1:   1. D; 2. B; 3. D; 4. B

Section 2:   1. D; 2. B; 3. B; 4. A

Section 3:   1. A; 2. D; 3. A; 4. C

Section 4:   1. D; 2. C; 3. A; 4. B

Section 5:   1. D; 2. C; 3. C; 4. B

glossary

A

abnormal behavior Behavior that is deviant, maladaptive, or personally distressful over a relatively long period of time.

absolute threshold The minimum amount of stimulus energy that a person can detect.

accommodation An individual's adjustment of his or her schemas to new information.

acquired immune deficiency syndrome (AIDS) A sexually transmitted infection, caused by the human immunodeficiency virus (HIV), that destroys the body's immune system.

acquisition The initial learning of the connection between the unconditioned stimulus and the conditioned stimulus when these two stimuli are paired.

action potential The brief wave of positive electrical charge that sweeps down the axon.

activation-synthesis theory Theory that dreaming occurs when the cerebral cortex synthesizes neural signals generated from activity in the lower part of the brain and that dreams result from the brain's attempts to find logic in random brain activity that occurs during sleep.

addiction A physical or a psychological dependence, or both, on a drug.

adrenal glands Glands at the top of each kidney that are responsible for regulating moods, energy level, and the ability to cope with stress.

aerobic exercise Sustained activity—jogging, swimming, or cycling, for example—that stimulates heart and lung functioning.

affectionate love or companionate love Love that occurs when an individual has a deep, caring affection for another person and desires to have that person near.

afferent nerves Also called sensory nerves; nerves that carry information about the external environment to the brain and spinal cord via sensory receptors.

aggression Social behavior whose objective is to harm someone, either physically or verbally.

agonist A drug that mimics or increases a neurotransmitter's effects.

alcoholism Disorder that involves long-term, repeated, uncontrolled, compulsive, and excessive use of alcoholic beverages and that impairs the drinker's health and social relationships.

algorithms Strategies—including formulas, instructions, and the testing of all possible solutions—that guarantee a solution to a problem.

all-or-nothing principle The principle that once the electrical impulse reaches a certain level of intensity (its threshold), it fires and moves all the way down the axon without losing any intensity.

altruism Giving to another person with the ultimate goal of benefiting that person, even if it incurs a cost to oneself.

amnesia The loss of memory.

amygdala An almond-shaped structure within the base of the temporal lobe that is involved in the discrimination of objects that are necessary for the organism's survival, such as appropriate food, mates, and social rivals.

androgens The class of sex hormones that predominate in males, produced by the testes in males and by the adrenal glands in both males and females.

anorexia nervosa Eating disorder that involves the relentless pursuit of thinness through starvation.

antagonist A drug that blocks a neurotransmitter's effects.

anterograde amnesia A memory disorder that affects the retention of new information and events.

antianxiety drugs Commonly known as tranquilizers, drugs that reduce anxiety by making individuals calmer and less excitable.

antidepressant drugs Drugs that regulate mood.

antipsychotic drugs Powerful drugs that diminish agitated behavior, reduce tension, decrease hallucinations, improve social behavior, and produce better sleep patterns in individuals with a severe psychological disorder, especially schizophrenia.

antisocial personality disorder (ASPD) Psychological disorder characterized by guiltlessness, law-breaking, exploitation of others, irresponsibility, and deceit.

anxiety disorders Disabling (uncontrollable and disruptive) psychological disorders that feature motor tension, hyperactivity, and apprehensive expectations and thoughts.

apparent movement The perception that a stationary object is moving.

applied behavior analysis or behavior modification The use of operant conditioning principles to change human behavior.

archetypes Jung's term for emotionally laden ideas and images in the collective unconscious that have rich and symbolic meaning for all people.

artificial intelligence (AI) A scientific field that focuses on creating machines capable of performing activities that require intelligence when they are done by people.

assimilation An individual's incorporation of new information into existing knowledge.

association cortex Sometimes called association areas, the region of the cerebral cortex that is the site of the highest intellectual functions, such as thinking and problem solving.

associative learning Learning that occurs when an organism makes a connection, or an association, between two events.

Atkinson-Shiffrin theory Theory stating that memory storage involves three separate systems: sensory memory, short-term memory, and long-term memory.

attention-deficit/hyperactivity disorder (ADHD) One of the most common psychological disorders of childhood, in which individuals show one or more of the following: inattention, hyperactivity, and impulsivity.

attitudes An individual's opinions and beliefs about people, objects, and ideas—how the person feels about the world.

attribution theory The view that people are motivated to discover the underlying causes of behavior as part of their effort to make sense of the behavior.

auditory nerve The nerve structure that receives information about sound from the hair cells of the inner ear and carries these neural impulses to the brain's auditory areas.

authoritarian parenting A restrictive, punitive parenting style in which the parent exhorts the child to follow the parent's directions and to value hard work and effort.

authoritative parenting A parenting style that encourages the child to be independent but that still places limits and controls on behavior.

autobiographical memory A special form of episodic memory, consisting of a person's recollections of his or her life experiences.

automatic processes States of consciousness that require little attention and do not interfere with other ongoing activities.

autonomic nervous system The body system that takes messages to and from the body's internal organs, monitoring such processes as breathing, heart rate, and digestion.

availability heuristic A prediction about the probability of an event based on the ease of recalling or imagining similar events.

aversive conditioning A form of treatment that consists of repeated pairings of a stimulus with a very unpleasant stimulus.

avoidance learning An organism's learning that it can altogether avoid a negative stimulus by making a particular response.

axon The part of the neuron that carries information away from the cell body toward other cells.

B

barbiturates Depressant drugs, such as Nembutal and Seconal, that decrease central nervous system activity.

basal ganglia Large neuron clusters located above the thalamus and under the cerebral cortex that work with the cerebellum and the cerebral cortex to control and coordinate voluntary movements.

base rate neglect The tendency to ignore information about general principles in favor of very specific but vivid information.

behavior Everything we do that can be directly observed.

behavior therapies Treatments, based on behavioral and social cognitive theories, that use principles of learning to reduce or eliminate maladaptive behavior.

behavioral approach An approach to psychology emphasizing the scientific study of observable behavioral responses and their environmental determinants.

behavioral genetics The study of the inherited underpinnings of behavioral characteristics.

behavioral medicine An interdisciplinary field that focuses on developing and integrating behavioral and biomedical knowledge to promote health and reduce illness; overlaps with and is sometimes indistinguishable from health psychology.

behaviorism A theory of learning that focuses solely on observable behaviors, discounting the importance of such mental activity as thinking, wishing, and hoping.

big five factors of personality The five broad traits that are thought to describe the main dimensions of personality: openness to experience, conscientiousness, extraversion, agreeableness, and neuroticism (emotional instability).

binding In the sense of vision, the bringing together and integration of what is processed by different neural pathways or cells.

binge-eating disorder (BED) Eating disorder characterized by recurrent episodes of consuming large amounts of food during which the person feels a lack of control over eating.

binocular cues Depth cues that depend on the combination of the images in the left and right eyes and on the way the two eyes work together.

biological approach An approach to psychology focusing on the body, especially the brain and nervous system.

biological rhythms Periodic physiological fluctuations in the body, such as the rise and fall of hormones and accelerated/decelerated cycles of brain activity, that can influence behavior.

biological therapies Also called *biomedical therapies*, treatments that reduce or eliminate the symptoms of psychological disorders by altering aspects of body functioning.

bipolar disorder Mood disorder characterized by extreme mood swings that include one or more episodes of mania, an overexcited, unrealistically optimistic state.

borderline personality disorder (BPD) Psychological disorder characterized by a pervasive pattern of instability in interpersonal relationships, self-image, and emotions, and of marked impulsivity beginning by early adulthood and present in a variety of contexts.

bottom-up processing The operation in sensation and perception in which sensory receptors register information about the external environment and send it up to the brain for interpretation.

brain stem The stemlike brain area that includes much of the hindbrain (excluding the cerebellum) and the midbrain; connects with the spinal cord at its lower end and then extends upward to encase the reticular formation in the midbrain.

broaden-and-build model Fredrickson's model of positive emotion, stating that the function of positive emotions lies in their effects on an individual's attention and ability to build resources.

bulimia nervosa Eating disorder in which an individual (typically female) consistently follows a binge-and-purge eating pattern.

bystander effect The tendency of an individual who observes an emergency to be less likely to help when other people are present than when the observer is alone.

C

Cannon-Bard theory The proposition that emotion and physiological reactions occur simultaneously.

case study or case history An in-depth look at a single individual.

catatonia State of immobility and unresponsiveness, lasting for long periods of time.

cell body The part of the neuron that contains the nucleus, which directs the manufacture of substances that the neuron needs for growth and maintenance.

central nervous system (CNS) The brain and spinal cord.

cerebral cortex Part of the forebrain, the outer layer of the brain, responsible for the most complex mental functions, such as thinking and planning.

chromosomes In the human cell, threadlike structures that come in 23 pairs, one member of each pair originating from each parent, and that contain DNA.

circadian rhythms Daily behavioral or physiological cycles that involve the sleep/wake cycle, body temperature, blood pressure, and blood sugar level.

classical conditioning Learning process in which a neutral stimulus becomes associated with an innately meaningful stimulus and acquires the capacity to elicit a similar response.

client-centered therapy Also called *Rogerian therapy or nondirective therapy,* a form of humanistic therapy, developed by Rogers, in which the therapist provides a warm, supportive atmosphere to improve the client's self-concept and to encourage the client to gain insight into problems.

clinical psychology An area of psychology that integrates science and theory to prevent and treat psychological disorders.

cognition The way in which information is processed and manipulated in remembering, thinking, and knowing.

cognitive affective processing systems (CAPS) Mischel's theoretical model for describing that individuals' thoughts and emotions about themselves and the world affect their behavior and become linked in ways that matter to that behavior.

cognitive appraisal Individuals' interpretation of the events in their life as harmful, threatening, or challenging and their determination of whether they have the resources to cope effectively with the events.

cognitive approach An approach to psychology emphasizing the mental processes involved in knowing: how we direct our attention, perceive, remember, think, and solve problems.

cognitive dissonance An individual's psychological discomfort (dissonance) caused by two inconsistent thoughts.

cognitive theory of dreaming Theory proposing that one can understand dreaming by applying the same cognitive concepts used in studying the waking mind.

cognitive therapies Treatments emphasizing that cognitions (thoughts) are the main source of psychological problems; therapies that attempt to change the individual's feelings and behaviors by changing cognitions.

cognitive-behavior therapy A therapy that combines cognitive therapy and behavior therapy with the goal of developing the client's self-efficacy.

collective unconscious Jung's term for the impersonal, deepest layer of the unconscious mind, shared by all human beings because of their common ancestral past.

comorbidity The simultaneous presence of two or more disorders in one person. The conditions are referred to as *"comorbid."*

concept A mental category that is used to group objects, events, and characteristics.

concrete operational stage Piaget's third stage of cognitive development, lasting from about 7 to 11 years of age, during which the individual uses operations and replaces intuitive reasoning with logical reasoning in concrete situations.

conditioned response (CR) The learned response to the conditioned stimulus that occurs after a conditioned stimulus–unconditioned stimulus pairing.

conditioned stimulus (CS) A previously neutral stimulus that eventually elicits a conditioned response after being paired with the unconditioned stimulus.

conditions of worth The standards that the individual must live up to in order to receive positive regard from others.

cones The receptor cells in the retina that allow for color perception.

confederate A person who is given a role to play in a study so that the social context can be manipulated.

confirmation bias The tendency to search for and use information that supports one's ideas rather than refutes them.

conformity A change in a person's behavior to coincide more closely with a group standard.

connectionism Also called parallel distributed processing (PDP), the theory that memory is stored throughout the brain in connections among neurons, several of which may work together to process a single memory.

consciousness An individual's awareness of external events and internal sensations under a condition of arousal, including awareness of the self and thoughts about one's experiences.

control group The participants in an experiment who are as much like the experimental group as possible and who are treated in every way like the experimental group except for a manipulated factor, the independent variable.

controlled processes The most alert states of human consciousness, during which individuals actively focus their efforts toward a goal.

convergence A binocular cue to depth and distance in which the muscle movements in an individual's two eyes provide information about how deep and/or far away something is.

convergent thinking Thinking that produces the single best solution to a problem.

coping Managing taxing circumstances, expending effort to solve life's problems, and seeking to master or reduce stress.

core knowledge approach A perspective on infant cognitive development that holds that babies are born with domain-specific knowledge systems.

corpus callosum The large bundle of axons that connects the brain's two hemispheres, responsible for relaying information between the two sides.

correlational research Research that examines the relationships between variables, whose purpose is to examine whether and how two variables change together.

counterconditioning A classical conditioning procedure for changing the relationship between a conditioned stimulus and its conditioned response.

couples therapy Group therapy involving married or unmarried couples whose major problem lies within their relationship.

creativity The ability to think about something in novel and unusual ways and to devise unconventional solutions to problems.

critical thinking The process of thinking deeply and actively, asking questions, and evaluating the evidence.

cross-cultural competence A therapist's assessment of his or her abilities to manage cultural issues in therapy and the client's perception of those abilities.

cross-sectional design A research design in which a group of people are assessed on a psychological variable at one point in time.

culture-fair tests Intelligence tests that are intended to be culturally unbiased.

D

decay theory Theory stating that when an individual learns something new, a neurochemical memory trace forms, but over time this trace disintegrates; suggests that the passage of time always increases forgetting.

decision making The mental activity of evaluating alternatives and choosing among them.

deductive reasoning Reasoning from a general case that is known to be true to a specific instance.

defense mechanisms Tactics the ego uses to reduce anxiety by unconsciously distorting reality.

deindividuation The reduction in personal identity and erosion of the sense of personal responsibility when one is part of a group.

delay of gratification Putting off the pleasure of an immediate reward in order to gain a larger, later reward.

delusions False, unusual, and sometimes magical beliefs that are not part of an individual's culture.

demand characteristics Any aspects of a study that communicate to the participants how the experimenter wants them to behave.

dendrites Treelike fibers projecting from a neuron, which receive information and orient it toward the neuron's cell body.

deoxyribonucleic acid (DNA) A complex molecule in the cell's chromosomes that carries genetic information.

dependent variable The outcome; the factor that can change in an experiment in response to changes in the independent variable.

depressants Psychoactive drugs that slow down mental and physical activity.

depressive disorders Mood disorders in which the individual suffers from depression—an unrelenting lack of pleasure in life.

depth perception The ability to perceive objects three-dimensionally.

development The pattern of continuity and change in human capabilities that occurs throughout life, involving both growth and decline.

difference threshold The degree of difference that must exist between two stimuli before the difference is detected.

discrimination An unjustified negative or harmful action toward a member of a group simply because the person belongs to that group.

discrimination (operant conditioning) Responding appropriately to stimuli that signal that a behavior will or will not be reinforced.

display rules Sociocultural standards that determine when, where, and how emotions should be expressed.

dissociative amnesia Dissociative disorder characterized by extreme memory loss that is caused by extensive psychological stress.

dissociative disorders Psychological disorders that involve a sudden loss of memory or change in identity due to the dissociation (separation) of the individual's conscious awareness from previous memories and thoughts.

dissociative identity disorder (DID) Formerly called multiple personality disorder, a dissociative disorder in which the individual has two or more distinct personalities or selves, each with its own memories, behaviors, and relationships.

divergent thinking Thinking that produces many solutions to the same problem.

divided attention Concentrating on more than one activity at the same time.

divided consciousness view of hypnosis Hilgard's view that hypnosis involves a splitting of consciousness into two separate components, one following the hypnotist's commands and the other acting as a "hidden observer."

dominant-recessive genes principle The principle that if one gene of a pair is dominant and one is recessive, the dominant gene overrides the recessive gene. A

recessive gene exerts its influence only if both genes of a pair are recessive.

double-blind experiment An experimental design in which neither the experimenter nor the participants are aware of which participants are in the experimental group and which are in the control group until the results are calculated.

dream analysis A psychoanalytic technique for interpreting a person's dreams.

drive An aroused state that occurs because of a physiological need.

DSM-5 The *Diagnostic and Statistical Manual of Mental Disorders (DSM-5)*, 5th ed.; the major classification of psychological disorders in the United States.

dyslexia A learning disability characterized by difficulty with learning to read fluently and with accurate comprehension, despite normal intelligence.

E

efferent nerves Also called motor nerves; nerves that carry information out of the brain and spinal cord to other areas of the body.

ego The Freudian structure of personality that deals with the demands of reality.

egoism Giving to another person to ensure reciprocity; to gain self-esteem; to present oneself as powerful, competent, or caring; or to avoid social and self-censure for failing to live up to society's expectations.

elaboration The formation of a number of different connections around a stimulus at a given level of memory encoding.

elaboration likelihood model Theory identifying two ways to persuade: a central route and a peripheral route.

electroconvulsive therapy (ECT) Also called *shock therapy*, a treatment, sometimes used for depression, that sets off a seizure in the brain.

emerging adulthood The transitional period from adolescence to adulthood, spanning approximately 18 to 25 years of age.

emotion Feeling, or affect, that can involve physiological arousal (such as a fast heartbeat), conscious experience (thinking about being in love with someone), and behavioral expression (a smile or grimace).

emotion-focused coping The coping strategy that involves responding to the stress that one is feeling—trying to manage one's emotional reaction—rather than focusing on the root problem itself.

empathy A feeling of oneness with the emotional state of another person.

empirical method Gaining knowledge through the observation of events, the collection of data, and logical reasoning.

empirically keyed test A type of self-report test that presents many questionnaire items to two groups that are known to be different in some central way.

encoding The first step in memory; the process by which information gets into memory storage.

endocrine system The body system consisting of a set of glands that regulate the activities of certain organs by releasing their chemical products into the bloodstream.

episodic memory The retention of information about the where, when, and what of life's happenings—that is, how individuals remember life's episodes.

estrogens The class of sex hormones that predominate in females, produced mainly by the ovaries.

ethnocentrism The tendency to favor one's own ethnic group over other groups.

evidence-based practice Integration of the best available research with clinical expertise in the context of client characteristics, culture, and preferences.

evolutionary approach An approach to psychology centered on evolutionary ideas such as adaptation, reproduction, and natural selection as the basis for explaining specific human behaviors.

executive attention The ability to plan action, allocate attention to goals, detect errors and compensate for them, monitor progress on tasks, and deal with novel or difficult circumstances.

executive function Higher-order, complex cognitive processes, including thinking, planning, and problem solving.

exercise Structured activities whose goal is to improve health.

experiment A carefully regulated procedure in which the researcher manipulates one or more variables that are believed to influence some other variable.

experimental group The participants in an experiment who receive the drug or other treatment under study—that is, those who are exposed to the change that the independent variable represents.

experimenter bias The influence of the experimenter's expectations on the outcome of research.

explicit memory or declarative memory The conscious recollection of information, such as specific facts or events and, at least in humans, information that can be verbally communicated.

external validity The degree to which an experimental design actually reflects the real-world issues it is supposed to address.

extinction (classical conditioning) The weakening of the conditioned response when the unconditioned stimulus is absent.

extinction (operant conditioning) Decreases in the frequency of a behavior when the behavior is no longer reinforced.

extrinsic motivation Motivation that involves external incentives such as rewards and punishments.

F

face validity The extent to which a test item appears to fit the particular trait it is measuring.

facial feedback hypothesis The idea that facial expressions can influence emotions as well as reflect them.

false consensus effect Observers' overestimation of the degree to which everybody else thinks or acts the way they do.

family therapy Group therapy with family members.

feature detectors Neurons in the brain's visual system that respond to particular features of a stimulus.

figure-ground relationship The principle by which we organize the perceptual field into stimuli that stand out (figure) and those that are left over (ground).

fixation Using a prior strategy and failing to look at a problem from a fresh new perspective.

flashbulb memory The memory of emotionally significant events that people often recall with more accuracy and vivid imagery than everyday events.

flat affect The display of little or no emotion—a common negative symptom of schizophrenia.

forebrain The brain's largest division and its most forward part.

formal operational stage Piaget's fourth stage of cognitive development, which begins at 11 to 15 years of age and continues through the adult years; it features thinking about things that are not concrete, making predictions, and using logic to come up with hypotheses about the future.

free association A psychoanalytic technique that involves encouraging individuals to say aloud whatever comes to mind, no matter how trivial or embarrassing.

frequency theory Theory on how the inner ear registers the frequency of sound, stating that the perception of a sound's frequency depends on how often the auditory nerve fires.

frontal lobes The portion of the cerebral cortex behind the forehead, involved in personality, intelligence, and the control of voluntary muscles.

functional fixedness Failing to solve a problem as a result of fixation on a thing's usual functions.

functionalism James's approach to mental processes, emphasizing the functions and purposes of the mind and behavior in the individual's adaptation to the environment.

fundamental attribution error Observers' overestimation of the importance of internal traits and underestimation of the importance of external situations when they seek explanations of another person's behavior.

G

gender The social and psychological aspects of being female or male.

gender identity A person's inner concept of themselves in relation to the ideas of being male, female, both or neither.

gender roles Roles that reflect the individual's expectations for how females and males should think, act, and feel.

gender similarities hypothesis Hyde's proposition that men and women (and boys and girls) are much more similar than they are different.

gene × environment (g × e) interaction The interaction of a specific measured variation in DNA and a specific measured aspect of the environment.

general adaptation syndrome (GAS) Selye's term for the common effects of stressful demands on the body, consisting of three stages: alarm, resistance, and exhaustion.

generalization (classical conditioning) The tendency of a new stimulus that is similar to the original conditioned stimulus to elicit a response that is similar to the conditioned response.

generalization (operant conditioning) Performing a reinforced behavior in a different situation.

generalized anxiety disorder Psychological disorder marked by persistent anxiety for at least six months, and in which the individual is unable to specify the reasons for the anxiety.

genes The units of hereditary information, consisting of short segments of chromosomes composed of DNA.

genotype An individual's genetic heritage; his or her actual genetic material.

gestalt psychology A school of thought interested in how people naturally organize their perceptions according to certain patterns.

gifted Possessing high intelligence (an IQ of 130 or higher) and/or superior talent in a particular area.

glands Organs or tissues in the body that create chemicals that control many bodily functions.

glial cells The second of two types of cells in the nervous system; glial cells (also called glia) provide support, nutritional benefits, and other functions and keep neurons running smoothly.

group polarization effect The solidification and further strengthening of an individual's position as a consequence of a group discussion or interaction.

group therapy A sociocultural approach to the treatment of psychological disorders that brings together individuals who share a particular psychological disorder in sessions that are typically led by a mental health professional.

groupthink The impaired group decision making that occurs when making the right decision is less important than maintaining group harmony.

H

habituation Decreased responsiveness to a stimulus after repeated presentations.

hallucinations Sensory experiences that occur in the absence of real stimuli.

hallucinogens Psychoactive drugs that modify a person's perceptual experiences and produce visual images that are not real.

hardiness A personality trait characterized by a sense of commitment rather than alienation and of control rather than powerlessness; a perception of problems as challenges rather than threats.

health behaviors Practices that have an impact on physical well-being.

health psychology A subfield of psychology that emphasizes psychology's role in establishing and maintaining health and preventing and treating illness.

heritability The proportion of observable differences in a group that can be explained by differences in the genes of the group's members.

heuristics Shortcut strategies or guidelines that suggest a solution to a problem but do not guarantee an answer.

hierarchy of needs Maslow's theory that human needs must be satisfied in the following sequence: physiological needs, safety, love and belongingness, esteem, and self-actualization.

hindbrain Located at the skull's rear, the lowest portion of the brain, consisting of the medulla, cerebellum, and pons.

hindsight bias The tendency to report falsely, after the fact, that one has accurately predicted an outcome.

hippocampus The structure in the limbic system that has a special role in the storage of memories.

homeostasis The body's tendency to maintain an equilibrium, or steady state.

hormones Chemical messengers that are produced by the endocrine glands and carried by the bloodstream to all parts of the body.

human sexual response pattern According to Masters and Johnson, the characteristic sequence of physiological changes that humans experience during sexual activity, consisting of four phases: excitement, plateau, orgasm, and resolution.

humanistic approach An approach to psychology emphasizing a person's positive qualities, the capacity for positive growth, and the freedom to choose any destiny.

humanistic perspectives Theoretical views stressing a person's capacity for personal growth and positive human qualities.

humanistic therapies Treatments that uniquely emphasize people's self-healing capacities and that encourage clients to understand themselves and to grow personally.

hypnosis An altered state of consciousness or a psychological state of altered attention and expectation in which the individual is unusually receptive to suggestions.

hypothalamic-pituitary-adrenal axis (HPA axis) The complex set of interactions among the hypothalamus, the pituitary gland, and the adrenal glands that regulate various body processes and control reactions to stressful events.

hypothalamus A small forebrain structure, located just below the thalamus, that monitors three pleasurable activities—eating, drinking, and sex—as well as emotion, stress, and reward.

hypothesis A testable prediction that derives logically from a theory.

I

id The part of the person that Freud called the "it," consisting of unconscious drives; the individual's reservoir of sexual energy.

implementation intentions Specific strategies for dealing with the challenges of making a life change.

implicit memory or nondeclarative memory Memory in which behavior is affected by prior experience without a conscious recollection of that experience.

independent variable A manipulated experimental factor; the variable that the experimenter changes to see what its effects are.

individual psychology Adler's view that people are motivated by purposes and goals and that perfection, not pleasure, is thus the key motivator in human life.

inductive reasoning Reasoning from specific observations to make generalizations.

infant attachment The close emotional bond between an infant and its caregiver.

infinite generativity The ability of language to produce an endless number of meaningful sentences.

informational social influence The influence other people have on us because we want to be right.

inner ear The part of the ear that includes the oval window, cochlea, and basilar membrane and whose function is to convert sound waves into neural impulses and send them to the brain.

insight learning A form of problem solving in which the organism develops a sudden insight into or understanding of a problem's solution.

instinct An innate (unlearned) biological pattern of behavior that is assumed to be universal throughout a species.

instinctive drift The tendency of animals to revert to instinctive behavior that interferes with learning.

integrative therapy Using a combination of techniques from different therapies based on the therapist's judgment of which particular methods will provide the greatest benefit for the client.

intellectual disability A condition of limited mental ability in which an individual has a low IQ, usually below 70 on a traditional intelligence test, and has difficulty adapting to everyday life.

intelligence All-purpose ability to do well on cognitive tasks, to solve problems, and to learn from experience.

intelligence quotient (IQ) An individual's mental age divided by chronological age multiplied by 100.

interference theory The theory that people forget not because memories are lost from storage but because other information gets in the way of what they want to remember.

internal validity The degree to which changes in the dependent variable are due to the manipulation of the independent variable.

interpretation A psychoanalyst's search for symbolic, hidden meanings in what the client says and does during therapy.

intrinsic motivation Motivation based on internal factors such as organismic needs (competence, relatedness, and autonomy), as well as curiosity, challenge, and fun.

investment model A model of long-term relationships that examines the ways that commitment, investment, and the availability of attractive alternative partners predict satisfaction and stability in relationships.

J

James-Lange theory The theory that emotion results from physiological states triggered by stimuli in the environment.

K

kinesthetic senses Senses that provide information about movement, posture, and orientation.

L

language A form of communication—whether spoken, written, or signed—that is based on a system of symbols.

latent content According to Freud, a dream's hidden content; its unconscious and true meaning.

latent learning or implicit learning Unreinforced learning that is not immediately reflected in behavior.

law of effect Thorndike's law stating that behaviors followed by positive outcomes are strengthened and that behaviors followed by negative outcomes are weakened.

learned helplessness Through experience with unavoidable aversive stimuli, an organism learns that it has no control over negative outcomes.

learning A systematic, relatively permanent change in behavior that occurs through experience.

levels of processing A continuum of memory processing from shallow to intermediate to deep, with deeper processing producing better memory.

limbic system A set of subcortical brain structures central to emotion, memory, and reward processing.

lithium The lightest of the solid elements in the periodic table of elements, widely used to treat bipolar disorder.

long-term memory A relatively permanent type of memory that stores huge amounts of information for a long time.

longitudinal design A special kind of systematic observation, used by correlational researchers, that involves obtaining measures of the variables of interest in multiple waves over time.

loss aversion The tendency to strongly prefer to avoid losses compared to attempting to acquire gains.

M

major depressive disorder (MDD) Psychological disorder involving a major depressive episode and depressed characteristics, such as lethargy and hopelessness, for at least two weeks.

manifest content According to Freud, the surface content of a dream, containing dream symbols that disguise the dream's true meaning.

medical model The view that psychological disorders are medical diseases with a biological origin.

meditation The attainment of a peaceful state of mind in which thoughts are not occupied by worry; the meditator is mindfully present to his or her thoughts and feelings but is not consumed by them.

memory The retention of information or experience over time as the result of three key processes: encoding, storage, and retrieval.

mental age (MA) An individual's level of mental development relative to that of others.

mental processes The thoughts, feelings, and motives that people experience privately but that cannot be observed directly.

mere exposure effect The phenomenon that the more individuals encounter someone or something, the more probable it is that they will start liking the person or thing even if they do not realize they have seen it before.

midbrain Located between the hindbrain and forebrain, an area in which many nerve-fiber systems ascend and descend to connect the higher and lower portions of the brain; in particular, the midbrain relays information between the brain and the eyes and ears.

middle ear The part of the ear that channels and amplifies sound through the eardrum, hammer, anvil, and stirrup to the inner ear.

mindfulness The state of being alert and mentally present for one's everyday activities.

Minnesota Multiphasic Personality Inventory (MMPI) The most widely used and researched empirically keyed self-report personality test.

monocular cues Powerful depth cues available from the image in one eye, either the right or the left.

morphology A language's rules for word formation.

motivated forgetting Forgetting that occurs when something is so painful or anxiety-laden that remembering it is intolerable.

motivation The force that moves people to behave, think, and feel the way they do.

motor cortex A region in the cerebral cortex, located just behind the frontal lobes, that processes information about voluntary movement.

myelin sheath A layer of fat cells that encases and insulates most axons.

N

natural selection Darwin's principle of an evolutionary process in which organisms that are best adapted to their environment will survive and produce offspring.

naturalistic observation The observation of behavior in a real-world setting.

nature An individual's biological inheritance, especially his or her genes.

need A deprivation that energizes the drive to eliminate or reduce the deprivation.

negative affect Negative emotions such as anger, guilt, and sadness.

negative punishment The removal of a stimulus following a given behavior in order to decrease the frequency of that behavior.

negative reinforcement The removal of a stimulus following a given behavior in order to increase the frequency of that behavior.

neglectful parenting A parenting style characterized by a lack of parental involvement in the child's life.

neocortex The outermost part of the cerebral cortex, making up 80 percent of the human brain's cortex.

nervous system The body's electrochemical communication circuitry.

neural networks Networks of nerve cells that integrate sensory input and motor output.

neurons One of two types of cells in the nervous system; neurons are the nerve cells that handle the information-processing function.

neuroscience The scientific study of the structure, function, development, genetics, and biochemistry of the nervous system, emphasizing that the brain and nervous system are central to understanding behavior, thought, and emotion.

neurotransmitters Chemical substances that are stored in very tiny sacs within the neuron's terminal buttons and involved in transmitting information across a synaptic gap to the next neuron.

noise Irrelevant and competing stimuli—not only sounds but also any distracting stimuli for the senses.

normal distribution A symmetrical, bell-shaped curve, with a majority of test scores (or other data) falling in the middle of the possible range and few scores (or other data points) appearing toward the extremes.

normative social influence The influence other people have on us because we want them to like us.

nurture An individual's environmental and social experiences.

O

obedience Behavior that complies with the explicit demands of the individual in authority.

object permanence Piaget's term for the crucial accomplishment of understanding that objects and events continue to exist even when they cannot directly be seen, heard, or touched.

observational learning Learning that occurs through observing and imitating another's behavior.

obsessive-compulsive disorder (OCD) Disorder in which the individual has anxiety-provoking thoughts that will not go away and/or urges to perform repetitive, ritualistic behaviors to prevent or produce some future situation.

occipital lobes Structures located at the back of the head that respond to visual stimuli.

Oedipus complex According to Freud, a boy's intense desire to replace his father and enjoy the affections of his mother.

olfactory epithelium The lining of the roof of the nasal cavity, containing a sheet of receptor cells for smell.

open-mindedness The state of being receptive to other ways of looking at things.

operant conditioning or instrumental conditioning A form of associative learning in which the consequences of a behavior change the probability of the behavior's occurrence.

operational definition A definition that provides an objective description of how a variable is going to be measured and observed in a particular study.

opioids A class of drugs that act on the brain's endorphin receptors. These include opium and its natural derivatives (sometimes called opiates) as well as chemicals that do not occur naturally but that have been created to mimic the activity of opium. These drugs (also called narcotics) depress activity in the central nervous system and eliminate pain.

opponent-process theory Theory stating that cells in the visual system respond to complementary pairs of red-green and blue-yellow colors; a given cell might be excited by red and inhibited by green, whereas another cell might be excited by yellow and inhibited by blue.

optic nerve The structure at the back of the eye, made up of axons of the ganglion cells, that carries visual information to the brain for further processing.

outer ear The outermost part of the ear, consisting of the pinna and the external auditory canal.

ovaries Sex-related endocrine glands that produce hormones involved in women's sexual development and reproduction.

overt aggression Physical or verbal behavior that directly harms another person.

P

pain The sensation that warns an individual of damage to the body.

pancreas A dual-purpose gland under the stomach that performs both digestive and endocrine functions.

panic disorder Anxiety disorder in which the individual experiences recurrent, sudden onsets of intense apprehension or terror, often without warning and with no specific cause.

papillae Rounded bumps above the tongue's surface that contain the taste buds, the receptors for taste.

parallel processing The simultaneous distribution of information across different neural pathways.

parasympathetic nervous system The part of the autonomic nervous system that calms the body.

parietal lobes Structures at the top and toward the rear of the head that are involved in registering spatial location, attention, and motor control.

perception The process of organizing and interpreting sensory information so that it makes sense.

perceptual constancy The recognition that objects are constant and unchanging even though sensory input about them is changing.

perceptual set A predisposition or readiness to perceive something in a particular way.

peripheral nervous system (PNS) The network of nerves that connects the brain and spinal cord to other parts of the body.

permissive parenting A parenting style characterized by the placement of few limits on the child's behavior.

person perception The processes by which an individual uses social stimuli to form impressions of others.

personality A pattern of enduring, distinctive thoughts, emotions, and behaviors that characterize the way an individual adapts to the world.

personality disorders Chronic, maladaptive cognitive-behavioral patterns that are thoroughly integrated into an individual's personality.

phenotype An individual's observable characteristics.

phonology A language's sound system.

physical dependence The physiological need for a drug that causes unpleasant withdrawal symptoms such as physical pain and a craving for the drug when it is discontinued.

pituitary gland A pea-sized gland just beneath the hypothalamus that controls growth and regulates other glands.

place theory Theory on how the inner ear registers the frequency of sound, stating that each frequency produces vibrations at a particular spot on the basilar membrane.

placebo In a drug study, a harmless substance that has no physiological effect, given to participants in a control group so that they are treated identically to the experimental group except for the active agent.

placebo effect The situation where participants' expectations, rather than the experimental treatment, produce an experimental outcome.

plasticity The brain's special capacity for change.

polygraph A machine, commonly called a lie detector, that monitors changes in the body, and is used to try to determine whether someone is lying.

population The entire group about which the researcher wants to draw conclusions.

positive affect Pleasant emotions such as joy, happiness, and interest.

positive illusions Favorable views of the self that are not necessarily rooted in reality.

positive punishment The presentation of a stimulus following a given behavior in order to decrease the frequency of that behavior.

positive reinforcement The presentation of a stimulus following a given behavior in order to increase the frequency of that behavior.

post-traumatic stress disorder (PTSD) Anxiety disorder that develops through exposure to a traumatic event, a severely oppressive situation, cruel abuse, or a natural or unnatural disaster.

pragmatics The useful character of language and the ability of language to communicate even more meaning than is verbalized.

preferential looking A research technique that involves giving an infant a choice of what object to look at.

prefrontal cortex An important part of the frontal lobes that is involved in higher cognitive functions such as planning, reasoning, and self-control.

prejudice An unjustified negative attitude toward an individual based on the individual's membership in a group.

preoperational stage Piaget's second stage of cognitive development, lasting from about 2 to 7 years of age, during which thought is more symbolic than sensorimotor thought.

preparedness The species-specific biological predisposition to learn in certain ways but not others.

primary reinforcer A reinforcer that is innately satisfying; one that does not take any learning on the organism's part to make it pleasurable.

priming The activation of information that people already have in storage to help them remember new information better and faster.

proactive interference Situation in which material that was learned earlier disrupts the recall of material that was learned later.

problem solving The mental process of finding an appropriate way to attain a goal when the goal is not readily available.

problem-focused coping The coping strategy of squarely facing one's troubles and trying to solve them.

procedural memory Memory for skills.

projective test A personality assessment test that presents individuals with an ambiguous stimulus and asks them to describe it or tell a story about it—to project their own meaning onto the stimulus.

prosocial behavior Behavior that is intended to benefit other people.

prospective memory Remembering information about doing something in the future; includes memory for intentions.

prototype model A model emphasizing that when people evaluate whether a given item reflects a certain concept, they compare the item with the most typical item(s) in that category and look for a "family resemblance" with that item's properties.

psychoactive drugs Drugs that act on the nervous system to alter consciousness, modify perception, and change moods.

psychoanalysis Freud's therapeutic technique for analyzing an individual's unconscious thoughts.

psychodynamic approach An approach to psychology emphasizing unconscious thought, the conflict between biological drives (such as the drive for sex) and society's demands, and early childhood family experiences.

psychodynamic perspectives Theoretical views emphasizing that personality is primarily unconscious (beyond awareness).

psychodynamic therapies Treatments that stress the importance of the unconscious mind, extensive interpretation by the therapist, and the role of early childhood experiences in the development of an individual's problems.

psychological dependence The strong desire to repeat the use of a drug for emotional reasons, such as a feeling of well-being and reduction of stress.

psychology The scientific study of behavior and mental processes.

psychoneuroimmunology A new field of scientific inquiry that explores connections among psychological factors (such as attitudes and emotions), the nervous system, and the immune system.

psychosis A state in which a person's perceptions and thoughts are fundamentally removed from reality.

psychosurgery A biological therapy, with irreversible effects, that involves removal or destruction of brain tissue to improve the individual's adjustment.

psychotherapy A nonmedical process that helps individuals with psychological disorders recognize and overcome their problems.

puberty A period of rapid skeletal and sexual maturation that occurs mainly in early adolescence.

punishment A consequence that decreases the likelihood that a behavior will occur.

R

random assignment Researchers' assignment of participants to groups by chance, to reduce the likelihood that an experiment's results will be due to preexisting differences between groups.

random sample A sample that gives every member of the population an equal chance of being selected.

reasoning The mental activity of transforming information to reach conclusions.

referential thinking Ascribing personal meaning to completely random events.

reflective speech A technique in which the therapist mirrors the client's own feelings back to the client.

reinforcement The process by which a stimulus or an event (a reinforcer) following a particular behavior increases the probability that the behavior will happen again.

reinforcement sensitivity theory A theory proposed by Jeffrey Gray identifying two biological systems linked to learning associations between behaviors and rewards or punishers. The behavioral activation system is sensitive to learning about rewards. The

behavioral inhibition system is sensitive to learning about punishers.

relapse A return to former unhealthy patterns.

relational aggression Behavior that is meant to harm the social standing of another person.

reliability The extent to which a test yields a consistent, reproducible measure of performance.

replication The process in which a scientist attempts to reproduce a study to see if the same results emerge.

representativeness heuristic The tendency to make judgments about group membership based on physical appearances or the match between a person and one's stereotype of a group rather than on available base rate information.

research participant bias In an experiment, the influence of participants' expectations, and of their thoughts on how they should behave, on their behavior.

resilience A person's ability to recover from or adapt to difficult times.

resistance A client's unconscious defense strategies that prevent the person from gaining insight into his or her psychological problems.

resting potential The stable, negative charge of an inactive neuron.

reticular activation system A network of structures including the brain stem, medulla, and thalamus that determine arousal, one aspect of consciousness.

reticular formation A system in the midbrain comprising a diffuse collection of neurons involved in stereotyped patterns of behavior such as walking, sleeping, and turning to attend to a sudden noise.

retina The multilayered light-sensitive surface in the eye that records electromagnetic energy and converts it to neural impulses for processing in the brain.

retrieval The memory process that occurs when information that was retained in memory comes out of storage.

retroactive interference Situation in which material that was learned later disrupts the retrieval of information that was learned earlier.

retrograde amnesia Memory loss for a segment of the past but not for new events.

retrospective memory Remembering information from the past.

risk factor Characteristics, experiences, or exposures that increase the likelihood that a person will develop a psychological disorder.

risky shift The tendency for a group decision to be riskier than the average decision made by the individual group members.

rods The receptor cells in the retina that are sensitive to light but not very useful for color vision.

romantic love or passionate love Love with strong components of sexuality and infatuation, often predominant in the early part of a love relationship.

Rorschach inkblot test A famous projective test that uses an individual's perception of inkblots to determine his or her personality.

S

sample The subset of the population chosen by the investigator for study.

schedules of reinforcement Specific patterns that determine when a behavior will be reinforced.

schema A preexisting mental concept or framework that helps people to organize and interpret information. Schemas from prior encounters with the environment influence the way individuals encode, make inferences about, and retrieve information.

schizophrenia Severe psychological disorder characterized by highly disordered thought processes; individuals suffering from schizophrenia may be referred to as psychotic because they are so far removed from reality.

science The use of systematic methods to observe the natural world, including human behavior, and to draw conclusions.

script A schema for an event, often containing information about physical features, people, and typical occurrences.

secondary reinforcer A reinforcer that acquires its positive value through an organism's experience; a secondary reinforcer is a learned or conditioned reinforcer.

secure attachment The ways that infants use their caregiver, usually their mother, as a secure base from which to explore the environment.

selective attention The act of focusing on a specific aspect of experience while ignoring others.

self-actualization The motivation to develop one's full potential as a human being—the highest and most elusive of Maslow's proposed needs.

self-determination theory Deci and Ryan's theory asserting that all humans have three basic, innate organismic needs: competence, relatedness, and autonomy.

self-efficacy The belief that one can master a situation and produce positive change.

self-fulfilling prophecy Social expectations that cause an individual to act in such a way that the expectations are realized.

self-perception theory Bem's theory on how behaviors influence attitudes, stating that individuals make inferences about their attitudes by perceiving their behavior.

self-regulation The process by which an organism effortfully controls its behavior in order to pursue important objectives.

self-report test Also called an objective test or an inventory, a method of measuring personality characteristics that directly asks people whether specific items describe their personality traits.

self-serving bias The tendency to take credit for one's successes and to deny responsibility for one's failures.

semantic memory A person's knowledge about the world.

semantics The meaning of words and sentences in a particular language.

semicircular canals Three fluid-filled circular tubes in the inner ear containing the sensory receptors that detect head motion caused when an individual tilts or moves the head and/or the body.

sensation The process of receiving stimulus energies from the external environment and transforming those energies into neural energy.

sensorimotor stage Piaget's first stage of cognitive development, lasting from birth to about 2 years of age, during which infants construct an understanding of the world by coordinating sensory experiences with motor (physical) actions.

sensory adaptation A change in the responsiveness of the sensory system based on the average level of surrounding stimulation.

sensory memory Memory system that involves holding information from the world in its original sensory form for only an instant, not much longer than the brief time it is exposed to the visual, auditory, and other senses.

sensory receptors Specialized cells that detect stimulus information and transmit it to sensory (afferent) nerves and the brain.

serial position effect The tendency to recall the items at the beginning and end of a list more readily than those in the middle.

set point The weight maintained when the individual makes no effort to gain or lose weight.

sexual orientation The direction of an individual's erotic interests, today viewed as a continuum from exclusive male–female relations to exclusive same-sex relations.

sexually transmitted infection (STI) An infection that is contracted primarily through sexual activity—vaginal intercourse as well as oral and anal sex.

shaping Rewarding successive approximations of a desired behavior.

short-term memory Limited-capacity memory system in which information is usually retained for only as long as 30 seconds unless strategies are used to retain it longer.

signal detection theory An approach to perception that focuses on decision making about stimuli in the presence of uncertainty.

sleep A natural state of rest for the body and mind that involves the reversible loss of consciousness.

social anxiety disorder or social phobia An intense fear of being humiliated or embarrassed in social situations.

social cognition The area of social psychology exploring how people select, interpret, remember, and use social information.

social cognitive behavior view of hypnosis The perspective that hypnosis is a normal state in which the hypnotized person behaves the way he or she believes that a hypnotized person should behave.

social cognitive perspectives Theoretical views emphasizing conscious awareness, beliefs, expectations, and goals.

social comparison The process by which individuals evaluate their thoughts, feelings, behaviors, and abilities in relation to others.

social contagion Imitative behavior involving the spread of behavior, emotions, and ideas.

social exchange theory The view of social relationships as involving an exchange of goods, the objective of which is to minimize costs and maximize benefits.

social facilitation Improvement in an individual's performance because of the presence of others.

social identity The way individuals define themselves in terms of their group membership.

social identity theory The view that social identity is a crucial part of self-image and a valuable source of positive feelings about oneself.

social loafing Each person's tendency to exert less effort in a group because of reduced accountability for individual effort.

social psychology The study of how people think about, influence, and relate to other people.

social support Information and feedback from others indicating that one is loved and cared for, esteemed and valued, and included in a network of communication and mutual obligation.

sociocultural approach An approach to psychology that examines the ways in which social and cultural environments influence behavior.

sociocultural therapies Treatments that acknowledge the relationships, roles, and cultural contexts that characterize an individual's life, often bringing them into the therapeutic context.

somatic nervous system The body system consisting of the sensory nerves, whose function is to convey information from the skin and muscles to the central nervous system about conditions such as pain and temperature, and the motor nerves, whose function is to tell muscles what to do.

somatic symptom and related disorders Psychological disorders characterized by bodily symptoms that are either very distressing or that interfere with a person's functioning along with excessive thoughts, feeling, and behaviors about the symptoms.

somatosensory cortex A region in the cerebral cortex that processes information about body sensations, located at the front of the parietal lobes.

specific phobia Psychological disorder in which an individual has an irrational, overwhelming, persistent fear of a particular object or situation.

spontaneous recovery The process in classical conditioning by which a conditioned response can recur after a time delay, without further conditioning.

stages of change model Theoretical model describing a five-step process by which individuals give up bad habits and adopt healthier lifestyles.

standardization The development of uniform procedures for administering and scoring a test, and the creation of norms (performance standards) for the test.

stem cells Unique primitive cells that have the capacity to develop into most types of human cells.

stereotype A generalization about a group's characteristics that does not consider any variations from one individual to another.

stereotype threat An individual's fast-acting, self-fulfilling fear of being judged based on a negative stereotype about his or her group.

stimulants Psychoactive drugs, including caffeine, nicotine, amphetamines, and cocaine, that increase the central nervous system's activity.

storage The retention of information over time and how this information is represented in memory.

stream of consciousness Term used by William James to describe the mind as a continuous flow of changing sensations, images, thoughts, and feelings.

stress The responses of individuals to environmental stressors.

stress management program A regimen that teaches individuals how to appraise stressful events, how to develop skills for coping with stress, and how to put these skills into use in everyday life.

stressors Circumstances and events that threaten individuals and tax their coping abilities and that cause physiological changes to ready the body to handle the assault of stress.

structuralism Wundt's approach to discovering the basic elements, or structures, of mental processes.

subgoals Intermediate goals or problems to solve that put one in a better position for reaching a final goal or solution.

subjective well-being A person's assessment of his or her own level of positive affect relative to negative affect, and an evaluation of his or her life in general.

subliminal perception The detection of information below the level of conscious awareness.

substance use disorder A psychological disorder in which a person's use of psychoactive drugs (such as alcohol or opiates) affects their health, ability to work, and engage in social relationships.

superego The Freudian structure of personality that serves as the harsh internal judge of the individual's behavior; what is often referred to as *conscience*.

suprachiasmatic nucleus (SCN) A small brain structure that uses input from the retina to synchronize its own rhythm with the daily cycle of light and dark; the body's way of monitoring the change from day to night.

sustained attention The ability to maintain attention to a selected stimulus for a prolonged period of time.

sympathetic nervous system The part of the autonomic nervous system that arouses the body to mobilize it for action and thus is involved in the experience of stress.

synapses Tiny spaces between neurons; the gaps between neurons are referred to as synaptic gaps.

syntax A language's rules for combining words to form acceptable phrases and sentences.

systematic desensitization A behavior therapy that treats anxiety by teaching the client to associate deep relaxation with increasingly intense anxiety-producing situations.

T

temperament An individual's behavioral style and characteristic way of responding.

temporal lobes Structures in the cerebral cortex that are located just above the ears and are involved in hearing, language processing, and memory.

testes Sex-related endocrine glands in the scrotum that produce hormones involved in men's sexual development and reproduction.

thalamus The forebrain structure that sits at the top of the brain stem in the brain's central core and serves as an important relay station.

Thematic Apperception Test (TAT) A projective test that is designed to elicit stories that reveal something about an individual's personality.

theory A broad idea or set of closely related ideas that attempts to explain observations and to make predictions about future observations.

theory of mind Individuals' understanding that they and others think, feel, perceive, and have private experiences.

theory of planned behavior Theoretical model that includes the basic ideas of the theory of reasoned action but adds the person's perceptions of control over the outcome.

theory of reasoned action Theoretical model stating that effective change requires individuals to have specific intentions about their behaviors, as well as positive attitudes about a new behavior, and to perceive that their social group looks positively on the new behavior as well.

therapeutic alliance The relationship between the therapist and client—an important element of successful psychotherapy.

thermoreceptors Sensory nerve endings under the skin that respond to changes in temperature at or near the skin and provide input to keep the body's temperature at 98.6 degrees Fahrenheit.

thinking The process of manipulating information mentally by forming concepts, solving problems, making decisions, and reflecting critically or creatively.

third variable problem The circumstance where a variable that has not been measured accounts for the relationship between two other variables. Third variables are also known as *confounds*.

tip-of-the-tongue (TOT) phenomenon A type of effortful retrieval associated with a person's feeling that he or she knows something (say, a word or a name) but cannot quite pull it out of memory.

tolerance The need to take increasing amounts of a drug to get the same effect.

top-down processing The operation in sensation and perception, launched by cognitive processing at the brain's higher levels, that allows the organism to sense what is happening and to apply that framework to information from the world.

trait theories Theoretical views stressing that personality consists of broad, enduring dispositions (traits) that tend to lead to characteristic responses.

tranquilizers Depressant drugs, such as Valium and Xanax, that reduce anxiety and induce relaxation.

transference A client's relating to the psychoanalyst in ways that reproduce or relive important relationships in the client's life.

triarchic theory of intelligence Sternberg's theory that intelligence comes in three forms: analytical, creative, and practical.

trichromatic theory Theory stating that color perception is produced by three types of cone receptors in the retina that are particularly sensitive to different, but overlapping, ranges of wavelengths.

two-factor theory of emotion Schachter and Singer's theory that emotion is determined by two factors: physiological arousal and cognitive labeling.

Type A behavior pattern A cluster of characteristics—including being excessively competitive, hard-driven, impatient, and hostile—that is related to a higher incidence of heart disease.

Type B behavior pattern A cluster of characteristics—including being relaxed and easygoing—that is related to a lower incidence of heart disease.

Type D behavior pattern A cluster of characteristics—including being generally distressed, having negative emotions, and being socially inhibited—that is related to adverse cardiovascular outcomes.

U

unconditional positive regard Rogers's construct referring to the individual's need to be accepted, valued, and treated positively regardless of his or her behavior.

unconditioned response (UR) An unlearned reaction that is automatically elicited by the unconditioned stimulus.

unconditioned stimulus (US) A stimulus that produces a response without prior learning.

unconscious thought According to Freud, a reservoir of unacceptable wishes, feelings, and thoughts that are beyond conscious awareness.

V

validity The soundness of the conclusions that a researcher draws from an experiment. In the realm of testing, the extent to which a test measures what it is intended to measure.

variable Anything that can change.

vestibular sense Sense that provides information about balance and movement.

visual cortex Located in the occipital lobe, the part of the cerebral cortex involved in vision.

volley principle Principle addressing limitations of the frequency theory of hearing, stating that a cluster of nerve cells can fire neural impulses in rapid succession, producing a volley of impulses.

vulnerability-stress hypothesis or diathesis-stress model A theory holding that preexisting conditions (genetic characteristics, personality dispositions, experiences, and so on) put an individual at risk of developing a psychological disorder.

W

Weber's law The principle that two stimuli must differ by a constant minimum percentage (rather than a constant amount) to be perceived as different.

wisdom Expert knowledge about the practical aspects of life.

working memory A combination of components, including short-term memory and attention, that allow individuals to hold information temporarily as they perform cognitive tasks; a kind of mental workbench on which the brain manipulates and assembles information to guide understanding, decision making, and problem solving.

Y

Yerkes-Dodson law The psychological principle stating that performance is best under conditions of moderate arousal rather than either low or high arousal.

references

A

Aalsma, M. C., Lapsley, D. K., & Flannery, D. J. (2006). Personal fables, narcissism, and adolescent adjustment. *Psychology in the Schools, 43*(4), 481-491.

Abadie, M., Waroquier, L., & Terrier, P. (2017). The role of gist and verbatim memory in complex decision making: Explaining the unconscious-thought effect. *Journal of Experimental Psychology: Learning, Memory, and Cognition, 43,* 694-705. doi:10.1037/xlm0000336

Abbate, C., Trimarchi, P. D., Salvi, G. P., Quarenghi, A. M., Vergani, C., & Luzzatti, C. (2012). Delusion of inanimate doubles: Description of a case of focal retrograde amnesia. *Neurocase, 18*(6), 457-477.

Abbott, L. S., & Elliott, L. T. (2017). Eliminating health disparities through action on the social determinants of health: A systematic review of home visiting in the United States, 2005-2015. *Public Health Nursing, 34*(1), 2-30. doi:10.1111/phn.12268

Abdollahi, A., Abu Talib, M., Yaacob, S. N., & Ismail, Z. (2014). Hardiness as a mediator between perceived stress and happiness in nurses. *Journal of Psychiatric and Mental Health Nursing, 21*(9), 789-796.

Abdullah, T., & Brown, T. L. (2011). Mental illness stigma and ethnocultural beliefs, values, and norms: An integrative review. *Clinical Psychology Review, 31*(6), 934-948.

Abi-Dargham, A. (2017). A dual hit model for dopamine in schizophrenia. *Biological Psychiatry, 81*(1), 2-4.

Abraham, M. A., Filippi, B. M., Kang, G. M., Kim, M. S., & Lam, T. K. (2014). Insulin action in the hypothalamus and dorsal vagal complex. *Experimental Physiology, 99*(9), 1104-1109.

Abram, S. V., & DeYoung, C. G. (2017). Using personality neuroscience to study personality disorder. *Personality Disorders: Theory, Research, and Treatment, 8*(1), 2-13. doi:10.1037/per0000195

Abramowitz, J. S., & Jacoby, R. J. (2015). Obsessive-compulsive and related disorders: A critical review of the new diagnostic class. *Annual Review of Clinical Psychology* (vol. 11). Palo Alto, CA: Annual Reviews.

Abrams, A. (Dec 04, 2016). Divorce rate in U.S. drops to nearly 40-year low. *Time magazine*. http://time.com/4575495/divorce-rate-nearly-40-year-low/

Abrams, D. (2014). Social identity and intergroup relations. In M. Mikulincer, P. R. Shaver, J. F. Dovidio, & J. A. Simpson (Eds.), *APA handbook of personality and social psychology* (vol. 2). Washington, DC: American Psychological Association.

Abrams, L., & Rodriguez, E. L. (2005). Syntactic class influences phonological priming of tip-of-the-tongue resolution. *Psychonomic Bulletin and Review, 12*(6), 1018-1023.

Abramson, C. I., Dinges, C. W., & Wells, H. (2016). Operant conditioning in honey bees (Apis mellifera L.): The cap pushing response. *PloS one, 11*(9), e0162347.

Abramson, L. Y., Seligman, M. E. P., & Teasdale, J. (1978). Learned helplessness in humans: Critique and reformulation. *Journal of Abnormal Psychology, 87*(1), 49-74.

Acabchuk, R. L., Kamath, J., Salamone, J. D., & Johnson, B. T. (2017). Stress and chronic illness: The inflammatory pathway. *Social Science & Medicine, 185,* 166-170. doi:10.1016/j.socscimed.2017.04.039

Accardi, M., Cleere, C., Lynn, S. J., & Kirsch, I. (2013). Placebo versus "standard" hypnosis rationale: Attitudes, expectancies, hypnotic responses, and experiences. *American Journal of Clinical Hypnosis, 56*(2), 103-114.

Adachi, P. C., Ryan, R. M., Frye, J., McClurg, D., & Rigby, C. S. (2017). 'I can't wait for the next episode!' Investigating the motivational pull of television dramas through the lens of self-determination theory. *Motivation Science,* in press. doi:10.1037/mot0000063

Adams, M. J., Majolo, B., Ostner, J., Schülke, O., De Marco, A., Thierry, B., et al. (2015). Personality structure and social style in macaques. *Journal of Personality and Social Psychology, 109*(2), 338-353. doi:10.1037/pspp0000041

Addington, J., & others. (2011). At clinical high risk for psychosis: Outcome for nonconverters. *American Journal of Psychiatry, 168*(8), 800-805.

Adelman, R. M., Herrmann, S. D., Bodford, J. E., Barbour, J. E., Graudejus, O., Okun, M. A., & Kwan, V. Y. (2017). Feeling closer to the future self and doing better: Temporal psychological mechanisms underlying academic performance. *Journal of Personality, 85*(3), 398-408. doi:10.1111/jopy.12248

Ader, R. (1974). Letter to the editor: Behaviorally conditioned immunosuppression. *Psychosomatic Medicine, 36,* 183-184.

Ader, R. (2000). On the development of psychoneuroimmunology. *European Journal of Pharmacology, 405*(1-3), 167-176.

Ader, R., & Cohen, N. (1975). Behaviorally conditioned immunosuppression. *Psychosomatic Medicine, 37*(4), 333-340.

Ader, R., & Cohen, N. (2000). Conditioning and immunity. In R. Ader, D. L. Felton, & N. Cohen (Eds.), *Psychoneuroimmunology* (3rd ed.). San Diego: Academic.

Adler, A. (1927). *The theory and practice of individual psychology.* Fort Worth, TX: Harcourt Brace.

Adolph, K. E., & Robinson, S. R. R. (2015). Motor development. In R. M. Lerner, L. S. Liben, & U. Mueller (Eds.), *Handbook of child psychology and developmental science* (7th ed., vol. 2). Hoboken, NJ: Wiley.

Ager, A. (2013). Annual research review: Resilience and child well-being—Public policy implications. *Journal of Child Psychology and Psychiatry, 54*(4), 488-500.

Aggarwal, N. K. (2018, in press). Integrating culture and psychotherapy through the DSM-5 cultural formulation interview. In D.J. Dewan, B.N. Steenbarger, & R.P. Greenberg (Eds.) *The art and science of brief psychotherapies: A practitioner's guide, 3rd ed.* Washington, DC: APA.

Agnew, C. R., Harvey, S. M., VanderDrift, L. E., & Warren, J. (2017). Relational underpinnings of condom use: Findings from the project on partner dynamics. *Health Psychology, 36*(7), 713-720. doi:10.1037/hea0000488

Agnew-Blais, J. C., Polanczyk, G., Danese, A., Wertz, J., Moffitt, T. E., & Arseneault, L. (2016). Persistence, remission and emergence of ADHD in young adulthood: results from a longitudinal, prospective population-based cohort. *JAMA Psychiatry, 73*(7), 713.

Ago, Y., Tanaka, T., Kita, Y., Tokumoto, H., Takuma, K., & Matsuda, T. (2012). Lithium attenuates methamphetamine-induced hyperlocomotion and behavioral sensitization via modulation of prefrontal monoamine release. *Neuropharmacology, 62*(4), 1634-1639.

Agorastos, A., Haasen, C., & Huber, C. G. (2012). Anxiety disorders through a transcultural perspective: Implications for migrants. *Psychopathology, 45*(2), 67-77.

Ahmann, E. (2014). Encouraging positive behavior in 'challenging' children: The nurtured heart approach. *Pediatric Nursing, 40*(1), 38-42.

Aichele, S., Rabbitt, P., & Ghisletta, P. (2015). Life span decrements in fluid intelligence and processing speed predict morality risk. *Psychology and Aging, 30,* 598-612.

Aichele, S., Rabbitt, P., & Ghisletta, P. (2016). Think fast, feel fine, live long: A 29-year study of cognition, health, and survival in middle-aged and older adults. *Psychological Science, 27,* 518-529. doi:10.1177/0956797615626906

Ainsworth, M. D. S. (1979). Infant-mother attachment. *American Psychologist, 34*(10), 932-937.

Ainsworth, M. S., Blehar, M. C., Waters, E., & Wall, S. (1978). *Patterns of attachment: A psychological study of the strange situation.* Oxford, UK: Erlbaum.

Ajzen, I. (2001). Nature and operation of attitudes. *Annual Review of Psychology* (vol. 52, pp. 27-58). Palo Alto, CA: Annual Reviews.

Ajzen, I. (2002). Perceived behavioral control, self-efficacy, locus of control, and the theory of planned behavior. *Journal of Applied Social Psychology, 32*(4), 665-683.

Ajzen, I. (2012a). Attitudes and persuasion. In K. Deaux & M. Snyder (Eds.), *The Oxford handbook of personality and social psychology.* New York: Oxford University Press.

Ajzen, I. (2012b). The theory of planned behavior. In P. A. M. Lange, A. W. Kruglanski, & E. T. Higgins (Eds.), *Handbook of theories of social psychology.* Thousand Oaks, CA: Sage.

Ajzen, I. (2015). The theory of planned behaviour is alive and well, and not ready to retire: A commentary on Sniehotta, Presseau, and Araújo-Soares. *Health Psychology Review, 9*(2), 131-137. doi:10.1080/17437199.2014.883474

Ajzen, I., & Albarracin, D. (2007). Predicting and changing behavior: A reasoned action approach. In I. Ajzen, D. Albarracin & R. Hornik (Eds.), *Prediction and change in health behavior.* Mahwah, NJ: Erlbaum.

Ajzen, I., & Fishbein, M. (1980). *Understanding attitudes and predicting social behavior.* Englewood Cliffs, NJ: Prentice-Hall.

Ajzen, I., & Fishbein, M. (2005). The influence of attitudes on behavior. In D. Albarracin, B. T. Johnson, & M. P. Zanna (Eds.), *The handbook of attitudes* (pp. 173-221). Mahwah, NJ: Erlbaum.

Ajzen, I., & Sheikh, S. (2013). Action versus inaction: Anticipated affect in the theory of planned behavior. *Journal of Applied Social Psychology, 43*(1), 155-162. doi:10.1111/j.1559-1816.2012.00989.x

Akhtar, S. (2006). Technical challenges faced by the immigrant psychoanalyst. *Psychoanalytic Quarterly, 75*(1), 21-43.

Aknin, L. B., & others. (2013). Prosocial spending and well-being: Cross-cultural evidence for a psychological universal. *Journal of Personality and Social Psychology, 104*(4), 635-652.

Akyürek, E. G., Kappelmann, N., Volkert, M., & van Rijn, H. (2017). What You See Is What You Remember: Visual Chunking by Temporal Integration Enhances Working Memory. *Journal of Cognitive Neuroscience, 29*(12), 2025–2036.

Al-Wer, E. (2012). *Understanding sociolinguistics.* New York: Oxford University Press.

Albarracin, D., Durantini, M. R., & Earl, A. (2006). Empirical and theoretical conclusions of an analysis of outcomes of HIV-prevention interventions. *Current Directions in Psychological Science, 15*(2), 73–78.

Albarracin, D., Durantini, M. R., Earl, A., Gunnoe, J., & Leeper, J. (2008). Beyond the most willing audiences: A meta-intervention to increase participation in HIV prevention intervention. *Health Psychology, 27*(5), 638–644.

Albarracin, D., Gillette, J. C., Earl, A. N., Glasman, L. R., Durantini, M. R., & Ho, M. (2005). A test of major assumptions about behavior change: A comprehensive look at the effects of passive and active HIV-prevention interventions since the beginning of the epidemic. *Psychological Bulletin, 131*(6), 856–897.

Alden, L. E., & Taylor, C. T. (2004). Interpersonal processes in social phobia. *Clinical Psychological Review, 24*(7), 857–882.

Alea, N., & Bluck, S. (2003). Why are you telling me that? A conceptual model of the social function of autobiographical memory. *Memory, 11,* 165–178.

Alexander, G. M., Wilcox, T., & Woods, R. (2009). Sex differences in infants' visual interest in toys. *Archives of Sexual Behavior, 38*(3), 427–433.

Alexander, M. G., & Fisher, T. D. (2003). Truth and consequences: Using the bogus pipeline to examine sex differences in self-reported sexuality. *Journal of Sex Research, 40*(1), 27–35.

Alford, C. F. (2016). *Trauma, Culture, and PTSD.* New York: Springer.

Alladin, A. (2014). Mindfulness-based hypnosis: Blending science, beliefs, and wisdoms to catalyze healing. *American Journal of Clinical Hypnosis, 56*(3), 285–302.

Allely, C. S., Minnis, H., Thompson, L., Wilson, P., & Gillberg, C. (2014). Neurodevelopmental and psychosocial risk factors in serial killers and mass murderers. *Aggression and Violent Behavior, 19*(3), 288–301.

Allen, K., & Diamond, L. M. (2012). Same-sex relationships. In M. Fine & F. Fincham (Eds.), *Family theories.* New York: Routledge.

Allen, M. S., Walter, E. E., & McDermott, M. S. (2017). Personality and sedentary behavior: A systematic review and meta-analysis. *Health Psychology, 36*(3), 255–263. doi:10.1037/hea0000429

Allen, R. J., Baddeley, A. D., & Hitch, G. J. (2014). Evidence for two attentional components in visual working memory. *Journal of Experimental Psychology: Learning, Memory, and Cognition, 40*(6), 1499–1509.

Allen, T.A., & DeYoung, C. G. (2017). Personality neuroscience and the five factor model. In T.A. Widiger (Ed.), *Oxford Handbook of the Five Factor Model.* New York: Oxford University Press.

Allik, J., Church, A. T., Ortiz, F. A., Rossier, J., Hřebíčková, M., de Fruyt, F., et al. (2017). Mean profiles of the NEO personality inventory. *Journal of Cross-Cultural Psychology, 48*(3), 402–420. doi:10.1177/0022022117692100

Alloy, L. B., Salk, R., Stange, J. P., & Abramson, L. Y. (2017). Cognitive vulnerability and unipolar depression. In R. J. DeRubeis & D. R. Strunk (Eds.), *The Oxford Handbook of Mood Disorders.* (pp. 142–153). New York: Oxford University Press.

Allport, G. W. (1961). *Pattern and growth in personality.* New York: Holt, Rinehart & Winston.

Allport, G. W., & Odbert, H. (1936). *Trait-names: A psycho-lexical study* (no. 211). Princeton, NJ: Psychological Review Monographs.

Alluri, V., Toiviainen, P., Burunat, I., Kliuchko, M., Vuust, P., & Brattico, E. (2017). Connectivity patterns during music listening: Evidence for action-based processing in musicians. *Human Brain Mapping, 38,* 2955–2970.

Alston, L. L., Kratchmer, C., Jeznach, A., Bartlett, N. T., Davidson, P. S., & Fujiwara, E. (2013). Self-serving episodic memory biases: Findings in the repressive coping styles. *Frontiers in Behavioral Neuroscience, 7,* 117.

Altemus, M. (2006). Sex differences in depression and anxiety disorders: Potential biological determinants. *Hormones and Behavior, 50*(4), 534–538.

Altenor, A., Volpicelli, J. R., & Seligman, M. E. P. (1979). Debilitated shock escape is produced by both short- and long-duration inescapable shock: Learned helplessness vs. learned inactivity. *Bulletin of the Psychonomic Society, 14*(5), 337–339.

Altszuler, A. R., Morrow, A. S., Merrill, B. M., Bressler, S., Macphee, F. L., Gnagy, E. M., et al. (2017). The effects of stimulant medication and training on sports competence among children with ADHD. *Journal of Clinical Child & Adolescent Psychology,* in press. https://doi.org/10.1080/15374416.2016.1270829

Alvarez, M. J., & Garcia-Marques, L. (2011). Cognitive and contextual variables in sexual partner and relationship perception. *Archives of Sexual Behavior, 40*(2), 407–417

American Academy of Ophthalmology. (2003). *Use of marijuana to treat glaucoma.* San Francisco: Author.

American Association on Intellectual and Developmental Disabilities (AAIDD). (2010). *Intellectual disability: Definition, classification, and systems of supports (11th edition).* Washington, DC: Author.

American Cancer Society. (2015). Cigarette smoking. *American Cancer Society.* www.cancer.org/cancer/cancercauses/tobaccocancer/cigarettesmoking/cigarette-smoking-toc (accessed January 13, 2015)

American Cancer Society. (2015). Health Risks of Smokeless Tobacco. https://www.cancer.org/cancer/cancer-causes/tobacco-and-cancer/smokeless-tobacco.html

American Foundation for Suicide Prevention. (2016). *Facts and figures.* www.afsp.org/understanding-suicide/facts-and-figures (accessed August 22, 2017)

American Psychiatric Association (APA). (2001). *Mental illness.* Washington, DC: Author.

American Psychiatric Association (APA). (2006). *American Psychiatric Association practice guidelines for the treatment of psychiatric disorders.* Washington, DC: Author.

American Psychiatric Association (APA). (2013). *Diagnostic and statistical manual of mental disorders (DSM-5).* Washington, DC: Author.

American Psychological Association. (2004, July 28). APA supports legalization of APA of same-sex civil marriages and opposes discrimination against lesbian and gay parents. *American Psychological Association.* www.apa.org/news/press/releases/2004/07/gay-marriage.aspx (accessed December 22, 2014)

American Psychological Association. (2012). Research shows psychotherapy is effective but underutilized. *APA.org.* www.apa.org/news/press/releases/2012/08/psychotherapy-effective.aspx (accessed January 7, 2015)

Amitai, M., Arnon, N., Shaham, N., Gur, S., Apter, A., Weizman, A., & Hermesh, H. (2017). Nonfunctional redundant acts characterize OCD, even in OCD-unrelated tasks: A demonstration in questionnaire completion. *Psychopathology.* In press. https://doi.org/10.1159/000479885

Amunts, K., Schlaug, G., Jancke, L., Steinmetz, H., Schleicher, A., Dabringhaus, A., & Zilles, K. (1997). Motor cortex and hand motor skills: Structural compliance in the human brain. *Human Brain Mapping, 5*(3), 206–215.

An, D., & Carr, M. (2017). Learning styles theory fails to explain learning and achievement: Recommendations for alternative approaches. *Personality and Individual Differences, 116,* 410–416. doi:10.1016/j.paid.2017.04.050

An, D., Song, Y., & Carr, M. (2016). A comparison of two models of creativity: Divergent thinking and creative expert performance. *Personality and Individual Differences, 90,* 78–84. doi:10.1016/j.paid.2015.10.040

Anacker, C., & Hen, R. (2017). Adult hippocampal neurogenesis and cognitive flexibility—linking memory and mood. *Nature Reviews Neuroscience, 18,* 335–346

Anastasi, A., & Urbina, S. (1996). *Psychological testing* (7th ed.). Upper Saddle River, NJ: Prentice-Hall.

Andel, R., Crowe, M., Pedersen, N. L., Mortimer, J., Crimmins, E., Johansson, B., & Gatz, M. (2005). Complexity of work and risk of Alzheimer's disease: A population-based study of Swedish twins. *Journals of Gerontology: Series B: Psychological Sciences and Social Sciences, 60*(5), 251–258.

Anders, P. L., Yaden, D. J., Iddings, A. S., Katz, L., & Rogers, T. (2016). Editorial: More words for the poor? Problematizing the 'language gap'. *Journal of Literacy Research, 48*(2), 131–133. doi:10.1177/1086296X16662391

Anderson, C. A., & Bushman, B. J. (2002). Human aggression. *Annual Review of Psychology* (vol. 53, pp. 27–51). Palo Alto, CA: Annual Reviews.

Anderson, C. A., & others. (2010). Violent video game effects on aggression, empathy, and prosocial behavior in Eastern and Western countries: A meta-analytic review. *Psychological Bulletin, 136*(2), 151–173.

Anderson, C. A., Anderson, K. B., Dorr, N., DeNeve, K. M., & Flanagan, M. (2000). Temperature and aggression. In M. P. Zanna (Ed.), *Advances in experimental social psychology* (vol. 32, pp. 63–133). San Diego: Academic.

Anderson, C. A., Benjamin, A. J., Jr., & Bartholow, B. D. (1998). Does the gun pull the trigger? Automatic priming effects of weapon pictures and weapon names. *Psychological Science, 9*(4), 308–314.

Anderson, J. R., Kuroshima, H., & Fujita, K. (2017). Observational learning in capuchin monkeys: a video deficit effect. *The Quarterly Journal of Experimental Psychology, 70*(7), 1254–1262.

Anderson, J. W. (2017). An interview with Henry A. Murray on his meeting with Sigmund Freud. *Psychoanalytic Psychology, 34*(3), 322–331. doi:10.1037/pap0000073

Anderson, M. C., & Hanslmayr, S. (2014). Neural mechanisms of motivated forgetting. *Trends in Cognitive Sciences, 18*(6), 279–292.

Anderson, N. D., & Craik, F. I. (2017). 50 years of cognitive aging theory. *The Journals of Gerontology: Series B, 72*(1), 1–6.

Anderson, V., & others. (2009). Childhood brain insult: Can age at insult help us predict outcome? *Brain, 132*(Pt. 1), 45–56.

Anderson, V., Catroppa, C., Morse, S., Haritou, F., & Rosenfeld, J. (2005). Functional plasticity or vulnerability after early brain injury? *Pediatrics, 116*(6), 1374–1382.

Andersson, G., & Hedmen, E. (2013). Effectiveness of guided Internet-based cognitive behavior therapy in regular clinical settings. *Verhaltenstherapie, 23,* 140–148.

Andersson, G., & others. (2013). Randomised controlled non-inferiority trial with 3-year follow-up of internet-delivered versus face-to-face group cognitive behavioural therapy for depression. *Journal of Affective Disorders, 151*(3), 986–994.

Andersson, G., & Titov, N. (2014). Advantages and limitations of Internet-based interventions for common mental disorders. *World Psychiatry, 13*(1), 4–11.

Andersson, O., Miettinen, T., Hytönen, K., Johannesson, M., & Stephan, U. (2017). Subliminal influence on generosity. *Experimental Economics, 20*(3), 531–555.

Andric, M., Davis, B., & Hasson, U. (2017). Visual cortex signals a mismatch between regularity of auditory and visual streams. *Neuroimage, 157,* 648–659. doi:10.1016/j.neuroimage.2017.05.028

Andries, A., Frystyk, J., Flyvbjerg, A., & Støving, R. K. (2014). Dronabinol in severe, enduring anorexia nervosa:

A randomized controlled trial. *International Journal of Eating Disorders, 47*(1), 18–23.

Ang, S., & van Dyne, L. (Eds.). (2009). *Handbook on cultural intelligence.* New York: M. E. Sharpe.

Ang, S., van Dyne, L., & Tan, M. L. (2011). Cultural intelligence. In R. J. Sternberg & S. B. Kaufman (Eds.), *The Cambridge handbook of intelligence.* New York: Cambridge University Press.

Angelucci, A., Bijanzadeh, M., Nurminen, L., Federer, F., Merlin, S., & Bressloff, P. C. (2017). Circuits and mechanisms for surround modulation in visual cortex. *Annual Review of Neuroscience.* in press.

Angermeyer, M. C., & Schomerus, G. (2017). State of the art of population-based attitude research on mental health: A systematic review. *Epidemiology and Psychiatric Sciences, 26*(3), 252–264.

Anjali J., Marshall, J., Buikema, A., Bancroft, T., Kelly, J.P., & Newschaffer, C.J. (2015). Autism occurrence by MMR vaccine status among US children with older siblings with and without autism. *JAMA, 313*(15): 1534–1540

Anjum, B., Verma, N., Tiwari, S., Mahdi, A. A., Singh, R., Naaz, Q., et al. (2017). 24 Hours chronomics of ambulatory blood pressure and its relation with circadian rhythm of 6-sulfatoxy melatonin in night shift health care workers. *International Journal of Research in Medical Sciences, 3*(8), 1922–1931.

Anstey, K.J., Mack, H.A., & von Sanden, C. (2006). The relationship between cognition and mortality in patients with stroke, coronary heart disease, or cancer. *European Psychologist, 11*, 224–235.

Antelmi, E., Pizza, F., Vandi, S., Neccia, G., Ferri, R., Bruni, O., et al. (2017). The spectrum of REM sleep-related episodes in children with type 1 narcolepsy. *Brain, 140*(6), 1669–1679.

Antonucci, T. C., Ajrouch, K. J., & Birditt, K. S. (2014). The convoy model: Explaining social relations from a multidisciplinary perspective. *Gerontologist, 54*(1), 82–92.

Anusic, I., Schimmack, U., Pinkus, R. T., & Lockwood, P. (2009). The nature and structure of correlations among Big Five ratings: The halo-alpha-beta model. *Journal of Personality and Social Psychology, 97*(6), 1142–1156.

Aoyama, Y., Uchida, H., Sugi, Y., Kawakami, A., Fujii, M., Kiso, K., et al. (2017). Immediate effect of subliminal priming with positive reward stimuli on standing balance in healthy individuals: A randomized controlled trial. *Medicine, 96*(28).

APA Presidential Task Force on Evidence-Based Practice. (2006). Evidence-based practice in psychology. *American Psychologist, 61*(4), 271–285.

Appleton, K. M., Woodside, J. V., Arveiler, D., Haas, B., Amouyel, P., Montaye, M., et al. (2016). A role for behavior in the relationships between depression and hostility and cardiovascular disease incidence, mortality, and all-cause mortality: The prime study. *Annals of Behavioral Medicine, 50*(4), 582–591. doi:10.1007/s12160-016-9784-x

Aptekar, J. W., & Frye, M. A. (2013). Higher-order figure discrimination in fly and human vision. *Current Biology, 23*(16), R694–R700.

Araujo-Cabrera, Y., Suarez-Acosta, M. A., & Aguiar-Quintana, T. (2017). Exploring the influence of CEO extraversion and openness to experience on firm performance: The mediating role of top management team behavioral integration. *Journal of Leadership & Organizational Studies, 24*(2), 201–215. doi:10.1177/1548051816655991

Arden, M., & Armitage, C. J. (2008). Predicting and explaining transtheoretical model stage transitions in relation to condom-carrying behavior. *British Journal of Health Psychology, 13*(Pt. 4), 719–735.

Areh, I. (2011). Gender-related differences in eyewitness testimony. *Personality and Individual Differences, 50*(5), 559–563.

Arisi, G. M. (2014). Nervous and immune systems signals and connections: Cytokines in hippocampus physiology and pathology. *Epilepsy & Behavior, 38*, 43–47.

Arkadir, D., Bergman, H., & Fahn, S. (2014). Redundant dopaminergic activity may enable compensatory axonal sprouting in Parkinson disease. *Neurology, 82*(12), 1093–1098.

Armitage, C. J., & Arden, M. A. (2016). Enhancing the effectiveness of alcohol warning labels with a self-affirming implementation intention. *Health Psychology, 35*(10), 1159–1163. doi:10.1037/hea0000376

Armstrong, T. (2017). *The Myth of the ADHD Child, Revised Edition: 101 Ways to Improve Your Child's Behavior and Attention Span Without Drugs, Labels, or Coercion.* New York: Penguin.

Arndt, J., & Goldenberg, J. L. (2017). Where health and death intersect: Insights from a terror management health model. *Current Directions in Psychological Science, 26*(2), 126–131.

Arnett, J. J. (2006). Emerging adulthood: Understanding the new way of coming of age. In J. J. Arnett & J. L. Tanner (Eds.), *Emerging adults in America.* Washington, DC: American Psychological Association.

Arnett, J. J. (2007). Socialization in emerging adulthood. In J. E. Grusec & P. D. Hastings (Eds.), *Handbook of socialization.* New York: Oxford University Press.

Arnett, J. J. (2010). Oh, grow up! Generational grumbling and the new life stage of emerging adulthood. *Perspectives on Psychological Science, 5*(1), 89–92.

Arnett, J. J. (Ed.). (2012). *Adolescent psychology around the world.* New York: Psychology Press.

Arnett, J. J. (2014). *Emerging adulthood: The winding road from the late teens through the twenties* (2nd ed.). New York: Oxford University Press.

Arnett, J. J., & Fischel, E. (2013). *When will my grown-up kid grow up?* New York: Workman.

Arnett, N., & Wagers, M. (2017). Subject encodings and retrieval interference. *Journal of Memory and Language, 93*, 22–54.

Arnold, P. D., Askland, K. D., Barlassina, C., Bellodi, L., Bienvenu, O. J., Black, D., et al. (2017). Revealing the complex genetic architecture of obsessive–compulsive disorder using meta-analysis. *Molecular Psychiatry,* mp2017154.

Arntz, A. (2005). Cognition and emotion in borderline personality disorder. *Journal of Behavior Therapy and Experimental Psychiatry, 36*(3), 167–172.

Aronson, J., Burgess, D., Phelan, S. M., & Juarez, L. (2013). Unhealthy interactions: The role of stereotype threat in health disparities. *American Journal of Public Health, 103*(1), 50–56.

Arrow, H. (2007). The sharp end of altruism. *Science, 318*(5850), 581–582.

Arrowood, R. B., Cox, C. R., Kersten, M., Routledge, C., Shelton, J. T., & Hood Jr, R. W. (2017). Ebola salience, death-thought accessibility, and worldview defense: A terror management theory perspective. *Death Studies, 41*, 585–591.

Aru, J., & Bachmann, T. (2014). Phenomenal awareness can emerge without attention. *Frontiers in Human Neuroscience, 7*, 891.

Arvey, R. D., Harpaz, I., & Liao, H. (2004). Work centrality and post-award work behavior of lottery winners. *The Journal of Psychology: Interdisciplinary and Applied, 138*(5), 404–420. doi:10.3200/JRLP.138.5.404-420

Asch, S. E. (1951). Effects of group pressure on the modification and distortion of judgments. In H. S. Guetzkow (Ed.), *Groups, leadership, and men: Research in human relations.* Pittsburgh: Carnegie University Press.

Ashcraft, M. H., & Radvansky, G. A. (2014). *Cognition* (6th ed.). Upper Saddle River, NJ: Pearson.

Asher, M., Asnaani, A., & Aderka, I. M. (2017). Gender differences in social anxiety disorder: A review. *Clinical Psychology Review, 56*, 1–12

Asherson, P., Adamou, M., Bolea, B., Muller, U., Dunn, S., Pitts, M., Thome, J., & Young, S. (2010). Is ADHD a valid diagnosis in adults? Yes. *British Medical Journal, 340*, 736–737.

Ashok, A. H., Mizuno, Y., Volkow, N. D., & Howes, O. D. (2017). Association of stimulant use with dopaminergic alterations in users of cocaine, amphetamine, or methamphetamine: A systematic review and meta-analysis. *JAMA Psychiatry, 74*(5), 511–519.

Ashrafian, H. (2014). Artificial intelligence and robot responsibilities: Innovating beyond rights. *Science and Engineering Ethics.* PMID: 24737482

Asnaani, A., & Hofmann, S. G. (2012). Collaboration in multicultural therapy: Establishing a strong therapeutic alliance across cultural lines. *Journal of Clinical Psychology, 68*(2), 187–197.

Aspinwall, L. G. (1998). Rethinking the role of positive affect in self-regulation. *Motivation and Emotion, 22*(1), 1–32.

Aspinwall, L. G. (2011). Future-oriented thinking, proactive coping, and the management of potential threats to health and well-being. In S. Folkman (Ed.), *The Oxford handbook of stress, health, and coping.* New York: Oxford University Press.

Aspinwall, L. G., & Pengchit, W. (2013). Positive psychology. In M. D. Gellman & J. R. Turner (Eds.). *Encyclopedia of behavioral medicine.* New York: Springer.

Aspinwall, L. G., Leaf, S. L., & Leachman, S. A. (2009). Meaning and agency in the context of genetic testing for familial cancer. In P. T. P. Wong (Ed.), *The human quest for meaning* (2nd ed.). Hillsdale, NJ: Erlbaum.

Atkinson, R. C., & Shiffrin, R. M. (1968). Human memory: A proposed system and its control processes. *Psychology of Learning and Motivation, 2*, 89–195.

Au, J., Buschkuehl, M., Duncan, G. J., & Jaeggi, S. M. (2016). There is no convincing evidence that working memory training is NOT effective: A reply to Melby-Lervåg and Hulme (2015). *Psychonomic Bulletin & Review, 23*(1), 331–337. doi:10.3758/s13423-015-0967-4

Augustine, R. A., Ladyman, S. R., Bouwer, G. T., Alyousif, Y., Sapsford, T. J., Scott, V., et al. (2017). Prolactin regulation of oxytocin neurone activity in pregnancy and lactation. *The Journal of Physiology, 595*(11), 3591–3605.

Austad, C. S. (2009). *Counseling and psychotherapy today.* New York: McGraw-Hill.

Avvenuti, G., Baiardini, I., & Giardini, A. (2016). Optimism's explicative role for chronic diseases. *Frontiers In Psychology, 7.*

Axelsson, M., Lötvall, J., Cliffordson, C., Lundgren, J., & Brink, E. (2012). Self-efficacy and adherence as mediating factors between personality traits and health-related quality of life. *Quality of Life Research, 22*(3), 567–575.

Azarbad, L., Corsica, J., Hall, B., & Hood, M. (2010). Psychosocial correlates of binge eating in Hispanic, African American, and Caucasian women presenting for bariatric surgery. *Eating Behaviors, 11*(2), 79–84.

Azmitia, M., Syed, M., & Radmacher, K. (2013). Finding your niche: Identity and emotional support in emerging adults' adjustment to the transition to college. *Journal of Research on Adolescence, 23*(4), 744–761.

B

Bąbel, P., Adamczyk, W., Świder, K., Bajcar, E. A., Kicman, P., & Lisińska, N. (2017). How classical conditioning shapes placebo analgesia: Hidden versus open conditioning. *Pain Medicine,* pnx177.

Babiloni, C., Marzano, N., Soricelli, A., Cordone, S., Millán-Calenti, J. C., Del Percio, C., & Buján, A. (2016). Cortical neural synchronization underlies primary visual consciousness of qualia: Evidence from event-related potentials. *Frontiers In Human Neuroscience, 10.*

Babiloni, C., Vecchio, F., Cappa, S., Pasqualetti, P., Rossi, S., Miniussi, C., & Rossini, P. M. (2006). Functional frontoparietal connectivity during encoding and retrieval processes follows HERA model: A high-resolution study. *Brain Research Bulletin, 68*(4), 203–212.

Bach, D. (April 15, 2015). Man with restored sight provides new insight into how vision develops. *UW News.*

http://www.washington.edu/news/2015/04/15/man-with-restored-sight-provides-new-insight-into-how-vision-develops/

Baddeley, A. (2013). On applying cognitive psychology. *British Journal of Psychology, 104*(4), 443-456.

Baddeley, A. D. (1993). Working memory and conscious awareness. In A. F. Collins, S. E. Gatherhole, M. A. Conway, & P. E. Morris (Eds.), *Theories of memory.* Mahwah, NJ: Erlbaum.

Baddeley, A. D. (1998). *Human memory* (rev. ed.). Boston, MA: Allyn & Bacon.

Baddeley, A. D. (2003). Working memory and language: An overview. *Journal of Communication Disorders, 36*(3), 189-208.

Baddeley, A. D. (2008). What's new in working memory? *Psychological Review, 13*(3), 2-5.

Baddeley, A. D. (2012). Working memory: Theories, models, and controversies. *Annual Review of Psychology* (vol. 64). Palo Alto, CA: Annual Reviews.

Baddeley, J. L., & Pennebaker, J. W. (2011). A postdeployment expressive writing intervention for military couples: A randomized controlled trial. *Journal of Traumatic Stress, 24*(5), 581-585.

Baddeley, J. L., & Singer, J. A. (2010). A loss in the family: Silence, memory, and narrative identity after bereavement. *Memory, 189*(2), 198-207.

Badin, A. S., Fermani, F., & Greenfield, S. A. (2017). The features and functions of neuronal assemblies: Possible dependency on mechanisms beyond synaptic transmission. *Frontiers in neural circuits, 10*, 114.

Badour, C. L., Resnick, H. S., & Kilpatrick, D. G. (2017). Associations between specific negative emotions and DSM-5 PTSD among a national sample of interpersonal trauma survivors. *Journal of Interpersonal Violence, 32*(11), 1620-1641.

Bagemihl, B. (1999). *Biological exuberance: Animal homosexuality and natural diversity.* New York: St. Martin's Press.

Bahrick, H. P. (1984). Semantic memory content in permastore: Fifty years of memory for Spanish learned in school. *Journal of Experimental Psychology, 113*(1), 1-29.

Bahrick, H. P. (2000). Long-term maintenance of knowledge. In E. Tulving & F. I. M. Craik (Eds.), *The Oxford handbook of memory* (pp. 347-362). New York: Oxford University Press.

Bahrick, H. P., Bahrick, P. O., & Wittlinger, R. P. (1974). Long-term memory: Those unforgettable high-school days. *Psychology Today, 8*(7), 50-56.

Bai, Y., Maruskin, L. A., Chen, S., Gordon, A. M., Stellar, J. E., McNeil, G. D., & ... Keltner, D. (2017, in press). Awe, the diminished self, and collective engagement: Universals and cultural variations in the small self. *Journal of Personality and Social Psychology,* doi:10.1037/pspa0000087

Bailey, A. P., Parker, A. G., Colautti, L. A., Hart, L. M., Liu, P., & Hetrick, S. E. (2014). Mapping the evidence for the prevention and treatment of eating disorders in young people. *Journal of Eating Disorders, 2,* 5.

Bailey, J. M. (2003). Biological perspectives on sexual orientation. In L. D. Garnets & D. C. Kimmel (Eds.), *Psychological perspectives on lesbian, gay, and bisexual experiences* (2nd ed., pp. 50-85). New York: Columbia University Press.

Bailey, T. D., & Brand, B. L. (2017). Traumatic dissociation: Theory, research, and treatment. *Clinical Psychology: Science and Practice, 24,* 170-185.

Baillargeon, R., Scott, R. M., & Bian, L. (2016). Psychological reasoning in infancy. *Annual Review of Psychology, 67,* 159-186. doi:10.1146/annurev-psych-010213-115033

Bais, M., Figee, M., & Denys, D. (2014). Neuromodulation in obsessive-compulsive disorder. *Psychiatric Clinics of North America, 37*(3), 393-413.

Baker, K. S., Georgiou-Karistianis, N., Gibson, S. J., & Giummarra, M. J. (2017). Optimizing cognitive function

in persons with chronic pain. *The Clinical Journal of Pain, 33*(5), 462-472. doi:10.1097/AJP.0000000000000423

Baker, M. R., Frazier, P. A., Greer, C., Paulsen, J. A., Howard, K., Meredith, L. N., et al. (2016). Sexual victimization history predicts academic performance in college women. *Journal of Counseling Psychology, 63*(6), 685-692.

Bakermans-Kranenburg, M. J., & van IJzendoorn, M. H. (2011). Differential susceptibility to rearing environment depending on dopamine-related genes: New evidence and a meta-analysis. *Development and Psychopathology, 23*(1), 39-52.

Bakotic, M., Radosevic Vidacek, B., & Koscec Bjelajac, A. (2017). Morningness-eveningness and daytime functioning in university students: The mediating role of sleep characteristics. *Journal of Sleep Research, 26*(2), 210-218. doi:10.1111/jsr.12467

Balantekin, K. N., Birch, L. L., & Savage, J. S. (2017). Eating in the absence of hunger during childhood predicts self-reported binge eating in adolescence. *Eating behaviors, 24,* 7-10.

Balcetis, E., & Dunning, D. (2010). Wishful seeing: More desired objects are seen as closer. *Psychological Science, 21*(1), 147-152.

Baldwin, C. L., Roberts, D. M., Barragan, D., Lee, J. D., Lerner, N., & Higgins, J. S. (2017). Detecting and quantifying mind wandering during simulated driving. *Frontiers in Human Neuroscience, 11*, 406. doi:10.3389/fnhum.2017.00406

Baldwin, D. S., Hou, R., Gordon, R., Huneke, N. T., & Garner, M. (2017). Pharmacotherapy in generalized anxiety disorder: Novel experimental medicine models and emerging drug targets. *CNS drugs, 31*, 307-317.

Ball, C. L., Smetana, J. G., & Sturge Apple, M. L. (2017). Following my head and my heart: Integrating preschoolers' empathy, theory of mind, and moral judgments. *Child Development, 88*(2), 597-611.

Ball, C. L., Smetana, J. G., Sturge-Apple, M. L., Suor, J. H., & Skibo, M. A. (2017). Moral development in context: Associations of neighborhood and maternal discipline with preschoolers' moral judgments. *Developmental Psychology, 53*(10), 1881.

Balliet, D. (2010). Conscientiousness and forgivingness: A meta-analysis. *Personality and Individual Differences, 48*(3), 259-263.

Balliet, D., Li, N. P., & Joireman, J. (2011). Relating trait self-control and forgiveness within prosocials and proselfs: Compensatory versus synergistic models. *Journal of Personality and Social Psychology, 101*(5), 1090-1105.

Balter, M. (2010). Did working memory spark creative culture? *Science, 328*(5975), 160-163.

Balthazart, J. & Court, L. (2017). Human sexual orientation: The importance of evidentiary convergence. *Archives of Sexual Behavior, 46,* 1595-1600.

Banas, J. A., & Richards, A. S. (2017). Apprehension or motivation to defend attitudes? Exploring the underlying threat mechanism in inoculation-induced resistance to persuasion. *Communication Monographs, 84*(2), 164-178. doi:10.1080/03637751.2017.1307999

Bandura, A. (1986). *Social foundations of thought and action.* Englewood Cliffs, NJ: Prentice-Hall.

Bandura, A. (1997). *Self-efficacy.* New York: Freeman.

Bandura, A. (2001). Social cognitive theory. *Annual Review of Psychology* (vol. 52, pp. 1-26). Palo Alto, CA: Annual Reviews.

Bandura, A. (2007). Social cognitive theory. In W. Donsbach (Ed.), *International encyclopedia of communication.* Thousand Oaks, CA: Sage.

Bandura, A. (2010). Self efficacy. In D. Matsumoto (Ed.), *Cambridge dictionary of psychology.* New York: Cambridge University Press.

Bandura, A. (2010). Vicarious learning. In D. Matsumoto (Ed.), *Cambridge dictionary of psychology.* New York: Cambridge University Press.

Bandura, A. (2011). Social cognitive theory. In P. A. M. van Lange, A. W. Kruglanski, & E. T. Higgins (Eds.),

Handbook of social psychological theories. Thousand Oaks, CA: Sage.

Bandura, A. (2011a). The social and policy impact of social cognitive theory. In M. Mark, S. Donaldson, & B. Campbell (Eds.), *Social psychology and evaluation.* New York: Guilford.

Bandura, A. (2012). Social cognitive theory. *Annual Review of Clinical Psychology* (vol. 8). Palo Alto, CA: Annual Reviews.

Bandura, A. (2016). *Moral disengagement: How people do harm and live with themselves.* New York: Worth Publishers.

Bandura, A. (2016b). The power of observational learning through social modeling. In R. J. Sternberg, S. T. Fiske, & D. J. Foss (Eds.), *Scientists making a difference: One hundred eminent behavioral and brain scientists talk about their most important contributions* (pp. 235-239). New York: Cambridge University Press.

Bandura, A., & Bussey, K. (2004). On broadening the cognitive, motivational, and sociostructural scope of theorizing about gender development and functioning: Comment on Martin, Ruble, and Szkrybalo (2002). *Psychological Bulletin, 130*(5), 691-701.

Bandura, A., Ross, D., & Ross, S. A. (1961). Transmission of aggression through imitation of aggressive models. *Journal of Abnormal and Social Psychology, 63*(3), 575-582.

Banyard, V. L., & Williams, L. M. (2007). Women's voices on recovery: A multi-method study of the complexity of recovery from child sexual abuse. *Child Abuse and Neglect, 31*(3), 275-290.

Banyard, V. L., Demers, J. M., Cohn, E. S., Edwards, K. M., Moynihan, M. M., Walsh, W. A., & Ward, S. K. (2017). Academic correlates of unwanted sexual contact, intercourse, stalking, and intimate partner violence: An understudied but important consequence for college students. *Journal of Interpersonal Violence,* in press.

Bard, P. (1934). Emotion. In C. Murchison (Ed.), *Handbook of general psychology.* Worcester, MA: Clark University Press.

Barkley, R. A. (1997). Behavioral inhibition, sustained attention, and executive functions: Constructing a unifying theory of ADHD. *Psychological Bulletin, 121*(1), 65-95.

Barloon, T., & Noyes, R., Jr. (1997). Charles Darwin and panic disorder. *Journal of the American Medical Association, 277*(2), 138-141.

Barlow, D. H., Bullis, J. R., Comer, J. S., & Ametaj, A. A. (2013). Evidence-based psychological treatments: An update and a way forward. *Annual Review of Clinical Psychology* (vol. 9, pp. 1-27). Palo Alto, CA: Annual Reviews.

Baron-Cohen, S. (1995). *Mindblindness: An essay on autism and theory of mind.* Cambridge, MA: MIT Press.

Baron-Cohen, S. (2008). Autism, hypersystemizing, and the truth. *Quarterly Journal of Experimental Psychology, 61*(1), 64-75.

Baron-Cohen, S. (2011). The empathizing-systemizing (E-S) theory of autism: A cognitive developmental account. In U. Goswami (Ed.), *Wiley-Blackwell Handbook of Childhood Cognitive Development (2nd edition).* (pp. 626-640). New York: Wiley-Blackwell.

Baron-Cohen, S. (2017). Editorial Perspective: Neurodiversity-a revolutionary concept for autism and psychiatry. *Journal of Child Psychology and Psychiatry, 58,* 744-747.

Barratt, B.B. (2017). Seven questions for Kleinian psychology. *Psychoanalytic Psychology, 34,* 332-345.

Barrera, M. E., & Maurer, D. (1981). Recognition of mother's photographed face by the three-month-old infant. *Child Development, 52*(2), 714-716.

Barron, L. G., Randall, J. G., Trent, J. D., Johnson, J. F., & Villado, A. J. (2017). Big Five traits: Predictors of retesting propensity and score improvement. *International Journal of Selection and Assessment, 25*(2), 138-148. doi:10.1111/ijsa.12166

Barrouillet, P. (2015). Theories of cognitive development: From Piaget to today. *Developmental Review, 38,* 1-12.

Bartholomew, T. T. (2017). Madness (Eemwengu) and its sources: conceptualizing mental illness in Namibian Ovambo culture. *Journal of Cross-Cultural Psychology, 48*(3), 421–437.

Bartholow, B. D. (2018). The aggressive brain: Insights from neuroscience. *Current Opinion in Psychology, 19*, in press.

Bartley, E. J., & Fillingim, R. B. (2016). Sex differences in pain: A brief review of clinical and experimental findings. *Survey of Anesthesiology, 60*(4), 175–176.

Bartolucci, C., & Lombardo, G. P. (2017). The pioneering work of Enrico Morselli (1852–1929) in light of modern scientific research on hypnosis and suggestion. *International Journal of Clinical and Experimental Hypnosis, 65*(4), 398–428. doi:10.1080/00207144.2017.13 48839

Baruš, I., & Rabier, V. (2014). Failure to replicate retrocausal recall. *Psychology of Consciousness: Theory, Research, and Practice, 1*(1), 82–91.

Basilio, C. D., Knight, G. P., O'Donnell, M., Roosa, M. W., Gonzales, N. A., Umaña-Taylor, A. J., & Torres, M. (2014). The Mexican-American Biculturalism Scale: Bicultural comfort, ease, and advantage for adolescents and adults. *Psychological Assessment, 26*(2), 539–554.

Bassil Morozow, H. (2015). Analytical psychology and cinema. *The Journal of Analytical Psychology, 60*(1), 132–136. doi:10.1111/1468-5922.12135

Batson, C. D. (2002). Addressing the altruism question experimentally. In S. G. Post, L. G. Underwood, J. P. Schloss, & W. B. Hurlbut (Eds.), *Altruism and altruistic love: Science, philosophy, and religion in dialogue* (pp. 89–105). New York: Oxford University Press.

Batson, C. D. (2006). Not all self-interest after all: Economics of empathy-induced altruism. In D. De Cremer, M. Zeelenberg, & J. K. Murnigham (Eds.), *Social psychology and economics* (pp. 281–299). Mahwah, NJ: Erlbaum.

Batson, C. D. (2012). A history of prosocial behavior research. In A. W. Kruglanski & W. Stroebe (Eds.), *Handbook of the history of social psychology* (pp. 243–264). New York: Psychology Press.

Batson, D., Lishner, D., & Stocks, E. (2015). The empathy-altruism hypothesis. In D. A. Schroeder & W. G. Graziano (Eds.). *The Oxford handbook of prosocial behavior.* New York: Oxford University Press.

Battaglia, M. (2017). Sensitivity to carbon dioxide and translational studies of anxiety disorders. *Neuroscience, 346*, 434–436.

Batterink, L. J., & Paller, K. A. (2017). Sleep-based memory processing facilitates grammatical generalization: evidence from targeted memory reactivation. *Brain and language, 167*, 83–93.

Bauer, J. J., McAdams, D. P., & Sakaeda, A. R. (2005). The crystallization of desire and the crystallization of discontent in narratives of life-changing decisions. *Journal of Personality, 73*(5), 1181–1213.

Bauer, P. J. (2013). Memory. In P. D. Zelazo (Ed.), *The Oxford handbook of developmental psychology* (vol. 1, pp. 505–541). New York: Oxford University Press.

Bauer, S. M., & others. (2011). Culture and the prevalence of hallucinations in schizophrenia. *Comprehensive Psychiatry, 52*(3), 319–325.

Baumeister, R. F. (2000). Gender differences in erotic plasticity: The female sex drive as socially flexible and responsive. *Psychological Bulletin, 126*(3), 347–374.

Baumeister, R. F., & Leary, M. R. (2000). The need to belong: Desire for interpersonal attachments as a fundamental human motivation. In E. T. Higgins & A. W. Kruglanski (Eds.), *Motivational science: Social and personality perspectives* (pp. 24–49). New York: Psychology Press.

Baumrind, D. (1991). Parenting styles and adolescent development. In J. Brooks-Gunn, R. Lerner, & A. C. Petersen (Eds.), *The encyclopedia of adolescence* (vol. 2). New York: Garland.

Baumrind, D. (1993). The average expectable environment is not good enough: A response to Scarr. *Child Development, 64*(5), 1299–1307.

Baxter, L. R., Jr., Phelps, M. E., Mazziotta, J. C., Schwartz, J. M., Gerner, R. H., Selin, C. E., & Sumida, R. M. (1985). Cerebral metabolic rates for glucose in mood disorders: Studies with positron emission tomography and fluorodeoxyglucose F 18. *Archives of General Psychiatry, 42*(5), 441–447.

Beare, R., Adamson, C., Bellgrove, M. A., Vilgis, V., Vance, A., Seal, M. L., & Silk, T. J. (2017). Altered structural connectivity in ADHD: a network based analysis. *Brain Imaging and Behavior, 11*(3), 846–858.

Beaty, J. J., & Pratt, L. (2015). *Early literacy in preschool and kindergarten* (4th ed.). Upper Saddle River, NJ: Pearson.

Beck, A. (1967). *Depression*. New York: Harper & Row.

Beck, A. T. (2005). The current state of cognitive therapy: A 40-year retrospective. *Archives of General Psychiatry, 62*(9), 953–959.

Beck, A. T. (2006). How an anomalous finding led to a new system of psychotherapy. *Nature Medicine, 12*(10), 1139–1141.

Beck, A. T., & Haigh, E. A. (2014). Advances in cognitive theory and therapy: The generic cognitive model. *Annual Review of Clinical Psychology* (vol. 10, pp. 1–24). Palo Alto, CA: Annual Reviews.

Becker, E. (1971). *The birth and death of meaning.* New York: Free Press.

Becker, S. P., Mehari, K. R., Langberg, J. M., & Evans, S. W. (2017). Rates of peer victimization in young adolescents with ADHD and associations with internalizing symptoms and self-esteem. *European Child & Adolescent Psychiatry, 26*(2), 201–214.

Becvar, R. J., & Becvar, D. S. (2017). *Systems theory and family therapy: A primer.* Guilford, CT: Rowman & Littlefield.

Beebe, K. R. (2014). Hypnotherapy for labor and birth. *Nursing and Women's Health, 18*(1), 48–58.

Beeftink, F., Van Eerde, W., Rutte, C. G., & Bertrand, J. W. (2012). Being successful in a creative profession: The role of innovative cognitive style, self-regulation, and self-efficacy. *Journal of Business Psychology, 27*(1), 71–81.

Beeli, G., Esslen, M., & Jancke, L. (2005). Synaesthesia: When coloured sounds taste sweet. *Nature, 434*(7029), 38.

Beh, H. G. (2015). The right to comprehensive sex education. In S. M. Coupet & E. Marrus (Eds.), *Children, sexuality, and the law* (pp. 163–185). New York: New York University Press. doi:10.18574/nyu/9780814723852.003.0007

Behnia, B., & others. (2014). Differential effects of intranasal oxytocin on sexual experiences and partner interactions in couples. *Hormones and Behavior, 65*(3), 308–318.

Behrman, B. W., & Davey, S. L. (2001). Eyewitness identification in actual criminal cases: An archival analysis. *Law and Human Behavior, 25*(5), 475–491.

Beidel, D. C., Frueh, B. C., Neer, S. M., Bowers, C. A., Trachik, B., Uhde, T. W., & Grubaugh, A. (2017). Trauma management therapy with virtual-reality augmented exposure therapy for combat-related PTSD: A randomized controlled trial. *Journal of Anxiety Disorders.* in press. https://doi.org/10.1016/j.janxdis.2017.08.005

Beike, D. R., Cole, H. E., & Merrick, C. R. (2017). Sharing specific "We" autobiographical memories in close relationships: The role of contact frequency. *Memory, 25*, 1425–1434.

Bell, A. P., Weinberg, M. S., & Hammersmith, S. K. (1981). *Sexual preference: Its development in men and women.* Bloomington: Indiana University Press.

Bell, M. R., De Lorme, K. C., Figueira, R. J., Kashy, D. A., & Sisk, C. L. (2013). Adolescent gain in positive valence of a socially relevant stimulus: Engagement of the mesocorticolimbic reward circuitry. *European Journal of Neuroscience, 37*(3), 457–468.

Belsky, D. W., Moffitt, T. E., Corcoran, D. L., Domingue, B., Harrington, H., Hogan, S., et al. (2016). The genetics of success: How single-nucleotide polymorphisms associated with educational attainment relate to life-course development. *Psychological Science, 27*(7), 957–972. doi:10.1177/0956797616643070

Beutler, L. E., Forrester, B., Gallagher-Thompson, D., Thompson, L., & Tomlins, J. B. (2012). Common, specific, and treatment fit variables in psychotherapy outcome. *Journal of Psychotherapy Integration, 22*(3), 255–281.

Bem, D. (1967). Self-perception: An alternative explanation of cognitive dissonance phenomena. *Psychological Review, 74*(3), 183–200.

Benedetti, F., Pollo, A., Lopiano, L., Lanotte, M., Vighetti, S., & Rainero, I. (2003). Conscious expectation and unconscious conditioning in analgesic; Motor and hormonal placebo/nocebo responses. *Journal of Neuroscience, 23*(10), 4315–4323.

Bennett, S. (2014, March 19). The year of the selfie—statistics, facts & figures. *Adweek.* http://www.adweek.com/socialtimes/selfie-statistics-2014/497309 (accessed March 3, 2016)

Benowitz-Fredericks, C. A., Garcia, K., Massey, M., Vasagar, B., & Borzekowski, D. L. (2012). Body image, eating disorders, and the relationship to adolescent media use. *Pediatric Clinics of North America, 59*(3), 693–704.

Bethlehem, R. A., Romero-Garcia, R., Mak, E., Bullmore, E. T., & Baron-Cohen, S. (2017). Structural covariance networks in children with autism or ADHD. *Cerebral Cortex, 27*(8), 4267–4276.

Bercovitz, K., Pagnini, F., Phillips, D., & Langer, E. (2017). Utilizing a creative task to assess Langerian mindfulness. *Creativity Research Journal, 29*(2), 194–199. doi:10.1080/10400419.2017.1304080

Berg, H., & Slaattelid, R. (2017). Facts and values in psychotherapy—A critique of the empirical reduction of psychotherapy within evidence based practice. *Journal of Evaluation in Clinical Practice.* http://onlinelibrary.wiley.com/doi/10.1111/jep.12739/full

Bergman, L. R., Corovic, J., Ferrer-Wreder, L., & Modig, K. (2014). High IQ in early adolescence and career success in adulthood: Findings from a Swedish longitudinal study. *Research In Human Development, 11*(3), 165–185. doi:10.1080/15427609.2014.936261

Bergmann, O., Liebel, J., Bernard, S., Alkass, K., Yeung, M.S.Y., Steier, P., Kutschera, W., Johnson, L., Landen, M., Druid, H., Spalding, K.L., & Frisen, J. (2012). The age of olfactory bulb neurons in humans. *Neuron, 74*, 634–639. doi:10.1016/j.neuron.2012.03.0.

Berk, M., Cowdery, S., Williams, L., & Malhi, G. S. (2017). Recalibrating the risks and benefits of lithium therapy. *The British Journal of Psychiatry, 211*, 1–2.

Berke, D. S., Reidy, D. E., Miller, J. D., & Zeichner, A. (2017). Take it like a man: Gender-threatened men's experience of gender role discrepancy, emotion activation, and pain tolerance. *Psychology of Men & Masculinity, 18*(1), 62–69.

Berko Gleason, J., & Ratner, N. B. (2013). *The development of language* (8th ed.). Upper Saddle River, NJ: Pearson.

Berkowitz, L. (1993). *Aggression.* New York: McGraw-Hill.

Berkowitz, L., & LePage, A. (1996). Weapons as aggression-eliciting stimuli. In S. Fein & S. Spencer (Eds.), *Readings in social psychology: The art and science of research* (pp. 67–73). Boston: Houghton Mifflin.

Bernard, S., Clément, F., & Mercier, H. (2016). Wishful thinking in preschoolers. *Journal of Experimental Child Psychology, 141*, 267–274.

Bernardi, G., Siclari, F., Yu, X., Zennig, C., Bellesi, M., Ricciardi, E., ... & Tononi, G. (2015). Neural and behavioral correlates of extended training during sleep deprivation in humans: evidence for local, task-specific effects. *Journal of Neuroscience, 35*(11), 4487–4500.

Bernardy, N. C., Lund, B. C., Alexander, B., & Friedman, M. J. (2012). Prescribing trends in veterans with posttraumatic stress disorder. *Journal of Clinical Psychiatry, 73*(3), 297–303.

Berndt, N. C., Hayes, A. F., Verboon, P., Lechner, L., Bolman, C., & De Vries, H. (2012). Self-efficacy mediates the impact of craving on smoking abstinence in low to moderately anxious patients: Results of a moderated mediation approach. *Psychology of Addictive Behaviors, 27*(1), 113–124.

Bernstein, E. E., & McNally, R. J. (2017). Acute aerobic exercise helps overcome emotion regulation deficits. *Cognition and Emotion, 31*(4), 834–843. doi:10.1080/02699931.2016.1168284

Bernstein, L., Burns, C., Sailer-Hammons, M., Kurtz, A., & Rohr, F. (2017). Multiclinic Observations on the simplified diet in PKU. *Journal of Nutrition and Metabolism, 2017*. Article # 4083293. https://doi.org/10.1155/2017/4083293

Berscheid, E. (1988). Some comments on love's anatomy. Or, whatever happened to an old-fashioned lust? In R. J. Sternberg & M. L. Barnes (Eds.), *Anatomy of love*. New Haven, CT: Yale University Press.

Berscheid, E. (2000). Attraction. In A. Kazdin (Ed.), *Encyclopedia of psychology*. Washington, DC, & New York: American Psychological Association and Oxford University Press.

Berscheid, E. (2006). Searching for the meaning of "love." In R. J. Sternberg & K. Weis (Eds.), *The new psychology of love* (pp. 171–183). New Haven, CT: Yale University Press.

Berscheid, E. (2010). Love in the fourth dimension. *Annual Review of Psychology* (vol. 61, pp. 1–25). Palo Alto, CA: Annual Reviews.

Berscheid, E., & Regan, P. C. (2005). *The psychology of interpersonal relationships*. New York: Prentice-Hall.

Berthoud, H. R., Münzberg, H., & Morrison, C. D. (2017). Blaming the brain for obesity: integration of hedonic and homeostatic mechanisms. *Gastroenterology, 152*(7), 1728–1738.

Bertoia, M. L., Rimm, E. B., Mukamal, K. J., Hu, F. B., Willett, W. C., & Cassidy, A. (2016). Dietary flavonoid intake and weight maintenance: Three prospective cohorts of 124,086 US men and women followed for up to 24 years. *BMJ: British Medical Journal, 352*.

Betancourt, T. S., Newnham, E. A., Birman, D., Lee, R., Ellis, B. H., & Layne, C. M. (2017). Comparing trauma exposure, mental health needs, and service utilization across clinical samples of refugee, immigrant, and US-origin children. *Journal of Traumatic Stress, 30*, 209–218

Bertrand, M., & Mullainathan, S. (2004). Are Emily and Greg more employable than Lakisha and Jamal? A field experiment on labor market discrimination. *American Economic Review, 94*(4), 991–1013.

Best, J. R., Rosano, C., Aizenstein, H. J., Tian, Q., Boudreau, R. M., Ayonayon, H. N., et al. (2017). Long-term changes in time spent walking and subsequent cognitive and structural brain changes in older adults. *Neurobiology of Aging, 57*, 153–161

Besedovsky, L., Lange, T., & Born, J. (2012). Sleep and immune function. *European Journal of Physiology, 463*(1), 121–137.

Betancur, C. (2011). Etiological heterogeneity in autism spectrum disorders: more than 100 genetic and genomic disorders and still counting. *Brain Research, 1380*, 42–77.

Beydoun, H. A., Beydoun, M. A., Chen, X., Chang, J. J., Gamaldo, A. A., Eid, S. M., & Zonderman, A. B. (2017). Sex and age differences in the associations between sleep behaviors and all-cause mortality in older adults: results from the National Health and Nutrition Examination Surveys. *Sleep Medicine, 36*, 141–151

Bidwell, L., Gray, J. C., Weafer, J., Palmer, A. A., de Wit, H., & MacKillop, J. (2017). Genetic influences on ADHD symptom dimensions: Examination of a priori candidates, gene-based tests, genome-wide variation, and SNP heritability. *American Journal of Medical Genetics Part B: Neuropsychiatric Genetics, 174*(4), 458–466.

Birch, L. L., Savage, J. S., & Fisher, J. O. (2015). Right sizing prevention. Food portion size effects on children's eating and weight. *Appetite, 88*, 11–16. doi:10.1016/j.appet.2014.11.021

Birkhofer, C. (2017). Theoretical diversity and pluralism in psychoanalysis: Change, challenges, and benefits. *Psychoanalytic Psychology, 34*, 114–121. doi.org/10.1037/pap0000045

Birnbaum, G. E., Mizrahi, M., Kaplan, A., Kadosh, D., Kariv, D., Tabib, D., ... & Burban, D. (2017). Sex Unleashes Your Tongue: Sexual Priming Motivates Self-Disclosure to a New Acquaintance and Interest in Future Interactions. *Personality and Social Psychology Bulletin, 43*(5), 706–715.

Birur, B., Kraguljac, N., Shelton, R., & Lahti, A. (2017). Brain structure, function, and neurochemistry across schizophrenia and bipolar disorder–A systematic review of the magnetic resonance neuroimaging literature. *Biological Psychiatry, 81*(10), S255–S256.

Biswas-Diener, R., Vittersø, J., & Diener, E. (2005). Most people are pretty happy, but there is cultural variation: The Inughuit, the Amish, and the Maasai. *Journal of Happiness Studies, 6*, 205–226.

Bjork, R. A., & Druckman, D. (1991). *In the mind's eye: Enhancing human performance*. Washington, DC: National Academy Press

Bjork, R. A., Dunlosky, J., & Kornell, N. (2013). Self-regulated learning: Beliefs, techniques, and illusions. *Annual Review of Psychology* (vol. 64). Palo Alto, CA: Annual Reviews.

Björklund, A., & Lindvall, O. (2017). Replacing dopamine neurons in Parkinson's disease: How did it happen? *Journal of Parkinson's Disease, 7*(s1), S23–S33.

Blackie, L. E., Jayawickreme, E., Tsukayama, E., Forgeard, M. J., Roepke, A. M., & Fleeson, W. (2017). Post-traumatic growth as positive personality change: Developing a measure to assess within-person variability. *Journal of Research in Personality, 69*, 22–32.

Blackmore, S. (2017). *Consciousness: A very short introduction*. New York: Oxford University Press.

Blagrove, M., & Akehurst, L. (2000). Personality and dream recall frequency: Further negative findings. *Dreaming, 10*(3), 139–148.

Blaine, B.E., & McClure, K.J. (2018). *Understanding the Psychology of Diversity* (3rd ed.). Thousand Oaks, CA: Sage.

Blair, K. S., Otero, M., Teng, C., Geraci, M., Ernst, M., Blair, R. J. R., et al. (2017). Reduced optimism and a heightened neural response to everyday worries are specific to generalized anxiety disorder, and not seen in social anxiety. *Psychological Medicine*, in press.

Blair, S. N., Kohl, H. W., Paffenbarger, R. S., Clark, D. G., Cooper, K. H., & Gibbons, L. W. (1989). Physical fitness and all-cause mortality: A prospective study of healthy men and women. *Journal of the American Medical Association, 262*(17), 2395–2401.

Blais, L. T., Mack, D. E., Wilson, P. M., & Blanchard, C. M. (2017). Challenging body weight: Evidence from a community-based intervention on weight, behaviour and motivation. *Psychology, Health & Medicine, 22*(7), 872–878. doi:10.1080/13548506.2016.1271440

Blakemore, J. E. O., Berenbaum, S. E., & Liben, L. S. (2009). *Gender development*. New York: Psychology Press.

Blakemore, S. J., & Mills, K. (2014). Is adolescence a sensitive period for sociocultural processing? *Annual Review of Psychology*, vol. 65 (pp. 187–207). Palo Alto, CA: Annual Reviews.

Blanco, M., & others. (2009). *Investigating critical incidents, driver restart period, sleep quantity, and crash countermeasures in commercial operations using naturalistic data collection: A final report* (Contract No. DTFH61-01-00049, Task Order #23). Washington, DC: Federal Motor Carrier Safety Administration.

Blanton, H., Jaccard, J., Strauts, E., Mitchell, G., & Tetlock, P. E. (2015). Toward a meaningful metric of implicit prejudice. *Journal of Applied Psychology, 100*(5), 1468–1481. doi:10.1037/a0038379

Blashfield, R. K., Keeley, J. W., Flanagan, E. H., & Miles, S. R. (2014). The cycle of classification: DSM-1 through DSM-5. *Annual Review of Clinical Psychology* (vol. 10, pp. 25–51). Palo Alto, CA: Annual Reviews.

Blass, R. (2017). Understanding Freud's conflicted view of the object-relatedness of sexuality and its implications for contemporary psychoanalysis: A re-examination of Three Essays on the Theory of Sexuality. In P. Van Haute, & H. Westerink (Eds.), *Deconstructing normativity? Re-reading Freud's 1905 Three Essays* (pp. 6–27). New York: Routledge/Taylor & Francis Group.

Blaszczyk, M. B. (2017). Boldness towards novel objects predicts predator inspection in wild vervet monkeys. *Animal Behaviour, 123*, 91–100. doi:10.1016/j.anbehav.2016.10.017

Blechert, J., Wilhelm, F. H., Meuret, A. E., Wilhelm, E. M., & Roth, W. T. (2013). Experiential, autonomic, and respiratory correlates of CO_2 reactivity in individuals with high and low anxiety sensitivity. *Psychiatry Research, 209*(3), 566–573.

Bleidorn, W. (2015). What account for personality maturation in early adulthood? *Current Directions in Psychological Science, 24*, 245–252.

Bleidorn, W., Klimstra, T. A., Denissen, J. A., Rentfrow, P. J., Potter, J., & Gosling, S. D. (2013). Personality maturation around the world: A cross-cultural examination of social-investment theory. *Psychological Science, 24*, 2530–2540.

Blickle, G., Wendel, S., & Ferris, G. R. (2010). Political skill as moderator of personality–Job performance relationships in socioanalytic theory: Test of the getting ahead motive in automobile sales. *Journal of Vocational Behavior, 76*(2), 326–335.

Block, J. (1982). Assimilation, accommodation, and the dynamics of personality development. *Child Development, 53*(2), 281–295.

Block, J. (2010). The five-factor framing of personality and beyond: Some ruminations. *Psychological Inquiry, 21*(1), 2–25.

Block, J., & Kremen, A. M. (1996). IQ and ego-resiliency: Conceptual and empirical connections and separateness. *Journal of Personality and Social Psychology, 70*(2), 349–361.

Bloom, B. (1985). *Developing talent in young people*. New York: Ballantine.

Bloom, P. (2004). Myths of word learning. In D. G. Hall & S. R. Waxman (Eds.), *Weaving a lexicon* (pp. 205–224). Cambridge, MA: MIT Press.

Bloor, C., & White, F. (1983). Unpublished manuscript. La Jolla: University of California, San Diego.

Bluck, S. (2017). Remember and review or forget and let go? Views from a Functional approach to autobiographical memory. *The International Journal of Reminiscence and Life Review, 4*(1), 3–7.

Blum, K., Febo, M., Fried, L., Li, M., Dushaj, K., Braverman, E. R., ... & Badgaiyan, R. D. (2017). Hypothesizing That Neuropharmacological and Neuroimaging Studies of Glutaminergic-Dopaminergic Optimization Complex (KB220Z) Are Associated With "Dopamine Homeostasis" in Reward Deficiency Syndrome (RDS). *Substance Use & Misuse, 52*(4), 535–547.

Blum, S. D., & Riley, K. C. (September 9, 2014). Selling the language gap. *Anthropology News*. http://linguisticanthropology.org/wp-content/uploads/2015/02/BlumRiley2014_SellingTheLanguageGap.pdf

Blume, C., Del Giudice, R., Lechinger, J., Wislowska, M., Heib, D. P., Hoedlmoser, K., & Schabus, M. (2017). Preferential processing of emotionally and self-relevant stimuli persists in unconscious N2 sleep. *Brain and Language, 167*, 72–82.

Boals, A., & Rubin, D. C. (2011). The integration of emotions in traumatic memories: Cognitive-emotional distinctiveness and posttraumatic stress disorder. *Applied Cognitive Psychology, 25*(5), 811–816.

Bockting, W., Coleman, E., Deutsch, M. B., Guillamon, A., Meyer, I., Meyer III, W., et al. (2016). Adult development and quality of life of transgender and gender nonconforming people. *Current Opinion in Endocrinology, Diabetes and Obesity, 23*(2), 188-197.

Boddice, R. (2017). *Pain: A very short introduction.* Oxford, UK: Oxford University Press.

Boeschoten, R. E., Braamse, A. M., Beekman, A. T., Cuijpers, P., van Oppen, P., Dekker, J., & Uitdehaag, B. M. (2017). Prevalence of depression and anxiety in Multiple Sclerosis: A systematic review and meta-analysis. *Journal of the Neurological Sciences, 372,* 331-341.

Bogaert, A. F. (2000). Birth order and sexual orientation in a national probability sample. *Journal of Sex Research, 37*(4), 361-368.

Bogdashina, O. (2016). *Sensory perceptual issues in autism and asperger syndrome: Different sensory experiences-different perceptual worlds.* Philadelphia: Jessica Kingsley Publishers.

Bohart, A. C., & Tallman, K. (2010). Clients: The neglected common factor in psychotherapy. In B. L. Duncan, S. D. Miller, B. E. Wampold, & M. A. Hubble (Eds.), *The heart and soul of change: Delivering what works in therapy* (2nd ed., pp. 83-111). Washington, DC: American Psychological Association.

Bohbot, V. D., Anderson, N., Trowbridge, A., Sham, R., Konishi, K., Kurdi, V., & Behrer, L. (2011, November 16). *A spatial memory intervention program aimed at stimulating the hippocampus while controlling for caudate nucleus-dependent response strategies led to significant improvements on independent virtual navigation tasks in healthy elderly.* Washington, DC: Society for Neuroscience Convention.

Böhm, R., & Buttelmann, D. (2017). The impact of resource valence on children's other-regarding preferences. *Developmental Psychology, 53*(9), 1656-1665. doi:10.1037/dev0000365

Bohn, A., Koppel, J., & Harris, C. B. (2017). Life happens when you are young: Reminiscence bump in cultural life scripts regardless of number of events elicited. *Journal of Applied Research in Memory and Cognition, 6*(3), 337-342.

Bokor, G., & Anderson, P. D. (2014). Obsessive-compulsive disorder. *Journal of Pharmacy Practice, 27*(2), 116-130.

Boldt, L. J., Kochanska, G., & Jonas, K. (2017). Infant attachment moderates paths from early negativity to preadolescent outcomes for children and parents. *Child Development, 88*(2), 584-596.

Bonanno, G. A. (2004). Loss, trauma, and human resilience: Have we underestimated the human capacity to thrive after extremely aversive events? *American Psychologist, 59*(1), 20-28.

Bonanno, G. A. (2005). Resilience in the face of potential trauma. *Current Directions in Psychological Science, 14*(3), 135-138.

Bonanno, G. A., Westphal, M., Mancini, A. D. (2011). Resilience to loss and potential trauma. *Annual Review of Clinical Psychology, 7,* 511-535.

Bonchek, A. (2009). What's broken with cognitive behavior therapy treatment of obsessive-compulsive disorder and how to fix it. *American Journal of Psychotherapy, 63*(1), 69-86.

Bond, M. A., Serrano-García, I. E., Keys, C. B., & Shinn, M. E. (2017). *APA handbook of community psychology: Theoretical foundations, core concepts, and emerging challenges, Vol. 1.* Washington, DC: American Psychological Association.

Bond, R., & Smith, P. B. (1996). Culture and conformity: A meta-analysis of studies using Asch's (1952, 1956) line judgment task. *Psychological Bulletin, 119*(1), 111-137.

Bonfatti, J. F. (2005). Finding inspiration: Hope holds the key. *NAMI.* www.nami.org/Template.cfm?Section=Spotlight_1&Template=/ContentManagement/ContentDisplay.cfm&ContentID=25281&lstid=537 (accessed January 6, 2015)

Bora, E., Aydın, A., Saraç, T., Kadak, M. T., & Köse, S. (2017). Heterogeneity of subclinical autistic traits among parents of children with autism spectrum disorder: Identifying the broader autism phenotype with a data driven method. *Autism Research, 10*(2), 321-326.

Bora, E., Yalincetin, B., Akdede, B. B., & Alptekin, K. (2017). Duration of untreated psychosis and neurocognition in first-episode psychosis: A meta-analysis. *Schizophrenia Research.* in press.

Borghi, A. M., & Cangelosi, A. (2014). Action and language integration: From humans to cognitive robots. *Topics in Cognitive Science, 6*(3), 344-358.

Borniger, J. C., Cisse, Y. M., & Nelson, R. J. (2017). Reciprocal Regulation of Circadian Rhythms and Immune Function. *Current Sleep Medicine Reports, 3*(2), 93-103.

Borza, L. (2017). Cognitive-behavioral therapy for generalized anxiety. *Dialogues in Clinical Neuroscience, 19,* 203-208.

Boteler, C. (May 5, 2017). 8 charged with manslaughter in fraternity hazing death at Penn State. *USA Today.* http://college.usatoday.com/2017/05/05/criminal-charges-announced-fraternity-hazing-death-student-penn-state-student/

Bott, N. T., Bettcher, B. M., Yokoyama, J. S., Frazier, D. T., Wynn, M., Karydas, A., et al. (2017). Youthful processing speed in older adults: Genetic, biological, and behavioral predictors of cognitive processing speed trajectories in aging. *Frontiers in Aging Neuroscience, 9.*

Bouchard, S. M., Brown, T. G., & Nadeau, L. (2012). Decision-making capacities and affective reward anticipation in DWI recidivists compared to non-offenders: A preliminary study. *Accident: Analysis and Prevention, 45,* 580-587.

Bouchard, S., Dumoulin, S., Robillard, G., Guitard, T., Klinger, É., Forget, H., et al. (2017). Virtual reality compared with in vivo exposure in the treatment of social anxiety disorder: a three-arm randomised controlled trial. *The British Journal of Psychiatry, 210*(4), 276-283.

Bouchard, T. J., Jr., & Loehlin, J. C. (2001). Genes, evolution, and personality. *Behavior Genetics, 31*(3), 243-273.

Bouchard, T. J., Lykken, D. T., Tellegen, A., & McGue, M. (1996). Genes, drives, environment, and experience. In D. Lubinski & C. Benbow (Eds.), *Psychometrics and social issues concerning intellectual talent.* Baltimore: Johns Hopkins University Press.

Bouris, A., & Hill, B. J. (2017). Exploring the mother-adolescent relationship as a promotive resource for sexual and gender minority youth. *Journal of Social Issues, 73*(3), 618-636.

Bouton, M.E., & Todd, T. P. (2014). A fundamental role for context in instrumental learning and extinction. *Behavioural Processes, 104,* 13-19.

Bouvard, M., Fournet, N., Denis, A., Sixdenier, A., & Clark, D. (2017). Intrusive thoughts in patients with obsessive compulsive disorder and non-clinical participants: a comparison using the International Intrusive Thought Interview Schedule. *Cognitive Behaviour Therapy, 46*(4), 287-299.

Bow, J. N., Flens, J. R., & Gould, J. W. (2010). MMPI-2 and MCMI-III in forensic evaluations: A survey of psychologists. *Journal of Forensic Psychology Practice, 10*(1), 37-52.

Bowlby, J. (1969). *Attachment and loss* (vol. 1). London: Hogarth.

Bowlby, J. (1989). *Secure and insecure attachment.* New York: Basic.

Boxer, P., Groves, C. L., & Docherty, M. (2015). Video games do indeed influence children and adolescents' aggression, prosocial behavior, and academic performance: A clearer reading of Ferguson (2015). *Perspectives on Psychological Science, 10*(5), 671-673. doi:10.1177/1745691615592239

Boywitt, C. D., & Meiser, T. (2012). The role of attention for context-context binding of intrinsic and extrinsic features. *Journal of Experimental Psychology: Learning, Memory, and Cognition, 38*(4), 1099-1107.

Brabec, J., & others. (2011). Volume of the amygdala is reduced in patients with narcolepsy—a structural MRI study. *Neuroendocrinology Letters, 32*(5), 652-656.

Bradizza, C. M., Stasiewicz, P. R., Zhuo, Y., Ruszczyk, M., Maisto, S. A., Lucke, J. F., et al. (2017). Smoking cessation for pregnant smokers: Development and pilot test of an emotion regulation treatment supplement to standard smoking cessation for negative affect smokers. *Nicotine & Tobacco Research, 19*(5), 578-584. doi:10.1093/ntr/ntw398

Bradley, J. M., & Hojjat, M. (2017). A model of resilience and marital satisfaction. *The Journal of Social Psychology, 157*(5), 588-601.

Brancaccio, M., Patton, A. P., Chesham, J. E., Maywood, E. S., & Hastings, M. H. (2017). Astrocytes control circadian timekeeping in the suprachiasmatic nucleus via glutamatergic signaling. *Neuron, 93*(6), 1420-1435.

Brand, B. L., Loewenstein, R. J., & Spiegel, D. (2014). Dispelling myths about dissociative identity disorder treatment: An empirically based approach. *Psychiatry, 77*(2), 169-189.

Brander, G., Pérez-Vigil, A., Larsson, H., & Mataix-Cols, D. (2016). Systematic review of environmental risk factors for Obsessive-Compulsive Disorder: a proposed roadmap from association to causation. *Neuroscience & Biobehavioral Reviews, 65,* 36-62.

Branley, D. B., & Covey, J. (2017). Pro-ana versus pro-recovery: A content analytic comparison of social media users' communication about eating disorders on Twitter and Tumblr. *Frontiers in Psychology, 8,* 1356.

Brannon, L. (1999). *Gender: Psychological perspectives* (2nd ed.). Boston: Allyn & Bacon.

Brase, G. L. (2014). The nature of thinking, shallow and deep. *Frontiers in Psychology, 5,* 435.

Bratman, G. N., Hamilton, J. P., Hahn, K. S., Daily, G. C., & Gross, J. J. (2015). Nature experience reduces rumination and subgenual prefrontal cortex activation. *Proceedings of the National Academy of Sciences, 112*(28), 8567-8572.

Braun, M. H., Lukowiak, K., Karnik, V., & Lukowiak, K. (2012). Differences in neuronal activity explain differences in memory forming abilities of different populations of Lymnaea stagnalis. *Neurobiology of Learning and Memory, 97*(1), 173-182.

Braunstein, G. D. (2007). Management of female sexual dysfunction in postmenopausal women by testosterone administration: Safety issues and controversies. *Journal of Sexual Medicine, 4*(4 Pt. 1), 859-866.

Bray, N. (2017). Learning and memory: Working out working memory. *Nature Reviews Neuroscience, 18*(2), 68-68.

Breedlove, S. M. (2017). Prenatal influences on human sexual orientation: Expectations versus data. *Archives of Sexual Behavior, 46,* 1583-1592.

Breland, K., & Breland, M. (1961). The misbehavior of animals. *American Psychologist, 16,* 681-684.

Brescoll, V. L. (2016). Leading with their hearts? How gender stereotypes of emotion lead to biased evaluations of female leaders. *The Leadership Quarterly, 27*(3), 415-428. doi:10.1016/j.leaqua.2016.02.005

Brewer, J. B., Zuo, Z., Desmond, J. E., Glover, G. H., & Gabrieli, J. D. E. (1998). Making memories: Brain activity that predicts how well visual experience will be remembered. *Science, 281*(5380), 1185-1187.

Brewer, N., & Wells, G. L. (2011). Eyewitness identification. *Current Directions in Psychological Science, 20*(1), 24-27.

Brewin, C.R. (2014). Episodic memory, perceptual memory, and their interaction: Foundations for a theory of posttraumatic stress disorder. *Psychological Bulletin, 140,* 69-97.

Brickman, P., & Campbell, D. T. (1971). Hedonic relativism and planning the good society. In M. H. Appley (Ed.), *Adaptation-level theory* (pp. 287-302). New York: Academic.

Bridge, J. A., Birmaher, B., Iyengar, S., Barbe, R. P., & Brent, D. A. (2009). Placebo response in randomized controlled trials of antidepressants for pediatric major depressive disorder. *American Journal of Psychiatry, 166*(1), 42–49.

Bridges, J.S., & Etaugh, C.A. (2017). *Women's Lives: A Psychological Exploration* (4th ed.). New York: Routledge.

Briggs, K. C., & Myers, I. B. (1998). *Myers-Briggs Type Indicator.* Palo Alto, CA: Consulting Psychologists Press.

Brigham, J. C. (1986). Race and eyewitness identifications. In S. Worschel & W. G. Austin (Eds.), *Psychology of intergroup relations.* Chicago: Nelson-Hall.

Brigham, J. C., Bennett, L. B., Meissner, C. A., & Mitchell, T. L. (2007). The influence of race on eyewitness memory. In R. C. L. Lindsay, D. F. Ross, J. D. Read, & M. P. Toglia (Eds.), *The handbook of eyewitness memory* (vol. 2). Mahwah, NJ: Erlbaum.

Briley, D. A., Domiteaux, M., & Tucker-Drob, E. M. (2014). Achievement-relevant personality: Relations with the big five and validation of an efficient instrument. *Learning and Individual Differences, 32,* 26–39.

British Psychological Society. (2011). Response to the American Psychiatric Association: DSM-5 development. http://apps.bps.org.uk/_publicationfiles/consultation-responses/DSM-5%202011%20-%20BPS%20response.pdf. (accessed January 3, 2015)

Brito, R. G., Rasmussen, L. A., & Sluka, K. A. (2017). Regular physical activity prevents development of chronic muscle pain through modulation of supraspinal opioid and serotonergic mechanisms. *Pain Reports, 2*(5), e618.

Brittian Loyd, A., & Williams, B. V. (2017). The potential for youth programs to promote African American youth's development of ethnic and racial identity. *Child Development Perspectives, 11*(1), 29–38.

Briñol, P., & Petty, R. E. (2012). History of attitudes and persuasion research. In A. W. Kruglanski & W. Stroebe (Eds.), *Handbook of the history of social psychology* (pp. 285–320). New York: Psychology Press.

Briñol, P., Petty, R. E., Durso, G. O., & Rucker, D. D. (2017). Power and persuasion: Processes by which perceived power can influence evaluative judgments. *Review of General Psychology, 21*(3), 223–241. doi:10.1037/gpr0000119

Broad, K. D. (2017). Mechanisms and potential treatments for declining olfactory function and neurogenesis in the ageing brain. *Journal of Gerontology and Geriatrics, 65*(2), 93–100.

Broberg, D. J., & Bernstein, I. L. (1987). Candy as a scapegoat in the prevention of food aversions in children receiving chemotherapy. *Cancer, 60*(9), 2344–2347.

Brockie, J., & others. (2014). EMAS position statement: Menopause for medical students. *Maturitas, 78*(1), 67–69.

Brockmole, J. R., & Logie, R. H. (2013). Age-related change in visual working memory: A study of 55,753 participants aged 8–75. *Frontiers in Psychology, 4,* 12.

Brody, G.H., Yu, T., & Shalev, I. (2017). Risky family processes prospectively forecast shorter telomere length. *Health Psychology, 36,* 438–444.

Brody, L. R. (1999). *Gender, emotion, and the family.* Cambridge, MA: Harvard University Press.

Brody, N. (2007). Does education influence intelligence? In P. C. Kyllonen, R. D. Roberts, & L. Stankov (Eds.), *Extending intelligence.* Mahwah, NJ: Erlbaum.

Brody, S., & Costa, R. M. (2009). Satisfaction (sexual, life, relationship, and mental health) is associated directly with penile-vaginal intercourse, but inversely with other sexual behavior frequencies. *Journal of Sexual Medicine, 6*(7), 1947–1954.

Bronfman, Z. Z., Brezis, N., Jacobson, H., & Usher, M. (2014). We see more than we can report: "Cost free" color phenomenality outside focal attention. *Psychological Science, 25*(7), 1394–1403.

Brooker, R. J., Widmaier, E. P., Graham, L., & Stiling, P. (2015). *Principles of Biology.* New York: McGraw-Hill.

Brooks, R., & Meltzoff, A. N. (2014). Gaze following: A mechanism for building social connections between infants and adults. In M. Mikulincer & P. R. Shaver (Eds.), *Mechanisms of social connection: From brain to group* (pp. 167–183). Washington, DC: American Psychological Association.

Brotto, L. A., & Yule, M. (2017). Asexuality: Sexual orientation, paraphilia, sexual dysfunction, or none of the above? *Archives of Sexual Behavior, 46*(3), 619–627. doi:10.1007/s10508-016-0802-7

Brown, D. (2007). Evidence-based hypnotherapy for asthma: A critical review. *International Journal of Clinical and Experimental Hypnosis, 55*(2), 220–249.

Brown, E. D., Lee, H., Scott, D., & Cummings, G. G. (2014). Efficacy of continuation/maintenance electroconvulsive therapy for the prevention of recurrence of a major depressive episode in adults with unipolar depression: A systematic review. *Journal of Electroconvulsive Therapy, 30*(3), 195–202.

Brown, J. T., Eum, S., Cook, E. H., & Bishop, J. R. (2017). Pharmacogenomics of autism spectrum disorder. *Pharmacogenomics, 18*(4), 403–414.

Brown, N. M., Brown, S. N., Briggs, R. D., Germán, M., Belamarich, P. F., & Oyeku, S. O. (2017). Associations Between Adverse Childhood Experiences and ADHD Diagnosis and Severity. *Academic Pediatrics, 17*(4), 349–355.

Brown, P., & Tierney, C. (2011). Media role in violence and the dynamics of bullying. *Pediatric Reviews, 32*(10), 453–454.

Brown, R. (1973). *A first language: The early stages.* Cambridge, MA: Harvard University Press.

Brown, R. L. (2017). Functional limitation and depressive symptomatology: Considering perceived stigma and discrimination within a stress and coping framework. *Stigma And Health, 2*(2), 98–109. doi:10.1037/sah0000042

Brown, S. D., Lent, R. W., Telander, K., & Tramayne, S. (2011). Social cognitive career theory, conscientiousness, and work performance: A meta-analytic path analysis. *Journal of Vocational Behavior, 79*(1), 81–90.

Brown, S. L., Nesse, R. N., Vinokur, A. D., & Smith, D. M. (2003). Providing social support may be more beneficial than receiving it: Results from a prospective study of mortality. *Psychological Science, 14*(4), 320–327.

Brownell, C. A., Lemerise, E. A., Pelphrey, K. A., & Roisman, G. I. (2015). Measuring socioemotional behavior and development. In R. M. Lerner & M. E. Lamb (Ed.), *Handbook of child psychology and developmental science* (7th ed., vol. 3). Hoboken, NJ: Wiley.

Brownley, K. A., Berkman, N. D., Peat, C. M., Lohr, K. N., & Bulik, C. M. (2017). Binge-Eating Disorder in Adults. *Annals of Internal Medicine, 166*(3), 231–232.

Broz, F., & others. (2014). The ITALK Project: A developmental robotics approach to the study of individual, social, and linguistic learning. *Topics in Cognitive Science, 6*(3), 534–544.

Bruce, C. R., Unsworth, C. A., Dillon, M. P., Tay, R., Falkmer, T., Bird, P., & Carey, L. M. (2017). Hazard perception skills of young drivers with Attention Deficit Hyperactivity Disorder (ADHD) can be improved with computer based driver training: An exploratory randomised controlled trial. *Accident Analysis & Prevention, 109,* 70–77.

Bruce, D. (1989). Functional explanations of memory. In L. W. Poon, D. C. Rubin, & B. A. Wilson (Eds.), *Everyday cognition in adulthood and late life* (pp. 44–58). Cambridge, UK: Cambridge University Press.

Bruck, M., & Ceci, S. J. (2012). Forensic developmental psychology in the courtroom. In D. Faust & M. Ziskin (Eds.), *Coping with psychiatric and psychological testimony.* New York: Cambridge University Press.

Bruck, M., & Ceci, S. J. (2013). Expert testimony in a child sex abuse case: Translating memory development research. *Memory, 21*(5), 556–565.

Bruehl, S., Burns, J. W., Gupta, R., Buvanendran, A., Chont, M., Orlowska, D., ... & France, C. R. (2017). Do resting plasma β-endorphin levels predict responses to opioid analgesics? *The Clinical Journal of Pain, 33*(1), 12–20.

Brug, J., Conner, M., Harré, N., Kremers, S., McKellar, S., & Whitelaw, S. (2005). The transtheoretical model and stages of change: A critique. Observations by five commentators on the paper by Adams, J. and White, M. (2004) Why don't stage-based activity promotion interventions work? *Health Education Research, 20*(2), 244–258.

Brummett, B. H., Boyle, S. H., Kuhn, C. M., Siegler, I. C., & Williams, R. B. (2008). Associations among central nervous system serotonergic function and neuroticism are moderated by gender. *Biological Psychology, 78*(2), 200–203.

Brunelin, J., & others. (2014). The efficacy and safety of low frequency repetitive transcranial magnetic stimulation for treatment-resistant depression: The results from a large multicentre French RCT. *Brain Stimulation, 7*(6), 855–863.

Brunetti, R., Indraccolo, A., Mastroberardino, S., Spence, C., & Santangelo, V. (2017). The impact of cross-modal correspondences on working memory performance. *Journal of Experimental Psychology: Human Perception And Performance, 43*(4), 819–831. doi:10.1037/xhp0000348

Brunstein, J., & Maier, G. W. (2005). Implicit and self-attributed motives to achieve: Two separate but interacting needs. *Journal of Personality and Social Psychology, 89*(2), 205–222.

Brunstein, J. C. (1993). Personal goals and subjective well-being: A longitudinal study. *Journal of Personality and Social Psychology, 65*(5), 1061–1070.

Brus, M., Keller, M., & Lévy, F. (2013). Temporal features of adult neurogenesis: Differences and similarities across mammalian species. *Frontiers in Neuroscience, 7,* 135.

Brust, V., & Guenther, A. (2017). Stability of the guinea pigs personality—Cognition—Linkage over time. *Behavioural Processes, 134,* 4–11. doi:10.1016/j.beproc.2016.06.009

Bryan, J. L., & Lu, Q. (2016). Vision for improvement: Expressive writing as an intervention for people with Stargardt's disease, a rare eye disease. *Journal of Health Psychology, 21*(5), 709–719. doi:10.1177/1359105314536453

Bryan, S. M. (2012, January 28). Wolves' senses tapped to keep them clear of cattle. Associated Press. http://bangordailynews.com/2012/01/28/outdoors/wolves-senses-tapped-to-keep-them-clear-of-cattle/ (accessed December 2, 2014)

Bucherelli, C., Baldi, E., Mariottini, C., Passani, M. B., & Blandina, P. (2006). Aversive memory reactivation engages in the amygdala only some neurotransmitters involved in consolidation. *Learning and Memory, 13*(4), 426–430.

Buetti, S., Cronin, D. A., Madison, A. M., Wang, Z., & Lleras, A. (2016). Towards a better understanding of parallel visual processing in human vision: Evidence for exhaustive analysis of visual information. *Journal Of Experimental Psychology: General, 145*(6), 672–707. doi:10.1037/xge0000163

Bukowski, W. M., Brendgen, M., & Vitaro, F. (2007). Peers and socialization: Effects on externalizing and internalizing problems. In J. E. Grusec & P. D. Hastings (Eds.), *Handbook of socialization: Theory and research* (pp. 355–381). New York: Guilford.

Bulganin, L., Bach, D. R., & Wittmann, B. C. (2014). Prior fear conditioning and reward learning interact in fear and reward networks. *Frontiers in Behavioral Neuroscience, 8,* 67.

Bureau of Labor Statistics. (June 27, 2017). *American Time Use Survey Summary.* https://www.bls.gov/news.release/atus.nr0.htm

Burgdorf, J. S., Panksepp, J., & Moskal, J. R. (2014). Animal neuroscience of positive emotion. In M. M. Tugade, M. N. Shiota, & L. D. Kirby (Eds.), *Handbook of positive emotions* (pp. 119–132). New York: Guilford Press.

Burger, J. (2009). Replicating Milgram: Would people still obey today? *American Psychologist, 64*(1), 1–11.

Burger, J. M. (2014). Situational features in Milgram's experiment that kept his participants shocking. *Journal Of Social Issues, 70*(3), 489–500. doi:10.1111/josi.12073

Burke, B. L., Martens, A., & Faucher, E. H. (2010). Two decades of terror management theory: A meta-analysis of mortality salience research. *Personality and Social Psychology Review, 14*(2), 155–195.

Burman, D. (2017). Sleep disorders: Circadian rhythm sleep-wake disorders. *FP essentials, 460*, 33–36.

Burnside, K., Wright, K., & Poulin-Dubois, D. (2017). Social motivation and implicit theory of mind in children with autism spectrum disorder. *Autism Research, 10*, 1834–1844

Burstein, M., Georgiades, K., He, J. P., Schmitz, A., Feig, E., Khazanov, G. K., & Merikangas, K. (2012). Specific phobia among U.S. adolescents: Phenomenology and typology. *Depression and Anxiety, 29*(12), 1072–1082.

Burton, C. M., & King, L. A. (2004). The health benefits of writing about peak experiences. *Journal of Research in Personality, 38*(2), 150–163.

Burton, C. M., & King, L. A. (2008). The effects of (very) brief writing on health: The 2-minute miracle. *British Journal of Health Psychology, 13*(1), 9–14.

Buscemi, J., Janke, E. A., Kugler, K. C., Duffecy, J., Mielenz, T. J., St. George, S. M., & Sheinfeld Gorin, S. N. (2017). Increasing the public health impact of evidence-based interventions in behavioral medicine: New approaches and future directions. *Journal of Behavioral Medicine, 40*(1), 203–213. doi:10.1007/s10865-016-9773-3

Bushman, B. J., Wang, M. C., & Anderson, C. A. (2005). Is the curve relating temperature to aggression linear or curvilinear? Assaults and temperature in Minneapolis reexamined. *Journal of Personality and Social Psychology, 89*(1), 62–66.

Bushman, L., & Huesmann, L. R. (2012). Effects of media violence on aggression. In D. G. Singer & J. L. Singer (Eds.), *Handbook of children and the media* (2nd ed.). Thousand Oaks, CA: Sage.

Buss, D. M. (2012). *Evolutionary psychology* (4th ed.). Boston: Allyn & Bacon.

Buss, D. M. (2015). *Evolutionary psychology* (5th ed.). Upper Saddle River, NJ: Pearson.

Buss, D. M. (2016). *The Handbook of Evolutionary Psychology (2nd Ed.)*. Hoboken, NJ: Wiley.

Busse, D., Yim, I.S., Campos, B., & Marshburn, C.K. (2017). Discrimination and the HPA axis: Current evidence and future directions. *Journal of Behavioral Medicine, 40*, 539–552.

Butcher, J. N. (2010). Personality assessment from the nineteenth century to the early twenty-first century: Past achievements and contemporary challenges. *Annual Review of Psychology* (vol. 61). Palo Alto, CA: Annual Reviews.

Butcher, J. N., Beutler, L. E., Harwood, T. M., & Blau, K. (2011). The MMPI-2. In T. M. Harwood, L. E. Beutler, & G. Groth-Marnat (Eds.), *Integrative assessment of adult personality* (3rd ed.). New York: Guilford.

Butcher, J. N., Hooley, J. M., & Mineka, S. M. (2013). *Abnormal psychology* (16th ed.). Upper Saddle River, NJ: Pearson.

Butler, A. C., Chapman, J. E., Forman, E. M., & Beck, A. T. (2006). The empirical status of cognitive-behavioral therapy: A review of meta-analyses. *Clinical Psychology Review, 26*(1), 17–31.

C

Cabeza, R. (2002). Hemispheric asymmetry reduction in older adults: The HAROLD model. *Psychology and Aging, 17*(1), 85–100.

Cadaret, M. C., Hartung, P. J., Subich, L. M., & Weigold, I. K. (2017). Stereotype threat as a barrier to women entering engineering careers. *Journal of Vocational Behavior, 99*, 40–51. doi:10.1016/j.jvb.2016.12.002

Cadoni, C., Pisanu, A., Simola, N., Frau, L., Porceddu, P. F., Corongiu, S., et al. (2017). Widespread reduction of dopamine cell bodies and terminals in adult rats exposed to a low dose regimen of MDMA during adolescence. *Neuropharmacology, 123*, 385–394.

Cai, L., Chan, J. S., Yan, J. H., & Peng, K. B. (2014). Brain plasticity and motor practice in cognitive aging. *Frontiers in Aging and Neuroscience, 6*, 31.

Caillouet, B. A., Boccaccini, M. T., Varela, J. G., Davis, R. D., & Rostow, C. D. (2010). Predictive validity of the MMPI-2 PSY-5 scales and facets for law enforcement officer employment outcomes. *Criminal Justice and Behavior, 37*(2), 217–238.

Cain Miller, C. (May 17, 2015). Do children of working moms benefit? *The New York Times*, SR5.

Cairney, J., Kwan, M. Y., Veldhuizen, S., & Faulkner, G. E. (2014). Who uses exercise as a coping strategy for stress? Results from a national study of Canadians. *Journal of Physical Activity and Health, 11*(5), 908–916.

Calabretta, G., Gemser, G., & Wijnberg, N. M. (2017). The interplay between intuition and rationality in strategic decision making: A paradox perspective. *Organization Studies, 38*, 225–261.

Callaghan, T., & Corbit, J. (2018). Early prosocial development across cultures. *Current Opinion in Psychology, 20*, 102–106.

Calmes, J. (2012, May 23). When a boy found a familiar feel in a pat of the head of state. *The New York Times*. www.nytimes.com/2012/05/24/us/politics/indelible-image-of-a-boys-pat-on-obamas- head-hangs-in-whitehouse.html (accessed December 2, 2014)

Calvillo, D. P., & Jackson, R. E. (2014). Animacy, perceptual load, and inattentional blindness. *Psychonomic Bulletin & Review, 21*(3), 670–675.

Cameron, C. A., McKay, S., Susman, E. J., Wynne-Edwards, K., Wright, J. M., & Weinberg, J. (2017). Cortisol stress response variability in early adolescence: Attachment, affect and sex. *Journal of Youth and Adolescence, 46*(1), 104–120.

Cameron, R. (2016). The paranormal as an unhelpful concept in psychotherapy and counselling research. *European Journal Of Psychotherapy And Counselling, 18*(2), 142–155. doi:10.1080/13642537.2016.1170060

Camos, V., Lagner, P., & Loaiza, V. M. (2017). Maintenance of item and order information in verbal working memory. *Memory, 25*(8), 953–968.

Campbell, J. D., Yoon, D. P., & Johnstone, B. (2009). Determining relationships between physical health and spiritual experience, religious practice, and congregational support in a heterogeneous sample. *Journal of Religion and Health, 21*(2), 127–136.

Campbell, L., Campbell, B., & Dickinson, D. (2004). *Teaching and learning through multiple intelligences*. Boston: Allyn & Bacon.

Campbell, L., Overall, N., Rubin, H., & Lackenhauer, S. D. (2013). Inferring a partner's ideal discrepancies: Accuracy, projection, and the communicative role of interpersonal behavior. *Journal of Personality and Social Psychology, 105*(2), 217–233.

Campos, R. C., Mesquita, I., Besser, A., & Blatt, S. J. (2014). Neediness and depression in women. *Bulletin of the Menninger Clinic, 78*(1), 16–33.

Canessa, N., Crespi, C., Baud-Bovy, G., Dodich, A., Falini, A., Antonellis, G., & Cappa, S. F. (2017). Neural markers of loss aversion in resting-state brain activity. *Neuroimage, 146*, 257–265. doi:10.1016/j.neuroimage.2016.11.050

Cannon, W. B. (1927). The James-Lange theory of emotions: A critical examination and an alternative theory. *American Journal of Psychology, 39*, 106–124.

Cantarero, K., Gamian-Wilk, M., & Dolinski, D. (2017). Being inconsistent and compliant: The moderating role of the preference for consistency in the door-in-the-face technique. *Personality and Individual Differences, 11*, 554–557. doi:10.1016/j.paid.2016.07.005

Canteras, N. S., & Graeff, F. G. (2014). Executive and modulatory neural circuits of defensive reactions: Implications for panic disorder. *Neuroscience and Biobehavioral Reviews, 46*(Pt. 3), 352–364.

Cantor, N., & Sanderson, C. A. (1999). Life task participation and well-being: The importance of taking part in daily life. In D. Kahneman, E. Diener, & N. Schwarz (Eds.), *Well-being: The foundations of hedonic psychology* (pp. 230–243). New York: Russell Sage Foundation.

Cantwell, J., Muldoon, O. T., & Gallagher, S. (2014). Social support and mastery influence the association between stress and poor physical health in parents caring for children with developmental disabilities. *Research In Developmental Disabilities, 35*(9), 2215–2223. doi:10.1016/j.ridd.2014.05.012

Caplan, R. (2017). ADHD in pediatric epilepsy: Fact or fiction? *Epilepsy Currents, 17*(2), 93–95.

Capoccia, S., Berry, A., Bellisario, V., Vacirca, D., Ortona, E., Alleva, E., & Cirulli, F. (2013). Quality and timing of stressors differentially impact on brain plasticity and neuroendocrine-immune function in mice. *Neural Plasticity, 2013*, 971817.

Cappelen, A. W., Charness, G., Ekström, M., Gneezy, U., & Tungodden, B. (2017). *Exercise Improves Academic Performance*. Discussion Paper. Norwegian School of Economics.

Caprara, G. V., Alessandri, G., Di Giunta, L., Panerai, L., & Eisenberg, N. (2010). The contribution of agreeableness and self-efficacy beliefs to prosociality. *European Journal of Personality, 24*(1), 36–55.

Caprara, G. V., Fagnani, C., Alessandri, G., Steca, P., Gigantesco, A., Cavalli Sforza, L. L., & Stazi, M. A. (2009). Human optimal functioning: The genetics of positive orientation towards self, life, and the future. *Behavior Genetics, 39*(3), 277–284.

Capraro, V., Jordan, J. J., & Rand, D. G. (2014). Heuristics guide the implementation of social preferences in one-shot Prisoner's Dilemma experiments. *Scientific Reports, 4*, 6790.

Carbon, M., Hsieh, C. H., Kane, J. M., & Correll, C. U. (2017). Tardive dyskinesia prevalence in the period of second-generation antipsychotic use: A meta-analysis. *Journal of Clinical Psychiatry, 78*, e264–e278. doi:10.4088/JCP.16r10832.

Cardno, A. G., & Gottesman, I. I. (2000). Twin studies of schizophrenia: From bow-and-arrow concordances to Star Wars Mx and functional genomics. *American Journal of Medical Genetics, 97*(1), 12–17.

Carey, B. (2009, August 9). After injury, fighting to regain a sense of self. *New York Times*. www.nytimes.com/2009/08/09/health/research/09brain.html (accessed December 5, 2014)

Carey, B. (2011, November 25). Finding purpose after living with delusion. *The New York Times*. www.nytimes.com/2011/11/26/health/man-uses-his-schizophrenia-to-gather-clues-for-daily-living.html?pagewanted=all (accessed January 6, 2015)

Carey, B. (2012, February 14). The therapist may see you anytime, anywhere. *New York Times*. www.nytimes.com/2012/02/14/health/feeling-anxious-soon-there-will-be-an-app-for-that.html?pagewanted=all (accessed January 9, 2015)

Cargas, S., Williams, S., & Rosenberg, M. (2017). An approach to teaching critical thinking across disciplines using performance tasks with a common rubric. *Thinking Skills and Creativity*. In press.

Carkhuff, R. (2017). *Toward effective counseling and psychotherapy: Training and practice*. New York: Routledge.

Carlson, K. A., & Winquist, J. R. (2018). *An Introduction to Statistics: An Active Learning Approach* (2nd ed.). Thousand Oaks, CA: Sage.

Carlson, L., Skubic, M., Miller, J., Huo, Z., & Alexenko, T. (2014). Strategies for human-driven robot comprehension of spatial descriptions by older adults in a robot fetch task. *Topics in Cognitive Science, 6*(3), 513–533.

Carman, C. A. (2011). Stereotypes of giftedness in current and future educators. *Journal for the Education of the Gifted, 34*(5), 790–812.

Carnahan, T., & McFarland, S. (2007). Revisiting the Stanford prison experiment: Could participant self selection have led to the cruelty? *Personality and Social Psychology Bulletin, 33*(5), 603–614.

Carney, D. R., Colvin, C. R., & Hall, J. A. (2007). A thin slice perspective on the accuracy of first impressions. *Journal of Research in Personality, 41*(5), 1054–1072.

Carney, E. F. (2017). The psychology of extraordinary altruism. *Nature Reviews Nephrology, 13*, 383.

Carothers, B. J., & Reis, H. T. (2013). Men and women are from earth: Examining the latent structure of gender. *Journal of Personality and Social Psychology, 104*(2), 385–407.

Carpenter, G., & Patil, M. (2017). Gender differences in pain. In M.A. Huntoon (Ed.), *Pain Medicine Board Review* (pp. 63–77). Oxford, UK: Oxford University Press.

Carpenter, J., Preotiuc-Pietro, D., Flekova, L., Giorgi, S., Hagan, C., Kern, M. L., et al. (2017). Real men don't say 'cute': Using automatic language analysis to isolate inaccurate aspects of stereotypes. *Social Psychological and Personality Science, 8*(3), 310–322. doi:10.1177/1948550616671998

Carpentieri, J. D., Elliott, J., Brett, C. E., & Deary, I. J. (2017). Adapting to aging: Older people talk about their use of selection, optimization, and compensation to maximize well-being in the context of physical decline. *The Journals of Gerontology: Series B, 72*(2), 351–361.

Carrard, I., Van der Linden, M., & Golay, A. (2012). Comparison of obese and nonobese individuals with binge eating disorder: Delicate boundary between binge eating disorder and non-purging bulimia nervosa. *European Eating Disorders Review, 20*(5), 350–354.

Carretti, B., Caldarola, N., Tencati, C., & Cornoldi, C. (2014). Improving reading comprehension in reading and listening settings: The effect of two training programs focusing on metacognition and working memory. *British Journal of Educational Psychology, 84*(Pt. 2), 194–210.

Carroll, J. L. (2013). *Sexuality now* (4th ed.). Boston: Cengage.

Carskadon, M. A. (2006, March). *Too little, too late: Sleep bioregulatory processes across adolescence.* Paper presented at the meeting of the Society for Research on Adolescence, San Francisco.

Carskadon, M. A. (2011a). Sleep in adolescents: The perfect storm. *Pediatric Clinics of North America, 58*(3), 637–647.

Carskadon, M. A. (2011b). Sleep's effects on cognition and learning in adolescence. *Progress in Brain Research, 190*, 137–143.

Carstensen, L. L. (2006). The influence of a sense of time on human development. *Science, 312*(5782), 1913–1915.

Carstensen, L. L., & others. (2011). Emotional experience improves with age: Evidence based on over 10 years of experience sampling. *Psychology and Aging, 26*(1), 21–33.

Carter, A. R., McAvoy, M. P., Siegel, J. S., Hong, X., Astafiev, S. V., Rengachary, J., et al. (2017). Differential white matter involvement associated with distinct visuospatial deficits after right hemisphere stroke. *Cortex, 88*, 81–97.

Carter, R. (1998). *Mapping the mind.* Berkeley: University of California Press.

Caruso, J. P., & Sheehan, J. P. (2017). Psychosurgery, ethics, and media: a history of Walter Freeman and the lobotomy. *Neurosurgical focus, 43*(3), E6.

Caruso, S., Mauro, D., Scalia, G., Palermo, C. I., Rapisarda, A. M. C., & Cianci, A. (2017). Oxytocin plasma levels in orgasmic and anorgasmic women. *Gynecological Endocrinology,* 1–4.

Carver, C. S., & Scheier, M. F. (2009). Optimism. In M. R. Levy & R. H. Hoyle (Eds.), *Handbook of individual differences in social behavior* (pp. 330–342). New York: Guilford.

Carver, C. S., & Scheier, M. F. (2014). Dispositional optimism. *Trends in Cognitive Science, 18*(6), 293–299.

Case, P., Sparks, P., & Pavey, L. (2016). Identity appropriateness and the structure of the theory of planned behaviour. *British Journal of Social Psychology, 55*(1), 109–125. doi:10.1111/bjso.12115

Caserta, T. A., Punamäki, R., & Pirttilä Backman, A. (2017). The buffering role of social support on the psychosocial wellbeing of orphans in Rwanda. *Social Development, 26*(2), 402–422. doi:10.1111/sode.12188

Casey, B. J. (2015). The adolescent brain and self-control. *Annual Review of Psychology* (vol. 66). Palo Alto, CA: Annual Reviews.

Casey, B. J., & others. (2011). Behavioral and neural correlates of delay of gratification 40 years later. *Proceedings of the National Academy of Sciences USA, 108*(36), 14998–15003.

Casey, E. A., Lindhorst, T., & Storer, H. L. (2017). The situational-cognitive model of adolescent bystander behavior: Modeling bystander decision-making in the context of bullying and teen dating violence. *Psychology of Violence, 7*(1), 33–44. doi:10.1037/vio0000033

Cash, R., Udupa, K., Gunraj, C., Mazzella, F., Daskalakis, Z. J., Wong, A. H., et al. (2017). Influence of the BDNF Val66Met polymorphism on the balance of excitatory and inhibitory neurotransmission and relationship to plasticity in human cortex. *Brain Stimulation: Basic, Translational, and Clinical Research in Neuromodulation, 10*(2), 502.

Caspi, A., & others. (2002). Role of genotype in the cycle of violence in maltreated children. *Science, 297*(5582), 851–854.

Cassels, L., & Barde, Y. A. (2017). Scaling pain threshold with microRNAs. *Science, 356*(6343), 1124–1125.

Castellanos, F. X. (2015). Is adult-onset ADHD a distinct entity? *American Journal of Psychiatry, 172*, 929–931.

Casteñeda, H., Holmes, S. M., Madrigal, D. S., DeTrinidad Young, M.-E., Beyeler, N., & Quesada, J. (2015). Immigration as a social determinant of health. *Annual Review of Public Health* (vol. 36). Palo Alto: Annual Reviews.

Castillo, A. (September 21, 2017). Meet Frida, the valiant Lab who's saved a dozen lives in Mexico. *Los Angeles Times.* http://www.latimes.com/world/mexico-americas/la-fg-mexico-earthquake-frida-dog-20170921-story.html

Cathers-Schiffman, T. A., & Thompson, M. S. (2007). Assessment of English- and Spanish-speaking students with the WISC-III and Leiter-R. *Journal of Psychoeducational Assessment, 25*(1), 41–52.

Cavadel, E. W., & Frye, D. A. (2017). Not Just Numeracy and Literacy: Theory of Mind Development and School Readiness Among Low-Income Children. *Developmental Psychology.* in press. doi: 10.1037/dev0000409

Cavanna, F., Vilas, M. G., Palmucci, M., & Tagliazucchi, E. (2017). Dynamic functional connectivity and brain metastability during altered states of consciousness. *Neuroimage,* in press. doi:10.1016/j.neuroimage.2017.09.065

Cavazza, N., Guidetti, M., & Butera, F. (2017). Portion size tells who I am, food type tells who you are: Specific functions of amount and type of food in same- and opposite-sex dyadic eating contexts. *Appetite, 112,* 96–101. doi:10.1016/j.appet.2017.01.019

Caverzasi, E., & others. (2008). Complications in major depressive disorder therapy: A review of magnetic resonance spectroscopy studies. *Functional Neurology, 23*(3), 129–132.

Caye, A., Swanson, J., Thapar, A., Sibley, M., Arseneault, L., Hechtman, L., et al. (2016). Life span studies of ADHD—conceptualchallenges and predictors of persistence and outcome. *Current Psychiatry Reports, 18*(12), 111.

Center for Behavioral Health Statistics and Quality. (2016). *Key substance use and mental health indicators in the United States: Results from the 2015 National Survey on Drug Use and Health* (HHS Publication No. SMA 16-4984, NSDUH Series H-51). Retrieved from http://www.samhsa.gov/data/

Centers for Disease Control and Prevention (CDC). (2014b). Overweight and obesity. *CDC.* www.cdc.gov/Obesity/ (accessed January 13, 2015)

Centers for Disease Control and Prevention (CDC). (2016). *Current Cigarette Smoking Among Adults in the United States .* https://www.cdc.gov/tobacco/data_statistics/fact_sheets/adult_data/cig_smoking/index.htm

Centers for Disease Control and Prevention (CDC). (2016). *Sexually transmitted disease surveillance 2015.* Atlanta: CDC. https://www.cdc.gov/std/stats15/default.htm

Centers for Disease Control and Prevention (CDC). (November 13, 2017). *ADHD Data and Statistics.* https://www.cdc.gov/ncbddd/adhd/data.html

Centers for Disease Control and Prevention (CDC). (May, 2017). *African American Health.* Atlanta, GA: CDC. https://www.cdc.gov/vitalsigns/aahealth/index.html

Centers for Disease Control and Prevention (CDC). (March 10, 2017). *Autism Spectrum Disorder: Facts, Screening and Diagnosis.* https://www.cdc.gov/ncbddd/autism/facts.html

Centers for Disease Control and Prevention (CDC). (2017). *Health Effects of Cigarette Smoking.* https://www.cdc.gov/tobacco/data_statistics/fact_sheets/health_effects/effects_cig_smoking/index.htm

Centers for Disease Control (CDC). (2017). *Health Effects of Secondhand Smoke.* Atlanta, GA: CDC. https://www.cdc.gov/tobacco/data_statistics/fact_sheets/secondhand_smoke/health_effects/index.htm

Centers for Disease Control and Prevention (CDC). (2017). *HIV Basics.* https://www.cdc.gov/hiv/basics/index.html

Cha, C. B., Franz, P. J., M Guzmán, E., Glenn, C. R., Kleiman, E. M., & Nock, M. K. (2018). Annual Research Review: Suicide among youth–epidemiology, (potential) etiology, and treatment. *Journal of Child Psychology and Psychiatry.* in press.

Cha, J., Guffanti, G., Gingrich, J., Talati, A., Wickramaratne, P., Weissman, M., & Posner, J. (2017). Effects of serotonin transporter gene variation on impulsivity mediated by default mode network: A family study of depression. *Cerebral Cortex,* in press. doi:10.1093/cercor/bhx097 .

Chabris, C. F., Lee, J. J., Cesarini, D., Benjamin, D. J., & Laibson, D. I. (2015). The fourth law of behavior genetics. *Current Directions in Psychological Science, 24*, 304–312. doi:10.1177/0963721415580430

Chaladze, G. (2016). Heterosexual male carriers could explain persistence of homosexuality in men: Individual-based simulations of an X-linked inheritance model. *Archives Of Sexual Behavior, 45*(7), 1705–1711. doi:10.1007/s10508-016-0742-2

Chambeaud, J. G., Martín, A., & Barraza, J. F. (2014). Effect of disparity on the perception of motion-defined contours. *Psychology & Neuroscience, 7*(2), 91–101. doi:10.3922/j.psns.2014.018

Chambless, D. L. (2002). Beware the dodo bird: The dangers of overgeneralization. *Clinical Psychology: Science and Practice, 9*(1), 13–16.

Chambless, D. L., Allred, K. M., Chen, F. F., McCarthy, K. S., Milrod, B., & Barber, J. P. (2017). Perceived criticism predicts outcome of psychotherapy for panic disorder: Replication and extension. *Journal of Consulting and Clinical Psychology, 85*(1), 37–44.

Chambon, V., Baudouin, J.-Y., & Franck, N. (2006). The role of configural information in facial emotion recognition in schizophrenia. *Neuropsychologia, 44*(12), 2437–2444.

Chan, C. M. H., Ng, C. G., Taib, N. A., Wee, L. H., Krupat, E., & Meyer, F. (2017). Course and predictors of post traumatic stress disorder in a cohort of psychologically distressed patients with cancer: A 4 year follow up study. *Cancer.* in press.

Chan, C., & Mogilner, C. (2017). Experiential gifts foster stronger social relationships than material gifts. *Journal of Consumer Research, 43*(6), 913–931.

Chandra, A., Mosher, W. D., Copen, C., & Sionean, C. (2011). Sexual behavior, sexual attraction, and sexual identity in the United States: Data from the 2006–2008 National Survey of Family Growth. *National Health Statistics Reports,* No. 36. www.cdc.gov/nchs/data/nhsr/nhsr036.pdf (accessed December 21, 2014)

Chang, A. K., Bijur, P. E., & Esses, D., Barnaby, D. F., & Baer, J. (2017). Effect of a Single Dose of Oral Opioid and Nonopioid Analgesics on Acute Extremity Pain in the Emergency Department. A Randomized Clinical Trial. *Journal of the American Medical Association, 318,* 1661–1667. doi:10.1001/jama.2017.16190

Chang, C. H., Yu, C. J., Du, J. C., Chiou, H. C., Chen, H. C., Yang, W., et al. (2018). The interactions among organophosphate pesticide exposure, oxidative stress, and genetic polymorphisms of dopamine receptor D4 increase the risk of attention deficit/hyperactivity disorder in children. *Environmental Research, 160,* 339–346.

Chang, M. X. L., Jetten, J., Cruwys, T., & Haslam, C. (2017). Cultural identity and the expression of depression: A social identity perspective. *Journal of Community & Applied Social Psychology, 27*(1), 16–34.

Chatters, L. M., Taylor, R. J., Woodward, A. T., & Nicklett, E. J. (2014). Social support from church and family members and depressive symptoms among older African Americans. *American Journal of Geriatric Psychiatry.* doi:10.1016/j.jagp.2014.04.008

Chaste, P., Roeder, K., & Devlin, B. (2017). The yin and yang of autism genetics: How rare de novo and common variations affect liability. *Annual Review of Genomics and Human Genetics, 18,* 167–187.

Charlesworth, L. A., Allen, R. J., Morson, S., Burn, W. K., & Souchay, C. (2014). Working memory and the enactment effect in early Alzheimer's disease. **ISRN Neurology.** doi:10.1155/2014/694761

Charney, A. W., Ruderfer, D. M., Stahl, E. A., Moran, J. L., Chambert, K., Belliveau, R. A., et al. (2017). Evidence for genetic heterogeneity between clinical subtypes of bipolar disorder. *Translational Psychiatry, 7*(1), e993.

Chartier, K. G., Thomas, N. S., & Kendler, K. S. (2017). Interrelationship between family history of alcoholism and generational status in the prediction of alcohol dependence in US Hispanics. *Psychological Medicine, 47*(1), 137–147.

Chaves, J. F. (2000). Hypnosis. In A. Kazdin (Ed.), *Encyclopedia of psychology.* Washington, DC, & New York: American Psychological Association and Oxford University Press.

Chellappa, S. L., Morris, C. J., & Scheer, F. A. (2017). Circadian misalignment impacts on human cognitive performance. *Journal of Sleep and Sleep Disorders Research, 40*(suppl_1), A77–A77.

Chen, C., Hewitt, P. L., & Flett, G. L. (2017). Ethnic variations in other-oriented perfectionism's associations with depression and suicide behaviour. *Personality and individual differences, 104,* 504–509.

Chen, F. R., Rothman, E. F., & Jaffee, S. R. (2017). Early puberty, friendship group characteristics, and dating abuse in US girls. *Pediatrics,* e20162847.

Chen, L., Mishra, A., Newton, A. T., Morgan, V. L., Stringer, E. A., Rogers, B. P., & Gore, J. C. (2011). Fine-scale functional connectivity in somatosensory cortex revealed by high-resolution fMRI. *Magnetic Resonance Imaging, 29*(10), 1330–1337.

Chen, P., & Jacobson, K. C. (2012). Developmental trajectories of substance use from early adolescence to young adulthood: Gender and racial/ethnic differences. *Journal of Adolescent Health, 50*(2), 154–163.

Cheng, C. H., Niddam, D. M., Hsu, S. C., Liu, C. Y., & Tsai, S. Y. (2017). Resting GABA concentration predicts

inhibitory control during an auditory Go-Nogo task. *Experimental Brain Research, 12,* 3833–3841.

Cheng, C. M., & Huang, C. L. (2011). Processes of conscious and unconscious memory: Evidence from current research on dissociation of memories within a test. *American Journal of Psychology, 124*(4), 421–440.

Cheng, M. F. (2017). Adult neurogenesis in injury-induced self-repair: Use it or lose it. *Brain Plasticity, 2*(2), 115–126.

Cheng, W., Rolls, E. T., Gu, H., Zhang, J., & Feng, J. (2015). Autism: reduced connectivity between cortical areas involved in face expression, theory of mind, and the sense of self. *Brain, 138*(5), 1382–1393.

Cherkasova, M. V., Faridi, N., Casey, K. F., Larcher, K., O'Driscoll, G. A., Hechtman, L., et al. (2017). Differential associations between cortical thickness and striatal dopamine in treatment-naïve adults with ADHD vs. healthy controls. *Frontiers in Human Neuroscience, 11,* 421.

Chess, S., & Thomas, A. (1977). Temperamental individuality from childhood to adolescence. *Journal of Child Psychiatry, 16*(2), 218–226.

Chevallier, C., Kohls, G., Troiani, V., Brodkin, E. S., & Schultz, R. T. (2012). The social motivation theory of autism. *Trends in Cognitive Sciences, 16,* 231–239.

Chiesa, P. A., Liuzza, M. T., Macaluso, E., & Aglioti, S. M. (2017). Brain activity induced by implicit processing of others' pain and pleasure. *Human Brain Mapping.* in press.

Chivers, M. L., & Brotto, L. A. (2017). Controversies of women's sexual arousal and desire. *European Psychologist, 22*(1), 5–26. doi:10.1027/1016-9040/a000274

Chivers, M. L., Seto, M. C., & Blanchard, R. (2007). Gender and sexual orientation differences in sexual response to sexual activities versus gender of actors in sexual films. *Journal of Personality and Social Psychology, 93*(6), 1108–1121.

Chivers, M. L. (2017). The specificity of women's sexual response and its relationship with sexual orientations: A review and ten hypotheses. *Archives of Sexual Behavior, 46*(5), 1161–1179.

Cho, H. J., Savitz, J., Dantzer, R., Teague, T. K., Drevets, W. C., & Irwin, M. R. (2017). Sleep disturbance and kynurenine metabolism in depression. *Journal of Psychosomatic Research, 99,* 1–7.

Cho, H., Gonzalez, R., Lavaysse, L. M., Pence, S., Fulford, D., & Gard, D. E. (2017). Do people with schizophrenia experience more negative emotion and less positive emotion in their daily lives? A meta-analysis of experience sampling studies. *Schizophrenia Research, 183,* 49–55.

Choi, B., & others. (2014). Very long (>48 hours) shifts and cardiovascular strain in firefighters: A theoretical framework. *Annals of Occupational and Environmental Medicine, 26*(1), 5.

Choi, D., Tsuji, H., & Watanuki, S. (2017). Association between oxytocin receptor gene rs53576 polymorphism and behavioral inhibition/activation system (bis/bas) sensitivity. *Personality And Individual Differences,* in press. doi:10.1016/j.paid.2017.09.001

Choi, H., Kensinger, E. A., & Rajaram, S. (2017). Mnemonic transmission, social contagion, and emergence of collective memory: Influence of emotional valence, group structure, and information distribution. *Journal of Experimental Psychology: General, 146*(9), 1247–1265. doi:10.1037/xge0000327

Choi, J. H., Chung, K., & Park, K. (2013). Psychosocial predictors of four health-promoting behaviors for cancer prevention using the stage of change of Transtheoretical Model. *Psycho-Oncology, 22*(10), 2253–2261.

Choi, J., Lisanby, S. H., Medalia, A., & Prudic, J. (2011). A conceptual introduction to cognitive remediation for memory deficits associated with right unilateral electroconvulsive therapy. *Journal of Electroconvulsive Therapy, 27*(4), 286–291.

Choi, K. R., Seng, J. S., Briggs, E. C., Munro-Kramer, M. L., Graham-Bermann, S. A., Lee, R. C., & Ford, J. D. (2017). The dissociative subtype of posttraumatic stress disorder (PTSD) among adolescents: co-occurring PTSD, depersonalization/derealization, and other dissociation symptoms. *Journal of the American Academy of Child & Adolescent Psychiatry, 56,* 1062–1072.

Choi-Kain, L. W., Finch, E. F., Masland, S. R., Jenkins, J. A., & Unruh, B. T. (2017). What works in the treatment of borderline personality disorder. *Current Behavioral Neuroscience Reports, 4*(1), 21–30.

Chomsky, N. (1975). *Reflections on language.* New York: Pantheon.

Chorney, Saryn. (October 19, 2017). Lulu the CIA's Bomb-Sniffing Dog Fails Out of School; Just Wasn't That Into It. *People Magazine.* http://people.com/pets/bomb-sniffing-cia-dog-fails-school/

Chou, H. T., & Edge, N. (2012). "They are happier and having better lives than I am": The impact of using Facebook on perceptions of others' lives. *Cyberpsychology, Behavior, and Social Networking, 15*(2), 117–121.

Chouinard, G. (2006). Interrelations between psychiatric symptoms and drug-induced movement disorder. *Journal of Psychiatry and Neuroscience, 31*(3), 177–180.

Chowdhury, T., Bindu, B., Singh, G. P., & Schaller, B. (2017). Sleep disorders: Is the trigemino-cardiac reflex a missing link? *Frontiers in Neurology, 8.*

Christ, C. C., Carlo, G., & Stoltenberg, S. F. (2016). Oxytocin receptor (OXTR) single nucleotide polymorphisms indirectly predict prosocial behavior through perspective taking and empathic concern. *Journal of Personality, 84*(2), 204–213. doi:10.1111/jopy.12152

Christensen, D. L., Bilder, D. A., Zahorodny, W., Pettygrove, S., Durkin, M. S., Fitzgerald, R. T., et al. (2016). Prevalence and characteristics of autism spectrum disorder among 4-year-old children in the autism and developmental disabilities monitoring network. *Journal of Developmental & Behavioral Pediatrics, 37*(1), 1–8.

Christensen, H., & others. (2010). Protocol for a randomized trial investigating the effectiveness of an online e-health application compared to attention placebo or sertraline in the treatment of generalized anxiety disorder. *Trials, 11,* 48.

Christensen, J., Grønborg, T.K., Sørensen, M.J., Schendel, D., Parner, E.T., Pedersen, L.H., & Vestergaard, M. (2013). Prenatal valproate exposure and risk of autism spectrum disorders and childhood autism. *JAMA, 309*(16):1696–1703. doi:10.1001/jama.2013.2270.

Christian, T. M. (2017). An appearance of the collective unconscious in a military mental health clinic. *Psychological Perspectives, 60*(2), 162–169.

Christiansen, J., Larsen, F. B., & Lasgaard, M. (2016). Do stress, health behavior, and sleep mediate the association between loneliness and adverse health conditions among older people? *Social Science & Medicine, 15,* 280–286. doi:10.1016/j.socscimed.2016.01.020

Christopherson, E. R., & VanScoyoc, S. M. (2013). *Treatments that work with children: Empirically supported strategies for managing childhood problems* (2nd ed.). Washington, DC: American Psychological Association.

Chu, J., & Leino, A. (2017). Advancement in the maturing science of cultural adaptations of evidence-based interventions. *Journal of Consulting and Clinical Psychology, 85*(1), 45–57.

Chuang, Y., & Wu, P. (2017). Kin altruism: Testing the predictions of evolutionary theories in Taiwan. *Evolutionary Behavioral Sciences, in press.* doi:10.1037/ebs0000094

Chun, S., Harris, A., Carrion, M., Rojas, E., Stark, S., Lejuez, C., et al. (2017). A psychometric investigation of gender differences and common processes across borderline and antisocial personality disorders. *Journal of Abnormal Psychology, 126*(1), 76–88.

Chung, J., Schriber, R. A., & Robins, R. W. (2016). Positive illusions in the academic context: A longitudinal study of academic self-enhancement in college. *Personality and Social Psychology Bulletin*, *42*(10), 1384–1401. doi:10.1177/0146167216662866

Cialdini, R. (2016). *Pre-suasion: A revolutionary way to influence and persuade.* New York: Simon & Schuster.

Cialdini, R. B. (1991). Altruism or egoism? That is (still) the question. *Psychological Inquiry, 2*(2), 124–126.

Cialdini, R. B. (1993). *Influence: Science and practice.* New York: HarperCollins.

Cialdini, R. B., Vincent, J. E., Lewis, S. K., Catalan, J., Wheeler, D., & Darby, B. L. (1975). Reciprocal concessions procedure for inducing compliance: The door-in-the-face technique. *Journal of Personality and Social Psychology, 31*(2), 206–215.

Ciao, A. C., Accurso, E. C., Fitzsimmons-Craft, E. E., Lock, J., & Le Grange, D. (2015). Family functioning in two treatments for adolescent anorexia nervosa. *International Journal of Eating Disorders, 48*(1), 81–90.

Ciardelli, L. E., Weiss, A., Powell, D. M., & Reiss, D. (2017). Personality dimensions of the captive California sea lion (Zalophus californianus). *Journal Of Comparative Psychology, 131*(1), 50–58. doi:10.1037/com0000054

Ciarrochi, J., Morin, A. S., Sahdra, B. K., Litalien, D., & Parker, P. D. (2017). A longitudinal person-centered perspective on youth social support: Relations with psychological wellbeing. *Developmental Psychology, 53*(6), 1154–1169. doi:10.1037/dev0000315

Cioffi, C.E., Levitsky, D.A., Pacanowski, C.R., & Bertz, F. (2015). A nudge in a healthy direction. The effect of nutrition labels on food purchasing behaviors in university dining facilities. *Appetite, 92,* 7–14. DOI: 10.1016/j.appet.2015.04.053

Cioffi, M. C., Banissy, M. J., & Moore, J. W. (2016). 'Am I moving?' An illusion of agency and ownership in mirror-touch synaesthesia. *Cognition, 146,* 426–430. doi:10.1016/j.cognition.2015.10.020

Cirstea, C.M., Choi, I., Lee, P., Peng, H., Kaufman, C.L., & Frey, S.H. (2017). Magnetic resonance spectroscopy of current hand amputees reveals evidence for neuronal-level changes in former sensorimotor cortex. *Journal of Neurophysiology, 117,* 1821–1830. doi: 10.1152/jn.00329.2016

Clark, A. J. (2016). Empathy and Alfred Adler: An integral perspective. *The Journal of Individual Psychology, 72*(4), 237–253. doi:10.1353/jip.2016.0020

Clark, J. L., & Green, M. C. (2017). Self-fulfilling prophecies: Perceived reality of online interaction drives expected outcomes of online communication. *Personality and Individual Differences,* in press. doi:10.1016/j.paid.2017.08.031

Clark, M. L., Barbaro, J., & Dissanayake, C. (2017). Continuity and change in cognition and autism severity from toddlerhood to school age. *Journal of Autism and Developmental Disorders, 47*(2), 328–339.

Clark, M. S., & Chrisman, K. (1994). Resource allocation in intimate relationships: Trying to make sense of a confusing literature. In M. J. Lerner & G. Mikula (Eds.), *Entitlement and the affectional bond: Justice in close relationships* (pp. 65–88). New York: Plenum.

Clark, R. D., & Hatfield, E. (1989). Gender differences in receptivity to sexual offers. *Journal of Psychology and Human Sexuality, 2*(1), 39–55.

Clarke, N., Mun, E. Y., Kelly, S., White, H. R., & Lynch, K. (2013). Treatment outcomes of a combined cognitive behavior therapy and pharmacotherapy for a sample of women with and without substance abuse histories on an acute psychiatric unit: Do therapeutic alliance and motivation matter? *American Journal of Addictions, 22*(6), 566–573.

Clarke, S. E., Longtin, A., & Maler, L. (2014). A neural code for looming and receding motion is distributed over a population of electrosensory ON and OFF contrast cells. *Journal of Neuroscience, 34*(16), 5582–5594.

Clarkin, J. F. (2012). An integrated approach to psychotherapy techniques for patients with personality disorder. *Journal of Personality Disorders, 26*(1), 43–62.

Clemens, N. A. (2010). Evidence base for psychotherapy: Two perspectives. *Journal of Psychiatric Practice, 16*(3), 183–186.

Cleveland, J. N., Barnes-Farrell, J. L., & Ratz, J. M. (1997). Accommodation in the workplace. *Human Resource Management Review, 7*(1), 77–107.

Clifford, S. M., & Dissanayake, C. (2008). The early development of joint attention in infants with autistic disorder using home video observations and parental interview. *Journal of autism and developmental disorders, 38*(5), 791–805.

Clore, G. L., & Palmer, J. (2009). Affective guidance of intelligent agents: How emotion controls cognition. *Cognitive Systems Research, 10*(1), 21–30.

Cobb, S., & Battin, B. (2004). Second-impact syndrome. *Journal of School Nursing, 20*(5), 262–267.

Cobianchi, S., de Cruz, J., & Navarro, X. (2014). Assessment of sensory thresholds and nociceptive fiber growth after sciatic nerve injury reveals the differential contribution of collateral reinnervation and nerve regeneration to neuropathic pain. *Experimental Neurology, 255,* 1–11.

Coburn, A., Vartanian, O., & Chatterjee, A. (2017). Buildings, Beauty, and the Brain: A Neuroscience of Architectural Experience. *Journal of Cognitive Neuroscience, 29,* 1521–1531.

Cohen, D. (2001). Cultural variation: Considerations and implications. *Psychological Bulletin, 127*(4), 451–471.

Cohen, D., Kim, E., & Hudson, N. W. (2017). Religion, repulsion, and reaction formation: Transforming repellent attractions and repulsions. *Journal of Personality and Social Psychology,* in press. doi:10.1037/pspp0000151

Cohen, D., Nisbett, R. E., Bowdle, B. F., & Schwarz, N. (1996). Insult, aggression, and the southern culture of honor: An "experimental ethnography." *Journal of Personality and Social Psychology, 70*(5), 945–960.

Cohen, S., & Lemay, E. (2007). Why would social networks be linked to affect and health practices? *Health Psychology, 26*(4), 410–417.

Cohen, S., Doyle, W. J., Alper, C. M., Janicki-Deverts, D., & Turner, R. B. (2009). Sleep habits and susceptibility to the common cold. *Archives of Internal Medicine, 169*(1), 62–67.

Cohen, S., Janicki-Deverts, D., Doyle, W. J., Miller, G. E., Frank, E., Rabin, B. S., & Turner, R. B. (2012). Chronic stress, glucocorticoid receptor resistance, inflammation, and disease risk. *Proceedings of the National Academy of Sciences USA, 109*(16), 5995–5999.

Cohen-Mansfield, J., & Perach, R. (2015). Interventions for alleviating loneliness among older adults: A critical review. *American Journal of Health Promotion, 29*(3), e109–e125.

Coifman, K. G., Bonanno, G. A., Ray, R. D., & Gross, J. J. (2007). Does repressing coping promote resilience? Affective-autonomic response discrepancy during bereavement. *Journal of Personality and Social Psychology, 92*(4), 745–758.

Colapinto, J. (2000). *As nature made him.* New York: HarperAcademic.

Cole, C. B. (2016). *Deductive reasoning exercises for attention and executive functions: Real-life problem solving.* San Diego, CA: Plural Publishing.

Cole, P. M., Bendezú, J. J., Ram, N., & Chow, S. (2017). Dynamical systems modeling of early childhood self-regulation. *Emotion, 17*(4), 684–699. doi:10.1037/emo0000268

Coles, B. A., & West, M. (2016). Weaving the internet together: Imagined communities in newspaper comment threads. *Computers In Human Behavior, 60,* 44–53. doi:10.1016/j.chb.2016.02.049

Collins, B., Breithaupt, L., McDowell, J. E., Miller, L. S., Thompson, J., & Fischer, S. (2017). The impact of acute stress on the neural processing of food cues in bulimia nervosa: Replication in two samples. *Journal of Abnormal Psychology, 126*(5), 540–551.

Colom, R., Martínez, K., Burgaleta, M., Román, F. J., García-García, D., Gunter, J. L., et al. (2016). Gray matter volumetric changes with a challenging adaptive cognitive training program based on the dual n-back task. *Personality and Individual Differences, 98,* 127–132. doi:10.1016/j.paid.2016.03.087

Colomer, C., Berenguer, C., Roselló, B., Baixauli, I., & Miranda, A. (2017). The impact of inattention, hyperactivity/impulsivity symptoms, and executive functions on learning behaviors of children with ADHD. *Frontiers in Psychology, 8.*

Commonwealth of Massachusetts v. Porter 31285–330 (1993, Massachusetts).

Compton, J., & Pfau, M. (2004). Use of inoculation to foster resistance to credit card marketing targeting college students. *Journal of Applied Communication Research, 32*(4), 343–364.

Compton, J., & Pfau, M. (2008). Inoculating against pro-plagiarism justifications: Rational and affective strategies. *Journal of Applied Communication Research, 36*(1), 98–119.

Comstock, G. (2012). The use of television and other film-related media. In D. G. Singer & J. L. Singer (Eds.), *Handbook of children and the media* (2nd ed.). Thousand Oaks, CA: Sage.

Conde, L. C., Amin, N., Hottenga, J. J., Gizer, I., Trull, T., van Duijn, C., et al. (2017). The first genome-wide association meta-analysis of borderline personality disorder features. *European Neuropsychopharmacology, 27,* S504–S505.

Conley, T. D. (2011). Perceived proposer personality characteristics and gender differences in acceptance of casual sex offers. *Journal of Personality and Social Psychology, 100*(2), 309–329.

Conley, T. D., Moors, A. C., Matsick, J. L., Ziegler, A., & Valentine, B. A. (2011). Women, men and the bedroom: Methodological and conceptual insights that narrow, reframe, and eliminate gender differences in sexuality. *Current Directions in Psychological Science, 20*(5), 296–300.

Connellan, J., Baron-Cohen, S., Wheelwright, S., Batki, A., & Ahluwalia, J. (2000). Sex differences in human neonatal social perception. *Infant Behavior & Development, 23*(1), 113–118.

Constantino, M. J., Westra, H. A., Antony, M. M., & Coyne, A. E. (2017). Specific and common processes as mediators of the long-term effects of cognitive-behavioral therapy integrated with motivational interviewing for generalized anxiety disorder. *Psychotherapy Research.* in press.

Conti, D., Di Nuovo, S., Cangelosi, A., & Di Nuovo, A. (2016). Lateral specialization in unilateral spatial neglect: A cognitive robotics model. *Cognitive Processing, 17*(3), 321–328. doi:10.1007/s10339-016-0761-x

Converse, P. D., Thackray, M., Piccone, K., Sudduth, M. M., Tocci, M. C., & Miloslavic, S. A. (2016). Integrating self-control with physical attractiveness and cognitive ability to examine pathways to career success. *Journal of Occupational and Organizational Psychology, 89*(1), 73–91. doi:10.1111/joop.12107

Conway, M., & Rubin, D. (1993). The structure of autobiographical memory. In A. F. Collins, S. E. Gathercole, M. A. Conway, & P. E. Morris (Eds.), *Theories of memory.* Hillsdale, NJ: Erlbaum.

Cook, A., Spinazzola, J., Ford, J., Lanktree, C., Blaustein, M., Cloitre, M., et al. (2017). Complex trauma in children and adolescents. *Psychiatric Annals, 35*(5), 390–398.

Coon, H., & others. (2013). Genetic risk factors in two Utah pedigrees at high risk for suicide. *Translational Psychiatry, 3,* e325.

Cooper, A. A., Kline, A. C., Graham, B., Bedard-Gilligan, M., Mello, P. G., Feeny, N. C., & Zoellner, L. A. (2017).

Homework "dose," type, and helpfulness as predictors of clinical outcomes in prolonged exposure for PTSD. *Behavior Therapy, 48*(2), 182–194.

Cooper, C. R., Gonzalez, E., & Wilson, A. R. (2015). Identities, cultures, and schooling: How students navigate racial-ethnic, indigenous, immigrant, social class, and gender identities on their pathways through school. In K. C. McLean & M. Syed (Eds.), *The Oxford handbook of identity development.* New York: Oxford University Press.

Cooper, E. A., Garlick, J., Featherstone, E., Voon, V., Singer, T., Critchley, H. D., & Harrison, N. A. (2014). You turn me cold: Evidence for temperature contagion. *PLoS One, 9*(12), e116126.

Cooper, R. M., & Zubek, J. P. (1958). Effects of enriched and restricted early environments on the learning ability of bright and dull rats. *Canadian Journal of Psychology, 12*(3), 159–164.

Cooper, S., & Bidaisee, S. (2017). Evaluation of risks and factors linked to precocious puberty. *Journal of Translational Diagnostic Technology, 2*(1), 27–29.

Copeland, C. S., Wall, T. M., Sims, R. E., Neale, S. A., Nisenbaum, E., Parri, H. R., & Salt, T. E. (2017). Astrocytes modulate thalamic sensory processing via mGlu2 receptor activation. *Neuropharmacology, 121*, 100–110. doi:10.1016/j.neuropharm.2017.04.019

Copen, C. E., Chandra, A., & Martinez, G. (2012). Prevalence and timing of oral sex with opposite-sex partners among females and males aged 15–24 years: United States, 2007–2010. *National Health Statistics Reports,* No. 56. www.cdc.gov/nchs/data/nhsr/nhsr056.pdf (accessed December 21, 2014).

Corey, G. (2016). *Theory & practice of group counseling* (9th ed.). Boston: Cengage.

Cornblatt, B. A., & others. (2012). Risk factors for psychosis: Impaired social and role functioning. *Schizophrenia Bulletin, 38*(6), 1247–1257.

Cornelius, T., & Kershaw, T. (2017). Perception of partner sexual history: Effects on safe-sex intentions. *Health Psychology, 36*(7), 704–712. doi:10.1037/hea0000474

Correll, J., Wittenbrink, B., Crawford, M. T., & Sadler, M. S. (2015). Stereotypic vision: How stereotypes disambiguate visual stimuli. *Journal of Personality and Social Psychology, 108*(2), 219–233.

Correll, J., Wittenbrink, B., Park, B., Judd, C. M., & Goyle, A. (2011). Dangerous enough: Moderating racial bias with contextual threat cues. *Journal of Experimental Social Psychology, 47*(1), 184–189.

Corrigan, P. W., & Penn, D. L. (2015). Lessons from social psychology on discrediting psychiatric stigma. *Stigma And Health, 1*(S), 2–17. doi:10.1037/2376-6972.1.S.2

Cosci, F. (2017). Withdrawal symptoms after discontinuation of a noradrenergic and specific serotonergic antidepressant: A case report and review of the literature. *Personalized Medicine in Psychiatry, 1*, 81–84.

Cosentino, A.C., & Solano, A.C. (2017). The high five: Associations of the five positive factors with the big five and well-being. *Frontiers in Physiology, 8*, art. no. 1250.

Cosmides, L. (2011). Evolutionary psychology. *Annual Review of Psychology* (vol. 62). Palo Alto, CA: Annual Reviews.

Costa, P. J., & McCrae, R. R. (2006). Age changes in personality and their origins: Comment on Roberts, Walton, and Viechtbauer (2006). *Psychological Bulletin, 132*(1), 26–28. doi:10.1037/0033-2909.132.1.26

Costa, P. T., & McCrae, R. R. (2010). *NEO Inventories, professional manual.* Lutz, FL: Psychological Assessment Resources.

Costa, P. T., & McCrae, R. R. (2013). A theoretical context for adult temperament. In T. D. Wachs, R. R. McCrae, & G. A. Kohnstamm (Eds.), *Temperament in context.* New York: Psychology Press.

Costa, P. T., Weiss, A., Duberstein, P. R., Friedman, B., & Siegler, I. C. (2014). Personality facets and all-cause mortality among Medicare patients aged 66 to 102 years:

A follow-on study of Weiss and Costa (2005). *Psychosomatic Medicine, 76*(5), 370–378.

Costa, S. P., & Neves, P. (2017). Forgiving is good for health and performance: How forgiveness helps individuals cope with the psychological contract breach. *Journal of Vocational Behavior, 100,* 124–136. doi:10.1016/j.jvb.2017.03.005

Costello, K., & Hodson, G. (2014). Explaining dehumanization among children: The interspecies model of prejudice. *British Journal of Social Psychology, 53*(1), 175–197. doi:10.1111/bjso.12016

Cotter, D., Mackay, D., Chana, G., Beasley, C., Landau, S., & Everall, I. P. (2002). Reduced neuronal size and glial density in area 9 of the dorsolateral prefrontal cortex in subjects with major depressive disorder. *Cerebral Cortex, 12*(4), 386–394.

Coubart, A., Izard, V., Spelke, E. S., Marie, J., & Streri, A. (2014). Dissociation between small and larger numerosities in newborn infants. *Developmental Science, 17*(1), 11–22.

Courtet, P., & others. (2004). Serotonin transporter gene may be involved in short-term risk of subsequent suicide attempts. *Biological Psychiatry, 55*(1), 46–51.

Courtin, E., & Knapp, M. (2017). Social isolation, loneliness and health in old age: A scoping review. *Health & Social Care In The Community, 25*(3), 799–812. doi:10.1111/hsc.12311

Coutaux, A. (2017). Non-pharmacological treatments for pain relief: TENS and acupuncture. *Joint Bone Spine.* in press.

Cowan, N. (2008). What are the differences between long-term, short-term, and working memory? In W. S. Sossin, L. C. Lacaille, V. F. Castellucci, & S. Belleville (Eds.), *Essence of memory: Progress in brain research* (vol. 169, pp. 323–338). New York: Elsevier.

Cowan, N. (2017) Working Memory: The Information You Are Now Thinking of. In J.T. Wixted (Ed.), *Cognitive Psychology of Memory, Vol. 2* (pp. 147–161.) Oxford: Academic Press

Cowan, N., Li, D., Moffitt, A., Becker, T. M., Martin, E. A., Saults, J. S., & Christ, S. E. (2011a). A neural region of abstract working memory. *Journal of Cognitive Neuroscience, 23*(10), 2852–2863.

Cowan, N., Morey, C. C., Aubuchon, A. M., Zwilling, C. E., Gilchrist, A. L., & Saults, J. S. (2011b). New insights into an old problem: Distinguishing storage from processing in the development of working memory. In P. Barrouillet & V. Gaillard (Eds.), *Cognitive development and working memory: A dialogue between neo-Piagetian theories and cognitive approaches* (pp. 137–150). Hove, UK: Psychology Press.

Cowan, N., Rouder, J. N., Blume, C. L., & Saults, J. S. (2012). Models of verbal working memory capacity: What does it take to make them work? *Psychological Review, 119*(3), 480–499.

Cowan, R. L., Roberts, D. M., & Joers, J. M. (2008). Neuroimaging in human MDMA (Ecstasy) users. *Annals of the New York Academy of Sciences, 1139,* 291–298.

Cowell, J. M., & Decety, J. (2015). Precursors to morality in development as a complex interplay between neural, socioenvironmental, and behavioral facets. *Proceedings of the National Academy of Sciences of the United States of America, 112,* 12657–12662. doi:10.1073/pnas.1508832112

Cox, R. E., & Bryant, R. A. (2008). Advances in hypnosis research: Methods, designs, and contributions of intrinsic and instrumental hypnosis. In M. R. Nash & A. J. Barnier (Eds.), *The Oxford handbook of hypnosis: Research theory and practice* (pp. 311–336). New York: Oxford University Press.

Coyne, J. C., & Tennen, H. (2010). Positive psychology in cancer care: Bad science, exaggerated claims, and unproven medicine. *Annals of Behavioral Medicine, 39*(1), 16–26.

Coyne, J. C., Tennen, H., & Ranchor, A. V. (2010). Positive psychology and cancer care: A story line resistant to evidence. *Annals of Behavioral Medicine, 39*(1), 35–42.

Craik, F. I. M., & Lockhart, R. S. (1972). Levels of processing: A framework for memory research. *Journal of Verbal Learning and Verbal Behavior, 11*(6), 671–684.

Craik, F. I. M., & Tulving, E. (1975). Depth of processing and retention of words in episodic memory. *Journal of Experimental Psychology, 104*(3), 268–294.

Cramer, P. (2008a). Longitudinal study of defense mechanisms: Late childhood to late adolescence. *Journal of Personality, 75*(1), 1–24.

Cramer, P. (2015). Defense mechanisms: 40 years of empirical research. *Journal of Personality Assessment, 97*(2), 114–122. doi:10.1080/00223891.2014.947997

Cramer, P., & Jones, C. J. (2007). Defense mechanisms predict differential lifespan change in self-control and self-acceptance. *Journal of Research in Personality, 41*(4), 841–855.

Crane, L., Chester, J. W., Goddard, L., Henry, L. A., & Hill, E. (2016). Experiences of autism diagnosis: A survey of over 1000 parents in the United Kingdom. *Autism, 20*(2), 153–162.

Crane, R. S., Brewer, J., Feldman, C., Kabat-Zinn, J., Santorelli, S., Williams, J. M. G., & Kuyken, W. (2017). What defines mindfulness-based programs? The warp and the weft. *Psychological Medicine, 47*(6), 990–999.

Cranney, S. (2017). Does asexuality meet the stability criterion for a sexual orientation? *Archives Of Sexual Behavior, 46*(3), 637–638. doi:10.1007/s10508-016-0887-z

Cratsley, K. (2016). Revisiting Freud and Kohut on narcissism. *Theory & Psychology, 26*(3), 333–359. doi:10.1177/0959354316638181

Crego, C., & Widiger, T. A. (2014). Psychopathy and the DSM. *Journal of Personality.* doi:10.1111/jopy.12115

Cressey, D. (2011, June 14). Psychopharmacology in crisis: Researchers warn of "withdrawal of hope" as funding shrivels. *Nature.* www.nature.com/news/2011/110614/full/news.2011.367.html (accessed January 9, 2015)

Crocker, J., Canevello, A., & Brown, A. A. (2017). Social motivation: Costs and benefits of selfishness and otherishness. *Annual Review of Psychology, 68,* 299–325. doi:10.1146/annurev-psych-010416-044145

Crocker, J., Major, B., & Steele, C. (1998). Social stigma. In D. T. Gilbert, S. T. Fiske, & G. Lindzey (Eds.), *The handbook of social psychology* (4th ed., vol. 2, pp. 504–553). New York: McGraw-Hill.

Crockett, M. J. (2009). The neurochemistry of fairness: Clarifying the link between serotonin and prosocial behavior. *Annals of New York Academy of Science, 1167,* 76–86.

Croft, W. (2012). *Verbs: Aspect and causal structure.* New York: Oxford University Press.

Crompton, E. (September 26, 2017). Under pressure from 9 to 5. *The New York Times,* D4.

Cronbach, L. J. (1957). The two disciplines of scientific psychology. *American Psychologist, 12*(11), 671–684.

Crowley, K., Pickle, J., Dale, R., & Fattal, O. (2008). A critical examination of bifrontal electroconvulsive therapy: Clinical efficacy, cognitive side effects, and directions for future research. *Journal of Electroconvulsive Therapy, 24*(4), 268–271.

Crowley, S. J., & Carskadon, M. A. (2010). Modifications to weekend recovery sleep delay circadian phase in older adolescents. *Chronobiology International, 27*(7), 1469–1492.

Csikszentmihalyi, M. (1990). *Flow: The psychology of optimal experience.* New York: Harper Perennial.

Csillag, C., Nordentoft, M., Mizuno, M., Jones, P. B., Killackey, E., Taylor, M., ... & McDaid, D. (2016). Early intervention services in psychosis: from evidence to wide implementation. *Early Intervention in Psychiatry, 10*(6), 540–546.

Cuesto, G., Everaerts, C., León, L. G., & Acebes, A. (2017). Molecular bases of anorexia nervosa, bulimia nervosa and binge eating disorder: shedding light on the darkness. *Journal of Neurogenetics,* in press.

Cuijpers, P., Turner, E. H., Mohr, D. C., Hofmann, S. G., Andersson, G., Berking, M., & Coyne, J. (2014). Comparison of psychotherapies for adult depression to pill placebo control groups: A meta-analysis. *Psychological Medicine, 44*(4), 685–695.

Cullen, K. (2010, January 24). The untouchable mean girls. *Boston Globe.* www.boston.com/news/local/massachusetts/articles/2010/01/24/the_untouchable_mean_girls/ (accessed February 13, 2015)

Cummings, J. R., Ji, X., Allen, L., Lally, C., & Druss, B. G. (2017). Racial and ethnic differences in ADHD treatment quality among Medicaid-enrolled youth. *Pediatrics, 139*(6), e20162444.

Cummings, M. (2016). *Human heredity* (11th ed.). Boston: Cengage.

Cunningham, R. L., & McGinnis, M. Y. (2007). Factors influencing aggression toward females by male rats exposed to anabolic androgenic steroids during puberty. *Hormones and Behavior, 51*(1), 135–141.

Curran, G., & Ravindran, A. (2014). Lithium for bipolar disorder: A review of the recent literature. *Expert Review of Neurotherapeutics, 14*(9), 1079–1098.

Curtin, S. C., Warner, M., & Hedegaard, H. (2016). *Increase in suicide in the United States, 1999-2014. NCHS data brief, no 241.* Hyattsville, MD: National Center for Health Statistics.

Curtiss, J., Andrews, L., Davis, M., Smits, J., & Hofmann, S. G. (2017). A meta-analysis of pharmacotherapy for social anxiety disorder: an examination of efficacy, moderators, and mediators. *Expert Opinion on Pharmacotherapy, 18*(3), 243–251.

Curtiss, S. (2014). The case of Chelsea: The effects of late age at exposure to language on language performance and evidence for the modularity of language and mind. In C. T. Schutze & L. Stockall (Eds.), Connections: Papers by and for Sarah Van Wagenen. *UCLA Working Papers in Linguistics, 18,* 115–146.

Cushing, D., Gazzaley, A., & Morsella, E. (2017). Externally controlled involuntary cognitions and their relations with other representations in consciousness. *Consciousness and Cognition, 55,* 1–10.

Cutter, M. G., Drieghe, D., & Liversedge, S. P. (2017). Is orthographic information from multiple parafoveal words processed in parallel: An eye-tracking study. *Journal of Experimental Psychology: Human Perception and Performance, 43*(8), 1550–1567. doi:10.1037/xhp0000408

Cuzzolaro, M. (2014). Eating and weight disorders: Studies on anorexia, bulimia, and obesity turn 19. *Eating and Weight Disorders, 19*(1), 1–2.

Cwik, A. J. (2017). What is a Jungian analyst dreaming when myth comes to mind? Thirdness as an aspect of the anima media natura. *The Journal Of Analytical Psychology, 62*(1), 107–129. doi:10.1111/1468-5922.12284

D

D'Arrigo-Patrick, J., Hoff, C., Knudson-Martin, C., & Tuttle, A. (2017). Navigating critical theory and postmodernism: Social justice and therapist power in family therapy. *Family Process, 56*(3), 574–588.

da Cunha-Bang, S., Hjordt, L. V., Perfalk, E., Beliveau, V., Bock, C., Lehel, S., et al. (2017). Serotonin 1B receptor binding is associated with trait anger and level of psychopathy in violent offenders. *Biological Psychiatry, 82*(4), 267–274. doi:10.1016/j.biopsych.2016.02.030

da Silva, K. K. M., De Martino, M. M. F., Cruz, G. K. P., Junior, M. A. F., de Carvalho Lira, A. L. B., Vitor, A. F., et al. (2017). Sleep disorders related to circadian rhythm in people with visual impairment: Integrative review. *International Archives of Medicine, 9.* In press. http://dx.doi.org/10.3823/2238

da Silva, W. R., Lisboa, T., Ferrari, E. P., de Freitas, K. T. D., & Cardoso, F. L. (2017). Opportunities for motor stimulation in the home environment of children. *Journal of Human Growth and Development, 27*(1), 84–90.

Dai, D., & others. (2014). Meta-analyses of 10 polymorphisms associated with the risk of schizophrenia. *Biomedical Reports, 2*(5), 729–736.

Daley, D., & DuPaul, G. (2016). Nonpharmacological interventions for preschool children with attention-deficit/hyperactivity disorder. *Journal of the American Academy of Child & Adolescent Psychiatry, 55*(10), S329–S330.

Damian, R. I., & Roberts, B. W. (2015a). The associations of birth order with personality and intelligence in a representative sample of U.S. high school students. *Journal of Research In Personality, 58,* 96–105. doi:10.1016/j.jrp.2015.05.005

Damian, R. I., & Roberts, B. W. (2015b). Settling the debate on birth order and personality. *PNAS: Proceedings of the National Academy of Sciences of the United States of America, 112,* 14119–14120, doi: 10.1073/pnas.1519064112

Damsa, C., Kosel, M., & Moussally, J. (2009). Current status of brain imaging in anxiety disorders. *Current Opinion in Psychiatry, 22*(1), 96–110.

Dane, E. (2017). Where is my mind? Theorizing mind wandering and its performance-related consequences in organizations. *Academy of Management Review,* in press.

Danner, D. D., Snowdon, D. A., & Friesen, W. V. (2001). Positive emotions in early life and longevity: Findings from the Nun Study. *Journal of Personality and Social Psychology, 80*(5), 804–813.

Darcy, E. (2012). Gender issues in child and adolescent eating disorders. In J. Lock (Ed.), *The Oxford handbook of child and adolescent eating disorders: Developmental perspectives.* New York: Oxford University Press.

Darley, J. M., & Latané, B. (1968). Bystander intervention in emergencies: Diffusion of responsibility. *Journal of Personality and Social Psychology, 8*(4), 377–383.

Darling, S., Allen, R. J., & Havelka, J. (2017). Visuospatial bootstrapping: when visuospatial and verbal memory work together. *Current Directions in Psychological Science, 26*(1), 3–9.

Darwin, C. (1965). *The expression of emotion in man and animals.* Chicago: University of Chicago Press. (original work published in 1872).

Dating Sites Reviews. (2017). Online dating statistics & facts. *Dating Sites Reviews.* https://www.datingsitesreviews.com/staticpages/index.php?page=Online-Dating-Industry-Facts-Statistics

Datta Gupta, N., Etcoff, N. L., & Jaeger, M. M. (2016). Beauty in mind: The effects of physical attractiveness on psychological well-being and distress. *Journal of Happiness Studies, 17*(3), 1313–1325. doi:10.1007/s10902-015-9644-6

Dauvilliers, Y., Roth, T., Guinta, D., Alvarez-Horine, S., Dynin, E., & Black, J. (2018). Effect of sodium oxybate, modafinil, and their combination on disrupted nighttime sleep in narcolepsy. *Sleep Medicine,* in press.

Davidson, R. J. (2000). Affective style, psychopathology, and resilience: Brain mechanisms and plasticity. *American Psychologist, 55*(11), 196–214.

Davidson, R. J., & Begley, S. (2012). *The emotional life of your brain.* New York: Hudson Street.

Davidson, R. J., & others. (2003). Alterations in brain and immune function produced by mindfulness meditation. *Psychosomatic Medicine, 65*(4), 564–570.

Davidson, R. J., Pizzagalli, D., Nietschke, J. B., & Kalin, N. H. (2003). Parsing the subcomponents of emotion and disorder of emotion: Perspectives from affective neuroscience. In R. J. Davidson, K. R. Scherer, & H. H. Goldsmith (Eds.), *Handbook of affective sciences* (pp. 8–24). New York: Oxford University Press.

Davies, G., & others. (2011). Genome-wide association studies establish that human intelligence is highly heritable and polygenic. *Molecular Psychiatry, 16,* 996–1005.

Davies, P. T., & Cicchetti, D. (2014). How and why does the 5-HTTLPR gene moderate associations between maternal unresponsiveness and children's disruptive problems? *Child Development, 85*(2), 484–500.

Davies, S. J., Nash, J., & Nutt, D. J. (2017). Management of panic disorder in primary care. *Prescriber, 28*(1), 19–26.

Davis, C. M., & Riley, A. L. (2010). Conditioned taste aversion learning: Implications for animal models of drug abuse. *Annals of the New York Academy of Sciences, 1187,* 247–275.

Davis, K. C., & Raizen, D. M. (2017). A mechanism for sickness sleep: lessons from invertebrates. *The Journal of Physiology.* doi:10.1113/JP273009

Davis, M. (2015). Empathy and prosocial behavior. In D. A. Schroeder & W. G. Graziano (Eds.), *The Oxford handbook of prosocial behavior.* New York: Oxford University Press.

Davis, M. A., Anthony, D. L., & Pauls, S. D. (2015). Seeking and receiving social support on Facebook for surgery. *Social Science & Medicine, 131,* 40–47.

Davis, R. L., & Zhong, Y. (2017). The biology of forgetting—a perspective. *Neuron, 95*(3), 490–503.

Davis, S. R. (2013). Androgen therapy in women, beyond libido. *Climacteric, 16,* Suppl. 1, 18–24.

Davydenko, M., & Peetz, J. (2017). Time grows on trees: The effect of nature settings on time perception. *Journal of Environmental Psychology, 54,* 20–26.

de Almeida Silva, V., Louzã, M. R., da Silva, M. A., & Nakano, E. Y. (2016). Ego defense mechanisms and types of object relations in adults with ADHD. *Journal of Attention Disorders, 20*(11), 979–987. doi:10.1177/1087054712459559

De Backer, M., Boen, F., De Cuyper, B., Høigaard, R., & Broek, G. V. (2015). A team fares well with a fair coach: Predictors of social loafing in interactive female sport teams. *Scandinavian Journal of Medicine & Science in Sports, 25*(6), 897–908. doi:10.1111/sms.12303

De Cort, K., Griez, E., Büchler, M., & Schruers, K. (2012). The role of "interoceptive" fear conditioning in the development of panic disorder. *Behavior Therapy, 43*(1), 203–215.

De Dreu, C. W. (2014). Oxytocinergic circuitry motivates group loyalty. In M. Mikulincer & P. R. Shaver (Eds.), *Mechanisms of social connection: From brain to group* (pp. 391–407). Washington, DC: American Psychological Association. doi:10.1037/14250-022

de Frias, C. M., & Dixon, R. A. (2014). Lifestyle engagement affects cognitive status differences and trajectories on executive functions in older adults. *Archives of Clinical Neuropsychology, 29*(1), 16–25.

de Guzman, N. S., & Nishina, A. (2014). A longitudinal study of body dissatisfaction and pubertal timing in an ethnically diverse adolescent sample. *Body Image, 11*(1), 68–71.

De Picker, L. J., Morrens, M., Chance, S. A., & Boche, D. (2017). Microglia and brain plasticity in acute psychosis and schizophrenia illness course: A meta-review. *Frontiers in Psychiatry, 8,* 238.

De Raad, B., & others. (2010). Only three factors of personality description are fully replicable across languages: A comparison of 14 trait taxonomies. *Journal of Personality and Social Psychology, 98*(1), 160–173.

De Roover, K., Vermunt, J.K., Timmerman, M.E., Ceulemans, E. (2017). Mixture simultaneous factor analysis for capturing differences in latent variables between higher level units of multilevel data. *Structural Equation Modeling, 24*(4), 506–523.

de Souto Barreto, P., Andrieu, S., Rolland, Y., Vellas, B., & DSA MAPT Study Group. (2018). Physical activity domains and cognitive function over three years in older adults with subjective memory complaints: Secondary analysis from the MAPT trial. *Journal of Science and Medicine in Sport, 21*(1), 52–57.

De Venter, M., Van Den Eede, F., Pattyn, T., Wouters, K., Veltman, D. J., Penninx, B. W., & Sabbe, B. G. (2017). Impact of childhood trauma on course of panic disorder: Contribution of clinical and personality characteristics. *Acta Psychiatrica Scandinavica, 135*(6), 554–563.

de Vondervoort, J. W., & Hamlin, J. K. (2016). Evidence for intuitive morality: Preverbal infants make sociomoral evaluations. *Child Development Perspectives, 10,* 143–148. https://doi.org/10.1111/cdep.12175.

De Vos, J. (2010). From Milgram to Zimbardo: The double birth of postwar psychology/psychologization. *History of the Human Sciences, 23*(5), 156–175.

de Vries, J., Byrne, M., & Kehoe, E. (2015). Cognitive dissonance induction in everyday life: An fMRI study. *Social Neuroscience, 10*(3), 268–281. doi:10.1080/1747091 9.2014.990990

DeAngelis, T. (2002, March). Binge-eating disorder: What's the best treatment? *Monitor on Psychology.* www. apa.org/monitor/mar02/binge.html (accessed January 5, 2015)

Deaux, K. (2001). Social identity. In J. Worell (Ed.), *Encyclopedia of gender and women.* San Diego: Academic.

Debiec, J., & LeDoux, J. E. (2006). Noradrenergic signaling in the amygdala contributes to the reconsolidation of fear memory: Treatment implications for PTSD. *Annals of the New York Academy of Science, 1071,* 521–524.

Decety, J., Meidenbauer, K. L., & Cowell, J. M. (2017). The development of cognitive empathy and concern in preschool children: A behavioral neuroscience investigation. *Developmental Science.* http://onlinelibrary.wiley.com/doi/10.1111/desc.12570/full

Deci, E. L. (2013). An interview with Dr. Edward L. Deci, codeveloper of self-determination theory. Interview by Paul Terry. *American Journal of Health Promotion, 27*(6), TAHP2-7.

Deci, E. L., & Ryan, R. M. (2000). The "what" and "why" of goal pursuits: Human needs and the self-determination of behavior. *Psychological Inquiry, 4*(11), 227–268.

Deci, E. L., & Ryan, R. M. (2012). Self-determination theory in health care and its relations to motivational interviewing: A few comments. *International Journal of Behavioral Nutrition and Physical Activity, 9,* 24.

Deci, E., & Ryan, R. (1994). Promoting self-determined education. *Scandinavian Journal of Educational Research, 38*(1), 3–14.

Deckert, J., Weber, H., Villmann, C., Lonsdorf, T. B., Richter, J., Andreatta, M., et al. (2017). GLRB allelic variation associated with agoraphobic cognitions, increased startle response and fear network activation: A potential neurogenetic pathway to panic disorder. *Molecular Psychiatry, 22,* 1431–1439.

Dehaene, S., & Changeux, J. P. (2011). Experimental and theoretical approaches to conscious processing. *Neuron, 70*(2), 200–207.

Dehaene, S., Lau, H., & Kouider, S. (2017). What is consciousness, and could machines have it? *Science, 358,* 486–492.

Dein, S., Cook, C. C., & Koenig, H. (2012). Religion, spirituality, and mental health: Current controversies and future directions. *Journal of Nervous and Mental Disease, 200*(10), 852–855.

Del Corso, J. J., & Rehfuss, M. C., & Galvin, K. (2011). Striving to adapt: Addressing Adler's work task in the 21st century. *Journal of Individual Psychology, 67*(2), 88–106.

DeLeon, I. G., Chase, J. A., Frank-Crawford, M. A., Carreau-Webster, A. B., Triggs, M. M., Bullock, C. E., & Jennett, H. K. (2014). Distributed and accumulated reinforcement arrangements: Evaluations of efficacy and preference. *Journal of Applied Behavior Analysis, 47*(2), 293–313.

Dell, P. F., & Eisenhower, J. W. (1990). Adolescent multiple personality disorder: A preliminary study of eleven cases. *Journal of the American Academy of Child & Adolescent Psychiatry, 29*(3), 359–366.

Dell'osso, B., & Lader, M. (2012). Do benzodiazepines still deserve a major role in the treatment of psychiatric disorders? A critical reappraisal. *European Psychiatry, 28*(1), 7–20.

Deloitte (2016). *Digital democracy survey, 10th edition.* Istanbul, Turkey: Author. https://www2.deloitte.com/tr/en/pages/technology-media-and-telecommunications/articles/digital-democracy-survey-generational-media-consumption-trends.html

Demiralay, C., Agorastos, A., Yassouridis, A., Jahn, H., Wiedemann, K., & Kellner, M. (2017). Copeptin–A potential endocrine surrogate marker of CCK-4-induced panic symptoms? *Psychoneuroendocrinology, 76,* 14–18.

Demiray, B., & Freund, A. M. (2014). Michael Jackson, Bin Laden, and I: Functions of positive and negative, public and private flashbulb memories. *Memory.* doi: 10.1080/09658211.2014.907428

Den Heijer, A. E., Groen, Y., Tucha, L., Fuermaier, A. B., Koerts, J., Lange, K. W., et al. (2017). Sweat it out? The effects of physical exercise on cognition and behavior in children and adults with ADHD: A systematic literature review. *Journal of Neural Transmission, 124*(1), 3–26.

Dennett, D. C. (2017). *Consciousness explained.* New York: Little, Brown.

Dennett, D. C. (2017). *From Bacteria to Bach and Back: The Evolution of Minds.* New York: W.W. Norton.

Denollet, J., & Conraads, V. M. (2011). Type D personality and vulnerability to adverse outcomes of heart disease. *Cleveland Clinic Journal of Medicine, 78,* Suppl. 1, S13–S19.

DePaoli, A. (2014). Leptin in common obesity and associated disorders of metabolism. *Journal of Endocrinology, 223*(1), T71–T81.

Depue, R. A., & Collins, P. F. (1999). Neurobiology of the structure of personality: Dopamine, facilitation of incentive motivation, and extraversion. *Behavioral and Brain Sciences, 22*(3), 491–569.

Depue, R. A., & Fu, Y. (2013). On the nature of extraversion: Variation in conditioned contextual activation of dopamine-facilitated affective, cognitive, and motor processes. *Frontiers in Human Neuroscience, 7,* 288.

Derntl, B., Habel, U., Robinson, S., Windischberger, C., Kryspin-Exner, I., Gur, R. C., & Moser, E. (2012). Culture but not gender modulates amygdala activation during explicit emotion recognition. *BMC Neuroscience, 13,* 54.

Devine, P. G., Forscher, P. S., Austin, A. J., & Cox, W. T. (2012). Long-term reduction in implicit race bias: A prejudice habit-breaking intervention. *Journal of Experimental Social Psychology, 48*(6), 1267–1278.

Devine, R. T., White, N., Ensor, R., & Hughes, C. (2016). Theory of mind in middle childhood: Longitudinal associations with executive function and social competence. *Developmental Psychology, 52*(5), 758–771

Devita, M., Montemurro, S., Zangrossi, A., Ramponi, S., Marvisi, M., Villani, D., ... & Mondini, S. (2017). Cognitive and motor reaction times in obstructive sleep apnea syndrome: a study based on computerized measures. *Brain and cognition, 117,* 26–32.

DeWall, C. N., Anderson, C. A., & Bushman, B. J. (2013). Aggression. In H. A. Tennen, J. M. Suls, & I. B. Weiner (Eds.), *Handbook of psychology* (2nd ed., vol. 5, pp. 449–466). New York: Wiley.

DeYoung, C. G. (2013). The neuromodulator of exploration: A unifying theory of the role of dopamine in personality. *Frontiers in Human Neuroscience, 7,* 762.

DeYoung, C. G. (2015). Cybernetic Big Five Theory. *Journal of Research in Personality, 56,* 33–58.

DeYoung, C. G. (2015). Openness/intellect: A dimension of personality reflecting cognitive exploration. In M. Mikulincer, P. R. Shaver, M. L. Cooper, & R. J. Larsen (Eds.), *APA Handbook of Personality and Social Psychology, Volume 4: Personality processes and individual differences* (pp. 369–399). Washington, DC: American Psychological Association. doi:10.1037/14343-017

DeYoung, C. G., & Clark, R. (2012). The gene in its natural habitat: The importance of gene–trait interactions. *Development And Psychopathology, 24*(4), 1307–1318. doi:10.1017/S0954579412000727

DeYoung, C. G., Hirsh, J. B., Shane, M. S., Papademetris, X., Rajeevan, N., & Gray, J. R. (2010). Testing predictions from personality neuroscience: Brain structure and the big five. *Psychological Science, 21*(6), 820–828.

Di Iorio, C. R., Carey, C. E., Michalski, L. J., Corral-Frias, N. S., Conley, E. D., Hariri, A. R., & Bogdan, R. (2017). Hypothalamic-pituitary-adrenal axis genetic variation and early stress moderates amygdala function. *Psychoneuroendocrinology, 80,* 170–178. doi:10.1016/j.psyneuen.2017.03.016

Di Narzo, A. F., & others. (2014). A unique gene expression signature associated with serotonin 2C receptor RNA editing in the prefrontal cortex and altered in suicide. *Human Molecular Genetics, 23*(18), 4801–4813.

Diamond, L. M. (2013a). Gender and same-sex sexuality. In D. T. Tolman & L. M. Diamond (Eds.), *APA handbook on sexuality and psychology.* Washington, DC: American Psychological Association.

Diamond, L. M. (2013b). Sexuality and same-sex sexuality in relationships. In J. Simpson & J. Davidio (Eds.), *Handbook of personality and social psychology.* Washington, DC: American Psychological Association.

Diamond, L. M., & Savin-Williams, R. C. (2015). Same-sex activity in adolescence: Multiple meanings and implications. In R. F. Fassinger & S. L. Morrow (Eds.), *Sex in the margins.* Washington, DC: American Psychological Association.

Diamond, L. M., Dickenson, J. A., & Blair, K. L. (2017). Stability of sexual attractions across different timescales: The roles of bisexuality and gender. *Archives of Sexual Behavior, 46*(1), 193–204. doi:10.1007/s10508-016-0860-x

Diamond, M., & Sigmundson, H. K. (1997). Sex reassignment at birth: Long-term review and clinical implications. *Archives of Pediatric and Adolescent Medicine, 151*(3), 298–304.

Diaz, M. T., Rizio, A. A., & Zhuang, J. (2016). The neural language systems that support healthy aging: Integrating function, structure, and behavior. *Language and Linguistics Compass, 10*(7), 314–334. doi:10.1111/lnc3.12199

Diaz-Morales, J. F., & Escribano, C. (2013). Circadian preference and thinking styles: Implications for school achievement. *Chronobiology International, 30,* 1231–1239,

Diekman, A. B., & Clark, E. K. (2015). Beyond the damsel in distress: Gender differences and similarities in enacting prosocial behavior. In D. A. Schroeder & W. G. Graziano (Eds.), *The Oxford handbook of prosocial behavior* (pp. 376–391). New York: Oxford University Press. doi:10.1093/oxfordhb/9780195399813.013.028

Diener, E. (1999). Introduction to the special section on the structure of emotion. *Journal of Personality and Social Psychology, 76*(5), 803–804.

Diener, E. (2000). Subjective well-being: The science of happiness and a proposal for a national index. *American Psychologist, 55*(1), 34–43.

Diener, E., & Chan, M. Y. (2011). Happy people live longer: Subjective well-being contributes to health and well-being. *Applied Psychology: Health and Well-Being, 3*(1), 1–43.

Diener, E., & Diener, C. (1996). Most people are happy. *Psychological Science, 7*(3), 181–185.

Diener, E., & Lucas, R. (2014). New findings on personality and well-being. In M. Mikulincer & P. Shaver (Eds.), *APA handbook of personality and social psychology.* Washington, DC: American Psychological Association.

Diener, E., Emmons, R. A., Larsen, R. J., & Griffin, S. (1985). The Satisfaction with Life Scale. *Journal of Personality Assessment, 49*(1), 71–75.

Diener, E., Ng, W., Harter, J., & Arora, R. (2010). Wealth and happiness across the world: Material prosperity predicts life evaluation, whereas psychosocial prosperity predicts positive feeling. *Journal of Personality and Social Psychology, 99*(1), 52–61.

Diener, E., Tay, L., & Oishi, S. (2013). Rising income and the subjective well-being of nations. *Journal of Personality and Social Psychology, 104*(2), 267–276.

Dietz, W. H. (2015). The response of the US Centers for Disease Control and Prevention to the obesity epidemic. *Annual Review of Public Health* (vol. 36). Palo Alto, CA: Annual Reviews.

Digman, J. M. (1990). Personality structure: Emergence of the five-factor model. *Annual Review of Psychology* (vol. 41, pp. 417–440). Palo Alto, CA: Annual Reviews.

Dijkhuizen, J., Gorgievski, M., Veldhoven, M., & Schalk, R. (2017). Well-being, personal success and business performance among entrepreneurs: A two-wave study. *Journal of Happiness Studie*s, in press. doi:10.1007/s10902-017-9914-6

Diller, J. (2015). *Cultural diversity* (5th ed.). Boston: Cengage.

Ding, Z., Mangino, M., Aviv, A., Spector, T., Durbin, R., & UK10K Consortium. (2014). Estimating telomere length from whole genome sequence data. *Nucleic Acids Research, 42*(9), e75.

Dirkx, M. F., den Ouden, H. E., Aarts, E., Timmer, M. H., Bloem, B. R., Toni, I., & Helmich, R. C. (2017). Dopamine controls Parkinson's tremor by inhibiting the cerebellar thalamus. *Brain, 140*(3), 721–734.

Distel, M. A., & others. (2008). Heritability of borderline personality disorder features is similar across three countries. *Psychological Medicine, 38*(9), 1219–1229.

Dixon, R. A., McFall, G. P., Whitehead, B. P., & Dolcos, S. (2013). Cognitive development in adulthood and aging. In R. M. Lerner, M. A. Easterbrooks, J. Mistry, & I. B. Weiner (Eds.), *Handbook of psychology* (2nd ed., vol. 6, pp. 451–474). Hoboken, NJ: Wiley.

Dixon, R. M. W. (2012). *Basic linguistic theory* (vol. 3). New York: Oxford University Press.

Dobson, R. (2005). "Fighting spirit" after cancer diagnosis does not improve outcome. *British Medical Journal, 330*(7456), 865.

Dodge, E. (2012). Family evolution and process during the child and adolescent years in eating disorders. In J. Lock (Ed.), *The Oxford handbook of child and adolescent eating disorders: Developmental perspectives.* New York: Oxford University Press.

Dodge, K. A., Coie, J. D., & Lynam, D. (2006). Aggression and antisocial behavior in youth. In W. Damon & R. Lerner (Eds.), *Handbook of child psychology* (6th ed.). New York: Wiley.

Dolan, M., & Fullam, R. (2006). Face affect recognition deficits in personality-disordered offenders: Association with psychopathy. *Psychological Medicine, 36*(11), 1563–1569.

Doll, B. B., Shohamy, D., & Daw, N. D. (2014). Multiple memory systems as substrates for multiple decision systems. *Neurobiology of Learning and Memory.* doi:10.1016/j.nlm.2014.04.014

Dollard, J., Doob, L. W., Miller, N. E., Mowrer, O. H., & Sears, R. R. (1939). *Frustration and aggression.* New Haven, CT: Yale University Press.

Domhoff, G. W. (2017). *The emergence of dreaming: Mind-wandering, embodied simulation, and the default network.* New York: Oxford University Press.

Domingue, B. W., Belsky, D. W., Conley, D., Harris, K. M., & Boardman, J. D. (2015). Polygenic influence on educational attainment. *AERA Open, 1*(3), 1–13. doi:10.1177/ 2332858415599972

Domjan, M. (2015). *Principles of learning and behavior* (7th ed.). Boston: Cengage.

Domjan, M. (2016). Elicited versus emitted behavior: Time to abandon the distinction. *Journal of the Experimental Analysis of Behavior, 105*(2), 231–245.

Donate Life (2017). *Living Donation.* https://www.donatelife.net/types-of-donation/living-donation/ downloaded 9/34/2017

Donatelle, R. J. (2015). *Access to health* (14th ed.). Upper Saddle River, NJ: Pearson.

Donatelle, R. J. (2015). *Health* (11th ed.). Upper Saddle River, NJ: Pearson.

Donnellan, M. B., Larsen-Rife, D., & Conger, R. D. (2005). Personality, family history, and competence in early adult romantic relationships. *Journal of Personality and Social Psychology, 88*(3), 562–576.

Donnellan, M. B., Lucas, R. E., & Fleeson, W. (2009). Introduction to personality and assessment at age 40: Reflections on the legacy of the person–situation debate and the future of person–situation integration. *Journal of Research in Personality, 43*(2), 117–119.

Donovan, B. M. (2017). Learned inequality: Racial labels in the biology curriculum can affect the development of racial prejudice. *Journal of Research in Science Teaching, 54*(3), 379–411. doi:10.1002/tea.21370

Dooley, L. N., Slavich, G. M., Moreno, P. I., & Bower, J. E. (2017). Strength through adversity: Moderate lifetime stress exposure is associated with psychological resilience in breast cancer survivors. *Stress and Health, 33,* 549–557.

Dorahy, M. J., & van der Hart, O. (2014). DSM-5's "PTSD with dissociative symptoms": Challenges and future directions. *Journal of Trauma and Dissociation.* PMID: 24983300

Dou, Y., Yang, X., Li, Z., Wang, S., Zhang, Z., Ye, A. Y., et al. (2017). Post-zygotic single-nucleotide mosaicisms contribute to the etiology of autism spectrum disorder and autistic traits and the origin of mutations. *Human Mutation, 38,* 1002–1013

Douglass, S., & Umaña-Taylor, A. J. (2017). Examining discrimination, ethnic-racial identity status, and youth public regard among Black, Latino, and White adolescents. *Journal of Research on Adolescence, 27*(1), 155–172.

Dovidio, J. F., Piliavin, J. A., Schroeder, D. A., & Penner, L. A. (2017). *The social psychology of prosocial behavior.* New York: Psychology Press.

Dovidio, J. F., Saguy, T., Gaertner, S. L., & Thomas, E. L. (2012). From attitudes to (in)action: The darker side of "we." In J. Dixon, M. Keynes, & M. Levine (Eds.), *Beyond prejudice.* New York: Cambridge University Press.

Dow, D., Guthrie, W., Stronach, S. T., & Wetherby, A. M. (2017). Psychometric analysis of the Systematic Observation of Red Flags for autism spectrum disorder in toddlers. *Autism, 21*(3), 301–309.

Doyle, A. E., Martin, J., Vuijk, P. J., Capawana, M. R., O'Keefe, S. M., Lee, B. A., et al. (2017). Translating discoveries in attention-deficit/hyperactivity disorder (ADHD) genomics to the clinic. *Journal of the American Academy of Child & Adolescent Psychiatry, 56*(10), S229.

Draguns, J. G., & Tanaka-Matsumi, J. (2003). Assessment of psychopathology across and within cultures: Issues and findings. *Behavior Research and Therapy, 41*(7), 755–776.

Dryman, M. T., Gardner, S., Weeks, J. W., & Heimberg, R. G. (2016). Social anxiety disorder and quality of life: How fears of negative and positive evaluation relate to specific domains of life satisfaction. *Journal of Anxiety Disorders, 38,* 1–8.

Duan, J., Sanders, A., Drigalenko, E., Göring, H. H., & Gejman, P. (2017). Transcriptomic signatures of schizophrenia revealed by dopamine perturbation of lymphoblastoid cell lines. *European Neuropsychopharmacology, 27,* S400.

Dudukovic, N. M., & Kuhl, B. A. (2017). Cognitive Control in Memory Encoding and Retrieval. In T. Egner (Ed.), *The Wiley Handbook of Cognitive Control.* (pp. 355–375). New York: Wiley.

Duggan, K. A., & Friedman, H. S. (2014). Lifetime biopsychosocial trajectories of the Terman gifted children: Health, well-being, and longevity. In D. K. Simonton (Ed.), *The Wiley-Blackwell handbook of genius* (pp. 488–510). New York: Wiley-Blackwell.

Duke, A. A., Bègue, L., Bell, R., & Eisenlohr-Moul, T. (2013). Revisiting the serotonin-aggression relationship in humans: A meta-analysis. *Psychological Bulletin, 139*(5), 1148–1172.

Duman, R. S., Li, N., Liu, R. J., Duric, V., & Aghajanian, G. (2012). Signaling pathways underlying the rapid antidepressant actions of ketamine. *Neuropharmacology, 62*(1), 35–41.

Dunbar, R. I. M., & Shultz, S. (2007). Evolution in the social brain. *Science, 317*(5843), 1344–1347.

Duncan, A. E., & others. (2006). Exposure to paternal alcoholism does not predict development of alcohol-use disorders in offspring: Evidence from an offspring-of-twins study. *Journal of Studies on Alcohol, 67*(5), 649–656.

Duncan, B. L., & Reese, R. J. (2013). Empirically supported treatments, evidence-based treatments, and evidence-based practice. In G. Stricker, T. A. Widiger, & I. B. Weiner (Eds.), *Handbook of psychology* (2nd ed., vol. 8, pp. 489–514). Hoboken, NJ: Wiley.

Duncan, B. L., Miller, S. D., Wampold, B. E., & Hubble, M. A. (Eds.). (2010). *The heart and soul of change: Delivering what works in therapy* (2nd ed.). Washington, DC: American Psychological Association.

Duncan, G. J., Magnuson, K., & Votruba-Drzal, E. (2015). Children and socioeconomic status. In M. H. Bornstein & T. Leventhal (Eds.), *Handbook of child psychology and developmental science* (7th ed., vol. 4). New York: Wiley.

Duncan, L., Yilmaz, Z., Gaspar, H., Walters, R., Goldstein, J., Anttila, V., et al. (2017). Significant locus and metabolic genetic correlations revealed in genome-wide association study of anorexia nervosa. *American Journal of Psychiatry, 174,* 850–858.

Dunlop, W. L., Bannon, B. L., & McAdams, D. P. (2017). Studying the motivated agent through time: Personal goal development during the adult life span. *Journal of Personality, 85*(2), 207–219.

Dunn, A. R., Stout, S. K. A., Ozawa, M., Lohr, K. M., Hoffman, C. A., Bernstein, A. I., et al. (2017). Synaptic vesicle glycoprotein 2C (SV2C) modulates dopamine release and is disrupted in Parkinson disease. *Proceedings of the National Academy of Sciences, 114*(11), E2253–E2262.

Dunn, E. W., Aknin, L. B., & Norton, M. I. (2008). Spending money on others promotes happiness. *Science, 319*(5870), 1687–1688.

Dunn, K., & Bremner, J. G. (2017). Investigating looking and social looking measures as an index of infant violation of expectation. *Developmental Science, 20*(6). e12452.

Dupin, L., Hayward, V., & Wexler, M. (2017). Generalized movement representation in haptic perception. *Journal of Experimental Psychology: Human Perception And Performance, 43*(3), 581–595. doi:10.1037/xhp0000327

Durantini, M. R., & Albarracin, D. (2009). Material and social incentives to participation in behavioral interventions: A meta-analysis of gender disparities in enrollment and retention in experimental HIV prevention interventions. *Health Psychology, 28*(5), 631–640.

Durantini, M. R., & Albarracin, D. (2012). Men and women have specific needs that facilitate enrollment in HIV-prevention counseling. *AIDS Care, 24*(10), 1197–1203.

Durkin, M. S., Maenner, M. J., Baio, J., Christensen, D., Daniels, J., Fitzgerald, R., et al. (2017). Autism spectrum disorder among US children (2002–2010): Socioeconomic, racial, and ethnic disparities. *American Journal of Public Health, 107,* 1818–1826.

Duvarci, S., Nader, K., & LeDoux, J. E. (2008). De novo mRNA synthesis is required for both consolidation and reconsolidation of fear memories in the amygdala. *Learning and Memory, 15*(10), 747–755.

Duverne, S., & Koechlin, E. (2017). Hierarchical control of behaviour in human prefrontal cortex. In T. Egner (Ed.), *The Wiley handbook of cognitive control* (pp. 207–220). New York: Wiley-Blackwell.

Dweck, C. S. (2012). Mindsets and human nature: Promoting change in the Middle East, the school yard, the racial divide, and willpower. *The American Psychologist, 67*(8), 614–622.

Dweck, C. S. (2013). Social development. In P. Zelazo (Ed.), *The Oxford handbook of developmental psychology* (vol. 2, pp. 167–190). New York: Oxford University Press.

Dweck, C. S. (2017). *Mindset: Changing the way you think to fulfill your potential.* New York: Random House.

Dworkin, E. R., Menon, S. V., Bystrynski, J., & Allen, N. E. (2017). Sexual assault victimization and psychopathology: A review and meta-analysis. *Clinical Psychology Review, 56,* 65–81.

Dworkin, E. R., Ullman, S. E., Stappenbeck, C., Brill, C. D., & Kaysen, D. (2017). Proximal relationships between social support and PTSD symptom severity: A daily diary study of sexual assault survivors. *Depression and Anxiety.* in press.

Dzokoto, V., Wallace, D. S., Peters, L., & Gentsi-Enchill, E. (2014). Attention to emotion and non-Western faces: Revisiting the facial feedback hypothesis. *Journal of General Psychology, 141*(2), 151–168.

E

Eagly, A. H. (2009). The his and hers of prosocial behavior: An examination of the social psychology of gender. *American Psychologist, 64*(8), 644–658.

Eagly, A. H. (2010). Gender roles. In J. Levine & M. Hogg (Eds.), *Encyclopedia of group processes and intergroup relations.* Thousand Oaks, CA: Sage.

Eagly, A. H. (2012). Science, feminism, and the investigation of gender. In R. W. Proctor & E. J. Capaldi (Eds.), *Psychology of science: Implicit and explicit reasoning.* New York: Oxford University Press.

Eagly, A. H. (2012). Women as leaders: Paths through the labyrinth. In M. C. Bligh & R. Riggio (Eds.), *When near is far and far is near: Exploring distance in leader-follower relationships.* New York: Wiley-Blackwell.

Eagly, A. H., & Antonakis, J. (2014). Leadership. In M. Mikulincer, P. R. Shaver, E. Borgida, & J. A. Bargh (Eds.), *APA handbook of personality and social psychology* (vol. 1). Washington, DC: American Psychological Association.

Eagly, A. H., & Crowley, M. (1986). Gender and helping behavior: A meta-analytic review of the social psychological literature. *Psychological Bulletin, 100*(3), 283–308.

Eagly, A. H., & Wood, W. (2011). Feminism and the evolution of sex differences and similarities. *Sex Roles, 64*(9–10), 758–767.

Eagly, A. H., & Wood, W. (2012). Social role theory. In P. A. M. Van Lange, A. W. Kruglanski, & E. T. Higgins (Eds.), *Handbook of theories of social psychology* (pp. 458–476). Thousand Oaks, CA: Sage.

Eagly, A. H., & Wood, W. (2013). The nature–nurture debates: 25 years of challenges in understanding the psychology of gender. *Perspectives on Psychological Science, 8*(3), 340–357.

Eagly, A. H., Gartzia, L., & Carli, L. L. (2014). Female advantage: Revisited. In S. Kumra, R. Simpson, & R. J. Burke (Eds.), *The Oxford handbook of gender in organizations.* New York: Oxford University Press.

Earnshaw, V. A., Reisner, S. L., Juvonen, J., Hatzenbuehler, M. L., Perrotti, J., & Schuster, M. A. (2017). LGBTQ bullying: Translating research to action in pediatrics. *Pediatrics,* e20170432.

Eaton, D. A., & others. (2012). Youth risk behavior surveillance–United States, 2011. *MMWR Surveillance Summaries, 61*(4), 1–162.

Eaton, R. W., Libey, T., & Fetz, E. E. (2016). Operant conditioning of neural activity in freely behaving monkeys with intracranial reinforcement. *Journal of Neurophysiology,* jn-00423.

Ecker, C., Andrews, D. S., Gudbrandsen, C. M., Marquand, A. F., Ginestet, C. E., Daly, E. M., et al. (2017). Association between the probability of autism spectrum disorder and normative sex-related phenotypic diversity in brain structure. *JAMA Psychiatry, 74*(4), 329–338.

Eckstein, M.P., Koehler, K., Welbourne, L.E., & Akbas, E. (2017). Humans, but not deep neural networks, often miss giant targets in scenes. *Current Biology, 27,* 2827–2832.

Eguchi, E., & others. (2012). Healthy lifestyle behaviors and cardiovascular mortality among Japanese men and women: The Japan collaborative cohort study. *European Heart Journal, 33*(4), 467–477.

Eich, E. (2007). Mood, memory, and the concept of context. In H. L. Roediger, Y. Dubai, & S. Fitzpatrick (Eds.), *Science of memory: Concepts.* New York: Oxford University Press.

Eilam, D. (2017). From an animal model to human patients: An example of a translational study on obsessive compulsive disorder (OCD). *Neuroscience & Biobehavioral Reviews, 76,* 67–76.

Eilertsen, E. M., Gjerde, L. C., Reichborn-Kjennerud, T., Ørstavik, R. E., Knudsen, G. P., Stoltenberg, C., et al. (2017). Maternal alcohol use during pregnancy and offspring attention-deficit hyperactivity disorder (ADHD): A prospective sibling control study. *International Journal of Epidemiology, 46,* 633–1640.

Eisenberg, D. P., Yankowitz, L., Ianni, A. M., Rubinstein, D. Y., Kohn, P. D., Hegarty, C. E., et al. (2017). Presynaptic dopamine synthesis capacity in schizophrenia and striatal blood flow change during antipsychotic treatment and medication-free conditions. *Neuropsychopharmacology, 42,* 2232–2241.

Eisenberg, M., Gower, A., Brown, C., Wood, B., & Porta, C. (2017). "They want to put a label on it:" Patterns and interpretations of sexual orientation and gender identity labels among adolescents. *Journal of Adolescent Health, 60*(2), S27–S28.

Eisenberg, N., & Spinrad, T. R. (2014). Multidimensionality of prosocial behavior: Re-thinking the conceptualization and development of prosocial behavior. In L. Padilla-Walker & G. Gustavo (Eds.), *Prosocial behavior.* New York: Oxford University Press.

Eisenberg, N., Eggum, N. D., & Spinrad, T. L. (2015). The development of prosocial behavior. In D. A. Schroeder & W. G. Graziano (Eds.), *The Oxford handbook of prosocial behavior.* New York: Oxford University Press.

Eisenstein, A. R., & others. (2011). Environmental correlates of overweight and obesity in community residing older adults. *Journal of Aging and Health, 23*(6), 994–1009.

Ekman, P. (1996). Lying and deception. In N. L. Stein, C. Brainerd, P. A. Ornstein, & B. Tversky (Eds.), *Memory for everyday emotional events.* Mahwah, NJ: Erlbaum.

Ekman, P., & Friesen, W. V. (1969). The repertoire of nonverbal behavior: Categories, origins, usage, and coding. *Semiotica, 1*(1) 49–98.

Ekman, P., & Friesen, W. V. (1971). Constants across cultures in the face and emotion. *Journal of Personality and Social Psychology, 17*(2), 124–129.

Ekman, P., Davidson, R. J., & Friesen, W. V. (1990). The Duchenne smile: Emotional expression and brain physiology: II. *Journal of Personality and Social Psychology, 58*(2), 342–353.

Ekman, P., Levenson, R. W., & Friesen, W. V. (1983). Autonomic nervous system activity distinguishes among emotions. *Science, 221*(4616), 1208–1210.

Ekman, P., & O'Sullivan, M. (1991). Facial expression: Methods, means, and moues. In R. S. Feldman and B. Rime (Eds.), *Fundamentals of nonverbal behavior.* Cambridge, UK: Cambridge University Press.

Ekman, P. (1980). *The face of man.* New York: Garland.

Ekman, P. (2003). Emotions inside out: 130 years after Darwin's "The expression of emotions in man and animal." *Annals of the New York Academy of Science, 1000,* 1–6.

El-Hai, J. (2005). *The lobotomist: A maverick medical genius and his tragic quest to rid the world of mental illness.* Hoboken, NJ: Wiley.

El-Sheikh, M. (2013). *Auburn university child sleep, health, and development center.* Auburn, AL: Auburn University.

Eldred, M. (2017). Love hormones and mental health. *Science, 355*(6330), 1170–1171.

Eldredge, J. H. (2016). Imagined interaction frequency and the five-factor model of personality. *Imagination, Cognition And Personality, 35*(4), 351–358. doi:10.1177/0276236616636215

Eley, T. C., & others. (2004). Gene–environment interaction analysis of serotonin system markers with adolescent depression. *Molecular Psychiatry, 9*(10), 908–915.

Elklit, A., Hyland, P., & Shevlin, M. (2014). Evidence of symptom profiles consistent with posttraumatic stress disorder and complex posttraumatic stress disorder in different trauma samples. *European Journal of Psychotraumatology.* doi:10.3402/ejpt.v5.24221

Ellins, E. A., Rees, D. A., Deanfield, J. E., Steptoe, A., & Halcox, J. P. (2017). Increased fibrinogen responses to psychophysiological stress predict future endothelial dysfunction implications for cardiovascular disease? *Brain, Behavior, And Immunity, 60,* 233–239. doi:10.1016/j.bbi.2016.10.017

Elliott, M. A., & Ainsworth, K. (2012). Predicting university undergraduates' binge-drinking behavior: A comparative test of the one- and two-component theories of planned behavior. *Addictive Behaviors, 37*(1), 92–101.

Ellis, A. (2005). Why I (really) became a therapist. *Journal of Clinical Psychology, 61*(8), 945–948.

Emberson, L. L., Boldin, A. M., Riccio, J. E., Guillet, R., & Aslin, R. N. (2017). Deficits in top-down sensory prediction in infants at risk due to premature birth. *Current Biology, 27*(3), 431–436.

Emmelkamp, P. M. (2011). Effectiveness of cybertherapy in mental health: A critical appraisal. *Studies in Health Technology and Informatics, 167,* 3–8.

Emmons, R. A., & Diener, E. (1986). Situation selection as a moderator of response consistency and stability. *Journal of Personality and Social Psychology, 51*(5), 1013–1019.

Emmons, R. A., & King, L. A. (1988). Conflict among personal strivings: Immediate and long-term implications for psychological and physical well-being. *Journal of Personality and Social Psychology, 54*(6), 1040–1048.

Emmons, R. A., & McCullough, M. E. (2003). Counting blessings versus burdens: An experimental investigation of gratitude and subjective well-being in daily life. *Journal of Personality and Social Psychology, 84*(2), 377–389.

Emmons, R. A., & McCullough, M. E. (Eds.). (2004). *The psychology of gratitude.* New York: Oxford University Press.

Endler, N. S. (1988). The origins of electroconvulsive therapy (ECT). *Convulsive Therapy, 4*(1), 5–23.

Eng, P. M., Fitzmaurice, G., Kubzansky, L. D., Rimm, E. B., & Kawachi, I. (2003). Anger expression and risk of stroke and coronary heart disease among male health professionals. *Psychosomatic Medicine, 65*(1), 100–110.

Engberg, H., Jeune, B., Andersen-Ranberg, K., Martinussen, T., Vaupel, J. V., & Christensen, K. (2013). Optimism and survival: Does an optimistic outlook predict better survival at advanced ages? A twelve-year follow-up of Danish nonagenarians. *Aging: Clinical and Experimental Research, 25*(5), 517–525.

Engel, A. K., & Singer, W. (2001). Temporal binding and the neural correlates of sensory awareness. *Trends in Cognitive Science, 5*(1), 16–25.

Enger, D. (January 26, 2016). The neurologist who hacked his brain–and almost lost his mind. *Wired.com.* https://www.wired.com/2016/01/phil-kennedy-mind-control-computer/

English, T., & Carstensen, L. (2014). Selective narrowing of social networks across adulthood is associated with improved emotional experience in daily life. *International Journal of Behavioral Development, 38*(2), 195–202.

Ensembl Human. (2010). *Explore the homo sapiens genome.* www.ensembl.org/Homo_sapiens/index.html (accessed November 9, 2014)

Ensink, K., Berthelot, N., Bégin, M., Maheux, J., & Normandin, L. (2017). Dissociation mediates the relationship between sexual abuse and child psychological difficulties. *Child Abuse & Neglect, 69,* 116–124.

Ent, M. R., & Gerend, M. A. (2016). Cognitive dissonance and attitudes toward unpleasant medical screenings. *Journal of Health Psychology, 21*(9), 2075–2084. doi:10.1177/1359105315570986

Entwistle, P. A., Webb, R. J., Abayomi, J. C., Johnson, B., Sparkes, A. C., & Davies, I. G. (2014). Unconscious agendas in the etiology of refractory obesity and the role of hypnosis in their identification and resolution: A new paradigm for weight-management programs or a paradigm revisited? *International Journal of Clinical and Experimental Hypnosis, 62*(3), 330–359.

Epel, E. S., & Lithgow, G. J. (2014). Stress biology and aging mechanisms: Toward understanding the deep connection between adaptation to stress and longevity. *Journals of Gerontology A: Biological Sciences and Medical Sciences, 69,* Suppl. 1, S10–S16.

Erickson, K. I., Miller, D. L., & Roecklein, K. A. (2012). The aging hippocampus: Interactions between exercise, depression, and BDNF. *Neuroscientist, 18*(1), 82–97.

Erikson, E. (1969). *Gandhi's truth.* New York: Norton.

Erikson, E. H. (1968). *Identity: Youth and crisis.* New York: Norton.

Erlikhman, G., & Kellman, P.J. (2016). From flashes to edges to objects: Recovery of local edge fragments initiates spatiotemporal boundary formation. *Frontiers in Psychology, 7*(910). doi: 10.3389/fpsyg.2016.00910

Espnes, G. A., & Byrne, D. (2016). Type A behavior and cardiovascular disease. In M. E. Alvarenga & D. Byrne (Eds.), *Handbook of psychocardiology* (pp. 645–664). New York, NY: Springer Science + Business Media. doi:10.1007/978-981-287-206-7_30

Esposito, E. A., Grigorenko, E. L., & Sternberg, R. J. (2012). The nature–nurture issue: An illustration using behavior-genetic research on cognitive development. In A. Slater & J. Gavin-Bremmer (Eds.), *An introduction to developmental psychology* (2nd ed.). New York: Wiley-Blackwell.

Etherton, J., Lawson, M., & Graham, R. (2014). Individual and gender differences in subjective and objective indices of pain: Gender, fear of pain, pain catastrophizing and cardiovascular reactivity. *Applied Psychophysiology and Biofeedback, 39*(2), 89–97. doi:10.1007/s10484-014-9245-x

Evans, B. G., & Iverson, P. (2007). Plasticity in vowel perception and production: A study of accent change in young adults. *Journal of the Acoustical Society of America, 121*(6), 3814–3826.

Evans, J. (2012). Dual-process theories of reasoning: Facts and fallacies. In K. J. Holyoak & R. G. Morrison (Eds.), *Oxford handbook of thinking and reasoning.* New York: Oxford University Press.

Evans, S., Ling, M., Hill, B., Rinehart, N., Austin, D., & Sciberras, E. (2017). Systematic review of meditation-based interventions for children with ADHD. *European Child & Adolescent Psychiatry,* in press.

Evans-Lacko, S., & others. (2014). The state of art in European research on reducing social exclusion and stigma related to mental health: A systematic mapping of the literature. *European Psychiatry, 29*(6), 381–389.

Everitt, B.J., & Robbins, T. W. (2016). Drug addiction: Updating actions to habits to compulsions ten years on. *Annual Review of Psychology, 67,* 23–50.

Eysenck, H. J. (1967). *The biological basis of personality.* Springfield, IL: Thomas.

F

Fagan, S. E., Zhang, W., & Gao, Y. (2017). Social adversity and antisocial behavior: Mediating effects of autonomic nervous system activity. *Journal of Abnormal Child Psychology, 45,* 1553–1564.

Fagundes, C. P., Glaser, R., Hwang, B. S., Malarkey, W. B., & Kiecolt-Glaser, J. K. (2013). Depressive symptoms enhance stress-induced inflammatory responses. *Brain, Behavior, and Immunity, 31,* 172–176.

Fairman, K. A., Peckham, A. M., & Sclar, D. A. (2017). Diagnosis and treatment of ADHD in the United States: Update by gender and race. *Journal of Attention Disorders,* doi:10.1177/1087054716688534

Faivre, N., Filevich, E., Solovey, G., Kühn, S., & Blanke, O. (2017). Behavioural, modeling, and electrophysiological evidence for supramodality in human metacognition. *Journal of Neuroscience,* in press. doi: 10.1523/JNEUROSCI.0322-17.2017

Farahani, M. N., De Raad, B., Farzad, V., & Fotoohie, M. (2016). Taxonomy and structure of Persian personality-descriptive trait terms. *International Journal of Psychology, 51*(2), 139–149. doi:10.1002/ijop.12133

Faraone, S. V., Perlis, R. H., Doyle, A. E., Smoller, J. W., Goralnick, J. J., Holmgren, M. A., & Sklar, P. (2005). Molecular genetics of attention-deficit/hyperactivity disorder. *Biological Psychiatry, 57*(11), 1313–1323.

Faraone, S.V., Asherson, P. A., Banaschewski, T., Biederman, J., Buitelaar, J.K. et al. (2015). Attention-decifict hyperactivty disorder. *Nature Reviews Disease Primers, 1,* 15020. doi:10.1038/nrdp.2015.20

Farr, R. H., & Patterson, C. J. (2013). Coparenting among lesbian, gay, and heterosexual couples: Associations with adopted children's outcomes. *Child Development, 84*(4), 1226–1240.

Farrar, M. J., Seung, H. K., & Lee, H. (2017). Language and false-belief task performance in children with autism spectrum disorder. *Journal of Speech, Language, and Hearing Research, 60*(7), 1999–2013.

Fastame, M. C., Hitchcott, P. K., & Penna, M. P. (2017). Does social desirability influence psychological well-being: Perceived physical health and religiosity of Italian elders? A developmental approach. *Aging & Mental Health, 21*(4), 348–353. doi:10.1080/13607863.2015.1074162

Fatemi, S. H., & Folsom, T. D. (2009). The neurodevelopmental hypothesis of schizophrenia, revisited. *Schizophrenia Bulletin, 35*(3), 528–548.

Fattinger, S., de Beukelaar, T. T., Ruddy, K. L., Volk, C., Heyse, N. C., Herbst, J. A., ... & Huber, R. (2017). Deep sleep maintains learning efficiency of the human brain. *Nature Communications, 8,* in press.

Fava, G. A., Guidi, J., Rafanelli, C., & Rickels, K. (2017). The clinical inadequacy of the placebo model and the development of an alternative conceptual framework. *Psychotherapy and Psychosomatics, 86*(6), 332–340.

Faymonville, M. E., Boly, M., & Laureys, S. (2006). Functional neuroanatomy of the hypnotic state. *Journal of Physiology, Paris, 99,* 463–469.

Fazakas-DeHoog, L. L., Rnic, K., & Dozois, D. J. (2017). A cognitive distortions and deficits model of suicide ideation. *Europe's Journal of Psychology, 13,* 178–193.

Fazio, R. H., & Olsen, A. (2007). Attitudes. In M. A. Hogg & J. Cooper (Eds.), *The Sage handbook of social psychology* (concise 2nd ed.). Thousand Oaks, CA: Sage.

Fazio, R. H., Chen, J.-M., McDonel, E. C., & Sherman, S. J. (1982). Attitude accessibility, attitude-behavior consistency, and the strength of the object-evaluation association. *Journal of Experimental Social Psychology, 18*(4), 339–357.

FBI (Federal Bureau of Investigation). (2016). Expanded homicide data. *FBI.* https://ucr.fbi.gov/crime-in-the-u.s/2015/crime-in-the.u.s.-2015/tables/expanded_homicide_data_table_3_murder_offenders_by_age_sex_and_race_2015.xls

Federal Communications Commission (FCC) (2017). The Dangers of Distracted Driving. https://www.fcc.gov/consumers/guides/dangers-texting-while-driving

Fei-Fei, L., Iyer, A., Koch, C., & Perona, P. (2007). What do we perceive in a glance at a real-world scene? *Journal of Vision, 7*(1), 10.

Fein, S., Goethals, G. R., Kassin, S. M., & Cross, J. (1993, August). *Social influence and presidential debates.* Paper presented at the meeting of the American Psychological Association, Toronto.

Feinberg, E., Abufhele, M., Sandler, J., Augustyn, M., Cabral, H., Chen, N., et al. (2016). Reducing disparities in timely autism diagnosis through family navigation: Results from a randomized pilot trial. *Psychiatric Services, 67*(8), 912–915.

Feinberg, T.E., & Mallatt, J.M. (2017). *The ancient origins of consciousness: How the brain created experience.* Cambridge, MA: MIT press.

Feinstein, E. C., Richter, L., & Foster, S. E. (2012). Addressing the critical health problem of adolescent substance use through health care, research, and public policy. *Journal of Adolescent Health, 50*(5), 431–436.

Feitosa-Santana, C. (2017). Understanding how the mind works: The neuroscience of perception, behavior, and creativity. In R. Zuanon (Ed.), *Projective processes and neuroscience in art and design* (pp. 239–252). Hershey, PA: Information Science Reference/IGI Global. doi:10.4018/978-1-5225-0510-5.ch014

Feldman, R., & Bakermans-Kranenburg, M. J. (2017). Oxytocin: a parenting hormone. *Current Opinion in Psychology, 15,* 13–18.

Feltham, C., Hanley, T., & Winter, L. A. (Eds.). (2017). *The SAGE handbook of counselling and psychotherapy.* Los Angeles: Sage.

Feng, Y., Herdman, M., van Nooten, F., Cleeland, C., Parkin, D., Ikeda, S., ... & Devlin, N. J. (2017). An exploration of differences between Japan and two European countries in the self-reporting and valuation of pain and discomfort on the EQ-5D. *Quality of Life Research,* in press.

Ferguson, C. J. (2015). Do angry birds make for angry children? A meta-analysis of video game influences on children's and adolescents' aggression, mental health, prosocial behavior, and academic performance. *Perspectives on Psychological Science, 10*(5), 646–666. doi:10.1177/1745691615592234

Ferguson, C. J., & Kilburn, J. (2010). Much ado about nothing: The misestimation and overinterpretation of violent video game effects in Eastern and Western nations: Comment on Anderson et al. (2010). *Psychological Bulletin, 136*(2), 174–178.

Ferguson, C. J., Rueda, S. M., Cruz, A. M., Ferguson, D. E., Fritz, S., & Smith, S. M. (2008). Violent video games and aggression: Causal relationship or byproduct of family violence and intrinsic violence motivation? *Criminal Justice and Behavior, 35*(3), 311–332.

Ferguson, E., & Bibby, P. A. (2012). Openness to experience and all-cause mortality: A meta-analysis and r(equivalent) from risk ratios and odds ratios. *British Journal of Health Psychology, 17*(1), 85–102.

Ferguson, S., Zimmer-Gembeck, M. J., & Duffy, A. L. (2016). A longitudinal study of relational aggression and victimisation in early adolescence: Gender differences in the moderating effects of social status. *Journal of Relationships Research, 7.* doi:10.1017/jrr.2016.9

Fernald, A., Marchman, V. A., & Weisleder, A. (2013). SES differences in language processing skill and vocabulary are evident at 18 months. *Developmental Science, 16*(2), 234–248. doi:10.1111/desc.12019

Ferrarelli, F., & others. (2013). Experienced mindfulness meditators exhibit higher parietal-occipital EEG gamma activity during NREM sleep. *PLoS One, 8*(8), e73417.

Ferrari, C., Lega, C., Vernice, M., Tamietto, M., Mende-Siedlecki, P., Vecchi, T., et al. (2016b). The dorsomedial prefrontal cortex plays a causal role in integrating social impressions from faces and verbal descriptions. *Cerebral Cortex, 26*(1), 156–165. doi:10.1093/cercor/bhu186

Ferrari, C., Vecchi, T., Todorov, A., & Cattaneo, Z. (2016). Interfering with activity in the dorsomedial prefrontal cortex via TMS affects social impressions updating. *Cognitive, Affective & Behavioral Neuroscience, 16*(4), 626–634. doi:10.3758/s13415-016-0419-2

Ferrari, M., & Westrate, N. (Eds.). (2013). *Personal wisdom*. New York: Springer.

Ferrer, E., Shaywitz, B. A., Holahan, J. M., Marchione, K., & Shaywitz, S. E. (2010). Uncoupling of reading and IQ over time: Empirical evidence for a definition of dyslexia. *Psychological Science, 21*(1), 93–101.

Ferrie, J. E., Shipley, M. J., Akbaraly, T. N., Marmot, M. G., Kivimäki, M., & Singh-Manoux, A. (2011). Change in sleep duration and cognitive function: Findings from the Whitehall II Study. *Sleep, 34*(5), 565–573.

Ferrières, J. (2004). The French paradox: Lessons for other countries. *Heart, 90*(1), 107–111.

Festinger, L. (1954). A theory of social comparison processes. *Human Relations, 7*(2), 117–140.

Festinger, L. (1957). *A theory of cognitive dissonance*. Evanston, IL: Row Peterson.

Festinger, L., & Carlsmith, J. M. (1959). Cognitive consequences of forced compliance. *Journal of Abnormal and Social Psychology, 58*(2), 203–211.

Fiacconi, C. M., Dekraker, J., & Köhler, S. (2015). Psychophysiological evidence for the role of emotion in adaptive memory. *Journal of Experimental Psychology: General, 144*(5), 925–933. doi:10.1037/xge0000097

Fielding, N.G., Lee, R.M., & Blank, G. (Eds.) (2017). *The SAGE Handbook of Online Research Methods* (2nd ed.). Thousand Oaks, CA: Sage.

Fields, R. (2013). *Drugs in perspective* (8th ed.). New York: McGraw-Hill.

Fillingim, R. B. (2017). Individual differences in pain: understanding the mosaic that makes pain personal. *Pain, 158*, S11–S18.

Finch, C. E. (2009). The neurobiology of middle-age has arrived. *Neurobiology and Aging, 30*(4), 515–520.

Finkel, A. G., Ivins, B. J., Yerry, J. A., Klaric, J. S., Scher, A., & Sammy Choi, Y. (2017). Which matters more? A retrospective cohort study of headache characteristics and diagnosis type in soldiers with MTBI/concussion. *Headache: The Journal of Head and Face Pain, 57*(5), 719–728.

Finkel, E. J., Cheung, E. O., Emery, L. F., Carswell, K. L., & Larson, G. M. (2015). The suffocation model: Why marriage in America is becoming an all-or-nothing institution. *Current Directions In Psychological Science, 24*(3), 238–244. doi:10.1177/0963721415569274

Finkel, E. J., Simpson, J. A., & Eastwick, P. W. (2017). The psychology of close relationships: Fourteen core principles. *Annual Review of Psychology, 68*, 383–411. doi:10.1146/annurev-psych-010416-044038

Finley, J. R., Benjamin, A. S., & McCarley, J. S. (2014). Metacognition of multitasking: How well do we predict the costs of divided attention? *Journal of Experimental Psychology: Applied, 20*(2), 158–165.

Fiori, M., Antonietti, J. P., Mikolajczak, M., Luminet, O., Hansenne, M., & Rossier, J. (2014). What is the Ability Emotional Intelligence Test (MSCEIT) good for? An evaluation using item response theory. *PLoS One, 9*(6), e08827.

Fischer, R. (2006). Congruence and functions of personal and cultural values: Do my values reflect my culture's values? *Personality and Social Psychology Bulletin, 32*(11), 1419–1431.

Fisher, C. M. (2017). An ounce of prevention or a pound of cure? Two experiments on in-process interventions in decision-making groups. *Organizational Behavior and Human Decision Processes, 13*, 859–873. doi:10.1016/j.obhdp.2016.11.004

Fisher, O., & Oyserman, D. (2017). Assessing interpretations of experienced ease and difficulty as motivational constructs. *Motivation Science, 3*, 133–163. doi:10.1037/mot0000055

Fisher, O., O'Donnell, S.C., Oyserman, D. (2017). Social class and identity-based motivation. *Current Opinion in Psychology, 18*, pp. 61–66.

Fisher, T. D., Moore, Z. T., & Pittenger, M. J. (2012). Sex on the brain? An examination of frequency of sexual cognitions as a function of gender, erotophilia, and social desirability. *Journal of Sex Research, 49*(1), 69–77.

Fishman, E. J., & Husman, J. (2017). Extending attribution theory: Considering students' perceived control of the attribution process. *Journal of Educational Psychology, 109*(4), 559–573. doi:10.1037/edu0000158

Fiske, S. T., & Tablante, C. B. (2014). Stereotyping: Processes and content. In M. Mikulincer, P. R. Shaver, E. Borgida & J. A. Bargh (Eds.), *APA handbook of personality and social psychology* (vol. 1). Washington, DC: American Psychological Association.

Fitzhugh, E. C., Bassett, D. R., & Evans, M. F. (2010). Urban trails and physical activity: A natural experiment. *American Journal of Preventive Medicine, 39*(3), 259–262.

Fitzpatrick, C., Archambault, I., Janosz, M., & Pagani, L. S. (2015). Early childhood working memory forecasts high school dropout risk. *Intelligence, 53*, 160–165.

Fitzpatrick, K. K. (2012). Developmental considerations when treating anorexia nervosa in adolescents and young adults. In J. Lock (Ed.), *The Oxford handbook of child and adolescent eating disorders: Developmental perspectives.* New York: Oxford University Press.

Fivush, R., Booker, J. A., & Graci, M. E. (2017). Ongoing Narrative Meaning-Making Within Events and Across the Life Span. *Imagination, Cognition and Personality, 37*(2), 127–152.

Flaccus, G. (2017, May 28). Mayor: 'Heroes' Died Protecting Women From Anti-Muslim Rant. Associated Press. http://hosted2.ap.org/APDEFAULT/386c25518f46 4186bf7a2ac026580ce7/Article_2017-05-28-US–Fatal%20 Stabbing-Portland/id-cc9d904c773345e792141b5737b3 ef15

Flamier, A., Singh, S., & Rasmussen, T. P. (2017). A standardized human embryoid body platform for the detection and analysis of teratogens. *PloS one, 12*(2), e0171101.

Flegal, K. M., Carroll, M. D., Kit, B. K., & Ogden, C. L. (2012). Prevalence of obesity and trends in the distribution of body mass index among U.S. adults, 1999–2010. *Journal of the American Medical Association, 307*, 491–497.

Fleming, K. A., Heintzelman, S. J., & Bartholow, B. D. (2016). Specifying associations between conscientiousness and executive functioning: Mental set shifting, not prepotent response inhibition or working memory updating. *Journal of Personality, 84*(3), 348–360.

Flor, H. (2014). Psychological pain interventions and neurophysiology: Implications for a mechanisms-based approach. *American Psychologist, 69*(2), 188–196.

Flynn, J. R. (1999). Searching for justice: The discovery of IQ gains over time. *American Psychologist, 54*(1), 5–20.

Flynn, J. R. (2006). The history of the American mind in the 20th century: A scenario to explain gains over time and a case for the irrelevance of *g.* In P. C. Kyllonen, R. D. Roberts, & L. Stankov (Eds.), *Extending intelligence.* Mahwah, NJ: Erlbaum.

Flynn, J. R. (2011). Secular changes in intelligence. In R. J. Sternberg & S. B. Kaufman (Eds.), *The Cambridge handbook of intelligence* (pp. 647–665). New York: Cambridge University Press.

Flynn, J. R. (2013). *Are we getting smarter?* New York: Cambridge University Press.

Focht, B. C. (2012). Exercise and health-related quality of life. In E. O. Acevedo (Ed.), *The Oxford handbook of exercise psychology.* New York: Oxford University Press.

Foels, R., & Pratto, F. (2014). The hidden dynamics of discrimination: How ideologies organize power and influence intergroup relations. In M. Mikulincer, P. R. Shaver, J. F. Dovidio, & J. A. Simpson (Eds.), *APA handbook of personality and social psychology* (vol. 2). Washington, DC: American Psychological Association.

Foer, J. (2008). The unspeakable odyssey of the motionless boy. *Esquire.* www.esquire.com/features/unspeakable-odyssey-motionless-boy-1008 (accessed November 26, 2014)

Fok, H., Hui, C., Bond, M. H., Matsumoto, D., & Yoo, S. H. (2008). Integrating personality, context, relationship, and emotion type into a model of display rules. *Journal of Research in Personality, 42*(1), 133–150.

Folkman, S., & Lazarus, R. S. (1980). An analysis of coping in a middle-aged community sample. *Journal of Health and Social Behavior, 21*(3), 219–239.

Fondell, E., Axelsson, J., Franck, K., Ploner, A., Lekander, M., Bälter, K., & Gaines, H. (2011). Short natural sleep is associated with higher T cell and lower NK cell activities. *Brain, Behavior, and Immunity, 25*(7), 1367–1375.

Fong, C.J., Kim, Y., Davis, C.W., Hoang, T., & Kim, Y.W. (2017). A meta-analysis on critical thinking and community college student achievement. *Thinking Skills and Creativity.* In press.

Foote, B., Smolin, Y., Kaplan, M., Legatt, M. E., & Lipschitz, D. (2006). Prevalence of dissociative disorders in psychiatric outpatients. *American Journal of Psychiatry, 163*(4), 566–568.

Foote, M. (2012). Freedom from high-stakes testing: A formula for small school success. In M. Hantzopoulos & A. R. Tyner-Mullings (Eds.), *Critical small schools: Beyond privatization in New York City urban educational reform* (pp. 121–133). Charlotte, NC: IAP Information Age Publishing.

Forbes, M. K., Eaton, N. R., & Krueger, R. F. (2017). Sexual quality of life and aging: A prospective study of a nationally representative sample. *The Journal of Sex Research, 54*(2), 137–148.

Forbes, T. A., & Gallo, V. (2017). All wrapped up: Environmental effects on myelination. *Trends in Neurosciences, 40*(9), 572–587.

Forbush, K., Heatherton, T. F., & Keel, P. K. (2007). Relationships between perfectionism and specific disordered eating behaviors. *International Journal of Eating Disorders, 40*(1), 37–41.

Ford, B. Q., Lam, P., John, O. P., & Mauss, I. B. (2017). The psychological health benefits of accepting negative emotions and thoughts: Laboratory, diary, and longitudinal evidence. *Journal of Personality and Social Psychology*, in press. doi:10.1037/pspp0000157

Forgas, J. P., Fiedler, K., & Sedikides, C. (Eds.). (2012). *Social thinking and interpersonal behavior.* New York: Psychology Press.

Forman-Hoffman, V. L., & Cunningham, C. L. (2008). Geographical clustering of eating disordered behaviors in U.S. high school students. *International Journal of Eating Disorders, 41*(3), 209–214.

Fornaciari, C. J., & Lund Dean, K. (2013). I, S, T, and J Grading Techniques for Es, Ns, Fs, and Ps: Insights from the MBTI on managing the grading process. *Journal of Management Education, 37*(6), 828–853. doi:10.1177/1052562912461737

Fortuna, K., & Knafo, A. (2014). Parental and genetic contributions to prosocial behavior during childhood. In L. M. Padilla-Walker & G. Carlo (Eds.), *Prosocial development: A multidimensional approach* (pp. 70–89). New York: Oxford University Press. doi:10.1093/acprof: oso/9780199964772.003.0004

Foss Sigurdson, J., Undheim, A. M., Lance Wallander, J., Lydersen, S., & Sund, A. M. (2017). The Longitudinal Association of Being Bullied and Gender with Suicide Ideations, Self-Harm, and Suicide Attempts from Adolescence to Young Adulthood: A Cohort Study. *Suicide and Life-Threatening Behavior.* in press.

Fountas, K. N., & Smith, J. R. (2007). Historical evolution of stereotactic amygdalotomy for the management of severe aggression. *Journal of Neurosurgery, 106*(4), 710–713.

Fournier, J. C., DeRubeis, R. J., Hollon, S. D., Dimidjian, S., Amsterdam, J. D., Shelton, R. C., & Fawcett, J. (2010). Antidepressant drug effects and depression severity: A patient-level meta-analysis. *Journal of the American Medical Association, 303*(1), 47–53.

Fox, H. C., Milivojevic, V., Angarita, G. A., Stowe, R., & Sinha, R. (2017). Peripheral immune system suppression in early abstinent alcohol-dependent individuals: Links to stress and cue-related craving. *Journal Of Psychopharmacology, 31*(7), 883–892.

Francis, N. A., & Kanold, P. O. (2017). Automated operant conditioning in the mouse home cage. *Frontiers in Neural Circuits*, 11.

Francis, R., Estlin, T., Doran, G., Johnstone, S., Gaines, D., Verma, V., Burl, M. Frydenvang, J., Montaño, S., Wiens, R.C., Schaffer, S. Gasnault, O. DeFlores, L., Blaney, D., & Bornstein, B. (2017). AEGIS autonomous targeting for ChemCam on Mars Science Laboratory: Deployment and results of initial science team use. *Science Robotics, 2*, eaan4582 DOI: 10.1126/scirobotics. aan4582

Franco, B., & Malgrange, B. (2017). Concise review: Regeneration in mammalian cochlea hair cells: Help from supporting cells transdifferentiation. *Stem Cells, 35*(3), 551–556.

Frank, D. W., & others. (2014). Emotion regulation: Quantitative meta-analysis of functional activation and deactivation. *Neuroscience and Biobehavioral Reviews, 45*, 202–211.

Frank, M. G. (2017). Sleep and plasticity in the visual cortex: more than meets the eye. *Current Opinion in Neurobiology, 44*, 8–12.

Franke, K., & Baden, T. (2017). General features of inhibition in the inner retina. *The Journal of Physiology, 595*(16), 5507–5515. doi:10.1113/JP273648

Frankl, V. E. (1946/1984). *Man's search for meaning* (3rd ed.). New York: First Washington Square Press. (original work published 1946)

Franklin, M. S., Smallwood, J., Zedelius, C. M., Broadway, J. M., & Schooler, J. W. (2016). Unaware yet reliant on attention: Experience sampling reveals that mind-wandering impedes implicit learning. *Psychonomic Bulletin & Review, 23*(1), 223–229.

Franssen, M., Claes, N., Vervliet, B., Beckers, T., Hermans, D., & Baeyens, F. (2017). Reinstatement after human feature-positive discrimination learning. *Behavioural processes*. in press.

Frattaroli, J. (2006). Experimental disclosure and its moderators: A meta-analysis. *Psychological Bulletin, 132*(6), 823–865.

Frazier, T. W., Strauss, M., Klingemier, E. W., Zetzer, E. E., Hardan, A. Y., Eng, C., & Youngstrom, E. A. (2017). A meta-analysis of gaze differences to social and nonsocial information between individuals with and without autism. *Journal of the American Academy of Child & Adolescent Psychology, 56*, 546–555

Fredrick, S., & Loewenstein, G. (1999). Hedonic adaptation. In D. Kahneman, E. Diener, & N. Schwarz (Eds.), *Well-being: The foundations of hedonic psychology* (pp. 302–329). New York: Russell Sage Foundation.

Fredrickson, B. L. (1998). What good are positive emotions? *Review of General Psychology, 2*(3), 300–319.

Fredrickson, B. L. (2013). Positive emotions broaden and build. In P. Devine & A. Plant (Eds.), *Advances in experimental social psychology* (vol. 47, pp. 1–53). New York: Elsevier.

Fredrickson, B. L., & Siegel, D. J. (2017). Broaden-and-build theory meets interpersonal neurobiology as a lens on compassion and positivity resonance. In P. Gilbert (Eds.), *Compassion: Concepts, research and applications* (pp. 203–217). New York: Routledge/Taylor & Francis Group.

Fredrickson, B. L., Cohn, M. A., Coffey, K. A., Pek, J., & Finkel, S. M. (2008). Open hearts build lives: Positive emotions, induced through loving-kindness meditation, build consequential personal resources. *Journal of Personality and Social Psychology, 95*(5), 1045–1062.

Fredrickson, B. L., Tugade, M. M., Waugh, C. E., & Larkin, G. R. (2003). What good are positive emotions in crisis? A prospective study of resilience and emotions

following the terrorist attacks on the United States on September 11th, 2001. *Journal of Personality and Social Psychology, 84*(2), 365–376.

Freedman, J. L., & Fraser, S. C. (1966). Compliance without pressure: The foot-in-the-door technique. *Journal of Personality and Social Psychology, 4*(2), 195–202.

Freeland, A., Manchanda, R., Chiu, S., Sharma, V., & Merskey, H. (1993). Four cases of supposed multiple personality disorder: Evidence of unjustified diagnoses. *Canadian Journal of Psychiatry, 38*(4), 245–247.

Freeman, L. M., Locke, J., Rotheram-Fuller, E., & Mandell, D. (2017). Brief report: Examining executive and social functioning in elementary-aged children with autism. *Journal of Autism and Developmental Disorders, 47*(6), 1890–1895.

French, B., & Neville, H. A. (2017). What is nonconsensual sex? Young women identify sources of coerced sex. *Violence Against Women, 23*(3), 368–394. doi:10.1177/1077801216641517

Frenda, S. J., Nichols, R. M., & Loftus, E. F. (2011). Current issues and advances in misinformation research. *Current Directions in Psychological Science, 20*(1), 20–23.

Frensch, K. M., Pratt, M. W., & Norris, J. E. (2007). Foundations of generativity: Personal and family correlates of emerging adults' generative life-story themes. *Journal of Research in Personality, 41*(1), 45–62.

Freud, S. (1911). *The interpretation of dreams* (3rd ed.). A. A. Brill (Trans.). New York: Macmillan. (original work published 1899).

Freud, S. (1917). *A general introduction to psychoanalysis.* New York: Washington Square Press.

Freud, S. (1996). Number 23091. In R. Andrews, M. Seidel, & M. Biggs (Eds.), *Columbia World of Quotations.* New York: Columbia University Press. (original work published in 1918).

Freund, A. M., Nikitin, J., & Riediger, M. (2013). Successful aging. In R. M. Lerner, M. A. Easterbrooks, J. Mistry, & I. B. Weiner (Eds.), *Handbook of psychology* (2nd ed., vol. 6, pp. 615–638). New York: Wiley.

Frewen, P. A., & Lanius, R. A. (2014). Trauma-related altered states of consciousness: Exploring the 4-D model. *Journal of Trauma and Dissociation, 15*(4), 436–456.

Fried, L. E., Williams, S., Cabral, H., & Hacker, K. (2013). Differences in risk factors for suicide attempts among 9th and 11th grade youth: A longitudinal perspective. *Journal of School Nursing, 29*(2), 113–122.

Fried, S. (2008, October 9). Commentary on "Think fat just hangs around, does nothing." *USA Today*, 6D.

Friedman, J. P., & Jack, A. I. (2017). Mapping cognitive structure onto the landscape of philosophical debate: An empirical framework with relevance to problems of consciousness, free will and ethics. *Review of Philosophy and Psychology*, in press.

Friedman, L. M., Rapport, M. D., Raiker, J. S., Orban, S. A., & Eckrich, S. J. (2017). Reading comprehension in boys with ADHD: The mediating roles of working memory and orthographic conversion. *Journal of Abnormal Child Psychology, 45*(2), 273–287.

Friedman, M., & Rosenman, R. (1974). *Type A behavior and your heart.* New York: Knopf.

Friedman, N. P., & Miyake, A. (2017). Unity and diversity of executive functions: Individual differences as a window on cognitive structure. *Cortex, 86*, 186–204.

Friedman, R., Myers, P., & Benson, H. (1998). Meditation and the relaxation response. In H. S. Friedman (Ed.), *Encyclopedia of mental health* (vol. 2). San Diego: Academic.

Frijda, N. H. (2007). *The laws of emotion.* Mahwah, NJ: Erlbaum.

Frohard-Dourlent, H., Dobson, S., Clark, B. A., Doull, M., & Saewyc, E. M. (2017). "I would have preferred more options": Accounting for non-binary youth in health research. *Nursing inquiry, 24*(1). http://onlinelibrary.wiley.com/doi/10.1111/ nin.12150/full

Fromm, E. (1947). *Man for himself.* New York: Holt, Rinehart & Winston.

Fromm, E. (1973). *The anatomy of human destructiveness.* New York: Fawcett.

Frosch, A. (2014). Psychoanalysis: The sacred and the profane. *American Journal of Psychoanalysis, 74*(2), 133–146.

Fu, Q., Liu, Y. J., Dienes, Z., Wu, J., Chen, W., & Fu, X. (2017). Neural correlates of subjective awareness for natural scene categorization of color photographs and line-drawings. *Frontiers in Psychology, 8.*

Fuertes, J. N., & Nutt Williams, E. (2017). Client-focused psychotherapy research. *Journal of Counseling Psychology, 64*(4), 369–375.

Fuglset, T. S., Endestad, T., Landrø, N. I., & Rø, Ø. (2014). Brain structure alterations associated with weight changes in young females with anorexia nervosa: A case series. *Neurocase, 21*(2), 169–177

Funder, D. C. (2009). Persons, behaviors, and situations: An agenda for personality psychology in the postwar era. *Journal of Research in Personality, 43*(2), 120–126.

Fung, M. T., Raine, A., Loeber, R., Lynam, D. R., Steinhauer, S. R., Venables, P. H., & Stouthamer-Loeber, M. (2005). Reduced electrodermal activity in psychopathy-prone adolescents. *Journal of Abnormal Psychology, 114*(2), 187–196.

Furaker, B., & Hedenus, A. (2009). Gambling windfall decisions: Lottery winners and employment behavior. *UNLV Gaming Research & Review Journal, 13*(2), 1–15.

Furley, P., & Schweizer, G. (2016). In a flash: Thin slice judgment accuracy of leading and trailing in sports. *Journal of Nonverbal Behavior, 40*(2), 83–100. doi:10.1007/s10919-015-0225-5

Furukawa, S., Fujita, T., Shimabukuro, M., Iwaki, M., Yamada, Y., Nakajima, Y., et al. (2017). Increased oxidative stress in obesity and its impact on metabolic syndrome. *The Journal of Clinical Investigation, 114*(12), 1752–1761.

Furukawa, T. A., Weitz, E. S., Tanaka, S., Hollon, S. D., Hofmann, S. G., Andersson, G., et al. (2017). Initial severity of depression and efficacy of cognitive–behavioural therapy: individual-participant data meta-analysis of pill-placebo-controlled trials. *The British Journal of Psychiatry, 210*(3), 190–196.

G

Gaffrey, M. S., Barch, D. M., Bogdan, R., Farris, K., Petersen, S. E., & Luby, J. L. (2018). Amygdala reward reactivity mediates the association between preschool stress response and depression severity. *Biological Psychiatry, 83*(2), 128–136.

Galambos, N. L., Howard, A. L., & Maggs, J. L. (2011). Rise and fall of sleep quality with student experiences across the first year of the university. *Journal of Research on Adolescence, 21*(2), 342–349.

Galderisi, S., Vignapiano, A., Mucci, A., & Boutros, N. N. (2014). Physiological correlates of positive symptoms in schizophrenia. *Current Topics in Behavioral Neuroscience, 21*, 103–128.

Gale, C. R., Booth, T., Möttus, R., Kuh, D., & Deary, J. J. (2013). Neuroticism and extraversion in youth predict mental wellbeing and life satisfaction 40 years later. *Journal of Research in Personality, 47*(6), 687–697.

Galilee, A., Stefanidou, C., & McCleery, J. P. (2017). Atypical speech versus non-speech detection and discrimination in 4 to 6-yr old children with autism spectrum disorder: An ERP study. *PloS one, 12*(7), e0181354.

Gallagher, A., Dagenais, L., Doussau, A., Décarie, J. C., Materassi, M., Gagnon, K., et al. (2017). Significant motor improvement in an infant with congenital heart disease and a rolandic stroke: The impact of early intervention. *Developmental Neurorehabilitation, 20*(3), 165–168.

Gallucci, A., Martin, R., Beaujean, A., & Usdan, S. (2015). An examination of the misuse of prescription stimulants among college students using the theory of planned behavior. *Psychology, Health & Medicine, 20*(2), 217–226. doi:10.1080/13548506.2014.913800

Gamond, L., Vecchi, T., Ferrari, C., Merabet, L. B., & Cattaneo, Z. (2017). Emotion processing in early blind and sighted individuals. *Neuropsychology, 31*(5), 516.

Gannon, T. A., Wood, J. L., Pina, A., Tyler, N., Barnoux, M. F., & Vasquez, E. A. (2014). An evaluation of mandatory polygraph testing for sexual offenders in the United Kingdom. *Sexual Abuse, 26*(2), 178–203.

Gantiva, C., Ballén, Y., Casas, M., Camacho, K., Guerra, P., & Vila, J. (2015). Influence of motivation to quit smoking on the startle reflex: Differences between smokers in different stages of change. *Motivation & Emotion, 39*(2), 293–298. doi:10.1007/s11031-014-9449-7

Garb, H. N., Wood, J. M., Nezworski, M. T., Grove, W. M., & Stejskal, W. J. (2001). Toward a resolution of the Rorschach controversy. *Psychological Assessment, 13*(4), 433–448.

Garcia, J. (1989). Food for Tolman: Cognition and cathexis in concert. In T. Archer & L. Nilsson (Eds.), *Aversion, avoidance, and anxiety.* Mahwah, NJ: Erlbaum.

Garcia, J., & Koelling, R. A. (1966). Relation of cue to consequence in avoidance learning. *Psychonomic Science, 4*(1), 123–124.

Garcia, J., & Koelling, R. A. (2009). Specific hungers and poison avoidance as adaptive specializations of learning. In D. Shanks (Ed.), *Psychology of learning.* Thousand Oaks, CA: Sage.

Garcia, J., Ervin, F. E., & Koelling, R. A. (1966). Learning with prolonged delay of reinforcement. *Psychonomic Science, 5*(3), 121–122.

Garcia, L. F., Aluja, A., Fibla, J., Cuevas, L., & Garcia, O. (2010). Incremental effect for antisocial personality disorder genetic risk combining 5-HTTLPR and 5-HTTVNTR polymorphisms. *Psychiatry Research, 177*(1–2), 161–166.

Garcia, R. (2017). Neurobiology of fear and specific phobias. *Learning & Memory, 24*(9), 462–471.

Gardner, H. (1983). *Frames of mind.* New York: Basic.

Gardner, H. (1993). *Multiple intelligences.* New York: Basic.

Gardner, H. (2002). The pursuit of excellence through education. In M. Ferrari (Ed.), *Learning from extraordinary minds.* Mahwah, NJ: Erlbaum.

Gardner, M. K. (2014). Theories of intelligence. In M. A. Bray & T. J. Kehle (Eds.), *Oxford handbook of school psychology.* New York: Oxford University Press.

Gardner, W. L., & Martinko, M. J. (1996). Using the Myers-Briggs Type Indicator to study managers: A literature review and research agenda. *Journal of Management, 22*, 45–83.

Garety, P., & others. (2014). Cognitive mechanisms of change in delusions: An experimental investigation targeting reasoning to effect change in paranoia. *Schizophrenia Bulletin.* PMID: 25053650

Garrett, B. L. (2011). *Convicting the innocent: Where criminal prosecutions go wrong.* Cambridge, MA: Harvard University Press.

Gartstein, M. A., Putnam, S. P., Aron, E. N., & Rothbart, M. K. (2016). Temperament and personality. In S. Maltzman (Ed.), The *Oxford handbook of treatment processes and outcomes in psychology: A multidisciplinary, biopsychosocial approach* (pp. 11–41). New York, NY: Oxford University Press.

Garver, D. L. (2006). Evolution of antipsychotic intervention in the schizophrenic psychosis. *Current Drug Targets, 7*(9), 1205–1215.

Gates, G. (2017). *In US, More Adults Identifying as LGBT.* Washington, DC: Gallup. http://news.gallup.com/poll/201731/lgbt-identification-rises.aspx

Geary, D. C. (2006). Evolutionary developmental psychology: Current status and future directions. *Developmental Review, 26*(2), 113–119.

Gedam, S. R., Patil, P. S., & Shivji, I. A. (2018). Childhood night terrors and sleepwalking: diagnosis and treatment. *Open Journal of Psychiatry & Allied Sciences, 9*(1), 73–74.

Geib, B. R., Stanley, M. L., Dennis, N. A., Woldorff, M. G., & Cabeza, R. (2017). From hippocampus to whole-brain: The role of integrative processing in episodic memory retrieval. *Human brain mapping, 38*(4), 2242–2259.

Geiser, C., Götz, T., Preckel, F., & Freund, P. A. (2017). States and traits: Theories, models, and assessment. *European Journal of Psychological Assessment, 33*(4), 219–223. doi:10.1027/1015-5759/a000413

Geller, E. S. (2002). The challenge of increasing proenvironmental behavior. In R. B. Bechtel & A. Churchman (Eds.), *Handbook of environmental psychology* (pp. 525–540). Hoboken, NJ: Wiley.

Geller, E. S. (2006). Occupational injury prevention and applied behavior analysis. In A. C. Gielen, D. A. Sleet, & R. J. DiClemente (Eds.), *Injury and violence prevention: Behavioral science theories, methods, and applications* (pp. 297–322). San Francisco: Jossey-Bass.

Gelo, O. C. G., Pritz, A., & Rieken, B. (Eds.). (2014). *Psychotherapy research: Foundations, process, and outcome.* Vienna/New York: Springer.

Generoso, M. B., Trevizol, A. P., Kasper, S., Cho, H. J., Cordeiro, Q., & Shiozawa, P. (2017). Pregabalin for generalized anxiety disorder: an updated systematic review and meta-analysis. *International Clinical Psychopharmacology, 32*(1), 49–55.

Genetics of Personality Consortium. (2015). Meta-analysis of genome-wide association studies for neuroticism, and the polygenic association with major depressive disorder. *JAMA Psychiatry, 72*(7), 642–650. doi:10.1001/jamapsychiatry.2015.0554

Gentile, D. A., Li, D., Khoo, A., Prot, S., & Anderson, C. A. (2014). Mediators and moderators of long-term effects of violent video games on aggressive behavior: Practice, thinking, and action. *JAMA Pediatrics, 168*(5), 450–457.

Geoffroy, M. C., Li, L., & Power, C. (2014). Depressive symptoms and body mass index: Co-morbidity and direction of association in a British birth cohort followed over 50 years. *Psychological Medicine, 44*(12), 2641–2652.

George, L. S., & Park, C. L. (2017). Does spirituality confer meaning in life among heart failure patients and cancer survivors? *Psychology of Religion and Spirituality, 9*(1), 131–136. doi:10.1037/rel0000103

Georgeson, M. A., Wallis, S. A., Meese, T. S., & Baker, D. H. (2016). Contrast and lustre: A model that accounts for eleven different forms of contrast discrimination in binocular vision. *Vision Research, 129*, 98–118. doi:10.1016/j.visres.2016.08.001

Geraerts, E., Lindsay, D. S., Merckelbach, H., Jelicic, M., Raymaekers, L., Arnold, M. M., & Schooler, J. W. (2009). Cognitive mechanisms underlying recovered-memory experiences of childhood sexual abuse. *Psychological Science, 20*(1), 92–98.

Gerashchenko, D., Pasumarthi, R. K., & Kilduff, T. S. (2017). Plasticity-Related Gene Expression During Eszopiclone-Induced Sleep. *Sleep, 40*, zsx098, doi:10.1093/sleep/zsx098

Germain, A. (2012). Parasomnias I: Nightmares. In C. M. Morin & C. A. Espie (Eds.), *Oxford handbook of sleep and sleep disorders.* New York: Oxford University Press.

Getahun, D., Fassett, M. J., Peltier, M. R., Wing, D. A., Xiang, A. H., Chiu, V., & Jacobsen, S. J. (2017). Association of perinatal risk factors with autism spectrum disorder. *American Journal of Perinatology, 34*, 295–304.

Geukes, K., Nestler, S., Hutteman, R., Dufner, M., Küfner, A. P., Egloff, B., et al. (2017). Puffed-up but shaky selves: State self-esteem level and variability in narcissists. *Journal of Personality and Social Psychology, 112*(5), 769–786. doi:10.1037/pspp0000093

Geuter, S., Koban, L., & Wager, T. D. (2017). The cognitive neuroscience of Placebo Effects: concepts, predictions, and physiology. *Annual Review of Neuroscience.* in press.

Ghosal, S., Hare, B. D., & Duman, R. S. (2017). Prefrontal cortex GABAergic deficits and circuit dysfunction in the pathophysiology and treatment of chronic stress and depression. *Current Opinion in Behavioral Sciences, 14*, 1–8.

Giang, D. W., Goodman, A. D., Schiffer, R. B., Mattson, D. H., Petrie, M., Cohen, N., & Ader, R. (1996). Conditioning of cyclophosphamide-induced leukopenia in humans. *Journal of Neuropsychiatry and Clinical Neuroscience, 8*(2), 194–201.

Gibbs, J. C. (2014). *Moral development and reality: Beyond the theories of Kohlberg and Hoffman* (3rd ed.). New York: Oxford University Press.

Gilbert, A. L., Regier, T., Kay, P., & Ivry, R. B. (2006). Whorf hypothesis is supported in the right visual field but not the left. *Proceedings of the National Academy of Sciences USA, 103*(2), 489–494.

Gilbert, D. T., & Malone, P. S. (1995). The correspondence bias. *Psychological Bulletin, 117*(1), 21–38.

Gilboa, A., & Marlatte, H. (2017). Neurobiology of schemas and schema-mediated memory. *Trends in Cognitive Sciences.* in press.

Gilboa-Schechtman, E., Keshet, H., Livne, T., Berger, U., Zabag, R., Hermesh, H., & Marom, S. (2017). Explicit and implicit self-evaluations in social anxiety disorder. *Journal of Abnormal Psychology, 126*(3), 285–290.

Gillet, R. (December, 7, 2016). The 50 best places to work in 2017, according to employees. *Business Insider.com.* http://www.businessinsider.com/best-places-to-work-2017-2016-12/#6-fast-enterprises-45

Gilligan, C. (1982). *In a different voice.* Cambridge, MA: Harvard University Press.

Gilmore, A. K., Walsh, K., Badour, C. L., Ruggiero, K. J., Kilpatrick, D. G., & Resnick, H. S. (2017). Suicidal ideation, posttraumatic stress, and substance abuse based on forcible and drug- or alcohol-facilitated/incapacitated rape histories in a national sample of women. *Suicide and Life-Threatening Behavior.* in press. DOI: 10.1111/sltb.12337

Gino, F., Kouchaki, M., & Galinsky, A. D. (2015). The moral virtue of authenticity: How inauthenticity produces feelings of immorality and impurity. *Psychological Science, 26*(7), 983–996.

Ginsburg, V., Archambeau, K., van Dijck, J. P., Chetail, F., & Gevers, W. (2017). Coding of serial order in verbal, visual and spatial working memory. *Journal of Experimental Psychology: General, 146*(5), 632–650.

Ginting, H., van de Ven, M., Becker, E. S., & Näring, G. (2014). Type D personality is associated with health behaviors and perceived social support in individuals with coronary heart disease. *Journal of Health Psychology.* doi: 10.1177/1359105314536750

Girgenti, M. J., Hare, B. D., Ghosal, S., & Duman, R. S. (2017). Molecular and Cellular Effects of Traumatic Stress: Implications for PTSD. *Current Psychiatry Reports, 19*(11), 85. https://doi.org/10.1007/s11920-017-0841-3

Gittelman, M. (2008). Editor's introduction: Why are the mentally ill dying? *International Journal of Mental Health, 37*(1), 3–12.

Glaw, X. M., Garrick, T. M., Terwee, P. J., Patching, J. R., Blake, H., & Harper, C. (2009). Brain donation: Who and why? *Cell and Tissue Banking, 10*(3), 241–246.

Glogger-Frey, I., Gaus, K., & Renkl, A. (2017). Learning from direct instruction: Best prepared by several self-regulated or guided invention activities? *Learning and Instruction, 51*, 26–35.

Glum, J. (2015, September 22). Millennials selfies: Young adults will take more than 25,000 pictures of themselves during their lifetimes: Report. *International Business Times.* http://www.ibtimes.com/millennials-selfies-young-adults-will-take-more-25000-pictures-themselves-during-2108417 (accessed March 3, 2016)

Godden, D. R., & Baddeley, A. D. (1975). Context-dependent memory in two natural environments: On land

and under water. *British Journal of Psychology, 66*(3), 325–331.

Goel, A. K., & Davies, J. (2011). Artificial intelligence. In R. J. Sternberg & S. B. Kaufman (Eds.), *The Cambridge handbook of intelligence.* New York: Cambridge University Press.

Goethals, G. R., & Demorest, A. P. (1995). The risky shift is a sure bet. In M. E. Ware & D. E. Johnson (Eds.), *Demonstrations and activities in teaching of psychology* (vol. 3). Mahwah, NJ: Erlbaum.

Golchert, J., Smallwood, J., Jefferies, E., Seli, P., Huntenburg, J. M., Liem, F., & … Margulies, D. S. (2017). Individual variation in intentionality in the mind-wandering state is reflected in the integration of the default-mode, fronto-parietal, and limbic networks. *Neuroimage, 146,* 226–235. doi:10.1016/j.neuroimage.2016.11.025

Goldin-Meadow, S. (2014a). Language and the manual modality: How our hands help us talk and think. In N. J. Enfield & others (Eds.), *The Cambridge handbook of linguistic anthropology.* New York: Cambridge University Press.

Goldin-Meadow, S. (2014b). Widening the lens: What the manual modality reveals about language, learning, and cognition. *Philosophical Transactions of the Royal Society, Series B, 369*(1651), 20130295.

Goldschmidt, A. B., Crosby, R. D., Cao, L., Pearson, C. M., Utzinger, L. M., Pacanowski, C. R., et al. (2017). Contextual factors associated with eating in the absence of hunger among adults with obesity. *Eating Behaviors, 26,* 33–39.

Goldsmith, A. A., Thompson, R. D., Black, J. J., Tran, G. Q., & Smith, J. P. (2012). Drinking refusal self-efficacy and tension-reduction alcohol expectancies moderating the relationship between generalized anxiety and drinking behaviors in young adult drinkers. *Psychology of Addictive Behaviors, 26*(1), 59–67.

Goldstein, B. I., Birmaher, B., Carlson, G. A., DelBello, M. P., Findling, R. L., Fristad, M., et al. (2017). The International Society for Bipolar Disorders Task Force report on pediatric bipolar disorder: Knowledge to date and directions for future research. *Bipolar Disorders.* In press. doi:10.1111/bdi.12556

Goldstein, E. B. (2015). *Cognitive psychology.* Boston: Cengage.

Goldstein, M. H., King, A. P., & West, M. J. (2003). Social interaction shapes babbling: Testing parallels between birdsong and speech. *Proceedings of the National Academy of Sciences USA, 100*(13), 8030–8035.

Goldstein, R. B., Chou, S. P., Saha, T. D., Smith, S. M., Jung, J., Zhang, H., et al. (2017). The epidemiology of antisocial behavioral syndromes in adulthood: Results from the National Epidemiologic Survey on Alcohol and Related Conditions-III. *The Journal of Clinical Psychiatry, 78*(1), 90–98.

Goldston, D. B., Molock, S. D., Whibeck, L. B., Murakami, J. L., Zayas, L. H., & Hall, G. C. (2008). Cultural considerations in adolescent suicide prevention and psychosocial treatment. *American Psychologist, 63*(1), 14–31.

Goldstrom, I. D., Campbell, J., Rogers, J. A., Lambert, D. B., Blacklow, B., Henderson, M. J., & Manderscheid, R. W. (2006). National estimates for mental health mutual support groups, self-help organizations, and consumer-operated services. *Administration and Policy in Mental Health, 33*(1), 92–103.

Goleman, D., Kaufman, P., & Ray, M. (1993). *The creative mind.* New York: Plume.

Golier, J. A., Yehuda, R., & Baker, D. (2017). A randomized clinical trial of a glucocorticoid receptor antagonist in PTSD. *Psychoneuroendocrinology, 83,* 87.

Gollan, T. H., Ferreira, V. S., Cera, C., & Flett, S. (2014). Translation-priming effects on tip-of-the-tongue states. *Language and Cognitive Processes, 29*(3), 278–288.

Golombok, S., Mellish, L., Jennings, S., Casey, P., Tasker, F., & Lamb, M. E. (2014). Adoptive gay father families: Parent–child relationships and children's psychological adjustment. *Child Development, 85*(2), 456–468.

Goltseker, K., Bolotin, L., & Barak, S. (2017). Counterconditioning during reconsolidation prevents relapse of cocaine memories. *Neuropsychopharmacology, 42,* 716–726.

Gomes, A. R., & Teixeira, P. M. (2014). Stress, cognitive appraisal, and psychological health: Testing instruments for health professionals. *Stress and Health.* doi: 10.1002/smi.2583

Gómez-Ariza, C. J., del Prete, F., Prieto del Val, L., Valle, T., Bajo, M. T., & Fernandez, A. (2017). Memory inhibition as a critical factor preventing creative problem solving. *Journal of Experimental Psychology: Learning, Memory, and Cognition, 43*(6), 986–996. doi:10.1037/xlm0000348

Gomez-Nicola, D., & Perry, V. H. (2014). Microglial dynamics and role in the healthy and diseased brain: A paradigm of functional plasticity. *Neuroscientist.* doi: 10.1177/1073858414530512

Gonda, X., & others. (2009). Association of the s allele of the 5-HTTLPR with neuroticism-related traits and temperaments in a psychiatrically healthy population. *European Archives of Psychiatry and Clinical Neuroscience, 259*(2), 106–113.

González, R., Lickel, B., Gupta, M., Tropp, L. R., Luengo Kanacri, B. P., Mora, E., et al. (2017). Ethnic identity development and acculturation preferences among minority and majority youth: Norms and contact. *Child Development, 88*(3), 743–760.

Gonzalez-Vallejo, C., Lassiter, G. D., Bellezza, F. S., & Lindberg, M. J. (2008). "Save angels perhaps": A critical examination of unconscious thought theory and the deliberation-without-attention effect. *Review of General Psychology, 12*(3), 282–296.

Goode, E., & Schwartz, J. (2011, August 28). Police lineups start to face fact: Eyes can lie. *New York Times,* A1.

Goode, T. D., Holloway-Erickson, C. M., & Maren, S. (2017). Extinction after fear memory reactivation fails to eliminate renewal in rats. *Neurobiology of Learning and Memory.* in press.

Goodman, M., Tomas, I. A., Temes, C. M., Fitzmaurice, G. M., Aguirre, B. A., & Zanarini, M. C. (2017). Suicide attempts and self-injurious behaviours in adolescent and adult patients with borderline personality disorder. *Personality and Mental Health, 11,* 157–163.

Goodson, M. L., Packard, A. B., Buesing, D. R., Maney, M., Myers, B., Fang, Y., et al. (2017). Chronic stress and Rosiglitazone increase indices of vascular stiffness in male rats. *Physiology & Behavior, 17,* 216–223. doi:10.1016/j.physbeh.2016.03.031

Goodvin, R., Thompson, R. A., & Winer, A. C. (2016). The individual child: Temperament, emotion, self, and personality. In M. H. Bornstein & M. E. Lamb (Eds.), *Developmental science* (7th ed.). New York: Psychology Press.

Goodwin, H., Yiend, J., & Hirsch, C. (2017). Generalized Anxiety Disorder, worry and attention to threat: A systematic review. *Clinical Psychology Review, 54,* 107–122.

Gooley, J. J. (2017). Light-induced Resetting of Circadian Rhythms in Humans. *Journal of Science and Technology in Lighting,* in press.

Goosens, K. A. (2011). Hippocampal regulation of aversive memories. *Current Opinion in Neurobiology, 21*(3), 460–466.

Gorbaniuk, O., Razmus, W., Slobodianyk, A., Mykhailych, O., Troyanowskyj, O., Kashchuk, M., et al. (2017). Searching for a common methodological ground for the study of politicians' perceived personality traits: A multilevel psycholexical approach. *Journal of Research in Personality, 70,* 27–44.

Gordon, A. M., & Chen, S. (2016). Do you get where I'm coming from? Perceived understanding buffers against the negative impact of conflict on relationship satisfaction. *Journal of Personality and Social Psychology, 110*(2), 239–260.

Gordon, B., Chen, S., & Durstine, J. L. (2014). The effects of exercise training on the traditional lipid profile and beyond. *Current Sports Medicine Reports, 13*(4), 253–259.

Gordon, I., Zagoory-Sharon, O., Leckman, J. F., & Feldman, R. (2010). Oxytocin and the development of parenting in humans. *Biological Psychiatry, 68*(4), 377–382.

Goritz, C., & Frisén, J. (2012). Neural stem cells and neurogenesis in the adult. *Cell: Stem Cell, 10*(6), 657–659.

Gosling, S. D. (2008). Personality in nonhuman animals. *Social and Personality Psychology Compass, 2*(2), 985–1001.

Gosling, S. D., & John, O. P. (1999). Personality dimensions in nonhuman animals: A cross-species review. *Current Directions in Psychological Science, 8*(3), 69–75.

Gosling, S. D., Kwan, V. S., & John, O. (2003). A dog's got personality: A cross-species comparison of personality judgments in dogs and humans. *Journal of Personality and Social Psychology, 85*(6), 1161–1169.

Gottfredson, L. S., & Deary, I. J. (2004). Intelligence predicts health and longevity, but why? *Current Directions in Psychological Science, 13,* 1–4.

Gottlieb, G. (2007). Probabilistic epigenesis. *Developmental Science, 10*(1), 1–11.

Gottman, J. M. (2006, April 29). Love special: Secrets of long-term love. *New Scientist, 2549,* 40.

Gottman, J. M., Swanson, C., & Swanson, K. (2002). A general systems theory of marriage: Nonlinear difference equation modeling of marital interaction. *Personality and Social Psychology Review, 6*(4), 326–340.

Goyal, M., & others. (2014). *Meditation programs for psychological and well-being.* Rockville, MD: Agency for Healthcare Research and Quality (U.S.).

Graber, J. A. (2013). Pubertal timing and the development of psychopathology in adolescence and beyond. *Hormones and Behavior, 64*(2), 262–269.

Graeff, F. G. (2017). Translational approach to the pathophysiology of panic disorder: Focus on serotonin and endogenous opioids. *Neuroscience & Biobehavioral Reviews, 76, Part A,* 48–55

Graham, J. R. (2012). *MMPI-2: Assessing personality and psychopathology.* New York: Oxford University Press.

Graham, J., Nosek, B. A., Haidt, J., Iyer, R., Koleva, S., & Ditto, P. H. (2011). Mapping the moral domain. *Journal of Personality and Social Psychology, 101*(2), 366–385.

Graham, S. (2017). Attention-deficit hyperactivity disorder (ADHD), learning disabilities (LD), and executive functioning: Recommendations for future research. *Contemporary Educational Psychology, 50,* 97–101. doi:10.1016/j.cedpsych.2017.01.001

Granacher, R. P. (2014). Commentary: Dissociative amnesia and the future of forensic psychiatry assessment. *Journal of the American Academy of Psychiatry and Law, 42*(2), 214–218.

Grand, J. A. (2017). Brain drain? An examination of stereotype threat effects during training on knowledge acquisition and organizational effectiveness. *Journal of Applied Psychology, 102*(2), 115–150. doi:10.1037/apl0000171

Grandin, T. (2006). *Thinking in pictures: My life with autism.* New York: Random House.

Grando, S. A. (2014). Connections of nicotine to cancer. *Nature Reviews. Cancer, 14*(6), 419–429.

Grant, B. F., & others. (2004). Prevalence and co-occurrence of substance use disorders and independent mood and anxiety disorders: Results from the National Epidemiologic Survey on Alcohol and Related Conditions. *Archives of General Psychiatry, 61*(8), 807–816.

Grant, L. K., Cain, S. W., Chang, A. M., Saxena, R., Czeisler, C. A., & Anderson, C. (2018). Impaired cognitive flexibility during sleep deprivation among carriers of the Brain Derived Neurotrophic Factor (BDNF) Val66Met allele. *Behavioural Brain Research, 338*, 51–55.

Gray, J. A. (1987). *The psychology of fear and stress.* Cambridge, UK: Cambridge University Press.

Gray, J. A., & McNaughton, N. (2000). *The neuropsychology of anxiety: An enquiry into the functions of the septo-hippocampal system.* Oxford: Oxford University Press.

Gray, J. M., & Diller, J. W. (2017). Evaluating the work of applied animal behaviorists as applied behavior analysis. *Behavior Analysis: Research And Practice, 17*(1), 33–41. doi:10.1037/bar0000041

Gray, S. A., Dueck, K., Rogers, M., & Tannock, R. (2017). Qualitative review synthesis: The relationship between inattention and academic achievement. *Educational Research, 59*(1), 17–35.

Gray, S., Green, S., Alt, M., Hogan, T., Kuo, T., Brinkley, S., & Cowan, N. (2017). The structure of working memory in young children and its relation to intelligence. *Journal of Memory and Language, 92*, 183–201.

Grayson, D. S., Bliss-Moreau, E., Bennett, J., Lavenex, P., & Amaral, D. G. (2017). Neural Reorganization Due to Neonatal Amygdala Lesions in the Rhesus Monkey: Changes in Morphology and Network Structure. *Cerebral Cortex, 27*(6), 3240–3253.

Graziano, W. G., & Habashi, M. M. (2015). Searching for the prosocial personality. In D. A. Schroeder & W. G. Graziano (Eds.), *The Oxford handbook of prosocial behavior.* New York: Oxford University Press.

Graziano, W.G., & Tobin, R.M. (2017). Agreeableness. In T.A. Widiger (Ed.), *Oxford Handbook of the Five Factor Model.* New York: Oxford University Press.

Greco, F. A., & Deutsch, C. K. (2017). Carl Gustav Jung and the psychobiology of schizophrenia. *Brain: A Journal Of Neurology, 140*(1).

Gredebäck, C., Kaduk, K., Bakker, M., Gottwald, J., Ekberg, T., Elsner, C., Reid, V., & Kenward, B. (2015). The neuropsychology of infants' pro-social preferences. *Developmental Cognitive Neuroscience, 12*, 106–113. doi:10.1016/j.dcn.2015.01.006

Green, J. P., Page, R. A., Handley, G. W., & Rasekhy, R. (2005). The "hidden observer" and ideomotor responding: A real–simulator comparison. *Contemporary Hypnosis, 22*(3), 123–137.

Greenbaum, C. A., & Javdani, S. (2017). Expressive writing intervention promotes resilience among juvenile justice-involved youth. *Children and Youth Services Review, 73*, 220–229. doi:10.1016/j.childyouth.2016.11.034

Greene, R. L. (2011). *MMPI-2/MMPI-2-RF: An interpretive manual* (3rd ed.). Upper Saddle River, NJ: Pearson.

Greenwald, A. G., Poehlman, T. A., Uhlmann, E., & Banaji, M. R. (2009). Understanding and using the Implicit Association Test: III. Meta-analysis of predictive validity. *Journal of Personality and Social Psychology, 97*(1), 17–41.

Greenwood, C. R., Carta, J. J., Walker, D., Watson-Thompson, J., Gilkerson, J., Larson, A. L., & Schnitz, A. (2017). Conceptualizing a public health prevention intervention for bridging the 30 Million Word Gap. *Clinical Child and Family Psychology Review, 20*, 3–24. doi:10.1007/s10567-017-0223-8

Greer, S., Morris, T., & Pettingale, K. W. (1979). Psychological response to breast cancer: Effect on outcome. *Lancet, 2*(8146) 785–787.

Greitemeyer, T. (2009). Effects of songs with prosocial lyrics on prosocial thoughts, affect, and behavior. *Journal of Experimental Social Psychology, 45*(1), 186–190.

Greitemeyer, T., & Osswald, S. (2010). Effects of prosocial video games on prosocial behavior. *Journal of Personality and Social Psychology, 98*(2), 211–221.

Greitemeyer, T., & Osswald, S. (2011). Playing prosocial video games increases the accessibility of prosocial thoughts. *Journal of Social Psychology, 151*(2), 121–128.

Griffin, B., & Hu, W. (2015). The interaction of socio-economic status and gender in widening participation in medicine. *Medical Education, 49*(1), 103–113.

Griffith, R. L., & Converse, P. D. (2011). The rules of evidence and the prevalence of applicant faking. In M. Ziegler, C. MacCann, & R. Roberts (Eds.), *New perspectives on faking in personality assessment.* New York: Oxford University Press.

Griffiths, J. D., Marslen-Wilson, W. D., Stamatakis, E. A., & Tyler, L. K. (2013). Functional organization of the neural language system: Dorsal and ventral pathways are critical for syntax. *Cerebral Cortex, 23*(1), 139–147.

Griggs, R. A., & Whitehead, G. I. (2015). Coverage of Milgram's obedience experiments in social psychology textbooks: Where have all the criticisms gone? *Teaching of Psychology, 42*(4), 315–322. doi:10.1177/0098628315603065

Grigorenko, E. L., Jarvin, L., Tan, M., & Sternberg, R. J. (2009). Something new in the garden: Assessing creativity in academic domains. *Psychology Science Quarterly, 50*(2), 295–307.

Grilo, C. M., Masheb, R. M., & White, M. A. (2010). Significance of overvaluation of shape/weight in binge-eating disorder: Comparative study with overweight and bulimia nervosa. *Obesity, 18*(3), 499–504.

Grimm, K. J., Davoudzadeh, P., & Ram, N. (2017). Developmental methodology: IV. Developments in the analysis of longitudinal data. *Monographs of the Society for Research in Child Development, 82*(2), 46–66. doi:10.1111/mono.12298

Groh, A. M., Narayan, A. J., Bakermans-Kranenburg, M. J., Roisman, G. I., Vaughn, B. E., Fearon, R. M., & IJzendoorn, M. H. (2017). Attachment and temperament in the early life course: A meta-analytic review. *Child Development, 88*(3), 770–795.

Gross, J. T., Stern, J. A., Brett, B. E., & Cassidy, J. (2017). The multifaceted nature of prosocial behavior in children: Links with attachment theory and research. *Social Development, 26*, 661–678.

Grossman, I., Na, J., Varnum, M. E. W., Park, D. C., Kitayama, S., & Nisbett, R. E. (2010). Reasoning about social conflicts improves into old age. *Proceedings of the National Academy of Sciences USA, 107*(16), 7246–7250.

Grubin, D., & Madsen, L. (2006). Accuracy and utility of post-conviction polygraph testing of sex offenders. *British Journal of Psychiatry, 188*, 479–483.

Grumet, R., & Fitzpatrick, M. (2016). A case for integrating values clarification work into cognitive behavioral therapy for social anxiety disorder. *Journal of Psychotherapy Integration, 26*(1), 11–21.

Grønli, J., Soulé, J., & Bramham, C. R. (2014). Sleep and protein-synthesis-dependent synaptic plasticity: Impacts of sleep loss and stress. *Frontiers in Behavioral Neuroscience, 7*, 224.

Guardino, C. M., Schetter, C. D., Hobel, C. J., Lanzi, R. G., Schafer, P., Thorp, J. M., & Shalowitz, M. U. (2017). Chronic stress and C-reactive protein in mothers during the first postpartum year. *Psychosomatic Medicine, 79*(4), 450–460.

Guerin, B. (2017). Deconstructing psychological therapies as activities in context: What are the goals and what do therapists actually do? *Revista Perspectivas, 8*(01), 097–119.

Gujjar, K. R., van Wijk, A., Sharma, R., & de Jongh, A. (2017). Virtual reality exposure therapy for the treatment of dental phobia: A controlled feasibility study. *Behavioural and Cognitive Psychotherapy*, doi:10.1017/S1352465817000534

Gunderson, J. (2008). Borderline personality disorder: An overview. *Social Work in Mental Health, 6*(1–2), 5–12.

Gunderson, J. G., & others. (2003). Plausibility and possible determinants of sudden "remissions" in borderline patients. *Psychiatry: Interpersonal and Biological Processes, 66*(2), 111–119.

Guo, Y. (2005). Filial therapy for children's behavioral and emotional problems in mainland China. *Journal of Child and Adolescent Psychiatric Nursing, 18*(4), 171–180.

Gutierrez, I. A., Park, C. L., & Wright, B. E. (2017). When the divine defaults: Religious struggle mediates the impact of financial stressors on psychological distress. *Psychology of Religion and Spirituality*, in press. doi:10.1037/rel0000119

Guttman, N., & Kalish, H. I. (1956). Discriminability and stimulus generalization. *Journal of Experimental Psychology, 51*(1), 79–88.

Guye, S., & von Bastian, C. C. (2017). Working memory training in older adults: Bayesian evidence supporting the absence of transfer. *Psychology And Aging, 32*(8), 732–746. doi:10.1037/pag0000206

Guzick, A. G., McNamara, J. P., Reid, A. M., Balkhi, A. M., Storch, E. A., Murphy, T. K., et al. (2017). The link between ADHD-like inattention and obsessions and compulsions during treatment of youth with OCD. *Journal of Obsessive-Compulsive and Related Disorders, 12*, 1–8.

Guéguen, N., Martin, A., Silone, F., & David, M. (2016). Foot-in-the-door technique and reduction of driver's aggressiveness: A field study. *Transportation Research Part F: Traffic Psychology and Behaviour*, 361–365. doi:10.1016/j.trf.2015.10.006

Guérin, E., Biagé, A., Goldfield, G., & Prud'homme, D. (2017). Physical activity and perceptions of stress during the menopause transition: A longitudinal study. *Journal of Health Psychology*, in press.

Gyurkovics, M., Balota, D. A., & Jackson, J. D. (2017). Mind-Wandering in Healthy Aging and Early Stage Alzheimer's Disease. *Neuropsychology*, in press. doi:10.1037/neu0000385

H

Haaker, J., Yi, J., Petrovic, P., & Olsson, A. (2017). Endogenous opioids regulate social threat learning in humans. *Nature Communications, 8*, 15495 doi: 10.1038/ncomms15495

Haase, L., Stewart, J. L., Youssef, B., May, A. C., Isakovic, S., Simmons, A. N., et al. (2016). When the brain does not adequately feel the body: Links between low resilience and interoception. *Biological Psychology, 11*, 337–345. doi:10.1016/j.biopsycho.2015.11.004

Habashi, M. M., Graziano, W. G., & Hoover, A. E. (2016). Searching for the prosocial personality: A big five approach to linking personality and prosocial behavior. *Personality And Social Psychology Bulletin, 42*(9), 1177–1192. doi:10.1177/0146167216652859

Haber, J. R., Koenig, L. B., & Jacob, T. (2011). Alcoholism, personality, religion/spirituality: An integrative review. *Current Drug Abuse Reviews, 4*(4), 250–260.

Haber, S.N., & Knutson, B. (2010). The reward circuit: Linking primate anatomy and human imaging. *Neuropsychopharmacology, 35*, 4–26.

Habermas, T., & Köber, C. (2014). Autobiographical reasoning in life narratives buffers the effects of biographical disruptions on the sense of self-continuity. *Memory, 9*, 1–11.

Hackett, R. A., Hamer, M., Endrighi, R., Brydon, L., & Steptoe, A. (2012). Loneliness and stress-related inflammatory and neuroendocrine responses in older men and women. *Psychoneuroimmunology, 37*(11), 1801–1809.

Hackman, C. L., & Knowlden, A. P. (2014). Theory of reasoned action and theory of planned behavior–based dietary interventions in adolescents and young adults: A systematic review. *Adolescent Health, Medicine, and Therapeutics, 5*, 101–114.

Haeffel, G. J., Hershenberg, R., Goodson, J. T., Hein, S., Grigorenko, E. L., & Chapman, J. (2017). The hopelessness theory of depression: Clinical utility and generalizability. *Cognitive Therapy and Research, 41*, 543–555.

Haesen, K., Beckers, T., Baeyens, F., & Vervliet, B. (2017). One-trial overshadowing: Evidence for fast specific fear learning in humans. *Behaviour Research and Therapy, 90*, 16–24.

Hagger-Johnson, G., Hamer, M., Stamatakis, E., Bell, J. A., Shahab, L., & Batty, G. D. (2014). Association between sitting time in midlife and common mental disorder symptoms: Whitehall II prospective cohort study. *Journal of Psychiatric Research, 57*, 182–184.

Haidle, M. N. (2010). Working memory capacity and the evolution of modern cognitive capacities—Implications from animal and early human tool use. *Current Anthropology, 51*, Suppl. 1 Wenner-Gren Symposium, S149–S166.

Hajek, A. & Helmut-König, H. (2017). The role of self-efficacy, self-esteem and optimism for using routine health check-ups in a population-based sample. A longitudinal perspective. *Preventive Medicine, 105*, 47–51.

Halberstadt, A. L. (2017). Hallucinogenic drugs: A new study answers old questions about LSD. *Current Biology, 27*(4), R156–R158.

Halberstadt, J. (2010). Intuition: Dumb but lucky: Fortuitous affect cues and their disruption by analytic thought. *Social and Personality Psychology Compass, 4*(1), 64–76.

Halberstadt, J., & Catty, S. (2008). Analytic thought disrupts familiarity-based decision making. *Social Cognition, 26*(6), 755–765.

Halfon N., & Forrest C.B. (2018) The emerging theoretical framework of life course health development. In N. Halfon, C. Forrest, R. Lerner, & E. Faustman (Eds.), *Handbook of life course health development.* Cham: Springer. in press.

Hall, J. A., Park, N., Song, H., & Cody, M. J. (2010). Strategic misrepresentation in online dating: The effects of gender, self-monitoring, and personality traits. *Journal of Social and Personal Relationships, 27*(1), 117–135.

Hall, W. J. (2017). Psychosocial risk and protective factors for depression among lesbian, gay, bisexual, and queer youth: A systematic review. *Journal of Homosexuality, 65*, 263–316.

Halldorsdottir, T., & Binder, E.B. (2017). Gene × Environment Interactions: From Molecular Mechanisms to Behavior. *Annual Review of Psychology, 68*, 215–241.

Haller, C. S., Bosma, C. M., Kapur, K., Zafonte, R., & Langer, E. J. (2017). Mindful creativity matters: trajectories of reported functioning after severe traumatic brain injury as a function of mindful creativity in patients' relatives: a multilevel analysis. *Quality of life research, 26*(4), 893–902.

Halpern, C. T., & Haydon, A. A. (2012). Sexual timetables for oral-genital, vaginal, and anal intercourse: Sociodemographic comparisons in a nationally representative sample of adolescents. *American Journal of Public Health, 102*(6), 1221–1228.

Hames, J. L., Hagan, C. R., & Joiner, T. E. (2013). Interpersonal processes in depression. *Annual Review of Clinical Psychology* (vol. 9, pp. 355–377). Palo Alto, CA: Annual Reviews.

Hamilton, B.E., Martin, J.A., Osterman, M.J.K., Driscoll, A.K., & Rossen, L. M. (2017). Births: Provisional data for 2016. *Vital Statistics Rapid Release, 2.* Atlanta: Center for Disease Control and Prevention.

Hamilton, J. L., Hamlat, E. J., Stange, J. P., Abramson, L. Y., & Alloy, L. B. (2014). Pubertal timing and vulnerabilities to depression in early adolescence: Differential pathways to depressive symptoms by sex. *Journal of Adolescence, 37*(2), 165–174.

Hamlin, J. K. (2013). Failed attempts to help and harm: Intention versus outcome in preverbal infants' social evaluations. *Cognition, 128*, 451–474. doi:10.1016/j.cognition.2013.04.004

Hamlin, J. K., & Wynn, K. (2011). Young infants prefer prosocial to antisocial others. *Cognitive Development, 26*, 30–39. doi:10.1016/j.cogdev.2010.09.001

Hamlin, J. K., Wynn, K., & Bloom, P. (2007). Social evaluation by preverbal infants. *Nature, 450*, 557–559. doi:10.1038/nature06288

Hamlin, J. K., Wynn, K., & Bloom, P. (2010). Three-month-olds show a negativity bias in their social evaluations. *Developmental Science, 13*, 923–929. doi:10.1111/j.1467-7687.2010.00951.x

Hammond, D., Lillico, H. G., Vanderlee, L., White, C. M., & Reid, J. L. (2015). The impact of nutrition labeling on menus: A naturalistic cohort study. *American Journal of Health Behavior, 39*(4), 540–548.

Hammond, S. I., Al-Jbouri, E., Edwards, V., & Feltham, L. E. (2017). Infant helping in the first year of life: Parents' recollection of infants' earliest prosocial behaviors. *Infant Behavior and Development, 47*, 54–57.

Hamon, M., & Blier, P. (2013). Monoamine neurocircuitry in depression and strategies for new treatments. *Progress in Neuro-Psychopharmacology & Biological Psychiatry, 45*, 54–63.

Han, S. (2016). Culture, self, and brain: Sociocultural influences on neurocognitive processes of the self. In M. J. Gelfand, C. Chiu, & Y. Hong (Eds.), *Handbook of advances in culture and psychology.* (pp. 77–112). New York: Oxford University Press.

Han, S., Han, S., Yu, F. H., Schwartz, M. D., Linton, J. D., Bosma, M. M., Hurley, J. B., Catterall, W. A., & de la Iglesia, H. O. (2012). Na(V)1.1 channels are critical for intercellular communication in the suprachiasmatic nucleus and for normal circadian rhythms. *Proceedings of the National Academy of Sciences USA.* doi: 10.1073/pnas.1115729109

Haney, C., Banks, C., & Zimbardo, P. (1973). Interpersonal dynamics in a simulated prison. *International Journal of Criminology and Penology, 1*(1), 69–97.

Hanna, E., Ward, L. M., Seabrook, R. C., Jerald, M., Reed, L., Giaccardi, S., & Lippman, J. R. (2017). Contributions of social comparison and self-objectification in mediating associations between Facebook use and emergent adults' psychological well-being. *Cyberpsychology, Behavior, And Social Networking, 20*(3), 172–179. doi:10.1089/cyber.2016.0247

Hannum, R. D., Rosellini, R. A., & Seligman, M. E. P. (1976). Learned helplessness in the rat: Retention and immunization. *Developmental Psychology, 12*(5), 449–454.

Hanowski, R. J., Olson, R. L., Hickman, J. S., & Bocanegra, J. (2009, September). *Driver distraction in commercial vehicle operations.* Paper presented at the First International Conference on Driver Distraction and Inattention, Gothenburg, Sweden.

Hanscombe, K. B., Trzaskowski, M., Haworth, C. M. A., Davis, O. S. P., Dale, P. S., & Plomin, R. (2012). Socioeconomic status (SES) and children's intelligence (IQ): In a UK-representative sample SES moderates the environmental, not genetic, effect on IQ. *PLoS One, 7*(2), e30320.

Harden, K. P., & Mendle, J. (2011). Adolescent sexual activity and the development of delinquent behavior: The role of relationship context. *Journal of Youth and Adolescence, 40*(7), 825–838.

Hardy, S. A., & Carlo, G. (2011). Moral identity: What is it, how does it develop, and is it linked to moral action? *Child Development Perspectives, 5*(3), 212–218.

Harker, L. A., & Keltner, D. (2001). Expressions of positive emotion in women's college yearbook pictures and their relationship to personality and life outcomes across adulthood. *Journal of Personality and Social Psychology, 80*(1), 112–124.

Harkin, B., Webb, T. L., Chang, B. I., Prestwich, A., Conner, M., Kellar, I., et al. (2016). Does monitoring goal progress promote goal attainment? A meta-analysis of the experimental evidence. *Psychological Bulletin, 142*(2), 198–229. doi:10.1037/bul0000025

Harlow, H. F. (1958). The nature of love. *American Psychologist, 13*(12), 673–685.

Harper, Q., Worthington, E. L., Jr., Griffin, B. J., Lavelock, C. R., Hook, J. N., Vrana, S. R., & Greer, C. L. (2014). Efficacy of a workbook to promote forgiveness: A randomized controlled trial with university students. *Journal of Clinical Psychology.* doi: 10.1002/jclp.22079

Harrell, P. T., Trenz, R. C., Scherer, M., Martins, S. S., & Latimer, W. W. (2013). A latent class approach to treatment readiness corresponds to a transtheoretical ("Stages of Change") model. *Journal of Substance Abuse Treatment, 45*(3), 249–256.

Harrington, B., & O'Connell, M. (2016). Video games as virtual teachers: Prosocial video game use by children and adolescents from different socioeconomic groups is associated with increased empathy and prosocial behaviour. *Computers In Human Behavior, 63*, 650–658. doi:10.1016/j.chb.2016.05.062

Harris, D. M., & Kay, J. (1995). I recognize your face but I can't remember your name: Is it because names are unique? *British Journal of Psychology, 86*(Pt. 3), 345–358.

Harris, J. A., Andrew, B. J., & Livesey, E. J. (2012). The content of compound conditioning. *Journal of Experimental Psychology: Animal Behavior and Processes, 38*(2), 157–166.

Harris, M. A., Donnellan, M. B., Guo, J., McAdams, D. P., Garnier-Villarreal, M., & Trzesniewski, K. H. (2017). Parental Co-Construction of 5- to 13-Year-Olds' Global Self-Esteem Through Reminiscing About Past Events. *Child Development, 88*(6), 1810–1822.

Harris, P. R., & others. (2014). Combining self-affirmation with implementation intentions to promote fruit and vegetable consumption. *Health Psychology, 33*(7), 729–736.

Harris, P. R., Brearley, I., Sheeran, P., Barker, M., Klein, W. M. P., Creswell, J. D., Levine, J.M., & Bond, R. (2017). Combining self-affirmation with implementation intentions to promote fruit and vegetable consumption. *Health Psychology, 36*, 729–736. http://dx.doi.org/10.1037/hea0000065

Harro, J., Merenäkk, L., Nordquist, N., Konstabel, K., Comasco, E., & Oreland, L. (2009). Personality and the serotonin transporter gene: Associations in a longitudinal population-based study. *Biological Psychology, 81*(1), 9–13.

Hart, B., & Risley, T.R. (1995). *Meaningful differences in the everyday experience of young American children.* Baltimore: Brookes.

Hart, C. L., & Ksir, C. J. (2015). *Drugs, society, and human behavior* (16th ed.). New York: McGraw-Hill.

Hartcher-O'Brien, J., Soto-Faraco, S., & Adam, R. (2017). Editorial: A Matter of Bottom-Up or Top-Down Processes: The Role of Attention in Multisensory Integration. *Frontiers in Integrative Neuroscience, 11*, 5. http://doi.org/10.3389/fnint.2017.00005

Hartenbaum, N., & others. (2006). Sleep apnea and commercial motor vehicle operators. *Chest, 130*(3), 902–905.

Hartmann, E. (1993). Nightmares. In M. A. Carskadon (Ed.), *Encyclopedia of sleep and dreams.* New York: Macmillan.

Hasan, A., Wobrock, T., Guse, B., Langguth, B., Landgrebe, M., Eichhammer, P., ... & Winterer, G. (2017). Structural brain changes are associated with response of negative symptoms to prefrontal repetitive transcranial magnetic stimulation in patients with schizophrenia. *Molecular Psychiatry, 22*(6), 857–864.

Hasan, F. M., & others. (2014). Hypnotherapy is more effective than nicotine replacement therapy for smoking cessation: Results of a randomized controlled trial. *Complementary Therapies in Medicine, 22*(1), 1–8.

Haselton, M. G. (2006, April 29). How to pick a perfect mate. *New Scientist, 2549*, 36.

Haslam, S. A., & Reicher, S. (2003). Beyond Stanford: Questioning a role-based explanation of tyranny. *SPSP Dialogue, 18*, 22–25.

Hasler, B. P., Buysse, D. J., & Germain, A. (2016). Shifts toward morningness during behavioral sleep interventions are associated with improvements in depression, positive affect, and sleep quality. *Behavioral Sleep Medicine, 14*(6), 624-635. doi:10.1080/15402002.2015.1048452

Hassabis, D., Kumaran, D., Summerfield, C., & Botvinick, M. (2017). Neuroscience-inspired artificial intelligence. *Neuron, 95*(2), 245-258.

Hassall, R. (2017) How should applied psychologists conceptualise an autism spectrum disorder diagnosis and its predictive validity? *Educational and Child Psychology, 34*(4). ISSN 0267-1611

Hauser, T. U., Iannaccone, R., Dolan, R. J., Ball, J., Hättenschwiler, J., Drechsler, R., et al. (2017). Increased fronto-striatal reward prediction errors moderate decision making in obsessive-compulsive disorder. *Psychological Medicine, 47*(7), 1246-1258.

Hawkley, L. C., & Cacioppo, J. T. (2012a). Loneliness and health. In M. Gellman & J. R. Turner (Eds.), *Encyclopedia of behavioral medicine.* New York: Springer.

Hawkley, L. C., & Cacioppo, J. T. (2012b). Social connection and relationships in successful aging. In J. M. Rippe (Ed.), *Encyclopedia of lifestyle medicine and health.* Thousand Oaks, CA: Sage.

Hawley, P. H. (2014). Evolution, prosocial behavior, and altruism: A roadmap for understanding where the proximate meets the ultimate. In L. M. Padilla-Walker & G. Carlo (Eds.), *Prosocial development: A multidimensional approach* (pp. 43-69). New York: Oxford University Press. doi:10.1093/acprof:o so/9780199964772.003.0003

Haws, K. L., & Liu, P. J. (2016). Half-size me? How calorie and price information influence ordering on restaurant menus with both half and full entrée portion sizes. *Appetite, 97,* 127-137. doi:10.1016/j.appet.2015.11.031

Hay, P. P., Bacaltchuk, J., Stefano, S., & Kashyap, P. (2009). Psychological treatments for bulimia nervosa and binging. *Cochrane Database of Systematic Reviews,* (4), CD000562.

Hayakawa, Y. (2012). Targeting NKG2D in tumor surveillance. *Expert Opinion on Therapeutic Targets, 16*(6), 587-599.

Hayama, S., Chang, L., Gumus, K., King, G. R., & Ernst, T. (2016). Neural correlates for perception of companion animal photographs. *Neuropsychologia, 85,* 278-286. doi:10.1016/j.neuropsychologia.2016.03.018

Hayes, J. E., & Keast, R. S. J. (2011). Two decades of supertasting: Where do we stand? *Physiology and Behavior, 104*(5), 1072-1074.

Hayflick, L. (1977). The cellular basis for biological aging. In C. E. Finch & L. Hayflick (Eds.), *Handbook of the biology of aging.* New York: Van Nostrand.

Hazelden Betty Ford Foundation (June 10, 2015). *Survey Finds Risky Opioid Use Among College-Age Youth, With Limited Knowledge of the Danger or Where to Get Help.* http://www.hazeldenbettyford.org/about-us/news-media/press-release/2015-opioid-use-among-college-youth

He, W., Fan, C., & Li, L. (2017). Transcranial magnetic stimulation reveals executive control dissociation in the rostral prefrontal cortex. *Frontiers In Human Neuroscience, 11.* doi:10.3389/fnhum.2017.00464

He, W., Qian, F., & Cao, J. (2017). Pinning-controlled synchronization of delayed neural networks with distributed-delay coupling via impulsive control. *Neural Networks, 85,* 1-9.

He, Y., Chen, J., Zhu, L. H., Hua, L. L., & Ke, F. F. (2017). Maternal smoking during pregnancy and ADHD: Results from a systematic review and meta-analysis of prospective cohort studies. *Journal of Attention Disorders,* in press. doi: 10.1177/1087054717696766.

Heal, D. J., Hallam, M., Prow, M., Gosden, J., Cheetham, S., Choi, Y. K., et al. (2017). Dopamine and μ-opioid receptor dysregulation in the brains of binge-eating female rats–possible relevance in the psychopathology and treatment of binge-eating disorder. *Journal of Psychopharmacology, 31*(6), 770-783.

Heap, M. (2017). Theories of hypnosis. In G. R. Elkins (Ed.), *Handbook of medical and psychological hypnosis: Foundations, applications, and professional issues* (pp. 9-18). New York: Springer.

Hearold, S. (1986). A synthesis of 1043 effects of television on social behavior. In G. Comstock (Ed.), *Public communication of behavior* (pp. 65-133). San Diego: Academic.

Heath, M., Manzone, J., Khan, M., & Davarpanah Jazi, S. (2017). Vision for action and perception elicit dissociable adherence to Weber's law across a range of 'graspable' target objects. *Experimental Brain Research, 235*(10), 3003-3012. doi:10.1007/s00221-017-5025-1

Hebb, D. O. (1949). *The organization of behavior: A neuropsychological theory.* New York: Wiley.

Hebb, D. O. (1980). *Essay on mind.* Mahwah, NJ: Erlbaum.

Heeger, D. J. (2017). Theory of cortical function. *PNAS Proceedings of the National Academy of Sciences of the United States of America, 114*(8), 1773-1782. doi:10.1073/pnas.1619788114

Heeren, A., Billieux, J., Philippot, P., De Raedt, R., Baeken, C., de Timary, P., et al. (2017). Impact of transcranial direct current stimulation on attentional bias for threat: A proof-of-concept study among individuals with social anxiety disorder. *Social Cognitive and Affective Neuroscience, 12*(2), 251-260.

Hegmans, J. P., & Aerts, J. G. (2014). Immunomodulation in cancer. *Current Opinion in Pharmacology, 17,* 17-21.

Hehman, E., Sutherland, C. M., Flake, J. K., & Slepian, M. L. (2017). The unique contributions of perceiver and target characteristics in person perception. *Journal of Personality and Social Psychology,* in press. doi:10.1037/pspa0000090

Heider, F. (1958). *The psychology of interpersonal relations.* Hillsdale, NJ: Erlbaum.

Heil, P., Matysiak, A., & Neubauer, H. (2017). A probabilistic poisson-based model accounts for an extensive set of absolute auditory threshold measurements. *Hearing Research, 353,* 135-161. doi:10.1016/j.heares.2017.06.011

Heineman, K. R., Schendelaar, P., van den Heuvel, E. R., & Hadders-Algra, M. (2017). Investigate associations between motor development measured with the Infant Motor Profile (IMP) in infancy and IQ at the age of 4 years. *European Journal of Paediatric Neurology, 21,* e156.

Heirman, W., & Walrave, M. (2012). Predicting adolescent perpetration in cyberbullying: An application of the theory of planned behavior. *Psicothema, 24*(4), 614-620.

Helgeson, V. S., & Zajdel, M. (2017). Adjusting to chronic health conditions. *Annual Review of Psychology, 68,* 545-571.

Hellmer, K., & Nyström, P. (2017). Infant acetylcholine, dopamine, and melatonin dysregulation: Neonatal biomarkers and causal factors for ASD and ADHD phenotypes. *Medical Hypotheses, 100,* 64-66.

Helmore, E. (August 20, 2017). 'He's trying to save lives': The ex-addict judge on the frontline of the opiate crisis. *The Guardian.* https://amp.theguardian.com/us-news/2017/aug/20/opioid-crisis-america-buffalo-new-york-trump-national-emergency

Henderson, M. (2008, February 18). Welcome to the town that will make you lose weight. *The Times.* www.thetimes.co.uk/tto/health/article1881007.ece (accessed January 13, 2015)

Hendrick, C., & Hendrick, S. S. (2006). Styles of romantic love. In R. J. Sternberg & K. Weis (Eds.), *The new psychology of love* (pp. 149-170). New Haven, CT: Yale University Press.

Hendrick, C., & Hendrick, S. S. (2009). Love. In S. Lopez & C. R. Snyder (Eds.), *The Oxford handbook of positive psychology* (2nd ed., pp. 447-454). New York: Oxford University Press.

Hendrickson, K. L., & Rasmussen, E. B. (2017). Mindful eating reduces impulsive food choice in adolescents and adults. *Health Psychology, 36*(3), 226-235. doi:10.1037/hea0000440

Hennessey, B. A. (2011). Intrinsic motivation and creativity: Have we come full circle? In R. A. Beghetto & J. C. Kaufman (Eds.), *Nurturing creativity in the classroom.* New York: Cambridge University Press.

Henry, J. D., MacLeod, M. S., Phillips, L. H., & Crawford, J. R. (2004). A meta-analytic review of prospective memory and aging. *Psychology and Aging, 19*(1), 27-39.

Hepach, R., Haberl, K., Lambert, S., & Tomasello, M. (2017). Toddlers help anonymously. *Infancy, 22*(1), 130-145.

Hepting, U., & Solle, R. (1973). Sex-specific differences in color coding. *Archiv fur Psychologie, 125*(2-3), 184-202.

Herman, C. P. (2017). The social facilitation of eating or the facilitation of social eating? *Journal of Eating Disorders, 5.* in press doi:10.1186/s40337-017-0146-2

Hermans, E. J., Battaglia, F. P., Atsak, P., de Voogd, L. D., Fernández, G., & Roozendaal, B. (2014). How the amygdala affects emotional memory by altering brain network properties. *Neurobiology of Learning and Memory, 112C,* 2-16.

Hermes, M., Hagemann, D., Naumann, E., & Walter, C. (2011). Extraversion and its positive emotional core—Further evidence from neuroscience. *Emotion, 11*(2), 367-378. doi:10.1037/a0021550

Herron, W. G. (2015). Transference, countertransference, and resistance. In D. O. Morris, R. A. Javier, & W. G. Herron, *Specialty competencies in psychoanalysis in psychology* (pp. 101-123). New York: Oxford University Press.

Hershfield, H. E., Scheibe, S., Sims, T. L., & Carstensen, L. L. (2013). When feeling bad can be good: Mixed emotions benefit physical health across adulthood. *Social Psychological And Personality Science, 4*(1), 54-61. doi:10.1177/1948550612444616

Herting, M. M., & Sowell, E. R. (2017). Puberty and structural brain development in humans. *Frontiers in Neuroendocrinology, 44,* 122-137.

Hertzog, C., Kramer, A. F., Wilson, R. S., & Lindenberger, U. (2009). Enrichment effects on adult cognitive development. *Psychological Perspectives in the Public Interest, 9*(1), 1-65.

Herzog, H. (2006). Forty-two thousand and one Dalmatians: Fads, social contagion, and dog breed popularity. *Society & Animals, 14*(4), 383-397.

Hevey, D., McGee, H. M., & Horgan, J. H. (2014). Comparative optimism among patients with coronary heart disease (CHD) is associated with fewer adverse clinical events 12 months later. *Journal of Behavioral Medicine, 37*(2), 300-307. doi:10.1007/s10865-012-9487-0

Heward, W. L. (2013). *Exceptional children* (10th ed.). Upper Saddle River, NJ: Pearson.

Hewison, D., Clulow, C., & Drake, H. (2014). *Couple therapy for depression: A clinician's guide to integrative practice.* New York: Oxford University Press.

Heyselaar, E., Segaert, K., Walvoort, S. J., Kessels, R. P., & Hagoort, P. (2017). The role of nondeclarative memory in the skill for language: Evidence from syntactic priming in patients with amnesia. *Neuropsychologia, 101,* 97-105.

Hibbard, S., Porcerelli, J., Kamoo, R., Schwartz, M., & Abell, S. (2010). Defense and object relational maturity on Thematic Apperception Test scales indicate levels of personality organization. *Journal of Personality Assessment, 92*(3), 241-253.

Hicks, J. A., Trent, J., Davis, W., & King, L. A. (2012). Positive affect, meaning in life, and future time perspective: An application of Socioemotional Selectivity Theory. *Psychology and Aging, 27*(1), 181-189.

Higa-McMillan, C. K., & Ebesutani, C. E. (2011). The etiology of social anxiety disorder in adolescents and young adults. In C. A. Alfano & D. C. Beidel (Eds.), *Social anxiety disorder in adolescents and young adults* (pp. 29–51). Washington, DC: American Psychological Association.

Highfield, R. (2008, April 30). Harvard's baby brain research lab. *The Telegraph.* www.telegraph.co.uk/science/science-news/3341166/Harvards-baby-brain-research-lab.html (accessed December 15, 2014)

Hilchey, M. D., Klein, R. M., & Satel, J. (2014). Returning to "inhibition of return" by dissociating long-term oculomotor IOR from short-term sensory adaptation and other nonoculomotor "inhibitory" cueing effects. *Journal of Experimental Psychology: Human Perception and Performance, 40*(4), 1603–1616.

Hildebrandt, T., Bacow, T., Markella, M., & Loeb, K. L. (2012). Anxiety in anorexia nervosa and its management using family-based treatment. *European Eating Disorders Review, 20*(1), e1–e16.

Hilgard, E. R. (1977). *Divided consciousness: Multiple controls in human thought and action.* New York: Wiley.

Hilgard, E. R. (1992). Dissociation and theories of hypnosis. In E. Fromm & M. R. Nash (Eds.), *Contemporary hypnosis research.* New York: Guilford.

Hilgard, J., Engelhardt, C. R., & Rouder, J. N. (2017). Overstated evidence for short-term effects of violent games on affect and behavior: A reanalysis of Anderson et al. (2010). *Psychological Bulletin, 143*(7), 757–774. doi:10.1037/bul0000074

Hilgard, J., Engelhardt, C. R., Bartholow, B. D., & Rouder, J. N. (2015). How much evidence is p > .05? Stimulus pre-testing and null primary outcomes in violent video games research. *Psychology of Popular Media Culture,* doi:10.1037/ppm0000102

Hill, E. M. (2016). Posthumous organ donation attitudes, intentions to donate, and organ donor status: Examining the role of the big five personality dimensions and altruism. *Personality and Individual Differences, 88,* 182–186. doi:10.1016/j.paid.2015.09.021

Hill, E. M. (2016). Quality of life and mental health among women with ovarian cancer: Examining the role of emotional and instrumental social support seeking. *Psychology, Health & Medicine, 21*(5), 551–561. doi:10.1080/13548506.2015.1109674

Hill, P. L., Jackson, J. J., Roberts, B. W., Lapsley, D. K., & Brandenberger, J. W. (2011). Change you can believe in: Changes in goal setting during emerging and young adulthood predict later adult well-being. *Social Psychological and Personality Science, 2*(2), 123–131.

Hill, P. L., Nickel, L. B., & Roberts, B. W. (2014). Are you in a healthy relationship? Linking conscientiousness to health via implementing and immunizing behaviors. *Journal of Personality, 82*(6), 485–492.

Hill, P. L., Turiano, N. A., Hurd, M. D., Mroczek, D. K., & Roberts, B. W. (2011). Conscientiousness and longevity: An examination of possible mediators. *Health Psychology, 30*(5), 536–541.

Hill, T. D., Burdette, A. M., Ellison, C. G., & Musick, M. A. (2006). Religious attendance and the health behaviors of Texas adults. *Preventive Medicine, 42*(4), 309–312.

Hill, T. D., Uchino, B. N., Eckhardt, J. L., & Angel, J. L. (2016). Perceived social support trajectories and the all-cause mortality risk of older Mexican American women and men. *Research On Aging, 38*(3), 374–398. doi:10.1177/0164027515620239

Hillebrandt, A., & Barclay, L. J. (2017). Comparing integral and incidental emotions: Testing insights from emotions as social information theory and attribution theory. *Journal of Applied Psychology, 102*(5), 732–752. doi:10.1037/apl0000174

Hiller, R. M., Meiser-Stedman, R., Fearon, P., Lobo, S., MacKinnon, A., Fraser, A., & Halligan, S. L. (2016). Changes in the prevalence and symptom severity of child PTSD in the year following trauma: A meta-analytic study. *Journal of Child Psychology and Psychiatry, 57*(8), 884–898.

Hindman, A. H., Wasik, B. A., & Snell, E. K. (2016). Closing the 30 million word gap: Next steps in designing research to inform practice. *Child Development Perspectives, 10,* 134–139. doi:10.1111/cdep.12177

Hines, M. (2013). Sex and sex differences. In P. D. Zelazo (Ed.), *The Oxford handbook of developmental psychology.* New York: Oxford University Press.

Hingson, R. W., Heeren, T., & Winter, M. R. (2006). Age at drinking onset and alcohol dependence: Age of onset, duration, and severity. *Archives of Pediatric and Adolescent Medicine, 160*(7), 739–746.

Hinojosa, A. S., Gardner, W. L., Walker, H. J., Cogliser, C., & Gullifor, D. (2017). A review of cognitive dissonance theory in management research: Opportunities for further development. *Journal of Management, 43*(1), 170–199. doi:10.1177/0149206316668236

Hinterberger, T., Schmidt, S., Kamei, T., & Walach, H. (2014). Decreased electrophysiological activity represents the conscious state of emptiness in meditation. *Frontiers in Psychology, 5,* 99.

Hinton, E. C., Brunstrom, J. M., Fay, S. H., Wilkinson, L. L., Ferriday, D., Rogers, P. J., & de Wijk, R. (2013). Using photography in 'The Restaurant of the Future'. A useful way to assess portion selection and plate cleaning? *Appetite, 63,* 31–35. doi:10.1016/j.appet.2012.12.008

Hirata, A., & Castro-Alamancos, M. A. (2010). Neocortex network activation and deactivation states controlled by the thalamus. *Journal of Neurophysiology, 103*(3), 1147–1157.

Hirschberger, G. (2015). Terror management and prosocial behavior: A theory of self-protective altruism. In D. A. Schroeder & W. G. Graziano (Eds.), *The Oxford handbook of prosocial behavior* (pp. 166–187). New York: Oxford University Press.

Hirsh-Pasek, K., & Golinkoff, R. M. (2014). Early language and literacy: Six principles. In S. Gilford (Ed.), *Head Start teacher's guide.* New York: Teacher's College Press.

Ho, C., & MacDorman, K. F. (2017). Measuring the uncanny valley effect: Refinements to indices for perceived humanness, attractiveness, and eeriness. *International Journal of Social Robotics, 9*(1), 129–139. doi:10.1007/s12369-016-0380-9

Ho, M. L., & Brass, S. D. (2011). Obstructive sleep apnea. *Neurology International, 3*(3), e15.

Hobson, A. J., & Maxwell, B. (2017). Supporting and inhibiting the well-being of early career secondary school teachers: Extending self-determination theory. *British Educational Research Journal, 43*(1), 168–191. doi:10.1002/berj.3261

Hobson, J. A. (1999). Dreams. In R. Conlan (Ed.), *States of mind.* New York: Wiley.

Hobson, J. A. (2000). Dreams: Physiology. In A. Kazdin (Ed.), *Encyclopedia of psychology.* Washington, DC, & New York: American Psychological Association and Oxford University Press.

Hobson, J. A. (2002). *Dreaming.* New York: Oxford University Press.

Hobson, J. A. (2004). Freud returns? Like a bad dream. *Scientific American, 290*(5), 89.

Hobson, J. A., & Voss, U. (2011). A mind to go out of: Reflections on primary and secondary consciousness. *Consciousness and Cognition, 20*(4), 993–997.

Hobson, J. A., Pace-Schott, E. F., & Stickgold, R. (2000). Dreaming and the brain: Toward a cognitive neuroscience of conscious states. *Behavior and Brain Sciences, 23*(6), 793–842.

Hockett, C. F. (1960). The origin of speech. *Scientific American, 203,* 88–96.

Hodapp, R. M., Griffin, M. M., Burke, M. M., & Fisher, M. H. (2011). Intellectual disabilities. In R. J. Sternberg & S. B. Kaufman (Eds.), *The Cambridge handbook of intelligence.* New York: Cambridge University Press.

Hodas, N. O., & Lerman, K. (2014). The simple rules of social contagion. *Scientific Reports, 4,* 4343.

Hodes, G. E., Walker, D. M., Labonté, B., Nestler, E. J., & Russo, S. J. (2017). Understanding the epigenetic basis of sex differences in depression. *Journal of Neuroscience Research, 95*(1–2), 692–702.

Hodgins, D. C. (2005). Weighing the pros and cons of changing change models: A comment on West (2005). *Addiction, 100*(8), 1042–1043.

Hoek, H. W. (2006). Incidence, prevalence and mortality of anorexia nervosa and other eating disorders. *Current Opinion in Psychiatry, 19*(4), 389–394.

Hoekzema, E., Barba-Müller, E., Pozzobon, C., Picado, M., Lucco, F., García-García, D., et al. (2017). Pregnancy leads to long-lasting changes in human brain structure. *Nature neuroscience, 20*(2), 287–296.

Hoff, E. (2014). *Language development* (5th ed.). Boston: Cengage.

Hofmann, S. G., & Barlow, D. H. (2014). Evidence-based psychological interventions and the common factors approach: The beginnings of rapprochement? *Psychotherapy, 51*(4), 510–513.

Hogan, R. (2009). Much ado about nothing: The person–situation debate. *Journal of Research in Personality, 43*(2), 249.

Hogg, M. A. (2012). Social identity and the psychology of groups. In M. R. Leary & J. P. Tangney (Eds.), *Handbook of self and identity* (2nd ed., pp. 502–519). New York: Guilford.

Holland, K. J., Rabelo, V. C., & Cortina, L. M. (2017). (Missing) knowledge about sexual assault resources: Undermining military mental health. *Violence and Victims, 32*(1), 60–77.

Holle, H., Banissy, M. J., & Ward, J. (2013). Functional and structural brain differences associated with mirror-touch synaesthesia. *Neuroimage, 83,* 1041–1050. doi:10.1016/j.neuroimage.2013.07.073

Hollingdale, J., & Greitemeyer, T. (2014). The effect of online violent video games on levels of aggression. *PLoS One, 9*(11), e111790.

Hollis, S., Heller, G., Stevenson, M., & Schofield, P. (2014). Recurrent mild traumatic brain injury among a cohort of rugby union players. *British Journal of Sports Medicine, 48*(7), 609.

Holmes, S. (1993). Food avoidance in patients undergoing cancer chemotherapy. *Support Care Cancer, 1*(6), 326–330.

Homan, K. J., Sim, L. A., Fargo, J. D., & Twohig, M. P. (2017). Five-year prospective investigation of self-harm/suicide-related behaviors in the development of borderline personality disorder. *Personality Disorders: Theory, Research, and Treatment, 8*(2), 183–188.

Hommel, B. (2017). Consciousness and action control. In T. Egner (Ed.), *The Wiley Handbook of Cognitive Control* (pp. 111–123). Hoboken, NJ: John Wiley & Sons.

Hoogman, M., Bralten, J., Hibar, D. P., Mennes, M., Zwiers, M. P., Schweren, L. S., et al. (2017). Subcortical brain volume differences in participants with attention deficit hyperactivity disorder in children and adults: A cross-sectional mega-analysis. *The Lancet Psychiatry, 4*(4), 310–319.

Hooker, S. A., Masters, K. S., & Park, C. L. (2017). A meaningful life is a healthy life: A conceptual model linking meaning and meaning salience to health. *Review of General Psychology,* in press. doi:10.1037/gpr0000115

Hooper, J., & Teresi, D. (1993). *The 3-pound universe.* New York: Tarcher/Putnam.

Hooper, N., Erdogan, A., Keen, G., Lawton, K., & McHugh, L. (2015). Perspective taking reduces the fundamental attribution error. *Journal of Contextual Behavioral Science, 4*(2), 69–72. doi:10.1016/j.jcbs.2015.02.002

Hoorn, J., Crone, E. A., & Leijenhorst, L. (2017). Hanging out with the right crowd: Peer influence on risk-taking behavior in adolescence. *Journal of Research on Adolescence, 27*(1), 189–200.

Hope, T. M., Leff, A. P., Prejawa, S., Bruce, R., Haigh, Z., Lim, L., ... & Seghier, M. L. (2017). Right hemisphere structural adaptation and changing language skills years after left hemisphere stroke. *Brain, 140*(6), 1718–1728.

Horney, K. (1945). *Our inner conflicts.* New York: Norton.

Horney, K. (1964). *The neurotic personality of our time.* New York, NY, US: W W Norton & Co.

Horney, K. (1967). *Feminine psychology: collected essays, 1922-1937.* H. Kelman (Ed.). New York: Norton.

Hornsey, M. J., & Fielding, K. S. (2017). Attitude roots and Jiu Jitsu persuasion: Understanding and overcoming the motivated rejection of science. *American Psychologist, 72*(5), 459–473. doi:10.1037/a0040437

Horvath, A. O. (2013). You can't step into the same river twice, but you can stub your toes on the same rock: Psychotherapy outcome from a 50-year perspective. *Psychotherapy, 50*(1), 25–32.

Horwitz, A. G., Berona, J., Czyz, E. K., Yeguez, C. E., & King, C. A. (2017). Positive and negative expectations of hopelessness as longitudinal predictors of depression, suicidal Ideation, and suicidal behavior in high-risk adolescents. *Suicide and Life-threatening Behavior, 47*(2), 168–176.

Hoss, R. A., & Langlois, J. H. (2003). Infants prefer attractive faces. In O. Pascalis & A. Slater (Eds.), *The development of face processing in infancy and early childhood: Current perspectives* (pp. 27–38). Hauppauge, NY: Nova Science.

Hotard, S. R., McFatter, R. M., McWhirter, R. M., & Stegall, M. E. (1989). Interactive effects of extraversion, neuroticism, and social relationships on subjective well-being. *Journal of Personality and Social Psychology, 57*(2), 321–331.

Hou, Y., Kim, S. Y., Hazen, N., & Benner, A. D. (2017). Parents' perceived discrimination and adolescent adjustment in Chinese American families: Mediating family processes. *Child Development, 88*(1), 317–331. doi:10.1111/cdev.12603

House, J. S., Landis, K. R., & Umberson, D. (1988). Social relationships and health. *Science, 241*(4865), 540–545.

House, R., Kalisch, D., & Maidman, J. (Eds.). (2017). *Humanistic psychology: Current trends and future prospects.* New York: Routledge.

Houser-Marko, L., & Sheldon, K. M. (2008). Eyes on the prize or nose to the grindstone? The effects of level of goal evaluation on mood and motivation. *Personality and Social Psychology Bulletin, 34*(11), 1556–1569.

Hovey, J. D., Morales, L. R., Hurtado, G., & Seligman, L. D. (2014). Religion-based emotional social support mediates the relationship between intrinsic religiosity and mental health. *Archives of Suicide Research, 18*(4), 376–391.

Hovick, S. R., & Bigsby, E. (2016). Heart disease and colon cancer prevention beliefs and their association with information seeking and scanning. *Journal of Health Communication, 21*(1), 76–84. doi:10.1080/10810730.2015.1049307

Howe, M. J. A., Davidson, J. W., Moore, D. G., & Sloboda, J. A. (1995). Are there early childhood signs of musical ability? *Psychology of Music, 23*(2), 162–176.

Howe, P. L., & Ferguson, A. (2015). The identity-location binding problem. *Cognitive Science, 39*(7), 1622–1645. doi:10.1111/cogs.12204

Howell, J. L., & Ratliff, K. A. (2017). Not your average bigot: The better-than-average effect and defensive responding to implicit association test feedback. *British Journal of Social Psychology, 56*(1), 125–145. doi:10.1111/bjso.12168

Howes, M. B. (2006). *Human memory.* Thousand Oaks, CA: Sage.

Howes, M. J. R., Fang, R., & Houghton, P. J. (2017). Effect of Chinese herbal medicine on Alzheimer's disease. *International Review of Neurobiology, in press.* doi: 10.1016/bs.irn.2017.02.003

Howes, O. D., McCutcheon, R., Owen, M. J., & Murray, R. M. (2017). The role of genes, stress, and dopamine in the development of schizophrenia. *Biological Psychiatry, 81*(1), 9–20.

Howland, R. H. (2012). The use of dopaminergic and stimulant drugs for the treatment of depression. *Journal of Psychosocial Nursing and Mental Health Services, 50*(2), 11–14.

Hoxmeier, J. C., Acock, A. C., & Flay, B. R. (2017). Students as prosocial bystanders to sexual assault: Demographic correlates of intervention norms, intentions, and missed opportunities. *Journal of Interpersonal Violence, in press.*

Hoyer, D., Hannon, J. P., & Martin, G. R. (2002). Molecular, pharmacological, and functional diversity of 5-HT receptors. *Pharmacology, Biochemistry, and Behavior, 71*(4), 533–554.

Hozo, I., Djulbegovic, B., Luan, S., Tsalatsanis, A., & Gigerenzer, G. (2017). Towards theory integration: Threshold model as a link between signal detection theory, fast-and-frugal trees and evidence accumulation theory. *Journal Of Evaluation In Clinical Practice, 23*(1), 49–65. doi:10.1111/jep.12490

Hsieh, L. T., Hung, D. L., Tzeng, O. J., Lee, J. R., & Cheng, S. K. (2009). An event-related potential investigation of the processing of remember/forget cues and item encoding in item-method directed forgetting. *Brain Research, 1250*, 190–201.

Hu, Y., Hitch, G. J., Baddeley, A. D., Zhang, M., & Allen, R. J. (2014). Executive and perceptual attention play different roles in visual working memory: Evidence from suffix and strategy effects. *Journal of Experimental Psychology: Human Perception and Performance, 40*(4), 1665–1678.

Huang, C. C., & Chang, Y. C. (2009). The long-term effects of febrile seizures on the hippocampal neuronal plasticity—clinical and experimental evidence. *Brain Development, 31*(5), 383–387.

Huang, K. Y., Calzada, E., Cheng, S., Barajas-Gonzalez, R. G., & Brotman, L. M. (2017). Cultural adaptation, parenting and child mental health among English speaking Asian American immigrant families. *Child Psychiatry & Human Development, 48*(4), 572–583.

Huang, Y., & Spelke, E. (2014). Core knowledge and the emergence of symbols: The case of maps. *Journal of Cognition and Development.* doi: 10.1080/15248372.2013.784975

Huart, C., Collet, S., & Rombaux, P. (2009). Chemosensory pathways: From periphery to cortex. *B-ENT, 5*, Suppl. 13, S3–S9.

Huart, C., Rombaux, P., & Hummel, T. (2013). Plasticity of the human olfactory system: The olfactory bulb. *Molecules, 18*(9), 11586–11600.

Hubbard, J., Harbaugh, W. T., Srivastava, S., Degras, D., & Mayr, U. (2016). A general benevolence dimension that links neural, psychological, economic, and life-span data on altruistic tendencies. *Journal of Experimental Psychology: General, 145*(10), 1351–1358. doi:10.1037/xge0000209

Hubbard, K., & Hegarty, P. (2016). Blots and all: A history of the Rorschach ink blot test in Britain. *Journal of the History of the Behavioral Sciences, 52*(2), 146–166. doi:10.1002/jhbs.21776

Hubble, M. A., & Miller, S. D. (2004). The client: Psychotherapy's missing link for promoting a positive psychology. In A. Linley & S. Joseph (Eds.), *Positive psychology in practice* (pp. 335–353). Hoboken, NJ: Wiley.

Hubel, D. H., & Wiesel, T. N. (1963). Receptive fields of cells in striate cortex of very young, visually inexperienced kittens. *Journal of Neurophysiology, 26*, 994–1002.

Hudson, A., & Jacques, S. (2014). Put on a happy face! Inhibitory control and socioemotional knowledge predict emotion regulation in 5- to 7-year-olds. *Journal of Experimental Child Psychology, 123*, 36–52.

Hudson, D. L., Bullard, K. M., Neighbors, H. W., Geronimus, A. T., Yang, J., & Jackson, J. S. (2012). Are benefits conferred with greater socioeconomic position undermined by racial discrimination among African American men? *Journal of Men's Health, 9*, 127–136.

Huey, S. J., Jr., Tilley, J. L., Jones, E. O., & Smith, C. A. (2014). The contribution of cultural competence to evidence-based care for ethnically diverse populations. *Annual Review of Clinical Psychology* (vol. 10, pp. 305–338). Palo Alto, CA: Annual Reviews.

Huff, C. R. (2002). What can we learn from other nations about the problem of wrongful conviction? *Judicature, 86*(2), 91–97.

Huffman, G., Rajsic, J., & Pratt, J. (2017). Ironic capture: Top-down expectations exacerbate distraction in visual search. *Psychological Research, in press.* doi:10.1007/s00426-017-0917-z

Hughes, A. E., Berg, C. A., & Wiebe, D. J. (2012). Emotional processing and self-control in adolescents with type 1 diabetes. *Journal of Pediatric Psychology, 37*(8), 925–934.

Hughes, A. M., Gordon, R., Chalder, T., Hirsch, C. R., & Moss-Morris, R. (2016). Maximizing potential impact of experimental research into cognitive processes in health psychology: A systematic approach to material development. *British Journal of Health Psychology, 21*(4), 764–780. doi:10.1111/bjhp.12214

Hull, E. M., & Dominguez, J. M. (2006). Getting his act together: Roles of glutamate, nitricoxide, and dopamine in the medial preoptic area. *Brain Research, 1126*(1), 66–75.

Hulst, B. M., Zeeuw, P., Bos, D. J., Rijks, Y., Neggers, S. F., & Durston, S. (2017). Children with ADHD symptoms show decreased activity in ventral striatum during the anticipation of reward, irrespective of ADHD diagnosis. *Journal of Child Psychology and Psychiatry, 58*(2), 206–214.

Hunsley, J., & Bailey, J. M. (2001). Whither the Rorschach? An analysis of the evidence. *Psychological Assessment, 13*(4), 472–485.

Hunsley, J., Lee, C. M., Wood, J. M., & Taylor, W. (2015). Controversial and questionable assessment techniques. In S. O. Lilienfeld, S. J. Lynn, & J. M. Lohr (Eds.), *Science and pseudoscience in clinical psychology, 2nd ed* (pp. 42–82). New York: Guilford Press.

Hunt, R. R., & Ellis, H. C. (2004). *Fundamentals of cognitive psychology* (7th ed.). New York: McGraw-Hill.

Huntjens, R. J. C., Wessel, I., Hermans, D., & van Minnen, A. (2014). Autobiographical memory specificity in dissociative identity disorder. *Journal of Abnormal Psychology, 123*(2), 419–428.

Hurme, M., Koivisto, M., Revonsuo, A., & Railo, H. (2017). Early processing in primary visual cortex is necessary for conscious and unconscious vision while late processing is necessary only for conscious vision in neurologically healthy humans. *Neuroimage, 150*, 230–238. doi:10.1016/j.neuroimage.2017.02.060

Hussey, E. K., & Novick, J. M. (2012). The benefits of executive control training and the implications for language processing. *Frontiers in Psychology: Cognition, 3*, 158.

Huttenlocher, P. R. (1999). Dendritic synaptic development in human cerebral cortex: Time course and critical periods. *Developmental Neuropsychology, 16*(3), 347–349.

Hutton, J. (2016). Does Rubella Cause Autism: A 2015 reappraisal? *Frontiers of Human Neuroscience, 10*, 25. doi: 10.3389/fnhum.2016.00025

Huuhka, K., & others. (2012). One-year follow-up after discontinuing maintenance electroconvulsive therapy. *Journal of Electroconvulsive Therapy, 28*(4), 225–228.

Hven, L., Frost, P., & Bonde, J. P. E. (2017). Evaluation of pressure pain threshold as a measure of perceived stress and high job strain. *PloS one, 12*(1), e0167257.

Hwang, A. C., Peng, L. N., Wen, Y. W., Tsai, Y. W., Chang, L. C., Chiou, S. T., & Chen, L. K. (2014). Predicting all-cause and cause-specific mortality by static and dynamic measurements of allostatic load: A 10-year population-based cohort study in Taiwan. *Journal of the American Medical Directors Association.* PMID: 24631353

Hwang, J. Y., & others. (2012). Multidimensional comparison of personality characteristics of the Big Five model, impulsiveness, and affect in pathological gambling and obsessive-compulsive disorder. *Journal of Gambling Studies, 28*(3), 351–362.

Hyde, J. S. (2005). The gender similarities hypothesis. *American Psychologist, 60*(6), 581–592.

Hyde, J. S. (2007). New directions in the study of gender similarities and differences. *Current Directions in Psychological Science, 16*(5), 259–263.

Hyde, J. S. (2014). Gender similarities and differences. *Annual Review of Psychology* (vol. 65). Palo Alto, CA: Annual Reviews.

Hyde, L. W., Shaw, D. S., & Moilanen, K. L. (2010). Developmental precursors of moral disengagement and the role of moral disengagement in the development of antisocial behavior. *Journal of Abnormal Child Psychology, 38*(2), 197–209.

Hyman, I. E., Sarb, B. A., & Wise-Swanson, B. M. (2014). Failure to see money on a tree: Inattentional blindness for objects that guided behavior. *Frontiers in Psychology, 5,* 356.

Hyman, S. (2001, October 23). *Basic and clinical neuroscience in the post-genomic era.* Paper presented at the centennial symposium on the Celebration of Excellence in Neuroscience, Rockefeller University, New York City.

I

Iacono, W. G., & Lykken, D. T. (1997). The validity of the lie detector: Two surveys of scientific opinion. *Journal of Applied Psychology, 82*(3), 426–433.

Iancu, I., Bodner, E., & Ben-Zion, I. Z. (2014). Self-esteem, dependency, self-efficacy, and self-criticism in social anxiety disorder. *Comprehensive Psychiatry.* doi: http://dx.doi.org/10.1016/j.comppsych.2014.11.018

Iannilli, E., Singh, P. B., Schuster, B., Gerber, J., & Hummel, T. (2012). Taste laterality studied by means of umani and salt stimuli: An fMRI study. *NeuroImage, 60*(1), 426–435.

Ida-Eto, M., Hara, N., Ohkawara, T., & Narita, M. (2017). Mechanism of auditory hypersensitivity in human autism using autism model rats. *Pediatrics International, 59*(4), 404–407.

Iemmola, F., & Ciani, A. C. (2009). New evidence of genetic factors influencing sexual orientation in men: Female fecundity increase in the maternal line. *Archives of Sexual Behavior, 38*(3), 393–399.

Iggena, D., Winter, Y., & Steiner, B. (2017). Melatonin restores hippocampal neural precursor cell proliferation and prevents cognitive deficits induced by jet lag simulation in adult mice. *Journal of Pineal Research, 62,* e12397.

Iglesias, P. A. (2012). A systems biology view of adaptation in sensory mechanisms. *Advances in Experimental Medicine and Biology, 736,* 499–516.

Ignácio, Z. M., Réus, G. Z., Abelaira, H. M., & Quevedo, J. (2014). Epigenetic and epistatic interactions between serotonin transporter and brain-derived neurotrophic factor genetic polymorphism: Insights in depression. *Neuroscience, 275,* 455–468.

Ikeda, B. E., Collins, C. E., Alvaro, F., Marshall, G., & Garg, M. L. (2006). Well-being and nutrition-related side effects in children undergoing chemotherapy. *Nutrition and Dietetics, 63*(4), 227–239.

Imada, T. (2012). Cultural narratives of individualism and collectivism: A content analysis of textbook stories in the United States and Japan. *Journal of Cross-Cultural Psychology, 43*(4), 576–591.

Imeri, L., & Opp, M. R. (2009). How (and why) the immune system makes us sleep. *Nature Reviews: Neuroscience, 10*(3), 199–210.

Inaba, A., Thoits, P. A., Ueno, K., Gove, W. R., Evenson, R. J., & Sloan, M. (2005). Depression in the United States and Japan: Gender, marital status, and SES patterns. *Social Science & Medicine, 61*(11), 2280–2292.

Ingersoll, R. E., & Rak, C. F. (2016). *Psychopharmacology for mental health professionals (2nd ed.).* Boston: Cengage.

Insko, C. A., & Wilson, M. (1977). Interpersonal attraction as a function of social interaction. *Journal of Personality and Social Psychology, 35*(12), 903–911.

Ion, A., Iliescu, D., Aldhafri, S., Rana, N., Ratanadilok, K., Widyanti, A., & Nedelcea, C. (2017). A cross-cultural analysis of personality structure through the lens of the HEXACO model. *Journal of Personality Assessment, 99*(1), 25–34. doi:10.1080/00223891.2016.1187155

Irwing, P., Booth, T., Nyborg, H., & Rushton, J. P. (2012). Are *g* and the general factor of personality (GFP) correlated? *Intelligence, 40*(3), 296–305.

Iscan, Z., Rakesh, G., Rossano, S., Yang, J., Zhang, M., Miller, J., et al. (2017). A positron emission tomography study of the serotonergic system in relation to anxiety in depression. *European Neuropsychopharmacology, 27*(10), 1011–1021.

Ishihara, T., Sugasawa, S., Matsuda, Y., & Mizuno, M. (2017). The beneficial effects of game-based exercise using age-appropriate tennis lessons on the executive functions of 6–12-year-old children. *Neuroscience Letters, 642,* 97–101.

Ishikawa, R., Ishigaki, T., Kikuchi, A., Matsumoto, K., Kobayashi, S., Morishige, S., et al. (2017). Cross-cultural validation of the cognitive biases questionnaire for psychosis in Japan and examination of the relationships between cognitive biases and schizophrenia symptoms. *Cognitive Therapy and Research, 41*(2), 313–323.

Ives, A. M., & Bertke, A. S. (2017). Stress Hormones Epinephrine and Corticosterone Selectively Modulate Herpes Simplex Virus 1 (HSV-1) and HSV-2 Productive Infections in Adult Sympathetic, but Not Sensory, Neurons. *Journal of Virology, 91*(13), e00582-17.

J

Jablensky, A. (2000). Epidemiology of schizophrenia: The global burden of disease and disability. *European Archives of Psychiatry and Clinical Neuroscience, 250*(6), 274–285.

Jablensky, A., & others. (1992). Schizophrenia: Manifestations, incidence and course in different cultures: A World Health Organization ten-country study. *Psychological Medicine, Monograph Suppl., 20,* 1–97.

Jackendoff, R. (2012). *A user's guide to thought and meaning.* New York: Oxford University Press.

Jackson, J. J., & Roberts, B. W. (2017). Conscientiousness. In T.A. Widiger (Ed.), *Oxford Handbook of the Five Factor Model.* New York: Oxford University Press.

Jackson, L. C., & Greene, B. (2000). *Psychotherapy with African-American women.* New York: Guilford.

Jackson, T. L., Braun, J. M., Mello, M., Triche, E. W., & Buka, S. L. (2017). The relationship between early childhood head injury and later life criminal behaviour: a longitudinal cohort study. *Journal of Epidemiology and Community Health, 71*(8), 800–805.

Jacobs, E. E., Schimmel, C. J., Masson, R. L., & Harvill, R. L. (2016). *Group counseling: Strategies and skills* (8th ed.). Boston: Cengage.

Jacobs, T. L., Epel, E. S., Lin, J., Blackburn, E. H., Wolkowitz, O. M., Bridwell, D. A., et al. (2011). Intensive meditation training, immune cell telomerase activity, and psychological mediators. *Psychoneuroendocrinology, 36*(5), 664–681.

Jacobsen, P. B., & others. (1993). Formation of food aversions in cancer patients receiving repeated infusions of chemotherapy. *Behavior Research Therapy, 31*(8), 739–748.

Jaeggi, S. M., Buschkuehl, M., Jonides, J., & Perrig, W. J. (2008). Improving fluid intelligence with training on working memory. *Proceedings of the National Academy of Sciences USA, 105*(19), 6829–6833.

Jafari, Z., Kolb, B. E., & Mohajerani, M. H. (2017). Effect of acute stress on auditory processing: a systematic review of human studies. *Reviews in the Neurosciences, 28*(1), 1–13.

James, G. M., Baldinger-Melich, P., Philippe, C., Kranz, G. S., Vanicek, T., Hahn, A., ... & Mitterhauser, M. (2017). Effects of selective serotonin reuptake inhibitors on interregional relation of serotonin transporter availability in major depression. *Frontiers in human neuroscience, 11.*

James, W. (1950). *Principles of psychology.* New York: Dover. (original work published 1890)

Jangraw, D. C., Gonzalez-Castillo, J., Handwerker, D. A., Ghane, M., Rosenberg, M. D., Panwar, P., & Bandettini, P. A. (2018). A functional connectivity-based neuromarker of sustained attention generalizes to predict recall in a reading task. *NeuroImage, 166,* 99–109.

Janis, I. (1972). *Victims of groupthink: A psychological study of foreign-policy decisions and fiascos.* Boston: Houghton Mifflin.

Janowsky, D. S., Addario, D., & Risch, S. C. (1987). *Psychopharmacology case studies* (2nd ed.). New York: Guilford.

Jansen, L.A., Mahadevan, D., Appelbaum, P.S., Klein, W.M.P., Weinstein, N.D., Mori, M., et al. (2017). Perceptions of control and unrealistic optimism in early-phase cancer trials *Journal of Medical Ethics,* in press. doi: 10.1136/medethics-2016-103724

Jaramillo, N., Buhi, E. R., Elder, J. P., & Corliss, H. L. (2017). Associations between sex education and contraceptive use among heterosexually active, adolescent males in the United States. *Journal of Adolescent Health, 60*(5), 534–540. doi:10.1016/j.jadohealth.2016.11.025

Jaremka, L. M., & others. (2014). Pain, depression, and fatigue: Loneliness as a longitudinal risk factor. *Health Psychology, 33*(9), 948–957.

Jaremka, L. M., Fagundes, C. P., Peng, J., Bennett, J. M., Glaser, R., Malarkey, W. B., & Kiecolt-Glaser, J. K. (2013a). Loneliness promotes inflammation during acute stress. *Psychological Science, 24*(7), 1089–1097.

Jaremka, L. M., Glaser, R., Malarkey, W. B., & Kiecolt-Glaser, J. K. (2013b). Marital distress prospectively predicts poorer cellular immune function. *Psychoneuroendocrinology, 38*(11), 2713–2719.

Jasaui, Y., Kirton, A., Wilkes, T. C., McLellan, Q., Kahl, C., Swansburg, R., & MacMaster, F. (2017). 647-glutamate and response to repetitive transcranial magnetic stimulation in youth with treatment resistant depression. *Biological Psychiatry, 81*(10), S262.

Jasiak, N. M., & Bostwick, J. R. (2014). Risk of QT/QTc prolongation among newer non-SSRI antidepressants. *Annals of Pharmacotherapy, 48*(12), 1620–1628.

Jaya, E. S., Hillmann, T. E., Reininger, K. M., Gollwitzer, A., & Lincoln, T. M. (2017). Loneliness and psychotic symptoms: The mediating role of depression. *Cognitive Therapy And Research, 41*(1), 106–116. doi:10.1007/s10608-016-9799-4

Jayawickreme, E. & Blackie, L.E.R. (2016). *Exploring the psychological benefits of hardship: A critical reassessment of posttraumatic growth.* Switzerland: Springer.

Jayawickreme, E., Brocato, N. W., & Blackie, L. E. (2017). Wisdom gained? Assessing relationships between adversity, personality and well-being among a late adolescent sample. *Journal of Youth and Adolescence, 46*(6), 1179–1199.

Jensen, H. H., Mortensen, E. L., & Lotz, M. (2014). Drop-out from a psychodynamic group outpatient unit. *Nordic Journal of Psychiatry, 68*(8), 594–604.

Jensen, K. P., Stein, M. B., Kranzler, H. R., Yang, B. Z., Farrer, L. A., & Gelernter, J. (2014). The α-endomannosidase gene (MANEA) is associated with panic disorder and social anxiety disorder. *Translational Psychiatry, 4,* e353.

Jensen, L. W., & Wadkins, T. A. (2007). Mental health success stories: Finding paths to recovery. *Issues in Mental Health Nursing, 28*(4), 325–340.

Jensen, M. P., & Patterson, D. R. (2014). Hypnotic approaches for chronic pain management: Clinical implications of recent research findings. *American Psychologist, 69*(2), 167–177.

Jensen-Campbell, L. A., & Malcolm, K. T. (2007). The importance of conscientiousness in adolescent interpersonal relationships. *Personality and Social Psychology Bulletin, 33*(3), 368–383.

Jessen, L., Smith, E. P., Ulrich-Lai, Y., Herman, J. P., Seeley, R. J., Sandoval, D., & D'alessio, D. (2017). Central nervous system GLP-1 receptors regulate islet hormone secretion and glucose homeostasis in male rats. *Endocrinology, 158*(7), 2124–2133.

Ji, X., Saha, S., Kolpakova, J., Guildford, M., Tapper, A. R., & Martin, G. E. (2017). Dopamine receptors differentially control binge alcohol drinking-mediated synaptic plasticity of the core nucleus accumbens direct and indirect pathways. *Journal of Neuroscience, 37*(22), 5463–5474.

Jiang, W., Li, G., Liu, H., Shi, F., Wang, T., Shen, C., et al. (2016). Reduced cortical thickness and increased surface area in antisocial personality disorder. *Neuroscience, 337*, 143–152.

Jimenez, M. E., Wade, R., Schwartz-Soicher, O., Lin, Y., & Reichman, N. E. (2017). Adverse Childhood Experiences and ADHD Diagnosis at Age 9 Years in a National Urban Sample. *Academic Pediatrics, 17*(4), 356–361.

Jin, K., & Baillargeon, R. (2017). Infants possess an abstract expectation of ingroup support. *PNAS Proceedings of the National Academy of Sciences of the United States of America, 114*(31), 8199–8204. doi:10.1073/pnas.1706286114

Jin, Y., & Li, J. (2017). When newbies and veterans play together: The effect of video game content, context and experience on cooperation. *Computers In Human Behavior, 68*, 556–563. doi:10.1016/j.chb.2016.11.059

Jin, Y., Hamiez, J., & Hao, J. (2017). Algorithms for the minimum sum coloring problem: A review. *Artificial Intelligence Review, 47*(3), 367–394. doi:10.1007/s10462-016-9485-7

Johannsson, M., Snaedal, J., Johannesson, G. H., Gudmundsson, T. E., & Johnsen, K. (2015). The acetylcholine index: An electroencephalographic marker of cholinergic activity in the living human brain applied to Alzheimer's disease and other dementias. *Dementia and Geriatric Cognitive Disorders, 39*, 132–142. doi:10.1159/000367889

John, S. G., Cisler, J. M., & Sigel, B. A. (2017). Emotion regulation mediates the relationship between a history of child abuse and current PTSD/depression severity in adolescent females. *Journal of Family Violence, 32*, 565–575.

Johnson, G. B. (2015). *The living world* (8th ed.). New York: McGraw-Hill.

Johnson, J., & Wood, A. M. (2017). Integrating positive and clinical psychology: Viewing human functioning as continua from positive to negative can benefit clinical assessment, interventions and understandings of resilience. *Cognitive Therapy And Research, 41*(3), 335–349. doi:10.1007/s10608-015-9728-y

Johnson, J. S., & Newport, E. L. (1991). Critical period effects on universal properties of language: The status of subjacency in the acquisition of a second language. *Cognition, 39*(3), 215–258.

Johnson, S. J. (2017). The art of health promotion: Linking research to practice. *American Journal of Health Promotion, 31*(4), 353–366. doi:10.1177/0890117117715321

Johnson, S. P., & Hannon, E. H. (2015). Perceptual development. In R. M. Lerner, L. S. Liben, & U. Mueller (Eds.), *Handbook of child psychology and developmental science* (7th ed., vol. 2). Hoboken, NJ: Wiley.

Johnson, W., & Bouchard, T. J. (2014). Genetics of intellectual and personality traits associated with creative genius: Could geniuses be cosmobian dragon kings? In

D. K. Simonton (Ed.), *The Wiley handbook of genius* (269–296). New York: Wiley-Blackwell.

Johnston, L. D., O'Malley, P. M., Bachman, J. G., & Schulenberg, J. E. (2016). *Monitoring the Future national survey results on adolescent drug use: Overview of key findings, 2016.* Ann Arbor: Institute of Social Research, University of Michigan.

Joiner, T. E. (2005). *Why people die by suicide.* Cambridge, MA: Harvard University Press.

Joiner, T. E., & Ribeiro, J. D. (2011). Assessment and management of suicidal behavior in children and adolescents. *Pediatric Annals, 40*(6), 319–324.

Joiner, T. E., Ribeiro, J. D., & Silva, C. (2012). Nonsuicidal self-injury, suicidal behavior, and their co-occurrence as viewed through the lens of the interpersonal theory of suicide. *Current Directions in Psychological Science, 21*(5), 342–347.

Jones, C., Barrera, I., Brothers, S., Ring, R., & Wahlestedt, C. (2017). Oxytocin and social functioning. *Dialogues in Clinical Neuroscience, 19*(2), 193–201.

Jones, D. E., Greenberg, M., & Crowley, M. (2015). Early social-emotional functioning and public health: The relationship between kindergarten social competence and future wellness. *American Journal of Public Health, 105*, 2283–2290.

Jones, E. E. (1998). Major developments in five decades of social psychology. In D. T. Gilbert, S. T. Fiske, & G. Lindzey (Eds.), *The handbook of social psychology* (4th ed., vol. 1). New York: McGraw-Hill.

Jones, E. E., & Harris, V. A. (1967). The attribution of attitudes. *Journal of Experimental Social Psychology, 3*(1), 1–24.

Jones, K. M., & Ruthig, J. C. (2015). The impact of positive thinking, gender, and empathy on social attributions for cancer outcomes. *Current Psychology: A Journal for Diverse Perspectives on Diverse Psychological Issues, 34*(4), 762–771. doi:10.1007/s12144-014-9288-4

Jones, N. P., Chase, H. W., & Fournier, J. C. (2016). Brain mechanisms of anxiety's effects on cognitive control in major depressive disorder. *Psychological Medicine, 46*(11), 2397–2409. doi:10.1017/S0033291716001185

Jooyoung, P., Lu, F., & Hedgcock, W. (2017). Forward and backward planning and goal pursuit. *Psychological Science.* in press. DOI:10.1177/0956797617715510

Jordano, M. L., & Touron, D. R. (2017). Stereotype threat as a trigger of mind-wandering in older adults. *Psychology And Aging, 32*(3), 307–313. doi:10.1037/pag0000167

Joseph, J. (2006). *The missing gene.* New York: Algora.

Joseph, J., Breslin, C., & Skinner, H. (1999). Critical perspectives on the transtheoretical model and stages of change. In J. A. Tucker, D. M. Donovan, & G. A. Marlatt (Eds.), *Changing addictive behavior: Bridging clinical and public health strategies* (pp. 160–190). New York: Guilford.

Joshi, G., Faraone, S. V., Wozniak, J., Tarko, L., Fried, R., Galdo, M., et al. (2017). Symptom profile of ADHD in youth with high-functioning autism spectrum disorder: a comparative study in psychiatrically referred populations. *Journal of Attention Disorders, 21*(10), 846–855.

Joshi, S., Mooney, S. J., Rundle, A. G., Quinn, J. W., Beard, J. R., & Cerdá, M. (2017). Pathways from neighborhood poverty to depression among older adults. *Health & Place, 43*, 138–143.

Jost, J. T., Gaucher, D., & Stern, C. (2014). "The world isn't fair": A system justification perspective on social stratification and inequality. In M. Mikulincer, P. R. Shaver, J. F. Dovidio, & J. A. Simpson (Eds.), *APA handbook of personality and social psychology* (vol. 2). Washington, DC: American Psychological Association.

Joy, J. E., Watson, J. S., & Benson, J. A. (Eds.). (1999). *Marijuana and medicine: Assessing the science base.* Institute of Medicine. Washington, DC: National Academy Press.

Jozaghi, E., & Carleton, R. (2015). The identification of subtypes among injection drug users: HIV and hepatitis C differences as indicated with the theory of planned behaviour. *Journal of Substance Use, 20*(2), 119–127. doi:10.3109/14659891.2013.866987

Judd, C. M., & Park, B. (2017). Social cognition about a collaboration in social cognition. In R. L. Zweigenhaft, & E. Borgida (Eds.), *Collaboration in psychological science: Behind the scenes* (pp. 79–91). New York, NY: Worth Publishers.

Julsing, J. E., Kromhout, D., Geleijnse, J. M., & Giltay, E. J. (2016). Loneliness and all-cause, cardiovascular, and noncardiovascular mortality in older men: The Zutphen Elderly Study. *The American Journal Of Geriatric Psychiatry, 24*(6), 475–484. doi:10.1016/j.jagp.2016.01.136

Jung, C. (1917). *Analytic psychology.* New York: Moffat, Yard.

Jung, C. G. (1921/1977). *The collected works of C. G. Jung. vol. 6. Psychological types.* Princeton, NJ: Princeton University Press.

Jury, M., Smeding, A., Stephens, N.M., Nelson, J.E., Aelenei, C., Darnon, C. (2017). The experience of low-SES students in higher education: Psychological bBarriers to success and interventions to reduce social-class inequality. *Journal of Social Issues, 73*(1), pp. 23–41. Cited 9 times.

K

Kaag, A. M., Schluter, R. S., Karel, P., Homberg, J., Van Den Brink, W., Reneman, L., & Van Wingen, G. A. (2016). Aversive counterconditioning attenuates reward signaling in the ventral striatum. *Frontiers in Human Neuroscience, 10*, 418.

Kabat-Zinn, J. (2006). *Coming to our senses: Healing ourselves and the world through mindfulness.* New York: Hyperion.

Kabat-Zinn, J. (2009, March 18). *This analog life: Reconnecting with what is important in an always uncertain world.* Presentation at the 7th Annual Conference at the Center for Mindful Meditation, Worcester, MA.

Kabat-Zinn, J., & Davidson, R. (Eds.). (2012). *The mind's own physician.* Berkeley, CA: New Harbinger.

Kabat-Zinn, J., & others. (1998). Influence of a mindfulness meditation-based stress reduction intervention on rates of skin clearing in patients with moderate to severe psoriasis undergoing phototherapy (UVB) and photochemotherapy (PUVA). *Psychosomatic Medicine, 60*(5), 625–632.

Kabat-Zinn, J., Lipworth, L., & Burney, R. (1985). The clinical use of mindfulness meditation for the self-regulation of chronic pain. *Journal of Behavioral Medicine, 8*(2), 163–190.

Kaboski, J., McDonnell, C. G., & Valentino, K. (2017). Resilience and autism spectrum disorder: Applying developmental psychopathology to optimal outcome. *Review Journal of Autism and Developmental Disorders, 4*, 175–189.

Kafashan, S., Sparks, A., Rotella, A., & Barclay, P. (2017). Why heroism exists: Evolutionary perspectives on extreme helping. In S. T. Allison, G. R. Goethals, & R. M. Kramer, (Eds.), *Handbook of heroism and heroic leadership* (pp. 36–57). New York: Routledge/Taylor & Francis Group.

Kagan, J. (2013). Temperamental contributions to inhibited and uninhibited profiles. In P. D. Zelazo (Ed.), *The Oxford handbook of developmental psychology.* New York: Oxford University Press.

Kahn, A., & others. (1992). Sleep and cardiorespiratory characteristics of infant victim of sudden death: A prospective case-control study. *Sleep, 15*(4), 287–292.

Kahneman, D., & Klein, G. (2009). Conditions for intuitive experience: A failure to disagree. *American Psychologist, 64*(6), 515–526.

Kahneman, D., & Tversky, A. (1984). Choices, values and frames. *American Psychologist, 39*(4), 341–350.

Kahneman, D., Knetsch, J. L., & Thaler, R. H. (1990). Experimental tests of the endowment effect and the coase theorem. *Journal of Political Economy, 98*(6), 1325-1348.

Kaiseler, M., Queirós, C., Passos, F., & Sousa, P. (2014). Stress appraisal, coping, and work engagement among police recruits: An exploratory study. *Psychological Reports, 114*(2), 635-646.

Kaiser, D., & Haselhuhn, T. (2017). Facing a Regular World: How Spatial Object Structure Shapes Visual Processing. *Journal of Neuroscience, 37*(8), 1965-1967.

Kajonius, P., Giolla, E.M. (2017). Personality traits across countries: Support for similarities rather than differences. *PLoS ONE, 12*(6), e0179646.

Kalichman, S. C. (2007). The theory of reasoned action and advances in HIV/AIDS prevention. In I. Ajzen, D. Albarracin, & R. Hornik (Eds.), *Prediction and change of health behavior*. Mahwah, NJ: Erlbaum.

Kaliman, P., Alvarez-López, M. J., Cosín-Tomás, M., Rosenkranz, M. A., Lutz, A., & Davidson, R. J. (2014). Rapid changes in histone deacetylases and inflammatory gene expression in expert meditators. *Psychoneuroendocrinology, 40*, 96-107.

Kalokerinos, E. K., Kjelsaas, K., Bennetts, S., & Hippel, C. (2017). Men in pink collars: Stereotype threat and disengagement among male teachers and child protection workers. *European Journal of Social Psychology*, in press. doi:10.1002/ejsp.2246

Kamin, L. J. (1968). Attention-like processes in classical conditioning. In M. R. Jones (Ed.), *Miami symposium on the prediction of behavior: Aversive stimuli*. Coral Gables, FL: University of Miami Press.

Kaminsky, Z., & others. (2014). DNA methylation and expression in KCNQ3 in bipolar disorder. *Bipolar Disorders*. doi: 10.1111/bdi.12230

Kammrath, L. K., & Scholer, A. A. (2013). The cognitive-affective processing system. In I. H. A. Tennen, J. Suls, & I. B. Weiner (Eds.), *Handbook of psychology* (2nd ed., vol. 5, pp. 161-182). New York: Wiley.

Kanazawa, S. (2017). Possible evolutionary origins of human female sexual fluidity. *Biological Reviews, 92*(3), 1251-1274.

Kandel, E. R., & Schwartz, J. H. (1982). Molecular biology of learning: Modulation of transmitter release. *Science, 218*(4571), 433-443.

Kane, J. M., Correll, C. U., Harvey, P. D., & Olfson, M. (2014). Clinical and cost implications of treating schizophrenia: Safety, efficacy, relapse prevention, and patient outcomes. *Journal of Clinical Psychiatry, 75*(8), e-20.

Kane, J. M., Robinson, D. G., Schooler, N. R., Mueser, K. T., Penn, D. L., Rosenheck, R. A., et al. (2015). Comprehensive versus usual community care for first-episode psychosis: 2-year outcomes from the NIMH RAISE early treatment program. *American Journal of Psychiatry, 173*(4), 362-372.

Kane, M. J., Gross, G. M., Chun, C. A., Smeekens, B. A., Meier, M. E., Silvia, P. J., & Kwapil, T. R. (2017). For whom the mind wanders, and when, varies across laboratory and daily-life settings. *Psychological Science, 28*(9), 1271-1289.

Kaneda, T., Shigemune, Y., & Tsukiura, T. (2017). Lateral and medial prefrontal contributions to emotion generation by semantic elaboration during episodic encoding. *Cognitive, Affective, & Behavioral Neuroscience, 17*(1), 143-157.

Kang, Y., Gray, J. R., & Dovidio, J. F. (2014). The nondiscriminating heart: Lovingkindness meditation training decreases implicit intergroup bias. *Journal of Experimental Psychology: General, 143*(3), 1306-1313.

Kanwisher, N. (2006). Neuroscience: What's in a face? *Science, 311*(5761), 617-618.

Kaplan, M. S., Huguet, N., McFarland, B. H., Caetano, R., Conner K. R., Giesbrecht, N., & Nolte, K. B. (2014). Use of alcohol before suicide in the United States. *Annals of Epidemiology, 24*(8), 588-592.

Kapur, S. (2003). Psychosis as a state of aberrant salience: A framework linking biology, phenomenology, and pharmacology. *American Journal of Psychiatry, 160*(1), 13-23.

Karantzas, G. C., & Gillath, O. (2017). Stress and wellbeing during chronic illness and partner death in later-life: The role of social support. *Current Opinion In Psychology, 13*, 75-80. doi:10.1016/j.copsyc.2016.05.009

Karapanagiotidis, T., Bernhardt, B. C., Jefferies, E., & Smallwood, J. (2017). Tracking thoughts: Exploring the neural architecture of mental time travel during mind-wandering. *Neuroimage, 147*, 272-281.

Karnath, H. O., & Rennig, J. (2017). Investigating structure and function in the healthy human brain: Validity of acute versus chronic lesion-symptom mapping. *Brain Structure and Function, 222*(5), 2059-2070.

Karpati, F.J., Giacosa, C., Foster, N.E.V., Penhune, V.B., Hyde, K.L. (2017). Dance and music share gray matter structural correlates. *Brain Research, 1657*, 62-3.

Kasemsap, K. (2017). Mastering cognitive neuroscience and social neuroscience perspectives in the information age. In M. A. Dos Santos (Ed.). *Applying neuroscience to business practice* (pp. 82-113). Hershey, PA: Business Science Reference/IGI Global. doi:10.4018/978-1-5225-1028-4.ch005

Kasser, T. (2011). Cultural values and the well-being of future generations: A cross-national study. *Journal of Cross-Cultural Psychology, 42*(2), 206-215.

Kasser, T., & Ryan, R. M. (1993). A dark side of the American dream: Correlates of financial success as a central life aspiration. *Journal of Personality and Social Psychology, 65*(2), 410-422.

Kasser, T., & Ryan, R. M. (1996). Further examining the American dream: Differential correlates of intrinsic and extrinsic goals. *Personality and Social Psychology Bulletin, 22*(3), 280-287.

Kasser, T., & Sharma, Y. S. (1999). Reproductive freedom, educational equality, and females' preference for resource-acquisition characteristics in mates. *Psychological Science, 10*(4), 374-377.

Kasser, T., Ryan, R. M., Couchman, C. E., & Sheldon, K. M. (2004). Materialistic values: Their causes and consequences. In T. Kasser & A. D. Kanner (Eds.), *Psychology and consumer culture: The struggle for a good life in a materialistic world* (pp. 11-28). Washington, DC: American Psychological Association.

Katonai, E. R., Szekely, A., Vereczkei, A., Sasvari-Szekely, M., Bányai, É. I., & Varga, K. (2017). Dopaminergic and serotonergic genotypes and the subjective experiences of hypnosis. *International Journal Of Clinical And Experimental Hypnosis, 65*(4), 379-397. doi:10.1080/00207144.2017.1348848

Kaufman, S. B., Quilty, L. C., Grazioplene, R. G., Hirsh, J. B., Gray, J. R., Peterson, J. B., & DeYoung, C. G. (2016). Openness to experience and intellect differentially predict creative achievement in the arts and sciences. *Journal of Personality, 84*(2), 248-258. doi:10.1111/jopy.12156

Kawabata, Y., Tseng, W. L., & Crick, N. R. (2014). Adaptive, maladaptive, mediational, and bidirectional processes of relational and physical aggression, relational and physical victimization, and peer liking. *Aggressive Behavior, 40*(3), 273-287.

Kawamoto, T., Van der Linden, D., & Dunkel, C. S. (2017). The general factor of personality (GFP) and moral foundations. *Personality and Individual Differences, 11*, 978-82. doi:10.1016/j.paid.2017.06.043

Kawasaki, M., Uno, Y., Mori, J., Kobata, K., & Kitago, K. (2014). Transcranial magnetic stimulation-induced global propagation of transient phase resetting associated with directional information flow. *Frontiers in Human Neuroscience, 8*, 173.

Kaye, W. H., Wierenga, C. E., Bailer, U. F., Simmons, A. N., & Bischoff-Grethe, A. (2013). Nothing tastes as good as skinny feels: The neurobiology of anorexia nervosa. *Trends in Neuroscience, 36*(2), 110-120.

Kayser, D. (2017). Using facial expressions of emotion as a means for studying music-induced emotions. *Psychomusicology: Music, Mind, and Brain, 27*(3), 219-222. doi:10.1037/pmu0000187

Kegel, A. F., & Flückiger, C. (2014). Predicting psychotherapy dropouts: A multilevel approach. *Clinical Psychology and Psychotherapy*. doi:10.1002/cpp.1899

Kell, H. J., & Lubinski, D. (2014). The study of mathematically precocious youth at maturity: Insights into elements of genius. In D. K. Simonton (Ed.), *The Wiley handbook of genius* (pp. 397-421). New York: Wiley-Blackwell.

Kellerman, A. L., & others. (1993). Gun ownership as a risk factor for homicide in the home. *New England Journal of Medicine, 329*(15), 1084-1091.

Kelley, H. H. (1973). The processes of causal attribution. *American Psychologist, 28*(2), 107-128.

Kellner, C. H. (2006). Continuation electroconvulsive therapy vs pharmacotherapy for relapse prevention in major depression: A multisite study from the Consortium for Research in Electroconvulsive Therapy (CORE). *Archives of General Psychiatry, 63*(12), 1337-1344.

Kelly, J. F. (2017). Is Alcoholics Anonymous religious, spiritual, neither? Findings from 25 years of mechanisms of behavior change research. *Addiction, 112*(6), 929-936.

Kelly, J. F., Hoeppner, B., Sout, R. L., & Pagano, M. (2012). Determining the relative importance of the mechanisms of behavior change within Alcoholics Anonymous: A multiplier mediator analysis. *Addiction, 107*(2), 289-299.

Kelly, K. M., & Mezuk, B. (2017). Predictors of remission from generalized anxiety disorder and major depressive disorder. *Journal of Affective Disorders, 208*, 467-474.

Keltner, D., Kogan, A., Piff, P. K., & Saturn, S. R. (2014). The sociocultural appraisals, values, and emotions (SAVE) framework of prosociality: Core processes from gene to meme. *Annual Review of Psychology* (vol. 65). Palo Alto, CA: Annual Reviews.

Kempe, M., Lycett, S. J., & Mesoudi, A. (2014). From cultural traditions to cumulative culture: Parameterizing the differences between human and nonhuman culture. *Journal of Theoretical Biology, 359*, 29-36.

Kendler, K. S., Gardner, C., & Dick, D. M. (2011). Predicting alcohol consumption in adolescence from alcohol-specific and general externalizing genetic risk factors, key environmental factors, and their interaction. *Psychological Medicine, 41*(7), 1507-1516.

Kendzierski, D., Ritter, R. L., Stump, T. K., & Anglin, C. L. (2015). The effectiveness of an implementation intentions intervention for fruit and vegetable consumption as moderated by self-schema status. *Appetite, 95*228-238. doi:10.1016/j.appet.2015.07.007

Kennison, R. F., Situ, D., Reyes, N., Ahacic, K. (2017) Cohort effects. In N.A. Pachana (Ed.), *Encyclopedia of geropsychology*. Singapore: Springer in press.

Keogh, R., & Pearson, J. (2017). The perceptual and phenomenal capacity of mental imagery. *Cognition, 162*, 124-132.

Kernis, M. H. (Ed.). (2013). *Self-esteem issues and answers: A sourcebook of current perspectives*. New York: Psychology Press.

Kerr, W. C., Kaplan, M. S., Huguet, N., Caetano, R., Giesbrecht, N., & McFarland, B. H. (2017). Economic recession, alcohol, and suicide rates: comparative effects of poverty, foreclosure, and job loss. *American Journal of Preventive Medicine, 52*(4), 469-475.

Kettenmann, H., & Verkhratsky, A. (2016). Glial cells: neuroglia. In D.W. Pfaff, N.D. Volkov (Eds.), *Neuroscience in the 21st century: From basic to clinical* (2nd ed., pp. 547-578). New York: Springer.

Khalighinejad, N., Kunnumpurath, A., Bertini, C., Ladavas, E., & Haggard, P. (2017). Subliminal modulation of voluntary action experience: A neuropsychological investigation. *Cortex, 90*, 58-70.

Khan, A., Fahl Mar, K., Faucett, J., Khan Schilling, S., & Brown, W. A. (2017). Has the rising placebo response impacted antidepressant clinical trial outcome? Data from the US Food and Drug Administration 1987-2013. *World Psychiatry, 16*(2), 181-192.

Khan, A., Faucett, J., & Brown, W. A. (2014). Magnitude of placebo response and response variance in antidepressant clinical trials using structured, taped and appraised rater interviews compared to traditional rating interviews. *Journal of Psychiatric Research, 51*, 88-92.

Khan, A., Khan, S., & Brown, W. A. (2002). Are placebo controls necessary to test new antidepressants and anxiolytics? *International Journal of Neuropsychopharmacology, 5*(3), 193-197.

Khan, A., Redding, N., & Brown, W. A. (2008). The persistence of placebo response in antidepressant clinical trials. *Journal of Psychiatric Research, 42*(10), 791-796.

Khan, A., Schmidt, L. A., & Chen, X. (2017). Cultural neuroscience of emotion: Toward a developmental framework. *Psychology & Neuroscience, 10*(1), 11-40. doi:10.1037/pne0000078

Khurana, V. G., & Kaye, A. H. (2012). An overview of concussion in sport. *Journal of Clinical Neuroscience, 19*(1), 1-11.

Kidd, E., & Arciuli, J. (2016). Individual differences in statistical learning predict children's comprehension of syntax. *Child Development, 87*(1), 184-193. doi:10.1111/cdev.12461

Kievit, R. A., Lindenberger, U., Goodyer, I. M., Jones, P. B., Fonagy, P., Bullmore, E. T. et al. (2017). Mutualistic coupling between vocabulary and reasoning supports cognitive development during late adolescence and early adulthood. *Psychological Science*, in press. doi: 10.1177/0956797617710785

Kihlstrom, J. (2005). Is hypnosis an altered state of consciousness or what?: Comment. *Contemporary Hypnosis, 22*(1), 34-38.

Killen, M., & Smetana, J. G. (Eds.). (2014). *Handbook of moral development* (2nd ed.). New York: Psychology Press.

Kilpatrick, D. G. (2000). *The Mental Health Impact of Rape*. Medical University of South Carolina: National Violence Against Women Prevention Research Center. https://mainweb-v.musc.edu/vawprevention/research/mentalimpact.shtml

Kim, E. S., Chopik, W. J., & Smith, J. (2014). Are people healthier if their partners are more optimistic? The dyadic effect of optimism on health among older adults. *Journal of Psychosomatic Research, 76*(6), 447-453.

Kim, E., Zeppenfeld, V., & Cohen, D. (2013). Sublimation, culture, and creativity. *Journal of Personality and Social Psychology, 105*(4), 639-666.

Kim, H. (2011). Differential neural activity in the recognition of old and new events: An activation likelihood estimation meta-analysis. *Human Brain Mapping, 34*(4), 814-836.

Kim, H. J., Yang, G. S., Greenspan, J. D., Downton, K. D., Griffith, K. A., Renn, C. L., et al. (2017). Racial and ethnic differences in experimental pain sensitivity: systematic review and meta-analysis. *Pain, 158*(2), 194-211.

Kim, H., Kim, B., Cho, J., Ryu, S., Shin, H., Sung, J., & ... Kim, H. (2015). Pathway analysis of genome-wide association datasets of personality traits. *Genes, Brain & Behavior, 14*(4), 345-356. doi:10.1111/gbb.12212

Kim, J. I., Kim, J. W., Lee, J. M., Yun, H. J., Sohn, C. H., Shin, M. S., et al. (2018). Interaction between DRD2 and lead exposure on the cortical thickness of the frontal lobe in youth with attention-deficit/hyperactivity disorder. *Progress in Neuro-Psychopharmacology and Biological Psychiatry*. in press.

Kim, S., & Bay, D. (2017). Cognitive dissonance as an explanation of goodwill write-offs. *Journal of Behavioral Finance, 18*(1), 14-28. doi:10.1080/15427560.2017.1274755

Kim, Y., Perova, Z., Mirrione, M. M., Pradhan, K., Henn, F. A., Shea, S., ... & Li, B. (2016). Whole-brain mapping of neuronal activity in the learned helplessness model of depression. *Frontiers in Neural Circuits, 10*.

Kim-Fuchs, C., & others. (2014). Chronic stress accelerates pancreatic cancer growth and invasion: A critical role for beta-adrenergic signaling in the pancreatic microenvironment. *Brain, Behavior, and Immunity, 40*, 40-47.

King, L. A. (2002). Gain without pain: Expressive writing and self-regulation. In S. J. Lepore & J. Smyth (Eds.), *The writing cure*. Washington, DC: American Psychological Association.

King, L. A. (2008). Personal goals and life dreams: Positive psychology and motivation in daily life. In W. Gardner & J. Shah (Eds.), *Handbook of motivation science* (pp. 518-532). New York: Guilford.

King, L. A., & Hicks, J. A. (2006). Narrating the self in the past and the future: Implications for maturity. *Research in Human Development, 3*(2-3), 121-138.

King, L. A., & Hicks, J. A. (2007). Whatever happened to "what might have been"? Regret, happiness, and maturity. *American Psychologist, 62*(7), 625-636.

King, L. A., & Hicks, J. A. (2012). Positive affect and meaning in life: The intersection of hedonism and eudaimonia. In P. T. Wong (Ed.), *The human quest for meaning* (2nd ed., pp. 125-142). New York: Routledge.

King, L. A., & Trent, J. (2012). Personality strengths. In H. Tennen & J. M. Suls (Eds.), *Handbook of psychology: Personality and social psychology* (vol. 5). New York: Wiley.

King, L. A., Hicks, J. A., & Abdelkhalik, J. (2009). Death, life, scarcity, and value: An alternative approach to the meaning of death. *Psychological Science, 20*(12), 1459-1462.

King, L. A., Hicks, J. A., Krull, J. L., & Del Gaiso, A. K. (2006). Positive affect and the experience of meaning in life. *Journal Of Personality And Social Psychology, 90*(1), 179-196. doi:10.1037/0022-3514.90.1.179

King, L. A., Hicks, J. A., Krull, J., & Del Gaiso, A. K. (2006). Positive affect and the experience of meaning in life. *Journal of Personality and Social Psychology, 90*(1), 179-196.

Kinney, H. C. (2009). Neuropathology provides new insight in the pathogenesis of the sudden infant death syndrome. *Acta Neuropathologica, 117*(3), 247-255.

Kinney, K. L., Boffa, J. W., & Amir, N. (2017). Gender difference in attentional bias toward negative and positive stimuli in generalized anxiety disorder. *Behavior Therapy, 48*(3), 277-284.

Kinsey, A. C., Martin, C. E., & Pomeroy, W. B. (1953). *Sexual behavior in the human female*. Philadelphia: Saunders.

Kinsey, A. C., Pomeroy, W. B., & Martin, C. E. (1948). *Sexual behavior in the human male*. Philadelphia: Saunders.

Kiosses, D. N., Gross, J. J., Banerjee, S., Duberstein, P. R., Putrino, D., & Alexopoulos, G. S. (2017). Negative emotions and suicidal ideation during psychosocial treatments in older adults with major depression and cognitive impairment. *The American Journal of Geriatric Psychiatry, 25*(6), 620-629.

Kirby, D. B. (2008). The impact of abstinence and comprehensive sex and STD/HIV education programs on adolescent sexual behavior. *Sexuality Research & Social Policy: A Journal of the NSRC, 5*(3), 18-27. doi:10.1525/srsp.2008.5.3.18

Kirk, H., Gray, K., Ellis, K., Taffe, J., & Cornish, K. (2017). Impact of attention training on academic achievement, executive functioning, and behavior: A randomized controlled trial. *American Journal on Intellectual and Developmental Disabilities, 122*(2), 97-117.

Kirkpatrick, K., & Balsam, P. D. (2016). Associative learning and timing. *Current opinion in behavioral sciences, 8*, 181-185.

Kirmayer, L. J., Gomez-Carrillo, A., & Veissière, S. (2017). Culture and depression in global mental health: An ecosocial approach to the phenomenology of psychiatric disorders. *Social Science & Medicine, 183*, 163-168

Kirsch, I. (2009). Antidepressants and the placebo response. *Epidemiology and Psychiatric Sciences, 18*(4), 318-322.

Kirsch, I. (2017). Placebo effects and hypnosis. In G. R. Elkins (Ed.), *Handbook of medical and psychological hypnosis: Foundations, applications, and professional issues* (pp. 679-685). New York: Springer Publishing Co.

Kirsch, I., Deacon, B. J., Huedo-Medina, T. B., Scoboria, A., Moore, T. J., & Johnson, B. T. (2008). Initial severity and antidepressant benefits: A meta-analysis of data submitted to the Food and Drug Administration. *PLoS Medicine, 5*(2), e45.

Kisely, S., Alichniewicz, K. K., Black, E. B., Siskind, D., Spurling, G., & Toombs, M. (2017). The prevalence of depression and anxiety disorders in indigenous people of the Americas: A systematic review and meta-analysis. *Journal of Psychiatric Research, 84*, 137-152.

Kjell, O. N., Nima, A. A., Sikström, S., Archer, T., & Garcia, D. (2013). Iranian and Swedish adolescents: Differences in personality traits and well-being. *Peer Journal, 1*, e197.

Kjellström, S., & Stålne, K. (2017). Adult development as a lens: Applications of adult development theories in research. *Behavioral Development Bulletin, 22*(2), 266-278.

Klahn, A. L., Klinkenberg, I. A., Lueken, U., Notzon, S., Arolt, V., Pantev, C., et al. (2017). Commonalities and differences in the neural substrates of threat predictability in panic disorder and specific phobia. *NeuroImage: Clinical, 14*, 530-537.

Klapper, A., Ramsey, R., Wigboldus, D., & Cross, E. S. (2014). The control of automatic imitation based on bottom-up and top-down cues to animacy: Insights from brain and behavior. *Journal of Cognitive Neuroscience, 26*(11), 2503-2513.

Klein, M., Onnink, M., van Donkelaar, M., Wolfers, T., Harich, B., Shi, Y., et al. (2017). Brain imaging genetics in ADHD and beyond- mapping pathways from gene to disorder at different levels of complexity. *Neuroscience & Biobehavioral Reviews, 80*, 115-155.

Klein, R. A., Ratliff, K. A., Vianello, M., Adams, R. J., Bahník, Š., Bernstein, M. J., & ... Nosek, B. A. (2014). Investigating variation in replicability: A 'many labs' replication project. *Social Psychology, 45*(3), 142-152. doi:10.1027/1864-9335/a000178

Klemanski, D. H., Curtiss, J., McLaughlin, K. A., & Nolen-Hoeksema, S. (2017). Emotion regulation and the transdiagnostic role of repetitive negative thinking in adolescents with social anxiety and depression. *Cognitive Therapy and Research, 41*(2), 206-219.

Klingman, K. J., Jungquist, C. R., & Perlis, M. L. (2017). Questionnaires that screen for multiple sleep disorders. *Sleep medicine reviews, 32*, 37-44.

Klocek, J. (2017). History of medical and psychological hypnosis. In G. R. Elkins (Ed.), *Handbook of medical and psychological hypnosis: Foundations, applications, and professional issues* (pp. 3-7). New York: Springer.

Klosterhalfen, S., & others. (2000). Pavlovian conditioning of taste aversion using a motion sickness paradigm. *Psychosomatic Medicine, 62*(5), 671-677.

Klucharev, V., Hytönen, K., Rijpkema, M., Smidts, A., & Fernández, G. (2009). Reinforcement learning signal predicts social conformity. *Neuron, 61*(1), 140-151.

Klöckner, C. A. (2017). A stage model as an analysis framework for studying voluntary change in food choices—The case of beef consumption reduction in Norway. *Appetite, 108* 434-449. doi:10.1016/j.appet.2016.11.002

Knafo, A., Israel, S., & Ebstein, R. P. (2011). Heritability of children's prosocial behavior and differential susceptibility to parenting by variation in the dopamine receptor D4 gene. *Development and Psychopathology, 23*(1), 53-67.

Knapp, S., & VandeCreek, L. (2000). Recovered memories of childhood abuse: Is there an underlying consensus. *Professional Psychology: Research and Practice, 31*(4), 365–371.

Knight, C. P., Basilio, C. D., Cham, H., Gonzales, N. A., Liu, Y., & Umaña-Taylor, A. J. (2014). Trajectories of Mexican American and mainstream cultural values among Mexican American adolescents. *Journal of Youth and Adolescence, 43*(12), 2012–2027.

Knight, R. (2014). A hundred years of latency: From Freudian psychoanalytic theory to dynamic systems nonlinear development in middle childhood. *Journal of the American Psychoanalytic Association, 62*(2), 203–235.

Knoll, A. R., Otani, H., Skeel, R. L., & Van Horn, K. R. (2017). Learning style, judgements of learning, and learning of verbal and visual information. *British Journal of Psychology, 108*(3), 544–563. doi:10.1111/bjop.12214

Knouse, L. E., Teller, J., & Brooks, M. A. (2017). Meta-analysis of cognitive–behavioral treatments for adult ADHD. *Journal of Consulting and Clinical Psychology, 85*(7), 737–750.

Knutsson, A. (2017). Mortality of shift workers. *Scandinavian Journal of Work, Environment & Health, 43*(2), 97–98.

Ko, H. J., Hooker, K., Geldhof, G. J., & McAdams, D. P. (2016). Longitudinal purpose in life trajectories: Examining predictors in late midlife. *Psychology and Aging, 31*(7), 693.

Kobasa, S. C., Maddi, S. R., Puccetti, M. C., & Zola, M. (1986). Relative effectiveness of hardiness, exercise, and social support as resources against illness. *Journal of Psychosomatic Research, 29*(5), 525–533.

Kobasa, S., Maddi, S., & Kahn, S. (1982). Hardiness and health: A prospective study. *Journal of Personality and Social Psychology, 42*(1), 168–177.

Kochanek, K.D., Murphy, S.L., Xu, J.Q. (2015). Deaths: Final data for 2011. *National Vital Statistics Reports, 63*, 3. Hyattsville,MD: National Center for Health Statistics. https://www.cdc.gov/nchs/data/nvsr/nvsr63/nvsr63_03.pdf

Koegel, R. L., Koegel, L. K., Vernon, T. W., & Brookman-Frazee, L. I. (2017). Pivotal response treatment for individuals with autism spectrum disorder. In J.R. Weisz & A.E. Kazdin (Eds.), *Evidence-Based Psychotherapies for Children and Adolescents, 3rd ed.* (pp 290–307). New York: Guilford.

Koelkebeck, K., Uwatoko, T., Tanaka, J., & Kret, M. E. (2017). How culture shapes social cognition deficits in mental disorders: A review. *Social Neuroscience, 12*(2), 102–112.

Koenig, A. M., & Butters, M. A. (2014). Cognition in late-life depression: Treatment considerations. *Current Treatment Options in Psychiatry, 1*(1), 1–14.

Koenig, A. M., Eagly, A. H., Mitchell, A. A., & Ristikari, T. (2011). Are leader stereotypes masculine? A meta-analysis of three research paradigms. *Psychological Bulletin, 137*(4), 616–642.

Koenis, M. M., Romeijn, N., Piantoni, G., Verweij, I., Van der Werf, Y. D., Van Someren, E. J., & Stam, C. J. (2011). Does sleep restore the topology of functional brain networks? *Human Brain Mapping, 34*(2), 487–500.

Koestner, R., & others. (2006). Bolstering implementation plans for the long haul: The benefits of simultaneously boosting self-concordance or self-efficacy. *Personality and Social Psychology Bulletin, 32*(11), 1547–1558.

Kohlberg, L. (1958). *The development on modes of moral thinking and choice in the years 10 to 16.* Unpublished doctoral dissertation, University of Chicago, Chicago, Illinois.

Kohlberg, L. (1986). A current statement on some theoretical issues. In S. Modgil & C. Modgil (Eds.), *Lawrence Kohlberg.* Philadelphia: Falmer.

Kohler, P. K., Manhart, L. E., & Lafferty, W. E. (2008). Abstinence-only and comprehensive sex education and the initiation of sexual activity and teen pregnancy. *Journal Of Adolescent Health, 42*(4), 344–351. doi:10.1016/j.jadohealth.2007.08.026

Köhler, W. (1925). *The mentality of apes.* New York: Harcourt Brace Jovanovich.

Kohut, H. (1977). *Restoration of the self.* New York: International Universities Press.

Koike, B. D. V., Farias, K. S., Billwiller, F., Almeida-Filho, D., Libourel, P. A., Tiran-Cappello, A., ... & Queiroz, C. M. (2017). Electrophysiological evidence that the retrosplenial cortex displays a strong and specific activation phased with hippocampal theta during paradoxical (REM) sleep. *Journal of Neuroscience, 37*(33), 8003–8013.

Kok, B. E., Catalino, L. I., & Fredrickson, B. L. (2008). The broadening, building, buffering effects of positive emotion. In S. J. Lopez (Ed.), *Positive psychology: Exploring the best of people* (vol. 3). Westport, CT: Greenwood.

Kok, B. E., Waugh, C. E., & Fredrickson, B. L. (2013). Meditation and health: The search for mechanisms of action. *Social and Personality Psychology Compass, 7*(1), 27–39.

Koletzko, S. H., Herrmann, M., & Brandstätter, V. (2015). Unconflicted goal striving: Goal ambivalence as a mediator between goal self-concordance and well-being. *Personality and Social Psychology Bulletin, 41*(1), 140–156.

Kong, L. L., Allen, J. J. B., & Glisky, E. L. (2008). Interidentity memory transfer in dissociative identity disorder. *Journal of Abnormal Psychology, 117*(3), 686–692.

Königs, M., Pouwels, P. J., Ernest van Heurn, L., Bakx, R., Jeroen Vermeulen, R., Carel Goslings, J., & ... Oosterlaan, J. (2017). Relevance of neuroimaging for neurocognitive and behavioral outcome after pediatric traumatic brain injury. *Brain Imaging And Behavior,* in press. doi:10.1007/s11682-017-9673-3

Kööts-Ausmees, L., Schmidt, M., Esko, T., Metspalu, A., Allik, J., & Realo, A. (2016). The role of the five-factor personality traits in general self-rated health. *European Journal of Personality, 30*(5), 492–504. doi:10.1002/per.2058

Kübler-Ross, E. (1969). *On death and dying.* New York: Simon & Schuster.

Koponen, A. M., Simonsen, N., & Suominen, S. (2017). Determinants of physical activity among patients with type 2 diabetes: The role of perceived autonomy support, autonomous motivation and self-care competence. *Psychology, Health & Medicine, 22*(3), 332–344. doi:10.10 80/13548506.2016.1154179

Koss, K. J., Hostinar, C. E., Donzella, B., & Gunnar, M. R. (2014). Social deprivation and the HPA axis in early development. *Psychoneuroendocrinology, 50*, 1–13.

Kosslyn, S. M., Thompson, W. L., Kim, I. J., Rauch, S. L., & Alpert, N. M. (1996). Individual differences in cerebral blood flow in Area 17 predict the time to evaluate visualized letters. *Journal of Cognitive Neuroscience, 8*(1), 78–82.

Kotter-Grühn, D., & Smith, J. (2011). When time is running out: Changes in positive future perception and their relationships to changes in well-being in old age. *Psychology and Aging, 26*(2), 381–387.

Kottler, J. A., & Shepard, D. S. (2015). *Introduction to counseling* (8th ed.). Boston: Cengage.

Koutsoklenis, A., & Gaitanidis, A. (2017). Interrogating the effectiveness of educational practices: A critique of evidence-based psychosocial treatments for children diagnosed with attention-deficit/hyperactivity disorder. *Frontiers in Education, 2*, 11.

Kovarski, K., Latinus, M., Charpentier, J., Cléry, H., Roux, S., Houy-Durand, E., et al. (2017). Facial expression related vMMN: Disentangling emotional from neutral change detection. *Frontiers in Human Neuroscience, 11.*

Koć-Januchta, M., Höffler, T., Thoma, G., Prechtl, H., & Leutner, D. (2017). Visualizers versus verbalizers: Effects of cognitive style on learning with texts and pictures—An eye-tracking study. *Computers In Human Behavior, 68*, 170–179. doi:10.1016/j.chb.2016.11.028

Kragel, J. E., Ezzyat, Y., Sperling, M. R., Gorniak, R., Worrell, G. A., & Berry, B. M., et al. (2017). Similar

patterns of neural activity predict memory function during encoding and retrieval. *NeuroImage, 155*, 60–71.

Kraus, C., Castrén, E., Kasper, S., & Lanzenberger, R. (2017). Serotonin and neuroplasticity-Links between molecular, functional and structural pathophysiology in depression. *Neuroscience & Biobehavioral Reviews, 77*, 317–326

Kraus, M. W., & Callaghan, B. (2016). Social class and prosocial behavior: The moderating role of public versus private contexts. *Social Psychological and Personality Science, 7*(8), 769–777. doi:10.1177/1948550616659120

Kraus, M. W., Piff, P. K., Mendoza-Denton, R., Rheinschmidt, M. L., & Keltner, D. (2012). Social class, solipsism, and contextualism: How the rich are different from the poor. *Psychological Review, 119*(3), 546–572. doi:10.1037/a0028756

Krause, A. J., Simon, E. B., Mander, B. A., Greer, S. M., Saletin, J. M., Goldstein-Piekarski, A. N., & Walker, M. P. (2017). The sleep-deprived human brain. *Nature Reviews Neuroscience, 18*, 404–418.

Krause, D., & Pogarell, O. (2017). Shrinking brain and schizophrenia: A review of current studies on the effect of antipsychotic medication on gray matter volume. *Psychiatry and Mental Disorders, 1*, 102–108.

Krause, E. D., Vélez, C. E., Woo, R., Hoffmann, B., Freres, D. R., Abenavoli, R. M., & Gillham, J. E. (2017). Rumination, depression, and gender in early adolescence: A longitudinal study of a bidirectional model. *The Journal of Early Adolescence,* in press.

Krause, N. (2006). Religion and health in late life. In J. E. Birren & K. W. Schaie (Eds.), *Handbook of the psychology of aging* (6th ed., pp. 500–515). San Diego: Elsevier.

Krause, N., & Hayward, R. D. (2014). Religious involvement, practical wisdom, and self-rated health. *Journal of Aging and Health, 26*(4), 540–558.

Kredlow, M. A., Szuhany, K. L., Lo, S., Xie, H., Gottlieb, J. D., Rosenberg, S. D., & Mueser, K. T. (2017). Cognitive behavioral therapy for posttraumatic stress disorder in individuals with severe mental illness and borderline personality disorder. *Psychiatry Research, 249*, 86–93.

Kretch, K. S., Franchak, J. M., & Adolph, K. E. (2014). Crawling and walking infants see the world differently. *Child Development, 85*(4), 1503–1518.

Krieger, I. (2017). *Counseling transgender and non-binary youth: The essential guide.* London: Jessica Kingsley Publishers.

Kringelbach, M. L. (2005). The human orbitofrontal cortex: Linking reward to hedonic experience. *Nature Reviews Neuroscience, 6*(9), 691–702.

Kristeller, J. L., & Epel, E. (2014). Mindful eating and mindless eating: The science and the practice. In A. le, C. T. Ngnoumen, & E. J. Langer (Eds.), *The Wiley Blackwell handbook of mindfulness, Vols. I and II* (pp. 913–933). New York: Wiley-Blackwell. doi:10.1002/9781118294895. ch47

Kroger, J., Martinussen, M., & Marcia, J. E. (2010). Identity change in adolescence and young adulthood: A meta-analysis. *Journal of Adolescence, 33*(5), 683–698.

Krone, L., Frase, L., Piosczyk, H., Selhausen, P., Zittel, S., Jahn, F., ... & Riemann, D. (2017). Top-down control of arousal and sleep: Fundamentals and clinical implications. *Sleep Medicine Reviews, 31*, 17–24.

Kross, E., Mischel, W., & Shoda, Y. (2010). Enabling self-control: A cognitive affective processing system (CAPS) approach to problematic behavior. In J. Maddux & J. Tangney (Eds.), *Social psychological foundations of clinical psychology.* New York: Guilford.

Kruse, E., Chancellor, J., Ruberton, P. M., & Lyubomirsky, S. (2014). An upward spiral between gratitude and humility. *Social Psychological and Personality Science, 5*(7), 805–814.

Kubo, H., Nakataki, M., Sumitani, S., Iga, J. I., Numata, S., Kameoka, N., et al. (2017). 1H-magnetic resonance spectroscopy study of glutamate-related abnormality in bipolar disorder. *Journal of Affective Disorders, 208,* 139–144.

Kucera, K. L., Yau, R. K., Register-Mihalik, Marshall, S. W., Thomas, L. C., et al. (2017). Traumatic brain and spinal cord fatalities among high school and college football players—United States, 2005–2014. *MMWR. Morbidity and mortality weekly report, 65,* 1465–1469

Kuchel, G. A. (2017). Function Begets Function and Resilience in Old Age: Is Precision Gerontology Possible? *Journal of the American Geriatrics Society.* In press. doi: 10.1111/jgs.14901

Kuhl, P. K. (1993). Infant speech perception: A window on psycholinguistic development. *International Journal of Psycholinguistics, 9,* 33–56.

Kuhl, P. K. (2012). Language learning and the developing brain: Cross-cultural studies unravel the effects of biology and culture. *Journal of the Acoustical Society of American, 131,* 3207.

Kuhle, C. L., Steffen, M. W., Anderson, P. J., & Murad, M. H. (2014). Effect of exercise on anthropometric measures and serum lipids in older individuals: A systematic review and meta-analysis. *BMJ Open, 4*(6), e005283.

Kuhn, D. (2008). Formal operations from a twenty-first century perspective. *Human Development, 51*(1), 48–55.

Kuipers, G. S., den Hollander, S., van der Ark, L. A., & Bekker, M. J. (2017). Recovery from eating disorder 1 year after start of treatment is related to better mentalization and strong reduction of sensitivity to others. *Eating And Weight Disorders, 22*(3), 535–547. doi:10.1007/s40519-017-0405-x

Kulacaoglu, F., Solmaz, M., Ardic, F. C., Akin, E., & Kose, S. (2017). The relationship between childhood traumas, dissociation, and impulsivity in patients with borderline personality disorder comorbid with ADHD. *Psychiatry and Clinical Psychopharmacology, 27*(4), 393–402.

Kulkofsky, S., Behrens, K. Y., & Battin, D. B. (2015). The bonds that remind us: Maternal reminiscing for bonding purposes in relation to perceived competence and social acceptance. *Infant and Child Development, 24*(5), 469–488.

Kumar, P. N., & George, B. (2013). Life events, social support, coping strategies, and quality of life in attempted suicide: A case-control study. *Indian Journal of Psychology, 55*(1), 46–51.

Kuo, M. C., Kiu, I. P., Ting, K. H., & Chan, C. C. (2014). Age-related effects on perceptual and semantic encoding in memory. *Neuroscience, 261,* 95–106.

Kurson, R. (2007). *Crashing through: A true story of risk, adventure, and the man who dared to see.* New York: Random House.

Kushnir, V., Godinho, A., Hodgins, D. C., Hendershot, C. S., & Cunningham, J. A. (2016). Motivation to quit or reduce gambling: Associations between Self-Determination Theory and the Transtheoretical Model of Change. *Journal Of Addictive Diseases, 35*(1), 58–65. doi:1 0.1080/10550887.2016.1107315

Kuvaas, B., Buch, R., Weibel, A., Dysvik, A., & Nerstad, C. L. (2017). Do intrinsic and extrinsic motivation relate differently to employee outcomes? *Journal of Economic Psychology, 61,* 244–258. doi:10.1016/j.joep.2017.05.004

Kuyper, P. (1972). The cocktail party effect. *Audiology, 11,* 277–282.

Kwan, V. S. Y., & Herrmann, S. D. (2014). The interplay between culture and personality. In M. Mikulincer & P. Shaver (Eds.), *APA handbook of personality and social psychology.* Washington, DC: American Psychological Association.

Kwok, D. W., & Boakes, R. A. (2012). Blocking of acquisition of a taste aversion by a context experienced prior to the taste. *Behavioral Processes, 89*(1), 27–29.

L

Labbe, D., Rytz, A., Godinot, N., Ferrage, A., & Martin, N. (2017). Is portion size selection associated with expected satiation, perceived healthfulness or expected tastiness? A case study on pizza using a photograph-based computer task. *Appetite, 108,* 311–316.

Labella, M. H., & Masten, A. S. (2018). Family influences on the development of aggression and violence. *Current Opinion in Psychology, 19,* 11–16.

Labouvie-Vief, G. (1986, August). *Modes of knowing and life-span cognition.* Paper presented at the meeting of the American Psychological Association, Washington, DC.

Labouvie-Vief, G. (2006). Emerging structures of adult thought. In J. J. Arnett & J. L. Tanner (Eds.), *Emerging adults in America* (pp. 60–84). Washington, DC: American Psychological Association.

Lachman, M. E., Röcke, C., Rosnick, C., & Ryff, C. D. (2008). Realism and illusion in Americans' temporal views of their life satisfaction: Age differences in reconstructing the past and anticipating the future. *Psychological Science, 19*(9), 889–897.

Lachman, M. E., Teshale, S., & Agrigoroaei, S. (2015). Midlife as a pivotal point in the life course: Balancing growth and decline at the crossroads of youth and old age. *International Journal of Behavioral Development, 39*(1), 20–31.

Lachman, M. E., Teshale, S., & Agrigoroaei, S. (2015). Midlife is a pivotal period in the life course: Balancing growth and decline at the crossroads of youth and old age. *International Journal of Behavioral Development, 39*(1), 20–31.

Lack, C.W., & Rousseau, J. (2016). *Critical Thinking, Science, and Pseudoscience: Why We Can't Trust Our Brains.* New York: Springer.

Laffont, C. M., Gomeni, R., Zheng, B., Heidbreder, C., Fudala, P. J., & Nasser, A. F. (2015). Population pharmacokinetic modeling and simulation to guide dose selection for RBP-7000, a new sustained-release formulation of risperidone. *Journal of Clinical Pharmacology, 55*(1), 93–103.

Lahti, A., White, D., Kraguljac, N., & Reid, M. (2017). Hippocampal glutamate and functional connectivity as biomarkers of treatment response to antipsychotic medication. *Schizophrenia Bulletin, 43*(suppl_1), S5–S5.

Laible, D. J., & Karahuta, E. (2014). Prosocial behaviors in early childhood: Helping others, responding to the distress of others, and working with others. In L. Padilla-Walker & G. Carlo (Eds.), *Prosocial behavior.* New York: Oxford University Press.

Laird, S. (July 21, 2016). Concussions ended his promising NFL career, so he became an Olympian instead. *Mashable.* http://mashable.com/2016/07/21/jahvid-best-nfl-olympics/#zBKcgSdyw5qx

Lam, R. (2012). *Depression* (2nd ed.). New York: Oxford University Press.

Lamb, M. E., Malloy, L. C., Hershkowitz, I., & La Rooy, D. (2015). Children and the law. In R. E. Lerner (Ed.), *Handbook of child psychology and developmental science* (7th ed., vol. 3). New York: Wiley.

Lambert, K., Hyer, M., Bardi, M., Rzucidlo, A., Scott, S., Terhune-Cotter, B., ... & Kinsley, C. (2016). Natural-enriched environments lead to enhanced environmental engagement and altered neurobiological resilience. *Neuroscience, 330,* 386–394.

Lambert, M. J. (2001). The effectiveness of psychotherapy: What has a century of research taught us about the effects of treatment. *Georgia Psychologist, 55*(2), 9–11.

Lambert, M. J. (2013). Outcome in psychotherapy: The past and important advances. *Psychotherapy, 50*(1), 42–51.

Laming, D. (2010). Serial position curves in free recall. *Psychological Review, 117*(1), 93–133.

Lamis, D. A., Ballard, E. D., & Patel, A. B. (2014). Loneliness and suicide ideation in drug-using college students. *Suicide and Life-Threatening Behavior, 44*(6), 629–640.

Lamkin, D. M., & others. (2012). Chronic stress enhances progression of acute lymphoblastic leukemia via ß-adrenergic signaling. *Brain, Behavior, and Immunity, 26*(4), 635–641.

Lampard, A. M., Byrne, S. M., McLean, N., & Fursland, A. (2012). The Eating Disorder Inventory-2 perfectionism scale: Factor structure and associations with dietary restraint and weight and shape concern in eating disorders. *Eating Behaviors, 13*(1), 49–53.

Lander, I. A. (2016). Exploring the place of forgiveness therapy in social work practice. *Journal of Social Work Practice, 30,* 69–80. doi:10.1080/02650533.2015.1081879

Landgren, S., & others. (2011). Reward-related gender and personality traits in alcohol-dependent individuals: A pilot case control study. *Neuropsychobiology, 64*(1), 38–46.

Landis, C., & Erlick, D. (1950). An analysis of the Porteus Maze Test as affected by psychosurgery. *American Journal of Psychology, 63*(4), 557–566.

Landler, M. (2012, January 30). From Biden, a vivid account of Bin Laden decision. The Caucus, *New York Times* blog. http://thecaucus.blogs.nytimes.com/2012/01/30/from-biden-a-vivid-account-of-bin-laden-decision/?_r=0 (accessed February 14, 2015)

Lane, A., Luminet, O., Nave, G., & Mikolajczak, M. (2016). Is there a publication bias in behavioural intranasal oxytocin research on humans? Opening the file drawer of one laboratory. *Journal of Neuroendocrinology, 28*(4).

Lane, A., Mikolajczak, M., Treinen, E., Samson, D., Corneille, O., de Timary, P., & Luminet, O. (2015). Failed replication of oxytocin effects on trust: The envelope task case. *Plos ONE, 10*(9),

Lane, S. M., & Schooler, J. W. (2004). Skimming the surface: Verbal overshadowing of analogical retrieval. *Psychological Science, 15*(11), 715–719.

Lange, C. G. (1922). *The emotions.* Baltimore, MD: Williams & Wilkins.

Lange, I., Goossens, L., Bakker, J., Michielse, S., van Amelsvoort, T., & Schruers, K. (2017). Fear extinction mechanisms and the link to exposure therapy outcome in specific phobia: A pilot study. *Biological Psychiatry, 81*(10), S186–S187.

Lange, I., Goossens, L., Michielse, S., Bakker, J., Lissek, S., Papalini, S., et al. (2017). Behavioral pattern separation and its link to the neural mechanisms of fear generalization. *Social Cognitive and Affective Neuroscience, 12*(11), 1720–1729.

Langer, E. J. (1997). *The power of mindful learning.* Reading, MA: Addison-Wesley.

Langer, E. J. (2000). Mindful learning. *Current Directions in Psychological Science, 9*(6), 220–223.

Langer, E. J. (2005). *On becoming an artist.* New York: Ballantine.

Langer, E., Blank, A., & Chanowitz, B. (1978). The mindlessness of ostensibly thoughtful action: The role of "placebic" information in interpersonal interaction. *Journal of Personality and Social Psychology, 36*(6), 635–642.

Langer, J. J. (1991). *Holocaust testimonies: The ruins of memory.* New Haven, CT: Yale University Press.

Langeslag, S. E., & Surti, K. (2017). The effect of arousal on regulation of negative emotions using cognitive reappraisal: An ERP study. *International Journal of Psychophysiology, 118,* 18–26. doi:10.1016/j.ijpsycho.2017.05.012

Langlois, J. H., Kalakanis, L., Rubenstein, A. J., Larson, A., Hallam, M., & Smoot, M. (2000). Maxims or myths of beauty? A meta-analytic and theoretical review. *Psychological Bulletin, 126*(3), 390–423.

Langlois, J. H., Roggman, L. A., & Musselman, L. (1994). What is average and what is not average about attractive faces? *Psychological Science, 5*(4), 214–220.

Langridge, M., & Betters, E. (August 3, 2017). What is Elon Musk's Hyperloop? The 700mph subsonic train explained. *Pocket-lint*. http://www.pocket-lint.com/news/132405-what-is-elon-musk-s-hyperloop-the-700mph-subsonic-train-explained

Langstrom, N., Rahman, Q., Carlstrom, E., & Lichtenstein, P. (2010). Genetic and environmental effects on same-sex sexual behaviour: A population study of twins in Sweden. *Archives of Sexual Behavior, 39*(1), 75–80.

Lapid, H., & others. (2011). Neural activity at the human olfactory epithelium reflects olfactory perception. *Nature Neuroscience, 14*(11), 1455–1461.

Laplana, M., Royo, J. L., García, L. F., Aluja, A., Gomez-Skarmeta, J. L., & Fibla, J. (2014). SIRPB1 copy-number polymorphism as candidate quantitative trait locus for impulsive-disinhibited personality. *Genes, Brain, and Behavior, 13*(7), 653–662.

Lashley, K. (1950). In search of the engram. In *Symposium of the Society for Experimental Biology* (vol. 4, pp. 454–482). New York: Cambridge University Press.

Latané, B. (1981). The psychology of social impact. *American Psychologist, 36*(4), 343–356.

Latchoumane, C. F. V., Ngo, H. V. V., Born, J., & Shin, H. S. (2017). Thalamic spindles promote memory formation during sleep through triple phase-locking of cortical, thalamic, and hippocampal rhythms. *Neuron, 95*(2), 424–435.

Lauer, J. E., Ilksoy, S. D., & Lourenco, S. F. (2018). Developmental stability in gender-typed preferences between infancy and preschool age. *Developmental Psychology.* in press.

Laurelut, M. H., Latif, S., Billington, T., Simon, G., Hassall, R., McCabe, B., et al. (2016). *Re-thinking autism: Diagnosis, identity and equality*. Philadelphia: Jessica Kingsley Publishers.

Laurent, H. K., Neiderhiser, J. M., Natsuaki, M. N., Shaw, D. S., Fisher, P. A., Reiss, D., & Leve, L. D. (2014). Stress system development from age 4.5 to 6: Family environment predictors and adjustment implications of HPA activity stability versus change. *Developmental Psychobiology, 56*, 340–354.

Lautenbacher, S., Peters, J. H., Heesen, M., Scheel, J., & Kunz, M. (2017). Age changes in pain perception: a systematic-review and meta-analysis of age effects on pain and tolerance thresholds. *Neuroscience & Biobehavioral Reviews.* in press.

Lavender, J. M., & others. (2014). Dimensions of emotion dysregulation in bulimia nervosa. *European Eating Disorders Review, 22*(3), 212–216.

Lavender, J. M., Goodman, E. L., Culbert, K. M., Wonderlich, S. A., Crosby, R. D., Engel, S. G., & et al. (2017). Facets of impulsivity and compulsivity in women with anorexia nervosa. *European Eating Disorders Review, 25*(4), 309–313. doi:10.1002/erv.2516

Law, J., Shaw, P., Earland, K., Sheldon, M., & Lee, M. (2014). A psychology based approach for longitudinal development in cognitive robotics. *Frontiers in Neurorobotics, 8*, 1.

Laws, H. B., Constantino, M. J., Sayer, A. G., Klein, D. N., Kocsis, J. H., Manber, R., et al. (2017). Convergence in patient–therapist therapeutic alliance ratings and its relation to outcome in chronic depression treatment. *Psychotherapy Research, 27*(4), 410–424.

Lazarus, R. S. (1991). On the primacy of cognition. *American Psychologist, 39*(2), 124–129.

Lazarus, R. S. (1993). Coping theory and research: Past, present, and future. *Psychosomatic Medicine, 55*(3), 234–247.

Lazarus, R. S. (2000). Toward better research on stress and coping. *American Psychologist, 55*(6), 665–673.

Lazarus, R. S. (2003). Does the positive psychology movement have legs? *Psychological Inquiry, 14*(2), 93–109.

Le, D., Holt, C. L., Hosack, D. P., Huang, J., & Clark, E. M. (2016). Religious participation is associated with increases in religious social support in a national longitudinal study of African Americans. *Journal of Religion and Health, 55*(4), 1449–1460. doi:10.1007/s10943-015-0143-1

Le Grange, D., Lock, J., Loeb, K., & Nicholls, D. (2010). Academy for Eating Disorders position paper: The role of the family in eating disorders. *International Journal of Eating Disorders, 43*(1), 1–5.

Le Texier, T. (2018). Histoire d'un mensonge. Enquête sur l'expérience de Stanford. Paris: Zones. (published in French).

Leahy, R. L., Holland, S. J. F., & McGinn, L. K. (2012). *Treatment plans and interventions for depression and anxiety disorders* (2nd ed.). New York: Guilford.

Leaper, C. (2015). Gender development from a social-cognitive perspective. In R. M. Lerner (Ed.), *Handbook of child psychology and developmental science* (7th ed., vol. 2). New York: Wiley.

Leary, M. R., & Guadagno, J. (2011). The sociometer, self-esteem, and the regulation of interpersonal behavior. In K. D. Vohs & R. F. Baumeister (Eds.), *Handbook of self-regulation: Research, theory, and applications* (2nd ed., pp. 339–354). New York: Guilford.

Leavy, P. (2017). *Research design: Quantitative, qualitative, mixed methods, arts-based, and community-based participatory research*. New York: Guilford.

LeBlanc, L. A., & Gillis, J. M. (2012). Behavioral interventions for children with autism spectrum disorders. *Pediatric Clinics of North America, 59*(1), 147–164.

LeBoeuf, R. A., & Shafir, E. (2012). Decision making. In K. J. Holyoak & R. G. Morrison (Eds.), *The Oxford handbook of thinking and reasoning*. New York: Oxford University Press.

Lecce, S., Caputi, M., Pagnin, A., & Banerjee, R. (2017). Theory of mind and school achievement: The mediating role of social competence. *Cognitive Development, 44*, 85–97.

LeDoux, J. E. (1996). *The emotional brain: The mysterious underpinnings of emotional life*. New York: Simon & Schuster.

LeDoux, J. E. (2001). Emotion, memory, and the brain. www.cns.nyu.edu/ledoux/overview.htm (accessed December 22, 2014)

LeDoux, J. E. (2002). *The synaptic self*. New York: Viking.

LeDoux, J. E. (2008). Amygdala. *Scholarpedia, 3*, 2698.

LeDoux, J. E. (2012). Evolution of human emotion: A view through fear. *Progress in Brain Research, 195*, 431–442.

LeDoux, J. E. (2013). The slippery slope of fear. *Trends in Cognitive Science, 17*(4), 155–156.

LeDoux, J. E. (2014). Coming to terms with fear. *Proceedings of the National Academy of Sciences USA, 111*(8), 2871–2878.

LeDoux, J. E., & Pine, D. S. (2016). Using neuroscience to help understand fear and anxiety: A two-system framework. *The American Journal of Psychiatry, 173*(11), 1083–1093. doi:10.1176/appi.ajp.2016.16030353

Lee, A. S., Azmitia, E. C., & Whitaker-Azmitia, P. M. (2017). Developmental microglial priming in postmortem autism spectrum disorder temporal cortex. *Brain, Behavior, and Immunity, 62*, 193–202

Lee, H. (2016). Which feedback is more effective for pursuing multiple goals of differing importance? The interaction effects of goal importance and performance feedback type on self-regulation and task achievement. *Educational Psychology, 36*(2), 297–322. doi:10.1080/01443410.2014.995596

Lee, I. S., Yoon, S. S., Lee, S. H., Lee, H., Park, H. J., Wallraven, C., & Chae, Y. (2013). An amplification of feedback from facial muscles strengthened sympathetic activations to emotional facial cues. *Autonomic Neuroscience, 179*(1–2), 37–42.

Lee, K., Quinn, P. C., Pascalis, O., & Slater, A. (2013). Development of face-processing ability in children. In P. D. Zelazo (Ed.), *The Oxford handbook of developmental psychology*. New York: Oxford University Press.

Lee, S. W., Kim, I., Yoo, J., Park, S., Jeong, B., & Cha, M. (2016). Insights from an expressive writing intervention on Facebook to help alleviate depressive symptoms. *Computers In Human Behavior, 62*, 613–619. doi:10.1016/j.chb.2016.04.034

Lee, W., & Reeve, J. (2017). Identifying the neural substrates of intrinsic motivation during task performance. *Cognitive, Affective & Behavioral Neuroscience, 17*(5), 939–953. doi:10.3758/s13415-017-0524-x

Lee-Bates, B., Billing, D. C., Caputi, P., Carstairs, G. L., Linnane, D., & Middleton, K. (2017). The application of subjective job task analysis techniques in physically demanding occupations: Evidence for the presence of self-serving bias. *Ergonomics, 60*(9), 1240–1249. doi:10.1080/00140139.2016.1262063

Leerkes, E. M., Su, J., Calkins, S. D., O'Brien, M., & Supple, A. J. (2017). Maternal physiological dysregulation while parenting poses risk for infant attachment disorganization and behavior problems. *Development and Psychopathology, 29*(1), 245–257.

Légal, J. B., Chekroun, P., Coiffard, V., & Gabarrot, F. (2017). Beware of the gorilla: Effect of goal priming on inattentional blindness. *Consciousness and Cognition, 55*, 165–171.

Legey, S., Aquino, F., Lamego, M. K., Paes, F., Nardi, A. E., Neto, G. M., et al. (2017). Relationship among physical activity level, mood and anxiety states and quality of life in physical education students. *Clinical Practice and Epidemiology in Mental Health, 13*, in press. doi:10.2174/1745017901713010082

Lehmkuhl Noer, C., Kjær Needham, E., Wiese, A., Johannes Skovbjerg Balsby, T., & Dabelsteen, T. (2016). Personality matters: Consistency of inter-individual variation in shyness-boldness across non-breeding and pre-breeding season despite a fall in general shyness levels in farmed American mink (Neovison vison). *Applied Animal Behaviour Science, 181*, 191–199. doi:10.1016/j.applanim.2016.05.003

Leibowitz, S., & de Vries, A. L. (2016). Gender dysphoria in adolescence. *International Review of Psychiatry, 28*(1), 21–35.

Leichsenring, F., & Leweke, F. (2017). Social Anxiety Disorder. *New England Journal of Medicine, 376*(23), 2255–2264.

Leiknes, K. A., Jarosh-von Schweder, L., & Høie, B. (2012). Contemporary use and practice of electroconvulsive therapy worldwide. *Brain and Behavior, 2*(3), 283–344.

Leippe, M. R., Bergold, A. N., & Eisenstadt, D. (2017). Prejudice and terror management at trial: Effects of defendant race/ethnicity and mortality salience on mock-jurors' verdict judgments. *The Journal of Social Psychology, 157*(3), 279–294.

Lemay, E. J., O'Brien, K. M., Kearney, M. S., Sauber, E. W., & Venaglia, R. B. (2017). Using conformity to enhance willingness to intervene in dating violence: A theory of planned behavior analysis. *Psychology of Violence,* doi:10.1037/vio0000114

Lenneberg, E. H., Rebelsky, F. G., & Nichols, I. A. (1965). The vocalization of infants born to deaf and hearing parents. *Human Development, 8*, 23–37.

Lepage, M., Sergerie, K., Benoit, A., Czechowska, Y., Dickie, E., & Armony, J. L. (2011). Emotional face processing and flat affect in schizophrenia: Functional and structural neural correlates. *Psychological Medicine, 41*(9), 1833–1844.

Leppma, M., Long, D., Smith, M., & Lassiter, C. (2017). Detecting Symptom Exaggeration in College Students Seeking ADHD Treatment: Performance Validity Assessment Using the NV-MSVT and IVA-Plus. *Applied Neuropsychology: Adult,* in press. https://doi.org/10.1080/23279095.2016.1277723

Lerner, B. H. (2005). Last-ditch medical therapy—Revisiting lobotomy. *New England Journal of Medicine, 353*(2), 119–121.

Lerner, I., & Shriki, O. (2014). Internally- and externally-driven network transitions as a basis for automatic and strategic processes in semantic priming: Theory and experimental validation. *Frontiers in Psychology, 5*, 314.

Lerner, J. E., & Hawkins, R. L. (2016). Welfare, liberty, and security for all? U.S. sex education policy and the 1996 Title V Section 510 of the Social Security Act. *Archives Of Sexual Behavior, 45*(5), 1027–1038. doi:10.1007/s10508-016-0731-5

Lerner, M. D., De Los Reyes, A., Drabick, D. A., Gerber, A. H., & Gadow, K. D. (2017). Informant discrepancy defines discrete, clinically useful autism spectrum disorder subgroups. *Journal of Child Psychology and Psychiatry*. in press.

LeRoy, A. S., Murdock, K. W., Jaremka, L. M., Loya, A., & Fagundes, C. P. (2017). Loneliness predicts self-reported cold symptoms after a viral challenge. *Health Psychology, 36*(5), 512–520. doi:10.1037/hea0000467

Leshinskaya, A., & Caramazza, A. (2016). For a cognitive neuroscience of concepts: Moving beyond the grounding issue. *Psychonomic Bulletin & Review, 23*, 991–1001. doi:10.3758/s13423-015-0870-z

Leung, A. K., Maddux, W. W., Galinsky, A. D., & Chiu, C. (2008). Multicultural experience enhances creativity: The when and how. *The American Psychologist, 63*(3), 169–181.

Leung, W. (2014). Infusions of allogeneic natural killer cells as cancer therapy. *Clinical Cancer Research, 20*(13), 3390–3400.

Lev-Ari, L., Baumgarten-Katz, I., & Zohar, A. H. (2014). Show me your friends, and I shall show you who you are: The way attachment and social comparisons influence body dissatisfaction. *European Eating Disorders Review, 22*(6), 463–469.

Lev-On, A., & Waismel-Manor, I. (2016). Looks that matter: The effect of physical attractiveness in low- and high-information elections. *American Behavioral Scientist, 60*(14), 1756–1771. doi:10.1177/0002764216676249

Leventhal, H., & Tomarken, A. J. (1986). Emotion: Today's problems. *Annual Review of Psychology* (vol. 37). Palo Alto, CA: Annual Reviews.

Levi, O., Shoval-Zuckerman, Y., Fruchter, E., Bibi, A., Bar-Haim, Y. and Wald, I. (2017), Benefits of a psychodynamic group therapy (PGT) model for treating veterans with PTSD. *Journal of Clinical Psychology, 73*, 1247–1258.

Levi-Belz, Y. (2016). To share or not to share? The contribution of self-disclosure to stress-related growth among suicide survivors. *Death Studies, 40*(7), 405–413. doi:10.1080/07481187.2016.1160164

Levine, B., Svoboda, E., Turner, G. R., Mandic, M., & Mackey, A. (2009). Behavioral and functional neuroanatomical correlates of anterograde autobiographical memory in isolated retrograde amnesic patient M.L. *Neuropsychologia, 47*(11), 2188–2196.

Levine, D. S., Taylor, R. J., Nguyen, A. W., Chatters, L. M., & Himle, J. A. (2015). Family and friendship informal support networks and social anxiety disorder among African Americans and Black Caribbeans. *Social Psychiatry and Psychiatric Epidemiology, 50*(7), 1121–1133.

Levine, M., Cassidy, C., & Jentzsch, I. (2010). The implicit identity effect: Identity primes, group size, and helping. *British Journal of Social Psychology, 49*(Pt 4), 785–802.

Levine, R. L. (2002). Endocrine aspects of eating disorders in adolescents. *Adolescent Medicine, 13*(1), 129–144.

Levis, D. L. (Ed.). (2017). *Foundations of behavioral therapy*. New York: Routledge. Originally published in 1970.

Levy, B. R., Slade, M. D., Kunkel, S. R., & Kasl, S. V. (2002). Longevity increased by positive self-perceptions of aging. *Journal of Personality and Social Psychology, 83*(2), 261–270.

Levy, H. C., Worden, B. L., Gilliam, C. M., D'Urso, C., Steketee, G., Frost, R. O., & Tolin, D. F. (2017). Changes in saving cognitions mediate hoarding symptom change in cognitive-behavioral therapy for hoarding disorder. *Journal of Obsessive-Compulsive and Related Disorders, 14*, 112–118.

Lewald, J., & Getzmann, S. (2011). When and where of auditory spatial processing in cortex: A novel approach using electromyography. *PLoS One, 6*(9), e25146.

Lewis, D. G., Al-Shawaf, L., Conroy-Beam, D., Asao, K., & Buss, D. M. (2017). Evolutionary psychology: A how-to guide. *American Psychologist, 72*(4), 353–373. doi:10.1037/a0040409

Lewkowicz, D. J. (2010). Infant perception of audiovisual speech synchrony. *Developmental Psychology, 46*(1), 66–77.

Lewkowicz, D. J., & Hansen-Tift, A. M. (2012). Infants deploy selective attention to the mouth of a talking face when learning speech. *Proceedings of the National Academy of Sciences USA, 109*(5), 1431–1436.

Li, A., MacNeill, B., Curiel, H., & Poling, A. (2017). Risperidone in combination with other drugs: Experimental research in individuals with autism spectrum disorder. *Experimental and Clinical Psychopharmacology, 25*(5), 434–439.

Li, G., Shao, C., Chen, Q., Wang, Q., & Yang, K. (2017). Accumulated GABA activates presynaptic GABAB receptors and inhibits both excitatory and inhibitory synaptic transmission in rat midbrain periaqueductal gray. *NeuroReport, 28*(6), 313–318.

Li, H., Huang, L., Zhang, Y., & Ni, S. (2016). Effects of intuition and deliberation on escape judgment and decision-making under different complexities of crisis situations. *Safety Science, 89*, 106–113. doi:10.1016/j.ssci.2016.06.006

Li, H., Ji, Y., & Chen, T. (2014). The roles of different sources of social support on emotional well-being among Chinese elderly. *PLoS One, 9*(3), e90051.

Li, S. H., & Graham, B. M. (2017). Why are women so vulnerable to anxiety, trauma-related and stress-related disorders? The potential role of sex hormones. *The Lancet Psychiatry, 4*(1), 73–82.

Li, S., Tian, J., Bauer, A., Huang, R., Wen, H., Li, M., ... & Jiang, G. (2016). Reduced integrity of right lateralized white matter in patients with primary Insomnia: a diffusion-tensor imaging study. *Radiology, 280*(2), 520–528.

Li, X., Chen, W., & Popiel, P. (2015). What happens on Facebook stays on Facebook? The implications of Facebook interaction for perceived, receiving, and giving social support. *Computers in Human Behavior, 51*, 106–113.

Li, Y., & Epley, N. (2009). When the best appears to be saved for last: Serial position effects on choice. *Journal of Behavioral Decision Making, 22*(4), 378–389.

Liang, B., Williams, L. M., & Siegel, J. A. (2006). Relational outcomes of childhood sexual trauma in female survivors: A longitudinal study. *Journal of Interpersonal Violence, 21*(1), 42–57.

Liang, P., Jia, X., Taaatgen, N. A., Zhong, N., & Li, K. (2014). Different strategies in solving series completion inductive reasoning problems: An fMRI and computational study. *International Journal of Psychophysiology, 93*(2), 253–260.

Liben, L. S., Bigler, R. S., & Hilliard, L. J. (2014). Gender development: From universality to individuality. In E. T. Gershoff, R. S. Mistry, & D. A. Crosby (Eds.), *Societal contexts of child development*. New York: Oxford University Press.

Light, S. N., Coan, J. A., Frye, C., Goldsmith, H. H., & Davidson, R. J. (2009). Dynamic variation in pleasure in children predicts nonlinear change in lateral frontal brain electrical activity. *Developmental Psychology, 45*(2), 525–533.

Light, S. N., Heller, A. S., Johnstone, T., Kolden, G. G., Peterson, M. J., Kalin, N. H., & Davidson, R. J. (2011). Reduced right ventrolateral prefrontal cortex activity while inhibiting positive affect is associated with improvement in hedonic capacity after 8 weeks of antidepressant treatment in major depressive disorder. *Biological Psychiatry, 70*(10), 962–968.

Lilienfeld, S. O., Wood, J. M., & Garb, H. N. (2000, November). The scientific status of projective techniques. *Psychological Science in the Public Interest, 1*(2), 27–66.

Lim, A., Nakamura, B. J., Higa-McMillan, C. K., Shimabukuro, S., & Slavin, L. (2012). Effects of workshop trainings on evidence-based practice knowledge and attitudes among youth community mental health providers. *Behavior Research and Therapy, 50*(6), 397–406.

Lin, J. Y., Arthurs, J., & Reilly, S. (2014). Conditioned taste aversion, drugs of abuse and palatability. *Neuroscience and Biobehavioral Reviews, 45*, 28–45.

Lin, P. (2016). Risky behaviors: Integrating adolescent egocentrism with the theory of planned behavior. *Review of General Psychology, 20*(4), 392–398. doi:10.1037/gpr0000086

Lin, Y., & others. (2014). Efficacy of REACH forgiveness across cultures. *Journal of Clinical Psychology, 70*(9), 781–793.

Lindberg, L.D., Santelli, J.S., & Desai, S. (2016). Understanding the decline in adolescent fertility in the United States, 2007–2012. *Journal of Adolescent Health, 59*, 577–583. doi: 10.1016/j.jadohealth. 2016.06.024

Lindeman, M. I., Zengel, B., & Skowronski, J. J. (2017). An exploration of the relationship among valence, fading affect, rehearsal frequency, and memory vividness for past personal events. *Memory, 25*(6), 724–735.

Lindholm, T., Sjöberg, R. L., & Memon, A. (2014). Misreporting signs of child abuse: The role of decision-making and outcome information. *Scandinavian Journal of Psychology, 55*(1), 1–9.

Lingjaerde, O., Føreland, A. R., & Engvik, H. (2001). Personality structure in patients with winter depression, assessed in a depression-free state according to the five-factor model of personality. *Journal of Affective Disorders, 62*(3), 165–174.

Linkovski, O., Katzin, N., & Salti, M. (2017). Mirror neurons and mirror-touch synesthesia. *The Neuroscientist, 23*(2), 103–108. doi:10.1177/ 1073858416652079

Lipnevich, A. A., Credè, M., Hahn, E., Spinath, F. M., Roberts, R. D., & Preckel, F. (2017). How distinctive are morningness and eveningness from the Big Five factors of personality? A meta-analytic investigation. *Journal of Personality and Social Psychology, 112*(3), 491–509. doi:10.1037/pspp0000099

Lippke, S., Schwarzer, R., Ziegelmann, J. P., Scholz, U., & Schüz, B. (2010). Testing stage-specific effects of a stage-matched intervention: A randomized controlled trial targeting physical exercise and its predictors. *Health Education & Behavior, 37*(4), 533–546. doi:10.1177/1090198109359386

Lippke, S., Ziegelmann, J. P., Schwarzer, R., & Velicer, W. F. (2009). Validity of stage assessment in the adoption and maintenance of physical activity and fruit and vegetable consumption. *Health Psychology, 28*(2), 183–193.

Lipsey, M. W., & Wilson, D. B. (1993). The efficacy of psychological, educational, and behavioral treatment: Confirmation from meta-analysis. *American Psychologist, 48*(12), 1181–1209.

Lissek, S., Bradford, D. E., Alvarez, R. P., Burton, P., Espensen-Sturges, T., Reynolds, R. C., & Grillon, C. (2014). Neural substrates of classically conditioned fear-generalization in humans: A parametric fMRI study. *Social Cognitive and Affective Neuroscience, 9*(8), 1134–1142.

Lissek, S., Rabin, S., Heller, R. E., Lukenbaugh, D., Geraci, M., Pine, D. S., & Grillon, C. (2010). Overgeneralization of conditioned fear as a pathogenic marker of panic disorder. *American Journal of Psychiatry, 167*(1), 47–55.

Liszkowski, U., Schaffer, M., Carpenter, M., & Tomasello, M. (2009). Prelinguistic infants, but not chimpanzees, communicate about absent entities. *Psychological Science, 20*(5), 654–660.

Litim, N., Morissette, M., & Di Paolo, T. (2017). Metabotropic glutamate receptors as therapeutic targets in Parkinson's disease: An update from the last 5 years of research. *Neuropharmacology, 115*, 166–179.

Littlefield, A. K., & Sher, K. J. (2010). Alcohol use disorders in young adulthood. In J. E. Grant (Ed.), *Young adult mental health* (pp. 292–310). New York: Oxford University Press.

Littleton, H. (2014). Interpersonal violence on college campuses: Understanding risk factors and working to find solutions. *Trauma Violence Abuse, 15*(4), 297–303.

Littrell, J. H., & Girvin, H. (2002). Stages of change: A critique. *Behavior Modification, 26*(2), 223–273.

Liu, C. Y., Huang, W. L., Kao, W. C., & Gau, S. S. F. (2017). Influence of disruptive behavior disorders on academic performance and school functions of youths with attention-deficit/hyperactivity disorder. *Child Psychiatry & Human Development, 48*, 870–880.

Liu, C.-M., & others. (2012). SOAP3: Ultra-fast GPU-based parallel alignment tool for short reads. *Bioinformatics, 28*(6), 878–879.

Liu, J. D., & Chung, P. (2016). Students' perceived autonomy support and psychological needs satisfaction in physical education and exercise intrinsic motivation. *Journal of Sport Behavior, 39*(4), 409–425.

Liu, J., Gong, P., Gao, X., & Zhou, X. (2017). The association between well-being and the COMT gene: Dispositional gratitude and forgiveness as mediators. *Journal of Affective Disorders, 214*, 115–121. doi:10.1016/j.jad.2017.03.005

Liu, S., & Spelke, E. S. (2017). Six-month-old infants expect agents to minimize the cost of their actions. *Cognition, 160*, 35–42.

Liu, S., Ullman, T. D., Tenenbaum, J. B., & Spelke, E. S. (2017). Ten-month-old infants infer the value of goals from the costs of actions. *Science, 358*(6366), 1038–1041.

Liu, W., Liu, J., Xia, J., Xue, X., Wang, H., Qi, Z., & Ji, L. (2017). Leptin receptor knockout-induced depression-like behaviors and attenuated antidepressant effects of exercise are associated with STAT3/ SOCS3 signaling. *Brain, Behavior, and Immunity, 61*, 297–305. doi:10.1016/j.bbi.2017.01.001

Livengood, J., Sytsma, J., & Rose, D. (2017). Following the FAD: Folk attributions and theories of actual causation. *Review of Philosophy and Psychology, 8*(2), 273–294. doi:10.1007/s13164-016-0316-1

Lo Sauro, C., Ravaldi, C., Cabras, P. L., Faravelli, C., & Ricca, V. (2008). Stress, hypothalamic-pituitary-adrenal axis, and eating disorders. *Neuropsychobiology, 57*(3), 95–115.

Loaiza, V. M., Duperreault, K. A., Rhodes, M. G., & McCabe, D. P. (2014). Long-term semantic representations moderate the effect of attentional refreshing on episodic memory. *Psychonomic Bulletin and Review.* doi:10.3758/s13423-014-0673-7

Loftus, E. F. (1975). Leading questions and the eye-witness report. *Cognitive Psychology, 7*(4), 560–572.

Loftus, E. F. (1993). Psychologists in the eyewitness world. *American Psychologist, 48*(5), 550–552.

Logan, A. M., Mammel, A. E., Robinson, D. C., Chin, A. L., Condon, A. F., & Robinson, F. L. (2017). Schwann cell-specific deletion of the endosomal PI 3-kinase Vps34 leads to delayed radial sorting of axons, arrested myelination, and abnormal ErbB2-ErbB3 tyrosine kinase signaling. *Glia, in press.* doi: 10.1002/glia.23173

Lombardi, D. R., Button, M. L., & Westra, H. A. (2014). Measuring motivation: Change talk and counter-change talk in cognitive behavioral therapy for generalized anxiety. *Cognitive Behavior Therapy, 43*(1), 12–21.

Lönnqvist, J., & Itkonen, J. A. (2014). It's all about Extraversion: Why Facebook friend count doesn't count towards well-being. *Journal of Research in Personality, 53*, 64–67. doi:10.1016/j.jrp.2014.08.009

Lonsdorf, E. V. (2017). Sex differences in nonhuman primate behavioral development. *Journal of Neuroscience Research, 95*(1–2), 213–221.

Lopez, J., Coll, J., Haimel, M., Kandasamy, S., Tarraga, J., Furio-Tari, P., et al. (2017). HGVA: the Human Genome Variation Archive. *Nucleic Acids Research.* in press.

Lopez-Rolon, A., Vogler, J., Howell, K., Shock, J., Czermak, S., Heck, S., ... & Bender, A. (2017). Severe disorders of consciousness after acquired brain injury: a single-centre long-term follow-up study. *NeuroRehabilitation, 40*(4), 509–517.

Lorant, V., Croux, C., Weich, S., Deliège, D., Mackenbach, J., & Ansseau, M. (2007). Depression and socio-economic risk factors: 7-year longitudinal population study. *British Journal of Psychiatry, 190*, 293–298.

Lorenzo-Blanco, E. I., Schwartz, S. J., Unger, J. B., Zamboanga, B. L., Des Rosiers, S. E., Baezconde-Garbanati, L., et al. (2016). Alcohol use among recent immigrant Latino/a youth: Acculturation, gender, and the Theory of Reasoned Action. *Ethnicity & Health, 21*(6), 609–627. doi:10.1080/13557858.2016.1179723

LoSavio, S. T., Cohen, L. H., Laurenceau, J.-P., Dasch, K. B., Parrish, B. P., & Park, C. L. (2011). Reports of stress-related growth from daily negative events. *Journal of Social and Clinical Psychology, 30*(7), 760–785.

Loveday, P. M., Lovell, G. P., & Jones, C. M. (2017). The best possible selves intervention: A review of the literature to evaluate efficacy and guide future research. *Journal of Happiness Studies,* in press. doi:10.1007/s10902-016-9824-z

Lovick, T. A. (2014). Sex determinants of experimental panic attacks. *Neuroscience and Biobehavioral Reviews, 46*(Pt. 3), 465–471.

Lovik, A., Nassiri, V., Verbeke, G., Molenberghs, G., & Sodermans, A. K. (2017). Psychometric properties and comparison of different techniques for factor analysis on the Big Five Inventory from a Flemish sample. *Personality And Individual Differences, 117*, 122–129. doi:10.1016/j.paid.2017.05.048

Lu, J., Sherman, D., Devor, M., & Saper, C. B. (2006). A putative flip-flop switch for control of REM sleep. *Nature, 441*, 589–594.

Lu, Y., Pouget, J. G., Andreassen, O. A., Djurovic, S., Esko, T., Hultman, C. M., et al. (2017). Genetic risk scores and family history as predictors of schizophrenia in Nordic registers. *Psychological Medicine.* in press.

Lubinski, D., Benbow, C. P., Webb, R. M., & Bleske-Rechek, A. (2006). Tracking exceptional human capital over two decades. *Psychological Science, 17*(3), 194–199.

Lubinski, D., Webb, R. M., Morelock, M. J., & Benbow, C. P. (2001). Top 1 in 10,000: A 10-year follow-up of the profoundly gifted. *Journal of Applied Psychology, 86*(4), 718–729.

Luborsky, L., & others. (2002). The dodo bird verdict is alive and well—mostly. *Clinical Psychology: Science and Practice, 9*(1), 2–12.

Lucas, R. E., & Baird, B. M. (2004). Extraversion and emotional reactivity. *Journal of Personality and Social Psychology, 86*(3), 473–485.

Lucas, T., Pierce, J., Lumley, M. A., Granger, D. A., Lin, J., & Epel, E. S. (2017). Telomere length and procedural justice predict stress reactivity responses to unfair outcomes in African Americans. *Psychoneuroendocrinology, 86*, 104–109.

Lucas, T., Wegner, R., Pierce, J., Lumley, M. A., Laurent, H. K., & Granger, D. A. (2017). Perceived discrimination, racial identity, and multisystem stress response to social evaluative threat among African American men and women. *Psychosomatic Medicine, 79*(3), 293–305. doi:10.1097/PSY.0000000000000406

Luciano, M. T., & McDevitt-Murphy, M. E. (2017). Posttraumatic stress and physical health functioning: Moderating effects of deployment and postdeployment

social support in OEF/OIF/OND veterans. *Journal Of Nervous And Mental Disease, 205*(2), 93–98.

Luh, D. L., & others. (2014, February 8). Stages of change, determinants, and mortality for smoking cessation in adult Taiwanese screenees. *Prevention Science.* doi: 10.1007/s11121-014-0471-5

Lui, J. H., Marcus, D. K., & Barry, C. T. (2017). Evidence-based apps? A review of mental health mobile applications in a psychotherapy context. *Professional Psychology: Research and Practice, 48*(3), 199–210.

Luijten, M., Schellekens, A. F., Kühn, S., Machielse, M. W., & Sescousse, G. (2017). Disruption of reward processing in addiction: an image-based meta-analysis of functional magnetic resonance imaging studies. *JAMA Psychiatry, 74*(4), 387–398.

Lumb, A. B., Beaudry, M., & Blanchard, C. (2017). Posttraumatic growth and bereavement: The contribution of self-determination theory. *Omega: Journal Of Death And Dying, 75*(4), 311–336. doi:10.1177/0030222816652971

Luminet, O., & Curci, A. (Eds.) (2018). *Flashbulb memories: New challenges and future perspectives. 2nd ed.* New York: Routledge.

Lund, H. G., Reider, B. D., Whiting, A. B., & Prichard, J. R. (2010). Sleep patterns and predictors of disturbed sleep in a large population of college students. *Journal of Adolescent Health, 46*(2), 124–132.

Lunde, B., Perry, R., Sridhar, A., & Chen, K. T. (2017). An evaluation of contraception education and health promotion applications for patients. *Women's Health Issues, 27*(1), 29–35. doi:10.1016/j.whi.2016.09.012

Lungu, A., & Linehan, M. M. (2017). Dialectical behavior therapy: Overview, Characteristics, and future directions. In S.G. Hofman & G.J.G. Asmundsen (Eds.), *The science of cognitive behavioral therapy* (pp. 429–459). San Diego: Academic press.

Luo, Y., Cao, Z., Wang, D., Wu, L., Li, Y., Sun, W., & Zhu, Y. (2014). Dynamic study of the hippocampal volume by structural MRI in a rat model of depression. *Neurological Sciences, 35*(11), 1777–1783.

Luo, Y., Hawkley, L. C., Waite, L. J., & Cacioppo, J. T. (2012). Loneliness, health, and mortality in old age: A national longitudinal study. *Social Science and Medicine, 74*(6), 907–914.

Luong, G., Wrzus, C., Wagner, G. G., & Riediger, M. (2016). When bad moods may not be so bad: Valuing negative affect is associated with weakened affect–health links. *Emotion, 16*(3), 387–401. doi:10.1037/emo0000132

Luppi, P. H., Peyron, C., & Fort, P. (2017). Not a single but multiple populations of GABAergic neurons control sleep. *Sleep medicine reviews, 32*, 85–94.

Luria, A. R. (1973). *The working brain.* New York: Penguin.

Lushington, K., Pamula, Y., Martin, J., & Kennedy, J. D. (2014). Developmental changes in sleep: Infancy and preschool years. In A. R. Wolfson & E. Montgomery-Downs (Eds.), *Oxford handbook of infant, child, and adolescent sleep and behavior.* New York: Oxford University Press.

Luttrell, A., Petty, R. E., Briñol, P., & Wagner, B. C. (2016). Making it moral: Merely labeling an attitude as moral increases its strength. *Journal of Experimental Social Psychology, 65*, 82–93. doi:10.1016/j.jesp.2016.04.003

Lydon, C. A., Rohmeier, K. D., Yi, S. C., Mattaini, M. A., & Williams, W. L. (2011). How far do you have to go to get a cheeseburger around here? The realities of an environmental design approach to curbing the consumption of fast-food. *Behavior and Social Issues, 20*, 6–23.

Lykken, D. (1999). *Happiness: What studies on twins show us about nature, nurture, and the happiness set-point.* New York: Golden Books.

Lykken, D. T. (1987). The probity of the polygraph. In S. M. Kassin & L. S. Wrightsman (Eds.), *The psychology of evidence and trial procedures.* Newbury Park, CA: Sage.

Lykken, D. T. (1998). *A tremor in the blood: Uses and abuses of the lie detector.* New York: Plenum.

Lykken, D. T. (2001). Lie detection. In W. E. Craighead & C. B. Nemeroff (Eds.), *The Corsini encyclopedia of psychology and behavioral science* (3rd ed.). New York: Wiley.

Lynam, D. R., Caspi, A., Moffitt, T. E., Loeber, R., & Stouthamer-Loeber, M. (2007). Longitudinal evidence that psychopathy scores in early adolescence predict adult psychopathy. *Journal of Abnormal Psychology, 116*(1), 155–165.

Lynch, A., Elmore, B., & Kotecki, J. (2015). *Choosing health* (2nd ed.). Upper Saddle River, NJ: Pearson.

Lyngs, U., Cohen, E., Hattori, W. T., Newson, M., & Levin, D. T. (2016). Hearing in color: How expectations distort perception of skin tone. *Journal of Experimental Psychology: Human Perception And Performance, 42*(12), 2068–2076. doi:10.1037/xhp0000235

Lynn, S. J., & Green, J. P. (2011). The sociocognitive and dissociation theories of hypnosis: Toward a rapprochement. *International Journal of Clinical and Experimental Hypnosis, 59*(3), 277–293.

Lynn, S. J., Maxwell, R., & Green, J. P. (2017). The hypnotic induction in the broad scheme of hypnosis: A sociocognitive perspective. *American Journal of Clinical Hypnosis, 59*(4), 363–384. doi:10.10 80/00029157.2016.1233093

Lynott, D., Corker, K. S., Connell, L., & O'Brien, K. S. (2017). The effect of haptic and ambient temperature experience on prosocial behavior. *Archives of Scientific Psychology, 5*(1), 10–18. doi:10.1037/arc0000031

Lyubomirsky, S. (2008). *The how of happiness: A scientific approach to getting the life you want.* New York: Penguin.

Lyubomirsky, S. (2011). *The way to happiness: Action plan for a happy life.* Yehuda, Israel: Kinneret.

Lyubomirsky, S. (2013). *The myth of happiness.* New York: Penguin.

Lyubomirsky, S., Boehm, J. K., Kasri, F., & Zehm, K. (2011a). The cognitive and hedonic costs of dwelling on achievement-related negative experiences: Implications for enduring happiness and unhappiness. *Emotion, 11*(5), 1152–1167.

Lyubomirsky, S., Dickerhoof, R., Boehm, J. K., & Sheldon, K. M. (2011b). Becoming happier takes both a will and a proper way: An experimental longitudinal intervention to boost well-being. *Emotion, 11*(2), 391–402.

M

Maccallum, F., Malgaroli, M., & Bonanno, G. A. (2017). Networks of loss: Relationships among symptoms of prolonged grief following spousal and parental loss. *Journal of Abnormal Psychology, 126*(5), 652–662.

Maccoby, E. E. (2002). Gender and group processes: A developmental perspective. *Current Directions in Psychological Science, 11*(2), 54–58.

Macdonald, J. S. P., & Lavie, N. (2008). Load induced blindness. *Journal of Experimental Psychology: Human Perception and Performance, 34*(5), 1078–1091.

Macfarlan, S. J., Walker, R. S., Flinn, M. V., & Chagnon, N. A. (2014). Lethal coalitionary aggression and long-term alliance formation among Yanomamö men. *Proceedings of the National Academy of Sciences USA, 111*(47), 16662–16669.

Mackenbach, J. D., Lakerveld, J., Van Lenthe, F. J., Teixeira, P. J., Compernolle, S., De Bourdeaudhuij, I., et al. (2016) Interactions of individual perceived barriers and neighbourhood destinations with obesity-related behaviours in Europe. *Obesity Reviews, 17,* 68–80. doi: 10.1111/obr.12374.

Maddi, S. (1998). Hardiness. In H. S. Friedman (Ed.), *Encyclopedia of mental health* (vol. 3). San Diego, CA: Academic.

Maddi, S. R., Matthews, M. D., Kelly, D. R., Villarreal, B. J., Gundersen, K. K., & Savino, S. C. (2017). The continuing role of hardiness and grit on performance and retention in West Point cadets. *Military Psychology, 29*(5), 355–358. doi:10.1037/mil0000145

Maddux, W. W., & Galinsky, A. D. (2007, September). *Cultural borders and mental barriers: Living in and adapting to foreign countries facilitates creativity.* Working Paper No. 2007/51/B. Fountainbleau, France: INSEAD.

Madhyastha, T. M., Hamaker, E. L., & Gottman, J. M. (2011). Investigating spousal influence using moment-to-moment affect data from marital conflict. *Journal of Family Psychology, 25*(2), 292–300.

Madras, B. K. (2013). History of the discovery of the antipsychotic dopamine D2 receptor: A basis for the dopamine hypothesis of schizophrenia. *Journal of the History of the Neurosciences, 22*(1), 62–78.

Madrid, H. P., & Patterson, M. G. (2016). Creativity at work as a joint function between openness to experience, need for cognition and organizational fairness. *Learning and Individual Differences, 51,* 409–416. doi:10.1016/j. lindif.2015.07.010

Maeda, U., Shen, B. J., Schwarz, E. R., Farrell, K. A., & Mallon, S. (2012). Self-efficacy mediates the association of social support and depression with treatment adherence in heart failure patients. *International Journal of Behavioral Medicine, 20*(1), 88–96.

Maes, H. H., Neal, M. C., & Eaves, L. J. (1997). Genetic and environmental factors in relative body weight and human adiposity. *Behavior Genetics, 27*(4), 325–351.

Maguire, E. A., Gadian, G. D., Johnsrude, I. S., Good, C. D., Ashburner, J., Frackowiak, R. S. J., & Frith, C. D. (2000). Navigation-related structural change in the hippocampi of taxi drivers. *Proceedings of the National Academy of Sciences USA, 97*(9), 4398–4403.

Mahmoud, F. A., Aktas, A., Walsh, D., & Hullihen, B. (2011). A pilot study of taste changes among hospice inpatients with advanced cancer. *American Journal of Hospice and Palliative Care, 28*(7), 487–492.

Mahmuda, F., Akhter, M., & Nath, R. K. (2017). Obesity in the pathogenesis of type 2 diabetes. *KYAMC Journal, 4*(1), 357–361.

Maholmes, V. (2014). *Fostering resilience and well-being in children and families in poverty: Why hope still matters.* New York: Oxford University Press.

Maier, N. R. F. (1931). Reasoning in humans. II. The solution of a problem and its appearance in consciousness. *Journal of Comparative Psychology, 12*(2), 181–194.

Mailey, E. L., & McAuley, E. (2014). Physical activity intervention effects on perceived stress in working mothers: The role of self-efficacy. *Women's Health, 54*(6), 552–568.

Mairs, H. J., & Bradshaw, T. (2013). Promoting mental and physical health in adults with psychosis. *Nursing Standard, 27*(47), 50–56.

Maitre, N. L., Key, A. P., Chorna, O. D., Slaughter, J. C., Matusz, P. J., Wallace, M. T., & Murray, M. M. (2017). The dual nature of early-life experience on somatosensory processing in the human infant brain. *Current Biology, 27*(7), 1048–1054.

Major, B., & Townsend, S. M. (2012). Meaning making in response to unfairness. *Psychological Inquiry, 23*(4), 361–366. doi:10.1080/1047840X.2012.722785

Major, B., Kunstman, J. W., Malta, B. D., Sawyer, P. J., Townsend, S. S., & Mendes, W. B. (2016). Suspicion of motives predicts minorities' responses to positive feedback in interracial interactions. *Journal of Experimental Social Psychology, 62,* 75–88. doi:10.1016/j.jesp.2015.10.007

Mak, C., Whittingham, K., Cunnington, R., & Boyd, R. N. (2017). Efficacy of mindfulness-based interventions for attention and executive function in children and adolescents—a systematic review. *Mindfulness.* in press.

Makovac, E., Watson, D. R., Meeten, F., Garfinkel, S. N., Cercignani, M., Critchley, H. D., & Ottaviani, C. (2016). Amygdala functional connectivity as a longitudinal biomarker of symptom changes in generalized anxiety. *Social Cognitive and Affective Neuroscience, 11*(11), 1719–1728.

Malaia, E., Tommerdahl, J., & McKee, F. (2014). Deductive versus probabilistic reasoning in healthy adults: An EEG analysis of neural differences. *Journal of Psycholinguistic Research.* PMID: 24866361

Malakh-Pines, A., & Maslach, C. (2002). *Experiencing social psychology* (4th ed.). New York: McGraw-Hill.

Malcolm-Smith, S., Solms, M., Turnbull, O., & Tredoux, C. (2008). Threat in dreams: An adaptation? *Consciousness and Cognition, 17*(4), 1281–1291.

Malhotra, R. K. (2017). Sleep, recovery, and performance in sports. *Neurologic Clinics, 35*(3), 547–557.

Malhotra, R. K., & Desai, A. K. (2010). Healthy brain aging: What has sleep got to do with it? *Clinics in Geriatric Medicine, 26*(1), 46–56.

Malin, D. H., Anderson, A. N., & Goyarzu, P. (2017). Transmitters and receptors in nicotine withdrawal syndrome. In F. S. Hall, J. W. Young, & A. Der-Avakian (Eds.), *Negative affective states and cognitive impairments in nicotine dependence* (pp. 133–151). San Diego, CA: Elsevier Academic Press. doi:10.1016/B978-0-12-802574-1.00008-9

Mamarde, A., Navkhare, P., Singam, A., & Kanoje, A. (2013). Recurrent dissociative fugue. *Indian Journal of Psychological Medicine, 35*(4), 400–401.

Mancini, M., Wade, A. G., Perugi, G., Lenox-Smith, A., & Schacht, A. (2014). Impact of patient selection and study characteristics on signal detection in placebo-controlled trials with antidepressants. *Journal of Psychiatric Research, 51,* 21–29.

Mandler, G. (1980). Recognizing: The judgment of previous occurrence. *Psychological Review, 87*(3), 252–271.

Mandler, G. (2007). *A history of modern experimental psychology: From James and Wundt to cognitive science.* Cambridge: MIT Press.

Mandy, W., & Lai, M. (2016). Annual research review: The role of the environment in the developmental psychopathology of autism spectrum condition. *Journal of Child Psychology and Psychiatry, 57*(3), 271–292. doi:10.1111/jcpp.12501

Mangino, M., Roederer, M., Beddall, M. H., Nestle, F. O., & Spector, T. D. (2017). Innate and adaptive immune traits are differentially affected by genetic and environmental factors. *Nature communications, 8.* in press.

Maniadakis, M., & Trahanias, P. (2014). Time models and cognitive processes: A review. *Frontiers in Neurobotics, 8,* 7.

Manning, R., Levine, M., & Collins, A. (2007). The Kitty Genovese murder and the social psychology of helping: The parable of the 38 witnesses. *American Psychologist, 62*(6), 555–562.

Mansfield, K. E., Sim, J., Jordan, J. L., & Jordan, K. P. (2016). A systematic review and meta-analysis of the prevalence of chronic widespread pain in the general population. *Pain, 157*(1), 55–64.

Mantonakis, A., Rodero, P., Lesschaeve, I., & Hastie, R. (2009). Order in choice: Effects of serial position on preferences. *Psychological Science, 20*(11), 1309–1312.

Mantovani, A., Simpson, H. B., D'Urso, G., Santarnecchi, E., Rossi, S., & Lisanby, S. H. (2017). Low-frequency repetitive transcranial magnetic stimulation for obsessive-compulsive disorder. *Brain Stimulation: Basic, Translational, and Clinical Research in Neuromodulation, 10*(2), 518.

Marcia, J. E. (1980). Ego identity development. In J. Adelson (Ed.), *Handbook of adolescent psychology.* New York: Wiley.

Marcia, J. E. (2002). Identity and psychosocial development in adulthood. *Identity: An International Journal of Theory and Research, 2*(1), 7–28.

Marcus, G. F. (2001). *The algebraic mind.* Cambridge, MA: MIT Press.

Mares, D. (2013). Climate change and levels of violence in socially disadvantaged neighborhoods. *Journal of Urban Health, 90*(4), 768-783.

Marin, M. F., Zsido, R. G., Song, H., Lasko, N. B., Killgore, W. D., Rauch, S. L., et al. (2017). Skin conductance responses and neural activations during fear conditioning and extinction recall across anxiety disorders. *JAMA Psychiatry, 74*, 622-631. doi:10.1001/jamapsychiatry.2017.0329

Marinkovic, K., & others. (2011). Right hemisphere has the last laugh: Neural dynamics of joke appreciation. *Cognitive and Affective Behavioral Neuroscience, 11*(1), 113-130.

Markovits, H., Brisson, J., & de Chantal, P. (2017). Logical reasoning versus information processing in the dual-strategy model of reasoning. *Journal Of Experimental Psychology: Learning, Memory, And Cognition, 43*(1), 72-80. doi:10.1037/xlm0000291

Marks, A. K., Ejesi, K., McCullough, M. B., & Garcia Coll, C. (2015). The implications of discrimination for child and adolescent development. In R. M. Lerner & M. E. Lamb (Eds.), *Handbook of child psychology and developmental science* (7th ed., vol. 3). New York Wiley.

Marsac, M. L. Kassam-Adams, N., Delahanty, D. L., Ciesla, J., Weiss, D., Widaman, K. F., & Barakat, L. P. (2017). An initial application of a biopsychosocial framework to predict posttraumatic stress following pediatric injury. *Health Psychology, 36*, 787-796. http://dx.doi.org/10.1037/hea0000508

Marsh, E. J., & Roediger, H. L. (2013). Episodic and autobiographical memory. In A. F. Healy, R. W. Proctor, & I. B. Weiner (Eds.), *Handbook of psychology* (2nd ed., vol. 4, pp. 472-494). Hoboken, NJ: Wiley.

Marshall, C. R., Howrigan, D. P., Merico, D., Thiruvahindrapuram, B., Wu, W., Greer, D. S., et al. (2018). Contribution of copy number variants to schizophrenia from a genome-wide study of 41,321 subjects. *Nature Genetics*. in press.

Marshall, D. S. (1971). Sexual behavior in Mangaia. In D. S. Marshall & R. C. Suggs (Eds.), *Human sexual behavior: Variations in the ethnographic spectrum* (pp. 103-162). New York: Basic.

Marshall, P. J., & Meltzoff, A. N. (2014). Neural mirroring mechanisms and imitation in human infants. *Philosophical Transactions of the Royal Society of London. Series B, Biological Sciences, 369*(1644), 20130620.

Marteau, T. (2015). Downsizing: policy options to reduce portion sizes to help tackle obesity. *British Medical Journal, 351*, h5863

Martin Ginis, K. A., Strong, H. A., Arent, S. M., Bray, S. R., & Bassett-Gunter, R. L. (2014). The effects of aerobic- versus strength-training on body image among young women with pre-existing body image concerns. *Body Image, 11*(3), 219-227.

Martin, A. J., & Elliot, A. J. (2016). The role of personal best (PB) goal setting in students' academic achievement gains. *Learning and Individual Differences, 45*, 222-227.

Martin, D., Cleghorn, E., & Ward, J. (2017). The lived experience of mirror-touch synaesthesia: A qualitative investigation of empathy and social life. *Journal of Consciousness Studies, 24*(1-2), 214-227.

Martin, G. L., & Pear, J. (2014). *Behavior modification* (10th ed.). Upper Saddle River, NJ: Pearson.

Martinelli, M. K., Mostofsky, S. H., & Rosch, K. S. (2017). Investigating the impact of cognitive load and motivation on response control in relation to delay discounting in children with ADHD. *Journal of Abnormal Child Psychology, 45*(7), 1339-1353.

Martinez, L., Falvello, V. B., Aviezer, H., & Todorov, A. (2016). Contributions of facial expressions and body language to the rapid perception of dynamic emotions. *Cognition and Emotion, 30*(5), 939-952. doi:10.1080/02699931.2015.1035229

Maruyama, Y., Pereira, M., Margolskee, R. F., Chaudhari, N., & Roper, S. D. (2006). Umami responses in mouse taste cells indicate more than one receptor. *Journal of Neuroscience, 26*(8), 2227-2234.

Marx, R. F., & Didziulis, V. (2009, February 27). A life, interrupted. *New York Times*. www.nytimes.com/2009/03/01/nyregion/thecity/01miss.html?pagewanted=all (accessed January 5, 2015)

Marzillier, J. (2014). *The trauma therapies*. New York: Oxford University Press.

Masdrakis, V. G., Papageorgiou, C., & Markianos, M. (2017). Associations of plasma leptin to clinical manifestations in reproductive aged female patients with panic disorder. *Psychiatry Research, 255*, 161-166.

Mashour, G. A., & Hudetz, A. G. (2017). Bottom-up and top-down mechanisms of general anesthetics modulate different dimensions of consciousness. *Frontiers in Neural Circuits, 11*. doi:10.3389/fncir.2017.0004444.

Maslow, A. H. (1954). *Motivation and personality*. New York: Harper & Row.

Maslow, A. H. (1971). *The farther reaches of human nature*. New York: Viking.

Massa, L. J., & Mayer, R. E. (2006). Testing the ATI hypothesis: Should multimedia instruction accommodate verbalizer-visualizer cognitive style? *Learning and Individual Differences, 16*(4), 321-336.

Masten, A. S. (2014). *Ordinary magic*. New York: Guilford.

Masters, N. T., Casey, E., Wells, E. A., & Morrison, D. M. (2013). Sexual scripts among young heterosexually active men and women: Continuity and change. *Journal of Sex Research, 50*(5), 409-420. doi:10.1080/00224499.2012.661102

Masters, W. H., & Johnson, V. E. (1966). *Human sexual response*. Boston: Little, Brown.

Masuda, T., & Nisbett, R. E. (2001). Attending holistically vs. analytically: Comparing the context sensitivity of Japanese and Americans. *Journal of Personality and Social Psychology, 81*(5), 922-934.

Masuda, T., & Nisbett, R. E. (2006). Culture and change blindness. *Trends in Cognitive Science, 30*(2), 381-399.

Mate, I., Madrid, J. A., & De la Fuente, M. D. (2014). Chronobiology of the neuroimmunoendocrine system and aging. *Current Pharmaceutical Design, 20*(29), 4642-4655.

Matheny, M., Strehler, K. Y., King, M., Tümer, N., & Scarpace, P. J. (2014). Targeted leptin receptor blockade: Role of ventral tegmental area and nucleus of the solitary tract leptin receptors in body weight homeostasis. *Journal of Endocrinology, 222*(1), 27-41.

Mathieson, L. C., Klimes-Dougan, B., & Crick, N. R. (2014). Dwelling on it may make it worse: The links between relational victimization, relational aggression, rumination, and depressive symptoms in adolescents. *Development and Psychopathology, 26*(3), 735-747.

Matkarimov, B. T., & Saparbaev, M. K. (2017). Aberrant DNA glycosylase-initiated repair pathway of free radicals induced DNA damage: implications for age-related diseases and natural aging. *Biopolymers and Cell, 33*(1), 3-23.

Matlin, M. W. (2012). *Psychology of women* (7th ed.). Boston: Cengage.

Matos, A. P., Ferreira, J. A., & Haase, R. F. (2012). Television and aggression: A test of a mediated model with a sample of Portuguese students. *Journal of Social Psychology, 152*(1), 75-91.

Matott, M. P., Kline, D. D., & Hasser, E. M. (2017). Glial EAAT2 regulation of extracellular nTS glutamate critically controls neuronal activity and cardiorespiratory reflexes. *The Journal of Physiology, 595*, 6045-6063.

Matsumoto, D., & Hwang, H. C. (2014). Judgments of subtle facial expressions of emotion. *Emotion, 14*(2), 349-357.

Matsumoto, D., & Juang, L. (2013). *Culture and psychology* (5th ed.). Boston: Cengage.

Matsumoto, D., & Juang, L. (2016). *Culture and psychology* (6th ed.). Boston: Cengage.

Matsumoto, M., Walton, N. M., Yamada, H., Kondo, Y., Marek, G. J., & Tajinda, K. (2017). The impact of genetics on future drug discovery in schizophrenia. *Expert Opinion on Drug Discovery, 12*, 673-686.

Matsunaga, H., & Seedat, S. (2011). Obsessive-compulsive spectrum disorders: Cross-national and ethnic issues. In E. Hollander, J. Zohar, P. J. Sirovatka, & D. A. Regier (Eds.), *Obsessive-compulsive spectrum disorders: Refining the research agenda for DSM-V* (pp. 205-221). Washington, DC: American Psychiatric Association.

Mattarozzi, K., Colonnello, V., De Gioia, F., & Todorov, A. (2017). I care, even after the first impression: Facial appearance-based evaluations in healthcare context. *Social Science & Medicine, 18*, 268-272. doi:10.1016/j.socscimed.2017.04.011

Matthews, A. J., Mackintosh, C., Williams, S., Williams, M., & Kirkby, K. C. (2017). Habituation of self-reported anxiety and cortical hyper-vigilance during image-based exposure to spiders. *Journal of Behavior Therapy and Experimental Psychiatry, 54*, 150-157.

Matthews, K. A., Gump, B. B., Harris, K. F., Haney, T. L., & Barefoot, J. C. (2004). Hostile behaviors predict cardiovascular mortality among men enrolled in the multiple risk factor intervention trial. *Circulation, 109*(1), 66-70.

Maule, J., Stanworth, K., Pellicano, E., & Franklin, A. (2017). Ensemble perception of color in autistic adults. *Autism Research, 10*(5), 839-851. doi:10.1002/aur.1725

Maxfield, M., Pyszczynski, T., Greenberg, J., Pepin, R., & Davis, H. P. (2012). The moderating role of executive functioning in older adults' responses to a reminder of mortality. *Psychology and Aging, 27*(1), 256-263.

Maxwell, A. L., Loxton, N. J., & Hennegan, J. M. (2017). Exposure to food cues moderates the indirect effect of reward sensitivity and external eating via implicit eating expectancies. *Appetite, 111*, 135-141.

Maxwell, W. L. (2012). Traumatic brain injury in the neonate, child, and adolescent human: An overview of pathology. *International Journal of Developmental Neuroscience, 30*(3), 167-183.

May, M. (2003, May 25). *Vision diary*. www.guardian.co.uk/g2/story/0,3604,1029268,00.html (accessed November 10, 2014)

Mayas, J., Parmentier, F. B. R., Andrés, P., & Ballesteros, S. (2014). Plasticity of attentional functions in older adults after non-action video game training: A randomized controlled Trial. *PLoS One, 9*(3), e92269.

Mayer, A. R., Quinn, D. K., & Master, C. L. (2017). The spectrum of mild traumatic brain injury: A review. *Neurology, 89*(6), 623-632.

Mazursky-Horowitz, H., Thomas, S. R., Woods, K. E., Chrabaszcz, J. S., Deater-Deckard, K., & Chronis-Tuscano, A. (2017). Maternal executive functioning and scaffolding in families of children with and without parent-reported ADHD. *Journal of Abnormal Child Psychology*. https://doi.org/10.1007/s10802-017-0289-2

McAbee, S. T., & Oswald, F. L. (2013). The criterion-related validity of personality measures for predicting GPA: A meta-analytic validity comparison. *Psychological Assessment, 25*(2), 532-544.

McAbee, S. T., Landis, R. S., & Burke, M. I. (2017). Inductive reasoning: The promise of big data. *Human Resource Management Review, 27*(2), 277-290. doi:10.1016/j.hrmr.2016.08.005

McAdams, D. P. (2001). The psychology of life stories. *Review of General Psychology, 5*(2), 100-122.

McAdams, D. P. (2006). *The redemptive self: Stories Americans live by*. New York: Oxford University Press.

McAdams, D. P. (2009). *The person* (5th ed.). New York: Wiley.

McAdams, D. P. (2011a). Life narratives. In K. L. Fingerman, C. A. Berg, J. Smith, & T. C. Antonucci (Eds.), *Handbook of lifespan development*. New York: Springer.

McAdams, D. P. (2011b). Narrative identity. In S. J. Schwartz, K. Luyckx, & V. L. Vignoles (Eds.), *Handbook of identity theory and research*. New York: Springer.

McBride, K. R., Sanders, S. A., Hill, B. J., & Reinisch, J. M. (2017). Heterosexual women's and men's labeling of anal behaviors as having "had sex". *The Journal of Sex Research.* in press.

McCarthy, M. J., Liang, S., Spadoni, A. D., Kelsoe, J. R., & Simmons, A. N. (2014). Whole brain expression of bipolar disorder associated genes: Structural and genetic analyses. *PLoS One, 9*(6), e100204.

McCaulley, M. H. (2000). Myers-Briggs Type Indicator: A bridge between counseling and consulting. *Consulting Psychology Journal:*
Practice and Research, 52, 117–132.

McClelland, J. L. (2011). Memory as a constructive process: The parallel-distributed processing approach. In S. Nalbantian, P. Matthews, & J. L. McClelland (Eds.), *The memory process.* Cambridge, MA: MIT Press.

McClelland, J. L., & Rumelhart, D. E. (2009). Why there are complementary learning systems in the hippocampus and neocortex: Insights from the successes and failures of connectionist models of learning and memory. In D. Shanks (Ed.), *Psychology of learning.* Thousand Oaks, CA: Sage.

McClelland, J. L., Botvinick, M. M., Noelle, D. C., Plaut, D. C., Rogers, T. T., Seidenberg, M. S., & Smith, L. B. (2010). Letting structure emerge: Connectionist and dynamical systems approaches to cognition. *Trends in Cognitive Sciences, 14*(8), 348–356.

McClure, V. S. (2017). *Infant massage: A handbook for loving parents.* New York: Bantam.

McCrae, R. R., Harwood, T. M., & Kelly, S. L. (2011). The NEO inventories. In T. M. Harwood, L. E. Beutler, & G. Groth-Marnat (Eds.), *Integrative assessment of adult personality* (3rd ed.). New York: Guilford.

McCullough, M. E., & Willoughby, B. L. (2009). Religion, self-regulation, and self-control: Associations, explanations, and implications. *Psychological Bulletin, 135*(1), 69–93.

McCullough, M. E., Emmons, R. A., & Tsang, J. (2002). The grateful disposition: A conceptual and empirical topography. *Journal of Personality and Social Psychology, 82*(1), 112–127.

McCullough, M. E., Luna, L. R., Berry, J. W., Tabak, B. A., & Bono, G. (2010). On the form and function of forgiving: Modeling the time-forgiveness relationship and testing the valuable relationships hypothesis. *Emotion, 10*(3), 358–376.

McCullough, M. E., Kurzban, R., & Tabak, B. A. (2011). Evolved mechanisms for revenge and forgiveness. In M. Mikulincer & P. R. Shaver (Eds.), *Human aggression and violence: Causes, manifestations, and consequences* (pp. 221–239). Washington, DC: American Psychological Association.

McCullough, M., Kurzban, R., & Tabak, B. A. (2013). Putting revenge and forgiveness in an evolutionary context. *Behavioral and Brain Sciences, 36*(1), 41–58.

McDaniel, M. A., & Einstein, G. O. (2007). *Prospective memory: An overview and synthesis of an emerging field.* Thousand Oaks, CA: Sage.

McDonald, R. J., & White, N. M. (2013). A triple dissociation of memory systems: Hippocampus, amygdala, & dorsal striatum. *Behavioral Neuroscience, 127*(6), 835–853.

McElvaney, R., Greene, S., & Hogan, D. (2014). To tell or not to tell? Factors influencing young people's informal disclosures of child sexual abuse. *Journal of Interpersonal Violence, 29*(5), 928–947.

McEwen, B. S. (2017). Neurobiological and systemic effects of chronic stress. *Chronic Stress, 1*, 1–11 http://journals.sagepub.com/doi/abs/10.1177/2470547017692328

McGough, J. J. (2016). Treatment controversies in adult ADHD. *American Journal of Psychiatry, 173*(10), 960–966.

McGregor, C., Riordan, A., & Thornton, J. (2017). Estrogens and the cognitive symptoms of schizophrenia: Possible neuroprotective mechanisms. *Frontiers in Neuroendocrinology, 47*, 19–33.

McGue, M., Rustichini, A., & Iacono, W. G. (2017). Cognitive, noncognitive, and family background contributions to college attainment: A behavioral genetic perspective. *Journal of Personality, 85*(1), 65–78.

McGuire, M. T., Wing, R. R., Klem, M. L., Lang, W., & Hill, J. O. (1999). What predicts weight regain in a group of successful weight losers? *Journal of Consulting and Clinical Psychology, 67*(2), 177–185.

McGuire, W. J. (2003). Doing psychology my way. In R. J. Sternberg (Ed.), *Psychologists defying the crowd: Stories of those who battled the establishment and won* (pp. 119–137). Washington, DC: American Psychological Association.

McGuire, W. J., & Papageorgis, D. (1961). The relative efficacy of various types of prior belief-defense in producing immunity against persuasion. *Journal of Abnormal and Social Psychology, 62*(2), 327–337.

McIntosh, R. C., & Rosselli, M. (2012). Stress and coping in women living with HIV: A meta-analytic review. *AIDS Behavior, 16*(8), 2144–2159.

McIntosh, W. D., Harlow, T. F., & Martin, L. L. (1995). Linkers and non-linkers: Goal beliefs as a moderator of the effects of everyday hassles on rumination, depression, and physical complaints. *Journal of Applied Social Psychology, 25*(14), 1231–1244.

McIntyre, C. C., Chaturvedi, A., Shamir, R. R., & Lempka, S. F. (2015). Engineering the next generation of clinical deep brain stimulation. *Brain Stimulation, 8*(1), 21–26.

McKay, K. M., Imel, Z. E., & Wampold, B. E. (2006). Psychiatrist effects in the psychopharmacological treatment of depression. *Journal of Affective Disorders, 92*(2–3), 287–290.

McKee, T. E. (2017). Peer relationships in undergraduates with ADHD symptomatology: Selection and quality of friendships. *Journal of Attention Disorders, 21*(12), 1020–1029.

McLachlan, N. M., & Wilson, S. (2010). The central role of recognition in auditory perception: A neurobiological model. *Psychological Review, 117*(1), 175–196.

McLaughlin, K. A., Aldao, A., Wisco, B. E., & Hilt, L. M. (2014). Rumination as a transdiagnostic factor underlying transitions between internalizing symptoms and aggressive behavior in early adolescents. *Journal of Abnormal Psychology, 123*(1), 13–23.

McMullen, V., Mahfood, S. L., Francis, G. L., & Bubenik, J. (2017). Using Prediction and Desensitization Techniques to Treat Dental Anxiety: A Case Example. *Behavioral Interventions, 32*(1), 91–100.

McNamara, T. P. (2013). Semantic memory and priming. In A. F. Healy, R. W. Proctor, & I. B. Weiner (Eds.), *Handbook of psychology* (2nd ed., vol. 4). Hoboken, NJ: Wiley.

McNicholas, F., Healy, E., White, M., Sherdian-Pereira, M., O'Connor, N., Coakley, S., & Dooley, B. (2014). Medical, cognitive, and academic outcomes of very low birth weight infants at 10–14 years in Ireland. *Irish Journal of Medical Science, 183*(4), 525–532.

McNicholas, P. J., Floyd, R. G., Woods, I. J., Singh, L. J., Manguno, M. S., & Maki, K. E. (2017). State special education criteria for identifying intellectual disability: A review following revised diagnostic criteria and Rosa's Law. *School Psychology Quarterly,* doi:10.1037/spq0000208

McNulty, J. K. (2011). The dark side of forgiveness: The tendency to forgive predicts continued psychological and physical aggression in marriage. *Personality and Social Psychology Bulletin, 37*(6), 770–783.

McNulty, J. K., & Russell, V. M. (2016). Forgive and forget, or forgive and regret? Whether forgiveness leads to less or more offending depends on offender agreeableness. *Personality and Social Psychology Bulletin, 42*, 616–631. doi:10.1177/0146167216637841

McNulty, J. K., Wenner, C. A., & Fisher, T. D. (2016). Longitudinal associations among relationship

satisfaction, sexual satisfaction, and frequency of sex in early marriage. *Archives of Sexual Behavior, 45*(1), 85–97.

Meaney M. J. (2017) Epigenetics and the biology of gene × environment interactions. In P. Tolan & B. Leventhal (Eds.), *Gene-environment transactions in developmental psychopathology. Advances in Development and Psychopathology: Brain Research Foundation Symposium Series, Vol 2.* (pp. 59–94). Cham: Springer.

Medda, P., Toni, C., & Perugi, G. (2014). The mood-stabilizing effects of electroconvulsive therapy. *Journal of Electroconvulsive Therapy, 30*(4), 275–282.

MedlinePlus. (2014). *Alcoholism.* www.nlm.nih.gov/medlineplus/alcoholism.html (accessed December 1, 2014)

Mehrabian, A. (2001). Characteristics attributed to individuals on the basis of their first names. *Genetic, Social, and General Psychology Monographs, 127*, 59–88.

Mehta, U. M., Thirthalli, J., Gangadhar, B. N., & Keshaven, M. S. (2011). Need for culture specific tools to assess social cognition in schizophrenia. *Schizophrenia Research, 133*(1–3), 255–256.

Meiri, N., Schnapp, Z., Ankri, A., Nahmias, I., Raviv, A., Sagi, O., et al. (2017). Fear of clowns in hospitalized children: prospective experience. *European Journal of Pediatrics, 176*(2), 269–272.

Melby-Lervåg, M., & Hulme, C. (2016). There is no convincing evidence that working memory training is effective: A reply to Au et al. (2014) and Karbach and Verhaeghen (2014). *Psychonomic Bulletin & Review, 23*(1), 324–330. doi:10.3758/s13423-015-0862-z

Melby-Lervåg, M., Redick, T. S., & Hulme, C. (2016). Working memory training does not improve performance on measures of intelligence or other measures of 'far transfer': Evidence from a meta-analytic review. *Perspectives on Psychological Science, 11*(4), 512–534. doi:10.1177/1745691616635612

Mele, P., Zammaretti, F., Longo, A., Panzica, G., Oberto, A., & Eva, C. (2016). Sex-dependent regulation of hypothalamic neuropeptide Y-Y1 receptor gene expression in leptin treated obese (ob/ob) or lean mice. *Brain Research, 1649*(Part A), 102–109. doi:10.1016/j.brainres.2016.07.022

Mele, S., Mattiassi, A. D., & Urgesi, C. (2014). Unconscious processing of body actions primes subsequent action perception but no motor execution. *Journal of Experimental Psychology: Human Perception and Performance, 40*(5), 1940–1962.

Melin, A.D., Khetpal, V., Matsushita, Y., Zhou, K., Campos, F.A., Welker, B., & Kawamura, S. (2017). Howler monkey foraging ecology suggests convergent evolution of routine trichromacy as an adaptation for folivory. *Ecology and Evolution, 7*, 1421–1434. doi:10.1002/ece3.2716

Mellor, J. M., & Freeborn, B. A. (2011). Religious participation and risky health behaviors among adolescents. *Health Economics, 20*(10), 1226–1240. doi:10.1002/hec.1666

Melton, L. (2005). How brain power can help you cheat old age. *New Scientist, 2530*, 32

Meltzer, A. L., & McNulty, J. K. (2016). Who is having more and better sex? The Big Five as predictors of sex in marriage. *Journal of Research in Personality, 63*, 62–66.

Meltzer, A. L., Makhanova, A., Hicks, L. L., French, J. E., McNulty, J. K., & Bradbury, T. N. (2017). Quantifying the sexual afterglow: The lingering benefits of sex and their implications for pair-bonded relationships. *Psychological Science, 28*(5), 587–598. doi:10.1177/0956797617691361

Melzack, R. (1973). *The puzzle of pain.* New York: Basic Books.

Mendes, N., Hanus, D., & Call, J. (2007). Raising the level: Orangutans use water as a tool. *Biology Letters, 3*(5), 453–455.

Mendes, W. B. (2007). Social facilitation. In R. Baumeister & K. Vohs (Eds.), *Encyclopedia of social psychology.* Thousand Oaks, CA: Sage.

Menozzi, D., Sogari, G., Veneziani, M., Simoni, E., & Mora, C. (2017). Eating novel foods: An application of the theory of planned behaviour to predict the consumption of an insect-based product. *Food Quality and Preference, 59,* 27–34. doi:10.1016/j.foodqual.2017.02.001

Mercier, H. (2017). Confirmation bias—Myside bias. In R. F. Pohl (Ed.), *Cognitive illusions: Intriguing phenomena in thinking, judgment and memory* (pp. 99–114). New York: Routledge/Taylor & Francis Group.

Mercier, H., & Sperber, D. (2011). Why do humans reason? Arguments for an argumentative theory. *Behavioral and Brain Sciences, 34*(2), 57–111.

Messenger, J. C. (1971). Sex and repression in an Irish folk community. In D. S. Marshall & R. C. Suggs (Eds.), *Human sexual behavior.* New York: Basic.

Metcalfe, J., & Mischel, W. (1999). A hot/cool system analysis of delay of gratification: Dynamics of will power. *Psychological Review, 106*(1), 3–19.

Mettler, F. A. (Ed.). (1952). *Psychosurgical problems.* Oxford, U.K.: Blakiston.

Metzger, B. A., Mathewson, K. E., Tapia, E., Fabiani, M., Gratton, G., & Beck, D. M. (2017). Regulating the access to awareness: Brain activity related to probe-related and spontaneous reversals in binocular rivalry. *Journal of Cognitive Neuroscience, 29,* 1089–1102.

Meuret, A. E., Kroll, J., & Ritz, T. (2017). Panic disorder comorbidity with medical conditions and treatment implications. *Annual Review of Clinical Psychology, 13,* 209–240.

Meyer, E. (2014). *The culture map.* New York: Public Affairs.

Meyer, P. J., Meshul, C. K., & Phillips, T. J. (2009). Ethanol- and cocaine-induced locomotion are genetically related to increases in accumbal dopamine. *Genes, Brain, and Behavior, 8*(3), 346–355.

Mez, J., Daneshvar, D. H., Kiernan, P. T., Abdolmohammadi, B., Alvarez, V. E., et al. (2017). Clinicopathological evaluation of chronic traumatic encephalopathy in players of American football. *Journal of the American Medical Association, 318,* 360–370.

Mhalhal, T. R., Washington, M. C., Newman, K., Heath, J. C., & Sayegh, A. I. (2017). Infusion of exogenous cholecystokinin-8, gastrin releasing peptide-29 and their combination reduce body weight in diet-induced obese male rats. *Appetite, 109,* 172–181. doi:10.1016/j.appet.2016.12.001

Micevych, P. E., & Meisel, R. L. (2017). Integrating neural circuits controlling female sexual behavior. *Frontiers In Systems Neuroscience, 11* doi:10.3389/fnsys.2017.00042

Michalik, N. M., Eisenberg, N., Spinrad, T. L., Ladd, B., Thompson, M., & Valiente, C. (2007). Longitudinal relations among parental emotional expressivity and sympathy and prosocial behavior in adolescence. *Social Development, 16*(2), 286–309.

Michel, M. (2017). A role for the anterior insular cortex in the global neuronal workspace model of consciousness. *Consciousness and Cognition, 49,* 333–346.

Middeldorp, C. M., de Geus, E. J., Beem, A. L., Lakenberg, N., Hottenga, J. J., Slagboom, P. E., & Boomsma, D. I. (2007). Family based association analyses between the serotonin transporter gene polymorphism (5-HTTLPR) and neuroticism, anxiety, and depression. *Behavior Genetics, 37*(2), 294–301.

Mihura, J. L., Meyer, G. J., Dumitrascu, N., & Bombel, G. (2013). The validity of individual Rorschach variables: Systematic reviews and meta-analyses of the comprehensive system. *Psychological Bulletin, 139*(3), 548–605. doi:10.1037/a0029406

Mikal, J. P., Rice, R. E., Kent, R. G., & Uchino, B. N. (2016). 100 million strong: A case study of group identification and deindividuation on Imgur.Com. *New Media & Society, 18*(11), 2485–2506.

Mikolajczak, M., Pinon, N., Lane, A., de Timary, P., Luminet O. (2010). Oxytocin not only increases trust when money is at stake, but also when confidential information is in the balance. *Biological Psychology, 85,* 182–184

Miksis, S. (2008). A review of the evidence comparing the human papillomavirus versus condoms in the prevention of human papillomavirus infections. *Journal of Obstetric, Gynecologic, and Neonatal Nursing, 37*(3), 329–337.

Milaneschi, Y., Lamers, F., Bot, M., Drent, M. L., & Penninx, B. H. (2017). Leptin dysregulation is specifically associated with major depression with atypical features: Evidence for a mechanism connecting obesity and depression. *Biological Psychiatry, 81*(9), 807–814. doi:10.1016/j.biopsych.2015.10.023

Milgram, S. (1965). Some conditions of obedience and disobedience to authority. *Human Relations, 18*(1), 56–76.

Milgram, S. (1974). *Obedience to authority.* New York: Harper & Row.

Miller, A. B., Esposito-Smythers, C., Weismoore, J. T., & Renshaw, K. D. (2013). The relation between child maltreatment and adolescent suicidal behavior: A systematic review and critical examination of the literature. *Clinical Child and Family Psychology Review, 16*(2), 146–172.

Miller, B. L., & Cummings, J. L. (Eds.). (2017). *The human frontal lobes: Functions and disorders.* New York: Guilford Publications.

Miller, D. B., & O'Callaghan, J. P. (2006). The pharmacology of wakefulness. *Metabolism, 55,* Suppl. 2, S13–S19.

Miller, G. A. (1956). The magical number seven, plus or minus two: Some limits on our capacity for processing information. *Psychological Review, 63*(2), 81–97.

Miller, J. G., & Hastings, P. D. (2016). Biopsychosocial models of prosociality: Compassionate love, vagal regulation, and children's altruism. In D. Narvaez, J. M. Braungart-Rieker, L. E. Miller-Graff, L. T. Gettler, & P. D. Hastings (Eds.), *Contexts for young child flourishing: Evolution, family, and society* (pp. 185–200). New York: Oxford University Press. doi:10.1093/acprof:oso/9780190237790.003.0009

Miller, J. J., Fletcher, K., & Kabat-Zinn, J. (1995). Three-year follow-up and clinical implications of a mindfulness meditation-based stress reduction intervention in the treatment of anxiety disorders. *General Hospital Psychiatry, 17*(3), 192–200.

Miller, N. E. (1985). The value of behavioral research on animals. *American Psychologist, 40*(4), 432–440.

Miller, N., Ament, S. A., Shekhtman, T., Roach, J. C., Study, T. B. G., & Kelsoe, J. R. (2017). Search for risk variants in TrkB and BDNF that predispose to lithium responsiveness in bipolar disorder. *Biological Psychiatry, 81*(10), S96.

Miller, S. D., Hubble, M. A., Chow, D. L., & Seidel, J. A. (2013). The outcome of psychotherapy: Yesterday, today, and tomorrow. *Psychotherapy, 50*(1), 88–97.

Miller, W. R., & Moyers, T. B. (2017). Motivational interviewing and the clinical science of Carl Rogers. *Journal of Consulting and Clinical Psychology, 85*(8), 757–766. doi:10.1037/ccp0000179

Milling, L. S., Coursen, E. L., Shores, J. S., & Waszkiewicz, J. A. (2010). The predictive utility of hypnotizability: The change in suggestibility produced by hypnosis. *Journal of Consulting and Clinical Psychology, 78*(1), 126–130.

Milner, A. D., & Goodale, M. A. (1995). *The visual brain in action.* New York: Oxford University Press.

Milojev, P., & Sibley, C. G. (2017). Normative personality trait development in adulthood: A 6-year cohort-sequential growth model. *Journal of Personality And Social Psychology, 112*(3), 510–526. doi:10.1037/pspp0000121

Miltenberger, R. G. (2016). *Behavior modification* (6th ed.). Boston: Cengage.

Mindell, J. A., Meltzer, L. J., Carskadon, M. A., & Chervin, R. D. (2009). Developmental aspects of sleep hygiene: Findings from the 2004 National Sleep in America Poll. *Sleep Medicine, 10*(7), 771–779.

Mineka, S., & Ohman, A. (2002). Phobias and preparedness: The selective, automatic, and encapsulated nature of fear. *Biological Psychiatry, 52*(10), 927–937.

Minges, M. V., Solomonov, N., & Barber, J. P. (2017). What makes psychodynamic psychotherapy work? A review of five perspectives. *Psychoanalytic Inquiry, 37*(3), 191–201.

Mischel, W. (2004). Toward an integrative science of the person. *Annual Review of Psychology* (vol. 55, pp. 1–22). Palo Alto, CA: Annual Reviews.

Mischel, W. (2009). From *Personality and Assessment* (1968) to personality science, 2009. *Journal of Research in Personality, 43*(2), 282–290.

Mischel, W., & Ayduk, O. (2011). Willpower in a cognitive-affective processing system: The dynamics of delay of gratification. In K. D. Vohs & R. F. Baumeister (Eds.), *Handbook of self-regulation* (2nd ed.). New York: Guilford.

Mischel, W., & Moore, B. S. (1980). The role of ideation in voluntary delay for symbolically presented rewards. *Cognitive Therapy and Research, 4*(2), 211–221.

Mischel, W., & Shoda, Y. (1999). Integrating dispositions and processing dynamics within a unified theory of personality: The cognitive-affective personality system. In L. A. Pervin & O. P. John (Eds.), *Handbook of personality: Theory and research* (2nd ed., pp. 197–218). New York: Guilford.

Mischel, W., Cantor, N., & Feldman, S. (1996). Principles of self-regulation: The nature of willpower and self-control. In E. T. Higgins & A. W. Kruglanski (Eds.), *Social psychology: Handbook of basic principles.* New York: Guilford.

Misra, U. K., Kalita, J., Tripathi, G., & Bhoi, S. K. (2017). Role of β endorphin in pain relief following high rate repetitive transcranial magnetic stimulation in migraine. *Brain Stimulation, 10*(3), 618–623.

Mistry, J., Contreras, M., & Dutta, R. (2013). Culture and child development. In R. M. Lerner, M. A. Easterbrooks, J. Mistry, & I. B. Weiner (Eds.), *Handbook of psychology* (2nd ed., vol. 6, pp. 265–286). Hoboken, NJ: Wiley.

Mitchell, J. (2014). *Individualism and moral character: Karen Horney's depth psychology.* Piscataway, NJ: Transaction Publishers.

Mitchell, R. L. C., & Kumari, V. (2016). Hans Eysenck's interface between the brain and personality: Modern evidence on the cognitive neuroscience of personality. *Personality and Individual Differences, 103,* 74–81.

Mittag, W., & Schwarzer, R. (1993). Interaction of employment status and self-efficacy on alcohol consumption: A two-wave study on stressful life transitions. *Psychology and Health, 8*(1), 77–87.

Miyamoto, Y., Nisbett, R. E., & Masuda, T. (2006). Culture and the physical environment. *Psychological Science, 17*(2), 113–119.

Moazen-Zadeh, E., Shirzad, F., Karkhaneh-Yousefi, M. A., Khezri, R., Mohammadi, M. R., & Akhondzadeh, S. (2017). Simvastatin as an adjunctive therapy to risperidone in treatment of autism: A randomized, double-blind, placebo-controlled clinical trial. *Journal of Child and Adolescent Psychopharmacology.* In press. doi: 10.1089/cap.2017.005

Moberg, C. A., Bradford, D. E., Kaye, J. T., & Curtin, J. J. (2017). Increased startle potentiation to unpredictable stressors in alcohol dependence: Possible stress neuroadaptation in humans. *Journal of Abnormal Psychology, 126*(4), 441–453. doi:10.1037/abn0000265

Moberly, A. C., Harris, MS., Boyce, L., & Nittrouer, S. (2017). Speech recognition in adults with cochlear implants: The effects of working memory, phonological sensitivity, and aging. *Journal of Speech, Language, and Hearsearch, 60*(4), 1046–1061.

Moberly, N. J., & Watkins, E. R. (2009). Negative affect and ruminative self-focus during everyday goal pursuit. *Cognition and Emotion, 24*(4), 1–15.

Moen, K. C., Miller, J. K., & Lloyd, M. E. (2017). Selective attention meets spontaneous recognition memory: Evidence for effects at retrieval. *Consciousness and Cognition, 49*, 181–189.

Moghimi, D., Zacher, H., Scheibe, S., & Van Yperen, N. W. (2017). The selection, optimization, and compensation model in the work context: A systematic review and meta-analysis of two decades of research. *Journal of Organizational Behavior, 38*(2), 247–275.

Mokhlesi, B., Grimaldi, D., Beccuti, G., & Van Cauter, E. (2017). Effect of one week of CPAP treatment of obstructive sleep apnoea on 24-hour profiles of glucose, insulin and counter-regulatory hormones in type 2 diabetes. *Diabetes, Obesity and Metabolism, 19*(3), 452–456.

Molina, B., & Pelham, W.E. (2014). The attention deficit/hyperactivity disorder (ADHD) substance use connection. *Annual Review of Clinical Psychology, 10*, 607–639.

Molloy, A., & Murphy, P. (September 18, 2016). Emotional moment these Irish best friends reunite after 43 years following international search. *The Independent.* http://www.independent.ie/life/family/family-features/emotional-moment-these-irish-best-friends-reunite-after-43-years-following-international-search-35058439.html

Molouki, S., & Pronin, E. (2014). Self and other. In M. Mikulincer, P. R. Shaver, E. Borgida, & J. A. Bargh (Eds.), *APA handbook of personality and social psychology* (vol. 1). Washington, DC: American Psychological Association.

Molyneaux, E., Howard, L. M., McGeown, H. R., Karia, A. M., & Trevillion, K. (2014). Antidepressant treatment for postnatal depression. *Cochrane Database of Systematic Reviews, 9*, CD002018.

Momtaz, Y. A., Hamid, T. A., Yusoff, S., Ibrahim, R., Chai, S. T., Yahaya, N., & Abdullah, S. S. (2012). Loneliness as a risk factor for hypertension in later life. *Journal of Aging and Health, 24*(4), 696–710.

Money, J., & Tucker, P. (1975). *Sexual signatures: On being a man or woman.* Boston: Little Brown.

Monnereau, C., Jansen, P. W., Tiemeier, H., Jaddoe, V. W., & Felix, J. F. (2017). Influence of genetic variants associated with body mass index on eating behavior in childhood. *Obesity, 25*(4), 765–772.

Monni, E., Cusulin, C., Cavallaro, M., Lindvall, O., & Kokaia, Z. (2014). Human fetal striatum-derived neural stem (NS) cells differentiate to mature neurons in vitro and in vivo. *Current Stem Cell Research and Therapy.* doi:10.2174/1574888X09666140321115803

Montenegro, G., Alves, L., Zaninotto, A. L., Falcão, D. P., & de Amorim, R. B. (2017). Hypnosis as a valuable tool for surgical procedures in the oral and maxillofacial area. *American Journal of Clinical Hypnosis, 59*(4), 414–421. doi:10.1080/00029157.2016.1172057

Montgomery, E. (2010). Trauma and resilience in young refugees: A 9-year follow-up study. *Developmental Psychology, 22*(2), 477–489.

Montgomery, G. H., Sucala, M., Baum, T., & Schnur, J. B. (2017). Hypnosis for symptom control in cancer patients at the end-of-life: A systematic review. *International Journal Of Clinical And Experimental Hypnosis, 65*(3), 296–307. doi:10.1080/00207144.2017.1314728

Montgomery, S. A., Lyndon, G., Almas, M., Whalen, E., & Prieto, R. (2017). Early improvement with pregabalin predicts endpoint response in patients with generalized anxiety disorder: an integrated and predictive data analysis. *International Clinical Psychopharmacology, 32*(1), 41–48.

Mooneyham, B. W., Mrazek, M. D., Mrazek, A. J., Mrazek, K. L., Ihm, E. D., & Schooler, J. W. (2017). An integrated assessment of changes in brain structure and function of the insula resulting from an intensive mindfulness-based intervention. *Journal of Cognitive Enhancement:* 1–10. doi: 10.1007/s41465-017-0034-3

Moore, D. S. (2013). Behavioral genetics, genetics, and epigenetics. In P. D. Zelazo (Ed.), *Handbook of Developmental Psychology.* New York: Oxford University Press.

Moore, M. T., Dawkins Jr, M. R., Fisher, J. W., & Fresco, D. M. (2016). Depressive realism and attributional style: Replication and Extension. *International Journal of Cognitive Therapy, 9*(1), 1–12.

Moran, J. M., Jolly, E., & Mitchell, J. P. (2014). Spontaneous mentalizing predicts the fundamental attribution error. *Journal of Cognitive Neuroscience, 26*(3), 569–576. doi:10.1162/jocn_a_00513

Moravčík, M., Schmid, M., Burch, N., Lisý, V., Morrill, D., Bard, N., et al. (2017). DeepStack: Expert-level artificial intelligence in heads-up no-limit poker. *Science, 356*(6337), 508–513. doi:10.1126/science.aam6960

Morawetz, C., Alexandrowicz, R. W., & Heekeren, H. R. (2017). Successful emotion regulation is predicted by amygdala activity and aspects of personality: A latent variable approach. *Emotion, 17*(3), 42–441.

Morawski, J. G., & Bayer, B. M. (2013). Social psychology. In D. K. Freedheim & I. B. Weiner (Eds.), *Handbook of psychology* (2nd ed., vol. 1, pp. 248–278). Hoboken, NJ: Wiley.

Moreira, J., Courtin, C., Geoffroy, P. A., Curis, E., Bellivier, F., & Cynthia, M. C. (2017). Lithium response in bipolar disorder: No difference in GADL1 gene expression between cell lines from excellent-responders and non-responders. *Psychiatry Research, 251*, 217–220.

Moreman, C. M. (2014). On the relationship between birds and spirits of the dead. *Society & Animals: Journal of Human-Animal Studies, 22*(5), 481–502. doi:10.1163/15685306-12341328

Morgan, C. A., & Southwick, S. (2014). Perspective: I believe what I remember, but it may not be true. *Neurobiology of Learning and Memory, 112*, 101–103.

Morgan, C. J., Coleman, M. J., Ulgen, A., Boling, L., Cole, J. O., Johnson, F. V., et al. (2017). Thought disorder in schizophrenia and bipolar disorder probands, their relatives, and nonpsychiatric controls. *Schizophrenia Bulletin, 43*(3), 523–535.

Morgan, S., Cooper, B., Paul, S., Hammer, M. J., Conley, Y. P., Levine, J. D., & … Dunn, L. B. (2017). Association of personality profiles with depressive, anxiety, and cancer-related symptoms in patients undergoing chemotherapy. *Personality and Individual Differences, 117*, 130–138. doi:10.1016/j.paid.2017.05.039

Morley, C. P., Rosas, S. R., Mishori, R., Jordan, W., Jarris, Y. S., & Prunuske, J. (2017). Essential public health competencies for medical students: Establishing a consensus in family medicine. *Teaching And Learning In Medicine, 29*(3), 255–267. doi:10.1080/10401334.2016.1268964

Morris, D. O., Javier, R. A., & Herron, W. G. (2015). *Specialty competencies in psychoanalysis in psychology.* New York: Oxford University Press.

Morris, J. K., Vidoni, E. D., Johnson, D. K., Van Sciver, A., Mahnken, J. D., Honea, R. A., et al. (2017). Aerobic exercise for Alzheimer's disease: A randomized controlled pilot trial. *Plos ONE, 12*(2).

Morris, M. W., & Peng, K. (1994). Culture and cause: American and Chinese attributions for social and physical events. *Journal of Personality and Social Psychology, 67*(6), 949–971.

Morrison, J. (2017). *DSM-5 made easy: The clinician's guide to diagnosis.* New York: Guilford Publications.

Morrison, J. D., & Mayer, L. (2017). Physical activity and cognitive function in adults with multiple sclerosis: An integrative review. *Disability and Rehabilitation, 39*(19), 1909–1920.

Mortimer, J. A., Snowdon, D. A., & Markesbery, W. R. (2009). The effect of APOE-epsilon4 on dementia is mediated by Alzheimer neuropathology. *Alzheimer Disease and Associated Disorders, 23*(2), 152–157.

Morton, J. (2017). Interidentity amnesia in dissociative identity disorder. *Cognitive Neuropsychiatry, 22*, 315–330.

Moscovici, S. (1985). Social influence and conformity. In G. Lindzey & E. Aronson (Eds.), *Handbook of social psychology* (3rd ed., vol. 2). New York: Random House.

Moscovitch, M. (2013). Brain and cognitive mechanisms in human episodic memory. *Annual Review of Psychology* (vol. 64). Palo Alto, CA: Annual Reviews.

Moscovitch, M., Cabeza, R., Winocur, G., & Nadel, L. (2016). Episodic memory and beyond: the hippocampus and neocortex in transformation. *Annual review of psychology, 67*, 105–134.

Moskowitz, D. S., & Fournier, M. A. (2014). The interplay of persons and situations: Retrospect and prospect. In M. Mikulincer & P. Shaver (Eds.), *APA handbook of personality and social psychology.* Washington, DC: American Psychological Association.

Moss-Racusin, C. A., Dovidio, J. F., Brescoll, V. L., Graham, M. J., & Handelsman, J. (2012). Science faculty's subtle gender biases favor male students. *PNAS Proceedings of the National Academy of Sciences of the United States of America, 109*(41), 16474–16479. doi:10.1073/pnas.1211286109

Mostofsky, E., Maclure, M., Sherwood, J. B., Tofler, G. H., Muller, J. E., & Mittleman, M. A. (2012). Risk of acute myocardial infarction after the death of a significant person in one's life: The Determinants of Myocardial Infarction Onset Study. *Circulation, 125*(3), 491–496.

Motivala, S. J., Arellano, M., Greco, R. L., Aitken, D., Hutcheson, N., Tadayonnejad, R., et al. (2017). Relationships between obsessive-compulsive disorder, depression and functioning before and after exposure and response prevention therapy. *International Journal of Psychiatry in Clinical Practice,* https://doi.org/10.1080/13651501.2017.1351991

Motti-Stefanidi, F., & Masten, A. S. (2017). A resilience perspective on immigrant youth adaptation and development. In N.J. Cabrera & B. Leyendecker (Eds.), *Handbook on Positive Development of Minority Children and Youth* (pp. 19–34). New York: Springer International Publishing.

Mõttus, R., Kandler, C., Bleidorn, W., Riemann, R., & McCrae, R. R. (2017). Personality traits below facets: The consensual validity, longitudinal stability, heritability, and utility of personality nuances. *Journal of Personality and Social Psychology, 112*(3), 474–490. doi:10.1037/pspp0000100

Moulton, S. T., & Kosslyn, S. M. (2008). Using neuroimaging to resolve the psi debate. *Journal of Cognitive Neuroscience, 20*, 182–192 10.1162/jocn.2008.20009

Mracsko, E., Liesz, A., Karcher, S., Zorn, M., Bari, F., & Veltkamp, R. (2014). Differential effects of sympathetic nervous system and hypothalamic-pituitary-adrenal axis on systemic immune cells after severe experimental stroke. *Brain, Behavior, and Immunity, 41*, 200–209.

Muehlenhard, C. L., Peterson, Z. D., Humphreys, T. P., & Jozkowski, K. N. (2017). Evaluating the one-in-five statistic: women's risk of sexual assault while in college. *The Journal of Sex Research, 54*(4–5), 549–576.

Mueller, D. L. (2010). Mechanisms maintaining peripheral tolerance. *Nature Immunology, 11*(1), 21–27.

Mueller, P. A., & Oppenheimer, D. M. (2014). The pen is mightier than the keyboard: Advantages of longhand over laptop note taking. *Psychological science, 25*(6), 1159–1168.

Muise, A., Schimmack, U., & Impett, E. A. (2016). Sexual frequency predicts greater well-being, but more is not always better. *Social Psychological and Personality Science, 7*(4), 295–302.

Müller, A. B., Valentini, N. C., & Bandeira, P. F. R. (2017). Affordances in the home environment for motor development: Validity and reliability for the use in daycare setting. *Infant Behavior and Development, 47*, 138–145.

Müller-Engelmann, M., & Steil, R. (2017). Cognitive restructuring and imagery modification for posttraumatic stress disorder (CRIM-PTSD): A pilot study. *Journal of Behavior Therapy and Experimental Psychiatry, 54,* 44–50.

Munafo, M. R., Yalcin, B., Willis-Owen, S. A., & Flint, J. (2008). Association of the dopamine D4 receptor (DRD4) gene and approach-related personality traits: Meta-analysis and new data. *Biological Psychiatry, 63*(2), 197–206.

Muris, P., & Merckelbach, H. (2012). Specific phobia: Phenomenology, epidemiology, and etiology. In T. E. Davis, T. H. Ollendick, & L.-G. Öst (Eds.), *Intensive one-session treatment of specific phobias.* New York: Springer.

Muris, P., Meesters, C., & Timmermans, A. (2013). Some youths have a gloomy side: Correlates of the dark triad personality traits in non-clinical adolescents. *Child Psychiatry and Human Development, 44*(5), 658–665.

Murphy, M. O., Cohn, D. M., & Loria, A. S. (2017). Developmental origins of cardiovascular disease: Impact of early life stress in humans and rodents. *Neuroscience and Biobehavioral Reviews, 74*(Part B), 453–465. doi:10.1016/j.neubiorev.2016.07.018

Murphy, N. A., Hall, J. A., Mast, M. S., Ruben, M. A., Frauendorfer, D., Blanch-Hartigan, D., et al. (2015). Reliability and validity of nonverbal thin slices in social interactions. *Personality and Social Psychology Bulletin, 41*(2), 199–213. doi:10.1177/0146167214559902

Mustoe, A. C., Taylor, J. H., Birnie, A. K., Huffman, M. C., & French, J. A. (2014). Gestational cortisol and social play shape development of marmosets' HPA functioning and behavioral responses to stressors. *Developmental Psychobiology, 56,* 1229–1243.

Mutschler, J., Grosshans, M., Soyka, M., & Rösner, S. (2016). Current findings and mechanisms of action of disulfiram in the treatment of alcohol dependence. *Pharmacopsychiatry, 49*(04), 137–141.

Myers, N. L. (2010). Culture, stress, and recovery form schizophrenia: Lessons from the field for global mental health. *Culture, Medicine, and Psychiatry, 34*(3), 500–528.

Myers, S. G., Grøtte, T., Haseth, S., Guzey, I. C., Hansen, B., Vogel, P. A., & Solem, S. (2017). The role of metacognitive beliefs about thoughts and rituals: A test of the metacognitive model of obsessive-compulsive disorder in a clinical sample. *Journal of Obsessive-Compulsive and Related Disorders, 13,* 1–6.

Myrick, A. C., Webermann, A. R., Loewenstein, R. J., Lanius, R., Putnam, F. W., & Brand, B. L. (2017). Six-year follow-up of the treatment of patients with dissociative disorders study. *European Journal of Psychotraumatology, 8*(1), Article 1344080.

N

Nabavi, S., Fox, R., Proulx, C. D., Lin, J. Y., Tsien, R. Y., & Malinow, R. (2014). Engineering a memory with LTD and LTP. *Nature, 511*(7509), 348–352.

Nakamura, T. J., Nakamura, W., Yamazaki, S., Kudo, T., Cutler, T., Colwell, C. S., & Block, G. D. (2011). Age-related decline in circadian output. *Journal of Neuroscience, 31*(28), 10201–10205.

Nakao, T., & others. (2005). A functional MRI comparison of patients with obsessive-compulsive disorder and normal controls during a Chinese character Stroop task. *Psychiatry Research: Neuroimaging, 139*(2), 101–114.

Nalepka, P., Kallen, R.W., Chemero, A., Saltzman, E., & Richardson, M.J. (2017). Herd those sheep: Emergent multiagent coordination and behavioral-mode switching. *Psychological Science 28,* 630–650.

Nash, M. R. (2001). The truth and the hype about hypnosis. *Scientific American, 285*(1), 46–49, 52–55.

Nasstasia, Y., Baker, A. L., Halpin, S. A., Lewin, T. J., Hides, L., Kelly, B. J., & Callister, R. (2017). Pilot study of an exercise intervention for depressive symptoms and associated cognitive-behavioral factors in young adults with major depression. *Journal of Nervous and Mental Disease, 205*(8), 647–655. doi:10.1097/NMD.0000000000000611

National Alliance on Mental Illness. (2013). Mental illness: Facts and numbers. *NAMI.* www.nami.org/factsheets/mentalillness_factsheet.pdf (accessed January 5, 2015)

National Center for PTSD. (2014). *PTSD.* Washington, DC: U.S. Department of Veterans Affairs.

National Human Genome Research Institute. (2012). Genome-wide association studies. *Genome.* www.genome.gov/12011238

National Institute of Mental Health (NIMH). (2014). Brain stimulation therapies. *NIMH.* www.nimh.nih.gov/health/topics/brain-stimulation-therapies/brain-stimulation-therapies.shtml (accessed January 9, 2015)

National Institute of Mental Health (NIMH). (2014c). What is schizophrenia? *NIMH.* www.nimh.nih.gov/health/topics/schizophrenia/index (accessed January 5, 2014)

National Institutes of Mental Health. (October, 2016). *Depression.* https://www.nimh.nih.gov/health/topics/depression/index.shtml#part_145398

National Institute of Mental Health (NIMH). (February, 2016b). *Eating disorders: Overview.* https://www.nimh.nih.gov/health/topics/eating-disorders/index.shtml

National Institute on Deafness and Other Communication Disorders (NIDCD). (2014). Cochlear implants. U.S. Department of Health and Human Services, National Institutes of Health. www.nidcd.nih.gov/health/hearing/pages/coch.aspx (accessed November 10, 2014)

National Institute on Drug Abuse (NIDA). (2009). *Research report series—MDMA (Ecstasy) abuse.* Bethesda, MD: Author.

National Institute on Drug Abuse (NIDA). (June, 2016). Fentanyl. https://www.drugabuse.gov/publications/drugfacts/fentanyl

National Institute on Drug Abuse (NIDA). (September, 2017). Overdose Death rates. https://www.drugabuse.gov/related-topics/trends-statistics/overdose-death-rates

National Sleep Foundation. (2011, March 7). *Annual Sleep in America Poll exploring connections with communications technology use and sleep.* Arlington, VA: author.

National Sleep Foundation. (2017). National Sleep Foundation recommends new sleep times. https://sleepfoundation.org/press-release/national-sleep-foundation-recommends-new-sleep-times/page/0/1

Naumann, L. P., Vazire, S., Rentfrow, P. J., & Gosling, S. D. (2009). Personality judgments based on physical appearance. *Personality and Social Psychology Bulletin, 35*(12), 1661–1671.

Nava, E., Romano, D., Grassi, M., & Turati, C. (2016). Skin conductance reveals the early development of the unconscious processing of emotions. *Cortex, 84,* 124–131. doi:10.1016/j.cortex.2016.07.011

Nave, C. S., Edmonds, G. W., Hampson, S. E., Murzyn, T., & Sauerberger, K. S. (2017). From elementary school to midlife: Childhood personality predicts behavior during cognitive testing over four decades later. *Journal of Research in Personality, 67,* 183–189.

Neale, D., & Pino-Pasternak, D. (2017). A review of reminiscing in early childhood settings and links to sustained shared thinking. *Educational Psychology Review, 29*(3), 641–665.

Needham, A. W., Wiesen, S. E., Hejazi, J. N., Libertus, K., & Christopher, C. (2017). Characteristics of brief sticky mittens training that lead to increases in object exploration. *Journal of Experimental Child Psychology, 164,* 209–224

Needham, A., Barrett, T., & Peterman, K. (2002). A pick-me-up for infants' exploratory skills: Early simulated experiences reaching for objects using "sticky mittens" enhances young infants' object exploration skills. *Infant Behavior and Development, 25*(3), 279–295.

Nehama, Y., Rabinowitz, I., Baruch, Y., Mandel, A., Lurie, I., & Barak, Y. (2014). Debunking the placebo effect in depression: The effect of patient and investigator expectation on escitalopram efficacy. *International Clinical Psychopharmacology, 29*(2), 106–110.

Neikrug, A. B., & Ancoli-Israel, S. (2010). Sleep disorders in the older adult: A mini-review. *Gerontology, 56*(2), 181–189.

Nelson, C. A. (2013). Brain development and behavior. In A. M. Rudolph, C. Rudolph, L. First, G. Lister, & A. A. Gersohon (Eds.), *Rudolph's pediatrics* (22nd ed.). New York: McGraw-Hill.

Nelson, J. C., Zhang, Q., Kelin, K., Eriksson, E., Deberdt, W., & Berk, M. (2013). Baseline patient characteristics associated with placebo remission and their impact on remission with duloxetine and selected SSRI antidepressants. *Current Medical Research and Opinion, 29*(7), 827–833.

Nelson, K. (1993). The psychological and social origins of autobiographical memory. *Psychological Science, 4*(1), 7–14.

Nelson, M. D., & Tumpap, A. M. (2017). Posttraumatic stress disorder symptom severity is associated with left hippocampal volume reduction: a meta-analytic study. *CNS Spectrums, 22*(4), 363–372.

Nelson, N. L., & Russell, J. A. (2014). Dynamic facial expressions allow differentiation of displays intended to convey positive and hubristic pride. *Emotion, 14*(5), 857–864.

Nelson, T. D. (Ed.). (2018). *Getting Grounded in Social Psychology: The Essential Literature for Beginning Researchers.* Abingdon, UK: Psychology Press Ltd.

Neniskyte, U., & Gross, C. T. (2017). Errant gardeners: glial-cell-dependent synaptic pruning and neurodevelopmental disorders. *Nature Reviews Neuroscience, 18*(11), 658–670.

Nesti, A., Beykirch, K. A., MacNeilage, P. R., Barnett-Cowan, M., & Bülthoff, H. H. (2014). The importance of stimulus noise analysis for self-motion studies. *PLoS One, 9*(4), e94570.

Nestler, S., Blank, H., & Egloff, B. (2010). Hindsight ≠ hindsight: Experimentally induced dissociations between hindsight components. *Journal of Experimental Psychology: Learning, Memory, and Cognition, 36*(6), 1399–1413.

Neubauer, D. N. (2014). New and emerging pharmacotherapeutic approaches for insomnia. *International Review of Psychiatry, 26*(2), 214–224.

Neufeld, J., Sinke, C., Dillo, W., Emrich, H. M., Szycik, G. R., Dima, D., Bleich, S., & Zedler, M. (2012). The neural correlates of coloured music: A functional MRI investigation of auditory-visual synesthesia. *Neuropsychologia, 50*(1), 85–89.

Neugebauer, J., Ray, D. G., & Sassenberg, K. (2016). When being worse helps: The influence of upward social comparisons and knowledge awareness on learner engagement and learning in peer-to-peer knowledge exchange. *Learning and Instruction, 44,* 41–52. doi:10.1016/j.learninstruc.2016.02.007

Neukrug, E. S., & Fawcett, R. C. (2015). *Essentials of testing and assessment* (3rd ed.). Boston: Cengage.

Neumaier, F., Paterno, M., Alpdogan, S., Tevoufouet, E. E., Schneider, T., Hescheler, J., & Albanna, W. (2017). Surgical approaches in psychiatry: a survey of the world literature on psychosurgery. *World Neurosurgery, 97,* 603–634.

Neville, H. J. (2006). Different profiles of plasticity within human cognition. In Y. Munakata & M. H. Johnson (Eds.), *Attention and performance.* Oxford, UK: Oxford University Press.

Newbury-Helps, J., Feigenbaum, J., & Fonagy, P. (2017). Offenders with antisocial personality disorder display more impairments in mentalizing. *Journal of Personality Disorders, 31*(2), 232–255.

Newell, F. N., & Mitchell, K. J. (2016). Multisensory integration and cross-modal learning in synaesthesia: A unifying model. *Neuropsychologia, 88,* 140–150. doi:10.1016/j.neuropsychologia.2015.07.026

Newman, E., Jernigan, T. L., Lisdahl, K. M., Tamm, L., Tapert, S. F., Potkin, S. G., et al. (2016). Go/No Go task performance predicts cortical thickness in the caudal inferior frontal gyrus in young adults with and without ADHD. *Brain Imaging and Behavior, 10*(3), 880–892.

Newman, I. R., Gibb, M., & Thompson, V. A. (2017). Rule-based reasoning is fast and belief-based reasoning can be slow: Challenging current explanations of belief-bias and base-rate neglect. *Journal of Experimental Psychology: Learning, Memory, and Cognition, 43*(7), 1154–1170. doi:10.1037/xlm0000372

Newton, E. K., Thompson, R. A., & Goodman, M. (2016). Individual differences in toddlers' prosociality: Experiences in early relationships explain variability in prosocial behavior. *Child Development, 87*(6), 1715–1726. doi:10.1111/cdev.12631

Nezami, B. T., Lang, W., Jakicic, J. M., Davis, K. K., Polzien, K., Rickman, A. D., et al. (2016). The effect of self-efficacy on behavior and weight in a behavioral weight-loss intervention. *Health Psychology, 35*(7), 714–722. doi:10.1037/hea0000378

Nezu, A. M., Nezu, C. M., Felgoise, S. H., & Greenberg, L. M. (2013). Psychosocial oncology. In A. M. Nezu, C. M. Nezu, P. A. Geller, & I. B. Weiner (Eds.), *Handbook of psychology* (2nd ed., vol. 9, pp. 271–291). Hoboken, NJ: Wiley.

Nguyen, T. V., Ducharme, S., & Karama, S. (2017). Effects of sex steroids in the human brain. *Molecular Neurobiology, 54*(9), 7507–7519.

Niaura, R., Todaro, J. F., Strood, L., Spiro, A., Ward, K. D., & Weiss, S. (2002). Hostility, the metabolic syndrome, and incident coronary heart disease. *Health Psychology, 21*(6), 588–593.

Nicholas, C. L., Jordan, A. S., & Trinder, J. (2017). The functions of sleep. In D. Mansfield, N. Antic, S. Rajaratnam, & M. Naughton (Eds.), *Sleep Medicine.* Victoria, Australia: IP Communications. In press.

Nicholson, A. A., Rabellino, D., Densmore, M., Frewen, P. A., Paret, C., Kluetsch, R., et al. (2017). The neurobiology of emotion regulation in posttraumatic stress disorder: Amygdala downregulation via real-time fMRI neurofeedback. *Human Brain Mapping, 38*, 541–560.

Nicholson, S. B., & Lutz, D. J. (2017). The importance of cognitive dissonance in understanding and treating victims of intimate partner violence. *Journal of Aggression, Maltreatment & Trauma, 26*(5), 475–492. doi:10.1080/10926771.2017.1314989

Nickels, N., Kubicki, K., & Maestripieri, D. (2017). Sex differences in the effects of psychosocial stress on cooperative and prosocial behavior: Evidence for 'flight or fight' in males and 'tend and befriend' in females. *Adaptive Human Behavior and Physiology, 3*(2), 171–183.

Nickerson, R. S., & Adams, M. J. (1979). Long-term memory for a common object. *Cognitive Psychology, 11*(3), 287–307.

Nie, Y., Chua, B. L., Yeung, A. S., Ryan, R. M., & Chan, W. Y. (2015). The importance of autonomy support and the mediating role of work motivation for well-being: Testing self-determination theory in a Chinese work organisation. *International Journal of Psychology, 50*(4), 245–255. doi:10.1002/ijop.12110

Niehorster, D. C., & Li, L. (2017). Accuracy and tuning of flow parsing for visual perception of object motion during self-motion. *I-Perception, 8*(3), doi:10.1177/2041669517708206

Niemiec, C. P., & Coulson, J. C. (2017). Need-supportive parenting and its role in the wellbeing and recovery of individuals: A self-determination theory perspective. In M. Slade, L. Oades, & A. Jarden (Eds.), *Wellbeing, recovery and mental health* (pp. 300–310). New York: Cambridge University Press. doi:10.1017/9781316339275.025

Nieß, C., & Zacher, H. (2015). Openness to experience as a predictor and outcome of upward job changes into managerial and professional positions. *Plos ONE, 10*(6).

Nigg, C. R., Jake-Schoffman, D. E., & Janke, E. A. (2017). Motivating future directions of behavioral

medicine. *Journal of Behavioral Medicine, 40*(1), 1–5. doi:10.1007/s10865-016-9817-8

Nijenhuis, E. R. (2017). Ten reasons for conceiving and classifying posttraumatic stress disorder as a dissociative disorder. *European Journal of Trauma & Dissociation, 1*(1), 47–61.

Nijstad, B. (2009). *Group performance.* New York: Psychology Press.

Nillni, Y. I., Berenz, E. C., Rohan, K. J., & Zvolensky, M. J. (2012). Sex differences in panic-relevant responding to a 10% carbon dioxide–enriched air biological challenge. *Journal of Anxiety Disorders, 26*(1), 165–172.

Nilsson, H., Juslin, P., & Olsson, H. (2008). Exemplars in the mist: The cognitive substrate of the representativeness heuristic. *Scandinavian Journal of Psychology, 49*(3), 201–212.

Nir, Y., Andrillon, T., Marmelshtein, A., Suthana, N., Cirelli, C., Tononi, G., & Fried, I. (2017). Selective neuronal lapses precede human cognitive lapses following sleep deprivation. *Nature Medicine,* in press. doi:10.1038/nm.4433

Nisbett, R. E., & Ross, L. (1980). *Human inference.* Upper Saddle River, NJ: Prentice-Hall.

Nisbett, R. E., Aronson, J., Blair, C., Dickens, W., Flynn, J., Halpern, D. F., & Turkheimer, E. (2012). Intelligence: New findings and theoretical developments. *American Psychologist, 67*(2), 130–159.

Norcross, J. C. (Ed.). (2011). *Psychotherapy relationships that work: Evidence-based responsiveness.* New York: Oxford University Press.

Norcross, J. C., Campbell, L. F., Grohol, J. M., Santrock, J. W., Selagea, F., & Sommer, R. (2013). *Self-help that works: Resources to improve emotional health and strengthen relationships* (4th ed.). New York: Oxford University Press.

Norcross, J. C., Krebs, P. M., & Prochaska, J. O. (2011). Stages of change. *Journal of Clinical Psychology, 67*(2), 143–154.

Nordahl, H., Nordahl, H. M., Hjemdal, O., & Wells, A. (2017). Cognitive and metacognitive predictors of symptom improvement following treatment for social anxiety disorder: A secondary analysis from a randomized controlled trial. *Clinical Psychology & Psychotherapy.* In press. Doi: 10.1002/cpp.2083

Nordstrom, B. R., & others. (2011). Neurocriminology. *Advances in Genetics, 75,* 255–283.

Nordt, C., Rossler, W., & Lauber, C. (2006). Attitudes of mental health professionals toward people with schizophrenia and major depression. *Schizophrenia Bulletin, 32*(4), 709–714.

Nosek, B. A., & Banaji, M. R. (2007). Implicit attitude. In P. Wilken, T. Bayne, & A. Cleeremans (Eds.), *The Oxford companion to consciousness.* Oxford: Oxford University Press.

Nosek, B. A., Bar-Anan, Y., Sriram, N., Axt, J., & Greenwald, A. G. (2014). Understanding and using the Brief Implicit Association Test: Recommended scoring procedures. *PLoS ONE, 9* (12), e110938.

Notman, M. T., & Nadelson, C. C. (2002). Women's issues. In M. Hersen & W. H. Sledge (Eds.), *Encyclopedia of psychotherapy.* San Diego: Academic.

Nouchi, R., & others. (2013). Brain training game boosts executive functions, working memory, and processing speed in the young adults: A randomized controlled trial. *PLoS One, 8*(2), e55518.

Novemsky, N., & Kahneman, D. (2005). The boundaries of loss aversion. *Journal of Marketing Research, 42*(May), 119–128.

Nowak, M. A., Page, K. M., & Sigmund, K. (2000). Fairness versus reason in the ultimatum game. *Science, 289*(5485), 1773–1775.

Nurnberger, J. I., Jr., & others. (2014). Identification of pathways for bipolar disorder: A meta-analysis. *JAMA Psychiatry, 71*(6), 657–664.

Nusbaum, E. C., Silvia, P. J., & Beaty, R. E. (2017). Ha ha? Assessing individual differences in humor production ability. *Psychology of Aesthetics, Creativity, and the Arts, 11*(2), 231–241. doi:10.1037/aca0000086

Nutt, D., & Goodwin, G. (2011). ECNP Summit on the future of CNS drug research in Europe 2011. *European Neuropsychopharmacology, 21*(7), 495–499.

Nystul, M. S. (1999). *Introduction to counseling.* Boston: Allyn & Bacon.

O

Oakley, D. A., & Halligan, P. W. (2011). Using hypnosis to gain insights into healthy and pathological cognitive functioning. *Consciousness and Cognition, 20*(2), 328–331.

Oakley, M., Farr, R. H., & Scherer, D. G. (2017). Same-sex parent socialization: Understanding gay and lesbian parenting practices as cultural socialization. *Journal of GLBT Family Studies, 13*(1), 56–75. doi:10.1080/1550428X.2016.1158685

Odeon, M. M., Yamauchi, L., Grosman, M., & Acosta, G. B. (2017). Long-term effects of repeated maternal separation and ethanol intake on HPA axis responsiveness in adult rats. *Brain Research, 1657,* 193–201. doi:10.1016/j.brainres.2016.11.034

O'Barr, W. M. (2006). Multiculturalism in the marketplace: Targeting Latinas, African American women, and gay consumers. Advertising and Society Review. https://muse.jhu.edu/journals/advertising_and_society_review/v007/7.4unit11.html (accessed December 22, 2014)

O'Brien, E., & Roney, E. (2017, June 7). Worth the wait? Leisure can be just as enjoyable with work left undone. Psychological Science. https://doi.org/10.1177/0956797617701749

O'Connor, C. (2017). Embodiment and the construction of social knowledge: Towards an integration of embodiment and social representations theory. *Journal for the Theory of Social Behaviour, 47*(1), 2–24.

O'Connor, D. B., Conner, M., Jones, F., McMillan, B., & Ferguson, E. (2009). Exploring the benefits of conscientiousness: An investigation of the role of daily stressors and health behaviors. *Annals of Behavioral Medicine, 37*(2), 184–196.

O'Connor, D., Potier, N. V., Kovacs, M., Xu, T., Ai, L., Pellman, J., et al. (2017). The healthy brain network serial scanning initiative: a resource for evaluating interindividual differences and their reliabilities across scan conditions and sessions. *GigaScience, 6*(2), 1–4.

O'Dell, K. R., Masters, K. S., Spielmans, G. I., & Maisto, S. A. (2011). Does type-D personality predict outcomes among patients with cardiovascular disease? A meta-analytic review. *Journal of Psychosomatic Research, 71*(4), 199–206.

Odermatt, J., Frommen, J. G., & Menz, M. H. (2017). Consistent behavioural differences between migratory and resident hoverflies. *Animal Behaviour, 127,* 187–195. doi:10.1016/j.anbehav.2017.03.015

Office of Adolescent Health. (2016). *Trends in teen pregnancy and childbearing.* Washington, DC: U.S. Department of Health and Human Services. Births https://www.hhs.gov/ash/oah/adolescent-development/reproductive-health-and-teen-pregnancy/teen-pregnancy-and-childbearing/trends/index.html

Ogden, C. L., & Carroll, M. D. (2010). Prevalence of overweight, obesity, and extreme obesity among adults: United States, trends 1960-1962 through 2007-2008. *NCHS Health E-Stat.* www.cdc.gov/nchs/data/hestat/obesity_adult_07_08/obesity_adult_07_08.pdf (accessed January 13, 2015)

Ogden, C. L., Carroll, M. D., Fryar, C.D., & Flegal K. M. (2015). *Prevalence of childhood and adult obesity in the United States, 2011-2014.* NCHS Data brief, #219. https://www.cdc.gov/nchs/data/databriefs/db219.pdf

Ogden, C. L., Carroll, M. D., Kit, B. K., & Flegal, K. M. (2012, January). Prevalence of obesity in the United States, 2009-2010. *NCHS Data Brief, (82)*, 1-8.

Ogilvie, R. D., & Wilkinson, R. T. (1988). Behavioral versus EEG-based monitoring of all-night sleep/wake patterns. *Sleep, 11*(2), 139-155.

Ohira, T., Diez Roux, A. V., Polak, J. F., Homma, S., Iso, H., & Wasserman, B. A. (2012). Associations of anger, anxiety, and depressive symptoms with carotid arterial wall thickness: The multi-ethnic study of atherosclerosis. *Psychosomatic Medicine, 74*(5), 517-525.

Ohman, A., & Mineka, S. (2001). Fears, phobias, and preparedness: Toward an evolved module of fear and fear learning. *Psychological Review, 108*(3), 483-522.

Ohman, A., & Mineka, S. (2003). The malicious serpent: Snakes as a prototypical stimulus for an evolved module of fear. *Current Directions in Psychological Science, 12*(1), 5-9.

Ohman, A., & Soares, J. J. P. (1998). Emotional conditioning to masked stimuli: Expectancies for aversive outcomes following nonrecognized fear-relevant stimuli. *Journal of Experimental Psychology, 127*(1), 69-82.

Oishi, S., & Diener, E. (2014). Residents of poor nations have a greater sense of meaning in life than residents of wealthy nations. *Psychological Science, 25*(2), 422-430.

Okun, B. F., & Kantrowitz, R. E. (2015). *Effective helping: Interviewing and counseling techniques* (8th ed.). Boston: Cengage.

Okun, M. A., Yeung, E. W., & Brown, S. (2013). Volunteering by older adults and risk of mortality: A meta-analysis. *Psychology and Aging, 28*(2), 564-577.

Olds, J. M. (1958). Self-stimulation experiments and differential reward systems. In H. H. Jasper, L. D. Proctor, R. S. Knighton, W. C. Noshay, & R. T. Costello (Eds.), *Reticular formation of the brain*. Boston: Little, Brown.

Olds, J. M., & Milner, P. M. (1954). Positive reinforcement produced by electrical stimulation of the septal area and other areas of the rat brain. *Journal of Comparative and Physiological Psychology, 47*(6), 419-427.

O'Leary, A. P., & Sloutsky, V. M. (2017). Carving metacognition at its joints: Protracted development of component processes. *Child Development, 88*(3), 1015-1032.

Oliva, J., Serrano, J. L., Del Castillo, M. D., & Iglesias, A. (2014). A methodology for the characterization and diagnosis of cognitive impairments–application to specific language impairment. *Artificial Intelligence in Medicine, 61*(2), 89-96.

Oliver, Z. J., Cristino, F., Roberts, M. V., Pegna, A. J., & Leek, E. C. (2017). Stereo viewing modulates three-dimensional shape processing during object recognition: A high-density ERP study. *Journal of Experimental Psychology: Human Perception and Performance*, in press. doi:10.1037/xhp0000444

Olivola, C. Y., & Todorov, A. (2017). The biasing effects of appearances go beyond physical attractiveness and mating motives. *Behavioral And Brain Sciences, 40*, in press. doi:10.1017/S0140525X16000595

Olooto, W. E. (2017). Infertility in male; risk factors, causes and management-A review. *Journal of Microbiology and Biotechnology Research, 2*(4), 641-645.

Oltmanns, T. F., & Powers, A. D. (2012). Gender and personality disorders. In T. Widiger (Ed.), *The Oxford handbook of personality disorders*. New York: Oxford University Press.

Omoto, A. M., & Snyder, M. (1995). Sustained helping without obligation: Motivation, longevity of service, and perceived attitude change among AIDS volunteers. *Journal of Personality and Social Psychology, 68*(4), 671-686.

Ong, G., Sewell, D. K., Weekes, B., McKague, M., & Abutalebi, J. (2017). A diffusion model approach to analysing the bilingual advantage for the flanker task: The role of attentional control processes. *Journal of*

Neurolinguistics, 43(Part A), 28-38. doi:10.1016/j.jneuroling.2016.08.002

Onishi, E., Kobayashi, T., Dexter, E., Marino, M., Maeno, T., & Deyo, R. A. (2017). Comparison of opioid prescribing patterns in the United States and Japan: primary care physicians' attitudes and perceptions. *The Journal of the American Board of Family Medicine, 30*(2), 248-254.

Open Science Collaboration. (2015). Estimating the reproducibility of psychological science. *Science, 349*, 943.

Ophir, E., Nass, C., & Wagner, A. D. (2009). Cognitive control in media multitaskers. *Proceedings of the National Academy of Sciences USA, 106*(37), 15583-15587.

Orchard, J., & Price, J. (2017). County-level racial prejudice and the black-white gap in infant health outcomes. *Social Science & Medicine, 181*, 191-198. doi:10.1016/j.socscimed.2017.03.036

Orellana Barrera, E., Arias, C., González, F., & Abate, P. (2017). Context-dependent extinction of an appetitive operant conditioned response in infant rats. *Developmental Psychobiology, 59*(3), 348-356.

Organisation for Economic Co-Operation and Development (OECD). (2017). Obesity update. *OECD.* http://www.oecd.org/els/health-systems/Obesity-Update-2017.pdf

Orlov, N. D., Tracy, D. K., Joyce, D., Patel, S., Rodzinka-Pasko, J., Dolan, H., et al. (2017). Stimulating cognition in schizophrenia: A controlled pilot study of the effects of prefrontal transcranial direct current stimulation upon memory and learning. *Brain Stimulation, 10*(3), 560-566.

Orom, H., & Cervone, D. (2009). Personality dynamics, meaning, and idiosyncrasy: Identifying cross-situational coherence by assessing personality architecture. *Journal of Research in Personality, 43*(2), 228-240.

Orpwood, R. (2017). Information and the origin of qualia. *Frontiers In Systems Neuroscience, 11*, doi:10.3389/fnsys.2017.00022

Osterling, J., & Dawson, G. (1994). Early recognition of children with autism: A study of first birthday home videotapes. *Journal of Autism and Developmental Disorders, 24*(3), 247-257.

Osterman, L. L., & Brown, R. P. (2011). Culture of honor and violence against the self. *Personality And Social Psychology Bulletin, 37*(12), 1611-1623. doi:10.1177/0146167211418529

Ostir, G. V., Markides, K. S., Black, S. A., & Goodwin, J. S. (2000). Emotional well-being predicts subsequent functional independence and survival. *Journal of the American Geriatrics Society, 48*(5), 473-478.

Otake, K., Shimai, S., Tanaka-Matsumi, J., Otsui, K., & Fredrickson, B. L. (2006). Happy people becoming happier through kindness: A counting kindnesses intervention. *Journal of Happiness Studies, 7*(3), 361-375.

O'Toole, S. E., Monks, C. P., & Tsermentseli, S. (2017). Executive function and theory of mind as predictors of aggressive and prosocial behavior and peer acceptance in early childhood. *Social Development, 26*, 907-920.

Otteson, D. C. (2017). Talkin' about my (re) generation: The who of intrinsic retinal stem cells. *Neuroscience, 346*, 447-449.

Owens, E. B., Zalecki, C., Gillette, P., & Hinshaw, S. P. (2017). Girls with childhood ADHD as adults: Cross-domain outcomes by diagnostic persistence. *Journal of Consulting and Clinical Psychology, 85*(7), 723.

Owens, R.E. (2015). *Language development: An introduction (9th ed.).* New York: Pearson.

Oxenham, A.J. (2018). How we hear: The perception and neural coding of sound. *Annual Review of Psychology, 69.* In press.

Oyserman, D., Elmore, K., & Smith, G. (2012). Self, self-concept, and identity. In M. R. Leary & J. P. Tangney (Eds.), *Handbook of self and identity* (2nd ed., pp. 69-104). New York: Guilford.

Öztekin, I., & Badre, D. (2011). Distributed patterns of brain activity that lead to forgetting. *Frontiers in Human Neuroscience, 5*, 86.

P

Pachai, A. A., Acai, A., LoGiudice, A. B., & Kim, J. A. (2016). The mind that wanders: Challenges and potential benefits of mind wandering in education. *Scholarship of Teaching and Learning in Psychology, 2*(2), 134-146. doi:10.1037/stl0000060

Packer, D. J. (2008). Identifying systematic disobedience in Milgram's obedience experiments: A meta-analytic review. *Perspectives on Psychological Science, 3*(4), 301-304.

Packer, D. J. (2009). Avoiding groupthink: Whereas weakly identified members stay silent, strongly identified members dissent about collective matters. *Psychological Science, 20*(5), 546-548.

Paglieri, F., & others. (2014). Nonhuman gamblers: Lessons from robots, primates, and robots. *Frontiers in Behavioral Neuroscience, 8*, 33.

Paivio, A. (1971). *Imagery and verbal processes.* New York: Holt, Rinehart & Winston.

Paivio, A. (1986). *Mental representations: A dual coding approach.* New York: Oxford University Press.

Paivio, A. (2007). *Mind and Its evolution: A dual coding theoretical approach.* Mahwah, NJ: Erlbaum.

Paivio, A., & Sadoski, M. (2011). Lexicons, contexts, events, and images: Commentary on Elman (2009) from the perspective of dual coding theory. *Cognitive Science, 35*(1), 198-209.

Pakhomov, S. V. S., & Hemmy, L. S. (2014). A computational linguistic measure of clustering behavior on semantic verbal fluency task predicts risk of future dementia in the Nun Study. *Cortex, 55*(1), 97-106.

Palmatier, J. J., & Rovner, L. (2014). Credibility assessment: Preliminary Process Theory, the polygraph process, and construct validity. *International Journal of Psychophysiology.* PMID: 24933412

Palmeri, A., Ricciarelli, R., Gulisano, W., Rivera, D., Rebosio, C., Calcagno, E., et al. (2017). Amyloid-β peptide is needed for cGMP-induced long-term potentiation and memory. *Journal of Neuroscience, 37*(29), 6926- 6937.

Palpacuer, C., Gallet, L., Drapier, D., Reymann, J. M., Falissard, B., & Naudet, F. (2017). Specific and non-specific effects of psychotherapeutic interventions for depression: Results from a meta-analysis of 84 studies. *Journal of Psychiatric Research, 87*, 95-104.

Pan, A., & others. (2012). Red meat consumption and mortality: Results from 2 prospective cohort studies. *Archives of Internal Medicine, 172*(7), 555-563.

Pansu, P., Régner, I., Max, S., Colé, P., Nezlek, J. B., & Huguet, P. (2016). A burden for the boys: Evidence of stereotype threat in boys' reading performance. *Journal of Experimental Social Psychology, 65*, 26-30. doi:10.1016/j.jesp.2016.02.008

Pant, S., & Ramaswamy, B. (2009). Association of major stressors with elevated risk of breast cancer incidence or relapse. *Drugs Today, 45*(2), 115-126.

Paradies, Y., Ben, J., Denson, N., Elias, A., Priest, N., Pieterse, A., Gupta, A., Kelaher, M., & Gee, G. (2015). Racism as a determinant of health: A systematic review and meta-analysis. *PLoS One, 10*(9), e0138511

Paralympic Movement. (2012). *Believe in yourself.* www.paralympic.org/believe-in-yourself/our-heroes (accessed December 22, 2014)

Parati, G., Lombardi, C., & Narkiewicz, K. (2007). Sleep apnea: Epidemiology, pathophysiology, and relation to cardiovascular risk. *American Journal of Physiology: Regulatory, Integrative and Comparative Physiology, 293*(4), R1671-R1683.

Parikh, S. V., & Huniewicz, P. (2015). E-health: an overview of the uses of the Internet, social media, apps, and websites for mood disorders. *Current opinion in psychiatry, 28*(1), 13-17.

Parish-Morris, J., Golinkoff, R. M., & Hirsh-Pasek, K. (2013). From coo to code: A brief story of language development. In P. D. Zelazo (Ed.), *The Oxford handbook of developmental psychology* (vol. 1, pp. 867–908). New York: Oxford University Press.

Park, C. L. (2012). Meaning making in cancer survivorship. In P. T. P. Wong (Ed.), *Handbook of meaning* (2nd ed.). Thousand Oaks, CA: Sage.

Park, D. C., & Bischof, G. N. (2011). The aging mind: Neuroplasticity in response to cognitive training. *Dialogues in Clinical Neuroscience, 15*(1), 109–119.

Park, D. C., Lodi-Smith, J., Drew, L., Haber, S., Hebrank, A., Bischof, G. N., & Aamodt, W. (2014). The impact of sustained engagement on cognitive function in older adults: The Synapse Project. *Psychological Science, 25*(1), 103–112.

Park, M. (2009, April 4). Teen tries to quiet the voices caused by schizophrenia. *CNN.* www.cnn.com/2009/ HEALTH/04/24/schizophrenia.soloist.brain/index.html (accessed January 6, 2015)

Park, M. J., Paul Mulye, T., Adams, S. H., Brindis, C. D., & Irwin, C. E., Jr. (2006). The health status of young adults in the United States. *Journal of Adolescent Health, 39*(3), 305–317.

Parker, P. S. (2006). *Race, gender, and leadership.* Mahwah, NJ: Erlbaum.

Parks, M. R. (2007). *Personal relationships and personal networks.* Mahwah, NJ: Erlbaum.

Parris, B. A. (2017). The role of frontal executive functions in hypnosis and hypnotic suggestibility. *Psychology Of Consciousness: Theory, Research, And Practice, 4*(2), 211–229. doi:10.1037/cns0000106

Parsons, T. D., Carlew, A. R., Magtoto, J., & Stonecipher, K. (2017). The potential of function-led virtual environments for ecologically valid measures of executive function in experimental and clinical neuropsychology. *Neuropsychological Rehabilitation, 27*(5), 777–807.

Pascalls, O., & Kelly, D. J. (2008). Face processing. In M. M. Haith & J. B. Benson (Eds.), *Encyclopedia of infant and early childhood development.* Oxford, UK: Elsevier.

Pascoe, E.A., & Smart-Richman, L. (2009). Perceived stigmatization and health: A meta-analytic review. *Psychological Bulletin, 135*, 531–544.

Pashler, H. & Harris, C. R. (2012). Is the replicability crisis overblown? Three arguments examined. *Perspectives on Psychological Science, 7*, 531–536.

Pashler, H., McDaniel, M., Rohrer, D., & Bjork, R. (2008). Learning styles: Concepts and evidence. *Psychological Science in the Public Interest, 9*(3), 105–119.

Passer, M. (2017). *Research Methods* (2nd ed.). New York: Macmillan Higher Education.

Patnode, C. D., Evans, C. V., Senger, C. A., Redmond, N., & Lin, J. S. (2017). Behavioral counseling to promote a healthful diet and physical activity for cardiovascular disease prevention in adults without known cardiovascular disease risk factors: Updated evidence report and systematic review for the US Preventive Services Task Force. *JAMA: Journal of the American Medical Association, 318*(2), 175–193.

Pattamadilok, C., Chanoine, V., Pallier, C., Anton, J., Nazarian, B., Belin, P., & Ziegler, J. C. (2017). Automaticity of phonological and semantic processing during visual word recognition. *Neuroimage, 149*, 244–255. doi:10.1016/j.neuroimage.2017.02.003

Patten, C. A., Goggin, K., Harris, K. J., Richter, K. P., Williams, K., Decker, P. A., et al. (2016). Relationship of autonomy social support to quitting motivation in diverse smokers. *Addiction Research & Theory, 24*(6), 477–482. doi:10.3109/16066359.2016.1170815

Patterson, A. C., & Veenstra, G. (2010). Loneliness and risk of mortality: A longitudinal investigation in Alameda County, California. *Social Science & Medicine, 71*(1), 181–186. doi:10.1016/j.socscimed.2010.03.024

Patterson, C. J. (2012). Family lives of lesbian and gay adults. In G. W. Petersen & K. R. Bush (Eds.), *Handbook of marriage and the family.* New York: Springer.

Patterson, C. J. (2013). Family lives of gay and lesbian adults. In G. W. Peterson & K. R. Bush (Eds.), *Handbook of marriage and the family* (3rd ed.). New York: Springer.

Patterson, C. J. (2014). Sexual minority youth and youth with sexual minority parents. In G. B. Melton, A. Ben-Arieh, J. Cashmore, G. S. Goodman, & N. K. Worley (Eds.), *Sage handbook of child research.* Thousand Oaks, CA: Sage.

Patterson, C. J., & Farr, R. H. (2012). Children of lesbian and gay parents: Reflections on the research-policy interface. In H. R. Schaffer & K. Durkin (Eds.), *Blackwell handbook of developmental psychology in action.* New York: Wiley-Blackwell.

Patterson, C. J., & Farr, R. H. (2014). Children of lesbian and gay parents: Reflections on the research-policy interface. In H. R. Schaffer & K. Durkin (Eds.), *Blackwell handbook of developmental psychology in action.* London: Blackwell.

Patterson, C. J., & Wainwright, J. L. (2010). Adolescents with same-sex parents: Findings from the National Longitudinal Study of Adolescent Health. In D. Brodzinsky, A. Pertman, & D. Kunz (Eds.), *Lesbian and gay adoption: A new American reality.* New York: Oxford University Press.

Patterson, C. J., Riskind, R. G., & Tornello, S. L. (2014). Sexual orientation and parenting: A global perspective. In A. Abela & J. Walker (Eds.), *Contemporary issues in family studies.* New York: Wiley.

Patterson, G. R., DeGarmo, D. S., & Knutson, N. (2000). Hyperactive and antisocial behaviors: Comorbid or two points in the same process? *Developmental Psychopathology, 12*, 91–106

Pattillo, R. (2010). Are students as good at multi-tasking as they think? *Nurse Educator, 35*(1), 24.

Paul, A., Chaker, Z., & Doetsch, F. (2017). Hypothalamic regulation of regionally distinct adult neural stem cells and neurogenesis. *Science,* in press.

Paul, E. D., Johnson, P. L., Shekhar, A., & Lowry, C. A. (2014). The Deakin/Graeff hypothesis: Focus on serotonergic inhibition of panic. *Neuroscience and Biobehavioral Reviews, 46* (Pt. 3), 379–396.

Paul, M. A., Gray, G. W., Lieberman, H. R., Love, R. J., Miller, J. C., Trouborst, M., et al. (2011). Phase advance with separate and combined melatonin and light treatment. *Psychopharmcology, 214*(2), 515–523.

Paulhus, D. L., & Jones, D. N. (2017). Individual differences in aggression: The role of dark personalities. In B. J. Bushman (Eds.), *Aggression and violence: A social psychological perspective* (pp. 105–118). New York: Routledge/Taylor & Francis Group.

Pauls, D. L., Abramovitch, A., Rauch, S. L., & Geller, D. A. (2014). Obsessive-compulsive disorder: An integrative genetic and neurobiological perspective. *Nature Reviews: Neuroscience, 15*(6), 410–424.

Paulus, P. B. (1989). An overview and evaluation of group influence. In P. B. Paulus (Ed.), *Psychology of group influence.* Mahwah, NJ: Erlbaum.

Paunonen, S., Jackson, D., Trzebinski, J., & Forserling, F. (1992). Personality structures across cultures: A multimethod evaluation. *Journal of Personality and Social Psychology, 62*(3), 447–456.

Pavani, J., Le Vigouroux, S., Kop, J., Congard, A., & Dauvier, B. (2016). Affect and affect regulation strategies reciprocally influence each other in daily life: The case of positive reappraisal, problem-focused coping, appreciation and rumination. *Journal Of Happiness Studies, 17*(5), 2077–2095. doi:10.1007/s10902-015-9686-9

Pavlov, I. P. (1927). *Conditioned reflexes.* G. V. Anrep (Trans.). New York: Dover.

Pavot, W., & Diener, E. (2008). The Satisfaction with Life Scale and the emerging construct of life satisfaction. *Journal of Positive Psychology, 3*(2), 137–152.

Payne, B. K. (2006). Weapon bias: Split-second decisions and unintended stereotyping. *Current Directions in Psychological Science, 15*(6), 287–291.

Peachman, R.R. (January 31, 2017). Raising a transgender child. *New York Times,* D4.

Pecina, P., & others. (2014). Adaptation of machine translation for multilingual information retrieval in the medical domain. *Artificial Intelligence in Medicine, 61*(3), 165–185.

Peich, M. C., Husain, M., & Bays, P. M. (2013). Age-related decline of precision and binding in visual working memory. *Psychology and Aging, 28*(3), 729–743.

Pejic, T., Hermann, A., Vaitl, D., & Stark, R. (2013). Social anxiety modulates amygdala activation during social conditioning. *Social Cognitive and Affective Neuroscience, 8*(3), 267–276.

Peleg, G., & others. (2006). Hereditary family signature of facial expression. *Proceedings of the National Academy of Sciences USA, 103*(43), 15921–15926.

Pelham, W. E., Smith, B. H., Evans, S. W., Bukstein, O., Gnagy, E. M., Greiner, A. R., & Sibley, M. H. (2017). The effectiveness of short-and long-acting stimulant medications for adolescents with ADHD in a naturalistic secondary school setting. *Journal of Attention Disorders, 21*(1), 40–45.

Pelleymounter, M. A., Cullen, M. J., Baker, M. B., Hecht, R., Winters, D., Boone, T., & Collins, F. (1995). Effects of the obese gene product on body weight regulation in ob/ob mice. *Science, 269*(5223), 540–543.

Pellicano, E., Kenny, L., Brede, J., Klaric, E., Lichwa, H., & McMillin, R. (2017). Executive function predicts school readiness in autistic and typical preschool children. *Cognitive Development, 43*, 1–13.

Penfield, W. (1947). Some observations in the cerebral cortex of man. *Proceedings of the Royal Society, 134*(876), 349.

Peng, P., Namkung, J., Barnes, M., & Sun, C. (2016). A meta-analysis of mathematics and working memory: Moderating effects of working memory domain, type of mathematics skill, and sample characteristics. *Journal Of Educational Psychology, 108*(4), 455–473. doi:10.1037/edu0000079

Pennebaker, J. W. (1997a). *Opening up: The healing power of expressing emotions* (rev. ed.). New York: Guilford.

Pennebaker, J. W. (1997b). Writing about emotional experiences as a therapeutic experience. *Psychological Science, 8*(3), 162–166.

Pennebaker, J. W. (2004). *Writing to heal: A guided journal for recovering from trauma and emotional upheaval.* Oakland, CA: New Harbinger.

Pennebaker, J. W., & Chung, C. K. (2007). Expressive writing, emotional upheavals, and health. In H. S. Friedman & R. C. Silver (Eds.), *Foundations of health psychology* (pp. 263–284). New York: Oxford University Press.

Pennebaker, J. W., & Chung, C. K. (2011). Expressive writing: Connections to physical and mental health. In H. S. Friedman (Ed.), *The Oxford handbook of health psychology* (pp. 417–437). New York: Oxford University Press.

Pennycook, G., & Thompson, V. A. (2017). Base-rate neglect. In R. F. Pohl (Ed.), *Cognitive illusions: Intriguing phenomena in thinking, judgment and memory* (pp. 44–61). New York: Routledge/Taylor & Francis Group.

Perera, F. P., Wheelock, K., Wang, Y., Tang, D., Margolis, A. E., Badia, G., et al. (2018). Combined effects of prenatal exposure to polycyclic aromatic hydrocarbons and material hardship on child ADHD behavior problems. *Environmental Research, 160*, 506–513.

Perkins, D. N. (1984). Creativity by design. *Educational Leadership, 42*(1) 18–25.

Perkins, S. C., Finegood, E. D., & Swain, J. E. (2013). Poverty and language development: Roles of parenting and stress. *Innovations In Clinical Neuroscience, 10*, 10–19.

Perogamvros, L., Baird, B., Seibold, M., Riedner, B., Boly, M., & Tononi, G. (2017). The phenomenal contents and neural correlates of spontaneous thoughts acrosswakefulness, NREM sleep, and REM sleep. *Journal of Cognitive Neuroscience, 29*, 1766–1777

Perry, A., Mankuta, D., & Shamay-Tsoory, S. G. (2015). OT promotes closer interpersonal distance among highly empathic individuals. *Social Cognitive and Affective Neuroscience, 10*(1), 3–9.

Perry, J., VanDenKerkhof, E. G., Wilson, R., & Tripp, D. A. (2017). Guided internet-based psycho-educational intervention using cognitive behavioral therapy and self-management for individuals with chronic pain: A feasibility study. *Pain Management Nursing, 18*(3), 179–189.

Perszyk, D.R., & Waxman, S. R., (2018). Linking Language and Cognition in Infancy. *Annual Review of Psychology, 69*. In press.

Pert, C. B. (1999). *Molecules of emotion.* New York: Simon & Schuster.

Pert, C. B., & Snyder, S. H. (1973). Opiate receptor: Demonstration in a nervous tissue. *Science, 179*(4077), 1011.

Petersen, J. L., & Hyde, J. S. (2010). A meta-analytic review of research on gender differences in sexuality, 1973–2007. *Psychological Bulletin, 136*(1), 21–38.

Petersen, J. L., & Hyde, J. S. (2011). Gender differences in sexual attitudes and behaviors: A review of meta-analytic results and large datasets. *Journal of Sex Research, 48*(2–3), 149–165. doi:10.1080/00224499.2011.551851

Peterson, A. C., Zhang, S., Hu, S., Chao, H. H., & Li, C. S. R. (2017). The effects of age, from young to middle adulthood, and gender on resting state functional connectivity of the dopaminergic midbrain. *Frontiers in Human Neuroscience, 11.*

Peterson, M. H., Griffith, R. L., Isaacson, J. A., O'Connell, M. S., & Mangos, P. M. (2011). Applicant faking, social desirability, and the prediction of counterproductive work behaviors. *Human Performance, 24*(3), 270–290.

Peterson, S. J., Van Tongeren, D. R., Womack, S. D., Hook, J. N., Davis, D. E., & Griffin, B. J. (2017). The benefits of self-forgiveness on mental health: Evidence from correlational and experimental research. *The Journal of Positive Psychology, 12*, 159–168. doi:10.1080/17439760.2016.1163407

Petrulis, A. (2013). Chemosignals and hormones in the neural control of mammalian sexual behavior. *Frontiers In Neuroendocrinology, 34*(4), 255–267.

Petticrew, M., Bell, R., & Hunter, D. (2002). Influence of psychological coping on survival and recurrence in people with cancer: Systematic review. *British Medical Journal, 325*(7372), 1066–1069.

Pettigrew, T. F., & Tropp, L. R. (2006). A meta-analytic test of intergroup contact theory. *Journal of Personality and Social Psychology, 90*(5), 751–783.

Petty, R. E., & Briñol, P. (2015). Processes of social influence through attitude change. In M. Mikulincer, P. R. Shaver, E. Borgida, & J. A. Bargh, M. (Eds.), *APA handbook of personality and social psychology, Volume 1: Attitudes and social cognition* (pp. 509–545). Washington, DC: American Psychological Association. doi:10.1037/14341-016

Petty, R. E., & Cacioppo, J. T. (1986). The elaboration likelihood of persuasion. In L. Berkowitz (Ed.), *Advances in experimental social psychology* (vol. 19). New York: Academic.

Pettygrove, D.M., Hammond, S.I., Karahuta, E.L., Waugh, W.E., & Brownell, C. (2013). From cleaning up to helping out: Parental socialization and children's early prosocial behavior. *Infant Behavior and Development, 36*, 843–846. doi:10.1016/j.infbeh.2013.09.005se

Peyton, C., Yang, E., Msall, M. E., Adde, L., Støen, R., Fjørtoft, T., et al. (2017). White matter injury and general movements in high-risk preterm infants. *American Journal of Neuroradiology, 38*(1), 162–169.

Pezdek, K. (2003). Event memory and autobiographical memory for the events of September 11, 2001. *Applied Cognitive Psychology, 17*(9), 1033–1045.

Pezzo, M. V. (2011). Hindsight bias: A primer for motivational researchers. *Social and Personality Psychology Compass, 5*(9), 665–678.

Peñate, W., Fumero, A., Viña, C., Herrero, M., Marrero, R. J., & Rivero, F. (2017). A meta-analytic review of neuroimaging studies of specific phobia to small animals. *The European Journal of Psychiatry, 31*(1), 23–36.

Pfeffer, M., Korf, H. W., & Wicht, H. (2017). Synchronizing effects of melatonin on diurnal and circadian rhythms. *General and Comparative Endocrinology.* In press.

Phelan, S., Hill, J. O., Lang, W., Dibello, J. R., & Wing, R. R. (2003). Recovery from relapse among successful weight maintainers. *American Journal of Clinical Nutrition, 78*(6), 1079–1084.

Phillips, D. A., & Lowenstein, A. (2011). Early care, education, and child development. *Annual Review of Psychology* (vol. 62, pp. 119–142). Palo Alto, CA: Annual Reviews.

Phillips, K. A., Osborne, R. H., Giles, G. G., Dite, G. S., Apicella, C., Hopper, J. L., & Milne, R. L. (2008). Psychosocial factors and survival of young women with breast cancer: A population-based prospective cohort study. *Journal of Clinical Oncology, 26*(28), 4666–4671.

Phillips, K. J., & Mudford, O. C. (2008). Functional analysis skills training for residential caregivers. *Behavioral Interventions, 23*(1), 1–12.

Piaget, J. (1952). *The origins of intelligence in children.* New York: Oxford University Press

Picchioni, D., Reith, R. M., Nadel, J. L., & Smith, C. B. (2014). Sleep, plasticity, and the pathophysiology of neurodevelopmental disorders: The potential roles of protein synthesis and other cellular processes. *Brain Sciences, 4*(1), 150–201.

Piekarski, D. J., Johnson, C. M., Boivin, J. R., Thomas, A. W., Lin, W. C., Delevich, K., et al. (2017). Does puberty mark a transition in sensitive periods for plasticity in the associative neocortex? *Brain research, 1654*, 123–144.

Pierz, K. A., & Thase, M. E. (2014). A review of vilazodone, serotonin, and major depressive disorder. *Primary Care Companion to the Journal of Clinical Psychiatry, 16*(1). doi:10.4088/PCC.13r01554

Pietschnig, J., & Voracek, M. (2015). One century of global IQ gains: A formal meta-analysis of the Flynn effect (1909–2013). *Perspectives On Psychological Science, 10*(3), 282–306. doi:10.1177/1745691615577701

Piff, P. K., Kraus, M. W., Côté, S., Cheng, B. H., & Keltner, D. (2010). Having less, giving more: The influence of social class on prosocial behavior. *Journal of Personality and Social Psychology, 99*(5), 771–784.

Pike, K. M., Yamamiya, Y., & Konishi, H. (2011). Eating disorders in Japan: Cultural context, clinical features, and future directions. In R. H. Striegel-Moore, S. A. Wonderlich, B. T. Walsh, & J. E. Mitchell (Eds.), *Developing an evidence-based classification of eating disorders: Scientific findings for DSM-5* (pp. 335–349). Washington, DC: American Psychiatric Association.

Pikhartova, J., Bowling, A., & Victor, C. (2016). Is loneliness in later life a self-fulfilling prophecy? *Aging & Mental Health, 20*(5), 543–549. doi:10.1080/13607863.2015.1023767

Pilecki, B., Arentoft, A., & McKay, D. (2011). An evidence-based causal model of panic disorder. *Journal of Anxiety Disorders, 25*(3), 381–388.

Piliavin, J. A., & Siegl, E. (2015). Health and well-being consequences of formal volunteering. In D. A. Schroeder & W. G. Graziano (Eds.), *The Oxford handbook of prosocial behavior.* New York: Oxford University Press.

Pillemer, D. B. (1998). *Momentous events: Vivid memories.* Cambridge, MA: Harvard University Press.

Pina, M. M., & Cunningham, C. L. (2017). Ethanol-seeking behavior is expressed directly through an extended amygdala to midbrain neural circuit. *Neurobiology of Learning And Memory, 13*, 783–791. doi:10.1016/j.nlm.2016.11.013

Pinciotti, C. M., & Orcutt, H. K. (2017). Rape aggression defense: Unique self-efficacy benefits for survivors of sexual trauma. *Violence against women,* in press. https://doi.org/10.1177/1077801217708885107780121770885.

Pinker, S. (1994). *The language instinct.* New York: HarperCollins.

Pinquart, M. (2017). Associations of parenting dimensions and styles with externalizing problems of children and adolescents: An updated meta-analysis. *Developmental Psychology, 53*(5), 873–932. http://dx.doi.org/10.1037/dev0000295

Pinquart, M., & Kauser, R. (2018). Do the associations of parenting styles with behavior problems and academic achievement vary by culture? Results from a meta-analysis. *Cultural Diversity and Ethnic Minority Psychology,* in press. doi:10.1037/cdp0000149

Piolino, P., Desgranges, B., Clarys, D., Guillery-Girard, B., Taconnat, L., Isingrini, M., & Eustache, F. (2006). Autobiographical memory, autonoetic consciousness, and self-perspective in aging. *Psychology and Aging, 21*(3), 510–525.

Piper, M. E., Cook, J. W., Schlam, T. R., Smith, S. S., Bolt, D. M., Collins, L. M., et al. (2017). Toward precision smoking cessation treatment II: Proximal effects of smoking cessation intervention components on putative mechanisms of action. *Drug and Alcohol Dependence, 17*, 150–158. doi:10.1016/j.drugalcdep.2016.11.027

Piqueras-Fiszman, B., & Spence, C. (2015). Sensory expectations based on product-extrinsic food cues: An interdisciplinary review of the empirical evidence and theoretical accounts. *Food Quality and Preference, 40*(Pt A), 165–179. doi:10.1016/j.foodqual.2014.09.013

Pittenger, D. J. (2005). Cautionary comments regarding the Myers-Briggs Type Indicator. *Consulting Psychology Journal: Practice and Research, 57*(3), 210–221. doi:10.1037/1065-9293.57.3.210

Pitts, B. L., Safer, M. A., Russell, D. W., & Castro-Chapman, P. L. (2016). Effects of hardiness and years of military service on posttraumatic stress symptoms in U.S. Army medics. *Military Psychology, 28*(4), 278–284. doi:10.1037/mil0000106

Place, S. S., Todd, P. M., Zhuang, J., Penke, L., & Asendorpf, J. B. (2012). Judging romantic interest of others from thin slices is a cross-cultural ability. *Evolution and Human Behavior, 33*(5), 547–550.

Plasencia, M. L., Taylor, C. T., & Alden, L. E. (2016). Unmasking one's true self facilitates positive relational outcomes: Authenticity promotes social approach processes in social anxiety disorder. *Clinical Psychological Science, 4*(6), 1002–1014.

Pliatsikas, C., Johnstone, T., & Marinis, T. (2014). FMRI evidence for the involvement of the procedural memory system in morphological processing of a second language. *PLoS One, 9*(5), e97298.

Plotnikoff, R. C., Lubans, D. R., Costigan, S. A., Trinh, L., Spence, J. C., Downs, S., & McCargar, L. (2011). A test of the theory of planned behavior to explain physical activity in a large population sample of adolescents from Alberta, Canada. *Journal of Adolescent Health, 49*(5), 547–549.

Poh, J. H., & Chee, M. W. (2017). Degradation of cortical representations during encoding following sleep deprivation. *Neuroimage, 153*, 131–138.

Poile, C. (2017). Why would I help my coworker? Exploring asymmetric task dependence and the self-determination theory internalization process. *Journal of Experimental Psychology: Applied, 23*(3), 354–368. doi:10.1037/xap0000128

Polverino, A., Grimaldi, M., Sorrentino, P., Jacini, F., D'Ursi, A. M., & Sorrentino, G. (2017). Effects of Acetylcholine on β-Amyloid-Induced cPLA2 Activation in the TB Neuroectodermal Cell Line: Implications for the Pathogenesis of Alzheimer's Disease. *Cellular and Molecular Neurobiology*, in press. doi: 10.1007/s10571-017-0555-4

Pomerantz, E. M., Saxon, J. L., & Oishi, S. (2000). The psychological trade-offs of goal investment. *Journal of Personality and Social Psychology*, 79(4), 617–630.

Pompili, M., & others. (2007). Suicide risk in schizophrenia: Learning from the past to change the future. *Annals of General Psychiatry*, 6, 10.

Poprac, P., Jomova, K., Simunkova, M., Kollar, V., Rhodes, C. J., & Valko, M. (2017). Targeting free radicals in oxidative stress-related human diseases. *Trends in Pharmacological Sciences*, 38, 592–607

Porcerelli, J. H., Cramer, P., Porcerelli, D. J., & Arterbery, V. E. (2017). Defense mechanisms and utilization in cancer patients undergoing radiation therapy: A pilot study. *Journal of Nervous and Mental Disease*, 205(6), 466–470. doi:10.1097/NMD.0000000000000674

Posner, J., Russell, J., & Peterson, B. S. (2005). The circumplex model of affect: An integrative approach to affective neuroscience, cognitive development, and psychopathology. *Developmental Psychopathology*, 17(3), 715–734.

Posporelis, S., Coughlin, J. M., Marsman, A., Pradhan, S., Tanaka, T., Wang, H., et al. (2017). Decoupling of brain temperature and glutamate in recent onset of schizophrenia: A 7T proton magnetic resonance spectroscopy study. *Biological Psychiatry: Cognitive Neuroscience and Neuroimaging. in press.* doi: 10.1016/j.bpsc.2017.04.003

Post, J. M., & Panis, L. K. (2011). Crimes of obedience: "Groupthink" at Abu Ghraib. *International Journal of Group Psychotherapy*, 61(1), 48–66.

Post, R. M., Altshuler, L. L., Kupka, R., McElroy, S. L., Frye, M. A., Rowe, M., et al. (2017). More childhood onset bipolar disorder in the United States than Canada or Europe: Implications for treatment and prevention. *Neuroscience & Biobehavioral Reviews*, 74, Part A, 204–213

Potter, C., Ferriday, D., Griggs, R. L., Hamilton-Shield, J. P., Rogers, P. J., & Brunstrom, J. M. (2017). Parental beliefs about portion size, not children's own beliefs, predict child BMI. *Pediatric Obesity. in press.*

Potter, N. N. (2012). Mad, bad, or virtuous? The moral, cultural, and pathologizing features of deviance. *Theory & Psychology*, 22(1), 23–45.

Powell, B., Cooper, G., Hoffman, K., & Marvin, B. (2014). *The circle of security intervention: Enhancing attachment in early parent–child relationships.* New York: Guilford.

Powell, R. A., & Honey, P. L. (2013). *Introduction to learning and behavior* (4th ed.). Boston: Cengage.

Power, R. A., Parkhill, J., & de Oliveira, T. (2017). Microbial genome-wide association studies: Lessons from human GWAS. *Nature Reviews Genetics*, 18(1), 41–50.

Poyatos-León, R., García-Hermoso, A., Sanabria-Martínez, G., Álvarez-Bueno, C., Cavero-Redondo, I., & Martínez-Vizcaíno, V. (2017). Effects of exercise-based interventions on postpartum depression: A meta-analysis of randomized controlled trials. *Birth: Issues In Perinatal Care*, in press. doi:10.1111/birt.12294

Preckel, F., Baudson, T. G., Krolak-Schwerdt, S., & Glock, S. (2015). Gifted and maladjusted? Implicit attitudes and automatic associations related to gifted children. *American Educational Research Journal*, 52(6), 1160–1184. doi:10.3102/0002831215596413

Preckel, F., Lipnevich, A. A., Boehme, K., Brandner, L., Georgi, K., Könen, T., & ... Roberts, R. D. (2013). Morningness-eveningness and educational outcomes: The lark has an advantage over the owl at high school.

British Journal of Educational Psychology, 83(1), 114–134. doi:10.1111/j.2044-8279.2011.02059.x

Preckel, K., Kanske, P., & Singer, T. (2018). On the interaction of social affect and cognition: empathy, compassion and theory of mind. *Current Opinion in Behavioral Sciences*, 19, 1–6.

Preller, K. H., Herdener, M., Pokorny, T., Planzer, A., Kraehenmann, R., Stämpfli, P., ... & Vollenweider, F. X. (2017). The fabric of meaning and subjective effects in LSD-induced states depend on serotonin 2A receptor activation. *Current Biology*, 27(3), 451–457.

Presti, D.E. (2016). *Foundational concepts in neuroscience: A brain-mind odyssey (Norton Series on Interpersonal Neurobiology) 1st ed.* New York: W.W. Norton.

Price, C. C., Garvan, C., Hizel, L. P., Lopez, M. G., Billings, I. V., & Frederic, T. (2017). Delayed recall and working memory MMSE domains predict delirium following cardiac surgery. *Journal of Alzheimer's Disease*, 59(3), 1027–1035.

Price, D. D., Finniss, D. G., & Benedetti, F. (2008). A comprehensive review of the placebo effect. *Annual Review of Psychology* (vol. 59). (pp. 565–590). Palo Alto, CA: Annual Reviews.

Price-Blackshear, M. A., Kamble, S. V., Mudhol, V., Sheldon, K. M., & Bettencourt, B. A. (2017). Mindfulness Practices Moderate the Association Between Intergroup Anxiety and Outgroup Attitudes. *Mindfulness*, 8, 1172–1183.

Prieto, G. A., Trieu, B. H., Dang, C. T., Bilousova, T., Gylys, K. H., Berchtold, N. C., et al. (2017). Pharmacological rescue of long-term potentiation in Alzheimer diseased synapses. *Journal of Neuroscience*, 37(5), 1197–1212.

Prochaska, J. O., & Norcross, J. C. (2013). *Systems of psychotherapy: A transtheoretical analysis* (8th ed.). Boston: Cengage.

Prochaska, J. O., Norcross, J. C., & DiClemente, C. C. (2013). Applying the stages of change. In G. P. Koocher, J. C. Norcross, & B. A. Greene (Eds.), *Psychologists' desk reference, 3rd ed* (pp. 176–181). New York: Oxford University Press.

Pronk, T. M., Karremans, J. C., Overbeek, G., Vermulst, A. A., & Wigboldus, D. H. J. (2010). What it takes to forgive: When and why executive functioning facilitates forgiveness. *Journal of Personality and Social Psychology*, 98(1), 119–131.

Protzko, J., Aronson, J., & Blair, C. (2013). How to make a young child smarter: Evidence from the Database of Raising Intelligence. *Perspectives on Psychological Science*, 8(1), 25–40.

Provenzo, E. F. (2002). *Teaching, learning, and schooling in American culture: A critical perspective.* Boston: Allyn & Bacon.

Przybylski, A. K., Deci, E. L., Rigby, C. S., & Ryan, R. M. (2014). Competence-impeding electronic games and players' aggressive feelings, thoughts, and behaviors. *Journal of Personality and Social Psychology*, 106(3), 441–457. doi:10.1037/a0034820

Pun, A., Ferera, M., Diesendruck, G., Hamlin, J.K., & Baron, A.S. (2017). Foundations of infants' social group evaluations. *Developmental Science. in press.* doi: 10.1111/desc.12586

Putilov, A. A. (2017). Owls, larks, swifts, woodcocks and they are not alone: A historical review of methodology for multidimensional self-assessment of individual differences in sleep-wake pattern. *Chronobiology International*, 34(3), 426–437. doi:10.1080/07420528.2017.1278704

Putnam, S. P., & Gartstein, M. A. (2017). Aggregate temperament scores from multiple countries: Associations with aggregate personality traits, cultural dimensions, and allelic frequency. *Journal of Research in Personality*, 67, 157–170.

Putz, Á., Palotai, R., Csertő, I., & Bereczkei, T. (2016). Beauty stereotypes in social norm enforcement: The effect of attractiveness on third-party punishment and reward.

Personality and Individual Differences, 88, 230–235. doi:10.1016/j.paid.2015.09.025

Pyszczynski, T., Greenberg, J., Solomon, S., Arndt, J., & Schimel, J. (2004). Why do people need self-esteem? A theoretical and empirical review. *Psychological Bulletin*, 130(3), 435–468.

Pyszora, N. M., Fahy, T., & Kopelman, M. D. (2014). Amnesia for violent offenses: Factors underlying memory loss and recovery. *Journal of the American Academy of Psychiatry and Law*, 42(2), 202–213.

Q

Qadri, M. A., Asen, Y., & Cook, R. G. (2014). Visual control of an action discrimination in pigeons. *Journal of Vision*, 14(5), 16.

Qayyum, A., Zai, C. C., Hirata, Y., Tiwari, A. K., Cheema, S., Nowrouzi, B., et al. (2015). The role of the catechol-o-methyltransferase (COMT) gene Val158Met in aggressive behavior, a review of genetic studies. *Current Neuropharmacology*, 13(6), 802–814. doi:10.2174/1570159X13666150612225836

Qi, Z., Beach, S. D., Finn, A. S., Minas, J., Goetz, C., Chan, B., & Gabrieli, J. D. (2017). Native-language N400 and P600 predict dissociable language-learning abilities in adults. *Neuropsychologia*, 98, 177–191. doi:10.1016/j.neuropsychologia.2016.10.005

Qiu, A., Mori, S., & Miller, M. I. (2015). Diffusion tensor imaging for understanding brain development: Why and how. *Annual Review of Psychology* (vol. 66). Palo Alto, CA: Annual Reviews.

Qiu, C., & others. (2014). Role of psychosocial factors and serotonin transporter genotype in male adolescent criminal activity. *Asia-Pacific Psychiatry*, 6(3), 284–291.

Qiu, X., Martin, G.B., & Blache, D. (2017). Gene polymorphisms associated with temperament. *Journal of Neurogenetics*, 31, 1–16.

Quilty, L. C., DeYoung, C. G., Oakman, J. M., & Bagby, R. M. (2014). Extraversion and behavioral activation: Integrating the components of approach. *Journal of Personality Assessment*, 96(1), 87–94. doi:10.1080/00223891.2013.834440

Quilty, L. C., Taylor, G. J., McBride, C., & Bagby, R. M. (2017). Relationships among alexithymia, therapeutic alliance, and psychotherapy outcome in major depressive disorder. *Psychiatry Research*, 254, 75–79.

R

Raabe, T., & Beelmann, A. (2011). Development of ethnic, racial, and national prejudice in childhood and adolescence: A multinational meta-analysis of age differences. *Child Development*, 82(6), 1715–1737. doi:10.1111/j.1467-8624.2011.01668.x

Rabeyron, T. (2014). Retro-priming, priming, and double testing: Psi and replication in a test-retest design. *Frontiers in Human Neuroscience.* doi: 10.3389/fnhum.2014.00154

Racine, M., Tousignant-Laflamme, Y., Kloda, L. A., Dion, D., Dupuis, G., & Choinière, M. (2012a). A systematic literature review of 10 years of research on sex/gender and experimental pain perception—Part 1: Are there really differences between women and men? *Pain*, 153(3), 619–635.

Racine, M., Tousignant-Laflamme, Y., Kloda, L. A., Dion, D., Dupuis, G., & Choinière, M. (2012b). A systematic literature review of 10 years of research on sex/gender and pain perception—Part 2: Do biopsychosocial factors alter pain sensitivity differently in women and men? *Pain*, 153(3), 619–635.

Racsmány, M., Conway, M. A., & Demeter, G. (2010). Consolidation of episodic memory during sleep: Long-term effects of retrieval practice. *Psychological Science*, 21(1), 80–85.

Radke, S., Hoffstaedter, F., Löffler, L., Kogler, L., Schneider, F., Blechert, J., & Derntl, B. (2017). Imaging the up's and down's of emotion regulation in lifetime depression. *Brain Imaging and Behavior*, in press.

Rai, T. S., & Fiske, A. P. (2011). Moral psychology is relationship regulation: Moral motives for unity, hierarchy, equality, and proportionality. *Psychological Review, 118*(1), 57–75.

Railo, H., Andersson, E., Kaasinen, V., Laine, T., & Koivisto, M. (2014). Unlike in clinical blindsight patients, unconscious processing of chromatic information depends on early visual cortex in healthy humans. *Brain Stimulation, 7*(3), 415–420.

Raine, A., & Venables, P. H. (2017). Adolescent daytime sleepiness as a risk factor for adult crime. *Journal of Child Psychology and Psychiatry, 58*(6), 728–735.

Raine, A., Venables, P. H., & Williams, M. (1990). Relationships between N1, P300, and contingent negative variation recorded at age 15 and criminal behavior at age 24. *Psychophysiology, 27*(5), 567–575.

Rais, M., Cahn, W., Schnack, H. G., Hulshoff Pol, H. E., Kahn, R. S., & van Haren, N. E. (2012). Brain volume reductions in medication-naïve patients with schizophrenia in relation to intelligence quotient. *Psychological Medicine, 42*(9), 1847–1856.

Rajsic, J., Taylor, J. T., & Pratt, J. (2017). Out of sight, out of mind: Matching bias underlies confirmatory visual search. *Attention, Perception, & Psychophysics, 79*(2), 498–507. doi:10.3758/s13414-016-1259-4

Ramberg, M., Stanley, B., Ystgaard, M., & Mehlum, L. (2014). Depressed suicide attempters with posttraumatic stress disorder. *Archives of Suicide Research.* PMID: 25058681

Ramirez-Esparza, N., Gosling, S. D., Benet-Martinez, V., Potter, J. P., & Pennebaker, J. W. (2006). Do bilinguals have two personalities? A special case of cultural frame switching. *Journal of Research in Personality, 40*(2), 99–120.

Ramsey, J. L., Langlois, J. H., Hoss, R. A., Rubenstein, A. J., & Griffin, A. M. (2004). Origins of a stereotype: Categorization of facial attractiveness by 6-month-old infants. *Developmental Science, 7*(2), 201–211.

Ramírez-Esparza, N., García-Sierra, A., & Kuhl, P. K. (2014). Look who's talking: Speech style and social context in language input to infants are linked to concurrent and future speech development. *Developmental Science, 17*(6), 880–891. doi:10.1111/desc.12172

Rand, D. G. (2016). Cooperation, fast and slow: Meta-analytic evidence for a theory of social heuristics and self-interested deliberation. *Psychological Science, 27*(9), 1192–1206. doi:10.1177/0956797616654455

Rand, D. G., Brescoll, V. L., Everett, J. C., Capraro, V., & Barcelo, H. (2016). Social heuristics and social roles: Intuition favors altruism for women but not for men. *Journal of Experimental Psychology: General, 145*(4), 389–396. doi:10.1037/xge0000154

Randler, C., Schredl, M., Göritz, A.S. (2017). Chronotype, sleep behavior, and the big five personality factors. *SAGE Open, 7*(3).

Ranebo, M. C., Hallgren, H. C. B., Norlin, R., & Adolfsson, L. E. (2017). Clinical and structural outcome 22 years after acromioplasty without tendon repair in patients with subacromial pain and cuff tears. *Journal of Shoulder and Elbow Surgery.* in press.

Rapaport, D. (1967). On the psychoanalytic theory of thinking. In M. M. Gill (Ed.), *The collected papers of David Rapaport.* New York: Basic.

Rapaport, S. (1994, November 28). Interview. *U.S. News and World Report,* 94.

Rappaport, S. J., Riddoch, M. J., Chechlacz, M., & Humphreys, G. W. (2016). Unconscious familiarity-based color-form binding: Evidence from visual extinction. *Journal of Cognitive Neuroscience, 28*(3), 501–516. doi:10.1162/jocn_a_00904

Rasga, C., Quelhas, A. C., & Byrne, R. M. (2017). How children with autism reason about other's intentions: False-belief and counterfactual inferences. *Journal of Autism and Developmental Disorders, 47*(6), 1806–1817.

Rasmussen, K. A., & Wingate, L. R. (2011). The role of optimism in the interpersonal-psychological theory of suicidal behavior. *Suicide and Life-Threatening Behavior, 41*(2), 137–148.

Rasskazova, E., Ivanova, T., & Sheldon, K. (2016). Comparing the effects of low-level and high-level worker need-satisfaction: A synthesis of the self-determination and Maslow need theories. *Motivation And Emotion, 40*(4), 541–555. doi:10.1007/s11031-016-9557-7

Ratcliff, R., & Van Dongen, H. P. A. (2017). The Effects of Sleep Deprivation on Item and Associative Recognition Memory. *Journal of Experimental Psychology: Learning, Memory, and Cognition.*in press. doi:10.1037/xlm0000452

Rathbone, C. J., O'Connor, A. R., & Moulin, C. J. (2017). The tracks of my years: Personal significance contributes to the reminiscence bump. *Memory & Cognition, 45*(1), 137–150.

Rathunde, K. (2010). Experimental wisdom and optimal experience: Interviews with three distinguished lifelong learners. *Journal of Adult Development, 17*(2), 81–93.

Ratner, K. G., & Way, B. M. (2013). Unselfish genes? The quest to uncover genomic influences on prosocial behavior. *Social Neuroscience, 8*(5), 397–399.

Ratner, N. B. (1993). Learning to speak. *Science, 262*(5131), 260.

Raven, F., Van der Zee, E. A., Meerlo, P., & Havekes, R. (2017). The role of sleep in regulating structural plasticity and synaptic strength: Implications for memory and cognitive function. *Sleep Medicine Review*s. in press.

Raver, C. C., Roy, A. L., & Pressler, E. (2015). Struggling to stay afloat: Dynamic models of poverty-related adversity and child outcomes. In S. McClanahan (Ed.), *Diverging destinies: Families in an era of increasing inequality.* New York: Springer.

Ravizza, S. M., Uitvlugt, M. G., & Fenn, K. M. (2017). The negative effects of laptop internet use during class. *Neuroscience Letters, 637,* 44–49.

Rawlins, W. K., & Russell, L. D. (2013). Friendship, positive being-with-others, and the edifying practices of storytelling and dialogue. In M. Hojjat & D. Cramer (Eds.), *Positive psychology and love.* New York: Oxford University Press.

Ray, J. V., Frick, P. J., Thornton, L. C., Wall Myers, T. D., Steinberg, L., & Cauffman, E. (2017). Callous-unemotional traits predict self-reported offending in adolescent boys: The mediating role of delinquent peers and the moderating role of parenting practices. *Developmental Psychology, 53*(2), 319–328.

Raynor, H. A., Jeffrey, R. W., Phelan, S., Hill, J. O., & Wing, R. R. (2005). Amount of food groups variety consumed in the diet and long-term weight loss maintenance. *Obesity Research, 13*(5), 883–890.

Raz, A., Schweizer, H. R., Zhu, H., & Bowles, E. N. (2010). Hypnotic dreams as a lens into hypnotic dynamics. *International Journal of Clinical and Experimental Hypnosis, 58*(1), 69–81.

Read, J., & Arnold, C. (2017). Is electroconvulsive therapy for depression more effective than placebo? A systematic review of studies since 2009. *Ethical Human Psychology and Psychiatry, 19*(1), 5–23.

Reber, R., & Greifeneder, R. (2017). Processing fluency in education: How metacognitive feelings shape learning, belief formation, and affect. *Educational Psychologist, 52*(2), 84–103.

Rebok, G. W., & others. (2014). Ten-year effects of the advanced cognitive training for independent and vital elderly cognitive training trial on cognition and everyday functioning in older adults. *Journal of the American Geriatrics Society, 62*(1), 16–24.

Recanzone, G. H., & Sutter, M. L. (2008). The biological basis of audition. *Annual Review of Psychology* (vol. 59). Palo Alto, CA: Annual Reviews.

Reese, E. (2013). *Tell me a story: Sharing stories to enrich your child's world.* New York, NY: Oxford University Press.

Reeve, C. L., & Charles, J. E. (2008). Survey of opinions on the primacy of g and social consequences of ability testing: A comparison of expert and non-expert views. *Intelligence, 36*(6), 681–688.

Reeves, A., McKee, M., & Stuckler, D. (2014). Economic suicides in the Great Recession in Europe and North America. *British Journal of Psychiatry, 205*(3), 246–247.

Regel, S., Kotz, S. A., Henseler, I., & Friederici, A. D. (2017). Left inferior frontal gyrus mediates morphosyntax: ERP evidence from verb processing in left-hemisphere damaged patients. *Cortex, 86,* 156–171.

Reggia, J. A. (2013). The rise of machine consciousness: Studying consciousness with computational models. *Neural Networks, 44,* 112–131.

Reichardt, C. S. (2009). Quasi-experimental designs. In R. E. Millsap & A. Maydeu-Olivares (Eds.), *The Sage handbook of quantitative methods* (pp. 46–71). Thousand Oaks, CA: Sage.

Reichel, J. M., Bedenk, B. T., Czisch, M., & Wotjak, C. T. (2017). Age-related cognitive decline coincides with accelerated volume loss of the dorsal but not ventral hippocampus in mice. *Hippocampus, 27*(1), 28–35.

Reid, V. M., Kaduk, K., & Lunn, J. (2018). Links between action perception and action production in 10-week-old infants. *Neuropsychologia.* in press.

Reidy, P. F., Kristensen, K., Winn, M. B., Litovsky, R. Y., & Edwards, J. R. (2017). The acoustics of word-initial fricatives and their effect on word-level intelligibility in children with bilateral cochlear implants. *Ear and Hearing, 38*(1), 42–56.

Reiman, E. M., Fusselman, M. J., Fox, P. T., & Raichle, M. E. (1989). Neuroanatomical correlates of anticipatory anxiety. *Science, 243*(4894 Pt. 1), 1071–1074.

Reimann, M., Bechara, A., & MacInnis, D. (2015). Leveraging the happy meal effect: Substituting food with modest nonfood incentives decreases portion size choice. *Journal of Experimental Psychology: Applied, 21*(3), 276–286. doi:10.1037/xap0000054

Reinders, M. J., Huitink, M., Dijkstra, S. C., Maaskant, A. J., & Heijnen, J. (2017). Menu-engineering in restaurants-adapting portion sizes on plates to enhance vegetable consumption: a real-life experiment. *International Journal of Behavioral Nutrition and Physical Activity, 14*(1), 41.

Reinoso Carvalho, F., Wang, Q., van Ee, R., Persoone, D., & Spence, C. (2017). 'Smooth operator': Music modulates the perceived creaminess, sweetness, and bitterness of chocolate. *Appetite, 108,* 383–390. doi:10.1016/j.appet.2016.10.026

Reinoso-Suárez, F., De Andrés, I., Rodrigo-Angulo, M. L., De la Roza, C., Nuñez, A., & Garzón, M. (2018). The anatomy of dreaming, and REM sleep. *European Journal of Anatomy, 3*(3), 163–175.

Reis, H. T., & Lee, K. Y. (2016). Promise, peril, and perspective: Addressing concerns about reproducibility in social-personality psychology. *Journal of Experimental Social Psychology, 66,* 148–152.

Reitz, A. K., Motti-Stefanidi, F., & Asendorpf, J. B. (2016). Me, us, and them: Testing sociometer theory in a socially diverse real-life context. *Journal of Personality and Social Psychology, 110*(6), 908–920. doi:10.1037/pspp0000073

Rendell, P. G., & Craik, F. I. M. (2000). Virtual week and actual week: Age-related differences in prospective memory. *Applied Cognitive Psychology, 14*(7), S43–S62.

Rennie, B., Beebe-Frankenberger, M., & Swanson, H. L. (2014). A longitudinal study of neuropsychological functioning and academic achievement in children with and without signs of attention-deficit/hyperpectivity disorder. *Journal of Clinical and Experimental Neuropsychology, 36*(6), 621–635.

Rescorla, R. A. (1966). Predictability and number of pairings in Pavlovian fear conditioning. *Psychonomic Science, 4*(11), 383-384.

Rescorla, R. A. (1988). Pavlovian conditioning: It's not what you think it is. *American Psychologist, 43*(3), 151-160.

Rescorla, R. A. (2003). Contemporary study of Pavlovian conditioning. *Spanish Journal of Psychology, 6*(2), 185-195.

Rescorla, R. A. (2005). Spontaneous recovery of excitation but not inhibition. *Journal of Experimental Psychology: Animal Behavior Processes, 31*(3), 277-288.

Rescorla, R. A. (2009). A theory of Pavlovian conditioning: Variations in the effectiveness of reinforcement and nonreinforcement. In D. Shanks (Ed.), *Psychology of learning.* Thousand Oaks, CA: Sage.

Rescorla, R. A., & Wagner, A. R. (2009). A theory of attention: Variations in the associability of stimuli with reinforcement. In D. Shanks (Ed.), *Psychology of learning.* Thousand Oaks, CA: Sage.

Resnik, K., Bradbury, D., Barnes, G. R., & Leff, A. P. (2014). Between thought and expression, a magnetoencephalography study of the "tip-of-the-tongue" phenomenon. *Journal of Cognitive Neuroscience, 26*(10), 2210-2223.

Reuter-Lorenz, P., & Davidson, R. J. (1981). Differential contributions of the two cerebral hemispheres to the perception of happy and sad faces. *Neuropsychologia, 19*(4), 609-613.

Revell, T. (May 31, 2017). AI will be able to beat us at everything by 2060, say experts. *New Scientist.* https://www.newscientist.com/article/2133188-ai-will-be-able-to-beat-us-at-everything-by-2060-say-experts/

Reyna, V. F., & Zayas, V. (Eds.). (2014). *The neuroscience of risky decision making.* Washington, DC: American Psychological Association.

Reynolds, G. (January 13, 2016). To better cope with stress, listen to your body. *The New York Times.* https://well.blogs.nytimes.com/2016/01/13/to-better-cope-with-stress-listen-to-your-body/?mcubz=3&_r=0

Reynolds, G. D., & Richards, J. E. (2018). Infant Visual Attention and Stimulus Repetition Effects on Object Recognition. *Child Development.* in press.

Reynolds, K. C., Patriquin, M., Alfano, C. A., Loveland, K. A., & Pearson, D. A. (2017). Parent-reported problematic sleep behaviors in children with comorbid autism spectrum disorder and attention-deficit/hyperactivity disorder. *Research in Autism Spectrum Disorders, 39*, 20-32.

Reznik, S. J., Nusslock, R., Pornpattananangkul, N., Abramson, L. Y., Coan, J. A., & Harmon-Jones, E. (2017). Laboratory-induced learned helplessness attenuates approach motivation as indexed by posterior versus frontal theta activity. *Cognitive, Affective, & Behavioral Neuroscience, 17*, 904-916.

Rheker, J., Winkler, A., Doering, B. K., & Rief, W. (2017). Learning to experience side effects after antidepressant intake-Results from a randomized, controlled, double-blind study. *Psychopharmacology, 234*(3), 329-338.

Richardson, K. M. (2017). Managing employee stress and wellness in the new millennium. *Journal Of Occupational Health Psychology, 22*(3), 423-428. doi:10.1037/ocp0000066

Rief, W., & Martin, A. (2014). How to use the new DSM-5 somatic symptom disorder diagnosis in research and practice: a critical evaluation and a proposal for modifications. *Annual Review of Clinical Psychology, 10*, 339-367.

Riggle, E. B., Rostosky, S. S., Black, W. W., & Rosenkrantz, D. E. (2017). Outness, concealment, and authenticity: Associations with LGB individuals' psychological distress and well-being. *Psychology of Sexual Orientation and Gender Diversity, 4*(1), 54-62. doi:10.1037/sgd0000202

Rihmer, Z., Dome, P., Baldwin, D. S., & Gonda, X. (2012). Psychiatry should not become hostage to placebo: An alternative interpretation of the antidepressant-placebo differences in the treatment response in depression. *European Neuropsychopharmacology, 22*(11), 782-786.

Rips, L. J. (2011). Causation from perception. *Perspectives on Psychological Science, 6*(1), 77-97.

Riske, L., Thomas, R. K., Baker, G. B., & Dursun, S. M. (2017). Lactate in the brain: An update on its relevance to brain energy, neurons, glia and panic disorder. *Therapeutic advances in psychopharmacology, 7*(2), 85-89.

Risley, T. R., & Hart, B. (2006). Promoting early language development. In N. F. Watt, C. Ayoub, R. H. Bradley, J. E. Puma, & W. A. LeBoeuf (Eds.), *The crisis in youth mental health: Critical issues and effective programs, vol. 4: Early intervention programs and policies* (pp. 83-88). Westport, CT: Praeger.

Ritskes, R., Ritskes-Hoitinga, M., Stodkilde-Jorgensen, H., Baerentsen, K., & Hartman, T. (2003). MRI scanning during Zen meditation: The picture of enlightenment? *Constructivism in the Human Sciences, 8*(1), 85-90.

Ritter, D., & Elsea, M. (2005). Hot sauce, toy guns, and graffiti: A critical account of current laboratory aggression paradigms. *Aggressive Behavior, 31*(5), 407-419.

Ritter, M. L., Guo, W., Samuels, J. F., Wang, Y., Nestadt, P. S., Krasnow, J., et al. (2017). Genome Wide Association Study (GWAS) between attention deficit hyperactivity disorder (ADHD) and obsessive compulsive disorder (OCD). *Frontiers in Molecular Neuroscience, 10.*

Rivas-Drake, D., Syed, M., Umaña-Taylor, A., Markstrom, C., French, S., Schwartz, S. J., & Lee, R. (2014). Feeling good, happy, and proud: A meta-analysis of positive ethnic-racial affect and adjustment. *Child Development, 85*(1), 77-102.

Rivers, A. M. (2017) The Weapons Identification Task: Recommendations for adequately powered research. *PLoS ONE, 12*(6): e0177857. https://doi.org/10.1371/journal.pone.0177857

Rivers, A. M., Calanchini, J., & Sherman, J. W. (2016). The self-regulation of implicit social cognition. In K. D. Vohs & R. F. Baumeister (Eds.), *Handbook of self-regulation: Research, theory and applications (3rd Ed.)* (pp. 62-75). New York: Guilford Press.

Robbins, B. D. (2016). The heart of humanistic psychology: Human dignity disclosed through a hermeneutic of love. *Journal Of Humanistic Psychology, 56*(3), 223-237. doi:10.1177/0022167815591408

Robbins, B. D., Kamens, S. R., & Elkins, D. N. (2017). DSM-5 reform efforts by the Society for Humanistic Psychology. *Journal of Humanistic Psychology, 57*, 602-624.

Roberto, A. J., Shafer, M. S., & Marmo, J. (2014). Predicting substance-abuse treatment providers' communication with clients about medication assisted treatment: A test of the theories of reasoned action and planned behavior. *Journal of Substance Abuse Treatment, 47*(5), 307-313. doi:10.1016/j.jsat.2014.06.002

Roberts, A. L., Koenen, K. C., Chen, Q., Gilsanz, P., Mason, S. M., Prescott, J., et al. (2017). Posttraumatic stress disorder and accelerated aging: PTSD and leukocyte telomere length in a sample of civilian women. *Depression and Anxiety, 34*(5), 391-400.

Roberts, B. W., Donnellan, M. B., & Hill, P. L. (2013). Personality trait development in adulthood: Findings and implications. In H. M. Tennen, J. M. Suls, & I. B. Weiner (Eds.), *Handbook of psychology* (2nd ed., vol. 5, pp. 183-196). Hoboken, NJ: Wiley.

Roberts, B. W., Wood, D., & Caspi, A. (2008). The development of personality traits in adulthood. In O. P. John, R. W. Robins, & L. A. Pervin (Eds.), *Handbook of personality: Theory and research, 3rd ed* (pp. 375-398). New York, NY: Guilford Press.

Robertson, C. E., & Baron-Cohen, S. (2017). Sensory perception in autism. *Nature Reviews Neuroscience, 18*, 671-684

Robertson, D. A., Savva, G. M., King-Kallimanis, B. L., & Kenny, R. A. (2015). Negative perceptions of aging and decline in walking speed: A self-fulfilling prophecy. *Plos ONE, 10*(4).

Rodgers, J. L. (2007). The shape of things to come: Diagnosing social contagion from adolescent smoking and drinking curves. In T. D. Little, J. A. Bovaird, & N. A. Card (Eds.), *Modeling contextual effects in longitudinal studies* (pp. 343-362). Mahwah, NJ: Erlbaum.

Rodin, J. (1984, December). Interview: A sense of control. *Psychology Today,* 38-45.

Rodrigue, K. M., & Kennedy, K. M. (2011). The cognitive consequences of structural changes to the aging brain. In K. W. Schaie & S. L. Willis (Eds.), *Handbook of the psychology of aging* (7th ed., pp. 73-92). New York: Elsevier.

Rogers, C. R. (1961). *On becoming a person.* Boston: Houghton Mifflin.

Rogers, C. R. (1980). *A way of being.* Boston: Houghton Mifflin.

Rogers, G., & others. (2009). The harmful health effects of recreational ecstasy: A systematic review of observational evidence. *Health Technology Assessment, 13*(6), 1-315.

Rogers, H., & Maytan, M. (2012). *Mindfulness for the next generation.* New York: Oxford University Press.

Rognum, I. J., & others. (2014). Serotonin metabolites in the cerebrospinal fluid in sudden infant death syndrome. *Journal of Neuropathology and Experimental Neurology, 73*(2), 115-122.

Rohrer, J. M., Egloff, B., & Schmukle, S. C. (2015). Examining the effects of birth order on personality. *PNAS Proceedings Of The National Academy Of Sciences Of The United States Of America, 112*(46), 14224-14229. doi:10.1073/pnas.1506451112

Rolls, E. T. (2017). The roles of the orbitofrontal cortex via the habenula in non-reward and depression, and in the responses of serotonin and dopamine neurons. *Neuroscience & Biobehavioral Reviews, 75*, 331-334.

Romano, A., & Bailliet, B. (2017). Reciprocity outperforms conformity to promote cooperation. *Psychological Science,* in press. doi: 10.1177/0956797617714828.

Romijnders, K. A., Wilkerson, J. M., Crutzen, R., Kok, G., Bauldry, J., & Lawler, S. M. (2017). Strengthening social ties to increase confidence and self-esteem among sexual and gender minority youth. *Health promotion practice, 18*(3), 341-347.

Roncancio, A. M., Ward, K. K., & Fernandez, M. E. (2013). Understanding cervical cancer screening intentions among Latinas using an expanded theory of planned behavior model. *Behavioral Medicine, 39*(3), 66-72. doi:10.1080/08964289.2013.799452

Roncero, M., Perpina, C., & Garcia-Soriano, G. (2011). Study of obsessive compulsive beliefs: Relationship with eating disorders. *Behavioral and Cognitive Psychotherapy, 39*(4), 457-470.

Rosano, C., Guralnik, J., Pahor, M., Glynn, N. W., Newman, A. B., Ibrahim, T. S., et al. (2017). Hippocampal response to a 24-month physical activity intervention in sedentary older adults. *The American Journal of Geriatric Psychiatry, 25*(3), 209-217.

Rose, N. S., & Craik, F. I. (2012). A processing approach to the working memory/long-term memory distinction: Evidence from the levels-of-processing span task. *Journal of Experimental Psychology: Learning, Memory, and Cognition, 38*(4), 1019-1029.

Rose, R. J., Koskenvuo, M., Kaprio, J., Sarna, S., & Langinvainio, H. (1988). Shared genes, shared experiences, and similarity of personality: Data from 14,228 adult Finnish co-twins. *Journal of Personality and Social Psychology, 54*(1), 161-171.

Rosellini, A. J., Street, A. E., Ursano, R. J., Chiu, W. T., Heeringa, S. G., Monahan, J., et al. (2017). Sexual assault victimization and mental health treatment, suicide attempts, and career outcomes among women in the US Army. *American Journal of Public Health, 107*(5), 732-739.

Rosen, C. S. (2000). Is the sequencing of change processes by stage consistent across health problems? A meta-analysis. *Health Psychology, 19*(6), 593–604. doi:10.1037/0278-6133.19.6.593

Rosen, K., & Garety, P. (2005). Predicting recovery from schizophrenia: A retrospective comparison of characteristics at onset of people with single and multiple episodes. *Schizophrenia Bulletin, 31*(3), 735–750.

Rosen, M. L., Sheridan, M. A., Sambrook, K. A., Dennison, M. J., Jenness, J. L., Askren, M. K., et al. (2017). Salience network response to changes in emotional expressions of others is heightened during early adolescence: Relevance for social functioning. *Developmental Science.* in press.

Rosenbaum, R. S., & others. (2005). The case of K.C.: Contributions of a memory-impaired person to memory theory. *Neuropsychologia, 43*(7), 989–1021.

Rosenhan, D. L. (1973). On being sane in insane places. *Science, 179*(4070), 250–258.

Rosenström, T., Ystrom, E., Torvik, F. A., Czajkowski, N. O., Gillespie, N. A., Aggen, S. H., et al. (2017). Genetic and environmental structure of DSM-IV criteria for antisocial personality disorder: A twin study. *Behavior Genetics, 47*(3), 265–277.

Rosental, B., Appel, M. Y., Yossef, R., Hadad, U., Brusilovsky, M., & Porgador, A. (2012). The effect of chemotherapy/radiotherapy on cancerous pattern recognition by NK cells. *Current Medicinal Chemistry, 19*(12), 1780–1791.

Rosenthal, R. (1966). *Experimenter effects in behavioral research.* New York: Appleton-Century-Crofts.

Rosmarin, D. H., Krumrei, E. J., & Andersson, G. (2009). Religion as a predictor of psychological distress in two religious communities. *Cognitive Behavior Therapy, 38*(1), 54–64.

Rosnow, R. L., & Rosenthal, R. (2012). *Beginning behavioral research* (7th ed.). Upper Saddle River, NJ: Prentice-Hall.

Ross, C. A., & Ness, L. (2010). Symptom patterns in dissociative identity disorder patients and the general population. *Journal of Trauma and Dissociation, 11*(4), 458–468.

Ross, C. A., & others. (2008). A cross-cultural test of the trauma model of dissociation. *Journal of Trauma & Dissociation, 9*(1), 35–49.

Ross, J. N., & Coleman, N. M. (2011). Gold digger or video girl: The salience of an emerging hip-hop sexual script. *Culture, Health, and Sexuality, 13*(2), 157–171.

Ross, J., & Melinger, A. (2017). Bilingual advantage, bidialectal advantage or neither? Comparing performance across three tests of executive function in middle childhood. *Developmental Science, 20*(4), 1–21. doi:10.1111/desc.12405

Ross, K., Handal, P. J., Clark, E. M., & Vander Wal, J. S. (2009). The relationship between religion and religious coping: Religious coping as a moderator between religion and adjustment. *Journal of Religion and Health, 48*(4), 454–467.

Rossom, R. C., Solberg, L. I., Magnan, S., Crain, A. L., Beck, A., Coleman, K. J., et al. (2017). Impact of a national collaborative care initiative for patients with depression and diabetes or cardiovascular disease. *General Hospital Psychiatry, 44*, 77–85.

Roten, R. G. (2007). DSM-IV and the taxonomy of roles: How can the taxonomy of roles complement the DSM-IV to create a more holistic diagnostic tool? *The Arts in Psychotherapy, 34*(1), 53–68.

Rotge, J. Y., & others. (2009). Inverse relationship between thalamic and orbitofrontal volumes in obsessive-compulsive disorder. *Progress in Neuro-Psychopharmacology & Biological Psychiatry, 33*(4), 682–687.

Roth, R. (2016, February 23). Telling the truth about mental illness. *The Jewish Week.* http://www.thejewishweek.com/editorial-opinion/opinion/telling-truth-about-mental-illness (accessed April 10, 2016)

Rothbaum, F., Kakinuma, M., Nagaoka, R., & Azuma, H. (2007). Attachment and AMAE: Parent–child closeness in the United States and Japan. *Journal of Cross-Cultural Psychology, 38*(4), 465–486.

Rothbaum, F., Weisz, J., Pott, M., Miyake, K., & Morelli, G. (2000). Attachment and culture: Security in the United States and Japan. *American Psychologist, 55*(10), 1093–1104.

Rothkirch, M., & Hesselmann, G. (2017). What we talk about when we talk about unconscious processing—A plea for best practices. *Frontiers In Psychology, 8.*

Rothmore, P., Aylward, P., & Karnon, J. (2015). The implementation of ergonomics advice and the stage of change approach. *Applied Ergonomics, 51*, 370–376. doi:10.1016/j.apergo.2015.06.013

Rouder, J. N., & Morey, R. D. (2009). The nature of psychological thresholds. *Psychological Review, 116*(3), 655–660.

Rowley, C. D., Sehmbi, M., Bazin, P. L., Tardif, C. L., Minuzzi, L., Frey, B. N., & Bock, N. A. (2017). Age-related mapping of intracortical myelin from late adolescence to middle adulthood using T1-weighted MRI. *Human Brain Mapping, 38*, 3691–3703.

Roy, A., & Pompili, M. (2016). Suicide risk in schizophrenia. In D. Wasserman (Ed.), *Suicide: An Unnecessary Death, 2nd edition.* (pp. 105–112). New York: Oxford University Press.

Rozenblat, V., Ong, D., Fuller-Tyszkiewicz, M., Akkermann, K., Collier, D., Engels, R. C., et al. (2017). A systematic review and secondary data analysis of the interactions between the serotonin transporter 5-HTTLPR polymorphism and environmental and psychological factors in eating disorders. *Journal of Psychiatric Research, 84*, 62–72.

Rozin, P., Kabnick, K., Pete, E., Fischler, C., & Shields, C. (2003). The ecology of eating: Smaller portion sizes in France than in the United States help explain the French paradox. *Psychological Science, 14*(5), 450–454.

Rozin, P., Scott, S., Dingley, M., Urbanek, J. K., Jiang, H., & Kaltenbach, M. (2011). Nudge to nobesity I: Minor changes in accessibility decrease food intake. *Judgment and Decision Making, 6*(4), 323–332.

Rubin, D. C. (2011). The coherence of memories for trauma: Evidence from posttraumatic stress disorder. *Consciousness and Cognition, 20*(3), 857–865.

Rubio-Fernández, P., Jara-Ettinger, J., & Gibson, E. (2017). Can processing demands explain toddlers' performance in false-belief tasks? *Proceedings of the National Academy of Sciences, 114*(19), E3750–E3750.

Rudy, D., & Grusec, J. E. (2006). Authoritarian parenting in individualist and collectivist groups: Associations with maternal emotion and cognition and children's self-esteem. *Journal of Family Psychology, 20*(1), 68–78.

Rueger, S. Y., & George, R. (2017). Indirect effects of attributional style for positive events on depressive symptoms through self-esteem during early adolescence. *Journal of Youth and Adolescence, 46*(4), 701–708.

Rusbult, C. E., Agnew, C. R., & Arriaga, X. B. (2012). The investment model of commitment processes. In P. A. M. van Lange, A. W. Kruglanski, & E. T. Higgins (Eds.), *Handbook of theories of social psychology.* Thousand Oaks, CA: Sage.

Ruscio, A. M., Hallion, L. S., Lim, C. C., Aguilar-Gaxiola, S., Al-Hamzawi, A., Alonso, J., et al. (2017). Cross-sectional comparison of the epidemiology of DSM-5 generalized anxiety disorder across the globe. *JAMA Psychiatry, 74*(5), 465–475.

Rutherford, B. R., & Roose, S. P. (2013). A model of placebo response in antidepressant clinical trials. *American Journal of Psychiatry, 170*(7), 723–733.

Ruthig, J. C., & Holfeld, B. (2016). Positive thinking and social perceptions of a male vs. female peer's cancer experience. *The Journal of Social Psychology, 156*(2), 154–167. doi:10.1080/00224545.2015.1052361

Ruybal, A. L., & Siegel, J. T. (2017). Increasing social support for women with postpartum depression: An application of attribution theory. *Stigma and Health, 2*(2), 137–156. doi:10.1037/sah0000047

Ruzich, E., Allison, C., Smith, P., Ring, H., Auyeung, B., & Baron-Cohen, S. (2017). The Autism-Spectrum Quotient in siblings of people with Autism. *Autism Research, 10*(2), 289–297.

Ryan, R. M., & Deci, E. L. (2000). Self-determination theory and the facilitation of intrinsic motivation, social development, and well-being. *American Psychologist, 55*(1), 68–78.

Ryan, R. M., & Deci, E. L. (2001). On happiness and human potentials: A review of research on hedonic and eudaimonic well-being. *Annual Review in Psychology* (vol. 52, pp. 141–166). Palo Alto, CA: Annual Reviews.

Ryan, R. M., & Deci, E. L. (2009). Promoting self-determined school engagement, motivation, learning, and well-being. In K. R. Wentzel & A. Wigfield (Eds.), *Handbook of research on schools, schooling, and human development.* New York: Routledge.

Ryan, R. M., & Deci, E. L. (2011). A self-determination theory perspective on social, institutional, cultural, and economic supports for autonomy and their importance for well-being. In V. I. Chirkov, R. M. Ryan, & K. M. Sheldon (Eds.), *Human autonomy in cross-cultural context: Perspectives on the psychology of agency, freedom, and well-being* (pp. 45–64). New York: Springer Science + Business Media.

Ryan, R. M., & Deci, E. L. (2013). Toward a social psychology of assimilation: Self-determination theory in cognitive development and education. In B. W. Sokol, F. M. E. Grouzet, & U. Müller (Eds.), *Self-regulation and autonomy: Social and developmental dimensions of human conduct* (pp. 191–207). New York: Cambridge University Press.

Ryan, R. M., & Deci, E. L. (2017). *Self-determination theory: Basic psychological needs in motivation, development, and wellness.* New York: Plenum Press.

Ryan, R. M., Huta, V., & Deci, E. L. (2008). Living well: A self-determination theory perspective on eudaimonia. *Journal of Happiness Studies, 9*(1), 139–170.

Rydberg, J. A. (2017). Research and clinical issues in trauma and dissociation: Ethical and logical fallacies, myths, misreports, and misrepresentations. *European Journal of Trauma & Dissociation, 1*, 89–99.

Rymer, R. (1993). *Genie.* New York: HarperCollins.

S

Sacco, S. J., Park, C. L., Suresh, D. P., & Bliss, D. (2014). Living with heart failure: Psychosocial resources, meaning, gratitude, and well-being. *Heart and Lung, 43*(3), 213–218.

Sacks, O. (2006, June 19). Stereo Sue. *New Yorker,* 64–73.

Sailor, K. A., Schinder, A. F., & Lledo, P. M. (2017). Adult neurogenesis beyond the niche: its potential for driving brain plasticity. *Current Opinion in Neurobiology, 42*, 111–117.

Saito, K. (2017). Effects of sound, vocabulary, and grammar learning aptitude on adult second language speech attainment in foreign language classrooms. *Language Learning,* in press. doi:10.1111/lang.12244

Sakaluk, J. K., Todd, L. M., Milhausen, R., Lachowsky, N. J., & Undergraduate Research Group in Sexuality (URGiS). (2014). Dominant heterosexual scripts in emerging adulthood: Conceptualization and measurement. *Journal of Sexual Research, 51*(5), 516–531.

Sale, A., Berardi, N., & Maffei, L. (2014). Environment and brain plasticity: Towards an endogenous pharmacotherapy. *Physiological Reviews, 94*(1), 189–234.

Sale, M.V., Reid, L.B., Cocchi, L., Pagnozzi, A.M., Rose, S.E., Mattingley, J.B. (2017). Brain changes following four weeks of unimanual motor training: Evidence from behavior, neural stimulation, cortical thickness, and functional MRI. *Human Brain Mapping, 38*, 4773–4787.

Sales, J., & Krause, K. (2017). Schools must include faculty and staff in sexual violence prevention efforts. *Journal of American College Health, 65*(8), 585–587.

Salk, R. H., Hyde, J. S., & Abramson, L. Y. (2017). Gender differences in depression in representative national samples: Meta-analyses of diagnoses and symptoms. *Psychological Bulletin, 143*(8), 783–822.

Salk, R. H., Petersen, J. L., Abramson, L. Y., & Hyde, J. S. (2016). The contemporary face of gender differences and similarities in depression throughout adolescence: Development and chronicity. *Journal of Affective Disorders, 205*, 28–35.

Salmon, K., & Reese, E. (2016). The benefits of reminiscing wth young children. *Current Directions in Psychological Science, 25*(4), 233–238.

Salthouse, T. A. (1994). The nature of the influence of speed on adult age differences in cognition. *Developmental Psychology, 30*(2), 240–259.

Salthouse, T. A. (2012). Consequences of age-related cognitive declines. *Annual Review of Psychology* (vol. 63). Palo Alto, CA: Annual Reviews.

Salthouse, T. A. (2017). Contributions of the individual differences approach to cognitive aging. *The Journals of Gerontology: Series B, 72*(1), 7–15.

Salthouse, T. A. (1993). Speed mediation of adult age differences in cognition. *Developmental Psychology, 29*, 722–735.

Samudra, P. G., Min, I., Cortina, K. S., & Miller, K. F. (2016). No second chance to make a first impression: The 'thin-slice' effect on instructor ratings and learning outcomes in higher education. *Journal of Educational Measurement, 53*(3), 313–331. doi:10.1111/jedm.12116

Samuelson, K. W., Bartel, A., Valadez, R., & Jordan, J. T. (2017). PTSD symptoms and perception of cognitive problems: The roles of posttraumatic cognitions and trauma coping self-efficacy. *Psychological Trauma: Theory, Research, Practice, And Policy, 9*(5), 537–544. doi:10.1037/tra0000210

Sanchez, D., & Awad, G. H. (2016). Ethnic group differences in racial identity attitudes, perceived discrimination and mental health outcomes in African American, Black Caribbean and Latino Caribbean college students. *International Journal of Culture And Mental Health, 9*(1), 31–43. doi:10.1080/17542863.2015.1081955

Sand, A., & Nilsson, M. E. (2016). Subliminal or not? Comparing null-hypothesis and Bayesian methods for testing subliminal priming. *Consciousness And Cognition: An International Journal, 44*, 29–40. doi:10.1016/j.concog.2016.06.012

Sand, A., & Nilsson, M. E. (2017). When perception trumps reality: Perceived, not objective, meaning of primes drives Stroop priming. *Psychological science, 28*(3), 346–355.

Sanders, A. R., Martin, E. R., Beecham, G. W., Guo, S., Dawood, K., Rieger, G., et al. (2015). Genome-wide scan demonstrates significant linkage for male sexual orientation. *Psychological Medicine, 45*(7), 1379–1388. doi:10.1017/S0033291714002451

Saneiro, M., Santos, O. C., Salmeron-Majadas, S., & Boticario, J. G. (2014). Towards emotion detection in educational scenarios from facial expressions and body movements through multimodal approaches. *Scientific World Journal, 2014.* doi:10.1155/2014/484873

SantaCruz, K. S., Sonnen, J. A., Pezhouh, M. K., Desrosiers, M. F., Nelson, P. T., & Tyas, S. L. (2011). Alzheimer disease pathology in subjects without dementia in 2 studies of aging: The Nun Study and the Adult Changes in Thought Study. *Journal of Neuropathology and Experimental Neurology, 70*(10), 832–840.

Santelli, J. S., Kantor, L. M., Grilo, S. A., Speizer, I. S., Lindberg, L. D., Heitel, J., et al. (2017). Abstinence-only-until-marriage: An updated review of U.S. policies and programs and their impact. *Journal of Adolescent Health, 61*(3), 273–280. doi:10.1016/j.jadohealth.2017.05.031

Santtila, P., Sandnabba, N. K., Harlaar, N., Varjonen, M., Alanko, K., & von der Pahlen, B. (2008). Potential for homosexual response is prevalent and genetic. *Biological Psychology, 77*(1), 102–105.

Sapolsky, R. M. (2004). *Why zebras don't get ulcers* (3rd ed.). New York: Henry Holt.

Sar, V., Akyuz, G., & Dogan, O. (2007). Prevalence of dissociative disorders among women in the general population. *Psychiatry Research, 149*(1–3), 169–176.

Sarkar, U., Ali, S., & Whooley, M. A. (2009). Self-efficacy as a marker of cardiac function and predictor of heart failure hospitalization and mortality in patients with stable coronary heart disease: Findings from the Heart and Soul Study. *Health Psychology, 28*(2), 166–173.

Saroglou, V. (2010). Religiousness as a cultural adaptation of basic traits: A five-factor model perspective. *Personality and Social Psychology Review, 14*(1), 108–125.

Sasser, T. R., Bierman, K. L., Heinrichs, B., & Nix, R. L. (2017). Preschool jntervention can promote sustained growth in the executive-function skills of children exhibiting early deficits. *Psychological Science, 28*, 1719–1730.

Sateia, M. J., Buysse, D. J., Krystal, A. D., Neubauer, D. N., & Heald, J. L. (2017). Clinical practice guideline for the pharmacologic treatment of chronic insomnia in adults: An American Academy of Sleep Medicine Clinical Practice Guideline. *Journal of Clinical Sleep Medicine, 13*(2), 307–349.

Satoh-Kuriwada, S., Kawai, M., Iikubo, M., Sekine-Hayakawa, Y., Shoji, N., Uneyama, H., & Sasano, T. (2014). Development of an umami sensitivity test and its clinical use. *PLoS One, 9*(4), e95177.

Saunders, F. W. (1991). *Katherine and Isabel: Mother's light, daughter's journey.* Palo Alto, CA: Consulting Psychologists Press.

Saurer, T. B., Ijames, S. G., Carrigan, K. A., & Lysle, D. T. (2008). Neuroimmune mechanisms of opioid-mediated conditioned immunomodulation. *Brain, Behavior, and Immunity, 22*(1), 89–97.

Savage, J. (2008). The role of exposure to media violence in the etiology of violent behavior: A criminologist weighs in. *American Behavioral Scientist, 51*(8), 1123–1136.

Savage, J. E., Long, E. C., Kuo, S. I. C., Cooke, M. E., Su, J., Barr, Pf. B., & Salvatore, J. E. (2017). Alcohol misuse across the life span: Insights from developmental studies in behavior genetics. *Policy Insights from the Behavioral and Brain Sciences, 4*(2), 186–193.

Savage, J., & Yancey, C. (2008). The effects of media violence exposure on criminal aggression: A meta-analysis. *Criminal Justice and Behavior, 35*(6), 772–791.

Savin, H. B. (1973). Professors and psychological researchers: Conflicting values in conflicting roles. *Cognition, 2*(1), 147–149.

Savin-Williams, R. C. (2015). The new sexual-minority teenager. In J. S. Kaufman & D. A. Powell (Eds.), *The meaning of sexual identity in the 21st century.* New York: Cambridge Scholars.

Saxe, L., & Ben-Shakhar, G. (1999). Admissibility of polygraph tests: The application of scientific standards post-Daubert. *Psychology, Public Policy and Law, 5*(1), 203–223.

Saxe, R., & Powell, L. J. (2006). It's the thought that counts: Specific brain regions for one component of theory of mind. *Psychological Science, 17*(8), 692–699.

Sbarra, D. A. (2015). Taking stock of loneliness: Introduction to the special section. *Perspectives on Psychological Science, 10*(2), 200–201. doi:10.1177/1745691615569603

Scammell, T. E., Arrigoni, E., & Lipton, J. O. (2017). Neural circuitry of wakefulness and sleep. *Neuron, 93*(4), 747–765.

Scarr, S. (1984, May). Interview. *Psychology Today, 18*(5), 59–63.

Schachter, S., & Singer, J. E. (1962). Cognitive, social, and physiological determinants of emotional state. *Psychological Review, 69*, 379–399.

Schacter, D. L. (2001). *The seven sins of memory.* Boston, MA: Houghton Mifflin.

Schaefer, J. D., Caspi, A., Belsky, D. W., Harrington, H., Houts, R., Israel, S., et al. (2016). Early-life intelligence predicts midlife biological age. *The Journals of Gerontology: Series B: Psychological Sciences and Social Sciences, 71*(6), 968–977. doi:10.1093/geronb/gbv035

Schaie, K. W. (1994). The course of adult intellectual development. *American Psychologist, 49*(4), 304–313.

Schaie, K. W. (2007). Generational differences: The age-cohort period model. In J. E. Birren & K. W. Schaie (Eds.), *Encyclopedia of gerontology.* Oxford, UK: Elsevier.

Schaie, K. W. (2010). Adult intellectual abilities. *Corsini encyclopedia of psychology.* New York: Wiley.

Schaie, K. W. (2012). *Developmental influences on adult intellectual development: The Seattle Longitudinal Study* (2nd ed.). New York: Oxford University Press.

Schalk, G., Kapeller, C., Guger, C., Ogawa, H., Hiroshima, S., Lafer-Sousa, R., et al. (2018). Facephenes and rainbows: Causal evidence for functional and anatomical specificity of face and color processing in the human brain. *Proceedings of the National Academy of Sciences,* in press.

Schaller, M., & Cialdini, R. B. (1988). The economics of empathic helping: Support for a mood management motive. *Journal of Experimental Social Psychology, 24*(2), 163–181.

Schank, R., & Abelson, R. (1977). *Scripts, plans, goals, and understanding.* Mahwah, NJ: Erlbaum.

Schein, S. S., & Langlois, J. H. (2015). Unattractive infant faces elicit negative affect from adults. *Infant Behavior & Development, 38,* 130–134. doi:10.1016/j.infbeh.2014.12.009

Schein, S. S., Trujillo, L. T., & Langlois, J. H. (2017). Attractiveness bias: A cognitive explanation. *Behavioral and Brain Sciences, 40,* doi:10.1017/S0140525X16000649

Schenk, A. M., Cooper-Lehki, C., Keelan, C. M., & Fremouw, W. J. (2014). Underreporting of bestiality among juvenile sex offenders: Polygraph versus self-report. *Journal of Forensic Science, 59*(2), 540–542.

Schifani, C., Sukhanov, I., Dorofeikova, M., & Bespalov, A. (2017). Novel reinforcement learning paradigm based on response patterning under interval schedules of reinforcement. *Behavioural Brain Research.* in press.

Schiff, W. J. (2015). *Nutrition for healthy living* (4th ed.). New York: McGraw-Hill.

Schiff, W. J. (2015a). *Nutrition essentials: A personal approach.* New York: McGraw-Hill.

Schirmer, A. (2013). Sex differences in emotion. In J. Armony & P. Vuilleumier (Eds.), *The Cambridge handbook of human affective neuroscience* (pp. 591–610). New York: Cambridge University Press.

Schirmer, A., & Adolphs, R. (2017). Emotion perception from face, voice, and touch: comparisons and convergence. *Trends in Cognitive Sciences, 21,* 216–228. doi: 10.1016/j.tics.2017.01.001

Schkade, D. A., & Kahneman, D. (1998). Does living in California make people happy? A focusing illusion in judgments of life satisfaction. *Psychological Science, 9*(5), 340–346.

Schlam, T. R., Wilson, N. L., Shoda, Y., Mischel, W., & Ayduk, O. (2013). Preschoolers' delay of gratification predicts body mass 30 years later. *Journal of Pediatrics, 162*(1), 90–93.

Schlinger, H. D. (2017). Commentary: Can inner experience be apprehended in high fidelity? Examining brain activation and experience from multiple perspectives. *Frontiers In Psychology, 8.*

Schlinger, H. D. (2017). The importance of analysis in applied behavior analysis. *Behavior Analysis: Research and Practice,* doi:10.1037/bar0000080

Schmader, T., Hall, W., & Croft, A. (2014). Stereotype threat in intergroup relations. In M. Mikulincer, P. R. Shaver, J. F. Dovidio, & J. A. Simpson (Eds.), *APA handbook of personality and social psychology* (vol. 2). Washington, DC: American Psychological Association.

Schmidt, D., Peterlik, D., Reber, S. O., Lechner, A., & Männel, D. N. (2016). Induction of suppressor cells and increased tumor growth following chronic psychosocial stress in male mice. *Plos ONE, 11*(7),

Schmidt, K. T., Schroeder, J. P., Foster, S. L., Squires, K., Smith, B. M., Pitts, E. G., ... & Weinshenker, D. (2017). Norepinephrine regulates cocaine-primed reinstatement via α1-adrenergic receptors in the medial prefrontal cortex. *Neuropharmacology, 119*, 134–140.

Schmidt, L. M., & Foli-Andersen, N. J. (2017). Psychotherapy and cognitive behavioral therapy supervision in Danish psychiatry: Training the next generation of psychiatrists. *Academic Psychiatry, 41*(1), 4–9.

Schneider, D., Slaughter, V. P., & Dux, P. E. (2017). Current evidence for automatic Theory of Mind processing in adults. *Cognition, 162*, 27–31.

Schneider, K. J. (2002). Humanistic psychotherapy. In M. Hersen & W. H. Sledge. (Eds.), *Encyclopedia of psychotherapy*. San Diego: Academic.

Schneider, K.J., Pierson, J.F., & Bugental, J.T. (Eds.). (2015). *The handbook of humanistic psychology: Theory, research, and practice, 2nd ed.* Thousand Oaks, CA: Sage Publications, Inc.

Schneider, S. M., & Valet, P. (2017). Relative standards and distributive justice: How social comparison orientations moderate the link between relative earnings and justice perceptions. *Social Psychology Quarterly, 80*(3), 276–287. doi:10.1177/0190272517708810

Schneider, W. (1998). Performance prediction in young children: Effects of skill, metacognition, and wishful thinking. *Developmental Science, 1*(2), 291–297.

Schneiderman, I., Kanat-Maymon, Y., Zagoory-Sharon, O., & Feldman, R. (2014). Mutual influences between partners' hormones shape conflict dialog and relationship duration at the initiation of romantic love. *Social Neuroscience, 9*(4), 337–351.

Schoenfeld, E. A., Loving, T. J., Pope, M. T., Huston, T. L., & Štulhofer, A. (2017). Does sex really matter? Examining the connections between spouses' nonsexual behaviors, sexual frequency, sexual satisfaction, and marital satisfaction. *Archives of Sexual Behavior, 46*(2), 489–501.

Schofield, G., Larsson, B., & Ward, E. (2017). Risk, resilience and identity construction in the life narratives of young people leaving residential care. *Child & Family Social Work, 22*(2), 782–791.

Schofield, P. E., Stockler, M.R., Zannino, D., et al. (2016). Hope, optimism and survival in a randomised trial of chemotherapy for metastatic colorectal cancer. *Support Care Cancer, 24*, 401–408. https://doi.org/10.1007/s00520-015-2792-8

Schooler, J. W. (2002). Re-representing consciousness: Dissociations between experience and metaconsciousness. *Trends in Cognitive Sciences, 6*(8), 339–344.

Schooler, J. W., & Eich, E. (2000). Memory for emotional events. In E. Tulving & F. I. M. Craik (Eds.), *The Oxford handbook of memory* (pp. 379–392). New York: Oxford University Press.

Schooler, J. W., Ambadar, Z., & Bendiksen, M. (1997). A cognitive corroborative case study approach for investigating discovered memories of sexual abuse. In J. D. Read & D. S. Lindsay (Eds.), *Recollections of trauma: Scientific evidence and clinical practice* (pp. 379–387). New York: Plenum.

Schooler, J. W., Ariely, D., & Loewenstein, G. (2003). The explicit pursuit and assessment of happiness can be self-defeating. In I. Brocas & J. Carrillo (Eds.), *The psychology of economic decisions*. Oxford, UK: Oxford University Press.

Schooler, J. W., Ohlsson, S., & Brooks, K. (1993). Thoughts beyond words: When language overshadows insight. *Journal of Experimental Psychology, 122*(2), 166–183.

Schoormans, D., Husson, O., Denollet, J., & Mols, F. (2017). Is Type D personality a risk factor for all-cause mortality? A prospective population-based study among 2625 colorectal cancer survivors from the PROFILES registry. *Journal Of Psychosomatic Research, 96*, 76–83. doi:10.1016/j.jpsychores.2017.03.004

Schrantee, A., Tamminga, H. G., Bouziane, C., Bottelier, M. A., Bron, E. E., Mutsaerts, H. J. M., et al. (2016). Age-dependent effects of methylphenidate on the human dopaminergic system in young vs adult patients with attention-deficit/hyperactivity disorder: A randomized clinical trial. *JAMA Psychiatry, 73*(9), 955–962.

Schreurs, B. G., Smith-Bell, C. A., Wang, D., & Burhans, L. B. (2013). Dietary cholesterol degrades rabbit long-term memory for discrimination learning but facilitates acquisition of discrimination reversal. *Neurobiology of Learning and Memory, 106*, 238–245.

Schroeder, B. L., & Sims, V. K. (2017). Texting as a multidimensional behavior: Individual differences and measurement of texting behaviors. *Psychology of Popular Media Culture*, in press. doi:10.1037/ppm0000148

Schroeder, D. A., & Graziano, W. G. (2015). The field of prosocial behavior: An overview. In D. A. Schroeder & W. G. Graziano (Eds.), *The Oxford handbook of prosocial behavior*. New York: Oxford University Press.

Schröder, A., Rehfeld, E., Ornbøl, E., Sharpe, M., Licht, R. W., & Fink, P. (2012). Cognitive-behavioural group treatment for a range of functional somatic syndromes: Randomised trial. *British Journal of Psychology, 200*(6), 499–507.

Schröder, T., & Wolf, I. (2017). Modeling multi-level mechanisms of environmental attitudes and behaviours: The example of carsharing in Berlin. *Journal of Environmental Psychology, 52*, 136–148. doi:10.1016/j.jenvp.2016.03.007

Schultz, D. P., & Schultz, S. E. (2016). *A history of modern psychology* (11th ed.). Boston, MA: Cengage.

Schultz, W., Stauffer, W. R., & Lak, A. (2017). The phasic dopamine signal maturing: from reward via behavioural activation to formal economic utility. *Current Opinion in Neurobiology, 43*, 139–148.

Schulz, R. (2007). Cardiovascular health study. In K. S. Markides (Ed.), *Encyclopedia of health and aging*. Thousand Oaks, CA: Sage.

Schulz-Stübner, S., Krings, T., Meister, I. G., Rex, S., Thron, A., & Rossaint, R. (2004). Clinical hypnosis modulates functional magnetic resonance imaging signal intensities and pain perception in a thermal stimulation paradigm. *Regional Anesthesia and Pain Medicine, 29*(6), 549–556.

Schunk, D. H. (2012). *Learning theories* (6th ed.). Upper Saddle River, NJ: Pearson.

Schuyler, B. S., Kral, T. R. A., Jacquart, J., Burghy, C. A., Weng, H. Y., Perlman, D. M., ... Davidson, R. J. (2014). Temporal dynamics of emotional responding: Amygdala recovery predicts emotional traits. *Social Cognitive and Affective Neuroscience, 9*(2), 176–181.

Schwartz, A. L. (2014). A review of the Rorschach inkblot test: An interpretive guide for clinicians. *Journal of Personality Assessment, 96*(4), 482–483.

Schwartz, B. L. (2011). The effect of being in a tip-of-the-tongue state on subsequent items. *Memory and Cognition, 39*(2), 245–250.

Schwartz, M., Hart, B., Weyrauch, D., Benson, M., Klug, M. G., & Burd, L. (2017). The hidden face of fetal alcohol spectrum disorder. *Current Women's Health Reviews, 13*(2), 96–102.

Schwartz, S. (2010). Life goes on in dreams. *Sleep, 33*(1), 15–16.

Schwartz, S. J., Vignoles, V. L., Brown, R., & Zagefka, H. (2014). The identity dynamics of acculturation and multiculturalism: Situating acculturation in context. In V. Benet-Martinez & Y. Y. Hong (Eds.), *The Oxford handbook of multicultural identity*. New York: Oxford University Press.

Schwartze, D., Barkowski, S., Strauss, B., Burlingame, G. M., Barth, J., & Rosendahl, J. (2017). Efficacy of group psychotherapy for panic disorder: Meta-analysis of randomized, controlled trials. *Group Dynamics: Theory, Research, and Practice, 21*(2), 77–93.

Schwarz, J. F., Åkerstedt, T., Lindberg, E., Gruber, G., Fischer, H., & Theorell-Haglöw, J. (2017). Age affects sleep microstructure more than sleep macrostructure. *Journal of sleep research, 26*(3), 277–287.

Schwebel, D.C., McClure, L. A., & Severson, J. (2017). Teaching children to cross streets safely: A randomized, controlled trial. *Health Psychology, 36*, 628–638. http://dx.doi.org/10.1037/hea0000032

Schyns, G., Roefs, A., Mulkens, S., & Jansen, A. (2016). Expectancy violation, reduction of food cue reactivity and less eating in the absence of hunger after one food cue exposure session for overweight and obese women. *Behaviour Research and Therapy, 76*, 57–64.

Schönfeld, S., & Ehlers, A. (2017). Posttraumatic stress disorder and autobiographical memories in everyday life. *Clinical Psychological Science, 5*(2), 325–340.

Schüz, B., Sniehotta, F. F., Mallach, N., Wiedemann, A. U., & Schwarzer, R. (2009). Predicting transitions from preintentional, intentional, and actional stages of change. *Health Education Research, 24*(1), 64–75.

Scocchia, L., Valsecchi, M., Gegenfurtner, K. R., & Triesch, J. (2014). Differential effects of visual attention and working memory on binocular rivalry. *Journal of Vision, 14*(5), 13.

Scola, C., Holvoet, C., Arciszewski, T., & Picard, D. (2015). Further evidence for infants' preference for prosocial over antisocial behaviors. *Infancy, 20*, 684–692. doi:10.1111/infa.12095

Scott, M. N., Hunter, S. J., Joseph, R. M., O'Shea, T. M., Hooper, S. R., Allred, E. N., et al. (2017). Neurocognitive correlates of attention-deficit hyperactivity disorder symptoms in children born at extremely low gestational age. *Journal of Developmental & Behavioral Pediatrics, 38*(4), 249–259.

Scott, R. M., & Baillargeon, R. (2013). Do infants really expect others to act efficiently? A critical test of the rationality principle. *Psychological Science, 24*(4), 466–474.

Scott, T. R. (2011). Learning through the taste system. *Frontiers in System Neuroscience, 5*, 87.

Scott-Sheldon, L. A. J., & Johnson, B. T. (2006). Eroticizing creates safer sex: A research synthesis. *Journal of Primary Prevention, 27*(6), 619–640.

Scrimgeour, M. B., Mariotti, E. C., & Blandon, A. Y. (2017). Children's physiological regulation and sbling conflict as correlates of children's conscience development. *Social Development, 26*(2), 329–348.

Seabrook, R. C., Ward, L. M., Cortina, L. M., Giaccardi, S., & Lippman, J. R. (2017). Girl power or powerless girl? Television, sexual scripts, and sexual agency in sexually active young women. *Psychology of Women Quarterly, 41*(2), 240–253. doi:10.1177/0361684316677028

Seara-Cardoso, A., & Viding, E. (2014). Functional neuroscience of psychopathic personality in adults. *Journal of Personality*. doi: 10.1111/jopy.12113

Searls, D. (2017). *The inkblots: Hermann Rorschach, his iconic test, and the power of seeing.* New York, NY: Crown Publishers/Random House.

Sedgh G, Finer LB, Bankole A, Eilers MA, Singh S. (2015). Adolescent pregnancy, birth, and abortion rates across countries: levels and recent trends. *Journal of Adolescent Health, 56*, 223–30.

Sedikides, C., Meek, R., Alicke, M. D., & Taylor, S. (2014). Behind bars but above the bar: Prisoners' consider themselves more prosocial than non-prisoners. *British Journal of Social Psychology, 53*(2), 396–403.

Seery, M. D., Holman, E. A., & Silver, R. C. (2010). Whatever does not kill us: Cumulative lifetime adversity, vulnerability, and resilience. *Journal of Personality and Social Psychology, 99*(6), 1025–1041.

Segal, D. L., & Coolidge, F. L. (2004). Objective assessment of personality and psychopathology. In M. Hersen (Ed.), *Comprehensive handbook of psychological assessment* (vol. 2). New York: Wiley.

Segal, N., & Fraley, R. C. (2016). Broadening the investment model: An intensive longitudinal study on attachment and perceived partner responsiveness in commitment dynamics. *Journal of Social and Personal Relationships, 33*(5), 581–599. doi:10.1177/ 0265407515584493

Segall, M. H., Campbell, D. T., & Herskovits, M. J. (1966). *The influence of culture on visual perception.* Indianapolis: Bobbs-Merrill.

Segerstrom, S. C. (2006). *Breaking Murphy's law: How optimists get what they want from life and pessimists can too.* New York: Guilford.

Segerstrom, S.C. (2017). Affect and self-rated health: A dynamic approach with older adults. *Health Psychology, 36,* 720–728.

Sekar, A., Bialas, A. R., de Rivera, H., Davis, A., Hammond, T. R., Kamitaki, N., et al. (2016). Schizophrenia risk from complex variation of complement component 4. *Nature, 530*(7589), 177–183.

Selby, E. A., Anestis, M. D., Bender, T. W., & Joiner, T. E. (2009). An exploration of the emotional cascade model of borderline personality disorder. *Journal of Abnormal Psychology, 118*(2), 375–387.

Self, M. W., van Kerkoerle, T., Goebel, R., & Roelfsema, P. R. (2017). Benchmarking laminar fmri: Neuronal spiking and synaptic activity during top-down and bottom-up processing in the different layers of cortex. *Neuroimage,* in press. doi:10.1016/j.neuroimage. 2017.06.045

Seligman, M. (2016). How positive psychology happened and where it is going. In R. J. Sternberg, S. T. Fiske, D. J. Foss (Eds.). *Scientists making a difference: One hundred eminent behavioral and brain scientists talk about their most important contributions* (pp. 478–480). New York: Cambridge University Press.

Seligman, M. E. P. (1970). On the generality of the laws of learning. *Psychological Review, 77*(5), 406–418.

Seligman, M. E. P. (1990). *Learned optimism.* New York: Knopf.

Seligman, M. E. P., & Csikszentmihalyi, M. (2000). Positive psychology: An introduction. *American Psychologist, 55*(1), 5–14.

Seligman, M. E. P., & Maier, S. F. (1967). Failure to escape traumatic shock. *Journal of Experimental Psychology, 74*(1), 1–9.

Seligman, M. E. P. (1975). *Helplessness: On depression, development and death.* San Francisco: Freeman.

Sellon, J. B., Ghaffari, R., & Freeman, D. M. (2017). Geometric requirements for tectorial membrane traveling waves in the presence of cochlear loads. *Biophysical Journal, 112*(6), 1059–1062.

Selye, H. (1974). *Stress without distress.* Philadelphia: Saunders.

Selye, H. (1983). The stress concept: Past, present, and future. In C. I. Cooper (Ed.), *Stress research.* New York: Wiley.

Senan, S., Ali, M. S., Vadivel, R., & Arik, S. (2017). Decentralized event-triggered synchronization of uncertain Markovian jumping neutral-type neural networks with mixed delays. *Neural Networks, 86,* 32–41.

Senaratna, C. V., Perret, J. L., Lodge, C. J., Lowe, A. J., Campbell, B. E., Matheson, M. C., et al. (2017). Prevalence of obstructive sleep apnea in the general population: A systematic review. *Sleep medicine reviews, 34,* 70–81.

Senechal, M., & Lefevre, J. A. (2014). Continuity and change in the home literacy environment as predictors of growth in vocabulary and reading. *Child Development, 85*(4), 1552–1568.

Senzaki, S., Masuda, T., & Ishii, K. (2014). When is perception top-down and when is it not? Culture, narrative, and attention. *Cognitive Science, 38*(7), 1493–506.

Serafini, K., Shipley, L., & Stewart, D. G. (2016). Motivation and substance use outcomes among adolescents in a school-based intervention. *Addictive Behaviors, 53,* 74–79. doi:10.1016/j.addbeh.2015.10.004

Sereno, M. I. (2017). Finding and understanding cortical maps using neuroimaging. *The Journal of the Acoustical Society of America, 141*(5), 3558–3558.

Serrat, R., Villar, F., Giuliani, M. F., & Zacarés, J. J. (2017). Older people's participation in political organizations: The role of generativity and its impact on well-being. *Educational Gerontology, 43*(3), 128–138.

Settles, R. E., Fischer, S., Cyders, M. A., Combs, J. L., Gunn, R. L., & Smith, G. T. (2012). Negative urgency: A personality predictor of externalizing behavior characterized by neuroticism, low conscientiousness, and disagreeableness. *Journal of Abnormal Psychology, 121*(1), 160–172.

Sewell, K. K., McGarrity, L. A., & Strassberg, D. S. (2017). Sexual behavior, definitions of sex, and the role of self-partner context among lesbian, gay, and bisexual adults. *The Journal of Sex Research, 54*(7), 825–831.

Seymour, T. L., Seifert, C. M., Shafto, M. G., & Mosmann, A. L. (2000). Using response time measures to assess "guilty knowledge." *Journal of Applied Psychology, 85*(1), 30–37.

Shadel, W. G., Martino, S. C., Setodji, C., Cervone, D., & Witkiewitz, K. (2017). Does self-efficacy causally influence initial smoking cessation? An experimental study. *Addictive Behaviors, 73,* 199–203. doi:10.1016/ j.addbeh.2017.05.018

Shalev, I., Entringer, S., Wadhwa, P. D., Wolkowitz, O. M., Puterman, E., Lin, J., & Epel, E. S. (2013). Stress and telomere biology: A lifespan perspective. *Psychoneuroendocrinology, 38,* 1835–1842. http://dx.doi. org/10.1016/j.psyneuen.2013.03.010

Shan, Y., & Yang, L. (2017). Fast and frugal heuristics and naturalistic decision making: A review of their commonalities and differences. *Thinking & Reasoning, 23*(1), 10–32. doi:10.1080/13546783.2016.1152999

Shankar, A., & Hinds, P. (2017). Perceived Discrimination: Associations With Physical and Cognitive Function in Older Adults. *Health Psychology, doi:10.1037/hea0000522*

Shapiro, R. (August 25, 2017). Dwayne 'The Rock' Johnson is wowed by boy who copied his skills to save toddler's life. *Huffington Post.* https://www.huffingtonpost. com/entry/dwayne-johnson-the-rock-boy-save-life-hero_ us_599fc670e4b06d67e336ce3b? ncid=tweetlnkushpmg00000041

Shapiro-Mendoza, C. K., & others. (2014). Classification system for the Sudden Unexpected Infant Death Case Registry and its application. *Pediatrics, 134*(1), e210–e219.

Sharma, R., Gupta, N., & Bijlani, R. L. (2008). Effect of yoga based lifestyle intervention on subjective well-being. *Indian Journal of Physiology and Pharmacology, 52*(2), 123–131.

Shaw, P., Eckstrand, K., Sharp, W., Blumenthal, J., Lerch, J. P., Greenstein, D. E. E. A., et al. (2007). Attention-deficit/hyperactivity disorder is characterized by a delay in cortical maturation. *Proceedings of the National Academy of Sciences, 104*(49), 19649–19654.

Shea, J. L., Wongt, P. Y., & Chen, Y. (2014). Free testosterone: Clinical utility and important analytical aspects of measurement. *Advances in Clinical Chemistry, 63,* 59–84.

Shechtman, Z., & Tutian, R. (2017). Feedback to semi-professional counselors in treating child aggression. *Psychotherapy Research, 27*(3), 338–349.

Sheeran, P., Klein, W.M.P., & Rothman, A. J. (2017). Health Behavior Change: Moving from Observation to Intervention. *Annual Review of Psychology, 68,* 573–600.

Sheikh, J. I., Leskin, G. A., & Klein, D. F. (2002). Gender differences in panic disorder: Findings from the National Comorbidity Survey. *American Journal of Psychiatry, 159*(1), 55–58.

Sheldon, K. M. (2002). The self-concordance model of healthy goal-striving: When personal goals correctly represent the person. In E. L. Deci & R. M. Ryan (Eds.), *Handbook of self-determination research* (pp. 65–86). Rochester, NY: University of Rochester Press.

Sheldon, K. M., & Elliot, A. J. (1998). Not all personal goals are personal: Comparing autonomous and controlled reasons for goals as predictors of effort and attainment. *Personality and Social Psychology Bulletin, 24*(5), 546–557.

Sheldon, K. M., & Lyubomirsky, S. (2007). Is it possible to become happier? (And if so, how?). *Social and Personality Psychology Compass, 1*(1), 129–145.

Sheldon, K. M., & Lyubomirsky, S. (2012). The challenge of staying happier: Testing the happiness adaptation model. *Personality and Social Psychology Bulletin, 38*(5), 670–680.

Sheldon, K. M., Kasser, T., Houser-Marko, L., Jones, T., & Turban, D. (2005). Doing one's duty: Chronological age, felt autonomy, and subjective well-being. *European Journal of Personality, 19*(2), 97–115.

Sheldon, K. M., Osin, E. N., Gordeeva, T. O., Suchkov, D. D., & Sychev, O. A. (2017). Evaluating the dimensionality of self-determination theory's relative autonomy continuum. *Personality And Social Psychology Bulletin, 43*(9), 1215–1238. doi:10.1177/0146167217711915

Sheldrick, R. C., Maye, M. P., & Carter, A. S. (2017). Age at first identification of autism spectrum disorder: an analysis of two US Surveys. *Journal of the American Academy of Child & Adolescent Psychiatry, 56*(4), 313–320.

Shelton, J. N., & Richeson, J. A. (2014). Interacting across racial lines. In M. Mikulincer, P. R. Shaver, J. F. Dovidio, & J. A. Simpson (Eds.), *APA handbook of personality and social psychology* (vol. 2). Washington, DC: American Psychological Association.

Shelton, R. C., Osuntokun, O., Heinloth, A. N., & Corya, S. A. (2010). Therapeutic options for treatment-resistant depression. *CNS Drugs, 24*(2), 131–161.

Shepard, R. N. (1967). Recognition memory for words, sentences, and pictures. *Journal of Verbal Learning and Verbal Behavior, 6,* 156–163.

Sheppes, G., Suri, G., & Gross, J. J. (2015). Emotion regulation and psychopathology. *Annual Review of Clinical Psychology* (vol. 11). Palo Alto, CA: Annual Reviews.

Sherif, M., Harvey, O. J., White, B. J., Hood, W. R., & Sherif, C. W. (1961). *Intergroup cooperation and competition: The Robbers Cave experiment.* Norman: University of Oklahoma Press.

Sherry, S. B., Sherry, D. L., Macneil, M. A., Smith, M. M., Mackinnon, S. P., Stewart, S. H., & Antony, M. M. (2014). Does socially prescribed perfectionism predict daily conflict? A 14-day daily diary study of romantic couples using self- and partner-reports. *Personality and Individual Differences, 61–62,* 24–27.

Shi, B., Cao, X., Chen, Q., Zhuang, K., & Qiu, J. (2017). Different brain structures associated with artistic and scientific creativity: a voxel-based morphometry study. *Scientific Reports, 7,* 42911.

Shields, S. A. (1991). Gender in the psychology of emotion. In K. T. Strongman (Ed.), *International review of studies of emotion* (vol. 1). New York: Wiley.

Shihata, S., McEvoy, P. M., & Mullan, B. A. (2017). Pathways from uncertainty to anxiety: An evaluation of a hierarchical model of trait and disorder-specific intolerance of uncertainty on anxiety disorder symptoms. *Journal of Anxiety Disorders, 45,* 72–79.

Shimizu, Y., Lee, H., & Uleman, J. S. (2017). Culture as automatic processes for making meaning: Spontaneous trait inferences. *Journal of Experimental Social Psychology, 69,* 79–85.

Shin, R. Q., Smith, L. C., Welch, J. C., & Ezeofor, I. (2016). Is Allison more likely than Lakisha to receive a callback from counseling professionals? A racism audit study. *The Counseling Psychologist, 44*(8), 1187-1211. doi:10.1177/0011000016668814

Shoda, Y., & Mischel, W. (2006). Applying meta-theory to achieve generalisability and precision in personality science: Comment. *Applied Psychology: An International Review, 55*(3), 439-452.

Shrout, P. E., & Rodgers, J. L. (2018). Psychology, Science, and Knowledge Construction: Broadening Perspectives from the Replication Crisis. *Annual Review of Psychology, 69*, in press.

Shu, L. L., Gino, F., & Bazerman, M. H. (2011). Dishonest deed, clear conscience: When cheating leads to moral disengagement and motivated forgetting. *Personality and Social Psychology Bulletin, 37*(3), 330-349.

Sibley, M. H., Pelham Jr., W. E., Molina, B. S. G., Gnagy, E. M., Waschbusch, D. A., Garefino, A. C., Kuriyan, A. B., Babinski, D. E., & Karch, K. M. (2012). Diagnosing ADHD in adolescence. *Journal of Consulting and Clinical Psychology, 80*, 139-150.

Sibley, M. H., Rohde, L. A., Swanson, J. M., Hechtman, L. T., Molina, B. S., Mitchell, J. T., et al. (2017). Late-onset ADHD reconsidered with comprehensive repeated assessments between ages 10 and 25. *American Journal of Psychiatry*, in press. https://doi.org/10.1176/appi.ajp.2017.17030298

Siebner, H. R., Hartwigsen, G., Kassuba, T., & Rothwell, J. C. (2009). How does transcranial magnetic stimulation modify neuronal activity in the brain? Implications for studies of cognition. *Cortex, 45*(9), 1035-1042.

Siegel, J. M. (2005). Clues to the functions of mammalian sleep. *Nature, 437*(7063), 1264-1271.

Siegel, J. M. (2011). REM sleep: A biological and psychological paradox. *Sleep Medicine Review, 15*(3), 139-142.

Siegel, S. (2016). The heroin overdose mystery. *Current Directions In Psychological Science, 25*(6), 375-379. doi:10.1177/0963721416664404

Sieswerda, S., Arntz, A., Mertens, I., & Vertommen, S. (2007). Hypervigilance in patients with borderline personality disorder: Specificity, automaticity, and predictors. *Behaviour Research and Therapy, 45*(5), 1011-1024.

Simmons, A. N., Fitzpatrick, S., Strigo, I. A., Potterat, E. G., Johnson, D. C., Matthews, S. C., et al. (2012). Altered insula activation in anticipation of changing emotional states: Neural mechanisms underlying cognitive flexibility in special operations forces personnel. *Neuroreport: For Rapid Communication Of Neuroscience Research, 23*(4), 234-239. doi:10.1097/WNR.0b013e3283503275

Simmons, J. P., & Simonsohn, U. (2017). Power posing: *P*-curving the evidence. *Psychological Science, 28*, 687-693.

Simon, E. J. (2015). *Biology.* Upper Saddle River, NJ: Pearson.

Simon, H. A. (1969). *The sciences of the artificial.* Cambridge, MA: MIT Press.

Simon-Thomas, E. R., Godzik, J., Castle, E., Antonenko, O., Ponz, A., Kogan, A., & Keltner, D. J. (2012). An fMRI study of caring vs self-focus during induced compassion and pride. *Social Cognitive Affective Neuroscience, 7*(6), 635-648.

Simone, A. N., Marks, D. J., Bédard, A. C., & Halperin, J. M. (2017). Low working memory rather than ADHD symptoms predicts poor academic achievement in school-aged children. *Journal of Abnormal Child Psychology*, in press. https://doi.org/10.1007/s10802-017-0288-3

Simons, D. J., & Chabris, C. F. (1999). Gorillas in our midst: Sustained inattentional blindness for dynamic events. *Perception, 28*(9), 1059-1074.

Simons, D. J., & Chabris, C. F. (2011). What people believe about how memory works: A representative survey of the U.S. population. *PLoS One, 6*(8), e22757.

Sin, N. L., & Lyubomirsky, S. (2009). Enhancing well-being and alleviating depressive symptoms with positive psychology interventions: A practice-friendly meta-analysis. *Journal of Clinical Psychology, 65*(5), 467-487.

Sinclair, S., Dunn, E., & Lowery, B. S. (2005). The relationship between parental racial attitudes and children's implicit prejudice. *Journal of Experimental Social Psychology, 41*(3), 283-289. doi:10.1016/j.jesp.2004.06.003

Singer, J. A., & Blagov, P. (2004). The integrative function of narrative processing: Autobiographical memory, self-defining memories, and the life story of identity. In D. R. Beike, J. M. Lampinen, & D. A. Behrend (Eds.), *The self and memory* (pp. 117-138). New York: Psychology Press.

Singer, J. A., & Conway, M. A. (2008). Should we forget about forgetting? *Memory Studies, 1*(3), 279-285.

Singer, J. A., & Conway, M. A. (2011). Reconsidering therapeutic action: Loewald, cognitive neuroscience, and the integration of memory's duality. *International Journal of Psychoanalysis, 92*(5), 1183-1207.

Singh, M., Spielman, D., Adleman, N., Alegria, D., Howe, M., Reiss, A., & Chang, K. (2010). Brain glutamatergic characteristics of pediatric offspring of parents with bipolar disorder. *Psychiatry Research, 182*(2), 165-171.

Singh, R., Chen, F., & Wegener, D. T. (2014). The similarity-attraction link: Sequential versus parallel multiple-mediator models involving inferred attraction, respect, and positive affect. *Basic and Applied Social Psychology, 36*(4), 281-298. doi:10.1080/01973533.2014.912583

Singhal, J. (2017). Why Behavioral Approaches to Fighting Poverty Are So Controversial. *New York Magazine.* http://nymag.com/scienceofus/2017/02/word-gap-controversy.html

Sivacek, J., & Crano, W. D. (1982). Vested interest as a moderator of attitude–behavior consistency. *Journal of Personality and Social Psychology, 43*(2), 210-221.

Siviter, H., Charles Deeming, D., Rosenberger, J., Burman, O. P., Moszuti, S. A., & Wilkinson, A. (2017). The impact of egg incubation temperature on the personality of oviparous reptiles. *Animal Cognition, 20*(1), 109-116. doi:10.1007/s10071-016-1030-1

Sjöwall, D., Bohlin, G., Rydell, A. M., & Thorell, L. B. (2017). Neuropsychological deficits in preschool as predictors of ADHD symptoms and academic achievement in late adolescence. *Child Neuropsychology, 23*(1), 111-128.

Skinner, B. F. (1938). *The behavior of organisms: An experimental analysis.* New York: Appleton-Century-Crofts.

Skinner, B. F. (1957). *Verbal behavior.* New York: Appleton-Century-Crofts.

Skolin, I., Wahlin, Y. B., Broman, D. A., Koivisto Hursti, U., Vikstrom, L. M., & Hernell, O. (2006). Altered food intake and taste perception in children with cancer after start of chemotherapy: Perspectives of children, parents, and nurses. *Supportive Care in Cancer, 14*(4), 369-378.

Sliwa, J., & Freiwald, W. A. (2017). A dedicated network for social interaction processing in the primate brain. *Science, 356*(6339), 745-749.

Slotnik, S. D. (2017). *Cognitive Neuroscience of Memory, 1st edition.* New York: Cambridge University Press.

Slotnick, S. D., & Schacter, D. L. (2006). The nature of memory related activity in early visual areas. *Neuropsychologia, 44*(14), 2874-2886.

Smallwood, J., & Schooler, J. W. (2015). The science of mind wandering: Empirically navigating the stream of consciousness. *Annual Review of Psychology, 66*, 487-518. doi:10.1146/annurev-psych-010814-015331

Smetana, J. G. (2011a). *Adolescents, families, and social development: How adolescents construct their worlds.* New York: Wiley-Blackwell.

Smetana, J. G. (2011b). Adolescents' social reasoning and relationships with parents: Conflicts and coordinations within and across domains. In E. Amsel & J. Smetana (Eds.), *Adolescent vulnerabilities and opportunities: Constructivist and developmental perspectives.* New York: Cambridge University Press.

Smetana, J. G. (2017). Current research on parenting styles, dimensions, and beliefs. *Current Opinion in Psychology, 15*, 19-25.

Smillie, L. D., Cooper, A., Wilt, J., & Revelle, W. (2012). Do extraverts get more bang for the buck? Refining the affective-reactivity hypothesis of extraversion. *Journal of Personality and Social Psychology, 103*(2), 306-326.

Smillie, L. D. (2013). Why does it feel good to act like an extravert? *Social and Personality Psychology Compass, 7*(12), 878-887.

Smith, A. R., Silva, C., Covington, D. W., & Joiner, T. E. (2013). An assessment of suicide-related knowledge and skills among health professionals. *Health Psychology, 33*(2), 110-119.

Smith, M. C., Bibi, U., & Sheard, D. E. (2003). Evidence for the differential impact of time and emotion on personal and event memories for September 11, 2001. *Applied Cognitive Psychology, 17*(9), 1047-1055.

Smith, R. E., Horn, S. S., & Bayen, U. J. (2012). Prospective memory in young and older adults: The effects of ongoing task load. *Neuropsychology, Development, and Cognition: Aging, Neuropsychology, and Cognition, 19*(4), 495-514.

Smith, R. E., Hunt, R. R., & Murray, A. E. (2017). Prospective memory in context: Moving through a familiar space. *Journal of Experimental Psychology: Learning, Memory, and Cognition, 43*(2), 189-204.

Smith, R. L., Rose, R. J., & Schwartz-Mette, R. A. (2010). Relational and overt aggression in childhood and adolescence: Clarifying mean-level gender differences and associations with peer acceptance. *Social Development, 19*(2), 243-269.

Smith, S. M., & Handy, J. D. (2014). Effects of varied and constant environmental contexts on acquisition and retention. *Journal of Experimental Psychology: Learning, Memory, and Cognition, 40*(6), 1582-1593.

Smith, T. C., & others. (2014). Longitudinal assessment of mental disorders, smoking, and hazardous drinking among a population-based cohort of U.S. service members. *Journal of Addiction Medicine, 8*(4), 271-281.

Smyth, J. (1998). Written emotional expression: Effect sizes, outcome types, and moderating variables. *Journal of Consulting and Clinical Psychology, 66*(1), 174-184.

Sneed, R., Cohen, S., Turner, R. B., & Doyle, W. A. (2012). Parenthood and host resistance to the common cold. *Psychosomatic Medicine, 74*(6), 567-573.

Snippe, E., Jeronimus, B. F., aan het Rot, M., Bos, E. H., de Jonge, P., & Wichers, M. (2017). The reciprocity of prosocial behavior and positive affect in daily life. *Journal of Personality*, in press. doi:10.1111/jopy.12299

Snow, J. (March 28, 2017). Computers learn to cooperate better than humans. *Science Magazine.* http://www.sciencemag.org/news/2017/03/computers-learn-cooperate-better-humans

Snowdon, D. A. (2003). Healthy aging and dementia: Findings from the Nun Study. *Annals of Internal Medicine, 139*(5 Pt. 2), 450-454.

Snowdon, D. A. (2007, April). *Aging with grace: Findings from the Nun Study.* Paper presented at the 22nd annual Alzheimer's regional conference, Seattle, Washington.

Snyder, C. R., & Lopez, S. J. (Eds.). (2007). *Positive psychology: The scientific and practical explorations of human strengths.* Thousand Oaks, CA: Sage.

So, S. H., Chau, A. K. C., Peters, E., Swendsen, J., Garety, P., & Kapur, S. (2017). Moment-to-moment associations between emotional disturbances, aberrant salience, and persecutory delusions. *European Psychiatry, 41*, S838.

Soares, M. S., & others. (2013). Psychosurgery for schizophrenia: History and perspectives. *Neuropsychiatric Disease and Treatment, 9*, 509-515.

Society for Community Research and Action (2017). *What is community psychology?* http://www.scra27.org/

Sohmer, H. (2014). Reflections on the role of traveling wave along the basilar membrane in view of clinical and experimental findings. *European Archives of Otorhinolaryngology,* PMID: 24740735

Soke, G. N., Maenner, M. J., Christensen, D., Kurzius-Spencer, M., & Schieve, L. A. (2017). Brief report: Estimated prevalence of a community diagnosis of autism spectrum disorder by age 4 years in children from selected areas in the United States in 2010: Evaluation of birth cohort effects. *Journal of Autism and Developmental Disorders, 47*(6), 1917–1922.

Sokolowski, H. M., Fias, W., Mousa, A., & Ansari, D. (2017). Common and distinct brain regions in both parietal and frontal cortex support symbolic and nonsymbolic number processing in humans: A functional neuroimaging meta-analysis. *NeuroImage, 146,* 376–394.

Solanto, M. V. (2017). Child vs Adult Onset of Attention-Deficit/Hyperactivity Disorder. *JAMA Psychiatry, 74*(4), 421–421.

Solmi, M., Veronese, N., Manzato, E., Sergi, G., Favaro, A., Santonastaso, P., & Correll, C. U. (2015). Oxidative stress and antioxidant levels in patients with anorexia nervosa: A systematic review and exploratory meta-analysis. *International Journal of Eating Disorders, 48*(7), 826–841. doi:10.1002/eat.22443

Solomon, S. (2013). Self-esteem is central to human well-being. In M. H. Kernis (Ed.), *Self-esteem issues and answers: A sourcebook of current perspectives* (pp. 254–259). New York: Psychology Press.

Solomon, S., Greenberg, J., & Pyszczynski, T. (1991). Terror management theory of self-esteem. In C. R. Snyder & D. R. Forsyth (Eds.), *Handbook of social and clinical psychology: The health perspective* (pp. 21–40). Elmsford, NY: Pergamon.

Soltis, S. L., Probst, J., Xirasagar, S., Martin, A. B., & Smith, B. H. (2017). Diagnostic and demographic differences between incarcerated and nonincarcerated youth (ages 6–15) with ADHD in South Carolina. *Journal of Attention Disorders, 21*(7), 554–560.

Sommer, D., Hajak, G., Dohnel, K., Schwerdtner, J., Meinhardt, J., & Muller, J. L. (2006). Integration of emotion and cognition in patients with psychopathy. *Progress in Brain Research, 156,* 457–466.

Sommer, V., & Vasey, P. L. (Eds.). (2006). *Homosexual behaviour in animals: An evolutionary perspective.* New York: Cambridge University Press.

Sommerville, J. A., Schmidt, M. F., Yun, J. E., & Burns, M. (2013). The development of fairness expectations and prosocial behavior in the second year of life. *Infancy, 18,* 40–66. doi:10.1111/j.1532-7078.2012.00129.x7.

Song, S. (2006, March 27). Mind over medicine. *Time, 167,* 13.

Soto, C. J. (2014). Is happiness good for your personality? Concurrent and prospective relations of the big five with subjective well-being. *Journal of Personality.* doi:10.1111/jopy.12081

Souders, D. J., Boot, W. R., Blocker, K., Vitale, T., Roque, N. A., & Charness, N. (2017). Evidence for narrow transfer after short-term Cognitive training in older adults. *Frontiers in Aging Neuroscience, 9.*

Sourial-Bassillious, N., Rydelius, P.-A., Aperia, A., & Aizman, O. (2009). Glutamate-mediated calcium signaling: A potential target for lithium action. *Neuroscience, 161*(4), 1126–1134.

South, S. C., & Krueger, R. F. (2008). An interactionist perspective on genetic and environmental contributions to personality. *Social and Personality Psychology Compass, 2*(2), 929–948.

South, S. C., Reichborn-Kjennerud, T., Eaton, N. R., & Krueger, R. F. (2014). Genetics of personality. In M. Mikuliner & P. Shaver (Eds.), *APA handbook of personality and social psychology.* Washington, DC: American Psychological Association.

Southwell, D. G., Nicholas, C. R., Basbaum, A., Stryker, M. P., Kriegstein, A. R., Rubenstein, J. L., & Alvarez-

Buylla, A. (2014). Interneurons from embryonic development to cell-based therapy. *Science, 344*(6180), 1240622.

Spain, D., Spain, D., Sin, J., Sin, J., Harwood, L., Harwood, L., et al. (2017). Cognitive behaviour therapy for social anxiety in autism spectrum disorder: A systematic review. *Advances in Autism, 3*(1), 34–46.

Spann, M. N., Sourander, A., Surcel, H. M., Hinkka-Yli-Salomäki, S., & Brown, A. S. (2017). Prenatal toxoplasmosis antibody and childhood autism. *Autism Research, 10*(5), 769–777.

Spanos, N. P. (1996). *Multiple identities and false memories: A sociocognitive perspective.* Washington, DC: American Psychological Association.

Sparrow, B., Liu, J., & Wegner, D. M. (2011). Google effects on memory: Cognitive consequences of having information at our fingertips. *Science, 333*(6043), 776–778.

Spearman, C. (1904). "General intelligence" objectively determined and measured. *American Journal of Psychology, 15*(2), 201–293.

Spelke, E. S. (2011). Natural number and natural geometry. In E. Brannon & S. Dehaene (Eds.), *Space, time, and number in the brain.* New York: Oxford University Press.

Spelke, E. S., Bernier, E. P., & Snedeker, J. (2013). Core social cognition. In M. R. Banaji & S. A. Gelman (Eds.), *Navigating the social world: What infants, children, and other species can teach us.* New York: Oxford University Press.

Spence, K. W. (1938). Gradual versus sudden solution of discrimination problems by chimpanzees. *Journal of Comparative Psychology, 25*(1), 213–224.

Spence, M., Stancu, V., Dean, M., Livingstone, M. E., Gibney, E. R., & Lähteenmäki, L. (2016). Are food-related perceptions associated with meal portion size decisions? A cross-sectional study. *Appetite, 103,* 377–385. doi:10.1016/j.appet.2016.04.039

Spencer, K. (November 5, 2017). Opioids on the Quad. *The New York Times,* ED22.

Spencer, K. B., Charbonneau, A. K., & Glaser, J. (2016). Implicit bias and policing. *Social and Personality Psychology Compass, 10*(1), 50–63.

Spencer, R. L., & Deak, T. (2017). A users guide to HPA axis research. *Physiology & Behavior, 17,* 843–865. doi:10.1016/j.physbeh.2016.11.014

Spengler, M., Brunner, M., Damian, R. I., Lüdtke, O., Martin, R., & Roberts, B. W. (2015). Student characteristics and behaviors at age 12 predict occupational success 40 years later over and above childhood IQ and parental socioeconomic status. *Developmental Psychology, 51*(9), 1329–1340. doi:10.1037/dev0000025

Sperling, G. (1960). The information available in brief visual presentations. *Psychological Monographs: General and Applied, 74*(11), 1–29.

Sperry, R. W. (1968). Hemisphere deconnection and unity in conscious awareness. *American Psychologist, 23*(10), 723–733.

Sperry, R. W. (1974). Lateral specialization in surgically separated hemispheres. In F. O. Schmitt & F. G. Worden (Eds.), *The neurosciences: Third study program.* Cambridge, MA: MIT Press.

Spiacci Jr, A., Vilela-Costa, H. H., Sant'Ana, A. B., Fernandes, G. G., Frias, A. T., da Silva, G. S. F., et al. (2018). Panic-like escape response elicited in mice by exposure to CO_2, but not hypoxia. *Progress in Neuro-Psychopharmacology and Biological Psychiatry, 81,* 178–186.

Spiegel, D. (2006). Editorial: Recognizing traumatic dissociation. *American Journal of Psychiatry, 163*(4), 566–568.

Spiegel, D. (2010). Hypnosis testing. In A. F. Barabasz, K. Olness, R. Boland, & S. Kahn (Eds.), *Medical hypnosis primer: Clinical and research evidence* (pp. 11–18). New York: Routledge/ Taylor & Francis.

Spiegler, M. D., & Guevremont, D. C. (2016). *Contemporary behavior therapy* (6th ed.). Boston: Cengage.

Spielberger, C. D. (2004, August). *Type A behavior, anger-hostility, and heart disease.* Paper presented at the 28th International Congress of Psychology, Beijing, China.

Spitzer, J., Schrager, S. M., Imagawa, K. K., & Vanderbilt, D. L. (2017). Clinician disparities in anxiety and trauma screening among children with ADHD: A pilot study. *Children's Health Care, 46*(4), 344–355.

Sprich, S. E., Safren, S. A., Finkelstein, D., Remmert, J. E., & Hammerness, P. (2016). A randomized controlled trial of cognitive behavioral therapy for ADHD in medication-treated adolescents. *Journal of Child Psychology and Psychiatry, 57*(11), 1218–1226.

Spuhler, K., Huang, C., Ananth, M., Bartlett, E., Ding, J., He, X., et al. (2017). Using PET and MRI to assess pretreatment markers of lithium treatment responsiveness in bipolar depression. *Journal of Nuclear Medicine, 58*(supplement 1), 138–138.

Squire, L. R. (1990). *Memory and brain systems.* Paper presented at the meeting of the American Psychological Society, Dallas, Texas.

Squire, L. R. (2007). Memory systems as a biological concept. In H. L. Roediger, Y. Dudai, & S. Fitzpatrick (Eds.), *Science of memory: Concepts.* New York: Oxford University Press.

Sridharan, D., Schwarz, J. S., & Knudsen, E. I. (2014). Selective attention in birds. *Current Biology, 24*(11), R510–R513.

Sroufe, L. A., Coffino, B., & Carlson, E. A. (2010). Conceptualizing the role of early experience: Lessons from the Minnesota Longitudinal Study. *Developmental Review, 30*(1), 36–51.

Stafford, B. K., & Huberman, A. D. (2017). Signal Integration in Thalamus: Labeled Lines Go Cross-Eyed and Blurry. *Neuron, 93*(4), 717–720.

Stanaway, J. D., Wald, A., Martin, E. T., Gottlieb, S. L., & Magaret, A. S. (2012). Case-crossover analysis of condom use and herpes simplex virus type 2 acquisition. *Sexually Transmitted Diseases, 39*(5), 388–393.

Stange-Marten, A., Nabel, A. L., Sinclair, J. L., Fischl, M., Alexandrova, O., Wohlfrom, H., et al. (2017). Input timing for spatial processing is precisely tuned via constant synaptic delays and myelination patterns in the auditory brainstem. *Proceedings of the National Academy of Sciences, 114*(24), E4851–E4858.

Stangor, C. (2016). The study of stereotyping, prejudice, and discrimination within social psychology: A quick history of theory and research. In T. D. Nelson (Ed.), *Handbook of prejudice, stereotyping, and discrimination, 2nd ed* (pp. 3–27). New York: Psychology Press.

Stankewitz, A., & May, A. (2011). Increased limbic and brainstem activity during migraine attacks following olfactory stimulation. *Neurology, 77*(5), 476–482.

Stanley, J. T., & Isaacowitz, D. M. (2011). Age-related differences in profiles of mood-change trajectories. *Developmental Psychology, 47*(2), 318–330.

Stanovich, K. E. (2012). On the distinction between rationality and intelligence: Implications for understanding individual differences in reasoning. In K. J. Holyoak & R. G. Morrison (Eds.), *The Oxford handbook of thinking and reasoning.* New York: Oxford University Press.

Stanovich, K. E. (2013). *How to think straight about psychology* (10th ed.). Upper Saddle River, NJ: Pearson.

Stanton, S. C., Campbell, L., & Loving, T. J. (2014). Energized by love: Thinking about romantic relationships increases positive affect and blood glucose levels. *Psychophysiology, 51*(10), 990–995.

Starcher, D., & Allen, S. L. (2016). A global human potential movement and a rebirth of humanistic psychology. *The Humanistic Psychologist, 44*(3), 227–241. doi:10.1037/hum0000032

Stasenko, A., Matt, G. E., & Gollan, T. H. (2017). A Relative Bilingual Advantage in Switching With Preparation: Nuanced Explorations of the Proposed Association Between Bilingualism and Task Switching. *Journal Of Experimental Psychology: General*, in press. doi:10.1037/xge0000340

Staudinger, U. M., & Gluck, J. (2011). Psychological wisdom research. *Annual Review of Psychology* (vol. 62). Palo Alto, CA: Annual Reviews.

Steblay, N., Dysart, J., & Wells, G. L. (2011). Seventy-two tests of the sequential lineup superiority effect: A meta-analysis and policy discussion. *Psychology, Public Policy, and Law, 17*(1), 99–139.

Steele, C. M., & Aronson, J. (1995). Stereotype threat and the intellectual test performance of African Americans. *Journal of Personality and Social Psychology, 69*(5), 797–811.

Steele, C. M., & Aronson, J. A. (2004). Stereotype threat does not live by Steele and Aronson (1995) alone. *American Psychologist, 59*(1), 47–48.

Steenhuis, I., & Poelman, M. (2017). Portion size: Latest developments and interventions. *Current Obesity Reports, 6*(1), 10–17.

Steenkamp, M. M., Schlenger, W. E., Corry, N., Henn-Haase, C., Qian, M., Li, M., et al. (2017). Predictors of PTSD 40 years after combat: Findings from the National Vietnam Veterans Longitudinal Study. *Depression and Anxiety, 34*,711–722

Steger, M. F., & Frazier, P. (2005). Meaning in life: One link in the chain from religion to well-being. *Journal of Counseling Psychology, 52*(4), 574–582.

Steger, M. F., Frazier, P., Oishi, S., & Kaler, M. (2006). The meaning in life questionnaire: Assessing the presence of and search for meaning in life. *Journal of Counseling Psychology, 53*(1), 80–93.

Steidl, S., O'sullivan, S., Pilat, D., Bubula, N., Brown, J., & Vezina, P. (2017). Operant responding for optogenetic excitation of Ldtg inputs to the Vta requires D1 and D2 dopamine receptor activation in the Nacc. *Behavioural Brain Research, 333*, 161–170.

Stein, D. J., Craske, M. A., Friedman, M. J., & Phillips, K. A. (2014). Anxiety disorders, obsessive-compulsive and related disorders, trauma- and stressor-related disorders, and dissociative disorders in DSM-5. *American Journal of Psychiatry, 171*(6), 611–613.

Stein, M. B. (2017). Genomics of Posttraumatic Stress Disorder: Sequencing Stress and Modeling Misfortune. *Biological Psychiatry*. in press. https://doi.org/10.1016/j.biopsych.2017.05.001

Stein, M. B., & others. (2014). SCORS-G stimulus characteristics of select Thematic Apperception Test cards. *Journal of Personality Assessment, 96*(3), 339–349.

Stein, M. B., Chen, C. Y., Jain, S., Jensen, K. P., He, F., Heeringa, S. G., ... & Sun, X. (2017). Genetic risk variants for social anxiety. *American Journal of Medical Genetics Part B: Neuropsychiatric Genetics, 174*(2), 120–131.

Stein, M. D., Flori, J. N., Blevins, C. E., Conti, M. T., Anderson, B. J., & Bailey, G. L. (2017). Knowledge, past use, and willingness to start medication-assisted treatment among persons undergoing alcohol detoxification. *The American Journal on Addictions, 26*(2), 118–121.

Stein, R. (2003, September 2). *Blinded by the light*. www.theage.com.au/articles/2003/09/01/1062403448264.html?from=storyrhs (accessed November 10, 2014)

Steinberg, L. (2015a). How should the science of adolescent brain pathology inform legal policy? In J. Bhabha (Ed.), *Coming of age: Reframing the approach to adolescent rights*. Philadelphia: University of Pennsylvania Press.

Steinberg, L. (2015b). The neural underpinnings of adolescent risk-taking: The roles of reward-seeking, impulse control, and peers. In G. Oettingen & P. Gollwitzer (Eds.), *Self-regulation in adolescence*. New York: Cambridge University Press.

Steinbrook, R. (1992). The polygraph test—A flawed diagnostic method. *New England Journal of Medicine, 327*(2), 122–123.

Steine, I. M., Winje, D., Krystal, J. H., Bjorvatn, B., Milde, A. M., Grønli, J., et al. (2017). Cumulative childhood maltreatment and its dose-response relation with adult symptomatology: Findings in a sample of adult survivors of sexual abuse. *Child Abuse & Neglect, 65*, 99–111.

Steketee, M. B., & others. (2014). Regulation of intrinsic axon growth ability at retinal ganglion cell growth cones. *Investigative Ophthalmology and Visual Science, 55*(7), 4369–4377.

Stellar, J. E., Manzo, V. M., Kraus, M. W., & Keltner, D. (2012). Class and compassion: Socioeconomic factors predict responses to suffering. *Emotion, 12*(3), 449–459.

Stephens, N. M., Townsend, S. S. M., Hamedani, M. G., Destin, M., & Manzo, V. (2015). A difference-education intervention equips first-generation college students to thrive in the face of stressful college situations. *Psychological Science, 26*(10), 1556–1566.

Steptoe, A., & Kivimaki, M. (2012). Stress and cardiovascular disease. *Nature Reviews: Cardiology, 9*, 360–370.

Stern, C., West, T. V., Jost, J. T., & Rule, N. O. (2013). The politics of gaydar: Ideological differences in the use of gendered cues in categorizing sexual orientation. *Journal of Personality and Social Psychology, 104*(3), 520–541.

Stern, E. R., Welsh, R. C., Gonzalez, R., Fitzgerald, K. D., Abelson, J. L., & Taylor, S. F. (2013). Subjective uncertainty and limbic hyperactivation in obsessive-compulsive disorder. *Human Brain Mapping, 34*(8), 1956–1970.

Stern, Y., Alexander, G. E., Prohovnik, I., & Mayeux, R. (1992). Inverse relationship between education and parietotemporal perfusion deficit in Alzheimer's disease. *Annals of Neurology, 32*(3), 371–375.

Stern, Y., Scarmeas, N., & Habeck, C. (2004). Imaging cognitive reserve. *International Journal of Psychology, 39*(1), 18–26.

Sternberg, R. J. (1986). *Intelligence applied*. Fort Worth, TX: Harcourt Brace.

Sternberg, R. J. (2008). The triarchic theory of human intelligence. In N. Salkind (Ed.), *Encyclopedia of educational psychology*. Thousand Oaks, CA: Sage.

Sternberg, R. J. (2011). The theory of successful intelligence. In R. J. Sternberg & S. B. Kaufman (Eds.), *The Cambridge handbook of intelligence*. New York: Cambridge University Press.

Sternberg, R. J. (2012). Human intelligence. In V. S. Ramachandran (Ed.), *Encyclopedia of human behavior* (2nd ed.). New York: Elsevier.

Sternberg, R. J. (2013). Searching for love. *The Psychologist, 26*(2), 98–101.

Sternberg, R. J. (2013a). Intelligence. In D. K. Freedheim & I. B. Weiner (Eds.), *Handbook of psychology* (2nd ed., vol. 1, pp. 155–176). Hoboken, NJ: Wiley.

Sternberg, R. J. (2013b). Contemporary theories of intelligence. In W. M. Reynolds, G. E. Miller, & I. B. Weiner (Eds.), *Handbook of psychology* (2nd ed., vol. 7, pp. 23–44). Hoboken, NJ: Wiley.

Sternberg, R. J. (2014a). Human intelligence: Historical and conceptual perspectives. In J. Wright (Ed.), *Encyclopedia of social and behavioral sciences* (2nd ed.). New York: Elsevier.

Sternberg, R. J. (2014b). Multiple intelligences in the new age of thinking. In S. Goldstein & J. Naglieri (Eds.), *Evolutionary theory*. New York: Springer.

Sternberg, R. J. (Ed.). (2004). *Definitions and conceptions of giftedness*. Thousand Oaks, CA: Corwin.

Sternberg, R. J., & Bridges, S. L. (2014). Varieties of genius. In D. K. Simonton (Ed.), *The Wiley handbook of genius* (pp. 185–197). New York: Wiley-Blackwell.

Sternberg, R. J., Grigorenko, E. L., & Kidd, K. K. (2005). Intelligence, race, and genetics. *American Psychologist, 60*(1), 46–59.

Stewart, A. D., & others. (2012). Body image, shape, and volumetric assessments using 3D whole body laser scanning and 2D digital photography in females with a diagnosed eating disorder: Preliminary novel findings. *British Journal of Psychology, 103*(2), 183–202.

Stice, E., Shaw, H., & Marti, C. N. (2006). A meta-analytic review of obesity prevention programs for children and adolescents: The skinny on interventions that work. *Psychological Bulletin, 132*(5), 667–691.

Stickgold, R. (2001). Watching the sleeping brain watch us: Sensory processing during sleep. *Trends in Neuroscience, 24*(6), 307–309.

Stier-Jarmer, M., Frisch, D., Oberhauser, C., Berberich, G., & Schuh, A. (2016). The effectiveness of a stress reduction and burnout prevention program: A randomized controlled trial of an outpatient intervention in a health resort setting. *Deutsches Ärzteblatt International, 113*(46), 781–788.

Stillman, T. F., Maner, J. K., & Baumeister, R. F. (2010). A thin slice of violence: Distinguishing violent from nonviolent sex offenders at a glance. *Evolution and Human Behavior, 31*(4), 298–303.

Stipek, D., & Mac Iver, D. (1989). Developmental change in children's assessment of intellectual competence. *Child Development, 60*(3), 521–538.

Stoel-Gammon, C., & Menn, L. (2013). Phonological development: Learning sounds and sound patterns. In J. Berko Gleason & N. B. Ratner (Eds.), *The development of language* (8th ed.). Upper Saddle River, NJ: Pearson.

Stoner, J. (1961). *A comparison of individual and group decisions, including risk*. Unpublished master's thesis, School of Industrial Management, MIT.

Stoppelbein, L., McRae, E., & Greening, L. (2017). A longitudinal study of hardiness as a buffer for posttraumatic stress symptoms in mothers of children with cancer. *Clinical Practice In Pediatric Psychology, 5*(2), 149–160. doi:10.1037/cpp0000168

Stott, C., Drury, J., & Reicher, S. (2012). From prejudice to collective action. In J. Dixon, M. Keynes, & M. Levine (Eds.), *Beyond prejudice*. New York: Cambridge University Press.

Stowell, J. R., Robles, T., & Kane, H. S. (2013). Psychoneuroimmunology: Mechanisms, individual differences, and interventions. In A. M. Nezu, C. M. Nezu, P. A. Geller, & I. B. Weiner (Eds.), *Handbook of psychology* (2nd ed., vol. 9, pp. 79–102). Hoboken, NJ: Wiley.

Strachan, E., Duncan, G., Horn, E., & Turkheimer, E. (2017). Neighborhood deprivation and depression in adult twins: Genetics and gene× environment interaction. *Psychological Medicine, 47*(4), 627–638.

Strachan, S. M., Perras, M. M., Brawley, L. R., & Spink, K. S. (2016). Exercise in challenging times: The predictive utility of identity, self-efficacy, and past exercise. *Sport, Exercise, and Performance Psychology, 5*(3), 247–258. doi:10.1037/spy0000064

Straub, R. H. (2014). Systemic disease sequelae in chronic inflammatory diseases and chronic psychological stress: Comparison and pathophysiological model. *Annals of the New York Academy of Sciences, 1318*, 7–17.

Streff, F. M., & Geller, E. S. (1986). Strategies for motivating safety belt use: The application of applied behavior analysis. *Health Education Research, 1*(1), 47–59.

Stripp, T. K., Jorgensen, M. B., & Olsen, N. V. (2017). Anaesthesia for electroconvulsive therapy–new tricks for old drugs: a systematic review. *Acta Neuropsychiatrica*, in press. https://www.cambridge.org/core/journals/acta-neuropsychiatrica/article/anaesthesia-for-electroconvulsive-therapy-new-tricks-for-old-drugs-a-systematic-review/3196A1565F953740A8D49B5C4F95FBDA

Stroessner, S. J., & Sherman, J. W. (Eds.). (2015). *Social perception from individuals to groups.* New York: Psychology Press.

Strother, L., Zhou, Z., Coros, A. K., & Vilis, T. (2017). An fMRI study of visual hemifield integration and cerebral lateralization. *Neuropsychologia, 100,* 35–43.

Stukas, A. A., Snyder, M., & Clary, E. G. (2015). Volunteerism and community involvement: Antecedents, experiences, and consequences for the person and the situation. In D. A. Schroeder & W. G. Graziano (Eds.), *The Oxford handbook of prosocial behavior.* New York: Oxford University Press.

Sturgeon, K. M., Schweitzer, A., Leonard, J. J., Tobias, D. K., Liu, Y., Cespedes Feliciano, E., et al. (2017). Physical activity induced protection against breast cancer risk associated with delayed parity. *Physiology & Behavior, 16,* 952–958. doi:10.1016/j.physbeh.2016.11.026

Sturmer, T., Hasselbach, P., & Amelang, M. (2006). Personality, lifestyle, and risk of cardiovascular disease and cancer: Follow-up of population-based cohort. *British Medical Journal, 332*(7554), 1359.

Substance Abuse and Mental Health Services of Administration. (SAMHSA) (2014). *Behavioral Health Trends in the United States: Results from the 2014 National Survey on Drug Use and Health.* Rockville, MD: Author.

Suddeath, E. G., Kerwin, A. K., & Dugger, S. M. (2017). Narrative family therapy: Practical techniques for more effective work with couples and families. *Journal of Mental Health Counseling, 39*(2), 116–131.

Sue, D., Sue, D. W., Sue, S., & Sue, D. M. (2016). *Understanding abnormal behavior* (11th ed.). Boston: Cengage.

Sueur, C., Deneubourg, J.-L., & Petit, O. (2012). From social network (centralized vs. decentralized) to collective decision-making (unshared vs. shared consensus). *PLoS One, 7*(2), e32566.

Suh, S., Yang, H., Kim, N., Yu, J. H., Choi, S., Yun, C., & Shin, C. (2017). Chronotype differences in health behaviors and health-related quality of life: A population-based study among aged and older adults. *Behavioral Sleep Medicine, 15*(5), 361–376. doi:10.1080/15402002.2016.1141768

Sui, X., LaMonte, M. J., Laditka, J. N., Hardin, J. W., Chase, N., Hooker, S. P., & Blair, S. N. (2007). Cardiorespiratory fitness and adiposity as mortality predictors in older adults. *Journal of the American Medical Association, 298*(21), 2507–2516.

Suinn, R. M. (1984). *Fundamentals of abnormal psychology.* Chicago: Nelson-Hall.

Sullivan, H. S. (1953). *The interpersonal theory of psychiatry.* New York: Norton.

Suls, J., & Swain, A. (1998). Type A–Type B personalities. In H. S. Friedman (Ed.), *Encyclopedia of mental health* (vol. 3). San Diego: Academic.

Sultzer, D. L., Melrose, R. J., Riskin-Jones, H., Narvaez, T. A., Veliz, J., Ando, T. K., ... & Mandelkern, M. A. (2017). Cholinergic Receptor Binding in Alzheimer Disease and Healthy Aging: Assessment In Vivo with Positron Emission Tomography Imaging. *The American Journal of Geriatric Psychiatry, 25*(4), 342–353.

Suma, K., Adamson, L. B., Bakeman, R., Robins, D. L., & Abrams, D. N. (2016). After early autism diagnosis: Changes in intervention and parent–child interaction. *Journal of Autism and Developmental Disorders, 46*(8), 2720–2733.

Sumontha, J., Farr, R. H., & Patterson, C. J. (2017). Children's gender development: Associations with parental sexual orientation, division of labor, and gender Ideology. *Psychology of Sexual Orientation and Gender Diversity,* in press. doi:10.1037/sgd0000242

Sun, J., Stevenson, K., Kabbani, R., Richardson, B., & Smillie, L. D. (2017). The pleasure of making a difference: Perceived social contribution explains the relation between extraverted behavior and positive affect. *Emotion, 17*(5), 794–810. doi:10.1037/emo0000273

Suo, C., Gates, N., Singh, M. F., Saigal, N., Wilson, G. C., Meiklejohn, J., ... & Baune, B. T. (2017). Midlife managerial experience is linked to late life hippocampal morphology and function. *Brain imaging and behavior, 11*(2), 333–345.

Suri, M. A. K., Suri, M. Adil, M. M, Qureshi, M. H., Malik, A. A., Suri, M. F. K., & Qureshi, A. I. (2015). Indicators for electroconvulsive therapy among patients hospitalized for depression. *Psychiatric Annals, 45,* 140–144.

Susann, W., Clemens, K., Carsten, B., & Katja, P. (2017). Cortisol stress response in post-traumatic stress disorder, panic disorder, and major depressive disorder patients. *Psychoneuroendocrinology, 83,* 135–141

Sutin, A.R. (2017). Openness. In T.A. Widiger (Ed.), *Oxford Handbook of the Five Factor Model.* New York: Oxford University Press.

Suzuki, H., Savitz, J., Teague, T. K., Gandhapudi, S. K., Tan, C., Misaki, M., et al. (2017). Altered populations of natural killer cells, cytotoxic T lymphocytes, and regulatory T cells in major depressive disorder: Association with sleep disturbance. *Brain, behavior, and immunity, 66,* 193–200.

Swanson, S. A., Saito, N., Borges, G., Benjet, C., Aguilar-Gaxiola, S., Medina-Mora, M. E., & Breslau, J. (2012). Change in binge eating and binge eating disorder associated with migration from Mexico to the U.S. *Journal of Psychiatric Research, 46*(1), 31–37.

Swartzman, S., Booth, J. N., Munro, A., & Sani, F. (2017). Posttraumatic stress disorder after cancer diagnosis in adults: A meta-analysis. *Depression and Anxiety, 34*(4), 327–339.

Sylvia, L. G., Salcedo, S., Peters, A. T., da Silva Magalhães, P. V., Frank, E., Miklowitz, D. J., et al. (2017). Do sleep disturbances predict or moderate the response to psychotherapy in bipolar disorder? *The Journal of Nervous and Mental Disease, 205*(3), 196–202.

Synard, J., & Gazzola, N. (2017). Happiness, eudaimonia, and other holy grails: What can job loss teach us about 'One-size-fits-all' theories of well-being? *The Journal of Positive Psychology, 12,* 246–262. doi:10.1080/17439760.2016.1225116

Syrjala, K. L., Jensen, M. P., Mendoza, M. E., Yi, J. C., Fisher, H. M., & Keefe, F. J. (2014). Psychological and behavioral approaches to cancer pain management. *Journal of Clinical Oncology, 32*(16), 1703–1711.

Sysko, R., Ojserkis, R., Schebendach, J., Evans, S. M., Hildebrandt, T., & Walsh, B. T. (2017). Impulsivity and test meal intake among women with bulimia nervosa. *Appetite, 11,* 21–28. doi:10.1016/j.appet.2017.01.005

Szocs, C., & Lefebvre, S. (2017). Spread or stacked? Vertical versus horizontal food presentation, portion size perceptions, and consumption. *Journal of Business Research, 75,* 249–257. doi:10.1016/j.jbusres.2016.07.022

T

Taber, J. M., Klein, W. P., Ferrer, R. A., Lewis, K. L., Biesecker, L. G., & Biesecker, B. B. (2015). Dispositional optimism and perceived risk interact to predict intentions to learn genome sequencing results. *Health Psychology, 34*(7), 718–728. doi:10.1037/hea0000159

Tabung, F. K., Daguisé, V. G., Lydiard, D., & Steck, S. E. (2017). An integrated approach to addressing chronic disease risk factors in financially disadvantaged women in South Carolina. *American Journal of Health Promotion, 31*(4), 325–332. doi:10.4278/ajhp.141010-QUAN-512

Tackett, J. L., & Lahey, B.B. (2017). Neuroticism. In T. A. Widiger (Ed.), *Oxford Handbook of the Five Factor Model.* New York: Oxford University Press.

Tackett, J. L., Herzhoff, K., Kushner, S. C., & Rule, N. (2016). Thin slices of child personality: Perceptual, situational, and behavioral contributions. *Journal of Personality and Social Psychology, 110*(1), 150–166. doi:10.1037/pspp0000044

Taga, K. A., Markey, C. N., & Friedman, H. S. (2006). A longitudinal investigation of associations between boys' pubertal timing and adult behavioral health and well-being. *Journal of Youth and Adolescence, 35*(3), 380–390.

Tait, R. J., Brinker, J., Moller, C. I., & French, D. J. (2014). Rumination, substance use, and self-harm in a representative Australian adult sample. *Journal of Clinical Psychology, 70*(3), 283–293.

Tajfel, H. (1978). The achievement of group differentiation. In H. Tajfel (Ed.), *Differentiation between social groups.* London: Academic.

Tajiri, N., & others. (2014). Behavioral and histopathological assessment of adult ischemic rat brains after intracerebral transplantation of NSI-566RSC cell lines. *PLoS One, 9*(3), e91408.

Takano, T., Nakamura, K., & Watanabe, M. (2002). Urban residential environments and senior citizens' longevity in megacity areas: The importance of walkable green space. *Journal of Epidemiology and Community Health, 56*(12), 913–916.

Takemura, H., Pestilli, F., Weiner, K.S., Keliris, G.A., Landi, S.M., Sliwa, J., et al. (2017). Occipital white matter tracts in human and macaque. *Cerebral Cortex, 27,* 3346–3359. doi: 10.1093/cercor/bhx070

Takmakov, P. A. (2017). Electrochemistry of a Robust Neural Interface. *The Electrochemical Society Interface, 26*(3), 49–51.

Tal, R., & Tal, K. (2017). Child-parent relationship therapy—A dialogue with Winnicott's theory. *International Journal Of Play Therapy, 26*(3), 151–159. doi:10.1037/pla0000051

Talamantes, E., & Moreno, G. (2015). Immigration policies and the U.S. medical education system: A diverse physician workforce to reduce health disparities. *Journal of General Internal Medicine, 30*(8), 1058–1059. doi:10.1007/s11606-015-3281-y

Tamm, L., Denton, C. A., Epstein, J. N., Schatschneider, C., Taylor, H., Arnold, L. E., et al. (2017). Comparing treatments for children with ADHD and word reading difficulties: A randomized clinical trial. *Journal of Consulting and Clinical Psychology, 85*(5), 434–446.

Tando, T., & others. (2014). Developmental changes in frontal lobe function during a verbal fluency task: A multi-channel near-infrared spectroscopy study. *Brain & Development, 36*(10), 844–852.

Tang, C., Hamilton, L. S., & Chang, E. F. (2017). Intonational speech prosody encoding in the human auditory cortex. *Science, 357,* 797–801.

Tang, R., & others. (2014). Candidate genes and functional noncoding variants identified in a canine model of obsessive-compulsive disorder. *Genome Biology, 15*(3), R25.

Tang, Y., & others. (2014). Neural stem cell protects aged rat brain from ischemia-reperfusion injury through neurogenesis and angiogenesis. *Journal of Cerebral Blood Flow and Metabolism.* doi: 10.1093/brain/awp174

Tarokh, L., & Carskadon, M. A. (2010). Developmental changes in the human sleep EEG during early adolescence. *Sleep, 33*(6), 801–809.

Tarter, R. E., Vanyukov, M., Kirisci, L., Reynolds, M., & Clark, D. B. (2006). Predictors of marijuana use in adolescents before and after illicit drug use: Examination of the gateway hypothesis. *American Journal of Psychiatry, 163*(12), 2134–2140.

Tas, C., Brown, E. C., Aydemir, O., Brüne, M., & Lysaker, P. H. (2014). Metacognition in psychosis: Comparison of schizophrenia with bipolar disorder. *Psychiatry Research, 219*(3), 464–469.

Taurines, R., Gerlach, M., Warnke, A., Thome, J., & Wewetzer, C. (2011). Pharmacotherapy in depressed children and adolescents. *World Journal of Biological Psychiatry, 12,* Suppl. 1, S11–S15.

Tay, C., Ang, S., & Van Dyne, L. (2006). Personality, biographical characteristics, and job interview success: A longitudinal study of the mediating effects of self-efficacy and the moderating effects of internal locus of causality. *Journal of Applied Psychology, 91*(2), 446–454.

Tay, L., & Diener, E. (2011). Needs and subjective well-being around the world. *Journal of Personality and Social Psychology, 101*(2), 354–365.

Tay, L., Li, M., Diener, E., & Myers, D. (2013). Religiosity and subjective well-being: An international perspective. In C. Kim-Prieto (Ed.), *The positive psychology of religion and spirituality.* New York: Springer.

Taylor, C. L., Mckay, A. S., & Kaufman, J. C. (2017). Creativity and personality: Nuances of domain and mood. In G. J. Feist, R. Reiter-Palmon, & J. C. Kaufman (Eds.), *The Cambridge handbook of creativity and personality research* (pp. 167–186). New York: Cambridge University Press.

Taylor, E. (2017). Attention deficit hyperactivity disorder: Overdiagnosed or diagnoses missed? *Archives of Disease in Childhood, 102*(4), 376–379.

Taylor, J. P., Ashworth, S. J., Petrovich, S., & Young, C. A. (2017). Inducing an availability heuristic on the Wason selection task overrides the matching bias. *Journal of Cognitive Psychology, 29*(4), 508–519. doi:10.1080/204459 11.2017.1281282

Taylor, M. J., Gillberg, C., Lichtenstein, P., & Lundström, S. (2017). Etiological influences on the stability of autistic traits from childhood to early adulthood: Evidence from a twin study. *Molecular Autism, 8*(1), 5.

Taylor, S. E. (2001). Toward a biology of social support. In C. R. Snyder & S. J. Lopez (Eds.), *Handbook of positive psychology.* New York: Oxford University Press.

Taylor, S. E. (2007). Social support. In H. S. Friedman & R. C. Silver (Eds.), *Foundations of health psychology.* New York: Oxford University Press.

Taylor, S. E. (2011). Positive illusions: How ordinary people become extraordinary. In M. A. Gernsbacher, R. W. Pew, L. M. Hough, & J. R. Pomerantz (Eds.), *Psychology and the real world: Essays illustrating fundamental contributions to society* (pp. 224–228). New York: Worth.

Taylor, S. E. (2011a). Tend and befriend theory. In A. M. van Lange, A. W. Kruglanski, & E. T. Higgins (Eds.), *Handbook of theories of social psychology.* Thousand Oaks, CA: Sage.

Taylor, S. E. (2011b). Affiliation and stress. In S. S. Folkman (Ed.), *Oxford handbook of stress, health, and coping.* New York: Oxford University Press.

Taylor, S. E. (2013). Social cognition and health. In D. E. Carlston (Ed.), *The Oxford handbook of social cognition.* New York: Oxford University Press.

Taylor, S. E. (2014). Social cognition and health. In M. Mikulincer, P. R. Shaver, E. Borgida, & J. A. Bargh (Eds.), *APA handbook of personality and social psychology* (vol. 1). Washington, DC: American Psychological Association.

Taylor, S. E. (2014a). *Health psychology* (9th ed.). New York: McGraw-Hill.

Taylor, S. E. (2018). *Health psychology* (10th ed.). New York: McGraw-Hill.

Taylor, S. E., & Sherman, D. K. (2008). Self-enhancement and self-affirmation: The consequences of positive self-thoughts for motivation and health. In W. Gardner & J. Shah (Eds.), *Handbook of motivation science* (pp. 57–70). New York: Guilford.

Taylor, V. A., Chang, L., Rainville, P., & Roy, M. (2017). Learned expectations and uncertainty facilitate pain during classical conditioning. *Pain, 158*(8), 1528–1537.

Taylor, Z. E., & Conger, R. D. (2017). Promoting strengths and resilience in single-mother families. *Child Development, 88*(2), 350–358.

Taylor, Z. E., Widaman, K. F., Robins, R. W., Jochem, R., Early, D. R., & Conger, R. D. (2012). Dispositional optimism: A psychological resource for Mexican-origin mothers experiencing economic stress. *Journal of Family Psychology, 26*(1), 133–139.

Tedesco, A. M., Bianchini, F., Piccardi, L., Clausi, S., Berthoz, A., Molinari, M., & ... Leggio, M. (2017). Does the cerebellum contribute to human navigation by processing sequential information? *Neuropsychology, 31*(5), 564–574. doi:10.1037/neu0000354

Teeny, J., Briñol, P., & Petty, R. E. (2017). The elaboration likelihood model: Understanding consumer attitude change. In C. V. Jansson-Boyd, M. & J. Zawisza (Eds.), *Routledge international handbook of consumer psychology* (pp. 390–410). New York: Routledge/Taylor & Francis Group.

Teichmann, A. L., Nieuwenstein, M. R., & Rich, A. N. (2017). Digit–color synaesthesia only enhances memory for colors in a specific context: A new method of duration thresholds to measure serial recall. *Journal of Experimental Psychology: Human Perception And Performance, 43*(8), 1494–1503. doi:10.1037/xhp0000402

Tekampe, J., van Middendorp, H., Meeuwis, S. H., van Leusden, J. W., Pacheco-López, G., Hermus, A. R., & Evers, A. W. (2017). Conditioning immune and endocrine parameters in humans: A systematic review. *Psychotherapy and Psychosomatics, 86*(2), 99–107.

ten Velden Hegelstad, W., & others. (2012). Long-term follow-up of the TIPS early detection in psychosis study: Effects on 10-year outcome. *American Journal of Psychiatry, 169*(4), 374–380.

Tennie, C., Call, J., & Tomasello, M. (2010). Evidence for emulation in chimpanzees in social settings using the floating peanut task. *PLoS One, 5*(5), e10544.

Teodorescu, M., & others. (2006). Correlates of daytime sleepiness in patients with asthma. *Sleep Medicine, 7*(8), 607–613.

Terman, L. (1925). *Genetic studies of genius: Vol. 1: Mental and physical traits of a thousand gifted children.* Stanford, CA: Stanford University Press.

Terr, L. C. (1988). What happens to early memories of trauma? A study of twenty children under age five at the time of documented traumatic events. *Journal of the American Academy of Child and Adolescent Psychiatry, 27*(1), 96–104.

Terracciano, A., Stephan, Y., Luchetti, M., Albanese, E., & Sutin, A. R. (2017). Personality traits and risk of cognitive impairment and dementia. *Journal of Psychiatric Research, 89,* 22–27. doi:10.1016/j.jpsychires.2017.01.011

Thagard, P. (2014). Artistic genius and creative cognition. In D. K. Simonton (Ed.), *The Wiley handbook of genius* (pp. 120–138). New York: Wiley-Blackwell.

Thake, J., & Zelenski, J. M. (2013). Neuroticism, BIS, and reactivity to discrete negative mood inductions. *Personality and Individual Differences, 54*(2), 208–213. doi:10.1016/j.paid.2012.08.041

Thapar, A., & Cooper, M. (2016). Attention-deficit hyperactivity disorder. *Lancet, 387,* 1240–1250.

The Week Staff. (2011, November 4). Is eyewitness testimony too unreliable to trust? *The Week.* http://theweek.com/article/index/221008/is-eyewitness-testimony-too-unreliable-to-trust (accessed December 5, 2014)

Thigpen, C. H., & Cleckley, H. M. (1957). *The three faces of Eve.* New York. McGraw-Hill.

Thijssen, S., & Kiehl, K. A. (2017). Functional connectivity in incarcerated male adolescents with psychopathic traits. *Psychiatry Research: Neuroimaging, 265,* 35–44.

Thill, S., Padó, S., & Ziemke, T. (2014). On the importance of rich embodiment in the grounding of concepts: Perspectives from embodied cognitive science and computational linguistics. *Topics in Cognitive Science, 6*(3), 545–558.

Thoma, M. V., Gianferante, D., Hanlin, L., Fiksdal, A., Chen, X., & Rohleder, N. (2017). Stronger hypothalamus-pituitary-adrenal axis habituation predicts lesser sensitization of inflammatory response to repeated acute stress exposures in healthy young adults. *Brain, Behavior, And Immunity, 61,* 228–235. doi:10.1016/j.bbi.2016.11.030

Thomas, J. G., Bond, D. S., Phelan, S., Hill, J. O., & Wing, R. R. (2014). Weight-loss maintenance for 10 years in the National Weight Control Registry. *American Journal of Preventive Medicine, 46,* 17–23.

Thomas, M. S. C., & Johnson, M. H. (2008). New advances in understanding sensitive periods in brain

development. *Current Directions in Psychological Science, 17*(1), 1–5.

Thompson, L. Y., & others. (2005). Dispositional forgiveness of self, others, and situations. *Journal of Personality, 73*(2), 313–359.

Thompson, R. A. (2015a). Early attachment and later development: New questions. In J. Cassidy & P. R. Shaver (Eds.), *Handbook of attachment* (3rd ed.). New York: Guilford.

Thompson, R. A. (2015b). Relationships, regulation, and development. In R. M. Lerner & Michael E. Lamb (Eds.), *Handbook of child psychology and developmental science* (7th ed., vol. 3). Hoboken, NJ: Wiley.

Thompson, R. A., Meyer, S., & McGinley, M. (2014). Understanding values in relationships: The development of conscience. In M. Killen & J. G. Smetana (Eds.), *Handbook of moral development* (2nd ed., pp. 267–298). New York: Psychology Press.

Thompson, T. (2013). Autism research and services for young children: History, progress, and challenges. *Journal of Applied Research on Intellectual Disabilities, 26*(2), 1–27.

Thompson, T., Mitchell, J. A., Johnson-Lawrence, V., Watkins, D. C., & Modlin, C. J. (2017). Self-rated health and health care access associated with African American men's health self-efficacy. *American Journal of Men's Health, 11*(5), 1385–1387. doi:10.1177/1557988315598555

Thomson, D. R., Besner, D., & Smilek, D. (2015). A resource-control account of sustained attention: Evidence from mind-wandering and vigilance paradigms. *Perspectives On Psychological Science, 10*(1), 82–96. doi:10.1177/1745691614556681

Thorell, L. B., Sjöwall, D., Diamatopoulou, S., Rydell, A. M., & Bohlin, G. (2017). Emotional functioning, ADHD symptoms, and peer problems: A longitudinal investigation of children age 6–9.5 years. *Infant and Child Development, 26*(4), E2008.

Thorndike, E. L. (1898). Animal intelligence: An experimental study of the associative processes in animals. *Psychological Review,* monograph supplements, no. 8. New York: Macmillan.

Thurston, M. D., Goldin, P., Heimberg, R., & Gross, J. J. (2017). Self-views in social anxiety disorder: The impact of CBT versus MBSR. *Journal of Anxiety Disorders, 47,* 83–90.

Thurstone, L. L. (1938). *Primary mental abilities.* Chicago: University of Chicago Press.

Tian, Q., Chastan, N., Bair, W. N., Resnick, S. M., Ferrucci, L., & Studenski, S. A. (2017). The brain map of gait variability in aging, cognitive impairment and dementia—A systematic review. *Neuroscience & Biobehavioral Reviews, 74,* 149–162

Tigani, X., Artemiadis, A. K., Alexopoulos, E. C., Chrousos, G. P., & Darviri, C. (2012). Self-rated health in centenarians: A nation-wide cross-sectional Greek study. *Archives of Gerontology and Geriatrics, 54*(3), e342–e348.

Timimi, S. (2017). Non-diagnostic based approaches to helping children who could be labelled ADHD and their families. *International Journal of Qualitative Studies on Health and Well-being, 12*(sup1), https://doi.org/10.1080/1 7482631.2017.1298270.

Tindle, H., & others. (2012). Optimism, response to treatment of depression, and rehospitalization after coronary artery bypass graft surgery. *Psychosomatic Medicine, 74*(2), 200–207.

Tinsley, J.N., Molodtsov, M.I., Prevedel, R., Wartmann, D., Espigulé-Pons J., Lauwers, M., & Vaziri, A. (2016). Direct detection of a single photon by humans. *Nature Communications, 7,* 12172. doi: 10.1038/ncomms12172.

Todd, A. R., Thiem, K. C., & Neel, R. (2016). Does seeing faces of young black boys facilitate the identification of threatening stimuli? *Psychological Science, 27*(3), 384–393.

Todd, A.R., Simpson, A.J., Thiem, K.C., & Neel, R. (2016). The generalization of implicit racial bias to young black boys: Automatic stereotyping or automatic prejudice? *Social Cognition, 34*, 4, 306-323

Todd, B. K., Fischer, R. A., Di Costa, S., Roestorf, A., Harbour, K., Hardiman, P., & Barry, J. A. (2018). Sex differences in children's toy preferences: A systematic review, meta-regression, and meta-analysis. *Infant and Child Development*. In press.

Todorov, A. (2017). *Face value: The irresistible influence of first impressions.* Princeton, NJ, US: Princeton University Press.

Todorov, A., Mandisodza, A. N., Goren, A., & Hall, C. C. (2005). Inferences of competence from faces predict election outcomes. *Science, 308*(5728), 1623-1626.

Todorov, A., Olivola, C. Y., Dotsch, R., & Mende-Siedlecki, P. (2015). Social attributions from faces: Determinants, consequences, accuracy, and functional significance. *Annual Review of Psychology* (vol. 66, pp. 519-545). Palo Alto, CA: Annual Reviews.

Toffalini, E., Pezzuti, L., & Cornoldi, C. (2017). Einstein and dyslexia: Is giftedness more frequent in children with a specific learning disorder than in typically developing children? *Intelligence*, in press. doi:10.1016/j.intell.2017.04.006

Tolman, E. C. (1932). *Purposive behavior in animals and man.* New York: Appleton-Century-Crofts.

Tolman, E. C., & Honzik, C. H. (1930). Degrees of hunger, reward and non-reward, and maze performance in rats. *University of California Publications in Psychology, 4,* 21-256.

Tomasello, M. (2014). *A natural history of human thinking.* Cambridge, MA: Harvard University Press.

Tong, E. W. (2015). Differentiation of 13 positive emotions by appraisals. *Cognition And Emotion, 29*(3), 484-503. doi:10.1080/02699931.2014.922056

Tong, E. W., & Jia, L. (2017). Positive emotion, appraisal, and the role of appraisal overlap in positive emotion co-occurrence. *Emotion, 17*(1), 40-54. doi:10.1037/emo0000203

Tong, L., Thumboo, J., Tan, Y. K., Wong, T. Y., & Albani, S. (2014). The eye: A window of opportunity in rheumatoid arthritis? *Nature Reviews: Rheumatology, 10*(9), 552-560.

Topolinski, S., & Strack, F. (2009). Scanning the "fringe of consciousness": What is felt and what is not felt in intuition about semantic coherence. *Consciousness and Cognition, 18*(3), 608-618.

Tornero, D., Tsupykov, O., Granmo, M., Rodriguez, C., Grønning-Hansen, M., Thelin, J., et al. (2017). Synaptic inputs from stroke-injured brain to grafted human stem cell-derived neurons activated by sensory stimuli. *Brain, 140*(3), 692-706.

Torrens Armstrong, A. (2017). Serving those that serve: A practitioner commentary on health promotion in the military. *Health Promotion Practice, 18*(2), 169-174. doi:10.1177/1524839916678405

Toumbourou, J. W. (2016). Beneficial action within altruistic and prosocial behavior. *Review of General Psychology, 20*(3), 245-258. doi:10.1037/gpr0000081

Toussaint, L. L., Shields, G. S., & Slavich, G. M. (2016). Forgiveness, stress, and health: A 5-week dynamic parallel process study. *Annals Of Behavioral Medicine, 50*(5), 727-735. doi:10.1007/s12160-016-9796-6

Townsend, S. M., Eliezer, D., Major, B., & Mendes, W. B. (2014). Influencing the world versus adjusting to constraints: Social class moderates responses to discrimination. *Social Psychological and Personality Science, 5*(2), 226-234. doi:10.1177/1948550613490968

Tran, T. B., & Joormann, J. (2015). The role of Facebook use in mediating the relation between rumination and adjustment after a relationship breakup. *Computers in Human Behavior, 49*, 56-61.

Trask, S., Thrailkill, E. A., & Bouton, M. E. (2017). Occasion setting, inhibition, and the contextual control of extinction in Pavlovian and instrumental (operant) learning. *Behavioural Processes, 137*, 64-72.

Travagin, G., Margola, D., & Revenson, T. A. (2015). How effective are expressive writing interventions for adolescents? A meta-analytic review. *Clinical Psychology Review, 36*, 42-55. doi:10.1016/j.cpr.2015.01.003

Trent, J., Lavelock, C., & King, L. A. (2013). Processing fluency, positive affect, and meaning in life. *Journal of Positive Psychology, 8*(2), 135-139.

Triandis, H. C. (2000). Cross-cultural psychology: History of the field. In A. Kazdin (Ed.), *Encyclopedia of psychology.* Washington, DC, & New York: American Psychological Association and Oxford University Press.

Trivedi, A. K., & Kumar, V. (2014). Melatonin: An internal signal for daily and seasonal timing. *Indian Journal of Experimental Biology, 52*(5), 425-437.

Trivedi, P., & Bhargava, N. (2017). Effect of left and right hemisphere of brain in both eye open and close state on minimum power values and frequency of alpha wave activity. *Brain, 6*, 233-237.

Tromholt, M. (2016). The Facebook experiment: Quitting Facebook leads to higher levels of well-being. *Cyberpsychology, Behavior, And Social Networking, 19*(11), 661-666. doi:10.1089/cyber.2016.0259

Troscianko, J., Wilson-Aggarwal, J., Griffiths, D., Spottiswoode, C.N., & Stevens, M. (2017). Relative advantages of dichromatic and trichromatic color vision in camouflage breaking. *Behavioral Ecology, 28*, 556-564. DOI: 10.1093/beheco/arw185

Trudel-Fitzgerald, C., Qureshi, F., Appleton, A. A., & Kubzansky, L. D. (2017). A healthy mix of emotions: Underlying biological pathways linking emotions to physical health. *Current Opinion In Behavioral Sciences, 15*, 16-21. doi:10.1016/j.cobeha.2017.05.003

Trudell, J. R., Messing, R. O., Mayfield, J., & Harris, R. A. (2014). Alcohol dependence: Molecular and behavioral evidence. *Trends in Pharmacological Sciences, 35*(7), 317-323.

Trujillo, L. T., Jankowitsch, J. M., & Langlois, J. H. (2014). Beauty is in the ease of the beholding: A neurophysiological test of the averageness theory of facial attractiveness. *Cognitive, Affective & Behavioral Neuroscience, 14*(3), 1061-1076. doi:10.3758/s13415-013-0230-2

Trull, T. J., & Brown, W. C. (2013). Borderline personality disorder: A five-factor model perspective. In T. A. Widiger & P. T. Costa (Eds.), *Personality disorders and the five-factor model of personality* (3rd ed., pp. 119-132). Washington, DC: American Psychological Association.

Trump, L. J., & Mendenhall, T. J. (2017). Couples coping with cardiovascular disease: A systematic review. *Families, Systems, & Health, 35*(1), 58-69. doi:10.1037/fsh0000232

Tryon, R. C. (1940). Genetic differences in maze-learning ability in rats. In *39th Yearbook, National Society for the Study of Education.* Chicago: University of Chicago Press.

Trzaskowski, M., Yang, J., Visscher, P. M., & Plomin, R. (2014). DNA evidence for strong genetic stability and increasing heritability of intelligence from age 7 to 12. *Molecular Psychiatry, 19*(3), 380-384.

Tskhay, K. O., Zhu, R., & Rule, N. O. (2017). Perceptions of charisma from thin slices of behavior predict leadership prototypicality judgments. *The Leadership Quarterly*, in press. doi:10.1016/j.leaqua.2017.03.003

Tuck, I., & Anderson, L. (2014). Forgiveness, flourishing, and resilience: The influences of expressions of spirituality on mental health recovery. *Issues in Mental Health Nursing, 35*(4), 277-282.

Tuck, N. L., Adams, K. S., & Consedine, N. S. (2017). Does the ability to express different emotions predict different indices of physical health? A skill-based study of physical symptoms and heart rate variability. *British Journal of Health Psychology, 22*(3), 502-523. doi:10.1111/bjhp.12242

Tucker-Drob, E. M. (2011). Individual differences methods for randomized experiments. *Psychological Methods, 16*(3), 298-318.

Tugade, M. M., Fredrickson, B. L., & Feldman Barrett, L. (2004). Psychological resilience and positive emotional granularity: Examining the benefits of positive emotions on coping and health. *Journal of Personality, 72*(6), 1161-1190.

Tulving, E. (1972). Episodic and semantic memory. In E. Tulving & W. Donaldson (Eds.), *Origins of memory.* San Diego: Academic.

Tulving, E. (1983). *Elements of episodic memory.* New York: Oxford University Press.

Tulving, E. (1989). Remembering and knowing the past. *American Scientist, 77*(4), 361-367.

Tulving, E. (2000). Concepts of memory. In E. Tulving & F. I. M. Craik (Eds.), *The Oxford handbook of memory.* New York: Oxford University Press.

Tuncay, T., & Musabak, I. (2015). Problem-focused coping strategies predict posttraumatic growth in veterans with lower-limb amputations. *Journal of Social Service Research, 41*(4), 466-483. doi:10.1080/01488376.2015.1033584

Turiano, N. A., Chapman, B. P., Agrigoroaei, S., Infurna, F. J., & Lachman, M. (2014). Perceived control reduces mortality risk at low, not high, education levels. *Health Psychology, 33*(8), 883-890.

Turiano, N. A., Chapman, B. P., Gruenewald, T. L., & Mroczek, D. K. (2015). Personality and the leading behavioral contributors of mortality. *Health Psychology, 34*(1), 51-60. doi:10.1037/hea0000038

Turiano, N. A., Pitzer, L., Armour, C., Karlamangla, A., Ryff, C. D., & Mroczek, D. K. (2012). Personality trait level and change as predictors of health outcomes: Findings from a national study of Americans (MIDUS). *Journal of Gerontology B: Psychological Sciences and Social Sciences, 67*(1), 4-12.

Turiano, N., Chapman, B. P., Agrigoroaei, S., Infurna, F. J., & Lachman, M. (2014). Perceived control reduces mortality risk at low, not high education levels. *Health Psychology, 33*(8), 883-890.

Turkewitz, J. (September 21, 2017). 'The Pills are Everywhere': The opioid crisis and its youngest victims. *New York Times*, A15.

Turkheimer, E. (2011). Genetics and human agency: Comment on Dar-Nimrod and Heine. *Psychological Bulletin, 137*(5), 825-828.

Turkheimer, E., Haley, A., Waldron, M., D'Onofrio, B., & Gottesman, I. I. (2003). Socioeconomic status modifies heritability of IQ in young children. *Psychological Science, 14*(6), 623-628.

Tussis, L., Sollmann, N., Boeckh-Behrens, T., Meyer, B., & Krieg, S. M. (2017). Identifying cortical first and second language sites via navigated transcranial magnetic stimulation of the left hemisphere in bilinguals. *Brain and Language, 168*, 106-116.

Tutone, M., Pantano, L., Lauria, A., & Almerico, A. M. (2014). Molecular dynamics, dynamic site mapping, and highthroughput virtual screening on leptin and the Ob receptor as anti-obesity target. *Journal of Molecular Modeling, 20*(5), 2247.

Twenge, J. M., Sherman, R. A., & Wells, B. E. (2017). Declines in sexual frequency among American adults, 1989-2014. *Archives of Sexual Behavior*, in press.

Twilley, N. (2015, November 2). Accounting for taste: How packaging can make food more flavorful. *The New Yorker*, 50-57.

Tyas, S. L., Salazar, J. C., Snowdon, D. A., Desrosier, M. F., Riley, K. P., Mendiondo, M. S., & Kryscio, R. J. (2007). Transitions to mild cognitive impairments, dementia, and death: Findings from the Nun Study. *American Journal of Epidemiology, 165*(11), 1231-1238.

U

U.S. Census Bureau (2017a). *Table UC1. Opposite Sex Unmarried Couples By Labor Force Status of Both Partners: 2016.* Washington, DC: Author. https://www.census.gov/data/tables/2016/demo/families/cps-2016.html

U.S. Census Bureau. (2017b). *Historical Marital Status Tables.* Washington, DC: Author. https://www.census.gov/data/tables/time-series/demo/families/marital.html

U.S. Department of Justice. (2015). *Overview of Title IX of the Education Amendments of 1972, 20 U.S.C. A§ 1681 Et. Seq.* https://www.justice.gov/crt/overview-title-ix-education-amendments-1972-20-usc-1681-et-seq

Uddin, M. S., Sufian, M. A., Hossain, M. F., Kabir, M. T., Islam, M. T., Rahman, M. M., & Rafe, M. R. (2017). Neuropsychological effects of caffeine: Is caffeine addictive. *Journal of Psychology and Psychotherapy, 7*(295), 2161-0487.

Uemura, K., Makizako, H., Lee, S., Doi, T., Lee, S., Tsutsumimoto, K., & Shimada, H. (2017). Behavioral protective factors of increased depressive symptoms in community-dwelling older adults: A prospective cohort study. *International Journal of Geriatric Psychiatry,* doi:10.1002/gps.4776

Ullman, A. D. (1952). Review of "Antabuse" in the treatment of alcoholism. *Psychological Bulletin, 49*(5), 557-558.

Ullrich, M., Weber, M., Post, A. M., Popp, S., Grein, J., Zechner, M., et al. (2017). OCD-like behavior is caused by dysfunction of thalamo-amygdala circuits and upregulated TrkB/ERK-MAPK signaling as a result of SPRED2 deficiency. *Molecular Psychiatry.* doi:10.1038/mp.2016.232

Uncapher, M. R., Lin, L., Rosen, L. D., Kirkorian, H. L., Baron, N. S., Bailey, K., ... & Wagner, A. D. (2017). Media multitasking and cognitive, psychological, neural, and learning differences. *Pediatrics, 140*(Supplement 2), S62-S66.

Underwood, M. K. (2011). Aggression. In M. K. Underwood & L. Rosen (Eds.), *Social development.* New York: Guilford.

Undurraga, J., & Baldessarini, R. J. (2012). Randomized, placebo-controlled trials of antidepressants for acute major depression: Thirty-year meta-analytic review. *Neuropsychopharmacology, 37*(4), 851-864.

Undurraga, J., & Baldessarini, R. J. (2017). Direct comparison of tricyclic and serotonin-reuptake inhibitor antidepressants in randomized head-to-head trials in acute major depression: Systematic review and meta-analysis. *Journal of Psychopharmacology, 31*(9), 1184-1189.

United Nations Office on Drugs and Crime (UNODC). (2017). Drug Use. https://www.unodc.org/unodc/en/data-and-analysis/statistics/drug-use.html

United Nations. (2011, July 19). Happiness should have greater role in development policy—UN Member States. *UN News Centre.* www.un.org/apps/news/story.asp?NewsID=39084 (accessed November 3, 2014)

Unkelbach, C. (2007). Reversing the truth effect: Learning the interpretation of processing fluency in judgments of truth. *Journal of Experimental Psychology: Learning, Memory, and Cognition, 33*(1), 219-230.

Unsworth, N., Brewer, G. A., & Spillers, G. J. (2011). Variation in working memory capacity and episodic memory: Examining the importance of encoding specificity. *Psychonomic Bulletin and Review, 18*(6), 1113-1118.

Unsworth, N., Spillers, G. J., & Brewer, G. A. (2012). The role of working memory in autobiographical retrieval: Individual differences in strategic search. *Memory, 20*(2), 167-176.

Urbina, S. (2011). Tests of intelligence. In R. J. Sternberg & S. B. Kaufman (Eds.), *The Cambridge handbook of intelligence.* New York: Cambridge University Press.

Urry, H. L., & others. (2004). Making a life worth living: Neural correlates of well-being. *Psychological Science, 15*(6), 367-372.

Uysal, A., Ascigil, E., & Turunc, G. (2017). Spousal autonomy support, need satisfaction, and well-being in individuals with chronic pain: A longitudinal study. *Journal of Behavioral Medicine, 40*(2), 281-292. doi:10.1007/s10865-016-9783-1

V

Vail, K. E., Juhl, J., Arndt, J., Vess, M., Routledge, C., & Rutjens, B. T. (2012). When death is good for life: Considering the positive trajectories of terror management. *Personality and Social Psychology Review, 16*(4), 303-329.

Vaillant, G. (2003). A 60-year follow-up of alcoholic men. *Addiction, 98*(8), 1043-1051.

Valenza, G., Citi, L., Lanata, A., Scilingo, E. P., & Barbieri, R. (2014, May 21). Revealing real-time emotional responses: A personalized assessment based on heartbeat dynamics. *Scientific Reports, 4,* 4998.

Van Boekel, M., Varma, K., & Varma, S. (2017). A retrieval-based approach to eliminating hindsight bias. *Memory, 25*(3), 377-390. doi:10.1080/09658211.2016.1176202

van Bokhoven, I., & others. (2006). Salivary testosterone and aggression, delinquency, and social dominance in a population-based longitudinal study of adolescent males. *Hormones and Behavior, 50*(1), 118-125.

Van de Vondervoort, J. W., Aknin, L. B., Kushnir, T., Slevinsky, J., & Hamlin, J. K. (2018). Selectivity in toddlers' behavioral and emotional reactions to prosocial and antisocial others. *Developmental Psychology.* in press.

van den Berg, S. M., de Moor, M. M., Verweij, K. H., Krueger, R. F., Luciano, M., Arias Vasquez, A., et al. (2016). Meta-analysis of genome-wide association studies for extraversion: Findings from the genetics of personality consortium. *Behavior Genetics, 46*(2), 170-182. doi:10.1007/s10519-015-9735-5

van der Kaap-Deeder, J., Audenaert, E., Vandevelde, S., Soenens, B., Van Mastrigt, S., Mabbe, E., & Vansteenkiste, M. (2017). Choosing when choices are limited: The role of perceived afforded choice and autonomy in prisoners' well-being. *Law and Human Behavior,* in press. doi:10.1037/lhb0000259

van der Ploeg, M. M., Brosschot, J. F., Verkuil, B., Gillie, B. L., Williams, D. P., Koenig, J., ... & Thayer, J. F. (2017a). Inducing unconscious stress: Cardiovascular activity in response to subliminal presentation of threatening and neutral words. *Psychophysiology.* in press.

van der Ploeg, M. M., Brosschot, J. F., Versluis, A., & Verkuil, B. (2017b). Peripheral physiological responses to subliminally presented negative affective stimuli: A systematic review. *Biological Psychology, 129,* 131-153.

van der Wal, R. C., Karremans, J. C., & Cillessen, A. N. (2014). It takes two to forgive: The interactive role of relationship value and executive control. *Personality and Social Psychology Bulletin, 40*(6), 803-815. doi:10.1177/0146167214525807

van Dinteren, R., Huster, R. J., Jongsma, M. L. A., Kessels, R. P. C., & Arns, M. (2017). Differences in cortical sources of the event-related P3 potential between young and old participants indicate frontal compensation. *Brain Topography,* 1-12. https://link.springer.com/article/10.1007/s10548-016-0542-y

van Doorn, G. S., & Taborsky, M. (2012). The evolution of generalized reciprocity on social interaction networks. *Evolution, 66*(3), 651-664.

van Duijl, M., Cardeña, E., & de Jong, J. (2005). The validity of DSM-IV dissociative disorders categories in south-west Uganda. *Transcultural Psychiatry, 42*(2), 219-241.

van Duijl, M., Kleijn, W., & de Jong, J. (2014). Unravelling the spirits' message: a study of help-seeking steps and explanatory models among patients suffering from spirit possession in Uganda. *International Journal of Mental Health Symptoms, 8,* 24.

Van Dyck, D., Cerin, El., Conway, T. L., De Bourdeaudhuij, I., Owen, N., Kerr, J., Cardon, G., & Sallis, J. F. (2017). Interacting psychosocial and environmental correlates of leisure-time physical activity: A three-country study. *Health Psychology, 36,* 699-709. http://dx.doi.org/10.1037/a0033516

Van Erum, J., Van Dam, D., & De Deyn, P. P. (2017). Sleep and Alzheimer's disease: A pivotal role for the suprachiasmatic nucleus? *Sleep Medicine Reviews.* in press. doi:10.1016/j.smrv.2017.07.005

van Geel, M., Goemans, A., Toprak, F., & Vedder, P. (2017). Which personality traits are related to traditional bullying and cyberbullying? A study with the Big Five, Dark Triad and sadism. *Personality and Individual Differences, 106,* 231-235. doi:10.1016/j.paid.2016.10.063

van Gerven, M.A.J. (2017). A primer on encoding models in sensory neuroscience *Journal of Mathematical Psychology, 76,* 172-183. DOI: 10.1016/j.jmp.2016.06.009

van Hulzen, K. J., Scholz, C. J., Franke, B., Ripke, S., Klein, M., McQuillin, A., et al. (2017). Genetic overlap between attention-deficit/hyperactivity disorder and bipolar disorder: Evidence from genome-wide association study meta-analysis. *Biological Psychiatry, 82*(9), 634-641.

Van Lange, P. A., Rusbult, C. E., Drigotas, S. M., Arriaga, X. B., Witcher, B. S., & Cox, C. L. (1997). Willingness to sacrifice in close relationships. *Journal of Personality and Social Psychology, 72*(6), 1373-1395.

van Leeuwen, T.M., Trautmann-Lengsfeld, S.A., Wallace, M.T., Engel, A.K., & Murray, M.M. (2016). Bridging the gap: Synaesthesia and multisensory processes. *Neuropsychologia, 88,* 1-4. doi: 10.1016/j.neuropsychologia.2016.06.007

van Maanen, A., Meijer, A. M., van der Heijden, K. B., & Oort, F. J. (2016). The effects of light therapy on sleep problems: A systematic review and meta-analysis. *Sleep medicine reviews, 29,* 52-62.

van Os, J., & Kapur, S. (2009). Schizophrenia. *Lancet, 374*(9690), 635-645.

Van Petegem, S., Vansteenkiste, M., Soenens, B., Zimmermann, G., Antonietti, J. P., Baudat, S., & Audenaert, E. (2017). When do adolescents accept or defy to maternal prohibitions? The role of social domain and communication style. *Journal of Youth and Adolescence, 46*(5), 1022-1037.

van Polanen, V., Bergmann Tiest, W. M., & Kappers, A. L. (2014). Parallel processing of shape and texture in haptic search. *Acta Psychologica, 150,* 35-40. doi:10.1016/j.actpsy.2014.04.004

Van Riper, M. (2007). Families of children with Down syndrome: Responding to "a change in plans" with resilience. *Journal of Pediatric Nursing, 22*(2), 116-128.

van Roekel, E., Verhagen, M., Engels, R. E., & Kuppens, P. (2017). Variation in the serotonin transporter polymorphism (5-HTTLPR) and inertia of negative and positive emotions in daily life. *Emotion. in press.* doi:10.1037/emo0000336

van Scheppingen, M. A., Jackson, J. J., Specht, J., Hutteman, R., Denissen, J. A., & Bleidorn, W. (2016). Personality trait development during the transition to parenthood: A test of social investment theory. *Social Psychological and Personality Science, 7*(5), 452-462. doi:10.1177/1948550616630032

van Viersen, S., Kroesbergen, E. H., Slot, E. M., & de Bree, E. H. (2016). High reading skills mask dyslexia in gifted children. *Journal Of Learning Disabilities, 49*(2), 189-199. doi:10.1177/0022219414538517

van Vliet, I. M., & others. (2013). An evaluation of irreversible psychosurgical treatment of patients with obsessive-compulsive disorder in the Netherlands, 2001-2008. *Journal of Nervous and Mental Disease, 201*(3), 226-228.

Vancampfort, D., Moens, H., Madou, T., De Backer, T., Vallons, V., Bruyninx, P., et al. (2016). Autonomous motivation is associated with the maintenance stage of behaviour change in people with affective disorders. *Psychiatry Research, 240,* 267-271. doi:10.1016/j.psychres.2016.04.005

Vandello, J. A., & Cohen, D. (2004). When believing is seeing: Sustaining norms of violence in cultures of honor. In M. Schaller & C. S. Crandall (Eds.), *The psychological foundations of culture* (pp. 281-304). Mahwah, NJ: Erlbaum.

Vandello, J. A., & Cohen, D. (2008). Culture, gender, and men's intimate partner violence. *Social and Personality Psychology Compass, 2*(2), 652-667.

Vandello, J. A., Cohen, D., Grandon, R., & Franiuk, R. (2009). Stand by your man: Indirect prescriptions for honorable violence and feminine loyalty in Canada, Chile, and the United States. *Journal of Cross-Cultural Psychology, 40*(1), 81-104.

Vanderwal, T., Eilbott, J., Finn, E. S., Craddock, R. C., Turnbull, A., & Castellanos, F. X. (2017). Individual differences in functional connectivity during naturalistic viewing conditions. *NeuroImage. in press.*

Vanini, G., Nemanis, K., Baghdoyan, H. A., & Lydic, R. (2014). GABAergic transmission in rat potine reticular formation regulates the induction phase of anaesthesia and modulates hyperalgesia caused by sleep deprivation. *European Journal of Neuroscience, 40*(1), 2264-2273.

Varela, F. J., Thompson, E., & Rosch, E. (2017). *The embodied mind: Cognitive science and human experience.* Cambridge, MA: MIT press.

Veale, D., Murphy, P., Ellison, N., Kanakam, N., & Costa, A. (2013). Autobiographical memories of vomiting in people with a specific phobia of vomiting (emetophobia). *Journal of Behavioral Therapy and Experimental Psychiatry, 44*(1), 14-20.

Vedder, P., & Phinney, J. S. (2014). Identity formation in bicultural youth: A developmental perspective. In V. Benet-Martinez & Y.-Y. Hong (Eds.), *The Oxford handbook of multicultural identity.* New York: Oxford University Press.

Velasquez, M. M., Crouch, C., Stephens, N. S., & DiClemente, C. C. (2016). *Group treatment for substance abuse: A stages-of-change therapy manual., 2nd ed.* New York: Guilford Press.

Velik, R. (2012). From simple receptors to complex multimodal percepts: A first global picture on the mechanisms involved in perceptual binding. *Frontiers in Psychology, 3,* 259.

Vena, J. (2015). Karen Horney. In D. L. Dobbert & T. X. Mackey (Eds.), *Deviance: Theories on behaviors that defy social norms* (pp. 48-57). Santa Barbara, CA: Praeger/ABC-CLIO.

Verberne, J., Risi, F., Campbell, L., Chambers, S., & O'Leary, S. (2017). The effect of scala tympani morphology on basilar membrane contact with a straight electrode array: A human temporal bone study. *Otology & Neurotology, 38*(1), 47-53.

Verduyn, P., Lee, D. S., Park, J., Shablack, H., Orvell, A., Bayer, J., Ybarra, O., Jonides, J., & Kross, E. (2015). Passive Facebook usage undermines affective well-being: Experimental and longitudinal evidence. *Journal of Experimental Psychology: General, 144*(2), 480-488.

Verguts, T., & Chen, Q. (2017). Numerical cognition: learning binds biology to culture. *Trends in Cognitive Sciences.* in press.

Vermetten, E., Schmahl, C., Lindner, S., Loewenstein, R. J., & Bremner, J. D. (2006). Hippocampal and amygdalar volumes in dissociative identity disorder. *American Journal of Psychiatry, 163*(4), 630-636.

Vernon, D., Hocking, I., & Tyler, T. C. (2016). An evidence-based review of creative problem solving tools: A practitioner's resource. *Human Resource Development Review, 15,* 230-259. doi:10.1177/1534484316641512

Vernon, D., Hocking, I., & Tyler, T. C. (2016). An evidence-based review of creative problem solving tools: A practitioner's resource. *Human Resource Development Review, 15*(2), 230-259. doi:10.1177/1534484316641512

Veroude, K., Zhang-James, Y., Fernàndez-Castillo, N., Bakker, M. J., Cormand, B., & Faraone, S. V. (2016). Genetics of aggressive behavior: An overview. *American Journal of Medical Genetics Part B: Neuropsychiatric Genetics, 171*(1), 3-43. doi:10.1002/ajmg.b.32364

Verschuere, B., Crombez, G., De Clercq, A., & Koster, E. H. (2005). Psychopathic traits and autonomic responding to concealed information in a prison sample. *Psychophysiology, 42*(2), 239-245.

Vickers, K., Ein, N., Koerner, N., Kusec, A., McCabe, R. E., Rowa, K., & Antony, M. M. (2017). Self-reported hygiene-related behaviors among individuals with contamination-related obsessive-compulsive disorder, individuals with anxiety disorders, and nonpsychiatric controls. *Journal of Obsessive-Compulsive and Related Disorders, 14,* 71-83.

Vihman, M. M. (2014). *Phonological development* (2nd ed.). New York: Wiley.

Vijayan, S., Lepage, K. Q., Kopell, N. J., & Cash, S. S. (2017). Frontal beta-theta network during REM sleep. *Elife, 6,* e18894.

Vinberg, M., Mellerup, E., Andersen, P. K., Bennike, B., & Kessing, L. V. (2010). Variations in 5-HTTLPR: Relation to familiar risk of affective disorder, life events, neuroticism, and cortisol. *Progress in Neuro-Psychopharmacology & Biological Psychiatry, 34*(1), 86-91.

Viswanath, B., Maroky, A. S., Math, S. B., John, J. P., Benegal, V., Hamza, A., & Chaturvedi, S. K. (2012). Psychological impact of the tsunami on elderly survivors. *American Journal of Geriatric Psychiatry, 20*(5), 402-407.

Vlaev, I., Crockett, M. J., Clark, L., Müller, U., & Robbins, T. W. (2017). Serotonin enhances the impact of health information on food choice. *Cognitive, Affective & Behavioral Neuroscience, 17*(3), 542-553. doi:10.3758/s13415-016-0496-2

Vogt, T. M., Mullooly, J. P., Ernst, D., Pople, C. R., & Hollis, J. F. (1992). Social networks as predictors of ischemic heart disease, cancer, stroke, and hypertension. *Journal of Clinical Epidemiology, 45*(6), 659-666.

Vohs, K. D., & Baumeister, R. F. (Eds.). (2016). *Handbook of self-regulation: Research, theory, and applications.* New York: Guilford.

Vohs, K. D., & Luce, M. F. (2010). Judgment and decision making. In R. F. Baumeister & E. J. Finkel (Eds.), *Advanced social psychology: The state of the science* (pp. 733-756). Oxford, UK: Oxford University Press.

Voigt, J., & Fink, H. (2015). Serotonin controlling feeding and satiety. *Behavioural Brain Research, 277,* 14-31. doi:10.1016/j.bbr.2014.08.065

Volkow, N. D., Compton, W. M., & Wargo, E. M. (2017). The risks of marijuana use during pregnancy. *JAMA, 317*(2), 129-130.

Volkow, N. D., Wang, G. J., Newcorn, J. H., Kollins, S. H., Wigal, T. L., Telang, F., et al. (2011). Motivation deficit in ADHD is associated with dysfunction of the dopamine reward pathway. *Molecular Psychiatry, 16*(11), 1147-1154.

von Békésy, G. (1960). Vibratory patterns of the basilar membrane. In E. G. Wever (Ed.), *Experiments in hearing.* New York: McGraw-Hill.

von Hippel, C., Henry, J. D., Terrett, G., Mercuri, K., McAlear, K., & Rendell, P. G. (2017). Stereotype threat and social function in opioid substitution therapy patients. *British Journal Of Clinical Psychology, 56*(2), 160-171. doi:10.1111/bjc.12128

Von Neumann, J. (1958). *The computer and the brain.* New Haven, CT: Yale University Press.

Voss, U., Holzmann, R., Hobson, A., Paulus, W., Koppehele-Gossel, J., Klimke, A., & Nitsche, M. A. (2014). Induction of self awareness in dreams through frontal low current stimulation of gamma activity. *Nature Neuroscience, 17*(6), 810-812.

Vouloumanos, A., & Curtin, S. (2014). Foundational tuning: How infants' attention to speech predicts language development. *Cognitive Science, 38,* 1675-1686.

Vrticka, P., Lordier, L., Bediou, B., & Sander, D. (2014). Human amygdala response to dynamic facial expressions of positive and negative surprise. *Emotion, 14*(1), 161-169. doi:10.1037/a0034619

Vukovic, J., Marmorstein, L. Y., McLaughlin, P. J., Sasaki, T., Plant, G. W., Harvey, A. R., & Ruitenberg, M. J. (2009). Lack of fibulin-3 alters regenerative tissue responses in the primary olfactory pathway. *Matrix Biology, 28*(7), 406-415.

Vyazovskiy, V. V., Olcese, U., Hanlon, E. C., Nir, Y., Cirelli, C. & Tononi, G. (2011). Local sleep in awake rats. *Nature, 472,* 443-447.

Vygotsky, L. S. (1962). *Thought and language.* Cambridge, MA: MIT Press.

W

Wachtel, P. L. (2017). Psychoanalysis and the Moebius strip: Reexamining the relation between the internal world and the world of daily experience. *Psychoanalytic Psychology, 34*(1), 58-68. doi:10.1037/pap0000101

Wacker, J. (2017). Effects of positive emotion, extraversion, and dopamine on cognitive stability-flexibility and frontal eeg asymmetry. *Psychophysiology*, in press. doi:10.1111/psyp.12727

Wacker, J., Mueller, E. M., Hennig, J., & Stemmler, G. (2012). How to consistently link extraversion and intelligence to the catechol-O-methyltransferase (COMT) gene: On defining and measuring psychological phenotypes in neurogenetic research. *Journal of Personality and Social Psychology, 102*(2), 427-444.

Wagner, A. D., & others. (1998). Building memories: Remembering and forgetting of verbal experiences as predicted by brain activity. *Science, 281*(5380), 1185-1187.

Wagner, M. T., Mithoefer, M. C., Mithoefer, A. T., MacAulay, R. K., Jerome, L., Yazar-Klosinski, B., & Doblin, R. (2017). Therapeutic effect of increased openness: Investigating mechanism of action in MDMA-assisted psychotherapy. *Journal of Psychopharmacology, 31*(8), 967-974.

Wai, J., Lubinski, D., & Benbow, C. P. (2005). Creativity and occupational accomplishments among intellectually precocious youths: An age 13 to age 33 longitudinal study. *Journal of Educational Psychology, 97*(3), 484-492.

Wakefield, J. C. (2015). Diagnostic issues and controversies in DSM-5. *Annual Review of Clinical Psychology* (vol. 11). Palo Alto, CA: Annual Reviews.

Wakefield, J. C. (2016). Diagnostic issues and controversies in DSM-5: return of the false positives problem. *Annual Review of Clinical Psychology, 12,* 105-132.

Walder, D. J., Ospina, L., Daly, M., Statucka, M., & Raparia, E. (2012). Early neurodevelopment and psychosis risk: Role of neurohormones and biological sex in modulating genetic, prenatal, and sensory processing factors in brain development. In X. Anastassion-Hadjicharalambous (Ed.), *Psychosis: Causes, diagnosis and treatment.* Hauppauge, NY: Nova Science.

Walker, B. R., Jackson, C. J., & Frost, R. (2017). A comparison of revised reinforcement sensitivity theory with other contemporary personality models. *Personality and Individual Differences, 109,* 232-236. doi:10.1016/j.paid.2016.12.053

Walker, E. R., & Druss, B. G. (2017). Cumulative burden of comorbid mental disorders, substance use disorders, chronic medical conditions, and poverty on health among adults in the USA. *Psychology, Health & Medicine, 22*(6), 727-735.

Walker, L. J. (2014a). Moral personality, motivation, and identity. In M. Killen & J. G. Smetana (Eds.), *Handbook of moral development* (2nd ed.). New York: Psychology Press.

Walker, L. J. (2014b). Prosocial exemplarity in adolescence and adulthood. In L. Padilla-Walker & G. Carlo (Eds.), *Prosocial behavior.* New York: Oxford University Press.

Walkup, J. T., & Mohatt, J. W. (2017). 1.2 Psychopharmacology of obsessive-compulsive disorder: Weighing the evidence versus the risk. *Journal of the American Academy of Child & Adolescent Psychiatry, 56*(10), S134.

Wallace, J., Covassin, T., Nogle, S., Gould, D., & Kovan, J. (2017). Knowledge of concussion and reporting behaviors in high school athletes with or without access to an athletic trainer. *Journal of Athletic Training, 52*(3), 228–235.

Wallien, M. S. C., Veenstra, R., Kreukels, B. P. C., & Cohen-Kettenis, P. T. (2010). Peer group status of gender dysphoric children: A sociometric study. *Archives of Sexual Behavior, 39*(2), 553–560.

Walsh, C. E., & Hitchcock, P. F. (2017). Progranulin regulates neurogenesis in the developing vertebrate retina. *Developmental Neurobiology, 77*(9), 1114–1129. doi:10.1002/dneu.22499

Walsh, Z., Callaway, R., Belle-Isle, L., Capler, R., Kay, R., Lucas, P., & Holtzman, S. (2013). Cannabis for therapeutic purposes: Patient characteristics, access, and reasons for use. *International Journal of Drug Policy, 24*(6), 511–516.

Walton, K. E., & Roberts, B. W. (2004). On the relationship between substance use and personality traits: Abstainers are not maladjusted. *Journal of Research in Personality, 38*(6), 515–535.

Wammes, J. D., Seli, P., Cheyne, J. A., Boucher, P. O., & Smilek, D. (2016). Mind wandering during lectures II: Relation to academic performance. *Scholarship of Teaching And Learning In Psychology, 2*(1), 33–48. doi:10.1037/stl0000055

Wampold, B. E. (2001). *The great psychotherapy debate: Models, methods, and findings.* Mahwah, NJ: Erlbaum.

Wampold, B. E. (2013). The good, the bad, and the ugly: A 50-year perspective on the outcome problem. *Psychotherapy, 50*(1), 16–24.

Wampold, B. E., & Brown, G. S. (2005). Estimating variability in outcomes attributable to therapists: A naturalistic study of outcomes of managed care. *Journal of Consulting and Clinical Psychology, 73*(5), 914–923.

Wampold, B. E., Flückiger, C., Del Re, A. C., Yulish, N. E., Frost, N. D., Pace, B. T., et al. (2017). In pursuit of truth: A critical examination of meta-analyses of cognitive behavior therapy. *Psychotherapy Research, 27*(1), 14–32.

Wang, B., Deveaux, L., Li, X., Marshall, S., Chen, X., & Stanton, B. (2014). The impact of youth, family, peer, and neighborhood risk factors on developmental trajectories of risk involvement from early through middle adolescence. *Social Science Medicine, 106,* 43–52.

Wang, C. C., Shih, H. C., Shyu, B. C., & Huang, A. C. W. (2017). Effects of thalamic hemorrhagic lesions on explicit and implicit learning during the acquisition and retrieval phases in an animal model of central post-stroke pain. *Behavioural brain research, 317,* 251–262.

Wang, M., Rieger, M. O., & Hens, T. (2017). The impact of culture on loss aversion. *Journal of Behavioral Decision Making, 30*(2), 270–281. doi:10.1002/bdm.1941

Wang, S., Tudusciuc, O., Mamelak, A. N., Ross, I. B., Adolphs, R., & Rutishauser, U. (2014). Neurons in the human amygdala selective for perceived emotion. *Proceedings of the National Academy of Sciences USA, 111*(30), E3110–E3119.

Wang, S., Yang, Y., Xing, W., Chen, J., Liu, C., & Luo, X. (2014). Altered neural circuits related to sustained attention and executive control in children with ADHD: An event-related fMRI study. *Clinical Neurophysiology, 124*(11), 2181–2190.

Wang, X., Zheng, L., Li, L., Zheng, Y., Sun, P., Zhou, F. A., & Guo, X. (2017). Immune to situation: The self-serving bias in unambiguous contexts. *Frontiers In Psychology, 8.*

Wang, Y., & Yu, C. (2017). Social interaction-based consumer decision-making model in social commerce: The role of word of mouth and observational learning. *International Journal of Information Management, 37*(3), 179–189.

Wang, Z., McGlynn, K. A., Rajpert-De Meyts, E., Bishop, D. T., Chung, C. C., Dalgaard, M. D., et al. (2017). Meta-analysis of five genome-wide association studies identifies multiple new loci associated with testicular germ cell tumor. *Nature Genetics.* in press.

Ward, J., & Banissy, M. J. (2015). Explaining mirror-touch synesthesia. *Cognitive Neuroscience, 6*(2–3), 118–133. doi:10.1080/17588928.2015.1042444

Ward, S. J., & King, L. A. (2016). Socrates' dissatisfaction, a happiness arms race, and the trouble with eudaimonic well-being. In J. Vittersø (Ed.), *Handbook of Eudaimonic Wellbeing.* (pp.523–531). New York: Springer.

Ward, S. J. & King, L.A. (2017). Individual differences in faith in intuition predict harsher moral judgments. *Journal of Personality and Social Psychology.* in press.

Wardenaar, K. J., Lim, C. C., Al-Hamzawi, A. O., Alonso, J., Andrade, L. H., Benjet, C., et al. (2017). The cross-national epidemiology of specific phobia in the World Mental Health Surveys. *Psychological Medicine, 47*(10), 1744–1760.

Ward-Fear, G., Thomas, J., Webb, J. K., Pearson, D. J., & Shine, R. (2017). Eliciting conditioned taste aversion in lizards: Live toxic prey are more effective than scent and taste cues alone. *Integrative Zoology, 12*(2), 112–120.

Warneken F. (2013). Young children proactively remedy unnoticed accidents. *Cognition, 126*(1), 101–108.

Warneken, F. (2015). Precocious prosociality: Why do young children help? *Child Development Perspectives, 9*(1), 1–6. doi:10.1111/cdep.12101

Warneken F. (2016). Insights into the biological foundation of human altruistic sentiments. *Current Opinion in Psychology, 7,* 51–56

Warneken, F. (2018). How children solve the two challenges of cooperation. *Annual Review of Psychology, 69.* in press.

Warneken, F., & Tomasello, M. (2007). Helping and cooperation at 14 months of age. *Infancy, 11,* 271–294. doi:10.1080/15250000701310389S.

Warnica, W., & others. (2014). Copy number variable microRNAs in schizophrenia and their neurodevelopmental gene targets. *Biological Psychiatry, 77*(2), 158–166.

Warrier, V., Grasby, K., Uzefovsky, F., Toro, R., Smith, P., Chakrabarti, B., et al. (2017). A meta-analysis of cognitive empathy: Heritability and correlates of the 'reading the mind in the Eyes' etest with psychiatric conditions, psychological traits and subcortical volumes. *European Neuropsychopharmacology, 27,* S503–S504.

Watanabe, H., & Mizunami, M. (2007). Pavlov's cockroach: Classical conditioning of salivation in an insect. *PloS One, 2*(6), e529.

Watanabe, S., & Aust, U. (2017). Object and picture perception. In J. Call, G. M. Burghardt, I. M. Pepperberg, C. T. Snowdon, & T. Zentall (Eds.), *APA handbook of comparative psychology: Perception, learning, and cognition* (pp. 117–140). Washington, DC: American Psychological Association. doi:10.1037/0000012-006

Waters, A. M., Peters, R.-M., Forrest, K. E., & Zimmer-Gembeck, M. (2014). Fear acquisition and extinction in offspring of mothers with anxiety and depressive disorders. *Developmental Cognitive Neuroscience, 7,* 30–42.

Watson, D. (2001). Positive affectivity: The disposition to experience pleasurable emotional states. In C. R. Snyder & S. J. Lopez (Eds.), *Handbook of positive psychology.* New York: Oxford University Press.

Watson, D. L., & Tharp, R. G. (2014). *Self-directed behavior* (10th ed.). Boston: Cengage.

Watson, J. B., & Rayner, R. (1920). Conditioned emotional reactions. *Journal of Experimental Psychology, 3*(1), 1–14.

Watson, M., Homewood, J., Haviland, J., & Bliss, J. M. (2005). Influence of psychological response on breast cancer survival: A 10-year follow-up of a population-based cohort. *European Journal of Cancer, 41*(12), 1710–1714.

Watson, N. F., Martin, J. L., Wise, M. S., Carden, K. A., Kirsch, D. B., Kristo, D. A., ... & Rowley, J. A. (2017). Delaying Middle School and High School Start Times Promotes Student Health and Performance: An American Academy of Sleep Medicine Position Statement. *Journal of Clinical Sleep Medicine, 13*(4), 623–625.

Watson, P., Raju, P., & Soklaridis, S. (2017). Teaching not-knowing: Strategies for cultural competence in psychotherapy supervision. *Academic Psychiatry, 41*(1), 55–61.

Waugh, W. E., & Brownell, C. A. (2017). "Help Yourself!" What can toddlers' helping failures tell us about the development of prosocial behavior? *Infancy, 22,* 665–680.

Way, B. M., & Gurbaxani, B. M. (2008). A genetics primer for social health research. *Social and Personality Psychology Compass, 2*(2), 785–816.

Webb, R. T., Kontopantelis, E., Doran, T., Qin, P., Creed, F., & Kapur, N. (2012). Suicide risk in primary care patients with major physical diseases: A case-control study. *Archives of General Psychiatry, 69*(3), 256–264.

Webb, W. B. (2000). Sleep. In A. Kazdin (Ed.), *Encyclopedia of psychology.* Washington, DC, & New York: American Psychological Association and Oxford University Press.

Wechsler, D. (1939). *The measurement of adult intelligence.* Baltimore, MD: Williams & Wilkins.

Wechsler, H., Lee, J. E., Kuo, M., & Lee, H. (2000). College binge drinking in the 1990s—A continuing health problem: Results of the Harvard University School of Public Health 1999 College Alcohol Study. *Journal of American College Health, 48*(5), 199–210.

Wechsler, H., Lee, J. E., Kuo, M., Seibring, M., Nelson, T. F., & Lee, H. (2002). Trends in college binge drinking during a period of increased prevention efforts: Findings from 4 Harvard School of Public Health college alcohol study surveys: 1993–2001. *Journal of American College Health, 50*(5), 203–217.

Weeks, J. C., & Hasher, L. (2017). Divided attention reduces resistance to distraction at encoding but not retrieval. *Psychonomic Bulletin & Review, 24*(4), 1268–1273.

Wegmann, K. M. (2017). 'His skin doesn't match what he wants to do': Children's perceptions of stereotype threat. *American Journal of Orthopsychiatry,* doi:10.1037/ort0000238

Wehbe-Alamah, H., & Wolgamott, S. (2014). Uncovering the mask of borderline personality disorder: Knowledge to empower primary care providers. *Journal of the American Association of Nurse Practitioners, 26*(6), 292–300.

Weidemann, G., Satkunarajah, M., & Lovibond, P. F. (2016). I think, therefore eyeblink: The importance of contingency awareness in conditioning. *Psychological Science, 27*(4), 467–475.

Weinbach, N., Sher, H., & Bohon, C. (2018). Differences in Emotion Regulation Difficulties Across Types of Eating Disorders During Adolescence. *Journal of Abnormal Child Psychology.* in press.

Weiner, B. (2006). *Social motivation, justice, and the moral emotions: An attributional approach.* Mahwah, NJ: Erlbaum.

Weiner, I. B. (2004). Rorschach assessment: Current status. In M. Hersen (Ed.), *Comprehensive handbook of psychological assessment* (vol. 2). New York: Wiley.

Weinstein, A., & Weinstein, Y. (2014). Exercise addiction—diagnosis, bio-psychological mechanisms, and treatment issues. *Current Pharmaceutical Design, 20*(25), 4062–4069.

Weir, W. (1984, October 15). Another look at subliminal "facts." *Advertising Age,* 46.

Weisleder, A., & Fernald, A. (2013). Talking to children matters: Early language experience strengthens processing and builds vocabulary. *Psychological Science, 24*(11), 2143–2152. doi:10.1177/0956797613488145

Weisman, O., Zagoory-Sharon, O., & Feldman, R. (2014). Oxytocin administration, salivary testosterone, and father-infant social behavior. *Progress in Neuro-Psychopharmacology and Biological Psychiatry, 49,* 47–52.

Weiss, A. (2017). Personality traits: A view from the animal kingdom. *Journal of Personality*, doi:10.1111/jopy.12310

Weiss, A., Baselmans, B. L., Hofer, E., Yang, J., Okbay, A., Lind, P. A., et al. (2016). Personality polygenes, positive affect, and life satisfaction. *Twin Research and Human Genetics, 19*(5), 407–417. doi:10.1017/thg.2016.65

Weiss, A., King, J. E., & Perkins, L. (2006). Personality and subjective well-being in orangutans (*Pongo pygmaeus and Pongo abelii*). *Journal of Personality and Social Psychology, 90*(3), 501–511.

Weissman, M. M., & Olfson, M. (1995). Depression in women: Implications for health care research. *Science, 269*(5225), 799–801.

Weitlauf, A. S., & others. (2014). *Therapies for children with autism spectrum disorder: Behavioral interventions update.* Comparative Effectiveness Review No. 137. AHRQ Publication No. 14-EHC036-EF. Rockville, MD: Agency for Healthcare Research and Quality. www.effectivehealthcare.ahrq.gov/reports/final.cfm (accessed January 8, 2015)

Weitlauf, A. S., Sathe, N., McPheeters, M. L., & Warren, Z. E. (2017). Interventions targeting sensory challenges in autism spectrum disorder: A systematic review. *Pediatrics, 139*(6), e20170347.

Welborn, B. L., Gunter, B. C., Vezich, I. S., & Lieberman, M. D. (2017). Neural correlates of the false consensus effect: Evidence for motivated projection and regulatory restraint. *Journal of Cognitive Neuroscience, 29*(4), 708–717. doi:10.1162/jocn_a_01084

Welcome, S. E., Paivio, A., McRae, K., & Joanisse, M. F. (2011). An electrophysiological study of task demands on concreteness effects: Evidence for dual coding theory. *Experimental Brain Research, 212*(3), 347–358.

Wellman, H. M., & Woolley, J. D. (1990). From simple desires to ordinary beliefs: The early development of everyday psychology. *Cognition, 35*(3), 245–275.

Wells, G. L. (1993). What do we know about eyewitness identification? *American Psychologist, 48*(5), 553–571.

Wells, G. L., Steblay, N. K., & Dysart, J. E. (2011). *A test of the simultaneous vs. sequential lineup methods: An initial report of the AJS National Eyewitness Identification Field Studies.* Des Moines, IA: American Judicature Society.

Wen, Z., Cheng, T. L., Yin, D. Z., Sun, S. B., Wang, Z., Yu, S. Y., et al. S. (2017). Identification of the genetic cause for childhood disintegrative disorder by whole-exome sequencing. *Neuroscience Bulletin, 33*(2), 251–254.

West, R. (2005). Time for a change: Putting the transtheoretical (stages of change) model to rest. *Addiction, 100*(8), 1036–1039.

Westerhof, G. J., Bohlmeijer, E. T., & McAdams, D. P. (2017). The relation of ego integrity and despair to personality traits and mental health. *The Journals of Gerontology: Series B, 72*(3), 400–407.

Weston, S. J., Hill, P. L., & Jackson, J. J. (2015). Personality traits predict the onset of disease. *Social Psychological and Personality Science, 6*, 309–317. doi:10.1177/1948550614553248

Wetherell, M. (2012). The prejudice problematic. In J. Dixon, M. Keynes, & M. Levine (Eds.), *Beyond prejudice.* New York: Cambridge University Press.

Wheeler, J. J., Mayton, M. R., & Carter, S. L. (2015). *Methods for teaching students with autism spectrum disorders.* Upper Saddle River, NJ: Pearson.

White, E. K., Warren, C. S., Cao, L., Crosby, R. D., Engel, S. G., Wonderlich, S. A., et al. (2016). Media exposure and associated stress contribute to eating pathology in women with anorexia nervosa: Daily and momentary associations. *International Journal of Eating Disorders, 49*(6), 617–621. doi:10.1002/eat.22490

White, J. W., & Frabutt, J. M. (2006). Violence against girls and women: An integrative developmental perspective. In J. Worell & C. D. Goodheart (Eds.), *Handbook of girls' and women's psychological health: Gender and well-being across the lifespan* (pp. 85–93). New York: Oxford University Press.

White, R. C., & Aimola Davies, A. (2008). Attention set for numbers: Expectation and perceptual load in inattentional blindness. *Journal of Experimental Psychology: Human Perception and Performance, 34*(5), 1092–1107.

White, R. E., Prager, E. O., Schaefer, C., Kross, E., Duckworth, A. L., & Carlson, S. M. (2017). The "Batman Effect": Improving perseverance in young children. *Child Development, 88*(5), 1563–1571.

White, R., Knight, G. P., Jensen, M., & Gonzales, N. A. (2017). Ethnic socialization in neighborhood contexts: Implications for ethnic attitude and identity development among Mexican-origin adolescents. *Child Development.* in press.

Whitman, J. B., North, C. S., Downs, D. L., & Spitznagel, E. L. (2013). A prospective study of the onset of PTSD symptoms in the first month after trauma exposure. *Annals of Clinical Psychiatry, 25*, 8E-17E.

Whorf, B. L. (1956). *Language, thought, and creativity.* New York: Wiley.

Wichman, S., Kirschbaum, C., Böhmec, C., & Petrowski, K. (2017). Cortisol stress response in post-traumatic stress disorder, panic disorder, and major depressive disorder patients. *Psychoneuroendocrinology, 83*, 135–141.

Wickersham, I. R., & Feinberg, E. H. (2012). New technologies for imaging synaptic partners. *Current Opinion in Neurobiology, 22*(1), 121–127.

Wiebe, R. P. (2004). Delinquent behavior and the Five Factor model: Hiding in the adaptive landscape? *Individual Differences Research, 2*(1), 38–62.

Wieder-Huszla, S., & others. (2014). Effects of socio-demographic, personality, and medical factors on quality of life of postmenopausal women. *International Journal of Environmental Research and Public Health, 11*(7), 6692–6708.

Wiemer, J., Gerdes, A. B., & Pauli, P. (2012). The effects of an unexpected spider stimulus on skin conductance responses and eye movements: An inattentional blindness study. *Psychological Research, 77*(2), 155–166.

Wiemerslage, L., Nilsson, E. K., Solstrand Dahlberg, L., Ence-Eriksson, F., Castillo, S., Larsen, A. L., et al. (2016). An obesity-associated risk allele within the FTO gene affects human brain activity for areas important for emotion, impulse control and reward in response to food images. *European Journal of Neuroscience, 43*(9), 1173–1180. doi:10.1111/ejn.13177

Wiernik, E., & others. (2014). Perceived stress, sex, and occupational status interact to increase the risk of future high blood pressure: The IPC cohort study. *Journal of Hypertension, 32*(10), 1979–1986.

Wiersma, D., Nienhuis, F. J., Slooff, C. J., & Giel, R. (1998). Natural course of schizophrenic disorders: A 15-year followup of a Dutch incidence cohort. *Schizophrenia Bulletin, 24*(1), 75–85.

Wilder-Smith, A., Mustafa, F. B., Earnest, A., Gen, L., & Macary, P. A. (2013). Impact of partial sleep deprivation on immune markers. *Sleep Medicine, 14*(10), 1031–1034.

Wilhelm, O., Hildebrandt, A., Manske, K., Schacht, A., & Sommer, W. (2014). Test battery for measuring the perception and recognition of facial expressions of emotion. *Frontiers in Psychology, 5*, 404.

Willard, G., Isaac, K. J., & Carney, D. R. (2015). Some evidence for the nonverbal contagion of implicit racial bias. *Organizational Behavior and Human Decision Processes.* (in press)

Willard, J., & Madon, S. (2016). Understanding the connections between self-fulfilling prophecies and social problems. In S. Trusz & P. Bąbel (Eds.), *Interpersonal and intrapersonal expectancies* (pp. 117–124). New York: Routledge/Taylor & Francis Group.

Willcox, B. J., & Willcox, D. C. (2014). Caloric restriction, caloric restriction mimetics, and healthy aging in Okinawa: Controversies and clinical implications. *Current Opinion in Clinical Nutrition and Metabolic Care, 17*(1), 51–58.

Willcox, D. C., Scapagnini, G., & Willcox, B. J. (2014). Healthy aging diets other than Mediterranean: A focus on the Okinawan diet. *Mechanisms of Aging and Development, 136–137*, 148–162.

Williams, C. L., & Lally, S. J. (2017). MMPI-2, MMPI-2-RF, and MMPI-A administrations (2007–2014): Any evidence of a 'new standard?' *Professional Psychology: Research And Practice, 48*(4), 267–274. doi:10.1037/pro0000088

Williams, J. D., & Gruzelier, J. H. (2001). Differentiation of hypnosis and relaxation by analysis of narrow band theta and alpha frequencies. *International Journal of Clinical and Experimental Hypnosis, 49*(3), 185–206.

Williams, J. L., Aiyer, S. M., Durkee, M. I., & Tolan, P. H. (2014). The protective role of ethnic identity for urban adolescent males facing multiple stressors. *Journal of Youth and Adolescence, 43*(10), 1728–1741.

Williams, L. M. (1995). Recovered memories of abuse in women with documented child sexual victimization histories. *Journal of Traumatic Stress, 8*(4), 649–673.

Williams, L. M. (2003). Understanding child abuse and violence against women: A life-course perspective. *Journal of Interpersonal Violence, 18*(4), 441–451.

Williams, L. M. (2004). Researcher-advocate collaborations to end violence against women. *Journal of Interpersonal Violence, 19*(11), 1350–1357.

Williams, R. B. (2001). Hostility (and other psychosocial risk factors): Effects on health and the potential for successful behavioral approaches to prevention and treatment. In A. Baum, T. A. Revenson, & J. E. Singer (Eds.), *Handbook of health psychology.* Mahwah, NJ: Erlbaum.

Williams, R. B. (2002). Hostility, neuroendocrine changes, and health outcomes. In H. G. Koenig & H. J. Cohen (Eds.), *The link between religion and health.* New York: Oxford University Press.

Williams, S. E., van Zanten, J. J. V., Trotman, G. P., Quinton, M. L., & Ginty, A. T. (2017). Challenge and threat imagery manipulates heart rate and anxiety responses to stress. International *Journal of Psychophysiology, 117*, 111–118.

Wilson, A. E., O'Connor, D. B., Lawton, R., Hill, P. L., & Roberts, B. W. (2016). Conscientiousness and fruit and vegetable consumption: Exploring behavioural intention as a mediator. *Psychology, Health & Medicine, 21*(4), 469–475. doi:10.1080/13548506.2015.1093644

Wilson, G. T., Grilo, C. M., & Vitousek, K. M. (2007). Psychological treatment of eating disorders. *American Psychologist, 62*(3), 199–216.

Wilson, H. E. (2015). Social and emotional characteristics and early childhood mathematical and literacy giftedness: Observations from parents and childcare providers using the ECLS-B. *Journal for the Education of the Gifted, 38*(4), 377–404. doi:10.1177/0162353215607323

Wilson, K. P., Carter, M. W., Wiener, H. L., DeRamus, M. L., Bulluck, J. C., Watson, L. R., et al. (2017). Object play in infants with autism spectrum disorder: A longitudinal retrospective video analysis. *Autism & Developmental Language Impairments, 2*, 1–12.

Wilson, R. S., Barnes, L. L., Aggarwal, N. T., Boyle, P. A., Hebert, L. E., Mendes de Leon, C. F., & Evans, D. A. (2010). Cognitive activity and the cognitive morbidity of Alzheimer disease. *Neurology, 75*(11), 990–996.

Wilt, J., & Revelle, W. (2017). Extraversion. In T.A. Widiger (Ed.), *Oxford Handbook of the Five Factor Model.* New York: Oxford University Press.

Wiltermuth, S. S., & Heath, C. (2009). Synchrony and cooperation. *Psychological Science, 20*(1), 1–5.

Winer, E. S., & Snodgrass, M. (2015). Signal detection theory. In M. Matthen, M. Matthen (Eds.), *The Oxford handbook of philosophy of perception* (pp. 717–733). New York, NY: Oxford University Press.

Winner, E. (2000). The origins and ends of giftedness. *American Psychologist, 55*(1), 159-169.

Winner, E. (2006). Development in the arts. In W. Damon & R. Lerner (Eds.), *Handbook of child psychology* (6th ed.). New York: Wiley.

Winter, D. G. (2005). Measuring the motives of political actors at a distance. In J. M. Post (Ed.), *The psychological assessment of political leaders: With profiles of Saddam Hussein and Bill Clinton* (pp. 153-177). Ann Arbor: University of Michigan Press.

Wirth, A., Holst, K., & Ponimaskin, E. (2017). How serotonin receptors regulate morphogenic signalling in neurons. *Progress in Neurobiology, 151*, 35-56.

Wiseman, R., & Watt, C. (2006). Belief in psychic ability and the misattribution hypothesis: A qualitative review. *British Journal of Psychology, 97*(Pt. 3), 323-338.

Witelson, S. F., Kigar, D. L., & Harvey, T. (1999). The exceptional brain of Albert Einstein. *Lancet, 353*(9174), 2149-2153.

Witherington, D. C., & Lickliter, R. (2017). Integrating development and evolution in psychological science: Evolutionary developmental psychology, developmental systems, and explanatory pluralism. *Human Development, 59*(4), 200-234. doi:10.1159/000450715

Wittayanukorn, S., Qian, J., & Hansen, R. A. (2014). Prevalence of depressive symptoms and predictors of treatment among U.S. adults from 2005 to 2010. *General Hospital Psychiatry, 36*(3), 330-336.

Woike, B. (2001). Working with free response data: Let's not give up hope. *Psychological Inquiry, 12*(3), 157-159.

Woike, B. A. (2008). The state of the story in personality psychology. *Social and Personality Psychology Compass, 2*(1), 434-443.

Womick, J., & King, L. A. (2018, in press). Personality and well-being. In B. J. Carducci (Editor-in-Chief) & J. S. Mio & R. E. Riggio (Vol. Eds.), *The Wiley-Blackwell encyclopedia of personality and individual differences: Vol. IV. Clinical, applied, and cross-cultural research*. Hoboken, NJ: John Wiley & Sons.

Wong, C. K., Marshall, N. S., Grunstein, R. R., Ho, S. S., Fois, R. A., Hibbs, D. E., et al. (2017). Spontaneous adverse event reports associated with Zolpidem in the United States 2003-2012. *Journal of clinical sleep medicine, 13*(2), 223-234.

Wong, D. L., & others. (2012). Epinephrine: A short- and long-term regulator of stress and developmental illness. *Cellular and Molecular Neurobiology, 32*(5), 737-748.

Wong, D., Kuwabara, H., Roberts, J., Gapasin, L., Mishra, C., Brasic, J., ... & Kem, W. (2017). Test-retest and DXMB-A occupancy of human alpha 7 nicotinic acetylcholine receptors measured by 18F-ASEM. *Journal of Nuclear Medicine, 58*(supplement 1), 134-134.

Wong, P. P. (2017). Meaning-centered approach to research and therapy, second wave positive psychology, and the future of humanistic psychology. *The Humanistic Psychologist, 45*(3), 207-216. doi:10.1037/hum0000062

WonPat-Borja, A. J., Yang, L. H., Link, B. G., & Phelan, J. C. (2012). Eugenics, genetics, and mental illness stigma in Chinese Americans. *Social Psychiatry and Psychiatric Epidemiology, 47*(1), 145-156.

Woo, C.C., & Leon, M. (2013). Environmental enrichment as an effective treatment for autism: A randomized controlled trial. *Behavioral Neuroscience, 127*, 487-497.

Wood, D., Harms, P., & Vazire, S. (2010). Perceiver effects as projective tests: What your perceptions of others say about you. *Journal of Personality and Social Psychology, 99*(1), 174-190.

Wood, S. K., & Valentino, R. J. (2017). The brain norepinephrine system, stress and cardiovascular vulnerability. *Neuroscience & Biobehavioral Reviews, 74*, 393-400.

Wood, W., & Rünger, D. (2016). Psychology of habit. *Annual Review of Psychology, 67*, 289-314.

Woodbury-Smith, M., Nicolson, R., Zarrei, M., Ryan, K., Yuen, C., Walker, S., et al. (2017). Variable phenotype expression in a family segregating microdeletions of the NRXN1 and MBD5 autism spectrum disorder susceptibility genes. *NPJ Genomic Medicine, 2*, 1. doi:10.1038/s41525-017-0020-9

Woodson, J., Niemeyer, A., & Bergan, J. (2017). Untangling the neural circuits for sexual behavior. *Neuron, 95*(1), 1-2.

Woody, W. D. & Viney, W. (2017). *A History of Psychology: The Emergence of Science and Applications,* (6th ed.). New York: Routledge.

Woolfolk, A. (2015). *Educational psychology* (13th ed.). Upper Saddle River, NJ: Pearson.

World Health Organization (WHO) (November, 2014). Information sheet on opioid overdose. http://www.who.int/substance_abuse/information-sheet/en/

World Health Organization (WHO). (2015). *Suicide rates per 100,000 by country.* World Health Organization. http://www.who.int/gho/mental_health/suicide_rates_crude/en/

World Health Organization. (June, 2016). *Obesity and overweight factsheet.* Geneva, Switzerland: WHO. http://www.who.int/mediacentre/factsheets/fs311/en/

Worthington, E. L., Davis, D. E., Hook, J. N., Miller, A. J., Gartner, A. L., & Jennings, D. J. (2011). Promoting forgiveness as a religious or spiritual intervention. In J. D. Aten, M. R. McMinn, & E. L. Worthington (Eds.), *Spiritually oriented interventions for counseling and psychotherapy* (pp. 169-195). Washington, DC: American Psychological Association.

Wraw, C., Deary, I. J., Der, G., & Gale, C. R. (2016). Intelligence in youth and mental health at age 50. *Intelligence, 58*, 69-79. doi:10.1016/j.intell.2016.06.005

Wright, J. H., Brown, G. K., Thase, M. E., & Basco, M. R. (2017). *Learning cognitive-behavior therapy: An illustrated guide.* Arlington, VA: American Psychiatric Association.

Wu, C.C., Samanez-Larkin, G.R., Katovich, K., & Knutson, K. (2014). Affective traits link to reliable neural markers of incentive anticipation. *NeuroImage, 84*, 279-289.

Wuest, D. A., & Fisette, J. L. (2015). *Foundations of physical education, exercise science, and sport* (18th ed.). New York: McGraw-Hill.

Wynn, T., & Coolidge, F. L. (2010). Beyond symbolism and language: An introduction to Supplement 1, working memory. *Current Anthropology, 51*, Suppl. 1, 5-16.

Wynn, T., Coolidge, F. L., & Bright, M. (2009). Hohlenstein-Stadel and the evolution of human conceptual thought. *Cambridge Archaeological Journal, 19*(1), 73-83.

X

Xiao, X., Dong, Q., Gao, J., Men, W., Poldrack, R. A., & Xue, G. (2017). Transformed neural pattern reinstatement during episodic memory retrieval. *Journal of Neuroscience, 37*(11), 2986-2998.

Xie, W., & Zhang, W. (2017). Familiarity speeds up visual short-term memory consolidation. *Journal of Experimental Psychology: Human Perception and Performance, 43*, 1207-1221. doi:10.1037/xhp0000355

Xu, H., & others. (2013). The function of BMP4 during neurogenesis in the adult hippocampus in Alzheimer's disease. *Ageing Research and Reviews, 12*(1), 157-164.

Xu, J., & others. (2014). Nondirective meditation activates default mode network and areas associated with memory retrieval and emotional processing. *Frontiers in Human Neuroscience, 8*, 86.

Xu, N., Zhou, W. J., Wang, Y., Huang, S. H., Li, X., & Chen, Z. Y. (2014). Hippocampal Wnt3a is necessary and sufficient for contextual fear memory acquisition and consolidation. *Cerebral Cortex.* PMID: 24904070

Y

Yaffe, R. B., Shaikhouni, A., Arai, J., Inati, S. K., & Zaghloul, K. A. (2017). Cued memory retrieval exhibits reinstatement of high gamma power on a faster timescale in the left temporal lobe and prefrontal cortex. *Journal of Neuroscience, 37*(17), 4472-4480.

Yakunchikov, D. Y., Olechowski, C. J., Simmonds, M. K., Verrier, M. J., Rashiq, S., McWilliams, L. A., et al. (2017). The effect of social observational learning, empathy and catastrophizing in chronic pain patients during acute pain Induction. *Pain Medicine, 18*(5), 871-878.

Yalom, I. D., & Leszcz, M. (2005). *The theory and practice of group psychotherapy* (5th ed.). New York: Basic Books.

Yamaguchi, M., Randle, J. M., Wilson, T. L., & Logan, G. D. (2017). Pushing typists back on the learning curve: Memory chunking improves retrieval of prior typing episodes. *Journal of Experimental Psychology: Learning, Memory, and Cognition, 43*(9), 1432-1447.

Yang, S., & Sternberg, R. J. (1997a). Conceptions of intelligence in ancient Chinese philosophy. *Journal of Theoretical and Philosophical Psychology, 17*(2), 101-119.

Yang, S., & Sternberg, R. J. (1997b). Taiwanese Chinese people's conceptions of intelligence. *Intelligence, 25*(1), 21-36.

Yang, X., Liu, J., Meng, Y., Xia, M., Cui, Z., Wu, X., et al. (2017). Network analysis reveals disrupted functional brain circuitry in drug-naive social anxiety disorder. *NeuroImage.* in press.

Yang, Y., & Raine, A. (2009). Prefrontal structural and functional brain imaging findings in antisocial, violent, and psychopathic individuals: A meta-analysis. *Psychiatry Research, 174*(2), 81-88.

Yang, Y., Raine, A., Lencz, T., Bihrle, S., LaCasse, L., & Colletti, P. (2005). Volume reduction in prefrontal gray matter in unsuccessful criminal psychopaths. *Biological Psychiatry, 57*(10), 1103-1108.

Yap, M. B., Pilkington, P. D., Ryan, S. M., & Jorm, A. F. (2014). Parental factors associated with depression and anxiety in young people: A systematic review and meta-analysis. *Journal of Affective Disorders, 156*, 8-23.

Yates, L. B., Djoussé, L., Kurth, T., Buring, J. E., & Gaziano, J. M. (2008). Exceptional longevity in men: Modifiable factors associated with survival and function to age 90 years. *Archives of Internal Medicine, 168*(3), 284-290.

Yeomans, J. S. (2012). Muscarinic receptors in the brain stem and mesopontine cholinergic arousal functions. *Handbook of Experimental Pharmacology, 208*, 243-259.

Yi, Y., & Friedman, D. (2011). Event-related potential (ERP) measures reveal the timing of memory selection processes and proactive interference resolution in working memory. *Brain Research, 1411*, 41-56.

Yoder, R. M., & Taube, J. S. (2014). The vestibular contribution to the head direction signal and navigation. *Frontiers in Integrative Neuroscience, 8*, ArtID: 32

Yoder, R. M., Chan, J. M., & Taube, J. S. (2017). Acetylcholine contributes to the integration of self-movement cues in head direction cells. *Behavioral Neuroscience, 131*(4), 312-324. doi:10.1037/bne0000205

Yong, A. D., Williams, M. M., Provan, H., Clarke, D., & Sinclair, G. (2015). How do offenders move through the stages of change? *Psychology, Crime & Law, 21*(4), 375-397. doi:10.1080/1068316X.2014.989166

Yong, Z., Hsieh, P., & Milea, D. (2017). Seeing the sound after visual loss: Functional MRI in acquired auditory-visual synesthesia. *Experimental Brain Research, 235*(2), 415-420. doi:10.1007/s00221-016-4802-6

Yonkers, K. A., Gilstad-Hayden, K., Forray, A., & Lipkind, H. S. (2017). Association of panic disorder, generalized anxiety disorder, and benzodiazepine treatment during pregnancy with risk of adverse birth outcomes. *JAMA Psychiatry, 74*(11), 1145-1152.

Yoon, E., Adams, K., Clawson, A., Chang, H., Surya, S., & Jérémie-Brink, G. (2017). East Asian adolescents' ethnic identity development and cultural integration: A qualitative investigation. *Journal of Counseling Psychology, 64*(1), 65-79.

Yu, S., Levesque-Bristol, C., & Maeda, Y. (2017). General need for autonomy and subjective well-being: A meta-analysis of studies in the us and east asia. *Journal Of Happiness Studies*, doi:10.1007/s10902-017-9898-2

Z

Zablotsky, B., Colpe, L. J., Pringle, B. A., Kogan, M. D., Rice, C., & Blumberg, S. J. (2017). Age of parental concern, diagnosis, and service initiation among children with autism spectrum disorder. *American Journal on Intellectual and Developmental Disabilities, 122*(1), 49–61.

Zadra, A., & Domhoff, G. W. (2010). The content of dreams: Methods and findings. In M. Kryger, T. Roth, & W. Dement (Eds.), *Principles and practices of sleep medicine* (5th ed., pp. 585–594). Philadelphia: Elsevier Saunders.

Zahn, D., Tug, S., Wenzel, M., Simon, P., & Kubiak, T. (2016). Glucose metabolism and self-regulation—Is insulin resistance a valid proxy of self-control? *Personality and Individual Differences, 99*, 38–45. doi:10.1016/j.paid.2016.04.070

Zahrt, O. H., & Crum, A. J. (2017). Perceived physical activity and mortality: evidence from three nationally representative U.S. samples. *Health Psychology*, in press. doi:10.1037/hea0000531

Zajonc, R. B. (1965). Social facilitation. *Science, 149*(3681), 269–274.

Zajonc, R. B. (1968). Attitudinal effects of mere exposure. *Journal of Personality and Social Psychology, 9*(2, Pt 2), 1–27.

Zajonc, R. B. (1984). On the primacy of affect. *American Psychologist, 39*(2), 117–123.

Zajonc, R. B. (2001). Mere exposure: A gateway to the subliminal. *Current Directions in Psychological Science, 10*(6), 224–228.

Zald, D. H., & Treadway, M. T. (2017). Reward Processing, Neuroeconomics, and Psychopathology. *Annual Review of Clinical Psychology, 13*, 471–495.

Žampachová, B., Kaftanová, B., Šimánková, H., Landová, E., & Frynta, D. (2017). Consistent individual differences in standard exploration tasks in the black rat (Rattus rattus). *Journal of Comparative Psychology, 131*(2), 150–162. doi:10.1037/com0000070

Zampini, M., & Spence, C. (2004). The role of auditory cues in modulating the perceived crispness and staleness of potato chips. *Journal of Sensory Studies, 19*, 347–363.

Zane, T., Carlson, M., Estep, D., & Quinn, M. (2014). Using functional assessment to treat behavioral problems of deaf and hard of hearing children diagnosed with autism spectrum disorder. *American Annals of the Deaf, 158*(5), 555–566.

Zanetidou, S., Belvederi Murri, M., Menchetti, M., Toni, G., Asioli, F., Bagnoli, L., et al. (2017). Physical exercise for late-life depression: Customizing an intervention for primary care. *Journal of the American Geriatrics Society, 65*(2), 348–355. doi:10.1111/jgs.14525

Zarkhin, F. (2017, May 31). Surviving victim of Friday train stabbing a poet and PSU student. The Oregonian/OregonLive . www.oregonlive.com/portland/index.ssf/2017/05/surviving_victim_of_friday_tra.html

Zedelius, C. M., & Schooler, J. W. (2015). Mind wandering 'Ahas' versus mindful reasoning: Alternative routes to creative solutions. *Frontiers In Psychology, 6*.

Zeidner, M., & Shani-Zinovich, I. (2011). Do academically gifted and nongifted students differ on the big-five and adaptive status? Some recent data and conclusions. *Personality and Individual Differences, 51*(5), 566–570. doi:10.1016/j.paid. 2011.05.007

Zemore, S. E. (2017). Implications for future research on drivers of change and alternatives to Alcoholics Anonymous. *Addiction, 112*(6), 940–942.

Zendarski, N., Sciberras, E., Mensah, F., & Hiscock, H. (2017). Academic achievement and risk factors for adolescents with attention-deficit hyperactivity disorder in middle school and early high school. *Journal of Developmental & Behavioral Pediatrics, 38*(6), 358–368.

Zhai, S., Tanimura, A., Graves, S. M., Shen, W., & Surmeier, D. J. (2018). Striatal synapses, circuits, and Parkinson's disease. *Current Opinion in Neurobiology, 48*, 9–16.

Zhang, A., & Jang, Y. (2017). The role of internal health locus of control in relation to self-rated health in older adults. *Journal of Gerontological Social Work, 60*(1), 68–78. doi:10.1080/01634372.2016.1267672

Zhang, H., Jiang, Y., Nguyen, H. D., Poo, D. C., & Wang, W. (2017). The effect of a smartphone-based coronary heart disease prevention (SBCHDP) programme on awareness and knowledge of CHD, stress, and cardiac-related lifestyle behaviours among the working population in Singapore: A pilot randomised controlled trial. *Health and Quality of Life Outcomes, 15*. in press.

Zhang, J., Paksarian, D., Lamers, F., Hickie, I. B., He, J., & Merikangas, K. R. (2017). Sleep patterns and mental health correlates in US adolescents. *The Journal of Pediatrics, 182*, 137–143.

Zhang, L. F., & Sternberg, R. J. (2012). Culture and intellectual styles. In L. F. Zhang, R. J. Sternberg, & S. Rayner (Eds.), *Handbook of intellectual styles.* New York: Springer.

Zhang, L., Mistry, K., Neoh, S. C., & Lim, C. P. (2016). Intelligent facial emotion recognition using moth-firefly optimization. *Knowledge-Based Systems, 111*, 248–267. doi:10.1016/j.knosys.2016.08.018

Zhang, X., Qiu, J., Zhang, Y., Han, S., & Fang, F. (2014). Misbinding of color and motion in human visual cortex. *Current Biology, 24*(12), 1354–1360.

Zhang, Y., Liang, W., Yang, S., Dai, P., Shen, L., & Wang, C. (2013). Repetitive transcranial magnetic stimulation for hallucination in schizophrenia spectrum disorders: A meta-analysis. *Neural Regeneration Research, 8*(28), 2666–2676.

Zhao, H., Seibert, S. E., & Lumpkin, G. T. (2010). The relationship of personality to entrepreneurial intentions and performance: A meta-analytic review. *Journal of Management, 36*(2), 381–404.

Zhao, J., Deng, B., Qin, Y., Men, C., Wang, J., Wei, X., & Sun, J. (2017). Weak electric fields detectability in a noisy neural network. *Cognitive Neurodynamics, 11*, 81–90. doi: 10.1007/s11571-016-9409-x

Zhaoyang, R., Martire, L. M., & Sliwinski, M. J. (2017). Morning self-efficacy predicts physical activity throughout the day in knee osteoarthritis. *Health Psychology, 36*(6), 568–576. doi:10.1037/hea0000479

Zheng, J., & Zhang, Q. (2016). Priming effect of computer game violence on children's aggression levels. *Social Behavior and Personality, 44*(10), 1747–1760. doi:10.2224/sbp.2016.44.10.1747

Zheng, Y., Manson, J. E., Yuan, C., Liang, M. H., Grodstein, F., Stampfer, M. J., et al. (2017). Associations of weight gain from early to middle adulthood with major health outcomes later in life. *JAMA, 318*(3), 255–269.

Zhou, B., Gao, W., Lv, J., Yu, C., Wang, S., Liao, C., & ... Li, L. (2015). Genetic and environmental influences on obesity-related phenotypes in Chinese twins reared apart and together. *Behavior Genetics, 45*(4), 427–437. doi:10.1007/s10519-015-9711-0

Zhou, S., & Shapiro, M. A. (2017). Reducing resistance to narrative persuasion about binge drinking: The role of self-activation and habitual drinking behavior. *Health Communication, 32*(10), 1297–1309. doi:10.1080/1041023 6.2016.1219931

Zhou, X., Saucier, G., Gao, D., & Liu, J. (2009). The factor structure of Chinese personality terms. *Journal of Personality, 77*(2), 363–400.

Zhu, L. X., Ho, S. C., Sit, J. W., & He, H. G. (2014). Retraction: Effects of a transtheoretical model-based exercise stage-matched intervention on exercise behaviour and quality of life in patients with coronary heart disease: A randomized controlled trial. *Journal of Advanced Nursing, 70*(10), 2414.

Zhu, W., Wadley, V. G., Howard, V. J., Hutto, B., Blair, S. N., & Hooker, S. P. (2016). Objectively measured physical activity and cognitive function in older adults. *Medicine and Science in Sports and Exercise, 49*(1), 47–53.

Zhu, Y., Liu, W., Li, Y., Wang, X., & Winterstein, A. G. (2017). Prevalence of ADHD in publicly insured adults. *Journal of Attention Disorders*, in press.

Zhu, Z., Ho, S. M., & Bonanno, G. A. (2013). Cultural similarities and differences in the perception of valence and intensity: A comparison of Americans and Hong Kong Chinese. *American Journal of Psychology, 126*(3), 261–273.

Ziegler, M., MacCann, C., & Roberts, R. (Eds.). (2011). *New perspectives on faking in personality assessment.* New York: Oxford University Press.

Zietsch, B. P., & others. (2008). Genetic factors predisposing to homosexuality may increase mating success in heterosexuals. *Evolution and Human Behavior, 29*(6), 424–433.

Zillikens, M. C., Demissie, S., Hsu, Y. H., Yerges-Armstrong, L. M., Chou, W. C., Stolk, L., et al. (2017). Large meta-analysis of genome-wide association studies identifies five loci for lean body mass. *Nature Communications, 8*(1), 80.

Zimbardo, P. G. (1971). *The power and pathology of imprisonment.* Congressional Record (No. 15, 1971-10-25). Hearings before Subcommittee No. 3, of the Committee on the Judiciary, House of Representatives, Ninety-Second Congress, First Session on Corrections, Part II, Prisons, Prison Reform and Prisoner's Rights: California. Washington, DC: Government Printing Office.

Zimbardo, P. G. (1972). Pathology of imprisonment. *Society, 9*(6), 4–8.

Zimbardo, P. G. (1973). On the ethics of intervention in human psychological research: With special reference to the Stanford Prison Experiment. *Cognition, 2*(2), 243–256.

Zimbardo, P. G. (1989). *Quiet rage: The Stanford prison study video.* Stanford, CA: Stanford University.

Zimbardo, P. G. (2007). *The Lucifer effect: Understanding how good people turn evil.* New York: Random House.

Zimbardo, P. G., Maslach, C., & Haney, C. (2000). Reflections on the Stanford prison experiment: Genesis, transformations, consequences. In T. Blass (Ed.), *Obedience to authority: Current perspectives on the Milgram paradigm* (pp. 193–237). Mahwah, NJ: Erlbaum.

Zimmerman, F. H. (2012). Cardiovascular disease and risk factors in law enforcement personnel: A comprehensive review. *Cardiology in Review, 20*(4), 159–166.

Zollig, J., Mattli, F., Sutter, C., Aurelio, A., & Martin, M. (2012). Plasticity of prospective memory through a familiarization intervention in old adults. *Neuropsychology, Development, and Cognition: Aging, Neuropsychology, and Cognition, 19*(1–2), 168–194.

Zollo, L., Pellegrini, M. M., & Ciappei, C. (2016). What sparks ethical decision making? The interplay between moral intuition and moral reasoning: Lessons from the scholastic doctrine. *Journal of Business Ethics*, doi:10.1007/s10551-016-3221-8

Zorthian, J. (August 24, 2017). The $759 million Powerball winner quit her job almost immediately. *Fortune Magazine.* http://fortune.com/2017/08/24/powerball-jackpot-winner-hospital-worker-massachusetts/

Zorumski, C. F., & Izumi, Y. (2012). NMDA receptors and metaplasticity: Mechanisms and possible roles in neuropsychiatric disorders. *Neuroscience and Biobehaviorial Reviews, 36*(3), 989–1000.

Zwebner, Y., Sellier, A., Rosenfeld, N., Goldenberg, J., & Mayo, R. (2017). We look like our names: The manifestation of name stereotypes in facial appearance. *Journal of Personality and Social Psychology, 112*(4), 527–554. doi:10.1037/pspa0000076

name index

Deloitte, 344
Dement, W. C., 137
Demeter, G., 134
Demiralay, C., 454
Demiray, B., 224
Demorest, A. P., 429
Deneubourg, J. L., 429
Den Heijer, A. E., 452
Dennett, D. C., 7, 125
Denollet, J., 534
Denys, D., 511
DePaoli, A., 330
De Picker, L. J., 475
Depue, R. A., 390
De Raad, B., 380
Derntl, B., 356
De Roover, K., 378
Desai, A. K., 139
Desai, S., 336
Descartes, R., 6
de Souto Barreto, P., 290
Deutsch, C. K., 369
De Venter, M., 454
Devine, P., 436
Devine, R. T., 299
Devita, M., 138, 141
Devlin, B., 447
De Vos, J., 427
de Vries, A. L., 313
de Vries, J., 410
DeWall, C. N., 419
DeYoung, C. G., 379, 389–392, 415
Diamond, L. M., 339, 340
Diamond, M., 316
Diaz, M. T., 270
Diaz-Morales, J. F., 381
Dick, D. M., 149
Dickenson, J. A., 339
Dickinson, D., 265
Dickman, A. B., 415
DiClemente, C. C., 521
Didziulis, V., 463
Diener, C., 19
Diener, E., 15, 19, 20, 31, 378, 382, 386
Dietz, W. H., 519
Di Iorio, C. R., 532
Dijkhuizen, J., 359
Diller, J., 515
Diller, J. W., 9
Di Narzo, A. F., 482
Ding, Z., 291
Dinges, C. W., 179
Di Paolo, T., 52
Dirkx, M. F., 52, 61
Dissanayake, C., 445, 446
Distel, M. A., 480
Dixon, R. A., 301
Dixon, R. M. W., 267
Dobson, R., 530
Dodge, E., 470
Dodge, K. A., 418
Doetsch, F., 73
Dogan, O., 462, 463
Dolan, M., 480
Dolinski, D., 412
Doll, B. B., 215
Dollard, J., 417
Domhoff, G. W., 128, 130, 142–144
Domingue, B. W., 259
Dominguez, J. M., 334
Domiteaux, M., 379
Domjan, M., 35, 165, 174, 178
Donate Life, 413
Donatelle, R. J., 133, 540
Donhoff, G. W., 142
Donnellan, M. B., 379, 386, 528
Donovan, B. M., 433
Dooley, L. N., 281
Dorahy, M. J., 462, 463
Dou, Y., 447
Douglas, S., 308
Dovidio, J. F., 161, 318, 431
Dow, D., 446
Doyle, A. E., 450

Dozois, D. J., 466
Draguns, J. G., 442, 465
Drake, H., 513
Dreary, I. J., 257
Drieghe, D., 101
Druckman, D., 370
Drury, J., 434
Druss, B. G., 442
Dryman, M. T., 498
Duan, J., 476
Ducharme, S., 288
Dudukovic, N. M., 203, 204, 220
Duffy, A. L., 418
Duggan, K. A., 263
Dugger, S. M., 513
Duke, A. A., 416
Duman, R. S., 466
Dunbar, R. I. M., 63
Duncan, A. E., 149
Duncan, B. L., 493, 494
Duncan, G. J., 11
Duncan, L., 471
Dunkel, C. S., 376
Dunlop, W. L., 280
Dunlosky, J., 190
Dunn, E., 433
Dunn, E. W., 14
Dunn, K., 52, 286
Dunning, D., 74
Dupaul, G., 452
Dupin, L., 101
Durantini, M. R., 545
Durkin, M. S., 446
Durstine, J. L., 541
Dutta, R., 304, 315
Duvarci, S., 351
Duverne, S., 64
Dux, P. E., 127, 128
Dweck, C. S., 196, 197, 262
Dworkin, E. R., 459, 460
Dysart, J., 227
Dzokoto, V., 353

E

Eagly, A. H., 11, 315, 415, 421
Earl, S., 545
Earnshaw, V. A., 309
Eastwick, P. W., 422
Eaton, D. A., 481
Eaton, N. R., 338
Eaton, R. W., 179
Eaves, L. J., 331
Ebbinghaus, H., 229
Ebesutani, C. E., 456
Ebstein, R. P., 414
Ecker, C., 446
Eckstein, M. P., 86
Edge, N., 251
Eggum, N. D., 413
Egloff, B., 251, 372
Eguchi, E., 542
Ehlers, A., 458, 462
Eich, E., 222–224
Eilertsen, E. M., 450
Einstein, A., 37, 193
Einstein, G. O., 218, 232
Eisenberg, D. P., 309, 507
Eisenberg, N., 318, 413
Eisenstadt, D., 320
Eisenstein, A. R., 543
Ekman, P., 55, 353–355
Eldred, M., 53
Eldredge, J. H., 379
Eley, T. C., 391, 466
El-Hai, J., 511
Elkins, D. N., 444
Elklit, A., 462
Ellins, E. A., 533
Elliot, A. J., 344
Elliott, A. J., 190
Elliott, L. T., 434
Elliott, M. A., 521

Ellis, A., 501
Ellis, H. C., 204
Elmore, B., 331, 542
Elmore, K., 125
Elsea, M., 419
El-Sheikh, M., 137
Emberson, L. L., 284
Emmelkamp, P. M., 504
Emmons, R. A., 360, 378, 386
Endler, N. S., 510
Eng, P. M., 534
Engel, A. K., 101
Enger, D., 124
Englehardt, C. R., 419
English, T., 311
Engvik, H., 380
Ensembl Human, 76
Ensink, K., 461
Ent, M. R., 410
Entwistle, P. A., 158
Epel, E., 332
Epel, E. S., 535
Epley, N., 220
Erickson, K. I., 237
Erikson, E. H., 18, 304–306, 309, 311, 312, 368
Erlick, D., 511
Ervin, F. E., 194
Escribano, C., 381
Espnes, G. A., 534
Esposito, E. A., 259, 260
Esslen, M., 87
Etaugh, C. A., 30
Etcoff, N. L., 404
Etherton, J., 117
Evans, B. G., 275
Evans, J., 248
Evans, M. F., 543
Evans, S., 452
Evans-Lacko, S., 484
Everitt, B. J., 174
Eysenck, H. J., 389

F

Fagan, S. E., 479
Fagundes, C. P., 533
Fahn, S., 73
Fahy, T., 462
Fairman, K. A., 449
Faivre, N., 125
Fan, C., 57
Fang, R., 52
Faraone, S. V., 449, 450
Farr, R. H., 36, 340, 341
Farrar, M.J., 447
Fastame, M. C., 527
Fatemi, S. H., 475
Fattinger, S., 133
Faucett, J., 508
Faucher, E. H., 320
Fave, G. A., 508
Fawcett, R. C., 255
Faymonville, M. E., 157
Fazakas-DeHoog, L. L., 466
Fazio, R. H., 409
Federal Bureau of Investigation, 418
Fei-Fei, L., 95
Feigenbaum, J., 479
Fein, S., 424
Feinberg, J., 446
Feinberg, E. H., 54
Feinberg, T. E., 126
Feinstein, E. C., 515
Feitosa-Santana, C., 10
Feldman, R., 53
Feldman, S., 386
Feldman Barrett, L., 358
Feltham, C., 492, 512
Feng, Y., 117
Fenn, K. M., 205, 206
Ferguson, A., 101
Ferguson, C. J., 417, 419
Ferguson, E., 379

Ferguson, S., 418
Fermani, F., 50
Fernald, A., 272, 273
Fernandez, M. E., 521
Ferrarelli, F., 160
Ferrari, C., 403
Ferrari, M., 301
Ferreira, J. A., 419
Ferrer, E., 269
Ferrie, J. E., 139
Ferris, G. R., 378
Festinger, L., 409, 410
Fetz, E. E., 179
Fiacconi, C. M., 348
Fiedler, K., 403
Fielding, K. S., 412
Fielding, N. G., 18
Fields, R., 505, 506
Figee, M., 511
Fillingim, R. B., 117
Finch, C. E., 302
Finegood, E. D., 272
Fink, H., 331
Finkel, A. G., 74
Finkel, E. J., 422
Finley, J. R., 203
Finniss, D. G., 190
Fiori, M., 265
Fischel, E., 309
Fischer, R., 355
Fisette, J. L., 539
Fishbein, M., 521
Fisher, C. M., 429
Fisher, J. O., 333
Fisher, O., 125, 400
Fisher, T. D., 338, 339
Fishman, E. J., 407
Fiske, A. P., 318
Fiske, S. T., 404
Fitzhugh, E. C., 543
Fitzpatrick, C., 298
Fitzpatrick, F., 226
Fitzpatrick, K. K., 470, 471
Fitzpatrick, M., 498
Fivush, R., 202
Flaccus, G., 1
Flamier, A., 284
Flannery, D. J., 299
Fleeson, W., 386
Flegal, K. M., 541
Fleming, K. A., 66
Flens, J. R., 394
Fletcher, K., 160
Flor, H., 158
Flückiger, C., 495
Flynn, J. R., 261
Focht, B. C., 541
Foels, R., 433
Foer, J., 124
Fok, H., 355
Foli-Anderson, N.J., 491
Folkman, S., 536
Folsom, T. D., 475
Fonagy, P., 479
Fondell, E., 133
Fong, C. J., 252, 253
Foote, B., 464
Foote, M., 253
Forbes, M. K., 338
Forbes, T. A., 287
Forbush, K., 470
Ford, B. Q., 538
Føreland, A. R., 380
Forgas, J. P., 403
Forman-Hoffman, V. L., 428
Fornacieri, C. J., 370
Forrest, C. B., 281
Fort, P., 137
Fortuna, K., 414
Foss Sigurdson, J., 482
Foster, S. E., 515
Fountas, K. N., 511
Fournier, J. C., 351, 508
Fournier, M. A., 380, 383

subject index

mere exposure effect, **420**–421
meta-analysis, 493, 495, 506, 508
metacognition, 125. *See also*
　consciousness
methamphetamine, 152–153
Mexican Americans, binge eating disorder
　in, 472
MHC (major histocompatibility com-
　plex), 120
mHealth apps, 504
midbrain, **60**
middle ear, 110*f*, **111**
mild traumatic brain injury (MTBI), 74
Milgram's obedience experiments,
　425–426, 425*f*
mind-body link, 520
mindfulness, **253**
mindfulness meditation, 159–160
mindset, 196–197
mind wandering, 129, 143
Minnesota Multiphasic Personality
　Inventory (MMPI), **394**
Minnesota Study of Twins Reared
　Apart, 78
minority influence, 430
mirror neurons, 46
mirror-neurons, 116
mirror-touch synaesthesia (MTS), 116
mis-gendered, 313
misperception, and stereotypes, 89
modeling, 188. *See also* observational
　learning
molecular genetics, 77
Monitoring the Future, 144
monkeys, attachment in infant, 303, 303*f*
monoamine oxidase (MAO)
　inhibitors, 506
monocular cues, **105**, 105*f*
moods, 415. *See also* emotions
　circumplex model of, 357*f*
moral development, 316–319
　Kohlberg's theory, 317–318
　socioemotional context of, 318
moro or startle reflex, 285*f*
morphemes, 267
morphine, 53
morphology, **267**
morphology, in language, 267
mortality, 320
motion perception, 106–107
motivated forgetting, 225
motivation, 326–329. *See also* emotions
　Adler on, 369, 371
　drive reduction theory and, 326–328
　evolutionary approach to, 326
　Freud on, 364
　happiness, 358–359
　hierarchy of needs and, 342–343, 343*f*
　Horney on, 369
　in hunger, 327, 329–330
　inner, 254
　intrinsic vs. extrinsic, 16, 345–347
　Jung on, 369
　Murray on, 395
　optimum arousal theory and, 327*f*,
　　328–329
　for positive life changes, 525
　self-actualization, 373–374
　in sex, 326, 332–339, 364
motivation research, 12*f*
motor cortex, 63*f*, **65**, 65*f*
motor nerves, 43, 45
motor reproduction, 188
motor skills, development of, 285–286,
　286*f*
motor tension, 452
MRI (magnetic resonance imaging), 56
MTBI (mild traumatic brain injury), 74
multiple intelligences, 264–266
multiple personality disorder, 463, 463*f*
multiple sclerosis (MS), 47
multitasking, 203
　inattentional blindness and, 93–94
musical intelligence, 265

myelination, 287
myelin sheath, **47**, 47*f*, 287
Myers-Briggs Type Indicator (MBTI),
　370–371
myoclonic jerks, 135
mysophobia, 455*f*

N

NAc. *See* nucleus accumbens (NAc)
names, stereotypes and, 406
narcissistic personality disorder, 478*f*
narcolepsy, 141
narcotics (opiates), **149**–151, 155*f*
NaSSAs (noradrenergic and specific
　serotonergic antidepressants), 506
National Weight Control Registry, 542
Native Americans, 442, 467, 483, 483*f*
nativist approach, 297–298
naturalistic observation, **32**
naturalist intelligence, 265
natural selection, **7**–8
nature, in development, **280**. *See also*
　genetic influences
　Piaget and, 297
Nazi prisoner experiments, 34
need, **326**
negative affect, 303, **356**
negative correlations, 20, 21*f*
negative emotions, 538
negative punishment, **184**, 185*f*
negative reinforcement, 179–181, **180**,
　181*f*, 185*f*
neglectful parenting, **307**
Nembutal, 149
neocortex, **63**
neologisms, 474
nervous system, 42–45, 81. *See also* brain;
　neurons
　characteristics of, 42–43
　defined, 42
　divisions of, 44–45, 44*f*
　embryological development of, 57,
　　58*f*, 59
　glial cells, 46
　neural impulse, 47–49, 48*f*, 49*f*
　neural networks, 43–44, 54, 54*f*, 134,
　　143–144, 216–217
　neurogenesis, 73
　neuron structure, 46–47, 47*f*
　pathways in, 43–44
　synapses and neurotransmitters in,
　　49–53, 50*f*
neural impulse, 47–49, 48*f*, 49*f*
neural networks, **43**–44, 54, 54*f*
　dreaming and, 143
　example of, 54*f*
　long-term memory and, 216–217
neural tube development, 283
neurobiological factors, in aggression, 416
neurochemical messengers, 51–53
neurodevelopmental disorders, 445–452
　attention-deficit/hyperactivity disorder,
　　449–452
　autism spectrum disorder, 445–449
neurodiversity, 446
neurogenesis, 73, 292
neuroleptics, 507–510, 509*f*
neurology, 84
neurons, **46**–54, 47*f*, 81
　binding by, 101
　cell structure of, 46–47, 47*f*
　collateral sprouting, 73
　feature detectors and, 100
　glial cells and, 46
　graded currents from sensory
　　receptors, 87
　memory and, 216–217
　mirror, 46
　neural impulse, 47–49, 48*f*, 49*f*
　in neural networks, 51, 51*f*
　neurogenesis, 73
　sleep and, 138
　sleep deprivation and, 139

synapses and neurotransmitters, 49–54,
　50*f*
　in visual processing, 100–101
neuroscience, **9**, 42
neuroscientists, 42
neuroticism
　genetics and, 78
　HPA and, 391
　neurotransmitters and, 390–391
　in reinforcement sensitivity theory, 390,
　　390*f*
　serotonin and, 391
　subjective well-being and, 382
　in trait theories, 378, 378*f*, 382
*Neuroticism Extraversion Openness
　Personality Inventory-Revised*
　(NEO-PI-R), 394
neurotransmitters, **50**–51. *See also specific
　neurotransmitters*
　action of, 50*f*
　cocaine and, 153, 153*f*
　depression and, 52, 466
　drugs and, 53, 149, 153, 153*f*
　emotions and, 350–352, 351*f*
　examples of, 51–54
　hunger and, 331
　midbrain and, 60
　panic attacks, 453–454
　personality and, 390
　reuptake of, 51
　schizophrenia and, 475
　sexual behavior and, 333
　sleep and, 136–137, 142
NFL players, and CTE, 74
nicotine, 151–152, 152*f*, 155*f*, 544. *See
　also* tobacco
nicotine gum, 544
nicotine patch, 544
nicotine spray, 544
nightmares, 141
night terrors, 141
nine-dot problem, 247*f*, 275*f*
9/11 terrorist attacks, 224, 224*f*, 358, 429
NK cells, 133
noise, in sensory perception, **91**
non-binary gender, 313
nonconscious thought. *See* unconscious
　thought
nondeclarative (implicit) memory,
　214–215, 215*f*
nondeclarative memory, **214**
noradrenergic and specific serotonergic
　antidepressants (NaSSAs), 506
norepinephrine, **52**
　adrenal glands and, 71
　bipolar disorder and, 469
　cocaine and, 153
　depression and, 52, 466, 467*f*, 506
　Ecstasy and, 153
　functions of, 52, 71
　panic disorder and, 453
　psychoactive drugs and, 153
　sleep and, 136
"normalcy," views of, 441
normal distribution, **257**, 257*f*
normative social influence, **424**
novel stimuli, 93
nucleus accumbens (NAc)
　addiction and, 145–146, 145*f*
　alcohol and, 147
　cocaine and, 153*f*
　in reward pathway, 145, 145*f*, 511
Nun Study, 292–293, 292*f*
nurture, **280**
nurture, in development, 280. *See also*
　environment
　Piaget on, 297
nyctophobia, 455*f*

O

obedience, **425**–427, 425*f*, 426*f*
obesity, 331–332. *See also* weight loss
　biology of, 331

classical conditioning and, 173
　diet and, 331, 541–542
　hypothalamus and, 331
　leptin and, 330, 330*f*
　portion size and, 332
　psychological factors in, 331–332
　sleep and, 139
obesogenic environments, 543
objective evaluation of work, 254
objectivity, 4, 254
object permanence, 294*f*, **295**
ob mice, 330, 331
observational learning, **166**, 187–189,
　189*f*, 384–385
　aggression and, 417
　Bandura's model of, 188, 189*f*, 384
observations
　in descriptive research, 17–18, 29*f*
　naturalistic, 32
　in the scientific method, 13–14, 14*f*
obsessions, 457
obsessive-compulsive disorder (OCD),
　452, 456–458, **457**, 478*f*
　operant conditioning and, 500
　related disorders, 457–458
occipital lobes, **63**, 63*f*, 88
　visual information in, 88
occupational therapist, 491*f*
Oedipus complex, **367**
Old Order Amish, 19, 20
Olds studies, 62
olfactory bulb, 73
olfactory epithelium, **119**, 120*f*
olfactory sense, 118–120, 120*f*
Omega-3 fatty acids, 260
On Death and Dying (Kübler-Ross), 321
One Flew Over the Cuckoo's Nest
　(film), 510
one-third rule for alcoholism, 149
online "selves," 33
online support groups, 514
On the Origin of Species (Darwin), 7
open-mindedness, **253**
openness, 378*f*, 379
　eveningness and, 381
　neurotranmitters and, 391
operant conditioning, 176–187, **177**
　applied behavior analysis, 186–187
　classical conditioning vs., 165–166,
　　166*f*
　extinction and spontaneous recovery
　　in, 182
　generalization, discrimination, and
　　extinction in, 182, 182*f*
　learning and, 166, 166*f*
　positive and negative reinforcement in,
　　179–181, 181*f*, 185*f*
　primary and secondary reinforcers
　　in, 181
　punishment in, 184, 185*f*
　reinforcement, 179–180, 182–184, 184*f*
　shaping in, 179
　Skinner's approach to, 178–179, 178*f*
　as therapy, 499–500, 503*f*, 517
　Thorndike's law of effect, 177–178,
　　178*f*
　timing of reinforcement and
　　punishment, 184–186
operational definitions, **15**–16
operations, in Piaget's theory, 294*f*,
　295, 296
ophidiophobia, 455*f*
ophthalmology, 84
opiates. *See* opioids
opioids, **149**–151, 155*f*
opium, 53
opponent-process theory, **102**–103, 103*f*
optic chiasm, 100, 101*f*
optic nerve, 98*f*, **99**, 99*f*, 100*f*
optimism, 529, 530, 536
optimistic attributional style, 467
optimum arousal theory, 327*f*, 328–329
oral sex, 337
oral stage, 367, 368*f*